BASIC CONCEPTS IN COMMERCIAL LAW

CASES AND MATERIALS

By

John F. Dolan
Professor of Law
Wayne State University Law School

Lawrence Ponoroff
Professor of Law and Vice Dean
Tulane Law School

AMERICAN CASEBOOK SERIES®

WEST GROUP

ST. PAUL, MINN., 1998

610 Opperman Drive
P.O. Box 64526
St. Paul, MN 55164–0526
1–800–328–9352

Printed in the United States of America

ISBN 0–314–21117–9

TEXT IS PRINTED ON 10% POST CONSUMER RECYCLED PAPER

FOR MY MOTHER AND IN MEMORY OF MY FATHER

JFD

FOR MY PARENTS, JEAN AND CHARLES PONOROFF

LP

Preface

OBJECTIVES

This casebook is designed to introduce you to commercial law and to provide you a modicum of Uniform Commercial Code learning.

Please note that we are not trying to turn you into commercial lawyers or even to make you proficient in the UCC. We don't do that because we can't.

The Code is an artifact of commercial law, a product of a process that antedates the UCC by hundreds of years and that enjoys a rich vitality outside the UCC. Thus we list learning the technical detail as a secondary objective, because we view developing an affinity and appreciation for the breadth and dynamism of the commercial law as more important to you as future lawyers.

We recognize that most of you will not become "UCC lawyers," but virtually all of you will need to be literate in commercial law. And becoming literate in commercial law is what we mean when we say that our first objective is to introduce you to commercial law.

Much of the text in this book emphasizes principles, rather than the *rules*, of commercial law. The reality is that the rules change from one revision of the Code to the next; they may differ from state to state; and, in point of fact, many of the rules are unremarkable and can even be rather arcane. The basic *principles*, on the other hand, stay just about the same. They embody the important commercial policies the rules are intended to serve and, thus, they facilitate an understanding of the rules of commercial law as those rules may exist from time to time and place to place. In short, to teach only the rules would give you a false sense and static understanding of what commercial law is all about and what makes it exciting to us.

We also think that law teachers should treat second- and third-year law students who study commercial law as graduate students who are sophisticated enough to familiarize themselves somewhat with the literature of the field. That familiarity serves not to advance a quest to become commercial law experts but to advance your education in commercial law as a dynamic enterprise in which scholars play a role. Most practicing lawyers have little time for scholarship; and if you do not see scholarship in law school as an enterprise that plays the energizing, criticizing, and moderating roles we think it plays, you may never see it, and may conclude, as many lawyers do, that we scholars largely waste our time when we write.

We don't try to teach commercial law without teaching any rules. This book is full of them (perhaps more than you would like), and many of your teachers will supplement the text with other rules that are the subject of contemporary controversy or misunderstanding. Learning about Code rules is, furthermore, instructive. This book engages in that instruction because it advances understanding of commercial law principles. Exercises in rules analysis is not the objective of the study, however. We make no attempt here to cover the Code exhaustively or even to cover some of the articles exhaustively. We have picked through the Code and emphasized some of the rules because we think those rules help you understand the basic concepts, hence, the title of the book.

SCOPE

There is not much Sales here and not much Leasing or Securities and only a little Bankruptcy. Most of the study deals with the UCC. The study here of Article 9 and Articles 3 and 5 covers the bulk of commercial law learning that you should have for the level of literacy that we strive to give you. Those articles are the emphasis of this book. But, we cover other sources of commercial law: Articles 4, 4A, and 7; the Bankruptcy Code; the Uniform Customs and Practice for Documentary Credits; and the UNCITRAL Convention on Independent Bank Guarantees and Stand-by Letters of Credit, among others.

In all events, however, we are not striving to give you anything more than an introduction to commercial law, and we use these sources as illustrations of that law in operation.

CODE REVISION

The revision of Article 9 of the UCC, the secured lending article, renders the study of that subject complex. One of us is hopeful that the revision will succeed; the other is less sanguine about the process but concedes its inevitability. Nevertheless, we both believe that the process will take time. Our approach, teaching basics rather than a lot of rules, reduces that problem to a manageable level. While the rules are changing in Revised Article 9, the basics remain pretty much the same; and basics are what we strive to teach here.

References to "Article 9" are to the current version unless otherwise noted. References to "Revised Article 9" are to the November 20, 1997, American Law Institute Council Draft No. 3. Undoubtedly, the final version of the revision will differ both in numbering and in content. Nonetheless, the basic thrust and direction of the revision effort is clear from the latest Council Draft which, at least as of this writing, was the most recent version of Revised Article 9 available, even though it does not reflect certain changes adopted by the Drafting Committee at its November 1997 and March 1998 meetings. Where appropriate, we note those changes in the text as well.

The same reference practice follows for other articles where the revision process has already been approved by the UCC's sponsoring agencies. When not clear from the context, we have attempted to indicate in editorial footnotes those opinions that cite versions of the UCC other than the current official version.

STYLE

In reproducing opinions, statutes, articles, and other textual material, we have deleted most footnotes, have renumbered those we did not delete, and have noted ellipses with asterisks. We have also deleted textual citations and italics in opinions and articles without any notation.

When we felt it was particularly important to do so, we reproduced statutory material directly in the casebook itself. In most instances, however, we simply cross-referenced to *Selected Commercial Statutes*, published annually by West Group, which we assume most teachers will assign along with the casebook.

THANKS

There are many who deserve our thanks in connection with this effort. We are particularly grateful to colleagues and their publishers who permitted us to excerpt their work. We acknowledge them in the pages that follow.

Dolan would also like to thank, for grants and other financial support, Dean James Robinson and the Charles Gershenson Fund; for research assistance, Amy Munerantz, R. Bryan Schneider, Mark Spitzley, and Alan Tucker; and for secretarial assistance, Nancy Shafer. Ponoroff would like to thank his students and colleagues at Tulane Law School for their support and encouragement, and, in particular, Kent S. Neumann and Dana Tamir for their able research assistance. He would also like to thank (he thinks) Dolan for drawing him into this project. While it is yet to be seen how the law school community will receive this work, the collaboration has already been a rewarding personal and professional experience. Finally, as we produced this text in camera-ready form (don't blame West for the mistakes), we would both like to acknowledge an enormous debt of gratitude to Lynn Becnel, Law Journal Production Coordinator at Tulane Law School, for her technical computer assistance.

JFD
Detroit, Michigan

LP
New Orleans, Louisiana

May 1998

Acknowledgements

Alces, Peter A. & Lloyd, Robert M., An Agenda for Reform of the Article 9 Filing System, 44 Okla. L. Rev. 99, 105-08 (1991). Reprinted with permission. (p. 275).

Alces, Peter A., Fraud Bases for Bulk Transferee Liability, 63 Temple L. Rev. 679, 684-86 (1990). Reprinted by permission. (p. 83).

Aronstein, Martin J., et al., Article 8 *Is* Ready, 93 Harv. L. Rev. 889, 890-94 (1980). Reprinted with permission. (p. 191).

Baird, Douglas G. & Jackson, Thomas H., Information, Uncertainty, and the Transfer of Property, 13 J. Legal Stud. 299, 312-15, 318-20 (1984). Copyright 1984 by the University of Chicago. All rights reserved. Reprinted with permission. (p. 324).

Baird, Douglas G. & Jackson, Thomas H., Possession and Ownership: An Examination of the Scope of Article 9, 35 Stan. L. Rev. 175, 178 (1983). Reprinted with permission. (p. 36).

Baird, Douglas G., Notice Filing and the Problem of Ostensible Ownership, 12 J. Legal Stud. 53, 53-54 (1983). Copyright 1983 by the University of Chicago. All rights reserved. Reprinted with permission. (p. 66).

Baird, Douglas G., The Elements of Bankruptcy 101-02 (Rev. ed. 1993). Reprinted by permission. (p. 101).

Barnes, Richard L., Tracing Commingled Proceeds: The Metamorphosis of Equity Principles into U.C.C. Doctrine, 51 U. Pitt. L. Rev. 281, 340-42 (1990). Reprinted with permission. (p. 201).

Beard, Benjamin D., Effectuating the Customer's Right to Stop Payment of a Check: The Forgotten Section 4-401, 37 Wayne L. Rev. 1815, 1815-19 (1991). Reprinted with permission. (p. 666).

Beard, Benjamin, The Purchase Money Security Interest in Inventory: If It Does Not Float, It Must be Dead, 57 Tenn. L. Rev. 437, 438-39 (1990). Reprinted with permission of the author and the Tennessee Law Review Association, Inc. (p. 162).

Bebchuk, Lucian A. & Fried, Jesse M., The Uneasy Case for the Priority of Secured Claims in Bankruptcy, 105 Yale L.J. 857, 896-97 (1996). Reprinted by permission of The Yale Law Journal Co. and Fred B. Rothman & Co. from The Yale Law Journal. (p. 307).

Boss, Amelia H., Lease Chattel Paper: Unitary Treatment of a Special Kind of Commercial Specialty, 1983 Duke L.J. 69, 83-84 (1983). Reprinted with permission. (p. 176).

Braucher, Robert, Reclamation of Goods from a Fraudulent Buyer, 65 Mich. L. Rev. 1281, 1282-84 (1967). Reprinted with permission from the Michigan Law Review Association. (p. 472).

Carlson David G. & Shupack, Paul M., Judicial Lien Priorities Under Article 9 of the Uniform Commercial Code: Part II—Creditor Representations, Bank Receivers, Fixtures, Crops, and Accessions, 5 Cardozo L. Rev. 823-25, 827 (1984). Reprinted with permission. (p. 353).

Carlson, David G., Death and Subordination Under Article 9 of the Uniform Commercial Code: Senior Buyers and Senior Lien Creditors, 5 Cardozo L. Rev. 547-48 (1984). Reprinted with permission. (p. 363).

Clark, Barkley, The Law of Secured Transactions Under the Uniform Commercial Code ¶ 10.03[2], at 10-45-46, ¶ 3.09, at 3-100 (Rev. ed. 1993). Reprinted with permission. (pp. 16, 202).

Coogan, Peter F., Article 9—An Agenda for the Next Decade, 87 Yale L.J. 1012, 1014-17 (1978). Reprinted by permission of The Yale Law Journal Co. and Fred B. Rothman & Co. from The Yale Law Journal. (p. 157).

Cook, Michael L. & Mendales, Richard E., The Uniform Fraudulent Transfer Act: An Introductory Critique, 62 Am. Bankr. L.J. 87, 88-89 (1988). Reprinted with the permission of the American Bankruptcy Law Journal, which holds the copyright. (p. 81).

Countryman, Vern, The Concept of a Voidable Preference in Bankruptcy, 38 Vand. L. Rev. 713, 822-23 (1985). Reprinted with permission. (p. 468).

DiMatteo, Larry A., The Counterpoise of Contracts: The Reasonable Person Standard and the Subjectivity of Judgment, 48 S.C. L. Rev. 293, 330, 338-41 (1997). Reprinted with permission. (pp. 613, 645).

Dolan, John F., Good Faith Purchase and Warehouse Receipts: Thoughts on the Interplay of Articles 2, 7, and of the UCC, 30 Hastings L.J. 1, 2-3 (1978). Copyright 1978 by University of California, Hastings College of Law. Reprinted with permission. (pp. 44, 182).

Dolan, John F., Section 9-307(1): The U.C.C.'s Obstacle to Agricultural Commerce in the Open Market, 72 Nw. U. L. Rev. 706 (1978). Reprinted by special permission of Northwestern University Law Review, Volume 72, Number 5, pp. 706-36. (p. 371).

Dolan, John F., The U.C.C. Framework: Conveyancing Principles and Property Interests, 59 B.U. L. Rev. 822, 813-14 (1979). Reprinted with permission. © 1979 Trustees of Boston University. Forum of original publication. Boston University bears no responsibility for any errors that have occurred in reprinting or editing. (p. 24).

Dolan, John F., The Uniform Commercial Code and the Concept of Possession in the Marketing and Financing of Goods, 56 Tex. L. Rev. 1147, 1161-64 (1978). Copyright 1978 by the Texas Law Review Association. Reprinted with permission. (pp. 31, 269).

Dole, Richard F., Jr., Receiving Bank Liability for Errors in Wholesale Wire Transfers, 69 Tul. L. Rev. 877, 912-16 (1995). Originally published in 69 Tulane Law Review 877, 912-16 (1995), copyright the Tulane Law Review Association. All rights reserved. (p. 659).

Ellinger, Edward, Fraud in Documentary Credit Transactions, 1981 J. Bus. L. 258, 262. Reprinted with permission. (p. 639).

Farber, Daniel A. & Matheson, John H., Beyond Promissory Estoppel: Contract Law and the "Invisible Handshake," 52 U. Chi. L. Rev. 903, 945-46 (1985). Reprinted with permission. (p. 480).

Farnsworth, E. Allan, Documentary Drafts Under the Uniform Commercial Code, 22 Bus. Law. 479 (1967). Copyright 1967 by the American Bar Association. Reprinted with permission. (p. 180).

Frisch, David, Buyer Status Under the UCC: A Suggested Temporal Definition, 72 Iowa L. Rev. 531, 534 (1987). Reprinted with permission. (p. 55).

Gilmore, Grant, The Commercial Doctrine of Good Faith Purchase, 63 Yale L.J. 1057 (1954). Reprinted by permission of The Yale Law Journal Co. and Fred B. Rothman & Co. from The Yale Law Journal, Vol. 63, pages 1057-1122. (p. 23).

Gilmore, Grant, The Good Faith Purchase Idea and the Uniform Commercial Code: Confessions of a Repentant Draftsman, 15 Ga. L. Rev. 605, 612-13, 619 (1981). Reprinted with permission. (p. 547).

Goode, R.M., Abstract Undertakings in International Transactions, 22 Brook. J. Int'l L. 1, 9-10 (1996). Reprinted with permission. (p. 630).

Goode, R.M., Commercial Law 400-01 (1982). Reprinted with permission. (p. 5).

Goode, R.M., Commercial Law 60 (2d ed. 1995). Reprinted with permission. (p. 8).

Hakes, Russell A., According Purchase Money Status Proper Priority, 72 Or. L. Rev. 323, 329 (1993). Reprinted with permission. Copyright © 1993 by University of Oregon. (p. 8).

Hansford, Nathaniel & Speegle, Jerry, Lien Creditor Status Under the UCC—Does the FDIC Qualify?, 16 UCC L.J. 13, 14-17 (1983). Reprinted with permission. (p. 354).

Harfield, Henry, Bank Credits and Acceptances 109 (5th ed. 1974). The author is of counsel at Shearman & Sterling, New York, New York. Reprinted with permission. (p. 668).

Harris, Steven L. & Mooney Charles W., Jr., A Property-Based Theory of Security Interests: Taking Debtors' Choices Seriously, 80 Va. L. Rev. 2021, 2034-37, 2051-53 (1994). Reprinted with permission. (pp. 203, 307).

Harris, Steven L., Article 6: The Process and the Product—An Introduction, 43 Ala. L. Rev. 549, 549-51 (1990). Reprinted with permission. (pp. 85, 366).

Harris, Steven L., The Interface Between Articles 2A and 9 Under the Official Text and the California Amendments, 22 U.C.C. L.J. 99, 144 n.50 (1989). Reprinted with permission. (p. 16).

Harris, Steven L., The Rights of Creditors Under Article 2A, 39 Ala. L. Rev. 803, 811 (1988). Reprinted with permission. (p. 150).

Henson, Ray, Documents of Title Under the Uniform Commercial Code 142 (2d ed. 1990). Reprinted with permission. (p. 45).

Holmes, Eric Mills, Stature and Status of a Promise Under Seal as a Legal Formality, 29 Willamette L. Rev. 617, 618-21 (1993). Reprinted with permission. (p. 477).

Jackson, Thomas H. & Kronman, Anthony T., Secured Financing and Priorities Among Creditors, 88 Yale L.J. 1143-46, 1166-67 (1979). Reprinted by permission of The Yale Law Journal Co. and Fred B. Rothman & Co. from The Yale Law Journal. (p. 347).

Jackson, Thomas H., Avoiding Powers in Bankruptcy, 36 Stan. L. Rev. 725, 757-60 (1984). Copyright 1984 by the Board of Trustees of the Leland Stanford Junior University. Reprinted with special permission. (p. 79).

Juenger, Friedrich K., Listening to Law Professors Talk About Good Faith: Some Afterthoughts, 69 Tul. L. Rev. 1253, 1255-56 (1995). Originally published in 69 Tulane Law Review 1253, 1255-56 (1995), copyright the Tulane Law Review Association. All rights reserved. Reprinted with permission. (p. 613).

Kennedy, Frank R., Secured Creditors Under the Bankruptcy Act, 15 Ind. L. Rev. 477, 492-93 (1982). Copyright 1982 by the Trustees of Indiana University. Reprinted with permission. (p. 463).

King, Donald B., New Conceptualism of the UCC: Ethics, Title and Good Faith Purchase, 11 St. Louis L.J. 15, 38-39 (1966). The author is Professor of Law, Saint Louis Univ. School of Law. Reprinted with permission. (p. 28).

Kripke, Homer, Current Assets Financing as a Source of Long-Term Capital, 36 Minn. L. Rev. 506, 510-11 (1952). Reprinted with permission. (p. 161).

Kripke, Homer, Law and Economics: Measuring the Economic Efficiency of Commercial Law in a Vacuum of Fact, 133 U. Pa. L. Rev. 929-33, 934-36 (1985). Copyright 1985 by the University of Pennsylvania Law Review. Reprinted by permission. (p. 302).

Lawrence, Lary, Making Cashier's Checks and Other Bank Checks Cost-Effective: A Plea for Revision of Articles 3 and 4 of the UCC, 64 Minn. L. Rev. 275, 282 (1980). Reprinted with permission. (p. 498).

Laycock, Douglas, The Death of the Irreparable Injury Rule, 103 Harv. L. Rev. 688, 689-92 (1990). Reprinted with permission. (p. 678).

Llewellyn, Karl. N., Through Title to Contract and a Bit Beyond, 15 N.Y.U. L.Q. Rev. 159, 165-68 (1938). Reprinted with permission by the New York University Law Review. (p. 107).

Lloyd, Robert M., The Absolute Bar Rule in UCC Foreclosure Sales: A Prescription for Waste, 40 UCLA L. Rev. 695, 698-700, 721-24, 728-31 (1993). Copyright 1993 by the Regents of the University of California. All rights reserved. Reprinted with permission. (p. 241).

LoPucki, Lynn M., The Unsecured Creditor's Bargain, 80 Va. L. Rev. 1887, 1963 (1994). Reprinted with permission. (p. 205).

Macintosh, Kerry L., Letters of Credit: Curbing Bad Faith Dishonor, 25 U.C.C. L.J. 3-4, 29-32 (1992). Reprinted with permission. (p. 603).

McCoid, John C., II., Bankruptcy, Preferences, and Efficiency: An Expression of Doubt, 67 Va. L. Rev. 249, 270-73 (1981). Reprinted with permission. (p. 434).

McCurdy, William E., Commercial Letters of Credit, 35 Harv. L. Rev. 539, 564-66 (1992). Reprinted with permission. (p. 498).

Miller, Frederick H., Is Revision Due of U.C.C. Article 9, Part 5?, 44 Okla. L. Rev., 125-26, 128-29 (1991). Reprinted with permission. (p. 210).

Mooney, Charles W., Jr., Introduction to U.C.C. Annual Survey, 41 Bus. Law. 1343, 1352 (1986). Copyright 1986 by the American Bar Association. Reprinted with permission. (p. 375).

Mooney, Charles W., Jr., The Mystery and Myth of "Ostensible Ownership" and Article 9 Filing: A Critique of Proposals to Extend Filing Requirements to Leases, 39 Ala. L. Rev. 683, 788-89 (1988). Reprinted with permission. (p. 37).

Murray, John E., Jr., The Revision of Article 2: Romancing the Prism, 35 Wm. & Mary L. Rev. 1447, 1497-99 (1994). Reprinted with permission. (p. 643).

Nyquist, Curtis, A Spectrum Theory of Negotiability, 78 Marq. L. Rev. 897, 897-903 (1995). Reprinted with permission. (p. 549).

Overby, A. Brooke, Bondage, Domination, and the Art of the Deal: An Assessment of Judicial Strategies in Lender Liability Good Faith Litigation, 61 Fordham L. Rev. 963, 1023-24, 1028-29 (1993). Reprinted with permission. (p. 626).

Pantaleo, Peter V., et al., Rethinking the Role of Recourse in the Sale of Financial Assets, 52 Bus. Law. 159, 159-63 (1996). Copyright 1996 by the American Bar Association. Reprinted with permission. (p. 573).

Patterson, Dennis M., A Fable from the Seventh Circuit: Frank Easterbrook on Good Faith, 76 Iowa L. Rev. 503, 511-12, 520-21 (1991) (reprinted with permission). (p. 625).

Phillips, David M., Flawed Perfection: From Possession to Filing Under Article 9—Part 1, 59 B.U. L. Rev. 1, 35-38, and Part 2, 59 B.U. L. Rev. 255-56 (1979). Reprinted with permission. Boston University bears no responsibility for any errors that may have occurred in reprinting or editing. (pp. 103, 270).

Phillips, David M., The Commercial Culpability Scale, 92 Yale L.J. 228-29 (1982). Reprinted by permission of The Yale Law Journal Co. and Fred B. Rothman & Co. from The Yale Law Journal, Vol. 92, pages 228-90. (p. 24).

Ponoroff, Lawrence, Evil Intentions and an Irresolute Endorsement for Scientific Rationalism: Bankruptcy Preferences One More Time, 1993 Wisc. L. Rev. 1439, 1480-82 (1993). Copyright 1993 by The Board of Regents of the University of Wisconsin. Reprinted by permission of the Wisconsin Law Review. (p. 442).

Ponoroff, Lawrence, Now You See It, Now You Don't: An Unceremonious Encore for Two-Transfer Thinking in the Analysis of Indirect Preferences, 69 Am. Bankr. L.J. 203, 236-40 (1995). Reprinted with the permission of the American Bankruptcy Law Journal, which holds the copyright. (p. 433).

Priest, George L., A Theory of the Consumer Product Warranty, 90 Yale L.J. 1297, 1307-10, 1313 (1981). Reprinted by permission of The Yale Law Journal Co. and Fred B. Rothman & Co. from The Yale Law Journal, Vol. 90, pages 1297-1352. (p. 507).

Reitz, John C., A History of Cutoff Rules as a Form of Caveat Emptor: Part 1—The 1980 U.N. Convention on the International Sale of Goods, 36 Am. J. Comp. L. 437, 437-43 (1988). Reprinted with permission. (p. 509).

Rogers, James Steven, The Irrelevance of Negotiable Instruments Concepts in the Law of Check-Based Payment, 65 Tex. L. Rev. 929, 929-34 (1987). Reprinted with permission. (p. 535).

Rosenthal, Albert J., Negotiability—Who Needs It?, 71 Colum. L. Rev. 375, 376-77 (1971). This article originally appeared at 71 Colum. L. Rev. 375 (1971). Reprinted with permission. (p. 42).

Rubin, Edward, Efficiency, Equity and the Proposed Revision of Articles 3 and 4, 42 Ala. L. Rev. 551, 561-63, 564-65, 566-70 (1991). Reprinted with permission. (p. 593).

Shenker, Joseph C. & Colletta, Anthony J., Asset Securitization: Evolution, Current Issues and New Frontiers, 69 Tex. L. Rev. 1369, 1376-80 (1991). Published originally in 69 Texas Law Review 1369 (1991). Copyright 1991 by the Texas Law Review Association. Reprinted with permission. (p. 576).

Sherwin, Emily L., Creditors' Rights Against Participants in a Leveraged Buyout, 72 Minn. L. Rev. 449-52 (1988). Reprinted by permission. (p. 77).

Snyder, Stephen E. & Ponoroff, Lawrence, Commercial Bankruptcy Litigation §§ 1.02 & 10.11 (1989, 1997). Reprinted with permission. (pp. 418, 462).

Summers, Robert S., "Good Faith" in General Contract Law and the Sales Provisions of the Uniform Commercial Code, 54 Va. L. Rev. 195, 196-99 (1968). Reprinted with permission. (p. 611).

Ward, Thomas M., Ordering the Judicial Process Lien and the Security Interest Under Article Nine: Meshing Two Different Worlds—Part I—Secured

Parties and Post Judgment Process Creditors, 31 Maine L. Rev. 223-24, 226-29 (1980). Reprinted with permission. (p. 219).

Warren, William D., Cutting Off Claims of Ownership Under the Uniform Commercial Code, 30 U. Chi. L. Rev. 469, 470 (1963). Reprinted with permission. (p. 6).

Weinberg, Harold R., Markets Overt, Voidable Titles, and Feckless Agents: Judges and Efficiency in the Antebellum Doctrine of Good Faith Purchase, 56 Tul. L. Rev. 1, 4-5 (1981). Originally published in 56 Tulane Law Review 1, 4-5 (1981), copyright the Tulane Law Review Association. All rights reserved. Reprinted with permission. (p. 24).

Weinberg, Harold R., Toward Maximum Facilitation of Intent to Create Enforceable Security Interests, 18 B.C. Indus. & Com. L. Rev. 1-9 (1976). Reprinted with permission. (p. 226).

White, James J. & Summers, Robert S., 4 Uniform Commercial Code 170-74 (4th ed. 1995). Reprinted with permission of the West Publishing Corp. (p. 195).

White, James J., Efficiency Justifications for Personal Property Security, 37 Vand. L. Rev. 473-75, 479-81 (1984). Reprinted with permission. (p. 305).

White, James J., Reforming Article 9 in Light of Old Ignorance and New Filing Rules, 79 Minn. L. Rev. 529, 560-63 (1995). Reprinted with permission. (p. 349).

White, James J., Revising Article 9 to Reduce Wasteful Litigation, 26 Loy. L.A. L. Rev. 823, 823-27. Reprinted with permission. (p. 360).

Williston, Samuel, The Law of Sales in the Proposed UCC, 63 Harv. L. Rev. 561, 566-72 (1950). Reprinted with permission. (p. 109).

Summary of Contents

PART III. PRIORITIES

PART IV. COMMERCIAL SYSTEMS

Table of Contents

Table of Cases

The principal cases are in bold type.
Cases cited or discussed in the text are roman type.

PART I

TRANSFERRING INTERESTS IN PROPERTY

INTRODUCTORY NOTE

Students of commercial law are aware that the commercial subculture worked together to fashion a remarkable source for the law, a source that unifies law in more than fifty jurisdictions and provides mechanisms for keeping that law modern all with the commercial practices the source governs as the polestar. That source is the Uniform Commercial Code.

But students may not be as aware that the Code is the product of centuries of lawmaking and that it rests on the work of English and continental courts, on legislation, and on rules that merchants made for themselves.

In order to understand commercial law, then, study must often move away from the Code. In fact, given the dynamism of late twentieth-century commerce and the Code's adaptability to those changes, it is sometimes a mistake to focus too narrowly on Code rules. Better time can be spent understanding the basic Code concepts, because the peculiar rule of today may not be the rule of tomorrow. Basic concepts in commercial law tend not to change; and if they do change, they change slowly.

This Part I considers three conveyancing rules common to all property regimes. They are helpful because the Code is filled with property transfer concepts. Understanding these transfer rules facilitates understanding of Code rules.

Chapter 1

SECURITY OF PROPERTY: THE FIRST PRINCIPLE OF CONVEYANCING LAW

SECTION 1. PROTECTING OWNERSHIP

INTRODUCTORY NOTE

The first rule of conveyancing law is the rule that an owner may transfer property without permission from the King or anybody else. It follows from that rule that the owner must be able to convey everything he owns; and, in fact, the assumption in any transfer is that the owner has, indeed, transferred all of his interest. To transfer less, he must limit the transfer to a part interest. This principle of property law has a number of implications and raises a few questions. Can a party transfer something he does not own? Can a transferee claim more than the transferor claimed? Or can the transferor's creditors claim that the transferee did not take all that the transferor owned but took something less or took nothing?

Under the first rule of conveyancing the conveyance is entirely derivative: The transferee gets what the transferor had; and if the transferor had nothing, the transferee gets nothing.

The story begins with some responses to lawlessness in Civil War Chicago and, earlier, on the high seas.

ALLSTATE INSURANCE CO. v. ESTES, 345 So.2d 265, 266 (Miss. 1977). "[A] thief has neither title nor the power to convey such."

FAWCETT v. OSBORN

Supreme Court of Illinois, 1863.
32 Ill. 411.

[Fawcett entrusted hides to Stevens for tanning. Under the arrangement, Stevens was to deliver the tanned leather to Fawcett in New York City. A principal of Stevens took the leather to Chicago where a confederate entered into a contract to sell the leather to Osborn. Fawcett sued Osborn in trover and conversion.]

BREESE, J.

* * *

It is a general rule that a person who has no title to property can convey none; but to this rule there are some exceptions. To create such exception, and to give a third person a better title and a superior equity to the true owner, such third person must have given value for the property, etc., and without notice of the fraud. Such innocent third person is a *bona fide* purchaser for a valuable consideration. In such a case, the vendor, who has been defrauded of his property, and the *bona fide* purchaser from the fraudulent vendee, are both innocent parties; and when one of two innocent parties must suffer from the fraud of a third, the loss should fall on him who enabled such third person to commit the fraud. Possession of personal property is *prima facie* evidence of property.

* * *

But this court, in that case said, the principle does not apply to sales on condition, and when the original owner has never consented to the transfer of the property, referring to Bradsen v. Brooks, 22 Maine, 463; Draper Manuf. Co. v. Waterston, 3 Met., 9; 2 Kent's Com., 497. And the court further said, that it is a universal and fundamental principle of the law of personal property, that no man can be divested of it without his own consent. Saltus v. Everett, 20 Wend,. 275; Arb v. Putnam, 1 Hill, 303. In all these cases, cited by the defendant's counsel, the property was transferred to the purchaser, by the consent of the owner, under the form of a regular sale and delivery, and therein differ in a most important particular from the case we are considering. Here has been no transfer of the property by the consent of the true owners, nor have they, voluntarily, under the form of a sale, delivered the property to the defendant's vendor, or clothed him with any of the indicia of ownership, in the sense and meaning of any of the cases cited. We apprehend no well considered case can be found in the books, where a party has been deprived of his property without his consent, or where a party selling has been adjudged competent to convey to a purchaser a better title than he himself possessed.

The general rule of law, sanctioned by common sense, is, that no man can, by his sale, transfer to another the right of ownership in a thing wherein he himself has not the right of property, except, and this for the sake of sustaining the currency, in the instances of cash, bank bills, checks and notes payable to bearer or transferable by delivery in the ordinary course of business, to a person taking it, *bona fide*, and paying value for it. The other exception, of title acquired by sale in *market overt*, of stolen property, though recognized in England, has been uniformly held to have no force in this country. No one can sell a right when he himself has none to sell. This is a proposition so self evident that argument cannot elucidate or strengthen it.

It is true, that possession of personal property is one indicium of ownership, and is *prima facie* evidence of title to the thing. The bare possession of goods is a strong inducement to believe that the possessor is the true owner, and when to that is added proof of an actual sale and delivery to him, by the real owner, though by fraudulent pretenses, a subsequent sale by such purchaser to a *bona fide* purchaser, without notice of any fraud in the alleged sale and delivery to his vendor has been held, as is seen by the case cited, and may be seen in a multitude of other cases, to confer title upon such subsequent *bona fide* purchaser. The maxim of "he who trusts most shall lose most" is held to obtain in such cases, as will be seen by Root v. French and Jennings v. Gage. This maxim, so generally accepted, may be open to some just criticism. Does a party who parts with the possession of property, or the use of a thing, capable of easy identification, trust more than he who pays his money to a vendor upon his affirmance or assurance that the thing sold is his own, and he a stranger? There being, upon the sale of personal property an implied warranty of title, the vendee has his action against the vendor, if his title proves deficient.

The buyer must then take care that he is not deceived by dealing for a pretended title, or that his vendor is able to respond in damages for any loss which may happen to the vendee.

The general rule is, beyond all controversy or dispute, that no man can acquire a title to chattels from a person who has himself no title to them. Wheelwright v. Depeyster, 1 Johns., 478, and authorities cited. The exceptions we have stated being those of cash and certain commercial paper, and of sales in *market overt.* Then, even if the property sold was obtained by a felony, unless the buyers knew that the property was not in the seller, or there was any other fraud in the transaction, the purchaser would get a good title against the real owner, except he should be the king.

* * *

R.M. GOODE, COMMERCIAL LAW 400-01 (1982). "The market overt rule, which now appears to be peculiar to English law, originated in the days when shops were few, most goods were bought and sold at markets and fairs, and private sales were severely discouraged as being likely to involve stolen goods. One who received stolen goods and was not able to show that he had acquired them in open market stood in considerable danger of being hanged. The owner, for his part, was expected to look for his goods in the market; and if he did not intervene at the market prior to the sale of the goods, the bona fide buyer was given an assurance of good title, subject to two exceptions, namely the revesting of the goods in the owner where they had been stolen and the thief was prosecuted to conviction and the special statutory provisions as to the sale of horses."

TEXTILE SUPPLIES, INC. v. GARRETT, 687 F.2d 123 (5th Cir. 1982). "When Couch stole the carpet from Textile Supplies he acquired only 'void title.' He could not have passed valid title even to a good faith purchaser. * * * '[E]ven though the sale of the property is made to a bona fide purchaser for value, if it is stolen property, the person from whom it was stolen is not divested of his title.'"

SECTION 2. *NEMO DAT*—AN EXERCISE IN LOGIC

(a) In General

INTRODUCTORY NOTE

The following material considers claims by transferees that they enjoy greater rights than the transferor enjoyed. This is an idea that offends clear thinkers. To take by transfer more than the transferor had to transfer is akin to magic.

BARTHELMESS v. CAVALIER, 2 Cal. App. 2d 477, 487, 38 P.2d 484, 490 (1934). "Title, like a stream, cannot rise higher than its source."

CUNDY v. LINDSAY, 3 App. Cas. 459, 463-64 (H.L. 1878). "[B]y the law of our country the purchaser of a chattel takes the chattel as a general rule subject to what may turn out to be certain infirmities in the title."

Warren, Cutting Off Claims of Ownership Under the Uniform Commercial Code, 30 U. Chi. L. Rev. 469, 470 (1963). "In America the market overt was never to open, and we were left with the stern law that no one can transfer to another better title to goods than he himself has. The good faith purchaser from a thief or a mere bailee took subject to claims of ownership, and Justice Story had no sympathy for him presuming that 'his loss is often the result of his negligence and want of scrutiny * * *.'"

MITCHELL v. HAWLEY, 83 U.S. 544, 549 (1872). "No one in general can sell personal property and convey a valid title to it unless he is the owner, or lawfully represents the owner. *Nemo dat quod non habet.*"

BARNARD v. NORWICH & W.R. CO., 2 F. Cas. 841, 845 (Cir. Ct. D. Mass. 1876). "No person can sell a thing he does not own, unless as the duly authorized agent of the owner. *Nemo dat quod non habet.*"

UNION TRANSPORT FINANCE LTD. v. BRITISH CAR AUCTIONS LTD., [1978] 2 All E.R. 385 (C.A.). "During the argument, Cairns, L.J. referred to the well known Latin tag '*nemo dat quod non habet*,' which may be translated into English as: 'You cannot give what you have not got.'"

WHEELWRIGHT v. DEPEYSTER

Supreme Court of Judicature, New York, 1806.
1 Johns. 471.

[Plaintiffs purchased a cargo of coffee in Haiti, which at the time was in revolt against France, and transported the coffee on their schooner, the *Peggy*. A French privateer captured the *Peggy* and her cargo on the high seas and sold it at St. Jago to the defendants pursuant to a sale ordered by an agency of the French government. Plaintiffs sued the defendants in trover.]

By Court, KENT, C.J.

This cause was very ably argued by the counsel, and the several points submitted have received, as they merited, the attentive consideration of the court.

It was contended that a *bona fide* purchase by the defendants at St. Jago, for a valuable consideration, and without notice, was an equivalent to a purchase in market-overt under the English law, and bound the property against the party who had right. As no local law is alleged, or proved, this question must be governed by the general principles of the law of sales, which we are to presume until the contrary be shown, are received and adopted in all commercial countries, at St. Jago as well as New York. It was the maxim of the civil law that *nemo plus juris in alium transferre potest quam ipse habet*, and this plain dictate of common sense is considered by Pothier, *Traite du Contrat de Vente*, part 1, n. 7; and Erskine, Inst. of the Law of Scotland, vol. 2, 481, as a fundamental doctrine of the contract of sale in France and Scotland; and there is good reason to conclude that it prevails in most of the countries in Europe which have felt the influence or obeyed the precepts of the civil law. Lord Kames, in his Historical Law Tracts, tit. History of Property, vindicates this principle in the transfer of chattels, and observes that when notions of property were slight, a *bona fide* purchase of stolen goods gave a good title against the original owner; but that in the progress of society, property acquired such stability and energy, as to affect the subject wherever found, and to exclude even an honest purchaser, when the title of his vendor was discovered to be defective. It was also a principle in the English common law, that a sale out of market-overt did not change the property against the rightful owner; and the custom of the city of London, which forms an exception to the general rule, has always been regarded and restricted by the courts with unusual jealousy and vigilance: Conyn's Dig., tit. Market, E. The effect of such a purchase made here is not strictly before us, but I have no difficulty in saying that I know of no usage or regulation within this state, no Saxon institution of markets-overt which controls or interferes with the application of the common law. The purchase by the defendants did not, therefore, of itself, and without reference to the title of the vender give them an indefensible right to the goods in question.

* * *

The hardship of this case upon a *bona fide* purchaser is calculated, upon the first impression, to strike the imagination. It was contended by the counsel, that such purchasers ought to have been favored; but, as an English judge has some where observed, arguments upon the hardship of a case are only quicksands in the law, which, if admitted, would soon choke and destroy all established principles. A steady adherence to rule in these cases, by requiring the purchaser of captured property to look at his peril to the title, and to derive it under a competent sentence, will tend to check the intemperate avidity and irregular proceedings of belligerent captors.

The opinion of the court, therefore, is, that the defendants take nothing by their motion.

Judgment for the plaintiffs.

R.M. GOODE, COMMERCIAL LAW 60 (2d ed. 1995). "*NEMO DAT QUOD NON HABET*. The rule of the common law is that only the legal owner of goods or one who has been authorized or otherwise held out as entitled to dispose of them can make a disposition which will be effective to divest the legal owner of his title or encumber his interest. * * * Numerous exceptions to the *nemo dat* rule have been made by statute, but the rule nevertheless retains considerable vigour."

(b) After Acquired Collateral and the Purchase Money Concept

HAKES, ACCORDING PURCHASE MONEY STATUS PROPER PRIORITY, 72 Ore. L. Rev. 323, 329 (1993). "A longstanding principle of property law was that people could not transfer property prior to the time that they acquired ownership. This is often expressed as the Latin rule of logic *nemo dat quod non habet.* As long as that rule reigned supreme, there was little need for a purchase money concept. By reserving an interest or having an interest granted simultaneously with the debtor's acquisition of property, a party financing the acquisition could ensure a superior interest in the property. However, parties can more readily facilitate their intentions in certain commercial transactions if they can contract in the present for a springing interest in unowned property to arise when the debtor acquires an interest in that property. In those transactions commercial interests pressured courts to recognize and thereby legitimate security in after-acquired property."

INTRODUCTORY NOTE ON *INTERNATIONAL HARVESTER*

The following case illustrates a measure of judicial animus toward the after-acquired property theory. The court's logic is quite good, but its commercial values are quite useless. This may sound harsh, but it isn't half as harsh as the Florida legislature's treatment of the *International Harvester* case.

INTERNATIONAL HARVESTER CREDIT CORP. v. AMERICAN NATIONAL BANK

Supreme Court of Florida, 1974.
296 So.2d 32, 14 U.C.C. Rep. Serv. 19.

[On April 8, 1969, Machek Farms, Inc. granted American National Bank a security interest in all of Machek's equipment, including after-acquired equipment. The security interest secured a loan from the bank to Machek. Subsequently, Machek acquired equipment from a farm implement dealer and granted the dealer a purchase money security interest in the equipment. The dealer assigned its security interest to International Harvester Credit Corp. When Machek defaulted on the bank loan and on the obligation to pay for the equipment, both creditors claimed the equipment. The following opinion by the Florida Supreme Court is remarkable in light of the fact that in a dissent not reproduced here Chief Justice Carlton made it clear that the court had before it arguments properly explaining the meaning of Article 9 with its clear validation of security agreements covering after acquired collateral and its grant of priority over a purchase money secured party unless the purchase money lender complies with section 9-312(4).]

DEKLE, Justice.

This certiorari review is based upon two questions certified to us by the First District Court of Appeal as being ones of great public interest. The stipulated facts are succinctly set forth in the District opinion at 269 So.2d 726 (1972).

The questions certified involve the Uniform Commercial Code, as adopted in Florida, and are as follows: 1. Under Florida Statute 679.302(1)(c), must a seller of farm equipment file a financing statement to perfect his security interest in farm equipment sold under one contract when the purchase price of each item is less than $2,500.00, but the total amount of the contract for all items exceeds $2,500.00? 2. Under Florida Statute 679.312(4) and (5), does a party with a security interest in after acquired property take priority over a party with a purchase money security interest which was not perfected within ten days after the debtor took possession of the collateral?

The district court answered both questions in the affirmative. We reverse and answer the first question in the negative and agree with the dissent of Rawls, Acting C.J., in modifying the district court's affirmative answer to the second question.

* * *

SECOND QUESTION

Concerning the second question regarding 'after acquired property' as to security priorities, we are in agreement with the district's majority position in recognizing the earlier creditor's priority of security in after-acquired property (unless the required financing statement has been timely filed on such subsequent purchase). Fla.Stat. § 679.312(4), F.S.A. However, we differ with the district majority and agree with Acting Chief Justice Rawls that this priority security protection to the earlier creditor must be limited to the debtor's equity in the after-acquired property. This position is consistent with contractual constitutional requirements and equitable principles. The new seller's contract rights with his purchaser and any ownership retained in the property sold must be respected; moreover, it would be an invidious preference to the earlier creditor-bank without so much as a showing that there was a compelling public interest or purpose served by such arbitrary requirement of outright priority to the earlier creditor in the total after-acquired property.

The contention is made that to restrict the prior creditor's priority in the after-acquired property to the debtor's equity therein renders meaningless the requirement for filing a financing statement. We do not think so. There really are no conflicting security interests in this situation. That security interest retained by the subsequent seller in the after-acquired property never passes to the buyer-debtor and thus never becomes subject to the earlier creditor's claim of security interest in such after-acquired property. On the other hand, the earlier (perfected) creditor does have his security in that interest which is after-acquired by his debtor.

In this respect we note that the statute grants the priority in the Debtor's after-acquired property; it refers to the respective security 'interest' as being thereby affected. The debtor, while acquiring the physical property, only acquires an interest therein under a credit sales contract; it is this interest only then which is 'after acquired' and thereby subject to the earlier security right. The remainder is upon credit from the new creditor who often also retains title thereto. It would be abhorrent to equity and justice that the earlier creditor should acquire the subsequent Creditor's property or 'interest' in this manner. Upon principles of equity and in the avoidance of unjust enrichment, the limitation to the debtor's equity in after-acquired property appears to be the better and more logical rule. We would accordingly agree with Acting Chief Judge Rawls in this respect.

The 'new value' section of the code, § 679.108, urged by petitioners, is not invoked in the circumstances sub judice. The earlier secured creditor, respondent, stands upon its original contract and not upon 'new value.'

Logical and traditional equitable reasons preclude a result which would allow the bank as mortgagee to subject the after-acquired farm equipment as its collateral, while not changing its position and giving no 'new value' because of the later sale of equipment; consequently, the bank was not misled by the failure of the seller of the equipment to record his purchase money security.

To give the prior creditor the seller's retained interest in such property simply because of such seller's failure to record and to permit the original creditor to replevin the sold equipment would be to give to such earlier creditor a windfall not favored by the code (see § 679.108 and U.C.C. Comment 19C F.S.A. 198) contrary to established principles. Compare County of Pinellas v. Clearwater Federal Savings & Loan Ass'n, 214 So.2d 525 (Fla.App.2d 1968).

Our viewpoint regarding a limitation (to the buyer's equity) of the security of the earlier creditor, allows a just result to such creditor and yet is consistent with constitutional requirements as to the subsequent seller. Our position acknowledges, yet modifies, the view expressed by Judge Wigginton and that of the other jurisdictions cited in his opinion.

We accordingly modify the district court holding as to question 2 to the extent of limiting the priority allowed by the commercial code to the first (perfected) creditor (absent timely filing) to the extent of that creditor's debtor's equity in the after-acquired property under whatever contract it was purchased, preserving to the new seller his retained interest in such after-acquired property.

It is so ordered.

QUESTION

As later study reveals, the Code gives considerable preference to purchase-money lenders and credit sellers but also treats generously the working capital lender, usually a bank that takes all of the debtor's property, including after-acquired property, as security for a loan. The working capital lender and the purchase-money lender frequently claim the same collateral, and the Code drafters faced the challenge of resolving those competing claims. They did so with the ten-day rule the *International Harvester* decision mentions. What happens to that ten-day rule if the *International Harvester* court is correct?

FURTHER NOTE ON *INTERNATIONAL HARVESTER*

The Florida legislature responded to the holding in *International Harvester* by amending the Florida version of Article 9 to make it crystal clear that in order to achieve priority over an after acquired collateral provision in a security agreement, a purchase money lender must comply with the provisions of section 9-312(4). The language of the Florida Senate Bill is edifying.

Chapter 78-222
Senate Bill No. 417

An ACT relating to the Uniform Commercial Code; reenacting

> § 671.201 (37) and amending § 679. 312 (3) and (4), Florida Statutes, providing for priorities among conflicting security interests in the same collateral; providing an effective date.

WHEREAS, in a situation where there are conflicting security interests in the same collateral and a purchase money security interest has not been perfected within 10 days after the debtor took possession of the collateral, the Florida Supreme Court, in International Harvester Credit Corporation v. American National Bank of Jacksonville (296 So.2d 32), recognized 'the earlier creditor's priority of security in after-acquired property,' but limited such priority to "the debtor's equity in after-acquired property," and

WHEREAS, the Uniform Commercial Code, as adopted by the Florida Legislature, and as interpreted in other jurisdictions, contains no such "debtor's equity" concept, and in fact provides for a complete and logical system of priorities, and

WHEREAS, it is the intent of the Legislature that the concept of 'debtor's equity' should not be applicable in the State of Florida, and that the clear language in the Uniform Commercial Code should be adhered to, NOW, THEREFORE,

Be It Enacted by the Legislature of the State of Florida:

* * *

SECTION 3. THE SHELTER OR UMBRELLA RULE: THE FLIP SIDE OF *NEMO DAT*

INTRODUCTORY NOTE

Nemo dat is really only half a rule. It tells us what a transferor cannot convey, but it does not tell us what the transferor can convey. The other half of the rule is the umbrella or shelter principle. This half tells us that a transferor can convey everything he has and will convey everything unless he crafts the transaction as a partial transfer. Professors Baird and Jackson put the two rules together and call them the derivation principle.

AIRCRAFT TRADING & SERVICES, INC. v. BRANIFF, INC.

United States Court of Appeals, Second Circuit, 1987.
819 F.2d 1227.

[In December of 1982 Northeast Airlines granted a security interest in an aircraft's engine to ATASCO. ATASCO failed to perfect its interest by filing with the FAA. In November 1984 Northeast sold the engine to Braniff which sold it in the following month to Condren. Both Braniff and Condren filed bills of sale with the FAA. In February 1985 Condren leased the engine to IAL under a lease that gave IAL an option to purchase. IAL exercised the option and filed its bill of sale with the FAA in August of 1985. By that time, however, ATASCO had filed its security agreement with the FAA—a fact known to IAL when it exercised the option. In ATASCO's suit against Braniff, Condren, and IAL for conversion, replevin, and forfeiture, the trial court granted summary judgment in favor of the defendants.]

MINER, Circuit Judge.

* * *

ATASCO brought suit for conversion, replevin, and forfeiture against Braniff, Condren and IAL. ATASCO's central contention before the district court was that its rights were superior to those of IAL because its chattel mortgage was filed prior to IAL's filing, and IAL had actual knowledge of the terms of the instrument when it exercised its option to purchase. The district court granted summary judgment in favor of IAL, Condren, and Braniff, noting that if the only transaction at issue were the sale to IAL, then ATASCO might prevail. However, the district court ruled that, because of the intermediate transfers to Braniff and Condren prior to ATASCO's filing of the chattel mortgage, Braniff received good title and passed good title to Condren, who in turn passed good title to IAL.

* * *

All parties concede that New York's Uniform Commercial Code applies to determine priority in this case. We therefore turn to an analysis of the New York U.C.C., particularly Article 9, to determine how ATASCO's late perfected security interest should be treated.

* * *

2. Priority Between ATASCO and Braniff and Condren

We now turn to a determination of the strength of ATASCO's claim as against Braniff and Condren. Section 9-301(1) provides that: (1) an unperfected security interest is subordinate to the rights of

* * *

(b) a person who becomes a lien creditor before the security interest is perfected; (c) in the case of goods, instruments, documents, and chattel paper, a person who is not a secured party and who is a transferee in bulk or other *buyer not in ordinary course of business* * * * to the extent that he gives value and receives delivery of the collateral without knowledge of the security interest and before it is perfected. N.Y.U.C.C. Law § 9-301(1) (McKinney Supp.1987) (emphasis added). Both Braniff and Condren bought without knowledge of ATASCO's security interest and before it was perfected. Therefore, as buyers not in the ordinary course of business, their respective rights to the engine were superior to ATASCO's, by application of section 9-301(1)(c).

* * *

3. Shelter Provision of Article 2, Sales

Appellees argue that if Braniff and Condren are buyers not in the ordinary course of business, their priority over ATASCO's security interest under section 9-301(1) would pass to IAL with the conveyance. Relying on the shelter provision of Article 2, Sales, section 2-403, appellees assert that Braniff conveyed title to Condren, and Condren conveyed that title to IAL, subject at most to ATASCO's subordinated unperfected security interest. Section 2-403 provides that: (1) [a] purchaser of goods acquires all title which his transferor had or had power to transfer except that a purchaser of a limited interest acquires rights only to the extent of the interest purchased. N.Y.U.C.C. Law § 2-403(1) (McKinney 1964). Appellees have directed us to no authority for their assertion that the shelter provision of Article 2 may be applied to immunize transferees from a buyer who is protected under section 9-301(1)(c). It is a novel theory that we believe must fail.

Appellees' reliance on In re Gary Aircraft Corp., 681 F.2d 365 (5th Cir.1982), is misplaced. In Gary Aircraft, the secured party contended that it was entitled to possession of an aircraft because the last purchaser in the chain of sale was not a purchaser for value without notice, and therefore could not escape the secured party's interest as a buyer in the ordinary course of business. Rejecting that analysis, the Fifth Circuit held that the last purchaser was not subject to the secured party's interest because an intervening purchaser qualified under section 9-307 as a buyer in the ordinary course of business. That special status of the intervening purchaser extinguished the security interest in the collateral such that a subsequent sale could not resurrect it, and the last purchaser therefore prevailed.

New York law is in agreement. See Marine Midland Bank, N.A. v. Smith Boys, Inc., 129 Misc.2d 37, 41, 492 N.Y.S.2d 355, 358 (Sup.Ct.1985) (if any party in the chain of title takes free of the security interest under section 9-307, "all succeeding buyers likewise take free of the security interest"). However, this is a narrow exception to the general rule stated in section 9-306(2) that a security interest in collateral continues upon the sale of the collateral unless the sale was authorized by the secured party. Id. at 43, 492 N.Y.S.2d at 360. The case before us does not fall within this narrow exception because ATASCO's security interest was not extinguished, but merely subordinated, by the sale to Braniff: Braniff did not "take free" of ATASCO's interest under section 9-307; it took subject to ATASCO's subordinated claim. See T.M. Quinn, Uniform Commercial Code Commentary and Law Digest P 9-306[A] [2], at 9-169 (1978) ("[A]nyone dealing with the collateral deals with it subject to the continuing security interest.").

As the Fifth Circuit recognized in Gary Aircraft, "the rule is that section [2-403(1)] is not available to save one who buys when the seller's title is subject to a security interest but who does not qualify under section [9-307]" for preferred status as a buyer in the ordinary course of business.[1] Gary Aircraft, 681 F.2d at 377. See Commercial Credit Equipment Corp. v. Bates, 159 Ga.App. 910, 285 S.E.2d 560 (1981). But see Executive Financial Services, Inc. v. Pagel, 238 Kan. 809, 715 P.2d 381 (1986) (buyer in the ordinary course of business may prevail on "entrustment" theory under sections 2-403(2) and (3) even though he could not prevail under section 9-307(1)). Similarly, in National Shawmut Bank v. Jones, 108 N.H. 386, 388, 236 A.2d 484, 486 (1967), the court recognized section 9-307 as the only provision of Article 9 "under which a buyer of goods can claim to take free of a security interest where a sale, exchange or other disposition of the collateral was without consent of the secured party. * * * . Article 9-306(2) gives the court no leeway to create any other exceptions to its dictates." Accord Matteson v. Harper, 297 Ore. 113, 117, 682 P.2d 766, 769 (1984). See J. White & R. Summers, Uniform Commercial Code § 25-15, at 1073 (2d ed. 1980).

---

[1] IAL purchased with knowledge of ATASCO's security interest after ATASCO filed and perfected its claim. Therefore IAL cannot invoke protection in its own right under section 9-301(1)(c).

We find further support for this rule in other sections of the U.C.C. Section 9-306(2) provides for continuance of a security interest upon sale of the collateral "[e]xcept where this Article otherwise provides." We interpret this clause as expressly limiting exceptions to those found within Article 9. Moreover, section 2-402(3)(a) specifies that "[n]othing in this Article shall be deemed to impair the rights of creditors of the seller * * * under the provisions of [Article 9]." We conclude that the general scheme of the U.C.C. contemplates that a security interest is to be governed by Article 9, unimpaired by Article 2. Furthermore, the drafters of the U.C.C. explicitly provided shelter elsewhere in Article 9. See N.Y.U.C.C. Law § 9-302(2) (McKinney Supp.1987) ("If a secured party assigns a perfected security interest, no filing under this Article is required in order to continue the perfected status of the security interest against creditors of and transferees from the original debtor."). "[T]heir failure to do so in section 9-301(1)(c) should be taken as significant." [citation omitted]

Finally, we note that the U.C.C. does not require a security interest to be filed immediately or promptly, although it is the most prudent course for a cautious lender. Delay in perfection does not preclude perfected status at a later time upon filing. While the secured party's interest may be subordinated to interests of others arising prior to filing, "[h]e can, of course, file, even after a delay, and protect himself against interests arising subsequent to such filing." 53 N.Y.Jur. Secured Transactions § 175, at 152 (1967). The rule appellees urge us to adopt effectively would freeze a secured party's priority status as of the time of the first intervening conveyance: If one failed to file a security interest the day of the sale, the buyer could, by immediately reselling, forever destroy the security interest. While appellees urge that their rule would result in an increment of certainty in such transactions, we believe that such an extreme result would discourage lenders from taking security interests and would thereby inhibit commerce. The U.C.C. does not attempt to remove all uncertainty from secured transactions. It provides automatic perfection in certain situations, see N.Y.U.C.C. Law §§ 9-302(1)(b) (10-day automatic perfection for documents, proceeds), 9-302(1)(d) (purchase money security interest in consumer goods), & 9-304(4) (21-day automatic perfection for certain instruments) (McKinney Supp.1987), and allows a filing to relate back to the time of attachment in others, see N.Y.U.C.C. Law §§ 9-103(1)(d), 9-103(3)(e) (McKinney Supp.1987) (in multistate transaction, secured party has four months to file in state to which collateral has been removed). The U.C.C. aims to balance the competing concerns of protection for secured lenders and encouragement of trade.

4. Priority Between ATASCO and IAL

Having determined that ATASCO's security interest was not extinguished by the subsequent conveyances to Braniff and Condren, we now address the priority in the engine as between ATASCO and IAL.

At the time the engine was conveyed from Northeastern to Braniff and then to Condren, ATASCO's claim was subordinate to Braniff's and Condren's under section 9-301, as discussed above, because it was unfiled and unperfected. However, ATASCO eventually did file and perfect its security interest, and therefore section 9-301, which determines priority where an interest is unperfected, has no bearing on the issue of priority as between ATASCO and IAL, who have competing perfected interests in the engine.

Section 9-312(5)(a), the catch-all priority section of Article 9, governs conflicts between competing perfected interests: Conflicting security interests rank according to priority in time of filing or perfection. Priority dates from the time a filing is first made covering the collateral or the time the security interest is first perfected, whichever is earlier, provided that there is no period thereafter when there is neither filing nor perfection. N.Y.U.C.C. Law § 9-312(5)(a) (McKinney Supp.1987). As previously discussed, section 1403 of the Federal Aviation Act requires filing with the Secretary of the FAA to perfect an interest in an aircraft engine. Therefore, time of filing is identical to time of perfection in the case before us. Under section 9-312(5)(a), the first to file an interest with the FAA will rank first in priority. It is undisputed that ATASCO filed its chattel mortgage with the FAA in March 1985, and IAL filed its interest on August 5, 1985. Therefore, under the first to file or perfect rule of section 9-312(5)(a), ATASCO's security interest in the engine has priority over IAL's interest. We therefore reverse the district court's grant of summary judgment in favor of IAL and the denial of ATASCO's motion for summary judgment as against IAL, and remand the case for a determination of damages.

B. CLARK, THE LAW OF SECURED TRANSACTIONS UNDER THE UNIFORM COMMERCIAL CODE ¶ 1.08[1][b], at 1-83 (Rev. ed. 1993). "The result [in *Aircraft Trading & Services*] seems wrong. Courts should read Articles 2 and 9 together whenever possible, and the court in this case should have done so by applying the shelter rule. In the case at hand, § 9-301(1)(c) clearly gave priority to [Braniff] and [Condren]. Why was this priority not passed on to [IAL] under the general notion that any right title or interest may be alienated unless some other legal provision prohibits it?"

HARRIS, THE INTERFACE BETWEEN ARTICLES 2A AND 9 UNDER THE OFFICIAL TEXT AND THE CALIFORNIA AMENDMENTS, 22 U.C.C. L.J. 99, 114 n.50 (1989). "Although the section 'subordinate[s]' the unperfected security interest to the rights of certain buyers, in that context subordination should be read as termination. * * * Aircraft Trading & Servs., Inc. v. Braniff, * * * which holds to the contrary, is wrong."

UCC § 2-403(1)

A purchaser of goods acquires all title which his transferor had or had power to transfer except that a purchaser of a limited interest acquires rights only to the extent of the interest purchased.

PEB COMMENTARY NO. 6, SECTION 9-301(1)

Underlying principles of fairness require a broad reading and a broad application of the shelter concept, even when not expressly stated. The importance of shelter is too great in the Code's scheme to support a narrow reading of the Code. Section 9-301(1) should be interpreted and applied in this circumstance to incorporate the shelter principle so that a member of a protected class who prevails thereunder can transfer what he has, even though the security interest which was unperfected when the transferor acquired his rights has since been perfected.

INTRODUCTORY NOTE ON *GARY AIRCRAFT*

The following case applies the shelter principle when a protected party, here a buyer in ordinary course, transfers his interest. As you read the case, assume, as the court held, that Stewart was a buyer who took free of the General Dynamic security interest. Given that holding, must the court not protect parties after Stewart? What good does it do to say that Stewart owns property, if the law does not protect his transferees? Would you buy property from someone who is an owner but who cannot guarantee that you will defeat adverse claimants? The right to transfer property is an integral feature of ownership.

GARY AIRCRAFT CORP. v. GENERAL DYNAMICS CORP. (IN RE GARY AIRCRAFT CORP.)

United States Court of Appeals, Fifth Circuit, 1982.
681 F.2d 365.

[Ayer, a dealer in airplanes, granted General Dynamics a security interest in all of its inventory under federal law, which governs the creation and perfection of security interests in aircraft. Subsequently, Ayer sold two of the planes to Stewart, who then transferred them, apparently without value, to his company, Gary Aircraft. When Ayer defaulted on its loan with General Dynamics, General Dynamics attempted to recover the two airplanes from Gary. Gary is in bankruptcy, and one of the planes was sold pursuant to the agreement of all parties with the understanding that the prevailing party would receive the proceeds of the sale.

The bankruptcy, district and appellate courts all held first that although federal law governs the creation and perfection of a security interest in an airplane, state law, in this case the UCC as enacted in Texas, governs priority disputes between secured parties such as General Dynamics and Gary, a purchaser of the airplanes. For that portion of the opinion dealing with the buyer in ordinary course rule of section 9-307(1), see page 51 infra.]

WISDOM, Circuit Judge.

* * *

The bankruptcy court, affirmed by the district court, held that Gary was entitled to the proceeds of the sale of Airplane N8222H and to the possession of Airplane N8221H, free of any interest asserted by General Dynamics. General Dynamics appeals, presenting three theories. First, it contends that the Federal Aviation Act grants it priority because it recorded its security interest with the Federal Aviation Administration before Stewart purchased the aircraft. Second, even if the FAA does not govern the priority question but instead remits it to Texas law, which protects a buyer in the ordinary course of business against the perfected security interest of his seller's creditor, General Dynamics argues that Stewart could not take free of its interest because, according to General Dynamics, Stewart could not qualify as a buyer in the ordinary course of business. Finally, General Dynamics contends that, even if Stewart did qualify as a buyer in the ordinary course, he could not transfer his status to Gary, and Gary did not qualify in its own right so, in Gary's hands, the aircraft are subject to the interest of General Dynamics. Concluding that the FAA does not govern priorities in interests in aircraft, that Stewart, as a buyer in the ordinary course of business, took free of General Dynamics's interest, and that Gary takes the title of its transferor, we affirm.

* * *

IV.

General Dynamics next argues that, even if Stewart qualifies as a buyer in the ordinary course of business, Gary cannot take good title for one of two reasons-first, the security interest was not created by Gary's seller and, second, Gary gave no consideration for the planes. Neither argument has merit.

The first argument is based on the limitation in section 9.307(a): a buyer in the ordinary course of business takes free of a security interest only if it was created by his seller. See, e.g., National Shawmut Bank v. Jones, 1967, 108 N.H. 386, 236 A.2d 484. General Dynamics, noting that the security interest it asserts was not created by Stewart (Gary's seller) but by Ayer, contends that Gary cannot be protected against that interest. This argument misses the mark, for Gary does not claim under section 9.307(a). On the contrary, its position is that Stewart took good title under section 9.307(a), and Gary, as Stewart's transferee, took whatever title Stewart had, under section 2.403(a), the "shelter" provision. It is therefore of no consequence that Gary's seller did not create the security interest. General Dynamics attempts to rebut this reasoning by relying on language in National Shawmut Bank stating that section 2-403 of the Uniform Commercial Code cannot provide an escape from the limitations of section 9-307. In National Shawmut Bank an individual sold a car, subject to a security interest, to a dealer, who then sold it to a buyer in the ordinary course of business. Since the security interest was not created by his seller, the last buyer in the chain could not take free and clear of the interest under section 9-307 of the UCC. Section 2.403(a) provides that a purchaser of goods acquires all title that his transferor had or had power to transfer, and that a seller with voidable title can transfer good title. If, under that provision, a retailer who bought subject to a security interest was one with voidable title and had the power to transfer good title, the "created by his seller" limitation of section 9.307(a) would be without any effect, so the National Shawmut Bank court held that section 2.403(a) does not provide an escape to section 9.307(a). That rule has been approved by the commentators, see J. White & R. Summers, Uniform Commercial Code § 25-15 (2d ed. 1980), and we do not question it. But the rule is that section 2.403(a) is not available to save one who buys when the seller's title is subject to a security interest but who does not qualify under section 9.307(a). It certainly does not mean that section 2.403(a) is not available to subsequent transferees from a successful section 9.307(a) buyer, as General Dynamics urges. See Skilton, Buyer in the Ordinary Course of Business under Article 9 of the Uniform Commercial Code, 1974 Wis.L.Rev. 1, 76 (viewing the point as "obvious"). If General Dynamics were correct, section 9.307(a) would be of scant benefit to the "protected" buyer in the ordinary course, for good title means little if one cannot transfer it. We hold that the lien of General Dynamics was extinguished upon the sale by Ayer to Stewart under section 9.307(a), and the subsequent sale to Gary could not resurrect it.

Finally, General Dynamics contends that Gary cannot take good title under section 2.403(a) because it furnished no consideration, receiving the aircraft as a gift.[1] We disagree. Section 2.403(a) applies to a "purchaser" of goods, and section 1.201 defines a "purchaser" as one who takes by "sale, discount, negotiation, mortgage, pledge, lien, issue or reissue, *gift* or any other voluntary transaction". §§ 1.201(32), (33) (emphasis added).[2] The language could not be clearer. When the draftsmen of the Code wished to require consideration, they used the terms "buyer", "seller", and "sale", defined in sections 2.106(a) and 2.103(a)(1) to require consideration, instead of "purchaser", "transferor", and "purchase". See, e.g., §§ 2.313, 2.314, 2.315. We cannot imagine applying any rule other than that a donee takes the title that his donor had.

PROBLEM

On May 1, Seller granted First Bank a security interest in a metal stamping machine. On May 2, Seller sold and delivered the machine to Buyer. [See UCC § 9-301(1)(c).] On May 3, Buyer granted a security interest to Second Bank. On May 4, First Bank perfected its security interest by filing. On May 5, Second Bank perfected its security interest by filing. [See UCC § 9-312(5)(a).] Both banks claim the machine.

---

1 It is not clear how this argument would help General Dynamics if we accepted it. As we have already established, the sale to Stewart extinguished General Dynamics's lien. Even if Gary took less than good title from Stewart, we do not see how that would resurrect an extinguished lien; it would mean that Stewart retained some interest.

2 Although chapter 2 is entitled "Sales", § 2.101, it expressly regulates purchasers in section 2.403, and adopts the general definition of "purchaser" from chapter 1, see § 2.103(d). Furthermore, under section 2.102, the scope of chapter 2 is defined as "transactions in goods", with no requirement of consideration. See generally J. White & R. Summers, Uniform Commercial Code § 1-1 at 22 (2d ed. 1980) (differentiating between "transactions in goods" and "sales"); T. Quinn, Uniform Commercial Code Commentary and Law Digest P 2.102(A) (1978).

If § 9-301(1)(c) applies, which bank wins?

If § 9-312(5)(a) applies, which bank wins?

When two statutory provisions yield different results, should the more specific govern?

QUESTIONS

1. Why do Professors Clark and Harris disagree with the result in *Aircraft Trading*? Would they apply § 9-301 or § 9-312 in the preceding problem? We think they were right about *Aircraft Trading* and that they would apply § 9-301(1)(c). [If you agree, you see that literal application of the Code or of rules for statutory construction, can yield the "wrong" commercial result.]
2. What do the following statutory excerpts and the *Vitols* case have in common?

UCC § 2A-301

Except as otherwise provided in this Article, a lease contract is effective and enforceable according to its terms between the parties, against purchasers of the goods and against creditors of the parties.

UCC § 3-203(b)

Transfer of an instrument, whether or not the transfer is a negotiation, vests in the transferee any right of the transferor to enforce the instrument, including any right as a holder in due course * * *.

VITOLS v. CITIZENS BANKING CO., 10 F.3d 1227 (6th Cir. 1993). Limited partners in a real estate development venture gave the partnership negotiable promissory notes with the understanding that the venture would use the notes as security for a loan to finance the project. This was a common device for financing "deals" in the '80s and has continued into the '90s. The partnership endorsed the notes to Fleet National Bank, which subsequently assigned them to Citizens Bank. When the partnership defaulted on its loan, the promisors on the notes sued for a declaratory judgment that the holder of the notes, Citizens, could not collect them. The plaintiffs argued that Citizens was "closely connected" to the partnership and that the close connectedness doctrine of negotiable instruments law applied against Citizens. Under that doctrine, the law of negotiable instruments denies to a holder the protection of a holder in due course on the theory that the holder was too closely involved in the underlying transaction to benefit from the full range of holder-in-due-course protection. "As to the notes executed by Mr. Vitols and most of the other plaintiffs in the case at bar, it may well be that the short answer to the close-connectedness question is this: the plaintiffs have pointed to no evidence whatever of any unusually close relationship between [the partnership] and the entity from which Citizens Banking acquired the notes in question, Fleet National Bank. If Fleet was a holder in due course, so was any subsequent holder that had not been a holder before and had not been a party to any fraud or illegality. U.C.C. 3-201(1)."

UCC § 7-504(1)

A transferee of a document, whether negotiable or non-negotiable, to whom the document has been delivered but not duly negotiated, acquires the title and rights which his transferor had or had actual authority to convey.

UCC § 9-201

Except as otherwise provided in this Act a security agreement is effective according to its terms between the parties, against purchasers of the collateral and against creditors.

UCC § 9-306(2)

Except where this Article otherwise provides, a security interest continues in collateral notwithstanding sale, exchange, or other disposition thereof . * * *

Chapter 2

GOOD FAITH PURCHASE

INTRODUCTORY NOTE

The second conveyancing rule, good faith purchase, sometimes called "security of purchase," is the law's response to commercial exigencies that conflict with security of property. Here we see courts and the Code doing deliberate damage to the security of property concept that was so indispensable in the war against brigands and frauds. Note also the willing violence good faith purchase doctrine deals to the logic of ownership.

This chapter is only an introduction to good faith purchase. Later chapters deal with it and its conflict with security of property, as the law fashions and refashions rules that balance these two irreconcilable features of conveyancing law.

SECTION 1. NECESSITY

2 BLACKSTONE'S COMMENTARIES *449. "But [title] may also in some cases be transferred by sale, though the vendor *hath none at all* in the goods; for it is expedient that the buyer, by taking proper precautions, may at all events be secure of his purchase; otherwise all commerce between man and man must soon be at an end." (Emphasis in original)

GILMORE, THE COMMERCIAL DOCTRINE OF GOOD FAITH PURCHASE, 63 Yale L.J. 1057, 1057 (1954).

The triumph of the good faith purchaser has been one of the most dramatic episodes in our legal history. In his several guises, he serves a commercial function: he is protected not because of his praiseworthy character, but to the end that commercial transactions may be engaged in without elaborate investigation of property rights and in reliance on the possession of property by one who offers it for sale or to secure a loan. * * *

The initial common law position was that equities of ownership are to be protected at all costs: an owner may never be deprived of his property rights without his consent. That worked well enough against a background of local distribution where seller and buyer met face to face and exchanged goods for cash. But as the marketplace became first regional and then national, a recurrent situation came to be the misappropriation of goods by a faithless agent in fraud of his principal. Classical theory required that the principal be protected and that the risks of agency distribution be cast on the purchaser. The market demanded otherwise.

SECTION 2. JUSTIFICATION

DOLAN, THE U.C.C. FRAMEWORK: CONVEYANCING PRINCIPLES AND PROPERTY INTERESTS, 59 B.U. L. Rev. 811, 813-14 (1979). "In direct opposition to the security of property postulate that one cannot give what one does not have, the good faith purchase rule permits the taker to receive interests greater than those his transferor possessed. Courts have rationalized this departure from the logic of the shelter principle in two ways. Some assert that it is a question of fault or negligence of the true owner or his creditor. These cases emphasize the culpability of a property owner who does not take care to protect his interest in the property when introducing it into the channels of commerce. He thereby misleads an innocent purchaser who relies on the appearance that the owner's negligence has created. Other courts view the issue as essentially an economic one. These cases opt for the good faith purchase principle as commercially convenient and regard indiscriminate use of the security of property approach as wasteful."

PHILLIPS, THE COMMERCIAL CULPABILITY SCALE, 92 Yale L.J. 228, 228-29 (1982). "[t]he Code provisions evince a pattern that I term the 'culpability scale.' The culpability scale identifies a hierarchical set of rules to allocate loss. These rules are based upon the mental state, conduct, or position of the parties involved. Most culpable are those who violate the 'intention principle': persons who intentionally create the event or situation that gives rise to possible loss by someone more innocent. If no one who intentionally created the loss-causing event can be discovered, loss is allocated based on a 'knowledge principle' to that party who knew of the relevant circumstances. In the absence of a party with intent or knowledge, loss is allocated according to the 'negligence principle' to that party who reasonably could have discovered the event or situation before acting or who otherwise failed to exercise due care. Finally, if no greater level of culpability is present, the loss is distributed under the 'strict liability principle' to that party who could have avoided the loss at least cost."

WEINBERG, MARKETS OVERT, VOIDABLE TITLES, AND FECKLESS AGENTS: JUDGES AND EFFICIENCY IN THE ANTEBELLUM DOCTRINE OF GOOD FAITH PURCHASE, 56 Tul. L. Rev. 1, 4-5 (1981).

Coke * * * wrote that "the common Law did hold it for a point of great policie, and [advantageous] for the Commonwealth, the Faires and Markets overt should be replenished and well furnished with all manner of commodities * * * for the necessary [sustenance] and use of the people." Markets and fairs were so beneficial that it was essential "to incourage men thereunto."

Blackstone and Coke also described two exceptions to the doctrine, both reflecting the impact of property crime. First, if a thief was prosecuted to conviction the owner was entitled to the return of his goods. Second, there were statutory formalities that had to be complied with in order to pass title to horses. Coke explained the first exception as intended to encourage the owner to pursue the felon so that he might be punished. He believed that the "old rule, Caveat emptor" was preferable in the "rare case" where the exception would result in a loss to a good faith purchaser. Coke's discussion also indicates that, in general, owners were expected to minimize the risk that stolen goods might pass into the hands of good faith purchasers by reclaiming them before they were sold. Stolen horses were the subject of the second exception because even vigilant owners could not act fast enough to prevent their sale in some distant market or fair.

Blackstone's and Coke's statements suggest an intuitive understanding of economic values, many of which were to be considered by antebellum judges deciding whether the market overt doctrine would be received in America. Their calculus reflects risks connected with the theft and the good faith purchase of stolen goods and the possibility that these costs might be reduced by both owners and purchasers through the adoption of protective measures. Their statements also recognize how a decision rule governing disputes between owners and good faith purchasers might affect criminal and legitimate commercial activity. All these considerations provide the ingredients for an economic rationale for or against good faith purchaser protection. Gains from trade must be balanced against the costs of increased criminal activity. The relative capacities of owners and good faith purchasers to reduce the risk that stolen goods might pass from the former group into the hands of the latter must also be considered.

SECTION 3. SALES OF GOODS

UCC § 2-403(1)

A person with voidable title has power to transfer a good title to a good faith purchaser for value. (Cf. UCC § 2A-304(1) (similar rule for leases).)

NOTE

The *Cundy* case that follows reflects an early attempt to link a good faith purchase rule (the doctrine of voidable title) to intent and to the logic of ownership. Ultimately the effort failed, as section 2-403(1) and the questions that follow *Cundy* illustrate.

CUNDY v. LINDSAY

House of Lords, 1878.
3 App. Cas. 459.

[In 1873 Alfred Blenkarn fraudulently induced Lindsay, a Belfast partnership, to ship to him in London linen handkerchiefs on credit. The jury found that Lindsay thought it was shipping to Blenkiron & Co., which was located in the neighborhood of Blenkarn, and that Blenkarn had used his similar address with the intention of confusing and fraudulently inducing Lindsay to ship the goods on credit. Subsequently, Blenkarn sold some of the goods to Cundy, who took the goods in good faith, for value, and without notice that they were obtained by Blenkarn through fraud. Blenkarn was apprehended, convicted and sentenced, all without paying Lindsay, who brought this action against Cundy for conversion of the goods.]

THE LORD CHANCELLOR (Lord Cairns).

My Lords, you have in this case to discharge a duty which is always a disagreeable one for any Court, namely, to determine as between two parties, both of whom are perfectly innocent, upon which of the two the consequences of a fraud practiced upon both of them must fall. My Lords, in discharging that duty your Lordships can do no more than apply, rigorously, the settled and well known rules of law. Now, with regard to the title to personal property, the settled and well known rules of law may, I take it, be thus expressed: by the law of our country the purchaser of a chattel takes the chattel as a general rule subject to what may turn out to be certain infirmities in the title. If he purchases the chattel in market overt, he obtains a title which is good against all the world; but if he does not purchase the chattel in market overt, and if it turns out that the chattel has been found by the person who professed to sell it, the purchaser will not obtain a title good as against the real owner. If it turns out that the chattel has been stolen by the person who has professed to sell it, the purchaser will not obtain a title. If it turns out that the chattel has come into the hands of the person who professed to sell it, by a *de facto contract*, that is to say, a contract which has purported to pass the property to him from the owner of the property, there the purchaser will obtain a good title, even although afterwards it should appear that there were circumstances connected with the contract, which would enable the original owner of the goods to reduce it, and to set it aside, because these circumstances so enabling the original owner of the goods, or of the chattel, to reduce the contract and to set it aside, will not be allowed to interfere with a title for valuable consideration obtained by some third party during the interval while the contract remained unreduced.

My Lords, the question, therefore, in the present case, as your Lordships will observe, really becomes the very short and simple one which I am about to state. Was there any contract which, with regard to the goods in question in this case, had passed the property in the goods from the *Messrs. Lindsay* to *Alfred Blenkarn*! If there was any contract passing that property, even although, as I have said, that contract might afterwards be open to a process of reduction, upon the ground of fraud, still, in the meantime, *Blenkarn* might have conveyed a good title for valuable consideration to the present Appellants.

Now, my Lords, there are two observations bearing upon the solution of that question which I desire to make. In the first place, if the property in the goods in question passed, it could only pass by way of contract; there is nothing else which could have passed the property. The second observation is this, your Lordships are not here embarrassed by any conflict of evidence, or any evidence whatever as to conversations or as to acts done, the whole history of the whole transaction lies upon paper. The principal parties concerned, the Respondents and *Blenkarn*, never came in contract personally—everything that was done was done by writing. What has to be judged of, and what the jury in the present case had to judge of, was merely the conclusion to be derived from that writing, as applied to the admitted facts of the case.

Now, my Lords, discharging that duty and answering that inquiry, what the jurors have found is in substance this: it is not necessary to spell out the words, because the substance of it is beyond all doubt. They have found that by the form of the signatures to the letters which were written by *Blenkarn*, by the mode in which his letters and his applications to the Respondents were made out, and by the way in which he left uncorrected the mode and form in which, in turn, he was addressed by the Respondents; that by all those means he led, and intended to lead, the Respondents to believe, and they did believe, that the person with whom they were communicating was not *Blenkarn*, the dishonest and irresponsible man, but was a well known and solvent house of *Blenkiron & Co.*, doing business in the same street. My Lords those things are found as matters of fact, and they are placed beyond the range of dispute and controversy in the case.

If that is so, what is the consequence? It is that *Blenkarn*—the dishonest man, as I call him—was acting here just in the same way as if he had forged the signature of *Blenkiron & Co.*, the respectable firm, to the applications for goods, and as if, when, in return, the goods were forwarded and letters were sent, accompanying them, he had intercepted the goods and intercepted the letters, and had taken possession of the goods, and of the letters which were addressed to, and intended for, not himself but the firm of *Blenkiron & Co.* Now, my Lords, stating the matter shortly in that way, I ask the question, how is it possible to imagine that in that state of things any contract could have arisen between the Respondents and *Blenkarn* the dishonest man? Of him they knew nothing, and of him they never thought. With him they never intended to deal. Their minds never, even for an instant of time rested upon him, and as between him and them there was no consensus of mind which could lead to any agreement of any contract whatever. As between him and them there was merely the one side to a contract, where, in order to produce a contract, two sides would be required. With the firm of *Blenkiron & Co.* of course there was no contract, for as to them the matter was entirely unknown, and therefore the pretence of a contract was a failure.

The result, therefore, my Lords, is this, that your Lordships have not here to deal with one of those cases in which there is *de facto* a contract made which may afterwards be impeached and set aside, on the ground of fraud; but you have to deal with a case which ranges itself under a completely different chapter of law, the case namely in which the contract never comes into existence. My Lords, that being so, it is idle to talk of the property passing. The property remained, as it originally had been, the property of the Respondents, and the title which was attempted to be given to the Appellants was a title which could not be given to them.

My Lords, I therefore move your Lordships that this appeal be dismissed with costs, and the judgment of the Court of Appeal affirmed.

LORD HATHERLEY: —

My Lords, I have come to the same conclusion as that which has just been expressed by my noble and learned friend on the woolsack.

* * *

LORD PENZANCE: —

* * *

I am not aware, my Lords, that there is any decided case in which a sale and delivery intended to be made to one man, has been held to be a sale and delivery so as to pass the property to another, against the intent and will of the vendor.

* * *

The appeal ought therefore, in my opinion, to be dismissed.

LORD GORDON Concurred.

Judgment appealed from affirmed; and appeal dismissed with costs.

QUESTIONS

Can you state the doctrine of voidable title? Do you learn the contours of the doctrine from the *Cundy* case or from section 2-403(1)? Do subsections (1)(a) through (1)(d) describe all of the situations that fall within the doctrine? If not, how do the Code drafters expect lawyers to understand the rule of the section; and why did the drafters only mention four instances of voidable title and not all instances? Does the Code presuppose a body of commercial law that exists outside the Code and assume that those using the Code are familiar with that body of law?

KING, NEW CONCEPTUALISM OF THE UNIFORM COMMERCIAL CODE: ETHICS, TITLE, AND GOOD FAITH PURCHASE, 11 St. Louis U. L.J. 15, 38-39 (1966). "Painstaking efforts were made to determine when there was 'voidable title.' * * * With the continued development of this concept, some rather ridiculous results occurred. Where an imposter wrongfully obtained goods in person, in a face-to-face transaction with the owner, it was said by some courts that the owner primarily intended to pass title to the particular 'person' in front of him, more than to the person of that real name. Therefore the imposter was said to have gained 'voidable' title which could be passed to a good faith purchaser. Upon this passage the purchaser cut off the former owner's equitable rights and gained good title. On the other hand if the imposter committed his deceit through the mails, it was said by some courts that the owner intended to pass title primarily to the real person mentioned in the letter rather than to the imposter himself. This being so, it was said that no title, not even voidable title, passed to the imposter. The good faith purchaser who then bought the goods did not gain good title."

NOTE

Cundy applies an early good faith purchase rule that courts adopted for the sale of goods and that the Code modifies somewhat. The next case applies a rule of good faith purchase in the sale of goods context that common law courts usually rejected but that the Code embraces in § 2-403(2).

CARLSEN v. RIVERA

Court of Appeals of Florida, 1980.
382 So.2d 825, 29 U.C.C. Rep. Serv. 500.

[Rivera, a Quebec auto lessor, leased a 1976 Mercedes Benz 450 SL to James McEnroe, an automobile dealer – a fact known to Rivera at the time of the lease transaction. Through fraud, McEnroe obtained a certificate of title for the vehicle, and he used that certificate in a contract to sell the car to Expo. Expo entered into a contract to sell it to Marlin, which entered into a contract to sell it in turn to Carlsen, who was in possession when McEnroe defaulted on the lease. Rivera brought an action in replevin against Carlsen.]

HERSEY, Judge.

* * *

The controlling provision of the Florida Uniform Commercial Code is Section 672.403, Florida Statutes (1977), which provides: Power to transfer; good faith purchase of goods; "entrusting." * * * (2) Any entrusting of possession of goods to a merchant who deals in goods of that kind gives him power to transfer all rights of the entruster to a buyer in ordinary course of business. (3) "Entrusting" includes any delivery and any acquiescence in retention of possession regardless of any condition expressed between the parties to the delivery or acquiescence and regardless of whether the procurement of the entrusting or the possessor's disposition of the goods have been such as to be larcenous under the criminal law.

Initially, it is necessary to determine whether there was an entrustment of the automobile. Both under the Code and under prior case law McEnroe could not convey good title or even voidable title if he had stolen the automobile. Section 672.403, Florida Statutes (1977); Avis Rent-A-Car, Inc. v. Harrison Motor Co., 151 So.2d 855 (Fla.2d DCA 1963). While it is true that McEnroe is said to have stolen the automobile, he acquired possession lawfully by virtue of the lease agreement. He then committed larceny by forging the title documents, and converted the automobile by selling it. The distinction is that he obtained possession lawfully and could therefore convey a voidable title which could be perfected upon a sale to a buyer in the ordinary course of business. The statutes make it very clear that any delivery of possession and any acquiescence in retention of possession constitutes entrustment under the statute. This would obviously include a lease arrangement.

Having concluded that there was an entrustment, the second question to be answered is whether McEnroe was a merchant who deals in goods of that kind.

The record discloses that McEnroe was actively engaged in the business of selling automobiles. The trial court apparently considered the fact that the lease recited McEnroe's home address rather than his business address as conclusively establishing the intention of the lessor to lease the automobile to McEnroe the individual rather than to McEnroe the automobile dealer. Even assuming this was the intention of the parties to that transaction, the statute clearly does not look to intent but to effect. It is undisputed that McEnroe was in the business of selling cars. In our view that is determinative of this issue. The purpose of this section of the Uniform Commercial Code is to protect the buyer in the ordinary course of business and thus to eliminate impediments to the free flow of commerce. One analysis of this area of the code expressed it in the following language:

> The use of * * * doctrines to protect the original owners was frequently criticized; to permit the owner's intent to dictate the decision appeared to ignore the rights of the good faith purchaser rather than to weigh them against the owner's rights. This was regarded as unfair to the purchasers and harmful to the commercial objective of fostering a free flow of goods.
>
> * * *
>
> The Code broadens the entrusting doctrine * * * (and) the intent of the owner, which had been respected in prior law, appears disregarded under this provision of the Code. Note, the Owners Intent and the Negotiability of Chattels: A Critique of Section 2-403 of the Uniform Commercial Code, 72 Yale Law J. 1205.

Quite clearly, then, there was an entrustment of the automobile to a merchant who dealt in goods of that kind.

If McEnroe had sold directly to Carlsen for valid consideration and without notice of the defect in title, then Carlsen would prevail as against the interests of the owner/entrustor. Should the result be any different because of the existence of intervening sales? We think not. Carlsen purchased the automobile from Marlin Imports, Inc., which was engaged in the business of selling automobiles. Carlsen had no notice of any defect in the title and in fact obtained a title certificate. Under these circumstances, Carlsen was clearly a buyer in the ordinary course of business. In pre-Code language, McEnroe conveyed voidable title to Expo, who conveyed voidable title to Marlin, who conveyed voidable title to Carlsen, a bona fide purchaser for value without notice. The Uniform Commercial Code does not change the result. The buyer in the ordinary course of business obtains good title by virtue of Subsection 2 of Section 672.403, Florida Statutes (1977).

We therefore reverse the final judgment and remand the cause for such further proceedings as may be necessary to enable the trial court to enter a judgment in accordance with the foregoing.

DOLAN, THE UNIFORM COMMERCIAL CODE AND THE CONCEPT OF POSSESSION IN THE MARKETING AND FINANCING OF GOODS, 56 Tex. L. Rev. 1147, 1170-71 (1978).

Commercial lawyers have also recognized the unfairness of permitting a true owner to clothe another with the appearance of ownership and then deny the implications of that appearance. Manifest in a number of separate rules, this recognition has roots in estoppel and agency doctrines and results directly from the notion that possession connotes ownership.

The development of this rule has been somewhat tortuous. Originally, the true owner lost to a buyer only if the owner permitted the entrustee to mislead the buyer. Possession alone was insufficient, but possession with a bill of sale or with the entrustee's name emblazoned on the goods sufficed. Gradually, commercial lawyers came to accept the view of Lord Ellenborough in *Pickering v. Busk*, that an entrustor who delivers goods to a merchant dealer in those goods will not be heard to say he delivered them without authority to sell. Section 2-403(2) codifies this rule.

It is customary to justify the rule in terms of fault. Both true owner and buyer are innocent of wrongdoing, the merchant being the culprit. Yet either the true owner or the buyer must suffer loss of the goods, with the merchant's fisc as his only resort. Courts rise to the occasion with relish and announce that the true owner, having put his trust in the wrongdoer, should bear the loss.

Some have rejected this analysis on the grounds that both buyer and true owner trusted the merchant and that the rule is essentially one of allocating loss in a fashion that facilitates commerce.

QUESTION

Is a good faith purchaser from a thief less innocent than a good faith purchaser from a fraud? How do you justify commercial law's differentiation between purchasers from thieves and purchasers from frauds? Does Professor Phillips' culpability scale apply here? Professor Weinberg's economic analysis?

PICKERING v. BUSK

Court of King's Bench, 1812.
104 Eng. Rep. 758.

LORD ELLENBOROUGH, C.J.

It cannot fairly be questioned in this case but that Swallow had an implied authority to sell. Strangers can only look to the acts of the parties, and to the external indicia of property, and not to the private communications which may pass between a principal and his broker: and if a person authorizes another to assume the apparent right of disposing of property in the ordinary course of trade, it must be presumed that the apparent authority is the real authority. I cannot subscribe to the doctrine, that a broker's engagements are necessarily and in all cases limited to his actual authority, the reality of which is afterwards to be tried by the fact. It is clear that he may bind his principal with the limits of the authority with which he has been apparently clothed by the principal in respect of the subject-matter; and there would be no safety in mercantile transactions if he could not. If the principal sends his commodity to a place, where it is the ordinary business of the person to whom it is confided to sell, it must be intended that the commodity was sent thither for the purpose of sale. If the owner of a horse sends it to a repository of sale, can it be implied that he sent it thither for any other purpose than that of sale? Or if one send goods to an auction-room, can it be supposed that he sent them thither merely for safe custody? Where the commodity is sent in such a way and to such a place as to exhibit an apparent purpose of sale, the principal will be bound, and the purchaser safe. The case of a factor not being able to pledge the goods of his principal confided to him for sale, though clothed with an apparent ownership, has been pressed upon us in the argument, and considerably distressed our decision. The Court, however, will decide that question when it arises, consistently with the principle on which the present decision is founded. It was a hard doctrine when the pawnee was told that the pledger of the goods had no authority to pledge them, being a mere factor for sale; and yet since the case of Paterson v. Tash, that doctrine has never been overturned. I remember Mr. Wallace arguing in Campbell v. Wright that the bills of lading ought to designate the consignee as factor, otherwise it was but just that the consignors should abide by the consequence of having misled the pawnees. The present case, however, is not the case of a pawn, but that of a sale by a broker having the possession for the purpose of sale. The sale was made by a person who had all the indicia of property: the hemp could only have been transferred into his name for the purpose of sale; and the party who has so transferred it cannot now rescind the contract. If the plaintiff had intended to retain the dominion over the hemp, he should have placed it in the wharfinger's books in his own name.

GROSE, J.

The question, whether the plaintiff is bound by the act of Swallow, depends upon the authority which Swallow had. This being a mercantile transaction, the jury were most competent to decide it; and if I had entertained any doubt, I should rather have referred the question to them for their determination: but I am perfectly satisfied: I think Swallow had a power to sell.

LEBLANC, J.

The law is clearly laid down, that the mere possession of personal property does not convey a title to dispose of it; and which is equally clear, that the possession of a factor or broker does not authorize him to pledge. But this is a case of sale. The question then is whether Swallow had an authority to sell. To decide this, let us look at the situation of the parties. Swallow was a general seller of hemp; the hemp in question was left in the custody of the wharfingers, part in the name of Swallow, and part in the name of the plaintiff or Swallow, which is the same thing. Now for what purpose could the plaintiff leave it in the name of Swallow, but that Swallow might dispose of it in his ordinary business as broker: if so, the broker having sold the hemp, the principal is bound. This is distinguishable from all the cases, where goods are left in the custody of person, whose proper business it is not to sell.

BAYLEY, J.

It may be admitted that the plaintiff did not give Swallow any express authority to sell; but an implied authority may be given: and if a person put goods into the custody of another, whose common business it is to sell, without limiting his authority, he thereby confers an implied authority upon him to sell them. Swallow was in the habit of buying and selling hemp for others, concealing their names. And now the plaintiff claims a liberty to rescind the contract, because no express authority was given to Swallow to sell. But is it competent to him so to do? If the servant of a horse-dealer with express directions not to warrant, do warrant, the master has not notified to the world that the general authority is circumscribed. This case does not proceed on the ground of a sale in market overt, but it proceeds on the principle, that the plaintiff having given Swallow an authority to sell, he is not at liberty afterwards, when there has been a sale, to deny the authority.

NOTE ON CERTIFICATE OF TITLE LAWS

At times, commercial rules run headlong into the police power. What happens, for instance, if the law of a jurisdiction requires buyers of automobiles to obtain a certificate of title from the seller (in the case of a used car) or a certificate of origin that the buyer uses to obtain a certificate of title from the State. In many jurisdictions, helpful automobile dealers take an application for certificate of title from their buyers and send the old title or the certificate of origin along with the application to the State, which issues the new certificate. For a number of reasons, that practice is efficient. What if the dealer or other seller is lax or dishonest? Does the policy of the Code or the legislative exercise of the police power determine the outcome? The following case and the note case that comes after it yield different answers.

THORN v. ADAMS

Court of Appeals of Oregon, 1993.
125 Ore. App. 257, 865 P.2d 417.

LEESON, Judge.

Defendant appeals from a judgment for plaintiff based on the trial court's grant of plaintiff's motion for summary judgment and its denial of her cross-motion for summary judgment. The issue is whether, under ORS 72.4030(3), a buyer in the ordinary course of business acquires legal title to an automobile purchased from a merchant entrusted with the vehicle, even though the buyer did not acquire the certificate of title. We hold that such a buyer acquires legal title, and affirm.

Defendant purchased a car in 1989. On April 15, 1992, her son-in-law, Richard, took the car to Gateley's Fairway Motors (Gateley's), a car dealership that also performed repairs. As defendant's authorized agent, Richard requested an estimate of the car's value, and left it for repairs. Several days later, plaintiff saw the car on Gateley's lot, next to several cars for sale. Gateley's allowed her to take the car for a test drive, and later sold it to her. Gateley's never informed plaintiff that it had no authority to sell the car, nor did it indicate that the car was anything other than inventory.

When Richard learned of the sale, he demanded that plaintiff return the car. She refused, and brought this action for an injunction requiring defendant to deliver the certificate of title to her. She also sought damages for conversion, based on defendant's refusal to surrender the certificate of title. Defendant counterclaimed for an order requiring plaintiff to surrender possession of the car, or, in the alternative, to require plaintiff to pay defendant the reasonable market value of the car.

Both parties moved for summary judgment. The trial court denied defendant's motion and granted plaintiff's motion. It ordered defendant to surrender the certificate of title and to take such other actions as reasonably necessary to register the vehicle in plaintiff's name.

Summary judgment should be granted only when there is no genuine issue of material fact and the moving party is entitled to judgment as a matter of law. The parties agree that there is no genuine issue of material fact. The only dispute is which party was entitled to judgment as a matter of law.

Plaintiff bases her claim of legal ownership on ORS 72.4030, the provision of the Oregon Uniform Commercial Code commonly known as the "entrustment principle." ORS 72.4030(3) provides: "Any entrusting of possession of goods to a merchant who deals in goods of that kind gives the merchant power to transfer all rights of the entruster to a buyer in ordinary course of business." Under ORS 72.4030(4), "'[e]ntrusting' includes any delivery and any acquiescence in retention of possession regardless of any condition expressed between the parties to the delivery or acquiescence and regardless of whether the procurement of the entrusting of the possessor's disposition of the goods have been such as to be larcenous under the criminal law." Plaintiff contends that defendant entrusted the car to Gateley's, which was a merchant that dealt in goods of that kind, and, therefore, that Gateley's had the power to transfer all rights in the car to her as a buyer in the ordinary course of business.

Defendant concedes that the entrustment principle gives merchants the power to pass good title even when the merchant has no authority to sell the goods, but argues that that principle does not apply. She contends that ORS 803.094(1) provides the exclusive method for transferring legal title to a vehicle that has a certificate of title. That statute provides, in part: "Except as otherwise provided in this section, *upon the transfer of any interest* shown on an Oregon certificate of title any person whose interest is released, terminated, assigned or transferred, shall release or assign that interest on the title certificate." (Emphasis supplied.) Nothing in the plain language of the statute describes or limits the methods that may be used to transfer an interest shown on an Oregon certificate of title. Rather, the statute describes what must be done once the transfer has occurred. By its terms, ORS 803.094(1) does not prevent or invalidate a transfer of interest that takes place under ORS 72.4030(3).

Defendant argues that, even if the entrustment principle of ORS 72.4030 applies, plaintiff still was not entitled to judgment as a matter of law, because she was not a buyer in the ordinary course of business. According to ORS 71.2010(9), "'[b]uyer in ordinary course of business' means a person who in good faith and without knowledge that the sale to the person is in violation of the ownership rights * * * of a third party in the goods buys in ordinary course from a person in the business of selling goods of that kind * * * ."

Good faith is defined as "honesty in fact in the conduct or transaction concerned." ORS 71.2010(19).

Defendant argues that plaintiff could not have acted with honesty in fact, because no legal title can be conveyed at the time of the purchase without a concurrent transfer of the certificate of title. She contends that plaintiff was put on notice that there was something unusual in the transaction when she failed to obtain a certificate of title at the same time she purchased the vehicle.

We disagree. Nothing in the motor vehicle statutes required plaintiff to take possession of the certificate of title at the moment she purchased the car in order to acquire legal title. Absent such a requirement, plaintiff's "failure" to obtain the certificate of title at the moment that she purchased the car is not unreasonable, and does not put plaintiff on notice that the transaction was "unusual." Defendant provides no other support for her contention that plaintiff was not a buyer in the ordinary course of business.

Finally, defendant argues that it is unfair to place motor vehicle owners at the mercy of the entrustment principle. That choice was made by the legislature when it adopted ORS 72.4030(3), which mirrors section 2-402(3) of the Uniform Commercial Code. 1 Bailey, *Oregon Uniform Commercial Code* § 2.92 (2d ed. 1990). The entrustment principle promotes one of the basic goals of commerce:

"In most cases the equities between the entruster-owner and the buyer in the ordinary course are equal, and the balance is tipped in favor of the latter because that frees the marketplace and promotes commerce. This goal, called 'security of transactions[,]' is an ideal of the commercial law. The protection of property rights * * * is not an ideal of the commercial law. * * * On the assumption that both the entruster and buyer have been equally victimized by the dishonesty of the merchant-dealer, section 2-403(2) resolves the issue so as to free the marketplace, rather than protect the original owner's property rights." 2 Hawkland, UCC Series § 2.403:07 (1992). The trial court did not err in granting plaintiff's motion for summary judgment and in denying defendant's motion.

Affirmed.

NOTE ON *THORN v. ADAMS*

Not all courts accept the rule that Code buyer protection rules trump vehicle certificate of title laws. In Ladd v. Ford Consumer Finance Co., 550 N.W.2d 826 (Mich. Ct. App. 1996), the court held that section 9-307(1) did not protect a buyer in ordinary course when the buyer did not insist that the seller comply with Michigan's certificate of title law relating to mobile homes.

At a drafting session the next January, the reporter for Article 2 made a change in the buyer in ordinary course rule of Article 2 providing that a buyer in ordinary course of goods subject to a certificate of title law would be protected even though the seller of the goods failed to comply with the certificate of title law. See § 2-104(a)(1) & cmt. 2 (Discussion Draft, April 14, 1997).

UCC § 9-307(1)

A buyer in ordinary course of business (subsection (9) of Section 1-201) * * * takes free of a security interest created by his seller even though the security interest is perfected and even though the buyer knows of its existence.

QUESTION

How can a court know whether to promote specific legislation such as certificate of title legislation over the Code? Many courts, in fact, most of them, have limited the title impact of the certificate laws by applying the Code's buyer protection rules. How might a lawyer arguing such a case fashion the question and what arguments can the lawyer raise in support of the proposition that the Code should govern?

SECTION 4. LEASES

BAIRD & JACKSON, POSSESSION AND OWNERSHIP: AN EXAMINATION OF THE SCOPE OF ARTICLE 9, 35 Stan. L. Rev. 175, 178 (1983). "Instead of either relying on metaphysical ideas about where 'title' to a particular property rests or deferring to contractual divisions of property rights between two parties, judges and legislators should be sensitive to the costs imposed on third parties by the separation of ownership and possession whenever those costs exist. * * * [A] failure to appreciate these costs is responsible for a number of the most troublesome problems that have arisen under Article 9. Yet, once one realizes that these problems have a common source, simple solutions to them become apparent. In proposing these simple solutions to problems that have consumed hundreds of pages of law review commentary, we are not advocating a radical departure from established wisdom. Rather, we are urging only that rulemakers apply more generally the principle that has shaped the law of security interests in personal property for four hundred years: A party who wishes to acquire or retain a nonpossessory interest in property that is effective against others must, as a general matter, make it possible for others to discover that interest."

UCC § 2A-301, Official Comment 2

The effectiveness or enforceability of the lease contract is not dependent upon the lease contract or any financing statement or the like being filed or recorded * * * .

MOONEY, THE MYSTERY AND MYTH OF "OSTENSIBLE OWNERSHIP" AND ARTICLE 9 FILING: A CRITIQUE OF PROPOSALS TO EXTEND FILING REQUIREMENTS TO LEASES, 39 Ala. L. Rev. 683, 788-89 (1988).

It is distressing that we know so little about the "real world" functions, effects, and operations of the existing Article 9 filing requirements. It is especially troublesome, therefore, to embrace an expansion of those requirements to other transactions beyond traditional bounds. There exist fundamental unresolved issues concerning the operation of credit markets and the role of possession of goods and the behavioral relationships between the two. The existing information base is too thin.

Further study of bailments, including leases, provides an exceptional opportunity for gaining greater understanding of the role of filing for secured transactions under Article 9. A bailment of goods and a security interest in goods each usually involves possession by a debtor or lessee. Existing law provides a laboratory for examination of both the impact of a filing requirement and the effects of an absence of a filing requirement.

QUESTION

Arguably, Article 9 imposes filing requirements on a secured party so that subsequent creditors will know that the debtor's goods have been transferred as security for a loan. A lender that takes a security interest in an aluminum fabricator's fabricating equipment, therefore, must file a financing statement in a public office, so that the fabricator's creditors know that the equipment is encumbered. A subsequent creditor, then, that sees a plant full of fabricating equipment is not mislead.

Over the last thirty years or so, equipment manufacturers have modified their marketing practices; and much of the equipment in the fabricator's plant today is there under leasing arrangements. Some of those arrangements are really sales with a secured transactions feature disguised as a lease. The lessors of the equipment, the manufacturer that "leases" the equipment to the fabricator, must file a financing statement. Much leasing, however, is not a sale disguised as a lease but is a true lease. In these true lease situations, there is no filing requirement. Article 2A does not require a "true" lessor to file, even though Article 9 does require a secured party to file.

Historically, lessors of personal property did not make public filings, while secured parties traditionally did. Is historical practice a valid reason for continuing the distinction today? What do you think Professors Baird and Jackson would say about leasing situations? Are creditors fooled by true leases as much as they might be fooled by unfiled security interests? What is Professor Mooney's point? Would you be surprised to learn that he supported the Article 2A decision not to require filing? To what extent do you suppose audited financial statements give prospective lenders the true picture of a borrower's interest in its equipment? If lenders do not need public records of leases, why do they need public records of security interests?

SECTION 5. NEGOTIABLE INSTRUMENTS

INTRODUCTORY NOTE

If a buyer of Blackacre wants to know the state of his seller's title, the buyer sends a lawyer off to the real estate records to do a title search, at the conclusion of which, the lawyer gives the buyer an opinion.

Buyers of goods, as the previous sections in this chapter illustrate, cannot secure a title opinion, because generally we have decided not to maintain records of personal property transfers. The reasons for that decision are obvious. Usually, the sale of goods cannot support the time and expense of a title search and of recording the transfer, though there are exceptions, the certificate of title laws being chief among them.

It is also inconvenient to maintain records of transfer of interests in other kinds of property that move in the markets with little inquiry.

This section and the two that follow deal with pieces of paper that stand for property interests that at times have assumed considerable value in commerce. In Chapter 11 we study the abstraction principle, that feature of commercial law that permits pieces of paper to stand for something. In this section the paper stands for a money obligation. Section 6 deals with commodity paper, paper that stands for goods; and in Section 7 with corporate paper, paper that stands for an interest in or an obligation of a business or municipal corporation. As the cases and scholarly excerpts testify, the process of achieving protection of purchasers of this paper was not free from conceptual difficulties.

UCC § 3-306

A person taking an instrument, other than a person having rights of a holder in due course, is subject to a claim of a property or possessory right in the instrument or its proceeds, including a claim to rescind a negotiation and recover the instrument or its proceeds. A person having rights of a holder in due course takes free of the claim to the instrument.

MILLER v. RACE

Court of King's Bench, 1758.
97 Eng. Rep. 398.

It was an action of trover against the defendant, upon a bank note, for the payment of twenty-one pounds ten shillings to one William Finney or bearer, on demand.

The cause came on to be tried before Lord Mansfield at the sittings in Trinity term last at Guildhall, London: and upon the trial it appeared that Williams Finney, being possessed of this bank note on the 11th of December 1756, sent it by the general post, under cover, directed to one Bernard Odenbarty, at Chipping Norton in Oxfordshire; that on the same night the mail was robbed, and the bank note in question (amongst other notes) taken and carried away by the robber; that this bank note, on the 12th of the same December, came into the bands and possession of the plaintiff, for a full and valuable consideration, and in the usual course and way of his business and without any notice of knowledge of this bank note being taken out of that mail.

It was admitted and agreed, that, in the common and known course of trade, bank notes are paid by and received of the holder or possession of them, and cash; and that in the usual way of negotiating bank notes, they pass from one person to another as cash, by delivery only and without any further inquiry or evidence of title, than what arises from the possession. It appeared that Mr. Finney, having notice of this robbery, on the 13th December, applied to the Bank of England, "to stop the payment of this note:" which was ordered accordingly, upon Mr. Finney's entering into proper security "to indemnify the bank."

Some little time after this, the plaintiff applied to the bank for the payment of this note; and for that purpose delivered the note to the defendant, who is a clerk in the bank: but the defendant refused either to pay the note, or to re-deliver it to the plaintiff. Upon which this action was brought against the defendant.

The jury found a verdict for the plaintiff, and the sum of 211.10s. damages, subject nevertheless to the opinion of this Court upon this question—"Whether under the circumstances of this case the plaintiff had a sufficient property in this bank note, to entitle him to recover in the present action?"

LORD MANSFIELD now delivered the resolution of the Court.

After stating the case at large, he declared that at the trial, he had no sort of doubt, but this action was well brought, and would lie against the defendant in the present case; upon the general course of business, and from the consequences to trade and commerce: which would be much incommoded by a contrary determination.

It has been very ingeniously argued by Sir Richard Lloyd for the defendant. But the whole fallacy of the argument turns upon comparing bank notes to what they do not resemble, and what they ought not to be compared to, viz. to goods, or to securities, or document for debt.

Now they are not goods, nor securities, nor documents for debts, nor are so esteemed: but are treated as money, as cash, in the ordinary course and transaction of business, by the general consent of mankind; which gives them the credit and currency of money, to all intents and purposes. They are as much money, as guineas themselves are; or any other current coin, that is used in common payments, as money or cash.

They pass by a will, which bequeaths all the testator's money or cash; and are never considered as securities for money, but itself. Upon Ld. Ailesbury's will, 900£ in bank-notes was considered as cash. On payment of them, whenever a receipt is required, the receipts are always given as for money; not as for securities or notes.

So on bankruptcies, they cannot be followed as identical and distinguishable from money: but are always considered as money or cash.

It is a pity that reporters sometimes catch at quaint expressions that may happen to be dropped at the Bar or Bench; and mistake their meaning. It has been quaintly said, "that the reason why money can not be followed is, because it has not car-mark:" But this is not true. The true reason is, upon account of the currency of it: it can not be recovered after it has passed in currency. So, in case of money stolen, the true owner can not recover it, after it has been paid away fairly and honestly upon a valuable and bona fide consideration: but before money has passed in currency, an action may be brought for the money itself.

* * *

Apply this to the case of a bank-note. An action may lie against the finder, it is true; (and it is not at all denied:) but not after it has been paid away in currency. And this point has been determined, even in the infancy of bank-notes; for 1 Salk. 126, M. 10 W. 3, at Nisi Prius, is in point. And Ld. Ch. J. Holt there says that it is "by reason of the course of trade; which creates a property in the assignee or bearer." (And "the bearer" is a more proper expression than assignee).

Here, an inn-keeper took it, bona fide, in his business from a person who made an appearance of a gentleman. Here is no presence or suspicion of collusion with the robber: for this matter was strictly inquired and examined into at the trial; and is so stated in the case, "that he took it for a full and valuable consideration, in the usual course of business." Indeed if there had been any collusion, or any circumstances of unfair dealing; the case had been much otherwise. If it had been a note for 1000£ it might have been suspicious" but this was a small note for 211.10s only: and money given in exchange for it.

A bank-note is constantly and universally, both at home and abroad, treated as money, as cash; and paid and received, as cash; and it is necessary, for the purposes of commerce, that their currency should be established and secured.

There was a case in the Court of Chancery, on some of Mr. Child's notes, payable to the person to whom they were given, or bearer. The notes had been lost or destroyed many years. Mr. Child was ready to pay them to the widow and administratrix of the person to whom they were made payable; upon her giving bond, with two responsible sureties, (as is the custom in such cases,) to indemnify him against the bearer, if the notes should ever be demanded. The administratrix brought a bill; which was dismissed because she either could not or would not give the security required. No dispute ought to be made with the bearer of a cash-note; in regard to commerce, and for the sake of the credit of these notes; though it may be both reasonable and customary, to stay the payment, till inquiry can be made, whether the bearer of the note came by it fairly, or not.

UCC § 3-305(b)

The right of a holder in due course to enforce the obligation of a party to pay the instrument is subject to defenses of the obligor stated in subsection (a)(1), but is not subject to defenses of the obligor stated in subsection (a)(2) or claims of recoupment stated in subsection (a)(3) against a person other than the holder.

PEACOCK v. RHODES

Court of King's Bench, 1781.
99 Eng. Rep. 402.

[In Halifax, the defendants drew a bill (draft" in UCC locution) on Smith & Co. payable to Ingham, or order. Ingham indorsed to Daltry, who indorsed to Fisher, from whom it was stolen in York. The thief, claiming to be "Brown" gave it to the plaintiff Peacock, a mercer, at Scarborough in return for a quantity of cloth, other articles, and change. Peacock took the draft claiming to know defendants' signature and sued as indorsee of the original payee, Ingham. The defendants refused to pay.]

Wood, for the plaintiff, argued, that the bill was taken, by Peacock, in the ordinary course of business, and there was no pretence that he had notice that it had been obtained unfairly. If he had, he admitted that he could not recover. A bill indorsed by the payee, is to be considered to all intents as cash, unless he chooses to restrain its currency, which he may do by a special indorsement, as "Pay the contents to William Fisher". The very object in view, in making negotiable securities, is, that they may serve the purposes of cash. The case of Miller v. Race although the question there arose upon a bank-note, establishes the principle just stated. If this bill had not been stolen, but lost, the owner might have maintained trover against the finder, but still the bona fide holder would have been entitled to recover upon it. This was determined, with respect to a note upon a banker payable to A or bearer, in the case of Grant v. Vaughan. Here, the bill was indorsed blank, but that was the same thing in effect, as if it had been made payable to the bearer. A blank indorsement is an indorsement to all the world; to any body who shall happen to be the bearer.

* * *

The argument on the part of the present defendants would extend to all cases of fraud and imposition, as well as theft, and would stop the currency of bills of exchange, because it would render it necessary for every indorsee to insist upon proof of all the circumstances, and the manner in which the bill came to the indorser. As the negligence, in this case, was on the part of the person who lost the bill, the loss ought to fall upon him; not the plaintiff.

Fearnly, for the defendants. * * *

No man is obliged to take a bill of exchange in payment. A trader should not, in prudence, take a bill, unless he know the person from whom he receives it. But if the law were as contended for on the part of the plaintiff, the temptations to theft would be increased.

Lord Mansfield told Wood, he need not reply, and delivered the opinion of the Court, as follows:

Lord Mansfield.—I am glad this question was saved, not for any difficulty there is in the case, but because it is important that general commercial points should be publicly decided. The holder of a bill of exchange, or promissory note, is not to be considered in the light of an assignee of the payee. An assignee must take the thing assigned, subject to all the equity to which the original party was subject. If this rule applied to bills and promissory notes, it would stop their currency. The law is settled, that a holder, coming fairly by a bill or note, has nothing to do with the transaction between the original parties; unless, perhaps, in the single case, (which is a hard one, but has been determined,) of a note for money won at play. I see no difference between a note indorsed blank, and one payable to bearer. They both go by delivery, and possession proves property in both cases. The question of mala fides was for the consideration of the jury. The circumstances, that the buyer and also the drawers were strangers to the plaintiff, and that he took the bill for goods on which he had a profit, were grounds of suspicion, very fit for their consideration. But they have considered them, and have found it was received in the course of trade, and, therefore, the case is clear, and within the principle of all those Mr. Wood had cited, from that of Miller v. Race, downwards, to that determined by me at Nisi Prius.

The postea to be delivered to the plaintiff.

ROSENTHAL, NEGOTIABILITY—WHO NEEDS IT?, 71 Colum. L. Rev. 375, 376-77 (1971).

When a question arises as to whether a holder in due course can cut off defenses or claims, a decision must be made as to which of two innocent parties must bear the entire loss. The problem usually arises only because there is a third party who is dishonest, impecunious, or both. There is theoretically a right over against such a party, but exercise of this right is generally inconvenient and often worthless. While it would be possible to divide the loss between the two innocent parties, this type of solution rarely finds favor in our law. And where both have behaved decently and honorably, the allocation of loss can scarcely be based upon a calculus of comparative nobility of character. The decision therefore almost inevitably has to rest upon the collateral effects of the rule to be enunciated—for example, its effect on commerce.

There has been a tendency to think, rather uncritically, of negotiability as a "Good Thing." It conforms to the trend, manifest in Anglo-American law over the past two centuries, of increasing the protection given to bona fide purchasers, at the expense of various kinds of victims. It is generally assumed, without careful inquiry, that protection of the good faith purchaser helps the flow of commerce. Perhaps some of the credit—or blame—for this attitude can be laid at the door of the teachers of law school courses in Negotiable Instruments. It is difficult to make the subject interesting to students, and instructors can hardly be blamed for introducing a bit of "gee whiz" into their approach. One starts with the proposition, theoretically learned in first-year Contracts and Property courses, that just as water cannot rise above its level, one generally cannot convey greater rights than he himself has; student interest can be whetted by showing how just that can happen when a negotiable instrument is employed. * * *

It may be in part because of this pedagogical approach that, although considerable attention has been paid in recent years to specific areas in which negotiability has given rise to unfortunate results—especially in connection with consumer paper—no comprehensive re-examination of the wide array of situations in which it applies has been made. Who really needs negotiability today? To what extent does the free flow of commerce actually depend on it? Are there other areas apart from consumer financing, where the advantages achieved may be outweighed by the damage done?

QUESTION

Some academics read Dean Rosenthal's question as rhetorical; that is, they think he is saying that in an age of quick, cheap information, nobody needs negotiability. Do you agree? Before you answer that question, you might want to consider the following problems.

PROBLEMS

1. Ace Developers Co. was a group of community leaders intent on revitalizing the inner city. Ace acquired a number of decaying buildings that were adjacent to a newly constructed civic center. The principals of Ace honestly believed that if they razed the decayed structures and replaced them with modern office and retail space, they would contribute to the revitalization of the city. Ace was cash poor, however, having only enough capital to design the project and hire marketing people to sell it to prospective tenants and to investors. Banks were not interested. The project was too risky.

Ace designed the buildings, lined up a number of tenants, and entered into an arrangement with a syndicator to raise the money. The syndicator, which operated a number of offices throughout the country, approached wealthy people who were relatively risk neutral and were interested in high return investments with some attractive tax features. Syndicators set up a limited partnership with Developers as the general partner and the investors as limited partners. Syndicators arranged for the investors to buy the limited partnership interests in the new project for $500,000, but Syndicators made the investment easy for the investors by letting them put up only 10% of the $500,000 purchase price with the balance due under a demand promissory note. Developers then took the notes and endorsed them to First Bank, which made a mortgage loan to the partnership to build the project.

An economic recession prompted the prospective tenants to breach their lease obligations, and the partnership was unable to service the mortgage debt. A mortgage foreclosure sale yielded less than one-half of the mortgage loan balance. The bank then called the notes and asked the investors to pay the balance due on their investments. The investors argued that the partnership violated Blue Sky laws and that the violation gave the investors a defense on the notes.

That defense is good against the partnership. Should it be good against the bank? Who should bear the loss of this "bad" investment, the investors or the financial intermediary?

2. Assume in the foregoing problem that the developer and the bank are controlled by the construction company and that the construction company had good reason to know that the prospective tenants would never live up to their lease commitments. Under these modified facts, who should bear the loss?

SECTION 6. NEGOTIABLE DOCUMENTS

DOLAN, GOOD FAITH PURCHASE AND WAREHOUSE RECEIPTS: THOUGHTS ON THE INTERPLAY OF ARTICLES 2, 7, AND 9 OF THE UCC, 30 Hastings L.J. 1, 2-3 (1978).

For some purchasers, delivery is not an essential part of the purchase transaction. Grain dealers, for example, frequently purchase from farm producers and sell to industry consumers without moving the grain from the elevators to which the producers delivered it for drying and storing after harvest. Customarily these buyers and sellers effect such transfers by negotiable warehouse receipts. * * * The last purchaser then surrenders the receipt to the elevator and takes delivery. * * *

In transactions similar to the foregoing * * * market conditions or production schedules may force a buyer to hold a commodity. During that interval the buyer owns a valuable asset but cannot utilize it and, therefore, may seek to borrow against it. Lenders will grant credit on the security of the stored commodity by taking the negotiable warehouse receipt. When the borrower finds a buyer for the commodity or is prepared to use it in its own production process, the borrower will pay off the loan, obtain the receipt from the creditor and surrender the receipt to the warehouse against delivery of the goods.

R. HENSON, DOCUMENTS OF TITLE UNDER THE UNIFORM COMMERCIAL CODE 142 (2d ed. 1990). "Unless the rights are diminished by Section 7-503 or by Section 7-205, a holder who takes by due negotiation gets the greatest bundle of rights conferred by Article 7. If the circumstances are such that a thief can transfer a stolen document to a holder who meets the requirements for due negotiation, such a holder obviously acquires title to the document and title to the goods under Section 7-502(1). Anyone taking by due negotiation, unless an exception is applicable, not only acquires title to the document and title to the goods but also whatever rights accrue under the law of agency or estoppel and the issuer's direct obligation to hold or deliver the goods."

SHAW v. RAILROAD CO.

United States Supreme Court, 1879.
101 U.S. 557, 25 L.Ed.892.

[The transaction in question is a classic documentary draft transaction. Norvell & Co. delivered cotton of considerable value to the railroad for shipment from St. Louis to Philadelphia. Norvell then took the bill of lading that the railroad had given it, attached the bill to a draft (thereby creating a "documentary draft") and delivered both pieces of paper to a bank, which discounted the draft. Presumably, though the opinion does not recite the fact, the draft was drawn on a buyer in Philadelphia who would honor the draft by accepting it in advance of its due date. Upon acceptance, the bank's Philadelphia correspondent would deliver the bill to the buyer. The buyer would then take the bill to the railroad when the cotton finally arrived in Philadelphia and obtain delivery of it from the railroad.

The transaction went awry when a member of a brokerage firm (Kuhn) managed to obtain the bill of lading indorsed in blank from the bank. The broker sold it to Miller & Brother, who used it to obtain the cotton from the railroad. Miller & Brother then sold the cotton to Shaw. The bank sued Shaw to recover the value of the cotton.]

MR. JUSTICE STRONG delivered the opinion of the court.

The defendants below, now plaintiffs in error, bought the cotton from Miller & Brother by sample, through a cotton broker. No bill of lading or other written evidence of title in their vendors was exhibited to them. Hence, they can have no other or better title than their vendors had.

The inquiry, therefore, is, what title had Miller & Brother as against the bank, which confessedly was the owner, and which is still the owner, unless it has lost its ownership by the fraudulent act of Kuhn & Brother. * * * The jury has found, however, that there was no negligence of the bank, or of its agents, in parting with possession of the bill of lading, and that Miller & Brother knew facts from which they had reason to believe it was held to secure the payment of an outstanding draft; in other words, that Kuhn & Brother were not the lawful owners of it, and had no right to dispose of it.

It is therefore to be determined whether Miller & Brother, by taking the bill of lading from Kuhn & Brother under these circumstances, acquired thereby a good title to the cotton as against the bank.

In considering this question, it does not appear to us necessary to inquire whether the effect of the bill of lading in the hands of Miller & Brother is to be determined by the law of Missouri, where the bill was given, or by the law of Pennsylvania, where the cotton was delivered. The statutes of both States enact that bills of lading shall be negotiable by indorsement and delivery. The statute of Pennsylvania declares simply, they 'shall be negotiable and may be transferred by indorsement and delivery;' while that of Missouri enacts that 'they shall be negotiable by written indorsement thereon and delivery, in the same manner as bills of exchange and promissory notes.' There is no material difference between these provisions. Both statutes prescribe the manner of negotiation; i.e., by indorsement and delivery. Neither undertakes to define the effect of such a transfer.

We must, therefore, look outside of the statutes to learn what they mean by declaring such instruments negotiable. What is negotiability? It is a technical term derived from the usage of merchants and bankers, in transferring, primarily, bills of exchange and, afterwards, promissory notes. At common law no contract was assignable, so as to give to an assignee a right to enforce it by suit in his own name. To this rule bills of exchange and promissory notes, payable to order or bearer, have been admitted exceptions, made such by the adoption of the law merchant. They may be transferred by indorsement and delivery, and such a transfer is called negotiation. It is a mercantile business transaction, and the capability of being thus transferred, so as to give to the indorsee a right to sue on the contract in his own name, is what constitutes negotiability. The term 'negotiable' expresses, at least primarily, this mode and effect of a transfer.

In regard to bills and notes, certain other consequences generally, though not always, follow. Such as a liability of the indorser, if demand be duly made of the acceptor or maker, and seasonable notice of his default be given. So if the indorsement be made for value to a bona fide holder, before the maturity of the bill or note, in due course of business, the maker or acceptor cannot set up against the indorsee any defence which might have been set up against the payee, had the bill or note remained in his hands.

So, also, if a note or bill of exchange be indorsed in blank, if payable to order, or if it be payable to bearer, and therefore negotiable by delivery alone, and then be lost or stolen, a bona fide purchaser for value paid acquires title to it, even as against the true owner. This is an exception from the ordinary rule respecting personal property. But none of these consequences are necessary attendants or constituents of negotiability, or negotiation. That may exist without them. A bill or note past due is negotiable, if it be payable to order, or bearer, but its indorsement or delivery does not cut off the defences of the maker or acceptor against it, nor create such a contract as results from an indorsement before maturity, and it does not give to the purchaser of a lost or stolen bill the rights of the real owner.

It does not necessarily follow, therefore, that because a statute has made bills of lading negotiable by indorsement and delivery, all these consequences of an indorsement and delivery of bills and notes before maturity ensue or are intended to result from such negotiation.

Bills of exchange and promissory notes are exceptional in their character. They are representatives of money, circulating in the commercial world as evidence of money, 'of which any person in lawful possession may avail himself to pay debts or make purchases or make remittances of money from one country to another, or to remote places in the same country. Hence, as said by Story, J., it has become a general rule of the commercial world to hold bills of exchange, as in some sort, sacred instrument in favor of bona fide holders for a valuable consideration without notice.' Without such a holding they could not perform their peculiar functions. It is for this reason it is held that if a bill or note, endorsed in blank or payable to bearer, be lost or stolen, and be purchased from the finder or thief, without any knowledge of want of ownership in the vendor, the bona fide purchaser may hold it against the true owner. He may hold it though he took it negligently, and when there were suspicious circumstances attending the transfer. Nothing short of actual or constructive notice that the instrument is not the property of the person who offers to sell it; that is, nothing short of mala fides will defeat his right. The rule is the same as that which protects the bona fide indorser of a bill or note purchased for value from the true owner. The purchaser is not bound to look beyond the instrument. * * * The rule was first applied to the case of a lost bank-note (Miller v. Race, 1 Burr. 452), and put upon the ground that the interests of trade, the usual course of business, and the fact that bank-notes pass from hand to hand as coin, require it. It was subsequently held applicable to merchants' drafts, and in Peacock v. Rhodes (2 Doug. 633), to bills and notes, as coming within the same reason.

The reason can have no application to the case of a lost or stolen bill of lading. The function of that instrument is entirely different from that of a bill or note. It is not a representative of money, used for transmission of money, or for the payment of debts or for purchases. It does not pass from hand to hand as bank-notes or coin. It is a contract for the performance of a certain duty. True, it is a symbol of ownership of the goods covered by it,—a representative of those goods. But if the goods themselves be lost or stolen, no sale of them by the finder or thief, though to a bona fide purchaser for value, will divest the ownership of the person who lost them, or from whom they were stolen. Why then should the sale of the symbol or mere representative of the goods have such an effect? It may be that the true owner by his negligence or carelessness may have put it in the power of a finder or thief to occupy ostensibly the position of a true owner, and his carelessness may estop him from asserting his right against a purchaser who has been misled to his hurt by that carelessness. But the present is no such case. It is established by the verdict of the jury that the bank did not lose its possession of the bill of lading negligently. There is no estoppel, therefore, against the bank's right.

Bills of lading are regarded as so much cotton, grain, iron, or other articles of merchandise. The merchandise is very often sold or pledged by the transfer of the bills which cover it. They are, in commerce, a very different thing from bills of exchange and promissory notes, answering a different purpose and performing different functions. It cannot be, therefore, that the statute which made them negotiable by indorsement and delivery, or negotiable in the same manner as bills of exchange and promissory notes are negotiable, intended to change totally their character, put them in all respects on the footing of instruments which are the representatives of money, and charge the negotiation of them with all the consequences which usually attend or follow the negotiation of bills and notes. Some of these consequences would be very strange if not impossible. Such as the liability of indorsers, the duty of demand ad diem, notice of non-delivery by the carrier or the loss of the owner's property by the fraudulent assignment of a thief. If these were intended, surely the statute would have said something more than merely make them negotiable by indorsement. No statute is to be construed as altering the common law, farther than its words import. It is not to be construed as making any innovation upon the common law which it does not fairly express. Especially is so great an innovation as would be placing bills of lading on the same footing in all respects with bills of exchange not to be inferred from words that can be fully satisfied without it. The law has most carefully protected the ownership of personal property, other than money, against misappropriation by others than the owner, even when it is out of his possession. This protection would be largely withdrawn if the misappropriation of its symbol or representative could avail to defeat the ownership, even when the person who claims under a misappropriation had reason to believe that the person from whom he took the property had no right to it.

We think, therefore, that the rule asserted in Goodman v. Harvey, Goodman v. Simonds, Murray v. Lardner (supra), and in Phelan v. Moss (67 Pa. St. 59), is not applicable to a stolen bill of lading. At least the purchaser of such a bill, with reason to believe that his vendor was not the owner of the bill, or that it was held to secure the payment of an outstanding draft, is not a bona fide purchaser, and he is not entitled to hold the merchandise covered by the bill against its true owner. In the present case there was more than mere negligence on the part of Miller & Brother, more than mere reason for suspicion. There was reason to believe Kuhn & Brother had no right to negotiate the bill. This falls very little, if any, short of knowledge. It may fairly be assumed that one who has reason to believe a fact exists, knows it exists. Certainly, if he be a reasonable being. * * *

NOTE ON *SHAW*

Those who have studied legal history know that judges are sometimes jealous of legislative prerogative, especially when the legislature alters judge-made law. One of the chief weapons judges used against legislative reform of the common law is an old saw: "statutes in derogation of the common law shall be strictly construed."

The drafters of the Code were aware of this judicial tendency and of that old saw. They addressed it directly in the first sentence of the first substantive provision of the Code, § 1-102. Note the imperative nature of the verb: "This

Act shall be liberally construed and applied to promote its underlying purposes and policies."

The Code drafters, the Uniform Bills of Lading Act that predated the Code, and federal legislators have given the death sentence to Shaw v. Railroad Co.

FEDERAL BILLS OF LADING ACT
49 U.S.C.A. §§ 80104-80180 (West 1994).

§ 80104. **Form and requirements for negotiation**

(3) A negotiable bill of lading may be negotiated by a person possessing the bill, regardless of the way in which the person got possession, if

(A) a common carrier, under the terms of the bill, undertakes to deliver the goods to that person; or

(B) when the bill is negotiated, it is in a form that allows it to be negotiated by delivery.

§ 80105. **Title and rights affected by negotiation**

(a) Title—When a negotiable bill of lading is negotiated—

(1) the person to whom it is negotiated acquires the title to the goods that—

(A) the person negotiating the bill had the ability to convey to a purchaser in good faith for value; and

(B) the consignor and consignee had the ability to convey to such purchaser; and

(2) the common carrier issuing the bill becomes obligated directly to the person to whom the bill is negotiated to hold possession of the goods under the terms of the bill the same as if the carrier had issued the bill to that person.

(b) Superiority of rights—When a negotiable bill of lading is negotiated to a person for value in good faith, that person's right to the goods for which the bill was issued is superior to a seller's lien or to a right to stop the transportation of the goods. This subsection applies whether the negotiation is made before or after the common carrier issuing the bill receives notice of the seller's claim. The carrier may deliver the goods to an unpaid seller only if the bill first is surrendered for cancellation.

SECTION 7. SECURITIES

INTRODUCTORY NOTE

The indirect holding system that brokers and securities issuers now use to effect the great bulk of securities transfers may have rendered the negotiability of securities a marginal concept in commercial law. That is not to say that there is no place for the doctrine, however. In the following case a rather good commercial lawyer finds sufficient justification in it to rule against an elderly litigant.

RUSSELL v. AMERICAN BELL TELEPHONE CO.

Supreme Judicial Court of Massachusetts, 1902.
180 Mass. 467, 62 N.E. 751.

[Justice Holmes, when he was sitting on the Massachusetts court, confronted the entrustment question in a case where the true owner of a negotiable security argued that possession and the property (title) were not the same and that a fraudfeasor could hold the former without the latter.]

HOLMES, C. J.

The plaintiff's intestate intrusted a certificate of stock, indorsed in blank, to a fraudulent agent, and he, instead of using it for the purpose for which it was intrusted to him, obtained an advance from the defendant by giving the certificate in pledge. The case, therefore, so far, falls within the general reasoning of Scollans v. Rollins (Mass.) 60 N. E. 983, and the usage referred to in that case was found to be proved.

In order to avoid the intimations of Scollans v. Rollins, the plaintiff sets up that in this case only the possession of the certificate, not the property, passed to the agent and that, as the possession was obtained by fraud, it was obtained by larceny in judgment of law. In Scollans v. Rollins, it is admitted that the general principle there laid down would not apply to an instrument indorsed in blank and stolen before it had been transferred. We shall not examine the premises of this defence because we cannot accept the conclusion. The qualification of the rule, as not applying when the instrument is stolen, is not based upon the name of the agent's crime but upon the fact that in the ordinary and typical case of theft the owner has not intrusted the agent with the document and therefore is not considered to have done enough to be estopped as against a purchaser in good faith. He certainly has not done enough if the estoppel is based upon the principle that when one of two innocent persons is to suffer the sufferer should be the one whose confidence put into the hands of the wrongdoer the means of doing the wrong. But in a case like the present the agent has been intrusted with the converted property, and it is totally immaterial whether by a stretch which extends larceny beyond the true field of trespass, his wrong has been brought within the criminal law or not. The ground of the estoppel is present and the estoppel arises.

The distinction is not new. On the one side are cases like Knox v. Eden Musee American Co., 148 N. Y. 441, 42 N. E. 988, 31 L. R. A. 779, 51 Am. St. Rep. 700, where an agent or servant simply had access to a document remaining in the possession of the owner; on the other, cases like Appeal of Pennsylvania R. Co., 86 Pa. 80, where possession is intrusted to the agent for one purpose and he uses it for another. It cannot matter in the latter class that the agent intended the fraud from the outset.

It is found by the court that the intestate did not know of the custom, and if the question before us were the construction of a contract, her knowledge might be important. But she knew that she was putting into her agent's hands an instrument which made actual deceit possible, and it is not argued for the plaintiff that, under such circumstances and considering the nature of the usage which has been adopted as law in many jurisdictions, she did not take the risk of the appearances being interpreted as it is usual for business men to interpret them.

UCC § 8-302(3)

In addition to acquiring the rights of a purchaser, a protected purchaser also acquires its interest in the security free of any adverse claim.

SECTION 8. SECURED TRANSACTIONS

INTRODUCTORY NOTE

In the last three sections, we dealt with the paper purchasers (the holder in due course in Article 3, the holder by due negotiation in Article 7, and the protected purchaser in Article 8). They are less important commercial personages today than they were prior to the information age when negotiability played a signal role in paper transactions.

As we saw in the study of good faith purchase in Article 2, however, the idea that a buyer takes more than his seller had is not foreign to buyer protection rules in the sales article. Study of Article 9 reveals that it is equally vital in the law of secured transactions. In the next case, we take a brief look at the application of this rule, which involves a priority conflict between the holder of an Article 9 security interest and a buyer in the ordinary course of business. Later, in Chapter 9, we will return to this topic in much greater detail.

GARY AIRCRAFT CORP. v. GENERAL DYNAMICS CORP. (IN RE GARY AIRCRAFT CORP.)

United States Court of Appeals, Fifth Circuit, 1982.
681 F.2d 365.

[For the facts of the *Gary Aircraft* case and that portion of the opinion dealing with the shelter principle, see page 17 supra]

* * *

III.

Under the Uniform Commercial Code, enacted as the Texas Business and Commerce Code, a buyer in the ordinary course of business is one who, in good faith and without knowledge that the sale to him is in violation of the ownership rights or security interest of a third party, buys from a person in the business of selling goods of that kind. Tex.Bus. & Com.Code Ann. § 1.201(9) (Vernon Supp.1982). Such a buyer takes free of a security interest created by his seller, even if that interest is perfected and even if the buyer knows of its existence. Id., § 9.307(a).

Since Gary claims its title through Stewart, it cannot hold the aircraft and the proceeds free of General Dynamics's lien unless Stewart held the aircraft free of the lien, as a buyer in the ordinary course of business under section 9.307(a). General Dynamics offers three arguments that it contends require reversal of the holding that Stewart qualified as a buyer in the ordinary course of business.

First, General Dynamics contends that the bankruptcy court misapplied the burden of proof. The burden on this issue does rest with the party claiming the status of a buyer in the ordinary course of business, as General Dynamics urges. See International Harvester Co. v. Glendenning, Tex.Civ.App.- Dallas 1974, 505 S.W.2d 320, 324. Nonetheless, General Dynamics cannot prevail on this argument, for we agree with the district court that an examination of the entire opinion of the bankruptcy court shows that it did not misapply the burden of proof. General Dynamics's contention to the contrary relies exclusively on one sentence in the opinion of the bankruptcy court: "The preponderance of the evidence simply does not establish or show that Stewart had any knowledge of any default by Ayer on his obligation to General Dynamics at the time he purchased these airplanes." Taken out of context, the sentence could be read as an allocation of the burden of proof, and such an allocation would be improper. But the sentence can just as easily be read as a description of the evidence. The sentence is at most ambiguous, and there is no other indication anywhere in the opinion that the bankruptcy judge misapplied the burden of proof. Consequently, we conclude that the bankruptcy judge placed the burden where it belonged—on Gary.

Second, General Dynamics contends that, even if the bankruptcy judge acted properly in his assignment of the burden of proof, the holding must be reversed because the bankruptcy court considered Stewart's knowledge on December 22, 1971 and January 4, 1972, the dates of purchase, rather than on August 3, 1972, the date of recordation. The district court found some merit in General Dynamics's argument that Stewart's knowledge was to be evaluated as of August 3 but declined to choose between the dates of purchase and the date of recordation, holding that use of the date of purchase would be harmless error because Stewart did not know of the default by Ayer even on August 3. General Dynamics argues to us that the district court's disposition of this issue was improper because August 3 was the relevant time, but the bankruptcy court had made no finding on the state of Stewart's knowledge in August. We disagree with General Dynamics on both grounds.

We conclude that the dates of purchase were the relevant dates. The rule of § 9.307(a) is designed to protect the innocent buyer against prior security interests in retail goods because he cannot be expected to discover those interests, while the secured party may generally be assumed to have authorized the sale of inventory by a retailer. See generally, e.g., J. White & R. Summers, Uniform Commercial Code § 25-14 at 1070 (2d ed. 1980). But this "protection" leaves the buyer vulnerable if he cannot be certain of it until he records. Were that the rule, a buyer who discovered a violated security agreement after purchasing but before recording could have given consideration, in good faith and without knowledge, and taken possession of the goods but he would take a position subordinate to that of the secured lender. Measuring knowledge at the time of sale or earlier, however, prevents any gap in protection, for a potential buyer who discovers a violated security interest at the time of purchase can always decide not to buy.[1]

In the alternative, we conclude that the bankruptcy judge did find that in August Stewart was without knowledge of any violation of the security agreement between Ayer and General Dynamics. His opinion stated that Stewart was unaware of the lien until after the time of purchase, "and even then the mortgage appeared to authorize Ayer to sell free of any lien * * *. Stewart became and remained a buyer in ordinary course of business." Bankruptcy Court Op. at 6.

Third, General Dynamics challenges the correctness of the holding that Stewart bought in good faith and without knowledge that the sale to him was in violation of the rights of General Dynamics.[2] Our holding above was based on

---

1 We find additional support for our conclusion that the dates of purchase are the relevant dates in the limited nature of the current controversy over when the protection of the buyer in the ordinary course attaches. Although there is some debate as to whether one who qualifies as a buyer in the ordinary course prevails over the secured lender if the lender attempts to foreclose before the buyer takes possession of the goods, no one seems to question that, from the time of delivery, the buyer prevails. Although one might argue that the buyer's qualification should be determined as of a date earlier than that on which the protection takes effect, surely the qualification should not be determined as of a later date. General Dynamics cites no authority for its view that knowledge must be determined as of the date of recordation. It seems to rely entirely on 49 U.S.C. § 1403(c), which provides that no conveyance shall be valid as against third parties until recorded. Thus, according to General Dynamics, it could not lose its rights by operation of section 9.307(a) until Stewart recorded the conveyance, and Stewart would have to be without knowledge at the moment when General Dynamics would lose its rights if he is to take under section 9.307(a). To the extent that this argument reiterates the preemption argument, we have rejected it in Part II. The validity of General Dynamics's interest is governed by state law, which as our discussion in text shows, subordinates General Dynamics to a buyer in the ordinary course as of the date of purchase. Of course section 1403(c) does not affirmatively grant interests to third parties simply on the basis of the failure of the parties to the conveyance to record, and General Dynamics has no other claim arising after the failure to record; it did not in any way deal in reliance on recorded title.

2 In its brief, General Dynamics urged that we hold these conclusions "clearly erroneous". At oral argument, though, it changed its position, now contending that the determination of buyer in the ordinary course status is a mixed question of law and fact, which would give us greater freedom to substitute our judgment for that of the trial judge. In support of its new position, it cites Associates Discount Corp. v. Rattan Chevrolet, Inc., Tex.1970, 462 S.W.2d 546. That case held that summary judgment was improper when supported only by conclusory assertions that the sale was in the ordinary course of business because whether a sale is in the ordinary course of business is a mixed question of law and fact. The case did not hold, and we likewise refuse to hold, that the question of the buyer's knowledge is a mixed question. Some aspects of buyer in the ordinary course status may be mixed questions, as is the case with the question of good faith, reviewed below. See id.;

alternative grounds—that the dates of purchase are the dates on which Stewart's knowledge is relevant and that the bankruptcy court found that Stewart acted in good faith and had no knowledge on the date of recordation. In keeping with that alternative holding, we will consider Stewart's knowledge and good faith on both dates, although General Dynamics's argument deals mainly with the date of recordation.

The holding that Stewart had no knowledge that the sale violated the security agreement between Ayer and General Dynamics is not clearly erroneous. There is nothing in the record to show any knowledge on the dates of purchase, for the results of the title search did not arrive until January 5, 1972, the day after the second purchase. Once those results arrived, there is nothing to indicate that Stewart saw the security agreement before August 3, 1972, and, even if he did, that agreement appeared to authorize the sale. The record supports the conclusion that Stewart first learned of the default by Ayer from General Dynamics's letter of May 28, 1976. We cannot re-evaluate Stewart's credibility in denying knowledge; that was a question for the trial judge.

General Dynamics also contends that Stewart did not act in good faith, suggesting that he knowingly bought the planes for less than their value and that, though he was experienced in the sale of aircraft, did not undertake a title search before purchasing. To show that Stewart purchased below market value, General Dynamics relies on the gain on the later sale of one of the planes and on the use of a higher value in the 1975 mortgage agreement between Gary and its bank. Stewart apparently made no profit on the sale of the group of planes, and, indeed, his profit on a sale four years down the line is but weak evidence that he originally paid less than fair value for the planes and even weaker evidence that he was aware that this was a bargain too good to be true. Similarly, the use of a higher value in a mortgage agreement consummated three years later is weak evidence of the 1972 market value.

Stewart's failure to undertake a title search presents a question only slightly more troublesome. The Texas courts have repeatedly stated that the test of good faith is not negligence or diligence and that it is immaterial that the buyer was aware of facts that would put a reasonably prudent person on inquiry. To lose his status as a buyer in the ordinary course, the buyer must have actual knowledge of facts or circumstances that amount to bad faith. Thus, although a reasonably prudent person with Stewart's experience might have conducted a title search with the FAA before purchasing, Stewart's failure to do so does not, without more, establish that he acted in bad faith. Nor did Stewart have actual knowledge of any circumstances that would put him in bad faith. We decline to overrule the holding that Stewart acted in good faith.

Skilton, Buyer in the Ordinary Course of Business under Article 9 of the Uniform Commercial Code, 1974 Wis.L.Rev. 1, 31.

FRISCH, BUYER STATUS UNDER THE U.C.C.: A SUGGESTED TEMPORAL DEFINITION, 72 Iowa L. Rev. 531, 534 (1987).

The recognition of private property requires a comprehensive and systematic body of detailed rules to permit and control the transfer of property. Although these rules must necessarily comprehend innumerable transfer scenarios and force choices implicating difficult value judgments, at the most basic level two problems must be confronted: (1) how to accomplish a transfer of an item of property or an interest therein; and (2) how to resolve competing claims to the same item or interest. To deal with the former problem, one finds a history rich in rules clothed in ceremonial garb. The play is everything: a transfer occurs only if properly performed. Assuming a transfer occurs, resolution of the latter problem often depends on a family of rules, all born from what can best be described as the first principle of Anglo-American property law: the transferee of property can receive no greater interest than that possessed by the transferor. This Article examines one facet of one exception to this first principle.

It has been trumpeted that "[t]he triumph of the good faith purchaser has been one of the most dramatic episodes in our legal history." With this victory came the correlative commercial doctrine of good faith purchase, a doctrine that allows for the chipping away of "security of ownership" in favor of "security of purchase." The doctrine makes it possible for the transferee of goods to receive under certain circumstances a property interest superior to that of the transferor.

It is not surprising that such a doctrine, antithetical as it is to traditional common-law theory, should have experienced difficulty establishing roots in the common law. Not until the early part of the nineteenth century and the sporadic passage of the nonuniform Factor's Acts was there any show of support for the notion of a good faith purchase doctrine. Softening of the judicial bias in favor of ownership interests soon followed, but was limited to situations in which the transferor had somehow acquired voidable title from the true owner. Voidable title would ripen into good title when the item was later acquired by a good faith purchaser. With the eventual codification of sales law, the good faith purchase doctrine found a home in the Uniform Sale Act and now resides in the Uniform Commercial Code * * *.

Sparsed throughout the Code one finds several characters with different names, but all entitled under appropriate circumstances to good faith purchase treatment. The primary focus of the Article is on one of the favorites in the dramatis personae of the UCC: the buyer in ordinary course of business. In particular, the Article asks *when* during the life of a sales transaction will a purchaser qualify as a protected buyer: On this temporal issue, as well as on others, the Code is conspicuously silent.

This Article attempts two different but complementary tasks. First, it offers an answer to the "by no means academic question" asked above. In so doing, the Article considers Code rules that affect the buyer-seller relationship and those that impact on the interests of third parties. The conclusion reached is that buyer status occurs at the moment the purchaser obtains the remedial right to the goods vis-a-vis the seller. In most instances, therefore, buyer status will inevitably coincide with the moment the remedy of specific performance or, in some cases, replevin becomes available to the buyer.

Chapter 3

CONVEYANCES INVOLVING FRAUD

SECTION 1. TRANSACTIONS PRESUMED TO BE FRAUDULENT

INTRODUCTORY NOTE

Sometimes, people who owe other people money will attempt to hide their assets by transferring them to a relative or friend for little or no consideration, often with the understanding that they will retain beneficial ownership of the assets so transferred and perhaps even the right to recover legal title once the present threat has passed. These attempts to defraud creditors have been regarded as unlawful, and the transactions giving rise to them as ineffective, since Roman times. Modern fraudulent conveyance law traces its origins back to the English Statute of 13 Elizabeth c.5, enacted by Parliament in 1571. All American jurisdictions follow 13 Elizabeth either as part of their common law or, increasingly, through specific statutory enactments, the most important of which is the Uniform Fraudulent Transfer Act ("UFTA"). The UFTA was approved by the National Conference of Commissioners on Uniform State Laws in 1984. It replaced the Uniform Fraudulent Conveyance Act of 1918, which had been adopted by about half the states. The UFTA has been very favorably received, replacing the UFCA in virtually all of the adopting states and achieving enactment in a number of jurisdictions that had never adopted the UFCA.

All fraudulent conveyance laws reflect a deeply rooted attitude that it is wrong for a debtor to fail to pay a debt or debts which the debtor is capable of paying in whole or part while still enjoying the beneficial use of assets that might be applied to that debt. The material in this section examines the circumstances under which a debtor's conveyance of her property will be presumed to have been made with intent to defraud her creditors and, as such, is recoverable from the person to whom the transfer was made. In Section 2 we will examine a different category of fraudulent conveyance, comprised of transactions that do not necessarily involve an actual attempt to defraud creditors, but which, because of their perceived unfairness to creditors, are deemed by law to be "fraudulent."

The rule in *Twyne's Case*, which was decided under the Statute of 13 Elizabeth, forms the basis for many of the provisions and principles of modern fraudulent transfer law. In turn, our present law of secured financing can in large measure be seen as a response to the rule established in *Twyne's Case* concerning prejudicial effects on other creditors when a debtor conveys title to his property but retains both possession and the right to enjoy that property. As you read the case, ask yourself (1) did Twyne have a valid debt against Pierce? (2) if so, what exactly was unlawful about the payment from Pierce to Twyne? (3) would the result have been different if the payment from Pierce had been in currency (pounds) rather than goods (sheep)?

TWYNE'S CASE

Star Chamber, 1601.
76 Eng. Rep. 809.

In an information by Coke, the Queen's Attorney General, against Twyne of Hampshire, in the Star Chamber, for making and publishing of a fraudulent gift of goods: the case on the stat. of 13 Eliz. cap. 5 was such; Pierce was indebted to Twyne in four hundred pounds, and was indebted also to C in two hundred pounds. C brought an action of debt against Pierce, and pending the writ, Pierce being possessed of goods and chattels of the value of three hundred pounds, in secret made a general deed of gift of all his goods and chattels real and personal whatsoever to Twyne, in satisfaction of his debt; notwithstanding that Pierce continued in possession of the said goods, and some of them he sold; and he shore the sheep, and marked them with his own mark: and afterwards C had judgment against Pierce, and had a Fieri Facias directed to the Sheriff of Southampton, who by force of the said writ came to make execution of the said goods; but divers persons, by the command of the said Twyne did with force resist the said sheriff claiming them to be the goods of the said Twyne by force of the said gift; and openly declared by the commandment of Twyne that it was a good gift, and made on a good and lawful consideration. And whether this gift on the whole matter, was fraudulent and of no effect by the said Act of 13 Eliz. or not, was the question. And it was resolved by Sir Thomas Egertoe Lord Keeper of the Great Seal, and by the Chief Justice Popham and Anderson, and the whole Court of Star Chamber, that this gift was fraudulent, within the statute of 13 Eliz. And in this case divers points were resolved:

1st. That this gift had the signs and marks of fraud, because the gift is general, without exception of his apparel, or any thing of necessity; for it is commonly said *quod dolus versatur in generalibus.*

2nd. The donor continued in possession and used them as his own; and by reason thereof he traded and trafficked with others, and defrauded and deceived them.

3rd. It was made in secret, *et dona clandestina sunt semper suspiciosa.*

4th. It was made pending the writ.

5th. Here was a trust between the parties, for the donor possessed all, and used them as his proper goods and fraud is always apparelled and clad with a trust, and a trust is the cover of fraud.

STURTEVANT v. BALLARD

Supreme Court of Judicature, New York, 1812.
9 Johns. 337.

KENT, C.J.

This case is not of much moment, in respect to the amount of property, but it is very important, as to the principle involved in the decision. The facts lie in a narrow compass. Mecker, on the second of August, 1810, obtained judgment against Holt. On the twenty-ninth of August, Holt sold his goods and chattels, being a quantity of blacksmith's tools, to the plaintiffs, partly for cash, and partly to satisfy a debt due to them. The articles were specified in the bill of sale, and the bill contained an agreement that Holt was to retain the use and occupation of the goods for the term of three months. Just before the expiration of the term, and while the goods continued in the possession of Holt, they were seized by the defendant, as sheriff, by virtue of an execution issued on the judgment in favor of Mecker. The question arising upon the case is, whether the sale to the plaintiffs, under the above circumstances, was valid in law, as against the judgment-creditor. As between the parties to it, a sale of chattels unaccompanied by possession may be valid. It may even be valid as against a creditor, who was knowing and assenting to the sale. It was so ruled in Steele v. Brown and Pary, 1 Taunt. 381, but this is not such a case. Here was a judgment-creditor affected by the sale.

The statute of 13 Eliz. and which has been re-enacted with us, Sess. 10, c. 44, s. 2, makes void all grants, and alienations of goods and chattels, made with intent to delay, hinder and defraud creditors. This statute, as it has been frequently observed, by the English judges, was declaratory of the common law; and the true principles of law, in relation to such sales, are to be found in a series of judicial decisions, both before and since the statute of Elizabeth.

The great point is, whether the fact of permitting the vendor to retain possession of the goods did not render this sale fraudulent in law, notwithstanding such permission was inserted in the deed as a condition of the contract. If there had been no such insertion, but the sale had been absolute on the face of it, and possession had not immediately accompanied and followed the sale, it would have been fraudulent as against creditors, and the fraud in such case would have been an inference or conclusion of law, which the court would have been bound to pronounce. This is a well settled principle in the English courts. It is to be met with in a variety of cases, and especially in that of Edwards v. Harben, 2 T.R. 597; and it has been recognized and adopted by some of the most respectable tribunals in this country: Hamilton v. Russell, 1 Cranch, 303; Davies v. Cope, 4 Binn. 258. But it by no means follows that such a sale, with such an agreement attached to it, and appearing on the face of the deed, is necessarily valid. There must be some sufficient motive, of which the court is to judge, for the non-delivery of the goods, or the law will still presume the sale to have been made with a view to "delay, hinder or defraud creditors." Delivery of possession is so much of the essence of the sale of chattels, that an agreement to permit the vendor to keep possession is an extraordinary exception to the usual course of dealing, and requires a satisfactory explanation. This was a voluntary sale, made by the debtor, soon after the judgment against him, and made to a creditor, partly for cash and partly to satisfy an old debt; and why was the sale made three months before possession was to be delivered, if it was not to defeat the intermediate execution of the judgment-creditor. There is no assignable reason appearing for the arrangement and the time of delivery might have been postponed for three years as well as for three months. The instances in which a sale of chattels, unaccompanied with delivery, has been held valid, are all founded upon special reasons, which have no application to this case.

* * *

The general principle involved in this discussion is extremely important to the commercial interests of the community, and to confidence and integrity in dealing. The law in every period of its history has spoken a uniform language, and has always looked with great jealousy upon a sale or appropriation of goods, without parting with the possession, because it forms so easy and so fruitful a source of deception. Lord Kenyon said that he lamented that it was ever decided that the possession and apparent ownership of personal property might be in one person, and the title in another, and he thought it would have been better for the public, if the possession of such property (except in the case of factors), were to carry the title: 7 T.R. 234. The value of the principle and its necessity were perceived and felt as early as the age of Glanville, for he observed, when speaking of pledges, Lib. 10, c. 8, that "when a thing is agreed to be placed in pledge, by a debtor to a creditor, and delivery does not follow, it becomes a question what shall be done for the creditor in that case, since the same thing may be pledged to other creditors, both before and after. And it is to be observed that the court will not regard such private arrangements, nor intermeddle with it, or sustain a suit thereon." This was acknowledging the mischief and admitting the remedy under the same enlightened view of public policy and private interest, which some of the decisions of Lord Mansfield announce, at the period of the full growth and maturity of the commercial system.

We may, therefore, safely conclude that a voluntary sale of chattels, with an agreement, either in or out of the deed, that the vendor may keep possession is, except in special cases, and for special reasons, to be shown to and approved of by the court, fraudulent and void as against creditors. This is clearly not one of those cases, and the defendant is, therefore, entitled to judgment.

Judgment for the defendant.

QUESTIONS

1. What kind of evidence, if offered, might have satisfied the court in *Sturtevant* that this sale of goods, although not immediately accompanied with delivery, was not made with a view to "hinder, delay or defraud creditors"?

2. What is the difference between a transfer made with "intent to defraud," and a transfer made with "intent to hinder or delay"? In Smiley v. First National Bank (In re Smiley), 864 F.2d 562 (7th Cir. 1989), the debtor-defendants

had secretly moved from Illinois to Kansas shortly before filing for bankruptcy. At the time, Kansas had no dollar limitation on the value of a homestead exemption which a debtor could claim. Exemptions represent statutorily enumerated categories of property that are immune from execution by creditors. In this case, the debtors' creditors had objected to the debtors' right to a discharge in bankruptcy based on Bankruptcy Code § 727(a)(2). That provision makes a transfer or concealment of assets occurring within one year of bankruptcy grounds for denial of discharge if it can be shown that conduct was undertaken with intent to hinder, delay, or defraud creditors. The court found that while the debtors' conduct evinced an intent to *hinder* and *delay* creditors, it was less clear that they also intended to *defraud*. Nevertheless, the court affirmed the lower courts' denial of discharge because the elements of § 727(a)(2) (like UFTA § 4(a)(1)) are phrased disjunctively. How would you distinguish conduct only intended to *hinder* or *delay* from conduct intended to *defraud*? Should the consequences be the same when the transfer is challenged as a fraudulent conveyance? Even if so, do you think it should make a difference when the occurrence of the fraudulent conveyance is being used not just to recover the property transferred but to challenge a debtor's right to discharge in bankruptcy?

3. The UFTA not only proscribes certain "transfers" of the debtor's property, but also certain "obligations incurred" by the debtor. What is an example of an obligation incurred that might have the effect of hindering, delaying, or defrauding creditors?

UFTA §§ 4(a)(1) & 4(b)
(*see Selected Commercial Statutes*)

NOTE ON "BADGES OF FRAUD"

Proving intent to defraud can be tricky business. Unless the debtor is prepared to cooperate, which is not often the case, direct proof of improper motive is almost impossible to adduce. Therefore, as the next case illustrates, courts have freely allowed proof of actual intent to be established through use of circumstantial evidence or inferences drawn from other extrinsic evidence of the defendant's actual conduct.

SELVAGE v. J.J. JOHNSON & ASSOCIATES

Court of Appeals of Utah, 1996.
282 Utah Adv. Rep. 16, 910 P.2d 1252.

[In 1987, Selvage sued J.J. Johnson & Associates ("Johnson") for breach of contract. While the case was pending, Sear-Brown Associates ("Sear-Brown") became the sole shareholder of Johnson. During 1988 and 1989, while Selvage's suit was pending, Sear-Brown caused Johnson to transfer all of its assets to Sear-

Brown, and, in 1990, Sear-Brown caused Johnson to file bankruptcy. In 1991, Selvage filed an amended complaint against Sear-Brown alleging that the transfers made by Johnson to Sear-Brown were made with actual intent to hinder, delay or defraud Selvage. At trial, the jury returned special interrogatories finding that Sear-Brown was liable to Selvage under the UFTA. The trial court entered judgment for Selvage and Sear-Brown appealed on the ground that the evidence did not support the jury verdict.]

GREENWOOD, Judge.

Sear-Brown contends that the evidence was insufficient to support the jury's findings of an intent to hinder, delay or defraud, because the only evidence submitted was evidence of a preferential transfer, which, standing alone, is insufficient to support such findings. Further, Sear-Brown argues that the jury did not understand that a preferential transfer is not the same as a fraudulent transfer—that the former may be set aside if the action is timely, without any fault finding, but that the latter may be voided only if there is actual intent to hinder, delay or defraud.[1]

Selvage counters that the jury was properly instructed and that the evidence presented supports the jury's determination. Selvage further argues that Sear-Brown has failed to properly marshal all the evidence supporting the jury's findings.

The trial court found that between September 30, 1988 and February 17, 1989, while Johnson was insolvent, Johnson transferred to Sear-Brown assets with a value of at least $504,478.94. The jury determined, by special interrogatories, that Selvage had shown by a preponderance of the evidence that the asset transfer was made with an actual intent to hinder or delay Johnson's creditors. The jury also determined, again by special interrogatories, that Selvage had shown by clear and convincing evidence, that the transfer was made with actual intent to defraud Johnson's creditors.

After review of the trial proceedings, we conclude there is substantial credible evidence to support the jury's determination that the transfer of Johnson's assets to Sear-Brown was made with an actual intent to hinder, delay or defraud. The pertinent statute states:

(1) A transfer made or obligation incurred by a debtor is fraudulent as to a creditor, whether the creditor's claim arose before or after the transfer was made or the obligation was incurred, if the debtor made the transfer or incurred the obligation:

---

[1] Sear-Brown also argues, in part, that the improper submission of the insider claim confused the jury. This contention fails for two reasons. First, the submission of the insider claim to the jury was not improper because, as discussed, the insider claim was not time-barred. Second, the fact that a transfer was to an insider is one of the enumerated statutory factors which the jury may consider in determining if there was actual intent to hinder, delay or defraud. See Utah Code Ann. § 25-6-5(2)(a) (1995). Therefore, even if the insider claim itself was time-barred, the evidence of an insider transfer was still properly before the jury.

(a) with actual intent to hinder, delay, or defraud any creditor of the debtor; * * *

Utah Code Ann. § 25-6-5(1) (1995) * * * The statute also enumerates factors which the fact-finder may consider, among others, to determine if "actual intent" existed. These include whether:

(a) the transfer or obligation was to an insider;

(b) the debtor retained possession or control of the property transferred after the transfer;

(c) the transfer or obligation was disclosed or concealed;

(d) before the transfer was made or obligation was incurred, the debtor had been sued or threatened with suit;

(e) the transfer was of substantially all the debtor's assets;

(f) the debtor absconded;

(g) the debtor removed or concealed assets;

(h) the value of the consideration received by the debtor was reasonably equivalent to the value of the asset transferred or the amount of the obligation incurred;

(i) the debtor was insolvent or became insolvent shortly after the transfer was made or the obligation was incurred;

(j) the transfer occurred shortly before or shortly after a substantial debt was incurred; and

(k) the debtor transferred the essential assets of the business to a lienor who transferred the assets to an insider of the debtor.

Utah Code Ann. § 25-6-5(2) (1995). These enumerated factors, along with others determined to be relevant in a given case, are termed "badges of fraud." See Dahnken, Inc. v. Wilmarth, 726 P.2d 420, 423 (Utah 1986) (applying former version of U.F.T.A., noting that "[a]lthough actual fraudulent intent must be shown * * * its existence may be inferred from the presence of certain indicia of fraud or 'badges of fraud.'") (citation omitted). Such indicators of fraud have been described as facts which "throw suspicion on a transaction and which call for an explanation * * * facts having a tendency to show the existence of fraud, although their value as evidence is relative not absolute." Territorial Sav. & Loan Ass'n v. Baird, 781 P.2d 452, 462 (Utah 1989) (citation omitted).

The existence of fraudulent intent is a factual question, which may be inferred from all of the attendant circumstances. See id. It necessarily involves weighing the evidence presented and assessing the credibility of witnesses—tasks largely within the province of the fact-finder * * *.

Substantial evidence was presented to the jury in the instant case, which met certain of the enumerated statutory factors, from which the jury could infer an actual intent to hinder, delay or defraud. We refer to some, but not all, of this evidence. The evidence established that between October 1, 1988 and February of 1989, all of Johnson's assets were transferred to Sear-Brown. Johnson was insolvent when these transfers occurred, as its liabilities exceeded its assets by $499,000. The jury heard testimony that Sear-Brown owned all of Johnson's stock at the time of the transfers, compelling the conclusion that Sear-Brown was an insider. Evidence was also presented that Sear-Brown waited almost two years after the transfers before placing Johnson into bankruptcy in July of 1990, and did not disclose the transfers on the bankruptcy schedules prepared by an attorney hired by and paid for by Sear-Brown. In fact, Leon Clary, Sear-Brown's president, testified at trial that part of the decision regarding the date for placing Johnson into bankruptcy was to allow the one-year statute of limitation to expire. The jury also heard evidence that Selvage sued Johnson in the spring of 1987, prior to the asset transfer, and that the transfers were made at or near the time that Selvage filed his motion for summary judgment on the promissory note executed by Johnson. Furthermore, as the trial court observed in its findings of fact, Selvage's pending lawsuit was discussed at a board meeting on August 6, 1988, and instructions were given to continue negotiations with Selvage to try to settle the litigation. The jury could have reasonably inferred that these negotiations were intended to buy time to complete the transfer of Johnson's assets to Sear-Brown.

As to the amount of consideration received by the debtor, the jury was presented with evidence from which it could infer that the consideration Johnson received was not equivalent to the value of the assets transferred to Sear-Brown. Selvage also presented evidence that Sear-Brown undervalued Johnson's business by excluding factors such as its value as an ongoing business and its good will. The jury could also consider that Johnson did not concede the validity of the debt to Selvage until the eve of trial, despite having been controlled by Sear-Brown for some time. The existence of even a single one of these factors "may establish and stamp a transaction as fraudulent."... Therefore, the jury properly found that Sear-Brown's actions indicated an intentional attempt to hinder, delay or defraud rather than merely a bona fide purpose to reduce Johnson's debt to Sear-Brown. See Georgia-Pac. Corp. v. Lumber Prods. Co., 590 P.2d 661, 665 (Okla.1979) (noting motivation is pivotal in determining actual intent). While the evidence was sufficient to meet the clear and convincing standard of proof necessary to establish fraud, it even more certainly meets the less stringent preponderance of the evidence standard necessary to prove an intent to hinder or delay.[2]

To the extent that Sear-Brown contends that the elements of preferential and fraudulent transfers are mutually exclusive, we disagree. The facts that establish a preferential transfer may also be relevant to a fraudulent transfer. In fact, the very first of the enumerated factors which the jury may consider is whether "the transfer or obligation was to an insider." Utah Code Ann. § 25-6-5(2)(a) (1995).

---

[2] In In re Estate of Reed, 566 P.2d 587 (Wyo.1977), the court construed similar language in the Uniform Fraudulent Conveyance Act, and noted that "[a]n intent to 'hinder or delay' is sufficient to void a transfer even though there is no actual fraud as contemplated following the disjunctive 'or.'" Id. at 590. The court also observed that intent can rarely be established directly, and therefore circumstantial evidence must be examined as to the circumstances surrounding the transactions in question. Id. at 590-91.

The critical added element is intent. In this case, the jury had before it the facts establishing an insider transfer, additional facts—most notably the existence of Selvage's lawsuit prior to the transfer and Sear-Brown's decision to place Johnson into bankruptcy—and an opportunity to listen to and observe witnesses testifying at trial. Based upon that experience, the jurors could reasonably have inferred an intent to hinder, delay or defraud. Accordingly, we affirm the trial court's determination that the transfer violated section 25-6-5(1) because it was made with an actual intent to hinder, delay or defraud.

PROBLEM

Paula Proud, a recent medical school graduate, has come to your office with a problem. She intends to do her residency in anesthesiology and eventually practice in that specialty. However, she has heard horror stories about the high rate of malpractice claims in the field, together with huge judgments, often in excess of the liability limits in the physician's insurance coverage. Her problem is this. Just recently she inherited, from her grandfather, the old family manse, which has been in her family for generations and now has a value of over one million dollars. Paula is prepared to place her medical income at risk in the event of future liability, but does not want to take the chance of losing the old house. After talking to some friends she has struck on a plan and wants your advice. Her plan consists of conveying title to the house to her spouse, Peter, as a gift. Of course she will continue to live there. What do you tell her? Do you need additional information to formulate your response? If so, what do you want to know? If you conclude that her scheme is flawed, do you have any other suggestions? Would it be safer to grant Peter a mortgage on the property? How about if Paula sells him the house for $100 instead of transferring title as a gift?

UCC § 2-401(1)

Title to goods cannot pass under a contract for sale prior to their identification to the contract (2-501), and unless otherwise explicitly agreed the buyer acquires by their identification a special property as limited by this Act. Any retention or reservation by the seller of the title (property) in goods shipped or delivered to the buyer is limited in effect to a reservation of a security interest * * *.

UCC § 2-402(2)

A creditor of the seller may treat a sale or an identification of goods to a contract for sale as void if as against him a retention of possession by the seller is fraudulent under any rule of law of the state where the goods are situated, except that retention of possession in good faith and current course of trade by a merchant-seller for a commercially reasonable time after a sale or identification is not fraudulent.

QUESTION

What is the relationship between § 2-401(1) and § 2-402(2)? Are these rules internally consistent? Are they consistent with the rule in *Twyne's Case*?

BAIRD, NOTICE FILING AND THE PROBLEM OF OSTENSIBLE OWNERSHIP, 12 J. Legal Stud. 53, 53-54 (1983). "Few principles of Anglo-American law have been so long-lived and so widely held, as the one in *Twyne's Case*. The principle that secret interests in property possessed by someone else are void has shaped the entire law of security interests in personal property. The common justification for the principle is that those who rely on the debtor's assets, such as the debtor's other creditors, need an easy way to tell what property the debtor owns. The easiest way to accommodate these parties is to hold transfers of property ineffective against third parties unless possession is also transferred. With this rule, a party knows that no one else has a superior interest in property in the debtor's possession."

FRAUDULENT TRANSFERS IN BANKRUPTCY

Not only does each state have its own fraudulent transfer law, but the federal Bankruptcy Code (11 U.S.C. §§ 101 *et seq.*) gives the trustee in bankruptcy the power to recover transfers made in violation of § 548(a) of the Code, which is substantially similar in structure and content to the UFTA. However, state fraudulent transfer law continues to play an important role in bankruptcy cases. Here's why. Under § 548, the trustee may only avoid a fraudulent transfer made within one year before the bankruptcy petition was filed. However, § 544(b) also permits the trustee to avoid any transfer that could have been avoided by an unsecured creditor of the debtor provided that such creditor is still in existence. In other words, the trustee's right is a derivative one. She is permitted to step into the shoes of an actual unsecured creditor and exercise the rights of that creditor for the benefit of the bankruptcy estate. One of those rights may be the right to set aside a fraudulent transfer made by the debtor more than one year prior to filing but still within the state statute of limitations, which under § 9(b) of the UFTA may extend to as long as four years following the transfer.

Moreover, § 544(b) codifies the rule established in Moore v. Bay, 284 U.S. 3 (1931), decided under the former Bankruptcy Act, which permits the full value of the property transferred to be recovered regardless of the amount of the claim of the creditor whose status is essential to the trustee's rights under § 544(b) in the first place. Perhaps an example would be helpful here. Assume that three years prior to filing bankruptcy, the debtor made a transfer, fraudulent under applicable state law, in the amount of $100,000. Assume further that, at the time of the transfer, the debtor was obligated to a creditor holding a $750 unsecured claim. The trustee cannot attack the transfer under § 548 because it occurred too long before filing. However, so long as that creditor's claim remains outstanding, the trustee can step into the shoes of the creditor under § 544(b) to avoid the entire transfer, even though the creditor, had it brought the claim under state law, could only have avoided the transfer to the extent of its $750 claim. It is for this reason that it is often said that the trustee steps not just into the shoes of the actual creditor under § 544(b), but into the "overshoes" of that creditor.

SECTION 2. FRAUD AT LAW—DEEMED TO BE FRAUDULENT

(a) CONSTRUCTIVELY FRAUDULENT CONVEYANCES

UFTA §§ 4(a) & 5(a)
(*see Selected Commercial Statutes*)

BANKRUPTCY CODE § 548(a)(2)
(*see Selected Commercial Statutes*)

INTRODUCTORY NOTE

There is an axiom in commercial law that a debtor must be "just before she is generous." Therefore, both the UFTA and the Bankruptcy Code set out three types of conveyances which are *deemed* to be fraudulent; they may be avoided without proof of actual intent to defraud. In each instance, the common requirement is that the transfer be made for less than "reasonably equivalent value." In many cases, of course, the debtor will also have made the transfer with intent to place those assets beyond the reach of creditors. The point, however, is that it is not necessary to prove bad intent in order to recover the property. Today, some of the most controversial issues arising in the commercial law arena involve application of the law governing constructively fraudulent transfers and, more specifically, the question of what constitutes "reasonably equivalent value."

CHRISTIANS v. CRYSTAL EVANGELICAL FREE CHURCH (IN RE YOUNG)

United States District Court, Minnesota, 1993.
152 B.R. 939.

HARRY H. MacLAUGHLIN, District Judge.

This matter is before the Court on defendant Crystal Evangelical Free Church's appeal of the bankruptcy court's order granting summary judgment in favor of plaintiff Julia A. Christians, the trustee. The bankruptcy court's order will be affirmed.

FACTS

The parties stipulated to the following facts. Bruce and Nancy Young (debtors) filed a Chapter 7 bankruptcy petition on February 3, 1992. Plaintiff Julia A. Christians is the trustee in their case. In the year immediately preceding the debtors' filing, debtors contributed a total of $13,450 to defendant Crystal Evangelical Free Church. Debtors were insolvent at the time the contributions were made. In addition to their financial contributions, debtors held a variety of volunteer positions in the church. At no time did the church require debtors to pay any membership or attendance fee, but the church does teach that people should make regular financial contributions.

The trustee brought an adversary proceeding seeking to recover the contributions as "fraudulent transfers" within the meaning of the Bankruptcy Code. The trustee and the church both moved for summary judgment. The bankruptcy court granted the trustee's motion and denied the church's motion. Christians v. Crystal Evangelical Free Church (In re Young), 148 B.R. 886, 897 (Bankr.D.Minn.1992). The church appeals.

DISCUSSION

* * *

II. Overview

The parties raise several issues. Initially, the Court must determine whether, as a matter of statutory interpretation, the bankruptcy court correctly concluded that debtors did not receive "reasonably equivalent value in exchange for" the contributions.

* * *

III. Fraudulent Transfers Under the Bankruptcy Code

A. Applicable Law

The first issue before the Court is whether the contributions to the church were avoidable transfers within section 548 of the Bankruptcy Code. Section 548 provides in pertinent part:

> (a) The trustee may avoid any transfer of an interest of the debtor in property, or any obligation incurred by the debtor, that was made or incurred on or within one year before the date of the filing of the petition, if the debtor voluntarily or involuntarily—

* * *

(2)(A) received less than a *reasonably equivalent value in exchange* for such transfer or obligation; and

(B)(i) was insolvent on the date that such transfer was made or such obligation was incurred, or became insolvent as a result of such transfer or obligation * * *.

11 U.S.C. § 548(a) (emphasis added). For the Court to find that a fraudulent transfer occurred, the trustee must prove the following:

1. there was a transfer of an interest of the debtor in property;

2. the transfer was made within one year before the date of the filing of the petition;

3. the debtor was insolvent on the date the transfer was made; and

4. the debtor received less than a reasonable equivalent value in exchange for the transfer.

First Nat'l Bank in Anoka v. Minnesota Utility Contracting, Inc. (In re Minnesota Utility Contracting, Inc.), 110 B.R. 414, 417 (D.Minn.1990). The parties stipulated that the first three elements were satisfied; the only issue is whether the debtors received "reasonably equivalent value in exchange for" the contributions. Christians, 148 B.R. at 890.

In determining whether the debtors received reasonably equivalent value, the Court must examine all aspects of the transaction and carefully measure the value of all benefits and burdens to the debtor, direct or indirect. Pembroke Develop. Corp. v. Commonwealth Savings & Loan Assoc. (In re Pembroke Develop. Corp.), 124 B.R. 398, 400 (Bankr.S.D.Fla.1991). In other words, a determination of whether the debtor received reasonably equivalent value depends on the facts and circumstances of each case. Minnesota Utility, 110 B.R. at 419; Joshua Slocum, Ltd. v. Boyle (In re Joshua Slocum, Ltd.), 103 B.R. 610, 618 (Bankr.E.D.Pa.), aff'd, 121 B.R. 442 (E.D.Pa.1989). The burden is on the trustee to establish that debtors did not receive reasonably equivalent value. Mellon Bank, N.A. v. Metro Communications, Inc., 945 F.2d 635, 650 (3d Cir.1991), cert. denied, 503 U.S. 937, 112 S.Ct. 1476, 117 L.Ed.2d 620 (1992); Minnesota Utility, 110 B.R. at 417-19.

The Court has previously addressed the issue of what constitutes reasonably equivalent value. In Minnesota Utility, a bank extended Minnesota Utility Contracting, a closely-held corporation, a revolving line of credit that was secured by assets of Minnesota Utility. Later, the bank agreed to extend additional credit to Minnesota Utility but only if another closely-held corporation, MUC Leasing, which was owned by the same shareholders that owned Minnesota Utility, granted the bank a security interest in its assets. Both Minnesota Utility and MUC Leasing filed for bankruptcy within one year of the extension of additional credit. The issue was whether MUC Leasing had received reasonably equivalent value for the security interest it granted the bank. The bankruptcy court held that indirect benefits, under certain circumstances, may constitute reasonably equivalent value but that there was no evidence that MUC Leasing received any indirect benefits.

On appeal, the Court stated that "[i]n determining whether a debtor has received fair consideration for the transfer, the Court should consider the purpose of the requirement, which is to conserve the debtor's estate for the benefit of creditors." Id. at 420. The Court then held that while indirect benefits could constitute reasonably equivalent value under some circumstances, the benefits received must be "fairly concrete." Id. The Court affirmed the bankruptcy court's order because there was no evidence in the record that MUC Leasing received "fairly concrete" indirect benefits.

B. The Bankruptcy Court's Order

The bankruptcy court described the analysis as two-fold. Did the debtors receive "value?" If so, was that "value" given "in exchange for" the contributions? In addressing the question of whether debtors received "value," the bankruptcy court looked to the statutory definition of that term. For the purposes of section 548—

> "value" means *property*, or satisfaction or securing of a present or antecedent debt of the debtor, but does not include an unperformed promise to furnish support to the debtor or to a relative of the debtor.

11 U.S.C. § 548(d)(2)(A) (emphasis added). Because the church did not satisfy or secure a present or antecedent debt of the debtors in exchange for the donations, the bankruptcy court refined the inquiry to address whether the debtors received "property" in return. 148 B.R. at 890-93.

Based on the following reasoning, the bankruptcy court held that the debtors did not receive "property." First, relying on dictionary definitions of the term "property," the bankruptcy court concluded that property consists of rights and things subject to ownership. Id. at 891. Second, based on this definition, the bankruptcy court rejected the church's argument that debtors received "property" in the form of religious services, theological programs, and access to the premises. Id. "The debtors did not receive legal or equitable rights nor did they obtain any ownership interest from their contributions." Id. Third, the bankruptcy court concluded that the contributions did not yield "value" because they were economically detrimental to the debtors' financial estate. Id. at 893. The bankruptcy court found that "it was the debtors individually and not their pre-petition financial estate or their post-petition bankruptcy estate that received any benefit." Id. Fourth, the bankruptcy court bolstered its conclusion that the church's services were not "property" by asserting that the Establishment Clause might prevent a court from placing a value on those services, a task the court would be required to perform to determine whether the value received was reasonably equivalent to the contributions. Id. at 894.

The bankruptcy court then assumed, arguendo, that the debtors did receive "value" from the services of the church. The bankruptcy court held that any "value" the debtors received was not "in exchange for" their contributions. Id. at 895. The bankruptcy court noted that the church welcomes all members to worship regardless of the size of contribution. The court found that the services offered by the church were in no way linked to the debtors' contributions. The bankruptcy court also looked to the Internal Revenue Code for guidance. The court concluded that under the Internal Revenue Code payments made to a religious organization in exchange for a quid pro quo are not deductible. 26 U.S.C. § 170(c)(4); Hernandez v. C.I.R., 490 U.S. 680, 109 S.Ct. 2136, 104 L.Ed.2d 766, reh'g denied, 492 U.S. 933, 110 S.Ct. 16, 106 L.Ed.2d 630 (1989). Finding that the church's argument that the debtors received services "in exchange for" the contributions called into question the right of all members to deduct donations, the bankruptcy court held that the same contribution that qualifies for a deduction under the Internal Revenue Code cannot also be "in exchange for" "value" under the terms of the Bankruptcy Code. 148 B.R. at 895.

Finally, the bankruptcy court was sharply critical of two cases finding that religious contributions were not avoidable under section 548. In Ellenberg v. Chapel Hill Harvester Church, Inc. (In re Moses), 59 B.R. 815 (Bankr.N.D.Ga.1986), it was undisputed that the debtors had transferred $4,733.50 to their church in the year preceding the filing of their bankruptcy petition and the transfers took place while the debtors were insolvent. One of the debtors served as a deacon at the church and was required to tithe as a holder of that office. The trustee sought to recover the contributions as fraudulent transfers. The bankruptcy court found that the issue was solely one of statutory interpretation. The bankruptcy court recognized that in order for the services to constitute "value," the court first had to find that the services constituted "property." The bankruptcy court held that the debtors received "property" based on the following reasoning. First, the bankruptcy court concluded that because the church required the contributions as a condition of one of the debtor's employment as a deacon, the contributions could be directly tied to the monetary compensation and benefits he received through his employment by the church. Second, the court found that the debtors received valuable services including marriage counseling and theological education. Third, the court found that the church provided heating, air conditioning, and electrical services for the debtors' comfort during the services they attended and those utility services could constitute exchangeable value. In the end, the bankruptcy court held that the trustee failed to meet his burden of proof because he did not offer adequate evidence that the debtors received less than a reasonably equivalent value in exchange for the contributions.

In reaching its decision in the case at bar, the bankruptcy court was very critical of the Ellenberg court. The bankruptcy court stated that Ellenberg's conclusion that services provided by a church could constitute "property" violated the plain language of the statute. Christians, 148 B.R. at 896. The bankruptcy court also charged the Ellenberg court with neglecting to address the issue of whether the services provided by the church were "in exchange for" the contributions. Id. at 895-96. In short, the bankruptcy court concluded that the Ellenberg court ignored the statutory language in order to reach the "right" result. Id. at 896.

The bankruptcy court was also critical of a case on which the Ellenberg court relied. In Wilson v. Upreach Ministries (In re Missionary Baptist Found. of Am.), 24 B.R. 973 (Bankr.N.D.Tex.1982), the debtor was the Missionary Baptist

Foundation of America (MBFA), a nonprofit corporation which donated money to Upreach Ministries, another nonprofit corporation, within one year of MBFA filing for bankruptcy. There was no doubt that MBFA was insolvent at the time the contributions were made. After the bankruptcy court pointed out that a finding of fraudulent intent was not necessary, the court nevertheless felt it was relevant to highlight the fact that there were no "badges of fraud" in that case. The bankruptcy court held that whether the challenged transfer was for "reasonably equivalent value" was largely a question of fact and considerable latitude should be afforded to the finder of fact. The court concluded that "reasonably equivalent value" did not require that a monetary equivalent be received in exchange. The bankruptcy court held that the "good will" MBFA received in return for the contributions satisfied the "reasonably equivalent value" requirement and the contributions could not be recovered as fraudulent transfers.

In the instant case, the bankruptcy court criticized Upreach Ministries for the same reasons it criticized Ellenberg. The bankruptcy court stated that equating "good will" with intangible property which could provide "reasonably equivalent value" ignored the plain language of the Bankruptcy Code. Christians, 148 B.R. at 896. The bankruptcy court sympathized with the desire to do what "feel[s] right," but charged the Upreach Ministries court with willingly ignoring the statutory language in order to reach that result. Id.

C. The Parties' Arguments

The church argues that the bankruptcy court improperly construed section 548. The church begins by arguing that the bankruptcy court disregarded the canon of statutory interpretation that a statute should not be construed in a fashion that raises constitutional issues if another reasonable construction is available. The church asserts that Congress must clearly express an affirmative intention to regulate religious conduct before a statute should be interpreted in a way that interferes with the Establishment Clause and Free Exercise Clause of the First Amendment. The church argues that Congress did not intend section 548 to regulate religious conduct.

Next, the church argues that the bankruptcy court failed to consider the purpose of section 548. The church argues that the title of the statute, "Fraudulent transfers and obligations," indicates that Congress was concerned with unscrupulous creditors and not bona fide charities. The church asserts that because neither the church nor the debtors intended to defraud creditors, the purpose of section 548 does not apply in this case.

The church also argues that debtors received "value" in return for their contributions for several reasons. First, the church attempts to distinguish Hernandez v. C.I.R., 490 U.S. 680, 109 S.Ct. 2136, 104 L.Ed.2d 766, reh'g denied, 492 U.S. 933, 110 S.Ct. 16, 106 L.Ed.2d 630 (1989), which held that any quid pro quo received in return for a contribution renders the contribution non-deductible, by asserting that the different purposes of the Internal Revenue Code and the Bankruptcy Code allow a finding that debtors received "value" in return for their charitable contributions. Second, the church argues that a tax deduction for charitable contributions is "value" received for the purposes of the

Bankruptcy Code. Third, the church claims that the spiritual counseling provided for debtors constituted "value." Fourth, the church argues that the debtors' donations allowed the church to pay operating expenses including electricity, heat, and air conditioning, and that debtors received "value" from those utilities while they were at the church. The church contends that there is no requirement in section 548 that the debtor be the only person to receive value or that others cannot enjoy benefits at the same time.

The church also objects to the bankruptcy court's conclusion that even if the debtors did receive "value," it was not "in exchange for" their donations. The church argues that the spiritual counseling, educational, and worship services were provided during the general time frame during which the donations were made and thus were "in exchange for" those services. The church also argues that the debtors received a tax deduction "in exchange for" the donations.

The trustee responds to most of the church's arguments by directing the Court's attention to the reasoning adopted by the bankruptcy court. In short, the trustee first argues that a finding that the debtors received "value" requires a finding that they received "property," and that debtors received no property in this case. Second, the trustee argues even if the debtors received "value," it was not "in exchange for" their contributions. Third, the trustee argues that a finding that the services provided by the church constituted "value" would force the bankruptcy court into the impossible position of having to place a dollar value on those services in order to determine whether they were of "reasonably equivalent value" to the contributions. Finally, the trustee objects to the church's argument that a tax deduction was "value" received "in exchange for" the contributions on the grounds that the argument is being raised for the first time on appeal.

D. Analysis

The Court finds that the bankruptcy court adopted the proper analytical framework and interpreted section 548 correctly. There are two issues: (1) did the debtors receive "reasonably equivalent value" for their contributions, and if so (2) were the contributions given "in exchange for" that "value."

1. Did Debtors Receive "Reasonably Equivalent Value"?

The Court concludes that debtors did not receive "reasonably equivalent value," within the meaning of the Bankruptcy Code, for their contributions. "Value" is defined by the Bankruptcy Code. "Value" must be either "property, or satisfaction or securing of a present or antecedent debt." 11 U.S.C. § 548(d)(2)(A). The parties agree that the key issue is whether debtors received some sort of property right. The Court finds that they did not. Debtors stipulated that they could have taken advantage of the services offered by the church regardless of whether they made any financial contributions, but that the church encouraged regular donations. In other words, debtors made the contributions out of a "sense of religious obligation." Appellant's Mem. at 13. A debtor cannot receive reasonably equivalent value for payments that are made out of a sense of moral obligation rather than legal obligation. See Whitlock v. Hause (In re Hause), 13 B.R. 75, 79 (Bankr.D.Mass.1981). Moreover, emotional support received in exchange for a transfer, without more, cannot satisfy the requirement for reasonably equivalent value. Walker v. Treadwell (Matter of Treadwell), 699 F.2d 1050, 1051 (11th Cir.1983). "The object of section 548 is to prevent the debtor from depleting the resources available to creditors through gratuitous transfers of the debtor's property." Id. Charitable contributions are clearly gratuitous transfers, despite the fact that debtors feel morally obligated to tithe. Strictly as a matter of statutory interpretation, there are no justifiable grounds to differentiate between religious donations and other gratuitous transfers, such as gifts to family members, which are clearly avoidable. Walker, 699 F.2d at 1051.

The Court concludes that the church's argument that the tax deduction debtors received for the contributions was "reasonably equivalent value" is also unpersuasive. The ability to deduct an amount of money from gross income cannot, in economic terms, be of "reasonably equivalent value" to that same amount in cash that has been removed from the estate. See Durrett v. Washington Nat. Ins. Co., 621 F.2d 201, 203 (5th Cir.1980) (establishing rule that any transfer for less than 70 percent of market value of the property is per se not reasonably equivalent value).

Finally, the bankruptcy court was correct to look to Supreme Court precedent in connection with the Internal Revenue Code for assistance. In Hernandez v. C.I.R., 490 U.S. 680, 109 S.Ct. 2136, 104 L.Ed.2d 766, reh'g denied, 492 U.S. 933, 110 S.Ct. 16, 106 L.Ed.2d 630 (1989), the Supreme Court addressed the issue of whether fixed-level donations to a religious organization can be deducted from taxable income when specific services are provided by the religious organization in return for the fixed donation. The Court found that a quid pro quo analysis was appropriate. Id. 490 U.S. at 691, 109 S.Ct. at 2145. The Court held that a charitable contribution is deductible only if it is without adequate consideration. Id. 490 U.S. at 690, 109 S.Ct. at 2144. Given this ruling, by definition if a charitable contribution is deductible, i.e. without adequate consideration, it cannot be in exchange for "reasonably equivalent value." See Rubin v. Manufacturers Hanover Trust Co., 661 F.2d 979, 991 (2d Cir.1981) (fair consideration for bankruptcy purposes is more than consideration needed to support a simple contract).

2. If Debtors Received "Reasonably Equivalent Value," Was It "In Exchange For" Contributions?

Even if the debtors received "reasonably equivalent value," the Court finds that the church did not provide that value "in exchange for" the debtors' contributions. The parties stipulated that the church's support and services are available to all, regardless whether contributions are made. This stipulation precludes a finding that the church provided its services "in exchange for" debtors' contributions. The church's argument that debtors received a tax deduction "in exchange for" the contributions is also unpersuasive. A charitable contribution is deductible only if there is no quid pro quo. Hernandez, 490 U.S. at 690, 109 S.Ct. at 2144. The Court declines to hold that although a tax deduction is not a quid pro quo for a donation, a tax deduction is given "in exchange for" a donation. See Rubin, 661 F.2d at 991.

3. Other Case Law

The Court agrees with the bankruptcy court's conclusion that the other cases addressing this issue have glossed-over the statutory requirements in order to reach the "right" result. In Wilson v. Upreach Ministries (In re Missionary Baptist Found. of Am.), 24 B.R. 973 (Bankr.N.D.Tex.1982), the bankruptcy court concluded that "reasonably equivalent value" did not require that a monetary equivalent be received in exchange. Id. at 979. The bankruptcy court held that the "good-will" received in return for the contributions satisfied the "reasonably equivalent value" requirement and the contributions could not be recovered as fraudulent transfers. Id. Upreach Ministries is inconsistent with this Court's precedent stating that the benefits received must be "fairly concrete." First Nat'l Bank in Anoka v. Minnesota Utility Contracting, Inc. (In re Minnesota Utility Contracting, Inc.), 110 B.R. 414, 420 (D.Minn.1990). Moreover, the Upreach Ministries court did not discuss whether the contributions were given "in exchange for" the good-will it received. For these reasons, the Court declines to follow Upreach Ministries.

Turning to Ellenberg v. Chapel Hill Harvester Church, Inc. (In re Moses), 59 B.R. 815 (Bankr.N.D.Ga.1986), while the Court finds that this case's analysis suffers from many of the same flaws of Upreach Ministries, it is also distinguishable from the case at bar. In Ellenberg, the bankruptcy court premised its holding in part on the fact that the church required the contributions as a condition of one of the debtor's employment as a deacon and thus the contributions could be directly tied to the monetary compensation and benefits he received through his employment by the church. Id. In this case, the debtors have stipulated that they were not required to tithe. Accordingly, the Court concludes that debtors did not receive value in exchange for their contributions.

4. Summary

The church states that it is offended at the characterization of the transfers as "fraudulent." Unfortunately, that is the label the Bankruptcy Code places on transactions that harm the interests of creditors in general, and fraudulent intent is not required. Ellenberg, 59 B.R. at 819. While describing the donations as "avoidable transfers" rather than "fraudulent transfers" may be more appropriate because it lessens the inference of culpability, the purpose of section 548 is where attention should be focused. The avoiding powers of the Bankruptcy Code are designed to maximize the size of the estate in order to maximize the distribution to innocent creditors. Minnesota Utility, 110 B.R. at 417. The fact that debtors made gratuitous transfers to their church rather than to, for example, family members or some non-religious charity does not materially alter the analysis. In short, the Court concludes that, as a matter of statutory interpretation, debtors did not receive "reasonably equivalent value" from the church's services and, even if the church's services constituted "reasonably equivalent value," the services were not provided "in exchange for" the debtors' $13,450 in donations.

NOTE ON *CHRISTIANS*

The Crystal Evangelical Free Church took its case to the Eighth Circuit where it managed to get the district court's decision above reversed, *but not* on the ground that the court had misapplied the fraudulent transfer statute. Christians v. Crystal Evangelical Free Church, 82 F.3d 1407 (1994). Rather, while the appeal was pending, President Clinton signed into law the Religious Freedom Restoration Act of 1993 (the "RFRA") (42 U.S.C. § 2000bb), which invalidated any governmental action that substantially burdens the free exercise of religion, unless the action is in furtherance of a compelling governmental interest and is the least restrictive means of furthering that interest. Although the Eighth Circuit agreed that the debtors *had not* received reasonable equivalent return value in exchange for their contributions to their church, the court concluded that recovery of those contributions would substantially burden the debtors' free exercise of religion and that the basic bankruptcy goals of allowing a debtor a financial fresh start and protecting the interests of creditors did not rise to the level of a compelling governmental interest so as to permit the interference. The RFRA was subsequently struck down by the U.S. Supreme Court as applied to the states as exceeding Congress' Fourteenth Amendment power to enforce constitutional rights. Boerne v. Flores, 117 Sup. Ct. 2157 (1997). The Court then remanded the Eighth Circuit's decision in *Christians* for reconsideration in light of *Boerne.* However, on remand, the Eighth Circuit concluded that the RFRA was not unconstitutional as applied to *federal law*, 1998 WL 166642. Accordingly, the court reinstated its earlier decision reversing the district court's judgment in favor of the trustee.

Subsequent to the Eighth Circuit's decision in *Christians,* the U.S. District Court for the District of Kansas held that the spiritual benefits derived from tithing did not rise to the level of reasonably equivalent value *and* that the fraudulent transfer law neither violated the RFRA nor the debtors' First Amendment rights. Morris v. Midway Southern Baptist Church (In re Newman), 203 B.R. 468 (1996). See also In re Bloch, 207 B.R. 944 (D. Colo. 1997) (holding that § 548(a) does not constitute a substantial burden on religion). Because of its interpretation of the RFRA, the Eighth Circuit never reached the constitutional issues in *Christians*, although the district court (in a portion of the decision omitted from your casebook) ruled that an order directing the Youngs' church to turn over the Youngs' contributions did not violate either the Free Exercise or the Establishment Clauses of the First Amendment. In light of the holdings in *Christians* and *Newman* on the issue of reasonably equivalent value, would your school have to forfeit a large alumnus/a gift if the other elements of a constructively fraudulent transfer were proven? How about the winnings of a casino that had provided the debtor with a night's "action" at the gaming tables. See Allard v. Flamingo Hilton (In re Chomakos), 69 F.3d 769 (6th Cir. 1995).

QUESTIONS ON PROTECTION OF GOOD FAITH TRANSFEREES

Sometimes an insolvent debtor will convey property to a third party in an arms-length transaction for substantial, but still less than reasonably equivalent, return value. Presumably the transfer can still be set aside in that case as constructively fraudulent. What rights does the innocent transferee have in those circumstances? Is she deprived of the benefit of her bargain? If she must return the property for the benefit of the debtor's creditors, what happens to the value given for the property? See UFTA § 8(d). Compare Bankruptcy Code §§ 548(c) and 550(e)(1). Both the UFTA and the Bankruptcy Code offer some protection for a transferee who took in "good faith." So long as the transferee has given substantial consideration why should good faith matter at all?

SHERWIN, CREDITORS' RIGHTS AGAINST PARTICIPANTS IN A LEVERAGED BUYOUT, 72 Minn. L. Rev. 449-52 (1988).

Leveraged buyout transactions can take a variety of forms. The common feature is that assets of the acquired corporation are used to finance the acquisition. For the purposes of this Article, it is helpful to distinguish between two categories of buyouts—those financed by selling shareholders and those financed by an independent lending institution.

In the first category, selling shareholders finance the buyout by accepting the buyers' note for most or all of the purchase price of the shares. Simultaneously with the purchase, the buyers cause the corporation to endorse the note or guarantee its payment and to grant the sellers a security interest in corporate assets. Corporate assets and earnings are expected to be the primary source for repaying the acquisition debt.

Within the second category, buyouts financed by an independent lender, a further distinction should be made between two methods of outside financing. First, a lending institution may advance the funds required for the acquisition to the buyers. Typically, the buyers give the lender their unsecured note. In a simultaneous transaction, the buyers acquire the shares, assume control, and cause the corporation to endorse or guarantee their note and to secure the obligation with a lien on corporate assets. This is similar to the buyout financed by selling shareholders except that an independent party receives corporate obligations and security.

Second, in an effort to reduce the risk of a challenge by creditors, the parties may structure the transaction so that the lender advances funds directly to the acquired corporation. There are several ways to do this. The corporation may borrow from the lender and then reloan the proceeds on an unsecured basis to the buyers or a parent corporation formed by the buyers. Another possibility is to complete the buyout through a merger. To do this the buyers form a new corporation to purchase the shares of the existing corporation they wish to acquire. In a simultaneous transaction, the new corporation borrows from a lender and delivers the proceeds to the sellers in return for the shares of the acquired corporation, the acquired corporation is merged into the new corporation, and the combined entity grants a security interest in its assets to the lender to secure repayment of the loan.

Whatever its form, a leveraged buyout reduces the assets available to general creditors of the corporation. The sellers' equity interest, which is subordinate to creditors' claims, is replaced with secured debt. Often, the purchase price in a buyout approximates the net worth of the corporation, and a highly leveraged transaction may threaten the creditors' ability to collect. If the corporation is left with a positive net worth and sufficient funds to pay debts and continue in business, the buyout does not harm the creditors' reasonable expectations of an adequate source of payment. But if the corporation is left insolvent or without the resources it needs to sustain its business, the buyout conflicts with the creditors' legally protected rights.

When a corporation is left in inadequate financial condition following a buyout and later fails, unpaid creditors may assert claims against parties who participated in the buyout. Although several grounds are available, the most effective remedy is provided by fraudulent conveyance statutes. These statutes enable creditors to set aside certain transfers or obligations defined by statute as fraudulent against creditors. In a number of cases, creditors have used fraudulent conveyance law successfully to avoid corporate obligations and security given to selling shareholders in buyout transactions. In several notable decisions, courts have also applied fraudulent conveyance law to set aside obligations and security in the hands of independent lenders who financed the buyouts.

NOTES AND QUESTIONS

1. Assume that you represent a bank that extended a loan to a company, the proceeds of which were to be used to finance the borrower's acquisition of the stock of another company. Your client received, as security for the loan, a lien (or "security interest") on all of the assets of the acquired company. That company is now experiencing financial difficulties and your client has heard that some of its unsecured creditors are considering suing the bank to avoid its lien as a fraudulent transfer. In addition, there are rumors that the acquired company might file bankruptcy. The bank wants to know what kind of exposure it may have and also wants you to advise it on what arguments or defenses might be raised on its behalf. What do you tell the bank? In formulating your response, think about what additional information you will want to review. See Bay Plastics, Inc. v. BT Commercial Corp., 187 B.R. 315 (Bankr. C.D. Cal. 1995); Baird & Jackson, *Fraudulent Conveyance Law and Its Proper Domain*, 38 Vand. L. Rev. 842 (1985).

2. Not uncommonly, the owners of a single business elect to conduct the business through a group of affiliated corporate entities. This may take the form of numerous sibling corporations (all owned by the same shareholders) as well as parent/subsidiary arrangements. There is certainly nothing unlawful about this practice, and in fact it often makes considerable practical sense from a tax, accounting, or administrative standpoint. However, Professor Blumberg has pointed out that the shift from the simple corporate form of organization to the complex corporate structure, that increasingly characterizes the structure of large companies doing business around the world, has effected decisive changes in the way that the law deals with the individual constituent companies in a single corporate group. P. BLUMBERG,

THE LAW OF CORPORATE GROUPS (1983 & 1985). One of these areas of rapid development entails the proper framework for analysis when one of the constituent members of this group of corporations seeks to borrow money. Typically, the lender will require the guarantee of one or more of the affiliated companies as a condition to the loan. Traditionally, courts have drawn a distinction based on whether the guarantee was "downstream" (parent corporation guaranteeing debt of subsidiary) versus "upstream" (subsidiary guaranteeing parent debt) or cross-stream (sibling company intercorporate guarantees). Can you articulate a reason for treating these various types of intercorporate guarantees differently from a fraudulent conveyance analysis point of view? Discussion of the issue can be found in Mellon Bank, N.A. v. Metro Communications, Inc., 945 F.2d 635 (3d Cir. 1991); Rubin v. Manufacturers Hanover Trust Co., 661 F.2d 979 (2d Cir. 1981); First National Bank in Anoka v. Minnesota Utility Contracting, Inc. (In re Minnesota Utility Contracting, Inc), 101 B.R. 71 (Bankr. D. Minn. 1989), *aff'd in part, rev'd in part,* 110 B.R. 414 (D. Minn. 1990); and Lawrence Paperboard Corp. v. Arlington Trust Co. (In re Lawrence Paperboard Corp.), 76 B.R. 866 (Bankr. D. Mass. 1987).

3. Often, an individual debtor who has decided to make a fraudulent conveyance will seek out the aid of his attorney to draft the documents of transfer. It is clear under prevailing ethical standards that a lawyer may not assist a client in conduct that the lawyer knows is criminal or fraudulent. ABA MODEL RULES OF PROFESSIONAL CONDUCT (1984), Rule 4.4. If the lawyer drafts the documents, knowing for example that the consideration for the transfer is inadequate, that the transfer will render the debtor insolvent, and that the debtor's aim is to hamper creditor collection efforts, should the lawyer also have liability to the debtor's creditors if she proceeds to prepare the transfer documents? In McElhanon v. Hing, 728 P.2d 256, 261-64 (Ariz. Ct. App. 1985), *vacated on other grounds,* 728 P.2d 273 (Ariz. 1986), *cert. denied*, 481 U.S. 1030 (1987), the lawyer was held liable for *conspiracy* to commit a fraudulent conveyance. Is this a proper ruling in your judgment? What other considerations bear on the issue?

4. If the transferee of a fraudulent transfer subsequently conveys the property for valuable consideration to an innocent third party, should the transferor's creditors be able to reach the property in the hands of the secondary transferee? If not, what remedy do the defrauded creditors have?

(b) INSIDER PREFERENCES

JACKSON, AVOIDING POWERS IN BANKRUPTCY, 36 Stan. L. Rev. 725, 757-60 (1984).

In their simplest form, preferences are transfers that favor one existing creditor over another. Debtor prefers Creditor A to Creditor B if Debtor pays Creditor A before he pays Creditor B. Such behavior is not conventionally thought to be a fraudulent conveyance—assuming Debtor is not motivated by an actual desire to delay, hinder, or defraud Creditor B—because Debtor's antecedent debt to Creditor A is considered fair consideration for the transfer (presumably of cash) that Debtor makes to him. In other words, Debtor plans to pay Creditor B eventually, but prefers to pay Creditor A first.

This can be stated in a more illuminating way. Preference law, unlike fraudulent conveyance law, is not a part of the arsenal of rights and remedies between a *debtor* and his *creditors*. Rather, preferences differ from fraudulent conveyances precisely because preference law focuses on relationships *among creditors* in light of the advantages of a collective proceeding, not on relationships *between creditors* and their debtor. So stated, it is easy to see that preferences generally are permitted outside bankruptcy because the relationships of creditors among themselves are inherently collective in nature; preferences are a source of concern only when the creditors perceive there may not be enough to go around. Not surprisingly, no conflict exists among creditors absent that worry.

The justification sometimes given for permitting preferences outside bankruptcy is that one cannot undo one creditor's preference at the behest of another creditor without creating a new preference. Given the possibility of a collective system, however, such an explanation is at best only partially correct. Upon undoing a preference, one could divide the assets retrieved among the creditors as a group. This practice, however, would inevitably require a collective proceeding for collection and disbursement of assets. Any system that prevented preferences, therefore, would necessarily be a collective system in which creditors could not recover from their debtor without accounting for the interests of other creditors. For this reason, preferences do not seem inherently objectionable outside bankruptcy (or other collective proceeding). Preference law is part and parcel of the substitution of collective remedies for individual remedies.

The essence of a collective proceeding such as bankruptcy is ratable distribution among those similarly situated. Creditors share in the property of a debtor according to the priorities they agreed to when they initially entered into their transactions with the debtor. Creditors view this as desirable ex ante because collectivizing the disbursement of assets after insolvency brings gains to the creditors as a group.

Yet while the creditors would agree to this system before they lent money, they face the usual problems of policing a deal after it is struck. Each creditor has incentives to advance his individual interests, even though doing so might work against the greater collective benefit. Once his debtor becomes insolvent, and without collective enforcement of the creditors' bargain, each creditor must race for assets, not necessarily just to grab more than his share but also simply to avoid being left with nothing. Accordingly, creditors need a mechanism to bind them to their presumptive ex ante agreement and to foil the attempts of each creditor to welsh on the agreement for individual gain.

NOTE ON THE DISTINCTION BETWEEN ORDINARY AND INSIDER PREFERENCES

As the foregoing excerpt describes, ordinary (non-insider) preferences are distinct from actually fraudulent conveyances in that there is no *mens rea* requirement. A preference is a strict liability offense; what matters is preferential *effect,* not *motive.* We will be discussing ordinary preferences in greater detail in Chapter 10, infra. However, special rules have always pertained in bankruptcy with respect to preferential transfers to "insiders"—persons deemed to have a special, close relationship to the debtor—recognizing that insider-creditors usually have advance warning of the debtor's deteriorating financial condition and are in a position to influence which creditors get paid first. The Bankruptcy Code's solution to this problem is to extend the period of time during which preferential transfers can be recovered from 90 days before the bankruptcy filing to one year in the case of insiders. For further discussion, see McCoid, *Corporate Preferences and Insiders*, 43 So. Car. L. Rev. 805 (1992).

Preferences are generally not actionable under state law because, unlike fraudulent transfers, they represent payments on debts legitimately due and owing. However, state law may take a different view of preferences when the transfer is to an insider. In large measure this is because there is a connection between constructive fraud—which prohibits transfers that are prejudicial to general unsecured creditors—and insider-preferences, which also have the effect of prejudicing arms-length creditors as a group rather than just *inter se.* Unlike in bankruptcy, however, the prevailing state law approach makes proof of the insider's state of mind an element of the offense.

UFTA § 5(b)

A transfer made by a debtor is fraudulent as to a creditor whose claim arose before the transfer was made if the transfer was made to an insider for an antecedent debt, the debtor was insolvent at that time, and the insider had reasonable cause to believe that the debtor was insolvent.

COOK & MENDALES, THE UNIFORM FRAUDULENT TRANSFER ACT: AN INTRODUCTORY CRITIQUE, 62 Am. Bankr. L.J. 87, 88-89 (1988).

A. TRANSFERS TO INSIDERS [SECTION 5(b)]

Section 5(b) of the UFTA enables a preexisting creditor to avoid, as constructively "fraudulent," a transfer to an "insider," a term broadly defined in UFTA § 1(7) and derived from the definition of that term in section 101(30) of the Code. To be voidable, the transfer must have been made to an insider, for an antecedent debt, when the debtor was insolvent, and when the insider had reasonable cause to believe the debtor was insolvent. Collusion or some degree of bad faith on the part of the insider is thus presumed. Unlike bankruptcy preferences (11 U.S.C. § 547(b)), there is no requirement that the transfer enable the insider to receive more than he would receive in a liquidation of the debtor's assets (11 U.S.C. § 547(b)(5)). The UFTA also does not make available to the insider all of the possible defenses to a preference enumerated in section 547(c) of the Code.

Defenses available to an insider are enumerated in UFTA § 8(e) and (f). Although some resemble the defenses to a preference attack in section 547(c) of the Code, they are not identical. UFTA § 8(e) provides that a transfer is not voidable if it results from lawful termination of a lease after a default by the debtor, or from enforcement of a security interest under Article 9 of the Uniform Commercial Code. UFTA § 8(f)(1) provides that a transfer is not voidable under section 5(b) to the extent that the insider gave new value to or for the benefit of the debtor after (not contemporaneous with) the transfer, unless the new value was itself "secured by a valid lien." The variation from the corresponding defense under the Code, dispensing with the Code's requirement for "a substantially contemporaneous exchange," may make this defense somewhat easier to establish than the defense created by Code section 547(c)(1).

Under UFTA § 8(f)(2), a transfer is not voidable "if made in the ordinary course of business or financial affairs of the debtor and the insider." This corresponds to the preference defense provided by section 547(c)(2) of the Code; but UFTA § 8(f)(2), unlike Code section 547(c)(2), inexplicably does not require that the transfer be made in payment of a debt incurred in the ordinary course of business, or that it be made according to ordinary business terms. Other defenses from Code section 547(c) are absent from UFTA § 8(f), but UFTA § 8(f)(3) creates a new defense: a transfer to an insider will be protected if made "pursuant to a good-faith effort to rehabilitate the debtor," and if it "secured present value given for that purpose as well as an antecedent debt of the debtor." Thus, the insider lender who continues financing a troubled debtor in a good faith workout effort should be insulated from fraudulent transfer liability. By enabling the insider to secure 'antecedent debt' as well, the statute also encourages the insider to invest new funds.

UFTA § 5(b) is doubly anomalous. Not only does it blur the distinction between a fraudulent transfer and a preference, but it also disregards the basic rationale for the trustee's ability to avoid preferences in bankruptcy: to (a) prevent aggressive creditors from dismembering the debtor during insolvency, and to (b) promote an equal distribution among creditors of the same class. Under the proposed statute, however, an individual creditor may avoid a transfer to an otherwise innocent insider in cases when the insider may have obtained no unfair advantage over other creditors. More importantly, the avoidance is not for the benefit of the debtor's creditors generally, but solely for the benefit of the plaintiff creditor. In effect, it enables the plaintiff creditor to avoid a preference to an insider so as to gain one for himself. Perhaps for these reasons, California did not include section 5(b) when it adopted the UFTA.

There are other practical consequences flowing from the enactment of UFTA § 5(b):

* * *

3. New Substantive Powers for Bankruptcy Trustees to Attack Insider Transfers

(a) A trustee will be able to attack transfers to insiders under section 544(b) of the Code, which makes state fraudulent transfer law applicable under certain conditions, although these transfers would not be voidable as preferences under Code section 547 (e.g., if the insider transferee did not realize more than he would have received, absent the transfers, in a chapter 7 liquidation of the debtor's assets).

(b) Although section 9(c) of the UFTA places a one-year statute of limitation on claims against insiders under section 5(b), it is possible that a state could adopt section 5(b), but not section 9(c), thereby making insider preferences voidable to the extent of the state's statute of limitations for other fraud claims (e.g., New York CPLR § 213 (six years)).

(c) BULK SALES

INTRODUCTORY NOTE

Bulk sales law, the subject of UCC Article 6, applies when a buyer purchases in bulk the inventory of a seller whose principal business is selling inventory from stock. §§ 6-102(c)(i); 6-103(1). In such a transaction, the buyer must give notice of the sale to all of the seller's unsecured creditors, whose names are provided in a sworn statement from the seller, or ensure that the proceeds of the sale are used to satisfy all such claims. § 6-104. If the buyer fails to comply with this requirement, she becomes personally liable in damages for the actual loss suffered by the creditors as a result of the sale. § 6-107. Prior to its revision in 1989, Article 6, like most nonuniform bulk sales laws, provided that the buyer who failed to comply with the statutory notice requirement took the goods subject to the claims of the seller's creditors. Thus, creditors of the seller in a noncomplying transfer would be permitted to execute against the assets in the hands of the buyer as if the sale had never occurred. See Verco Industries v. Spartan Plastics (In re Verco Industries), 704 F.2d 1134 (9th Cir. 1983), holding that the transfer, while good as between the parties to the transaction, is void as against the transferor's creditors.

ALCES, FRAUD BASES OF BULK TRANSFEREE LIABILITY, 63 Temp. L. Rev. 679, 684-86 (1990).

In several important ways, bulk sales liability is akin to constructive fraud liability. That is, a transfer may be rendered "ineffective" merely because the plaintiff did not receive proper notice of the bulk sale. Liability does not arise because the parties to the bulk transfer schemed to deprive the creditor of its property or of its interest in the property of the transferor. To prevail in the bulk sales action, the plaintiff need not establish the animus of the bulk transferor or transferee. Prejudice to the interests of the creditor is presumed notwithstanding evidence that the transfer was not the efficient cause of the prejudice to the creditor's position. There is also no requirement that the plaintiff creditor demonstrate prejudice in fact. In that way, bulk sales liability accrues in much the same way as constructive fraudulent disposition liability accrues under the uniform state law on fraudulent transfers and the Bankruptcy Code. So long as the claimant in a fraudulent disposition action establishes the bases of avoidance (generally impaired financial condition of debtor and debtor's receipt of inadequate consideration from the transferee), the law does not care whether the plaintiff-creditor was in fact harmed; prejudice is presumed, as it is in the bulk sales law.

Given the misrepresentation basis of bulk sales liability, the breadth of the class of potential plaintiffs under the current bulk sales law confirms that constructive fraud principles support the imposition of liability. Section 6-109 of Article 6 provides that all creditors "holding claims based on transactions or events occurring before the bulk transfer" are entitled to prior notice of the bulk sale and have standing to attack the sale if they do not receive the required notice. Thus, in addition to the contract creditors of the transferor, tort claimants (nonconsensual creditors) may set aside the bulk sale. That is so even though the nonconsensual creditors never relied on the corpus of the transferor's assets, and notwithstanding the fact that their claims may not be liquidated.

The next step in the analysis is to describe the elements of actual fraud in the fraudulent disposition setting, focusing on their evolution in terms that will be relevant when applying the general fraudulent disposition law to bulk sales. That survey, combined with the foregoing conclusions regarding the nature of bulk sales fraud liability, foreshadows the effort to draw parallels between the constructive fraud and actual fraud law. An appreciation of those parallels is a prerequisite to determining transferee liability issues under the proposed bulk sales regime.

* * *

Fraudulent disposition law developed early in commercial jurisprudence, claiming roots in the Roman statutes, and assuming the form we would perhaps first recognize in the Statute of 13 Elizabeth, a penal statute. Accordingly, liability under the specific language of the statute was actual fraud liability. The statute proscribed all conveyances effected with the "actual intent to hinder, delay, or defraud" creditors of the transferor. Recognition of constructive fraud liability began in earnest with *Twyne's Case*. In that case, the court enumerated the so-called "badges of fraud" as an adjunct of actual fraud liability. The badges of fraud focused on *indicia* of prejudice to the creditors of the grantor rather than on any specific showing that prejudice had in fact resulted. Development of the badges, and, therefore, the bases of constructive fraud liability, resulted from an evidentiary predicament: how to prove an actual intent to hinder, delay, or defraud. So conceived, actual and constructive fraud liability are symbiotically related avoidance theories. That relationship underlies the formulation of actual and constructive fraud liability from the Statute of 13 Elizabeth, through the Uniform Fraudulent Conveyance Act ("UFCA"), to the most recent enactments, Bankruptcy Code Section 548 and the Uniform Fraudulent Transfer Act ("UFTA").

HARRIS, ARTICLE 6: THE PROCESS AND THE PRODUCT—AN INTRODUCTION, 41 Ala. L. Rev. 549, 549-51 (1990).

Despite its small size and limited applicability, nearly every aspect of Article 6 has been the subject of continuing controversy. Lawyers and other commentators have questioned the wisdom of virtually every one of the Article's provisions, from its scope to its remedial scheme. Many have questioned whether the Article properly belongs in the Uniform Commercial Code or, indeed, anywhere in the statute books.

The controversy surrounding Article 6 is not new. Early bulk sales legislation was challenged, sometimes successfully, as being unconstitutional; it was attacked as special interest legislation; it was belittled as unnecessary. The century-long history of bulk sales law has been characterized by strong differences of opinion over basic issues: Is there really a "bulk sales risk" worthy of legislative attention? If so, what is the precise nature of the risk and how serious is it? What is the most effective and appropriate way in which to minimize the risk?

Mindful of the controversy surrounding Article 6 and of the nearly universal view that the language of Article 6 is in need of improvement, the Code's sponsors, the National Conference of Commissioners on Uniform State Laws * * * and the American Law Institute * * * set out in 1984 to revise the Article. By the time the dust settled five years later, the sponsors had withdrawn their support for Article 6 and encouraged those states that had enacted the Article to repeal it. For those states that may be disinclined to repeal Article 6, the sponsors promulgated a revised version of the Article, which is designed to afford better protection to creditors while minimizing the impediments to good-faith transaction.

QUESTION

You represent a buyer in a bulk sales law jurisdiction who proposes to purchase the assets of a retail company, including substantially all of the company's stock-in-trade. Your client does not wish to incur the expense of giving the § 6-105 notice of sale to the seller's creditors. In light of the provisions of § 6-107, how would you propose to protect your client against liability to the claimants entitled to notice?

SECTION 3. FRAUDULENT CONVEYANCE LAW AND THE PROBLEM OF OSTENSIBLE OWNERSHIP

INTRODUCTION

At common law, the only recognized form of personal property security interest was the "pledge" involving the physical delivery of the mortgaged goods to the lender. Of course, transfer of possession was impossible in circumstances where the collateral was wholly incorporeal, and, while not impossible, certainly impracticable in situations where the debtor needed the collateral in order to run its business. The next two cases illustrate the common law's inhospitable reception to debtors' attempts to use either their intangible personal property or their inventory as a basis for obtaining commercial financing. In a post-industrial society however, where large economies of scale made businesses increasingly dependent on debt financing, the pressure to allow debtors to use all of their property as a source of obtaining commercial financing was too great to resist. During the first half of the twentieth century state legislatures passed a variety of statutory security devices designed to permit creditors to take effective security interests in collateral like inventory and accounts receivable. Volume I of Professor Grant Gilmore's classic treatise SECURITY INTERESTS IN PERSONAL PROPERTY is the definitive work on the various and sundry pre-Code security devices. The excerpt from Gilmore's treatise which follows the next two cases describes the Uniform Commercial Code's solution to the problem of ostensible ownership.

BENEDICT v. RATNER

United States Supreme Court, 1925.
268 U.S. 353, 45 S.Ct. 566, 69 L.Ed. 991.

Proceeding by Aaron Ratner against Wallace Benedict, receiver, and later trustee in bankruptcy, of the Hub Carpet Company. To review a decree of the Circuit Court of Appeals (282 F. 12), affirming a decree of the District Court for plaintiff, defendant brings certiorari. Reversed.

* * *

Mr. Justice BRANDEIS delivered the opinion of the Court.

The Hub Carpet Company was adjudicated bankrupt by the federal court for Southern New York in involuntary proceedings commenced September 26, 1921. Benedict, who was appointed receiver and later trustee, collected the book accounts of the company. Ratner filed in that court a petition in equity praying that the amounts so collected be paid over to him. He claimed them under a writing given May 23, 1921—four months and three days before the commencement of the bankruptcy proceedings. By it the company purported to assign to him, as collateral for certain loans, all accounts present and future. Those collected by the receiver were, so far as appears, all accounts which had arisen after the date of the assignment, and were enumerated in the monthly list of accounts outstanding which was delivered to Ratner September 23. Benedict resisted the petition on the ground that the original assignment was void under the law of New York as a fraudulent conveyance; that, for this reason, the delivery of the September list of accounts was inoperative to perfect a lien in Ratner; and that it was a preference under the Bankruptcy Act (Comp. St. §§ 9585-9656). He also filed a cross-petition in which he asked that Ratner be ordered to pay to the estate the proceeds of certain collections which had been made by the company after September 17 and turned over to Ratner pursuant to his request made on that day. The company was then insolvent and Ratner had reason to believe it to be so. These accounts also had apparently been acquired by the company after the date of the original assignment.

The District Judge decided both petitions in Ratner's favor. He ruled that the assignment executed in May was not fraudulent in law; that it created an equity in the future acquired accounts; that, because of this equity, Ratner was entitled to retain, as against the bankrupt's estate, the proceeds of the accounts which had been collected by the company in September and turned over to him; that by delivery of the list of the accounts outstanding on September 23, this equity in them had ripened into a perfect title to the remaining accounts; and that the title so perfected was good as against the supervening bankruptcy. Accordingly, the District Court ordered that, to the extent of the balance remaining unpaid on his loans, there be paid Ratner all collections made from accounts enumerated in any of the lists delivered to Ratner; and that the cross-petition of Benedict be denied. There was no finding of fraud in fact. On appeal, the Circuit Court of Appeals affirmed the order. 282 F. 12. A writ of certiorari was granted by this Court. 259 U. S. 579, 42 S. Ct. 591, 66 L. Ed. 1073.

The rights of the parties depend primarily upon the law of New York. It may be assumed that, unless the arrangement of May 23 was void because fraudulent in law, the original assignment of the future acquired accounts became operative under the state law, both as to those paid over to Ratner before the bankruptcy proceedings and as to those collected by the receiver; and that the assignment will be deemed to have taken effect as of May 23. That being so, it is clear that, if the original assignment was a valid one under the law of New York, the Bankruptcy Act did not invalidate the subsequent dealings of the parties. The sole question for decision is, therefore, whether on the following undisputed facts the assignment of May 23 was in law fraudulent.

The Hub Carpet Company was, on May 23, a mercantile concern doing business in New York City and proposing to continue to do so. The assignment was made there to secure an existing loan of $15,000, and further advances not exceeding $15,000 which were in fact made July 1, 1921. It included all accounts receivable then outstanding and all which should thereafter accrue in the ordinary course of business. A list of the existing accounts was delivered at the time. Similar lists were to be delivered to Ratner on or about the 23d day of each succeeding month containing the accounts outstanding at such future dates. Those enumerated in each of the lists delivered prior to September aggregated between $100,000, and $120,000. The receivables were to be collected by the company. Ratner was given the right, at any time, to demand a full disclosure of the business and financial conditions; to require that all amounts collected be applied in payment of his loans; and to enforce the assignment although no loan had matured. But until he did so, the company was not required to apply any of the collections to the repayment of Ratner's loan. It was not required to replace accounts collected by other collateral of equal value. It was not required to account in any way to Ratner. It was at liberty to use the proceeds of all accounts collected as it might see fit. The existence of the assignment was to be kept secret. The business was to be conducted as theretofore. Indebtedness was to be incurred, as usual, for the purchase of merchandise and otherwise in the ordinary course of business. The amount of such indebtedness unpaid at the time of the commencement of the bankruptcy proceedings was large. Prior to September 17, the company collected from accounts so assigned about $150,000, all of which it applied to purposes other than the payment of Ratner's loan. The outstanding accounts enumerated in the list delivered September 23 aggregated $90,000.

Under the law of New York a transfer of property as security which reserves to the transferor the right to dispose of the same, or to apply the proceeds thereof, for his own uses, is, as to creditors, fraudulent in law and void. This is true whether the right of disposition for the transferor's use be reserved in the instrument or by agreement in pais, oral or written; whether the right of disposition reserved be unlimited in time or be expressly terminable by the happening of an event; whether the transfer cover all the property of the debtor or only a part; whether the right of disposition extends to all the property transferred or only to a part thereof; and whether the instrument of transfer be recorded or not.

If this rule applies to the assignment of book accounts, the arrangement of May 23 was clearly void; and the equity in the future acquired accounts, which it would otherwise have created, did not arise. Whether the rule applies to accounts does not appear to have been passed upon by the Court of Appeals of New York. But it would seem clear that whether the collateral consist of chattels or of accounts, reservation of dominion inconsistent with the effective disposition of title must render the transaction void. Ratner asserts that the rule stated above rests upon ostensible ownership, and argues that the doctrine of ostensible ownership is not applicable to book accounts. That doctrine raises a presumption of fraud where chattels are mortgaged (or sold) and possession of the property is not delivered to the mortgagee (or vendee). The presumption may be avoided by recording the mortgage (or sale). It may be assumed, as Ratner contends, that the doctrine does not apply to the assignment of accounts. In their transfer there is nothing which corresponds to the delivery of possession of chattels. The statutes which embody the doctrine and provide for recording as a substitute for delivery do not include accounts. A title to an account good against creditors may be transferred without notice to the debtor or record of any kind. But it is not true that the rule stated above and invoked by the receiver is either based upon or delimited by the doctrine of ostensible ownership. It rests not upon seeming ownership because of possession retained, but upon a lack of ownership because of dominion reserved. It does not raise a presumption of fraud. It imputes fraud conclusively because of the reservation of dominion inconsistent with the effective disposition of title and creation of a lien.

The nature of the rule is made clear by its limitations. Where the mortgagor of chattels agrees to apply the proceeds of their sale to the payment of the mortgage debt or to the purchase of other chattels which shall become subject to the lien, the mortgage is good as against creditors, if recorded. The mortgage is sustained in such cases 'upon the ground that such sale and application of proceeds is the normal and proper purpose of a chattel mortgage, and within the precise boundaries of its lawful operation and effect. It does no more than to substitute the mortgagor as the agent of the mortgagee to do exactly what the latter had the right to do, and what it was his privilege and his duty to accomplish. It devotes, as it should, the mortgaged property to the payment of the mortgage debt.' The permission to use the proceeds to furnish substitute collateral 'provides only for a shifting of the lien from one piece of property to another taken in exchange.' Brackett v. Harvey, 91 N. Y. 214, 221, 223. On the other hand, if the agreement is that the mortgagor may sell and use the proceeds for his own benefit, the mortgage is of no effect although recorded. Seeming ownership exists in both classes of cases because the mortgagor is permitted to remain in possession of the stock in trade and to sell it freely. But it is only where the unrestricted dominion over the proceeds is reserved to the mortgagor that the mortgage is void. This dominion is the differentiating and deciding element. The distinction was recognized in Sexton v. Kessler, 225 U. S. 90, 98, 32 S. Ct. 657, 56 L. Ed. 995, where a transfer of securities was sustained. It was pointed out that a reservation of full control by the mortgagor might well prevent the effective creation of a lien in the mortgagee and that the New York cases holding such a mortgage void rest upon that doctrine.

The results which flow from reserving dominion inconsistent with the effective disposition of title must be the same whatever the nature of the property transferred. The doctrine which imputes fraud where full dominion is reserved must apply to assignments of accounts although the doctrine of ostensible ownership does not. There must also be the same distinction as to degrees of dominion. Thus, although an agreement that the assignor of accounts shall collect them and pay the proceeds to the assignee will not invalidate the assignment which it accompanies, the assignment must be deemed fraudulent in law if it is agreed that the assignor may use the proceeds as he sees fit.

In the case at bar the arrangement for the unfettered use by the company of the proceeds of the accounts precluded the effective creation of a lien and rendered the original assignment fraudulent in law. Consequently the payments to Ratner and the delivery of the September list of accounts were inoperative to perfect a lien in him, and were unlawful preferences. On this ground, and also because the payment was fraudulent under the law of the State, the trustee was entitled to recover the amount.

Stackhouse v. Holden, 66 App. Div. 423, 73 N. Y. S. 203, is relied upon by Ratner to establish the proposition that reservation of dominion does not invalidate an assignment of accounts. The decision was by an intermediate appellate court, and, although decided in 1901, appears never to have been cited since in any court of that state. There was a strong dissenting opinion. Moreover, the case is perhaps distinguishable on its facts, page 426. Greey v. Dockendorff, 231 U. S. 513, 34 S. Ct. 166, 58 L. Ed. 339, upon which Ratner also relies, has no bearing on the case at bar. It involved assignment of accounts, but there was no retention of dominion by the bankrupt. The sole question was whether successive assignments of accounts by way of security, made in pursuance of a contract, were bad because the contract embraced all the accounts. The lien acquired before knowledge by either party of insolvency was held good against the trustee.

Reversed.

BROWN v. LEO

United States Court of Appeals, Second Circuit, 1926.
12 F.2d 350.

[The debtor in a bankruptcy proceeding had granted to his sister a mortgage on the real estate comprising his grocery business. The mortgage included all of the stock of the business, that is, all of the inventory in the grocery store. The facts indicate that after the grant, the debtor continued to operate the business, selling items from inventory, replenishing inventory, and taking some of the proceeds from the sale of inventory for himself. The trial court held the mortgage, to the extent it covered the inventory, to be a fraudulent conveyance avoidable by the trustee.]

HAND, Circuit Judge.

* * *

It has been the law of New York since 1837, at least, that a chattel mortgage, under which the mortgagor not only remains in possession, but is authorized to sell the goods and use the proceeds on his own behalf, is a fraud on creditors. Wood v. Lowry, 17 Wend. 492. Just why this should be so we are not altogether clear. A person in possession of a stock of goods, from which he is free to sell as he pleases, may perhaps deceive creditors into supposing that they are unconditionally his. Again, it is possible to reason that this inference is stronger when he replenishes the stock, at least as to the substituted goods. But the last is not a necessary element in the fraud, and, as we shall show, the doctrine has nothing to do with ostensible ownership. Therefore it can rest only upon some supposed conceptual repugnancy between the mortgage and the reserved power, quite regardless of any evils which may result from their coupling.

At any rate it is thoroughly well established, though it requires an actual agreement creating the power; mere acquiescence of the mortgagee not being enough, and though it yields when the mortgagor agrees to pay the proceeds of any sale upon the debt. But the agreement may be dehors the mortgage, and it makes the lien invalid not only as to the stock of goods to which it applies, but even as to separate stocks or fixtures which the mortgagor has no power to touch.

In Benedict v. Ratner, 268 U.S. 353, 45 S.Ct. 566, 69 L.Ed. 991, the Supreme Court considered the doctrine in a case involving assigned accounts. We had held it a part only of the general doctrine of reputed or ostensible ownership, and therefore inapplicable to intangibles. But the court said no; that the law of New York made the agreement a fraud merely because of the repugnancy of which we spoke just above, and quite independently of whether its exercise gave to the mortgagor a false credit. Just before the decision in Benedict v. Ratner, we decided the only case in which, so far as we can find, the doctrine was urged in the case of a mortgage of real and personal property. Hammond v. Carthage, etc., (C.C.A.) 8 F.(2d) 35. The discussion there was not necessary to the decision, because the mortgage was carefully drawn, apparently with the purpose of excluding from the lien all property over which the mortgagor retained a power of sale.

So far, however, as we said that a single mortgage of land and chattels might be valid as to the land and void as to the chattels, when the mortgagor was given the right to dispose of the chattels on his own account, we think that our decision must be regarded as overruled by Benedict v. Ratner, supra. We thought that in such cases there was no actual fraud, but that the possession of the chattels by the mortgagor, being 'strongly repugnant' to the common law, if coupled with a power to sell, in effect left no mortgage at all. These considerations did not, in our judgment, apply to so much of the instrument as incumbered the land, especially as a mortgage of land in New York does not pass title. Hence there was no reason why the same instrument should not be good as a mortgage as to the land and bad as to the chattels. It was like the case of a mortgage, bad as to chattels for lack of filing, but good as to land because recorded. As there was no fraud to taint the whole, it might be good so far as it was a mortgage at all.

We cannot take this position after Benedict v. Ratner, supra. That case declared that the law of New York made such an agreement actually fraudulent, quite independently of any dislike of the common law for continued possession by the mortgagor as ostensible ownership. Thus we think that we may no longer distinguish between a mortgage covering land and chattels and one covering two stocks of chattels. As authoritatively construed for us, the law of New York finds an obliquity in coupling with the lien a beneficial power in the mortgagor to sell the goods, quite aside from any false credit he may so procure. This pervades and taints the instrument as a whole, and there can be no difference whether the property to which the power does not extend is land, or an independent stock of chattels, or fixtures.

Therefore we must say that the mortgage is void as to the land, as the trial court found it as to the chattels. It must be set aside in both respects, and the trustee declared entitled to the land free and clear, not only of the deed of June 23, 1916, but of the mortgage of October 28, 1915.

Decree reversed, and case remanded for further proceedings in accordance with the foregoing.

---

1 G. GILMORE, SECURITY INTERESTS IN PERSONAL PROPERTY 260 (1965).

To escape from *Benedict*, the lender was required to exercise "dominion" over his security. What came to be accepted as the proper way of asserting dominion in non-notification financing was a requirement that the proceeds of collection be remitted daily by assignor to assignee. Nothing was to go directly into the assignor's bank account; all checks, notes and acceptances must be indorsed and delivered to the assignee. Of course, following the remittance, there would be what was sometimes referred to as a "re-remittance": after having passed through the assignee's hands, the proceeds would end up in the assignor's bank account. Since receivables were (and are) typically assigned to secure a working capital loan, it was of course necessary that the proceeds be eventually made available for the assignor's use. But, under *Benedict* theory, it was fatal for the assignor to take them immediately; they had to be channeled *into* his bank account through the assignee.

Another aspect of post-*Benedict* receivables financing was that, instead of a term loan, a so-called revolving credit was used. That is, the lender agreed to advance a specified percentage (say, 75 percent) of the aggregate amount of the assigned receivables, adjustments of the loan to be made at frequent intervals—weekly or even daily. If at any time the assigned receivables fell below the agreed ratio of collateral to loan, the borrower had to pay down on the loan or assign new receivables until the ratio was restored. The amount of the loan would thus fluctuate as the mass of receivables expanded or contracted. It is hard to see a logical connection between *Benedict* and the revolving credit, although it could perhaps be argued that gearing the loan to the face amount of receivables assigned at any one time was still another indication that the assignee was exercising his "dominion." The revolving credit practice may well have been taken over from the pre-*Benedict* factoring arrangements.

UCC § 9-205

A security interest is not invalid or fraudulent against creditors by reason of liberty in the debtor to use, commingle or dispose of all or part of the collateral * * * or to collect or compromise accounts or chattel paper * * *.

Official Comment

1. This Article expressly validates the floating charge or lien on a shifting stock. * * * This section provides that a security interest is not invalid or fraudulent by reason of liberty in the debtor to dispose of the collateral without being required to account for proceeds or substitute new collateral. It repeals the rule of Benedict v. Ratner * * *.

SECTION 4. AN INTRODUCTION TO ARTICLE 9

OVERVIEW

Article 9 of the UCC governs all transfers, except for those expressly excluded, which are intended to create a *security interest* in personal property or fixtures. The scope provision is § 9-102 and the excluded transactions are catalogued in § 9-104. The term "security interest" is defined in § 1-201(37). At this time there is a process under way to revise Article 9, as well as conforming changes in Articles 1, 5, and 8. A Drafting Committee, appointed by the National Conference of Commissioners on Uniform State Laws (NCCUSL) and the American Law Institute (ALI) has produced a series of drafts that will be evaluated and, if successful, adopted by NCCUSL, the ALI and, eventually, by the individual states. We distinguish references to the revision from the current version of Article 9 by use of the convention "Revised § 9-101." Because as of this writing it is the most recent draft of Revised Article 9 available, the one we cite to in this book is Council Draft No. 3, submitted to the ALI Council in December 1997. While further changes in section numbering and even content are inevitable, and indeed some have already occurred, we nevertheless anticipate that the final draft will look substantially similar to this one. One of the most important features of the revision process is inclusion under Revised Article 9 of a number of transactions that are now excluded. Compare Revised § 9-112 with §§ 9-102 and 9-104. We will return to this topic in later chapters.

The object of a creditor that takes a security interest under Article 9 is to be able to satisfy its debt upon default out of the proceeds from the sale of its collateral. In many respects, the security interest is a hedge against the debtor's insolvency and it functions as the personal property analogue to the real estate mortgage or trust deed. Of course, the creditor that holds a security interest (called a "secured party") wants not only to be able to look to the property comprising the collateral for payment, but to be able to do so to the exclusion of other creditors claiming an interest in the same property.

To understand the operation of Article 9 it is critical to understand the key Article 9 concepts of "attachment" and "perfection". Attachment establishes the secured party's *default* rights in the property against the debtor. This includes the right to seize and sell the property without the need to resort to judicial process of any kind. Perfection establishes the secured party's *priority* rights against other parties that may claim an interest in the property. These parties may include other creditors, buyers, lessors, and, the secured party's most frequent competitor, the trustee in bankruptcy. Section 9-303 describes when a security interest is perfected. We discuss the mechanics of attachment and perfection in Chapter 7, infra. For present purposes, it is important only to appreciate that it is attachment that enables the secured party the right to look to the collateral for payment in the first place, and perfection that permits the secured party to enjoy the value of that property to the exclusion of other parties until the secured party has been paid in full.

(a) THE ARTICLE 9 STATUTE OF FRAUDS—THE "ATTACHMENT" CONCEPT

UCC § 9-201
(*see Selected Commercial Statutes*)

UCC § 9-203(1)
(*see Selected Commercial Statutes*)

DURHAM v. MOUNTAIN AMERICA CREDIT UNION (IN RE DURHAM)

United States Court of Appeals, Tenth Circuit, 1991.
935 F.2d 1160.

[In 1986 Durham and his wife borrowed $150,000 from Mountain America Credit Union and assigned, as security for the debt, Durham's interest in an annuity purchased for him by the Travelers Insurance Company in settlement of an injury claim. In 1987 the Durhams borrowed an additional $40,000 and later an additional $20,000 and executed two new notes at the time of each loan, each note being for the cumulative amount of the Durhams' indebtedness, prior notes not being retired, however. In 1989 the Durhams filed in bankruptcy, took the position that their debt to the credit union was discharged and asked for a declaratory judgment that the credit union had no interest in the annuity. The court held that Article 9 applied.]

BRORBY, Circuit Judge.

* * *

We now turn our attention to the dispositive issue: Was the original $150,000 debt and accompanying assignment extinguished by the subsequent transactions?

The Supreme Court of Utah has held, "'[T]he giving of a new note in renewal of another note [does not] extinguish the debt for which the original note was given unless it clearly appears that it was the intention of the parties that the execution of the new note and the cancellation of the old note should extinguish the debt represented by the old note.'" Jones v. American Coin Portfolios, Inc., 709 P.2d 303, 306 (Utah 1985) (quoting First Security Bank v. Proudfit Sporting Goods Co., 552 P.2d 123, 124 (Utah 1976)). When a note is given in renewal of another debt, Utah law specifically provides there is no presumption of extinguishment of the underlying debt.

In the case before us it is difficult to find that either of the subsequent notes was given in renewal of the original $150,000 note. From the loan proceeds of the second note (of $190,000), Credit Union drew a check to itself which completely paid off the original note (of $150,000). As Credit Union's president testified, this retired and extinguished the note and completely paid off the initial loan. There exists some evidence that might be labeled contrary on this point, this evidence being Credit Union's failure to act, i.e., failure to stamp the original note "paid." However, Mr. Bagley testified the Credit Union does not stamp a loan as "paid"; rather, all that is done is to review documentation to establish the status of the transaction "accounting wise."

In reviewing a decision by a district court granting summary judgment, we review de novo. In addition, all facts and reasonable inferences derived therefrom must be construed in a light most favorable to the party opposing the summary judgment. Our review of the facts reveals the Credit Union issued itself a check from the loan proceeds, and that a statement of purpose made by its president indicated this action served to completely pay off the initial note. We have searched the record for contrary evidence and have found none.

The essence of Credit Union's argument is that it had no intent to release its security. The evidence, however, does not support this alleged intent. Rather, the evidence in this case overwhelmingly supports but one conclusion: The proceeds from the second loan were used to pay off and extinguish the first loan.

The assignment was automatically extinguished when the underlying debt was extinguished. No subsequent assignment or security interest was created nor was such an assignment even attempted.

Credit Union also argues Durhams are equitably estopped from denying that the assignment extends to the subsequent notes. The doctrine of equitable estoppel prevents a person from benefitting from his own wrong where an innocent party changed its position or acted in reliance upon the first party's wrongful conduct. The facts of this case fail to support an estoppel claim. No evidence of misconduct by Durhams appears in the record.

* * *

We have sympathy for the position of Credit Union. It loaned $214,000, which was spent by Durhams, and through the bankruptcy laws, Durhams have retained their principal asset. Our sympathy, however, does not allow us to rewrite the law. Accordingly, the judgment of the district court is AFFIRMED.

(b) THE CONSEQUENCES OF A FAILURE TO PERFECT—AN INTRODUCTION

UCC § 9-301
(*see Selected Commercial Statutes*)

EARL DUBEY & SONS v. MACOMB CONTRACTING CO.

Court of Appeals of Michigan, 1980.
97 Mich.App. 553, 296 N.W.2d 582.

[Macomb Concrete Corporation entered into a contract with the state as part of a highway construction project. On April 26, 1976 Dubey, the plaintiff in this action, obtained judgment against Macomb in connection with another matter. In March of 1978 Macomb granted Western Bank a security interest in all of Macomb's accounts. Western perfected its security interest by filing a financing statement on March 13, 1978. On July 31, 1978 Dubey served a garnishment writ on the state in an attempt to garnish sums due Macomb from the state. Both Western and Dubey claim the sum due from the state, which paid the money into the court.]

KELLY, Presiding Judge.

* * *

With respect to intervening defendant Western Bank's claim to the contested funds we find that under the priority provisions of the Uniform Commercial Code its interest is superior to that of plaintiffs. Although the record does not include the security agreement between Western and Macomb, a copy of the filed financing statement indicates Western's interest in all property and assets of Macomb, including accounts. The money held by the state, reserved for progress payments to Macomb, clearly falls within the UCC's definition of an account: "'Account' means any right to payment for goods sold or leased or for services rendered which is not evidenced by an instrument or chattel paper whether or not it has been earned by performance."

Defendants contend that since Western Bank perfected its security interest prior to the date that plaintiffs achieved lien creditor status[1] by judgment and writ of garnishment Western should prevail. M.C.L. § 440.9301; M.S.A. § 19.9301 provides in part:

"(1) Except as otherwise provided in subsection (2), an unperfected security interest is subordinate to the rights of: * * * (b) A person who becomes a lien creditor before the security interest is perfected."

Conversely, one who becomes a lien creditor after another's security interest is perfected is subordinate to that perfected security interest. A recent amendment to the code, though not in effect at the time this dispute arose, confirms defendant's position:

"A person who becomes a lien creditor while a security interest is perfected takes subject to the security interest only to the extent that it secures advances made before he becomes a lien creditor or within 45 days thereafter or made without knowledge of the lien or pursuant to a commitment entered into without knowledge of the lien." M.C.L. § 440.9301(4); M.S.A. § 19.9301(4). (Emphasis added.)

Western Bank perfected its security interest in Macomb's accounts approximately four months prior to the date of plaintiff's service of the writ of garnishment.

Whether Macomb's default occurred before or after service of the writ is immaterial. It is correctly argued that until default is a reality the secured party cannot claim possession or otherwise assert rights in the collateral securing the loan, M.C.L. § 440.9501; M.S.A. § 19.9501; however, another creditor who subsequently perfects an interest in the same collateral takes that security subject to the interest of the first secured party. When Macomb did default in its payments to Western Bank, Western appropriately pursued its remedy under the UCC by seeking discharge of Macomb's obligation via the collateral (accounts). To deprive Western of its priority status would contravene the express provisions and purpose of the Uniform Commercial Code. Plaintiffs' interest in Macomb's accounts is second in time and right to that of Western Bank; therefore, the order granting turnover of the funds to plaintiffs is reversed.

Reversed.

---

1 "Lien Creditor" is defined at M.C.L. § 440.9301(3); M.S.A. § 19.9301(3): "A 'lien creditor' means a creditor who has acquired a lien on the property involved by attachment, levy or the like * * *."

BANKRUPTCY CODE § 544(a)(1) —The "Strong-Arm Clause"

(*see Selected Commercial Statutes*)

PACIFIC EXPRESS, INC. v. TEKNEKRON INFOSWITCH CORP. (IN RE PACIFIC EXPRESS, INC.)

United States Court of Appeals, Ninth Circuit, 1985.
780 F.2d 1482.

MERRILL, Circuit Judge.

Creditor Teknekron Infoswitch Corp. ("Teknekron") appeals the approval of the sale of certain telecommunications equipment by bankrupt debtor Pacific Express, Inc. ("Pacific"). The case requires us to resolve conflicting claims of title to two separate sets of equipment. We affirm as to one set, but reverse as to the other.

I. Facts and the Proceedings Below

On or around June 17, 1983, creditor Teknekron agreed to deliver to debtor Pacific certain telecommunications equipment (the "Original Equipment"). Teknekron is located in Texas; Pacific is in California. Later that year, on August 12, the parties executed a document denominated a "Lease Agreement." Under that "Lease Agreement," Pacific undertook to pay Teknekron $9,250 a month for the succeeding five years in exchange for the use of the Original Equipment. At the time of the execution of this document, the Original Equipment was worth in excess of $416,000. Teknekron has never filed a financing statement relating to the Original Equipment, now in Pacific's possession.

At approximately the same time, Pacific and Teknekron entered into a Maintenance Agreement in which Teknekron agreed to service the Original Equipment for a fee of $1,750 a month. As part of the Maintenance Agreement, Teknekron gave Pacific a non-exclusive license to use the software that was necessary to run the Original Equipment.

On October 7, 1983, in a separate and distinct transaction, Teknekron shipped to Pacific certain other telecommunications equipment (the "Additional Equipment"). Teknekron agreed to sell and Pacific agreed to buy this Additional Equipment for $112,060.

On February 2, 1984, before having paid any of the amounts owed to Teknekron, Pacific filed a petition as debtor-in-possession under Chapter 11 of the Bankruptcy Code. In the bankruptcy court, Teknekron applied for relief from the automatic stay triggered by the bankruptcy filing so that it could regain possession of both the Original Equipment and the Additional Equipment. * * *

For its part, Pacific asserted that the "Lease" was intended as security. It therefore did not reserve title in Teknekron and created only a security interest. Under section 544(a)(1) of the Bankruptcy Code, 11 U.S.C. § 544(a)(1), Pacific sought to avoid what it claimed to be Teknekron's unperfected security interest in the Original Equipment.[1] Pacific also claimed that it owned the Additional Equipment free of any interest of Teknekron.

On cross-motions for summary judgment, the bankruptcy court ruled that the "lease" represented only a security interest avoidable under section 544(a)(1) and that Pacific, as debtor-in-possession, therefore owned the Original Equipment free of Teknekron's interest. It also ruled that Pacific held title to the Additional Equipment. Accordingly, it denied Teknekron's motions. The bankruptcy court subsequently authorized Pacific to sell all of the equipment in question. Upon Teknekron's tender of a deposit, that sale has been held in abeyance pending the resolution of this dispute.

Teknekron appealed the bankruptcy court's orders to the district court, which affirmed the bankruptcy court in all respects.

* * *

II. The Original Equipment

With regard to the Original Equipment, application of section 544(a) * * * depends on characterization of the "Lease Agreement." If the "Lease" only secures payments due under an installment sale, then Pacific owns the Original Equipment, and Teknekron's unperfected security interest is subject to avoidance under section 544(a)(1). If, however, the "Lease" is a true lease, then Teknekron retains a reversionary ownership interest and is entitled to the return of the Original Equipment. In re J.A. Thompson & Son, Inc., 665 F.2d 941, 945 (9th Cir.1982).

A. Security Lease vs. True Lease

Paragraph 15 of the Lease Agreement provides that Texas law shall govern the interpretation of the document. Like its Uniform Commercial Code equivalent, Tex.Bus. & Com.Code Ann. § 1.201(37) (Vernon 1984) states that whether a lease is a true lease or a security agreement depends on the intention of the parties. The formal retention of title in a security lease serves to reserve only a security interest. The statute then continues:

> Whether a lease is intended as security is to be determined by the facts of each case; however, (a) the inclusion of an option to purchase does not of itself make the lease one intended for security, and (b) an agreement that upon compliance with the terms of the lease the lessee shall become or has the option to become the owner

---

[1] 11 U.S.C. § 544(a)(1) allows the bankruptcy trustee or debtor-in-possession to avoid any security interest that would be voidable by "a creditor that extends credit to the debtor at the time of the commencement of the case, and that obtains, at such time and with respect to such credit, a judicial lien on all property on which a creditor on a simple contract could have obtained such a judicial lien, whether or not such a creditor exists."

If the "Lease" is a security interest, Teknekron's failure to file a financing statement brings section 544(a)(1) into play. See Cal.Com.Code § 9301(1)(b) (West 1985). California Com.Code § 9302(1) requires the filing of such a statement to perfect a security interest of the type involved here. The filing requirement serves the purpose of providing future creditors with notice of the encumbrance on the collateral.

of the property for no additional consideration or for a nominal consideration does make the lease one intended for security.

The statute mandates that we "must determine the parties' intent in the light of the facts and circumstances of each case," and that "the substance of the document rather than mere formality of wording must be examined to determine whether the transaction involved a lease, a conditional sale, or a security interest." Davis Brothers v. Misco Leasing, Inc., 508 S.W.2d 908, 912-13 (Tex.Civ.App.1974). Here, that factual examination discloses that the parties intended the purported lease to serve as security for Pacific's installment purchase of the Original Equipment from Teknekron.

As both parties have stipulated, the parties initially agreed on or around June 17, 1983, that Pacific would buy the Original Equipment from Teknekron. Only with the written formalization of that agreement on August 12 did the transaction take on the trappings of a lease. The "Equipment Order Schedule Detail" incorporated into the "Lease Agreement" lists the individual items of Original Equipment by "Purchase Price." The stipulated value of the equipment at that time, $416,000 or more, approximates the sum of those prices. Pacific was unconditionally obligated to pay $9,250 a month for five years. Its payments would have amounted to $555,000, which appears to represent the stipulated original value plus interest over five years. Thus, the economic substance of the transaction is that of an installment sale.

Moreover, the evidence suggests that Teknekron did not anticipate regaining the use of the Original Equipment. Teknekron's own evidence, consisting of an affidavit from one of its employees, Steven Gwilliam, showed that advances in technology would render the equipment obsolescent by the end of the five-year lease period. A lease term spanning the effective useful life of the equipment is a sign that the parties intended a sale. In re Marhoefer Packing Co., 674 F.2d 1139, 1145 (7th Cir.1982); In re Peacock, 6 B.R. 922, 926 (Bankr.N.D.Tex.1980); In re Teel, 9 B.R. 85, 88-89 (Bankr.N.D.Tex.1981).

Other provisions of the "lease" indicate that the parties intended to pass actual ownership to Pacific and to reserve only a security interest for Teknekron. Pacific had the right to purchase the Original Equipment for its fair market value, not to exceed $20,000, at the end of the five-year term. Pacific agreed to pay all sales, use and property taxes pertaining to the Original Equipment. It also agreed to insure the equipment in favor of the lessor. Pacific bore the risk of loss or damage of the equipment, and it agreed to post a substantial deposit. The "lease" gave Teknekron the rights of a secured party under the Uniform Commercial Code upon default by Pacific. In case of default, Teknekron would have the right to sell the equipment, with Pacific liable for any deficiency after application of the sales proceeds to the payments due.

These facts support a finding that the parties intended to create a security interest rather than a true lease. Davis Brothers, 508 S.W.2d at 913; In re Tulsa Port Warehouse Co., 690 F.2d 809, 811-12 (10th Cir.1982); American Standard Credit v. National Cement Co., 643 F.2d 248, 265-66 (5th Cir.1981); United States v. Federal Insurance Co., 634 F.2d 1050, 1052-53 (10th Cir.1980); White and Summers, Handbook of the Law under the Uniform Commercial Code

882-83 (2d ed. 1980). Of course, any one of these facts alone might not suffice to justify that finding. In the aggregate, however, they point persuasively to the conclusion that the "lease" was actually a disguised security agreement.[2]

Because the purported "lease" was not a true lease but a security arrangement, Pacific owned the Original Equipment on the date of bankruptcy, and Teknekron's rights were limited to the retention of a security interest. Teknekron has never taken steps to perfect that security interest. Upon the filing of the bankruptcy petition, therefore, Pacific obtained the right to avoid Teknekron's interest under 11 U.S.C. 544(a)(1), leaving Teknekron with an unsecured claim for the amounts due it for the Original Equipment.

* * *

NOTE ON LEASE/SECURITY INTEREST DISTINCTION

One of the most litigated issues under Article 9 arises when a transaction structured as a lease of goods is really a disguised installment sale subject to the provisions of Article 9. In 1987, in connection with the enactment of Article 2A, the definition of a "security interest" in 1-201(37) was amended to provide the courts with more definitive guidelines for making the determination of whether a "lease" transaction is governed by Article 9 or Article 2A. Prior to 1987, the issue turned on the intent of the parties and whether the lessee had an option to purchase the goods at the expiry of the lease for nominal consideration. See footnote 2 in *Pacific Express.* Amended 1-201(37) shifts the focus from intent to the economic realities of the transaction, with an emphasis on whether there is substantial residual value at the end of the lease term and who has the right to that residual value. The key factors distinguishing a disguised "finance lease" from a true "bailment lease" are: (i) the parties economic expectations at the onset of the transaction; (ii) their rights and obligations at the end of the lease term; and (iii) the required term of the lease. In short, the courts look to see whether the purported lessor has retained any realistic residual value and whether the purported lessee has built up any equity in the "leased" goods. The courts consider the lessee to have equity in the goods if the lessee has the right to purchase the goods at the end of the lease term for less than fair market value, measured as of the beginning of the lease relationship. Correspondingly, the lessor is deemed to have retained a meaningful interest in the residual value of the goods if the lessee has reserved the right to terminate the lease before the stipulated expiration of the lease term. We will return to the issue of when Article 9 applies to transactions structured by the parties as a lease again in Chapter 4, infra.

---

2 Section 1.201(37) also deems a lease to be intended as security if it gives the lessee an option to purchase the goods for a nominal consideration. Because the evidence without regard to the size of the option purchase price shows that the parties intended to create a security interest, we find it unnecessary to decide under the facts here whether this provision provides additional support for the determination that the lease was a security agreement. In re Fashion Optical, Ltd., 653 F.2d 1385, 1389 (10th Cir. 1981).

IN RE MURRAY, 191 B.R. 309 (E.D. Pa. 1996). In this case, an automobile lease provided that the debtor could terminate the lease at any time. Moreover, the lessee had an option to purchase the leased vehicle for a price at least equal to the predicted fair market value of the car at the time of exercise. Applying amended 1-201(37) the court concluded, quite correctly, that this was a "true" lease, refusing to consider other evidence offered to show that the *intent* of the parties was otherwise. How, if at all, would it have affected the outcome of the case if the purchase option was for substantial consideration but less than estimated fair market value? Would it have mattered if the purchase option was for one dollar? If the transaction is a "true" lease, not subject to the public notice provisions of Article 9, are the ostensible ownership issues any less prevalent than if the transaction were determined to be a disguised security interest? If not, what accounts for the difference in treatment for purposes of § 544(a)(1) of the Bankruptcy Code?

NOTE ON CONSUMER CAR LEASES

Today, most new car consumer leases are structured as "closed-end" leases where the lessee's option at the end of the lease term is either to return the vehicle to the dealer or purchase it for a set price established at the onset of the lease, and expressed as a percentage of the original sticker price. These transactions are generally regarded as "true" leases. By contrast, in the typical "open-end" lease the vehicle is sold at the end of the lease term and, if the proceeds received are less than a preset depreciated value, the customer is liable for the deficiency. Conversely, if the proceeds exceed that value, the excess is remitted to the customer. These transactions are generally treated as financing arrangements even though there is no purchase option at all. See In re Tulsa Port Warehouse Co., 689 F.2d 809 (10th Cir. 1989). Can you identify what factors account for this difference in treatment?

D. BAIRD, THE ELEMENTS OF BANKRUPTCY 101-02 (Rev. ed. 1993).

Understanding section 544(a) depends critically on understanding the vulnerability of a transfer of property by third persons. Section 544 strikes down the property rights of a party if the party has not taken the steps necessary to gain a *priority* right. At this point, however, we need to ask why the trustee enjoys the powers of a lien creditor while representing general creditors. An unperfected secured creditor beats general creditors outside of bankruptcy, yet by virtue of the trustee's "strong-arm power," the unperfected secured creditor loses to them in bankruptcy. This result seems to depart from the usual rule that bankruptcy tracks nonbankruptcy law. Closer examination, however, shows that it does not.

Let's look at the relative positions of unperfected secured creditors and general creditors outside of bankruptcy. Section 9-301 of the Uniform Commercial Code and other state statutes suggest that the unperfected secured creditors beat general creditors. Section 9-301 tells us only that the secured creditor will win against a general creditor if the secured creditor perfects * * * .

Section 9-301 embraces a broad principle. The unperfected secured creditor claims an interest in property that is invisible to third parties. As a general matter Anglo-American law does not recognize much ownership interests vis-à-vis third parties unless public notice is given or some other step is taken to cure the ostensible ownership problem that arises from the separation of ownership and possession * * * .

Outside of bankruptcy * * * the outcome of the race between the unperfected secured creditor and the general creditor is uncertain because neither has cured the ostensible ownership problem and we have no way to know who would have cured it first. The effect of giving the trustee the power to avoid the unperfected secured creditor's interest is to declare a tie. In bankruptcy, the trustee represents the interests of all the general creditors, and an unperfected secured creditor whose lien is avoided becomes one of them. (You are never worse off trying to get a security interest and failing than you would have been if you had never tried at all.) To say that the trustee wins is to say that all creditors share equally. The bankruptcy rule, in other words, preserves the nonbankruptcy rule in the sense that, in the presence of uncertainty, the creditors share equally.

SECTION 5. CRITICISM OF THE OSTENSIBLE OWNERSHIP DOCTRINE

J. DOLAN, COMMERCIAL LAW: ESSENTIAL TERMS AND TRANSACTIONS § 3.1, 15-16 (2d ed. 1997).

Farmers and other merchants who sell to nonconsumer buyers have devised the open account sale as an efficient mechanism. It involves massive amounts of goods and billions of dollars of sales yearly in the domestic economy. Significantly, the open account sale is a credit transaction, and the existence of inexpensive, accurate, and easily accessible credit reporting has helped to make the open account sale possible with all its attendant savings for the small, thinly capitalized enterprise. In the overwhelmingly large percentage of merchant-to-merchant sales transactions, the parties will resort to the cheap, efficient device of the open account sale. A bit of history is helpful to understand open account sales.

There was a time when merchants were not often able to sell on open account. Credit reporting was slow and often unreliable. A New York manufacturer in the nineteenth century was not willing to ship on credit to a buyer way off in Tennessee unless the manufacturer had hard facts supporting the buyer's credit standing. The manufacturer certainly would not extend credit (i.e., ship on open account) on the basis of an order on the buyer's letterhead. Some manufacturers, however, were large enough to support a network of sales personnel ("drummers" who "drummed" up business) who would visit the buyer's establishment, talk to local merchants about the buyer, and report back to the manufacturer with a recommendation on credit. That system was expensive, and the volatile nature of many industries and many local economies rendered it imprecise and rendered the information generated by it of doubtful validity after short periods of time.

The day of the drummer is over. We encounter him in Meredith Wilson's catchy lyrics from *The Music Man* or in tired jokes modernized into stories about "traveling salesmen." Time has transmuted that commercial personage into a "marketing analyst" or the like. With the advent of accurate, reliable credit reporting agencies, sellers were in a better position to know the current state of a potential buyer's economic strength and, especially, to know when danger (usually foretold by late payments on current accounts) lurked. Specialized *credit agencies* accumulate data on customers in an industry and reported that information for a fee that is far less than the cost of maintaining a cadre of drummers * * * .

In the past, sellers had to acquire periodic, written credit reports from the credit-reporting agencies. That process was slow enough that the information could lose its value as circumstances changed and the report's data became dated. The advent of computerized communications, however, has generally guarded against data obsolescence and has rendered the credit-reporting process more immediate and therefore more reliable. Today, any high-volume, open account seller will have access to the credit-reporting agency's database. When a seller needs information about an account, a clerk in the seller's credit department will access the base by satellite, or by telephone wire and see on a computer terminal up-to-date credit information on the account in question.

The development of such credit reporting, faster communications methods, and the general standardization of many industries permitted sellers to do away with their costly in-house system of monitoring accounts and permitted them to sell to a vastly greater number of potential buyers. By the same token, the open account sale gives buyers tremendous advantages to the extent that it encourages sellers to sell on industry credit terms to new accounts and to new ventures that have in some way established a good credit rating.

It is important to understand that the open account sale is a credit sale. At the very least, the seller is giving the buyer credit during the time it takes for the seller's invoice to arrive at buyer's office and for buyer's purchasing people to forward payment to seller. In most industries, the credit terms are longer. Sellers in these industries ship on the understanding that payment is not due until the end of the month or 30 or even 60 days after the invoice date or after the end of the month. Many sellers, moreover, quote their prices in terms of discounts to those buyers that pay early.

PHILLIPS, FLAWED PERFECTION: FROM POSSESSION TO FILING UNDER ARTICLE 9—PART 1, 59 B.U. L. Rev. 1, 35-38 (1979). "Criticism of the doctrine of ostensible ownership finds its strongest behavioral support in the actions of parties who extend secured or unsecured credit subsequent to the secured transaction. Even with respect to creditors, one can poke holes in this criticism but its case seems incontrovertible—business people look to written, not possessory evidence of ownership. And this view leads generally to recognizing filing, but not possession, as a means of notice."

NOTE ON OSTENSIBLE OWNERSHIP

In a primitive credit system, possession of goods connotes ownership; and legal rules must accommodate the expectations that connotation engenders. The doctrine of voidable title; the rule of *Twyne's Case*; the rule for consignments in Article 2 [§ 2-326]; the buyer in ordinary course rules in Article 2 [§ 2-403(2)] and Article 9 [§ 9-307(1)]; and, arguably, the Article 9 filing and priority rules themselves stem from the law's desire to fashion rules in accord with ostensible ownership assumptions.

It may be time to question those assumptions. There is evidence that in the commercial setting [merchant to merchant sales, loans to commercial enterprises, the purchase and sale of a commercial enterprise], parties do not rely on the possession of goods as an indication of ownership. There are a number of factors that contribute to the unreliability of possession: (1) widespread equipment leasing practices in the manufacturing and service sectors, (2) fabricating or finishing by one company of another company's work in process, (3) rapid turnover of inventories, (4) rapid obsolescence of equipment and inventory in many industries, and (5) just in time inventory practices. But most important of all is the advent of reliable credit reporting.

Even in a primitive credit system, possession of goods is a poor substitute for an independent audit. Experience seems to suggest that a reliable system of credit reporting is more accurate; more reliable; and, often, a sufficient substitute for the CPA's audit. A combination of audits and credit reports is even a better alternative. When the cost of error is high [a $10,000,000 line of credit to a manufacturing concern] the parties will pay for the audit. When the cost is relatively low [monthly sales on open account averaging $10,000], they will use credit reports. Though inventory levels and the age and efficiency of equipment may be matters of concern to a commercial banker, in neither case will anybody rely primarily on the debtor's possession of equipment or inventory.

If these suggestions are correct, much of commercial law may be ready for rejection or revision. If trade creditors and commercial lenders do not rely on possession, perhaps the law should not reward them or penalize true owners when the debtor holds goods that do not belong to the debtor. Perhaps we should take another look at the priority of the trustee in bankruptcy over the unperfected secured party. Should the priority rules in Article 9 turn on the date of filing or on other criteria such as the contribution of value or the time of delivery? Or should all creditors share pro rata in the assets of a defaulting enterprise?

In all of this inquiry, we may find that fraud plays a greater role than it played in the ostensible ownership era, for fraud remains a problem for commerce.

PART II

DEFINING PROPERTY INTERESTS

INTRODUCTORY NOTE

In the first Part of the book we examined the basic property conveyancing rules common to all property regimes. It is important for students who are new to the commercial law to appreciate that, historically, property concepts have been central to resolving commercial law issues. One of the Code's most important innovations, however, has been to shift the focus under the law away from static property-based concepts, such as the location of title, to a more functional, dynamic approach.

One of the consequences of this shift in orientation is that, often, Code rules confer rights and impose obligations unrelated necessarily to formal questions of "ownership." For example, if a seller's reservation of title to goods delivered to a buyer has the *effect* of creating a security interest in those goods, the Code treats the seller's interest as a security interest in those goods and not as a title claim. Likewise, where a buyer's interest in specific goods can be *identified*, the Code recognizes that interest, even though the buyer has yet to receive either title to or possession of those goods.

Despite this orientation to the dynamic and away from the static, and indeed to a certain degree because of it, property concepts remain important under the Code. As we will see, significant legal consequences turn on the nature and character of a party's property rights. Thus, in the next two chapters we classify and consider the different categories of interests in personal property formally recognized under the Code. Later, we will see how the classification of a property interest affects the priority in that property to which the holder of the interest is entitled.

CHAPTER 4

GENERAL PROPERTY CATEGORIES

INTRODUCTORY NOTE

The first three chapters introduce conveyancing rules. This chapter introduces the stuff that is conveyed, property interests. There are six of them: title, the special property, the security interest created by law, the Article 9 security interest, the leasehold, and a catchall category, the lien.

SECTION 1. PROPERTY (TITLE)

INTRODUCTORY NOTE

Most students have met Professor Williston in the Contracts course and know the story of the debate between him and his friend Professor Corbin over promissory estoppel. Here is another Willistonian debate—this one between Williston and Professor Llewellyn, the chief architect of the Uniform Commercial Code.

There are those who think that Corbin won the promissory estoppel debate and that Llewellyn won this debate over the role of title in commercial transactions. Willistonians, of which there remain a few, will argue that the outcome of both the promissory estoppel debate and the controversy over the role of title remain inconclusive. In the case of title, Llewellyn won the drafters of the Code over to his position; but realists will point to cases where title remains a forceful concept.

LLEWELLYN, THROUGH TITLE TO CONTRACT AND A BIT BEYOND, 15 N.Y.U. L.Q. Rev. 159, 165-68 (1938).

NATURE AND UTILITY OF THE TITLE-CONCEPT

Nobody ever saw a chattel's Title. Its location in Sales cases is not discovered, but created, often *ad hoc*. In real-property matters, to be sure, it is a meaningful concept, because a chain of documents is there for art to construe; it is possible, objectively and definitely, to determine and agree in the great run of cases just where title to a disputed piece of land lies. Not so in Sales disputes, if Title be treated as one fixed whole. The reason for this is clear, though neglected. But before discussing it, let it be remembered that we have in chattel matters availed ourselves of the mass of conceptual inventions already worked out in the law of real property only as one or another of them has been casually found and almost unlawfully detained. Is there an unambiguous chain of documents which would afford a firm base line? In the common law of trust receipts such a chain has been seen and seized on, but then, repeatedly, with disregard of what the realty lawyer could offer as a tool to help the buyer out, to wit, the full interest of a mortgagor in possession. Elsewhere, as in the statutes requiring the original bill of sale to be indorsed, etc., when second-hand cars are sold, or in the shipment of goods under straight or order bill of lading, we let the chain-of-title evidence run into curious confusion with unseen, intangible intention. We do not, I repeat, in chattel matters, lay hold on a firm objective basis for allocating title when we have one—nor have we consistently utilized or remodeled the available concepts about divided interests. The quarrel thus is, first, with the use of Title for purposes of decision as if the *location* of Title *were* determinable with certainty; and second, with the insistence on reaching for a single lump to solve all or most of the problems between seller and buyer—and even in regard to third parties.

Why is a one-lump Title not determinable with certainty in Sales cases? It is because such a Title is a static concept, a something which is conceived as continuing in somebody. Its type is the book or handkerchief or dog or house, lastingly owned. A pledgor is "owner" not only before and after the pledge, but also after redemption; so is one whose rights are subjected to a common-law lien. You know in such cases where you start from, you know whither to return; you have your base-point firm and fixed. From that base-point courts can work out the rights and powers making up the particular "special property," in terms of what and how much is needed; from that base-point courts can see how much *not* to give. There is no great occasion for confusion on the point of ownership. This is, I think, one reason why the law of chattel mortgage in some "title" states, or of chattel mortgagee in possession where title is held to pass on such possession, runs into difficulty: a lump-title is conceived to rest where, from the angle of recurring in due course to the original static situation, it does not belong.

But in Sales cases, no static concept is at home. The essence of the Sales transaction is dynamic. Lump-title fits only in that rare case in which our economy resembles that of three hundred years ago: where the whole transaction can be accomplished at one stroke, shifting possession along with title, no strings being left behind—as in cash purchase of an overcoat worn home. But the contract for sale on credit, the shifting of goods to market via a factor, the shipment against draft, the installment sale, the delivery or shipment on approval, the agreement to sell goods lying in warehouse under non-negotiable receipt—these are not one-stroke transactions. They involve, each one, a complicated *series* of actions of varying significance. They involve a period, often an extended period, during which matters are in temporary suspension or are in active flux between the parties; over considerable periods of time there is no such Title in *either* party as the static picture of Title suggests. Take non-commercial shipbuilding. Admit that the builder has much or most of what we know as ownership. Yet is he "*free* to use," if buyer's inspector is on the job, checking on what goes on? Or if a possible action for specific delivery, or injunction against sale to another, is in the offing? Should the buyer who makes contract payments as building proceeds be regarded as bare of interest simply because the time has not yet come when the transaction will be wholly over and the vessel "his" and his alone? One needs no passing of Title to the vessel, plank by plank, nor does one need a vessel that is buyer's up to six feet from the keel, and seller's in what has been built since. One needs only, on the price and security side, a concept akin to equitable charge. But I do not want to linger on one illustration. The important point is to see the seller-buyer relation, save where a single stroke severs it utterly, as dynamic movement to which the Whole-Title concept applies on *neither side*. What other meaning have such concepts as specification, assent of seller and assent of buyer to appropriation, lien, stoppage in transit, goods not readily remarketable, delay in delivery, installment, severability? Where the transaction proceeds in a series of lesser actions, often long drawn-out, no static legal whole-hog concept can fit comfortably, unless some almost violently vital step in the series can be seen to shift the whole scene—as perhaps when a letter of acceptance drops into the mailbox. Such a violently vital step, in Sales transactions, is almost nonexistent. Even open shipment on credit remains subject to stoppage in transit—an idea which the United States Postal Regulations seem not to have been faced with when they entered court. *De facto*, then, Sales questions move much along the motto of the most orthodox of modern economists: *Natura non facit saltum.* Which can be rendered: It takes legal fiat to give little facts huge meaning.

WILLISTON, THE LAW OF SALES IN THE PROPOSED UNIFORM COMMERCIAL CODE, 63 Harv. L. Rev. 561, 566-72 (1950).

Confusion Caused by Fixing Rights of Buyer and Seller Irrespective of Title.

Certainly many of the most important questions in the law of property, both real and personal, have always turned on the requisites for the transfer of title, the moment when the transfer occurs, and the consequences of transfer. The English Sale of Goods Act and the American Sales Act, following established common law rules, make elaborate provisions for answering these questions. The primary requirement both for transfer and for fixing the time when it takes place is based on the intention of the parties. Since intention in regard to title is frequently not expressed or, indeed, considered by the parties to a bargain, rules of presumption as to intention, based on attributes of title upon which the parties have agreed, were developed by the common law, and these presumptions have been enacted into both the English and American statutes. If neither actual nor presumed intention to transfer title can be found, it is not transferred.

Although a sale is necessarily defined in the Code as consisting of "the passing of title from the seller to the buyer," and although Article 2 of the Code is devoted to the subject of sales, yet at the outset, in the Comment to Section 2-101 it is said that "legal consequences are stated as following directly from the contract and action taken under it without resorting to the idea of when property or title passed or was to pass as the determining factor."

Nevertheless an elaborate section (and only one) is devoted to title. This section, 2-401, is not expressed in any respect in the words of the existing Sales Act. The first provision of the section is the general one, that title "can" pass on any conditions to which the parties explicitly agree, except as qualified by the negative provisions discussed below. More specific affirmative provisions are that unless the contrary is explicitly agreed, title passes (1) when the seller completes his performance with reference to the physical delivery of the goods, and in particular (a) when goods are shipped, under a contract which does not require delivery, and (b) where the contract does require delivery, then on tender at destination; (2) where delivery is to be made without moving the goods, then at the time and place of contracting unless documents of title are to be delivered; and (3) in that case, on delivery of the documents.

It is further provided that if the buyer refuses to receive the goods, whether he is justified or unjustified, title is revested in the seller by operation of law. * * *

Section 2-401 does not purport to cover the whole question of transfer of title, in the absence of express agreement. In particular the section does not state the present comprehensive rule that title passes if the parties so intend actually or by presumption, and that otherwise it does not pass. Nor does the section state any other comprehensive rule. Particular situations only are covered. Indeed, it is the purpose of the Code to make the question of title immaterial, so far as possible, with reference to the rights of the parties. Doubtless the reason is because the intention of the parties to pass or retain title, which is controlling under the present law, is often not manifested and can be determined only by presumption. But no other general rule governing title is or can be suggested.

The principle upon which the Code is drawn is stated in the first sentence of the section and is emphasized in the following extracts from the Comment:

> This article [i.e., the portion of the Code regarding sales] deals with the issues between seller and buyer in terms of step-by-step performance or nonperformance under the contract for sale and not in terms of whether or not "title" to the goods has passed. Similarly, the presence or absence of externally observable and determinable facts, and not the location of "title," controls the rights of the seller's creditors and of good faith purchasers from either the buyer or the seller.

The Comment further states: "This section, however, in no way intends to indicate which line of interpretation should be followed in cases where the applicability of 'public' regulation depends upon a 'sale' or upon location of 'title' without further definition." Again, in Comment 1 to Section 2-709 it is stated: "Neither the passing of title to the goods nor the appointment of a day certain for payment is now material to a price action." It is true that it is stated in Comment 2 to Section 2-606 (which relates to acceptance) that acceptance always includes "acceptance of title." I find no warrant for that unqualified statement in the Code itself, but, in any event, the rights of the parties under the Code do not depend upon title.

The attempt to make title unimportant is unsatisfactory and can result only in confusion, when taken in connection with other laws. Under the express words of the Bankruptcy Act for instance, the trustee shall be vested "by operation of law with the title of the bankrupt as of the date of the filing of the petition * * * ." In using the word "title" without more, the Bankruptcy Act gives the possessor of title the attributes of the existing law. Therefore, if either buyer or seller becomes bankrupt, their rights under the Bankruptcy Act must depend upon which of them has title, not on the provisions of the Code, which would fix their rights irrespective of title. Again, whether a sale of liquor or of other prohibited goods is legal often depends on when and where there was a "sale," that is, when and where title passed; and the rights of the parties must depend upon the answer to these questions. But the Code inconsistently provides that the rights of the parties do not depend upon title. In questions of conflict of laws the determination of the applicable state law may depend upon title. In the devolution of the property of a deceased buyer or seller and in the taxation of automobiles and other goods of buyer and seller, title determines the rights of the parties. Even the rights of a good faith purchaser are confused when made to depend not upon title but upon a buyer's rights under the Code. Another question, who may recover from third persons who convert the goods, the Code seeks to answer in a subsequent section.

If it were intended under the novel terminology of the Code that the rights and duties of seller and buyer should be the same as under the hitherto accepted terminology which bases rights and duties on ownership, and makes intention the vital basis for transfer of title, the wording is so different that much litigation would be necessary to establish the fact. But the Code expressly repudiates title as determining the rights and duties of the parties and seeks to substitute particular rules instead of the inclusive principle based on intention. The provisions of the Code apply "irrespective of title." The Code gives no indication of what is to be done where rights of buyer and seller, under such laws as I have referred to, vary the rights provided for in the Code.

As Maitland wrote, the law is a "seamless web." The most fundamental feature of the law of property cannot be made immaterial in a statute on the sale of goods without tearing the seamless web. This misfit with other legislation and with the common law seems to me fatal.

UCC § 2-401

Each provision of this Article with regard to the rights, obligations and remedies of the seller, the buyer, purchasers or other third parties applies irrespective of title to the goods except where the provision refers to such title.

UCC § 9-202

Each provision of this Article with regard to rights, obligations and remedies applies whether title to collateral is in the secured party or in the debtor.

NOTE ON THE ROLE OF TITLE

Section 2-401, the Code's title section, sets out a series of rules for determining the location of title. Note, however, that the section's preamble limits the relevance of those rules to issues where the governing Code provision specifically refers to title.

Some courts have resisted, consciously or not, the Code's attempt to deprive them of a concept so central to their common law traditions and so responsive to the human longing to be able to say without condition, "This is *mine* and that is *yours*." We lawyers frequently begin the analysis of a dispute by saying that the seller "sold" the goods or that the buyer "bought" them. Precise analysis begins by saying that the seller and the purchaser entered into a contract for the sale of goods.

In the following cases, note the reluctance of some courts to untether property interest inquiry from title. The difficulty lies in the fact that the Code is itself an allocation of property rights, and the Code operates largely without reference to title. The lawyer who knows the Code goes directly to the applicable provisions without lingering over title issues.

WOOD CHEVROLET CO. v. BANK OF THE SOUTHEAST

Supreme Court of Alabama, 1977.
352 So.2d 1350, 23 U.C.C. Rep. Serv. 290.

BLOODWORTH, Justice.

Appellant, Wood Chevrolet Company, Inc. (Wood), appeals from a judgment for various appellees. We affirm.

Wood, a Birmingham retail automobile dealership, entered into an arrangement with United Motorists Association (UMA), a Birmingham business offering leasing, financing, and related services, whereby UMA would secure new automobiles, for its customers at a fleet discount, which Wood would then deliver to UMA's customers. Concurrent with the delivery of each automobile to each customer, a promissory note and security agreement were executed in favor of UMA whereby each customer agreed to pay UMA for the automobile and granted UMA a security interest therein. These notes and security agreements were assigned to appellee, Bank of the Southeast (Bank), which paid UMA by depositing funds into its general checking account at the Bank.

Testimony by Allison Turner Yeackle, corporate secretary of UMA, indicates that Wood expected UMA, rather than UMA's customers, to pay for the vehicles. However, after UMA went bankrupt, Wood brought suit against the Bank and the individual customers of UMA who had possession of the automobiles, praying, inter alia, for payment for the vehicles or their return.

Trial was held, ore tenus, and a final decree was entered for the appellees, holding, inter alia : that the customers of UMA, in possession of the vehicles, were innocent of any wrongdoing, although each is fully bound to the terms of the written contracts and the security agreements entered into; that appellee,

Bank, parted with valuable consideration in reliance upon a course of dealing between Wood and UMA, and is, therefore, the proper and legal holder of the contracts, documents, and security agreements, and is entitled to enforce them according to their terms; that all payments and credits made or provided by each customer to the Bank shall be applied to the indebtedness due the Bank, and should any of these contracts be in default, the Bank shall make further application to the court for relief; that Wood must return Coggin's vehicle, which it is allegedly holding under a mechanic's lien for repairs; that Wood must deliver all evidences of title in its possession to the Bank and furnish the Bank with whatever is necessary to fix title in the customers or owners, subject to the respective liens of the Bank; and, that all other relief requested is denied.

Wood's motion for new trial was overruled. Hence, this appeal.

Appellant Wood makes three main contentions on appeal. First, Wood contends that UMA acted as agent for the appellee-owners, whom Wood alleges were "principals," and that because these alleged principals retained the automobiles, they were liable to pay for them. Second, Wood contends, in the alternative, that a "sale" of these vehicles did not occur in that title was retained in Wood. Third, Wood contends that the Bank has no valid or enforceable security interests in these vehicles, since it "acquired no interests" in the instruments from its assignor, UMA, and thus, they are unenforceable. We cannot agree with any of these contentions.

We will now proceed to answer these contentions seriatim.

First, in Alabama, the question of agency is one of fact. See Riley v. Ford Motor Co., 442 F.2d 670 (5th Cir. 1971); Nearhos v. Keith, 221 Ala. 643, 130 So. 409 (1930). As such, it is subject to the more tenuous rule. Here, of course, the trial judge did not make specific findings of fact. Where, as here, however, the trial judge does not make express findings of fact, the Supreme Court must, nevertheless, assume that the trial judge found facts which would support his judgment, unless such a finding would be clearly erroneous and against the great weight and preponderance of the evidence. In this case, we do not think the great weight of the evidence supports a finding of agency.

It has been said that there can be no agency relationship absent a right of control by the principal over his agent. 2A C.J.S. Agency § 6, pp. 560-562. Cf. Hodges & Company, Inc. v. Albrecht, 288 Ala. 281, 259 So.2d 829 (1972). It is not essential that the right of control be exercised so long as that right actually exists. Id. Here, it seems apparent that the various owners exercised no control over the dealings between the alleged agent, UMA, and Wood. UMA apparently sought out the relationship with Wood and worked out the details, including the financing plan, prior to contacting the alleged principals, the owners, who then merely agreed to the terms of the plan in order to acquire automobiles at a discount. Such a factual setting clearly negates Wood's assertion that the owners were principals since they failed to exercise that degree of control essential to establish an agency relationship. Thus, it cannot be said that the owners, as principals, must answer for the debt of their alleged agent, UMA, since no agency relationship existed.

Second, Wood's next contention is that no valid "sale" of these vehicles occurred, because of lack of consideration and because Wood retained the Manufacturer's Statement of Origin, which Wood apparently equates with retaining title. Again, we cannot agree. Tit. 7A, § 2-106, Code of Alabama 1940 (§ 7-2-106, Code 1975), provides: "A 'sale' consists in the passing of title from the seller to the buyer for a price."

Passage of title is governed by Tit. 7A, § 2-401 (§ 7-2-401, Code 1975), which provides, in pertinent part:

> * * * "title to goods passes from the seller to the buyer in any manner and on any conditions explicitly agreed on by the parties.
>
> "(2) Unless otherwise explicitly agreed title passes to the buyer at the time and place at which the seller completes his performance with reference to the physical delivery of the goods, despite any reservation of a security interest and even though a document of title is to be delivered at a different time or place * * * ."

Wood argues that its retention of the Manufacturer's Statement of Origin evidences an explicit agreement to retain title until payment in full of the invoice was received. We disagree.

It has been held that nondelivery of a certificate of title at the time of a sale does not prevent the passage of title from the seller to the buyer. See, e. g., A. C. Rent-A-Car, Inc. v. American National Bank & Trust Co. of Mobile, 339 F.Supp. 506 (S.D.Ala.1972); Bunch v. Signal Oil and Gas Co., 505 P.2d 41 (Colo.App.1972). This is true even where a state's certificate of title act provides that no title can be acquired in an automobile until the certificate of title has been issued. See id. Thus, it is that retention of the Manufacturer's Statement of Origin does not evidence a clear intention that title remain in Wood. Instead, we hold that title passed when the cars were picked up by or delivered to the individual owners.

Wood's third contention is that the Bank has neither a valid nor enforceable security interest in any of these automobiles insofar as the Bank was the transferee of the notes and security agreements from UMA, which Wood contends had no interest in the notes and instruments. Wood cites Tit. 7A, § 3-201 Code 1940 (§ 7-3-201 Code 1975) for this proposition. Wood's argument is erroneous. We have already held that title had passed to the owners and therefore they could grant UMA a security interest in the vehicles, which UMA, in turn could assign to the Bank. See Tit. 7A, § 2-401 supra.

Having disposed of the major contentions on this appeal, we turn to several ancillary contentions raised for a brief discussion.

Wood further contends the Bank is guilty of "fraud" in that it acted in concert with UMA to suppress material facts from Wood. We cannot agree with this contention nor will the evidence support any such theory.

Wood finally contends it is entitled to recover the amounts the Bank deposited into UMA's general account by virtue of its alleged status as a "third party beneficiary." In Alabama, for a contract to be for the benefit of a third person, the contract must have been intended for the direct benefit of the third person, as distinguished from mere incidental benefit to him. Harris v. Board of Water and Sewer Commissioners of the City of Mobile, 294 Ala. 606, 320 So.2d 624 (1975). In the case at bar, however, it is clear that the arrangement between the Bank and UMA was not intended for the direct benefit of Wood. Rather, the agreement was to be for the mutual benefit of the Bank and UMA. Moreover, the cases Wood cites for this proposition do not support it. Nor, does the evidence support Wood in this respect.

WEISBART & CO. v. FIRST NATIONAL BANK

United States Court of Appeals, Fifth Circuit, 1978.
568 F.2d 391.

[On October 30, 1971 Gallo, who purchased cattle from breeders and fattened them, entered into a contract with Weisbart to deliver 3500 heifers to Weisbart between May 1 and October 1, 1972. Gallo had granted First National Bank a perfected security interest in all of his cattle whenever owned. When Gallo had difficulty meeting his contract with Weisbart, he negotiated extensions. The bank participated in those negotiations. Before Gallo delivered all of the cattle to Weisbart, the bank called his loan and seized the cattle remaining on his feed lots.

Section 9-306(2) provides that a security interest follows collateral when the debtor sells or otherwise transfers it to a third party. There are exceptions to that rule, however, one of them appearing in the subsection itself, which provides that a sale, exchange or other disposition is free of the security interest if the secured party authorizes it.]

INGRAHAM, Circuit Judge.

* * *

In May and June of 1973, the bank foreclosed upon seventeen hundred and sixty-three head of cattle in Gallo's possession after coming to the realization that the proceeds from the sale of the cattle under the contract would be insufficient to pay off the loan. Weisbart purchased the seventeen hundred and sixty-three head of cattle from the bank. Then, invoking the court's diversity jurisdiction, Weisbart sued the bank in federal district court for the difference between the price it paid the bank for the cattle and the original contract price. Judgment was rendered for the bank upon jury issues, after which Weisbart appealed.

Weisbart pursued its action under a theory of contractual interference, alleging that the bank "willfully, intentionally and without legal justification or excuse caused or brought about a breach of the contract by Gallo." The issue of waiver forms the linchpin of Weisbart's argument, for if the bank did not waive its security interest, its repossession of the livestock was fully justified.

In order to establish waiver by the bank, the trial court required a showing of intent. This requirement was reflected in jury issue 1(b): Do you find from a preponderance of the evidence that by consenting and acquiescing in the (renewed and extended contract for sale between Al Gallo and Weisbart & Co.)

that the bank intended that its mortgage and lien on the cattle would be subject to and inferior to Weisbart's contract to buy the cattle? ANSWER: It did not so intend.

Weisbart contests the submission of this issue on the ground that it is superfluous. The bulwark of Weisbart's position lies in § 9.306 of the UCC: (b) Except where this Article otherwise provides, a security interest continues in collateral notwithstanding sale, exchange or other disposition thereof unless the disposition was authorized by the secured party in the security agreement or otherwise, and also continues in any identifiable proceeds including collections received by the debtor. Tex.Bus. & Com. Code Ann. § 9.306(b) (1968). Weisbart argues that by consenting to or acquiescing in the contract extensions, the bank authorized the disposition of its collateral, thus subordinating its security interest to Weisbart's contract.[1]

The threshold inquiry in this case is whether or not there was a "sale, exchange, or other disposition," so as to trigger the operation of § 9.306(b). For the purposes of Article 9, § 9.105 adopts the definition of sale set out in § 2.106. This section defines a "sale" as "the passing of title from the seller to the buyer for a price." Tex.Bus. & Com. Code Ann. § 2.106 (1968); Allen v. Ortho Pharmaceutical Corp., 387 F.Supp. 364, 367 (S.D.Tex.1974); First National Bank v. Joseph T. Ryerson & Son, Inc., 487 S.W.2d 377, 381 (Tex.Civ.App. Texarkana, 1972, writ ref'd n.r.e.). Section 2.401 specifies when title passes: (b) Unless otherwise explicitly agreed title passes to the buyer at the time and place at which the seller completes his performance with reference to the physical delivery of the goods * * *. (2) if the contract requires delivery at destination, title passes on tender there. Tex. Bus. & Com. Code Ann. § 2.401 (1968).

The contracts in the instant case did not state when title was to pass. Title would therefore pass in accordance with § 2.401. Since the contract calls for delivery at Weisbart's ranch if it so desires, title could not pass until this delivery was effected. See Gehl Bros. Mfg. Co. v. Price's Producers, Inc., 319 S.W.2d 955, 958 (Tex.Civ.App. El Paso, 1958, no writ).

Neither was there an "exchange" of the livestock. Because the UCC does not define this term, we are relegated by § 1.103 to the general principles of law and equity for its definition. Under Texas law, the difference between a sale and exchange is purely technical. An exchange occurs when "one party passes his property to another and in turn receives from the latter his property without having an agreed value placed on (either)." Griswold v. Tucker, 216 S.W.2d 276, 278 (Tex.Civ.App. Ft. Worth, 1948, no writ). This type of transaction is to be distinguished from a sale where the property of each is transferred at an agreed value. Id. Significantly, an exchange requires at least a transfer of goods like

---

[1] This case does not implicate § 9.307 which permits the buyer in the ordinary course of business to take free of a security interest created by his seller. By its express terms § 9.307 does not apply to "a person buying farm products from a person engaged in farming operations." Tex.Bus. & Com. Code Ann. § 9.307(a) (1968). There can be no dispute that the cattle Weisbart contracted to buy were "farm products" and that Gallo was engaged in "farming operations." See Tex.Bus. & Com. Code Ann. § 9.109 (1968).

that required for sale. The contract in the instant case therefore does not constitute an "exchange."

The UCC likewise does not define "other disposition." The meaning of this term, however, may be distilled by applying the canon of statutory construction known as *ejusdem generis*. Employment of the doctrine mandates that "other disposition" refer to a transaction of the same general type as a sale or exchange. Therefore, though "other disposition" cannot technically be characterized as a sale or exchange, at the minimum it must meet the threshold test of these two transactions by effecting a transfer of property. See Barnard v. Barnard, 91 Ga.App. 502, 502-503, 86 S.E.2d 533, 536 (1955) (holding that since the word "sell" means to "divest one's self of all rights and interest in a thing sold," the doctrine of *ejusdem generis* compels that "exchange" and "dispose" also carry that connotation).

Thus the language of § 9.306 compels us to find that Weisbart's contract of sale did not constitute a "sale, exchange or other disposition." This conclusion accords with the policy sought to be furthered by the drafters of this section. Following acquiescence in and sale of the collateral, the farm products lender stands on the same footing as the inventory financier. Neither has a continuing security interest in the collateral. §§ 9.306(b), 9.307(a). Each, however, retains a threshold of protection, because his security interest attaches to the proceeds of the sale. § 9.306(a) & Comment 2(a).

To hold that there was a "sale, exchange, or other disposition" for the purpose of applying § 9.306 would be to emasculate the protection that the UCC grants the bank. Because Weisbart had not received the sale price of the cattle, there were no proceeds (excluding the down payment) to which the bank's security interest could attach. See In re Kittyhawk Television Corp., 383 F.Supp. 691, 693 (S.D.Ohio, 1974) (finding stock received in exchange for assets to be proceeds and thereby rejecting claim that there were no proceeds and hence no sale). We therefore hold that the contract of sale between Gallo and Weisbart does not spark the operation of § 9.306.

* * *

SECTION 2. SPECIAL PROPERTY

INTRODUCTORY NOTE

Code drafters recognized that certain commercial events turn on the existence in the buyer of a property interest in the goods being sold. Under Article 9, a debtor cannot grant a security interest in goods in which the debtor has no interest; and under insurance law, an insured cannot insure goods in which it has no interest. The Code drafters were adamant, however, that title not play the role in modern commercial law that it had played in pre-Code law. They eschewed title. That much is clear from the preamble to § 2-401. What is not always clear to the courts is that the substitute they fashioned for title is the special property.

MILLER v. RACE, 97 Eng. Rep. 398, 400 ((K.B. 1758). "I agree that the holder of the [stolen] note has a special property: but it does not follow that he can maintain trover for it, against the true owner."

WATERMAN v. ROBINSON, 5 Mass. 302, 303 (1809). "Upon these facts, we are to decide whether the property of the goods, so that he might lawfully replevy them, was in the plaintiff.

Trover may be maintained by him who has the possession; but replevin cannot be maintained but by him who has the property, either general or special. Admitting the commission, and the proceedings under it, to be regular, what property had the plaintiff in the goods? The general property was in the commissioners until the assignment and then in the assignee. The messenger, if any person, had the special property, and not the plaintiff, who had no interest in the goods, but merely had the care of them for safekeeping. If his possession was violated, he might maintain trespass or trover, but he had no special property, by which he could maintain replevin; in which the question is not of possession, but of property, although possession may be *prima facie* evidence of property."

O.W. HOLMES, THE COMMON LAW 244 (1881). "[T]he special property which was requisite to maintain the possessory actions was supposed to mean a qualified interest in the goods."

UCC § 2-501(1)

The buyer obtains a special property and an insurable interest in goods by identification of existing goods as goods to which the contract refers even though the goods so identified are non-conforming and he has an option to return or reject them. Such identification can be made at any time and in any manner explicitly agreed to by the parties.

NOTE ON SPECIAL PROPERTY

The special property has always denoted an interest inferior to the general property, that is, title, but sufficient to give the holder of the special property enforceable rights in the goods. Courts did not encumber the special property concept with what Llewellyn saw as the rigid theoretical accretions that they had fastened on the title concept. Without that rigidity, the special property survives as a flexible notion that can serve the Code pattern well. The special property arises at the time of identification and signals the beginning of the buyer's legally cognizable interest in the goods. The dimensions of the interest depend to a significant degree on Code sections other than those that speak directly of the special property.

We don't know too much about the special property. Most importantly, we do know that it is a property interest that can be conveyed. On the seller's breach, the special property will support a right of replevin of goods for which the buyer is unable to effect cover. § 2-716(3). Courts have had some difficulty in determining the point at which a party who would otherwise qualify as a buyer in ordinary course has sufficient interest in the goods to defeat a secured creditor. Many have succumbed to the temptation of looking to delivery, because it is the point at which title passes.

In the next two cases, the courts wrestle with property concepts. In the first, the court properly rejects title analysis; in the second, the court invokes the special property deftly.

CHRYSLER CREDIT CORP. v. SHARP

Supreme Court, Erie County, New York, 1968.
288 N.Y.S.2d 525, 56 Misc.2d 261.

[On February 16, 1966 Dorothy Mae Sharp entered into a retail installment contract to purchase an automobile from Heintzman-McRae Motors in Buffalo. Under the retail installment sales contract, Mrs. Sharp granted Heintzman a security interest in the car. Heintzman had earlier granted Marine Midland Trust Company a security interest in all of its inventory of automobiles. On February 17, Heintzman took the retail contract to Chrysler Credit and obtained a loan from Chrysler, granting Chrysler a security interest in the contract and assigning to Chrysler Heintzman's security interest in the vehicle that Mrs. Sharp had granted it. Chrysler duly perfected its security interest in the contract (chattel paper as we will see in the next chapter) by taking possession of it and perfected its assigned security interest in the motor vehicle as required by New York law. Before Mrs. Sharp obtained delivery of the car, Marine Midland closed Heintzman and took possession of all of its inventory, including the car in question. Apparently Mrs. Sharp abandoned any claim to the vehicle. Chrysler, claiming that it had an interest superior to that of Marine Midland sued Marine Midland for the value of the car.]

WILLIAM W. SERRA, J.

* * *

This Court is inclined to feel that while title questions may be of significance in determining many issues under the UCC, the theory of the act and its relation to the problem relegates the issue of title in this case to a subordinate position. The UCC is the result of the rapid expansion of credit operations in the business world, both wholesale and retail to the position where traditional paper in the form of chattel mortgages, conditional sales forms, and even trust receipt floor planning do not, in large, fast moving operations, meet the needs of a rapid flow of credit. The financing of inventories, particularly, has long baffled those accustomed to the country store with its annual inventory and slow movement of goods. A car dealer with hundreds of transactions a month, or a major appliance shop with transactions running into the thousands must keep inventory controls by modern business machinery and have a constant flow of cash and credit. To meet these demands the UCC provides for greater flexibility and in some respects to the uninitiated, will, during the transition of its ultimate form, seem to create new risks.

* * *

Applying the definitions and constructions indicated above, we find that Mrs. Sharp entered into a contract with the dealer to purchase the car by (1) delivery of her trade-in or exchange of property, (2) by cash, not actually paid but secured by a deferred delivery of the vehicle under a collateral oral agreement, (3) by cash, unsecured, to be paid at a later date, and, (4) by a secured credit agreement sold by the dealer to the plaintiff. The dispute, arising out of the attempt to enforce the secured credit agreement or retail installment contract comes from the contention of the defendant bank that the entire transaction with Mrs. Sharp was executory only, that it was never consummated, title did not pass and it was null and void. The plaintiff, as a retail financer, on the other hand, contends that Mrs. Sharp was a buyer out of inventory in the ordinary course of business on her partly performed contract.

Applying the definitions to the evidence, it may be said that Mrs. Sharp entered into a specific written contract to purchase the car owned by the dealer. She gave valuable consideration in goods, she traded in her old vehicle, and she signed a binding installment contract. She agreed to pay in cash a down payment and a deferred payment. By agreement, orally, she specified the course of her down payment, an anticipated income tax refund, and she certainly, in good faith expected to receive the car and to make her payments upon the evidence, UCC 1-102(3). According to the testimony, she attempted to pay her cash deficiency a few days after the repossession by the bank, but, finding the car gone, abandoned her rights. The sales manager testified without contradiction, that they frequently took and negotiated contracts with the car to be held for a time for the cash down payment, that it was common practice in his twenty years experience in the car business to take contracts without actual receipt of the recited cash down payment. He said he would fire a salesman who failed to do so and that in his experience and opinion a number of dealers would go out of business if they failed to follow this practice.

It is agreed by the parties that both the plaintiff and the defendant have formally perfected security interests and that the value of the collateral is \$1,200.00. The question, therefore, becomes one of the priority of rights in the proceeds of the sale of the 1963 Chevrolet automobile. A security interest is an interest in property which secures payment or performance of an obligation, UCC 1-201(37), Article 9, the security article, does not adopt a title or lien theory of security interests and rights. Obligations and remedies are not determined by the location of the title but rather on function, compliance with statutory requirements and the nature of the transaction. (See 'Official Comment' under UCC 9-101, Part 3, McKinney's Consolidated Laws of New York, Uniform Commercial Code, Volume 62 ½, pp. 318-321) It is clear that the automobiles of the dealer were inventory held for sale to the public, UCC 9-109(4). Under the agreement between the defendant bank and the dealer entitled 'Floor-Plan Agreement and Signatory Authorization (Inventory),' it is provided in the opening paragraph that the purpose is to finance the dealer's acquisition and/or holding goods, i.e., motor vehicles for use and resale in the course of the dealer's business. It further provides, paragraph 8, as follows '(8) The Dealer agrees that when any item of Goods is sold or otherwise disposed of, the Dealer will account to the Bank for the Proceeds and will deliver to the Bank such Proceeds and such assignments or indorsements as may be requisite or requested by the Bank. The Bank shall be entitled to the Proceeds and shall have a security interest in them. Pending such accounting and delivery, the Dealer will hold the Proceeds in trust for the Bank as the Bank's property, but at the Dealer's risk, in the identical form received and separate and apart from the Dealer's property. Proceeds as used herein means cash and non-cash proceeds, immediate and remote, and includes any debts owing to the Dealer by reason of the sale or other disposition of any Collateral and any cash, checks, trade-ins, accounts, chattel paper, notes, drafts, or other instruments whenever received and any items of Collateral disposed of by the Dealer which are returned to or repossessed by the Dealer.'

This is the very type of floating lien contemplated by UCC 9-204, and by UCC 9-205 which offsets the restrictive rulings of Benedict v. Ratner, 268 U.S. 353, 45 S.Ct. 566, 69 L.Ed. 991. Pursuant to this clause in the contract, the dealer received the funds obtained by assignments of Mrs. Sharp's retail installment contract and deposited these moneys to the dealer's account in the defendant bank. If it became commingled by the time of the insolvency, having, however, been traced into the bank account, it still remained a part of the gross remaining assets of the dealer inuring to the benefit of the bank on its seizure, under the provisions of UCC 9-306(4). The bank should, then, have a prior right to such funds even against the trustee in bankruptcy, since the claim is an equitable substitution authorized by the statute for the original inventory lien and relates back to the perfection of such lien. Howarth v. Universal C.I.T. Credit Corporation (W.D.Pa.1962) 203 F.Supp. 279. This theory is extensively discussed by R. D. Henson in 65 Columbia Law Review 232 (1965).

Under its floor plan agreement, paragraph 12, the bank is completely subrogated to all rights of the dealer in the business transactions and assets of the dealer on insolvency in implementation of the 'floating lien' type transaction and for the protection of its rights thereunder. This includes its rights in and to the trade-in and its proceeds, if any, in the rights, if any, and in the contract rights of the dealer against Mrs. Sharp, had they been pursued on the contract, or for damages, (Howarth, supra.).

By the same token, the plaintiff finance company, having furnished new value which has been paid to the dealer on the assignment, and having purchased the chattel paper in due course, is entitled to the returned or repossessed goods under UCC 9-306(5)(b), (c) and (d) and UCC 9-308, provided, as in this case, its interest has been perfected, UCC 9-306(5)(d), UCC 9-302(1)(d), UCC 9-401(1)(b) and UCC 9-312(1). See also 2 William D. Hawkland, a Transactional Uniform Commercial Code, pages 730 to 732, pages 700 to 701; 1 Anderson's Uniform Commercial Code, pages 562 to 566 inclusive, for discussions of this point.

In making this determination, the Court has, of course, by inference, determined that the buyer of goods was a buyer in the ordinary course of business out of inventory. A discussion of this has been left to the close of this memorandum by reason of the fact that the entire relation of the parties as indicated above relates to whether the irregularities of the transaction would make Mrs. Sharp other than such a buyer. As indicated at the beginning, UCC 1-102 requires a construction of all terms to carry out the underlying purposes and policies set forth in the statute, which is discussed at length in the practice commentaries of McKinney's Consolidated Laws of New York and in the Official Comments. Any interpretation of the entire transaction, where both the retail financer and bank entruster acted in good faith which became so technical as to abort the intention of the Act and where a dealer has acted in relation to all the other parties, buyer, entruster and financer, in such manner as to leave each with damage would undermine the ultimate success of the Act. If there is a usage of trade which exposes an entruster on floor plan to certain risks, these are risks against which he can guard by audits and accounting procedures or he can refuse to knowingly expose himself to the risk with the particular dealer. To fail to place the exposure of such risk with the entruster in such situation would make it impossible for retail finance companies to do business with any dealer unless the entruster were directly a participant. To hold otherwise, would expose the retail financer to a double loss as against at most a partial loss for both. The proliferation of paper work would be a giant step backwards in modern commercial practice. The Court feels a buyer who makes a purchase on a printed form contract in good faith with a full understanding it is a binding contract, who knowingly signs a retail installment payment obligation and trades in an old car in addition must, certainly as to a retail financer furnishing new value on the strength of such contract and as to an entruster giving the dealer wide latitude of sale goods, be deemed a buyer in the ordinary course of business, without regard to the technicalities of when title is to pass pursuant to collateral oral agreements or as to time of delivery and without the necessity of determining whether such delay brings about technically, a bailment, a non-delivery, a repossession or whatever. (See UCC 1-205, Practice Commentary, by Lester E. Denonn, McKinney's Consolidated Laws of New York, Volume 62 ½, Part 1, Page 56, regarding the use of printed forms, usage of trade and side agreements.) This is especially so where Article 9, UCC provides such a finely integrated plan for the determination of the priorities and equities of the parties to secured transactions. This Court does not, therefore, consider the title cases prior to the UCC as controlling on the facts of the instant litigation.

FIRST NATIONAL BANK v. SMOKER

Court of Appeals of Indiana, 1972.
153 Ind. App. 71, 286 N.E.2d 203.

[On February 16, 1966 Whisler granted a perfected security interest to First National Bank in all inventory then owned and thereafter acquired and all accounts receivable, then existing and thereafter arising, other collateral and proceeds and products of the foregoing categories of collateral. Subsequently, the Bank made a series of working capital loans to Whisler. Smoker, who sold cattle to Whisler claimed that the bank converted his cattle when they called Whistler's loan and seized his collateral.]

SHARP, J.

This action, initiated by Dwight Smoker (Smoker), plaintiff-appellee, against the First National Bank of Elkhart County (Bank), defendant-appellant, is for an alleged conversion by the Bank of sides of beef and hides from 85 head of cattle and for misappropriation of the proceeds from the sale of said cattle. The conversion allegedly occurred when the Bank exerted dominion and control over the cattle when they were in the hands of its debtor, J. L. Whisler and Sons, Inc. (Whisler) but when title to said cattle remained with Smoker. Trial was had before the court without the intervention of a jury and resulted in a judgment for Smoker in the sum of $17,576.40. The Bank duly filed its motion to correct errors, which was overruled, and this appeal was then taken.

* * *

There are two separate and distinct transactions which precipitated this action. The first involves the perfected security agreement between the bank and Whisler creating a security interest in all the inventory, accounts receivable, after acquired property and proceeds of Whisler. The second transaction is the oral contract for sale of eighty-five head of cattle to Whisler by Smoker, said oral contract being based upon custom and usage in the trade and the course of dealing between the immediate parties. We are concerned with the interrelation of these two separate transactions and the legal efficacy of each vis-a-vis the interests of third parties. The issue is one of priority of interests between a secured party with a 'floating lien' and a supplier of raw materials to the debtor. The fundamental issue is whether an oral agreement between a buyer and seller, relying heavily on custom and usage in the trade, can delay the passage of title to goods already delivered to the buyer so as to defeat the rights of third party secured creditors of the buyer and transform such a creditor into a convertor of goods in the possession of the buyer. To put it another way, will a secured party holding a perfected security interest in a buyer's inventory, accounts receivable, after-acquired property and proceeds, when liquidating the buyer's inventory upon default, be deemed to have converted the property of a subsequent unperfected seller who delivers goods to the buyer before default but who reserved title until a specified time after delivery? Although we are concerned with the common law action of conversion, we must look to the Uniform Commercial Code, I.C.1971, 26-1-1-101 et seq.; Ind.Ann.Stat. § 19-1-101 et seq. (Burns 1964), to determine the legal effect of the transactions and to ascertain the respective rights and interests of the parties involved. Once the respective rights of the parties have been established, we must then apply the applicable principles embodied in the action for tortious conversion.

The argument advanced by Smoker in favor of the judgment below is essentially that the parties to the contract for the sale of the cattle intended title to pass only after the cattle had been graded on the day following delivery. Smoker contends that the law prior to the passage of the Uniform Commercial Code was that passage of title depended upon the intentions of the parties to the contract, and that custom and usage in the trade and course of dealing, when applicable, were to be given effect in determining the intentions of the parties. Allegedly, the Code left this prior law unchanged and thus title remained in Smoker at the time the Bank made demand for payment of its note. The subsequent exercise of dominion or control by the Bank over the cattle was a conversion by the Bank.

Smoker's argument, bereft of glossing and reduced to essentials, is that custom and usage in the trade plus the course of dealing between Smoker and Whisler amounted to an express agreement as to when title to the goods was to pass. This explicit agreement, because it is based on the above ingredients, negates and prevents the application of I.C.1971, 26-1-2-401; Ind.Ann.Stat. § 19-2-101 (Burns 1964), and the applicable sections of the Article on Secured Transactions (Article 9). An ancillary argument is that the cattle, although in the possession of Whisler, were not identified to the contract prior to grading. Since goods must be identified to the contract before the buyer can obtain a special property in the goods and before title passes, Whisler did not have an interest in the cattle at the time of demand so as to allow the security interest to attach under I.C.1971, 26-1-9-204; Ind.Ann.Stat. § 19-9-204 (Burns 1964).

* * *

Under I.C.1971, 26-1-9-204; Ind.Ann.Stat. § 19-9-204 (Burns 1964), a security interest cannot attach to specific goods or collateral until there is an agreement that it attach and value is given and the debtor acquires rights in the collateral. It is uncontroverted that the first two requirements were met by the bank in this case. Nor does Smoker specifically and directly argue that Whisler did not have such rights in the cattle as to allow the Bank's security interest to attach thereto. Thus, although not specifically mentioned by either party, we deem it necessary to determine what rights Whisler had in the cattle and whether the rights were sufficient to allow the Bank's security interest to attach to the same.

Several courts have considered the question in the context of whether absolute ownership in and title to collateral was the requisite right necessary to permit the attachment of the secured creditor's interest. They uniformly have held that the location of the nebulous concept 'title' was immaterial in ascertaining whether a debtor had sufficient rights in specific collateral.

* * *

Thus, it would follow that when a debtor acquires possession of collateral under a contract, he has acquired such rights in the collateral as to allow the security interest of his creditor to attach to the collateral, and this is true regardless of who may be deemed to have title to and ownership of such collateral.

This line of reasoning is further supported by the fact that once the cattle come into the possession of Whisler, they cease to be classified as 'farm products' and become 'inventory.' The official comments to I.C.1971, 26-1-9-109; Ind.Ann.Stat. § 19-9-109, while not binding, are persuasive and read in pertinent part as follows: 'Goods are 'farm products' only if they are in the possession of a debtor engaged in farming operations. 'When crops or livestock or their products come into the possession of a person not engaged in farming operations they cease to be 'farm products.' If they come into possession of a marketing agency for sale or distribution or a manufacturer or processor as raw materials, they become inventory.'

Thus, regardless of whether Whisler had obtained title to the cattle, they became part of his inventory upon their coming into his possession pursuant to a contract for sale. As inventory, Whisler acquired such rights in and to the cattle so that the security interest of the Bank attached.

Having determined that the Bank had a perfected security interest in the eighty-five head of cattle as part of the inventory of Whisler, it remains to be determined if the oral agreement between Smoker and Whisler, in conjunction with the provisions of Article 2, in any way negate or vitiate the security interest of the bank. We must determine the legal efficacy of the retention of title by a seller after delivery of goods upon a prior perfected security interest.

* * *

Absent an explicit agreement, title to goods under § 19-2-401(2), supra, passes to the buyer at the time and place at which the seller completes his performance with reference to physical delivery of the goods. Thus, if Smoker and Whisler had not entered into an explicit agreement concerning when title was to pass, said title would have passed upon the physical delivery of the goods and Smoker would have had, at most, a purchase money security interest, I.C.1971, 26-1-9-107; Ind.Ann.Stat. § 19-9-107 (Burns 1964). But, as was pointed out earlier, Smoker argues that there was an explicit agreement based on custom and usage in the trade and the course of dealing between the parties, and that this explicit agreement prevents the application of § 19-2-401(2) supra, and allows title to remain in Smoker after delivery.

The evidence introduced at trial showed an oral agreement by telephone between Whisler and Smoker with respect to sale of the cattle in controversy. The record is devoid of any evidence indicating an explicit oral or written agreement between Whisler and Smoker concerning the retention of title in the cattle after they were delivered to Whisler, except as reference may be made to custom and usage of the trade. However, the drafters of the Uniform Commercial Code recognized that when dealing with a usage of the trade, it should be incorporated into a contract, whether oral or written, as an explicit agreement only: 'where a usage of the trade has previously been made explicit by reduction to a standard set of 'rules and regulations' currently incorporated by reference into the contract of the parties, a relevant provision of those 'rules and regulations' is 'explicit' within the meaning of the second.' (Comment 3 to the official text of the Uniform Commercial Code following Burns Ind.Stat.Annot. § 19-2-501, 1964 Repl.)

Nowhere in the record of this case is there found any evidence relating to a standard set of 'rules and regulations' in the packing industry with respect to the retention of title in a farmer after the cattle have been delivered to a packer. The most we have in this case is an implicit understanding between the parties, as well as within the industry as a whole, as when title is to pass. The implicit understanding is insufficient to meet the demands of the provisions of the Code and we, therefore, hold that there was not an explicit agreement between the parties as to when title would pass so as to remove the oral contract from the provisions of § 19-9-401(2).

But even assuming that the evidence of custom and usage and the course of dealing between the parties was sufficient to establish an explicit agreement, it is of no avail to Smoker. The argument of Smoker ignores the sentences in § 19-2-401(1), supra, regarding explicit agreements concerning retention of title to the effect that 'any retention or reservation by the seller of the title (property) in goods shipped or delivered to the buyer is limited in effect to a reservation of security interest.' The definition of 'agreement' as found in § 19-1-201(3), supra, now becomes important since it specifically states that whether any agreement, even those based upon course of dealing or usage, of trade, has legal consequences is determined by the provisions of the Act. Thus, the legal effect of retention of title by a seller is only the reservation of a security interest and therefore, the seller must comply with the provisions of Article 9, wherein § 19-9-202 specifically states that each provision of the article apply whether title to the collateral is in the secured party or the debtor.

The final question to be answered concerns the definition and scope of the term 'identification,' and whether the cattle in question were identified to the contract prior to grading. * * *

Title cannot pass before identification but the two are not synonymous. Identification is of limited importance under the Code although it does determine the earliest point at which title may pass. While § 19-2-501 does provide that identification may be made at any time and in any manner explicitly agreed to by the parties; this does not mean that the parties may delay the passage of title by the simple expedient of agreeing that the goods are not yet identified to the contract when, in fact, they have already been delivered to the buyer. Identification refers to when the goods are still in the possession of the seller. Thus, by explicit agreement, the parties may decide that the goods are identified at a point in time earlier than those enunciated in § 19-2-501, but in no event can they delay such identification after the goods are in the possession of the buyer. This case does not deal with identification but rather with I.C.1971, 26-1-2-305; Ind.Ann.Stat. 19-2-305 (Burns 1964) concerning open price terms. Our view is supported by other sections of the Code dealing with the remedies of the seller upon default by the buyer.

Pursuant to the above cited provisions, we hold, as a matter of law, that Smoker retained only a purchase money security interest in the eighty-five head of cattle upon the delivery of such cattle to Whisler under an oral contract for sale. To have effectively reserved his rights, Smoker would have had to proceed under Article 9, § 19-9-101 et seq., concerning secured transactions, specifically I.C.1971, 26-1-9-312(3); Ind.Ann.Stat. § 19-9-312(3). Since Smoker failed to perfect his security interest in the inventory of Whisler, his rights in the eighty-five head of cattle or the proceeds thereof are subordinated to the rights of the Bank, which had a prior perfected security interest, § 19-9-312(5), and this is true regardless of whether Smoker, by explicit agreement, retained title to the goods.

NOTE ON THE PACKERS & STOCKYARDS ACT

In 1979 in response to cases such as *Smoker*, the cattleman's lobby succeeded in having Congress amend the Packers & Stockyards Act to provide that packers hold all livestock and their proceeds in trust for the benefit of cash sellers and that the seller's interest in the trust is superior to claims of the packer's creditors. The statute defines a cash sale as one in which the seller does not expressly extend credit to the packer. See 7 U.S.C. § 196.

SECTION 3. NONCONSENSUAL SECURITY INTERESTS

INTRODUCTORY NOTE

Much study of commercial law deals with the Article 9 security interest, which is, by definition, a consensual security interest in personal property or fixtures. There are, in addition, security interests that arise by operation of law, that is, that arise without any agreement of the parties. Two of these nonconsensual security interests are in Article 2, and one is in Article 4.

UCC § 1-201(37)

"Security interest" means an interest in personal property or fixtures which secures payment or performance of an obligation.

UCC § 4-210

A collecting bank has a security interest in an item and any accompanying documents or the proceeds of either * * * .

PROBLEM

A New York seller has entered into a contract with a Parisian buyer for shipment of a container of aluminum ingots, CIF Le Havre, payment against documents. In this contract, the seller must arrange for the shipment from New York to Le Havre and must insure the goods during transport. Next he must see that documents are presented to the French buyer. Upon presentation of the proper documents, the buyer must pay.

The seller arranged to ship the documents on the New York Line and obtained a negotiable document of title from the line. The seller took the bill of lading and a draft (a negotiable order instrument drawn on the buyer) to the seller's bank in New York. The New York bank gave the seller credit for the draft and sent it through banking channels to Paris. When the Paris bank presented the draft to the buyer, the buyer dishonored; and the Paris bank returned the documents to the New York bank, whose officer was displeased to learn that the seller was now bankrupt.

The ingots are in the middle of the North Atlantic. Does the bank have any interest in them? See § 4-210.

UCC § 2-505(1)

Where the seller has identified goods to the contract by or before shipment: (a) his procurement of a negotiable bill of lading to his own order or otherwise reserves in him a security interest in the goods. * * * (b) a non-negotiable bill of lading to himself or his nominee reserves possession of the goods as security * * * .

NOTE ON *SAWYER v. DEAN*

Sellers that ship goods off to a distant destination before they are paid must have a twinge of regret as the ship sails off into the sunset. There go the goods; and, if the shipment is on open account, payment must abide their arrival at the buyer's port. Merchants developed the documentary draft transaction in order to insure that the buyer did not obtain possession of the goods until she either paid for them (against a sight draft) or signed a negotiable instrument promising to pay for them (accepting a time draft). Note that many of Code's delivery terms assume payment against documents. See §§ 2-319(4), 2-320(4), 2-513(3).

These provisions are clearly pro-seller. They require the buyer to pay for goods before she sees them. At common law, the seller's shipment of the goods sometimes caused title to pass to the buyer—a clear pro-buyer rule. The common law effected some balance to that rule in a fashion reflected in the following case.

SAWYER v. DEAN

Court of Appeals of New York, 1889.
114 N.Y. 469, 21 N.E. 1012.

[Plaintiff's assignor entered into a contract to sell the defendant, Dean, 500 hides to be shipped from the seller's place of business in Chicago to the buyer's tannery in Oswego, New York. Seller shipped the goods under a documentary draft. When the bank presented the draft to the buyer for payment, the buyer refused to honor it, claiming that he had the right to examine the hides when they arrived at Oswego. The seller declined to permit the inspection, caused the hides to be returned to Chicago, sold them, and sued the defendant for the difference between the selling price and the contract price.]

POTTER, J.

* * *

Upon the ordinary agreement to sell and to purchase personal property, in the absence of any agreement or provision in the agreement as to the time or manner of payment, delivery and payment are simultaneous acts; and, as a tender is equivalent in law to performance, a tender of delivery or payment by one person to the other gives the person making the tender the right to enforce the performance of the contract by the other. Hayden v. Demets, 53 N. Y. 426, 428, 429. In the case under consideration, defendant made no objection that the hides were not of good quality or of the quality specified in the terms of purchase, nor in the number of hides. He simply insisted that he had a right, under the contract, to an examination of the hides before acceptance and payment. Under such a contract, as I think the trial judge might have well found from the evidence in this case, it results, as in the case of Higgins v. Murray, 4 Hun, 565, and as was in the opinion in that case expressed by Judge DANIELS, that the plaintiff's assignor, by shipping in his own name, was simply keeping the possession of the property, as he had the right to do, until it had been accepted and paid for by the defendant. By shipping in that manner he retained and kept the lien of possession as his security for the payment of the property. The effect of the contract was to transfer the title of the property from plaintiff's assignor to the defendant, subject only to the right of possession of the assignor to retain possession until payment should be made, as long as no credit was to be given, or had been provided for, by the terms of the agreement. After the making of the contract he became the agent of the defendant, save in retaining possession of the property as security for the payment of the purchase money, while title to the property was vested in the defendant. To the same effect is the case of Bank v. Pfeiffer, 22 Hun, 327. Also the case of Morey v. Medbury, 10 Hun, 540. If the law in this case is not as above stated, the effect would be that a person who under a valid contract has sold his property, sent it to a distant place to the manufacturing establishment of the purchaser, has received no payment, and has parted with the possession of the property and that means of securing payment, must rely upon the responsibility of the purchaser, and his disposition to pay for the property. If this is not satisfactory to the purchaser, he should have made a different bargain. He could have done as he was advised by the plaintiff's assignor, viz., have appointed a hide broker or expert to have made the selection. Then both the buyer and the seller would have been bound by the selection made—the buyer to accept and pay for, and the seller to deliver. But the defendant chose to make the seller his agent to select, and he must abide by the selection made for him, especially in the absence of any evidence that the hides were not just what he ordered. Indeed, the defendant did not base his refusal to pay upon any allegation, much less upon any proof that the hides were not in accordance with his specification and order, but upon the simple pretext that he wanted to examine them, and that, too, after he had authorized the plaintiff's assignor to select the hides for him.

While the trial court might, and I think should, have found as above indicated, it has found substantially in that way, but with the qualification that the plaintiff's assignor gave the defendant the right to examine the hides before accepting them. This right the learned trial court bases upon expressions in the letters of October 27th and November 4th, and which, I think, were subsequent to the correspondence which constitutes the contract between the parties. The examination referred to in those letters is not to be an examination which should determine whether the defendant should receive these 500 hides, but the examination of this lot was to determine whether he was so well suited with this lot that he would make further and larger orders; besides, it seems very plain that the plaintiff's assignor did not mean to change the terms of the contract for this shipment, but at all times, and upon the stand as a witness upon the trial, he insisted that the defendant was not entitled as a matter of right to an examination before an acceptance of the hides. There was no consideration for such change of contract, or 'waiver' as it is called by the trial court, and it therefore imposed no new or different obligation upon the plaintiff than existed under the former contract. But the trial court made a finding that the contract was so modified as to allow the defendant an examination before acceptance. The trial court also found that plaintiff's assignor had offered to defendant an opportunity to examine the hides, outside of the car in which they were contained, upon the platform or in the store-house; that such opportunity was a just and reasonable one; and that defendant refused, and thus defendant broke the contract; and that the plaintiff's assignor was justified in the course he pursued thereafter. I can see no error in this finding or conclusion. It would afford a fair and reasonable opportunity for the defendant to determine the quality of the hides. None could be better for the purpose of an examination, unless they should be taken to defendant's tannery and there be worked as well as examined. Of course business of this kind could not be practically or successfully carried on in this way; certainly not to the vendor of hides living hundreds, if not thousands, of miles away, and receiving many, if not the most, of the hides he sells from dealers and butchers living and carrying on business as many more miles from the plaintiff's assignor.

UCC § 2-711(3)

On rightful rejection or justifiable revocation of acceptance a buyer has a security interest in goods in his possession or control for any payments made on their price and any expenses reasonably incurred in their inspection, receipt, transportation, care, and custody and may hold such goods and resell them in like manner as an aggrieved seller * * * .

SECTION 4. ARTICLE 9 SECURITY INTERESTS

UCC § 9-102(1)

Except as otherwise provided in Section 9-104 on excluded transactions, this Article applies (a) to any transaction (regardless of its form) which is intended to create a security interest in personal property or fixtures * * * and also (b) to any sale of accounts or chattel paper.

(a) REGARDLESS OF ITS FORM

NOTE ON CONSIGNMENTS

Once the law recognized the notion that title was a concept independent of possession, trouble brewed. And the trouble is fraud, for if title can be separated from possession, parties will find reason to put title in one party and possession in another and, sometimes, to let the party in possession accept the risks and the party with title keep his title a secret. This is the secret lien that Article 9 abhors. It is also the consignment.

Consignments were common in the 19th century and earlier. Usually they were inventory financing arrangements. Sellers marketing goods far from their plants, used what we would now call "sales representatives" and what they called "factors," old factors, that is, because we still have factors in commerce but the new factor is an account financer. Factors of the old variety took possession of merchandise and traveled with it through the territory, selling to customers as they went. In an even earlier era, the possessor of the goods was a ship's captain or its equivalent, who took the goods to distant ports and sold them. Early in this century, a truck manufacturer might "consign" trucks to a dealer. The largest manufacturer of worsted products used to "consign" wool to its distributors.

The Code largely prevents these practices unless the parties comply with the Article 9 filing requirements or unless the world knows that the consignee is holding merchandise belonging to others. See § 2-326(3). The trouble is that the possession of the goods can create expectations contrary to reality. The law has for a long time protected purchasers from factors. See § 2-403(2). But, creditors of factors are the ones who complain, for they do not know who will claim the factors' inventory.

Today, consignments survive in the jewelry trade and book publishing and distribution. It is not unusual for a jewelry wholesaler to consign diamond rings, for example, to a retail jeweler who will return them if he doesn't sell them. Bookstores take books on consignment and return them to publishers (for the remainder market) or, in the case of paperback books, destroy them if they are not sold.

Revised Article 9 eliminates the current distinction between "true" consignments (bailments for purpose of sale—subject to Article 2) and consignments which are really disguised financing devices (subject to Article 9) by amending § 1-201(37) to include even a true consignor's interest in the consigned goods as a security interest. See also Revised § 9-112. Thus, the rights and interests of creditors of, and purchasers from, the consignee are determined under Article 9. See Revised § 9-315A, although the relationship between the consignor and the consignee in a "true" consignment will continue to be governed by the consignment agreement between the parties and not the provisions of Part 6 of Revised Article 9 dealing with enforcement of the security interest. See Revised § 9-601(d).

LIEBOWITZ v. VOIELLO

United States Court of Appeals, Second Circuit, 1939.
107 F.2d 914.

CLARK, Circuit Judge.

The present case presents another variation of the repeated attempts of creditors to secure insulation from financial loss in continuing business dealings with a failing concern. The defendant wanted to deliver flour to the bankrupt concern (or those identified with it) for manufacture into macaroni, distribution, and sale; the legal device resorted to was a consignment contract supposed to create only an agency for the processing of the flour and the sale of the completed product. The device was adjudged successful by the District Court, which directed a defendant's verdict when the bankruptcy trustee brought this action for conversion of the bankrupt's assets. We do not believe, however, that under the circumstances the device was sufficiently ingenious to deserve the award of a judicial imprimatur.

The facts as presented to the jury disclose that the defendant, eastern agent of flour companies, had for some years sold flour to the bankrupt corporation. The corporation manufactured the flour into macaroni in its New Jersey factory and then sold it throughout the New York metropolitan area. The officers of the corporation were Peter Cassinelli and Emilio Zuccarini, who, together with their wives, owned all of its capital stock. The bankrupt's finances were never quite healthy, as the defendant well knew. On occasion he had exchanged his own check for that of the corporation, and permitted his own check to be sent to the flour companies in payment for the flour. As the condition of the bankrupt became even more questionable, a plan was worked out and a written agreement prepared with the competent assistance of defendant's lawyer. Under this agreement, defendant was, for his own account, to purchase flour from the companies for which he was agent, and deliver the flour to the individuals Cassinelli and Zuccarini on consignment. They were to convert the raw materials into macaroni and to sell the finished products for the defendant's account. Upon delivery of the flour the individuals were to pay defendant 50 per cent of its value; they were to pay the remainder after the flour was sold, any surplus which they obtained on sale to be their compensation for the processing. By the terms of the contract, the flour and its products were to remain defendant's property; they were to be segregated from other articles on the premises; Cassinelli and Zuccarini were to keep separate inventories ready for defendant's examination; sales accounts were to be kept in separate books; and so on. This agreement was duly signed, with the corporation playing no part therein other than the substantial one of signing (through its president, Cassinelli) an attached guaranty that the individuals would fulfill their obligations under the contract.

In spite of its carefully drawn limitations and restrictions aimed to show a retention of title by the defendant, the validity of this contract, with the corporate guaranty of the individual action, and under all the circumstances, might itself present a problem. But we are not limited to interpretation of an elaborate document, for during the period from the signing of the contract May 15, 1936, until the situation became hopeless in February, 1937, the parties followed a course of conduct more instructive as to their real intent than any written word could possibly be. True, though Voiello continued to deliver flour to the corporation's factory, he carefully addressed his invoices to Cassinelli and Zuccarini 'personally' and marked each invoice with the notation, 'Contract of May 15.' But actually things progressed much as before: the flour was manufactured into macaroni on the corporation's premises; when sales were completed, the corporation made entries on its own books; and the proceeds when collected were invariable commingled with other deposits in the corporation's bank account.

As it sank deeper into debt the company received all of its flour from Voiello whereas previously it had obtained raw materials from many sources. Cassinelli and Zuccarini found themselves unable to make the required 50 per cent cash payment upon delivery of the flour. Accordingly a supplemental agreement was drafted, in the form of a letter, stating that the two individuals would give their personal notes to Voiello as flour was delivered. These notes were to be for the entire purchase price, but the individuals were to be relieved from their obligations thereunder upon sale of the macaroni and remission of the proceeds to Voiello. In practice when collections were made, the corporation wrote its check to the individuals and they in turn endorsed the checks to the defendant to take up their personal notes. On certain occasions, the defendant, in order to avoid dishonor of the notes by the banks to whom he had transferred them, gave his own check to the corporation to take up these notes.

By February 11, 1937, when he realized that the situation was beyond repair, defendant removed from the premises some $1,200 worth of flour and $6,000 worth of finished macaroni. He also secured an assignment of the accounts receivable, executed by the bankrupt corporation. He claims that the merchandise and accounts transferred represented flour delivered by him to the individuals Cassinelli and Zuccarini under the written agreement of May 15, 1936. On February 18, 1937, a week after the transfer, the company filed its voluntary petition in bankruptcy in the District Court for the District of New Jersey.

The bulk of the record consists of the testimony of Cassinelli and the defendant, Voiello. Both these witnesses contradicted themselves and each other repeatedly, and it took the combined efforts of opposing counsel and the trial judge to elicit from them even the semblance of an orderly story. At the close of the case, both sides moved for a directed verdict, and the plaintiff also moved that the case be sent to the jury if plaintiff's motion for a directed verdict was denied. The trial court denied plaintiff's motions and granted that of defendant.

We think that under the testimony presented, the plaintiff had proven a case strongly indicating that the defendant had conveyed his merchandise to the bankrupt, and that his attempt to reserve an interest therein was in fraud of creditors. Indeed, upon the record made below, the only proper question for the jury was the amount of plaintiff's damages.

It is not readily apparent why any consignment arrangement is not a secret lien against creditors of a shaky consignee, as harmful as an unfiled chattel mortgage or conditional sale. But that matter has been settled for us, for the Supreme Court has held that a consignment contract fairly entered into and carried out is valid against a trustee in bankruptcy. Ludvigh v. American Woolen Co., 231 U.S. 522, 34 S.Ct. 161, 58 L.Ed. 345. In that case, however, the Court stressed the good faith of the parties and their adherence to the terms of their bargain. See pages 528-530 of 231 U.S., 34 S.Ct. 161, 58 L.Ed. 345. It is well settled that the real character of the agreement is to be determined from all the circumstances, notably from the conduct of the parties rather than by express statements of a written contract. Taylor v. Fram, 2 Cir., 252 F. 465.

Hence the conduct of the parties herein is of the utmost importance. True, the claimed arrangement was that the individuals Cassinelli and Zuccarini, not the corporation, were to be the ostensible processors. But in fact the corporation did continue as before to manufacture the macaroni, for its machinery and factory were used for that purpose. Following manufacture, distribution, sale, and even payment took place substantially in accordance with the corporation's previous practice. Under these circumstances the direct interest of the corporation, even beyond its guaranty of performance of the agreement (a strange-enough circumstance if the agreement were bona fide) is apparent, and we cannot respect the asserted anonymity of the corporation in the consignment arrangement.

The consignment document did not really govern the actions of the parties. It is true that on each delivery of flour the defendant made reference on his invoice to the written contract. Further he claims he made periodic visits of inspection, examined the accounts, and identified the flour by the mark 'FV' on the bags. But upon each delivery he received notes for the full purchase price. No term of the contract provided that the 'consignees' were privileged to return the flour in its native or processed state. Cassinelli and Zuccarini were apparently free to select their own customers for the macaroni that supposedly belonged to Voiello. Nothing in the appearance of the finished and packaged macaroni indicated that it was or ever had been Voiello's property. Purchasers believed they were buying from the Macaroni Company, and their obligations to pay were carried on the corporation's books as the corporation's accounts receivable. And, as stated, payments by purchasers were made to the corporation, and mingled with other funds of the Macaroni Company.

We do not see how the behavior of the parties could have been very different had the arrangement been one of outright or conditional sale. It is neither easy nor practical to say where a consignment ends and a sale begins. In the light of the Ludvigh case, however, there is a line to be drawn. When the rights and duties created by the contract (as actually performed) are substantially the same as the rights and duties that would be created by a sale, the arrangement must be deemed a sale. The asserted intent of the parties that there be a consignment and not a sale cannot prevail when, as here, the rights of creditors intervene.

Under the circumstances, therefore, the device must be considered in fact not a bailment, but a transfer to the bankrupt of an outright interest in the flour. Since there was no recording, it matters little for present purposes whether the transaction be considered an outright sale or something else, such as a conditional sale or a chattel mortgage. Defendant, in his brief, expressly repudiated any claim of conditional sale or chattel mortgage. Numerous cases have held invalid as against a bankruptcy trustee similar courses of dealings, whatever the name they go by. Thus, in Taylor v. Fram, supra, a quite similar case, the transaction was assimilated to a chattel mortgage; in Yarn v. Lieberman, D.C., 46 F.2d 464, to an outright sale (compare also Scott County Milling Co. v. Grayson, 5 Cir., 88 F.2d 190); in In re United States Electrical Supply Co., D.C., 2 F.2d 378, and In re Leflys, 7 Cir., 229 F. 695, to a conditional sale. In re Leflys contains a resume of indicated badges of fraud to be looked for in determining whether a transaction is in truth a consignment or conditional sale. The similarities are close to the case at bar. Of course, following the Ludvigh case, supra, where the courts have found on all the evidence that there were bona fide consignments, as in In re Klein, 2 Cir., 3 F.2d 375, and Kemp-Booth Co. v. Calvin, 9 Cir., 84 F.2d 377, the transactions must be sustained. But under the circumstances presented here, the action of the court below in holding that in effect as a matter of law there was a bona fide consignment was error.

The parties were not in agreement as to how to prove the value of the accounts receivable claimed to have been appropriated by the defendant. Should the point become in issue hereinafter, we state that it seems to us incumbent upon the defendant to show a value less than their face if he intends to rely on the point.

The judgment is reversed and the action is remanded for a new trial.

UCC § 2-401(1)

* * * Any retention or reservation by the seller of the title (property) in goods shipped or delivered to the buyer is limited in effect to a reservation of a security interest. * * *

NOTE ON LEASING

Currently, equipment leasing is a growth industry. For a number of reasons, many companies prefer to lease equipment rather than buy it. First, equipment often becomes obsolete quickly. Second, companies treat lease obligations on their balance sheets differently from the way they treat the long term obligations they incur when they borrow money to buy equipment. For purposes of the balance sheets they present to rating agencies when they borrow in the financial markets, then, they may prefer to lease equipment rather than buy it. Finally, companies that borrow on an unsecured basis or even on a secured basis often must, under their loan agreements observe financial ratios that are affected by long term equipment borrowing but may not be affected by lease obligations. These differences may strike some as accounting legerdemain, but the finance people seem comfortable with the distinction between the five-year lease and the five-year installment note.

Commercial law is more concerned with a different aspect of equipment leasing, that is, the distinction between the true lease and the sale disguised as a lease. The latter involves, of course, a delivery pursuant to a sale with the seller's retention of title. We all know what that means in commercial law: that the seller has only a security interest and must comply with Article 9. Thus, the lessor will often claim that the arrangement is a true lease, and the lessee's trustee in bankruptcy will claim otherwise as the following case illustrates.

IN RE MARHOEFER PACKING CO.

United States Court of Appeals, Seventh Circuit, 1982.
674 F.2d 1139.

[Marhoefer, the debtor in bankruptcy, leased equipment from Reiser under a lease that contained two options. Under the first, Marhoefer had the right after making lease payments for four years to purchase the equipment for $9,968. Under the second, Marhoefer had the right to continue the lease for an additional four years and to purchase the equipment at the end of the second four year term for $1.]

PELL, Circuit Judge.

This appeal involves a dispute between the trustee of the bankrupt Marhoefer Packing Company, Inc., ("Marhoefer") and Robert Reiser & Company, Inc., ("Reiser") over certain equipment held by Marhoefer at the time of bankruptcy. The issue presented is whether the written agreement between Marhoefer and Reiser covering the equipment is a true lease under which Reiser is entitled to reclaim its property from the bankrupt estate, or whether it is actually a lease intended as security in which case Reiser's failure to file a financing statement to perfect its interest renders it subordinate to the trustee.

* * *

Marhoefer never exercised either option. Approximately one year after the Vemag stuffer was delivered to its plant, it ceased all payments under the lease and shortly thereafter filed a voluntary petition in bankruptcy.

* * *

The dispute in this case centers on section 1-201(37) of the Uniform Commercial Code, I.C. 26-1-1-201. In applying this section, the bankruptcy court concluded that "the presence of the option to renew the lease for an additional four years and to acquire the Vemag Stuffer at the conclusion of the second four-year term by the payment of One Dollar ($1.00) did not, in and of itself, make the lease one intended for security." Section 1-201(37) of the Uniform Commercial Code states: "'Security interest' means an interest in personal property or fixtures which secures payment or performance of an obligation * * *. Unless a lease or consignment is intended as security, reservation of title thereunder is not a 'security interest' but a consignment is in any event subject to the provisions on consignment sales. Whether a lease is intended as security is to be determined by the facts of each case; however, (a) the inclusion of an option, to purchase does not of itself make the lease one intended for security, and (b) an agreement that upon compliance with the terms of the lease the lessee shall become or has the option to become the owner of the property for no additional consideration or for a nominal consideration does make the lease one intended for security."

The district court disagreed. It held that the presence of an option to purchase the stuffer for one dollar gave rise to a conclusive presumption under clause (b) of section 1-201(37) that the lease was intended as security. Although it acknowledged that the option to purchase the stuffer for only one dollar would not have come into play unless Marhoefer chose to renew the lease for an additional four-year term, the district court concluded that this fact did not require a different result. "It would be anomalous," said the court, "to rule that the lease was a genuine lease for four years after its creation but was one intended for security eight years after its creation."

Reiser, relying on Peter F. Coogan's detailed analysis of section 1-201(37), Coogan, Hogan & Vagts, Secured Transactions Under the Uniform Commercial Code, ch. 4A, (1981) (hereinafter "Secured Transactions Under U.C.C."), argues that the district court erred in construing clause (b) of that section as creating a conclusive presumption that a lease is intended as security where the lease contains an option for the lessee to become the owner of the leased property for no additional consideration or for only nominal consideration. It contends that by interpreting clause (b) in this way, the district court totally ignored the first part of that sentence which states that "(w)hether a lease is intended as security is to be determined by the facts of each case." Reiser claims that because the totality of facts surrounding the transaction indicate that the lease was not intended as security, notwithstanding the presence of the option to purchase the stuffer for one dollar, the district court erred in reversing the bankruptcy court's determination. We agree that the district court erred in concluding that because the Lease Agreement contained an option for Marhoefer to purchase the Vemag stuffer at the end of a second four-year term, it was conclusively presumed to be a lease intended as security. However, in our view, the district court's error lies not in its reading of clause (b) of section 1-201(37) as giving rise to such a presumption, but rather in its conclusion that clause (b) applies under the facts of this case.

The primary issue to be decided in determining whether a lease is "intended as security" is whether it is in effect a conditional sale in which the "lessor" retains an interest in the "leased" goods as security for the purchase price. 1C Secured Transactions Under U.C.C. § 29A.05(1)(C), p. 2939. By defining the term "security interest" to include a lease intended as security, the drafters of the Code intended such disguised security interests to be governed by the same rules that apply to other security interests. See U.C.C., Art. 9. In this respect, section 1-201(37) represents the drafter's refusal to recognize form over substance.

Clearly, where a lease is structured so that the lessee is contractually bound to pay rent over a set period of time at the conclusion of which he automatically or for only nominal consideration becomes the owner of the leased goods, the transaction is in substance a conditional sale and should be treated as such. It is to this type of lease that clause (b) properly applies. Here, however, Marhoefer was under no contractual obligation to pay rent until such time as the option to purchase the Vemag stuffer for one dollar was to arise. In fact, in order to acquire that option, Marhoefer would have had to exercise its earlier option to renew the lease for a second four-year term and pay Reiser an additional $11,960 in "rent." In effect, Marhoefer was given a right to terminate the agreement after the first four years and cease making payments without that option ever becoming operative.

Despite this fact, the district court concluded as a matter of law that the lease was intended as security. It held that, under clause (b) of section 1-201(37), a lease containing an option for the lessee to purchase the leased goods for nominal consideration is conclusively presumed to be one intended as security. This presumption applies, the court concluded, regardless of any other options the lease may contain.

We think the district court's reading of clause (b) is in error. In our view, the conclusive presumption provided under clause (b) applies only where the option to purchase for nominal consideration necessarily arises upon compliance with the lease. See 1C Secured Transactions Under U.C.C. § 29.05(2)(b) pp. 2947-49. It does not apply where the lessee has the right to terminate the lease before that option arises with no further obligation to continue paying rent. But see In re Vaillancourt, supra, 7 U.C.C.Rep. 748; In re Royers Bakery, Inc., 1 U.C.C.Rep. 342 (Bankr.E.D.Pa.1963). For where the lessee has the right to terminate the transaction, it is not a conditional sale.

Moreover, to hold that a lease containing such an option is intended as security, even though the lessee has no contractual obligation to pay the full amount contemplated by the agreement, would lead to clearly erroneous results under other provisions of the Code. Under section 9-506 of the Code, for example, a debtor in default on his obligation to a secured party has a right to redeem the collateral by tendering full payment of that obligation. The same right is also enjoyed by a lessee under a lease intended as security. A lessee who defaults on a lease intended as security is entitled to purchase the leased goods by paying the full amount of his obligation under the lease. But if the lessee has the right to terminate the lease at any time during the lease term, his obligation under the lease may be only a small part of the total purchase price of the goods leased. To afford the lessee a right of redemption under such circumstances would clearly be wrong. There is no evidence that the drafters of the Code intended such a result.

We therefore hold that while section 1-201(37)(b) does provide a conclusive test of when a lease is intended as security, that test does not apply in every case in which the disputed lease contains an option to purchase for nominal or no consideration. An option of this type makes a lease one intended as security only when it necessarily arises upon compliance with the terms of the lease.

Applying section 1-201(37), so construed, to the facts of this case, it is clear that the district court erred in concluding that the possibility of Marhoefer's purchasing the stuffer for one dollar at the conclusion of a second four-year term was determinative. Because Marhoefer could have fully complied with the lease without that option ever arising, the district court was mistaken in thinking that the existence of that option alone made the lease a conditional sale. Certainly, if Marhoefer had elected to renew the lease for another term, in which case the nominal purchase option would necessarily have arisen, then the clause (b) test would apply. But that is not the case we are faced with here. Marhoefer was not required to make any payments beyond the first four years. The fact that, at the conclusion of that term, it could have elected to renew the lease and obtain an option to purchase the stuffer for one dollar at the end of the second term does not transform the original transaction into a conditional sale.

This fact does not end our inquiry under clause (b), however, for the trustee also argues that, even if the district court erred in considering the one dollar purchase option as determinative, the lease should nevertheless be considered a conditional sale because the initial option price of $9,968 is also nominal when all of the operative facts are properly considered. We agree that if the clause (b) test is to apply at all in this case, this is the option that must be considered. For this is the option that was to arise automatically upon Marhoefer's compliance with the lease. We do not agree, however, that under the circumstances presented here the $9,968 option price can properly be considered nominal.

It is true that an option price may be more than a few dollars and still be considered nominal within the meaning of section 1-201(37). Because clause (b) speaks of nominal "consideration" and not a nominal "sum" or "amount," it has been held to apply not only where the option price is very small in absolute terms, but also where the price is insubstantial in relation to the fair market value of the leased goods at the time the option arises.

Here, however, the evidence revealed that the initial option price of $9,968 was not nominal even under this standard. George Vetie, Reiser's treasurer and the person chiefly responsible for the terms of the lease, testified at trial that the purchase price for the Vemag stuffer at the time the parties entered into the transaction was $33,225. He testified that the initial option price of $9,968 was arrived at by taking thirty percent of the purchase price, which was what he felt a four-year-old Vemag stuffer would be worth based on Reiser's past experience.

The trustee, relying on the testimony of its expert appraiser, argues that in fact the stuffer would have been worth between eighteen and twenty thousand dollars at the end of the first four-year term. Because the initial option price is substantially less than this amount, he claims that it is nominal within the meaning of clause (b) and the lease is therefore one intended as security.

Even assuming this appraisal to be accurate, an issue on which the bankruptcy court made no finding, we would not find the initial option price of $9,968 so small by comparison that the clause (b) presumption would apply. While it is difficult to state any bright line percentage test for determining when an option price could properly be considered nominal as compared to the fair market value of the leased goods, an option price of almost ten thousand dollars, which amounts to fifty percent of the fair market value, is not nominal by any standard.

Furthermore, in determining whether an option price is nominal, the proper figure to compare it with is not the actual fair market value of the leased goods at the time the option arises, but their fair market value at that time as anticipated by the parties when the lease is signed. Here, for example, Vetie testified that his estimate of the fair market value of a four-year-old Vemag stuffer was based on records from a period of time in which the economy was relatively stable. Since that time, a high rate of inflation has caused the machines to lose their value more slowly. As a result, the value of a machine may turn out to be significantly more than the parties anticipated it would be several years earlier. When this occurs, the lessee's option to purchase the leased goods may be much more favorable than either party intended, but it does not change the true character of the transaction. We conclude, therefore, that neither option to purchase contained in the lease between Marhoefer and Reiser gives rise to a conclusive presumption under section 1-201(37)(b) that the lease is one intended as security. This being so, we now turn to the other facts surrounding the transaction.

III

Although section 1-201(37) states that "(w)hether a lease is intended as security is to be determined by the facts of each case," it is completely silent as to what facts, other than the option to purchase, are to be considered in making that determination. Facts that the courts have found relevant include the total amount of rent the lessee is required to pay under the lease; whether the lessee acquires any equity in the leased property; the useful life of the leased goods; the nature of the lessor's business; and the payment of taxes, insurance and other charges normally imposed on ownership. Consideration of the facts of this case in light of these factors leads us to conclude that the lease in question was not intended as security.

First, Marhoefer was under no obligation to pay the full purchase price for the stuffer. Over the first four-year term, its payments under the lease were to have amounted to $31,920. Although this amount may not be substantially less than the original purchase price of $33,225 in absolute terms, it becomes so when one factors in the interest rate over four years that would have been charged had Marhoefer elected to purchase the machine under a conditional sale. The fact that the total amount of rent Marhoefer was to pay under the lease was substantially less than that amount shows that a sale was not intended.

It is also significant that the useful life of the Vemag stuffer exceeded the term of the lease. An essential characteristic of a true lease is that there be something of value to return to the lessor after the term. Where the term of the lease is substantially equal to the life of the leased property such that there will be nothing of value to return at the end of the lease, the transaction is in essence a sale. Here, the evidence revealed that the useful life of a Vemag stuffer was eight to ten years.

Finally, the bankruptcy court specifically found that "there was no express or implied provision in the lease agreement dated February 28, 1977, which gave Marhoefer any equity interest in the leased Vemag stuffer." This fact clearly reveals the agreement between Marhoefer and Reiser to be a true lease. See Hawkland, The Impact of the Uniform Commercial Code on Equipment Leasing, 1972 Ill.L. Forum 446, 453 ("The difference between a true lease and a security transaction lies in whether the lessee acquires an equity of ownership through his rent payments."). Had Marhoefer remained solvent and elected not to exercise its option to renew its lease with Reiser, it would have received nothing for its previous lease payments. And in order to exercise that option, Marhoefer would have had to pay what Reiser anticipated would then be the machine's fair market value. An option of this kind is not the mark of a lease intended as security.

Although Marhoefer was required to pay state and local taxes and the cost of repairs, this fact does not require a contrary result. Costs such as taxes, insurance and repairs are necessarily borne by one party or the other. They reflect less the true character of the transaction than the strength of the parties' respective bargaining positions. See also Rainier National Bank, supra, 631 P.2d at 395 ("The lessor is either going to include those costs within the rental charge or agree to a lower rent if the lessee takes responsibility for them.").

* * *

(b) SALES OF ACCOUNTS, CHATTEL PAPER, AND GENERAL INTANGIBLES

UCC § 1-201(37)

* * * The term ["security interest"] also includes any interest of a buyer of accounts or chattel paper which is subject to Article 9. * * *

BLACK, ROBERTSHAW, FREDERICK, COPPLE & WRIGHT v. UNITED STATES

Court of Appeals of Arizona, 1981.
130 Ariz. 110, 634 P.2d 398.

[On January 6, 1976 Regal assigned to its law firm $11,316.50 that was due Regal from Kealy on two construction contracts. On January 16 at 1:00 p.m. the federal government filed a notice of federal tax lien on all of Regal's property. On January 16 at 3:00 p.m. the law firm filed a financing statement perfecting its security interest in the assigned sum of money. Both the law firm and the government claimed the funds, and Kealy filed an interpleader action, depositing the funds in court.]

EUBANK, Judge.

* * *

Following the filing of the interpleader action and discovery, both parties moved for summary judgment. The United States' motion and memorandum of law claims a priority of lien over the Law Firm based on the Internal Revenue Code of 1954, 26 U.S.C.A. §§ 6321, 6322 (as amended 1966), and 6323(a) and (h) (as amended 1966). In addition, the memorandum argues that A.R.S. § 44-3123 A.5. (U.C.C. § 9-302), as amended, required the Law Firm to file a financing statement since, inferentially, the assignments constituted a significant part of Regal's outstanding accounts. The Law Firm's motion and memoranda did not address the A.R.S. § 44-3123 A.5. (U.C.C. § 9-302) issue, but instead claimed that the "assignment was absolute and divested Regal of any rights whatsoever to the claims against Kealy and passed to (the Law Firm) * * * the sole ownership of those claims." Thus, they argued, since Regal's assignments to the Law Firm were made on January 6, 1976, which was 10 days prior to the effective date of the United States' lien filed on January 16, the Law Firm was entitled to a priority over the United States and summary judgment. In a supplemental memorandum, the Law Firm reiterated the argument that the uncontradicted evidence constituted an "absolute assignment" and argued that because of the "absolute assignment" by Regal to the Law Firm, the Law Firm was not required to file a financing statement with the Secretary of State "since such a filing would only be required if the assignment was for security or collection purposes."[1] No supporting authority was cited for the Law Firm's argument.

In the United States' response, it again raised the A.R.S. § 44-3123 A.5. (U.C.C. § 9-302) issue. The Law Firm, the first time in its reply, directly addressed the issue, stating that "the filing of a financing statement was not required because the assignments were absolute in nature and were not for the purpose of perfecting a security interest in and to the receivables." Again no authority supporting the Law Firm's contention was cited.

On the basis of these pleadings and following argument, the trial court granted the Law Firm partial summary judgment "as a matter of law" and included Rule 54(b), Rules of Civil Procedure, 16 A.R.S., language making the judgment immediately appealable. Thus the United States has appealed from the partial summary judgment in favor of the Law Firm contending that the trial court erred as a matter of law. We agree.

Our analysis begins with the question of whether the Law Firm was ever obligated to file a financing statement with the Secretary of State because of Regal's assignment of accounts to it. Prior to Arizona's adoption of the Uniform Commercial Code in 1967, notice of any sale or assignment of an account was required to be filed in order for the assignee to obtain a priority over present and future creditors. A.R.S. § 44-801 et seq. (repealed, 1967). Thus prior to January 1, 1968, the effective date of the Arizona U.C.C., the Law Firm would have been required to file a notice of assignment with the Secretary of State in order to perfect its interest in the account and to obtain a priority over the United States tax lien.

With our adoption of the Uniform Commercial Code in 1968, the assignment of accounts statutes were repealed. Such assignments, with certain exceptions, are now covered by Article 9 of the Code, A.R.S. § 44-3101 et seq. Turning to the Code, "security interest", is defined, in part, as including "any interest of a buyer of accounts * * * which is subject to Article 9." (A.R.S. § 44-2208 (37) (U.C.C. § 1-201)). In Article 9, an "account" is defined as "any right to payment for * * * services rendered which is not evidenced by an instrument or chattel paper whether or not it has been earned by performance."

---

1 Assignment for collection is expressly excluded from Article 9 coverage by A.R.S. § 44-3104.6. (U.C.C. § 9-104).

A.R.S. § 44-3106 (U.C.C. § 9-106), as amended. A.R.S. § 44-3102 A.2. (U.C.C. § 9-102(1)(b)) states that Article 9 applies "to any sale of accounts or chattel paper." The only exceptions are detailed in A.R.S. § 44-3104.6. (U.C.C. § 9-104), none of which are claimed to be applicable here. Finally, A.R.S. § 44-3123 A.5. (U.C.C. § 9-302(1)(e)) requires the filing of a financing statement "to perfect all security interests except * * *, (5) An assignment of accounts which does not alone or in conjunction with other assignments to the same assignee transfer *a significant part* of the outstanding accounts of the assignor." (Emphasis added). Thus, the legislative intent is clear and we conclude that the Law Firm was required to file a financial statement to perfect its security interest in Regal's assigned accounts unless the assignment did not constitute a "significant part of the outstanding accounts" of Regal.

The complete answer, however, lies in determining whether "a significant part" of Regal's accounts was assigned and which party bears the burden of proving significance or insignificance. The courts have recognized three tests in determining the significant account question. They are, (1) a percentage of accounts test, (2) a "casual and isolated transaction" test, and (3) a combination of both (1) and (2). Representative cases of the test are analyzed and collected in Annot., 85 A.L.R.3d 1050, When is Filing of Financial Statement Necessary to Perfect an Assignment of Accounts Under U.C.C. § 9-302(1)(e). White & Summers, Uniform Commercial Code, § 23-8 (1972) discusses the tests and comes down on the side of certainty, the percentage test. * * *

A second approach is to disregard the professional status of the assignee and to ask only what percentage of the total accounts of the assignor were assigned and whether those accounts as percentage of the whole constitute a "significant" part.

* * *

Although we find White & Summer's discussion above persuasive, it is not necessary for us to select a specific test for Arizona because such evidence was not presented in support of the motion for summary judgment by the Law Firm. As we pointed out in some detail earlier in this opinion, the Law Firm took the position that Article 9 did not apply to its transaction with Regal. Thus, no effort was made to present evidence regarding the "significant part" of the assignment of Regal's outstanding accounts of the assignor Regal even though the United States specifically raised the issue. In U.C.C. § 9-302(1) (e) determinations, the courts have viewed "significant part" evidence as defense matter and have placed the burden of proving "insignificance" on the assignee, in this case, the Law Firm. In Professor Grant Gilmore's book, Security Interests in Personal Property, § 19.6 (1965), he tends to agree, stating:

> Section 9-302(1)(e) exempts from filing "an assignment of accounts or contract rights which does not alone or in conjunction with other assignments to the same assignee transfer a significant part of the outstanding accounts or contract rights of the assignor."
>
> The paragraph (e) filing exemption is to be contrasted with § 9-104(f), which makes "the Article" inapplicable to certain transfers of accounts,

> contract rights and chattel paper which are not made in anything that could reasonably be described as a financing transaction for example, transfers for collection only. The transactions described in § 9-302(1)(e) remain subject to the provisions of the Article and are exempted only from the filing requirement which means that a security interest arising from such a transaction is automatically perfected when it attaches.
>
> *Paragraph (e) seems to provide more a line of defense in litigation or bankruptcy proceedings than a guide for prospective action.* At the time of taking an assignment no assignee can know that this assignment, together with others which may be made to him in the future, will not result in the "transfer (of) a significant part" of the assignor's receivables; certainly no sane assignee will take the risk that he could convince a judge, jury or referee of his own insignificance. All right-minded assignees will, therefore, file. The reason for the paragraph (e) exemption lies in the fact that Article 9, like the pre-Code accounts receivable statutes, covers sales as well as security transfers of receivables. As a general rule there are sound reasons for what seems to be, at first blush, an unnecessarily broad coverage. However, when the net is spread so wide, some strange fish may be caught. (Emphasis added). (Footnotes omitted).

The general rule governing the burden of proof in Arizona is that a party who asserts the affirmative of an issue has the burden of proving it. The same rule is applicable to a defense where confession and avoidance, an affirmative defense or a counterclaim is pled by the defendant. As indicated above, regardless of which test for "significant part" is used, the burden of establishing "insignificance" is on the assignee Law Firm. As already discussed, because of the legal theory that the Law Firm relied on, the firm presented no evidence of "insignificance". Thus, the Law Firm did not carry its burden of proving the A.R.S. § 44-3123 A.5. (U.C.C. § 9-302(1)(e)) exception and was not, therefore, entitled to partial summary judgment as a matter of law.

The same cannot be said for the United States. Its motion for summary judgment demonstrated that its tax lien had been perfected, pursuant to Internal Revenue Code of 1954, § 6323(a) and (h), and was prior in time to the financial statement filed by the Law Firm. Therefore, the United States was entitled to partial summary judgment on its motion, pursuant to our priority statute, A.R.S. § 44-3122 (U.C.C. § 9-301), as a matter of law.

---

1 G. GILMORE, SECURITY INTERESTS IN PERSONAL PROPERTY 308-09 (1965).

The inclusion of sales of certain intangibles is no novelty. In this respect Article 9 merely follows the pre-Code accounts receivable statutes. In our discussion of those statutes, this broad coverage was explained on the ground that it was necessary to include both straight accounts receivable financing and the closely related factoring operation in which the assignee buys receivables without recourse against the assignor. The same reason explains the inclusion of such sales within Article 9. It should be noted that the "sale" provision of § 9-102(1)(b) does not extend to the types of intangibles which are known in Article 9 terminology as instruments, documents of title and general intangibles; only security transfers of such intangibles are covered. Article 9 goes beyond the accounts receivable statutes in including sales of "chattel paper"—the accounts receivable statutes did not in general apply to this type of intangible. The principal effect of making the Article applicable to sales of the types of intangibles which are covered by § 9-102(1)(b) is that a transferee must file or otherwise perfect his interest in order to have protection against his transferor's creditors and subsequent assignees: the default provisions sharply differentiate the situation of a buyer from that of a security transferee.

One defect of the accounts receivable statutes was that on a literal reading many transfers would be included (and thus subjected to filing requirements) which were not financing operations, which it made no sense to file, and which no one would ever think of filing. Article 9 attempts to remedy this defect by excluding non-financing sales.

NOTE ON OUTSOURCING

Often a manufacturer will send partially manufactured goods (inventory) to another firm which will process the goods further. A Seattle aircraft manufacturer might send components to Mexico for assembly and then reimport them to a facility in California for further processing and ultimate incorporation into a product. At other times a manufacturer may have the outside firm drop ship completed goods to the manufacturer's customers. In these and many other instances, we encounter the commercially problematic situation of possession in one party and "title" in another.

Compare the next opinion with the *Liebowitz* case, supra.

MEDOMAK CANNING v. WILLIAM UNDERWOOD CO. (IN RE MEDOMAK CANNING CO.)

United States Bankruptcy Court, District of Maine, 1977.
25 U.C.C. Rep. Serv. 437.

[Underwood was exceeding its capacity to produce canned pork and beans at its B & M plant in Portland. Medomak, on the other hand, was losing money and had excess capacity. The parties entered into an arrangement by which Underwood purchased the ingredients for the pork and the beans, the cans into which the ingredients were mixed, and the cartons in which the cans were to be shipped. Underwood caused the purchased supplies to be delivered to Medomak which, under the agreement, would prepare the canned beans, place them in the cartons, and ship them to Underwood. Underwood claimed that it paid Medomak for a "service" and that it had only entrusted its goods to Medomak. Medomak, as debtor in possession in the Chapter 11 Bankruptcy claimed that Underwood sold the ingredients and shipping materials to Medomak and agreed to repurchase them when Medomak completed manufacturing the product. Medomak's inventory lender which had a perfected security interest in all of Medomak's inventory characterized the transaction in the same fashion.]

CYR, Bankruptcy Judge.

* * *

In these circumstances Medomak's theory of the case settles securely into place only if, from the outset, it acquired the raw ingredients and other materials from Underwood by sale, either conditional or absolute. If by conditional sale, Underwood runs afoul of 11 MRSA §§ 1-201(37) and 2-401(1), which limit the legal effect of an attempt to retain title by the seller to the reservation of a security interest subject to the perfection requirements of Uniform Commercial Code Article 9. Since Underwood failed to comply with the filing requirements of 11 MRSA § 9-401(1), its security interest would have been voidable either by the debtor in possession, by virtue of Bankruptcy Act §§ 70c & e, 302, 341 & 342, or by Depositors Trust Company, the holder of a perfected security interest in Medomak's after-acquired inventory. If there had been an absolute sale, 11 MRSA § 2-401(1) would have vested title to the ingredients and other materials in Medomak upon their identification to the contract, which certainly occurred no later than the date of their delivery to Medomak by the third-party suppliers through whom they were ordered by Underwood. The security interest of Depositors Trust Company would then have attached to the ingredients and other materials upon the vesting of title in Medomak, thereby assuring priority to the lien of Depositors Trust Company (and perhaps the debtor in possession) over Underwood in both the finished and unfinished goods in Medomak's possession at the date of the initiation of the Chapter XI proceedings. Were Medomak held to have been a seller of the finished product to Underwood, it is entirely possible that its retention of the finished product for more than three months after pork and bean production ceased may have been considered commercially unreasonable, within the meaning of 11 MRSA § 2-402(2), and perhaps voidable by an attaching creditor of Medomak under Maine law.

[The court analyzed the terms of the agreement and concluded that the parties did not intend to effect a sale from Underwood to Medomak and, therefore, that section 1-201(37) and 2-401(1) did not operate to defeat Underwood's claim.]

Title 11 MRSA § 2-326(3), which preserves the rights of a buyer's creditors in goods held on "sale or return," is also unavailing to Medomak in these circumstances. Section 2-326 "* * * presupposes that a contract for sale is contemplated by the parties although that contract may be of the peculiar character here described." In addition, the peculiar characteristics of the types of transactions dealt with by § 2-326 were not present here, since the parties contemplated merely that Medomak would process the goods entrusted to it by Underwood for later sale *by Underwood* to its own customers.

The final contention requiring discussion is that the entrustment of the ingredients and other materials constituted a bailment or consignment intended for security, within the meaning of 11 MRSA § 1-201(37), subject to the perfection of Article 9. The merits of that position depend upon whether a security interest was intended by the parties. It is clear that it was not so intended. * * *

The potential for abuse posed by a retention of possession by a merchant in circumstances indicating ostensible ownership, such as the entrustment here involved, may well warrant, but has escaped, Uniform Commercial Code regulation. Uniform Commercial Code § 2-402(2), which empowers creditors of the seller to void a sale where a retention of possession by the seller would be fraudulent under other state law, does not extend to the case where the merchant in possession is a mere bailee.

* * *

UCC § 2-326 extends protection to the "buyer's" creditors only where the goods were delivered in contemplation of some sort of sale. It is not clear why the creditors of "* * * a person [maintaining] a place of business at which he deals in goods of the kind involved, under a name other than the name of the person making delivery * * *" should not be entitled to prevail over the person making delivery, whether the delivery constitutes a sale or a mere entrustment, where the person making delivery fails to comply either with the perfection requirements of Article 9 or with the provisions governing consignments.

Reasonable men may well differ as to the wisdom or equity of these Code policies, but not, it would seem, as to their sway under present law.

NOTE ON CHATTEL PAPER AND PAYMENT INTANGIBLES

Article 9 treats chattel paper much as it treats accounts in that it does not distinguish sales of chattel paper from transactions involving only the grant of a security interest in chattel paper. Much chattel paper arises in the consumer setting when a consumer purchases an automobile or mobile home. In those transactions the consumer (1) agrees to pay for the goods over time and (2) grants the seller a security interest as security for that promise. It is the combination of those elements of the transaction that brings it within the section 9-105(1)(b) definition of chattel paper. Note that the definition also includes leases. Sales disguised as leases probably fit the first part of the definition. True leases fall within the definition by virtue of that fact that the definition includes a "lease of specific goods." The equipment leasing industry generates significant amounts of chattel paper, and equipment lessors frequently transfer it and thereby invoke Article 9.

Revised Article 9 includes sales of payment intangibles in that category of collateral to which Article 9 applies regardless of the fact that the parties have entered into a contract to sell or assign the collateral rather than create a security interest in it. See Revised §§ 9-112(a)(3), 1-201(37). Payment intangibles include the obligation of an account debtor to pay money when that obligation arises out of a general intangible. See Revised § 9-103(c). Thus a publisher's obligation to pay royalties to an author or a corporation's obligation to pay a dividend to a shareholder would if assigned or sold come within Article 9 for much the same reasons that sales and assignments of chattel paper and accounts come within it.

SECTION 5. LIENS

INTRODUCTORY NOTE

In any categorization scheme, the careful crafter will create a catchall category. In the property interest regime this book fashions, the catchall category is the lien. Liens are clearly property interests and their features tend to be unique. Thus the category is rough. Discussion of a few of them, some rather important, follows.

(a) SELLER'S LIEN

INTRODUCTORY NOTE

The seller's lien is known better for its features than as a discrete property concept. There is something to learn, however, from an examination of those features. First, to an extent, the seller's lien is a response to the unfortunate effects of rigorous title rules. Second, characterizing the seller's right to reclaim as a feature of the seller's lien or an extension of it makes sense of that rather extraordinary property interest—a lien when the lienor is out of possession—and explains the good faith purchase limits on the right to reclaim and the ten-day demand requirement.

SAWYER v. DEAN

Court of Appeals of New York, 1889.

See page 128, supra

UCC § 2-507(2)

(*see Selected Commercial Statutes*)

UCC § 2-702(2)

(*see Selected Commercial Statutes*

BANKRUPTCY CODE § 546(c)

(*see Selected Commercial Statutes*)

(b) JUDGMENT CREDITOR'S LIEN

EARL DUBEY & SONS v. MACOMB CONTRACTING CO.

Court of Appeals of Michigan, 1980.
Page 95, supra

(c) MECHANIC'S LIEN

WILLIAMSPORT NATIONAL BANK v. SHREY

Superior Court of Pennsylvania, 1991.
417 Pa. Super. 563, 612 A.2d 1081.

[Shrey borrowed from the plaintiff bank and granted the bank a security interest in his boat and trailer. When Shrey defaulted on the loan, the bank attempted to repossess the goods, which were in the possession of J.J. Heavy Repair, Inc. J.J. had been working on the boat and the trailer which were damaged in an accident. This action is one in replevin by the bank to recover the goods.]

MONTEMURO, Judge.

* * *

On appeal * * * we address only the issue relating to the trial court's finding that J.J. did not receive consent from the bank prior to doing repairs to the boat. The trial court stated that since the bank, the holder of a perfected security interest in the boat, did not consent to the repair work done to the boat by J.J., its security interest had priority over J.J.'s repairman's lien. Since we find, however, that such consent is not needed under the Uniform Commercial Code, we reverse.

* * *

In the instant case, J.J. is claiming a common law possessory repairman's lien. Since this is a lien created by rule of law, 13 Pa.C.S.A. Section 9310 governs the outcome of the case. The record establishes that J.J. did not receive the implied or express consent of the bank before doing the repair work to the boat. Under the common law, this failure to receive the bank's consent would be fatal to J.J.'s claim that his lien was superior to that of the bank. Under the U.C.C., however, no consent is needed in order to obtain a possessory lien.

* * *

The implications of failing to follow the U.C.C. as explained above would seriously impede upon the ability of repairmen, such as J.J., to exist in today's commercial market. The ability of the repairman to protect himself by seeking the permission of a lienholder is commercially unrealistic. * * * Checking for a recorded financing statement could end up being a cumbersome task. To be completely protected, the repairman would necessarily have to check for a financing statement in the county in which the boat owner lives (or with an out of state debtor, in the office of the prothonotary where the boat is kept). See 13

Pa.C.S.A. § 9401. Imagine the situation where a Pennsylvania boat owner takes his boat to Florida for a fishing trip. While in Florida, the boat breaks down and the owner takes the boat to a repair shop in Florida. Must the Florida repairman go to Pennsylvania, to the county where the boat owner lives, go to the office of the prothonotary, and check to see if a security interest has been recorded? Suppose the boat breaks down on Friday afternoon, does the boat owner have to wait until Monday morning so that the repairman can check the office of the prothonotary? Even if the repairman finds a recorded financing statement, and can identify the secured party, what steps must he then take to get permission to complete the repairs? If the secured party has more than one office, which office must the repairman get permission from? Furthermore, what type of permission need the repairman get? A verbal approval on the telephone? A written approval? And who must the repairman get the approval from? From anyone in the office? Clearly, such a result would impede upon the repairman's ability to function and exist in today's commercial market. This type of absurd situation is exactly what Section 9310 is designed to prevent, and demonstrates the necessity of following the rule that gives repairmen priority, regardless of whether or not they receive permission from a secured party.

Accordingly, in keeping with the intended purpose of Section 9310 and the law among the various other jurisdictions cited herein, we now hold that the common law repairman's lien given by rule of law within the purview of Uniform Commercial Code § 9310 has priority over a prior security interest, even if perfected, regardless of whether or not consent for the repairs was given by the holder of the security interest. Thus, in the instant case, we find that as a result of the repair work J.J. performed on Mr. Shrey's boat, he acquired a common law possessory lien in the boat. This lien, under 13 Pa.C.S.A. § 9310, takes priority over the security interest of Williamsport National Bank, whether or not that interest was perfected.

(d) TAX LIEN

BLACK, ROBERTSHAW, FREDERICK, COPPLE & WRIGHT v. UNITED STATES

Court of Appeals of Arizona, 1981.
Page 141, supra

SECTION 6. LEASEHOLD

HARRIS, THE RIGHTS OF CREDITORS UNDER ARTICLE 2A, 39 U. Ala. L. Rev. 803, 811 (1988). "Perhaps because it was drafted at a time when personal property leasing was not a significant part of the economy, Article 9 contains only a few provisions specifically addressed to leasing transactions. As a consequence, under existing law the rights of a secured party with a security interest in goods that the debtor subsequently leases are somewhat uncertain. To determine whether and to what extent the security interest survives the creation of the lessee's leasehold interest, one first must distinguish between the lessor's residual interest, which the lessor retains, and the right to use the goods during the lease term, which the lessor transfers to the lessee. That the security interest in the residual interest survives is beyond dispute. The lease of the goods to the lessee does not affect that aspect of the secured party's collateral. The lessee has bargained for the use of the property only during the lease term and acquires no interest in the residual interest, which remains subject to the security interest. Any other result would enable a debtor to deprive a secured party of its entire security interest by transferring only some of the debtor's rights in the collateral."

FELDMAN v. FIRST NATIONAL CITY BANK (IN RE LEASING CONSULTANTS, INC.)

United States Court of Appeals, Second Circuit, 1973.
486 F.2d 367.

[Leasing Consultants leased heavy equipment to Plastimetrix, and assigned the leases (chattel paper) to the bank as collateral for a loan to Leasing. Plastimetrix had held the equipment in New Jersey. Leasing Consultants was located in New York. The bank perfected its security interest in the leases by taking possession of them, as Article 9 permits, see § 9-305, and by making an informational filing in New York, as Article 9 also permits. See § 9-408. When Leasing Consultants became bankrupt and when Plastimetrix defaulted on the leases, Leasing Consultant's trustee in bankruptcy claimed that the bank's only interest in the equipment was an unperfected security interest, although the trustee conceded that the bank held a perfected security interest in the leases themselves.]

JAMESON, District Judge.

* * *

As the district court recognized, the aim of Article 9 of the Uniform Commercial Code, relating to "Secured Transactions", is "to provide a simple and unified structure within which the immense variety of present day secured financing transactions can go forward with less cost and with greater certainty." Uniform Commercial Code, § 9-101, Official Comment. The drafters of this article eliminated many distinctions among security devices based on form alone. On the other hand, distinctions based on the type of property constituting the collateral were retained. Id.

Based on the stipulation of counsel, the court assumed that the agreements between Leasing and Plastimetrix were "true leases" and not "conditional sales agreements" or devices intended to create only a security interest.[1] Accordingly the court found that the Bank acquired "a security interest in both the right to

---

[1] Where a lease is intended as a security device the lessee usually becomes the owner or has the option to become the owner of the property at the end of the lease term. U.C.C. § 1-201(37). The lessor holds merely a security interest and has no reversionary right in the leased property.

receive rental payments under the lease and in the reversionary interest in the underlying equipment."

The court held, and the parties agree, that the leases themselves were "chattel papers" (U.C.C. § 9-105(1)(b)) and that the Bank's security interest in the chattel paper was perfected by filing financing statements in New York and taking possession of the leases. U.C.C. § 9-304(1), 9-305, and 9-102(1).

The court held further: "By contrast, the machines themselves constituted 'equipment' located in New Jersey and hence, for perfection purposes, came within the scope of the New Jersey requirements." The Bank having failed to perfect its interest in the reversion in New Jersey, the court concluded that the Trustee "-a lien creditor within the meaning of Uniform Commercial Code § 9-301(3)-has priority over an unperfected security interest under § 9-301(1)(b)."

Emphasizing the distinction between rights under the chattel paper and the reversionary interest in the equipment, the court quoted from Professor Levie as follows: "In one situation the purchaser of a security agreement may have an advantage over the purchaser of a lease. Where [he] purchases equipment leases, he takes only an assignor's interest in the equipment lease itself. If [he] wishes to be secured by an interest in the goods as well, he must obtain a security interest * * * [in the goods] and perfect it." Levie, Security Interests in Chattel Paper, 78 Yale L.J. 935, 940 (1969).[2]

The district court concluded: "The distinction between the rights represented by the lease and those represented by the reversionary interest in the equipment is a real one, supported by logic and precedent. To ignore the distinction contributes neither to clarity nor uniformity under the Uniform Commercial Code. Moreover, it may mislead third party creditors. The simple solution for a bank in the situation of petitioner is to file notices as to its interest in the reversion in accordance with the law of the state where the equipment is located."

* * *

In contending that the filing and physical possession of the lease instruments in New York were sufficient to cover the leased equipment located in New Jersey, appellant argues that the "reversionary interest" of Leasing is "an intangible interest, sited at Leasing's domicile in New York, and not in New Jersey." If the reversionary interest in the equipment were characterized as a "general intangible", the Bank's security interest in the equipment would have

---

2 The court continued: "Practical considerations support this conclusion. The property leased was heavy manufacturing equipment. A potential creditor observing these complicated and non-portable machines should be entitled to believe that he could discover all non-possessory interests by consulting the files in the state where the equipment is located. The equipment was obviously of great value; the New Jersey files revealed only that the lessee held it under a lease. Since the lease agreement required each piece of equipment to have a plate affixed indicating that it was the 'property' of the lessor, judgment creditors of the lessor might assume that its reversionary interest in the equipment was of substantial value. Not being alerted to the diminution of value which would be effected by the creditor's security interest, they might then, for example, attach the lessor's interest, relying on an apparently unencumbered and valuable reversionary interest."

been perfected when it filed with the New York Department of State and in the county in which Leasing had a place of business. N.Y.U.C.C. §§ 9-103 (2), 9-401(1)(c) (McKinney 1964).

The policies of the Code, however, militate against such an interpretation. We agree with the district court that the reversionary interest is an interest in "goods" rather than an interest in intangibles, and that to perfect the security interest in the reversionary interest in the equipment it was necessary to file a financing statement in New Jersey where the equipment was located. N.J.Stat.Anno. 12A:9-102(1) (1962), 9-302, 9-401(1)(c) (Supp.1972).

Obviously the leased property itself is "goods". We conclude, as did the district court, that the future reversionary interest is likewise an interest in goods, whether it represents "equipment" or "inventory" collateral. The drafters of the Code classified collateral mainly according to the nature or use of the underlying entity, rather than the character of its ownership at any given time. Significantly, the examples of "general intangibles" given in the Official Comment to § 9-106 are all types of property that are inherently intangible. And several Code sections and comments suggest that a collateral interest in "goods" remains such even when the goods are leased.

We conclude accordingly that if the instruments were "true leases", the security interest in the leased equipment was not perfected because of the failure of the Bank to file financing statements in New Jersey.

[The court then remanded the matter to determine whether the leases were in fact true leases.]

PROBLEM

Lessor has two pieces of earth moving equipment that it wants to lease to Lessee. On May 1, it had granted Bank a security interest in the first piece of equipment. On May 2, it leased both pieces to Lessee. On May 3, it assigned both leases to the bank, which took possession of the leases. On May 4, Lessor granted the bank a security interest in the second piece of equipment.

(a) If the leases are true leases, how should the bank perfect its various interests?

(b) Can the lessee grant its bank a security interest in the equipment? If so, what does lessee's bank get?

Chapter 5

ARTICLE 9 PROPERTY CATEGORIES

SECTION 1. EVOLUTION OF PERSONAL PROPERTY SECURITY

INTRODUCTION

Sometimes people cannot or do not pay their debts. Lenders and finance sellers are acutely aware of this fact and, therefore, often they will want something more than the debtor's naked promise to pay as a condition to the extension of credit in the first place. Such assurances could take the form of a guarantee from a more financially stable party or a bank letter of credit. Traditionally, however, the lender or seller will demand an interest in the debtor's assets which can be foreclosed upon (seized and liquidated) should the debtor default on the underlying debt. The proceeds from the foreclosure sale are then applied to the debt. Article 9 applies when the asset in question is personal, as distinguished from real, property. Prior to the widespread adoption of the Uniform Commercial Code, personal property security interests were governed by common law and a complex array of nonuniform state statutes that permitted creditors to take an effective nonpossessory security interest in a debtor's tangible and intangible personal property. In general, different categories of personal property, and different types of financing transactions, were subject to different regulatory regimes—*chattel mortgage statutes* for durable, tangible property like equipment; *factor's liens* and *field warehousing statutes* for a debtor's stock-in-trade; and *conditional sales acts* for credit sale transactions. Each of these pre-Code security devices used its own terminology, established its own procedures and rules of priority, and set forth its own remedies. Perhaps the single most important achievement of the Code (as important as the goal of making the law uniform from state to state) was to standardize, and bring together under a single law, the practice and the rules governing all forms of personal property security interests, although a few vagaries and some of the old terminology have survived.

You will recall from the discussion in the last chapter that Article 9 applies to all consensual security interests *regardless of form*. Official Comment 1 to § 9-102, however, makes clear that Article 9 "does not abolish existing security devices. The conditional sale or bailment lease, for example, is not prohibited; but even though it is used, the rules of this Article govern." You will also recall that Article 9 applies only to *consensual* security interests, those created by *contract*. See § 9-102(b). This excludes liens arising out of judicial proceedings and various forms of common law and statutory liens, such as mechanics', garagemen's, and innkeepers' liens. The various types of nonconsensual liens were also examined in greater detail in the last Chapter.

Revised Article 9, as originally proposed, would have included within its scope *nonpossessory* statutory liens—those liens conferred by statute that do not depend on the lienholder's possession of the personal property for their effectiveness. See Revised §§ 9-102(53)(A) and 9-112(a)(2). The rationale was that the present rules governing perfection and priority of these liens are often vague and at times inconsistent. This inevitably promotes costly uncertainty and wasteful litigation. By bringing these liens under the umbrella of Article 9 it was hoped that clear and unambiguous standards would develop. However, inclusion of all forms of statutory liens under Article 9 proved controversial, and at its November, 1997, meeting, the Drafting Committee decided to remove from the scope of the revision nonagricultural, nonpossessory statutory liens.

EXPLANATORY NOTE ON TYPES OF LENDERS

Commercial and consumer lending has changed dramatically over the course of the last century. Although today there are many different types of financing entities, for our purposes there are five basic kinds of lenders:

1. *Financing Sellers.* These are merchants who not only sell their product to a buyer, but who also, on request, will lend their buyer all or a portion of the purchase price for the goods sold. Often, but not always, the finance seller will then *discount* the buyer's note or account to a bank or finance company in order to receive immediate cash. The term discount is used because the assignee will pay less than face for these obligations to reflect both the time value of money and the risk of the buyer/borrower's default.

2. *Commercial Banks.* Unlike other more specialized kinds of banks and financial institutions, commercial banks are "full service" financial institutions that accept both time (savings) and demand (checking) deposits, provide payment and collection services, make commercial and consumer loans, offer trust services, and, increasingly, brokerage services to their customers. Commercial banks, which can be chartered under either state or federal law, dominate in the area of inventory and equipment lending.

3. *Finance Companies.* Traditionally, finance companies would make asset-based (secured) loans that were, for whatever reason, unappealing to commercial banks. In other instances, finance companies would purchase the paper (notes and account debt) generated by a financing seller or lessor. Today, it is not uncommon for large manufacturers of products mass distributed to consumers, such as new cars, to set up their own finance companies to provide their customers with the credit necessary to purchase their products. In addition to consumer loans, finance companies play an active and important role in commercial equipment sale and lease financing transactions.

4. *Small Loan Companies.* These are companies, sometimes national in scope, that typically made small (often under $1,000) loans to consumers, secured by either a security interest in the borrower's personal, family and household goods

or some type of assignment of wages. Over the past forty years, this type of lending has been severely restricted by state and federal regulatory legislation. Because of these restrictions, small loan companies today are not an important source of secured credit.

5. *Thrifts.* This term is generally used to refer to savings and loan associations, credit unions, and similar kinds of banks that were, by regulation, prohibited from accepting demand deposits but which could offer somewhat higher interest rates on time accounts. Traditionally, thrifts' activities were in the area of consumer loans and, in particular, home mortgage loans. The advent of deregulation in the banking industry has blurred the distinction between commercial banks and thrifts considerably, although thrifts continue to emphasize real estate-based lending.

COOGAN, ARTICLE 9—AN AGENDA FOR THE NEXT DECADE, 87 Yale L.J. 1012, 1014-17 (1978).

The idea that paramount significance attends the possession of property is the oldest concept of chattel security law. Until the early nineteenth century, the only way to create a valid security interest in personal property was by physical pledge—the transfer of possession of the property (collateral) by the debtor (the pledgor) to the creditor or secured party (the pledge). An attempt to transfer a security interest in property that remained in the debtor's possession was considered fraudulent and invalid against third parties. This historic antipathy to nonpossessory security interests has two aspects crucial to my thesis. The first is the rationale for holding such interests fraudulent. It was assumed that potential creditors and purchasers would rely on a debtor's apparent ownership of assets physically in his possession; this was part of the basic common law doctrine of protecting creditors against undisclosed interests in property. In other words, it was a requirement that there be public notice of the creation of a security interest; physical pledge, presumably, gave that public notice. The second important aspect was the especial hostility reserved for a particular kind of nonpossessory security interest—the interest in after-acquired property, particularly in the form of inventory and accounts receivable. This hostility resulted less directly from the status attributed to possession but nonetheless may be traced to that source.

During the late nineteenth and early twentieth centuries, there developed an increasingly pressing need for credit secured by collateral that remained in the debtor's possession, especially after-acquired collateral and especially in the form of inventory and receivables. Slowly, debtors and creditors devised ways to overcome the obstacles posed by the two aspects of the possession idea noted above. The history of this struggle, manifested by a proliferation of security devices, is a fascinating story well told by Professor Gilmore; it need not be repeated here. The outcome, on the eve of the drafting of the U.C.C., was that nonpossessory interests could usually be successfully created; in the process, however, "the law of personal property security transactions [had come] to resemble the obscure wood in which Dante once discovered the gates of hell."

Article 9 brought this "labyrinthine" mélange of personal property security law under one roof. It legitimized the status of nonpossessory interests and provided a workable mechanism—filing in a public office—for satisfying the requirement that potential creditors be put on notice that certain assets of the debtor might be subject to claims by others. The draftsmen, however, did not abandon established doctrine; indeed, they accepted "without question" the distinction between possessory and nonpossessory security interests. Article 9 retains a category of exclusively possessory security interests: certain types of collateral must be pledged, essentially in the old fashion. It likewise designates a category of exclusively nonpossessory security interests: for certain types of collateral, one cannot use the pledge. For most types of collateral, however, either method is permissible. On its face, then, Article 9 only slightly reduces the role of possession. But commercial developments in the years since its drafting suggest that its nonpossessory interests are of major importance and that its retention of exclusively possessory interests is of questionable utility and, indeed, sometimes proves to be little more than a stumbling block.

Article 9 rejected *in toto* the old notion that nonpossessory interests in after-acquired property are suspect. It dramatically expanded the parties' freedom to create security interests in all kinds of after-acquired collateral, regardless of the ultimate nature of the collateral. The best-known example, and perhaps the most widely used financing device under Article 9, is the security interest in present and future inventory and accounts receivable. This is the so-called "floating lien," which secures a debt that may change in size and covers collateral that is amorphous and likewise changeable. The floating lien has two characteristics that are important here: it is inherently nonpossessory, and the collateral to which it is "attached" is "fluid" or interchangeable.

DOLAN, CHANGING COMMERCIAL PRACTICES AND THE UNIFORM COMMERCIAL CODE, 26 Loy. L.A. L. Rev. 579, 592-95 (1993).

There have been four major developments in the landscape of secured lending: (1) the rise of equipment leasing, (2) the demise of secured consumer sales, (3) the diminishing role of inventory as security, and (4) the increase of non-asset based lending in the middle market.

A. History

Until the end of the last century or the beginning of this one, commercial bankers thought all loans should be self liquidating. A banker might finance a merchant-to-merchant sale on a secured basis, but the loan related to that discrete sale and usually was against assets generated by the sales transaction. First came the negotiable document representing the goods sold. Next came the negotiable instrument—the buyer's promissory note or trade acceptance.

This was the real bills theory of banking, and it gradually gave way to the realization that collateral, especially inventory and accounts, could revolve. The open-account sale provided significant credit for the buyer, but it was short term credit, and it was sometimes insufficient for the buyer to turn the merchandise over. Buyers, furthermore, needed working capital, and the discrete loan did not accommodate it.

Thus there developed the concept of the working capital loan, which was not discrete or self-liquidating in any way but was usually secured by revolving collateral and was evidenced by a demand, not a time note. Under the revolving loan, the borrower granted the lender security in a variety of assets and made payments as it suited the borrower's cash flow and the lender's patience.

Originally, trust companies made these daring loans that challenged commercial banking orthodoxy, but eventually the commercial banker saw their attractiveness and ventured into secured lending. As this new brand of secured commercial lending commenced, the borrower was the marginal operation or at least the new one. Borrowers longed to borrow on the credit of their reputation and their history of profits rather than on the marketability of their assets. As Kripke put it, they wanted to get out of the finance companies and into the banks. Commercial bankers were more inclined to lend to the enterprise that was at minimal risk of default and, therefore, did not need to post collateral; it was the finance company that made the asset based loan.

By the 1950s, the picture had begun to change, as the good credit risks, in order to avoid bank charges, moved out of the banks directly into the money markets. At the same time the asset based borrower moved to the banks. Clearly, one of the objects of the Code was to validate in all respects loans secured by revolving inventory and accounts. Article 9 faced two challenges to that loan concept, one a Supreme Court opinion by Justice Brandeis, another the anti-preference rule of the Bankruptcy Act. The drafters successfully overturned the first, a matter of state law, but failed as to the second, a matter of federal law. The courts relieved the pressure from the second challenge until Congress itself refashioned the bankruptcy statute in a way that renders it hospitable to these revolving loans.

Secured lending has played a major role in consumer finance. The middle of this century witnessed the rise of consumer credit. Unfortunately for all involved, the consumer credit transaction initially drew its form from the merchant credit sale and involved negotiable instruments and their holder in due course feature. The effect of these rules was to force consumers to pay for goods that failed to conform to reasonable expectations.

With the end of the Second World War and the burgeoning sales of consumer durables, consumer credit virtually always entailed a purchase money security interest in the durables. By dint of that security interest, the consumer not only had to pay the holder of his paper but faced the loss of the goods in the case of default. This double threat admitted no commercial defenses, since the holder of the paper took it free of defenses.

The Code drafters' successful attempts to fashion strong warranty terms in the sales transaction did not completely avail the consumer since the negotiability rules of Article 3 and the imputation doctrine of Article 9 rendered the consumer defenseless in the event institutional lenders entered the transaction.

B. Today

Developments since the 1950s alter the picture. First, in both the consumer and the commercial setting unsecured credit has grown and secured credit diminished markedly. Second, equipment leasing has become in its true lease form or its disguised sale form a critical source of credit in the equipment trade. Third, inventory has become relatively less important as collateral. Fourth, intellectual property, currently the subject of federal law, has become an important, valuable commercial asset.

Today most consumer credit, except for automobile or mobile home transactions, is unsecured. Quick, reliable credit reporting has once again worked considerable change on the face of commerce. Credit card issuers can rely on those reports when they issue the card, increase its limits, and honor merchant charges. Except for the automobile or mobile home transaction, the chattel paper that has been such a source of consumer credit and consumer dissatisfaction has assumed a much more modest role in the consumer credit picture. The Code, of course, does not govern credit card transactions, which are largely the domain of federal law or of the contracts between the various parties to the credit card transaction.

Since the 1950s, furthermore, many business enterprises that formerly obtained credit from banks now seek it in the money markets. It is true that some of those enterprises would have borrowed from banks on an unsecured basis, but others would have had to grant security interests in assets in order to secure their loans. Today, larger businesses are obtaining credit via commercial paper, much of it enhanced by guarantees of one sort or another, including the bank issued standby letter of credit. Commercial paper borrowing is unsecured and is not within the province of the Code. Even smaller businesses, the classic asset-based borrowers, are avoiding collateralized loans. Some of them reduce inventory through various mechanisms. They use just-in-time inventory planning and point-of-sale inventory control; and they bargain vigorously for longer credit terms from their larger suppliers, using them as sources of credit. The credit crunch of the 1970s taught some hard lessons. Borrowers became wary of credit charges and of bankers that suddenly demanded payment of notes that in the past had been refinanced with regularity. Some finance companies have responded to business wariness of asset based lending and its transaction costs by making unsecured advances, though usually on the very shortest of terms.

Leasing is probably still a growth industry. It is an industry, however, characterized by adhesion contracts, large merchant lessors and large merchant lessees. The leasing article codifies the best of the cases and provides what amounts in some instances to regulations for the gray areas of leasing law, not the least of which is the law that determines whether a transaction is a sale or a lease. One suspects that the number of leasing cases will be quite small and that the impact of Article 2A will be largely reflected or deflected in the drafting of the lease forms that the industry is using and will continue to use.

Durable assets characterize the balance sheet of the manufacturing sector. The 1990s are witnessing the relative decline of that sector and the corresponding growth of the service sector. Service industries are not durable asset rich. The great increase in assets over the last decade and the growth that one would expect will continue into the next one has been in the area of intellectual property. With the relative decline in manufacturing and the relative rise in services has come a dramatic increase in the economy's intellectual property. Durables, then, asinventory and as consumer goods, comprise a relatively less important part of the lending picture; and with their demise has come the spectacular rise of intellectual property assets.

SECTION 2. GOODS

(a) REVOLVING COLLATERAL (INVENTORY)

KRIPKE, CURRENT ASSETS FINANCING AS A SOURCE OF LONG-TERM CAPITAL, 36 Minn. L. Rev. 506, 510-11 (1952).

The Permanent Nature of Current Assets

The other two types of financing to be dealt with are inventory and accounts receivable. Both of these types of assets are classified by accountants as current assets. They show "above the line," in an accountant's financial statement, and they enter into his computations of "current assets," "net current assets," and "net quick worth." Because of this accountant's classification and because each item of inventory and each account receivable is itself of short duration, these types of assets are sometimes thought of as ephemeral. The price level changes since the end of World War II, however, and the heightened pace of industrial activity have served to impress the lesson that even though the individual item of inventory or the individual account receivable is of short duration, the aggregate investment in accounts receivable and the aggregate investment in inventory are permanent. It has been learned, sometimes painfully, that it requires more dollars of permanent investment to maintain a given physical quantity of inventory at a higher price level. Persons who have lengthened their trade credit terms after World War II, including such devices as the 4-pay, 6-pay, or 12-pay revolving credits of the department stores, have discovered that the change requires a vastly increased amount of permanent capital. The conclusion is that the accountant's classification, when we take it too literally, leads us astray and conceals from us the permanent long-term fixed character of the investment of a business enterprise in its normal inventory and in its normal amount of accounts receivable. The enterprise needs long-term capital for these purposes just as much as it needs long-term capital for its plant and machinery, which the accountant recognizes as fixed assets.

To the extent that the conventional forms of equity financing and long-term capital financing are available, there is, of course, no problem, except for devices to take up the slack during periods of maximum need for funds. But for the small businessman who is chronically undercapitalized, and to whom the conventional long-term sources of funds are not available, credit devices by which he is enabled to obtain the capital with which to carry his inventory or his accounts receivable, may, in fact, be credit devices for extending long-term credit even though the arrangements are nominally for the short term and are quickly terminable.

BEARD, THE PURCHASE MONEY SECURITY INTEREST IN INVENTORY: IF IT DOES NOT FLOAT, IT MUST BE DEAD!, 57 Tenn. L. Rev. 437, 438-39 (1990).

Article 9 has succeeded, as a general proposition, in providing a uniform and smoothly functioning system for securing commercial credit. This unified system of securing credit has perhaps no greater significance than in the area of inventory financing. Through the validation of the "floating lien" and the related exception for the purchase money security interest (PMSI), Article 9 has made the vast inventories of business more easily and readily available as a source of credit. Despite the current debate about whether a system of secured credit constitutes the most efficient means for obtaining and extending credit, Article 9 facilitates the provision of working capital and acquisition financing in a manner that permits the expansion of capital in business.

Through the combination of a unitary device, the "security interest," and the validation of the floating lien, Article 9 permits lenders to obtain security in the inventory of the borrower simply, at relatively low cost, and without the necessity of extensive, technical and burdensome on-going monitoring and paper work for purposes of maintaining priority. The creation of a single form of consensual lien simplified the task of obtaining security by eliminating the overly technical distinctions between the various forms of chattel security that existed prior to the Code. Equally important to the financing of inventory, the Code validated the floating lien. Unlike equipment and consumer goods that the borrower generally retains during the life of the financing, the borrower buys, sells and replenishes inventory in the ordinary course of business. This posed great difficulties under pre-Code chattel security law because of the requirement that the creditor retain significant controls over its collateral in order to maintain its security. Such controls required technical and burdensome monitoring in order to satisfy the creditor's need for security while at the same time permitting the debtor the necessary freedom to carry on business. Though complicated and difficult, it was possible to accommodate the business needs of the debtor and the security needs of the creditor under pre-Code chattel security laws.

UCC § 9-109

(*see Selected Commercial Statutes*)

IN RE MAYO

United States Bankruptcy Court, District of Vermont, 1990.
112 B.R. 607.

[Mayo, a boat dealer and the debtor in bankruptcy, purchased a 48-foot Chris-Craft 480 Corinthian on credit from the manufacturer. Mayo granted a security interest in all of his boat inventory to Borg Warner Acceptance Corp., a finance company. Thereafter, Mayo granted Midlantic Bank a security interest in the boat, telling Midlantic that the boat was his personal boat. In Mayo's bankruptcy case both Borg Warner and Midlantic claimed the proceeds for the sale of the boat.]

FRANCIS G. CONRAD, Bankruptcy Judge.

[Section] 9-312(5) sets out the priorities between two Article 9 secured creditors when their security interests are claimed in the same collateral. Subsection (5) is the quintessence of § 9-312's priority scheme. Its language translates to a rule of first in time, first in right. No party here denies that BWAC was the first to dance with Mayo. What Midlantic questions is whether the Boat was inventory and carried by Mayo as the "Business Groom" or by Mayo as the "consumer groom."

Section 9-109(4) defines inventory if it is "held by a person who holds them for sale * * * in a business. Inventory of a person is not to be classified as his equipment." "Each thing is what it is," said the poet, T.S. Eliot, "and not some other thing." T.S. Eliot never envisioned the Uniform Commercial Code, however. A boat could be an inventory item, a consumer item, or some combination of both. The UCC cautions that classes of goods are mutually exclusive, and in borderline cases, the principal use to which the property is put should be determined.

The evidence presented to us shows the Boat was inventory, and we so find. To support our finding we suggest several facts:

—Our observation of Mayo during his testimony tells us he would do anything to obtain what he wants.[1]

—The Boat was always maintained as an inventory item by BWAC and under normal floor plan arrangements.

—Mayo himself acknowledges the Boat was for sale.

—Chris-Craft wanted the Boat on Lake Champlain for commercial purposes.

—Carrying the Boat in his inventory caused Mayo to be over his credit line approval with [Borg Warner].

—Chris-Craft obtained a credit overline approval for Mayo.

—Mayo conducted the [Midlantic] transaction as if he was buying from his inventory.

Thus, we find [Borg Warner] has a valid perfected security interest in the Boat, which is a first priority position compared to all other secured lenders in this proceeding. The facts satisfy 9-312(5).

---

1 We believe Mayo lied when he wrote the marina on May 8, 1986 (MB-53) and informed them the Boat was not for sale and was for his personal use. There are any number of instances in his testimony that support our conclusion including using the Boat as bait to snare more customers.

IN RE BROWER

United States Bankruptcy Court, District of North Dakota, 1988.
104 B.R. 226.

[Rohweder entered into a "lease" with Brower, a dairy farmer, whereby Brower took possession of cattle and agreed to make lease payments to Rohweder. At the end of the lease term, Brower had the right to buy the cattle for $1.00 per head. The court found that the "lease" was in fact a disguised installment sales agreement. Rohweder had previously granted a bank a security interest in the cows. Brower became unable to continue his dairy operations and, just prior to filing bankruptcy, he relinquished possession of the cattle to Rohweder. The trustee in Brower's bankruptcy case sought possession of the cows free and clear of all liens, arguing that the bank was unperfected because it filed in the wrong office.]

WILLIAM A. HILL, Bankruptcy Judge.

* * *

The other party claiming an ownership interest in the cattle is the Bank. The trustee asserts that the Bank's interest was unperfected as of the date of filing. Section 544 gives the trustee the hypothetical status of a judicial lien holder as of the date of filing. Thus if the Bank was unperfected at the time of filing the trustee primes the Bank. Section 41-09-40(1)(a) of the North Dakota Century Code (U.C.C. § 9-401) provides that a creditor must perfect a security interest in farm products by filing a financing statement with the county register of deeds. A security interest in inventory is perfected by filing a financing statement with the North Dakota Secretary of State. In the current case the Bank initially filed a financing statement covering the cattle with the register of deeds but not the secretary of state. The financing statement at the register of deeds was continued in May of 1985, well after Rohweder began leasing cattle. At the time of the continuation the Bank still did not file a financing statement with the secretary of state. The Bank eventually did file with the secretary of state, however, the filing came after the Debtors filed their bankruptcy petition and has no bearing on this case because the trustee's status as a hypothetical judicial lien creditor arises on the date the bankruptcy petition is filed. Thus the question becomes whether the cattle constituted inventory or farm products. Section 41-09-09 of the North Dakota Century Code (U.C.C. § 9-109), in part, provides: Goods are:

* * *

3. "Farm products" if they are * * * livestock * * * used or produced in farming operations * * * and if they are in possession of a debtor engaged in raising, fattening, grazing, or other farming operations. If goods are farm products they are neither equipment nor inventory. 4. "Inventory" if they are held by a person who holds them for sale or lease * * * .

The North Dakota Supreme Court has reasoned that "[t]he intrinsic nature of the goods does not classify them [for purposes of section 41-09-09]; rather, it is the use to which the owner puts the goods, or intends to put them that determines their classification." Thus when livestock is placed by a farm debtor into the hands of a marketing agent for sale it becomes inventory. The United States

Court of Appeals for the Tenth Circuit has determined, in accord with the North Dakota court's decision in Central Livestock, that intent is dispositive with regard to classifications made pursuant to U.C.C. § 9-109. See First State Bank v. Maxfield, 485 F.2d 71, 74 (10th Cir.1973). In Maxfield the court concluded that certain cattle present on the Debtor's farm were inventory. The disputed cattle were not part of the farmer's cattle fattening operation. Rather he purchased them with the intent to immediately resell them as part of his secondary business as a cattle trader. Id. Official Comment No. 3 to U.C.C. § 9-109 provides that: "[w]hen an enterprise is engaged in the business of leasing a stock of products to users * * * that stock is also included within the definition of 'inventory.'"

In the instant case Rohweder was in the business of leasing dairy cows. In the transaction with the Debtor, as was determined in section 1, he was actually in the business of selling cows. The language of section 41-09-09(4) is clear that property which is held for sale or lease is inventory. Additionally, the statute requires that in order for property to be a farm product it must be in the possession of a debtor engaged in farming. Thus if the goods are not in the possession of the farm debtor they cannot be farm products. In the instant case the cattle were not in Rohweder's possession.

* * *

In the instant case Rohweder was not pursuing any farming activity with the cattle, instead he was leasing and selling the cattle to other farmers who used them for milk production. This court concludes that the cattle were inventory and the Bank did not properly perfect its security interest in inventory by a timely filing with the secretary of state. Thus the trustee, in his status as a hypothetical judicial lien creditor, primes the Bank's lien.

Accordingly, * * * IT IS ORDERED * * * that the security interest of * * * [the bank] is subject to the trustee's lien in the cattle.

QUESTIONS

1. How would you classify, for collateral purposes, feed purchased by the debtor in *Brower* for the purpose of fattening the cattle prior to sale?
2. If, as the court suggested in *Brower*, classification of collateral depends not on the intrinsic nature of the goods, but rather "the use to which the owner puts the goods, or intends to put them that determines their classification," what happens when the use to which the goods are put changes? See § 9-401(3).

(b) DISCRETE COLLATERAL, I.E., NONREVOLVING (EQUIPMENT, CONSUMER GOODS, AND FARM PRODUCTS)

WOODSON v. UTICA SQUARE NATIONAL BANK (IN RE McCLAIN)

United States Court of Appeals, Tenth Circuit, 1971.
447 F.2d 241.

BREITENSTEIN, Circuit Judge.

In this voluntary bankruptcy proceeding the question is whether the appellee Utica Square National Bank of Tulsa is a secured or an unsecured creditor. Over the objections of the trustee, the referee held that the bank was a secured creditor and the district court affirmed.

The bankrupt purchased a Chevrolet pickup truck from an automobile dealer in February, 1969, and executed a promissory note and a separate security agreement-financing statement. In that statement he warranted, by checking a box thereon, that the pickup was to be used primarily 'In Business.' The dealer assigned the note and the purchase-money security interest to the bank for value. In reliance on the 'In Business' designation the bank filed the security agreement in Oklahoma County, Oklahoma.

The bankruptcy proceedings were begun in April, 1970. The bank filed a proof of secured claim and the trustee objected thereto on the ground that the security agreement had not been filed in the proper county. The trustee contends that despite the 'In Business' designation the pickup had always been used as consumer goods and that the security agreement had to be filed in Tulsa County, the county of the debtor's residence. The trustee offered evidence that the bankrupt never used the pickup for business purposes and, hence, his intent at the time of purchase was not to use it primarily for business purposes. The bank objected on the ground that parol evidence was inadmissible to vary the terms of the written security agreement. The referee sustained the objection and the district court affirmed.

Oklahoma has adopted the Uniform Commercial Code. See 12A Okl.St.Ann. An automobile comes within the term 'goods' as there defined. See 9-105(1)(f) and Osborn v. First National Bank of Holdenville, Okl., 472 P.2d 440, 441-442. Goods are classified into four categories: consumer goods, equipment, farm products, and inventory. 9-109. The classes are mutually exclusive, and the goods cannot be in two categories at the same time as to the same person. 9-109, Comment 2.

The perfection of a security interest by filing requires the determination of the proper county in which to file. If the collateral is classified as consumer goods, the proper county in which to file is the county of the debtor's residence, in this case Tulsa County. 9-401(1)(a). If business equipment, the security agreement is to be filed with the county clerk of Oklahoma County. 9-401(1)(c). In the case before us the bank filed in Oklahoma County.

* * *

Finally, the bank argues that the warranty of use in the security agreement is conclusive. We believe that this is foreclosed by National Bank of Commerce v. First National Bank and Trust Company of Tulsa, Okl., 446 P.2d 277, a case involving priority of security interests as affected by the filing requirements of 9-401. The court there said that the primary issue was 'the classification of the (automobile) as equipment, consumer goods or inventory, to determine the proper place of filing.' Ibid. at 280. In making the determination the court looked to extrinsic facts and did not give conclusive effect to the warranty in the security agreement. This expression of Oklahoma law is binding on us. * * *

The National Bank of Commerce decision comports with Comment 2 to 9-109 which says that 'the principal use to which the property is put should be considered determinative.' Further, in bankruptcy situations involving the Uniform Commercial Code the courts have independently inquired into the classification and filing of collateral. The difficult position in which the bank is placed results from Oklahoma law. The only answer would seem to be that a creditor in doubt about the proper classification of collateral should file in all possible counties where filing might be required.

Our decision herein is limited to (1) the evidence offered by the trustee should be received, and (2) the warranty of use in the security agreement is not conclusive. The question of proper classification is one to be determined in accordance with the usual bankruptcy procedures. Problems which may arise in connection therewith are not before us at this time.

NOTES AND QUESTIONS

1. The *McClain* case is not uniformly followed. Some jurisdictions accept the argument that the creditor should be able to rely on the borrower's warranty concerning the use of the collateral. Also, in all U.S. jurisdictions today, motor vehicles are subject to certificate of title laws, and states have adopted versions of section 9-302(3)(b) that exempt such vehicles from the filing requirements of Article 9 and substitute the motor vehicle act's procedures for noting security interests on the certificate of title itself. See, e.g., Okla. Stat. Ann. tit. 47, § 1110 (West 1994).

2. In *McClain* the debtor misrepresented how he intended to use the collateral, i.e., for business or personal purposes. It is also possible that a debtor may *intend* to use particular goods for one purpose but *actually* use them for another. Because the definitions in § 9-109 for "consumer goods" and "equipment" refer to both intended and actual use, it is not clear which controls in those cases. White and Summers suggest that "[h]ow one resolves the intended use versus actual use dispute depends ultimately on whether one values more highly secured creditors' interests or third party creditors' interests." WHITE & SUMMERS, UNIFORM COMMERCIAL CODE § 22-11, at 784 (4th ed. 1995). Is this a fair statement? Which do you think ought to control? Consider that question in light of the next case.

COMMERCIAL CREDIT EQUIPMENT CORP. v. CARTER

Supreme Court of Washington, 1973.
83 Wash.2d 136, 516 P.2d 767.

BRACHTENBACH, Associate Justice.

The sole issue raised by this appeal is whether the airplane purchased by defendant from plaintiff's assignor and secured by a contemporaneously executed security agreement constitutes 'consumer goods' within the meaning of RCW 62A.9-501, so that defendant (the defaulting debtor) is not liable for any deficiency after plaintiff (the secured party) has disposed of the airplane pursuant to RCW 62A.9-504.

The defendant husband purchased an airplane from the plaintiff's assignor. The purchase price was $23,955, with the balance, after application of a down payment, being secured by a contemporaneously executed purchase money security agreement. After defendant had been in default in the monthly payments for some months, the plaintiff took possession of the airplane and disposed of it in a reasonably commercial manner. The parties admit that the sale was effected in accordance with RCW 62A.9-504, the out-of-court realization methods accorded to a secured party. There remained a deficit of $2,382.51.

The trial court held that the defendant purchased the airplane with the intent that it be for his own personal use only, rather than for commercial purposes, and that originally it was so used.

However, the court concluded that the airplane was not within the definition of 'consumer goods.' Consequently, judgment was entered against the defendant for the deficiency, plus costs and attorney's fees. We reverse.

Whether the defendant is liable for the deficiency depends upon a determination of the classification of the airplane under the Uniform Commercial Code. RCW 62A.9-109 segregates goods into four categories: (1) consumer goods, (2) equipment, (3) farm products and (4) inventory. These classifications not only determine the issue in this case, but have other ramifications such as fixing the place of filing (RCW 62A.9-401), controlling certain questions of priority (RCW 62A.9-312) and other consequences as mentioned in the official comment to Uniform Commercial Code § 9-109. As pointed out in that comment, the classes are mutually exclusive so that the same property cannot at the same time and as to the same person fit into more than one category.

RCW 62A.9-109(1) states that goods are "'consumer goods' if they are used or bought for use primarily for personal, family or household purposes." If the collateral herein falls within this definition the defendant is not liable for any deficiency because the Washington version of the Uniform Commercial Code contains the following addition to the proposed official text of the Code: Notwithstanding any other provision of this Code, in the case of a purchase money security interest in consumer goods taken or retained by the seller of such collateral to secure all or part of its price, the debtor shall not be liable for any deficiency after the secured party has disposed of such collateral under RCW 62A.9-504 or has retained such collateral in satisfaction of the debt under subsection (2) of RCW 62A.9-505. RCW 62A.9-501(1). This is somewhat akin to prior Washington law which held that if a conditional sale vendor repossessed, he could not obtain a deficiency judgment against the vendee. Washington Cooperative Check Ass'n v. Jacobs, 42 Wash.2d 460, 256 P.2d 294 (1953).

The trial court found that defendant purchased the airplane with the intent that it be used for personal rather than commercial purposes. The court further found that the aircraft was in fact used solely for personal purposes until 3 months after the purchase. Defendant then changed jobs and upon occasion thereafter used the airplane to fly to other cities in the course of his new employment, for which use he was compensated by his new employer. Still later, when faced with the financial inability to meet the monthly payments, defendant rented the plane to third persons.

Upon these facts the trial court concluded that the airplane did not constitute 'consumer goods' because (1) the defendant failed to meet the burden of showing that the aircraft was used primarily for personal purposes; and (2) 'consumer goods' as defined in the Uniform Commercial Code were not intended to cover expensive hobby items such as airplanes. We disagree with both conclusions.

First, we hold that the intent of the defendant at the time the plaintiff's security interest attached to the collateral is controlling and necessitates the conclusion that the airplane came within the code definition of consumer goods. We recognize, but do not reach, since they are not present here, such questions as the legal effect of the situation where there is a declaration of intent by the debtor which is false or where there is an actual use then made which is contrary to that declared.

The plaintiff, however, urges an alternate theory to support the trial court's result, contending that the defendant, when faced with the financial inability to meet the monthly payments, rented the airplane to third parties. In fact the testimony and findings of fact do show that about 9 months after executing the security agreement, the defendant did make the plane available for rental. This was a course suggested by plaintiff in an effort to generate funds to meet the payments. In terms of overall use of the plane from purchase until taking of possession by plaintiff, the evidence indicates more hours for rental use than for plaintiff's personal use. From these facts, the plaintiff concludes that the plane was not used primarily for personal purposes within the meaning of RCW 62A.9-109(1).

It is true that the cited statute refers to goods used primarily for personal, family or household purposes. Uniform Commercial Code § 9-109, Comment 2 states: 'In borderline cases—a physician's car or a farmer's jeep which might be either consumer goods or equipment—the principal use to which the property is put should be considered as determinative.' Unfortunately neither section 9-109 nor the comment is precise in stating the point of time at which the principal use is to be measured. Conceivably it could be either the principal use at the time the security interest attaches, such use at the time the debtor takes possession upon default, or the principal use to which the collateral has been put between the attachment of the security interest and taking of possession.

It is the underlying purpose and policy of the code of 'simplify, clarify and modernize the law governing commercial transactions.' RCW 62A.1-102(2). It is inconsistent with this declared underlying purpose and policy to require a creditor to monitor use of the collateral in order to ascertain its proper classification. The uncertainty caused by the potentially shifting status of the goods is not desirable in the commercial world. Also, there exists a potential mischief by debtors facing default who might endeavor to convert goods from the category of equipment to consumer goods to avoid a deficiency and, likewise, by creditors making the opposite claim in order to benefit from a deficiency.

Our holding that the use or intent at the time the security interest attaches controls does no violence to the language of U.C.C. § 9-109. If the code dealt only with purchase money security interests we would have difficulty rationalizing the primary use test since these would exist little or no use to establish the classification at the time the security interest attached. However, the collateral may be owned already and put to use at the time the security interest attaches. The principal use is more relevant to classification than the antecedent intent or purpose when the debtor bought the goods months or perhaps years earlier.

* * *

We turn therefore to the second basis for the trial court's conclusion that the airplane was not 'consumer goods.' The trial court reasoned that the aircraft fell within the definition of 'equipment' under U.C.C. § 9-109(2) because consumer goods were not intended to cover expensive hobby items such as airplanes. The court explained that since it could not interpret consumer goods to include this expensive hobby item, it necessarily came within the catchall definition of equipment under § 9-109(2) as goods not otherwise included in any of the other three categories. We disagree since we find nothing in the statute to imply any exclusion dependent upon cost or nature of the goods. Rather, the decisive factor is whether the goods are used or bought for use primarily for personal, family or household purposes.

In accord with this interpretation is Atlas Credit Corp. v. Dolbow, 193 Pa.Super. 649, 165 A.2d 704 (1960), in which the court held, without analysis, that a boat purchased for $5,980 was consumer goods. Indeed, it has been observed that (t)he classifications of Sec 9-109 are based solely on use or function and it is almost, if not impossible, to conceive of an item of tangible personal property that cannot be a consumer goods. Even the recently retired 'Queen Mary' could qualify as a consumer goods if purchased by a billionaire for his own personal use and one recalls that the late Henry Ford, at one time, bought up entire factories for his personal museum.

The finding that the defendant intended the airplane for personal use conclusively brings it within the Code definition of consumer goods. We do note but reject the rationale of two cases decided by a referee in bankruptcy which held that mobile homes were not consumer goods since the words 'consume' and 'consumer' imply the using up, wasting or destroying of the goods. We cannot read into the language or concept of the code any basis for such reasoning or results.

NOTE ON PERFECTING SECURITY INTERESTS IN AIRCRAFT

Under the Federal Aviation Act, 49 U.S.C. App. § 1403 (1994), the Secretary of Transportation is charged to maintain procedures for filing notice of security interests in airplanes. Under current Federal Regulations, such notices must be filed in Oklahoma City, Oklahoma. See 14 C.F.R. § 49.11 (1994). The Code anticipates such federal law and provides that federal rules such as this trump Code filing rules. See UCC § 9-104(a). Bear in mind, however, that while federal law controls the validity of a creditor's security interest in an aircraft by requiring recordation in accordance with the Federal Aviation Act, the priority conferred by virtue of that recordation is still governed by Article 9. See Philco Aviation, Inc. v. Shacket, 462 U.S. 406 (1983).

SECTION 3. INTANGIBLE PROPERTY RIGHTS

(a) ACCOUNTS

BENEDICT v. RATNER

United States Supreme Court, 1925.
Page 86, supra.

OVERVIEW

An "account" is defined as "any right to payment for goods sold or leased or for services rendered which is not evidenced by an instrument or chattel paper, whether or not it has been earned by performance." § 9-106. The 1962 version of the Code distinguished between earned and unearned rights to payment, treating only the former as "accounts" and denominating the latter as "contract rights." That distinction was eliminated with the 1972 amendments to the Code. In addition to being able to effectively assign unearned rights to payment under existing contracts, it is clear that a debtor can also make a present assignment of rights to accounts under future contracts not yet entered into. § 9-204(1). The ability of a creditor to take an effective interest in property not yet owned by the debtor (a so-called "floating lien") is particularly important with respect to inventory and accounts receivable financing where it is anticipated that the collateral will be constantly turning over in the ordinary course of the debtor's business.

As in *Benedict v. Ratner*, the quintessential "account" is short-term credit extensions made by the debtor to its customers (known as the "account debtors") in connection with the sale of the debtor's inventory. Permitting the purchase of inventory on thirty or sixty-day credit, often with a discount for earlier repayment, is referred to as "trade credit" from the perspective of the account debtor. From the perspective of the debtor, who is actually the creditor in the transaction with its customer, the right to payment appears on its books as an "account receivable." To the secured party who takes the receivable as collateral for a loan (usually in the form of a revolving line of credit to the debtor), the collateral is classified as an account. Even though individual accounts are usually paid off in relatively short order, because the debtor is constantly generating new accounts, in a mature business the level of outstanding accounts receivable will typically remain more-or-less constant within a narrow range. Therefore, the ability to borrow against this ever-shifting mass of accounts is an important source of working capital, particularly for small businesses that generally do not receive significant amounts of unsecured credit and whose fixed assets will typically already be hypothecated to secure long-term loans. For more detailed discussion of receivables financing, see Kripke, *Current Assets as a Source of Long-Term Capital*, 36 Minn. L. Rev. 506 (1952).

There are many varieties of accounts receivable financing. In the revolving credit arrangement generally described above, sometimes called "non-notification financing," the account debtor is oblivious of the debtor's financing transactions unless and until there is a default under the loan secured by the accounts. In other instances, the lender will notify the account debtors to make their remittances directly to a post office box which is under the secured party's control. Although these remittances may be made available by the secured party to the debtor in the absence of a default, this type of arrangement obviously gives the secured party a much greater ability to monitor the level of accounts receivable and to control their application. While less common, there is also nothing that prevents a debtor from borrowing against only a single account or a specified batch of accounts. Finally, another type of accounts lending is described in the excerpt below.

J. DOLAN, COMMERCIAL LAW: ESSENTIAL TERMS AND TRANSACTIONS 148-49 (2d ed. 1997).

The factor, the third of the account lenders * * *, is more prevalent in some industries than in others. In those industries, notably the garment industry, manufacturers are often small and yet are faced with the problem of selling to numerous buyers located, perhaps, all over the country. The cost of maintaining credit information on a national industry as widespread and full of recent entries as the retail clothing industry would impose a serious burden on small garment manufacturers. It is economically efficient and, therefore, not surprising that in such an industry certain account financers undertake to evaluate and collect a seller's accounts. Factors, the name these industries have given to the finance company that performs these functions, traditionally "buy" accounts from their customers, notify the account debtors (the buyers from the manufacturers), and collect the accounts by instructing the account debtors to make payment directly to the factor.

Factors, given their size and their access to credit information, are in a position to evaluate the accounts they purchase, which they usually purchase on a without recourse basis. By evaluating the credit strength of the various buyers, the factor determines the value to it of a given manufacturer's accounts and will price them accordingly. Some manufacturers may sell their accounts at a small discount; others may have to pay a larger discount.

Note that these transactions involve discrete accounts and differ somewhat from the revolving account arrangement described above. That is not to say that the factoring industry is unwilling to engage in revolving account financing. It is, but the traditional factoring arrangement involves the transfer of discrete accounts.

NOTE ON SALES OF ACCOUNTS

In situations where a factor actually "buys" the account, without recourse back against the assignor if the account debtor fails to pay, a student new to the area might be inclined to wonder whether Article 9 applies at all. After all, where the assignment of accounts is "absolute," not merely for collateral purposes, the transaction would not seem to fit the traditional concept of a *security interest*, and indeed it does not. However, as we saw in Chapter 4, § 1-201(37) includes the interest of a buyer of accounts within the statutory definition of "security interest," and § 9-102(b) brings such sale transactions under the umbrella of Article 9, thereby requiring the buyer to make its interest publicly known or risk losing the accounts to another creditor of the assignor. Sales of chattel paper, discussed in Section 4 of this chapter, are treated in the same way. Why should outright sales of accounts and chattel paper be made subject to the requirements of Article 9? See Official Comment 2 to 9-102. In answering this question, look at § 9-104(f) which *excludes* four kinds of account assignment transactions from Article 9. What do all of these excluded transactions have in common, and what distinguishes them from the sale of accounts to a factor or the collateral assignment of accounts to a lender as collateral for a loan?

(b) GENERAL INTANGIBLES

Section 9-106 defines "general intangibles" as meaning "any personal property (including things in action) other than goods, accounts, chattel paper, documents, instruments, investment property, rights to proceeds of written letters of credit, and money." Thus, the concept of "general intangible" serves as a catch-all category for intangible property rights not falling within the definition of an "account." Consider the limits of that definition in light of the next case.

CRICHTON v. HIMLIE PROPERTIES

Supreme Court of Washington, 1986.
105 Wash.2d 191, 713 P.2d 108.

UTTER, Justice.

This matter has been certified to this court from the United States District Court for the Western District of Washington. See RCW 2.60.010-.030; RAP

16.16. The parties dispute the proper security classification of assignments of a vendor's interest in real estate contracts. The appellants contend the assignments are "contract rights" and, thus, exempt from the Uniform Commercial Code (U.C.C.) filing requirement under the recently eliminated exception, R.C.W. 62A.9-302(1)(e). We disagree and hold for the respondents that the security interest in a real estate contract is a "general intangible" and, therefore, subject to the filing requirement. The effect of our holding is to make the appellant-creditors general unsecured creditors in the ensuing bankruptcy proceeding.

On May 11, 1981, the assignor-respondent, Himlie Properties (Assignor) sought relief under Chapter 11 of the Bankruptcy Code (11 U.S.C. § 101 et seq.). This led to a stay of all proceedings against Assignor. On June 15, 1983, the assignee-appellants, Helen and Frank Crichton, who held notes from Assignor secured by assignments of real estate contracts, sought relief from the stay by filing an adversary proceeding in the United States Bankruptcy Court for the Western District of Washington. The Official Creditors' Committee intervened and filed a third party complaint and counterclaim against all similarly situated real estate contract assignees. There being no factual dispute, both parties moved for summary judgment.

The bankruptcy judge granted the creditors' committee's summary judgment motion. He held that the assignments were "general intangibles" and had to be filed pursuant to RCW 62A.9-302 to be perfected. Thus, the Crichtons and other third party defendants (together, "Assignees") were not secured creditors. In re Himlie Properties, Inc., 36 B.R. 32 (1983). Assignees appealed to the federal district court and subsequently moved to certify to this court the issue of the U.C.C. article 9 classification of the assignments. Pursuant to RCW 2.60.020, the federal district court certified the following question to this court: In Freeborn v. Seattle Trust & Savings Bank, 94 Wn.2d 336 [617 P.2d 424] (1980), the Washington State Supreme Court held that a vendor's interest in a real estate contract given as collateral was subject to the provisions of Article 9 of the Uniform Commercial Code. Article 9 provides different rules and procedures for different classifications of collateral. In this case the issue is whether a real estate contract given as collateral is a "general intangible" or a "contract right" under the provisions of Article 9.

The stipulated facts are these: Assignor engaged in the business of selling and financing real estate. Assignees are not in the business of assigning real estate contracts. Assignees loaned money to Assignor. "* * * [a]s part of each transaction, [Assignor] executed a Seller's Assignment of Real Estate Contract and Deed as security for the loan. These documents were prepared by [Assignor] and recorded pursuant to RCW 65.08.070 with the appropriate county auditor." Record on Appeal, Stipulation 3. None of Assignees filed a financing statement relating to the original vendor's interest in the subject real estate contract. That interest is subject to article 9 of the U.C.C., RCW 62A.9-101 et seq.

With one possible exception, not significant here, we find Judge Treadwell's analysis to be correct and agree with the authorities cited. The review committee for article 9, in broadening the § 9-106 term "accounts" to include "contract rights," understood that contract rights differed from "accounts" only in that the former had not been earned by performance. See discussion of 1972 amendments, U.C.C. app. 2, topic E-8, at 886 (Official Text, 1978). Further, we note that the committee declined, at the same time, "to broaden the definition of accounts to include all rights for the payment of money," preferring the more limited definition which included "only traditional accounts arising from the sale of goods or services, and not miscellaneous rights for the payment of money." U.C.C. app. 2, topic E-15, at 888. This implies that "contract rights" were also viewed as arising from the sale of goods and services.

Concededly, the category "general intangibles" was originally intended "primarily to cover rights in intangibles * * * which are neither rights to payment nor rights arising under contracts * * *" (Italics ours.) 1B P. Coogan, J. McDonnell & N. Gordon, Secured Transactions Under the Uniform Commercial Code § 15.05, at 15-19 n.1 (1983). Nevertheless, contrary to creditors' contention, "general intangibles" included "miscellaneous rights for the payment of money." U.C.C. app. 2, topic E-15, at 888. Given the narrow scope of "contract rights" implicit in the committee's treatment of the term in 1972 and the much broader scope of "general intangibles," we agree with Judge Treadwell's analysis of the disputed classifications.

* * *

We hold that a security interest in a real estate contract is a "general intangible" and subject to the filing requirement.

NOTE ON "PAYMENT INTANGIBLES" AND "COMMERCIAL TORT CLAIMS"

Unlike the rule pertaining to accounts and chattel paper, Article 9 currently contains no provision that would subject *sales* of intangible property rights to the creation and perfection requirements of Article 9. As Chapter 4 mentions, Revised Article 9 creates a new category of collateral referred to as a "payment intangible," defined in Revised § 9-103(c) as "a general intangible under which the account debtor's principal obligation is to pay money." The scope provision would then be expanded to include sales of payment intangibles as well as accounts and chattel paper. However, to avoid interference in the high-volume, high-velocity world of loan participation transactions, Revised § 9-308A(3) provides that a sale of a payment intangible may be perfected without filing. See PEB Study Group UCC Article 9 Report, at 47 (1992).

In addition, Revised Article 9 limits the exclusion for a transfer of any claim arising in tort so as not to include a transfer of a "commercial tort claim." Revised § 9-112(d)(12)(A). Presently, all tort claims are excluded from the scope of Article 9. See § 9-104(k). The term "commercial tort claims" is intended to encompass the tort claims of organizations and business-related tort claims of individuals (claims not involving bodily injury or death). See Revised § 9-102(a)(9). The ability to take an effective security interest in commercial tort claims is limited in two respects. First, no such interest may arise in the absence of a specific reference to "tort claims" in the security agreement. Revised § 9-111(e). Second, a creditor will only be permitted to take an effective interest in existing, not after-acquired, tort claims. Revised § 9-204(b)(2).

SECTION 4. PAPER

(a) CHATTEL PAPER

1 G. GILMORE, SECURITY INTERESTS IN PERSONAL PROPERTY 378-79 (1965).

"Chattel paper" is a novel term coined by the Code draftsmen to describe a species of property which had previously managed to exist without a name. The simplest illustration of what is meant is the pre-Code conditional sale contract, used with or without a separate note for the price. It will be remembered that the "instrument" definition excludes "writings" which evidence both a money claim and an interest in property. The writings thus excluded show up as "chattel paper," when the accompanying property interest relates to "specific goods": "chattel paper" might be described as a "secured instrument." The reason why the draftsmen felt it necessary to invent, or at least to christen, this new species of intangible relates to the provisions on perfection and priority. As we shall see presently, "chattel paper" occupies a sort of halfway house between the pure intangibles, on the one hand, and "instruments" on the other.

BOSS, LEASE CHATTEL PAPER: UNITARY TREATMENT OF A SPECIAL KIND OF COMMERCIAL SPECIALTY, 1983 Duke L.J. 69, 83-84 (1983).

Lease financing is the second step in a two-step transaction. First, the lessor transfers the right to use and possess the goods under an ordinary lease, which is sometimes represented by a lease document. The lessor then assigns the lease to a financer, in a second and distinct transaction to which Article 9 applies. In Code parlance, the lessor-assignor is the "debtor," the financer-assignee is the "secured party," and the lessee in the underlying lease transaction, who is obligated to make rental payments, is the "account debtor."

When a lease is assigned by the lessor to a third party, the assignment transaction can take any of numerous forms. The assignment may be part of an outright sale of the lease in return for operating capital. Although the parties may not intend to create a security interest, Article 9 governs this transaction because it applies to "any sale of chattel paper," and leases generally fit the definition of chattel paper. The drafters included sales of chattel paper in Article 9 because these sales, like secured loans, are a form of commercial financing, and often the sale of chattel paper is indistinguishable from its assignment as security. The assignment may also be made to secure "payment or performance of an obligation," as is the case if the lessor assigns the lease to a creditor as collateral for a loan. This transaction is intended to create a security interest and is also covered by Article 9.

UCC § 9-105(1)(b)

"Chattel paper" means a writing or writings which evidence both a monetary obligation and a security interest in or a lease of specific goods * * * .

IN RE DILLARD FORD, INC.

United States Court of Appeals, Eleventh Circuit, 1991.
940 F.2d 1507.

[Ford Motor Credit floor planned inventory of Dillard Ford, a Ford dealer. Under the arrangement, Ford Credit made two types of loans. The first, the inventory loan, consisted of payments Ford Credit made to the manufacturer for automobiles delivered to the dealer. When the dealer sold a car to a customer, the customer either paid cash or purchased under a retail installment sales agreement. If the customer paid cash, the dealer would take as much of the cash as necessary to satisfy the advance under the inventory loan for that vehicle and pocket the balance as profit. If the customer purchased under a retail installment sales contract, Ford Credit made a series of advances under the second type of loan—the chattel paper loan.

Under the second type of loan, Ford Credit took the paper from the dealer, and made an advance sufficient to pay off the inventory loan on the vehicle, paid a portion to a dealer reserve account that dealer maintained with Ford Credit, and paid what was left to the dealer.

A simplified transaction illustrates this typical automobile dealer financing arrangement. On May 1 Dealer bought a new Ford from Ford Motor for \$15,000. Ford Credit paid Ford Motor \$15,000, thereby generating a \$15,000 advance under the floor plan loan. On May 2 Dealer sold the car to a customer for \$16,000, \$500 of which was a down payment, and the balance of which was payable in 48 monthly installments. The customer signed a retail installment sales agreement promising to make the payments and granting Dealer a security interest in the vehicle to secure the obligation. That same day Dealer took the paper to Ford Credit and "assigned it" or "sold it" or "granted a security interest in it" to Ford Credit. Whatever form this transfer of the paper took does not matter, because form notwithstanding, Article 9 governs. See § 9-102(1)(b). Ford Credit then paid Dealer \$15,500 for the paper. That \$15,500 payment was divided, part of it went to satisfy the inventory advance of May 1; part of it went into a DPW (Dealer Proceeds Withheld) account, as security against customer default, and the balance went to Dealer.]

JOHNSON, Circuit Judge.

* * *

A. The Dealer Proceeds Withheld Account

One of the two disputes in this case involves the dealer proceeds withheld (DPW) account. The DPW account is held by Ford Credit to cover any losses that it incurs when it provides the financing for a consumer's purchase of a car. The bankruptcy and district courts held that while Ford Credit had a security interest in the DPW account, it failed to properly perfect this security interest. The trustee argues that the lower courts erred because there was no security interest in the DPW account. Ford Credit argues that the lower courts erred because the security interests were properly perfected.

1. Definitions

Before it is possible to determine whether there was a security agreement or whether this agreement was properly perfected, we must first determine the proper definitions, under Article 9 of the Uniform Commercial Code, of each component part of this transaction. Clearly the dealer creates, and then sells to Ford Credit, chattel paper when the customer enters an agreement to finance a purchase of a car. According to the Uniform Commercial Code, chattel paper is "a writing * * * which evidence[s] both a monetary obligation and a security interest in [a] specific good[ ]." U.C.C. § 9-105(1)(b). Neither party seriously disputes the fact that these consumer financing contracts are chattel paper.

It is also obvious that any security interest in the DPW account constitutes a security interest in a general intangible. A general intangible is "any personal property * * * other than goods, accounts, chattel paper, documents, instruments, and money." U.C.C. § 9-106. Nonetheless, both parties erroneously assume that the DPW account is an account. An account is a "right to payment for goods sold * * * or for services rendered which is not evidenced by an instrument or chattel paper," U.C.C. § 9-106. The dealer's contingent right to the money in the DPW account is a right to payment for the sale of chattel paper. The sale of chattel paper is neither the sale of a good nor the rendering of a service. Compare U.C.C. § 9-105(1)(b) (defining chattel paper) with U.C.C. § 9-105(1)(h) (defining goods). It also is clear that Ford Credit's obligation to repay the dealers is neither a document, see U.C.C. § 9-105(1)(f), an instrument, see U.C.C. § 9-105(1)(i), nor money, see U.C.C. § 1-201(24).

In order for Ford Credit's security interest in the DPW account to be valid against the trustee in bankruptcy, the security interest must comply with two basic requirements. First, the security interest must attach to the property in order to be enforceable. U.C.C. § 9-203. Second, the security interest must be perfected in order to prevail over a trustee in bankruptcy's claim in a priority battle. U.C.C. § 9-301(1)(b) and § 9-301(3).

2. The Security Agreement

A security interest attaches when three conditions have been met. First, "the debtor[, Dillard Ford, must sign] a security agreement which contains a description of the collateral." U.C.C. § 9-203(1)(a). Second, "value [must be] given." U.C.C. § 9-203(1)(b). Third, the debtor [must have] rights in the collateral." U.C.C. § 9-203(1)(c).

The lower courts were correct in concluding that a security interest has attached to the DPW account. The financing agreement, which was signed by both parties, contains a description of the collateral in that it states that Ford Credit has a security interest in the DPW account. Value has been given in that Ford Credit gave the dealer money to finance its inventory. Finally, the debtor has rights in the collateral, albeit the rights are contingent.

3. Perfection

The lower courts held that this security interest is not enforceable against the trustee in bankruptcy because it was not properly perfected. See U.C.C. § 9-301(1)(b) and § 9-301(3). Ford Credit filed a UCC-1 financing statement which stated that Ford Credit had a security interest in Dillard Ford's general intangibles and in other property rights owned by the dealer. The lower courts found that this financing statement was inadequate because it was too vague to place other hypothetical creditors on notice.

The lower courts are mistaken in their reading of Article 9 of the Uniform Commercial Code. A financing statement is sufficient if it includes (1) the name and address of both the creditor and debtor; (2) "a statement indicating the types, or describes the items, of collateral;" and (3) the debtor's signature. U.C.C. § 9-402(1). There is no dispute that this financing statement complied with the first and third requirements of section 9-402. The only dispute is over the second requirement. The question presented in this appeal is whether this financing statement's use of the term "general intangibles" complies with the description requirement found in section 9-402. We hold that it does. Section 9-402 allows a secured party to file a financing statement which describes the property only by its "type." Although the term "type" is not defined in the Uniform Commercial Code, it is clear from the usage of the term in section 9-401(1) that a type of collateral is, for example, goods, accounts, chattel paper, general intangibles, etc. Moreover, the official comments state that the drafters of the UCC envisioned the filing system to be only a "notice filing" system which provides broad notice to other creditors. Later creditors who find the broadly worded financing statement are expected to inquire into the exact terms of the security agreement by reading the agreement or obtaining assurances from the debtor or creditor. U.C.C. § 9-402 official comment 2. Finally, the Georgia Supreme Court has stated, in dicta, that section 9-402 is to be read in a manner consistent with official comment 2.

PROBLEM

On February 1, Locke sells his home to Hobbes for $150,000. The terms of the sale are that Hobbes will pay $50,000 in cash at closing and deliver his promissory note for the balance to be secured by a first mortgage on the property. Subsequently, Locke decides that he needs cash and approaches the Devonshire Bank about a loan. The bank is willing to extend a $80,000 credit to Locke provided that Locke transfers the Hobbes note and mortgage as collateral. Do these writings constitute chattel paper within the meaning of § 9-105(1)(b)? Does Article 9 apply to this transaction at all? See §§ 9-104(j) and 9-102(3). If so, how would you classify the collateral? How, if at all, would it change your answer if the transaction had involved an installment land contract for the purchase and sale of the house rather than a note and mortgage? See Security Bank v. Chiapuzio, 304 Or. 438, 747 P.2d 335 (1987).

(b) DOCUMENTS

INTRODUCTORY NOTE

Students new to the area are frequently confused by the use of the term "document" referring to one of the categories of collateral under Article 9. In most cases, the reference is to a "document of title" as defined in § 1-201(15). Conceptually, it is not inaccurate to think of a document of title as simply a receipt issued by a bailee, such as a carrier or a warehouseperson, temporarily in possession of goods owned by another. The most frequently encountered documents of title thus are the bill of lading (§ 1-201(6)) and the warehouse receipt (§ 1-201(45)). The relationship among parties to a transaction involving the storage and transport of goods under a document of title is governed by Article 7 of the UCC. Like instruments, documents of title may be negotiable or nonnegotiable, depending on whether the document provides that the goods covered by the document are to be delivered to bearer or the order of a named person. See § 7-104(1). As discussed in the next two excerpts, documents of title play a vital role in facilitating domestic and international sales transactions; thus it is essential that Article 9 provide a mechanism for financing goods when they are in the hands of a bailee who has issued either a negotiable or nonnegotiable document therefor.

FARNSWORTH, DOCUMENTARY DRAFTS UNDER THE UNIFORM COMMERCIAL CODE, 84 Banking L.J. 189, 191-97 (1967), reprinted from 22 Bus. Law. 479 (1967).

Many domestic and some foreign sales of goods are made on open credit, with payment to be made in 30, 60 or 90 days. But credit must be bargained for and a seller lacking faith in the buyer's credit may refuse to agree to a credit term. In the absence of such an agreement, the Code provides that the buyer must pay when he receives the goods. In the simplest case, where the seller and the buyer carry out the exchange face to face, five consequences follow. First, the seller is assured of payment when he gives up control of the goods. Second, the buyer is assured of control of the goods when he pays. Third, the seller finances the transaction only until the goods leave his hands. Fourth, the buyer finances the transaction only after the goods reach his hands. And fifth, the buyer can inspect the goods before he pays.

When the parties are at a distance the situation changes and some means must be found to give each party a measure of the advantages which he enjoys in the simple face-to-face exchange. The traditional method is the documentary exchange, calling for payment by the buyer against a draft with a bill of lading attached. The immediate purpose of this discussion is to inquire into how the Uniform Commercial Code affects such a transaction.

* * *

Shipment of the Goods. When the parties have agreed to a documentary exchange, the seller will ordinarily place the goods in the hands of a carrier, obtaining a negotiable bill of lading to his own order. According to the Code, the effect of this "shipment under reservation" is to reserve in him "a security interest in the goods". Beyond this, the bill of lading must satisfy the requirements of the sales article, Article 2, of the Code. * * *

The seller, having obtained the negotiable bill of lading to his own order, then attaches it, together with an invoice and any other documents required by the contract, to a sight, or demand, draft for the amount due him drawn by him as drawer upon the buyer as drawee to the seller's own order. * * * The seller then indorses the draft and bill of lading and takes them to his bank.

Collection of the Draft. The bank, known as a "collecting bank" and more specifically as the "depositary bank", is required to "present or send the draft and accompanying documents for presentment", which it will normally do by forwarding them through "customary banking channels". Most important, it will treat the draft as a "collection" item rather than a "cash" item. Checks, the most common items handled by banks, are dealt with in bulk as "cash" items on the assumption that they will be honored in the overwhelming majority of cases; provisional credits are entered immediately for a check at all stages of the collection process and automatically become final without further action upon payment by the drawee bank. Documentary drafts, on the other hand, are handled as "collection" items and dealt with individually, rather than in bulk, and since no assumption is made that they will be honored, no credits, not even provisional credits, are given until the item has been paid by the buyer. Ultimately the draft will reach the "presenting" bank, which will undertake to present the documentary draft to the buyer.

The presenting bank will know the identity and location of the buyer, who will be indicated on the bill of lading as the person to be notified of the arrival of the goods as well as on the draft as the drawee. Unless otherwise instructed, the bank may make presentment to the buyer by sending him a written notice that it holds the item. In the event that the buyer does not honor the draft before the close of business on the third banking day after the notice was sent, the bank may treat it as dishonored. The buyer may, however, within this time require exhibition of the draft and documents by the bank so that he can determine whether it is properly payable. If direct presentment is made to the buyer, instead of presentment by notice, it must be made at the place specified in the draft, or if there be none at his place of business or residence, and he then has until the close of business on that day to pay. Absent contrary instructions, a collecting bank may have an additional day "in a good faith effort to secure payment"; it may also be excused for delay caused by circumstances beyond its control.

As already pointed out, under the face-to-face transaction, which the documentary exchange is designed to supplant, the buyer had the right to inspect the goods before paying for them. Since the goods will normally travel much more slowly than the documents, they will not ordinarily be available for inspection at the time that the buyer is required to pay under the rules just discussed. Therefore, absent agreement to the contrary, the buyer has no right to inspect the goods before he pays when the contract provides for payment against documents of title, except in the case, to be discussed later, where payment is due only after the goods are to become available for inspection. Indeed, the negotiable railway bill of lading typically bears the legend: "Inspection of property covered by this bill of lading will not be permitted unless provided by law or unless permission is indorsed on this original bill of lading or given in writing by the shipper." The Code goes on to prove that where, as in the transaction under discussion, the contract calls for payment before inspection, even the non-conformity of the goods does not, with rare exceptions, excuse the buyer from paying. But it makes it clear that such payment does not amount to an acceptance of the goods by the buyer and that the buyer retains his right to inspect the goods upon delivery and all of his remedies against the seller for breach of contract. He merely loses the opportunity to inspection before payment, an opportunity that gave him the advantage of refusing to pay, rather than the disadvantage of having to sue to recover his payment, in the event of a non-conformity.

Since the draft under discussion is a sight draft, the buyer is called upon to pay, rather than to accept it, before he gets the documents. Only when the draft is payable more than three days after presentment may the presenting bank release the documents against the buyer's acceptance rather than his payment. * * * The proceeds received from the buyer are then remitted by the presenting bank through banking channels.

When the buyer honors the draft, he receives the bill of lading. When the goods arrive, he is notified by the carrier and surrenders the bill of lading in return for the goods. At this point the buyer will be able to inspect the goods. Should he find them to be defective, his only recourse will ordinarily be to journey to the seller's jurisdiction and there litigate the issues of breach and damages.

DOLAN, GOOD FAITH PURCHASE AND WAREHOUSE RECEIPTS: THOUGHTS ON THE INTERPLAY OF ARTICLES 2, 7, AND 9 OF THE UCC, 30 Hastings L.J. 1, 2-3 (1978).

Historically, documents of title such as warehouse receipts facilitated the practice of storing and transporting commodities. More recently, the receipt has taken on significant marketing and financing features.

The Marketing Function

For some purchasers, delivery is not an essential part of the purchase transaction. Grain dealers, for example, frequently purchase from producers and sell to industry consumers without moving the grain from the elevators to which the producers delivered it for drying and storing after harvest. Customarily these buyers and sellers effect such transfers by negotiable warehouse receipts. The producer obtains the receipt, which describes the grain according to industry standards; the grain dealer then purchases the receipt and transfers it, perhaps through a series of buyers, to a buyer who desires to ship or otherwise take possession of the grain. This last purchaser then surrenders the receipt to the elevator and takes delivery. The result is that the parties have achieved the marketing of the grain without incurring unnecessary transportation expenses.

Similarly, in the cotton industry a producer will deliver cotton to a gin for processing and storing. The gin will issue a negotiable receipt for the cotton with a sample attached. Brokers then display the samples to buyers who may be located in markets distant from the gin. Upon receipt of a satisfactory offer, the broker forwards the receipt with a draft through banking channels. When the purchaser honors the draft the bank delivers the receipt; the purchaser, unless he desires to resell the cotton without taking possession, will surrender the receipt to the gin and take delivery of the goods. Again, the receipt simplifies the marketing process and saves transportation costs.

The Financing Function

In transactions similar to the foregoing illustrations, market conditions or production schedules may force a buyer to hold a commodity. During that interval the buyer owns a valuable asset but cannot utilize it and, therefore, may seek to borrow against it. Lenders will grant credit on the security of the stored commodity by taking the negotiable warehouse receipt. When the borrower finds a buyer for the commodity or is prepared to use it in its own production process, the borrower will pay off the loan, obtain the receipt from the creditor and surrender the receipt to the warehouse against delivery of the goods.

These models illustrate typical patterns through which business people employ warehouse receipts to save transaction costs and to achieve liquidity. The models also forecast the potential conflicts in these commodity paper transactions. With respect to each purchase, for example, there is the classic tension between the purchaser, on the one hand, and the seller's secured lender, on the other. Conflicts between purchasers and lenders claiming an interest in the same goods may also arise because some sellers will enter into a contract of sale with more than one buyer or grant a security interest to more than one lender.

HENDRIES, INC. v. AMERICAN EXPRESS CO.

Supreme Court of New York, Appellate Division, 1971.
316 N.Y.S.2d 554, appeal dismissed, 324 N.Y.S.2d 92.

MACKEN, Justice.

December 19, 1967 appellant Banque de Commerce et de Financement Bancofin S.A. (Bancofin), a Swiss bank, issued an irrevocable letter of credit in favor of Mercantile Commodities Corporation (Mercantile) at the request and for the account of appellant B.N.S. International Sales Corporation (B.N.S.) for the ostensible purpose of financing a purchase by B.N.S. from Mercantile of some 15,000 cartons of an imported ice cream and bake mix. Under the letter of credit

Bancofin agreed to pay sight drafts to the extent of $255,075 presented by Mercantile on or before December 29, 1967 provided the drafts were accompanied by a commercial invoice, insurance certificates, and negotiable warehouse receipts 'endorsed to the order of a New York bank, at the option of Bancofin' covering the mix to be purchased by B.N.S. which was then stored in a warehouse of defendant National Cold Storage Co. (National).

Thereafter, Mercantile duly presented its sight draft to appellant American Express Company (American), designated by Bancofin as its agent, together with the stipulated documents including an invoice evidencing sale of the mix by Mercantile to B.N.S. and negotiable warehouse receipts endorsed to the order of American. The draft was honored. Bancofin advised American that the receipts were to be the source for repayment of the moneys advanced to Mercantile under the letter of credit and instructed American to release the receipts to B.N.S. or to any party designated by B.N.S. upon payment of the amounts allocated by Bancofin to each receipt.

Respondents contracted to purchase from B.N.S. quantities of mix of the same brand as that covered by the warehouse receipts held by American, Hendries 4,000 cartons on December 11, 1967 and Peter Pan Ice Cream Company 2,100 cartons on April 3, 1968. The contracts called for future delivery. The location of the goods was not specified nor were there any other indicia of identification of specific merchandise. By November 1968 B.N.S. had delivered 3,459 cartons to Hendries and 700 cartons to Peter Pan at which time B.N.S. failed to deliver the remaining 541 cartons to Hendries and 1,300 cartons to Peter Pan. Upon learning that a lot of 1,941 cartons, the exact number allegedly undelivered to respondents, was stored in National's warehouse and that the receipt covering it was held by American, respondents commenced these actions as against American to recover possession of the warehouse receipt which at the time was the only unredeemed receipt remaining in American's possession. Subsequently, Bancofin was made a party defendant; B.N.S. confessed judgment and is bankrupt, and the actions were discontinued against National.

Special Term granted respondents summary judgment awarding them possession of the warehouse receipt and the respective quantities of goods claimed thereunder. Appellants' cross motions for summary judgment were denied. In the meantime and shortly after commencement of the actions respondents had obtained possession of the warehouse receipt and mix by replevin pursuant to CPLR 7102.

With the exception of the ordering dates and amounts, both actions involve identical issues of law and fact and the parties have so treated them. At issue is whether respondents as buyers in the ordinary course of business (U.C.C. § 1-201(9)) acquired title superior to appellants'. While apparently conceding that on their face the documents evidence an extension of credit to B.N.S. to finance the purchase of mix from Mercantile, respondents assert that in fact the purchase was fictitious and the intent of the parties was to secure payment of a direct loan by Bancofin to B.N.S., thereby creating a 'security interest' within the purview of Section 9-307 of the Uniform Commercial Code. They claim that in any event appellants 'entrusted' possession of the mix to B.N.S. as defined by Section 2-403 of the Code. Unless these contentions have merit, the documents submitted give Bancofin title to the mix and the right to its possession. Delivery of the warehouse receipts to Bancofin's agent American gave it possession just as effectively as if the mix had been transferred to another warehouse of its choice. As was said in Moors v. Kidder, supra, 106 N.Y. p. 40, 12 N.E. p. 819: '* * * where a commercial correspondent, however set in motion by a principal for whom he acts, advances his own money or credit for the purchase of property and takes the bill of lading in his own name, looking to such property as the reliable and safe means of reimbursement up to the moment when the original principal shall pay the purchase price, he becomes the owner of the property instead of its pledgee, and his relation to the original mover in the transaction is that of an owner under a contract to sell and deliver when the purchase price is paid.'

* * *

In support of the claim that appellants entrusted possession of the mix to B.N.S. it is said 'defendants permitted B.N.S. to send instructions to the warehouse with respect to disposition of the goods' and 'defendants permitted B.N.S. to contract to sell the goods to plaintiffs and others and to represent that it owned the goods and that it could make delivery at the warehouse'. In support of these conclusions respondents submit evidence of a sale by B.N.S. to one Fountain Foods, Inc. and three letters from B.N.S. to National dated September 27, 1968 requesting National to release to Hendries on three future dates 1,894 cartons of mix contained in three separate lots.

Upon examination it is found that the Fountain Foods sale was made over a month before the Bancofin transaction and it may be noted that in contrast to the contracts between B.N.S. and respondents, the Fountain Foods contract provided for delivery 'as soon as possible' and that the merchandise was 'available immediately' at a specified warehouse of National. From respondents' papers it appears that, far from being permitted by appellants, the letters from B.N.S. to National were sent at respondents' insistence and National refused to turn over the goods. While not specifically so stated, it may be gathered from the record that the mix described in the letters was eventually delivered to plaintiffs after payment to American as required by the Bancofin agreement.

Respondents point to a letter allegedly sent by B.N.S. to American (receipt of which American denies) directing American to release to respondents the mix here at issue. The letter is dated coincidentally with the commencement of these actions and aside from the legal conclusions contained therein, the agreement with Bancofin is confirmed by the direction that transfer of title be 'against payments only'. The evidence not only fails to establish, but effectively negates that possession of the mix was entrusted to B.N.S. The facts here bear no resemblance to instances where a true owner gives physical and visible possession of goods to a known dealer of similar merchandise.

The orders appealed from should be reversed on the law with costs and disbursements and the judgments entered thereon vacated. Respondents' motions for summary judgments should be denied and summary judgment granted appellants awarding them possession of the warehouse receipt or, in the alternative, judgment for the value of the goods thereby represented in an amount to be determined by the Court below. * * *

NOTE ON *HENDRIES*

The important point in *Hendries* for the moment is that it illustrates the bill of lading and the warehouse receipt as vehicles for marketing and financing goods. A subsidiary point relates to the way in which the Code facilitates sound commercial practices. Ask yourself whether Hendries or the bank was in the better position to protect itself from the conflicting claim. Hendries paid for goods that it never saw; without taking delivery; without inquiring whether the goods were pledged to a bank, as imports often are; and without obtaining a negotiable document covering them. The bank maintained control of the goods by holding the documents that stood for them.

Professor Skilton has argued that while the result in *Hendries* is correct, the analysis is wrong. See Skilton, *Buyer in Ordinary Course of Business Under Article 9 of the Uniform Commercial Code*, 1974 Wis. L. Rev. 1, 49. Skilton felt that title was not material but that a buyer relying on § 9-307(1) cannot defeat a holder to whom a negotiable document has been duly negotiated. Such a holder is the good faith purchaser of Article 7. See § 7-502. Under the Skilton analysis, that good faith purchaser is protected from the buyer in ordinary course rule of § 9-307(1) by virtue of a provision in Article 9 that makes Article 9 rules subject to the rights of the good faith purchaser of Article 7. See § 9-309. In other words, under § 9-309, Skilton maintained that the Article 7 good faith purchaser (the holder to whom a negotiable document of title has been duly negotiated) trumps the Article 9 good faith purchaser (the buyer in ordinary course). Note that under either the court's analysis or Professor Skilton's analysis, the method of financing imports under letters of credit survives. In fact the import financing arrangement described in *Hendries* remains quite common.

(c) INSTRUMENTS

INTRODUCTORY NOTE

Article 9's definition of an "instrument" in § 9-105(i) is neither limited by nor coincident with the concept of negotiability. Unlike Article 3, where the use of the term "instrument" is limited to negotiable instruments (§ 3-104(b)), Article 9 encompasses both negotiable and nonnegotiable instruments. On the other hand, as discussed in the materials that follow, it excludes negotiable securities and other forms of investment property. The quintessential "instrument" for purposes of Article 9, as elsewhere, is the promissory note.

EXPLANATORY NOTE ON CONTEMPORARY USES OF PROMISSORY NOTES

A common form of instrument, the promissory note is usually associated with a borrowing transaction, and indeed most financial institutions and financing sellers require that their borrower/buyer's obligation be evidenced by a promissory note meeting the § 3-104(a) requirements for negotiability. Despite being negotiable in form, often these notes simply rest in the lender's vault until maturity. Sometimes, however, lenders will pool their loans and sell participations to other lenders or in the securities markets. Because of the effective elimination of the holder in due course doctrine in consumer transactions, and more effective mechanisms, such as credit reporting, to assure a note's quality, the concept of negotiability in respect of instruments has become less important during the last half of the twentieth century.

In addition to routine borrowing transactions, promissory notes are used in a number of other contexts as well. A bank certificate of deposit, for example, is nothing more than a promissory note issued by a bank to its customer. See § 3-104(j). These, too, may be negotiable or nonnegotiable in form. In addition, promissory notes are often used as part of the financing of a limited partnership syndication. These transactions usually involve risky business undertakings that cannot be financed through conventional lending sources, such as banks and allied financial institutions. Therefore, the promoters of the venture will generate "venture capital" by forming a limited partnership, or other limited liability entity, and syndicating (selling) fractional interests in the entity to numerous small investors willing to speculate on the high stakes enterprise. To make the transaction more palatable to investors, the syndicators may require that only a portion of the initial investment be paid in cash. The balance of the obligation will then be paid with a negotiable promissory note, typically backed by a standby letter of credit from the investor's bank. The syndicators can then use these notes, made more valuable by the letters of credit which assure payment upon an investor's default, as collateral for a loan from a conventional financial institution. Limited partnerships, financed in this manner, were very popular in the 1970s and early 1980s as tax shelters, ventures designed to generate deductible depreciation and losses far in excess of the amount of cash invested by individual investors. After the Tax Reform Act of 1986, those kinds of investment became much more risky and less attractive, but limited partnership syndications involving the use of promissory notes continue to the present.

Another transaction, of much more recent origin, which also requires the use of negotiable promissory notes involves the practice known as *forfaiting*. In these transactions, exporters of goods will take negotiable notes from their foreign buyers. After shipment, the seller will negotiate the notes, without recourse, to a local bank where the buyer is located, known as the "forfaiting bank." The bank will then enforce the note against the buyer when it comes due. From the exporting seller's point of view, the arrangement allows the seller to offer credit to its foreign buyers, but because the indorsement of the notes is made "without recourse," the seller avoids the risk of the buyer's default and assures itself of prompt payment of the purchase price. The forfaiting bank makes its money on the difference between the face amount of the note and what it pays the seller. Moreover, because the promissory notes are transferred by negotiation, the bank takes free of any defenses the buyer may have arising out of the underlying sales transaction.

CORAL PETROLEUM, INC. v. BANQUE PARIBAS (IN RE CORAL PETROLEUM, INC.)

United States Bankruptcy Court, Southern District of Texas, 1985.
50 B.R. 830.

[Coral Petroleum was the payee of a $30 million promissory note from Tricentrol Resources. The Tricentrol Note was expressly made "nonnegotiable" and restricted assignment except by pledge to a bank approved by Tricentrol Resources. Coral did pledge the note to First National Bank of Chicago ("First Chicago"), an approved bank, as security for a $27 million credit accommodation. Subsequently, Coral entered into a loan agreement with Banque Paribas ("Paribas") which, as security for the loan, took a blanket security interest in all of Coral's assets, including instruments and general intangibles. Paribas properly filed a financing statement which included "general intangibles" as part of the collateral description. After Coral filed for protection under chapter 11 of the Bankruptcy Code, an action was brought by Coral to have Paribas' interest in the Tricentrol Note set aside under Bankruptcy Code § 544(a)(1). The court ruled that Paribas was not in possession of the Tricentrol Note by virtue of First Chicago's possession. However, Paribas argued that the Tricentrol Note should be classified as a general intangible, in which case Paribas' interest would be perfected by virtue of its filed financing statement and immune from avoidance under § 544(a)(1).]

MANUEL D. LEAL, Bankruptcy Judge.

* * *

An instrument is defined in U.C.C. § 9-105(1)(i) as:

> a negotiable instrument or a certified security or any other writing which evidences a right to the payment of money and is not itself a security agreement or lease and is of a type which is in ordinary course of business transferred by delivery with any necessary indorsement or assignment.

A general intangible is defined in U.C.C. § 9-106 as:

> any personal property (including things in action) other than goods, accounts, chattel paper, documents, instruments and money.

The question of whether a particular document qualifies as an instrument under the U.C.C. is a question of law. * * *

The parties agree that the Tricentrol Note is not negotiable because it is not payable to bearer, and it is not a certified security. However, Coral alleges it is an instrument because it evidences a right to the payment of money and is not itself a security agreement or lease. The Banks' argue that the note is not an instrument because of its limitations on transferability and its unique nature, that is, its extremely limited incorporation of the law of the United Kingdom, in so far as the definition of excluded subsidiaries.

The language "of a type which is in the ordinary course of business transferred by delivery with any necessary endorsement or assignment" is to be "construed broadly to include any writing which is treated as a token of the rights it represents and therefore is normally delivered to any person to whom the rights are transferred." First National Bank in Grand Prairie v. Lone Star Insurance Co., supra at 533. In that case, the bank argued that a certificate of deposit which bore the restrictive legend "non-negotiable" prevented the certificate from being transferred in the ordinary course of business by delivery or endorsement. The court rejected this argument and held as a matter of law that the certificate is "of a type which is in ordinary course of business transferred by delivery with any necessary indorsement or assignment" because "it may easily be delivered by one party to another in the course of a commercial transaction." Id. at 534. The Arkansas Supreme Court relied heavily on the First National Bank case when it ruled, under Arkansas law, that "the fact that the certificates were non-negotiable and non-transferable in no way prevents them from being instruments." General Electric Co. v. M & C Manufacturing, Inc., 283 Ark. 110, 671 S.W.2d 189, 190 (1984). * * * A commentator has suggested that the test to determine whether a writing is transferable in the ordinary course of business turns on what professionals ordinarily would do to transfer an interest in the claim evidenced by the writing in question. Harris, Non-negotiable Certificates of Deposits: An Article 9 Problem, 29 U.C.L.A.L.Rev. 330,372 (1981). The test turns on findings as to the current usage of the market place. Id. If professionals who deal with a writing attach importance to possession of the writing, then the law likewise should attach significance to possession. Id. at 376.

* * *

The Bank's argument that the Tricentrol Note is a general intangible must be rejected for the parties have cited no caselaw to support this view. The Second Circuit has stated:

> The drafters of the Code classified collateral mainly according to the nature or use of the underlying entity, rather that the character of its ownership at any given time. Significantly, the examples of "general intangibles" given in the official comments are all types of property that are inherently intangible.

Feldman v. First National City Bank, 486 F.2d 367, 372 (2d Cir.1973).

* * *

PROBLEM

Appleby's Appliances sells televisions, refrigerators, microwave ovens, and other home appliances to consumer purchasers. Frequently, Appleby's will sell these items to customers on credit. In those cases, Appleby's always obtains a signed promissory note from the customer and, in instances where the customer's credit report reveals a delinquency within the last three years, Appleby's also reserves a security interest in the item or items subject to the credit sale. In order to meet its current cash needs, each month Appleby's "discounts" notes generated during the month to Central National Bank for 85% of cash value. The 15% discount represents a combination of time value of money and the anticipated default rate by Appleby's customers. Just recently, Appleby's filed for bankruptcy. The trustee in Appleby's bankruptcy case has filed a complaint to have Central Bank's interest in the outstanding unpaid notes set aside under Bankruptcy Code § 544(a) as an unperfected security interest. In order to evaluate its position, Central Bank has contacted you and asked that you respond to the following questions.

(a) Are these transactions subject to Article 9 at all?

(b) If so, how are the customer promissory notes classified for collateral purposes?

(d) INVESTMENT PROPERTY

INTRODUCTORY NOTE

Debt and equity securities issued by corporations and other forms of business organization like limited partnerships, were originally made subject to Article 9. In most instances, it was assumed that the investment interest would be represented by a certificate, usually negotiable in form, and thus properly classified and treated in the same manner as negotiable instruments. By the middle of the twentieth century however, people in the financial community became convinced that, in the future, investment rights would no longer be evidenced by a formal, written certificate. Anticipating this development, in 1977 the drafters of the UCC recommended that the states move the law governing security interests in investment securities, both certificated and uncertificated, out of Article 9 and into a newly revised Article 8, dealing with "Investment Securities." The reason for that change, which is still the prevailing law in some states, is discussed in the next excerpt, and its consequences are explored in the case that follows. As it happens, however, the much expected shift to uncertificated securities as the norm in the financial world never materialized. Instead, most broker-dealers and banks dealing in securities today simply hold the securities they purchase for customer accounts through a centralized depository. Therefore, in the vast majority of cases, a physical certificate is never delivered to the customer. This has eliminated the "paperwork crunch" that at one time threatened the industry. Recognizing that commercial practices had evolved differently from what had been contemplated in the late 1970s, in 1994, the drafters took steps to bring investment securities back under Article 9, but subject to a very different set of rules from those that pertain for other forms of collateral, thus creating a new property classification under Article 9 known as "investment property." We consider investment property, a term that actually encompasses more than just investment securities in the traditional sense, at the end of this section.

ARONSTEIN, HAYDOCK & SCOTT, ARTICLE 8 *IS* READY, 93 Harv. L. Rev. 889, 890-94 (1980).

I. History of the 1977 Amendments

The "paperwork crunch" in the securities industry in the 1960s almost brought that industry to a standstill. A number of committees of the American Bar Association's Section of Corporation, Banking, and Business Law had individually addressed themselves to various aspects of the problem. In 1971, the Section Council decided to form a Committee on Stock Certificates (the Committee), made up of representatives of all other interested committees. The Committee was charged with recommending what legislation, if any, was desirable to facilitate the elimination or reduction in use of negotiable stock certificates and with submitting drafts of such legislation. One of the Committee's principal recommendations was that a legal framework to govern the relationships, rights, and duties of issuers and other parties who deal with uncertificated securities was an absolute prerequisite to the development of any system that could effectively dispense with certificates.

Article 8 of the pre-1977 U.C.C. was a comprehensive statute that set forth a coherent legal framework for "securities." But, by its very terms, a "security" was an "instrument" and, when no instrument existed, article 8 had no application. The legal position of the issuers, buyers, and sellers of uncertificated stock was addressed by neither article 8 nor any other part of the U.C.C.

Notwithstanding the absence of a governing statute, a substantial volume of quasi-certificateless stock had been utilized by mutual funds and the growing dividend reinvestment plans. Transactions in this stock, typically between the issuer and the owner, were justified by assuming that the owner's certificate was being held by the issuer or the transfer agent for the owner's benefit. So long as those transactions were confined to two parties, the assumption sufficed. But when a third party appeared, such as a lender or buyer who wanted to acquire an interest in the stock, the only safe procedure was to demand that a real certificate be issued to the owner and then to seek refuge in the legal certainties of article 8.

The developing depository system was another approach to the problem. By immobilizing certificates under the control of a securities depository, which became the nominal owner, transfers and pledges could be effected by entries on the depository's books, without certificate delivery. Indeed, in the intervening years, the depository system has enabled the securities industry to handle, quite effortlessly, a volume of trading which, a decade ago, would have engendered chaos. But even the depository system has its paperwork problems. Safekeeping facilities, deliveries between depositories and issuers, deliveries among depositories, and deliveries between depositories and nonparticipants are all time-consuming and expensive procedures that could be eliminated or greatly reduced by a truly certificateless system. Furthermore, the benefits of the depository system, as presently constituted, are available only to brokers, banks, and other institutional investors. The individual investor who chooses not to deposit his securities with a broker or custodian bank must continue to employ stock certificates to implement the majority of his transactions.

The committee did not conclude, as some had suggested, that the legislated elimination of certificates was the only answer to the industry's problems. Rather, it concluded that the development of a truly certificateless system was one of several promising approaches that were not mutually exclusive. More important, it concluded that the full potential of certificateless systems could not be realized, or even tested, absent a suitable framework of commercial law. It was that framework that emerged as the 1977 amendments.

The Committee's report, published in 1975 after several years of study and deliberation, contained a draft of the Committee's proposals for amendments to the U.C.C. That draft was submitted for consideration by the PEB which, in turn, referred it to its 3-4-8 Committee for study. After careful scrutiny and substantial revision by the 3-4-8 Committee, the proposed amendments were examined and further revised by the full PEB at several two-day sessions. The proposals were then reviewed before the Council of the American Law Institute, the 1977 annual meeting of the ALI and, in both 1976 and 1977, the National Conference of Commissioners on Uniform State Laws (NCCUSL). A number of suggestions were received at each of these presentations and many were ultimately incorporated in the proposed statute. After a final revision by the NCCUSL Committee on Style, the amended statute was published as part of the U.C.C. Official Text. Contrary to Professor Coogan's implication that the 1977 amendments were intended to spring "from the minds of the draftsmen onto the statute books," they were rather "the product of an extensive period of examination, criticism, and revision" extending over several years—a process in which Professor Coogan, as a member of the PEB and ALI, had ample opportunity to and did, in fact, participate.

II. The Initial Premise—Parallelism

One cannot properly evaluate either the drafters' approach or their product without first analyzing the objective they sought to attain. Article 8 had established a reasonably satisfactory legal framework with which the securities industry had learned to live quite comfortably. The primary problem was mechanical—how to eliminate or reduce the delivery of specific pieces of paper that necessarily accompanied virtually every securities transaction. The legal problem was secondary—how to structure the relationships of the parties in the absence of those pieces of paper upon which the existing legal framework was based. Early in its deliberations, the committee determined that its objective, the elimination or reduction in the use of certificates, could best be attained by preserving, as nearly as possible, the existing legal relationships.

The fundamental decision to parallel existing law was not based on a lack of imagination nor on any unwillingness to depart from the seemingly easy path of following established practice. Rather, it was based on the considered judgment that, if uncertificated securities were to have any significant impact on the use of certificates, their most important attribute would be commercial acceptability.

Little would be achieved by inducing newly organized corporations to experiment with the issuance of uncertificated stock. Real progress would result only when the giant publicly held corporations could be persuaded to issue their stock in uncertificated form and, even more importantly, when the constituents of the industry—brokers, buyers, sellers, and others—could feel comfortable about holding and dealing with it. In the Committee's view, no uncertificated system, however appealing in theory, had much chance of widespread adoption unless the prospective issuers and shareholders perceived that they could use it with a degree of confidence and comfort comparable to that provided by certificates.

There is another, more practical, reason for parallelism. Even assuming that uncertificated securities will some day totally displace certificates, the process of transition will inevitably span a period of years or even decades. During that period, both forms of securities will necessarily coexist within the same issues. Whether to employ one form or the other is a decision that should be based solely on considerations of cost and efficiency, and not on which form produces a more advantageous result for a party to a particular transaction. If, for example, the use of certificates were to produce a stronger legal position for the secured lender, knowledgeable lenders would likely attempt to negotiate the use of certificates as a condition of the transaction, despite the additional cost and effort that might be entailed. If, as many believe, significant economies can be obtained by the elimination of certificates, the realization of these savings should not be impeded by avoidable disparities in the legal consequences.

Had the Committee adopted the view that it was free to disregard current law and practice in favor of theoretical purism, it might have produced a statute that would have been more agreeable to many of its own members. It would not, however, have produced a statute expressly designed "to facilitate the elimination of negotiable stock certificates"—the task with which it was charged.

F.D.I.C. v. W. HUGH MEYER & ASSOCIATES, INC.

United States Court of Appeals, Fifth Circuit, 1989.
864 F.2d 371.

PATRICK E. HIGGINBOTHAM, Circuit Judge.

In 1982, Hugh Meyer signed an agreement pledging some stock to the First National Bank of Midland. The pledge agreement entitled the bank to a security interest in the dividends upon the stock, but neither the bank nor the FDIC, the bank's successor in interest, registered the pledged shares in the bank's name. As a result, dividends from the pledged stock were delivered to Meyer. Among these dividends was a stock dividend worth about $500,000. Meyer eventually pledged these dividend shares to his law firm, Grambling & Mounce, to secure payment of a $125,000 retainer. Meyer then went bankrupt. His total indebtedness to the bank is in the neighborhood of $3 million. First Midland became insolvent and went into receivership. The FDIC sued Meyer and Grambling & Mounce to get the dividend shares. The district court held that the law firm had a perfected security interest in the shares up to the amount of its retainer, and that the FDIC was an unsecured creditor of the Meyer estate. The

FDIC appeals. Because we find that possession is essential under Texas law to obtain a secured interest in securities, and because the bank never obtained possession of the contested securities, we affirm.

* * *

II

The outcome of this case turns upon interpretation of Article 8 of the Uniform Commercial Code, as amended in 1977 and enacted into Texas law in 1983. See Tex.Bus. & Com.Code Ann.§8.101-8.408 (Vernon 1988 Supp.). That article governs security interests in securities. The key question is whether the Code recognizes a security interest in stock shares—more precisely, in the language of the code, "certificated securities"[1]—if the holder of the putative security interest has never possessed the shares. If not, then the FDIC is an unsecured creditor with respect to the dividend shares, and Grambling & Mounce is apparently the only secured creditor. Resolving this question of UCC law requires this court to write upon a rather clean slate.

There is a preliminary dispute between the parties as to the proper order of the issues. The FDIC asks the Court to consider first whether Grambling & Mounce took the stock as a bona fide purchaser, and then, if the Court finds that Grambling & Mounce did not, whether the FDIC had a perfected security interest in the stock. Meyer and the law firm contend that if the District Court was correct in its finding that the FDIC had no security interest in the stock and that Grambling & Mounce did have a perfected security interest, it is irrelevant whether or not Grambling & Mounce took without notice of any claims that the FDIC was trying to make.

We agree that we should first determine which, if any, parties developed security interests in the stock, and that we may thereby avoid the bona fide purchaser issue. * * *

Our analysis of this case thus depends upon the interaction between §§ 8.313(a)(1) and 8.321. The implication of these two sections is that no party in this case can have acquired a security interest in shares of (certificated) stock without having taken actual possession of the stock certificates. The district court reached the same conclusion. Although there is little case law on this point, the relevant decisions do seem to assume that physical delivery is necessary to create a secured interest in certificated securities under the relevant provisions of Article 8. See, e.g., United States v. Doyle, 486 F.Supp. 1214, 1220 (D.Minn.1980) (applying amended version of UCC as enacted into Minnesota law; the case involves a "financial intermediary"). Every security interest transferred for value pursuant to § 8.313(a)(1), and thus any security interest created in this case, is a perfected security interest.

* * *

---

1 Both the base stock and the dividend stock in this case were represented by certificates—i.e., were certificated. The UCC speaks of "security interests in securities." For the sake of clarity, we will refer to the contested dividend stock as stock, or as stock shares, except where it is necessary to invoke the exact language of the UCC.

The district court concluded from the evidence that Grambling & Mounce possessed the shares and developed a perfected security interest in them. First Midland never possessed the shares. In light of the analysis developed above, the district court's determination that Grambling & Mounce has a perfected security interest in the shares while First Midland is an unsecured creditor is both consistent with the law and supported by the evidence. The decision of the district court is therefore

AFFIRMED.

NOTE ON *W. HUGH MEYER*

The court correctly pretermitted the bona fide purchaser discussion in *W. Hugh Meyer*. If, in fact, the FDIC, as successor in interest to the failed bank, did have a perfected security interest in the stock dividend, the law firm could have used § 9-309 to defeat that interest, since under that provision nothing in Article 9 (the bank's security interest) could limit the rights of a bona fide purchaser as defined in § 8-302 of the pre-1994 version of Article 8. Under old Article 8, the bona fide purchaser took free and clear of adverse claims such as the bank's security interest. *W. Hugh Meyer* illustrates that prior to 1994, the filing of a financing statement was simply not an effective method for perfecting a security interest in certificated securities just as it is not a permissible means of perfecting a security interest in any other form of negotiable paper. As the next excerpt explains, after the 1994 revisions of Articles 8 and 9, filing does become a permitted means of perfecting a security interest in investment securities in most cases, but it is still not sufficient to defeat the rights of a "protected purchaser" within the meaning of § 8-303. See § 9-309.

---

4 J. WHITE & R. SUMMERS, UNIFORM COMMERCIAL CODE 170-74 (4th ed. 1995).

Because the 1977 [amendments to Articles 8 and 9] missed the target, the National Conference of Commissioners on Uniform State Laws has proposed a new Article 8 [and conforming amendments of Article 9]. This new Article 8 goes before the legislatures in 1995. Barring unforeseen opposition, we expect it to be the law everywhere before the end of the century. [By mid-1997, 30 states had already enacted Revised Article 8, Eds.].

The 1995 revision returns the rules on security interests in investment securities to Article 9. It proposes a new section 9-115. * * * Revised Articles 8 and 9 retain possessory pledge as a means of perfecting a security interest in a certificated security, but in the words of the reporter, they abandon "the conceptual structure of the common law pledge" as to security in general. "There is no requirement of a 'transfer,' 'delivery,' or any similar action, physical or metaphysical, for the creation of an effective security interest." The reporter describes the new system that will prevail when revised Article 8 is adopted as follows:

The perfection methods for security interests in investment securities are set out in revised 9-115(4). The basic rule is that a security interest may be perfected by "control." The concept of control, defined in Section 8-106, plays an important role in both Article 8 and 9. * * *

Except where the debtor is itself a securities firm, the filing of an ordinary Article 9 financing statement is also a permissible alternate method of perfection. However, filing with respect to investment property does not assure the lender of the same protections as for other forms of collateral, since the priority rules provide that a secured party who obtains control has priority over a secured party who does not obtain control. * * *

* * *

When perfection of security interests in stocks, bonds, and other investment property returns to Article 9 * * * the primary scope provision will be 9-115(4). It provides that perfection of a security interest in "investment property" is governed by the rules set out in 9-115. Investment property, in turn, is defined in 9-115(1)(f) as follows:

"Investment Property," means:

(i) a security, whether certificated or uncertificated;

(ii) a security entitlement;

(iii) a securities account;

(iv) a commodity contract; or

(v) a commodity account.

The last two terms in (f) are defined in 9-115(a) and (b) * * *. The first three (security, security entitlement, and securities account) are defined in 8-102 and 8-103. * * *

NOTE ON NEGOTIABLE PAPER AS COLLATERAL

Lenders that take a security interest in negotiable paper, i.e., negotiable instruments, negotiable documents, and securities, often rely on their rights not as secured parties but as good faith purchasers of the paper. The articles governing the paper, Articles 3, 7, and 8, give good faith purchasers sufficient protection to render the paper valuable collateral. Section 9-309 makes it clear, moreover, that nothing in Article 9 detracts from the rights afforded by the paper articles, though presumably, Article 9 may add to the rights of such holders.

This feature of Code law often strikes observers as typical pro-bank legislation, further evidence of the banking lobby at work in the legislative process. Some academics, tracing the rules to the common law, complain that judges sympathetic to the moneyed class fashioned these rules to the detriment of the debtor class. In the consumer setting, much of this criticism is telling, and reform in the legislature and the courts has virtually extinguished negotiability rules in that context. Whatever the motivation in the legislative or common law processes for extant negotiability rules, their result is to make paper attractive media for investment thereby loosening the purse strings of tightfisted lenders. For the merchant class, chronically starved for capital, this loosening of credit was and remains a godsend.

SECTION 5. PROCEEDS

(a) WHAT ARE PROCEEDS?

UCC § 9-306(1)

"Proceeds" include whatever is received upon the sale, exchange, collection, or other disposition of collateral or proceeds. * * * Money, checks, deposit accounts, and the like are "cash proceeds". All other proceeds are "non-cash proceeds."

FARMERS COOPERATIVE ELEVATOR CO. v. UNION STATE BANK

Supreme Court of Iowa, 1987.
409 N.W.2d 178.

LARSON, Justice.

Rodger Cockrum operated a farm and hog confinement operation in Madison County, Iowa. For several years financing for a substantial portion of the operation came from Union State Bank of Winterset (Union State). In February 1981, Union State loaned Cockrum a large sum of money and took a security agreement covering

> all equipment and fixtures, including but not limited to sheds and storage facilities, used or acquired for use in farming operations, whether now or hereafter existing or acquired; all farm products including but not limited to, *livestock, and supplies used or produced in farming operations whether now or hereafter existing or acquired* * * * . (Emphasis added.)

In December 1983 and January 1984, Cockrum entered into several purchase money security agreements with Farmers Cooperative Elevator Company (CO-OP) for livestock feed. See Iowa Code § 554.9312 (1983). For each transaction, CO-OP filed a financing statement with the Secretary of State, which stated:

> This is a purchase money security interest which covers Collateral described as all feed sold to Debtors by Secured Party and all of Debtors' feeder hogs now owned or hereafter acquired including * * * additions, replacements, and substitutions of such livestock, including

> all issues presently or hereafter conceived and born, the products thereof, and the proceeds of any of the described Collateral.

Cockrum defaulted on his obligations to both Union State and the CO-OP. CO-OP commenced an action against Cockrum seeking possession of collateral. (International Barter Corporation was also joined as a defendant, but its petition under chapter 11 of the Bankruptcy Act stayed further proceedings against it, and it is not involved in the present action.)

Union State filed a statement of indebtedness and requested that its security interests be established as a first security lien on Cockrum's hog inventory and any sale proceeds therefrom. CO-OP responded by filing an amendment to its petition, joining Union State as a defendant and alleging that its right to the hogs is superior to Union State's.

On CO-OP's motion to adjudicate law points, the district court ruled that Union State's security interest in the hogs was prior and superior to the CO-OP's. CO-OP has appealed from that decision.

We first address CO-OP's argument that its interest in the livestock and proceeds therefrom is superior to Union State's under section 554.9312(4). That section provides:

> A purchase money security interest in collateral other than inventory has priority over a conflicting security interest in the same collateral or its proceeds if the purchase money security interest is perfected at the time the debtor receives possession of the collateral or within twenty days thereafter.

"Purchase money security interests" are defined in section 554.9107:

> A security interest is a "purchase money security interest" to the extent that it is
>
> a. taken or retained by the seller of the collateral to secure all or part of its price; or
>
> b. taken by a person who by making advances or incurring an obligation gives value to enable the debtor to acquire rights in or the use of collateral if such value is in fact so used.

Union State concedes that CO-OP held a purchase money security interest in the feed. The question, however, is whether such a priority interest continues in livestock which consume the feed.

In essence, one who takes a purchase money security interest under section 554.9107(a) is the equivalent of the old conventional vendor—a seller who has, in effect, made a loan by selling goods on credit. See J. White & R. Summers, Uniform Commercial Code § 25-5, at 1043 (2d ed. 1980). Put more simply, a purchase money security interest "is a secured loan for the price of new collateral." Henderson, Coordination of the Uniform Commercial Code With Other State and Federal Law in the Farm Financing Context, 14 Idaho L.Rev. 363, 375 (1978). In this case, CO-OP took the purchase money security interests to secure the price of the feed, not the hogs. Consequently, by definition, CO-OP does not have a purchase money security interest in the hogs.

CO-OP, nevertheless, argues that their priority interest in the feed continues to be superior in the hogs pursuant to section 554.9203(3) because the hogs are "proceeds" of the feed. That section provides, "[u]nless otherwise agreed a security agreement gives the secured party the rights to proceeds provided by section 554.9306." Subsection 1 of section 554.9306 defines proceeds to include "whatever is received upon the sale, exchange, collection or other disposition of collateral or proceeds."

CO-OP contends that the "other disposition of collateral" language in section 554.9306 includes ingestion and the biological processes involved when livestock consume feed, and as a result, fattened livestock are proceeds of the feed they consume. Such an argument was rejected in a case on all four hooves, so to speak. In First National Bank of Brush v. Bostron, 39 Colo.App. 107, 564 P.2d 964, 966 (1977), the court emphasized that "[the livestock producer] received nothing when he disposed of the collateral by feeding it to the * * * cattle * * * the collateral was consumed, and there are no traceable proceeds to which the security interest may be said to have attached."

We agree with the result reached by the Colorado court. Ingestion and biological transformation of feed is not a type of "other disposition" within the contemplation of section 554.9306. For UCC purposes, the hogs are not proceeds of the feed.

* * *

AFFIRMED.

(b) THE SECURED PARTY'S RIGHT TO PROCEEDS

UCC § 9-306(2)

Except where this Article otherwise provides, a security interest continues in the collateral notwithstanding sale, exchange or other disposition thereof, unless the disposition was authorized by the secured party in the security agreement or otherwise, and also continues in any identifiable proceeds including collections received by the debtor.

PROBLEM

Rodney Rollins purchased a nontitled sailboat from Anchors Away Boats six months ago. Rodney paid $10,000 and financed the balance of the purchase price, some $40,000, by signing a five-year installment sales agreement with Anchors under which he also granted Anchors a security interest in the boat. Anchors perfected its security interest by properly filing a financing statement. Last month, Rodney traded the boat to Sally Sails in exchange for a high speed skiing boat that Sally had purchased a number of years ago for $65,000. Sally had no knowledge of Anchors' security interest and agreed to an "even swap." When Rodney failed to make his regularly scheduled monthly payment, Anchors went to repossess the sailboat. Its repossession agent reported that the boat was no longer in Rodney's slip at the Marina, although there was a power boat there, and that he was sure he saw the sailboat subject to Anchors' security interest in another slip registered to Sally Sails. Confused, but undaunted, the repo man grabbed the sailboat from Sally's slip. Sally is now demanding its return and threatening to sue for conversion if Anchors does not promptly comply. Anchors has now approached you with the following questions.

1. Will it be liable for conversion if it does not return the sailboat to Sally?

2. If not, can it also sue Sally for the deficiency if the sale of the boat does not generate enough money to pay off Rodney's loan?

3. Regardless of whether it must relinquish the sailboat, can it also seize Rodney's new ski boat?

4. If you conclude that Anchors does not have to return Sally's boat, does she have any claims against Rodney?

5. How would the situation be different if instead of exchanging the sailboat, Rodney had sold it to Sally for a check which Rodney had deposited into his bank account? In answering this last question, consider the following discussion.

(c) TRACING CASH PROCEEDS

Section 9-306(2) provides that a secured party's interest continues in proceeds, including cash collateral, as long as those proceeds are *identifiable*. If those proceeds are deposited in the debtor's general bank account into and from which other deposits and withdrawals are occurring on a regular basis, the proceeds, although they can be traced into the account, are arguably no longer identifiable (and therefore not subject to the secured party's proceeds security interest) since it is physically impossible to determine which of the commingled funds remaining in the account at any given time are the deposited proceeds and which are funds attributable to either the existing balance at the time of the proceeds deposit or subsequent nonproceeds deposits.

Nevertheless, in non-insolvency situations, most courts permit the secured party to claim an interest in the balance of the deposited proceeds which can still be "identified" under common law tracing principles, originally developed as a mechanism to provide an equitable remedy where, for example, a trustee has appropriated and commingled fiduciary funds. These tracing principles, derived from basic accounting conventions, establish a fictional rule for determining when subsequent account activities involve the funds in question. The most widely used tracing mechanism is the "lowest intermediate balance rule" (LIBR) which consists of two basic principles: (1) that withdrawals from a commingled depository account are deemed to come *first* out of unencumbered funds; and (2) subsequent deposits are *not* deemed to be in restoration of previously withdrawn encumbered funds. By way of example, consider a debtor that receives $1,000 in cash proceeds from the sale of the secured creditor's collateral. The debtor deposits that $1,000 in its general banking account which, just prior to the deposit, has an existing balance of $2,000. Thereafter, the debtor makes one withdrawal of $2,500, and an additional deposit of $500, leaving a balance of $1,000. If, at that point, the secured party makes claim to the account, its proceeds security interest would be limited to $500, the amount it could trace under LIBR. The $2,500 withdrawal would be deemed to come first from the $2,000 of unencumbered funds and thereafter from the proceeds. Thus, only $500 of proceeds would remain in the account and, under LIBR, the $500 deposit would not be treated as restoring the withdrawn encumbered funds. Finally, note that although Article 9 does not apply to security interests in deposit accounts if taken as original collateral (§ 9-104(l)), bank deposits that qualify as proceeds are subject to the Code in the manner herein described. The decision generally given credit as establishing these principles is Universal C.I.T. Credit Corp. v. Farmers Bank of Portageville, 385 F.Supp. 317 (D. Mo. 1973). As discussed in the Note which follows the next excerpt, Revised Article 9 proposes to bring deposit account financing under the umbrella of Article 9 in all cases.

BARNES, TRACING COMMINGLED PROCEEDS: THE METAMORPHOSIS OF EQUITY PRINCIPLES INTO U.C.C. DOCTRINE, 51 U. Pitt. L. Rev. 281, 340-42 (1990).

In the dispute between the secured party and the general creditor, the very nature of the fictional accounting device is to distinguish and to discriminate among levels of creditors. The unsecured creditor is lower in position under Article Nine. Article Nine tacitly recognizes the contract between the secured party and the debtor; in this recognition, the inherent result is a failure to recognize the unsecured parties' rights. The general creditor will go without payment to the extent that the secured party is paid. There is no random assignment of rights between creditors at the same level. If the lowest intermediate balance or some other accounting system is used, the secured party, to the extent that it establishes its right, will eliminate the right of the unsecured creditor. The whole basis of this elimination is not that the parties had an equal chance, but that the secured party is somehow entitled to greater rights than the unsecured creditor by virtue of its security agreement. This system of distinction is suspect.

One should be suspicious of the system because of its source in the commingling rule. Funds were traceable at common law in a system of trusts, constructive trusts and restitution because of fraud or other wrongdoing by the person on whom the trust was impressed or against whom restitution was granted. * * * In every case, the defendant was a wrongdoer. * * * In a commercial commingling case there is no wrongdoing. At most there is negligence by the debtor in commingling the account. * * * The secured party loses because of a foreseeable and rather ordinary risk of financing. He or she is unable to identify in species his or her collateral. As the secured party's proceeds are commingled, she comes closer to the position of a general unsecured creditor, that is, one who extends credit without the reliance upon any specific asset. It is only the fiction of accounting which ameliorates this inability to link the commingled fund to her collateral. The fictional accounting methods create by analogy the "real" link we would like to see. It is an analogy only. There is no direct relationship between the original collateral and the commingled mass. If this is true, there is no particular reason to favor the secured party. The secured party could have required the debtor to segregate the proceeds. Absent such an agreement, or unless there is a higher equity in the secured party supporting the common law of constructive trusts, there is little basis for granting a new link lost by commingling. While there may be such a link, the drafters did not articulate it. Professor Gilmore in his landmark treatise did not suggest one. Nor have any of the courts suggested such a link. They are simply relying, without analysis, upon the existence of a common law group of cases which draw an obviously flawed analogy. * * *

B. CLARK, THE LAW OF SECURED TRANSACTIONS UNDER THE UNIFORM COMMERCIAL CODE § 10.03[2], 10-45 to 10-46 (Rev. ed. 1993).

Even if the floating lien proceeds commingled in a bank account are generally protected under tracing principles, the debtor's insolvency can cause special problems.

* * *

[U]nder § 9-306(4)(d)(ii), the security interest is limited to an amount not greater than the total cash proceeds received by the debtor within 10 days before insolvency. This provision is confusingly worded, to say the least. No one knows for sure the meaning of "deposit accounts * * * in which proceeds have been commingled with other funds." Moreover, it is uncertain that the provision would stand up in bankruptcy, particularly when the 10-day rule enhances the creditor's position over what it would have been outside bankruptcy. In this regard, the provision might constitute an invalid statutory lien or preference. Finally, the 10-day rule is bad public policy because there is no good justification for giving the creditor either a more expansive position or more restricted security interest in bankruptcy under the 10-day rule than outside under tracing principles. In any revision of Article 9, the 10-day rule of § 9-306(4)(d) should be eliminated.[*]

NOTE ON DEPOSIT ACCOUNT FINANCING

Traditionally, a secured creditor's proceeds security interest in a debtor's deposit account, whether segregated or commingled, has been afforded priority over the depository bank's common law right of setoff against the account for amounts owed to it by the debtor. See Citizens National Bank of Whitley County

---

[*] Revised Article 9 indeed eliminates this provision. See Revised § 9-313(d) [eds.].

v. Mid-States Development Co., 380 N.E. 2d 1243 (Ind. Ct. App. 1978). One of the major changes proposed as part of the Article 9 revision process is to bring consensual security interests within the ambit of Article 9 and to permit perfection of that interest by control alone. See Revised §§ 9-310(a)(2), 9-312. One of the effects of this change will be to allow banks and other depository institutions to reverse this priority rule by simply reserving a prior security interest in customers' accounts in the original account documentation executed when the account is initially established. Moreover, Revised § 9-337(a) expressly subordinates a secured party's interest in a deposit account to "any right of recoupment and any right of set-off" to which the depository institution at which the deposit account is maintained is entitled under state law.

QUESTION

Suppose a secured party can trace the cash proceeds from its collateral *beyond* the debtor's bank account. For instance, if the secured party can show that the debtor wrote a check on encumbered funds to an open account supplier that had sold the debtor goods on 30 days credit, can the secured creditor assert a claim to those funds in the hands of the supplier? Would it make a difference if the check was written as a charitable donation to a local orphanage? How about if the proceeds were never deposited in the debtor's bank account, but instead consisted of a check received by the debtor from the sale of the secured party's collateral which the debtor simply indorsed over to the supplier in payment on the debtor's open account or to the orphanage as a donation? See § 9-309, Official Comment 2(c) to § 9-306, and PEB Commentary No. 7. How would your answer to this question be affected, if at all, under Revised § 9-329(b)?

SECTION 6. THE FUTURE DIRECTION OF ARTICLE 9

HARRIS & MOONEY,* A PROPERTY-BASED THEORY OF SECURITY INTERESTS: TAKING DEBTORS CHOICES SERIOUSLY, 80 Va. L. Rev. 2021, 2051-53 (1994).

It seems enough that security interests, under Article 9 and real estate law alike, are interests in property. The legal regime for security interest reflects property law functionally as well as doctrinally. We believe it follows that the law should honor the transfer or retention of security interests on the same normative grounds on which it respects the alienation of property generally.

* * *

---

* The authors of this article are the Reporters for the Drafting Committee to revise Article 9 [eds.].

The positive value of permitting debtors to give security freely and effectively suggests two important rules of thumb to be followed in the process of revising Article 9. First, the drafters should purge Article 9 of obstacles to the creation of effective security interests. Because there is nothing generally unsound or suspect about the creation of effective security interests, formalistic requirements that upset the intentions of the parties and prove to be traps for the unwary should be eliminated. Second, the scope of Article 9 should be expanded. Many of the common-law rules governing the creation of security interests in personal property are uncertain and cumbersome. Insofar as the creation of security interests is easier, less costly, and more certain under Article 9 than under common-law rules, expansion of the statute is likely to serve the overarching goal of effectuating the will of the parties. The drafters should add limitations and restrictions only when they are demonstrably warranted in particular circumstances. Moreover, the presumption against interference with party autonomy should expand to existing impediments (e.g., public notice requirements) as well as to proposed new ones.

NOTE ON THE SCOPE OF ARTICLE 9

Not everyone agrees that Article 9 should be expanded. One of the concerns with making it easier for secured lenders to take a "blanket" security interest in all of the debtor's assets is that it effectively renders the debtor "judgment proof" to claims by unsecured creditors, such as trade creditors, tort victims, employees, etc. This has led some commentators, including Professor Elizabeth Warren of Harvard, to argue that, despite the principle of free alienability of property rights, perhaps there ought to be some limits on a business debtor's ability to hypothecate all of its assets to a single creditor or that the same goal might be achieved by reserving some portion of the debtor's assets for unsecured creditors in the event the business fails. This notion that there ought to be some limit to the reaches of Article 9 draws powerful historical support from its principal drafter, Grant Gilmore, who—speaking in the context of assignments of future accounts—expressed the idea as follows:

> Considerations of policy and common sense suggest that there must be a limiting point somewhere. Borrowers should not be encouraged or allowed to hypothecate all that they may ever own in the indefinite future in favor of a creditor who is willing to make the loan now. * * * And ways should be found to penalize a lender who, after allowing his borrower to pile up an intolerable weight of debt, then claims all the assets of the insolvent estate, leaving nothing to satisfy other claims.

1 G. GILMORE, SECURITY INTERESTS IN PERSONAL PROPERTY § 7.12, 248-49 (1965). See also Woodward, The Realist and Secured Credit: Grant Gilmore, Common-Law Courts, and the Article 9 Reform Process, 82 Cornell L. Rev. 1511 (1997).

LoPucki, The Unsecured Creditor's Bargain, 80 Va. L. Rev. 1887, 1963 (1994). "Article 9 artificially and unjustifiably advantages the institution of security over unsecurity. It holds involuntary unsecured creditors to an entirely fictitious bargain. It holds voluntary unsecured creditors to the terms of security agreements to which they did not in fact agree and to which they did not have access. The terms of those agreements are binding regardless of how unreasonable they may be. This bizarre scheme subsidizes the institution of security, causing more secured lending than is optimal."

FINAL THOUGHTS ON SECURED CREDIT

It is helpful in analyzing questions of secured lending policy to identify the unsecured creditor, for the nature of that creditor affects evaluation of the manner in which the law treats him. The unsecured creditor we meet in case reports can be a pathetic creature: tort claimants, consumers who do not understand the Code's rules for creating a security interest, and enterprises whose clerks made technical errors in a financing statement. These parties often suffer in a way that strikes some as unfair. They are unsecured or unperfected not because they chose to be. In the case of tort, the claimant did not choose to have a claim; the consumer did not know how to secure himself; and the enterprise intended to be secured but loses by virtue of the technicalities of the filing rules.

In fact, these three characters are not representative of unsecured creditors. Unsecured credit is a major source of credit in the economy, but the unsecured creditors usually do not make claims against the assets of the businesses to which they extend credit. Most unsecured credit, trade credit extended by suppliers that sell on open account, is not asset based lending. The seller is relying not on the accumulated assets of the buyer but on the buyer's success as an enterprise, success that is reflected in the enterprise's credit reputation. Many, probably most, and perhaps all but a few, commercial enterprises have relatively few assets available for their creditors upon the demise of the enterprise. The strength of a commercial enterprise, unlike that of many consumers, lies not in its assets but in its value as a healthy enterprise that generates not the goods or services it sells but profits. Thinly capitalized businesses with little inventory and few accounts will find unsecured credit available as long as they are profitable and pay their suppliers. Inventory and account rich enterprises that have a history of slow payments will not find unsecured credit.

When an enterprise files a petition in bankruptcy, usually its trade creditors are not surprised; and if they are, the trade creditors usually have small losses. They may have a month's worth of deliveries, but probably that is all. Many of them will have switched the buyer to cash on delivery or a similar arrangement before bankruptcy ensues.

It may be a mistake, then, to fashion secured lending law with an eye to promoting unsecured credit without understanding that most unsecured credit is not asset based and does not depend on the availability of assets in the event of the debtor's insolvency. On the other hand, if the object of treating unsecured creditors in bankruptcy is to effect fairness for tort claimants, an insurance scheme might better address the need than allocating priorities in the debtor's assets. Whatever the object, it is best to keep in mind that most unsecured creditors were paid before the debtor called his bankruptcy lawyer.

PART III

PRIORITIES

INTRODUCTORY NOTE

Having a security interest in the debtor's property is valuable and important to a creditor if the debtor is unable to satisfy its obligation when it comes due. However, there can be multiple security interests in the same property and, as we have seen, there are ways other than by acquiring an Article 9 security interest that a party can obtain an interest in the debtor's property. If the debtor becomes insolvent, these claims in and to the same property must be sorted out in a more or less hierarchical fashion. Determining the relative order of claims involves the rules of priority, found both in the Code and, occasionally, under applicable non-Code law.

In this Part III we examine primarily the rules governing priority set out in Article 9. We begin by examining the rules governing a secured party's enforcement of a security interest, which itself reflects the priority that secured creditors enjoy over their unsecured counterparts. Enforcement does not depend on perfection, but in most (albeit not all) cases, the party enforcing the security interest will also be the party with first priority in the collateral. Perfection is the key to establishing priority under Article 9, and that is where we turn next. We then examine the rules that govern the battles for priority that occur between the holder of a perfected security interest under Article 9 and a wide variety of other claimants in the collateral. To facilitate your understanding of the detailed rules that control priority disputes, we have separated these various claimants into two broad categories. First, we consider priority among parties all claiming an interest under Article 9. Next, we shift focus and examine the rules governing priority battles between an Article 9 security interest and various other kinds of claimants, including buyers, lessees, nonconsensual lienors, and even the IRS.

There are many different justifications for specific priority rules. Some of these rules can be seen as protecting reasonable reliance interests, while others implement important policy considerations that arise outside of Article 9. In still other cases, the rules are simply "traffic rules"; it does not really matter what the rule is as much as that there is a clear rule by which everyone is bound. These rules promote certainty and efficiency, which are important values in commercial law. Sometimes, however, application of a clear rule will produce what seems to be an unfair result. This raises the question of the extent to which, if any, these rules ought to be imbued with a dose of equity as applied in specific cases. As you go through the priority rules, see if you can identify any common themes and, in particular, evaluate whether the rule satisfactorily resolves the tension that occasionally arises between certainty and equity.

Chapter 6

RIGHTS AND OBLIGATIONS ON DEFAULT

SECTION 1. EVENTS OF DEFAULT

INTRODUCTORY NOTE

A creditor that has taken an Article 9 security interest in the debtor's property has to be concerned with two sets of rights. First, the creditor must be concerned with her rights vis-à-vis the debtor to seize and sell the collateral in order to obtain payment of the debt should the debtor default in his obligations under the security agreement or the instrument(s) of indebtedness which are secured by the security agreement. Those rights, sometimes referred to as the secured party's *default rights*, are the focus of this chapter. In addition, however, the secured party must also be concerned with her rights vis-à-vis other creditors and persons claiming an interest in the collateral. These rights, which are the subject of Chapters 8 and 9, are sometimes referred to as the creditor's *priority rights.* Priority rights are established by *perfection*, the mechanics of which are discussed in Chapter 7. The secured party's rights to look to her collateral for repayment of the debt are governed by Part 5 of Article 9 and, in most cases, are triggered by the occurrence of "an event of default."

Default Paragraph in Standard Form Promissory Note

Upon default in payment of this Note or of any other indebtedness of the Borrower to Bank or if there is a default under any security agreement, mortgage, loan-agreement or document given in connection with the Collateral or if the security afforded by the Collateral at any time subject to any lien or security interest in the sole opinion of the Bank becomes insufficient, or if any material representation made by the Borrower to Bank for the purpose of obtaining credit appears to the Bank to be untrue, or the commencement of a case under any federal or state bankruptcy or insolvency law by or against the Borrower or if Borrower fails generally to pay its debts as such debts become due or if proceedings are taken to attach, garnish or levy on any deposits, credits, funds or other property of the Borrower or the Borrower fails to notify the Bank of any material change in its financial status, or if the Bank at any time for any reason deems itself insecure, this Note and all other indebtedness of the Borrower shall, at the option of the Bank, become immediately due and payable in full without notice, presentation or demand for payment, all such being hereby waived by the Borrower and in such event, it is agreed that the Bank may exercise all rights and remedies available to it under any security agreement, mortgage, loan agreement, or document relating to or otherwise securing any of the indebtedness of Borrower or, which may be available to Bank under the Uniform Commercial Code as in effect in the State of Michigan or other applicable law.

Default Paragraph in Standard Form Security Agreement

Default and Remedies

Whenever a Default shall be existing, each Note and all other Indebtedness may (notwithstanding any provisions hereof), at the option of the Bank, and without demand or notice of any kind, be declared, and thereupon immediately shall become due and payable, and the Bank may, without notice to Borrower, notify any parties obligated on any of the Collateral to make payment to the Bank of any amounts due or to become due thereunder and enforce all or any part thereof, or compromise or extend or renew for any period (whether or not longer than the original period), any indebtedness thereunder or evidenced thereby. Upon request of the Bank, Borrower will, at its own expense, notify any parties obligated to Borrower on any of the collateral, to make payment to the Bank of any amounts due or to become due thereunder. In addition, Bank may take possession of the Collateral and any records concerning same wherever they may be found, with or without process of law and may dispose of the Collateral or any portion thereof in any manner permitted by the Michigan Uniform Commercial Code or other applicable laws. Any notification of intended disposition of any of the Collateral required by law shall be deemed reasonably and properly given if given at least ten days before such disposition. Any proceeds of any collection or disposition by the Bank of any of the Collateral may be applied by the Bank in the order following to the reasonable expense of retaking, conserving, collection (by suit or otherwise) or disposing of (by sale or otherwise) the Collateral, including reasonable attorneys' fees and legal expenses incurred, and then to the satisfaction of all the indebtedness in such order of application, as Bank elects. After such application, Bank will account to Borrower for any surplus and Borrower shall remain liable to Bank for any deficiency.

MILLER, IS REVISION DUE OF U.C.C. ARTICLE 9, PART 5?, 44 Okla. L. Rev. 125-26, 128-29 (1991).

Default

The key concept under part 5 of U.C.C. article 9 is "default." Because article 9 of the U.C.C. does not define "default," the security agreement must state when default has occurred. Of course there is no difficulty in contemplating and reaching agreement on certain events as defaults—for example, if there has been a failure to pay as agreed. However, this and whatever else may constitute a default is a matter of agreement between the parties entering into the security agreement. Thus, if a creditor desires that a failure to pay either principal or interest, a failure to keep the collateral insured, a failure to pay taxes on the property that is collateral, or any number of other things should constitute a default, these events must be defined in the security agreement as defaults. If an event is not declared a default in the security agreement, the creditor may not have the right to use that event to invoke a remedy.

Common events of default specified in many security agreements include:

— any payment provided in the security agreement and in any note is not made when due;

— failure to perform any other obligation, or failure to abide by any other provision, in the security agreement;

— failure to make any payment due or to perform any other obligation in any other transaction between the debtor and the secured party, or any other party;

— if any warranty made to the secured party is breached, or if any representation or financial information given is false;

— if any of the debtor's property is subjected to levy, garnishment or other legal process, or if any interest of the debtor in the collateral is transferred by way of sale, security interest or otherwise without the prior written consent of the secured party;

— if any of the collateral is stolen, damaged or destroyed;

— when in the judgment of the secured party the collateral becomes unsatisfactory or insufficient in character or value and the debtor upon request fails to provide additional collateral;

— upon the death, dissolution, termination of existence or insolvency of the debtor, the appointment of a receiver over any part of the debtor's property, the occurrence of any assignment for the benefit of the debtor's creditors, or the commencement of any proceedings under any bankruptcy or insolvency law against or by the debtor;

— upon the happening of any of the above events to a guarantor of the debt; and

— any time the secured party in its sole discretion believes the prospect of payment or performance is impaired or that the collateral is in jeopardy.

The last event of default listed above is a general catch-all that allows a secured party to proceed even though no *specific* event of default may have transpired. An example might be an attempt by the debtor to sell the collateral to a third party, even though no sale has in fact yet occurred. A creditor should not, however, exercise rights pursuant to a claimed default under this general type of clause unless it reasonably believes a significant risk of nonpayment or loss of collateral exists as shown by prior or general experience. The reason is that all actions to enforce the security agreement must be taken in good faith.

Acceleration

After a default occurs, a creditor has the rights and remedies provided in article 9 and, except as limited by statute, in the security agreement. One right universally provided in installment contracts is the right of acceleration. Indeed, if it is not provided the creditor may well have to wait until each installment is due and not paid before a default occurs. Thus, any security agreement and note need an acceleration clause accompanying the default clause. The acceleration clause should provide that upon default the entire obligation becomes due and payable at the creditor's option without need to give notice to the debtor of the exercise of the option. It must be recognized, however, that generally courts do not view acceleration clauses with favor. * * *

Clearly, acceleration is likely to impose hardship on a debtor. While there is a right to redeem, the right to accelerate is unlikely to be exercised if the default itself is due to financial distress, as a majority of defaults are. It also is clear that few creditors immediately invoke acceleration and its consequences because workout returns usually are superior to the return on collection. Thus, many contracts have grace periods and rights to cure or to reinstate written into them. Even when the contracts do not contain these provisions, in many transactions workouts will be arranged. Finally, debtors often default due to circumstances beyond their control and, if given leeway, may be able to cure the default or abide by a restructured agreement. Thus, on balance, there appears to be reason to give the debtor who is likely to be in the inferior bargaining position the legal leverage to move negotiation in the direction of salvaging the transaction, rather than leaving that option with the secured party as the U.C.C. now does.

GREENBERG v. SERVICE BUSINESS FORMS INDUSTRIES, INC.

United States Courts of Appeals, Tenth Circuit, 1989.
882 F.2d 1538.

PER CURIAM.

Service Business Forms Industries, Inc. (Service Business) and Service Computer Forms Industries, Inc. (Service Computer), defendants, appeal the district court's order granting plaintiffs partial summary judgment on their claim for recovery of an accelerated debt allegedly due under Service Business' promissory note. The district court determined that there were no material issues of fact as to Service Business' default under the terms of the promissory note and that plaintiffs properly exercised their right to accelerate the unpaid principal balance and accrued interest. On appeal, defendants contend there are genuine issues of fact regarding each of its defenses.

* * *

Plaintiffs brought this action to recover the accelerated amount of the principal and accrued interest under the note. In its answer, defendants raised several defenses, including waiver, estoppel, and lack of default under the terms of the note. * * * Plaintiffs moved for summary judgment and, after a hearing, the district court granted partial summary judgment in their favor. The court found that the terms of the contract clearly designated the payments to be due on October 29th of each year, by virtue of the date of the note's execution and the fact that annual payments were calculated on the basis of a twenty-year amortization. The court further held that there were no material issues of fact as to waiver, estoppel, or default and found that Business Service had defaulted on its payment obligations, that the Trust had the right to accelerate the balance owing upon default, and that the Trust properly exercised its right to accelerate. * * *

On appeal, Service Business contends that there are several genuine issues of fact which precluded the granting of partial summary judgment. First, Service Business contends that it did not default on its obligations under the note because the document did not specify a date on which payment was due, and argues under Oklahoma law that payment was thereby due within a reasonable time. We disagree. Oklahoma statute dictates that contracts are to be interpreted according to the intent of the parties at the time the instrument was executed. Okla.Stat. tit. 15, §§ 152, 153 (1981). Intent must be determined by construing the contract as a whole, and the court must construe the contract so as to give effect to each provision. Amoco Prod. Co. v. Lindley, 609 P.2d 733, 741 (Okla.1980). The language of the note setting the date of final payment as October 29, 1992, and the method for calculating the amount of annual payments clearly indicate that the parties intended that payments were to have been made on the anniversary date of the note.

Second, Service Business asserts that plaintiffs did not accelerate the note in good faith. Service Business claims the duty of good faith arises both under the Uniform Commercial Code (UCC), Okla.Stat. tit. 12A, § 1-208 (1981), and under the common law doctrine of good faith in the performance of a contract. Section 1-208 provides: A term providing that one party * * * may accelerate payment or performance or require collateral or additional collateral "at will" or "when he deems himself insecure" or in words of similar import shall be construed to mean that he shall have power to do so only if he in good faith believes that the prospect of payment or performance is impaired. The burden of establishing lack of good faith is on the party against whom the power has been exercised. Id.; see also Mitchell v. Ford Motor Credit Co., 688 P.2d 42, 44-45 (Okla.1984) (acceleration by a secured party). In finding that plaintiffs properly exercised their power of acceleration, the district court implicitly found that the good faith requirement set forth in § 1-208 does not apply to notes that permit acceleration at the option of the holder upon default by the debtor. We agree.

The only Oklahoma case we have located which addresses the question of whether the good faith requirement under the UCC applies to acceleration on default clauses is Knittel v. Security State Bank, Mooreland, Okla., 593 P.2d 92 (Okla.1979). The case did not directly address the issue; however, it upheld a challenged jury instruction which stated that the good faith requirement under § 1-208 did not apply to an acceleration on default clause. Id. at 97. Because a court must determine whether a challenged jury instruction properly states the applicable law, see Big Horn Coal Co. v. Commonwealth Edison Co., 852 F.2d 1259, 1271 (10th Cir.1988), it logically follows that Knittel supports the position that the UCC good faith requirement does not apply to acceleration on default clauses.

Several states have similarly held that the UCC good faith requirement is not applicable when the acceleration clause is based on an event in the debtor's complete control. Because of the ruling in Knittel and the general consensus in other jurisdictions, we conclude that Oklahoma would not apply the good faith requirement in § 1-208 to the acceleration on default clause at issue in this case.

* * *

The Oklahoma Supreme Court has ruled on two occasions that an acceleration clause contained in a mortgage will not be enforced where the conduct of the mortgagee has been unconscionable or inequitable. Continental Fed. Sav. & Loan Ass'n v. Fetter, 564 P.2d 1013, 1019 (Okla.1977); Murphy v. Fox, 278 P.2d 820, 826 (Okla.1955). In Continental, the court denied a bank's request to accelerate and foreclose on a mortgage based on a due-on-transfer clause when the bank refused to consent to a transfer solely because the mortgagor would not pay a substantial transfer fee. The transfer fee was an additional condition unilaterally imposed by the bank and was not contained in the original mortgage agreement. The court held the bank's conduct in demanding additional payment was unconscionable and denied its requested relief.

In Murphy, the court refused to permit a mortgagee to accelerate the maturity of a promissory note because the court found that the mortgagee had attempted to hinder timely payment by the mortgagor and had encouraged its default. 278 P.2d at 824. The court determined that this conduct was motivated solely by the mortgagee's desire to accelerate the maturity of the entire debt and held that the technical default of tendering late payment of taxes was insufficient to justify acceleration when the mortgagee had acted unconscionably.

According to our reading of these cases, whether the Oklahoma court permits acceleration depends on the conduct of the mortgagee and whether he has dealt fairly with the debtor or has acted oppressively or unconscionably. This view is consistent with that of several other jurisdictions. See Phipps v. First Fed. Sav. & Loan Ass'n, 438 N.W.2d 814, 819 (S.D.1989) (an acceleration clause will be enforced absent fraud, bad faith, or other conduct on part of the mortgagee which would make it unconscionable to enforce the clause); Key Int'l Mfg., Inc. v. Stillman, 103 A.D.2d 475, 480 N.Y.S.2d 528, 530 (1984) (absent some element of fraud, exploitative overreaching or unconscionable conduct by the creditor, the court should enforce an acceleration clause), aff'd as modified, 66 N.Y.2d 924, 498 N.Y.S.2d 795, 489 N.E.2d 764 (1985); Bowen v. Danna, 637 S.W.2d at 564 (a court in equity can relieve a debtor from the hardship of acceleration based on accident, mistake, fraud, or inequitable conduct of the creditor); First Fed. Sav. & Loan Ass'n v. Ram, 135 Ariz. 178, 659 P.2d 1323, 1325 (Ct.App.1982) (same); Ciavarelli v. Zimmerman, 122 Ariz. 143, 593 P.2d 697, 698-99 (Ct.App.1979) (same).

Nothing in the record warrants an application of these equitable principles in the instant case. Plaintiffs did not exercise their option to accelerate after a considerable delay. See, e.g., Brown, 603 F.2d at 1379; Caspert v. Anderson Apartments, Inc., 196 Misc. 555, 94 N.Y.S.2d 521, 526 (Sup.Ct.1949). Nor did the default concern a technical, secondary obligation such as payment of taxes. Rather, the default violated the essence of the written agreement, timely payment of principal and interest. Finally, no evidence was presented that Greenberg attempted to hinder or otherwise cause the default so as to make his conduct unconscionable. Defendants had complete control over the event which triggered plaintiffs' right to accelerate. The mere fact that the plaintiffs' interest might not have been in jeopardy, without some misconduct on the part of the plaintiffs, does not warrant a refusal to enforce an acceleration clause which was a bargained-for element of the contract between the parties. Under the circumstances of this case, we conclude that there are no material issues of fact under the applicable Oklahoma law regarding the enforceability of the acceleration clause and the issue of good faith.

* * *

JENSEN v. STATE BANK OF ALLISON, 518 F.2d 286 (8th Cir. 1975). The bank loaned the debtor money under two promissory notes containing standard general insecurity clauses. The loans were secured by a security interests in the debtor's livestock. Upon learning that another creditor had filed a financing statement against the same collateral, the bank deemed itself insecure and set off the debtor's checking account. The existence of the other financing statement did not impair the bank's priority in the collateral, and after the debtor filed for bankruptcy the trustee in the debtor's case sought to recover the amount of the set off on the ground, *inter alia*, that the bank had not acted in good faith. Although the court agreed that the bank's deeming itself insecure was "clearly open to question, and its heavy-handed treatment of its customer without prior notification is cause for dismay," it upheld the lower court's determination that the bank had acted in good faith because of the absence of any finding of dishonesty on the bank's part.

UCC § 1-201(19)

"Good faith" means honesty in fact in the conduct or transaction concerned.

REVISED § 9-102(27)

"Good faith" means honesty in fact and the observance of reasonable commercial standards of fair dealing.

QUESTION

How would *Jensen* be decided under the revised definition of "good faith"?

SECTION 2. GENERAL CREDITORS' RIGHTS UPON DEFAULT

NOTE ON STATE COLLECTION LAW

Subject only to an unpaid seller's limited right of reclamation under UCC § 2-702(2), general unsecured creditors' only recourse in the event of default is to initiate suit against the debtor and reduce their claim to judgment. They may not help themselves to the debtor's property either before or even after reducing their claim to judgment. Rather, they must enlist the aid of the state, through an appropriate law enforcement agency, to execute on the judgment. In fact, unless and until the debtor's property is seized (levied upon) by an officer of the state pursuant to a court issued writ of execution, the judgment creditor has no interest in specific items of personal property owned by the debtor. In the meantime, unsecured creditors run the risk that the debtor will discharge his debt in bankruptcy or otherwise prove nonamenable to suit. They also run the risk of having their claims against the debtor's property subordinated to the claims of prior secured creditors and to the debtor's claim of *exemption* from execution for certain categories of property, real and personal. Each state, by statute or state constitution, has declared certain types of property, often up to a maximum dollar amount, to be immune from the claims of the debtor's creditors.

SUN COUNTRY DISTRIBUTORS OF LOUISIANA v. STARKEY

Court of Appeal of Louisiana, First Circuit, 1994.
637 So.2d 739.

EDWARDS, Judge.

The plaintiff, Sun Country Distributors of Louisiana, Inc., appeals a judgment which held that certain items seized by the Sheriff of Tangipahoa Parish are necessary tools or instruments of the defendant's trade and thereby exempt from seizure pursuant to LSA-R.S. 13:3881. After a thorough review of the record, we affirm.

The record establishes that the defendant, Greg Starkey, owned and operated Starkey Boat Works and manufactured fiberglass boats for various boat dealers around the state for approximately ten years prior to this litigation. Mr. Starkey testified that the manufacturing process employed by his company uses raw materials, a wax solution which is poured into a boat mold, and a chopper gun, which is used to spray a gel coat onto the boats.

In January, 1993, the plaintiff obtained a writ of fieri facias in an attempt to collect on a default judgment against the defendant, as a result of an action to collect on a promissory note. Pursuant to plaintiff's writ, the Sheriff of Tangipahoa Parish went to Starkey Boat Works and seized five boat molds[1] and a

---

[1] The molds seized were the following:
1—16' skiff mounted on wheels mold

Binks fiberglass spray unit, or a chopper gun. The defendant then filed a petition seeking to enjoin the sale of this equipment, claiming that the boat molds and chopper gun are necessary tools of his trade as a boatmaker and exempt from seizure.

Plaintiff's primary contention on appeal is that the trial court's conclusion is erroneous in light of the testimony of two persons, one a qualified expert in boatmaking, to the effect that fiberglass boats could be made without the particular equipment seized. Plaintiff contends that this testimony established that the equipment was not "necessary" to the defendant's trade.

The test of whether an object qualifies as a tool or instrument of the trade or profession under LSA-R.S. 13:3881 is whether or not the tool or instrument is necessary for the exercise of the profession, that is, whether or not the debtor will be prevented from exercising his trade or profession if he is deprived of the tool or instrument. The latter question turns upon the former, and the debtor cannot be deprived of the tools or instruments if the profession or trade cannot be practiced without them without severe hardship. Finley v. Graves, 393 So.2d 345 (La.App. 1st Cir.1980); Ladnier v. Villafranco, 525 So.2d 1191, 1193 (La.App. 5th Cir.1988).

Mr. Starkey testified that when the boat molds and chopper gun were seized, he essentially went out of business, because he cannot make the boats without this equipment. He testified that he imagined there is probably a way to make the boats without the molds and the chopper gun, but that he, personally, had never done so and he does not know how to do so. Mr. Starkey's brother who was an employee of Starkey Boat Works prior to the seizure, testified that it is possible to make a fiberglass boat by hand, without the molds and the chopper gun, but that this method could not be employed to make a profit, as it is time consuming and not cost efficient.

The plaintiff is in the business of distributing raw materials to boat builders. Mr. Anthony Chisesi, vice president of Sun Country Distributors, testified that the application of raw materials to a boat mold could be effectuated manually, without the use of a chopper gun. However, he admitted that the same work could be accomplished much more efficiently with the use of a chopper gun. Finally, Mr. Carl Burney, a qualified expert in boat building, testified that it is possible to make fiberglass boats without the use of boat molds and a chopper gun, but he, too, admitted that it would be a lot more time consuming and costly to make the boats by hand.

Plaintiff/appellant claims that the testimony of Mr. Chisesi and Mr. Burney establishes that the equipment seized is not "necessary" to the defendant's trade, since the boats can be made manually. We disagree. In Finley v. Graves, supra, we held that a word processor typewriter was necessary to the practice of law and exempt under the statute. In Finley, as in the case before us, the appellant argued

---

1—18' fantail mold
1—21' fantail deep v mold
1—21' tri hull mold
1—19' tri hull mold

that since there were other, less expensive means of typing, that the word processor typewriter which was seized was not "necessary" to the lawyer's practice. In Finley we rejected that argument. In this case, we reject it also. The record convinces us that it would be a severe hardship for Mr. Starkey to engage in his trade of making boats without the necessary equipment, just as we found it would be a severe hardship for a lawyer to practice his trade without a typewriter. Arguably, a lawyer's work could also be performed manually, as appellant argues Mr. Starkey's boats can be made. However, the exemption statute does not contemplate imposing such a severe hardship on a person's trade or profession.

For the foregoing reasons, we find no error in the trial court's judgment ordering the items seized from Mr. Starkey's business exempt from seizure. Accordingly, that judgment is affirmed; appellant is assessed all costs of this appeal.

AFFIRMED.

NOTES AND QUESTIONS

1. At common law, all of a debtor's property was available to satisfy his debts. What public policies can you identify that warrant the decision by state legislatures to enact statutes shielding certain kinds of property from collection efforts by the debtor's creditors? Should it matter who the debtor is or what kind of debt is involved?

2. Suppose a debtor signs a promissory note which contains a provision in the default paragraph of the note which provides as follows: *"Debtor hereby waives the right to claim as exempt any property in an action to enforce this Note by payee or any subsequent holder."* Is there any reason not to enforce this provision if debtor subsequently defaults on the Note and thereafter attempts to claim an exemption for his automobile up to the amount allotted under applicable state law? Does it make a difference if the payee of the note also took a security interest in the automobile to secure payment of the obligation represented by the note? See, e.g., Bankruptcy Code § 522(e).

3. Most states' exemption statutes limit exemptions not only by type (e.g., tools of the trade, the family bible, medical appliances, etc.), but by dollar value as well. Thus, not uncommonly, a state will grant an exemption for an automobile to the extent of $2,500 or a wedding ring to the extent of $5,000. What happens when the debtor owns exempt property but with a value *in excess* of the dollar value limitation? What method should be used to value exempt property and who should make the valuation?

4. Suppose Darrin Debtor has just had a large judgment taken against him by Cathy Creditor. Darrin has enough money sitting in his bank account to pay the judgment. He is worried, however, how he will provide for his family if his accumulated wealth is lost to Cathy. Therefore, Darrin uses the money in his bank account to purchase life insurance and annuity contracts which

are, in the state where Darrin resides, exempt without limitation. If Cathy contests Darrin's exemption claim, how should the court rule?

WARD, ORDERING THE JUDICIAL PROCESS LIEN AND THE SECURITY INTEREST UNDER ARTICLE NINE: MESHING TWO DIFFERENT WORLDS—PART I—SECURED PARTIES AND POST JUDGMENT PROCESS CREDITORS, 31 Maine L. Rev. 223-24, 226-29 (1980).

The clash between a creditor with a consensual security interest in personal property and a general creditor with a judicially created lien in the same property generates fundamental problems for the commercial lawyer. The respective rights of these two parties hinge upon a determination of priority. Because the interests of the parties are governed by distinct bodies of state law whose interrelationship remains unclarified, the resolution of priority problems in this context is difficult. Article Nine of the Uniform Commercial Code, which purportedly contains a comprehensive priority system, regulates the consensual security transfer, and a variety of independent state statutory provisions define the lien acquired by resort to judicial process.

* * *

A. Judicial Process Creditor

The judicial process creditor seeking to satisfy a favorable judgment has access to a range of post-judgment enforcement procedures, the most common of which are execution and levy, and garnishment in aid of execution. Alternatively, a creditor may commence a creditor's bill, an action rooted in equity, if assets are either concealed by the debtor or in such a form as to require the court's aid in realizing on them. If provided by statute, a summary procedure can be utilized for discovering and applying all of the debtor's assets. At some stage, these collection devices generate what is loosely referred to as a "lien" in favor of the initiating judgment creditor. Though in this context the word "lien" lacks exact definition, it generally marks the time at which the initiating creditor is afforded a measure of judicial protection against the interest of third parties in the debtor's property. Modern summary procedure remedies, which assume various forms from state to state, have a particularly ill-defined "lien" generating function.

B. Secured Party

Matched against the creditor with a judicial process lien is the secured party, whose interest in the debtor's personal property arises by agreement. Section 1-201(37) of the Commercial Code defines "security interest" broadly as "an interest in personal property or fixtures which secures payment or performance of an obligation* * *. The term* * * includes any interest of a buyer of accounts or chattel paper which is subject to Article 9." While the section 1-201(37) definition is broad enough to include the creditor who acquires a lien by resort to judicial process, Article Nine applies only to those security interests which are consensual. Section 9-102(1)(a) refers "to any transaction (regardless of its form) which is *intended* to create a security interest in personal property," and section 9-102(1)(b) refers to any *sale* of accounts or chattel paper. The official comments add by way of explanation that "[t]he main purpose of this Section is to bring all consensual security interests in personal property and fixtures under this Article .* * * ."

C. Judicial Process Creditor Versus Secured Party: Levying on Encumbered Chattels

The most common conflict between the judicial process creditor and the secured party occurs when the creditor seeks to satisfy a judgment out of the debtor's encumbered property. At common law the mortgagor of chattels held an equitable interest that was not subject to execution. Long before the Uniform Commercial Code, however, courts began to recognize that the mortgagor was the real owner of the chattel, and that encumbered personal property in his possession could be levied on and sold at execution. Codifying this approach, section 9-311 of the Code clearly acknowledges the creditor's right to reach the debtor's mortgaged property through the judicial process, but leaves to the law of each state the manner in which this access may be accomplished. In keeping with the free alienability principle of section 9-311, the Code rejects the common law notion that the secured party reserves some form of title in the chattel. Instead, the more precise concept of a "security interest" is adopted and refined by the rules governing consensual interests in Article Nine.

The enabling effect of section 9-311, however, should not be confused with the concept of priority. If the Article Nine secured party has priority over a judicial process creditor, the creditor's ability to realize on the collateral is severely restricted, although not entirely blocked. Although section 9-311 permits the judicial process creditor to encumber and sell the debtor's property (despite contrary provisions in the security agreement), the secured party with a prior interest (i.e. perfected before the creditor's lien arises) is well protected under Article Nine. Property sold in satisfaction of a judgment creditor's claim remains subject to the interest of a prior secured party. Some states protect the secured party even further by requiring that the judicial process creditor satisfy the senior secured party before sale. Failure to satisfy the secured party could result in the creditor's liability for conversion.

By contrast, the secured party with priority can foreclose and sell after the judicial process creditor obtains a lien under state law. Section 9-504(3) of the Code does not require the secured party to notify the judicial process creditor of the sale, or to satisfy the creditor out of any surplus generated. Therefore, unless the judicial process creditor can establish a right in subject property prior to the secured party's, his ability to recover on the judgment is significantly hampered. Priority is a critical initial question, the answer to which may establish the particular rights of the secured party and the judicial process creditor.

IN RE CONTINENTAL MIDWAY CORP.

United States District Court, District of Maryland, 1960.
185 F. Supp. 867.

CHESNUT, District Judge.

This petition to review an order of the Referee has required a close consideration of the Maryland law and practice with regard to determining whether the judgment creditor in this case, who claims priority in payment, validly acquired a lien on personal property of the judgment debtor as against the Trustee in Bankruptcy. The order of the Referee determined that the creditor did not effectively obtain a lien and therefore was not entitled to priority in payment over general creditors. The controlling facts of the case as contained in the certificate of the Referee, and not here substantially challenged by counsel for the judgment creditor, are as follows:

1. The Chenille Manufacturing Company, Inc., obtained in due course a judgment against the Continental Midway Corporation (now the bankrupt) for $1490.01 with interest and costs in the Court of Common Pleas of Baltimore City on July 19, 1956.

2. On July 26, 1956 counsel for the creditor issued a fi. fa. on the judgment and had it delivered to the sheriff for service. The next return day in the court was the first Monday of August 1956, and at that time the sheriff made a return of nulla bona on the writ.

3. On August 14, 1956 counsel for the judgment creditor delivered a second fi. fa. to the sheriff which again was returned nulla bona on the next return day, the first Monday of September 1956.

4. Again on September 11, 1956 counsel for the judgment creditor delivered a third fi. fa. to the sheriff, the return day for which was the first Monday in October 1956, and it also was returned nulla bona.

5. On November 23, 1956 the Circuit Court of Baltimore (an equity court) appointed receivers for the debtor corporation who promptly took possession of the assets. The involuntary petition in bankruptcy in this case was filed December 13, 1956. Subsequently the Trustee, having taken possession of certain personal property of the bankrupt, sold the property consisting of office furniture, fixtures and equipment located at 1500 N. Chester Street, Baltimore, Maryland, for the net sum of $1330.

6. On January 30, 1957 the creditor filed its claim as an unsecured creditor (that is, stating that it held no security for its claim) in the amount of $1519.96, representing the amount of the judgment plus interest and costs. On July 26, 1957 the creditor filed a petition alleging in substance that he was entitled to priority in payment by reason of a lien on the personal property above referred to which had been sold by the Trustee. And with respect to the fi. fa. issued September 11, 1956, it appears from correspondence filed in the case that the creditor requested or demanded that the sheriff levy on certain furniture and equipment in the premises 1500 N. Chester Street, alleged to be the property of the debtor. But the sheriff refused to do so saying that his deputy was informed

when he started to make such a levy that the property did not belong to the debtor, and the sheriff then declined to make the levy unless the creditor would take 'supplemental proceedings' in court or furnish the sheriff with an indemnity bond. This not being done the sheriff in due course returned this third writ of fi. fa. nulla bona. The Referee in his certificate stated that by virtue of testimony produced before him after the bankruptcy intervened, he found as a fact that as of September 11, 1956 there was office equipment and furniture in the premises 1500 N. Chester Street belonging to the debtor which could have been levied on by the sheriff. The Referee held hearings on the creditor's petition on September 19, 1957, August 6, 1959, which was adjourned until November 13, 1959, and finally on January 15, 1960, concluded the matter by the order of that date denying priority.

* * *

The contention of counsel for the Trustee is that even assuming that the issuance of a fi. fa. from the Clerk of the Court and the delivery of the same to the sheriff under Maryland laws constitutes a lien on personal property of the debtor thereafter levied and scheduled by the sheriff in due course of return, nevertheless as there was no actual levy in this case on any of the furniture of the debtor and no schedule made or returned, and more particularly because the return to the first and each of the subsequent fi. fas. made by the sheriff was nulla bona, therefore any inchoate lien which might have arisen on the issuance of the fi. fa. was terminated and dissolved upon an official return of nulla bona; and that the lien could only have been revived by another fi. fa. on which the sheriff made a return of goods levied and scheduled and as no such return was ever made by him but there was a return of nulla bona in due course of time on all three writs and as the judgment creditor made thereafter no effort to subject the debtor's property to a lien until after the intervention of bankruptcy, the creditor has no proper basis for claiming priority in payment as a claim secured by a lien.

In a succinctly worded opinion the Referee decided that the creditor in this case has not established a lien and therefore denied priority in payment. I agree with the conclusion of the Referee, but think it will be worth while to develop the law applicable to the decision in more detail.

We must first turn to the Bankruptcy Act itself. It is not disputed that the Trustee in Bankruptcy succeeds in title to the assets of the bankrupt only to the extent that they have not been previously voluntarily or involuntarily by operation of law, subjected to valid claims of third persons. Section 67 (11 U.S.C.A.§ 107) provides that liens obtained against the property of the bankrupt within four months prior to the bankruptcy are invalidated if obtained when the debtor was insolvent. The section does not expressly deal with liens obtained more than four months prior to the bankruptcy but it has been held by the Supreme Court in Straton v. New, 1931, 283 U.S. 318, 51 S.Ct. 465, 75 L.Ed. 1060 that it is the clear implication of the law that such latter liens are valid and enforceable and that the determination of their validity is dependent upon the laws of the State where the property is situated. There is no dispute on this point in this case. It therefore follows that the question at to the validity of the liens here claimed by the creditor must be determined by the applicable and controlling Maryland law and practice.

In beginning the examination of the latter question it must first be borne in mind that Maryland is a so-called 'common law' State. That is, by the first Constitution of the State in 1776 the law of England was adopted, insofar as was compatible with our institutions. And a similar declaration has been made in subsequent Constitutions, including the latest of 1867, whereby it is provided in Art. 5 of the Declaration of Rights, shortly stated, that the English law as it prevailed in 1776 continues to be the Maryland law subject, however, to the statutes of this State thereafter enacted subject to Maryland constitutional provisions. This is, of course, well known but possibly it is not always sufficiently borne in mind in particular cases.

With respect to the effect of judgments against a debtor, it had long ago been provided by a Maryland statute that the judgment itself constituted a lien on real property including certain leaseholds. But I am not aware that it has ever been thought or held that a judgment constituted ex propria vigora a lien of any kind on tangible personal property. By the early English law this could be done only by issuing from the court where the judgment was obtained a writ of fieri facias (shortly, popularly called a fi. fa.). This was an early English writ and was in effect an order to the sheriff of the court to enforce a judgment against the debtor by levy, seizure and sale of his personal property to the extent needed to satisfy the judgment. I understand that in practice the sheriff, after receiving the writ, proceeded thereunder to seize the goods of the debtor and to schedule them and report to the court what he had done. This report, it is said, should have been made in time to allow the parties in interest to file objections thereto; but in practice, at least in Maryland, it has been customary for the sheriff to make his return to the court of what he has done at the next succeeding return day of the court which, in Baltimore City, has generally been the first Monday of the succeeding month. And if the sheriff is unable to locate and seize and schedule the goods of the debtor, he made a return of nulla bona. When such a latter return is made the function of the writ has been completely discharged. But the creditor thereafter can obtain another fi. fa. order to the sheriff for other proceedings thereon and possibly be more successful.

* * *

By many early decisions it is said that the date of the attachment of the lien under a fi. fa. begins when the sheriff receives the writ; but there are decisions to the effect that it is an implied condition that the creditor has the obligation to see that the writ should be promptly complied with by the sheriff and if there is undue delay the lien in favor of the particular judgment creditor may be lost by more active diligence on the part of some other creditor issuing a fi. fa. and securing an earlier levy and scheduling of goods seized by the sheriff. But where the creditor obtaining the writ of fi. fa. is properly diligent in having it executed by the sheriff, there are numerous Maryland cases which state in effect that the lien thereby secured dates from the receipt of the writ by the sheriff.

More importantly, however, in the instant case the sheriff never successfully executed any of the three successive writs of fi. fa. but in due course thereafter made the return of *nulla bona* in each case.

* * *

The duties of the sheriff with regard to the return of writs delivered to him are stated in the Md. Code of 1957, Art. 87, §§ 5, 10, 11, 12 and 14. In this case the sheriff duly made returns on each of the three fi. fas. handed to him; and the creditor at no time challenged the return of nulla bona so made by the sheriff. Counsel have not been able to call to my attention any Maryland statute changing the English law and practice as it was in 1776 affecting the duties of the sheriff in respect to writs of fi. fa. and I have not been able to find any. Counsel for the creditor calls attention to the correspondence with the sheriff regarding the writ of fi. fa. issued September 11, 1956 in which the creditor urged the sheriff to levy on certain alleged personal property of the debtor and asked the sheriff to confer with counsel for the debtor in support of the creditor's assertion, to which the sheriff replied that he could not accept that suggestion and requested that the creditor furnish him a bond of indemnity against foreseeable liability in making a mistaken seizure, or take supplementary proceedings in court to establish the ownership of the goods as those of the debtor. The creditor did not comply with either request. I have always understood that the sheriff had the right to insist upon a bond from the creditor where there was reasonable doubt as to the ownership of the goods, and it was so held in Robey v. State, Use of Mallery, 1901, 94 Md. 61, 50 A. 411 in an opinion by Chief Judge McSherry after an extended review of the English and American authorities on the point.

I therefore conclude that the Referee correctly decided the case and his opinion is affirmed.

SECTION 3. SECURED PARTIES' RIGHTS UPON DEFAULT (MORE ON ATTACHMENT)

UCC § 9-501

(1) When a debtor is in default under a security agreement, a secured party has the rights and remedies provided in this Part and except as limited by subsection (3) those provided in the security agreement. He may reduce his claim to judgment, foreclose or otherwise enforce the security interest by any available judicial procedure * * *. The rights and remedies referred to in this subsection are cumulative. * * *

(5) When a secured party has reduced his claim to judgment the lien of any levy which may be made upon his collateral by virtue of any execution based upon the judgment shall relate back to the date of the perfection of the security interest in such collateral. * * *

(a) WITHOUT ATTACHMENT

AMERICAN CARD CO. v. H.M.H. CO.

Supreme Court of Rhode Island, 1963.
97 R.I. 59, 196 A.2d 150.

CONDON, Chief Justice.

This is a partnership creditors' claim for priority as a valid security interest under the uniform commercial code, G.L.1956, Title 6A. The claim was duly filed in the above-entitled equity receivership proceeding and upon consideration the receivers recommended disallowance as a secured claim but allowed it as a general claim. After a hearing thereon in the superior court, a decree adopting the recommendation of the receivers was entered and from that decree the claimants have appealed to this court.

The sole question for our determination is whether the superior court erred in holding that § 6A-9-203(1)(b) of the code requires in a case of this kind a written security agreement between the debtor and the secured party before a prior security interest in any collateral can attach. The claimants, Oscar A. Hillman & Sons, a copartnership, contend that a separate agreement in writing is not necessary if the written financing statement which was filed contains the debtor's signature and a description of the collateral. In support of that position they point out that G.L.1956, § 6A-9-402, recognizes that a security agreement and a financing statement can be one and the same document. They further argue that "under the unique circumstances that exist in this case" the minimum requirements of § 6A-9-203 are satisfied by the agreed statement of facts and by exhibits A, B, and C appended thereto.

Those circumstances may be summarized as follows. On February 21, 1962 the debtor corporation executed a promissory note in the sum of $12,373.33 payable to claimants. On March 14, 1962 the corporation as debtor and claimants as secured parties signed a financing statement form provided by the office of the secretary of state and filed it in that office in accordance with the provisions of the uniform commercial code, G.L.1956, § 6A-9-402.

On July 2, 1962 Melvin A. Chernick and George F. Treanor were appointed co-receivers of the debtor corporation. On October 6, 1962 claimants duly filed their proof of debt and asserted therein a security interest against certain tools and dies of the debtor which were mentioned in the financing statement as collateral. Finally, there is in addition to the agreed statement of facts testimony of claimants' agent who attempted to collect the debt. He testified that the treasurer of the debtor corporation admitted the inability of the debtor to pay the debt and agreed to the execution of the promissory note and to the designation of the tools and dies as collateral security therefor.

The claimants argue that the code requires no "'magic words', no precise, formalistic language which must be put in writing in order for a security interest to be enforceable." And they further argue that "the definition of a security agreement indicates the question of whether or not a security interest is 'created or provided for' is a question of fact which must be decided upon the basis of the words and deeds of the parties." They rely on the definition of "agreement" in § 6A-9-105(1)(h) for support of this latter contention.

Upon consideration of those provisions of the code, we are of the opinion that they are not decisive of the special problem posed in the instant case. The receivers contend here, as they did successfully before the superior court, that the controlling section of the code is, in the circumstances, § 6A-9-203(1)(b) and that in order to establish a security interest in any collateral the secured party must show that "the debtor has signed a security agreement which contains a description of the collateral * * *." They concede that such a signed agreement may serve as a financing statement if it also contains the requirements thereof, but they deny that a financing statement, absent an agreement therein, can be treated as the equivalent of a security agreement.

The pertinent language of § 6A-9-402 in this regard is, "A copy of the security agreement is sufficient as a financing statement if it contains the above information and is signed by both parties." In other words, while it is possible for a financing statement and a security agreement to be one and the same document as argued by claimants, it is not possible for a financing statement which does not contain the debtor's grant of a security interest to serve as a security agreement.

In our opinion there is merit in the receivers' contention, and since the financing statement filed here contains no such grant it does not qualify as a security agreement.

* * *

The financing statement which the claimants filed clearly fails to qualify also as a security agreement because nowhere in the form is there any evidence of an agreement by the debtor to grant claimants a security interest. As for the testimony of the claimants' agent upon which they also rely to prove the intention of the debtor to make such a grant, our answer is that his testimony is without probative force to supply the absence of a required security agreement in writing. Therefore the trial justice did not err in holding as she did that the financing statement and the evidence before her did not prove the existence of a security agreement within the contemplation of the language of the statute.

The claimants' appeal is denied and dismissed, the decree appealed from is affirmed, and the cause is remanded to the superior court for further proceedings.

WEINBERG, TOWARD MAXIMUM FACILITATION OF INTENT TO CREATE ENFORCEABLE SECURITY INTERESTS, 18 B.C. Indus. & Com. L. Rev. 1-9 (1976).

Article Nine of the Uniform Commercial Code generally facilitates individual autonomy in the creation of consensual security interests by imposing limited form and content requirements on security agreements. Private autonomy is subordinated, however, where the Article's draftsmen believed that certain other policies required a degree of regulation. Through the process of interpreting and applying a number of Code provisions which set forth the requirements for creating security interests, a court can effectuate what it considers to be the appropriate balance between facilitating the parties' intent to create a security interest and insuring that regulatory policies, such as protecting creditors and debtors from fraud and mistake, are enforced. A court may also effectuate its view of the appropriate balance through the manner in which it treats evidence which is offered by a litigant to demonstrate the parties' intent to create a security interest and to interpret the provisions of an alleged security agreement.

* * *

I. AN OVERREGULATION EXEMPLAR

A. *Overregulation Through Interpretation of Article Nine*

The basic rule under Article Nine is one of validation for privately agreed terms: "Except as otherwise provided by this Act a security agreement is effective according to its terms between the parties, against purchasers of the collateral and against creditors." The draftsmen thus intended to allow individual secured parties and debtors to create customized security agreements. Three of Article Nine's provisions, however, provide a framework for the creation of an enforceable security interest which places some limits on this basic rule. The central provision which limits individual autonomy in the creation of Article Nine security interests is section 9-203(1)(a). This section provides that:

> [A] security interest is not enforceable against the debtor or third parties with respect to the collateral and does not attach unless * * * the collateral is in the possession of the secured party pursuant to agreement, or *the debtor has signed a security agreement which contains a description of the collateral*. * * *

The second limit to the basic rule is found in section 9-105(1)(l) which defines a security agreement as "an agreement which creates or provides for a security interest." This provision is expanded by the general definition of agreement in Article One as "the bargain of the parties in fact as found in their language or by implication from other circumstances including course of dealing or usage of trade or course of performance * * *." Section 9-110, the third Article Nine provision which limits private autonomy in the creation of security interests, states that "any description of personal property or real estate is sufficient whether or not it is specific if it reasonably identifies what is described." A number of courts have construed these provisions to demand a high degree of formalism and specificity for nonpossessory security agreements. A sampling of these cases provides a basis from which to strike a more appropriate balance between facilitation and regulation of privately created security interests.

1. Granting Clause Requirement Cases

The question of whether a particular signed writing sufficiently evidences an agreement which "creates or provides for a security interest" has been a frequent source of litigation under Article Nine. The cases addressing this issue have involved the sufficiency of promissory notes, financing statements, corporate resolutions, and other writings which do not contain typical security agreement language. A substantial number of these cases, beginning with the 1963 decision of the Rhode Island Supreme Court in American Card Co. v. H.M.H. Co., have concluded that a writing must contain a grant or conveyance of a security interest to constitute a security agreement even when the intent to create a security interest is certain. A more recent example of the reasoning employed in cases such as *American Card* can be found in the opinion of the United States Court of Appeals for the Eighth Circuit in Shelton v. Erwin.[1]

* * *

2. Inadequate Description Cases

Courts have also thwarted the intent of parties to create nonpossessory security agreements by focusing on the requirement imposed by sections 9-203(1)(a) and 9-110 that the agreement contain a reasonable description of the collateral. A recent example of a case in which a court found the temporal boundaries of the collateral insufficiently described is In re Middle Atlantic Stud Welding Co.[2] There the debtor had executed a security agreement which granted the secured party a security interest in "all Receivables and the proceeds thereof as security for the Liabilities." The agreement defined receivables as "all of Debtor's Accounts Receivable" and liabilities as "any and all indebtedness of Debtor to Secured Party of every kind and description, now existing or hereafter arising. The issue before the United States Court of Appeals for the Third Circuit was whether the phrase "all accounts receivable" was sufficient for purposes of Section 9-110 to "reasonably" identify after-acquired accounts as part of the described collateral.

The Third Circuit initially noted the lower court's finding that the debtor and secured party had intended to create a security interest in after-acquired accounts. With the recognition that floating liens on accounts receivable were widely used in current commercial practice, the reviewing court then concluded that there was a rational basis for the premise that "many" prospective lenders who read the security agreement "would be alerted that the parties may well have intended to include after-acquired accounts" in the collateral. The Third Circuit decided, however, that the description was insufficient to meet the requirement of section 9-110 because an express reference to after-acquired property was necessary to protect those few prospective lenders who might possibly be misled by the parties' description.

* * *

B. *Overregulation Through Restrictive Interpretation of Security Agreement Language—"Tunnel Vision" Cases*

Cases such as those previously discussed are examples of the way in which a court can actualize a regulatory bias through the interpretation and application of the statutory formalities for the creation of an enforceable security interest.

1 72 F.2d 1118 (8th Cir. 1973).

2 503 F.2d 1133 (3d Cir. 1974).

An illustration of how a court can also give effect to this bias through the interpretation of security agreement language is to be found in Mitchell v. Shepherd Mall State Bank.[1] There, Section D of the form security agreement contained the heading "COLLATERAL" and subsection D.1 thereunder stated: "The security interest is granted in the following collateral: Describe collateral." In the space provided for the description appeared the typed statement: "See EQUIPMENT LIST attached hereto and made a part hereof, describing equipment, furniture and fixtures located at [certain] * * * stores." A two-page list of equipment, furniture, and fixtures was attached to the security agreement. Subsection D.2 of the section on "COLLATERAL" directed the parties to "[c]lassify goods under (one or more of) the following Uniform Commercial Code categories," and contained five boxes labeled "Consumer Goods," "Equipment (business use)," "Inventory," "Accounts Receivable," and "Contract Rights." All of the boxes, except the first one, were checked. Therefore, the collateral "described" (equipment, furniture and fixtures) in subsection D.1 was not the same as the collateral "classified" (equipment, inventory, accounts receivable and contract rights) in subsection D.2. Financing statements covering all machinery, equipment, fixtures, furniture, inventory, accounts receivable and contract rights were properly filed. After the debtor filed for bankruptcy the trustee contested the secured party's claim that the agreement secured inventory, accounts receivable and contract rights.

The district court held that since the description of the collateral in subsection D.1 was unambiguous, parol evidence to the effect that the parties intended to include inventory, accounts receivable and contract rights as collateral, should not have been received by the referee in bankruptcy. Furthermore, the court refused to find that subsection D.2 extended the security interest to inventory, accounts receivable and contract rights or that it even so clouded the intent of the parties that it was necessary to resort to parol evidence for clarification. The court stated that under the UCC the purpose of a classifications section such as subsection D.2 was to determine the answers to questions such as where a financing statement must be filed, and not to describe or to create a security interest. Accordingly, a third party, who tried to determine what property was secured by this agreement, would be unlikely to regard subsection D.2 as determining the dimensions of the security interest. Thus, the district court essentially decided that a third party should not be required to study and interpret all the provisions of a security agreement at the peril of not learning the full extent of the security interest it creates when an unambiguous provision, in this case subsection D.1. is clearly designated in the agreement as containing a description of the collateral.

The affirming opinion of the United States Court of Appeals for the Tenth Circuit, while acknowledging the district court's considerations, focused on what it perceived to be a lack of language "creating or providing for" a security interest in accounts, contract rights and inventory in the security agreement. The court reasoned that the language in subsection D.1, that "[t]he security interest is granted in the following collateral," referred only to the items mentioned in the

---

[1] 458 F.2d 700 (10th Cir. 1972).

space provided below subsection D.1, while subsection D.2 contained no "granting' language of its own. In determining what extrinsic evidence, if any, might be considered to illuminate the actual intent of the immediate parties, the court held that, despite the unambiguous reference to inventory, accounts receivable and contract rights in the financing statements, these statements could have no bearing on the case, since a financing statement cannot serve as a security agreement absent explicit "granting" language. The court also agreed with the district court that the uncontroverted testimony of the bank's vice president, which was introduced in support of the secured party's contentions, was inadmissible because the description of collateral in subsection D.1 was unambiguous and, even if the form security agreement was ambiguous, it should be construed against the secured party draftsman.

The opinions in *Mitchell* demonstrate how restrictions on the admissibility of clarifying extrinsic evidence can define the legal effect of a security agreement in a manner which may be inconsistent with the actual intention of the parties. This restrictive approach flowed from an equally regulatory construction and application of the Article Nine formalities.

(b) WITH ATTACHMENT

IN RE BOLLINGER

United States Court of Appeals, Third Circuit, 1980.
614 F.2d 924.

ROSENN, Circuit Judge.

This appeal from a district court review of an order in bankruptcy presents a question that has troubled courts since the enactment of Article Nine of the Uniform Commercial Code (U.C.C.) governing secured transactions. Can a creditor assert a secured claim against the debtor when no formal security agreement was ever signed, but where various documents executed in connection with a loan evince an intent to create a security interest? The district court answered this question in the affirmative and permitted the creditor, Zimmerman & Jansen, to assert a secured claim against the debtor, bankrupt Bollinger Corporation in the amount of $150,000. We affirm.

I.

The facts of this case are not in dispute. Industrial Credit Company (ICC) made a loan to Bollinger Corporation (Bollinger) on January 13, 1972, in the amount of $150,000. As evidence of the loan, Bollinger executed a promissory note in the sum of $150,000 and signed a security agreement with ICC giving it a security interest in certain machinery and equipment. ICC in due course perfected its security interest in the collateral by filing a financing statement in accordance with Pennsylvania's enactment of Article Nine of the U.C.C.

Bollinger faithfully met its obligations under the note and by December 4, 1974, had repaid $85,000 of the loan leaving $65,000 in unpaid principal. Bollinger, however, required additional capital and on December 5, 1974, entered into a loan agreement with Zimmerman & Jansen, Inc. (Z&J), by which Z&J agreed to lend Bollinger $150,000. Z&J undertook as part of this transaction to pay off the $65,000 still owed to ICC in return for an assignment by ICC to Z&J of the original note and security agreement between Bollinger and ICC. Bollinger executed a promissory note to Z&J, evidencing the agreement containing the following provision: Security. This Promissory Note is secured by security interests in a certain Security Agreement between Bollinger and Industrial Credit Company * * * and in a Financing Statement filed by (ICC) * * *, and is further secured by security interests in a certain security agreement to be delivered by Bollinger to Z and J with this Promissory Note covering the identical machinery and equipment as identified in the ICC Agreement and with identical schedule attached in the principal amount of Eighty-Five Thousand Dollars ($85,000). No formal security agreement was ever executed between Bollinger and Z&J. Z&J did, however, in connection with the promissory note, record a new financing statement signed by Bollinger containing a detailed list of the machinery and equipment originally taken as collateral by ICC for its loan to Bollinger.

Bollinger filed a petition for an arrangement under Chapter XI of the Bankruptcy Act in March, 1975 and was adjudicated bankrupt one year later. In administrating the bankrupt's estate, the receiver sold some of Bollinger's equipment but agreed that Z&J would receive a $10,000 credit on its secured claim.

Z&J asserted a secured claim against the bankrupt in the amount of $150,000, arguing that although it never signed a security agreement with Bollinger, the parties had intended that a security interest in the sum of $150,000 be created to protect the loan. The trustee in bankruptcy conceded that the assignment to Z&J of ICC's original security agreement with Bollinger gave Z&J a secured claim in the amount of $65,000, the balance owed by Bollinger to ICC at the time of the assignment. The trustee, however, refused to recognize Z&J's asserted claim of an additional secured claim of $85,000 because of the absence of a security agreement between Bollinger and Z&J. The bankruptcy court agreed and entered judgment for Z&J in the amount of $55,000, representing a secured claim in the amount of $65,000 less $10,000 credit received by Z&J.

Z&J appealed to the United States District Court for the Western District of Pennsylvania, which reversed the bankruptcy court and entered judgment for Z&J in the full amount of the asserted $150,000 secured claim. The trustee in bankruptcy appeals.

II.

Under Article Nine of the U.C.C., two documents are generally required to create a perfected security interest in a debtor's collateral. First, there must be a "security agreement" giving the creditor an interest in the collateral. Section 9-203(1)(b) contains minimal requirements for the creation of a security agreement. In order to create a security agreement, there must be: (1) a writing (2) signed by the debtor (3) containing a description of the collateral or the types of collateral. Section 9-203, Comment 1. The requirements of section 9-203(1)(b) further two basic policies. First, an evidentiary function is served by requiring a signed security agreement and second, a written agreement also obviates any Statute of Frauds problems with the debtor-creditor relationship. Id. Comments 3, 5. The second document generally required is a "financing statement," which is a document signed by both parties and filed for public record. The financing statement serves the purpose of giving public notice to other creditors that a security interest is claimed in the debtor's collateral.

* * *

In the case before us, the district court * * * held that the promissory note executed by Bollinger in favor of Z&J, standing alone, was sufficient to act as the security agreement between the parties. In so doing, the court implicitly rejected the * * * rule requiring grant language before a security agreement arises under section 9-203(1)(b). The parties have not referred to any Pennsylvania state cases on the question and our independent research has failed to uncover any. But although we agree that no formal grant of a security interest need exist before a security agreement arises, we do not think that the promissory note standing alone would be sufficient under Pennsylvania law to act as the security agreement. We believe, however, that the promissory note, read in conjunction with the financing statement duly filed and supported, as it is here, by correspondence during the course of the transaction between the parties, would be sufficient under Pennsylvania law to establish a valid security agreement.

III.

We think Pennsylvania courts would * * * reject the * * * rule imposing the requirement of a formal grant of a security interest before a security agreement may exist. When the parties have neglected to sign a separate security agreement, it would appear that the better and more practical view is to look at the transaction as a whole in order to determine if there is a writing, or writings, signed by the debtor describing the collateral which demonstrates an intent to create a security interest in the collateral.

* * *

IV.

The minimal formal requirements of section 9-203(1)(b) were met by the financing statement and the promissory note, and the course of dealing between the parties indicated the intent to create a security interest. The judgment of the district court recognizing Z&J's secured claim in the amount of $150,000 will be affirmed.

NOTE ON REPOSSESSION AND SALE

Section 9-503 authorizes a creditor that has created a valid security interest in the debtor's property to seize the collateral upon default without prior notice to the debtor or judicial process of any kind. So-called "self-help" repossession has withstood several constitutional challenges. Although the U.S. Supreme Court has not ruled directly on the question, in Flagg Bros. v. Brooks, 436 U.S. 149 (1978), the Court rejected a due process challenge to a warehouse's sale pursuant to UCC § 7-210 which, like § 9-503, authorizes private action. The Court ruled that where self-help remedies are merely authorized by the legislature, and not compelled, there is no state action within the meaning of the due process clause of the Fourteenth Amendment. Id. at 161-62. The only limitation then on the secured creditor's ability to repossess is that it must occur without a "breach of the peace." The phrase "breach of the peace" is not defined in the Code, thus precipitating considerable litigation over its meaning in particular cases. Clearly the taking may not involve violence or even the threat of violence. Moreover, most courts agree that if the situation creates a "risk of invoking violence," the creditor must back off and seek to obtain possession of the collateral by means of a replevin action in state court. Some courts sensibly interpret this standard to mean that anytime there is a confrontation with the debtor, continuation of the repossession would be in breach of the peace and a conversion of the debtor's property. Other courts tend to make the determination based on an assessment of how likely it is that the debtor will resort to violence. These differing views are sharply contrasted in the majority and dissenting opinions in Williams v. Ford Motor Credit Co., 674 F.2d 717 (8th Cir. 1982). This uncertainty and lack of uniformity has lead one commentator to argue that the Code should define a "breach of the peace" and provide a specific remedial response when it occurs. Braucher, *The Repo Code: A Study of Adjustment to Uncertainty in Commercial Law*, 75 Wash. U. L. Rev. 549 (1997).

Once the secured party has repossessed the collateral, through either self-help or judicial process, it is not free simply to keep the property. Instead it must foreclose its interest by means, in most cases, of a public or private sale. Foreclosure is intended to protect the debtor's equity in the property, although in most cases it has the effect of fixing the amount of the deficiency for which the debtor remains personally liable. See § 9-504(2). There are two exceptions to foreclosure by sale. First, where the collateral consists of instruments or accounts, the secured party may, after default, notify the account debtor or obligor, as applicable, that future payments are to be made directly to the secured party. § 9-502. Second, in certain circumstances that we consider later in Section 5, a secured party that complies with the procedural steps set forth in § 9-505 may retain the collateral in full and complete satisfaction of the debt.

In most cases, however, the secured party will proceed with public or private sale under 9-504(3). The procedures for each differ slightly and the secured party is prohibited from being the purchaser in a private sale. In addition, except in circumstances where the collateral is perishable, threatens to decline speedily in value, or is of a type customarily sold on a recognized market (mostly stocks and bonds), the secured party must provide the debtor, and in some instances others, with advance notice of the sale. As with other provisions that give rights to the debtor and impose duties on the secured party, the notice requirement may not be waived prior to default. § 9-501(3). As illustrated by the next case, bear in mind that the rights of the secured parties with respect to the collateral do *not* depend on perfection of the security interest.

KANSAS STATE BANK v. OVERSEAS MOTORSPORT, INC.

Supreme Court of Kansas, 1977.
222 Kan. 26, 563 P.2d 414.

MILLER, Justice.

This is an action for the recovery of damages based upon a claim of breach of contract, commenced by the Kansas State Bank against Overseas Motorsport, Inc. The bank prevailed in the district court, and Overseas appeals.

Overseas admits that it breached the contract, and that the bank's loss is $1,500. The question before us is whether the breach caused the loss or, stated another way, whether the damages are such as may fairly and reasonably be considered as arising naturally, according to the usual course of things, from the breach of the contract itself.

* * *

The activity out of which this controversy arose commenced in May, 1974, when Steven C. Hunter applied for a loan from the Kansas State Bank. The bank made the usual credit checks, found that Hunter was serving in the U. S. Army, and approved the credit. On July 16, 1974, Hunter returned to the bank and signed a note and security agreement. The agreement described the collateral as a 1974 Suzuki GT-750, SN #52811. The bank accepted the note and security agreement, and issued its cashier's check in the amount of $1500, payable to Hunter and Overseas. Stamped on the back of the check, above the endorsement, was the following legend: "The endorsers of this money order guarantee that the Kansas State Bank of Manhattan, Kansas, has a recorded first lien against 1974 Suzuki GT-750, #52811."

The bank called Overseas and was assured that Overseas would show the bank's lien when title was delivered to Hunter.

The motorcycle sold for $2033.43. Overseas accepted the bank's check for $1500, and carried the balance of $523.43 on an open charge. It delivered title to Hunter, but inadvertently showed itself as the lien holder. The bank's lien was not shown. Overseas admits that this was a breach of its agreement with the bank.

Hunter's first payment to the bank was due on August 15, 1974. When this was not paid, the bank mailed notices to Hunter on August 20 and August 30; there was no response. About this time, the bank discovered that Hunter was AWOL, and that he had been AWOL since before July 16, when the loan was made. Thereafter, the bank tried to find him.

Between September 7 and 15, one of the bank officers located Hunter and the motorcycle in Manhattan. Hunter refused to surrender possession of the motorcycle, and stated that the bank couldn't do anything about it because he was sure the bank did not have a lien on the cycle. The bank checked with the motor vehicle department and found that it had no recorded lien. The bank then erroneously concluded that it could not foreclose because it had no perfected lien. About the middle of October, the bank discovered that Overseas was listed on the title as a lien holder. The bank continued its efforts to locate Hunter, but could find neither Hunter nor the motorcycle. On December 20 the bank commenced this action.

The bank argued to the trial court, and argues here, that the defendant's breach resulted in the bank having no enforceable lien on the motorcycle, and thus no legal avenues were open to it to secure possession of the motorcycle. The trial court found that this was not the paramount issue; that the omission of the bank's lien on the title caused the bank to delay foreclosure or take other action, and that the delay thus caused by the defendant was the proximate cause of the loss. The court did not decide whether the bank in fact had an enforceable lien.

* * *

The UCC does not require that a security interest be perfected by filing or otherwise in order to be valid. * * *

Here, Hunter signed a security agreement. It contained a description of the collateral. Hunter agreed that the security interest attach to the vehicle. Value was given by the bank. The title to the vehicle, and physical possession of it, were given to Hunter by Overseas, and thus Hunter acquired rights in the collateral. It is clear that the security interest of the bank attached * * *. Upon Hunter's default, the bank had the right to possession of the collateral pursuant to section 9-503.

We should emphasize that we are concerned here with the rights of only the original parties to a secured transaction-Hunter and the bank. So far as the record discloses, Hunter remained the owner of the vehicle. He did not sell it; he did not transfer the title; he did not mortgage, pledge, or otherwise encumber the vehicle to third parties; nor did he cause the cycle to become subject to the lien of a repairman.

The bank acquired its security interest—its lien on the vehicle—pursuant to the terms of its security agreement and the provisions of the Uniform Commercial Code. A security interest is created by a security agreement, and attaches as provided by sec. 9-204. Priority is established and protected by recording the lien on the title; but we are not here concerned with priorities or the rights of third parties. No third party is claiming an interest superior to that of the bank.

The bank confused 'security interest' with 'priority.' It misunderstood the law, and took no action. Hunter absconded with the motorcycle after the bank contacted him in early September. Neither the bank's misconception of the law nor Hunter's flight can be laid at the door of Overseas.

There is no evidence that Hunter or the motorcycle remained in Manhattan for any period of time after the bank made contact with Hunter in early September. Thus there is nothing in the evidence to support a finding that the bank could have foreclosed its lien anytime after that contact, or that delay by the bank caused its loss.

Upon the record before us we conclude that Hunter's flight, and his concealment of the motorcycle, caused the loss. As a matter of law, then, the loss was not caused by defendant's breach.

Accordingly, the judgment of the district court is reversed.

UCC § 9-504(3)

* * * Sale or other disposition may be as a unit or in parcels and at any time and place and on any terms but every aspect of the disposition including the method, manner, time, place, and terms must be *commercially reasonable.* * * * [Emphasis added.]

UCC § 9-507(2)

The fact that a better price could have been obtained by a sale at a different time or in a different method from that selected by the secured party is not itself sufficient to establish that the sale was not made in a commercially reasonable manner. * * *

REVISED § 9-626(b)

A disposition of collateral is made in a commercially reasonable manner if the disposition is made:

(1) in the usual manner on any recognized market therefor;

(2) at the price current in any recognized market at the time of disposition; or

(3) otherwise in conformity with the reasonable commercial practices among dealers in the type of property that was the subject of the disposition.

NOTE ON COMMERCIAL REASONABLENESS AND NOTICE

The relationship between the secured party's specific duty to give reasonable notification of sale and the secured party's overriding duty to conduct a commercially reasonable sale is a difficult one. If the secured party failed to give the required notice of sale, does that mean that the sale was by definition commercially unreasonable? Even if not, what difference does it make since the consequence to the secured party in either case is potential liability to the debtor under § 9-507(1) for any actual loss suffered as a result of the noncompliance? As a practical matter, in most cases, the challenge to the secured party's procedures will be raised as an affirmative defense in the secured party's deficiency action. However, § 9-507(2), cited above, makes the fact that the secured party did not receive the *best* price for the collateral legally irrelevant, at least standing by itself.

One thoughtful attempt to parse this relationship can be found in Judge Easterbrook's analysis in Matter of Excello Press, 890 F.2d 896 (7th Cir. 1989). In *Excello*, the secured party, Metlife Capital Credit Corp., had a security interest in two webb presses securing an indebtedness of approximately $2.7 million at the time the debtor filed bankruptcy. Pursuant to an order of the bankruptcy court, the presses were released to Metlife under an agreement that permitted Metlife to sell the presses and apply the proceeds to its indebtedness, but capped Metlife's deficiency claim against the debtor at $900,000 regardless of the amount received from the sale of the presses. Metlife sold the presses at a private sale for a total of $1.1 million, leaving an actual deficiency of $1.8 million. Pursuant to the agreement, Metlife filed a claim in the debtor's bankruptcy case for only $900,000, the maximum permitted under the agreement. Nonetheless, other creditors objected to the claim, asserting that Metlife had not given reasonable notification of the sale or conducted a commercially reasonable sale. The bankruptcy court found that proper notice had not been given and that, therefore, the prices received by Metlife at the sale could not be considered evidence of fair market value. The district court affirmed.

On further appeal Judge Easterbrook first addressed the lower courts' findings that the Code requires *written* notice. Stating that the purpose of notice is "to allow the debtor to ensure that the sale is commercially reasonable, find another buyer, or redeem the debt," the court concluded that the only issue was whether the debtor acquired knowledge of the sale in time to protect these interests. Since the bankruptcy court had made no finding on that issue, assuming formal written notice was required, the court remanded on that question.

On the issue of commercial reasonableness, the court rejected the view that the failure to give notice, even if established on remand, made the sale commercially unreasonable. Instead, Judge Easterbrook instructed the bankruptcy court that the failure to give notice was, at most, a factor which could be used to inform the court's assessment of commercial reasonableness. Noting that the Code does not define the concept of commercial reasonableness, Judge Easterbrook offered as a rule of thumb that a sale is to be considered commercially reasonable if the secured party has done "what a reasonable business would have done to maximize the return on the collateral." This approach eliminates the need for the secured party to offer secondary evidence in the form of third party appraisals to establish market value, because, according to the court; "The product of a commercially reasonable sale *is* the fair market value." In light of this standard, consider what the debtor's damages would be in a case where the creditor fails to give the required notice but is nevertheless able to establish, by showing that the process it went through to sell the collateral was prudent and careful in all other respects, that the sale was commercially reasonable.

PROBLEMS

1. John Minor approached State Street Bank about a loan for a new car. Concerned about John's lack of a credit history and his young age, Bank insisted on both a security interest in the car, a used Mazda Miata, and a personal guarantee from a party with a credit record acceptable to Bank. The next day, John showed up at Bank's offices with his wealthy Uncle August, who agreed to guarantee the note. Satisfied, Bank made the loan to John, had August sign a guarantee agreement, and took and perfected a security interest in the Miata by having its lien noted on the certificate of title. For a year, John faithfully made the scheduled payments required under Bank's note. At that point, however, he began to encounter some financial problems and, in order to keep the loan current, borrowed some money from his cousin Boone. Being no fool, Boone also insisted on a security interest in the Miata, which John agreed to, and Boone sent Bank a notice of his junior interest in the car. Alas, even with Boone's help, John just could not make it. He began missing payments on the loan and eventually Bank sent Scrooge, a local repo man, out to snatch John's Miata. Late one night, Scrooge found John's car in his unlocked garage. After making sure no one was around, Scrooge snatched the car and turned it over to Bank. Bank sent John a notice two days later telling him that the car would be sold in a private sale sometime after the first of the month. John rushed down to Bank with a certified check for all of the past due payments on the loan, plus interest, and pleaded for the return of his car. However, Bank insisted on full payment of the loan before it would release the car to John. In fact, several weeks later, Bank sold the car to a Mazda dealership for wholesale book value. The proceeds, however, were still less than the balance of the loan and Bank has now demanded payment of the deficiency from both John and August. In evaluating the position of the parties, consider the following questions under both current and Revised Article 9:

(a) Did Bank, through its agent Scrooge, commit a breach of the peace in repossessing the car?

(b) Was Bank obligated to return the car when John showed up with all of the back payments? See § 9-506 and Revised § 9-622.

(c) Was August entitled to notice of the sale? See §§ 9-504(3), 9-105(1)(d) and Revised §§ 9-602, 9-611(b).

(d) Was Boone entitled to notice of the sale? See § 9-504(3) and Revised § 9-611(b).

(e) Did the Mazda dealership take subject to Boone's security interest? See § 9-504(4) and Revised § 9-615(a), (c)

(f) Was the sale at wholesale price unreasonable? See § 9-507(2) and Revised §§ 9-626(a), 9-614(f).

(g) If the car had sold for more than the amount of the loan, to whom would Bank be required to remit the excess? See § 9-504(1) and (2) and Revised § 9-614(a).

(h) If John had defaulted on his loan to Boone, rather than Bank, and Boone had foreclosed, how would the proceeds of sale be allocated? See § 9-504(1), (4) and Revised § 9-614 (b), (g).

2. Assume that, in the previous problem, six months after the sale to the Mazda dealership, John files for bankruptcy and the trustee in John's case seeks to set aside the sale of John's Miata to the dealership on the basis that the debtor received "less than a reasonably equivalent value in exchange for such transfer." Assuming that John was insolvent at the time of the sale, what result in the trustee's action? See Bankruptcy Code § 548(a)(2) and UFTA § 3(b).

SECTION 4. DEBTORS' RIGHTS ON DEFAULT

INTRODUCTORY NOTE

Section 9-507(1) provides that if the secured party has failed to comply with any of its obligations under Part 5, the debtor has a right to recover for "any loss caused" by the secured party's failure to comply. This claim can be raised in a direct action against the secured party but, as a practical matter, is likely to be asserted as a counterclaim to the secured party's action for a deficiency. Ordinarily, the loss to the debtor will be measured by the difference between what the secured party would have received in a complying sale and the amount of proceeds actually received. As noted earlier in connection with our discussion of the *Excello* case, however, proving damages attributable to failure to give reasonable notice may be a nearly impossible task. Thus, the courts have contrived various ways to apply § 9-507(1) in a manner that maximizes the prospects that creditors will behave. On the other hand, given the expense, delay, and risk of litigation, don't creditors already have every incentive to obtain the highest price reasonably possible on resale of their collateral?

FEDERAL DEPOSIT INSURANCE CORP. v. FARRAR

Supreme Court of Iowa, 1975.
231 N.W.2d 602.

MOORE, Chief Justice.

* * *

In Division I of its petition FDIC sought a deficiency judgment of $1694.42, plus interest, on the note secured by Farrar's mobile home and in Division II a deficiency judgment of $445, plus interest, on the note secured by Farrar's automobile. FDIC further prayed for statutory attorney fees and costs.

Farrar's answer alleged, inter alia, plaintiff had taken possession of his 1964 mobile home and 1964 Chevrolet automobile which were worth more than the balance owing on his notes and sold them with no notice to him of the time and place of any public or private sale thereof. Farrar sought the surplus and denied plaintiff's claim to a deficiency judgment.

Plaintiff's reply admitted sale of the collateral but denied it was required to give notice of any public or private sale. It asserted the collateral was of a type customarily sold on a recognized market.

* * *

On or before June 8, 1971 FDIC sold the 1964 Hillcrest mobile home for $990. On or before August 6, 1971 FDIC sold the 1964 Chevrolet automobile for $25. FDIC gave Farrar no prior notice of the time and place of either sale.

Application of the mobile home sale proceeds to the unpaid balance of the first note left a deficiency balance of $1694.42 plus interest as provided in the note.

After the proceeds from the sale of the automobile were applied to the unpaid balance of the second note there remained a deficiency balance of $445, plus interest, as provided in the note.

* * *

We, like the trial court, refer to section 554.9504(3), Code 1973. The identical applicable provisions are in the 1966 and 1971 Codes. We are not concerned with statutory changes made after the trial of this case.

Section 554.9504(3) of Iowa's Uniform Commercial Code, as pertinent here, provides: "Disposition of the collateral may be by public or private proceedings and may be made by way of one or more contracts. Sale or other disposition may be as a unit or in parcels and at any time and place and on any terms but every aspect of the disposition including the method, manner, time, place and terms must be commercially reasonable. Unless collateral is perishable or threatens to decline speedily in value or is of a type customarily sold on a recognized market, reasonable notification of the time and place of any public sale or reasonable notification of the time after which any private sale or other intended disposition is to be made shall be sent by the secured party to the debtor, * * *."

FDIC concedes here as it did in the trial court it gave no notice to Farrar prior to the sale of the collateral and that if under the circumstances notice was required then it would not be entitled to a deficiency judgment. We held in Twin Bridges Truck City, Inc. v. Halling, Iowa, 205 N.W.2d 736, lack of notice required by section 554.9504 defeats any claim to a deficiency judgment.

* * *

The purpose of notice under section 554.9504(3) is to permit the debtor to bid at the sale or to protect himself from an inadequate sale price. A debtor unable or unwilling to exercise his section 554.9506 redemption right may still wish to bid on the property or encourage others to do so to insure a fair sale price which would minimize or eliminate a deficiency. A debtor who forfeits his right to redeem and willingly agrees to pay any deficiency remaining after sale has good reason to appear at the sale of his property. This is clearly demonstrated by the fact Farrar's Chevrolet appraised as worth $130 was sold for $25.

FDIC also contends no notice prior to sale was required as the collateral was 'of a type customarily sold in a recognized market' as exempted under section 554.9504(3). This contention is untenable as in Beneficial Finance Co. of Black Hawk County v. Reed, supra, Iowa, 212 N.W.2d 454, 459, we held: " * * * a used automobile does not fall within the category of collateral 'of a type customarily sold on a recognized market.'" There being no recognized market for used automobiles, it follows no recognized market exists for the sale of used mobile homes.

We have examined the contentions of the parties and cited authorities. We are convinced the trial court erred in entering the deficiency judgment against appellant Farrar.

This case is reversed and remanded to the trial court for order setting aside the judgment against Farrar and for judgment against FDIC for costs.

Lloyd, The Absolute Bar Rule in UCC Foreclosure Sales: A Prescription for Waste, 40 UCLA L. Rev. 695, 698-700, 721-24, 728-31 (1993).

When the debtor defaults on a secured loan, the Uniform Commercial Code allows the secured party to take possession of the collateral and to liquidate it towards satisfying the debt. Conversely, the UCC provides the debtor with several remedies in the event that the secured party fails to follow the prescribed procedures in disposing of the collateral. The debtor may sue for damages, or she may get a court to enjoin the secured party from proceeding further. Debtors seek these remedies only on rare occasions. As a practical matter, there is only one real sanction against the secured party who fails to follow the law. The court will reduce or deny the secured party's judgment for the difference between the loan balance and the amount realized upon disposition of the collateral.

Courts have taken three distinct approaches to the issue of secured parties' deficiency judgments. A small minority of courts have taken a conservative approach and have adopted what is known as the "setoff rule." The setoff rule strictly follows the Code language and general principles of law. Courts adopting the setoff rule read UCC section 9-504(2) as giving the secured party a deficiency judgment as a matter of right. The secured party merely has to prove the amount of the debt and the amount that was received upon disposition of the collateral. Under section 9-507 the debtor thereupon has the opportunity to prove that the secured party failed to follow the Code requirements and then to prove the damages suffered because of the secured party's failure. If the debtor is able to prove damages, these are offset against the amount of the deficiency.

A large number of courts have recognized that this approach places an unfair burden on the debtor. These courts require that the secured party affirmatively prove that he complied with the Code when he disposed of the collateral. If the secured party fails to prove this, these courts apply a rebuttable presumption that the value of the collateral was equal to the amount of the debt. Thus, the amount of the deficiency becomes equal to the amount of the damages from the improper disposition, so the creditor is entitled to no deficiency. However, the presumption is rebuttable, so the creditor may still recover a deficiency judgment if he proves that the value of the collateral was less than the amount of the debt and that the debtor's damages were therefore less than the full amount of the deficiency.

* * *

The Code does not say what happens if the secured party fails to follow the prescribed procedures for giving notice and selling the collateral. Prior to the enactment of the Code, failure to follow the prescribed procedures made the sale invalid and therefore subjected the creditor to potential liability for conversion. There was a certain logic to this result. The creditor was selling the debtor's property. She was empowered to do this only by particular provisions of law. If she failed to comply with the requirements of the applicable law, be it statutory or common law, her sale was invalid.

In theory, this was a nice, logical system, but in practice it created problems. The formalities were often complex, and creditors were often sloppy. As a result, third parties who might have wanted to bid on the collateral could never be sure that their purchases would not be taken back because the creditor had sent a required notice a day too late (or even a day too early). The result was to chill bidding at foreclosure sales. To avoid this, the drafters of Article 9 specifically provided that an innocent purchaser at a foreclosure sale (public or private) takes the collateral free of all rights of the debtor and any junior creditors.

Having addressed that problem, the drafters failed to give adequate attention to what sanctions should apply when the secured party fails to follow the prescribed procedures. Superficially, section 9-507(1) appears to deal with the issue. The first sentence of the section provides that if the secured party is not complying with the statutory requirements, the debtor may go to court and obtain an order compelling it to do so. The second sentence allows the debtor to recover damages for any loss resulting from the secured party's failure to follow the statute. And the third sentence provides for a monetary penalty in consumer transactions.

What the drafters seem to have failed to anticipate is that the real lever for making the secured party satisfy the Code requirements is denial of its deficiency judgment. Suits enjoining improper dispositions or seeking damages against secured parties are very rare, but secured parties seeking deficiency judgments are the norm, and denial of the deficiency is what gets secured parties' attention.

The drafters' failure to resolve the deficiency judgment question left the matter to the courts. As noted above, the courts have developed three distinct approaches to the question: the setoff rule, the rebuttable presumption rule, and the absolute bar rule.

A. The Setoff Rule

The setoff rule offers the most straightforward approach. The secured party gets his deficiency judgment as a matter of right, and the debtor simply sues for his damages under section 9-507(1) and sets them off against the deficiency. The setoff rule is also the only one of the three rules that follows the express language of the statute. Section 9-504(2) gives the secured party the right to a deficiency judgment, and section 9-507(1) provides that the debtor may be awarded damages if the secured party fails to follow the prescribed procedures. As in any situation where each party has a claim against the other, the court simply sets off one claim against the other.

Though clearly sound as a matter of statutory interpretation, the setoff rule gives the secured party an unfair advantage. The facts necessary to prove the debtor's damage claim are much more readily available to the secured party than they are to the debtor. This has been so widely recognized that courts seldom apply the setoff rule anymore.

B. The Rebuttable Presumption Rule

The rebuttable presumption rule originated in an Arkansas case, *Norton v. National Bank of Commerce*, where the court eloquently explained the reasoning that led it to create the presumption:

> [S]imple considerations of fair play cast the burden of proof upon the bank. It was the bank which wrongfully disposed of the car without notice to the debtors. Thus it was the bank's action that made it at least difficult, if not impossible, for Norton to prove the extent of his loss with reasonable certainty. A chattel such as a car may well be a thousand miles away before the debtor learns of its sale without notice. It would be manifestly unfair for the creditor to derive an advantage from its own misconduct. We think the just solution is to indulge the presumption in the first instance that the collateral was worth at least the amount of the debt, thereby shifting to the creditor the burden of proving the amount that should reasonably have been obtained through a sale conducted according to law.

At present twenty-six jurisdictions appear to apply the rebuttable presumption rule.

C. The Absolute Bar Rule

Most of the courts that do not subscribe to the rebuttable presumption rule go beyond it and hold that the secured party's failure to give proper notice and sell in a commercially reasonable manner is an absolute bar to any right to recover a deficiency.

The development of the absolute bar rule paralleled that of the rebuttable presumption rule. Its initial development appears to have been based primarily on the misconception that the pre-Code law absolutely barred a deficiency when the formalities were not followed and that the Code's drafters sought to perpetuate this practice. * * * [T]he absolute bar rule is wrong, both as a matter of history and as a matter of policy.

* * *

If we accept the proposition that Article 9's default provisions are intended to minimize losses, the absolute bar rule fails miserably. It encourages and rewards wasteful behavior, both on the part of the debtor and on the part of the secured party.

The absolute bar rule is, in effect, an *in terrorem* rule, a rule intended to force the secured party to spend enough time and money selling the collateral. Like all *in terrorem* rules, it compels people to overcompensate. If the secured party does not spend enough time and money selling the collateral, he loses his entire deficiency. Whether he spent enough of these commodities will not be decided until after the fact, often by a jury that has no understanding of commercial practices. The secured party's explanation of what he did and why will be attacked at every turn by the debtor's (or, more likely, the guarantor's) attorney.

The defendants will have the opportunity to bring in appraisers to say that the price paid by the successful bidder was too low, to bring in dealers to say that they would have bought the collateral for more, and to introduce many other kinds of evidence, all equally damaging. What will the secured party do to protect his deficiency? If the deficiency is large, the secured party will normally go overboard to protect himself. There will be unnecessary appraisals, unnecessary advertising, and unnecessary fix-up costs. It may be that no one is likely to travel more than one hundred miles to attend the sale and that there are only thirty potential buyers in that hundred-mile radius. Nevertheless, a mere mailing of thirty brochures does not sound impressive. By contrast, a mailing of thirty thousand brochures to every member of the International Widget Dealers Association (in all fifty states and twenty-nine foreign countries) sounds extraordinarily impressive.

Significantly, the costs of the secured party's excessive caution will be paid by the debtor and the guarantors, at least to the extent that those parties are solvent. The Code provides that the proceeds of the sale go *first* to the reasonable expenses of preparing and selling the collateral. And courts have been very reluctant to find secured parties' expenses unreasonable. As a leading treatise describes: "Except in cases of obvious overreaching, the courts are rather generous with respect to front-end fees [i.e., expenses of preparing and selling the collateral, legal fees, and the like] which can be added to a deficiency claim under section 9-504(1)(a)."

Even if the secured party does overspend, all he risks losing is the excess money spent. A review of hundreds of collateral sale opinions revealed no cases in which a sale was held to be commercially unreasonable because the secured party spent too much money preparing and selling the collateral. One case went so far as to say that excessive expenses are "irrelevant" to the issue of the commercial reasonableness of the sale and that the only sanction for running up excessive expenses is to deny recovery of those expenses.

Because it is virtually impossible to lose one's right to a deficiency judgment by overspending, and because the burden is on the secured party to prove that its sale of the collateral was commercially reasonable, the rational secured creditor will often incur expenses that he would never consider if he were selling his own property and bearing his own expenses.

REPORT OF THE PERMANENT EDITORIAL BOARD UCC ARTICLE 9 STUDY GROUP 199, Dec. 1, 1992. "Article 9 should be revised to set forth clearly the extent to which a secured party's failure to comply with Part 5 of the Article affects the secured party's right to a deficiency. The baseline rule should be the "rebuttable presumption" rule: Once it is established that a secured party has not complied with Part 5, the aggrieved party should be entitled to a rebuttable presumption that compliance with Part 5 would have yielded an amount sufficient to satisfy the secured debt in full. A secured party who seeks to recover a deficiency notwithstanding its failure to comply with Part 5 should have the burden of establishing the amount that would have been recovered had the secured party complied with Part 5, and the secured party's deficiency recovery should be limited to the difference between the amount of the secured debt and that amount."

REVISED § 9-625(2)(b)

[T]he liability of a debtor or other secondarily liable party for a deficiency is limited to an amount by which the sum of the secured obligation, expenses, and attorney's fees exceeds the greater of the proceeds of the collection, enforcement, disposition, or acceptance or the amount of proceeds that would have been realized had the noncomplying secured party proceeded in accordance with * * * [the provisions of this part relating to collection, enforcement, disposition, or acceptance]. However, the amount that would have been realized is equal to the sum of the secured obligation, expenses, and attorney's fees unless the secured party meets the burden of establishing that the amount is less than that sum.

NOTE ON RIGHTS AND LIABILITIES OF PURCHASERS

If the secured party fails to comply with the requirements of Part 5 of Article 9 in its public or private sale of the collateral, we have seen that its right to recover a deficiency from the debtor may be curtailed and that the secured party may be exposed to affirmative liability for damages under § 9-507(1). In contrast, however, a debtor's rights against the *purchaser* of the collateral at foreclosure are severely limited by § 9-504(4). That provision operates to confer title to the property on a purchaser for value free and clear of the security interest under which the sale occurred and all subordinate liens, notwithstanding the secured party's noncompliance with Part 5. In a public sale, the purchaser must take without knowledge of any defects in the sale, and must not have acted in collusion with the secured party or any other person conducting the sale, in order to qualify for this protection. In a private sale, the only limitation is that the purchaser must have acted in "good faith." Moreover, if the foreclosure sale is not flawed in any way, even a purchaser that failed to act in good faith will be protected under § 9-504(4). Thomas v. Price, 975 F.2d 231 (5th Cir. 1992). The rule in § 9-504(4) is designed to encourage potential purchasers at UCC foreclosure sales by assuring them of the quality of the title they receive to the property without having to investigate the regularity of the secured party's repossession and foreclosure procedures. Thus, the debtor's only recourse to protect its interest in the collateral in the event of creditor misbehavior is, if the debtor can act quickly enough, to seek to enjoin the sale under § 9-507(1).

The rule in § 9-504(4) is consistent with the general commercial law principle that a purchaser of assets (unlike a purchaser of stock) does not assume the liabilities of the transferor. However, an exception to this rule is recognized in circumstances involving special policy considerations, such as products liability and environmental contamination. In addition, under corporate law, when a transferee-corporation is deemed to be a "mere continuation" of the transferor-corporation, or in the case of a so-called "de facto merger" (a doctrine that recasts a sale transaction into a merger when in fact it is, in substance, identical in economic effect), courts have permitted the selling corporation's creditors to pursue their claims against the purchasing corporation. The question has arisen whether these exceptions to the rule that a transferee of assets does not assume the liabilities of its transferor apply in a secured creditor's sale of collateral under Article 9. Although Article 9 itself contains no such exceptions, many courts, employing supplemental equitable principles under § 1-103, have held that an Article 9 foreclosure sale of a debtor's assets does not act as an absolute bar to application against the purchaser of those assets of successor liability doctrines under applicable non-Code law. See Glynwed v. Plastimatic, Inc., 869 F. Supp. 265 (D.N.J. 1994). The effect of a finding of successor liability is to expose the purchaser to liability for the debts and obligations of the debtor. For this reason, in most cases in which successor liability is imposed, there will be a substantial continuity of ownership between the debtor and the purchaser as well as inadequate consideration for the purchase or some other element evidencing bad faith. See G.P. Publications, Inc. v. Quebecor Printing-St. Paul, Inc., 481 S.E.2d 674 (N.C. App. 1997).

NOTE ON "CONSUMER GOODS SECURED TRANSACTIONS"

Article 9, like most of the rest of the UCC, does not distinguish between commercial and consumer transactions, although there are a number of important qualifications to this general rule. Perhaps the most significant of these qualifications is in § 9-507(1), the last sentence of which provides: "If the collateral is consumer goods, the debtor has a right to recover in any event an amount not less than the credit service charge plus ten percent of the principal amount of the debt or the time price differential plus 10 per cent of the cash price."

Among the most controversial reforms in revised Article 9 are new provisions applicable only to "consumer goods secured transactions," statutorily defined as "a transfer in which (A) an individual incurs an obligation primarily for personal, family, or household purposes and the collateral is held for those purposes; and (B) a security interest in consumer goods secures the obligation." Revised § 9-102(15). See also Revised § 9-102(17), defining a "consumer secured transaction." Many of these provisions may not find their way into the final draft as consumer advocates and consumer credit groups continue to battle over whether it is appropriate to do any meaningful consumer protection inside of Article 9. In any event, among these new provisions is Revised § 9-613(b)(1), which requires that a notification of disposition in a consumer goods secured transaction must contain certain specific information, including the amount that must be paid to redeem the obligation under Revised § 9-621, and the amount necessary to reinstate the obligation under Revised § 9-622. In addition, Revised § 9-614A imposes a duty on the secured party in a consumer goods secured transaction to respond to a request for an explanation of the calculation of any surplus to which the debtor is entitled, or any deficiency for which the debtor is liable, upon disposition of the collateral. Failure to comply with this duty may expose the secured party to a $500 statutory penalty as well as to liability for any actual damages suffered. See Revised § 9-624(b), (e).

Revised § 9-625(2)(A) [Alternative A] imposes the "absolute bar rule" with respect to recovery of a deficiency in any consumer goods secured transaction in which the secured party failed to comply with its obligations under the new rules governing default and enforcement of security interests. Another provision, Revised § 9-622, permits the debtor in a consumer goods secured transaction, under certain conditions, to reinstate the secured obligation after default, notwithstanding acceleration by the secured party, upon tender of all past due installments, plus applicable late charges and fees. This is a one-time right. Finally, Revised § 9-628 confers discretion on the court to award attorney's fees if a secured party's "compliance with Article 9 is placed in issue in an action with respect to a consumer secured transaction," and the consumer prevails. Moreover, if the secured party would have been entitled to attorney's fees had it prevailed, the award of attorney's fees to the prevailing consumer becomes mandatory. Revised § 9-628(1).

The issue of whether special provisions aimed at protecting the interests of consumers ought to be incorporated into the UCC has been very controversial in the revision of the UCC generally, including Article 9. In evaluating how far the Code should go in distinguishing consumer transactions from other forms of commercial transactions, consider the following thoughts from Professor James J. White in his article *Work and Play in Revising Article 9*, 80 Va. L. Rev. 2089, 2095 (1994):

> The consumer threat rests upon the consumer's inalienable and inexhaustible right to legislative sympathy. One should not forget that every single resident of Leavenworth and San Quentin is a consumer. And each of those sweet persons who used to live in your house and lie to you so boldly and without remorse in their teenage years is now a consumer. However, deceitful and nasty the behavior of Bank of America or Citicorp and their ilk, the number of evil acts of all American banks from the beginning of time is equaled daily by the frauds and evil acts of consumers. So a starting point in answer to consumer requests for

generous treatment in Article 9 is to recognize that the consumer class overflows with lies and cheats. The drafters should purge the idea of the noble consumer who borrows in ignorance, and who is surprised by repossession and deficiency judgment, and who claims incredible promises by his creditor.

Ultimately, whether consumer transactions are afforded special protection under Article 9 or not, consumer credit transactions remain subject to a considerable body of suppletory state and federal legislation. For example, about 10 states have adopted the Uniform Consumer Credit Code which contains an integrated system for state consumer credit regulation. Other states have their own non-uniform legislation regulating retail installment sale and consumer loan transactions. Article 9 defers to both this uniform and nonuniform legislation whenever applicable. See § 9-203(4). Revised Article 9 continues this practice. See Revised § 9-115. In addition, the unevenness of state regulation has contributed to enactment of a steady stream of preemptive, largely disclosure-oriented federal legislation, such as the Consumer Credit Protection Act (15 U.S.C. §§ 1601 et seq.), which includes, among other provisions, the "Truth in Lending" Act (Title I of the CCPA), the Equal Credit Opportunity Act (Title VII of the CCPA), and the Fair Debt Collection Practice Act (Title VIII of CCPA). While the spate of federal consumer protection legislation has abated in recent years, certainly no seller or lender considering foreclosure of an Article 9 security interest in consumer goods would be well-advised to proceed without carefully consulting the supplementary duties and obligations imposed by these laws.

SECTION 5. STRICT FORECLOSURE

INTRODUCTORY NOTE

Section 9-505 codifies the Article 9 version of a strict foreclosure, which has historical antecedents in the law of real property finance. It represents an option sometimes available to a secured party in lieu of sale under § 9-504 to retain the collateral in full satisfaction of the debtor's obligation. The benefits of a strict foreclosure are that it avoids the additional costs of a sale where no deficiency is expected or where a deficiency will not be recoverable and insulates the secured party from having its disposition of the collateral challenged on commercial reasonableness grounds. On the other hand, the secured party can only *propose* to retain the collateral in exchange for abandoning any deficiency claim, and the debtor or any other party entitled to notice has the right to object, in which case the secured party must proceed with sale under § 9-504. In addition, the secured party is statutorily precluded from even proposing a strict foreclosure in any case where the collateral is consumer goods and more than 60 percent of the loan or cash price in the case of a purchase money security interest has been paid. See § 9-505(1).

Revised Article 9 not only continues strict foreclosure in its present form, it also permits a secured party to propose to retain the seized collateral in *partial* satisfaction of the debtor's obligation. In that case, however, the debtor must affirmatively agree to the proposal, which is to say mere acquiescence (which is all that is required when the proposal is to retain the collateral in full satisfaction) would not be sufficient. Revised § 9-618(b)(1), (d). At this time, the availability of partial strict foreclosure in consumer goods secured transactions is under discussion. While both current and Revised Article 9 contemplate only creditor-initiated strict foreclosures, as discussed in the next case, some courts have used strict foreclosure as a remedy to sanction creditor misconduct in the foreclosure process.

LAMP FAIR, INC. v. PEREZ-ORTIZ

United States Court of Appeals, First Circuit, 1989.
888 F.2d 173.

BREYER, Circuit Judge.

Does Article 9 of the Uniform Commercial Code permit a secured creditor, over the objection of the debtor, both to retain collateral for the creditor's own use and also to obtain a deficiency judgment? We believe that, in the circumstances of the present case, the answer is "no." Accordingly, we reverse the judgment of the district court.

I.

Relevant Background Facts

The plaintiff in this diversity case, Lamp Fair, Inc., sold its store to the defendant, Pedro Perez Ortiz, and Perez Ortiz failed to pay the full price. Lamp Fair then repossessed the store, kept it, and sued Perez Ortiz for the "deficiency" between Lamp Fair's valuation of the store and what Perez Ortiz still owed. * * *

The Security Agreement set out what would happen if Perez Ortiz defaulted on his obligation to pay the remainder of the purchase price (as he did). It provided that Lamp Fair could require Perez Ortiz to assemble the collateral, and that Lamp Fair could then take possession of it (i.e., the store), which is just what happened. The Agreement also provided that Lamp Fair would have "all the remedies of a Secured Party under the Uniform Commercial Code of Connecticut." In light of this last statement in the Agreement the magistrate should have looked to the Uniform Commercial Code (as adopted by Connecticut) to determine whether or not Lamp Fair was entitled to more than it had already received—the $50,000 down payment, the monthly payments through December, and the returned store. The magistrate failed to do this. We have examined Connecticut law ourselves, however, and we conclude that Lamp Fair cannot recover a deficiency.

A.

Article 9 of the Uniform Commercial Code sets forth the remedies available to a secured party. It gives a secured party, such as Lamp Fair, three basic options after default. See 2 J. White and R. Summers, Uniform Commercial Code 570 (3d ed. 1988). Each of these options, while permitting the creditor under some circumstances to obtain the collateral, contains safeguards to assure the debtor that the secured party will not take unfair advantage of the situation and that the value of the collateral will be fairly ascertained.

* * *

[The first option the court described was simply for the secured party to bring suit for judgment on the note itself. Because Lamp Fair did not choose this option, however, the court concluded that it could not support its claim for a deficiency based on the "judgment option".]

2. Retention. The secured party's second option after default is to "retain the collateral in satisfaction of the obligation." U.C.C. § 9-505(2). The Code makes clear, however, that retention of the collateral normally completely satisfies the debt; the secured party must abandon any claim for deficiency (unless the debtor signs a written statement permitting such a claim, which Perez Ortiz did not do). U.C.C. § 9-505, comment 1; 2 J. White and R. Summers, Uniform Commercial Code 585; Tanenbaum v. Economics Laboratory, Inc., 628 S.W.2d 769, 771 (Tex.1982). The Code also states that the secured party must give notice of its intention to retain the collateral in satisfaction of the obligation, so that the debtor may object to retention and demand that the collateral be sold. Lamp Fair did not give this notice; it did not consciously choose this option.

3. Disposition. Section 9-504 sets forth the secured creditor's remaining option. It says that he "may sell, lease or otherwise dispose of any or all of the collateral * * * by public or private proceedings." After doing so, he must "account to the debtor for any surplus," and "the debtor is liable for any deficiency." Every aspect of the disposition must be "commercially reasonable." In addition, the secured creditor must give the debtor notice of when the sale or other disposition will take place. The secured creditor can buy the collateral himself at any "public sale," but he cannot buy it at a "private sale" unless the collateral is "of a type customarily sold in a recognized market or * * * the subject of widely distributed standard price quotations." U.C.C. § 9-504(1)-(3). These rules in part seek to protect the debtor, for they help prevent the creditor from acquiring the collateral himself at less than its true value or unfairly understating its value to obtain a greater-than-warranted deficiency judgment. 2 J. White and R. Summers, Uniform Commercial Code 590, 599 (3d ed. 1988); 1A P. Coogan, W. Hogan, D. Vagts & J. McDonnell, Secured Transactions Under the Uniform Commercial Code § 8.04(2)(c) at 8-97, § 8.06(2) at 8-123 (1989); Ocean National Bank of Kennebunk v. Odell, 444 A.2d 422, 425 (Me.1982).

B.

Given these provisions of Connecticut law, Lamp Fair, in our view, cannot both retain the collateral and also obtain a deficiency judgment. We can reach this conclusion through either of two alternative lines of reasoning.

First, the majority of courts that have dealt with this issue would simply hold that Lamp Fair's conduct in retaining and operating the store on a permanent basis brings the transaction within the scope of the § 9-505(2) "retention option," irrespective of whether or not Lamp Fair consciously chose to invoke this option. See, e.g., Shultz v. Delaware Trust Co., 360 A.2d 576, 578 (Del.Super.1976) (retention of collateral for five years may be found to be in satisfaction of obligation despite secured party's protestations to the contrary); Millican v. Turner, 503 So.2d 289, 291 (Miss.1987) (adopting "majority position" that creditor who retains collateral for unreasonably long period is deemed to have retained in satisfaction); Swanson v. May, 40 Wash.App. 148, 697 P.2d 1013, 1015-16 (1985) (same); Schmode's, Inc. v. Wilkinson, 219 Neb. 209, 361 N.W.2d 557, 559 (1985) (secured party who used collateral for nearly three years elected to retain in satisfaction); Haufler v. Ardinger, 28 U.C.C. Rep. Serv. 893, 896-97 (Mass.App.1979) (use of collateral for 38 months is election to retain barring deficiency); In re Boyd, 73 B.R. 122, 124-25 (Bankr.N.D.Tex.1987) (use of collateral for three months deemed retention in satisfaction). See also 2 J. White and R. Summers, Uniform Commercial Code 588. These courts reason that the Code intends "to put the creditor to an election to either sell the repossessed collateral pursuant to Section 9.504 or to retain the collateral in complete satisfaction of the debt pursuant to Section 9.505." Tanenbaum v. Economics Laboratory, Inc., 628 S.W.2d at 771-72 (creditor who retained and then scrapped collateral deemed to have retained in satisfaction of debt). The secured creditor cannot both avoid a more "objective," market-based, valuation of the collateral and also obtain an additional "deficiency judgment" remedy (unless the debtor expressly consents).

We note, however, that a minority of courts, including the Second Circuit in a rather different context, have written that § 9-505(2) does not apply when the secured creditor, wishing it not to apply, does not fulfill its procedural prerequisites (i.e., does not give notice). See Warnaco, Inc. v. Farkas, 872 F.2d 539, 544-45 (2d Cir.1989) (Winter, J.) (predicting Connecticut would not follow cases applying § 9-505(2) where creditor did not give written notice of intent to retain collateral in satisfaction of debt); S. M. Flickinger Co. v. 18 Genesee Corp., 71 A.D.2d 382, 423 N.Y.S.2d 73, 76 (1979); In re Nardone, 70 B.R. 1010, 1016-17 (Bankr.D.Mass.1987). In effect, these courts have refused to "force" § 9-505(2) upon an unwilling secured creditor. Since Lamp Fair wishes to obtain a deficiency judgment, it is such an "unwilling creditor."

Our second, alternative, line of reasoning would accept this minority view; it would start from Warnaco's premise that § 9-505(2)'s "retention option" does not apply because an unwilling Lamp Fair did not give the required notice. Following this line of reasoning, we should note that the transaction must fall within the scope of the remaining "disposition option." This option, under § 9-504, does permit a creditor to obtain a deficiency judgment. But, regardless, Lamp Fair failed to satisfy § 9-504's preconditions for obtaining such a judgment because Lamp Fair did not "sell, lease or otherwise dispose" of the store. Lamp Fair did not hold a "public sale," at which it could have bid for the collateral. Nor could it have purchased the collateral itself by means of "private sale," for the store is not of the "type customarily sold in a recognized market or * * * the subject of widely distributed standard price quotations." And, whatever the meaning of the words "otherwise dispose of," they do not include permanent retention of the collateral for the secured party's own use. Appeal of Copeland, 531 F.2d 1195, 1207 (3d Cir.1976). Cf. National Equipment Rental, Ltd. v. Priority Electronics Corp., 435 F.Supp. 236, 240 (E.D.N.Y.1977) (repossession and conversion to own use by plaintiff's agent not "disposition" under § 9-504, so § 9-505 applies); Black's Law Dictionary 423 (5th ed.1979) (defining "disposition" as "transferring to the care or possession of another * * * parting with, alienation of, or giving up property"). (Consider, as well, the contrasting use of "disposition" in section 9-504 and "retention" in section 9-505. Copeland, 531 F.2d at 1207.)

* * *

We need not decide which alternative line of reasoning Connecticut would follow, whether Connecticut would hold 1) that § 9-505(2) governs, or 2) that the transaction falls within the scope of, but fails to meet the necessary prerequisites of, § 9-504. Either way the law denies Lamp Fair its deficiency judgment. We can predict with reasonable assurance, Meredith v. Winter Haven, 320 U.S. 228, 236-38, 64 S.Ct. 7, 11-13, 88 L.Ed. 9 (1943), that Connecticut would follow one or the other of these paths to this result. Therefore the judgment of the district court must be

Reversed.

SNYDER v. BANK ONE, 113 F.3d 774 (7th Cir. 1996). Bank One sent the defaulting debtors a letter that it intended to sell the bank stock that had been pledged as security, but, before a sale was arranged, the stock was rendered worthless when the office of the Comptroller of the Currency ordered the bank closed and its assets liquidated. The debtors contended that Bank One had elected its remedy, to retain the collateral in full satisfaction of the debt, and could not thereafter press for recovery of the unpaid balance of the loan from the debtors. The court disagreed, on the following basis: "Bank One did not at any time send written notice of intent to accept the collateral in satisfaction of the debt. Holding the collateral for a one month period while making at least some efforts to sell it is a very different matter from holding and controlling a business for eighteen months. Bank One used reasonable care for the month that it was possible to do so any contrary conclusion would be unreasonable."

PATRICK v. WIX AUTO COMPANY, INC.

Appellate Court of Illinois, First District, Fourth Division, 1997.
288 Ill. App.3d 846, 681 N.E.2d 98.

Justice CERDA delivered the opinion of the court.

Plaintiff, Catherine Patrick, filed a class action against defendant, Wix Auto Company, alleging that defendant failed to comply with the satisfaction by repossession notice requirements of section 9-505(2) of the Illinois Commercial Code (810 ILCS 5/9-505(2)(West 1994)) after it repossessed her automobile.

Defendant filed a section 2-615 motion to dismiss the complaint (735 ILCS 5/2-615 (West 1994)), which was granted. The trial court found that the notice sent by defendant was sufficient as a matter of law. For the following reasons, we reverse and remand.

Plaintiff purchased a used 1987 Cadillac automobile from defendant on March 22, 1995, for $6,995 plus finance charges. Pursuant to the retail installment contract, plaintiff was required to maintain insurance on the automobile. Defendant repossessed the automobile on April 26, 1995, and sent a letter entitled "Notice of Repossession" to plaintiff on May 2, 1995.

On September 29, 1995, plaintiff filed a class action against defendant for failure to comply with either section 9-504 or 9-505(2) of the Illinois Commercial Code (810 ILCS 5/9-504, 9-505(2)(West 1994)). The complaint sought statutory damages pursuant to section 9-507 of the Code. 810 ILCS 5/9-507(West 1994).

On December 5, 1995, defendant filed a section 2-615 motion to dismiss for failure to state a cause of action. The motion claimed that the notice sent to plaintiff on May 2, 1995, satisfied section 9-505(2)'s requirements. The trial court granted defendant's motion.

On appeal, plaintiff asserts that the complaint adequately pleaded a cause of action because (1) it established that defendant was a secured creditor who, after repossessing the secured collateral, was required by section 505(2) to send a written notice that it proposed to retain the collateral in satisfaction of the obligation; (2) it alleged that the notice did not comply with the requirements of section 505(2); and (3) it set out the damages for defendant's violation, which is a statutory penalty under section 507.

The main issue on appeal is whether plaintiff stated a cause of action pursuant to section 505(2), which reads, in pertinent part, as follows:

> "In any other case involving consumer goods or any other collateral a secured party in possession may, after default, propose to retain the collateral in satisfaction of the obligation. Written notice of such proposal shall be sent to the debtor if he has not signed after default a statement renouncing or modifying his rights under this subsection. In the case of consumer goods no other notice need be given. * * * [I]f the secured party receives objection in writing from a person entitled to receive notification within twenty-one days after the notice was sent, the secured party must dispose of the collateral under Section 9-504. In the absence of such written objection the secured party may retain the collateral in satisfaction of the debtor's obligation." 810 ILCS 5/9-505(2)(West 1994).

After repossessing a debtor's collateral, the secured creditor can either dispose of the collateral and seek a deficiency judgment (810 ILCS 5/9-504(West 1994)) or accept it in discharge of the obligation (810 ILCS 5/9-505(2)(West 1994)). In either case, the secured creditor must send notice of its action to the debtor. 810 ILCS 5/9-504, 505(2)(West 1994).

* * *

The notice stated as follows:

"Date: May 2, 1995

NOTICE OF REPOSSESSION

Catherine Patrick	VEHICLE	1987 Fleetwood Cadillac
921 W. Wilson		
Chicago, IL 60640	SERIAL NO #:	1G6CB5189H4249770
	BALANCE DUE:	$260.45

Dear Customer:

Our records indicate that you have failed to keep your contractual obligation. Despite our efforts to notify you of such, the contract still remains in default of insurance.

Therefore, we have repossessed the above mentioned vehicle. Please be advised that you may redeem at any time until it is restocked. If you fail to bring proof of insurance, the vehicle will be restocked and we will retain all monies thus far.

THIS IS A FINAL NOTICE." (emphasis in original)

The parties have cited no Illinois cases that interpret section 505(2) and we have found none. When there is a lack of Illinois cases interpreting the Illinois Commercial Code, this court has looked to Uniform Commercial Code decisions in other jurisdictions. Rebaque v. Forsythe Racing, Inc., 134 Ill.App.3d 778, 781, 89 Ill.Dec. 595, 480 N.E.2d 1338 (1985); First Nat. Bank of Thomasboro v. Lachenmyer, 131 Ill.App.3d 914, 921, 87 Ill.Dec. 53, 476 N.E.2d 755 (1985).

Defendant urges this court to adopt a broad standard of notice so that the facts and circumstances surrounding the written notice would be relevant. Defendant asserts that the notice was adequate because plaintiff did not allege that defendant later resold the automobile or pursued plaintiff to collect a deficiency after any sale. Based on relevant cases in other jurisdictions, we decline to adopt the broad standard defendant suggests.

Section 505(2) contains specific requirements for a strict foreclosure and should not be liberally construed so that a forfeiture can occur. In re McNair, 90 B.R. 912, 917 (Bankr.N.D.Ill.1988). If, upon default, a creditor elects to retain the collateral as full satisfaction of the debtor's obligations, he must comply with the terms of section 505(2) (Fletcher v. Cobuzzi, 499 F.Supp. 694, 699 (W.D.Pa.1980)), which requires that the creditor notify the debtor of the creditor's proposal to retain the collateral as full satisfaction of the debt (Fletcher, 499 F.Supp. at 699; Pan Ocean Navigation, Inc. v. Rainbow Navigation, Inc., No. 8674 (Del. Ch. July 8, 1987), slip op. at 6, 1987 WL 13519). The written notice must clearly and explicitly inform the debtor that the creditor is retaining the collateral in satisfaction of the indebtedness. Chen v. Profit Sharing Plan of Dr. Donald H. Bohne, P.A., 216 Ga.App. 878, 456 S.E.2d 237, 240 (1995); In re Alcom America Corporation, 154 B.R. 97, 113 (Bankr.D.D.C.1993).

Further, the notice must be of strict foreclosure in particular, not simply of an intent to foreclose. Fletcher, 499 F.Supp. at 699. A notice of default and request for payment is inconsistent with strict foreclosure and does not satisfy the statutory requirement of section 505(2). In re Alcom America Corporation, 154 B.R. at 113. Failure to comply with the requirements of section 505(2) makes the purported foreclosure ineffective. Pan Ocean Navigation, Inc., slip op. at 6.

We find that the notice in this case was deficient under section 505(2) as a matter of law. It did not give adequate notice because it was confusing, contradictory, and failed to inform plaintiff that defendant proposed to retain the automobile in full satisfaction of the debt. First, the notice indicated that defendant intended to "restock" the automobile, not retain the automobile in full satisfaction of the debt. Although no magic words are needed, it is insufficient to state that the automobile will be "restocked," which can be interpreted as meaning that it will be put back on the car lot to be resold, which would require following section 504. In its brief, defendant states that custom and usage of a commercial business indicates that "restock" means to put the car back on the lot to resell, and at oral argument, defendant stated that "'restocked' means we're going to put [the automobile] back on the lot to sell." It is not clear what would happen to the debt after the car is restocked and sold. Perhaps the plaintiff would have to pay a deficiency.

Further, the notice conveyed information that was inconsistent with a strict foreclosure: (1) it informed plaintiff that there was a balance due of $260.45; (2) it invited plaintiff to "redeem [the] vehicle at any time until it is restocked;" and (3) it stated only that defendant would "retain all monies received thus far" if plaintiff failed to cure the default.

A helpful case is In re Leeling, 129 B.R. 637, 16 U.C.C. Rep.Serv.2d 267, 271 (Bankr.D.Colo.1991), where the court found the notice to be improper under section 505(2). The notice in In re Leeling stated in part:

> "I have, concurrently herewith, delivered a Certificate of Default to Greg Van Wagner, and have instructed him to Smiths pay [sic] all payments hereafter due * * * until Mr. Leeling's Note obligation to the Smiths is fully paid * * * although not required by the Note, demand is hereby made for Mr. Leeling's full payment * * * please contact me if Mr. Leeling intends to pay off the Note."

The bankruptcy court stated:

> "Most importantly, it was inconsistent to have stated in the Kerst letter that the Van Wagner note would be retained in full satisfaction of the debt, and then two sentences later demand full payment by the debtor on the outstanding note he owed to the Smiths. If the Smiths were retaining the Van Wagner note in full satisfaction, then the debtor need not have made any more payments on his outstanding debt to the Smiths, and the demand for full payment could certainly be viewed as an ambiguity as to the Smith's intentions. Further, while it might not be necessary to use the magic words 'foreclosure' or 'retain in full satisfaction of the indebtedness' the intent to retain must be such that a reasonable person

> would understand that intent, and it must be clearly manifested by the secured creditor. [Cite omitted.] The court does not believe that such a clear intent was manifested by the Smiths and consequently, there was no foreclosure pursuant to § 4-9-505(2), as its notice requirements have not been complied with." In re Leeling, 129 B.R. 637, 16 U.C.C. Rep.Serv.2d at 272.

* * *

Similarly, in this case, the notice did not comply with section 505(2) as a matter of law because it did not clearly and explicitly inform plaintiff that defendant was retaining the automobile in full satisfaction of the debt. Therefore, the complaint adequately stated a valid cause of action.

Based on the foregoing, we reverse the circuit court judgment and remand this cause for further proceedings.

———

Chapter 7

THE MECHANICS OF PERFECTION

SECTION 1. THE NEED FOR ATTACHMENT

INTRODUCTORY NOTE

You may recall that earlier we distinguished between "attachment" and "perfection" on the basis that the former establishes the secured creditor's default rights against the debtor, while the later confers priority rights vis-à-vis other claimants with an interest in the collateral. In fact, however, attachment is also a prerequisite to perfection. Section 9-303(1) provides that a security interest is perfected when (1) it has attached, and (2) all steps necessary for perfection have been taken. These requirements can occur in any order or even simultaneously; however, even if the steps necessary for perfection have occurred, if the security interest has not attached, not only is the claim unperfected, it is *unsecured* as well. The first case in this chapter illustrates the relationship between the two requisites for perfection.

NBD-SANDUSKY BANK v. RITTER

Supreme Court of Michigan, 1991.
437 Mich. 354, 471 N.W.2d 340.

[In May of 1985 Mr. and Mrs. Ritter granted NBD a security interest in all their farm equipment, then owned or thereafter acquired. The bank filed a proper financing statement on May 30, 1985. On July 23 of that year Mr. Ritter took delivery of farm equipment purchased from Laethem Farm Service Co., a John Deere dealer. On July 31, Mr. Ritter executed a security agreement in favor of John Deere to secure his obligations under contracts to purchase the equipment he had received on the 23rd. The agreement recited that it was not effective until accepted by John Deere. On August 7, Deere filed a financing statement; but Deere did not execute the security agreement until August 15. Deere gave value to Laethem when it paid the purchase price of the equipment on July 31.]

BOYLE, J.

This is a priority dispute between two commercial lenders, each holding a perfected security interest in the same collateral. Appellant, John Deere, claims priority as a purchase money lender, and NBD claims priority under its "after-acquired property" clause. Resolution of the dispute is governed by the Uniform Commercial Code.

The Uniform Commercial Code must be "liberally construed and applied to promote its underlying purposes and policies." M.C.L. § 440.1102(1); M.S.A. § 19.1102(1). The court is to apply the language under a particular section of the code to further both that section's specific purpose and policies and the general underlying purposes of the code. U.C.C. § 1-102(1), Official Comment (1). Two of the code's general purposes are to simplify, clarify, and modernize commercial law and to permit the continued expansion of commercial practices through custom, usage, and agreement of the parties. M.C.L. § 440.1102(2)(a), (b); M.S.A. § 19.1102(2)(a), (b). One authority has acknowledged that an additional underlying purpose of the code is to make "the law of commercial transactions be, so far as reasonable, liberal and nontechnical." 1 White & Summers, Uniform Commercial Code (3d ed.), § 64, p. 15.

A priority contest between two parties holding a perfected security interest in the same collateral is usually determined according to which party either was the first to properly file a financing statement covering the subject collateral or was the first to perfect its security interest. M.C.L. § 440.9312(6); M.S.A. § 19.9312(6). NBD filed its financing statement on May 30, 1985. Thus, unless another rule applies, the bank's security interest has priority. John Deere claims that it holds a perfected purchase money security interest in the debtor's noninventory collateral and therefore its security interest in the subject farm equipment should enjoy the special priority status granted under M.C.L. § 440.9312(5); M.S.A. § 19.9312(5).

There is no real dispute that John Deere's security interest falls within the statutory definition of a purchase money security interest since it was "taken by a person who by making advances or incurring an obligation gives value to enable the debtor to acquire rights in or the use of collateral if such value is in fact so used." M.C.L. § 440.9107(b); M.S.A. § 19.9107(b).

Under the three-party transaction involved here, John Deere, as lender, paid Laethem, the seller, the amount Mr. Ritter owed under the purchase agreement with Laethem, and received a purchase money security interest in the goods acquired. The money advanced to Laethem became the purchase money debt, and the acquired goods became the purchase money collateral.

M.C.L. § 440.9312(5); M.S.A. § 19.9312(5) provides: "A purchase money security interest in collateral other than inventory has priority over a conflicting security interest in the same collateral or its proceeds *if the purchase money security interest is perfected at the time the debtor receives possession of the collateral or within 20 days thereafter*." (Emphasis added.) Thus, the central issue here is whether John Deere complied with the Uniform Commercial Code's requirements so as to allow it to enjoy special priority status over competing claimants. The code focuses on two critical dates: when the debtor received possession of the collateral and when John Deere's purchase money security interest was perfected. In addition to these requirements, we recognize both the code's preference for purchase money security interests as evidenced in §§ 9301(2), 9312(4), and 9312(5) and its condition that, in order to enjoy special priority status, the purchase money security interest holder must cure the ostensible ownership problem that its security interest creates shortly after the problem arises. U.C.C. § 9-312, Official Comment (3).

It is uncontested that Mr. Ritter received physical possession of the farm equipment on July 23, 1985. Thus, we turn to the date John Deere perfected its purchase money security interest in the subject equipment. Perfection is a two-step process requiring that the security interest "attach" and that all the applicable steps for "perfection" have been taken. The sequence of events is not determinative. M.C.L. § 440.9303(1); M.S.A. § 19.9303(1) specifically provides "[i]f such steps [for perfection] are taken before the security interest attaches, it is perfected at the time when it attaches."

John Deere complied with the second step in this process by filing a properly executed financing statement covering the subject equipment with the Sanilac County Register of Deeds on August 7, 1985. M.C.L. §§ 440.9302, 440.9401(1)(a); M.S.A. §§ 19.9302, 19.9401(1)(a). The filing was made fifteen days after the debtor took physical possession of the collateral. Thus, we can further narrow our inquiry to the date John Deere's purchase money security interest attached.

"Attachment" is a term of art used in the code to identify the steps necessary to create a security interest that is enforceable against the debtor. In this case, John Deere (the secured party) did not have possession of the collateral. Therefore, four steps were necessary for its security interest to "attach" to the collateral. John Deere was required to: (1) enter into a "security agreement" with the debtor, (2) reduce the agreement to a writing signed by the debtor and containing a description of the collateral, and (3) give value, and the debtor was required to (4) have rights in the collateral. M.C.L. § 440.9203(1)(a)-(c); M.S.A. § 19.9203(1)(a)-(c). As soon as all these events took place, attachment occurred unless the parties explicitly agreed to postpone the time of attaching. M.C.L. § 440.9203(2); M.S.A. § 19.9203(2).

The Court of Appeals focused on the language of the parties' loan contract and security agreement and held that the "agreement" and "value" elements of "attachment" were not satisfied until August 15, 1985, the date the document was executed by a John Deere representative. The Court emphasized that the document was worded as an application for financing, was conditioned upon John Deere's acceptance, and John Deere's signature clause was prefaced with the words "accepted by" and contained a space for an authorized signature and date.

In reaching its conclusion, the Court rejected John Deere's argument that the loan contract and security agreement was accepted by performance, finding that the claim was unsupported by the evidence presented at trial. Finally, in support of its decision, the Court stated that "[a]mbiguities in the loan contract and security agreement must be construed against Deere Company, which drafted it [and] Deere cannot now claim that it accepted by performance contrary to the terms of its own contract." 179 Mich.App. at 587, 446 N.W.2d 340. In other words, the Court reached its conclusion that there was no "agreement" or "value given" until August 15, 1985, by strictly construing the loan contract and security agreement against John Deere.

John Deere does not dispute that the loan contract and security agreement was conditioned upon its acceptance. It argues, however, that the document did not specify the method of acceptance and that it accepted by performance earlier than the August 15, 1985, signature date. It argues that the Court of Appeals erred when it stated this claim was not supported by the evidence presented at trial. We agree.

The code's definition sections provide the necessary guidance for establishing the date the parties reached an agreement to create a security interest and the date John Deere "gave value."

M.C.L. § 440.9105(1)(l); M.S.A. § 19.9105(1)(l) defines a security agreement as: "an agreement which creates or provides for a security interest." For guidance regarding the nature of the "agreement" between the parties, we look to how that term is defined. M.C.L. § 440.1201(3); M.S.A. § 19.1201(3) provides: " 'Agreement' means the bargain of the parties in fact as found in their language or by implication from other circumstances including course of dealing or usage of trade or course of performance as provided in this act (sections 1205 and 2208)." We have considered the parties' written security agreement and the course of performance and course of dealing testimony presented at trial, and find the parties' "bargain in fact" was that John Deere could accept by performance and that it did so earlier than the August 15, 1985, signature date on the loan contract and security agreement.

First, we underscore that the loan contract and security agreement document does not specify a method of acceptance, i.e., that it may only be accepted by John Deere's signature on the document. Second, we find convincing the uncontroverted testimony presented at trial which established that it is John Deere's practice to accept a security agreement prior to the date the financing statement is filed. John Deere filed its financing statement on August 7, 1985. Thus, we conclude that John Deere both "accepted" the loan contract and security agreement and satisfied the "agreement" element of attachment as of August 7, 1985. Moreover, when John Deere filed its financing statement, it cured any ostensible ownership problem created by Mr. Ritter's possession of the collateral. Consequently, there is no reason not to give effect to the Uniform Commercial Code's policy favoring purchase money security interests.

The record also indicates that on July 31, 1985, John Deere authorized Laethem to take an immediate credit on its account with John Deere. This is additional evidence of John Deere's acceptance of the agreement by performance. It is also uncontroverted evidence that John Deere "gave value" as required under M.C.L. § 440.9203(1)(b); M.S.A. § 19.9203(1)(b). By allowing Laethem to take a credit off its account, John Deere satisfied the definition of "value." M.C.L. § 440.1201(44)(a) and (d); M.S.A. § 19.1201(44)(a) and (d) provide that a party gives "value" when it gives "a binding commitment to extend credit" or it gives "any consideration sufficient to support a simple contract." See In re Reliable Mfg. Corp., 703 F.2d 996, 1000 (CA 7, 1983). Thus, we agree with Judge MacKenzie's conclusion in her dissenting opinion in the Court of Appeals that "[t]he record indicates that immediately after Ritter signed the contract and security agreement on July 31, Laethem received a retail note credit from John Deere and thus received its money for Ritter's purchase of the equipment [and] this transaction constitutes the giving of value by John Deere." NBD-Sandusky Bank, supra at 588, 446 N.W.2d 340.

SECTION 2. THE PLEDGE

CODE OF HAMMURABI §§ 117-119

If a man be in debt and sell his wife, son, or daughter, or bind them over to service, for three years they shall work in the house of their purchaser or master; in the fourth year they shall be given their freedom.

If he bind over to service a male or female slave, and if the merchant transfer or sell such slave, there is no cause for complaint.

If a man be in debt and he sell his maid servant who has borne him children (i.e., the man in debt) shall repay the money which the merchant paid (him), and he shall ransom his maid servant.

FERGUS KELLY, 3 A GUIDE TO EARLY IRISH LAW 164 n.55 (1988). "In the Celtic languages there is a close connection between the ideas of 'pledge' and 'hostage'. The [Old Irish] term *gell* 'pledge' * * * is from the same root as *giall* 'hostage'* * *. The [Welsh] cognate of *giall* is *gwystl*, which is normally used of a pledge, but also of a hostage * * *. [Irish] *gell* is also occasionally used of a hostage."

DASHIELL HAMMETT, THE MALTESE FALCON, IN THE NOVELS OF DASHIELL HAMMETT 397 (1965).

"Then the bird does not belong to any of you?" Spade asked, "but to a General Kemidov?"

"Belong?" the fat man said jovially, "Well, sir, you might say it belonged to the King of Spain, but I don't see how you can honestly grant anybody else clear title to it—except by right of possession." He clucked. "An article of that value that has passed from hand to hand by such means is clearly the property of whoever can get hold of it."

UCC § 9-304(1)

A security interest in chattel paper or negotiable documents may be perfected by filing. A security interest in the rights to proceeds of a written letter of credit can be perfected only by the secured party's taking possession of the letter of credit. A security interest in money or instruments (other than instruments which may constitute part of chattel paper) can be perfected only by the secured party's taking possession * * *.

REVISED UCC § 9-310(a)

(1) A security interest in instruments, chattel paper, investment property, or negotiable documents may be perfected by filing. * * *

IN RE PHOENIX STEEL CORP.

United States Bankruptcy Court, District of Delaware, 1987.
76 B.R. 373.

HELEN S. BALICK, Bankruptcy Judge.

On July 30, 1985, approximately two years after filing a Chapter 11 case, Phoenix Steel Corporation sued Rittenhouse Organization to recover an alleged preference of $50,625. Following discovery, pre-trial conference and several rescheduled trial dates, the court, on request of counsel, permitted the parties to submit a stipulation of facts in lieu of trial.

Phoenix paid $50,625 to Rittenhouse on July 5, 1983. Phoenix claims that this payment, made within the 90 days preceding the filing of Phoenix' Chapter 11 case, falls within the purview of 11 U.S.C. § 547(b).[1]

The July 5 payment was the third payment due under a purchase order from Phoenix to Rittenhouse issued on or about May 5 in connection with the purchase for $135,000 of a used shot blaster line located on property of Bethlehem Steel Corp. in Pottstown, Montgomery County, Pennsylvania. The terms of sale, embodied in an agreement of sale dated May 4 and 6, 1983, were:

TERMS:

"AS IS, WHERE IS"

Removal: Not to exceed 60 (sixty) days.

Payment Schedule:

Upon Receipt of Agreement	— $33,750
Due And Payable 5/16/83	— $50,625

---

[1] Under § 547(b) of the Code, a trustee/debtor in possession may avoid certain transfers of property. A preference is a transfer of an interest in debtor's property to or for the benefit of a creditor for or on account of an antecedent debt owing by the debtor before the transfer was made. The transfer must have been made while the debtor was insolvent and within 90 days before the filing of the bankruptcy petition. Further, as a result of the transfer the creditor must have received more than such creditor would receive in a liquidation had the transfer not been made and such creditor shared in the proceeds of the liquidation.

Balance Due And Payable
Before Completion of Removal — $50,625

Phoenix made the first two payments, disassembled the equipment and requested its release before making the final payment. The request was refused. Phoenix paid the $50,625 on July 5 and removed the equipment.

Phoenix filed a Chapter 11 case on August 12, 1983. Phoenix characterizes the transaction as a sale on credit and contends that but for the July 5 payment Rittenhouse, as an unsecured creditor, would have received something less than 100% in a liquidation case. Rittenhouse on the other hand contends that it had a security interest in the equipment.

If on the filing date, Rittenhouse was a creditor holding a security interest in the equipment, it could exercise rights under the Code to collect the amount of the final payment from its collateral. Since the equipment was worth $135,000, it is clear that Rittenhouse would have been paid in full. Thus, the nature of the debt, secured or unsecured, is of critical importance. That determination requires an examination of the entire transaction. The agreement, reached no later than May 6, requires Phoenix to pay 66% of the purchase price within 10 days. Phoenix did this and began to disassemble the equipment which was to take nearly two months. The agreement clearly states that removal of the equipment was not to take place before Rittenhouse received final payment. It is clear that although Rittenhouse was selling the equipment to Phoenix, it intended to retain control subject to final payment.

The language of the agreement together with Phoenix' request to remove the equipment before final payment and Rittenhouse's denial reinforces the court's conclusion that Rittenhouse intended to retain title. In doing this, it created a security interest in its favor. Gillespie v. Great Atlantic and Pacific Tea Co., 10 U.C.C.Rep.Serv. 754, 758 (N.C.App., 1972). In Gillespie, seller was a supermarket seeking to enforce its security interest in merchandise which debtor-buyer physically possessed. More specifically buyer physically held the merchandise but could not leave the store without paying for it. In the case at bar, the facts are similar. Phoenix physically disassembled the equipment but it could not take the equipment from the Bethlehem Plant until it had made the final payment.

Before Rittenhouse could prevail as a creditor holding a security interest in a liquidation case, that security interest would have to have been perfected. Security interests arising from sales transactions are governed by Title 13 Pa.C.S. § 9113 which provides: A security interest arising solely under Division 2 (relating to sale) is subject to the provisions of this Division except to the extent that and so long as debtor does not have or does not lawfully obtain possession of the goods. (1) No security agreement is necessary to make the security interest enforceable. (2) No filing is required to perfect the security interest. (3) The rights of the secured party on default by the debtor are governed by Division 2. This raises the question of whether Phoenix or Rittenhouse was in possession of the equipment.

At first blush, it would seem that Phoenix was in possession. The goods were identified at the time the contract was signed and the contract did not specifically provide a delivery date. However, if Phoenix had not fully paid the sales price, Rittenhouse had such control over the equipment that it could have exercised remedies under 13 Pa.C.S. § 2703—withheld delivery, resell and recover damages, cancel, etc. In order to exercise these rights, Rittenhouse itself would have to have been in possession of the equipment. The question of "possession" is further complicated by the fact that the equipment was at all relevant times at Bethlehem Steel's Pottstown location. The parties did not address the relationship of Rittenhouse and Bethlehem Steel in their stipulation of fact; nor is there anything in the record to indicate that Bethlehem Steel made any claim whatsoever with respect to the equipment. From its size, Bethlehem Steel had to know the equipment was there and acquiesced in permitting its disassembly and removal by Phoenix. Consequently, the known facts as well as what can be inferred from those facts suggest that Bethlehem Steel was a bailee with knowledge of Rittenhouse's rights in the property which equates to Rittenhouse's "possession" under 13 Pa.C.S. § 9305, which perfects a security interest without filing.

This sale involved the transfer of heavy equipment requiring progressive disassembly. The terms of the agreement prohibited Phoenix from taking possession of the equipment until after the purchase price had been paid. The actions of the parties and the nature of the goods sold make 13 Pa.C.S. § 2401(3)(ii) inapplicable and 13 Pa.C.S. § 2401(2) requiring physical delivery applicable. Mechanics National Bank of Worcester v. Gaucher, 25 U.C.C.Rep.Serv. 1313 (Mass.App., 1979). This result is derived from an exception carved out by the Gaucher court which held that in the case of heavy equipment requiring progressive disassembly, the provisions of UCC 2-401(3)(b) are inapplicable and UCC 2-401(2) (adopted in Pennsylvania as 13 Pa.C.S. § 2401(3)(ii) and 13 Pa.C.S. § 2401(2)) must be followed. * * *

Thus, Rittenhouse maintained a security interest in the equipment subject to the final payment and did not receive more than it would have received in a liquidation proceeding. Moreover, the transaction would be exempt from avoidance under 11 U.S.C. § 547(c)(1). It is specifically recognized that "relinquishment of an inchoate lien right constitutes new value" under the Bankruptcy Code. In re Advances Contractors, 44 B.R. 239 (Bankr. M.D.Fla., 1984). Thus, on July 5, 1983, when Rittenhouse released to Phoenix the equipment in exchange for the final payment, it released a lien right which was a contemporaneous exchange for new value.

Even if Phoenix had been able to meet its burden of proof, the equities demand a judgment in favor of Rittenhouse. Phoenix' estate was not depleted. It paid $135,000 and received equipment of equal value. Phoenix waited almost two years to file its complaint which if successful would have resulted in Rittenhouse being an unsecured creditor. Rittenhouse was not listed in Phoenix' schedules, did not receive notice of the bankruptcy case and would have been deprived of any participation in the case inasmuch as Phoenix was successful in obtaining an order confirming its plan the same day it filed this action.

For all of the foregoing reasons, judgment will be entered in favor of the defendant Rittenhouse.

PROBLEMS

1. Debtor borrows $10,000 from SP #1 granting an oral security interest in a note from X to Debtor in the amount of $25,000. SP #1 takes possession of the note. Subsequently Debtor borrows an additional $10,000 from SP #2 using his equity in the X note as collateral. Does SP #1 have a valid security interest in the note? If SP #2 and Debtor send SP #1 a letter notifying SP #1 of SP #2's interest in the note and requesting that SP #1 turn the note over to SP #2 if the SP #1 loan is paid-off, or that SP #1 remit any amounts received in excess of SP #1's loan to SP #2 in the event of collection, is SP #2's security interest perfected? See § 9-305 and Official Comment 2. Must SP #1 respond to SP #2's letter? See Coral Petroleum, Inc. v. Banque Paribas, 50 B.R. 830 (Bankr. S.D. Tex. 1985). Does it matter if SP #2's security interest is also oral? Does it change your analysis if SP #1 responds to the letter by advising SP #2 that it considers itself under no duty to SP #2 with respect to the note? How would these questions be resolved under Revised § 9-311?

2. Debtor grants Bank an oral security interest in her antique gun collection, which Bank perfects by obtaining possession of the collection. Subsequently, Debtor borrows $10,000 from Finance Co. and grants Finance Co. a security interest in, among other collateral, the same gun collection. Finance Co. files a proper financing statement containing a description of the gun collection. Later, at Debtor's insistence, Bank allows Debtor to retake possession of the gun collection temporarily so that Debtor can obtain for insurance purposes an appraisal of its worth from a nationally-renowned antique gun dealer who happens to be coming into town for a convention. Debtor assures Bank that it will promptly return the collection, and, true to her word, Debtor delivers the collection back to Bank the next day. Three months later, Debtor defaults on both loans and Bank and Finance Co. each claim a priority interest in the gun collection. Assuming that priority is determined under the first to file or perfect rule, which of the creditors has priority in the gun collection? Would it change your answer if, before releasing the gun collection, Bank had filed a financing statement covering the collection?

NOTE ON PERFECTION BY "CONTROL"

With the addition in 1994 of § 9-115, governing security interests in investment property, came the introduction of "control" as a new Article 9 method of perfection related to, but different in certain critical respects, from possession. Section 9-115(1)(e) defines control, incorporating by reference the definition of that term in § 8-106 with respect to investment securities and security entitlements. In general, a secured party has "control" when it is in a position to have the collateral struck off and sold without the need to obtain the debtor's further cooperation. Can a secured party be in possession, but not have control over a certificated security? Conversely, can a secured party have control without having possession? See § 8-106(b)-(d).

Revised Article 9 expands the concept of perfection by control. Specifically, Revised §§ 9-310(a)(2) and 9-312 continue the current practice of permitting perfection of a security interest in investment property by control or filing. In addition, however, control is designated as the exclusive method of perfection for security interests in deposit accounts and letter-of-credit rights. Revised § 9-310(a)(2)(B), (C). The meaning of "control" with respect to each of these types of property interests is then defined in Revised §§ 9-109 and 9-110, respectively. The meaning of control with respect to securities and security entitlements continues to rely on § 8-106. See Revised § 9-108(a). The revision also revises § 8-106 to conform with the changes made in Article 9. Finally, as in the case of possession, perfection by control exists as of the time the creditor obtains control and continues, without relation back, only so long as control is retained. Revised § 9-312(b).

TANBRO FABRICS CO. v. DEERING MILLIKEN, INC.

Court of Appeals of New York, 1976.
39 N.Y.2d 632, 350 N.E.2d 590.

BREITEL, Chief Judge.

In an action for the tortious conversion of unfinished textile fabrics (greige goods), plaintiff Tanbro sought damages from Deering Milliken, a textile manufacturer. Tanbro, known in the trade as a 'converter', finishes textile into dyed and patterned fabrics. The goods in question had been manufactured by Deering, and sold on a "bill and hold" basis to Mill Fabrics, also a converter, now insolvent. Mill Fabrics resold the goods, while still in Deering's warehouse, also on a bill and hold basis, to Tanbro.

Deering refused to deliver the goods to Tanbro on Tanbro's instruction because, although these goods had been paid for, there was an open account balance due Deering from Mill Fabrics. Deering under its sales agreements with Mill Fabrics claimed a perfected security interest in the goods.

At Supreme Court, Tanbro recovered a verdict and judgment of $87,451.68 for compensatory and $25,000 for punitive damages. The Appellate Division, by a divided court, modified to strike the recovery for punitive damages, and otherwise affirmed. Both parties appeal.

The issue is whether Tanbro's purchase of the goods was in the ordinary course of Mill Fabrics' business, and hence free of Deering's perfected security interest.

There should be an affirmance. Mill Fabrics' sale to Tanbro was in the ordinary course of business, even though its predominant business purpose was, like Tanbro's, the converting of greige goods into finished fabrics. All the Uniform Commercial Code requires is that the sale be in ordinary course associated with the seller's business (§ 9-307, subd. (1)). The record established that converters buy greige goods in propitious markets and often in excess of their requirements as they eventuate. On the occasion of excess purchases, converters at times enter the market to sell the excess through brokers to other converters, and converters buy such goods if the price is satisfactory or the particular goods are not available from manufacturers. Both conditions obtained here.

Tanbro and Mill Fabrics were customers of Deering for many years. Goods would be purchased in scale on a 'bill and hold' basis, that is, the goods would be paid for and delivered as the buyers instructed. When the goods were needed, they were delivered directly where they were to be converted, at the buyers' plants or the plants of others if that would be appropriate. Pending instructions, the sold and paid for goods were stored in the warehouses of the manufacturer, both because the buyers lacked warehousing space and retransportation of the goods to be processed would be minimized.

Mill Fabrics, like many converters, purchased greige goods from Deering on credit as well as on short-term payment. Under the sales notes or agreements, all the goods on hand in the seller's warehouse stood as security for the balance owed on the account. Tanbro was familiar with this practice. It was immaterial whether or not particular goods had been paid for. If the goods were resold by Deering's customers, Deering obtained for a period a perfected security interest in the proceeds of resale for the indebtedness on the open account (Uniform Commercial Code, § 9-306, subds. (2), (3)).

Deering's sales executives advised Tanbro that it had discontinued production of a certain blended fabric. Upon Tanbro's inquiry, the Deering sales executives recommended to Tanbro that it try purchasing the blended fabric from Mill Fabrics, which Deering knew had an excess supply. Ultimately, Tanbro purchased from Mill Fabrics through a broker 267,000 yards at 26 cents per yard. Tanbro paid Mill Fabrics in full.

During October and November of 1969, approximately 57,000 yards of the blended fabric was released by Deering on Mill Fabrics' instructions and delivered to a Tanbro affiliate. There remained some 203,376 yards at the Deering warehouse.

In early January of 1970, Tanbro ordered the remaining fabric delivered to meet its own contractual obligation to deliver the blended fabric in finished state at 60 cents per yard. Deering refused.

By this time Mill Fabrics was in financial trouble and its account debit balance with Deering at an unprecedented high. In mid-January of 1970, a meeting of its creditors was called and its insolvency confirmed.

As noted earlier, under the terms of the Deering sales agreements with Mill Fabrics, Deering retained a security interest in Mill Fabrics' 'property' on a bill and hold basis, whether paid for or not. This security interest was perfected by Deering's continued possession of the goods (Uniform Commercial Code, § 1-201, subd. (37); § 9-305). Tanbro argued that if it had title by purchase its goods were excluded from the security arrangement which was literally restricted to the "property of the buyer", that is, Mill Fabrics. In any event, unless prevented by other provisions of the code, or the sale was not unauthorized, Tanbro took title subject to Deering's security interest.

Under the code (§ 9-307, subd. (1)) a buyer in the ordinary course of the seller's business takes goods free of even a known security interest so long as the buyer does not know that the purchase violates the terms of the security agreement. As defined in the code (§ 1-201, subd. (9)) "a buyer in ordinary course" is "a person who in good faith and without knowledge that the sale to him is in violation of the ownership rights or security interest of a third party in the goods buys in ordinary course from a person in the business of selling goods of that kind but does not include a pawnbroker. 'Buying' may be for cash or by exchange of other property or on secured or unsecured credit and includes receiving goods or documents of title under a preexisting contract for sale but does not include a transfer in bulk or as security for or in total or partial satisfaction of a money debt." Critical to Tanbro's claim is that it purchased the goods in the ordinary course of Mill Fabrics' business and that it did not purchase the goods in knowing violation of Deering's security interest.

Under the code whether a purchase was made from a person in the business of selling goods of that kind turns primarily on whether that person holds the goods for sale. Such goods are a person's selling inventory. (Uniform Commercial Code, § 1-201, subd. (9); § 9-307, subd. (1); Official Comment, at par. 2.) Note, however, that not all purchases of goods held as inventory qualify as purchases from a person in the business of selling goods of that kind. The purpose of section 9-307 is more limited. As indicated in the Practice Commentary to that section, the purpose is to permit buyers 'to buy goods from a dealer in such goods without having to protect himself against a possible security interest on the inventory' (Kripke, Practice Commentary, McKinney's Cons.Laws of N.Y., Book 62 1/2 , Uniform Commercial Code, § 9-307, p. 491, par. 1). Hence, a qualifying purchase is one made from a seller who is a dealer in such goods.

A former Mill Fabrics' employee testified that there were times when Mill Fabrics, like all converters, found itself with excess goods. When it was to their business advantage, they sold the excess fabrics to other converters. Although these sales were relatively infrequent they were nevertheless part of and in the ordinary course of Mill Fabrics' business, even if only incidental to the predominant business purpose. Examples of a nonqualifying sale might be a bulk sale, a sale in distress at an obvious loss price, a sale in liquidation, a sale of a commodity never dealt with before by the seller and wholly unlike its usual inventory, or the like.

The combination of stored, paid for goods, on a hold basis, and the retention of a security interest by Deering makes commercial sense. Mill Fabrics' capacity to discharge its obligation to Deering was in part made possible because it sold off or converted the goods held at the Deering warehouse. Mill Fabrics, as an honest customer, was supposed to remit the proceeds from resale or conversion to Deering and thus reduce, and eventually discharge its responsibility to Deering. Thus, so long as it was customary for Mill Fabrics, and in the trade for converters, to sell off excess goods, the sale was in the ordinary course of business. Moreover, on an alternative analysis, such a sale by Mill Fabrics was therefore impliedly authorized under the code if its indebtedness to Deering was to be liquidated.

All subdivision (1) of section 9-307 requires is that the sale be of the variety reasonably to be expected in the regular course of an on-going business. This was such a case.

Hempstead Bank v. Andy's Car Rental System, 35 A.D.2d 35, 312 N.Y.S.2d 317, stands for no contrary principle. Rightly or wrongly, it was there held as a matter of law, unlike the situation here, that the selling of used rental cars was not in the ordinary course of business for an auto rental company. It may be significant that the used cars were in no sense an "inventory" of a sales business, but the capital inventory of a leasing company, usually subject to extended term financing.

* * *

[The court then ruled that there were no grounds for punitive damages.]

Accordingly, the order of the Appellate Division should be affirmed, with costs to plaintiff Tanbro.

DOLAN, THE UNIFORM COMMERCIAL CODE AND THE CONCEPT OF POSSESSION IN THE MARKETING AND FINANCING OF GOODS, 56 Tex. L. Rev. 1147, 1161-64 (1978).

Tanbro unsettles commercial lawyers, not because it favors buyers over lenders, but because it ignores the reasonable expectations of lenders and promotes careless or even deceptive conduct on the part of buyers. The case will not inevitably undermine the structure of commercial finance or increase transaction costs dramatically. It will, however, disturb modern commercial practices and needlessly reward unsuspecting parties, without any concomitant benefit. Widespread commercial practices presuppose that possession of goods signifies power to sell the goods and that lack of possession signifies want of that power. This presupposition is manifest in both the marketing and financing of goods.

* * *

The pledge, an ancient personal property security device, is an arrangement whereby the creditor deprives his debtor of possession of the collateral. It is the general rule that a pledge fails absent delivery to the creditor or his agent, and expires when the creditor surrenders the collateral to the debtor. The Code recognizes these rules in sections 9-203 and 9-305, which permit creation and perfection of a security interest by possession. Significantly, these provisions do not extend to the types of collateral, accounts and general intangibles, possession of which cannot be transferred. Pledge rules rest not on metaphysical considerations but on the realities of commercial expectations. It was reasonable for a medieval creditor to assume that his merchant debtor could not sell wares held by the creditor and equally reasonable for the medieval buyer to resist sales efforts by a peddler with an empty cart. Modern creditors have found safety in possession of collateral and modern buyers are reluctant to pay cash for goods they cannot see. By protecting the creditor in possession, the common law and the Code defer to these realities.

Possession by the creditor or his agent and lack of possession by the debtor serve the twofold purpose of any security device: they protect the creditor against use or sale of the collateral by the debtor and warn purchasers against giving value for goods subject to a security interest.

The common-law pledge permitted a number of exceptions to the general rule that the creditor must deprive the debtor of possession. As a general rule, the release of collateral to the debtor for services that benefited the creditor did not terminate the pledge. Common-law courts, however, recognized the commercial peril of permitting the lender to surrender the collateral and mislead third parties who might rely on the debtor's possession. It was the rule, therefore, that these third parties would defeat the pledge. Article 9 greatly limits the circumstances in which a pledgee may surrender possession to the debtor and still retain a security interest. In various circumstances, the purchaser's ignorance or incomplete knowledge of the security interest defeats or subordinates that interest.

The implications of *Tanbro* for the pledge are obvious. If the trier of fact finds it "ordinary" in a given industry for parties to effect purchases and sales without the buyer's taking delivery, the pledge becomes no better than a security interest perfected by filing. Neither perfection by possession nor perfection by filing protect the creditor from sales by the debtor—a conclusion contrary to the reasonable expectations of the parties.

NOTE ON REVISED ARTICLE 9

Revised § 9-316(d) provides that: "This section [dealing with the rights of a buyer in the ordinary course of business] does not affect a security interest in goods in the possession of the secured party under Section 9-311." How, if at all, would this provision affect the outcome in *Tanbro*?

PHILLIPS, FLAWED PERFECTION: FROM POSSESSION TO FILING UNDER ARTICLE 9—PART 2, 59 Boston U. L. Rev. 255-56 (1979).

The importance of possession as a means of perfection under Article 9 will continue to diminish. The costs of maintaining possession as an alternative to filing include an imperfect and less efficient filing system, doctrinal inconsistency within Article 9 and unfairness based on the false assumption that secured party possession accurately apprises others of the risks attending their commercial relations with the debtor. In response to these pressures, commercial law is inexorably moving from a filing system based on possession to one freed from its limitations. This development has already begun concerning place of filing, with the nascent abandonment of the requirement that in a multistate transaction filing must be effected in every jurisdiction in which collateral is physically present. Evidence of this movement also includes the development of uncertificated securities and the abandonment of the preference accorded possessory security interests over filed security interests in the context of future advances. The notion that possession itself perfects will probably linger longest because of the difficulty in abandoning the conception that possession best denotes a right to take possession. Freeing ourselves of this conception, however, should enable us to ask questions more appropriate to our commercial age: what functions does filing really serve? Are those functions worth the price of filing? How do we best improve the filing system to deter mistaken reliance, reduce transaction costs and increase certainty?

The filing system is worth its price. Even as presently constituted, it substantially aids in correcting or understanding a host of predominantly unaudited financial statements. A more fully evolved system might even result in the filing of a financial statement by a debtor, accompanied by the creditor's claimed security interest signed by the debtor. At least in the case of business debtors, both certainty and reduction of costs would ensue from eliminating the dual system of perfection, tailoring the time of filing to financial practice and seller knowledge, and fixing the filing location according to the debtor's location rather than the more transient location of collateral. These changes would promote the abstraction and, therefore, the manageability of the security interest, resulting in a simplified and more rational Article 9.

SECTION 3. THE FINANCING STATEMENT AND THE FILING SYSTEM

INTRODUCTORY NOTE

Perfection by filing is by far the most common way of perfecting an Article 9 security interest. In the case of accounts and general intangibles it is the only permissible way to perfect. Even with respect to other categories of collateral where perfection by possession is permitted, as a practical matter perfection by filing will be the norm since in most cases the debtor will not be able to relinquish possession and still operate her business or conduct her personal affairs. On the other hand, in the case of commercial paper which is either negotiable or of the type that ordinarily moves through the channels of commerce by indorsement and delivery, perfection by filing, although permitted, involves risk for the secured lender that would not exist if the lender perfected by possession. See §§ 9-308 and 9-309.

Perfection by filing is intended to be simple. The object of a filed financing statement is simply to put subsequent creditors on notice of the need to investigate further. Nevertheless, even sophisticated creditors routinely fail to satisfy the minimal mandatory requirements of a filed financing statement, as the cases in this section bear witness to. In addition, we will consider in this section some criticisms of the Article 9 filing system which many people believe is archaic and in serious need of a major overhaul in light of the technological advances of the past 30 years.

UCC § 9-402(1)

A financing statement is sufficient if it gives the names of the debtor and the secured party, is signed by the debtor, gives an address of the secured party from which information concerning the security interest may be obtained, gives a mailing address of the debtor and contains a statement indicating the types, or describing the items of collateral.

IN RE NOWLING

United States Bankruptcy Court, Northern District of Florida, 1991.
124 B.R. 858.

ROGER VINSON, District Judge.

Pending is the appeal of John E. Venn, Jr., as bankruptcy trustee, from the bankruptcy judge's ruling on the parties' cross motions for summary judgment. The bankruptcy judge granted summary judgment for Roberts Supply Co., Inc. ("Roberts"), defendant below, and denied the trustee's motion. For the reasons stated below, I REVERSE and REMAND for further proceedings.

The debtors, Billy and Brenda Nowling, operated a lawnmower shop prior to filing for bankruptcy under Chapter 7 of the Bankruptcy Code in August 1987. The Nowlings did business as "B & B Equipment." All of their business stationery, invoices, and business cards were in the name "B & B Equipment." On June 26, 1986, the Nowlings executed a security agreement in the name of "B & B Equipment" with Roberts, along with a financing statement (form UCC-1), which was promptly filed with the Secretary of State of Florida. The financing statement listed "B & B Equipment" as the debtor.

This controversy involves various merchandise sold by Roberts to the Nowlings on credit, and returned by the Nowlings to Roberts for credit, prior to the bankruptcy filing. Venn, as trustee, sought to avoid this transfer as a preference under Section 547 of the Bankruptcy Code, which allows the trustee to avoid transfers to "unsecured" creditors. See 11 U.S.C. § 547. If Roberts was a "secured" creditor of the debtors, then the return of items for credit would not be a voidable preference under Section 547.

As the bankruptcy judge indicated and the parties acknowledge, the narrow issue in this case is whether the UCC-1 Financing Statement filed by Roberts solely in the trade name of the debtors (and not in their individual names) is sufficient to perfect a security interest in the merchandise returned by the Nowlings. The parties also agree that this issue turns on whether the financing statement filed by Roberts adequately identified the debtor under Florida law. Venn argues that the financing statement failed to do so, because it identified the debtor simply as "B & B Equipment," without identifying the individual debtors, Billy and Brenda Nowling.

To determine the adequacy of the notice provided by the financing statement, it is necessary to look to the Uniform Commercial Code as adopted in Florida. Article 9 of the Uniform Commercial Code, adopted as Chapter 679 of the Florida Statutes, sets out the law on the perfection and priority of security interests. Section 679.402(1), Florida Statutes, provides that: (1) A financing statement is sufficient if it gives the names of the debtor and the secured party, is signed by the debtor, gives an address of the secured party from which information concerning the security interest may be obtained, gives a mailing address of the debtor, and contains a statement indicating the types, or describing the items, of collateral.

Regarding the identification of the debtor, Section 679.402(6) provides in pertinent part that: (6) A financing statement sufficiently shows the name of the debtor if it gives the individual, partnership, or corporate name of the debtor, whether or not it adds other trade names or names of partners.

A third subsection of Section 679.402 also provides generally that: (7) A financing statement substantially complying with the requirements of this section is effective even though it contains minor errors which are not seriously misleading.

In his order, the bankruptcy judge correctly noted that the purpose of the UCC filing system is to give notice to interested parties that a security interest exists in the property of the debtor. Further, a financing statement is effective so long as it puts any searcher on inquiry. As the bankruptcy judge noted, the trustee is also "considered to be in the position of a hypothetical but prudent creditor." Quoting Matter of Glasco, Inc., 642 F.2d 793, 796 (5th Cir.1981). He then concluded that "Any reasonably prudent creditor conducting a search with the Secretary of State would have discovered the Defendant's financing statement." He reached this conclusion for two reasons.

His first reason was based on the language of Section 679.402(7), which excuses technical defects if they are "not seriously misleading:" A filing in the name in which a debtor does business is not seriously misleading and does not render the financing statement ineffective where the debtor's checks, stationery and bank account all included the name under which the debtor did business, and the same name was used in the debtor's bills, contracts and telephone listing. In so construing the name filing requirement, the bankruptcy judge relied upon the former Fifth Circuit's opinion in In re Glasco, Inc., 642 F.2d 793 (5th Cir.1981). In that case, the former Fifth Circuit ruled that a financing statement listing the debtor by the name in which it did business, in addition to its legal corporate name, was sufficient. The bankruptcy trustee had failed to find the security interest in question because the debtor's name had been indexed as "Elite Boats, Division of Glasco, Inc." The trustee had searched under the debtor's correct corporate name of "Glasco, Inc."

However, as appellant points out, the former Fifth Circuit expressly distinguished cases holding that a financing statement listing only the trade name as the debtor will be insufficient to perfect a security interest effective against the individual. Id. at 796, citing In re Leichter, 471 F.2d 785 (2d Cir.1972); Citizens Bank v. Ansley, 467 F.Supp. 51 (M.D.Ga.1979), aff'd without opinion, 604 F.2d 669 (5th Cir.1980).

Moreover, the rationale of the Glasco holding, although equitable under the facts, seem to be inconsistent with the notice-filing system of the UCC. Others agree. See, e.g., In re Vital Breathing Products, Inc., 98 B.R. 97 (N.D.Ga.1988); B. Clark, The Law of Secured Transactions Under the Uniform Commercial Code § 2.09[1][b] (1988); Schinner, Examining the Integrity of a Notice-Filing System: Are Financing Statements Filed Solely Under Debtor's Trade Name Sufficient to Perfect a Security Interest Under UCC Section 9-402?, 94 Com.L.J. 176 (Spring 1988). Therefore, although Glasco is controlling precedent in this circuit [see Bonner v. City of Prichard, 661 F.2d 1206 (11th Cir.1981)], it should be narrowly applied. I note, however, that Glasco is within the plain language of Section 679.402(6) since both the corporate name and the trade name were on the filed UCC-1.

More importantly, the commentary to the statute indicates that filing solely in a trade name is not sufficient. The Uniform Commercial Code Comment to the 1972 Revision of Section 9-402(7) flatly states that, "In the case of individuals, it contemplates filing only in the individual's name, not in a trade name. * * * Trade names are deemed to be too uncertain and too likely not to be known to the secured party or person searching the record, to form the basis for a filing system." § 679.402, Fla.Stat.Ann., UCC Comment to 1972 Revision, P 7 (1990). In 1979, Florida adopted this amendment to the Uniform Commercial Code as the present Section 679.401(6).

The other basis for the bankruptcy judge's decision was that the debtors filed their bankruptcy petition as "Billy and Brenda Nowling, d/b/a B & B Equipment." Thus, the trustee was on notice to search for a financing statement under both the trade and individual names.

However, as the trustee points out, Section 544 of the Bankruptcy Code, the so-called "strong arm clause," permits a trustee to avoid a transfer of property to an unsecured creditor "without regard to any knowledge of the trustees or of any creditor." 11 U.S.C. § 544 (1979). Thus, even actual knowledge on the part of the trustee will not suffice as notice if the financing statement is defective.

Further, Section 679.301, Florida Statutes, was amended in 1979 so that creditors with knowledge would have priority over unperfected security interests. This section applies to Venn; the parties agree with the bankruptcy judge that the Bankruptcy Act puts the trustee in the place of a hypothetical lien creditor. The Sponsors' Notes to Section 679.301 explain that subordinating a lien creditor because of his actual knowledge of an encumbrance is inconsistent with the priority rules of Chapter 679, "where knowledge is not a relevant consideration." See § 679.301, Fla.Stat.Ann., & Sponsors' Notes to 1979 Amendment (1990). The Sponsors' Notes explain further that this elimination of knowledge as a relevant factor reconciled a conflict with the Bankruptcy Act "wherein there is a presumption of no knowledge even if all have knowledge and the trustee is the hypothetical or perfect creditor." Id.

Roberts acknowledges that the trustee's knowledge of the encumbrance is irrelevant to the question of the perfection of the security interest. But Roberts asserts that knowledge of the fact that the Nowlings operated their business in the name of B & B is relevant. Since the trustee had this information, Roberts argues, he had a duty to inquire into recordings under both names.

Roberts cites no authority for this proposition, with which I cannot agree. If actual knowledge of the encumbrance itself is insufficient to defeat a lien creditor's priority over an unperfected security interest, then constructive notice of the fact that a debtor goes by two different names should be a fortiori insufficient.

Finally, Roberts argues that B & B is a partnership under Florida law. Therefore, the financing statement was sufficient under Section 679.402(6), because it gives the "partnership * * * name of the debtor." Roberts argues that B & B fits the definition of partnership set out in Section 620.585(1), Florida Statutes: an "association of two or more person to carry on a business for profit as co-owners." Although it possibly could have been a partnership, that's not what the record indicates. No partnership tax returns were filed, and the security agreement which forms the basis of the filing specifically describes B & B Equipment as a "sole proprietorship."

Moreover, the bankruptcy judge never made a determination that B & B was a partnership; it seems to have been treated as a sole proprietorship, which was how the Nowlings filed for bankruptcy. As the trustee points out, the issue of whether a business is a partnership under Florida law is a question for the factfinder. Spencer v. Young, 63 So.2d 334 (Fla.1953). There is no basis for deciding otherwise on appeal.

Finding that neither of the grounds relied upon below support the decision appealed from, and that the UCC-1 filed in only a trade name (and not in the individual names of the debtors) was insufficient to perfect a security interest in the subject property, the order below is REVERSED. The matter is remanded to the Bankruptcy Division for further proceedings.

QUESTION

How would Revised § 9-503 affect the reasoning of the court in *Nowling*?

ALCES & LLOYD, AN AGENDA FOR REFORM OF THE ARTICLE 9 FILING SYSTEM, 44 Okla. L. Rev. 99, 105-08 (1991).

The Study has disclosed myriad problems with the filing systems presently in use. We have grouped these under three major headings: speed, accuracy and cost. A major item in the cost category is the attorney time spent attempting to achieve the necessary degree of certainty concerning the client's perfection and priority.

A. *Speed*

Because of U.C.C. section 9-312's first-to-file-or-perfect rule, a secured party is assured priority only if it searches through the date of its filing. This means that before disbursing funds the secured party must file it financing statement, wait for the financing statement to be indexed and searchable, and then obtain a search showing its financing statement filed with no competing financing statement ahead of it. In most jurisdictions this is not a problem. The delay between the time the financing statement and search request are first filed and the time the search showing priority is received is only a few days — fast enough for all but the most urgent transactions. In some states, however, the volume of filings that the central filing office must handle results in delays of several weeks from the time the secured party files its financing statement to the time it receives a search showing the priority of that financing statement. It has been asserted that this delay causes a great number of secured lenders to close transactions without assurance of their priority.

A simple solution to this problem may be for the filing offices to hire more people. This is not realistic, however, given the fact that state governments throughout the country are facing severe budget problems. Even if the money were available, it might be better spent on technology than on additional salaries. Moreover, because the volume of searches and filings ebbs and flows, having a staff large enough to keep current during the peak periods might mean having people idle during the slack ones.

Another solution would be better education for secured lenders and their attorneys. An informal survey suggests that, in spite of the time lag in the filing offices, experienced commercial lawyers seldom close important transactions without a search through the date of filing. Most of the cases in which funds are disbursed without obtaining a search through the date of filing are situations in which the lender and its counsel either failed to realize soon enough the need to file early or simply did not care enough to do so.

B. *Accuracy*

Accuracy is another concern of secured lenders. Properly filed financing statements can be misindexed or searchers can overlook properly indexed statements. The results can be large losses for secured lenders. In some jurisdictions, the lender who has suffered a loss may have no recourse. In most jurisdictions, however, the lender can recover for losses caused by the filing officer's failure to perform properly a ministerial duty, but this will often entail further expensive litigation. Moreover, because filing officers in many jurisdictions do not issue certificates, lenders may encounter difficulty in proving that they in fact received an inaccurate search.

Another important source of potential errors is the policy of some filing officers of backdating improperly rejected documents. When a secured party is able to convince a filing officer that its financing statement was improperly rejected, filing officers in some states will backdate the filing date to the date the document was originally submitted. This is a potential trap for later secured parties who may get a clean search in the gap between the original submission date and the date the financing statement is finally accepted.

It should be noted, however, that in spite of the huge potential for losses caused by inaccurate filings and searches, *actual losses appear to be extremely rare. An informal survey of lawyers in a state where searches are notoriously inaccurate revealed no one who had suffered a loss or personally knew anyone who had.* [Emphasis added.]

C. *Cost*

Although the charges made for searching and filing are minimal, the inefficiencies of the present system impose enormous hidden costs on both borrowers and lenders. Perhaps the most obvious of these is the cost of search firms. In many jurisdictions, the response time on a search request submitted to the central filing office is so long that lenders are forced to employ private search firms to make their searches. For large transactions, this cost is insignificant, but for small transactions it can become important. The result in some cases is that searches that should be made are, in fact, not. For example, some major commercial lenders when taking purchase money security interests fail to search after filing to make sure their financing statement is properly on file.

Another example is trade name filings. Because of cases such as *In re Glasco, Inc.* and *In re McBee*, there is uncertainty in some jurisdictions whether filings under trade names are valid. As a result, lenders must take time to discover trade names and search against them. Because this is attorney time, it is expensive.

Another uncertainty, one that is reduced to manageable proportions only at significant cost, is similar names. Many computerized systems do not pick up any name other than the exact name under which the search is entered. For example, in some systems, a search under the name "Allstate Enterprises" would not reveal a document filed under "All State Enterprises" or "All-State Enterprises." Similarly, a search under "Bijou Theater" would not reveal documents filed under "Bijou Theatre." Some computer systems will pick up some similar names, but none available will find them all. This means, first of all, that an attorney must take extra pains to be sure she has the exact name of the debtor. In addition, she would be well advised to search under any likely "near misses" that a court might decide were "minor errors which are not seriously misleading" under U.C.C. section 9-402(8).

Finally, local filing and dual filing also present problems. Lawyers have to take time to determine whether local filing is necessary and, if so, in what county or counties the filings must be made.

IN RE LINTZ WEST SIDE LUMBER, INC., 655 F.2d 786, 791 (7th Cir. 1981). "As a duly constituted corporation, Lintz West Side Lumber, Inc., is a legal entity separate and distinct from John and Mayella Lintz (whose names appear on the financing statement). A creditor would ordinarily, and could reasonably, assume that *corporate* assets would not be encumbered by a security interest filed under the names of these individuals despite the similarity in the names."

HIXON v. CREDIT ALLIANCE CORP.

Supreme Court of Virginia, 1988.
235 Va. 466, 369 S.E.2d 169.

CARRICO, Chief Justice.

This case involves an application of the Uniform Commercial Code in the context of a dispute between the holders of competing security interests in a piece of road construction machinery or equipment known as a "flusher." The litigation began when Virginia Tractor Company, Inc., through its trustees under a liquidating trust created by its shareholders (Virginia Tractor), filed a motion for judgment seeking damages against Credit Alliance Corporation, C-A Leasing Service Corporation, and Philip D. Cooper, regional vice president of Credit Alliance Corporation (collectively, Credit Alliance).

The motion for judgment alleged that Credit Alliance had wrongfully converted the flusher by selling it to satisfy its claim in violation of Virginia Tractor's rights. The trial court granted summary judgment in favor of Credit Alliance. Virginia Tractor has appealed.

The record shows that the flusher was purchased by Rodgers Brothers Construction Company, Inc., of Fairfax, Virginia, on April 29, 1982. It was installed on Rodgers' truck in Oregon, Illinois, and delivered to Rodgers at that location on May 28, 1982.

On the latter date, Rodgers executed a promissory note payable to Credit Alliance for $1,404,000. Rodgers also executed a security agreement giving Credit Alliance a security interest in all "the goods, chattels and property described in the annexed Schedule A and all other * * * machinery [and] equipment * * * now or hereafter belonging to [Rodgers]." On the attached schedule, 86 items of machinery and equipment were listed. The flusher in question, then still in Illinois or en route to Virginia, was not on the list. Credit Alliance perfected its security interest by filing financing statements with the State Corporation Commission on June 3, 1982, and the Clerk of the Circuit Court of Fairfax County on June 7, 1982.

On December 1, 1982, Rodgers executed a promissory note payable to Virginia Tractor for $44,000, together with a security agreement specifically naming the flusher as one of the items of equipment covered by the agreement. Virginia Tractor perfected its security interest by filing financing statements with the State Corporation Commission on December 7, 1982, and the Clerk of the Circuit Court of Fairfax County on December 9, 1982.

On October 5, 1983, Rodgers filed a petition for relief under Chapter 11 of the United States Bankruptcy Code. On December 5, 1983, the bankruptcy court permitted Virginia Tractor to pursue "whatever nonbankruptcy rights and remedies it had with respect to the flusher."

Virginia Tractor did not take possession of the flusher, but permitted it to remain on Rodgers' premises. In April 1984, Credit Alliance gave notice of its intent to sell the flusher on April 27, 1984. On that day, despite Virginia Tractor's protest, Credit Alliance took possession of the flusher and sold it for approximately $34,750. The filing of this action soon followed.

Virginia Tractor contends that the sale of the flusher was invalid and constituted an unlawful conversion because Credit Alliance had not perfected its security interest according to law. Virginia Tractor emphasizes the language of Paragraph 8 of the financing statement, which defines "the collateral" as: "All machinery, inventory, equipment and goods as described in attached entire Agreement &/or in any Schedule prepared in connection therewith. This UCC form together with the attached Security Agreement &/or Schedule are being submitted for filing herewith as a financing statement."

Virginia Tractor points out that Code § 8.9-402 allows a creditor's financing statement to describe collateral by item or by type. Virginia Tractor submits that had Credit Alliance wanted to claim a security interest in all equipment owned or later acquired by Rodgers, it could have done so simply by describing the collateral by type, saying in the financing statement that the collateral consisted of all "machinery, inventory, equipment, and goods now or hereafter belonging to Rodgers."

Virginia Tractor then asserts that when Credit Alliance added the words "as described" after the listing of "machinery, inventory, equipment and goods," it chose to describe the collateral by item rather than type and thus limited the collateral to what was listed on the attached Schedule A. Because the flusher was not listed on the schedule, Virginia Tractor concludes, Credit Alliance did not have "a perfected security interest in it."

We disagree with Virginia Tractor. What its argument amounts to is that a creditor may describe collateral by type or by name, but not both. As indicated in note 2, however, Code § 8.9-402, which sets forth the "[f]ormal requisites of financing statements," provides in subsection (1) that "[a] financing statement is sufficient if it * * * contains a statement indicating the types, or describing the items, of collateral." We see nothing in this statutory language which would either mandate or justify a holding that, if a creditor describes part of the collateral by item, he cannot describe another part by type.

Virginia Tractor cautions, however, that a "reasonably diligent title searcher" would look only to Schedule A "to determine what specific 'items' of collateral were described." The searcher would find a list of 86 items of equipment, Virginia Tractor says, specifically identified by name, make, and serial number, but would find the flusher nowhere on the list. The title searcher would not look to the security agreement itself, Virginia Tractor maintains, because it is "a fine print, boilerplate, printed form" on which no one "would reasonably expect to find an itemization of the particular collateral claimed."

We do not think a reasonably diligent title searcher would limit his examination to Schedule A. Instead, we think he would read Paragraph 8 of the financing statement and realize that the security agreement is made part of the financing statement and that the two must be read together to determine what is included in collateral.

* * *

Virginia Tractor argues, however, that the "multi-document financing statement" employed in this case "is 'seriously misleading'" and hence in violation of Code § 8.9-402(8). This subsection reads: A financing statement substantially complying with the requirements of [Code § 8.9-402] is effective even though it contains minor errors which are not seriously misleading. This provision, however, is intended to demonstrate "clearly that the purpose of [Code § 8.9-402] is to create a system of notice filing which contemplates further inquiry by a party in order to determine whether a particular asset is covered by a security agreement."

This view is consistent with the Official Comment to Code § 8.9-402. Paragraph 2 of the Official Comment states: This section adopts the system of "notice filing" which proved successful under the Uniform Trust Receipts Act. What is required * * * is * * * only a simple notice which may be filed before the security interest attaches or thereafter. The notice itself indicates merely that the secured party who has filed may have a security interest in the collateral described. Further inquiry from the parties concerned will be necessary to disclose the complete state of affairs.

In awarding summary judgment in this case, the trial court held that because the security interest of Credit Alliance was validly perfected and was prior in time to the security interest of Virginia Tractor, the sale of the flusher by Credit Alliance did not amount to a conversion or otherwise violate Virginia Tractor's rights. These holdings are plainly correct, and, accordingly, we will affirm them as well as the final judgment of the trial court.

Affirmed.

NOTE ON REVISED ARTICLE 9

Revised Article 9 changes the filing requirements in several important respects. First, to facilitate the gradual shift to an entirely electronic filing system, the revision eliminates the requirement that the debtor sign the "initial" financing statement. Instead it calls for the debtor to "authorize" the filing in a signed writing. Revised § 9-508(a), (b). Ordinarily, this authorization would be contained in the security agreement itself, and the financing statement could be communicated to the filing office in the form of an electronic "record." Revised § 9-102(43). In addition, Revised § 9-504 renders a generic reference to "all assets" or "all personal property" as sufficient to satisfy the collateral description requirement in the financing statement, although a more specific description is still required in the security agreement. Revised § 9-506 continues the "minor error" rule of current § 9-402(8), although an error in the debtor's name is deemed seriously misleading *unless* a search under the debtor's correct name would reveal the financing statement.

The revision also incorporates an "open drawer" approach, meaning that, among other things, the filing office would be obligated to link all subsequent filings (e.g., notices of assignment, amendments, continuation statements, etc.) to the initial financing statement to which they relate. See Revised §§ 9-520 and 9-520A. Furthermore, Revised § 9-521 contains a "National Financing Statement" form, along with related "Addendum" and "Change" forms. By using these forms, the secured party would be assured that its filing was proper in form and could not be refused except for one of the statutorily enumerated reasons set forth in Revised § 9-515(b). Finally, responding to the criticism that there are simply too many filing offices, and that the reasons articulated in Official Comment 1 to § 9-401(a) for local filing are no longer valid, Revised § 9-501(a) eliminates local filing, except with respect to collateral, like crops, mineral and fixtures, closely associated with the underlying realty. Read Official Comment 1 and consider the proposal to eliminate local filing in light of the materials in the next section.

SECTION 4. THE PLACE TO FILE IN GENERAL

UCC § 9-401(1)
(*see Selected Commercial Statutes*)

IN RE KALINOSKI

United States District Court, Western District of Wisconsin, 1973.
13 U.C.C. Rep. Serv. 387.

LEONARD BESSMAN, Referee in Bankruptcy.

Petitions for reclamation were filed in this matter by Kasten Manufacturing Corporation, Sperry Rand Corporation, John Miller Supply Company, Inc., and Avco Distributing Corporation, all secured creditors of the bankrupt. The trustee contends that the security interests were not perfected and that he is therefore entitled to retain the property in question as an asset of the estate.

The facts are undisputed. The bankrupt, who had been engaged in the farm implement business, had his place of business in Cuba City, Wisconsin. The greater part of Cuba City is located in Grant County with a small area in adjacent LaFayette County. The bankrupt's place of business was in that small area, about the thousand feet from the county line dividing LaFayette and Grant Counties. All of the petitioners filed financing statements in the office of the Wisconsin Secretary of State and in the office of the register of deeds for Grant County.

Section 409.401(1)(c), Wisconsin Statutes, the Wisconsin version of § 9-401 of the Uniform Commercial Code, requires that the financing statement be filed both in the secretary of state's office and in the register of deeds' office where the debtor's principal place of business is located. The question is whether the petitioners perfected their security interests in view of the fact that they filed their financing statements in Grant County rather than in LaFayette County, where the bankrupt had his place of business.

The testimony established that the petitioners generally refer to postal directories to determine the county in which a business is located. The postal directory, as well as the State of Wisconsin Blue Book, reports that Cuba City is located in Grant County. It does not indicate that part of the city is in LaFayette County. Similarly, the official Wisconsin highway map places Cuba City entirely in Grant County.

Under the circumstances, it is not at all surprising that the petitioners made an erroneous filing. Nevertheless, a few of the bankrupt's secured creditors somehow discovered that the debtor's place of business was in LaFayette County and properly perfected their security interests by filing financing statements with its register of deeds.

However understandable the plight of the petitioners, the statute leaves no opportunity for discretion. Its requirements are plain, as the Supreme Court of Wisconsin observed in In re Federal Wholesale Meats & Frozen Foods, 43 Wis.2d 21, 24 (1969) § 409.401(1)(c), and they must be satisfied with exactitude. The good faith of the petitioners in their attempt to comply with the statutory requirements cannot excuse their error, as pointed out in the cases cited in the trustee's brief.

Under § 70a of the Bankruptcy Act, the trustee has the status of a judgment creditor with an execution returned unsatisfied, and he is vested with all the property upon which a creditor of the bankrupt could have obtained a lien on the date of bankruptcy, regardless whether such a creditor exists. 4A Collier on Bankruptcy § 70.04 p 59. An unperfected security interest is subordinate to a trustee in bankruptcy under § 409.301(3) Wisconsin Statutes, as well as under the Bankruptcy Act.

The controlling facts in P. S. Products Corp. v. Equilease Corp., 435 F.2d 781 (2d Cir 1970), are virtually identical with those in the present case. Like Cuba City, the town of Farmingdale, New York, is situated in two counties, the larger part in Nassau County and a small part in Suffolk County. The bankrupt had his place of business in Suffolk County, but the secured creditor, in addition to filing with the New York Secretary of State, filed its financing statement in Nassau County. Notwithstanding, the bankrupt was listed in the Nassau County telephone directory and had leased a post office box in that county.

The New York statute, adopted without variation from the Uniform Commercial Code, requires filing "in the department of state and in addition, if the debtor has a place of business in this state and in only one county of this state, also in the office of the filing officer of such county." More liberal than the Wisconsin version, the New York creditor need file only with the secretary of state if the debtor has a place of business in more than one county. The court held that the circumstances could not justify the improper filing since the bankrupt's sole place of business was in Suffolk County and filing in that county was essential to perfection of a security interest. Accordingly, the court affirmed the judgment of the district court dismissing the creditor's petition for reclamation.

For the reasons given, the petitions for reclamation are dismissed.

NORTHWEST ACCEPTANCE CORP. v. MCCLELLAN EQUIPMENT CO.

Court of Appeals, Oregon, 1986.
79 Ore. App. 405, 719 P.2d 887.

BUTTLER, Presiding Judge.

Plaintiff seeks a judicial declaration that its security interest in construction equipment leased by defendant to Erosion Control, Inc. (debtor) is superior to defendant's security interest in the same equipment; it also seeks injunctive relief and damages. The trial court dismissed plaintiff's complaint and entered judgment for defendant. The sole issue on appeal is whether defendant, by filing in good faith, in the wrong state, a financing statement covering the equipment, perfected its security interest in the equipment as against plaintiff, which had actual knowledge of the erroneous filing and of its contents before it perfected its own security interest in the equipment and advanced funds to the debtor.

The facts are undisputed. On May 7, 1982, defendant "leased" to the debtor eight pieces of heavy equipment in which it retained a security interest that was subject to the filing requirements of Article 9 of the UCC (ORS 79.1010 et seq.). ORS 71.2010(37). In accordance with the terms of the lease agreements, the equipment was delivered to the debtor in Wrangell, Alaska, where the debtor allegedly had a contract to build roads. On May 17 and 24, 1982, defendant, in a good faith attempt to perfect its security interest, filed financing statements in Alaska covering the equipment. It did not file in Oregon, where it was required to file in order to perfect its security interest. ORS 79.1030(3).[1]

In April, 1983, plaintiff, which previously had financed the debtor's purchase of other equipment, advanced additional funds to it and filed a financing statement in Oregon, under which it perfected a security interest in all of the debtor's equipment, including the equipment in question. The debtor then defaulted on its debts to both creditors and filed a voluntary petition in bankruptcy. This action ensued after defendant was granted relief from the resulting stay and recovered possession of the leased equipment.

On appeal, plaintiff contends that, because defendant failed to file in Oregon as required by ORS 79.1030(3) and 79.4010, the filing was ineffectual to perfect defendant's security interest. Accordingly, it argues that its perfected security interest has priority under ORS 79.3120(5)(a), which provides the general rule that priority dates from the time when a filing covering the collateral is first made or the time when the security interest is first perfected, regardless of whether the party that files or perfects first has knowledge of a conflicting, preexisting security interest in the property. Defendant does not contest that general rule, but

---

[1] * * * On appeal, defendant concedes that the debtor was located in Oregon at the time of the transactions.

contends that the following exception to that rule, as provided in ORS 79.4010(2), is applicable:

> "A filing which is made in good faith in an improper place or not in all of the places required by this section is nevertheless effective with regard to any collateral as to which the filing complied with the requirements of ORS 79.1010 to 79.5070 and is also effective with regard to collateral covered by the financing statement against any person who has knowledge of the contents of such financing statement."

It is agreed that defendant filed in Alaska in good faith and that plaintiff knew of the contents of that financing statement before it acquired and perfected its own security interest in the same collateral. Plaintiff contends, however, that, given the general policy of the UCC that priority is given to the first to perfect a security interest, the ORS 79.4010(2) exception should be construed to apply only to financing statements filed in an improper place in Oregon, not to those improperly filed in another state.

Determining the proper place to file a financing statement to perfect a security interest under the UCC requires consideration of myriad diffuse and complex sections of the code. As one authoritative treatise has stated: " * * * Mistakes are inevitable in a system where the proper location for filing hinges upon such factors as classification of goods, location of the debtor, the proper time to determine status, place of business, and status of the debtor. The draftsmen wisely recognized that, despite their best intentions, pitfalls await the hapless traveler through the UCC. They provided a saving clause in 9-401(2), and judges should construe it in accord with its spirit." White and Summers, Uniform Commercial Code 951, § 23-15 (2d ed. 1980).

We see no benefit to be derived from restricting the applicability of the "saving clause" to in-state filing errors; neither do we perceive any justification for doing so. The pitfalls that a creditor must avoid in order to determine the state in which a financing statement must be filed to perfect a security interest are at least as formidable as those that must be confronted in order to determine the proper place to file within a particular state. ORS 79.1030, which governs the perfection of security interests in multi-state transactions, is among the longest and most complicated sections of the code. We do not believe, therefore, that the drafters of the code, or the Oregon legislature which adopted it, intended the ORS 79.4010(2) exception to apply only to in-state filing errors. If that was the intention, they could have said so. The legislature provided two conditions to the applicability of the exception: improper filing in good faith and the subsequent creditor's knowledge of the contents of that filing. Both conditions are satisfied here.

Plaintiff argues that it would be anomalous to apply the ORS 79.4010(2) exception to improper filings out of state when knowledge of a proper out of state filing under ORS 79.1030(3)(e) is irrelevant. That statute, however, does not cover improper filings made in good faith; it relates to proper filings that have expired after the debtor's move to another state and the creditor's failure to perfect in the new jurisdiction. See In re Miller, 14 UCC Rep Serv 1042

(Bankr.D.Or.1974). We perceive no anomaly, because the keystone of ORS 79.4010(2), a good faith attempt to perfect a security interest, is lacking.

Plaintiff also contends that applying the saving clause to interstate filing errors will impair the degree of certainty in determining priority intended to follow from the pure "race to file" aspects of the code. We perceive no reason why that certainty will be any more impaired than it would be by limiting the exception to improper filings in Oregon. Plaintiff had no obligation to search the records in Alaska, unless it was uncertain as to the proper place to file. However, plaintiff did conduct a search for relevant UCC filings and obtained a copy of the erroneously filed financing statement before it advanced funds secured by its blanket security interest. It then had a choice either to deal with defendant or to take its chances on priority. Its decision to extend the debtor's line of credit was, therefore, a fully informed choice and not one influenced by any uncertainty concerning the existence of defendant's claimed interest in the collateral. If it did consider the applicability of ORS 79.4010(2), the plain language of the statute should have forewarned it of a potential problem.

Affirmed.

PROBLEM

On February 1, Debtor grants SP a lien on a lathe used by Debtor in his woodworking business. SP has Debtor sign a financing statement that complies in all respects with § 9-402(1). SP sends the financing statement, together with the required fee, to the appropriate office for filing under the version of § 9-401(1) applicable in the state, but the filing officer, who was busy at the time with some other matters, set the financing statement aside where it got lost under a stack of papers and was never indexed in the records of the office. Subsequently, Debtor offered to sell the lathe to Peter Purchaser who, after searching the filing office records, paid full value for the lathe. When SP learned of the sale, it sought to replevy the lathe from purchaser. Did purchaser take subject to SP's security interest? See § 9-403(1). If so, what recourse does Purchaser have? What if, instead of losing the secured party's financing statement, the filing officer returned it as "improper in form"? How would the result differ under the revision? See Revised §§ 9-515(a) and 9-518(b).

SECTION 5. THE PLACE TO FILE IN MULTIPLE STATE TRANSACTIONS

INTRODUCTORY NOTE

Although we deal with a single, uniform version of Article 9 in this course, in reality, each state has its own version of Article 9. This creates a choice of law question—whose version of Article 9 controls—in any transaction in which the parties are located in different states or the goods move from one state to another. Section 1-105 leaves the parties free to specify by agreement the law that will govern the transaction *except* with respect to questions bearing on perfection or lack of perfection. As to those questions, the conflict rules in § 9-103 take the matter out of the hands of the parties. These rules are technical and complex, supplying different results depending on the classification of the collateral. One of the major changes in the revision is to replace these rules with a single "debtor location" rule. The operation of the basic rules governing ordinary goods and intangible property rights are examined below, along with the proposals to alter these rules in a manner that would provide greater clarity and certainty in the vast bulk of multi-state transactions.

(a) ORDINARY GOODS

UCC § 9-103(1)
(*see Selected Commercial Statutes*)

IN RE SLIPPERY ROCK FORGING, INC.

United States Bankruptcy Court, Western District of Pennsylvania, 1989.
99 B.R. 679.

JOSEPH L. COSETTI, Bankruptcy Judge.

A Motion for Relief from Stay by Citizens National Bank of Evans City, Pennsylvania, is before the court at this time. Citizens National Bank seeks, among other things, an Order compelling debtor Slippery Rock Forging, Inc. to pay over to it the net proceeds of a settlement of an adversary proceeding between debtor and Quanex Corporation.

The motion will be denied for reasons set forth below.

I.

The following facts are not in dispute.

Debtor purchased steel bars from Quanex Corporation, which is located in Michigan, on an open account basis. The steel bars were to be used by debtor as raw material in its forging facility located in Slippery Rock, Pennsylvania.

Before they could be forged, however, the steel bars had to be sheared. The bars were shipped in June of 1987 by Quanex at debtor's direction to Advanced Cutting Service in Cleveland, Ohio. The bars never reached Pennsylvania. Quanex repossessed the bars from Advanced Cutting Service in August of 1987 and issued a credit memo to debtor for $40,815.50, the total purchase price of the bars.

On October 13, 1987, approximately two months after Quanex had repossessed the bars, debtor filed a voluntary petition under chapter 11 of the Bankruptcy Code. Debtor subsequently brought an adversary proceeding against Quanex in which debtor claimed that Quanex's unilateral recovery of the bars amounted to a preferential transfer. Debtor demanded damages in the amount of $40,815.50.

Debtor and Quanex ultimately reached a settlement of the adversary proceeding. Quanex agreed to pay debtor the sum of $25,000.00.

Citizens National Bank became a creditor of debtor on December 11, 1985. Citizens National Bank and debtor executed a Direct Loan Security Agreement on that date. Citizens National Bank was granted a security interest in certain assets of debtor. Specifically, Citizens National Bank was granted interest in: All inventory of the debtor of every description, whether new or hereafter existing or acquired; all accounts, contract rights, and documents of title whether new or hereafter existing or acquired; all chattel paper and instruments, whether now or hereafter existing or acquired, evidencing any obligation to Debtor for payment of goods sold or leased or services rendered; and in all guaranties and other property securing the payment of or performance under any accounts, contract rights, or any such chattel paper or instruments; and all products and proceeds of any of the foregoing.

Citizens National Bank filed UCC-1 financing statements with the Secretary of the Commonwealth of Pennsylvania and the Prothonotary of the Court of Common Pleas of Butler Country, Pennsylvania, where debtor has its principal place of business, in December of 1985. The description in the financing statements of the property of debtor subject to the security interest of Citizens National Bank is identical to the above description contained in the security agreement.

II.

It is apparent that Citizens National Bank takes the position that it is entitled to the net proceeds of the settlement between Quanex and debtor. Unfortunately, it is not as apparent why Citizens National Bank believes that it is entitled to those proceeds.

Citizens National Bank appears to rely on two arguments, both of which are without merit. Neither supports the inference that Citizens is entitled to the proceeds of the settlement.

A multi-state transaction concerning goods is present in this case. Debtor, a Pennsylvania corporation, purchased steel bars from Quanex, a Michigan corporation, for use at debtor's facility in Pennsylvania. At debtor's direction, Quanex shipped the bars to Ohio for shearing. Before they were shipped to Pennsylvania, however, Quanex repossessed the bars in Ohio and took them back to Michigan.

The basic rule concerning perfection of a security interest in goods involved in multi-state transactions is set forth at 13 Pa.C.S.A. § 9103(a)(2) (Purdon's 1984). It provides that: [P]erfection and the effect of perfection or non-perfection of a security interest in collateral are governed by the law of the jurisdiction where the collateral is when the last event occurs on which is based the assertion that the security interest is perfected or unperfected.

It is not clear what the "last event" is upon which Citizens National Bank is relying in support of its claim that its security interest in the steel bars had been perfected prior to their being repossessed by Quanex in August of 1987.

The "last event" on which Citizens National Bank's alleged perfection of its security interest in the steel bars was not the filing of the UCC-1 financing statements in Pennsylvania in December of 1985. Presumably, this event antedates (by more than a year) the manufacturing of the steel bars which were purchased from Quanex. It strains credulity to maintain that the filing of these financial statements was the "last event" to perfect a security interest in goods which had not yet been produced. It appears that the "last event" in this case, for purposes of 13 Pa.C.S.A. § 9103(a)(2), was the manufacturing of the bars in Michigan. It therefore follows that the law of Michigan determines whether Citizens National Bank's security interest was perfected and, if it was not, the effect thereof.

The law of Michigan on such matters is identical to that of Pennsylvania. Michigan, like Pennsylvania, has adopted the 1972 version of the Uniform Commercial Code.

According to Michigan law, a financing statement must be filed in order to perfect a security interest. See Mich.Comp.Laws Ann. 440.9302(1)(a). More precisely Citizens National Bank's security interest in the steel bars had to be filed in the office of the Secretary of State of Michigan in order to be perfected. See Mich.Comp.Laws Ann. 440.9401(1)(c). While there is no dispute that Citizens National Bank filed financing statements with the Secretary of the Commonwealth of Pennsylvania and the Prothonotary of the Court of Common Pleas of Butler County, Pennsylvania, there is no evidence of record that Citizens National Bank filed a financing statement with the Secretary of State of Michigan. It therefore follows that Citizens National Bank's security interest in the steel bars was unperfected and that its security interest is subordinate to the rights of lien creditors. See Mich.Comp.Laws Ann. 440.9301(1)(a), (2).

According to Citizens National Bank, once Quanex wrongfully repossessed the bars, debtor was entitled either to replevy them or to receive their equivalent value. Citizens National Bank's second argument is that it is entitled to the net proceeds of the settlement because those proceeds constitute an "account receivable" or a "contract right," in which it had a perfected security interest.

An "account" is defined as: Any right to payment for goods sold or leased or for services rendered which is not evidenced by an instrument or chattel paper, whether or not it has been earned by performance. 13 Pa.C.S.A. § 9106 (Purdon's 1984).

Debtor's adversary proceeding against Quanex does not fall within this definition of "account". Debtor brought suit against Quanex pursuant to 11 U.S.C. § 547(b). According to debtor, Quanex's taking possession of the steel bars from Advanced Cutting Services was a preferential transfer. An action brought under 11 U.S.C. § 547(b) is not predicated on a claimed right of a debtor to payment for goods sold or leased or for services rendered.

The same reasoning applies to the contention that the proceeds of the settlement constitute a contract right. The most recent version of the Uniform Commercial Code does not contain a definition of "contract right". The term has been eliminated because it was thought of as an account and has been rendered superfluous by the expanded definition of "account". See Official U.C.C. Reasons for 1972 Change, 13 Pa.C.S.A. § 9106 (Purdon's 1984).

There is yet a final, and most compelling reason, why Citizens National Bank's request that debtor be compelled to pay over to it the net proceeds of the settlement between debtor and Quanex must be denied. As has been indicated, the settlement in question was of a cause of action brought against Quanex pursuant to 11 U.S.C. § 547(b). A cause of action is a general intangible. 13 Pa.C.S.A. § 9106 (Purdon's 1984). Neither the security agreement nor the financing statements filed by Citizens National Bank stated that it had a security interest in general intangibles and the proceeds derived therefrom.

An appropriate Order will be issued.

NOTES AND QUESTIONS

1. The location of the goods test, or "situs theory," measured as of the time of the last event on which the assertion of perfection or lack of perfection is based, has been controversial in a number of circumstances including the case where a creditor takes, and properly perfects in State A, a floating lien on the debtor's inventory. When the debtor later purchases new inventory from a vendor in State B and the goods are identified to the contract while still in the vendor's possession, what is the status of the creditor's security interest if the goods are levied upon before they reach State A? See Coogan, *The New UCC Article 9*, 86 Harv. L. Rev. 477, 539-41 (1973).

2. Assume that Debtor purchased a large commercial-quality copier from Seller on credit in State X and that Seller reserved a security interest in the copier. Buyer maintains offices in both State X and State Y, but intends to use this particular copier in its State Y office. Assume further that Debtor took delivery of the copier at its office in State X intending to ship it to State Y the next week, and on the same day Seller filed in State Y its financing statement covering the copier. Before being able to arrange for transport of the copier, however, Debtor succumbs to mounting financial pressure and files a petition in bankruptcy. Is Seller's security interest in the copier perfected? See § 9-103(1)(c).

3. Choice of law questions arise not only at the onset of the transaction, but also in circumstances where the initial perfection is proper but the goods are thereafter moved to another jurisdiction. Section 9-103(1)(d) creates a four-month grace period within which the secured party has to re-perfect in the state to which the goods have been relocated. What is the effect of the secured party's refiling or failure to refile as against (i) another secured party who takes and perfects a security interest in the new jurisdiction after removal but before the expiration of the four-month period, and (ii) an

unsecured creditor who obtains a judgment and levies on the goods after removal but before the expiration of the four-month period?

4. Revised § 9-301 establishes a bifurcated approach to choice of law issues for nonpossessory security interests in goods, documents, and instruments. Specifically, subsection (1) provides that questions of perfection are determined by the law of the jurisdiction where the debtor is located, while subsection (3) establishes that the law of the state where the collateral is located controls questions relating to the *effect* of perfection or nonperfection (i.e., priority). The law of the debtor's location continues to govern perfection and the effect of perfection of intangible property rights. For all of these purposes, a "registered entity" (defined in Revised § 9-102(45) as any organization organized under the laws of a state where a public record of the organization is maintained) is located in its state of organization, while individual nonbusiness debtors are deemed located at the debtor's residence. Revised § 9-307. If the debtor moves to another jurisdiction, Revised § 9-314(a) continues the effectiveness of the original perfection for four months, but if the security interest is not perfected in the new jurisdiction within that time it is thereafter deemed unperfected against all persons, *but* the unperfection is not retroactive as against a purchaser for value. This generally follows the current distinction in § 9-103(1)(d) and (3)(e) between "purchasers" and all other persons. Under the revision, the location of the collateral—so-called "situs theory" of current § 9-103(1)(b)—only controls perfection in the case of *possessory* security interests, although the troublesome "last event" test is eliminated. See Revised § 9-301(2). How would these rules, if applied, affect the analysis and outcome in *Slippery Rock*? In the case of a nonpossessory security interest, if the debtor moves to another jurisdiction, and the creditor fails to perfect in that other jurisdiction, what happens to the creditor's security interest should the debtor file bankruptcy two months after the change in location? Is the result different if the bankruptcy filing does not occur until five months after the move?

(b) MOBILE GOODS AND INTANGIBLE PROPERTY

UCC § 9-103(3)
(*see Selected Commercial Statutes*)

IN RE A.J. GIBBONS ROOFING & SHEET METAL, INC.

United States Bankruptcy Court, Northern District of Ohio, 1991.
139 B.R. 654.

[Gibbons Roofing borrowed $17,535.77 from Ohio Citizens Bank ("OC"), the defendant. In connection with the loan, Gibbons executed a promissory note, a security agreement, and a financing statement, all of which indicated that Gibbons was located in Temperance, Michigan. The bank filed with the Ohio secretary of state and the recorder of deeds in Lucas County, Ohio. Gibbons made payments of $500 on four separate occasions to the bank. Subsequently,

Gibbons filed in bankruptcy, and its trustee is challenging those payments as preferences. The trustee is also attempting to deprive the bank of certain setoffs it exercised against Gibbon's checking account. The bank claims that it is protected by virtue of the fact that it holds a perfected security interest. The court characterized the issue as one of determining the proper place for the bank to perfect its security interest in the debtor's accounts, general intangibles and mobile goods.]

RICHARD L. SPEER, Bankruptcy Judge.

* * *

LAW

Because the power to regulate commercial transactions belongs to the state, the Court must look to state law to determine whether OC properly perfected its security interest. O.R.C. Section 1309.03(C) provides some guidance on where to file a security interest in accounts, general intangibles, and certain mobile goods: [The court then quoted from section 9-103(3).]

Because mobile goods may not stay in one place very long, and because intangibles have no corporeal existence, perfection cannot depend upon their location. The law of the debtor's location governs perfection. The Official Comments to that section indicate that the "location" of the debtor "means the place from which in fact the debtor manages the main part of this[sic] business operations. This is the place where persons dealing with the debtor would normally look for credit information, and is the appropriate place for filing." Ohio Rev.Code § 1309.03, Comment 5(c) (Baldwin 1988).

Turning to the case at bar, testimony was presented as to the location of the Debtor at the time the financing statement was signed, as well as all times subsequent thereto. At the Trial, only two witnesses testified: Arthur J. Gibbons, former president, director, and sole stockholder of Gibbons Roofing and James R. Thornbury, Vice-president of Special Loans at Ohio Citizens Bank. Based upon the testimony and the exhibits presented, the Court makes the following factual findings:

1. The Debtor was engaged in roofing projects mainly in Ohio; however, he did not maintain an office in Ohio.

2. The Debtor maintained an office in Michigan, as evidence by a telephone, an answering machine, a typewriter, and filing cabinets being located at Temperance, Michigan.

3. The Debtor's president was located in, and operated out of, Michigan, and was responsible for all of the Debtor's roofing projects.

4. That portion of the Debtor's business which was conducted in Ohio was managed from and run by the Michigan office.

5. The Debtor's president frequently met with the foremen of the roofing projects at the Michigan office.

6. The majority of creditors were located in Ohio.

7. Inquiries and invoices from creditors in Ohio were received by the Michigan office.

8. Since the late 1970's, the Debtor maintained an office in Michigan.

9. Since 1987, the Debtor had been incorporated under the laws of Ohio.

10. On October 3, 1989, the Debtor designated its Temperance, Michigan address as its principal place of business on a security agreement signed with the Defendant.

11. The financing statement filed by the Defendant on October 19, 1989, with the Secretary of State for Ohio and the Lucas County Recorder's office reflects the Debtor's address as Temperance, Michigan.

12. In the Statement of Affairs filed by the Debtor in these proceedings on April 19, 1990, the Debtor stated its address as 3200 West Temperance, Temperance, Michigan.

13. The Debtor maintained a checking account with OC. The checks on that business account reflect the Michigan address.

14. At the Trial, Mr. Thornbury testified that the documents in OC's collateral file reflect the Michigan address.

The Court considered these facts as persuasive that the chief executive office of Gibbons Roofing was located in Michigan, during the relevant time period. The Court cannot find that this company was being managed and operated from Ohio, when the totality of the evidence is considered. Although the largest volume of business was primarily in Ohio, business volume is not the sine qua non of chief executive office location. Consequently, the Court must look to Michigan law for perfection requirements as that was the Debtor's location.

M.S.A. Section 19.9401 [M.C.L.A. § 440.9401] instructs one on where to file a security interest for proper perfection: "[I]n the office of the secretary of state." Mich. Statutes Ann. § 19.9401(1)(c) [M.C.L.A. § 440.9401(1)(c)] (Callaghan 1991-92 Supp.). OC did not comply with this section as they failed to file with the Michigan Secretary of State's office. Thus, its security interest in the accounts and general intangibles is not superior as to the Trustee.

In some instances, strict compliance with requirements of the filing statute is excused. "A filing which is made in *good faith* in an improper place or not in all of the places required by this section is nevertheless effective with regard to any collateral as to which the filing complied with the requirements of this article and is also effective with regard to collateral covered by the financing statement against any person who has knowledge of the contents of such financing statement." Mich. Statutes Ann. § 19.9401(2) [M.C.L.A. § 440.9401(2)] (Callaghan 1991-92 Supp.) (emphasis added). The Court does not believe that OC made a good faith attempt to perfect its security interest in the Debtor's property. Based upon OC's own records, OC should have filed in Michigan. This would not have caused the bank an undue burden. OC was in a position to know of the Debtor's location and in fact, the evidence adduced at trial indicated that it possessed actual knowledge that the Debtor was located in Michigan. "Where a creditor is uncertain as to the filing requirements, the logical and better practice is for the creditor to file security interests in all possible places where filing might be required." Ledford v. Farmers State Bank and Trust Co. (In re Reier), 53 B.R. 395, 399 (S.D. Ohio, W.D.1985) (quoting In re Burgess, 30 B.R. 364, 366 (W.D.Okla.1983)).

In reaching these conclusions, the Court has considered all the evidence and arguments of counsel, regardless of whether or not they are specifically referred to in this Opinion.

Accordingly, it is ORDERED that the Debtor's location for purposes of perfecting a security interest at the time the transaction occurred be, and is hereby, Michigan.

It is FURTHER ORDERED that OC's security interest be, and is hereby, declared ineffective as to the Trustee. * * *

NOTES AND QUESTIONS

1. Determining the location of a multi-state business is governed by § 9-103(3)(d), which provides that a business debtor's location shall be deemed to be where the business maintains its "chief executive office." The theory behind this rule is that even if the debtor maintains operations in other states, and even conducts the greatest volume of business in another state, the place where the debtor manages the main part of its business is where creditors are most likely to search for credit information. See Mellon Bank v. Metro Communications, Inc., 945 F.2d 635 (3d Cir. 1991). The state where a business has its chief executive office is not necessarily its state of incorporation. As noted earlier, Revised Article 9 would change the location of any "registered entity" (which would include limited partnerships and limited liability companies as well as corporations) from "chief executive office" to the jurisdiction of organization. Revised § 9-307(a). Will this rule provide more certainty for secured creditors? See LoPucki, *Why the Debtor's State of Incorporation Should be the Proper Place for Article 9 Filing: A Systems Analysis*, 79 Minn. L. Rev. 577 (1995).

2. Bank perfected its security interest in certain landscaping equipment owned by a Pennsylvania debtor by filing its financing statement in Pennsylvania. The equipment was also located in Pennsylvania at the time. Thereafter, the debtor, who was engaged in the landscaping and nursery business, moved the equipment to New Jersey. Two years later the debtor filed for bankruptcy and the trustee sought to set aside Bank's security interest, which had never been refiled in New Jersey, as unperfected. What argument would you make in Bank's behalf in response to the trustee's claim? See PNC Bank N.A. v. Varsity Sodding Service, Inc. (In re Varsity Sodding Service, Inc.), 1998 WL 1070982 (3d Cir. 1998).

3. Under both current and Revised Article 9 separate rules continue to govern perfection of security interests in goods (usually cars, pleasure boats, trailer, etc.) covered by a certificate of title. This is due in part to the fact that perfection of a security interest in titled vehicles (except when held as inventory by a person in the business of selling goods of that type) requires physical notation of the lien on the title itself rather than filing or possession. See § 9-302(3). The basic rule can be found in § 9-103(2)(b) which makes the law of the jurisdiction issuing the title applicable until four months after the vehicle has been removed from the state and thereafter until the vehicle is registered in another state, but in no event beyond surrender of the title. What happens under this language to the lien of a creditor that has its interest properly noted on the title issued by State A when the debtor takes the vehicle to State B, registers it in that state, but does not cause a new title certificate to be issued? See J. WHITE & R. SUMMERS, UNIFORM COMMERCIAL CODE § 22-18 (4th ed. 1994). See also Revised § 9-303(d).

SECTION 6. TEMPORARY AND AUTOMATIC PERFECTION RULES

In addition to perfection by possession, control, and filing, Article 9 contains a dizzying array of both "temporary" and "automatic" perfection rules. We discuss just a couple of the more important ones in this section. In general, however, it is important to bear in mind that although a creditor that relies on one of these rules is *perfected*, and therefore protected, for example, from the trustee's strong-arm powers in the event of the debtor's bankruptcy, the perfection is not as "firm," in terms of protection against other claimants in the collateral as it would be if the creditor were to perfect using one of the more notorious methods; i.e., filing or possession. Therefore, reliance on temporary and automatic perfection rules is best viewed as a back-up and should never be used as a substitute by a creditor that seeks to obtain the maximum possible protection of its security interest.

Temporary perfection rules are really automatic perfection rules that expire after a set period of time. Most important among them are the twin 21-day perfection rules in §§ 9-304(4) and (5). The former provides that a security interest in instruments, certificated securities, or negotiable documents of title is perfected for 21 days from the time of attachment, without the need for further action of any kind, provided that it arises for new value and under a written security agreement. Similarly, § 9-304(5) states that a possessory security interest in instruments, negotiable documents, certificated securities, and goods held by a bailee under a nonnegotiable document remains perfected for 21 days following relinquishment of possession of the collateral for one of the purposes stated in subsections 5(a) and (b). In either case, after the 21-day period expires, the secured party must be perfected by another method. Another type of temporary perfection rule is the provision in § 9-312(4) allowing a purchase money creditor ten days from the time the debtor comes into possession of the collateral to perfect in order to claim the purchase money priority over a conflicting security interest.

Section 9-302(1) lists several other types of security interests which are perfected automatically upon attachment. Among the most significant of these exceptions to the public notice requirement is the automatic perfection rule in § 9-302(1)(d) for purchase money security interest in consumer goods. This exemption from the filing requirement spares the creditor the expense and the filing system the burden of having to file with respect to numerous small consumer credit sales transactions where the collateral is likely to depreciate quickly and other lenders unlikely to have much interest. In fact, by FTC Regulation Rule (16 CFR Pt. 444), lenders are prohibited from taking a nonpurchase money security interest in most types of consumer goods. Certain items that qualify as consumer goods, however, can have significant value, including jewelry, antiques, electronic equipment, and nontitled boats and trailers. The rationale for the exemption from filing is far less compelling in these circumstances, but Revised § 9-308A(1) continues the exemption without limitation except with respect to goods that are subject to statute or treaty under Revised § 9-309(c).

Chapter 8

PRIORITIES AMONG SECURED CREDITORS

SECTION 1. THE UNPERFECTED SECURED PARTY

(a) PRIORITY

BARWELL, INC. v. FIRST OF AMERICA BANK—LAPORTE, NA

United States District Court, Northern District of Indiana, 1991.
768 F. Supp. 1312.

ROBIN D. PIERCE, Magistrate Judge.

On January 3, 1989, Barwell, Inc. submitted a quotation to McMann Golf Ball Company, Inc. for the price of a Rebuilt Barwell Precision Performer to be used in McMann's golf ball manufacturing operations. Barwell's quoted price for the Performer was $52,650. In a letter attached to the quotation, Barwell's President, Dean Reusser, also informed McMann that the monthly rate for a five-year lease of the equipment would be $1,226 per month. In addition, Reusser quoted a figure of $1,750 per month for a three-year lease. At the end of the lease period, McMann would have the option to buy the machine for $1.00.

On January 16, 1989, McMann issued a purchase order for the Performer. The total price of the unit and its accessories came to $55,184.58. The following day McMann wrote a check for $3,000 as a "deposit" on the equipment. McMann's former President, Peter Mandich, characterizes the $3,000 deposit as a "down payment" on the Performer. Dean Reusser, Barwell's president, attests that a 50 percent deposit is normally required under Barwell's credit terms for a sale. Further, he states that he was not willing to sell the Performer to McMann under these terms. Ronald Cordeau, McMann's former vice-president, testifies that he does not believe that Reusser informed him of Barwell's requirement of a 50 percent deposit as a condition of sale. He does say that Reusser told him that Barwell's ordinary credit terms required the balance on a purchase to be paid within 30 days of the delivery of the equipment.

Cordeau does not recall offering to pay Barwell directly for the Performer. He states that the parties understood that he would attempt to locate a leasing company who would then purchase the equipment from Barwell and lease it back to McMann. Cordeau, however, also states that it was McMann's original intention upon receiving the quote from Barwell to purchase the Performer. Further, he agreed with the proposition that whether McMann obtained the

Performer through a direct purchase or ultimately from a leasing company, "one way or the other, McMann was buying this equipment."

Dean Reusser, Barwell's president, says that he never agreed to sell the Performer directly to McMann, and that McMann never offered to pay the purchase price of the Performer. Further, he states that all of his discussions with Cordeau centered around a leasing arrangement, whereby Barwell would sell the Performer to a leasing company. Nevertheless, on January 20, 1989, Barwell issued an acknowledgment of McMann's purchase order for the Performer. Following a heading marked "Terms," Barwell typed "50% deposit with official order, balance net 30 days." The total price on the transaction was listed as $55,184.58, with a $3,000 deposit credited to McMann, leaving a balance due of $52,184.58.

Barwell shipped the Performer to McMann on February 20, 1989. On February 21, Barwell sent McMann an invoice stating a balance due on the Performer of $52,150.38. At no time did Barwell file U.C.C. financing statements with respect to the Performer. Immediately afterward, McMann began using the machine in its golf ball manufacturing processes. On March 1, 1989, McMann and First of America Bank entered into a loan agreement providing McMann with $350,000 to purchase equipment to be used in its business. In conjunction with the loan agreement, McMann signed a security agreement giving First of America rights in its presently owned and after-acquired property.

First of America perfected its security interest in McMann's equipment by timely filing a U.C.C. financing statement with the Indiana Secretary of State on March 2, 1989, and with the Recorder of LaPorte County on March 3. * * *

Throughout the month of March, McMann continued to use the Performer in its daily operations, but made no further payment on its account with Barwell. On March 30, 1989, Barwell's Controller, Nancy DeGroff, sent a letter to McMann directed to the attention of "Accounts Payable." This letter showed a balance due of $52,187.93 on McMann's account with Barwell. When McMann failed to make payment, Barwell sent additional letters on June 23, 1989 and August 2, 1989, demanding full payment of the balance due on the account. McMann continued to offer no remuneration to Barwell.

On August 23, 1989, McMann filed a bankruptcy petition under Chapter 11 of the United States Bankruptcy Code. On September 19, 1989, Barwell sent a letter to McMann demanding the return of its equipment, because of its failure to make an "arrangement with a leasing company who would take title and make payment in full to Barwell." On November 22, 1989, Barwell and First of America executed a written agreement for relief from stay and abandonment of the Performer, with the condition that the proceeds from the sale of the equipment be deposited in an interest bearing escrow account with First Source Bank. The proceeds from the sale of the Performer were $54,000. Ultimately, on September 17, 1990, the Bankruptcy Court determined that the abandonment of the Performer from the bankruptcy estate deprived it of jurisdiction to decide whether Barwell or First of America was entitled to the proceeds from the sale.

On October 4, 1990, Barwell filed a complaint for declaratory judgment in this court. First of America filed a motion for summary judgment on January 3, 1991. Barwell filed its own motion for summary judgment on January 16, 1991. For the reasons below, the court concludes that defendant First of America's motion for summary judgment should be granted and that the motion of plaintiff Barwell should be denied.

* * *

In a nutshell, Barwell's argument is that a sale of the Performer to McMann never took place. Instead, Barwell characterizes the transaction as a bailment, with the understanding that McMann would find a third-party purchaser to buy the equipment and then lease it back to McMann. First of America, on the other hand, claims that it is entitled to the proceeds from the sale of the Performer because of the "first in time, first in line" tenet of secured transactions law, as enunciated in IND.CODE 26-1-9-312(5). First of America argues that since it properly perfected its security interest in McMann's after-acquired equipment, and because Barwell failed to file a financing statement with respect to the sale or lease of the equipment, it is entitled to the proceeds from the sale of the Performer. First of America disputes Barwell's contention that the transaction involving the Performer was a bailment. In the alternative, it argues that even if the transaction was a bailment, its perfected security interest would still prevail against Barwell's interest as a bailor.

The crucial question in this case concerns the nature and effect of the transaction which took place between Barwell and McMann. First, was Barwell's transfer of the Performer to McMann a sale, a lease, or a bailment? Second, depending upon the nature of the transfer, did First of America's security interest attach to the equipment following its delivery to McMann? Finally, if the transaction was indeed a sale, does First of America's or Barwell's security interest in the equipment prevail?

* * *

The testimony regarding the negotiations between McMann and Barwell indicates that there was never any question that Barwell intended to sell the Performer. The only unclear aspect of the verbal negotiations was whether McMann itself would pay for the equipment, or whether a third party would pay for the equipment and then lease it back to McMann. The written documentation concerning the transaction strongly indicates a sale of the Performer to McMann by Barwell. It severely strains credulity that an equipment manufacturer as well-versed in sales transactions as Barwell would allow a newly-formed company such as McMann to possess and use an expensive piece of equipment simply on a dubious understanding that McMann would try to find a buyer for it at some indefinite point in the future.

What is more likely, and what the objective evidence indicates, is that Barwell intended a sale of the Performer to McMann; the only matter not explicitly agreed upon was where the financing for the purchase would come from. Apparently, Barwell was content to rely on a $3,000 deposit or down payment from McMann as sufficient consideration for delivering the equipment to McMann. Barwell then left it up to McMann to work out the details for the financing of the sale. When several months passed and Barwell learned that McMann had failed to procure a buyer for the Performer, Barwell's patience ran out, and the company began sending McMann collection letters demanding payment in full.

Barwell's collection action is the most revealing piece of evidence before the court, for it shows that Barwell understood that a sale of the equipment had indeed been made, and it was holding McMann ultimately responsible for payment on the Performer. Barwell could easily have protected its interest in the Performer by filing a U.C.C. financing statement to perfect its purchase money security interest. It failed to do so, however, and the court will not accept Barwell's attempt to rectify its oversight by recharacterizing the nature of the transaction involving the Performer.

* * *

The fact that Barwell retained in its possession the title to the Performer does not change the result under the law. IND.CODE 26-1-2-401(1) provides that "any retention or reservation by the seller of the title in goods shipped or delivered to the buyer is limited in effect to a reservation of a security interest." The Indiana Court of Appeals has upheld this proposition in several cases, among them National Bank and Trust Company of South Bend v. Moody Ford, Inc., 149 Ind.App. 479, 273 N.E.2d 757 (1971), and First National Bank of Elkhart County v. Smoker, 153 Ind.App. 71, 286 N.E.2d 203 (1972).

* * *

Barwell, by its failure to file such a financing statement to fully protect its interest in the Performer, took just such a risk (whether calculated or otherwise) and the law mandates that it must suffer such a loss. The transaction between Barwell and McMann involving the Performer must be characterized as a sale. There is nothing in the record before the court, either in the affidavits and depositions concerning the pre-transaction negotiations, or in the documentation concerning the transaction, which indicates that a lease or a bailment agreement was consummated between Barwell and McMann. Defendant First of America properly perfected its security interest in the Performer, McMann's after-acquired equipment. Plaintiff Barwell failed to file a financing statement perfecting its purchase money security interest in the Performer. Thus, pursuant to IND.CODE 26-1-9-312(5)(a), First of America's perfected security interest in the Performer takes priority over Barwell's unperfected security interest in the equipment. As a result, First of America is entitled to all proceeds from the sale of the Performer as are now held in an escrow account with First Source Bank.

* * *

NOTES AND QUESTIONS

1. In *Barwell* the court found that the purported bailment between McMann and Barwell was actually a sale with reservation of a security interest. Because

Barwell had not filed a financing statement, its security interest was unperfected. Applying Indiana's version of § 9-312(5)(a), the court concluded that First of America Bank had priority in the Performer as the first to file or perfect. A more complete analysis, however, requires consideration of § 9-301(1)(a), which subordinates the rights of a holder of an unperfected security interest to a person entitled to priority under § 9-312. What would the result have been if Barwell had filed a financing statement? See Deutsche Credit Corp. v. Lowe (In re Torgerson), 114 B.R. 899 (Bankr. W.D. Tex. 1990).

2. The basic rule of priority governing Article 9 security interests is set forth in § 9-201, which essentially declares that the security interest is effective not only against the debtor but against all other parties as well, *except as otherwise provided* in Article 9. Thus, the specific priority rules in Part 3 of Article 9 can be viewed as exceptions to the basic rule of priority in § 9-201. Among the most important of these rules is § 9-301(1) which renders the rights of a holder of an unperfected security interest subject to the claims of a variety of other parties including, under subsection (b), a lien creditor whose lien arises before the security interest can be perfected. This provision, it will be recalled, permits the trustee in bankruptcy to avoid the unperfected security interest.

3. Section 9-312(5) is the basic rule resolving the issue of priority between secured creditors who are either both perfected or both unperfected. In the former case, subsection (a) applies the first to file or perfect rules applied in *Barwell.* If both interests are unperfected, subsection (b) confers priority on the first to attach. Why is it unlikely, however, that the first to attach rule will ever resolve an actual priority contest?

4. The first to file or perfect rule in § 9-312(5)(a) contemplates that as between two creditors with perfected security interests in the same collateral, priority might be conferred on the last to perfect. Under what circumstances might this happen? Does this rule make sense? Does the manner in which perfection is accomplished matter? The revision continues to follow the rule in § 9-312(5)(a). See Revised § 9-319(a). Priority between and among secured creditors is explored further in Section 2, infra.

(b) THEORY OF SECURED DEBT

INTRODUCTORY NOTE

There is no argument that by imposing certainty and uniformity into the area of personal property financing, Article 9 has facilitated and promoted the institution of secured credit. There has been considerable disagreement among commentators, however, over the fairness, efficiency, and social value of Article 9. The revision process has intensified the debate as we saw earlier in connection with the discussion in Chapter 5 concerning the future direction of Article 9. The traditional justification for secured credit has been that it simultaneously reduces the internal cost of borrowing and increases the aggregate amount of credit available for debtors. Therefore, the ability to acquire a security interest easily in the debtor's assets benefits not only the secured party, but the debtor and other creditors, including unsecured creditors as well. But some have questioned the fairness of a regime that permits the debtor to prefer some creditors over others and, in the process, limit the debtor's liability to unsecured creditors in the event of insolvency. Others have taken the position that if the advantages Article 9 confers on secured creditors come at the expense of unsecured creditors—that there is a transfer of value from one group to the other—then Article 9 may actually produce more secured lending than is optimal, resulting in wasteful inefficiencies. This discussion has profound implications not only insofar as the scope of Article 9 is concerned, but also in terms of whether it is appropriate to afford full priority to the first-in-time security interest.

We offer the following materials to give you the flavor of the debate about secured debt and to encourage you to develop your own thoughts as you consider these materials relating to priorities. In the first two excerpts, Professors Kripke and White, respectively, respond to the efforts of law and economics writers to justify security as economically efficient. The next excerpt is from Professors Bebchuk and Fried who have advanced the position that according full priority to secured creditors leads to inefficiencies that could be controlled by only according partial priority to secured claims. Finally, we provide an excerpt from an article by Professors Harris and Mooney, the reporters to the project to revise Article 9, who argue that the debate about the efficiency of secured lending misses the point.

KRIPKE, LAW AND ECONOMICS: MEASURING THE ECONOMIC EFFICIENCY OF COMMERCIAL LAW IN A VACUUM OF FACT, 133 U. Pa. L. Rev. 929-33, 934-36 (1985).

This Article originated in my perusal of a new casebook on commercial transactions. A portion of the book is derived from and concentrated my attention on two articles: *Security Interests and Bankruptcy Priorities: A Review of Current Theories* by Alan Schwartz, and *Secured Financing and Priorities Among Creditors* by Thomas Jackson and Anthony Kronman. Both articles apply economic analysis to the questions why chattel security is permitted to exist and whether its protections should be changed under article 9 of the Uniform Commercial Code (UCC) and the Bankruptcy Code.

Professors Jackson & Kronman set out to explore the justification and proper scope of the purchase money priority under U.C.C. § 9-312. As a preliminary matter, they consider whether any chattel security is justified. They conclude that taking security is economically efficient and, therefore, justified because security serves as a monitoring device and can reduce the total monitoring cost for all creditors. I agree with the conclusion, but not with their reasoning.

Professor Schwartz questions the priorities accorded to security interests under the Bankruptcy Code. As a preface, he also considers the justification for chattel security. He rejects Jackson & Kronman's reliance on monitoring costs because he sees no need for monitoring in the case of short-term loans, yet he finds that security is nevertheless taken. After canvassing other economic theories for possible explanations, he concludes that the taking of security cannot be pronounced either efficient or inefficient and, therefore, that inadequate grounds exist to tamper with the present law of secured credit.

There is nothing wrong with the questions these articles ask. Indeed, I always ask my classes essentially the same question: why should the law allow discrimination in favor of certain creditors, through the device of contractual security, while invalidating discrimination in favor of other creditors through contractual arrangement with the debtor for preferred payment? This question becomes more difficult to answer as broadly encompassing security arrangements, such as after-acquired property clauses, future advance clauses, and the "floating lien," come into wider usage. Professors Countryman and Coogan, for example, have expressed their disapproval of increasingly expanded security interests.

Since both Jackson & Kronman and Schwartz conclude by proposing to leave the law unchanged for the present, I have no call to take issue with their conclusions. Rather, I write because these articles proceed in a world of academic reasoning reminiscent of the cloister and unfounded on any discussion of the factual world of commerce. They do not display an understanding of the role played by the system of secured financial credit in developing a distribution system for the great outpouring of goods that has occurred in the past century. In my opinion, they are unconvincing for that reason.

I suspect, however, that these articles are not much different from other articles that apply the techniques of law and economics to the commercial world. I am concerned because these abstractions, and reliance on secondary sources for an understanding of the business world, are very different from the techniques that Robert Braucher and I applied as drafters of the present form of UCC article 9, and very different from the kind of reasoning that we submitted to the Review Committee composed of practicing lawyers, judges, and academics of an older generation. My present colleagues and I on the Permanent Editorial Board continue to apply to the U.C.C. "conventional" reasoning of the sort that these articles reject in favor of economic analysis and belittle as "the accepted wisdom."

My concern is not based on any broad opposition to the application of economic analysis to law. Elsewhere I have strongly advocated the application of economics to regulatory problems and have criticized the Securities and Exchange Commission for not incorporating into its own system the conclusions of economic studies of capital markets. Conversely, Schwartz and Jackson & Kronman have demonstrated a sound ability to use conventional legal analysis in their other writings. Their rejection of that approach in the two articles considered here suggests a point of view later articulated by Professor Edmund W. Kitch:

> The principal "intellectual foundation" of law and economics was its success vis-a-vis the competition. Yet there has been no discussion of the

> competition. The reason is that there is none that offers anything like the range of methods, insights, and institutions that law and economics has, nor is there any competition that has been associated with a comparable quantity and quality of useful scholarly work on law.

This point of view is a cause for alarm in the older generation, and calls for a response.

* * *

My essential starting point is the obvious rule that, unless otherwise agreed, tender of payment is a condition of the seller's duty to deliver the goods. This is codified in U.C.C. § 2-511(1). Section 2-507(1) states the equally obvious converse: tender of the goods is a condition of the buyer's duty to pay. Many present-day secured credit arrangements developed directly form this basic principle.

When credit entered the picture, it was historically an easy step to the concept that, despite physical surrender of the goods, the seller retained title until paid. This was the origin of the conditional sale contract, which was initially thought to be different from a chattel mortgage loan and did not require the same publicity by filing.

Although we are long past that primitive point, the concept remains that security taken for purchase money is not only legitimate, but also entitled to favorable treatment. This recognition showed up in early cases protecting purchase money security against floating mortgages and against the federal tax lien—originally, in the latter case, without a filing requirement. Similarly, in the 1962 edition of U.C.C. § 9-313 the purchase money security interest in fixtures taken before accession to the real property had priority even without any filing against prior real estate creditors. Here too, we now require filing, but the purchase money security interest continues to receive favorable treatment in the present version of the UCC.

Recognition of the purchase money priority of a seller's security interest leads readily to the further recognition that the same rights must be accorded to a bank or other financial institution that, at the time of the transaction, provides the buyer with funds to pay off the seller—as provided in U.C.C. § 9-107(b).

Many types of chattel security not directly covered by the U.C.C.'s narrow definition of purchase money are nevertheless essentially equivalent to purchase money security for purposes of this discussion. Thus, a loan for refinancing purchase money security interests does not technically fit the definition of purchase money, but logically should be given the same recognition in the law. In fact, there is already a close analogy in the UCC: the construction mortgage is recognized as a purchase money type of loan and accorded favorable treatment, and refinancing of the construction mortgage receives the same treatment.

Finally, much long-term financing has as its purpose the acquisition of new facilities by the debtor. The security taken may not fall within the definition of a purchase money security interest or the definition of a refinancing mortgage. As financing intended to facilitate the acquisition of new assets by the debtor, however, such a loan deserves to be treated like the purchase money security interests for purposes of our inquiry into the legitimacy of secured credit.

Surprisingly, neither Schwartz nor Jackson & Kronman seem to realize that these priorities represent a recognition that one who contributes new assets to the debtor is entitled to be paid for them and should not be required to give up a hold on the assets until paid. Instead, much of the discussion in these two articles proceeds on the assumption that what the secured creditor gets is taken away from unsecured creditors and, therefore, does not increase either the debtor's or the creditors' welfare. Seemingly, these authors view secured credit as a zero-sum game.

None of the authors explicitly recognizes that in purchase money situations the secured party has *added to the assets* of the debtor, and that since the purchase money priority requires the secured creditor's funds to be traced into new assets, the secured creditor and the debtor have taken nothing away from the unsecured creditors.

* * *

WHITE, EFFICIENCY JUSTIFICATIONS FOR PERSONAL PROPERTY SECURITY, 37 Vand. L. Rev. 473-75, 479-81 (1984).

In February of 1983 Pan American World Airways issued 100 million dollars of convertible secured notes. As security for these notes it put up three Boeing 747 SP aircraft, two 747-100 aircraft, and one McDonnell Douglas DC10-30. The appraised value of these aircraft was 157 million dollars. To the extent possible under the law, Pan American made these aircraft subject to the claims of the owners of the new notes. On default, the note holders would have the first claim on these aircraft, would have the right to repossess them outside of bankruptcy, and would have the right to the value of these assets or to the assets themselves in bankruptcy. At least in theory, the effect of the security agreement was to remove the six aircraft from the pool of assets that would have been available to the general creditors of Pan American had it gone into bankruptcy without granting such a security interest. To that extent at least, the general creditors of Pan American, whether they be owners of other Pan American debt securities, trade creditors, employees, or others, now apparently have diminished status just as the purchasers of the notes have enhanced claims.

The conventional justification for granting such secured creditors superiority over unsecured creditors is the assertion that, but for such security, Pan American would not have been able to borrow. Of course, it is not intuitively obvious that Pan American would have been incapable of borrowing or raising the money by other methods had it not been able to give security, nor is it clear that the common welfare has been improved by Pan American's ability to borrow. All who recently have written about these matters have found this conventional justification for security to be too facile. Yet if it is not more efficient to give preferential treatment to secured creditors in bankruptcy, a persuasive justification for security will be hard to find. Secured creditors tend to be well informed, well represented, and powerful. Our traditional notions of fairness and concern for the underdog would suggest that the banks and other secured creditors should not receive better treatment than the general creditors.

Is society better off because bankruptcy law, Article 9 of the Uniform Commercial Code, and common law rules have made the taking and perfection of security simple, inexpensive, and efficacious? I believe that the answer is "yes." First, compared to the theoretical state in which no security interest is recognized in bankruptcy or other default proceedings, it is probably more efficient to grant priority to the claims of secured creditors over the claims of unsecured creditors than to do otherwise. Second, even if one rejects the first conclusion, one should nevertheless adopt the Article 9 position as the most efficient, practical alternative under an economic system that recognizes and protects private rights of ownership.

* * *

Although I cannot prove that the granting of personal property security is economically efficient, intuition, the available evidence, and defects in the challenges to security's efficiency make it seem likely that it is efficient. Note first that the various forms of personal property security in accounts, inventory, equipment, farm products, and a variety of other assets have grown up and persisted in a relatively free economy over a long period of time. There has been no obvious compulsion by the government for creditors and debtors to adopt this mode of operation, and it is one that has been tested and refined over decades of practice and through hundreds of thousands of disputes between creditors and debtors. One might ask why it has persisted in a free economy for so long if it is not efficient. Perhaps only because its efficiency and utility seem so obvious are the arguments on security's behalf so poorly developed in the literature. More to the point, those who have questioned the efficiency of security have based their challenges on a variety of assumptions that are probably not true and have omitted consideration of arguments and evidence that can be marshalled to support the efficiency of security.

Consider four criticisms one can make of the usual arguments against the efficiency of security in general and particularly against differential risk aversion as an efficiency explanation. First, the fundamental premise that forms the basis for the challenge to an efficiency argument—namely, that unsecured creditors would lend at lower rates if no one could receive security—may be untrue. If so, the presumed savings from the abolition of security mostly disappear, and a persuasive challenge to the efficiency of security becomes difficult to mount. Second, it is possible to overestimate the cost of granting security. Third, the arguments too narrowly define the efficiency equation by failing to consider benefits other than interest rate differentials—such as an expansion in the total credit granted to risky debtors. Last, by looking to the firm and not to the employee of the firm, Professor Schwartz and others may have focused on the wrong entity in an endeavor to measure risk aversion. Specifically, these commentators have looked to the creditor's overall firm when searching for risk aversion rather than the firm's individual employee who actually decides whether to extend credit in a given situation. Even if the firm is the correct entity, evidence other than the taking of security itself reveals that certain firms are less risk averse than others.

BEBCHUK & FRIED, THE UNEASY CASE FOR THE PRIORITY OF SECURED CLAIMS IN BANKRUPTCY, 105 Yale L.J. 857, 896-97 (1996).

As we saw in Part IV, a borrower and a secured creditor may have incentives under full priority to expend resources inefficiently encumbering an asset merely to transfer bankruptcy value from nonadjusting creditors. That is, a borrower and a secured creditor may adopt a security interest that gives the two parties a larger slice of the pie at the expense of nonadjusting creditors even though the security interest at the same time reduces the size of the total pie. This is the first efficiency cost of full priority.

Returning to our hypothetical Firm and Bank, suppose that Firm borrows $1 million each from three sources: Bank, a nonadjusting creditor, and an adjusting creditor. Suppose further that there is a 5% chance that Firm will fail by the end of the year and leave $600,000 of assets to its creditors. Assume that to obtain a security interest in the $600,000 worth of assets, Bank would be required to spend $2,000 [in contracting costs], and that use of the security interest would affect neither the probability of Firm's failure nor the amount of assets that would be available to Firm's creditors in the event of default. Thus, creating the security interest would be inherently inefficient because it would reduce the total value captured by all of the parties by $2,000.

Consider the case in which the use of a security interest would not confer any priority on Bank's claim. In such a case, Bank and Firm would have no incentive to spend $2,000 to create the security interest because Bank would receive $200,000 (1/3 of $600,000) in bankruptcy whether or not the security interest had been created. Thus Bank and Firm would act efficiently under a rule of no priority by choosing not to adopt the security interest.

Now consider the case in which the security interest would confer full priority on Bank's claim against Firm. Under a rule of full priority, the security interest would reduce Bank's risk of loss by $20,000 and would increase the other creditors' risk of loss by $10,000 each. Since Bank would incur $20,000 in contracting costs in connection with the security interest, and its risk of loss would be reduced by $20,000, it would charge Firm $18,000 less in interest while the adjusting creditor would charge Firm $10,000 more in interest. Thus, full priority will give the Firm an incentive to create an inefficient security interest merely to transfer value from its nonadjusting creditors.

HARRIS & MOONEY, A PROPERTY-BASED THEORY OF SECURITY INTERESTS: TAKING DEBTORS' CHOICES SERIOUSLY, 80 Va. L. Rev. 2021, 2034-37 (1994).

One of the central questions that the Efficiency Literature addresses is whether the granting of security under current law promotes efficiency. To date the Efficiency Literature has not provided any consensus theory concerning the efficiency of secured credit; however, several contributors who followed [Professor Alan] Schwartz claimed a solution of sorts to the "puzzle" [of secured credit] after having accepted it largely on its own terms. Our analysis acknowledges that * * * unsecured creditors are better off if their debtor incurs unsecured rather than secured debt (on the assumption that the present value of each unsecured creditor's claim in insolvency would be slightly larger in the former case). Nevertheless, unsecured creditors *can* be better off if their debtor borrows on a secured basis than if their debtor is unable to borrow at all. In short, extension of secured credit may be a "second best" result for unsecured creditors.

We agree with those who doubt that any single explanation could be adequate to address the efficiency of secured transactions across the board. * * * Whether the benefits of secured credit outweigh its costs in a few, many, or most of the circumstances in which security interests are granted is an empirical question that cannot be answered with any certainty using existing information.

In the absence of empirical data it is also impossible to conclude whether giving security generally transfers wealth from unsecured creditors to secured creditors. Research that focuses on creditors of debtors that actually become insolvent cannot possibly answer the question; everyone knows that collateral provides a comparative advantage to the secured creditor in that situation. But once one acknowledges that in the real world a substantial amount of credit would not be extended without collateral and that most recipients of secured credit do not become insolvent, benefits of secured credit appear—benefits that accrue to unsecured creditors and must be weighed against the costs imposed on those creditors in the comparatively few cases of insolvency.

Secured transactions are neutral. Like many types of transactions in property (and human behavior generally), security interests can foster both good and bad for debtors and third parties. Even if it cannot be proved that secured transactions necessarily have beneficial results, secured transactions *can and sometimes do* promote efficiency and social welfare. To the extent that secured transactions bear a tarnished reputation from inferences about the *general* effects of secured transactions, drawn solely from observing the effects in insolvencies, their good name should be cleared.

SECTION 2. PERFECTED SECURITY INTERESTS

(a) IN GENERAL

UCC § 9-312(5)(a)

Conflicting security interests rank according to priority in time of filing or perfection. Priority dates from the time a filing is first made covering the collateral or the time a security interest is first perfected, whichever is earlier, provided that there is no period thereafter when there is neither filing nor perfection.

UCC § 9-403(2)

* * * The effectiveness of a filed financing statement lapses on the expiration of the five-year period unless a continuation statement is filed prior to the lapse. * * *

FRANK v. JAMES TALCOTT, INC.

United States Court of Appeals, Eleventh Circuit, 1982.
692 F.2d 734.

[Land Services, Inc. ("LSI") was in the business of subdividing land in Florida into a development known as Orange Blossoms Estates. LSI sold lots in Orange Blossoms Estates under installment land contracts which called for payment of the purchase price over a period not to exceed ten years. In 1969, Frank sold property constituting units one through eleven in Orange Blossoms Estates to LSI in return for a mortgage on the land and, purportedly, an assignment of the land contracts on the subdivided lots as they came into existence. A financing statement covering Frank's interest in the installment land contracts was duly filed with the Florida Secretary of State in 1969. In 1973, Talcott agreed to lend to LSI up to 50% of the amounts due under the land contracts from lots sold on units twelve through nineteen. Talcott filed a mortgage on the land and a financing statement describing the collateral as "all present and hereafter acquired land sales contracts * * *." Subsequently, LSI and Talcott amended their loan agreement to include installment land contracts generated from the sale of lots in units one through eleven.

LSI eventually failed and, following foreclosure of the parties' interest in the land, an action was brought to determine priority in payments that had been received under land contracts for lots in units one through eleven. The district court held for Talcott on the basis that Frank's security interest lapsed in 1974 upon his failure to file a continuation statement, and that, in any event, Frank's security interest did not explicitly extend to "proceeds" of the land contracts in addition to the contracts themselves. Frank appealed.]

ALBERT J. HENDERSON, Circuit Judge.

* * *

We agree with the district court's conclusion that Frank is not entitled to priority over Talcott's claim and also find it unnecessary to ascertain whether LSI ever granted Frank a security interest in the installment sales contracts. Moreover, we concur in the determination that Talcott's knowledge is not relevant to this dispute. Our decision to affirm, however, rests on somewhat different reasoning than that relied upon by the district court.

Frank correctly argues that the failure to file a continuation statement in 1974 did not extinguish his security interest. The purpose of filing a financing statement is to perfect a security interest, and, thus, attain additional protection against conflicting claims in the same collateral. Having initially filed a financing statement, the creditor must file a continuation statement with the proper state authority within the statutory period in order to preserve its perfected status. Section 679.9-403 of Florida's Uniform Commercial Code provides that:

> A filed financing statement * * * is effective for a period of five years from the date of filing. The effectiveness of a filed financing statement lapses * * * on the expiration of such five year period * * * unless a continuation statement is filed prior to lapse.

Therefore, when Frank did not file a continuation statement in 1974, five years from the date of his original filing, the effectiveness of his filed financing statement lapsed. Allowing a financing statement to lapse does not invalidate the security interest, but, rather, under Section 679.9-403 of the Florida Uniform Commercial Code "[u]pon such lapse the security interest becomes *unperfected*." (Emphasis supplied.) Frank's unperfected interest would still be enforceable as between Frank and LSI, but could lose priority as against third party creditors such as Talcott.

Having established that Frank could have been an unperfected secured creditor if he, in fact originally had such an interest, the next step in our analysis is to classify Talcott's interest. The evidence available from the trial record that sheds light on the nature of Talcott's interest in the proceeds of the contracts discloses that (1) Talcott and LSI entered into a loan agreement in 1973 providing Talcott with a security interest in the contracts from units twelve through nineteen and their proceeds; (2) Talcott filed a financing statement in 1973 describing the collateral as all of LSI's present and future installment sales contracts, including the proceeds thereof; and, (3) Talcott and LSI amended the 1973 loan agreement in 1974 granting Talcott a security interest in the contracts from units one through eleven and their proceeds. There was also evidence that Talcott loaned money to LSI over the course of the loan agreement.

Section 679.9-204 of Florida's Uniform Commercial Code provides that a creditor's security interest attaches to the collateral when there is an agreement that it attach, value is given by the creditor and the debtor has rights in the collateral. The facts recited above clearly establish Talcott's security interest attached to LSI's contracts and their proceeds. The 1974 amendment to the 1973 loan agreement satisfies the agreement requirement. The debtor, LSI, acquired rights in the collateral, the contracts and their proceeds, when the installment sales contracts were executed with the purchasers. Finally, Talcott gave value to LSI by providing financing over the term of the loan. Thus, Talcott obtained a security interest in the unit one through eleven contracts and their proceeds, the same collateral in which Frank asserts an unperfected interest.

An examination of the provisions of the Florida Uniform Commercial Code also leads to the conclusion that Talcott's 1973 financing statement perfected its interest in this collateral. Section 679.9-302(1) governs the method of perfection of a security interest in installment sales contracts. This section stipulates that a financing statement must be filed in order to perfect such an interest; the version of section 679.9-306(3)(a) applicable to Talcott's interest states that proceeds are similarly perfected by filing as long as "[a] filed financing statement covering the original collateral also covers proceeds." A financing statement is sufficient to perfect a security interest if, among other things, it "contains a statement indicating the types, or describing the items of collateral." Section 679.9-402(1). It is generally accepted that a description of collateral in a financing statement as "all accounts, present and hereafter acquired," is sufficient to perfect an interest in the accounts. It is not necessary to list specific accounts. See, e.g., Richmond Crane Rigging & Drayage Co., Inc. v. Golden Gate National Bank, 27 Cal.App.3d 968, 104 Cal.Rptr. 277 (1972); Heights v. Citizens National Bank, 463 Pa. 48, 342 A.2d 738 (1975); Industrial Packaging Products Co. v. Fort Pitt Packaging International, Inc., 399 Pa. 643, 161 A.2d 19 (1960).

Although some courts have questioned whether a financing statement filed to perfect an earlier security interest can also perfect a later acquired security interest in collateral which comes within the same description, see, e.g. Coin-O-Matic Service Co. v. Rhode Island Hospital Trust Co., 3 U.C.C. Rep.Serv. (Callaghan) 1112 (R.I.Super.Ct.1966), the Uniform Commercial Code mandates the opposite conclusion. Section 679.9-402(1) specifies that "[a] financing statement may be filed before a security agreement is made or a security interest otherwise attaches." The Uniform Commercial Code contains no requirement that a financing statement refer to any security agreement that may exist between the parties designated in the financing statement. The central purpose of filing a financing statement is to provide notice that the creditor may have a security interest in the named collateral, the details of which can be ascertained upon further inquiry of the named parties. Owen v. McKesson & Robbins Drug Co., 349 F.Supp. 1327, 1334 (N.D.Fla.1972), aff'd mem., 486 F.2d 1401 (5th Cir. 1973). Moreover, consideration of the commercial realities of modern day financing militates against a requirement that a secured creditor must refile each time it enters into a new loan agreement with a debtor to whom the creditor lends money on a regular basis. Therefore, we agree that a financing statement which adequately describes the collateral can serve to perfect a security interest not contemplated by the parties at the time of the initial filing. See, e.g., In re Gilchrist Co., 403 F.Supp. 197 (E.D.Pa.1975), aff'd mem., 535 F.2d 1246 (3d Cir. 1976); Richmond Crane Rigging & Drayage Co., Inc. v. Golden Gate National Bank, 27 Cal.App.3d 968, 104 Cal.Rptr. 277 (1972); Chrysler Credit Corp. v. Community Banking Co., 35 Conn.Supp. 73, 395 A.2d 727 (Super.Ct.1978); In re Will of Gruder, 89 Misc.2d 477, 392 N.Y.S.2d 203 (Sur.Ct.1977).

Thus, Talcott's 1973 financing statement covering all installment sales contracts, "present and hereafter acquired" and the proceeds thereof, was sufficient to perfect its interest in the contracts from units one through eleven and their proceeds. The fact that the statement was originally filed to perfect an interest in the contracts from units twelve through nineteen does not change this conclusion. The filed financing statement certainly gave adequate notice to potential creditors that some, if not all, of LSI's contracts were encumbered by Talcott. When Talcott obtained an interest in the contracts in 1974, the interest was automatically perfected by virtue of the 1973 filing without need for additional filings.

The final stage in this analysis is to compare Frank's unperfected security interest to Talcott's later-acquired perfected security interest under the priority rules of Florida's Uniform Commercial Code. At the time that Talcott obtained a perfected security interest, Frank had a UCC-1 financing statement on file with the Florida Secretary of State. If Frank had filed a continuation statement at the proper time, his interest might have been superior to Talcott under the priority rule governing conflicting claims of perfected secured creditors. See § 679.9-312(5)(a). However, as earlier discussed, Frank became unperfected in 1974. A Florida court recognizes that, as a general rule, "[i]t is black letter law that an unperfected security interest is subordinate to a perfected security interest." Suburbia Federal Savings & Loan Association v. Bel-Air Conditioning Co., Inc., 385 So.2d 1151, 1153 (Fla.Dist.Ct.App.1980); see §§ 679.9-301(1), .9-312(5)(a). The only question that remains, then, is whether the fact that Talcott became perfected after Frank would cause Talcott to lose its priority even though Frank's filing lapsed and his interest became unperfected.

Although the Florida courts have not yet addressed this question, the drafters of the Uniform Commercial Code anticipated this problem and explained in Comment 3 to Section 9-403:

> [u]nder * * * subsection (2) [of section 9-403] the security interest becomes unperfected when filing lapses. Thereafter, the interest of the secured party is subject to defeat by those persons who take priority over an unperfected security interest * * * and under Section 9-312(5) the holder of a perfected conflicting security interest is such a person *even though before lapse the conflicting interest was junior*.

U.C.C. § 9-403 Comment 3 (1962) (emphasis supplied). Hence, although a creditor files a financing statement after another creditor has filed a financing statement covering the same collateral, if the first creditor allows its financing statement to lapse, the claim of the second creditor becomes superior as long as his security interest remains perfected. This interpretation advanced by the code drafters in Comment 3 comports with the decisions reached by other jurisdictions. See, e.g., Eastern Indiana Production Credit Association v. Farmers State Bank, 31 Ohio App.2d 252, 287 N.E.2d 824 (1972); Morse Electro Products Corp. v. Beneficial Industrial Loan Co., 90 Wash.2d 195, 579 P.2d 1341 (1978) (en banc). For this reason, it is clear to us that Talcott's perfected security interest takes priority over Frank's unperfected security interest. This conclusion is supported by the Code Comment and the decisions in other jurisdictions and is consistent with the rule in Florida that a creditor's knowledge of conflicting security interests is not relevant to a priority dispute under article nine of the Florida Uniform Commercial Code. See National Bank of Sarasota v. Dugger, 335 So.2d 859 (Fla.Dist.Ct.App.1976).

From our examination of the Florida Uniform Commercial Code, it becomes evident that Talcott should prevail in its claim against Frank. Because Frank's security interest became unperfected upon the lapse of his financing statement, no factual determination concerning his interest could give him priority over Talcott's perfected security interest in the same collateral. As between the parties, the record mandates the finding that Talcott is entitled to the payments on the LSI installment sales contracts held in the "disputed-disputed account."

The judgment of the district court is

AFFIRMED.

NOTE ON THE "DOUBLE DEBTOR DILEMMA"

Section 9-312(5)(a) operates smoothly and equitably in the usual situation where the there are multiple secured parties claiming an interest in the same collateral of a single debtor. A problem arose, however, in the more extraordinary situation where there were not only two secured creditors but also *two debtors*. Each creditor was the first to file or perfect with respect to its debtor, and claimed an interest in existing and after acquired collateral. Debtor #1 would then sell the collateral to Debtor #2 who, under the general rule in § 9-306(2), would take subject to the security interest granted to SP #1 by Debtor #1. At the same time, SP #2's security interest in the collateral would attach as soon as Debtor #2 acquired rights in the collateral. This scenario has been termed the "double debtor dilemma" by Barkley Clark. See B. CLARK, THE LAW OF SECURED TRANSACTIONS UNDER THE UNIFORM COMMERCIAL CODE § 3.08[3] (Rev. ed. 1993). It is possible to resolve the double debtor debacle under § 9-312(5)(a), but the policies that justify that rule do not pertain in this situation. Thus, as illustrated below, the Ninth Circuit has taken a different approach. Revised Article 9 deals with the "double debtor" problem in Revised §§ 9-323, 9-323A, largely following the lead of the Ninth Circuit.

BANK OF THE WEST v. COMMERCIAL CREDIT FINANCIAL SERVICES, INC.

United States Court of Appeals, Ninth Circuit, 1986.
852 F.2d 1162.

[Bank of the West had a security interest in all of Allied's existing and after acquired inventory and accounts which was properly perfected in 1982. CCFS had a security interest in all of BCI's existing and after acquired inventory and receivables, perfected by filing in 1984. Subsequently, Allied purchased BCI's beverage business and, as part of that transaction, acquired the collateral subject to CCFS's security interest. The issue in the case revolved around priority between Bank of the West and CCFS as to the actual inventory and accounts transferred to Allied by BCI and still in existence, as well as accounts that arose from the sale of former BCI inventory, which CCFS claimed as proceeds.]

THOMPSON, Circuit Judge.

* * *

* * * The difficulty * * * is this: Before the transfer from BCI to Allied, CCFS (the transferor's creditor) had a perfected security interest in the collateral. After the transfer, CCFS's perfected security interest suddenly is subordinated to the perfected security interest of Bank of the West (the transferee's creditor).

CCFS, which had taken all steps required of it by the commercial code to announce its interest in the collateral to potential creditors of the transferor (BCI), now finds its security interest subordinated to that of the transferee's (Allied's) creditor, (Bank of the West), whose security interest came into play only because BCI made an unauthorized disposition of the collateral to which the Bank's security interest attached solely by operation of an after-acquired collateral clause. * * *

We agree with the commentators that applying section 9312(5) to resolve this priority dispute produces an unsatisfactory result. The principal reason that section 9312(5) fails to produce a proper result is that it does not appear the drafters contemplated what Professor Clark calls the "dual debtor dilemma." See B. Clark, supra, ¶ 3.8[4]. Certainly the official comments to the Uniform Commercial Code, which offer several illustrations of the operation of section 9312(5), do not address the situation in which the competing security interests are between creditors of different debtors. See Cal.Com.Code § 9312 Uniform Commercial Code Comments 4-8. In Mr. Coogan's seminal article, The New UCC Article 9, 86 Harv.L.Rev. 477 (1973), no mention of the dual debtor scenario is made in the thoughtful portion of the article addressing the drafters' reasons for adopting section 9312(5). See id. at 507-11. Because section 9312(5) does not contemplate the dual debtor scenario, we must resolve this priority dispute by returning to first principles.

As a general rule of construction, the commercial code "shall be liberally construed and applied to promote its underlying purposes and policies." Cal.Com.Code § 1102(1). The commercial code is intended to be flexible. "It is intended to make it possible for the law embodied in this Act to be developed by the courts in the light of unforeseen and new circumstances and practices. However, the proper construction of the Act requires that its interpretation and application be limited to its reason." Id. Uniform Commercial Code Comment 1. There are two reasons behind the rule of section 9312(5)(a). First, the "first to file or first to perfect" rule serves to modify the common law notion of "first in time, first in right." Harris, supra, 39 Vand.L.Rev. at 222. Section 9312(5) places a premium on prompt filing of financing statements as a means of protecting future creditors of the debtor. The financing statement alerts potential creditors that collateral against which they are contemplating making a loan already is encumbered. Thus, section 9312(5)(a) penalizes a creditor who has a security interest but who does not promptly file a financing statement by awarding priority to a later creditor who acquires a security interest in the same collateral and who more promptly files a financing statement. The "first to file or first to perfect" rule of 9312(5)(a) thus addresses the problem of secret security interests that so concerned pre-Code courts. See id. But in the present case, the notice giving function of 9312(5)(a) does not apply. Bank of the West is a creditor of another debtor entity, and the Bank's interest in the collateral arises solely out of an after-acquired property clause. Bank of the West cannot claim that it has relied to its detriment on the absence of a filed financing statement by CCFS.

A second purpose behind section 9312(5)(a) is an implied commitment to a secured creditor who has filed a financing statement that, absent special considerations such as a purchase money security interest, see, e.g., Cal.Com.Code § 9312(3), (4), no subsequent creditor will be able to defeat the complying creditor's security interest. This notion finds support in comment 5 to section 9402(7), which reads in pertinent part: "The justification for this rule lies in the necessity of protecting the filing system—that is, of allowing the secured party who has first filed to make subsequent advances without each time having, as a precondition of protection, to check for filings later than his." Cal.Com.Code § 9312 Uniform Commercial Code Comment 5; see also Harris, supra, 39 Vand.L.Rev. at 223-24 (discussing same). This has been described as the "claim staking" function of the financing statement. See Knippenberg, supra, 52 Mo.L.Rev. at 61 & n. 22. What this means is that by filing a proper financing statement in the proper place, a secured creditor has staked a claim to its collateral and knows that, absent special considerations, its claim will prevail against subsequently arising interests in the same property. By complying with the Code, the creditor is relieved of much of the responsibility of monitoring its debtor's collateral—the Code has allocated the burden of discovering prior filed financing statements to later lenders. Cf. Cal.Com.Code § 9402 Uniform Commercial Code Comment 8 ("[A]ny person searching the condition of ownership of a debtor must make inquiry as to the debtor's source of title, and must search in the name of a former owner if the circumstances seem to require it.").

Applying section 9312(5)(a) to the present case serves neither of the rationales behind the "first to file or first to perfect" rule. The notice giving function is irrelevant because the creditor of a different debtor whose sole interest in disputed collateral arises from an after-acquired property clause has no incentive to check for financing statements against the property of another debtor. Certainly the burden is on a transferee's creditor to search the title to property, but this duty arises only when the transferee's creditor first appears on the scene after the transfer. Likewise, it makes no sense to use section 9312(5)(a) to defeat CCFS's perfected security interest when CCFS has taken all steps required of it by the Code to proclaim its interest in the collateral. CCFS is entitled to rely on the Code's promise that a creditor who fully complies usually may expect its security interest to be given priority in a dispute with another secured creditor. To apply section 9312(5)(a) to this case would produce an undesirable result that does not follow from the principles that the section is meant to promote.[1]

---

[1] It is possible to argue, of course, that our analysis does violence to the interest of the transferee's creditor, whose security interest has been perfected by filing just the same as the transferor's creditor. But it is important to remember that the situation we consider is one in which the transferee's creditor's security interest attaches to the transferred collateral solely by operation of an after-acquired property clause. Although the Uniform Commercial Code expressly validates after-acquired property clauses, see Cal.Com.Code § 9204(1), these "floating liens" still have not been whole-heartedly accepted by the drafters. * * *

To the extent our opinion results in holders of after-acquired property clauses not being able to prevail against the perfected security interest of a transferor's secured creditor, this is consistent with the drafters intention in validating after-acquired property clauses but not granting them an assurance of absolute priority in all cases.

* * *

We think the correct result is reached in this case by applying the common sense notion that a creditor cannot convey to another more than it owns. Put another way, the transferee, Allied, cannot acquire any greater rights in the beverage business's assets than its transferor, BCI, had in them. Cf. Cal.Com.Code § 2403(1) ("A purchaser of goods acquires all title which his transferor had or had power to transfer except that a purchaser of a limited interest acquires rights only to the extent of the interest purchased."); * * * The drafters tell us that "[i]n most cases when a debtor makes an unauthorized disposition of the collateral, the security interest, under * * * this Article, continues in the original collateral in the hands of the purchaser or other transferee. That is to say, * * * the transferee takes subject to the security interest.* * *. Subsection [9306(2)] codifies this rule." Cal.Com.Code § 9306(2) Uniform Commercial Code Comment 3. If the transferee (Allied) takes the transferred collateral subject to the transferor's creditor's (CCFS's) security interest, certainly the transferee's creditor (Bank of the West) can have no greater rights in the collateral than does its debtor (Allied). Because section 9402(7) preserves CCFS's perfected security interest in the collateral actually transferred as well as in the property acquired in the four months after the transfer, CCFS's security interest continues to be superior to Bank of the West's interest during this period, even though Bank of the West's interest also is perfected. This result is consistent with the principles of the filing system that we have previously discussed. If the notice giving function does not apply because Bank of the West has no reason to check for filings against BCI, the claim-staking function that protects CCFS should be enforced. CCFS has done all that the Code asks of it to protect its interest. Absent some countervailing consideration, CCFS should be entitled to rely on its perfected security interest.

* * *

REVERSED AND REMANDED.

(b) PROCEEDS

OVERVIEW

Earlier we saw that, unless authorized by the secured creditor, a security interest continues in collateral notwithstanding sale, exchange, or other disposition of the collateral and also continues in any identifiable proceeds in the hands of the debtor. § 9-306(2). Continuation of the security interest in identifiable proceeds does not, however, assure *perfection* of the security interest in proceeds. That question is governed by § 9-306(3). Consider that provision in connection with the following problems.

PROBLEMS

Problem 1

Bone's Quality Used Cars ("BQUC") has granted First ABC Bank a floating lien on its inventory to secure a revolving line of credit. First ABC has perfected by filing a financing statement with the Secretary of State's Office. Consider whether, and if so for how long, First ABC's security interest in proceeds is perfected in each of the following situations:

> Case #1 BQUC sells a used car to Adam in return for a trade-in of Adam's pick-up truck and a personal check from Adam for the balance of the purchase price.
>
> Case #2 BQUC trades Adam's pick-up with Harley's Truck World for a 1988 Honda. While at Harley's BQUC's manager also sees a 1979 Volkswagen which he purchases on BQUC's behalf by indorsing Adam's check to Harley.
>
> Case #3 BQUC sells a used car to Barnes and accepts in payment a black velvet portrait of Elvis, which BQUC hangs in its business office, and a promissory note for the balance of the purchase price.
>
> Case #4 While delivering bottled water to BQUC, Smyth, an amateur collector of Elvis memorabilia, sees the Elvis portrait and offers to trade a 1979 Volkswagen he owns for the portrait. BQUC makes the deal.
>
> Case #5 BQUC sells a used car to Charles, accepting in payment Charles' promissory note, which is to be secured by the car.
>
> Case #6 BQUC sells the Charles' note to First Finance in order to raise cash needed to pay some overdue bills. Does it matter if First Finance is aware of First ABC's security interest at the time of the sale?

Problem 2

Debtor is a retailer of office supplies which it sells primarily to business purchasers on 90-days open credit terms. Although Debtor's business offices are in State X, its store is just across the line in State Y and all of its inventory is housed at the store. Debtor has established a line of credit with Bank to finance the purchase of new inventory, and Bank has taken and perfected by filing in State Y a security interest in "all existing and after acquired inventory and accounts." Subsequently, Debtor assigns several months of accounts generated from the sale of its inventory to Finance Co. in return for desperately needed cash. Finance Co. has taken and perfected by filing in both State X and State Y, a security interest in "all existing and hereafter acquired inventory and accounts" of Debtor. If Debtor defaults on both loans, who has priority with respect to existing inventory and accounts. How, if at all, would your answer change, if Debtor's business offices were in State Y rather than State X?

CROCKER NATIONAL BANK v. CLARK EQUIPMENT CREDIT CORP.

United States Court of Appeals, Eighth Circuit, 1984.
724 F.2d 696.

[DLE granted Clark a security interest in all of DLE's inventory of heavy equipment. DLE also borrowed money from Credit Alliance. In this case Clark and Credit Alliance both claim a Hough Wheel Loader that DLE sold and later repossessed. DLE is insolvent.]

LAY, Chief Judge.

* * *

Prior to 1981, DLE sold a Hough Wheel Loader to its customer Joe Horner. This sale cut off Clark's security interest as an inventory creditor in the wheel loader. However, Clark had a security interest in the chattel paper (as proceeds) generated by the sale. DLE sold the chattel paper to Credit Alliance. Horner subsequently defaulted on his payments and Credit Alliance repossessed the item. Credit Alliance returned the wheel loader to DLE's inventory taking from DLE a "dealer trust letter" acknowledging Credit Alliance's interest in the unit. As in the other items of contested inventory, Credit Alliance claims that it retained a security interest in the wheel loader when the unit was returned to DLE's inventory and that this security interest had priority over the security interest of Clark (which reattached when the inventory was returned, UCC § 9-306(5)(a)). The fundamental difference between the other items of inventory previously discussed and the wheel loader is that Credit Alliance filed a financing statement on the other repossessed items but did not file on the wheel loader.

Subsection (d) of § 9-306(5) warns that the interest of the transferee must be perfected "for protection against creditors of the transferor." Clark contends that it is a creditor of the transferor and therefore Credit Alliance was required to perfect (by filing or possession) its security interest in the unit itself in order to be "protected." The district court agreed with this argument and held that Clark had priority over Credit Alliance's unperfected security interest in the wheel loader.

The purpose of § 9-306(5)(d) is to protect the transferor's creditors who are unaware of the chattel paper sale and the repossession of the inventory. By requiring the chattel paper holders to file on repossessed goods, creditors of the transferor are protected from relying on goods in the inventory of the transferor that are subject to a prior security interest (that of the transferee). Commentators on the Code insist, however, that an inventory financier such as Clark is not a "creditor" of the transferor within the meaning of § 9-306(5)(d). See, B. Clark, The Role of Secured Transactions under the UCC, § 10.2[2]; G. Gilmore, Security Interests in Personal Property, 738-39.

Although interpretation of the Code by knowledgeable commentators is often helpful in ascertaining the meaning of a provision, such interpretation cannot prevail over the plain wording of the statute when the two are in conflict. In the instant case, this court cannot reconcile the plain language of the statute with the interpretation given by the commentators. Section 9-306(5) refers to "creditors" of the transferor; the provision does not exempt any type of creditor from its protection. Clark is an inventory creditor of DLE and as such may properly demand that Credit Alliance file in order to maintain its priority in the wheel loader. Credit Alliance did not file. Thus, Credit Alliance's security interest was subordinate to Clark's. We therefore affirm the district court's award of priority in the wheel loader to Clark.[1]

* * *

PEB COMMENTARY NO. 5

"Creditors" and "purchasers" as used in § 9-306(5)(d) do not include the original secured inventory financer of the seller of the goods under subsection (a). Accordingly, a purchaser of chattel paper generated by a sale of the goods by that seller, attaining priority over the inventory financer under § 9-308, retains that priority in the event the goods covered by the chattel paper are returned to the seller, without having to further perfect against that inventory financer.

(c) FUTURE ADVANCES

KIMBELL FOODS, INC. v. REPUBLIC NATIONAL BANK

United States Court of Appeals, Fifth Circuit, 1977.
557 F.2d 491, aff'd, 440 U.S. 715 (1979).

GEE, Circuit Judge.

On this appeal we must decide which creditor of a mercantile chain enjoys priority to repayment from the proceeds of the sale of assets of three supermarkets, aggregating $86,672. One of these is the Small Business Administration (hereinafter SBA), an avatar of the United States, serving as the guarantor of a private loan to the debtor. SBA claims the special priority enjoyed by the sovereign in collecting taxes and the debts owed it by insolvents. We conclude that the SBA lacks priority under either state or federal law.

---

1 As author of this opinion, I dissent on this point. Though extrinsic interpretational aids may not supersede the clear and unambiguous language of a statute, they are useful in divining the intended meaning of the statute. This is particularly true where, as here, one of the interpreters was one of the original drafters of the relevant document. See generally G. Gilmore, Security Interests in Personal Property. In the instant case, Clark was put on notice, through § 9-308, of the vulnerability of the proceeds to a supervening security interest. When DLE sold the chattel paper to Credit Alliance, Credit Alliance obtained priority in the proceeds. The default of the buyer of the underlying collateral should not affect the relative priority between Clark and Credit Alliance. Modern commercial practice requires that the inventory financier, the party most able to guard against the risk, be exposed to the consequences of a sale of the proceeds in which it has a security interest and a subsequent default by the buyer of the underlying collateral. If this risk were not on the inventory financier, chattel paper purchasers such as Credit Alliance would be forced to go through elaborate and expensive auditing procedures to insure the security of their credit extensions. The increased risk of the subordination of those security interests would have serious and adverse repercussions to all dealers seeking commercial financing.

The other parties are the debtor, O. K. Supermarkets, Inc. (hereinafter O.K.), and a private lender, Kimbell Foods, Inc. (hereinafter Kimbell). O.K. is a Dallas supermarket chain. The bulk sale of fixtures, equipment and inventory of three of its stores forms the fund to which the parties seek priority. O.K. owed Kimbell because of weekly inventory sales to O.K. on open account. Much of the factual background from which the claims of the parties emerge is undisputed.

O.K. executed three security agreements and financing statements to Kimbell. The first was in August 1966, securing a $20,000 promissory note from Kimbell. The collateral listed included supermarket equipment and fixtures and "(a)ll goods, wares and merchandise and any and all additions or accessions thereto." In April and November of 1968, O.K. executed the remaining security agreements and financing statements to secure a $27,000 promissory note from Kimbell. The collateral for these two agreements was again specifically identified equipment normally used in a supermarket and "(a)ll goods, wares, merchandise and stock in trade and accessions." Each of the security agreements was duly filed, and no termination statement was filed on any of the agreements. It is of particular importance to this case that each of the security agreements included the provision that "said security interest also being given to secure the payment of all other indebtedness at any time hereafter owing by Debtor to Secured Party as well as the discharge of all obligations imposed upon Debtor hereunder."

On February 2, 1969, O.K. borrowed $300,000 from Republic National Bank of Dallas (hereinafter Republic). The SBA guaranteed 90% of this loan. On February 18, 1969, Republic filed with the Secretary of State of the State of Texas a security agreement and financing statement executed by O.K. to Republic granting it a security interest in all of the debtor's machinery, fixtures, equipment, inventory and all additions and accessions thereto. When O.K. defaulted on this note the SBA paid Republic 90% of the outstanding indebtedness, some $252,313.93, and on January 21, 1971, Republic assigned the SBA 90% of the note and financing statement.

Events subsequent to the 1969 loan of $300,000 form perhaps the most important part of this tableau. When Republic made its loan, O.K. owed Kimbell $24,893.10 on the 1968 note for $27,000. O.K. paid off this note from the Republic loan proceeds. Thus, both the 1966 note and the 1968 note between O.K. and Kimbell had been satisfied. O.K. still, however, owed Kimbell $18,390.93 on open account for inventory purchases. After February 12, 1969, O.K. paid Kimbell $18,390.93 against that debt—payments Kimbell credited to O.K.'s oldest outstanding balances. O.K. kept on making inventory purchases from Kimbell on open account until January 15, 1971. By then the balance of O.K.'s account with Kimbell was $18,258.57. On January 15, 1971, Kimbell filed suit in Texas courts to recover that amount and, on January 31, 1972, obtained a judgment for $24,445.37 $18,258.57 principal, $1,186.80 interest and $5,000 attorneys' fees.

Both the SBA and Kimbell claimed priority in the $86,672 proceeds of the sale of three O.K. Supermarkets. After hearing the evidence and considering the stipulations of the parties the court ruled that the SBA had priority superior to all inchoate liens by virtue of its special status as a federal lien creditor. The district court ruled Kimbell's lien inchoate because Kimbell had not reduced its lien to judgment before the SBA guaranteed Republic's note or before the SBA made good on its guarantee. The court went on to rule that Kimbell did not have a good security interest in the goods sold at bulk sale, a fact that certainly rendered its lien inchoate. Kimbell appeals.

Kimbell's Lien

We must first determine whether the district court properly held that Kimbell's security agreements securing the 1966 and 1968 notes did not cover the advances Kimbell made to O.K. on open account. The security agreements provide that the security interest also secures the payment of future indebtedness between the parties. Texas law countenances such so-called "dragnet clauses." See Tex.Bus. & Com.Code § 9.204(e) (Tex.U.C.C.). Acknowledging this apparent approval of future advance clauses, the district court ruled that the future advance clause did not operate in this case. It relied on pre-Code Texas cases and U.C.C. cases from other jurisdictions to restrict the application of the future advance clause to future debts clearly contemplated by the parties. So reasoning, it ruled that in this case the parties meant the security agreements to cover only the notes for which they were executed, not later purchases on open account. We view the transactions differently.

Although the district court correctly stated the law of Texas, it arrived at the wrong conclusion in light of Texas' application of its law. Texas courts do not recognize the application of a future advance clause unless the future advance to be secured was "reasonably within the contemplation of the parties to the mortgage at the time it was made." Wood v. Parker Square State Bank, 400 S.W.2d 898, 901 (Tex.1966).

[The court then held, contrary to the holding of the trial court, that the evidence supported a finding that the parties had indeed intended to secure the future advances.]

We now consider whether Kimbell had priority under state law. * * * As the assignee of Republic's 1969 note and security agreement, the SBA may assert whatever priority that note might command under state law. The district court did not directly address the question of Republic's priority qua noteholder because of its view that Kimbell's security agreements with O.K. did not secure future advances. We find that they did, but even so the security agreement of February 18, 1969, between Republic and O.K. might be thought prior for two reasons. First, Republic may have established a security interest superior to that of Kimbell. Second, the 1969 note might be thought prior to secured future advances made after February 18, 1969. After reviewing the Texas law, we conclude that neither of these theories accords the SBA, standing in the shoes of Republic, priority in the proceeds from the bulk sale.

Republic could obtain a superior security interest in the collateral, notwithstanding Kimbell's previously filed security agreement, if Republic attained a purchase money security interest in the collateral. The Uniform

Commercial Code, adopted in Texas, provides that a purchase-money security interest in collateral except inventory has priority over a conflicting security interest in the same collateral if the purchase money security interest is properly perfected. Tex.Bus. & Com.Code § 9.314(d) (1968) (Tex.U.C.C.). Unfortunately for Republic and the SBA, the record reflects no purchase of goods by O.K. with the proceeds of the $300,000 note that could give rise to a purchase-money security interest in any items sold at the bulk sale except inventory.

O.K. used some of the funds from the $300,000 note to purchase inventory. Texas law affords Republic a purchase-money security interest in that inventory and grants Republic priority: if the security interest was perfected at the time the debtor received possession; if the holder of the purchase-money security interest notified the holders of prior security interests before the debtor received possession of the collateral; and if that notice stated that the person giving notice had or expected to acquire a purchase-money security interest in the specifically described goods. Tex.Bus. & Com.Code § 9.312(c) (1968) (Tex.U.C.C.). Republic did not give the required notice to Kimbell so as to establish priority in the inventory. See Borg Warner Acceptance Corp. v. Wolfe City National Bank, 544 S.W.2d 947, 951 (Tex.Civ.App. Dallas 1976, no writ). Kimbell was vaguely aware that Republic was planning to loan O.K. funds and would expect to acquire a lien, but Republic never gave Kimbell the notification requisite for priority under the Code. Republic never notified Kimbell that it expected to acquire a lien on the inventory, nor did it describe the inventory by item or type. Republic thus forfeited whatever priority it could have attained. Republic had priority, therefore, only if its lien was prior in time to Kimbell's.

Here we again inquire into the nature of the future advance clause and the security interest it creates, a particularly important endeavor when, as here, the inquiry determines the status of the lien of an intervening secured creditor. The Texas U.C.C. provides in § 9.312(e)(1) that the first filed of conflicting security interests perfected by filing prevails. Tex.Bus. & Com.Code § 9.312(e)(1) (1968) (Tex.U.C.C.). In this case both Kimbell's and Republic's security interests were perfected by filing; Kimbell would normally have priority unless the future advance did not qualify because of the creation of an intervening security interest. The circumstance of a future advance after an intervening filed security interest does not alter the scheme, however. When both interests are filed security interests, we interpret section 9.312(e) of the U.C.C. to adopt the relation-back position so that the first-to-file rule awards priority even to an advance made after an intervening security interest. See Tex.Bus. & Com.Code § 9.312(e)(1) and Example 4 (1968) (Tex.U.C.C.); Cohen, The Future Advance Interest Under the Uniform Commercial Code: Validity and Priority, 10 B.C. Ind. & Com. L. Rev. 1, 13 (1968); Comment, Priority of Future Advances Lending Under the Uniform Commercial Code, 35 U. Chi. L. Rev. 128, 133-34 (1967). The 1972 amendments to the U.C.C., adopted by Texas in 1973, effective in 1974, explicitly adopted the relation-back position for future advances. See Tex.Bus. & Com.Code § 9.312(g) (Supp.1976) (Tex.U.C.C.). Under Texas law, Kimbell retained a superior lien to Republic, and the SBA, as Republic's assignee, held an inferior state lien.

* * *

COIN-O-MATIC SERVICE CO. v. RHODE ISLAND HOSPITAL TRUST CO., 3 U.C.C. Rep. Serv. 1112, 1120 (R.I. Super. 1966). "Section [9-312(5)] deals with priority between conflicting security interests in the same collateral and gives a priority in the order of the filing but that obviously does not relate to separate and distinct security transactions. Moreover, a careful examination of [§ 9-312] and the other applicable provisions of the Code lead to the conclusion that the reasonable interpretation of [§ 9-312] is that a security agreement which does not provide for future advances is a single transaction and in the case of subsequent security agreements there is required a new financing statement."

UCC § 9-312, Official Comment 7*

"On February 1 A makes an advance against machinery in the debtor's possession and files his financing statement. On March 1 B makes an advance against the same machinery and files his financing statement. On April 1 A makes a further advance, under the original security agreement, against the same machinery (which is covered by the original financing statement and thus perfected when made). A has priority over B both as to the February 1 and as to the April 1 advance and it makes no difference whether or not A knows of B's intervening advance when he makes his second advance.

A wins, as to the April 1 advance, because he first filed even though B's interest attached, and indeed was perfected, before the April 1 advance. The same rule would apply if either A or B had perfected through possession. Section 9-204(3) and the Comment thereto should be consulted for the validation of future advances.

The same result would be reached even though A's April 1 advance was not under the original security agreement, but was under a new security agreement under A's same financing statement or during the continuation of A's possession."

QUESTION

How would these priority issues addressed in the above example be resolved under the revision? See Revised §§ 9-319(a), 9-320(a).

---

* The last paragraph of this comment was added in the 1972 amendments to Article 9 [eds.].

BAIRD & JACKSON, INFORMATION, UNCERTAINTY, AND THE TRANSFER OF PROPERTY, 13 J. Legal Stud. 299, 312-15, 318-20 (1984).

Actual Knowledge and Priority Entitlements

The main difference among the various filing systems in use today turns on the role of actual knowledge. The three principal recording systems, both in real property law and in pre-Code chattel security law, are "notice," "race-notice," and "race" statutes. Under a notice statute, only a subsequent purchaser with neither record notice nor actual or constructive knowledge of an existing property claim at the time of his purchase transaction prevails over a prior purchaser holding such existing property claim. Under such a system, however, the subsequent purchaser without knowledge or notice of an earlier party's interest will prevail over that party regardless of whether either ever files.

Under a race-notice statute, a subsequent purchaser, if he has neither actual nor constructive knowledge of the claim of a prior purchaser at the time he enters into a purchase transaction, will prevail if, but only if, he records his claim first. Notice and race-notice schemes differ only in the posttransaction period: while the notice statute treats events occurring after that transaction as irrelevant for purposes of determining the priority between these two purchasers, the race-notice statute imposes an additional race requirement in that posttransaction period before priority is ultimately determined.

Under a race statute, knowledge gained outside the filing system (or from possession) is irrelevant. The first party to file—and hence the first party to give record notice—wins. The race system, while it is the purest system in regarding as exclusive the information in the files, exists in very few states with respect to real property. And while article 9 of the Uniform Commercial Code has, with a few exceptions, adopted a race system for security interests in personal property, this itself is a deviation from most pre-Code chattel mortgage systems. Indeed, prior to the 1956 revisions of article 9, courts usually read a knowledge requirement into statutes that were otherwise silent.

Two considerations, however, lead us to conclude that the knowledge of the claims of those not in possession, who have failed to record or who have recorded improperly should be irrelevant. First, even if there are advantages from insisting that subsequent purchasers meet the traditional requirement of being without knowledge, these advantages seem to pale beside the costs they impose. Any inquiry into knowledge is likely to be expensive and time consuming. It is simply much easier to live in a world in which everyone knows that he must comply with a few simple formalities or lose than to live in a world in which the validity of someone's property rights turns on whether certain individuals had knowledge at some particular time in the past. Those who are required to make appropriate filings, in the main, either are professionals or engage the services of professionals. We think it likely that everyone is ultimately better off with a clear rule than with a legal regime that is somewhat more finely tuned but much more expensive to operate. Ferreting out those who took with knowledge despite a defective filing generally is not worth the uncertainty and the litigation it generates.

Second, and less obvious but perhaps even more important, the virtues of punishing those with knowledge are more apparent than real. We think there are few advantages to be gained by incorporating a knowledge requirement, even apart from a consideration of its costs. Acting with knowledge, without more, is not the same as acting in bad faith. We deny thieves the right to convey any title at all to third parties, because we want to discourage theft. We refuse to recognize the rights of those who lie or are otherwise in bad faith, because we want to discourage fraud. We should not, however, penalize those with knowledge just for having knowledge. Other things being equal, we want to encourage people to gather information, while we do not want to encourage people to steal or lie. Because making rights turn on knowledge is always costly and because having knowledge is generally good, those who want to justify the common-law rule bear a heavy burden.

* * *

Reliance and Priorities

Even in regimes in which a subsequent party's knowledge of an earlier, unfiled claim will defeat his interest, a subsequent party does not need to show that, in addition to being unaware of the prior interest, he was affirmatively misled because he actually checked the filing system and found nothing. He is entitled to priority regardless of whether he "relied" on the files before acquiring his property claim to the asset in question. In a case such as this, the prior party has failed to file or to file properly, while the subsequent party has failed to check the files or to check the files properly.

We find no particular reason to believe that either of the parties is better able to bear the risk, by preventing it from occurring or by insuring against it. But incorporating the concept of reliance into a filing system for evidencing the transfer of ownership claims to assets imposes two costs that seem to tip the balance against a reliance requirement. The first and less substantial reason involves the costs of determining whether a party checked the files. One approach would be to incorporate this information into the filing system as well. A filing system requires a mechanism for determining the presence and accuracy of a filing. As a corollary of this, a filing system requires a mechanism for recording *who* claims *what* ownership rights to a particular asset. Thus, embodied in the concept of a filing system itself is the notion of a mechanism for keeping track of who files. The concept of a filing system does not embody—and the existing systems do not otherwise incorporate—a mechanism for determining whether or not the files were inspected, and by whom, but it would be possible to require the recording of such information. This method of incorporating reliance seems cheaper than an investigation after the fact into whether someone checked the filing system. Yet regardless of how one proved whether someone checked the files, a new cost, however slight, would be introduced.

A more substantial reason for failing to incorporate reliance into the filing system is the presence of other proof costs such incorporation would entail. To say that a purchaser has not checked the files is not to say that he has not relied, perhaps indirectly, on the presence or absence of information in those files. A lender, for example, may have knowledge from other sources about what is in the files, thus obviating the need to check the files himself. More abstractly, a lender may "rely" on the information in the files without checking simply by observing the competitive rate for the acquisition of the interest in the property from the debtor. In this way, the lender free rides off information garnered by others, much as participants in a stock market are gaining the benefits of research by others. Whatever the indirect method of obtaining information about competing claims, these forms of reliance do not lend themselves easily to proof. A reliance requirement would increase costs to purchasers, in that they could no longer safely use these other forms of information, but would have to check the files themselves to be certain that they could show reliance after the fact.

SECTION 3. PURCHASE MONEY SECURITY INTERESTS

(a) THE PURCHASE MONEY PRIORITY

B. CLARK, THE LAW OF SECURED TRANSACTIONS UNDER THE UNIFORM COMMERCIAL CODE § 3.09, at 3-100 (Rev. ed. 1993). "The most important exception to the first-to-file rule is the superpriority claimed by a purchase money security interest under §§ 9-312(3) and 9-312(4). The former subsection protects a supplier of inventory against an earlier filer whose interest includes after-acquired inventory; the latter protects those who finance equipment, consumer goods, and farm products against a floating lien that would otherwise have priority under the first-to-file rule. Without the purchase money priority, secondary sources of credit would be chilled out of the picture unless they were willing and able to obtain subordination agreements from the floating lienor. The purchase money priority, an outgrowth of conditional sales financing, breaks up what would otherwise be a complete monopoly on the debtor's collateral. In exchange for this superpriority, however, the purchase money creditor must jump through various hoops under §§ 9-312(3) and 9-312(4). If it fails to jump through these hoops, the prior filer will latch on to the collateral under an after-acquired property clause."

KUNKEL v. SPRAGUE NATIONAL BANK

United States Court of Appeals, Eighth Circuit, 1997.
128 F.3d 636.

JOHN R. GIBSON, Circuit Judge.

* * *

Beginning in 1990, Sprague made a number of loans to John and Dorothy Morken pursuant to certain loan agreements and promissory notes. The Morkens executed a security agreement in favor of Sprague covering their inventory, farm products, equipment, and accounts receivable presently owned or thereafter acquired. Sprague filed with the Kansas Secretary of State a UCC-1 financing statement regarding the collateral located in Kansas. Sprague contends that the Morkens' debt to Sprague currently exceeds $1.9 million.

Hoxie is in the business of financing and selling cattle and operating a feedlot near Hoxie, Kansas. In five transactions between February and April 1994, John Morken purchased interests in approximately 1900 head of cattle from Hoxie. Hoxie financed Morken's cattle purchases. For each transaction, Morken executed a loan agreement and promissory note in favor of Hoxie and a security agreement granting Hoxie a purchase money security interest (PMSI) in the cattle, which were identified by lot number when the documents were executed. In addition, Hoxie was paid $100 per head by either Morken or a company in which he owned an interest. The invoices for the cattle transactions recited that the cattle were shipped to Morken, Hoxie, or both.

Hoxie did not file a UCC-1 financing statement with the Kansas Secretary of State but instead perfected its security interest by taking possession of the cattle pursuant to feedlot agreements between Morken and Hoxie. The feedlot agreements stated that the cattle belonged to "the Party of the First Part," meaning Morken, and acknowledged that Morken had delivered the cattle to Hoxie, although Morken never had physical possession of the cattle. Under the feedlot agreements, the cattle were to remain on Hoxie's feedlot for purposes of care and feeding. The feedlot and loan agreements authorized Hoxie to sell the cattle in its own name for slaughter, to receive direct payment from the packing house, and to deduct the feeding and purchase expenses from the sale proceeds and then remit the balance to Morken. Hoxie's general manager acknowledged, however, that he needed Morken's authority to sell the cattle, and that Morken determined at what price the cattle would be sold. The loan agreements recited that Morken bore all risk as to the profit or loss generated by feeding and selling the cattle.

On June 10, 1994, Morken and his wife filed a Chapter 11 bankruptcy case under Title 11 of the United States Bankruptcy Code. After the bankruptcy case was commenced, Hoxie sold the cattle to Iowa Beef Processors for slaughter. After deducting amounts owed to Hoxie for the care and feeding of the cattle, approximately $550,000 in sale proceeds remained. It is these funds which are the subject of competing claims by Sprague and Hoxie.

* * *

The bankruptcy court granted Hoxie's motion for summary judgment and denied Sprague's motion. It held that both Sprague and Hoxie had perfected security interests in the cattle but Hoxie's interest had first priority under the Kansas UCC, Kan. Stat. Ann. § 84-9-312(3). This UCC provision gives "superpriority" to a creditor with a PMSI in inventory if certain conditions are met, including the requirement that the creditor must send a specified notification to any competing secured party. The competing secured party must receive the notification within five years before the debtor receives possession of the inventory. Although Sprague did not send its statutory notification to Hoxie until

March 1995,[1] long after the cattle had been sold and slaughtered and the adversary proceeding commenced, the bankruptcy court held that the timing of the notification was nevertheless sufficient because "the Debtor never obtained possession and never will."

Sprague appealed to the district court, which affirmed the bankruptcy court's summary judgment in favor of Hoxie. The district court held that a creditor that has perfected its security interest in inventory through possession, rather than by filing, is not required to provide notification of its PMSI to competing secured creditors to attain "superpriority." According to the district court, the "superpriority" provision presumes that the creditor perfected by filing and that the debtor has possession of the inventory. The court concluded that this presumption was strong evidence that the notification requirement did not apply to a PMSI creditor that perfects by possession. 198 B.R. at 737-38.

As an alternative holding, the district court ruled that Sprague did not even have a security interest in the cattle because delivery of the cattle to Morken had not been completed and, therefore, no "present sale" had occurred. The court explained:

> Under Kansas law, a delivery may be completed although the goods remain in the possession of the seller if the seller's possession "is as an agent or at the request of the buyer under an agreement to store or care for the property, and nothing further remains to be done by either party to complete the sale." Lakeview Gardens, Inc. v. Kansas, 221 Kan. 211, 557 P.2d 1286, 1290-91 (1976) (emphasis added). Here, something further was required, payment to Hoxie under the loan agreement.

Id. at 739. Because the transactions were not a "present sale," the court reasoned that Morken did not have "rights in the collateral," as required by the Kansas UCC, Kan. Stat. Ann. § 84-9-203(1)(c), to convey a security interest in the cattle to Sprague. Morken's interest in the cattle was only a "remedial" interest against Hoxie; such an interest was inadequate to support Morken's alleged grant of a security interest to Sprague. Id. at 739-40.

I.

On appeal, the district court's grant of summary judgment is reviewed under a de novo standard. See Miller v. Citizens Sec. Group, Inc., 116 F.3d 343, 345 (8th Cir.1997). Summary judgment is proper if there are no genuine issues of material fact and Hoxie is entitled to judgment as a matter of law. See Fed.R.Civ.P. 56(c). We view the evidence in the light most favorable to Sprague and give it the benefit of all reasonable inferences. See Miller, 116 F.3d at 345. If Sprague can present evidence that would permit a reasonable fact finder to find in its favor, summary judgment is inappropriate. See Anderson v. Liberty Lobby, Inc., 477 U.S. 242, 248, 106 S.Ct. 2505, 2510, 91 L.Ed.2d 202 (1986).

We also apply a de novo standard of review to the questions of law raised by the parties, including the interpretation and application of the UCC. See Affeldt v. Westbrooke Condominium Ass'n (In re Affeldt), 60 F.3d 1292, 1294

---

1 Presumably the court meant that Hoxie gave notice to Sprague [eds.].

(8th Cir.1995).

The issues on appeal are: (a) did Sprague have a perfected security interest in the cattle?; (b) did Hoxie have a "superpriority" purchase money security interest which had priority over Sprague's interest in the cattle?; and (c) was Hoxie entitled to the proceeds from the sale of the cattle to IBP?

II.

The district court held that Sprague did not have a security interest in the cattle because Morken did not have "rights in the collateral" sufficient for a security interest to attach. We reverse on this issue.

Under the UCC, a security interest is not enforceable against the debtor or third parties, and does not attach, unless and until the following three requirements are met: (a) either the secured party has possession of the collateral by agreement with the debtor (as is the case here) or the debtor has signed a security agreement; (b) value has been given; and (c) "the debtor has rights in the collateral." Kan. Stat. Ann. § 84-9-203(1). Only the last requirement is at issue in this case.

The phrase "rights in the collateral" is not defined in the UCC. "If the debtor owns the collateral outright, it is obvious that the security interest may attach...." B. Clark, The Law of Secured Transactions Under the Uniform Commercial Code ¶ 2.04[1], at 2-43 (Rev. ed.1993). It is also well-settled, however, that "rights in the collateral" may be an interest less than outright ownership, but must be more than the mere right of possession. See id.; see also 4 J. White & R. Summers, Uniform Commercial Code 126 (4th ed. 1995) ("It follows that almost any 'rights in the collateral' will suffice under 9-203."). The concept of "title" is not determinative. See Kan. Stat. Ann. § 84-9-202. "An agreement to purchase can give rise to sufficient rights in the debtor to allow a security interest to attach, regardless of whether the debtor has technically obtained title to the property." United States v. Ables, 739 F.Supp. 1439, 1444 (D.Kan.1990). Courts consider factors such as the extent of the debtor's control over the property and whether the debtor bears the risk of ownership. See, e.g., Kinetics Tech. Int'l Corp. v. Fourth Nat'l Bank, 705 F.2d 396, 399 (10th Cir.1983) (debtor's control); Chambersburg Trust Co. v. Eichelberger, 403 Pa.Super. 199, 588 A.2d 549, 552-53 (1991) (debtor had risk of ownership). The debtor need not have possession in order to pledge the property; the UCC expressly contemplates that the secured party may retain possession of the collateral. See Kan. Stat. Ann. § 84-9-305.

The district court looked to Article 2 of the UCC, which governs sales, to determine whether Morken had "rights in the collateral." It was appropriate to consider Article 2 principles. "In many cases the secured creditor may turn to Article 2 of the UCC to measure the debtor's 'rights' with respect to collateral." Kan. Stat. Ann. § 84-9-203 Kan. cmt. (1996). The district court erred, however, in its interpretation of Article 2 and its conclusion that the cattle transactions did not bestow Morken with "rights in the collateral." As will be seen, the cattle were sold and delivered by Hoxie to Morken and Morken thus acquired "rights in the collateral."

A "sale" is the passing of title from buyer to seller for a price. Kan. Stat. Ann. § 84-2-106(1). Where delivery of the goods is made without moving the goods, title passes from buyer to seller at the time parties contracted if the goods are identified at that time. Id. § 84-2-401(3)(b). When identification occurs, the buyer acquires a "special property" and, importantly, any title interest retained by the seller is limited to the reservation of a security interest. Id. § 84-2-401(1). Physical receipt of the goods by the debtor is not necessary; rather, a sale may take place if the goods are constructively delivered to the buyer through delivery to the buyer's agent or bailee. "Delivery is not required for a 'sale' to take place, and the buyer does not even need any right to possession of the goods in question." B. Clark, The Law of Secured Transactions ¶ 3.04[2], at 3-48.

In this case, the cattle were identified in the invoices and other transaction documents, and the parties agreed that delivery would be made to Morken by delivering the cattle to Hoxie at its feedlot. The feedlot agreements recited that the cattle belonged to Morken. Morken solely bore the risk that the venture would not generate a profit. Hoxie became a bailee of the cattle because it took "delivery of property for some particular purpose on an express or implied contract that after the purpose has been fulfilled the property will be returned to the bailor, or dealt with as he directs." M. Bruenger & Co., Inc. v. Dodge City Truck Stop, Inc., 234 Kan. 682, 675 P.2d 864, 868 (1984) (quoting 8 C.J.S. Bailments § 1). Even though Hoxie had the right to deduct the costs of purchasing and caring for the cattle from the sale proceeds, the parties viewed Morken as owner of the cattle, and Morken determined when cattle would be sold and at what price. In sum, Morken became the owner of an interest in the cattle, and Hoxie's interest in the cattle was therefore limited to that of a bailee and secured party.

* * *

III.

Having determined that Sprague held a perfected security interest in the cattle, we now turn to the priority dispute between the two secured creditors, Sprague and Hoxie. We hold that Hoxie attained purchase money security interest "superpriority" under the Kansas UCC, Kan. Stat. Ann. § 84-9-312(3), and has priority over Sprague's interest.

Section 9-312 of the UCC sets forth rules for determining priorities among conflicting security interests in the same collateral. See Kan. Stat. Ann. § 84-9-312. The general priority scheme is that the first creditor to perfect its security interest beats later perfected security interests. See Kan. Stat. Ann. § 84-9-312(5)(a). There is an important exception to this "first-to-perfect" rule for a purchase money security interest. A PMSI in inventory has "superpriority" over an earlier perfected interest if: (a) the PMSI is perfected at the time the debtor receives possession of the inventory; (b) the PMSI creditor gives written notification to all holders of competing security interests which had UCC-1 financing statements on file when the PMSI creditor filed its UCC-1; (c) the competing secured creditor receives the notification within five years before the debtor receives possession of the inventory; and (d) the notification states "that the person giving the notice has or expects to acquire a purchase money security interest in inventory of the debtor, describing such inventory by item or type." Id. § 84-9-312(3).

Sprague contends that the Section 84-9-312(3)'s "superpriority" status cannot be attained by a creditor that has perfected its security interest in inventory by possession, rather than by filing a UCC-1 financing statement. It emphasizes language in this UCC section and its commentary that refers to perfection by filing and the debtor receiving possession of the inventory. See Kan. Stat. Ann. § 84-9-312(3) & Official UCC cmt. 3. We observe, however, that there is no language expressly excluding a creditor that has perfected by possession from taking advantage of this UCC section. More importantly, there is no sound policy reason to distinguish between perfection by filing and possession, and to provide the former, but not the latter, the opportunity to attain "superpriority." The common law of pledge-perfection by possession-predates, and was incorporated by, the UCC. In addition, pre-UCC law afforded special priority to purchase money security interests, and this has been carried over into the UCC. See B. Clark, The Law of Secured Transactions ¶ 3.09[1], at 3-100 ("the purchase money priority ... breaks up what would otherwise be a complete monopoly on the debtor's collateral"). Thus, the UCC, as it stands today, does not reflect any intent to penalize a PMSI creditor by depriving it of the opportunity to attain "superpriority" simply because of its means of perfection.

We believe that there is a more logical explanation for UCC § 9-312(3)'s contemplation that a creditor with a security interest in inventory would likely perfect by filing rather than possession. Inventory are goods "held for immediate or ultimate sale." Kan. Stat. Ann. § 84-9-109 Official UCC cmt. 3. The debtor typically needs its inventory to run its business and is not in a position to allow a third party, such as its lender, to possess the inventory. Therefore, the situation here-in which the creditor has possession of the inventory-will arise only rarely. The fact that the "superpriority" provision of Section 84-9-312(3) does not expressly refer to perfection by possession does not establish that its scope is limited to perfection by filing. The UCC was not drafted to address every possible factual situation, but, rather, was "intentionally designed to allow room to grow," Kan. Stat. Ann. § 84-1-102 Kan. cmt. 1 (1996), and to accommodate the "expansion of commercial practices." Id. Official UCC cmt. 1.

* * *

Having concluded that it was possible for Hoxie to use Section 84-9-312(3) to attain "superpriority," we must now decide whether it did so by fulfilling the statutory requirements. The only requirement at issue here is the timing of Hoxie's PMSI notice, which was received after the cattle were sold and slaughtered and this litigation was commenced. We believe that this issue turns on the meaning of "possession" in the context of Section 84-9-312(3). As explained above, the UCC treats constructive possession as analogous to actual possession in certain circumstances. If Morken's constructive possession triggered the notification requirement, then Hoxie's notification was untimely because Sprague received the notification after Morken received constructive possession of the cattle. On the other hand, if "possession" is limited to actual possession, Hoxie's notice was timely because Sprague received it before

Morken could ever receive actual possession.

Professor Grant Gilmore, the primary drafter of UCC Article 9, provides guidance on the meaning of "receives possession" in Section 84-9-312(3). Professor Gilmore's treatise Security Interests in Personal Property has been described as "an invaluable source of legislative intent because he is the fountainhead in this area." B. Clark, The Law of Secured Transactions ¶ 1.01 [2][c], at 1-8. In that treatise, Professor Gilmore states that "'[r]eceives possession' is evidently meant to refer to the moment when the goods are physically delivered at the debtor's place of business-not to the possibility of the debtor's acquiring rights in the goods at an earlier point by identification or appropriation to the contract or by shipment under a term under which the debtor bears the risk." II G. Gilmore, Security Interests in Personal Property § 29.3, at 787 (1965). In light of Professor Gilmore's comments, we interpret UCC § 9-312(3)'s notification requirement to be triggered by actual possession of the inventory by the debtor. Because Sprague received Hoxie's notification within five years before Morken could have received actual possession, that notification was timely.

Sprague complains that the purpose of Section 84-9-312(3) is frustrated by granting "superpriority" to a PMSI without requiring pre-perfection notification to prior filed secured creditors. It contends that debtors on the brink of insolvency will now have the motive to create "secret liens" to the detriment of prior-perfected secured creditors. The notification requirement, however, was not intended to allow other secured creditors veto power over the extension of new credit because the notification does not have to be given before the PMSI is acquired. The notification is required to state "that the person giving the notice has or expects to acquire a purchase money security interest in inventory of the debtor, describing such inventory by item or type." Kan. Stat. Ann. § 84-9-312(3)(d) (emphasis added). Thus, the PMSI creditor can wait to notify competing secured creditors after it has acquired and perfected its security interest. The Official UCC Comment explains that the notification protects the inventory financier from making additional advances to the debtor in the mistaken belief that it is secured by inventory which, in fact, has been financed by a third party with a PMSI in that inventory. If the inventory financier "has received notification, he will presumably not make an advance; if he has not received notification (or if the other interest does not qualify as a purchase money interest), any advance he may make will have priority." Kan. Stat. Ann. § 84-9-312 Official UCC cmt. 3.

Our holding is consistent with this purpose in the context of this case. Sprague did not extend further credit in reliance on the cattle serving as its collateral; in fact, Sprague had not made any loans to Morken since at least a year before Morken acquired an interest in these particular cattle. We stop short, however, of holding, as did the district court, that a PMSI creditor that perfects by possession of inventory does not ever have to send a statutory notification. It is not necessary to reach that issue because Hoxie timely sent its statutory notification. A different fact pattern in another case might justify a different conclusion. See Scallop Petroleum Co. v. Banque Trad-Credit Lyonnais, 690 F.Supp. 184, 192 (S.D.N.Y.1988) (PMSI creditor was required to send notification even though debtor never had possession of the inventory).

IV.

The "superpriority" of the purchase money security interest extends to inventory and "identifiable cash proceeds received on or before the delivery of the inventory to a buyer." Kan. Stat. Ann. § 84-9-312(3). Sprague argues that Hoxie does not have "superpriority" as to the proceeds from the cattle sales to IBP because Hoxie received payment "two or three days" after delivering the cattle to IBP. We hold that Hoxie has priority over Sprague as to the proceeds from the cattle sales.

The "on or before delivery" language in this UCC provision was discussed by the Fourth Circuit in Sony Corp. of America v. Bank One, West Virginia, Huntington NA, 85 F.3d 131 (4th Cir.1996). The court explained that this language "was meant to distinguish between cash proceeds and accounts proceeds." Id. at 136 (citing UCC § 9-312 Official UCC cmt. 3). The court concluded that "[t]he drafters of the U.C.C. decided to protect accounts financers over inventory financers, and they limited the priority of purchase money secured creditors to the cash proceeds of inventory collateral." Id. at 137 (citing UCC § 9-312 Official UCC cmt. 8); see also B. Clark, The Law of Secured Transactions ¶ 3.09[3][c], at 3-121 (describing the drafters' favorable treatment of the account lender over the PMSI creditor). Thus, the issue here turns on whether cattle sales generated an account receivable or cash proceeds.

The answer is found in the Packers and Stockyards Act, 1921, 7 U.S.C. §§ 181-229. The Act provides that for purposes of livestock sales to packers, "a cash sale means a sale in which the seller does not expressly extend credit to the buyer." 7 U.S.C. § 196(c) (1976). Even if there is a delay in payment, the transaction is a "cash sale" unless there is an express agreement extending credit from the seller to the buyer. See The First State Bank v. Gotham Provision Co., Inc. (In re Gotham Provision Co., Inc.), 669 F.2d 1000, 1004-05 (5th Cir. Unit B), cert. denied, 459 U.S. 858, 103 S.Ct. 129, 74 L.Ed.2d 111 (1982). There was no written credit agreement here; therefore, the cattle transactions between Hoxie and IBP were cash sales and not accounts receivable.

Even if these were cash sales, Sprague argues that PMSI "superpriority" does not extend to the sale proceeds because Hoxie did not receive them "on or before the delivery of the inventory to the buyer." The Fourth Circuit faced a similar issue in Sony Corp., in which payment was received one day after delivery. 85 F.3d at 136. The court refused to construe UCC § 9-312(3) to limit the PMSI creditor's "superpriority" in inventory proceeds to only those proceeds received on the same day as delivery because such a construction would lead to arbitrary results. Id. at 137. Instead, the court adopted a "reasonably contemporaneous" standard and held that the creditor had priority in the sale proceeds received one day after delivery. Id.

When cattle are sold on a "weigh and grade" basis, the purchase price is determined after the cattle are slaughtered and the meat is graded and weighed. This explains the delay between delivery and payment. See In re Gotham Provision Co., 669 F.2d at 1005 n. 3 (discussing the difference between "grade and yield" and "live weight" purchases). We follow the reasoning of the Fourth

Circuit in Sony Corp. and hold that, in the circumstances of the sales here, Hoxie's receipt of the cash proceeds was reasonably contemporaneous with delivery. Accordingly, Hoxie's "superpriority" extends to those proceeds.

In conclusion, we reverse the district court's holding that Sprague did not have a security interest in the cattle, but affirm its judgment that Hoxie's security interest has priority over Sprague's security interest.

MBANK ALAMO, N.A. v. RAYTHEON CO.

United States Court of Appeals, Fifth Circuit, 1989.
886 F.2d 1449.

REAVLEY, Circuit Judge.

MBank Alamo National Association ("MBank") and E.I. DuPont de Nemours Company, Inc. ("DuPont") pressed this conversion action against Raytheon Company ("Raytheon"), claiming that Raytheon collected certain accounts receivable, in which MBank and DuPont had security interests superior to those of Raytheon. Raytheon's defense was that it had a purchase money security interest in the accounts receivable. Concluding that Raytheon had no purchase money security interest in the accounts, the district court held that Raytheon's security interests were subordinate to those of MBank and DuPont, and granted MBank's and DuPont's motions for summary judgment. We affirm.

I. Background

MBank and DuPont entered various security agreements with Howe X-ray ("Howe"). By January 10, 1983, in accordance with these agreements, both DuPont and MBank held perfected liens in Howe's present and future accounts receivable. MBank also held a perfected security interest in Howe's present and after acquired inventory.

Beginning in January 1983, Raytheon, an x-ray equipment manufacturer, entered a series of transactions with Howe who was one of its distributors. Raytheon agreed to ship x-ray equipment to Howe after Howe contracted with one of its customers for the sale, delivery, and installation of certain Raytheon equipment. In exchange, Howe agreed to assign the specific accounts receivable to Raytheon. Subsequent to the assignments, Raytheon filed financing statements in specific accounts receivable of Howe. Between July 1983 and December 1984, Raytheon collected over $850,000.00.

By November 1984, Howe had defaulted on its obligations to MBank and DuPont. MBank and DuPont, pursuant to their security interests, demanded payment from Raytheon from the accounts receivable that it had collected. Raytheon refused, claiming that it had a purchase money security interest ("PMSI") in the accounts receivable and that its interests were therefore superior to those of MBank and DuPont.

In addition to its contention that it had a PMSI in the accounts receivable, Raytheon claimed that even if it did not have a PMSI in those accounts, MBank waived its security interest in the accounts. The district court granted MBank's and DuPont's motions for summary judgment, deciding that Raytheon had no PMSI in the accounts receivable and that Raytheon had not raised an issue of MBank's alleged waiver.

Raytheon appeals the district court's determination that it did not have a PMSI in the accounts receivable. In the alternative, Raytheon contends that if our construction of the PMSI statutory provisions excludes the Raytheon-Howe transaction, the ruling should not apply to this case under the doctrine of nonretroactivity. Raytheon also appeals the district court's finding that Raytheon failed to produce sufficient evidence of waiver to overcome MBank's motion for summary judgment.

II. Analysis

A. Purchase Money Security Interests

* * *

Raytheon claims the district court erred by not recognizing its priority in the accounts receivable as a PMSI under § 9.312(d).[1] Section 9.312(d) provides that "[a] purchase money security interest in collateral other than inventory has priority over a conflicting security interest in the same collateral or its proceeds if the purchase money security interest is perfected at the time the debtor receives possession of the collateral or within 20 days thereafter."

As a threshold matter, Raytheon must establish that it meets the statutory definition of a PMSI. Raytheon contends that it fits the statutory requirements of a PMSI under § 9.107(2), which provides: [Here the court quotes the provision.] To meet these requirements Raytheon must show: (1) that it gave value; (2) that the value given enabled Howe to acquire rights in the accounts receivable; and (3) that the accounts receivable qualify as collateral within the meaning of the statute.

* * *

To create a PMSI, the value must be given in a manner that enables the debtor to acquire interest in the collateral. * * *

The collateral at issue here is the accounts receivable. In an attempt to force its interest into the PMSI mold, Raytheon has characterized the transaction as follows: "Raytheon, by agreeing to extend credit on its equipment, enabled Howe X-Ray to enter into subsequent contracts of sale with its customers, thereby acquiring rights in the contract accounts which, upon the specific advance and delivery of equipment, blossomed into a right to the collateral accounts receivable." Raytheon, however, cannot force this transaction to fit. To accept this characterization, we would have to close our eyes to the true nature of the transaction.

---

1 Raytheon claims a PMSI in the accounts receivable and not in the inventory. Raytheon cannot claim a PMSI in this inventory because it did not comply with § 9.312(c)(2), which requires a PMSI holder to notify in writing the holder of a conflicting security interest in the same inventory.

Raytheon, in essence, is claiming that it advanced x-ray machines to Howe on credit, which then enabled Howe to purchase accounts receivable from its customers. This, however, does not comport with our view of commercial reality. While, as Raytheon suggests, it may be theoretically possible to create a PMSI in accounts receivable by advancing funds for their purchase, the same cannot be done by advancing x-ray machines. We view this as a two-step transaction in which Raytheon first advanced machines to Howe for retail sale and, once these machines were sold, Howe then assigned the accounts receivable to Raytheon. Through the credit advance, Howe acquired an interest in the machines, not the accounts receivable. Raytheon's credit advance, therefore, did not enable Howe to acquire an interest in the accounts receivable, as collateral within the meaning of the statute.

Additionally, in its characterization of the transaction, Raytheon is attempting to benefit from the PMSI's preferred status in a manner that was not contemplated by the U.C.C. drafters. PMSIs provide an avenue for heavily burdened debtors to obtain credit for specific goods when creditors who have previously loaned money to the debtor may be unwilling to advance additional funds. By giving a PMSI holder a priority interest in the specific goods purchased, there is some incentive for a lender to advance funds or credit for the specific transaction. The scope of a PMSI holder's preferred interest, however, is specifically limited by the Code.

Under § 9.312(c), a PMSI in inventory is limited to that inventory or to "identifiable cash proceeds received on or before the delivery of the inventory to a buyer * * *." The drafters noted that general financing of an inventory business is based primarily on accounts resulting from inventory, chattel paper and other proceeds. § 9.312, Official U.C.C. Reasons for 1972 Change comment (4). Reasoning that "[a]ccounts financing is more important in the economy than the financing of the kinds of inventory that produce accounts, and [that] the desirable rule is one which makes accounts financing certain as to its legal position," id., they specifically excluded accounts resulting from the sale of inventory from the protections of a PMSI. Thus, financing statements that are filed on a debtor's accounts take precedence over any subsequent claim to accounts as proceeds of a PMSI in inventory. Additionally, to protect lenders who make periodic advances against incoming inventory, the PMSI holder is required to notify other secured parties before it can take priority. § 9.312(c)(2); see id., 1972 Official U.C.C. Comment 3.

The priority scheme, however, differs in the context of collateral other than inventory. Under § 9.312(d), a PMSI in collateral other than inventory entitles the holder to a superior interest in both the collateral and its proceeds regardless of any intervening accounts. The differing entitlement to proceeds is due to differences in the expectations of the parties with respect to the collateral involved.

Collateral other than inventory generally refers to equipment used in the course of business. Since, unlike inventory, "it is not ordinarily expected that the collateral will be sold and that proceeds will result, [the drafters found it] appropriate to give the party having a purchase money security interest in the original collateral an equivalent priority in its proceeds." § 9.312, Official U.C.C. Reasons for 1972 Change comment (3).

Howe's business primarily involved the sale of inventory, which included the Raytheon x-ray machines. The accounts receivable are proceeds resulting from the sale of the machines. MBank and DuPont took security interests in the accounts receivable, in accordance with their expectation that sale of the inventory would generate the accounts. If we were to accept Raytheon's argument that it holds a PMSI in Howe's accounts receivable, we would be giving Raytheon a priority interest in the proceeds of inventory, in direct contravention to the express intent of the drafters. Additionally, Raytheon would have successfully avoided the notice requirements of § 9.312(c)(2).

Raytheon argues, however, that the policies underlying PMSIs actually favor recognizing Raytheon's priority interest in Howe's accounts. It points out that Howe could find no other source of financing besides Raytheon and that "MBank and DuPont benefited by the financing arrangements because the extension of [credit] by Raytheon helped Howe X-ray stay in business thereby servicing its debts." Raytheon also contends that if the Code is interpreted to limit the security interests of creditors, such as Raytheon, to a mere promise of repayment and the grant of a PMSI in inventory, a "valuable source of credit" to similarly encumbered debtors would "dry up." This is because the risk of default is too great in the face of prior liens on the debtor's accounts.

The Code itself, however, answers this argument. The drafters were apparently well aware that the failure to extend a PMSI holder's priority status to the resulting accounts would provide less incentive for inventory financiers to provide credit. See § 9.312, 1972 Official U.C.C. Comment comment 8. Yet, they did not extend the protections of a PMSI and merely noted that "[m]any parties financing inventory are quite content to protect their first security interest in the inventory itself, realizing that when inventory is sold, someone else will be financing the accounts and the priority for inventory will not run forward to the accounts." Id. The drafter's recognition of the problem and the statutory favoring of accounts financing demonstrate that the drafters were not overly concerned that this source of financing would "dry up."

Additionally, Raytheon had alternative means of securing its right to receive payment. Besides obtaining a PMSI in the inventory by complying with the § 9.312(c)(2) notice requirements, it could have entered subordination agreements with MBank and DuPont on the specific accounts resulting from the sale of Raytheon's x-ray machines. It also could have sold the machines to Howe's customers who would have paid Raytheon directly, with Howe receiving a commission on the sale. If Raytheon had followed either of these courses, it would not have subverted the notice and filing requirements of the Code. As this transaction goes beyond that contemplated by the PMSI provisions, we decline "to expand the scope of special protection afforded a purchase money security interest, lest in so doing we defeat the underlying purposes of the Code: to bring predictability to commercial transactions." Mark Prod. U.S., Inc. v. Interfirst Bank Houston, N.A., 737 S.W.2d 389, 393 (Tex.App.-Houston [14th Dist.] 1987).

Since Raytheon did not have a PMSI in Howe's accounts receivable, the first-to-file priority rules govern. See Ford Motor Credit Co. v. First State Bank of Smithville, 679 S.W.2d 486, 487 (Tex.1984). As the last to file, Raytheon's interest is subordinate to those of MBank and DuPont.

* * *

[The dissent of Goldberg, Circuit Judge, is omitted.]

JOHN DEERE CO. v. PRODUCTION CREDIT ASSOCIATION

Court of Appeals of Tennessee, 1984.
686 S.W.2d 904, 39 U.C.C. Rep. Serv. 684.

NEARN, Presiding Judge, Western Section.

This appeal involves a dispute between two commercial lenders, John Deere Company and Production Credit Association (P.C.A.), over their interests in the proceeds from the sale of a piece of farm equipment purchased by James Willis. The Chancellor held that neither had priority over the other under Article 9 of the U.C.C. (T.C.A. § 47-9-101, et seq.), and that their rights in the proceeds were pro rata, according to the amount each loaned to Willis.

The facts are not disputed. In a transaction prior to the one in question here, P.C.A. acquired a security interest in "all farm machinery and equipment, including but not limited to all tractors, tilling and harvesting equipment" owned by Willis and in all such property acquired in the future. The financing statement was properly filed on December 10, 1980. At that time, Willis owned a John Deere 6600 combine.

In September, 1981, this combine burned. The insurance proceeds on the combine were turned over to P.C.A. and applied to Willis' debt. Shortly thereafter, Willis borrowed $17,859.03 from P.C.A. to be used as a down payment on the purchase of a new combine and flex head from General Equipment Company (hereinafter "General").

To provide these funds, a sight draft made payable to General, drawn on a P.C.A. account and signed by Willis, was given to Willis by P.C.A. The face of the draft contained wording that it was to be used for the purchase of a John Deere 6620 combine, with a specific serial number. At the time of the issuance of this draft, P.C.A. did not obtain a new security agreement from Willis, nor was a new financing statement filed. However, the P.C.A. financing statement filed on December 10, 1980, contained both a future advances clause and an after-acquired property clause.

The same day that the sight draft was issued by P.C.A—October 14, 1981—Willis signed a retail installment contract for the purchase of a new John Deere 6620 combine and a new John Deere 215 flex head from General for $59,000.00 less a down payment of $17,800.00. At the same time, he also signed a security agreement and financing statement in favor of General, which was properly filed on October 23, 1981. General accepted the draft of P.C.A. as down payment on the combine. Shortly after the transaction was completed between Willis and

General, General assigned the security agreement and financing statement to the John Deere Company. John Deere accepted the assignment from General on October 29, 1981.

Subsequently, Willis defaulted on both the debts to P.C.A. and to John Deere. He voluntarily released the combine and flex head to P.C.A. At the time of the default, the balance owed to Deere was $52,216.28 and the balance owed to P.C.A. was $17,859.03. Deere filed suit against Willis and P.C.A., seeking possession and sale of the combine, that the proceeds be paid into the Court for a determination of the interests of P.C.A. and Deere and that a judgment for any deficiency be entered against Willis. P.C.A. surrendered the collateral with a reservation of its rights in the proceeds and filed a cross-claim against Willis and John Deere claiming a purchase money security interest in the combine in the amount loaned to Willis by P.C.A. for the down payment, $17,859.03. P.C.A. based its claim upon the draft dated September 14, 1981, issued by it to General and upon its original financing statement and security agreement filed in December, 1980.

Willis neither appeared nor filed any pleading. In a non-jury trial, the Chancellor gave John Deere a judgment against Willis in the sum of $52,216.28 as the unpaid balance of the promissory note, plus attorney's fees in the amount of $3,600.00.

As to P.C.A.'s claim against John Deere, the Chancellor held that each of the creditors had a purchase money security interest in the collateral and that to the extent of its $17,859.03 loan to Willis, P.C.A. had an equal priority in the combine or in the proceeds therefrom with John Deere. Based on the percentage ratio of the amount of the down payment to the purchase price, he awarded P.C.A. judgment against John Deere in the sum of $16,860.00.

John Deere Company appeals and insists that P.C.A. could not have a purchase money security interest in the collateral based on the filing of their financing statement of December 1980 that contained an after-acquired property clause. We hold that P.C.A. does have a purchase money security interest in the collateral and because their financing statement was filed prior to Deere's, they also have priority over Deere's interest. We therefore must affirm in part and reverse in part.

Pursuant to T.C.A. § 47-9-204, a party has a valid security interest in collateral when there is an agreement between the debtor and the secured party that the secured party has an interest in the collateral, when the secured party gives value and when the debtor has rights in the collateral. In order to perfect a security interest in farm equipment to insure that it will be superior to interests of third parties, the secured party must file a financing statement in the county of the debtor's residence. See T.C.A. § 47-9-401(1). If the value given is used by the debtor to purchase the collateral, then the secured party has a purchase money security interest in the collateral, which normally would give him priority over any other security interest in the same collateral, as long as he perfected his interest by filing a financing statement within twenty days of the debtor receiving possession of the collateral. See T.C.A. §§ 47-9-107(b) and 47-9-312(4).

In this case we have two secured parties fighting over the same collateral, now converted to money. It is undisputed that Deere has a perfected purchase money security interest in the collateral. It is also undisputed that P.C.A. gave the debtor money to purchase the collateral. The problem is that the security agreement and financing statement that P.C.A. is relying on were filed earlier, in another loan transaction. However, both of these instruments include an after-acquired property clause that we believe is sufficient to accomplish the purpose of giving P.C.A. a purchase money security interest in the combine. This is especially true in this case because the recorded financing statement specifically describes farm equipment. The purpose of the financing statement is to put third parties who check the filings on notice. We believe the financing statement P.C.A. had on file would have alerted Deere to the possibility that P.C.A. had an interest in the collateral. After thus being notified, it was incumbent upon Deere to look into the matter further if they wanted to make sure that they had the highest priority interest in the collateral. That is the purpose of notice filing. The burden is upon the party seeking a purchase money security interest to check recorded filings. Such task certainly should be performed when the credit advanced is substantially less than the purchase price of the collateral. Such fact clearly opens up the distinct possibility that someone else has advanced the debtor funds and will therefore be claiming a purchase money security interest in that collateral.

* * *

In the case at bar, as far as we can determine from record, P.C.A. had a security agreement and a prior recorded financing statement and based thereon advanced to the debtor $17,859.03. The draft for $17,859.03 was given to the debtor, who in turn gave it to Deere, who applied it as a down payment for the new collateral. The undisputed testimony of P.C.A. was that no payments were made on the new loan. There is no difficulty in determining what portion of the loan was represented by the purchase money.

Additionally, P.C.A. is not claiming a purchase money security interest in the collateral any greater than the purchase money it loaned. They are claiming a purchase money security interest to the extent of the present consideration they advanced for the purchase of the combine, not for any prior loans they made. If they were, different results might be reached. See T.C.A. § 47-9-107, comment 2.

Therefore, we hold that P.C.A. has a purchase money security interest in the combine only up to the amount of the value they gave that was used for the purchase, that is, for $17,859.03. It is not our view that in all cases where a financing statement is filed and the lender has an after-acquired property clause in the financing statement that a purchase money security interest is retained in whatever the borrower purchases. A security interest yes, but the type will depend upon the circumstances. Where the funds are delivered by the lender for the specific purpose of purchasing specific equipment that is specifically covered by the prior financing statement of the parties, that security interest is a purchase money security interest when the funds are so used. Such are the provisions of T.C.A. § 47-9-107(b).

Deere asserts that a new financing statement had to be filed for P.C.A. to obtain a purchase money security interest in the combine. We see no reason for a second filing of a financing statement by P.C.A. to insure a purchase money security interest. The first filing was notice to the world of a security interest in farm equipment and after-acquired property, and any further notice filing would be, in our opinion, supererogation.

Since we hold that both parties have a perfected purchase money security interest in the combine, it must be determined which has priority.

Both interests attached at the same time, that is, when the debtor acquired rights in the collateral. P.C.A. had, in essence, a pre-filing and Deere's filing related back to the day the debtor obtained possession under T.C.A. § 47-9-312(4). Since this section does not assist us in determining which party has priority, we must look to the "clean up" section, § 47-9-312(5). Since both parties perfected by filing, the first to file has priority. See T.C.A. § 47-9-312(5)(a). Therefore, P.C.A.'s purchase money security interest is superior to Deere's.

Accordingly, P.C.A. is entitled to $17,859.03 of the disputed fund and John Deere is entitled to the balance.

The result is that the holding of the Chancellor that both P.C.A. and Deere possess purchase money security interests in the collateral is affirmed. However, his holding that the interests are held equally on a pro rata basis is reversed. Costs below are as there adjudged. Since the assessment of costs of appeal are not governed by the U.C.C., we adopt in principal the policy of the Chancellor and assess them on an equal, pro rata basis of one-half to each.

Done at Nashville in the two hundred and eighth year of our Independence and in the one hundred and eighty-ninth year of our Statehood.

NOTES AND QUESTIONS

1. Revised § 9-322(a) carries over the rule applied in *MBank Alamo* that a purchase money priority in inventory does not extend to accounts receivable or trade-ins generated by the sale of such inventory.

2. Revised § 9-322(e) addresses the issue of priority between competing purchase money security interests by affording a security interest securing the price of the collateral priority over a security interest securing an obligation incurred to enable the debtor to acquire rights in the collateral. In all other cases, priority is resolved under the first to file or perfect rule of Revised § 9-319(b). How would *John Deere* be decided under the revision?

3. Under § 9-312(4) a purchase money creditor has ten days to perfect from the date the debtor acquires possession of the collateral in order to qualify for the purchase money priority. But when does a debtor come into *possession* for purposes of § 9-312(4)? Assume Buyer accepts goods on a "sale on approval basis" (§ 2-326) and 30 days later elects to purchase the goods by signing a note and security agreement with Seller. Assume further that Buyer had

previously granted a security interest to Bank in all existing and after acquired goods of the type purchased from Seller. If Seller perfects with ten days after the security agreement is executed, will it qualify for priority under § 9-312(4)? See Brodie Hotel Supply, Inc. v. United States, 431 F.2d 1316 (9th Cir. 1970).

4. Apparently, all of the parties in *Kunkel* conceded that the cattle were "inventory" for purposes of analyzing Hoxie's purchase money priority. Do you agree? Hoxie was holding the cattle for Morken for purposes of "care and feeding." See § 9-109(3). How would a different classification of the collateral affect the analysis?

5. A number of states have adopted a more generous grace period in their local version of § 9-312(4), most typically 20 days. Revised § 9-322(d) follows suit.

(b) Determining the Purchase Money Character of Security Interests

SOUTHTRUST BANK OF ALABAMA, N.A. v. BORG-WARNER ACCEPTANCE CORP.

United States Court of Appeals, Eleventh Circuit, 1985.
760 F.2d 1240.

TUTTLE, Senior Circuit Judge.

Borg-Warner Acceptance Corporation ("BWAC") appeals from a decision of the district court denying its motion for summary judgment and granting summary judgment to Southtrust Bank ("the Bank") in a diversity suit. The Bank filed a declaratory judgment action to ascertain which of the parties has priority in the inventory of four debtors, Molay Brothers Supply Company, Inc., Gulf City Distributors, Inc., Standard Wholesale Supply Company and Crest Refrigeration, Inc. These debtors, which are no longer in existence, defaulted on obligations they owed to one or the other party.

Both the Bank and BWAC have perfected security interests in the inventory of the debtors. In each case, the Bank filed its financing statement first. BWAC contends that as a purchase money lender it falls within the purchase money security interest exception to the first to file rule and therefore is entitled to possession of the inventory. The Uniform Commercial Code (UCC) as adopted in both Alabama and Georgia, provides in pertinent part:

> A security interest is a "purchase money security interest" to the extent that it is:
> (a) Taken or retained by the seller of the collateral to secure all or part of its price; or
> (b) Taken by a person who by making advances or incurring an obligation gives value to enable the debtor to acquire rights in or the use of collateral if such value is in fact so used.

Ala.Code § 7-9-107 (1975); O.C.G.A. § 11-9-107 (1981).

BWAC engages in purchase money financing. Here, BWAC purchased invoices from vendors who supplied inventory items to the debtors in question. The security agreements between BWAC and each of the debtors contained the following provision:

> In order to secure repayment to Secured Party of all such extensions of credit made by Secured Party in accordance with this Agreement, and to secure payment of all other debts or liabilities and performance of all obligations of Debtor to Secured Party, whether now existing or hereafter arising, Debtor agrees that Secured Party shall have and hereby grants to Secured Party a security interest in all Inventory of Debtor, whether now owned or hereafter acquired, and all Proceeds and products thereof.

The term "Inventory" was defined as "all inventory, of whatever kind or nature, wherever located, now owned or hereafter acquired * * * when such inventory has been financed by Borg-Warner Acceptance Corporation."

BWAC and the debtors employed a scheduled liquidation arrangement to reduce the debt owed BWAC. Under this arrangement a debtor was permitted to pay a percentage of the invoice each month, without regard to whether the item was actually sold. If an unpaid item was sold, then the remaining inventory served as collateral to secure the unpaid balance.

The key issue for decision by this Court is whether inclusion of an after-acquired property clause and a future advances clause in BWAC's security agreements converted its purchase money security interest (PMSI) into an ordinary security interest.

The district court held that inclusion of after-acquired property and future advances clauses ("the clauses") in the security agreement converted BWAC's PMSI into an ordinary security interest. The court relied on In re Manuel, 507 F.2d 990 (5th Cir.1975) (holding, in a consumer bankruptcy context, that PMSI must be limited to the item purchased at time of the agreement and cannot exceed the price of that item); In re Norrell, 426 F.Supp. 435 (M.D.Ga.1977) (same); and In re Simpson, 4 U.C.C.Rep.Serv. 243 (W.D.Mich.1966) (inclusion of future advances clause in security agreement for farm equipment destroys PMSI).

BWAC argues that the cases relied on by the court are distinguishable. First, BWAC notes that almost all the cases following the "transformation" rule (i.e., inclusion of the clauses transforms a PMSI into an ordinary security interest) are consumer bankruptcy cases. It argues that the rationale of those cases, which is to protect the consumer, does not apply in commercial cases such as the case at bar. See In re Mid-Atlantic Flange, 26 U.C.C.Rep.Serv. 203, 208 (E.D.Pa.1979). BWAC argues that the policy considerations in a commercial setting, promoting commercial certainty and encouraging credit extension, do not support the application of the transformation rule. According to BWAC, applying the transformation rule to inventory financiers would require them to police inventory constantly and to see that inventory corresponds on an item-by-item basis with debt.

The Bank argues that the transformation rule is not a product of special bankruptcy considerations, and that if the drafters had intended to limit the rule to consumer transactions, they would have said so, as they did in other sections of the Code. The Bank contends that a holding that inclusion of the clauses destroys a PMSI would not have a serious negative effect on inventory financiers. It points out that such financiers could retain priority by obtaining a subordination agreement from the first-to-file creditor.

We see no reason to limit the holding of In re Manuel to consumer bankruptcy cases. In that case, the Fifth Circuit stated:

> A plain reading of the statutory requirements would indicate that they require the purchase money security interest to be in the item purchased, and that, as the judges below noted, the purchase money security interest cannot exceed the price of what is purchased in the transaction wherein the security interest is created. * * *

Id. at 993. Nothing in the language of U.C.C. § 9-312(3) or § 9-107 distinguishes between consumer and commercial transactions or between bankruptcy and nonbankruptcy contexts. We see no policy reasons for creating a distinction where the drafters have not done so.

Second, BWAC contends that the cases supporting the transformation rule involve situations in which the clauses were actually exercised, e.g., Manuel (agreement covered pre-existing debt); Simpson (future advances actually made). BWAC argues that mere inclusion of the clauses does not void a PMSI. In re Griffin, 9 B.R. 880 (Bankr.N.D.Ga.1981) (when creditor is seller, mere existence of unexercised future advances clause does not destroy PMSI); Mid Atlantic Flange (same). We need not reach the issue of whether mere inclusion of unexercised future advances and after-acquired property clauses voids a PMSI because we find that BWAC exercised the clauses here. After entering the security agreements with the debtors, BWAC regularly purchased inventory for the debtors and now claims that the debtors' BWAC-financed inventory secures these purchases. This is an exercise of the future advances clause. Similarly, BWAC claims as collateral not only the inventory purchased at the time the security agreements were entered, but all BWAC-financed inventory. This is an exercise of the after-acquired property clause. We hold, therefore, that BWAC's exercise of the future advances and after-acquired property clauses in its security agreements with the debtors destroyed its PMSI.

We note, as did the district court, that BWAC retains a security interest in the goods. It merely loses its priority status as a purchase money secured lender. The concept of the floating lien under the U.C.C. remains intact. We hold, merely, that such a floating lien is inconsistent with a PMSI. A PMSI requires a one-to-one relationship between the debt and the collateral.

BWAC's final argument is that the court should adopt a "to the extent" rule, based on the literal language of UCC, § 9-107:

> A security interest is a "purchase money security interest" *to the extent* that it is * * * (b) Taken by a person who by making advances or incurring an obligation gives value to enable the debtor to acquire rights in or the use of collateral if such value is in fact so used. (emphasis added.)

Some courts have held that the clauses, even if exercised, do not invalidate a PMSI if there is some method for determining the extent of the PMSI. For example, in In re Staley, 426 F.Supp. 437 (M.D.Ga.1977), the court held that the PMSI was valid because the security agreement specified that payments be allocated first to items bought first. Thus, it was easy for the court to ascertain which items had been fully paid for and hence no longer served as collateral. Here, however, nothing in the contract or in state law allocates payments to particular items of inventory. BWAC, in fact, claims all BWAC-financed inventory as its collateral without regard to payments made by the debtors. We agree with the court in In re Coomer, 8 B.R. 351, 355 (Bankr.E.D.Tenn.1980), that

> Without some guidelines, legislative or contractual, the court should not be required to distill from a mass of transactions the extent to which a security interest is purchase money.

Unless a lender contractually provides some method for determining the extent to which each item of collateral secures its purchase money, it effectively gives up its purchase money status.

Because we hold that BWAC's exercise of the after-acquired property and future advances clauses in its security agreements voided its PMSI, we need not reach the other issues raised by the Bank. We also do not reach the issue raised by BWAC concerning the district court's reference to proceeds from sales of the inventory being held "in trust." Whether the proceeds are held "in trust" is relevant only to the issue of damages. The district court entered final judgment only on the claim for declaratory relief and referred the damage claim to a magistrate. Because no final judgment has been entered as to damages, that issue is not properly before this Court.

AFFIRMED.

NOTE ON *SOUTHTRUST*

Southtrust illustrates what has come to be known as the "transformation" rule, which operates to transform a security interest from purchase money to nonpurchase money. The transformation rule has been applied in circumstances like *Southtrust* where the security agreement contains an after acquired property and a future advance clause. The reasoning being that once the security interest extends to advances other than those used to acquire the collateral, the purchase money character of the security interest is lost. Similarly, even if all the advances are used to purchase new collateral, as appears to have been the case in *Southtrust*, the transaction can no longer be treated as purchase money because, under the cross collateralization clause, each item of collateral is securing not only its own debt but the debts incurred to purchase the other items of collateral. Thus, unless there is separate documentation and accounting for each transaction, the creditor cannot claim a purchase money priority. The transformation rule has also been applied in circumstances where the original purchase money debt is refinanced, particularly if new credit is extended as part of the refinance transaction. See Citizens Savings Bank of Hawkeye v. Miller, 515 N.W.2d 7 (Iowa 1994). The rationale is that the security interest now secures the restructured debt rather than "its price." However, it should be observed that the "its price" language appears only in § 9-107(a) and not § 9-107(b).

Southtrust, and other decisions applying the transformation rule, rely on cases decided under § 522(f)(1) of the Bankruptcy Code, a provision that permits debtors to set aside nonpurchase money security interests in exempt consumer goods. In those cases, the beneficiary of a narrow interpretation of when a security interest qualifies as purchase money is a consumer debtor seeking to protect property from the reaches of a consumer finance company. Section 522(f)(1) reflects a congressional sentiment that such security interests are most frequently taken in order to obtain leverage over the debtor rather than for their economic value. Thus many commentators, as well as other courts, have questioned the relevance of that authority in cases involving priority disputes between two commercial creditors and, as set forth below, these dissenting views have had their influence on the Article 9 revision process. See Borg-Warner Acceptance Corp. v. Tascosa National Bank, 784 S.W.2d 129 (Tex. Ct. App. 1990) (refusing to extend the transformation rule into the question of establishing priorities among creditors under Article 9).

REVISED § 9-104(e)

A purchase money security interest does not lose its status as such if:

(1) the purchase money collateral also secures an obligation that is not a purchase money obligation;

(2) collateral that is not purchase money collateral also secures the purchase money obligation; or

(3) the purchase money obligation has been renewed, refinanced, or restructured.

PROBLEM

Your client, First State Bank ("FSB"), is planning to loan one of its regular and valued customers, a large oilfield supplier of drilling pipe and casing, the funds it needs to purchase, from a Japanese manufacturer, a new, state-of-the-art machine for threading pipe ends so that the pipe can be securely joined for deep well drilling. The cost is $32 million. FSB is aware that the borrower has already granted a security interest in its existing and after acquired equipment to another lender that has perfected by filing. However, FSB is also aware of the special priority for purchase money loans and plans to reserve a security interest in the threader as collateral for the loan and to perfect no later than ten days after the borrower takes possession. The borrower, which has an office in Osaka, has proposed that, in the interest of expediency, it will lay out the cash for the threader and that FSB can reimburse the expense by disbursing the loan proceeds into the borrower's FSB operating account while the threader is in route. Do you see any problems with this plan?

(c) RECONSIDERING THE PURCHASE MONEY PRIORITY

JACKSON & KRONMAN, SECURED FINANCING AND PRIORITIES AMONG CREDITORS, 88 Yale L.J. 1143-46, 1166-67 (1979).

One of the principal advantages of a secured transaction is the protection it provides against the claims of competing creditors. A creditor asserting a security interest in his debtor's property is likely to find himself in competition with a wide assortment of other claimants. For example, his security interest may be challenged by another creditor with a consensual security interest, by a creditor with a judgment or execution lien, by a creditor claiming a right to the collateral under some general statutory entitlement such as a repairman's lien, by a seller to or buyer from the debtor, or by the debtor's trustee in bankruptcy. To a considerable extent, the value of a security interest depends upon the degree to which it insulates the secured party from the claims of the debtor's other creditors.

Article 9 of the Uniform Commercial Code contains detailed rules for resolving conflicts between secured creditors and various third parties—rules that tell the secured party what he must do in order to prevent his security interest form being overridden by a competing claimant, or, conversely, what a competitor must do in order to circumvent an existing security interest in the debtor's property. These rules are called "priority" rules, since it is their function to determine the order in which competing creditors may satisfy their claims from particular assets belonging to their common debtor's estate. Taken together, they define the principal advantages and limitations of a consensual security interest in the debtor's personal property.

One of Article 9's most striking innovations is its relatively comprehensive and systematic treatment of priority questions. In this regard, Article 9 represents a distinct improvement over the various pre-Code chattel security statues, which treated priority problems in an ad hoc and inconsistent fashion. Nevertheless, the analytic justification for many of Article 9's most important priority rules remains obscure. This is especially true of the overriding priority enjoyed by purchase money lenders. Established long before the enactment of the Code and carried forward in Code sections 9-107 and 9-312(3) and (4), the purchase money priority enables a lender or seller who has financed the debtor's acquisition of an asset to create a security interest in the asset that is superior to any prior interest claimed by another secured party. The overriding priority afforded purchase money lenders occupies an especially important place in the Article 9 scheme because it constitutes an exception to the general rule that competing security interests are to be ranked temporally, with earlier interests prevailing over later ones.

Viewed uncritically, the purchase money priority may appear to strike a sensible balance between the interests of prior lenders, who retain their priority with respect to their original collateral, and the interests of the new lender, who obtains a special priority in the particular item or items of property the acquisition of which he has financed. It has been said that a rule of this sort prevents prior secured creditors from "tying their debtor's hands," thereby making it impossible for him to obtain fresh capital. But such an explanation is ultimately unsatisfying. It not only rests upon the questionable premise that a debtor's existing creditors wish to cripple him financially, but also fails to explain one of the most prominent features of the purchase money security interest, its limitation to loans that are used to finance the acquisition of identifiable new collateral.

The purpose of this article is to develop a unified theory that explains several of the most important priority rules in Article 9. More particularly, our theory attempts to explain three salient features of the Article 9 priority scheme: why, generally speaking, the claims of secured creditors are ranked in temporal order, the first in time being first in right; why purchase money lenders are excepted from this rule; and why this exception is itself limited to loans that can be traced to identifiable collateral, rather than applying more broadly to all subsequent advances that increase the value of the debtor's estate. We also examine the particular form given to the first-in-time rule by the Code's system of "notice filing."

* * *

It is sometimes assumed that the principal function of an after-acquired property clause is to decrease the riskiness of a particular claim by expanding the pool of collateral that secures it. If this were the only advantage of such a clause, however, it is hard to see what incentive the parties to a credit transaction would have to include an after-acquired property clause in their contract. For while the clause makes one creditor's claim less risky, it simultaneously increases the riskiness of loans made by the debtor's other creditors. In fact, in the absence of transaction costs, we would expect these effects to exactly offset one another, leaving the total cost of credit to the debtor unchanged; what the debtor gained by having the interest rate on one loan reduced, he would lose in increased payments to his remaining creditors.

When transaction costs are taken into account, however, both the advantages of an after-acquired property clause and a basis for predicting when such a clause will be used emerge more clearly. If the collateral securing a loan is a type of property, such as inventory or receivables, that is turned over rapidly in the ordinary course of the debtor's business, both the debtor and his creditor are likely to view an after-acquired property clause as a cost-saving device. In a case of this sort, the clause saves the parties the expense of writing a new contract, or rewriting their original one, whenever individual items of collateral are liquidated and replaced by new items of the same kind. Because it allows transaction cost savings, a legal regime that recognizes the validity of after-acquired property clauses is more efficient than one that does not.

* * *

Although the after-acquired property clause saves costs, it also creates what economists call a "situational monopoly," in that a creditor with a security interest in after-acquired property enjoys a special competitive advantage over other lenders in all his subsequent dealings with the debtor. In our view, the purchase money priority is best thought of as a device for alleviating the situational monopoly created by an after-acquired property clause. Therefore, when a debtor and his creditor have an incentive to include such a clause in their contract, they are also likely to favor the inclusion of a provision empowering the debtor to create an overriding purchase money priority in subsequently acquired assets.

WHITE, REFORMING ARTICLE 9 IN LIGHT OF OLD IGNORANCE AND NEW FILING RULES, 79 Minn. L. Rev. 529, 560-63 (1995).

c. Purchase Money Security Interests in Sections 9-312(3) and (4)

Exactly why a purchase money secured creditor who comes later in time and is on notice of prior perfected security interests deserves priority over that interest is not clear. Yet purchase money secured creditors are the most direct challengers of the King and enjoy most the best recognized priority of all those considered in this paper. Their rights are specifically set out in very same section that anoints the King and recognizes his pure race rights. What justifies this purchase money priority?

Perhaps fairness commands priority for purchase money lenders. It might be argued that a seller, less likely a financer, naturally expects to have priority as to the assets that it sells to a debtor. An intelligent business person who is ignorant of Article 9 might reflect: "I own this commodity. No one else has any claim to it; therefore, I must be able to control the rights in it. If I retain rights, such as a security interest, I must have priority over all others because that security interest is merely a lesser right than I hold now." Of course, if that expectation is the basis for the purchase money priority rule, section 9-312(3), which requires notice to the prior filers, and section 9-312(4), which depends on prompt filing or retention of possession, are without justification because they already violate that expectation. Given those limitations on the rights of the purchase money lender, it is hard to justify them on the grounds that we are merely conforming to the expectation of the clear thinking business person.

A second justification for purchase money priority relates to efficiency. By giving the debtor the possibility of granting first priority to a subsequent purchase money lender, one may facilitate socially desirable transactions that would not otherwise occur. Conceivably, a secured creditor who has a perfected security interest in all of the debtor's inventory, or inventory and equipment, including after-acquired property, might refuse to make a new loan for the purchase of new assets. Yet a seller or another financer of the debtor might make a different evaluation of the debtor's creditworthiness and thus be willing to finance a new acquisition—at least if it could be assured of priority in the assets to be acquired. Assuming these transactions are socially desirable, they should be facilitated.

Although that efficiency often is asserted, I have never seen it proven. First, one must assume the original lender will not lend on the same terms as the purchase money lender. Second, one must assume that the second lender does not intend to buy out and thus replace the first lender, for that would be possible even without the purchase money rules. Third, one must assume the second lender is unwilling to lend unsecured, or that it would charge an additional interest fee that would exceed the costs (on others) of granting a prior perfected security interest. Fourth, one must assume the potential injury to the first filer, from suffering a purchase money lender with priority, is outweighed by the potential gain from the new transaction.

Finally, one must assume the transaction—which the new lender will finance, but the old lender will not—is more likely to increase the wealth of the parties than to decrease it. Conceivably the first lender has declined to lend, not out of vindictiveness, but because of its view that the debtor is already as deeply in debt as it should be. It is possible that an empirical examination of purchase money loans would show that the debtor's optimism is unwarranted and that most purchase money loans that would not have been made by the original debtor lead to bankruptcy, not to riches.

Note, too, that there are costs to the King in allowing purchase money priority. First is the possibility that the original lender and the purchase money lender's assets or proceeds will become commingled, causing a dispute between them. Second is the possibility that both the original lender and the subsequent lender will ultimately be partially unsecured, and thus the first lender will suffer injury by a reduction of the percentage it will be paid on its unsecured portion.

Furthermore, the transaction could take place even in the absence of a particular priority rule that favors purchase money lenders. In the absence of sections 9-312(3) and (4), the second lender would have to negotiate for subordination of the first lender.

To me, the most persuasive claim for purchase money priority is the fairness argument—that reasonable business people expect to have priority when they sell goods from their own stock. Perhaps this idea is embedded so deeply in mercantile expectation that it must be recognized by the Code in order to meet the legitimate expectations of our honest but ill informed mercantile actor.

Even so, the question remains whether purchase money rights should be extended beyond the seller. Conceivably section 9-107 ought to be limited to sellers and should exclude financers. Presumably those financers would not be misled. They would know the need to get subordination agreements and the same fairness arguments could not be made on their behalf as would be made on behalf of the seller. Of course, modifying section 9-107 could produce silly behavior, such as the financer's purchasing the goods and then purporting to sell them to the debtor to fit within the purchase money rules. Note that we are now on uneasy ground where the intelligent but uninformed business person may be injured because of failure to give notice under section 9-312(3) or failure promptly to perfect under section 9-312(4).

I suspect that the status quo is too powerful to challenge here. Perhaps the widespread recognition of purchase money priority says that it is either fair or efficient or both. I still have my doubts. At least the drafters should appreciate that the case for priority of purchase money loans over earlier filed creditors has always been uneasy. I would not shed a tear over the abolition of sections 9-312(3) and (4).

Chapter 9

SECURED CREDITORS AND THIRD PARTIES

SECTION 1. JUDICIAL LIEN CREDITORS

(a) HISTORY

CARLSON & SHUPACK, JUDICIAL LIEN PRIORITIES UNDER ARTICLE 9 OF THE UNIFORM COMMERCIAL CODE: PART II—CREDITOR REPRESENTATIVES, BANK RECEIVERS, FIXTURES, CROPS, AND ACCESSIONS, 5 Cardozo L. Rev. 823-25, 827 (1984).

The Uniform Commercial Code (UCC) equates assignees for the benefit of creditors (general assignees), bankruptcy trustees, and receivers in equity with lien creditors. Their appearance in the UCC section 9-301(3) definition of lien creditors is a holdover from the Uniform Trust Receipts Act and the Uniform Conditional Sales Act, each of which also lumped these creditor representatives together with judicial lien creditors.

The concept of making creditor representatives into lien creditors was introduced in 1910, when Congress, reacting to a then recent Supreme Court opinion, made bankruptcy trustees into lien creditors as of the day of bankruptcy. Such a power was quite a useful tool for destroying the unperfected security interests. Without it, the trustee would have had to prove that the unperfected security interest was a voidable preference. In 1910, a preference was voidable only if, at that time, the creditor had reason to know of the debtor's insolvency—a requirement often difficult to prove. Because the Bankruptcy Reform Act (Bankruptcy Code) drops this element of voidable preference law, the hypothetical lien power retains its importance only in unusual circumstances.

Hypothetical lien creditor status accords well with the trustee's capacity as representative of general creditors. The debtor is deemed to transfer all of his property to the trustee on the day of bankruptcy. This transfer resembles a lien in that it terminates the debtor's power of alienation and the power of subsequent creditors to obtain liens against the transferred property. In addition, the trustee's lien creditor power operates as an equitable replacement for the loss of each individual creditor's ability under state law to obtain a lien that would be superior to the unperfected security interest.

After Congress vested the bankruptcy trustee with lien creditor powers, the drafters of the Uniform Conditional Sales Act, adopted in 1918, and the Uniform Trust Receipt Act, adopted in 1933, vested similar powers in both assignees for the benefit of creditors and equity receivers. Equity receiverships were particularly important in the era when bankruptcy legislation did not include the rehabilitative chapters. At that time, reorganization was accomplished through the enforcement of judgments (often contrived in collusion with a failing debtor) by means of a creditor's bill in equity. The ability of receivers and assignees for the benefit of creditors to avoid security interests was a natural complement to the ability of the bankruptcy trustee to do the same.

* * *

Although bankruptcy trustees make a cameo appearance in section 9-301(3), the drafters of the UCC need hardly have bothered to equip the trustees with the strong-arm power they already possessed under federal law. One of the earlier drafts of the UCC recognized this and deleted the trustee from the definition of "lien creditor." In the subsequent drafts, however, the bankruptcy trustee appeared again, and he remains there to this day.

HANSFORD & SPEEGLE, LIEN CREDITOR STATUS UNDER THE UCC—DOES THE FDIC QUALIFY?, 16 UCC L.J. 13, 14-17 (1983).

Lien Creditor Priority Over Unperfected Interests

Section 9-301 of the UCC governs the priority rights of an unperfected security interest. The general rule of that section is that the unperfected security interest will lose to most other creditors or transferees. Purchasers in and out of the ordinary course of business of the debtor defeat the prior unperfected security interest. A perfected security interest that a creditor creates after the debtor has granted another a security interest that is not perfected takes priority over it. Finally, a lien creditor that is prior or subsequent to the unperfected security interest defeats it. In the last analysis, the unperfected secured party is superior to two types of claimants: a general creditor without any grant of security and another unperfected secured party that is subsequent in time.

Although many third-party claimants fit neatly into one of the categories set out in Section 9-301, some competing parties are more difficult to categorize. One area of concern, of course, is who qualifies as what the UCC calls a "lien creditor." The Code gives assistance in identifying lien creditors by providing in Section 9-301(3) that

> [A] lien creditor means a creditor who has acquired a lien on the property involved by attachment, levy or the like and includes an assignee for the benefit of creditors from time of assignment, and a trustee in bankruptcy from the date of the filing of the petition or a receiver in equity from the time of appointment.

Thus, there are four types of Section 9-301 lien creditors: (1) the judicial lien creditor; (2) the assignee for benefit of creditors; (3) the receiver in equity; and (4) the trustee in bankruptcy. The fourth is the easiest to identify, since federal statutory law governs who is the trustee in bankruptcy and when the bankruptcy petition is filed. The first three parties, however, are more difficult to recognize because they arise through state law, and thus the qualifications and existence of each vary from jurisdiction to jurisdiction.

The judicial lien creditor arises by operation of law and, depending upon the jurisdiction, may come into existence at the time of levy, execution, or judgment. It is clear that the notion of the lien creditor under Section 9-301(3) is more closely connected to the judicial lien creditor than any of the other three types. This is the claimant that is most often seen in a priority conflict with an Article 9 secured party. Indeed, the bankruptcy laws increased the frequency of this kind of conflict, since Section 544(a) of the Bankruptcy Reform Act gives the trustee in bankruptcy the rights of a judicial lien creditor under state law as of the time of the filing of the petition in bankruptcy. Therefore, the trustee is making most of his claims under Section 9-301 clothed with the rights of a state judicial lien creditor.

Although the concept of the assignment for the benefit of creditors developed in the case law as a state-sanctioned technique of insolvency administration, in many jurisdictions statutes now govern this device. Because the procedures closely resemble bankruptcy, an insolvent debtor rarely uses the assignment for the benefit of creditors for protection or to equalize distribution of the debtor's estate to all the creditors. The more common approach is a bankruptcy proceeding, which offers wider protection to a debtor, rather than an assignment for the benefit of creditors.

The final class of Section 9-301(3) lien creditors is the receiver in equity. Of all the four subtypes listed in Section 9-301, the equitable receiver is the most difficult to define. This is true for several reasons: (1) the receiver in equity arises from the equity case law and does not arise or operate under the set rules of a statute; (2) the equitable receivership today is one of the least used forms of creditor protection; and (3) the appointment and nature of an equitable receiver vary from state to state.

(b) Application

MOTTAZ v. KEIDEL (IN RE KEIDEL)

United States Court of Appeals, Seventh Circuit, 1980.
613 F.2d 172.

CUDAHY, Circuit Judge.

This is an appeal by a putative secured creditor from an order of the district court affirming the decision of a bankruptcy judge requiring appellant First National Bank of Wood River to turn over to the trustee in bankruptcy $3,500, representing the value of a mobile home. The issue presented is the priority in bankruptcy between the holder of the security interest in the mobile home and the trustee.

On May 17, 1977, the bankrupt, Esther Keidel, borrowed $3,500 from the First National Bank of Wood River to finance the purchase of a mobile home.

Keidel signed a security agreement with the Bank and executed a promissory note. She received from the Bank a check for $3,500 payable jointly to her, to Kenneth and Rose Mitchell (the sellers) and to Olin Employees' Credit Union (the prior lienholder). When the check was issued by the Bank it was taken to the business office of the Credit Union, where the money changed hands, and various notations were made on the old certificate of title. The bankrupt was advised immediately to apply for a new certificate of title.

The mobile home was purchased by the bankrupt from the Mitchells by assignment of the old certificate of title. The old certificate showed by notation the assignment, the release of its lien by the Credit Union and the existence of a security agreement in favor of the First National Bank of Wood River. The bankrupt attempted to apply for a new certificate of title but failed in (and finally desisted from) her efforts.

The petition in bankruptcy was filed on November 7, 1977. About one month later, the Bank delivered an application for a new certificate of title to the Secretary of State of Illinois. A new certificate was issued on December 15, 1977. Subsequently, the trustee filed a complaint for turnover, which was sustained by the bankruptcy judge. The district court approved the bankruptcy judge's order. We affirm.

Under Illinois law, security interests in personal property are, in general, governed by the Uniform Commercial Code as adopted in Illinois. Ill.Rev.Stat. ch. 26, § 9-101 Et seq. With respect to the means of Perfection of security interests in motor vehicles (including mobile homes), however, the Illinois Vehicle Code exclusively controls. Thus, the Illinois Vehicle Code provides that: A security interest is perfected by delivery to the Secretary of State of the existing certificate of title, if any, an application for a certificate of title containing the name and address of the lienholder and the date of his security agreement and the required fee. It is perfected as of the time of its creation if the delivery is completed within 21 days thereafter, otherwise as of the time of the delivery.

In the instant case the old certificate of title and an application for a new certificate were not delivered to the Secretary of State until shortly before December 15, 1977. But the security interest of the First National Bank of Wood River was created on May 17, 1977, when the security agreement and the promissory note were signed. Therefore, since the security interest was not perfected within 21 days of its creation, it was not perfected until the application was delivered to the Secretary of State well after the date of bankruptcy (Nov. 7, 1977). On November 7, 1977, therefore, the security interest of the Bank was unperfected.

But the trustee in bankruptcy came into the position of a lien creditor of the bankrupt (whether or not such a creditor actually existed) as of the date of bankruptcy that is, on November 7, 1977. The Illinois Vehicle Code, as of the date of bankruptcy, spells out the respective rights of holders of unperfected security interests and the trustee in bankruptcy (standing in the shoes of a lienholder) as follows:

> * * * a security interest in a vehicle of a type for which a certificate of title is required is not valid against subsequent transferees or lienholders of the vehicle unless perfected as provided in this Act.

Hence, as of the date of the bankruptcy, the rights of the Bank, as the holder of an unperfected security interest, were subordinate to those of the trustee in bankruptcy, who stood in the position of a lien creditor or lienholder. This result illustrates the general rule that a lien creditor or lienholder (in whose shoes the trustee stands) prevails over the holder of an unperfected security interest but is defeated by the holder of a perfected security interest. Under the Uniform Commercial Code, the rule, which is intended to reward diligence in perfection, applies even when the competing creditor has knowledge of the unperfected security interest.

In the instant case, the First National Bank of Wood River failed to perfect its security interest by carrying out its statutory duty of "immediately, [after execution and delivery by the bankrupt, causing] the certificate, application and the required fee to be mailed or delivered to the Secretary of State." Ill.Rev.Stat. ch. 95 1/2, § 3-203(b). In fact, such delivery to the Secretary of State did not take place until after bankruptcy. Hence, the interest of the Bank cannot be sustained against that of the trustee.

* * *

The Bank contends that the result here produces a windfall for the bankrupt's estate at the expense of the secured creditor, which furnished the purchase price of the mobile home. This may indeed be the result in this case, but the Bank has only itself to blame for failure to perform its statutory duty prescribing application for a new title. The Illinois law applicable to secured transactions in personal property, including motor vehicles, places strong emphasis on the need for diligence in perfection of the security interest in accordance with the statutory method. See Ill.Rev.Stat. ch. 26, § 9-301, ch. 95 1/2, § 3-202. The strong policy favoring diligence in perfection (and the consequent gain in certainty and regularity) outweighs the possibility here of "unjust enrichment" or a "windfall."

AFFIRMED.

LEDFORD v. EASY LIVING FURNITURE (IN RE JACKSON)

United States Bankruptcy Court, Southern District of Ohio, 1985.
52 B.R. 706.

WILLIAM A. CLARK, Bankruptcy Judge.

[In November of 1983 the debtor purchased furniture from Easy Living Furniture on credit and granted Easy Living a security interest. Easy Living did not file a financing statement. In February of 1984, debtor filed her petition in bankruptcy, and the trustee challenges the security interest.]

The issue is simply whether the trustee may avoid pursuant to 11 U.S.C. § 544 a purchase money security interest in furniture, when a financing statement has not been filed.

11 U.S.C. § 544(a), the so-called "strong-arm" clause of the Bankruptcy Code, grants to the trustee broad powers, which enable him to defeat certain interests of parties in property of the bankruptcy estate. However, these powers are not without limit and they do not render the trustee omnipotent, capable of defeating any claimant to property of the estate. Instead, the trustee is able to assume three distinct postures, which place him in the role of a hypothetical judicial lien creditor, an unsatisfied execution creditor, or a bona fide purchaser of real property.

"While it is federal law which provides the trustee with his 'strong arm' powers, his exercise of those powers is controlled by the substantive law of the jurisdiction governing the property in question." In re Roman Crest Fruit, Inc., 35 B.R. 939, 946 (Bankr.S.D.N.Y.1983). Section 544 of the Bankruptcy Code does not bestow upon the trustee any greater rights than those accorded by applicable law to a creditor possessing the same status as the trustee. "Thus, if under applicable state law a judgment lien creditor would prevail over an adverse claimant, the trustee in bankruptcy will prevail; if not, he will not." Angeles Real Estate Co. v. Kerxton, 737 F.2d 416 (4th Cir.1984).

The trustee admits that Easy Living Furniture was granted a valid purchase money security interest by the debtor as provided by OHIO REV. CODE § 1309.05 [U.C.C. § 9-107] and that the purchase money security interest "attached" to debtor's furniture pursuant to OHIO REV. CODE § 1309.14 [U.C.C. § 9-203]. There are, depending on the circumstances, four modes for perfecting a security interest: filing of a financing statement, possession of the collateral by the secured party, notation on a certificate of title, and automatic perfection.

When a security interest is a purchase money security interest and the collateral consists of consumer goods, OHIO REV. CODE § 1309.21(A)(4) [U.C.C. § 9-302(d)] specifically excuses a secured party from filing a financing statement. Although the non-filing of a financing statement results in the creation of a "secret lien," the drafters of the U.C.C. in providing for automatic perfection yielded to pre-Code practices (See Official Comment No. 4 to U.C.C. § 9-302) and apparently to practical economic concerns. Once the security interest of Easy Living Furniture had attached and the provisions of OHIO REV. CODE § 1309.21 [U.C.C. § 9-302] were complied with in November of 1983, the purchase money security interest was perfected. OHIO REV. CODE § 1309.22(A) [U.C.C. § 9-303(1)]. It was and is valid against almost all subsequent claims.

* * *

The trustee concedes that the defendant was not required to file a financing statement, but states in his memorandum that "This is true as long as no other creditor, including the perfect lien creditor—a bankruptcy trustee, or a buyer without knowledge of the security interest, for value, and for his own personal, family or household purposes enters on the scene." The trustee is partially correct. While the security interest of Easy Living Furniture was perfected without filing, it was vulnerable to a narrow class of buyers of goods. In the case of consumer goods, a buyer takes free of a security interest even though perfected if he buys without knowledge of the security interest, for value, and for his own personal, family, or household purposes, unless prior to the purchase the secured party has filed a financing statement covering such goods. OHIO REV. CODE § 1309.26(C) [U.C.C. § 9-307(2)].

To protect itself against this type of buyer, the secured party in a purchase money transaction for consumer goods must file a financing statement. But in the instant proceeding, whether or not the secured party filed a financing statement is irrelevant. The trustee does not occupy the position of a bona fide purchaser of consumer goods for personal use under the provisions of § 544 of the Bankruptcy Code. Notwithstanding this broad grant of power to the trustee, it is well settled that the trustee does not have the rights of a bona fide purchaser of personalty. Moreover, subsections 544(a)(1) and 544(a)(2) do not specifically confer upon the trustee bona fide creditor status with respect to personalty. This omission is underscored by the grant of such status to the trustee under subsection 544(a)(3) with regard to real estate.

The remaining portion of the trustee's assertion, above, that a secured party must file a financing statement to protect its interest from any "other creditor, including the perfect lien creditor—a bankruptcy trustee * * *" is simply incorrect. The trustee's interpretation would render the automatic perfection provisions for purchase money security interests a nullity and the secured party would be granted a security interest of little value. Against whom besides the debtor would the security interest of the secured party be perfected?

* * *

For the foregoing reasons it is hereby ORDERED that plaintiff's motion for summary judgment is DENIED and defendant's motion for summary judgment is SUSTAINED AND JUDGMENT IS AWARDED TO DEFENDANT.

PROBLEMS

1. On March 1, Bank takes and properly perfects a security interest in all of Debtor's existing and after acquired inventory. On April 1, Supplier obtains a judgment against Debtor based on a delinquent open account debt. The judgment was entered by a court of competent jurisdiction in a state that permits a judgment lien to be created against personalty by filing a transcript of the judgment with the county clerk's office where the property is located. On April 10, Supplier files its judgment in the county where all of Debtor's equipment is located. On May 1 and June 1 of the same year Bank, unaware of Supplier's judgment lien, makes additional advances to Debtor. In July, Debtor defaults on its obligation to Bank, and Bank seizes all of Debtor's equipment, which it intends to sell at a public auction. Supplier, upon learning of Bank's action, has sent Bank a demand that all proceeds received in excess of the amount of

Debtor's debt to Bank as of April 10 be remitted to Supplier. How should Bank respond? See § 9-301(4).

2. On September 10, Seller sells on credit and delivers to Debtor, a lumberyard operator, a new forklift for moving inventory around the yard. Seller has Debtor execute a security agreement and financing statement, both of which describe the collateral as the forklift subject to the sale. Seller then mails the financing statement to the Secretary of State's Office for filing. However, because of a delay in the mail, the financing statement does not reach the Secretary of State's Office until February 18, at which point it is properly indexed in the UCC records under Debtor's name. In the meantime, however, on February 15, Judgment Creditor had the sheriff levy on Debtor's inventory and equipment, including the forklift. As between Seller and Judgment Creditor, who has priority in the forklift? See §§ 9-312(4) and 9-301(2). How, if at all, would it change your answer if what happened on February 15 was that Debtor sold the forklift to another lumberyard operator who took without knowledge of Seller's security interest?

WHITE, REVISING ARTICLE 9 TO REDUCE WASTEFUL LITIGATION, 26 Loy. L.A. L. Rev. 823, 823-27 (1993).

II. THE PROPOSAL AND ITS LEGAL EFFECT

I propose that the drafters of Article 9 repeal section 9-301(1). That subsection provides:

> Except as otherwise provided in subsection (2), an unperfected security interest is subordinate to the rights of * * * (b) a person who becomes a lien creditor before the security interest is perfected * * *.

To one unfamiliar with Article 9 of the UCC, the consequences of such revision will not be obvious. To begin to understand those consequences, consider the first sentence of section 9-201:

> Except as otherwise provided by this Act a security agreement is effective according to its terms between the parties, against purchasers of the collateral and against creditors.

Section 9-201 makes even an unperfected security interest king of the hill "[e]xcept as otherwise provided by this Act." Unless some other rule contained in Article 9 deposes an unperfected security interest, it is king. Section 9-301(1)(b) does subordinate unperfected security interests to the rights of lien creditors. If that subsection were removed, the priority would be reversed and an unperfected security interest would be superior to a lien creditor's claim.

The direct and most obvious effect of the repeal of section 9-301(1)(b) would be to subordinate a creditor who had procured a judicial lien—usually after judgment and levy—to an unperfected secured creditor who had a security interest in the personal property on which the lien creditor levied. Because creditors with judicial liens on personal property are more scarce than wise men in President Clinton's Cabinet, this consequence would be unimportant. I predict that subordination of the judicial lien creditor's claim to an unperfected secured creditor's claim in Article 9 and outside of bankruptcy would go almost unnoticed by lawyers and courts.

Because trustees in bankruptcy are as ubiquitous as judicial lienors are scarce, the principal effect of the repeal of section 9-301(1)(b) would be in bankruptcy. As every commercial lawyer knows, § 544(a) of the Bankruptcy Code makes the trustee in bankruptcy a hypothetical lien creditor on the date the petition is filed. From that date the trustee in bankruptcy has the rights that a hypothetical lien creditor would have under state law. Indirectly, the combination of § 544(a) and section 9-301(1)(b) elevates not only the trustee in bankruptcy—our hypothetical lien creditor—but also his or her flock of unsecured creditors of the bankrupt debtor over unperfected secured creditors. Because the trustee in bankruptcy uses § 544(a) to strike down the unperfected security interest, the unsecured creditors who have claims against the bankruptcy estate are enriched. This is because the collateral that is released from the avoided security interest is treated merely as an asset of the estate and, thus, subject to all of the claims of the unsecured creditors.

Section 544(a)(1) rides on state law; it gives the federally created trustee in bankruptcy only the rights that a lien creditor has under state law. Therefore, a repeal of section 9-301(1)(b), that subordinates the lien creditor to the unperfected secured creditor in state law, also subordinates the trustee in bankruptcy. Nothing in § 544(a) or in any other section of the Bankruptcy Code gives the trustee in bankruptcy an independent right under federal law to strike down an unperfected security interest.

Before one considers the arguments for and against my proposal, understand how limited its effect is. Mostly it will impose the same priority on unsecured creditors in bankruptcy that would apply to them outside bankruptcy. Section 9-201 now grants priority to unperfected secured creditors over unsecured creditors unless the former procure a lien. Only a minuscule part of all unsecured creditors in and out of bankruptcy ever procure judicial liens. Therefore, my proposal would merely put these unsecured creditors in bankruptcy in the same status that they would suffer outside of bankruptcy, namely, a status subordinate to the unperfected secured creditors.

Note, too, that many creditors under the current version of the Uniform Commercial Code achieve perfection and the attendant priority without filing, taking possession of the collateral or performing any other public act. For example, a secured purchase money seller of consumer goods has an automatically perfected security interest superior not only to unsecured creditors, but also to subsequently secured creditors and to lien creditors. Section 9-302(1) gives a series of less important examples of creditors who achieve priority over others simply by executing a security agreement with the debtor. Therefore, superiority of one who has done no public perfecting act is not unknown to Article 9, nor has such priority caused any obvious difficulties for the credit market.

Understand what the repeal of section 9-301(1)(b) would not do. It would not give an unperfected secured creditor priority over a perfected secured creditor under section 9-312. Thus, if secured creditors wished to have protection against other secured creditors, they would still have to perfect their security interest, usually by a filing. For that reason, many secured creditors would file financing statements even under the regime I propose.

The basic argument for my proposal is straightforward—to eliminate waste. This waste is the cost of unnecessary filings and needless litigation over the efficacy of secured creditors' perfection. I also argue that fairness supports my proposal; on that question I would expect reasonable people to differ. Consider the arguments.

III. FAIRNESS

Does fairness dictate that unperfected secured creditors be subordinated to lien creditors? To subsequent unsecured creditors? Although the section that I would repeal, section 9-301(1)(b), nominally subordinates unperfected secured creditors to lien creditors, its real impact in the law as practiced in today's bankruptcy and commercial courts is to subordinate the unperfected secured creditors to unsecured creditors who have no lien. The perverse effect of the combination of § 544(a) and section 9-301(1)(b) is a reversal of the priority in bankruptcy between an unperfected secured creditor and an unsecured creditor that would prevail under section 9-201 outside of bankruptcy. Therefore, in evaluating the fairness of my proposal, I argue that one should view the competitors as an unperfected secured creditor on one side, and an unsecured creditor without a lien on the other. To suggest that the true competitor is a lien creditor is to ignore today's reality in which judicial liens are few and bankruptcies are many.

REVISED UCC § 9-315(a)

An unperfected security interest * * * is subordinate to the rights of:

* * *

(2) a person who becomes a lien creditor before the security interest * * * is perfected and before a financing statement covering the collateral is filed.

QUESTION

Under what circumstances does Revised § 9-315(a)(2) offer protection to a secured creditor against a lien creditor that is not available under the current version of Article 9?

SECTION 2. BUYERS AND LESSEES

(a) OF GOODS

CARLSON, DEATH AND SUBORDINATION UNDER ARTICLE 9 OF THE UNIFORM COMMERCIAL CODE: SENIOR BUYERS AND SENIOR LIEN CREDITORS, 5 Cardozo L. Rev. 547-48 (1984).

A comparison between section 9-301 and section 9-307(1) will make the point with regard to buyers. Section 9-307(1) is that all-important provision governing sales in the ordinary course of business. Such a sale (by anyone but a farmer selling farm products) kills any security interest created by the seller. This can be seen from the drafters' use of the term "takes free": "A buyer in ordinary course of business * * * takes free of a security interest created by his seller even though the security interest is perfected and even though the buyer knows of its existence." The basic idea is expressed clearly enough. After a sale to a buyer in the ordinary course of business, any security interest in the goods sold ceases to exist. The death penalty is imposed upon security interests that are, for whatever reason, junior to the rights of these buyers. They are dead, and appropriately so.

Section 9-301(1)(c) expresses the subordination idea. This section provides:

> [A]n unperfected security interest is subordinate to the rights of * * *
>
> (c) in the case of goods, instruments, documents, and chattel paper, a person who is not a secured party and who is a transferee in bulk or other buyer not in ordinary course of business or is a buyer of farm products in ordinary course of business, to the extent that he gives value and receives delivery of the collateral without knowledge of the security interest and before it is perfected.

This provision deals predominantly with buyers who are not protected by the death-dealing section 9-307(1). As against unperfected security interests, the language of section 9-301(1)(c) indicates that the buyer's rights (whatever they may be) are merely senior to the secured party's rights, provided both payment and receipt of possession by the buyer occur at a time when the buyer has the requisite ignorance. Subordination is not death, or at least not obviously so. Most people would assume that a junior security interest is distinguishable from no security interest. Perhaps the security interest lives on. Thus, whereas section 9-307(1) kills perfected security interests, section 9-301(1)(c) may allow unperfected security interests to survive.

UCC § 9-307(1)

(1) A Buyer in ordinary course of business * * * takes free of a security interest * * * even though the security interest is perfected * * * .

(2) In the case of consumer goods, a buyer takes free of a security interest even though perfected if he buys without knowledge of the security interest, for value and for his own personal, family or household purposes * * * .

(i) The Bulk Buyer

NATIONAL BANK v. FRYDLEWICZ

Court of Appeals of Michigan, 1976.
67 Mich. App. 417, 241 N.W.2d 471.

PER CURIAM.

Defendant National Unclaimed Furniture Showrooms (National) appeals a judgment of $17,356.76 granted in plaintiff's favor after a bench trial in Oakland County Circuit Court.

This litigation arose out of the transfer by Edward Frydlewicz to National of inventory in which plaintiff had a security interest. In December, 1968, Edward Frydlewicz asked plaintiff for a loan in the total amount of $20,027 to pay for inventory for his business, King Furniture & Appliance Mart. This business establishment, located at 126 East 14 Mile Road, Clawson, Michigan, was a retail outlet for King Distributors, Inc., which sold furniture wholesale and was owned and operated by Frydlewicz.

The security agreement gave plaintiff a security interest in all inventory located at King Furniture & Appliance Mart, 126 East 14 Mile Road. The security interest attached on December 31, 1968. Plaintiff filed a financing statement for the inventory with the Oakland County register of deeds. * * * The repayment of the loan was to be by 60 monthly installments commencing in February, 1969. Monthly installment payments, totalling $2,670.24, were made as scheduled through September, 1969, after which Frydlewicz was declared bankrupt.

In the interim on March 6, 1969, Frydlewicz contracted with National to lease the King Furniture & Appliance Mart. As a pre-condition to the agreement to lease the premises, National agreed to purchase all of the King Furniture & Appliance Mart inventory. Accordingly, an item-by-item inventory was conducted by the parties of the merchandise which consisted of damaged furniture and odds and ends. Defendant purchased this entire inventory for $13,603.24. When defendant purchased this inventory and leased the premises in Clawson, it changed the name of the business establishment to National Unclaimed Furniture Showrooms and removed all of the old King Furniture signs.

* * *

At trial and on appeal, the dispute requires the interaction of the Uniform Commercial Code (UCC) provisions on secured transactions and bulk transfers. Plaintiff's status under article 9 of the UCC is that of an unperfected secured creditor. Plaintiff failed to perfect its interest when it filed the financing statement with the Oakland County register of deeds rather than with the Secretary of State, as M.C.L.A. § 440.9401; M.S.A. § 19.9401 requires.

National's status is the dispositive issue in the case. Under the instant facts, one of three legal positions could be ascribed to National: (1) a buyer in ordinary course of business, (2) a buyer not in ordinary course of business or (3) a transferee in bulk. If National is a buyer in the ordinary course of business, UCC § 9-307(1), M.C.L.A. § 440.9307(1); M.S.A. § 19.9307(1), would give its interest in the disputed merchandise priority over plaintiff's unperfected security interest. As a buyer not in the ordinary course of business, National's interest would be subordinated to plaintiff's interest.

Normally, as a transferee in bulk, National would be entitled to priority over plaintiff's unperfected security interest. Pursuant to UCC § 9-301(1) (c), M.C.L.A. § 440.9301(1)(c); M.S.A. § 19.9301(1)(c), "an unperfected security interest is subordinate to the rights of in the case of goods, * * *, a person who is not a secured party and who is a transferee in bulk". However, National failed to satisfy the requirements necessary under the bulk transfer provisions of UCC art. 6 to assert a claim of priority as a transferee in bulk. Specifically, UCC § 6-104(1) requires: "Except as provided with respect to auction sales (section 6-108), a bulk transfer subject to this article is ineffective against *any creditor* of the *transferor* unless:

> (a) The transferee requires the transferor to furnish a list of his existing creditors prepared as stated in this section; and
> (b) The parties prepare a schedule of the property transferred sufficient to identify it; and
> (c) The transferee preserves the list and schedule for 6 months next following the transfer and permits inspection of either or both and copying therefrom at all reasonable hours by any creditor of the transferor, or files the list and schedule in the office of the secretary of state." M.C.L.A. § 440.6104(1); M.S.A. § 19.6104(1). (Emphasis supplied.)

It was undisputed at trial that National did not request Frydlewicz to furnish a list of his creditors.

The trial court found National to be a transferee in bulk and, therefore, to be subordinate to plaintiff's rights in the disputed merchandise. The court relied in part on an admission in National's trial brief that it was not a "buyer in ordinary course of business".

While we do not rely on this ill-conceived admission, we find from the record that National was, as the trial court held, a transferee in bulk. A bulk transfer is "any transfer in bulk and not in the ordinary course of the transferor's business of a major part of the materials, supplies, merchandise or other inventory (section 9-109) of an enterprise subject to this article." M.C.L.A. § 440.6102(1); M.S.A. § 19.6102(1). The items transferred must be inventory, i.e. held 'for sale or lease.' M.C.L.A. § 440.9109(4); M.S.A. § 19.9109(4). Here, the furniture transferred clearly represented the entire inventory held for sale by the King Furniture and Appliance Mart.

The transferor enterprise must have as its 'principal business * * * the sale of merchandise from stock.' M.C.L.A. § 440.6102(3); M.S.A. § 19.6102(3). Here, the transferor was a retail furniture store. The transfer must not be in the ordinary course of the transferor's business, and the items transferred must constitute a 'major part' of the transferor's inventory. 'Major part' has been defined as 'meaning something more than 50%'. Coogan, Hogan, Vagts, Secured Transactions Under the UCC, § 22.06(1)(c), p. 2287. Whether 'major' is a quantitative or qualitative determination remains an open question; one which courts have approached on an ad hoc basis. Id. Ordinary course means day-to-day operation. The bulk sale must be an extraordinary event, one occurring a few times in the life of a merchant. First National Bank of Martinsville v. Crone, 301 N.E.2d 378 (Ind.App., 1973). 'The plain meaning of the statute is that when a storekeeper disposes of a substantial part of his stock in trade in bulk, and selling in bulk sales is not the usual and ordinary way in which he conducts his business from day to day, the sale falls within the statute.' Jubas v. Sampsell, 185 F.2d 333, 334 (C.A. 9, 1950).

The closing of a retail store and bulk sale of its stock, both whole and damaged items, constitutes such an extraordinary transaction. Further, the instant case is prototypical of the situation which the bulk sales law was promulgated to remedy. The law attempts to protect a creditor from a 'merchant, owing debts, who sells out his stock in trade to anyone for any price, pockets the proceeds, and disappears leaving the creditors unpaid.' UCC § 6-101, Official Comment 2(b). Here Frydlewicz sold his inventory for less than its value and declared bankruptcy. But for the bulk sales law plaintiff might be without a remedy.

* * *

Affirmed. Costs to plaintiff.

HARRIS, ARTICLE 6: THE PROCESS AND THE PRODUCT—AN INTRODUCTION, 41 Ala. L. Rev. 549-51 (1990).

Despite its small size and limited applicability, nearly every aspect of Article 6 has been the subject of continuing controversy. Lawyers and other commentators have questioned the wisdom of virtually every one of the Article's provisions, from its scope to its remedial scheme. Many have questioned whether the Article properly belongs in the Uniform Commercial Code or, indeed, anywhere in the statute books.

The controversy surrounding Article 6 is not new. Early bulk sales legislation was challenged, sometimes successfully, as being unconstitutional, it was attacked as special interest legislation, it was belittled as unnecessary. The century-long history of bulk sales law has been characterized by strong differences of opinion over basic issues: Is there really a "bulk sales risk" worthy of legislative attention? If so, what is the precise nature of the risk and how serious is it? What is the most effective and appropriate way in which to minimize the risk?

Mindful of the controversy surrounding Article 6 and of the nearly universal view that the language of Article 6 is in need of improvement, the Code's sponsors, the National Conference of Commissioners on Uniform State Laws (the "Conference") and the American Law Institute (the "ALI" or "Institute") set out in 1984 to revise the Article. By the time the dust settled five years later, the sponsors had withdrawn their support for Article 6 and encouraged those states that had enacted the Article to repeal it. For those states that may be disinclined to repeal Article 6, the sponsors promulgated a revised version of the Article, which is designed to afford better protection to creditors while minimizing the impediments to good-faith transactions.

(ii) The Buyer in Ordinary Course

OCEAN COUNTY NATIONAL BANK v. PALMER

Superior Court of New Jersey, 1983.
188 N.J. Super. 509, 457 A.2d 1225

BOTTER, P.J.A.D.

This appeal concerns the priority of liens on a boat which was sold twice by the same merchant to two different purchasers and was pledged as collateral for two loans without the first lien having been satisfied and discharged. The trial judge gave priority to the lien held by First Commercial Corporation (First Commercial) which had financed the second sale. Based upon our interpretation of the pertinent provisions of Title 12A, N.J.S.A. 12A:9-306(2) and N.J.S.A. 12A:9-307(1), we are compelled to reverse, giving priority to the first secured creditor, notwithstanding the hardship to the innocent purchasers in the second sale.

On October 30, 1978 respondent Charles Palmer (Palmer) purchased a 22-foot Penn Yan boat from Normandy Beach Marina (Normandy Beach) for $13,400. Palmer made a down-payment of $1,900 and financed the balance with Normandy Beach, which took a security interest in the boat. Normandy Beach then assigned all of its rights to the Ocean County National Bank (Ocean County Bank), which timely filed a UCC financing statement with the Monmouth County Clerk's Office and the Secretary of State. The financing statement listed Ocean County Bank as the secured party and was signed by Palmer as the debtor. See N.J.S.A. 12A:9-105(1)(m); N.J.S.A. 12A:9-402(1).

Sometime thereafter, Palmer returned the boat to Normandy Beach with the understanding that it would be sold on his behalf and the Ocean County Bank lien satisfied. On April 30, 1979 respondents Guy and Mary Hess (Hess) purchased the boat from Normandy Beach, apparently out of inventory, for $11,500. Hess made a $4,500 down payment and financed the balance with Normandy Beach, which took a security interest in the boat. The retail installment contract named Normandy Beach as the seller. Normandy Beach thereafter assigned its rights to First Commercial.

Normandy Beach did not satisfy Palmer's debt to Ocean County Bank and did not obtain a discharge of that bank's lien. When Palmer later discovered that the boat had been sold, he stopped making payments on his loan. Ocean County Bank declared the loan in default and, after locating the boat at the Hess home, repossessed it on May 2, 1980. Following a textbook scenario, Normandy Beach filed for bankruptcy.

Ocean County Bank brought this action to determine the priority of the two outstanding liens. Each of the parties also sought damages and various other remedies. The trial judge fixed the order of priorities in a partial summary judgment, subordinating Ocean County Bank's lien to that of First Commercial. Because some damage claims were not addressed, no final judgment was entered as to all parties. We have determined, however, that the interlocutory nature of this appeal ought not preclude disposition of the merits of the controversy. Therefore, we now grant leave to appeal nunc pro tunc on our own motion. See Butler v. Bonner & Barnewall, Inc., 56 N.J. 567, 573, n. 2, n. 3, 267 A.2d 527 (1970).

The problem here is that neither Hess nor First Commercial knew that the boat bought by Hess was owned by Palmer. They had no reason to search for a financing statement signed by Palmer as debtor and had no notice that the boat being sold by Normandy Beach was encumbered by a lien previously created by Palmer.[1] Thus, all parties agree that Mr. and Mrs. Hess were buyers in the ordinary course of business, having purchased the boat in good faith and without knowledge of Ocean County Bank's security interest. See N.J.S.A. 12A:1-201(9).

Nevertheless, the general rule governing the sale of encumbered collateral is found in N.J.S.A. 12A:9-306(2), which provides: Except where this Chapter otherwise provides, a security interest continues in collateral notwithstanding sale, exchange or other disposition thereof unless the disposition was authorized by the secured party in the security agreement or otherwise, and also continues in any identifiable proceeds including collections received by the debtor. The resale of the boat by Palmer or Normandy Beach was not authorized by the secured party, Ocean County Bank. Therefore, by reason of § 9-306(2), Ocean County Bank's perfected security interest in the boat continued unless another provision of chapter 9 permitted Hess to take free of that interest or gave First Commercial priority for its lien. See Chemical Bank v. Miller Yacht Sales, supra, 173 N.J.Super. at 101, n. 2, 413 A.2d 619.

Hess and First Commercial rely on N.J.S.A. 12A:9-307(1) as a basis for their claimed exception from the general rule established by § 9-306(2). N.J.S.A. 12A:9-307(1) provides, in pertinent part: "A buyer in the ordinary course of business ... takes free of a security interest created by his seller even though the security interest is perfected and even though the buyer knows of its existence." Hess and First Commercial contend that the security interest held by Ocean County Bank was created to some extent by Normandy Beach. Therefore, they argue that § 9-307(1) allowed Hess to purchase the boat free of that security interest. The issue, then, is whether the security interest held by Ocean County

---

[1] We assume that the federal Ship Mortgage Act of 1920, 46 U.S.C.A. § 921 et seq., does not apply since the parties have not relied upon nor asserted that the boat in question was federally documented. * * *

Bank was created by Normandy Beach within the meaning of N.J.S.A. 12A:9-307(1). The trial judge held that it was. In his oral opinion he said that Normandy Beach "participated and [was] instrumental" in creating the encumbrance and therefore, as between the second innocent consumer, Hess, and the innocent lienholder, Ocean County Bank, he would interpret § 9-307(1) to protect the second innocent consumer. * * *

The purpose of N.J.S.A. 12A:9-307(1) is to protect a bona fide purchaser who buys goods in the ordinary course of business from a dealer against the claim of a secured party who has financed the dealer's floor inventory. See N.J.S.A. 12A:9-307(1), New Jersey Study Comment P 2, which states that the concept follows that expressed in R.S. 46:32-12 (§ 9 of the Uniform Conditional Sales Act), namely, that the security interest is lost when the holder leaves the goods with a dealer in those goods with the expectation that they will be sold by the dealer in the ordinary course of business. See Cunningham v. Camelot Motors, 138 N.J.Super. 489, 495-496, 351 A.2d 402 (Ch.Div.1975). In Muir v. Jefferson Credit Corp., 108 N.J.Super. 586, 262 A.2d 33 (Law Div.1970), Justice Handler, then-Judge Handler explained: Section 9-307(1) is for the exclusive protection of those who buy from merchants in the ordinary course of business and out of inventory. Nevertheless, 9-307(1) limits its protection of such buyers against only a security interest which was "created by [the buyer's] seller." [at 593, 262 A.2d 33] Addressing the same issue presented in the case at hand, the court in Commercial Credit Equip. Corp. v. Bates, 154 Ga.App. 71, 74, 267 S.E.2d 469, 472 (Ct.App.1980), said that § 9-307(1) "is intended to protect buyers in the ordinary course from the lien claims of creditors who have financed 'floor-plan' (inventory) arrangements for the dealer." Therefore, the court held that the security interest in the goods was not created by the dealer within the meaning of § 9-307(1) but was created by the original purchaser (in our case, Palmer). See, also Dugan, "Buyer-Secured Party Conflicts Under Section 9-307(1) of the Uniform Commercial Code," 46 U.Colo.Rev. 333, 345 (1975); Sexton, "Section 9-307(1) of the U.C.C.: The Scope of the Protection Given a Buyer in Ordinary Course of Business," 9 B.C.Indus. & Com.L.Rev. 985-993 (1968). Thus, the "security interest created by his seller" as used in § 9-307(1), refers only to a security interest given by the seller as debtor and does not include any other security interest even though it was created in an agreement to which the seller was a non-debtor party. First Am. Bank v. Hunning, 218 Va. 530, 238 S.E.2d 799 (Sup.Ct.1977). A contrary conclusion would create an anomalous impact upon the alienability of collateral, depending upon whether the retail buyer finances the purchase through the seller (who then assigns the security interest) or directly with the institutional lender. While innocent purchasers are at risk if goods subject to a lien are entrusted to a dealer for resale, the Georgia court noted in the Commercial Credit case, supra, on subsequent appeal after remand, 159 Ga.App. 910, 911, 285 S.E.2d 560, 561 (Ct.App.1981), that lenders must have protection for their liens despite subsequent resale of the collateral in order to induce them to finance consumer purchases. Allowing the resale through a dealer to overcome a lien held by a third party, other than one financing a floor plan, would make it too easy to defeat such liens. * * *

We also find unavailing respondents' alternative argument that Normandy Beach was Palmer's agent in reselling the boat and that Hess bought the boat from Palmer who had created the security interest. But this cannot impair Ocean County's Bank lien because Palmer was not in the boat-selling business. See Security Pacific Nat'l Bank v. Goodman, 24 Cal.App.3d 131, 135-137, 100 Cal.Rptr. 763, 766-767 (D.Ct.App.1972). Although the boat was consumer goods in Palmer's hands, a buyer from him could not take free of a security interest perfected prior to that sale. N.J.S.A. 12A:9-307(2). Thus, Ocean County Bank's lien was protected against the resale to Hess whether sold by Palmer or Normandy Beach. To the extent that Palmer may have had any equity in the boat, however, it was transferred to Hess by operation of N.J.S.A. 12A:2-403(2), Palmer having entrusted the boat to Normandy Beach, a merchant who dealt in boats. Adams v. City Nat'l Bank & Trust Co., supra.

We conclude, therefore, that as between Ocean County Bank and First Commercial, Ocean County Bank's lien has priority under N.J.S.A. 12A:9-312(5) based upon the order of filing. See, also, Chemical Bank v. Miller Yacht Sales, supra, 173 N.J.Super. at 100-101, 413 A.2d 619. The judgment below is reversed and the matter is remanded for further proceedings not inconsistent with this opinion.

UCC § 2-403(2)

Any entrusting of possession of goods to a merchant who deals in goods of that kind gives him power to transfer all rights of the entruster to a buyer in the ordinary course.

NOTE ON THE RELATIONSHIP BETWEEN THE ENTRUSTING DOCTRINE AND § 9-307(1)

Near the end of the opinion in *Palmer* the court mentions that, although Hess took subject to Ocean Bank's lien, any equity that Palmer may have had in the boat was transferred to Hess by operation of § 2-403(2) because Palmer had "entrusted" the boat to Normandy Beach, a boat dealer. Ordinarily, § 2-403(2) and § 9-307(1) operate to ensure the same result; namely, that a person who buys goods in the ordinary course from a dealer's stock-in-trade will take title and possession of those goods free from the claims of prior owners and lienors. In certain instances, however, § 2-403(2) may cut-off a secured party's as well as an owner's rights in the goods under circumstances where § 9-307(1) does not apply. Which provision takes precedence in those cases?

For example, where the secured party either entrusts the goods subject to its security interest to a merchant in the business of selling goods of that type, or acquiesces in the debtor's entrusting of the goods, a buyer in the ordinary course of those goods would *not* take free of the security interest under § 9-307(1) because the security interest was not *created* by *his seller*. However, there is no such limitation in § 2-403(2). But see § 2-403(4) and the last sentence of Off. Cmt. 2.

In its 1992 Report, at 192, the PEB Study Group on Article 9 recommended that the Code be revised to make clear that a buyer in the ordinary course would prevail in these situations, noting as follows: "In the view of the Committee and the Article 2 Study Group, if a secured party itself entrusts goods to a merchant who is a dealer in goods of that kind, that merchant should have the power to transfer the goods to a buyer in the ordinary course free of the security interest even though the merchant-seller is not the secured party's debtor (*i.e.*, even though the merchant, the buyer's seller, did not create the security interest)." For an example of a case taking this approach, see In re Woods, 25 B.R. 924 (Bankr. E.D. Tenn. 1982).

DOLAN, SECTION 9-307(1): THE U.C.C.'S OBSTACLE TO AGRICULTURAL COMMERCE IN THE OPEN MARKET, 72 Nw. U. L. Rev. 706 (1978).

The Uniform Commercial Code provides a general open market rule in the Secured Transactions article which permits certain good faith purchasers to take goods free of perfected security interests. That general rule, however, excepts from its application sales of farm products by persons engaged in farming operations. Defenders of the exception proffer two justifications. Some feel that farm producers would not find ample credit if farm lenders faced the possibility of losing collateral to buyers. Others argue that the exception enjoys widespread support among state legislatures and among the federal agencies which account for a significant share of agricultural credit. Thus, this second argument continues, adoption of a rule in the Code which treats farm sales in the same fashion as it treats nonfarm sales would invite deviation from the Code rule by both state and federal systems with a resulting loss of uniformity.

[T]he farm exception grows out of archaic notions of agriculture and agricultural finance; * * * the exception is basically unfair in that it penalizes unwary buyers who reasonably expect they will buy free of security interests; * * * the exception creates uncertainty and thereby increases transaction costs to the detriment of farm producer and farm lender; and * * * the farm exception itself has so contributed to a lack of uniformity that its abrogation could hardly cause more.

UNITED STATES v. PROGRESSIVE FARMERS MARKETING AGENCY

United States Court of Appeals, Seventh Circuit, 1986.
788 F.2d 1327.

[Darrell M. Newman and JoAnn Newman borrowed from the Farmers Home Administration (FmHA) and granted the FmHA a perfected security interest in their hogs. In 1981 the Newmans made a series of hog deliveries to Progressive, a livestock marketing agency. Progressive sold the hogs to buyers in ordinary course and remitted the proceeds of the sales, less commissions, to the Newmans. Progressive was unaware of the FmHA security interest. The FmHA brings this suit against Progressive in conversion.]

HANSON, Senior District Judge.

* * *

In denying Progressive's motion for summary judgment in its May 7, 1985 order, the district court held that it would not relieve Progressive of liability for conversion. The court noted:

> [T]he practical effect of ruling for the defendant is that a farmer-debtor would be given the unilateral power to extinguish a secured party's perfected security interest in farm products by choosing a particular method of marketing. If the farmer chose to sell his hogs through a marketing agency, the secured creditor would not have rights in the collateral once it was in the hands of the third parties. * * * Alternatively, if the farmer chose to sell his farm products directly to the buyer, the security interest would continue in the hogs and the secured party would have enforceable rights in the hogs even though they were processed to the extent of being pork chops on a grocery shelf.

The court, although recognizing the inherent harshness of its ruling on marketing agencies and auctioneers, asserted that, on balance, the equities lean in favor of the secured party in cases such as this.

In United States v. Kimbell Foods, Inc., 440 U.S. 715, 99 S.Ct. 1448, 59 L.Ed.2d 711 (1979), the Supreme Court held that the federal government's priority rights are decided by federal law, but that the state law—the U.C.C.—applies to determine priority conflicts between the federal government and private lenders if no federal law has set the priorities. Id. at 740, 99 S.Ct. at 1464-65. Because there was no federal law in effect at the time of the alleged conversion as to the liability of commission merchants to the FmHA for selling mortgaged farm products, the content of the federal rule is determined by incorporating state law.

Until July 1, 1985, Progressive's liability for conversion of the debtor's hogs was governed by an interpretation of the interplay between the farm products exception in Iowa Code § 554.9307(1) and the definition of "farm products" and "inventory" set out in §§ 554.9109(3) and (4). Section 554.9307(1) provided that: (1) A buyer in ordinary course of business (subsection 9 of Section 554.1201) other than a person buying farm products from a person engaged in farming operations takes free of a security interest created by his seller even though the security interest is perfected and even though the buyer knows of its existence.

The key issue on this appeal is whether the hogs were "inventory" or "farm products." The district court found that Progressive, as the marketing agent for the debtors, was liable for the conversion of the hogs just as if the debtors had sold the hogs directly to the buyers without using the intervening agent. The difficulty with the district court's rationale for imposing liability on Progressive is that it does not square with the intent of the U.C.C. to alter the definition of the collateral at issue when it comes into the hands of the commission merchant. Official Comment 4 of 9-109 states: When crops or livestock or their products come into the possession of a person not engaged in farming operations they cease to be "farm products." If they come into the possession of a marketing agency for sale or distribution or of a manufacturer or processor as raw materials, they become inventory.

The district court was troubled with the application of this change in the nature of the collateral because it believed that this would enable the farmer-debtor to extinguish the security interest in farm products simply by choosing to sell his goods through a commission merchant rather than selling directly to the buyer himself. The court found that when it balanced the equities of forcing the commission merchant to search the U.C.C. records at the office of the Secretary of State for outstanding liens, as opposed to forcing the secured party to police its outstanding loans, public policy seemed to lean in favor of protecting the secured party. However, the holding of the district court is difficult to rationalize in light of the express language set out in Comment 4 of § 554.9109. It appears that the drafters of the U.C.C. contemplated the kind of problems that would arise when collateral comes into the hands of commission merchants by providing that they are outside the farm products exception.

Moreover, the Iowa legislature has squarely confronted the issues in this case by clarifying that it did not intend to include within the farm products exception commission merchants by its amended § 554.9307(1), effective July 1, 1985. The revised statute states: (1) Except as provided in subsection 4, a buyer in ordinary course of business as defined in § 554.1201, subsection 9, takes free of a security interest created by that person's seller even though the security interest is perfected. For purposes of this section, a buyer or buyer in ordinary course of business includes any commission merchant, selling agent, or other person engaged in the business of receiving livestock as defined in section 189A.2 on commission for or on behalf of another. Section 554.9307(4)(a) states in pertinent part: (4)(a) A buyer in ordinary course of business buying farm products from a person engaged in farming operations takes free of a security interest created by that person's seller even though the security interest is perfected, unless the buyer receives prior written notice of the security interest, or unless the buyer purchases the farm products outside of the seller's trade area, or the buyer's principal place of business is located outside of the seller's trade area. The "seller's trade area" consists of the county in which the seller resides or a county that is contiguous to or corners upon the county where the seller resides. * * *[1]

Although the revised statute may not be applicable in this case because the statute became effective after the district court had rendered its opinion, there can be little doubt that these changes reflect the prevailing public policy of the State of Iowa. Indeed, it appears that more than one third of the states, including many major agricultural states, have altered their commercial codes within the last

---

[1] In this case the "seller's trade area" provision is met in that Ida County, the Newmans' county of residence, is contiguous to Woodbury County, Iowa, the county where Progressive does business.

three years to address the growing dissatisfaction with the farm products exception. See Uchtmann, Bauer & Dudek, "The U.C.C. Farm Products Exception—A Time to Change," 69 Minnesota Law Review 1315, 1315-16 nn. 3-4 (1985).[2] These changes have been brought about because of the problems caused by the farm products exception and the need to provide greater protection to the buyers of farm products. These statutes eliminate the harsh result contemplated by the district court of transforming buyers and commission merchants into sureties on the farmers' debts.

If the changes made by the Iowa legislature were not enough to establish the public policy in favor of protecting commission merchants from liability for outstanding security interests, the Court also takes judicial notice that Congress in the Food Security Act of 1985, Pub.L. No. 99-198, § 1324(g), 99 Stat. 1354 (Dec. 23, 1985), provided that commission merchants or selling agents who sell in the ordinary course of business "shall not be subject to a security interest created by the seller in such farm product even though the security interest is perfected and even though the commission merchant or selling agent knows of the existence of such interest." Although the Food Security Act provisions will not be effective until December 23, 1986, the changes made by Congress further aid the Court in establishing public policy. There can be little doubt that Congress intends, in its repeal of the farm products exception, to allocate the loss resulting when a borrower defaults on the farm products lender.

In light of the statutory changes made by the Iowa legislature and the Congress, as well as what appears to have been the original intent of the drafters of the U.C.C. as set out in Comment 4 of § 9-109, the public policy in the instant case is well-settled. It is not for this Court to rebalance the equities in order to determine what public policy should apply. Although there is no doubt that the district court did not have the advantage of these subsequently enacted legislative materials, its judgment nonetheless must be reversed and remanded.

NOTE ON THE FOOD SECURITY ACT OF 1985

Section 9-307(1) protects buyers of ordinary course against perfected security interests created by their sellers but exempts from that protection buyers of farm products from a person engaged in farming operations. The nature of farm sales differs from many buyer in ordinary course sales. In the buyer in ordinary course paradigm, a wholesaler buys from a manufacturer, a retailer from a wholesaler, or a consumer from a retailer. Thus, buyers are small; sellers are big. In the farm sale, however, the model seller is a family farmer; the buyer a grain company.

---

2 Uchtmann, Bauer, and Dudek provide an especially comprehensive overview of the law as it relates to the farm products exception. Their careful study makes it apparent that the farm products exception is of dubious continued vitality. See Uchtmann, Bauer & Dudek, "The Farm Products Exception—A Time to Change," 69 Minn.L.Rev. 1315, 1325 (1985).

While it was controversial in 1950, when the drafters completed their work on the Code, to argue that the Code's farm sale paradigm was outmoded, everyone must agree that the paradigm is less accurate today if not wholly out of date. As long ago as 1972 when the Code sponsors named a committee of distinguished practitioners and academics to revise Article 9, that Committee reported that it despaired of fashioning a rule for farm sales in § 9-307(1) that could achieve national uniformity when the states were to adopt the 1972 revisions to the article. Thus the farm products exception survived the 1972 revision.

In ensuing years, however, buyers of farm products suffered unfairly at the hands of the rule. Grain elevators and livestock brokers that purchased from farmers in the ordinary course of business sometimes learned that they took subject to security interests. Auctioneers that sold livestock learned that the law of conversion made them liable to banks and production credit associations with security interests. In view of the Article 9 rules for filing as to farm products, which rules usually call for local filings, these commercial enterprises in the agricultural sector found it difficult to search for filings, which buyers in ordinary course from nonfarm producers did not have to search for anyway.

The losses mounted sufficiently that there was strong sentiment for legislative reform. While some thought, and still think, that simple deletion of the farm products exception from § 9-307(1) would solve the problem best, Congress responded differently with the Food Security Act. The Act creates a new central filing system and a notice regime, defines terms and personages new to secured lending (e.g., commission merchant, effective financing statement, selling agent), fashions a criminal penalty, and orders the Secretary of Agriculture to prescribe regulations to aid the states in erecting the new filing system. The Drafting Committee for Revised Article 9 has not yet reached a decision whether to retain the farm products exception. See Revised § 9-316(a).

MOONEY, INTRODUCTION TO U.C.C. ANNUAL SURVEY, 41 Bus. Law. 1343, 1352 (1986).

A recent example of federal intervention in commercial law is section 1324 of the Food Security Act of 1985. Section 1324 repeals (in the absence of compliance with one of two specified alternative methods) the farm products exception to U.C.C. section 9-307(1). It is beyond the scope of this article to discuss the merits, or absence thereof, of the U.C.C. exception to section 9-307(1) for certain sales of farm products to a "buyer in ordinary course of business." However, the goals, methods, and likely results of section 1324 illustrate the non-U.C.C. statutory assault. Recent years have witnessed in many states the enactment of modifications (within and without the U.C.C.) to the farm products exception in section 9-307(1), each attempting to balance the competing interests of farmers, buyers of farm products, and lenders secured by farm products. Section 1324 stemmed from a desire to facilitate interstate commerce by providing a uniform rule. It will more than likely result in a burden to interstate commerce.

Section 1324 includes elaborate provisions relating to notices to buyers of farm products and the establishment of optional state "central filing systems" for "effective financing statements," as alternative methods of ensuring that a buyer of farm products will buy subject to existing security interests in the farm products. Although even the most pejorative hyperbole is inadequate to fully express what section 1324 deserves, the following is a frail attempt: Section 1324 is internally inconsistent, unintelligible, and unworkable. It was drafted and enacted without apparent knowledge or understanding of present and past systems of public notice and secured financing. It ignores the issues involved in multistate transactions. It does not draw upon, acknowledge, or include many matters that are adequately covered in the U.C.C. and in judicial decisions that treat such U.C.C. provisions. It is a disaster. No buyer or financer of farm products should tolerate such incompetence from its legal counsel, yet these disgraceful provisions have now been imposed upon agricultural commerce and finance. What is worse, in attempts to set up "central filing systems" under section 1324, some state legislatures may expand the harm by unnecessarily disrupting the existing U.C.C. article 9 filing systems and thereby interfering with secured transactions unrelated to farm products.

(b) Of Paper

(i) Chattel Paper

UCC § 9-308

A purchaser of chattel paper * * * who gives new value and takes possession of it in the ordinary course of his business has priority over a security interest in the chattel paper * * *

(a) which is perfected * * * if he acts without knowledge * * *
(b) which is claimed merely as proceeds of inventory * * *.

CROCKER NATIONAL BANK v. CLARK EQUIPMENT CREDIT CORP.

United States Court of Appeals, Eighth Circuit, 1984.
Page 318, supra

NOTE ON REVISED ARTICLE 9

Under § 9-308(a), a purchaser of chattel paper who has knowledge that the specific paper is subject to a prior perfected security interest will not obtain priority even though he obtains possession, takes for value, and in the ordinary course of his business. An exception to this rule pertains, however, if the security interest is "claimed merely as proceeds" of an inventory financer's security interest, in which case § 9-308(b) affords the purchaser of chattel paper priority even if he has knowledge of the inventory financing arrangement and the fact that the chattel paper is subject to that security interest as proceeds. PEB Commentary No. 8 explains the distinction as intending to protect an inventory financer who gives new value against the paper from one whose interest is merely as proceeds of an inventory lien. In the former case, the financer who leaves the debtor in possession of the paper for collection purposes can protect itself against a subsequent purchaser by having notice of its interest stamped or legended directly on the paper.

The drafters of Revised Article 9 initially concluded that the distinction between the two situations was unclear in many instances and, thus, proposed to eliminate it entirely. However, the current draft retains the distinction between earlier-perfected security interests in chattel paper that are claimed "merely as proceeds" and those claimed as original collateral. Specifically, Revised § 9-327(a) deals with the situation where the chattel paper is claimed merely as proceeds of inventory (current § 9-308(b)), but it eliminates any reference to the purchaser's knowledge, instead relying on the concept that the purchaser will be protected unless the chattel paper has been stamped with a legend indicating that it has been assigned. Subsection (b) basically continues the rule of current § 9-308(a), although it adds the requirement that the purchaser take in "good faith," and substitutes for the current requirement that the purchaser take without knowledge that the "specific paper" is subject to a security interest the standard that the purchaser take without *actual* knowledge "that the purchase violates the rights of the secured party." Revised § 9-327(c) makes clear that, for purposes of subsection (b), knowledge of the secured party's rights in the paper is imparted to a purchaser of chattel paper if the paper itself indicates that "it has been assigned to an identified assignee." Finally, Revised § 9-102(38) contains a somewhat different definition of "new value" from that contained in current § 9-108.

(ii) Negotiable Instruments, Documents, and Securities

UCC § 9-309

Nothing in this Article limits the rights of a holder in due course of a negotiable instrument (Section 3-302) or a holder to whom a negotiable document of title has been duly negotiated (Section 7-501) or a protected purchaser of a security (Section 8-303) and the holders or purchasers take priority over an earlier security interest even though perfected. * * *

ALLSTATE FINANCIAL CORP. v. FINANCORP, INC.

United States Court of Appeals, Fourth Circuit, 1991.
934 F.2d 55.

ERVIN, Chief Judge.

In March 1989, Allstate Financial Corporation ("Allstate") filed an amended complaint against Financorp, Incorporated ("Financorp") in the United States District Court for the District of Maryland. Allstate sought damages for unjust enrichment, conversion, and trespass to chattels allegedly suffered when Financorp negotiated two checks made payable to Kane Delivery Limited, d.b.a.

Advance Disposal Service ("Kane"). Allstate asserted that it had superior rights to the checks as they represented proceeds of collateral in which Allstate had a prior perfected security interest.

The parties conducted discovery in the case. Afterwards, on November 3, 1989, Allstate moved for summary judgment. Financorp moved for summary judgment three days later. The district court determined that a hearing was not necessary in order to rule on the summary judgment motions. On July 30, 1990, the district court entered an order granting summary judgment in favor of Financorp, denying Allstate's motion. Allstate appealed from this order. On review, we find that the district court properly granted summary judgment in favor of Financorp. Therefore, we affirm.

* * *

This suit arises out of the competing claims of Allstate and Financorp as to two checks which were received by Kane, a debtor of both Allstate and Financorp. Three contracts are involved in this suit.

The first contract was between Allstate and Kane. Under this contract, Allstate advanced monies to Kane and financed, or purchased, Kane's accounts receivable from Kane's delivery business. This contract was conducted in two stages. The first was between August 1987 and February 1988. The second was between July 1, 1988 and October 27, 1988. Allstate advanced a total of $192,749.06 to Kane during those periods. Approximately $114,000 remains outstanding. Under this contract, Allstate received a security interest in Kane's accounts receivable. At the time of the contract, Kane was located in Washington, D.C. Therefore, on September 23, 1987, Allstate filed a financing statement with the Recorder of Deeds of Washington, D.C. Kane subsequently moved to Maryland. Within four months of Kane's move, Allstate filed a financing statement in Maryland to maintain its perfected security interest in the accounts receivable.

The second contract was between Kane and Laidlaw Waste Systems, Inc. Under this contract, Kane became a subcontractor for Laidlaw. Laidlaw made all payments under this contract by check made payable to the order of Kane.

The third contract was between Kane and Financorp. Under this contract, Financorp made loans to Kane and received an assignment of the Laidlaw accounts receivable in exchange. Financorp advanced to Kane a total of $301,279.45, and $157,636 remains unpaid. Prior to entering this contract with Kane, Financorp searched the Maryland UCC lien filings to ascertain whether there were any prior liens on the accounts receivable. The search revealed no such filing, as Allstate did not file in Maryland until after this search was conducted. Financorp did not search the Washington, D.C., UCC filings.

Periodically, Laidlaw made payments by check to Kane. Then, pursuant to its contract with Financorp, Kane indorsed some of the checks to Financorp. Two of those checks are at issue in this case. They totalled $96,888.33. Financorp negotiated the checks and applied them to the amount due from Kane. Allstate claims that it had a superior right to those two checks because of its contract with Kane whereby it obtained a security interest in Kane's accounts receivable.

The district court found that Financorp had a right to the checks that was superior to Allstate's because Financorp was a "holder in due course" as defined by the UCC. Under § 9-309 of the UCC, a holder in due course has priority over an earlier security interest, even if that prior interest was perfected. Therefore, the court determined that Financorp was entitled to summary judgment, and this appeal followed.

* * *

Allstate * * * attacks the district court's determination that Financorp, as a holder in due course, had superior rights to a prior secured party. Section 3-305(1) of the UCC provides that a holder in due course takes an instrument "free from all claims to it on the part of any person." Md.Commercial Law Code Ann. § 3-305(1) (1975). Thus, under Article 3, it appears that Financorp as a holder in due course took the two checks free of Allstate's claims to them.

Allstate claims that Article 3 is subject to Article 9, and that the priority scheme of Article 9 controls and gives Allstate priority as a prior secured party. The district court found that the controlling provision of the UCC in this case was § 9-309. We agree with the district court. Section 9-309 sets out the relative priority between Article 9 and Article 3 concerning the rights of a holder in due course and a secured party.

* * *

Under the plain language of § 9-309, Financorp had priority over the checks at issue in this case because of its status as holder in due course. As a result, summary judgment in favor of Financorp was proper because as a matter of law, Financorp had priority over the checks at issue in this case.

AFFIRMED.

PROBLEM

Newell Pipe Supply, a plumbing contractor, granted successive security interests in its accounts receivable and proceeds to Bank and Lender. Bank perfected its security interest first by filing a proper financing statement with the secretary of state. Subsequently, Newell began to experience financial difficulties and Lender demanded that, in the future, Newell direct its customers to issue their checks payable jointly to Newell and Lender. Newell complied and, thereafter, when customer checks were received, Newell would duly indorse them and deliver them to Lender who applied the proceeds to Newell's outstanding indebtedness. Upon discovering this arrangement several months later, Bank demanded that Lender turn over the collections it had received from these accounts, and when Lender refused, Bank brought suit for conversion. Explain the basis for Bank's claim. On what basis might Lender defend this suit? See PEB Commentary No. 7. Does it matter to your analysis if or when Lender became aware of Bank's prior security interest? How about if the checks had been made payable solely to Newell who then indorsed them over to Lender? Is there any question as to who has priority with respect to payments made by Newell's account debtors in the future? How would these cases be resolved under Revised Article 9? See Revised § 9-328.

NOTE ON LESSEES

In Chapter 3, we examined the priority conflict that rages between a lessor of goods and a bankruptcy trustee (representing unsecured creditors of the lessee) when the lessee files for bankruptcy. Because the UCC does not require true personal property lessors to record notice of their interests, these battles are usually decided on the basis of whether the purported lease transaction is a true bailment lease, governed by Article 2A, or a finance lease subject to Article 9. Sometimes, however, the secured party will be a creditor of the lessor of goods. If the borrower/lessor should default on its obligation for which the security interest was granted, now the battle will be between the secured party and the lessee. In these instances, § 2A-307 controls, and the rules are roughly parallel to the rules governing conflicts between buyers and secured parties. For example, § 2A-307(3) permits a "lessee in the ordinary course of business" (defined in § 2A-103(1)(o)) to take the leasehold interest free of even a prior security interest in the leased goods created by her lessor. This corresponds with the buyer rule in § 9-307(1). See also Revised § 9-317. Section 2A-307(2)(b), in turn, is the analog of 9-301(1)(c), which makes an unperfected security interest subordinate to the rights of a nonordinary course buyer who took for value and without knowledge of the security interest. Similarly, just as a nonordinary course buyer takes subject to a perfected security interest, § 2A-307(2)(c) makes the lessee's interest subject to a security interest in the goods that was perfected before the lease became enforceable. However, because under the language of § 2A-307(2)(c), the security interest must be perfected *before* the lease becomes enforceable, if the perfection of the security interest and the effectiveness of the lease occur at the *same* time, the lessee will take free of the security interest. How might this come about? Suppose, for example, a debtor has granted a security interest in existing and after acquired equipment to a lender who properly perfects by filing. Thereafter, the debtor agrees to lease its equipment to lessee. The lessee's leasehold interest is subject to the lender's security interest. However, if the debtor later acquires a new piece of equipment that is immediately made subject to the existing lease, arguably the lender's security interest is not perfected *before* the lease contract becomes enforceable. In that case, if the lessee, which has given value, receives the new equipment without knowledge of the lender's security interest, it takes free of that interest. Another difference between the "buyer" and "lessee" rules is that Article 2A contains no relation back for purchase money security interests comparable to § 9-301(2) for buyers in bulk.

SECTION 3. RECLAIMING SELLERS

(a) THE CASH SELLER

BURNS BROTHERS v. BIGELOW

Supreme Court of New York, Appellate Term, 1910.
122 N.Y.S. 253.

LEHMAN, J.

The plaintiffs have replevined coal, which they sold and delivered to defendant, and which defendant has not paid for. The sole questions in the case are whether the sale of the coal was upon the condition that the bill should be paid upon delivery, and whether the delivery without payment waived this condition and vested title in the defendant.

While the defendant claims that the sale to her was upon credit, it seems to me that the plaintiffs have established beyond any question that this is not true. The defendant says that the order for the coal was given to the plaintiffs' solicitor, who called upon her without request from her; that at that time she had a credit account with the plaintiffs, and owed them a balance of $22.50, which the solicitor asked her to pay, and which she told him she would pay when she got ready. She then testified that he took her order, and agreed to deliver the coal some time during the summer, and that later he called again and said they would rather wait until the fall, and, when she complained that the price of $6.50 was not fair, he said he would see about it, and call her up, and let her know if they would let her have it for $6, and they did call her up, and said they would rather put it in at $6. She testified positively that she was never called up on the phone and told that she should pay cash for the coal, and that she had no conversation on the subject with any person, and that the first time she knew anything about such a demand was when a man came, the day after the coal was delivered, and said if it was not paid for they would take it out.

The plaintiffs' solicitor, on the other hand, testified: That he called on defendant at her request on June 15th, and that she told him she wanted to order her coal at the prevailing June price, and that he said:

> "All right; I will take your order, and I will submit it; and if they accept it, of course, we will take the order."

That he called on her a day or two later, and told her the firm did not want to put the coal in unless she paid for it. After some conversation he said he would go back again and see what he could do. That he then spoke to Mr. Burns, the president of plaintiff's corporation, and then telephoned her that he could not give her the coal in the spring and wait until the fall for the money; but that he would put it in the fall, about September 15th, at the spring price, and that she should pay for it then. He claims that she then asked him to put it in writing, to which he agreed, and that Mr. Burns then wrote her a letter, which was put in evidence without objection. This letter was produced by the defendant, and therefore contradicts her testimony that she knew nothing of any claim that she would pay cash, and completely corroborates the plaintiff in regard to the whole transaction, stating:

> "In view of the understanding between our Mr. Pinetti and yourself regarding the financial situation, we have entered this order to be delivered some time between now and September 15, 1909, at that same price, i.e., $6.00 per ton, with the understanding that when you take the coal you are to pay cash for it."

It seems to me that under all the circumstances of the case the contract was not complete until the giving of this letter. Even if the solicitor booked the order without stating that it was to be submitted to the firm, he could not be presumed to have authority to make a contract for an unusual credit, and the letter constitutes the contract. In any event, however, it so completely contradicts the defendant as to the whole transaction, and especially as to her lack of knowledge that the delivery was intended to be for cash, and explanation of why the coal was sold to her for $6, instead of $6.50, that any finding that the goods were sold on credit would be completely against the weight of evidence.

The more serious question in the case, however, is whether, upon the delivery of the coal, the condition of payment was waived. There is no contradiction of the testimony as to the circumstances of the delivery. The plaintiff's driver says that before delivering the last load of the order he presented the bill, and a ticket for the coal, saying, "Here is the bill for $118;" that he then completed the delivery, and waited for 15 minutes, but defendant did not come down again, and the gate was locked. He rang the bell, and a boy came to the door, and said Mrs. Bigelow was upstairs, and he then told the boy he had presented the bill and did not get the money. After that he drove off and reported to the office. The plaintiff's bill collector said he called a few days after the delivery, and asked to see Mrs. Bigelow. He heard a woman's voice say that Mrs. Bigelow was out, and would not be back till 6 o'clock, and he told the boy who opened the door that if they did not get the money they would be compelled to take out the coal.

Under these circumstances I think the court erred in finding that the condition was waived by the delivery. It is quite true that, where goods to be paid for in cash upon delivery are delivered to the purchaser without the cash being given or demanded at the time, the presumption is that the condition is waived and that a complete title vests in the purchaser; but this presumption may be rebutted by proof of such declarations or acts of the parties connected with the circumstances of the case as show an intention that the delivery should not be considered complete until the performance of the condition, and the question with what intention the delivery is made, where any doubt arises, is one of fact. It is also true, however, that where the testimony of such declarations and acts is undisputed, and, connected with the surrounding circumstances, allows the inference only that the condition was not waived, this testimony is controlling, and requires the trial justice to find that the delivery was conditional, and renders his finding to the contrary erroneous as a matter of law. Parker v. Baxter, 86 N. Y. 586, at pages 593, 594.

In this case the sale was for cash; the coal was delivered, and the bill presented at the same time; an attempt to demand payment was made at the completion of the delivery, and a further demand for the money or the goods was made thereafter. In spite of the fact that the bill presented was not indorsed with the words "Received payment," as is customary where the driver is to receive the payment, it is impossible to find from the circumstances any basis for the inference that the plaintiff intended an absolute delivery.

Judgment should be reversed, and a new trial granted, with costs to the appellant to abide the event. All concur.

UCC § 2-507(2)

Where payment is due and demanded on the delivery to the buyer of goods or documents of title, his right as against the seller to retain or dispose of them is conditional upon his making the payment due.

(b) The Credit Seller

STOWERS v. MAHON (IN RE SAMUELS & CO.)

United States Court of Appeals, Fifth Circuit, 1976.
526 F.2d 1238, cert. denied, 429 U.S. 834.

[It was the practice for cattle producers to deliver cattle to Samuels & Co., a meatpacking firm, under an arrangement whereby Samuels took possession of the cattle, slaughtered, graded, and weighed it, and then paid the producer by check the day after delivery. Although the court saw the transaction as a cash sale, it is clear under § 2-511, cmt. 6 (delivery against check post dated by even one day is delivery on credit.) that the sale was on credit. C.I.T. held a floating lien on all of Samuels' inventory, given to secure a revolving line of credit. Before the producers' checks were presented for payment, C.I.T., concerned about Samuels' financial condition, cutoff the company's line of credit. Thus, the checks were returned for insufficient funds. Based on its perfected security interest, C.I.T. claimed priority in the producers' cattle. The producers argued that they could defeat C.I.T. under their right to reclaim goods delivered for which they were not paid. The simplest issue in the case, then, is whether the sellers' right to reclaim defeats the security interest of C.I.T. in Samuels' after acquired inventory.]

PER CURIAM:

The action of the panel is reversed and the judgment of the District Court is affirmed.

The court en banc adopts as its opinion the dissenting opinion of Judge Godbold with the additional comments which we set out in the margin.

APPENDIX

Opinion of Circuit Judge GODBOLD (510 F.2d at 154).

I dissent.

This case raises one primary question: under the Uniform Commercial Code as adopted in Texas, is the interest of an unpaid cash seller in goods already delivered to a buyer superior or subordinate to the interest of a holder of a perfected security interest in those same goods? In my opinion, under Article Nine, the perfected security interest is unquestionably superior to the interest of the seller. Moreover, the perfected lender is protected from the seller's claims by two independent and theoretically distinct Article Two provisions. My result is not the product of revealed truth, but rather of a meticulous and dispassionate reading of Articles Two and Nine and an understanding that the Code is an integrated statute whose Articles and Sections overlap and flow into one another in an effort to encourage specific types of commercial behavior. The Code's overall plan, which typically favors good faith purchasers, and which encourages notice filing of nonpossessory security interests in personalty through the imposition of stringent penalties for nonfiling, compels a finding that the perfected secured party here should prevail.

My brothers have not concealed that their orientation in the case before us is to somehow reach a result in favor of the sellers of cattle, assumed by them to be 'little fellows,' and against a large corporate lender, because it seems the 'fair' thing to do. We do not sit as federal chancellors confecting ways to escape the state law of commercial transactions when that law produces a result not to our tastes. Doing what seems fair is heady stuff. But the next seller may be a tremendous corporate conglomerate engaged in the cattle feeding business, and the next lender a small town Texas Bank. Today's heady draught may give the majority a euphoric feeling, but it can produce tomorrow's hangover.

I. Rights under § 2.403

My analysis begins with an examination of the relative rights of seller and secured party under § 2.403(a).

Section 2.403 gives certain transferors power to pass greater title than they can themselves claim. Section 2.403(a) gives good faith purchasers of even fraudulent buyers-transferors greater rights than the defrauded seller can assert. This harsh rule is designed to promote the greatest range of freedom possible to commercial vendors and purchasers.

The provision anticipates a situation where (1) a cash seller has delivered goods to a buyer who has paid by a check which is subsequently dishonored, § 2.403(a)(2), (3), and where (2) the defaulting buyer transfers title to a Code defined 'good faith purchaser.' The interest of the good faith purchaser is protected pro tanto against the claims of the aggrieved seller. §§ 2.403(a); 2.403, Comment 1. The Code expressly recognizes the power of the defaulting buyer to transfer good title to such a purchaser even though the transfer is wrongful as against the seller. The buyer is granted the power to transfer good title despite the fact that under § 2.507 he lacks the right to do so.

The Code definition of 'purchaser' is broad, and includes not only one taking by sale but also covers persons taking by gift or by voluntary mortgage, pledge or lien. § 1.201(32), (33). It is therefore broad enough to include an Article Nine secured party. §§ 1.201(37); 9.101, Comment; 9.102(a), (b). Thus, if C.I.T. holds a valid Article Nine security interest, it is by virtue of that status also a purchaser under § 2.403(a).

While I shall discuss in detail infra, the implications of C.I.T.'s security interest under Article Nine and under other Article Two provisions, I here note that C.I.T. is the holder of a perfected Article Nine interest which extends to the goods claimed by the seller Stowers.

Attachment of an Article Nine Interest takes place when (1) there is agreement that the interest attach to the collateral; (2) the secured party has given value; and (3) the debtor has rights in the collateral sufficient to permit attachment. § 9.204(a).

(1) The agreement: In 1963, Samuels initially authorized C.I.T.'s lien in its after-acquired inventory. The agreement between these parties remained in effect throughout the period of delivery of Stowers' cattle to Samuels.

(2) Value: At the time of Stowers' delivery, Samuels' indebtedness to C.I.T. exceeded $1.8 million. This preexisting indebtedness to the lender constituted 'value' under the Code. § 1.201(44).

(3) Rights in the collateral: Finally, upon delivery, Samuels acquired rights in the cattle sufficient to allow attachment of C.I.T.'s lien. The fact that the holder of a voluntary lien—including an Article Nine interest—is a 'purchaser' under the Code is of great significance to a proper understanding and resolution of this case under Article Two and Article Nine. The Code establishes that purchasers can take from a defaulting cash buyer, § 2.403(a). Lien creditors are included in the definition of purchasers, § 1.201(32), (33). A lien is an Article Nine interest, §§ 9.101, Comment; 9.102(b); 9.102, Comment. The existence of an Article Nine interest presupposes the debtor's having rights in the collateral sufficient to permit attachment, § 9.204(a). Therefore, since a defaulting cash buyer has the power to transfer a security interest to a lien creditor, including an Article Nine secured party, the buyer's rights in the property, however marginal, must be sufficient to allow attachment of a lien. And this is true even if, arguendo, I were to agree that the cash seller is granted reclamation rights under Article Two.

If the Article Nine secured party acted in good faith, it is prior under § 2.403(a) to an aggrieved seller. Under the facts before us, I think that C.I.T. acted in good faith. The Code good faith provision requires 'honesty in fact', § 1.201(19), which, for Article Two purposes, is 'expressly defined as * * * reasonable commercial standards of fair dealing.' §§ 1.201, Comment 19; 2.103(a)(2). There is no evidence that C.I.T. acted in bad faith in its dealings with Samuels, or that Stowers' loss resulted from any breach of obligation by C.I.T. There is no claim that the 1963 security agreement was the product of bad faith. The lender's interest had been perfected and was of record for six years when Stowers' delivery to Samuels occurred. There is no suggestion that the

$1.8 million debt owing from Samuels to C.I.T. was the result of bad faith or of a desire to defeat Stowers' $50,000 claim. There is no claim that C.I.T. exercised or was able to exercise control over Samuels' business operations. There is no evidence that C.I.T. authorized or ordered or suggested that Samuels dishonor Stowers' check. There is no contention that C.I.T.'s refusal to extend credit on May 23, the date Samuels filed a voluntary petition on bankruptcy at a time when it owed C.I.T. more than $1.8 million, was violative of an obligatory future advance clause. The Code's good faith provision requires 'honesty in fact', § 1.201(19); it hardly requires a secured party to continue financing a doomed business enterprise.

* * *

II. Rights under § 2.507

The majority opinion devotes much of its concentration and energy to an analysis of the sellers' 'reclamation right' under § 2.507 and § 2.702. Relying on an expansive reading of these Sections, the opinion concludes that a cash seller whose right to payment is frustrated through a check ultimately dishonored can 'reclaim' proceeds of goods delivered to the buyer despite an interim third-party interest, and despite a year long delay in seeking reclamation. I am unable to accept this reading of Code policy and requirements.

Although the Code expressly grants a credit seller the right and power to reclaim goods from a breaching buyer, the right is triggered only by specific and limited circumstances; it can be asserted only if an exacting procedure is followed; and the right can never be asserted to defeat the interests of certain third parties who have dealt with the defaulting buyer. § 2.702(b), (c). There is no Code Section expressly granting a similar reclamation right to a cash seller.

The seller's remedies upon breach are enumerated in § 2.703. These provisions do not include or suggest a right of power in a cash seller to recover goods already delivered to a breaching buyer. Nevertheless the courts have read a reclamation right into the Code. It is this judicially-confected right to reclaim goods in which the majority's reclamation analysis is grounded. However, the majority take the reclamation right beyond anything intimated by the Code or heretofore permitted by courts recognizing a cash seller's reclamation right.

The cash seller's right to reclaim has been drawn from the language of § 2.507(b) and § 2.507, Comment 3. I note, first, that the remedy granted by § 2.507(b) is one of seller against buyer. It does not concern rights of seller against third parties. Section 2.507, Comment 3 explains that the seller's rights under § 2.507 must 'conform with the policy set forth in the bona fide purchase section of this Article,' i.e., with § 2.403. As I have noted above, under this provision the rights of an aggrieved cash seller are subordinated to those of the buyer's good-faith purchasers, including Article Nine lenders such as C.I.T. Thus, the Code provisions supporting a cash seller's reclamation right expressly preclude recovery by Stowers as against C.I.T. See §§ 2.507(b); 2.507, Comment 3; 2.702(b), (c).

Moreover, those courts which have permitted reclamation under § 2.507 have invariably adhered to § 2.507, Comment 3's express requirement that demand for return be made within ten days after receipt by the buyer or else be lost.

In the instant case, demand was not made within ten days or ten weeks; it came a full year after delivery to Samuels. The majority excuse this gross noncompliance by finding that the sellers' failure was the product of innocent error, and, in any event, was not required since the 'purpose' of the demand rule—protection of purchasers of the delivered goods—was served through C.I.T.'s alleged intimate knowledge of Samuels' business operations.

The Code's ten-day provision is an absolute requirement. There is no exception in the Code Sections or Comments, express or implied, to the statutory period. I would be hesitant to read any extension into a statute of limitations clear and unambiguous on its face, and particularly unwilling to allow an extension some 36 times greater than the statutory maximum. My reluctance is all the greater where the right at issue is not granted by the Code but is rather the product of judicial interpretation of a Comment which, whatever grant of power it may suggest, expressly limits that right to a ten-day life.

The spirit in which the rule was broken seems to me irrelevant. Even conceding that Stowers' noncompliance occurred in absolute good faith, it was nonetheless noncompliance. Mistake of law does not constitute excuse of mistake.

C.I.T.'s apocryphal intimate knowledge of Samuels' business operations is, I believe, also irrelevant to a determination of the validity of Stowers' claim. The majority find the purpose of the ten-day rule to be one of notice to third parties that a claim exists. I have somewhat greater difficulty than my brothers in pinpointing the purpose of the ten-day rule. But I am convinced that the goal is not one of protection or notice to third-party purchasers, for their rights are secure under the Code as against the aggrieved seller even if demand is timely made. §§ 2.507, Comment 3; 2.702(c). The Code does not condition the purchasers' rights on a lack of knowledge of the seller's interest. With or without knowledge, the purchaser rests secure. I am therefore forced to conclude that the ten-day rule serves some function other than notifying third-party takers, and, consequently, that even if C.I.T. knew of Stowers' claim, the sellers' obligation under the ten-day rule would not have been excused. And even if knowledge by the purchaser suspended the sellers' duty to make a timely demand, the record in this case is devoid of any hint that C.I.T. knew of Samuels' breach and Stowers' reclamation right.

Moreover, § 2.507 and § 2.702 speak of a right to reclaim goods. Neither provision grants a right to go after proceeds of those goods. Where a right or interest in proceeds is recognized by the Code it is recognized expressly. See e.g., § 9.306. The right granted by § 2.507 is narrowly defined. I am unwilling to imply an extension to such a short-lived and precisely drawn remedy.

Finally, even if there were a right to reclaim proceeds, even if the right had been timely exercised, and even if it could have been exercised despite the transfer of interest to C.I.T., Stowers would have taken subject to C.I.T.'s perfected Article Nine interest. See §§ 9.201, 9.301, 9.306, 9.312. See also my discussion of C.I.T.'s rights and interest under Article Nine, infra.

NOTE ON THE PACKERS AND STOCKYARDS ACT

Texas cattle ranchers did not take *Samuels* lying down. In 1976 Congress amended the Packers and Stockyards Act to give sellers of livestock a super lien that defeats secured parties such as C.I.T. See Packers and Stockyards Act, 7 U.S.C.A. § 196 (West 1980). See The First State Bank v. Gotham Provision Co., Inc. (In re Gotham Provision Co., Inc.), 699 F.2d 1000, 1004-05 (5th Cir.) (holding that under the amended Act even if there is a delay in payment, the transaction is a "cash sale" unless there is an express agreement extending credit from the seller to the buyer), *cert. denied*, 459 U.S. 858 (1982). Some states enacted similar legislation that protected farm sellers on credit of other agricultural commodities when the farmer sells them to a slaughterhouse or grain elevator.

SECTION 4. OTHER LIENORS

(a) FEDERAL TAX LIENS

LITTON INDUSTRIAL AUTOMATION SYSTEMS, INC. v. NATIONWIDE POWER CORPORATION

United States Court of Appeals, Eleventh Circuit, 1997.
106 F.3d 366.

BIRCH, Circuit Judge.

The issue in this appeal is whether an unperfected security interest in interpleaded funds is entitled to priority over a competing federal tax lien. The district court held that the federal tax lien is entitled to priority. We affirm.

I. BACKGROUND

The facts in this appeal are essentially undisputed. Plaintiff Litton Industrial Automation Systems, Inc. ("Litton") filed this interpleader action in the United States District Court for the Eastern District of Michigan, from which it was transferred to the United States District Court for the Middle District of Florida. Litton deposited in the registry of the court $572,627.46, which it owed to Nationwide Power Corporation ("Nationwide") pursuant to a judgment obtained by Nationwide on August 15, 1989. The real parties in interest are Highlander International Corporation ("Highlander") and the United States.

Highlander's interest in the interpleaded funds stems from an agreement between Nationwide and Highlander, pursuant to which Nationwide sought to secure a debt it owed to Highlander. In this agreement, Nationwide granted to Highlander a security interest in certain "cash collateral," including Nationwide's cause of action against Litton, which eventually resulted in the money judgment here in dispute. This interest arose on the date of the agreement, April 15, 1986. Highlander did not file a UCC-1 statement until August 1989, however. The Government's interest in the interpleaded funds arose from a tax assessment on June 9, 1986 of tax penalties exceeding $700,000 against Nationwide. On July 3, 1986, the Internal Revenue Service ("IRS") filed a notice of federal tax lien in Broward County, Florida, in which Nationwide had its principal executive office.

On July 27, 1989, the IRS served a notice of levy on Litton's attorney, directing him to deliver to the IRS any monies owed to Nationwide. After judgment was entered in favor of Nationwide in its suit against Litton, Litton initiated the instant interpleader action to determine which party is entitled to the funds. The district court granted summary judgment to the Government, holding that the federal tax lien was entitled to priority over Highlander's security interest. This appeal followed.

II. DISCUSSION

* * *

A. Applicable Law

Before we address the contentions of the parties, we briefly outline the applicable law. Under the Internal Revenue Code, a tax lien arises at the time of assessment, 26 U.S.C. § 6322, on "all property and rights of property, whether real or personal, belonging to" a delinquent taxpayer, id. § 6321. The FTLA provides, however, that the tax lien "shall not be valid as against any * * * holder of a security interest * * * until notice thereof which meets the requirements of subsection (f) has been filed." Id. § 6323(a). Therefore, any "security interest" which arises prior to the proper filing of a federal tax lien takes priority over the tax lien. See United States v. McDermott, 507 U.S. 447, 449, 113 S.Ct. 1526, 1528, 123 L.Ed.2d 128 (1993). The FTLA defines a "security interest" as

> any interest in property acquired by contract for the purpose of securing payment or performance of an obligation or indemnifying against loss or liability. A security interest exists at any time (A) if, at such time, the property is in existence and the interest has become protected under local law against a subsequent judgment lien arising out of an unsecured obligation, and (B) to the extent that, at such time, the holder has parted with money or money's worth.

26 U.S.C. § 6323(h)(1). The dispute in this case is whether Highlander's interest qualifies as a security interest as defined by the FTLA.

B. District Court Opinion and Contentions of the Parties

It is undisputed in this appeal that a tax lien arose upon all Nationwide's property on June 9, 1986, the first date of the tax penalty assessments against Nationwide. It is also undisputed that the IRS properly filed a notice of this tax lien in Nationwide's county of residence, as required by 26 U.S.C. § 6323(f)(2)(B), on July 3, 1986. Therefore, for Highlander's interest to take priority over the tax lien, Highlander must have been the holder of a "security interest," as that term is defined in the FTLA, on July 3, 1986. To do so,

Highlander must establish that its interest satisfies four conditions:

> (1) that the security interest was acquired by contract for the purpose of securing payment or performance of an obligation or indemnifying against loss; (2) that the property to which the security interest was to attach was in existence at the time the tax lien was filed; (3) that the security interest was, at the time of the tax lien filing, protected under state law against a judgment lien arising out of an unsecured obligation; and (4) that the holder of the security interest parted with money or money's worth.

Haas v. Internal Revenue Serv. (In re Haas), 31 F.3d 1081, 1085 (11th Cir.1994), cert. denied, 115 S.Ct. 2578, 132 L.Ed.2d 828 (1995). As in Haas, the only issue on appeal in this case is whether the third condition is satisfied. In other words, this case turns on whether Highlander's interest was protected under Florida law—the applicable local law—against a judgment lien arising out of an unsecured obligation on July 3, 1986.

Relying on the "hypothetical judgment lien creditor test" adopted by this court in Haas, the district court held that Highlander's interest was not protected under Florida law against a judgment lien.

> [T]he hypothetical judgment lien creditor test operates to put the IRS in the shoes of any subsequent judgment creditor, including the most favorable shoes. Thus, if any subsequent judgment creditor could prevail over [Highlander], then the IRS prevails.

Haas, 31 F.3d at 1089 (footnote omitted). The district court reasoned that a class of judgment creditors, those who qualify as "lien creditors" as defined in U.C.C. § 9-301(3) and who have no notice of Highlander's previous unperfected interest, could have prevailed over Highlander's interest under Florida law. The court concluded that the Government prevails here.

Highlander contends, however, that under Florida law a "judgment lien" does not attach to intangible assets, such as the funds at issue in this case, until the judgment creditor has taken further judicial action—by way of garnishment or an independent suit to enforce the debt. See Peninsula State Bank v. United States, 211 So.2d 3, 5 (Fla.1968). Highlander concludes that the holder of a simple "judgment lien" on intangibles does not qualify as a UCC "lien creditor" under Florida law. Thus, Highlander's security interest, though unperfected, prevails over the judgment lien because Highlander's interest was the first to attach. See Fla. Stat. ch. 679.312(5)(b) (1995).

Highlander argues that Haas is distinguishable. The priority contest in Haas was between a mortgagee who had mistakenly released its mortgage on the contested real property and a federal tax lien. The applicable local law was Alabama law, which provided that the mortgagee's interest is subordinate to that of a "judgment creditor without notice." Haas, 31 F.3d at 1086. The issue decided in that case was whether knowledge on the part of the IRS of the mistakenly released mortgage affected the hypothetical priority contest—we decided that it did not—, not whether the IRS should be treated as a UCC lien creditor. In other words, the IRS would have won the priority contest in Haas, whether it was a UCC lien creditor or not, because it was the hypothetical holder of a "judgment lien" and thus a judgment creditor entitled to priority under Alabama law. Highlander acknowledges that, in Haas, we noted: "In interpreting the phrase 'protected under local law against a subsequent judgment lien,' courts and commentators have determined the phrase is equivalent to being protected against a 'lien creditor' as defined in U.C.C. § 9-301(3)." Haas, 31 F.3d at 1087. Highlander contends, however, that this statement is dictum, in light of the discussion of the specific type of interest and applicable local law at issue in Haas.

Highlander also distinguishes Dragstrem v. Obermeyer, 549 F.2d 20 (7th Cir.1977), which is the first decision of a United States Court of Appeals to adopt the hypothetical judgment creditor test and upon which we relied heavily in Haas. Dragstrem involved facts analogous to those we face here. The priority contest in Dragstrem was between an unperfected security interest and a subsequent tax lien over an interpleaded fund. Id. at 22. The difference between Dragstrem and this case lies, however, in the applicable local law. The relevant local law in Dragstrem was U.C.C. § 9-301(1)(b), which, as adopted in Indiana at the time, provided that "an unperfected security interest is subordinate to the rights of * * * (b) a person who becomes a lien creditor *without knowledge* of the security interest and before it is perfected." Id. at 23 (omission in original) (emphasis added). The equivalent provision of Florida law is a newer version of section 9-301(1)(b) that omits the knowledge requirement. See Fla. Stat. ch. 679.301(1)(b). Therefore, the central issue decided in Haas and Dragstrem, whether knowledge on the part of the IRS affects the priority of the tax lien, is not relevant in this case.

More importantly, a judgment lien attaches to intangible property in Indiana upon docketing of a judgment and the delivery of a writ of execution to the sheriff, Dragstrem, 549 F.2d at 27, without any additional judicial proceeding as required in Florida. Highlander argues that the holder of a "simple judgment lien" is therefore a UCC lien creditor under Indiana law but not under Florida law. Compare id. ("Upon delivery [of the writ to the sheriff], the lien would attach to the debtor's property and the creditor would become a 'lien creditor' under the UCC.") with Peninsula State Bank, 211 So.2d at 5 ("The only way a simple judgment creditor can reach [intangible property] owed to his debtor is by way of a separate and independent judicial proceeding * * *."). According to Highlander, that such holder of a simple judgment lien prevailed under Indiana law does not mean that it should prevail under Florida law.

The Government contends, however, that the additional procedural steps that a Florida judgment creditor must take for its judgment lien to attach to intangible property are no different from the lack of knowledge requirement that was at issue in Haas. In order to be in "the most favorable shoes," Haas, 31 F.3d at 1089, the hypothetical judgment creditor must be assumed to have completed whatever additional steps are required under local law for the judgment lien to attach. Highlander responds that there is an important distinction between the knowledge requirement in Haas and the additional steps necessary under Florida law for a judgment lien to attach to intangible property. The underpinning of the hypothetical judgment creditor test is that the FTLA

> "does not put the government in the position of a competing holder of a security interest or judgment lien, but rather describes the legal status which security interests must obtain under state law in order to have priority over later filed or unfiled federal tax liens."

Haas, 31 F.3d at 1087 (quoting Dragstrem, 549 F.2d at 26). Therefore, whether the IRS had knowledge of the security interest is irrelevant to the inquiry of whether that security interest achieved a given legal status. Under Haas, we do not engage in "a case-by-case inquiry into whether the IRS had 'notice.'" Haas, 31 F.3d at 1088. Instead, we compare the security interest at issue to a given legal construct, namely a hypothetical "judgment lien." Just what the phrase "judgment lien" means was not an issue in Haas, although it was addressed in dicta. See id. at 1087 (noting that "courts and commentators have determined the phrase is equivalent to * * * a 'lien creditor' as defined in the U.C.C. § 9-301(3)"). Highlander argues that the plain meaning of the phrase "judgment lien" is a "simple" judgment lien that arises, but not necessarily attaches to intangible property, upon the entry of a judgment. Highlander argues further that whether such "judgment lien" should be considered to have attached to the property in dispute is a matter of state law. If state law requires separate judicial action for the lien to attach to the property, then a "judgment lien" in that state, even a hypothetical judgment lien, has not attached and its holder is not a UCC lien creditor. Cf. Peninsula State Bank, 211 So.2d at 5. Highlander adds that defining a "judgment lien" in this fashion does not defeat the congressional purpose, implemented in the hypothetical judgment creditor test, of avoiding a case-by-case inquiry into whether the IRS actually complied with certain state law requirements—i.e., had no notice (as in Haas) or performed the actions necessary under state law for the judgment lien to attach to the property in question.

C. Analysis

We agree with Highlander that Haas does not necessarily dictate the result in this case. To determine whether the language of Haas should be extended to encompass the additional steps needed under Florida law for a "simple judgment lien" to attach, we must construe the statute and ascertain what the phrase "judgment lien," as used by Congress in section 6323(h)(1), means.

In a case involving statutory construction, our starting point always is the language of the statute, and we assume that Congress expressed its intent by the ordinary meaning of the words it used. American Tobacco Co. v. Patterson, 456 U.S. 63, 68, 102 S.Ct. 1534, 1537, 71 L.Ed.2d 748 (1982); Gulf Life Ins. Co. v. Arnold, 809 F.2d 1520, 1522 (11th Cir.1987). The FTLA does not define the phrase "judgment lien." Highlander relies primarily on the Florida Supreme Court's decision in Peninsula State Bank to argue that the plain meaning of the phrase "judgment lien" is a "simple unperfected judgment lien." Peninsula State Bank, 211 So.2d at 7. The gist of this argument is that, under Florida law, a simple money judgment against a defendant creates a "lien" on all of its property. Such a lien, "a simple judgment lien" in the terminology used by the Florida Supreme Court, does not attach to the defendant's intangible personal property until further judicial action is taken. Id. at 5. Highlander's argument is unconvincing.

Federal law, not state law, governs a priority contest between a security interest and a federal tax lien. Haas, 31 F.3d at 1084-85 (citing Aquilino v. United States, 363 U.S. 509, 513-15, 80 S.Ct. 1277, 1280-81, 4 L.Ed.2d 1365 (1960)). Thus, although the FTLA resolves such a contest by comparing the security interest to a judgment lien under state priority rules, what constitutes a "judgment lien" within the meaning of section 6323(h)(1) is a matter of federal law. We are concerned with what Congress intended that phrase to mean, not with what state law labels as a judgment lien. Cf. id. at 1088 n. 10 (definition of "judgment creditor" in a predecessor to the FTLA is a matter of federal law).

The phrase "judgment lien" does not have a generally understood meaning. See Texas Oil & Gas Corp. v. United States, 466 F.2d 1040, 1047 (5th Cir.1972) ("The phrase 'protected against a judgment lien' is not a term of art * * *."), cert. denied, 410 U.S. 929, 93 S.Ct. 1367, 35 L.Ed.2d 591 (1973); Peter F. Coogan, The Effect of the Federal Tax Lien Act of 1966 Upon Security Interests Created Under the Uniform Commercial Code, 81 Harv. L. Rev. 1369, 1389 (1968) ("The term 'judgment lien' is not generally used in chattel security statutes* * *."). For example, in contrast to Florida, there appears to be no such thing as a "judgment lien," whether labeled "simple" or not, on personal property in some states. See, e.g., Keep Fresh Filters, Inc. v. Reguli, 888 S.W.2d 437, 443 (Tenn.Ct.App.1994) (Under Tennessee law, "judgment creditors * * * may obtain two significantly different liens against the judgment debtor's property. The first is [a] judgment lien * * * that attaches to * * * real property. The second is [an] execution lien * * * that attaches to * * * personal property."); Franchise Tax Bd. v. Danning (In re Perry), 487 F.2d 84, 89 (9th Cir.1973) (Zirpoli, J., dissenting) (explaining that "no provision of California law ever permits that a judgment lien attach to personal property" and that only an "execution lien" can reach such property), cert. denied, 415 U.S. 978, 94 S.Ct. 1565, 39 L.Ed.2d 874 (1974). In other states, a simple judgment creates no lien at all on personal property, and a judgment lien does not arise until certain additional action is taken by the judgment creditor. See, e.g., Fore v. United States, 339 F.2d 70, 72 (5th Cir.1964) (Under Texas law, "[t]he filing and indexing of [a] judgment in * * * Harrison County entitled [the judgment creditor] to a lien upon all of the real estate of the defendant * * * situated in the county. It gave him no lien on the personal property of the defendant."); First Security Bank v. Friese Mfg., Inc., 489 N.W.2d 342, 345 (N.D.1992) ("Under North Dakota law, a judgment lien on personal property only arises upon the 'actual levy' of the property in question.").[1]

---

1 The inconsistency between what these courts from other states refer to as a judgment lien or execution lien and what the Florida Supreme Court refers to as a "simple judgment lien" in Peninsula State Bank appears to stem from a different understanding of the word "lien." For the Reguli, Fore, and First Security Bank courts, and the dissenting judge in Perry, a lien is an interest that has actually attached to the defendant's property. The Florida court uses the word "lien" to mean a claim arising from a judgment but that has not necessarily attached to the subject property. This inconsistency may be a good example of what Massachusetts Justice H.T. Lummus said: "The word 'lien' hardly admits of definition. It is used to describe various kinds of interests in property or rights over it, and is frequently used in a very loose way." H.T. Lummus, The Law of Liens with Especial

Even the Florida Supreme Court's opinion upon which Highlander relies is confusing in defining a judgment lien. Although the court eventually concluded in that opinion that the term "judgment lien" used in 26 U.S.C. § 6323(c)(1)(B) means a "simple judgment lien" under Florida law, it also stated: "[I]nsofar as what we call a 'simple judgment creditor' is concerned, there simply is *no such thing* as a judgment lien against [intangible property] in this state." Peninsula State Bank, 211 So.2d at 5 (emphasis added). What the court was referring to in its opinion as a "simple judgment lien" is therefore nothing more than a simple money judgment. This interpretation of the phrase "judgment lien," which Highlander invites us to adopt, in fact reads the word "lien" out of the statute. As the Eighth Circuit did in a similar case, we decline this invitation. See International Fidelity Ins. Co. v. United States, 949 F.2d 1042, 1045 (8th Cir.1991).

We conclude that the phrase "judgment lien" has no ordinary meaning so as to compel Highlander's interpretation of the phrase within the context of the FTLA. The Government argues that "judgment lien," as used in the FTLA, is equivalent to the interest of a UCC lien creditor. This interpretation is one that has been adopted almost unanimously by the commentators, see, e.g., Timothy R. Zinnecker, When Worlds Collide: Resolving Priority Disputes Between the IRS and the Article Nine Secured Creditor, 63 Tenn. L. Rev. 585, 605-06 & nn.89-90 (1996) (collecting cases); Coogan, supra, at 1382-83, and by the courts—though arguably in dicta, see, e.g., Haas, 31 F.3d at 1087; Dragstrem, 549 F.2d at 25. The rationale for adopting this interpretation is that one of Congress's main goals in enacting the FTLA was "to conform the lien provisions of the internal revenue laws to the concepts developed in [the] Uniform Commercial Code." H.R.Rep. No. 89-1884, at 1-2 (1966), reprinted in Committee on Ways and Means, 89th Cong., Legislative History of H.R. 11256: Federal Tax Lien Act of 1966, at 443-44 (1966) [hereinafter Legislative History]. The only way in which the UCC gives effect to the interest of a judgment creditor is the "lien creditor" concept embodied in section 9-301(3) of the UCC. See Coogan, supra, at 1382-83. The logical conclusion, though by no means an inevitable one, is that Congress intended the phrase "judgment lien" to mean the interest, arising from a judgment (as opposed to assignment, for example), that a lien creditor has in a given property.[2] This conclusion is further supported by the fact that it gives

---

Reference to Massachusetts & Maine I (1904), quoted in Coogan, supra, at 1371 n. 11. Unfortunately, Congress did not define the word "lien" or the phrase "judgment lien" in the FTLA.

2 Highlander's strongest attack on this conclusion is that a previous version of the bill that eventually became the FTLA defined "security interest" in terms equivalent to those used in the UCC, but that this language was deleted from the bill. Compare 26 U.S.C. § 6323(h)(1) (enacted definition of security interest) with H.R. 11256, 89th Cong. § 101 (1966) (version initially introduced by Rep. Mills) (providing in 26 U.S.C. § 6323(h)(4) that "[a] security interest shall be deemed to arise at the time when it becomes protected under local law as against a subsequent lien upon such property obtainable by legal or equitable proceedings on a simple contract"), reprinted in Legislative History, supra, at 50. Highlander infers that Congress must have intended to develop the law in a way that is inconsistent with the UCC lien creditor analysis. Congress, however, could have modified the language for other reasons. According to Coogan, "[a]pparently, in an effort to conform the language of

effect to Congress's "specific legislative intent * * * to enable creditors to protect certain types of security interests against subsequent federal tax liens, and to do so by taking the same steps already necessary under state law to protect their interests against various other types of competing claims." Dragstrem, 549 F.2d at 26.

In short, we are faced with two possible interpretations of an ambiguous phrase that Congress used in the FTLA. Cf. Texas Oil & Gas Corp., 466 F.2d at 1047 ("The phrase 'protected against a judgment lien' is not a term of art easily adaptable to the sometimes equally unartful language of the Uniform Commercial Code."); David G. Epstein & Steve H. Nickles, Debt: Bankruptcy, Article 9 and Related Laws, 521 n.56 (1994) (stating that "[t]he use of the term 'judgment lien' was unfortunate") quoted in Zinnecker, supra, at 606 n. 90; Coogan, supra, at 1388 (characterizing the phrase "judgment lien" as "baffling language"). Although we believe that the interpretation offered by the Government is the better one,[3] we need not resolve this case solely on the basis of the statutory analysis described above. Congress has entrusted the administration of the Internal Revenue Code, which includes the FTLA, to the United States Department of Treasury and the IRS. In construing an administrative (or regulatory) statute, we are guided by the framework of analysis set out by the Supreme Court in Chevron, U.S.A., Inc. v. Natural Resources Defense Council, Inc., 467 U.S. 837, 104 S.Ct. 2778, 81 L.Ed.2d 694 (1984). "First, always, is the question whether Congress has directly spoken to the precise question at issue. If the intent of Congress is clear, that is the end of the matter; for the court, as well as the agency, must give effect to the unambiguously expressed intent of Congress." Id. at 842-43, 104 S.Ct. at 2781.

---

other parts of section 6323 to that of subsection (a), where 'judgment lien creditor' is not inappropriate, the language was changed by Treasury draftsmen who understandably knew more tax law than lien law." Coogan, supra, at 1389. Moreover, that the drafters of the statute substituted ambiguous language for more accurate language in a previous version of the bill does not inevitably lead to the conclusion that Congress rejected the analysis consistent with the more accurate language. Congress might have failed to realize that the new language is ambiguous and might have intended no change in the substantive provision. In short, while the change in statutory language casts some doubt on the Government's interpretation, it is not dispositive of the issue in this case, at least in light of the total absence of any explanation of the change in the voluminous legislative history of the FTLA.

3 We reach this conclusion because the Government's interpretation is logical and comports with the stated purpose of the statute, while Highlander's interpretation is unconvincing. As presented by Highlander, the meaning of the phrase "judgment lien" in section 6323(h)(1) is derived from what the Supreme Court of Florida labels as a judgment lien. Accepting Highlander's interpretation leads to two equally unlikely results: First, Congress could have chosen Florida's interpretation as the federal standard, a result that has no support whatsoever in the statute or elsewhere. Moreover, as we already discussed, this result essentially reduces the phrase "judgment lien" to "simple judgment," thus reading the word "lien" out of the statute. Second, Congress could have intended for the meaning of the phrase to be governed by each state's understanding of what a judgment lien is, a result that defeats the FTLA's purpose of uniformity. Cf. United States v. Gilbert Assocs., 345 U.S. 361, 364, 73 S.Ct. 701, 703, 97 L.Ed. 1071 (1953) (stating, in the context of a predecessor to the FTLA, "A cardinal principle of Congress in its tax scheme is uniformity, as far as may be. Therefore, a 'judgment creditor' should have the same application in all the states.").

If Congress did not express its intent unambiguously, we defer to the agency's interpretation if it "is based on a permissible construction of the statute." Id. at 843, 104 S.Ct. at 2782.

As we have already stated, we believe that Congress did not express its intent unambiguously when it used the phrase "judgment lien" in section 6323(h)(1). Department of Treasury regulations, however, define "judgment lien" as "a lien held by a judgment lien creditor." Treas. Reg. § 301.6323(h)-1(a)(2).

> The term "judgment lien creditor" means a person who has obtained a valid judgment, in a court of record and of competent jurisdiction, for the recovery of specifically designated property or for a certain sum of money. In the case of a judgment for the recovery of a certain sum of money, a judgment lien creditor is a person who has perfected a lien under the judgment on the property involved * * *. If recording or docketing is necessary under local law before a judgment becomes effective against third parties acquiring liens on real property, a judgment lien under such local law is not perfected * * * until the time of such recordation or docketing. If under local law levy or seizure is necessary before a judgment lien becomes effective against third parties acquiring liens on personal property, then a judgment lien under such local law is not perfected until levy or seizure of the personal property involved.

Treas. Reg. § 301.6323(h)-1(g). In short, the regulation codifies the interpretation of "judgment lien" that the Government advocates in this case and that we have already determined is not only permissible, but also is the better interpretation. This interpretation holds that a judgment lien is equivalent to the interest of a UCC lien creditor. Under the second step of Chevron, we must defer to the Department's interpretation.

Because Highlander's interest in the interpleaded funds was unperfected under Florida law on July 3, 1986, it was subordinate to that of a UCC lien creditor. See Fl. Stat. ch. 679.301(1)(b). Highlander's interest, therefore, was not protected under local law against a judgment lien arising on that date; it was not a "security interest" within the meaning of 26 U.S.C. § 6323(h)(1). The Government's tax lien is entitled to priority.

III. CONCLUSION

This appeal involves a priority contest between an unperfected security interest and a federal tax lien. The district court held that the tax lien takes priority. The case turns on whether the security interest is protected under local law against a "judgment lien"; if the answer is no, the tax lien takes priority. Because we hold that a judgment lien is equivalent to the interest of a UCC lien creditor, we conclude that the unperfected security interest at issue here is subordinate to a judgment lien under local law. Therefore, the federal tax lien is entitled to priority. Accordingly, we AFFIRM.

NOTE ON FEDERAL TAX LIENS AND FLOATING LIENS

Under § 6323(a) of the Federal Tax Lien Act (the "FTLA"), a tax lien is not valid against the holder of a security interest until notice of the lien is filed. As *Litton* makes clear, however, in a priority contest between an Article 9 security interest and a federal tax lien, the federal definition of security interest in FTLA § 6323(h)(1) controls. This is why an unperfected security interest is subordinate to a tax lien. In addition, under § 6323(h)(1) a security interest is deemed to exist only to the extent the property is in existence and the holder has parted with money or money's worth. Effectively, this means that both after acquired property and future advances are not protected against a filed federal tax lien. There is, however, a limited general exception for disbursements made to and property acquired by the debtor post-tax lien filing. Specifically, FTLA § 6323(d) affords priority to future advances made within 45 days following filing of the tax lien, *provided*, (i) the creditor had not obtained actual knowledge of the tax lien filing prior to making the advance, and (ii) the advance is protected under state law against a judgment lien arising as of the time of filing out of an unsecured obligation. FTLA § 6323(c) then contains a similar 45-day grace period for after acquired property, regardless of the secured party's knowledge. However, this exception for after acquired property applies only to "qualified property," a term defined in the FTLA to include most forms of commercial financing security *except* for equipment and farm products. See FTLA § 6323(c)(2)(B). For banks and finance companies, the operation of these twin 45-day rules eliminates the need to check for tax lien filings before making each advance or permitting any substitution of collateral. Instead, a creditor that conducts a proper search every 45 days will be fully protected. The Problem below illustrates the operation of these two rules.

PROBLEM

On February 10, Bank made a $15,000 loan to Debtor secured by a properly perfected lien on Debtor's inventory and receivables. The security agreement provided that the lien secured both the $15,000 loan and "any subsequent indebtedness of Debtor to Bank." On the same day, unbeknownst to Bank, the IRS assessed Debtor with a $25,000 delinquency for unpaid taxes. On March 1, the IRS filed its notice of tax lien in the office designated under state law for that purpose. On March 15, Debtor acquired new inventory and Bank made an optional advance to Debtor of $10,000. On April 17, Debtor acquired more new inventory and Bank made another advance of $5,000. On April 20, the IRS seized all of the Debtor's assets. What is the extent and priority of Bank's lien in Debtor's inventory?

(b) STATUTORY LIENS

UCC § 9-310

When a person in the ordinary course of his business furnishes services or materials with respect to goods subject to a security interest, a lien upon goods in the possession of such person given by statute or rule of law for such materials or services takes priority over a perfected security interest unless the lien is statutory and the statute expressly provides otherwise.

CHEMICAL BANK v. COMMUNICATIONS DATA SERVICES, INC.

United States District Court, Southern District of Iowa, 1991.
765 F. Supp. 1401.

VIETOR, Chief Judge.

This is a diversity of citizenship action for declaratory judgment by one creditor of the Mother Earth News Partners ("MEN") against another creditor of MEN that presents an issue of lien priorities. The property in question is MEN's master file of subscribers ("subscription list"). Plaintiff Chemical Bank ("Chemical") seeks a preliminary injunction against defendant Communications Data Services, Inc. ("CDS"), to stop CDS from foreclosing its purported artisan's lien on the subscription list by sale of the list.

On February 15, 1991, I issued a temporary restraining order prohibiting the sale by CDS of the subscription list pending hearing and ruling on Chemical's motion for preliminary injunction. The hearing was held on March 27, 1991.

FINDINGS OF FACT

CDS is an Iowa corporation that entered into several subscription fulfillment agreements with MEN; the most recent agreement (as amended) is dated October 1, 1985. Pursuant to the agreements, CDS has had possession of MEN's subscription list in Iowa since 1979, and provided subscription fulfillment services to Mother Earth News Magazine from 1979 to December 31, 1990. The services CDS provided, according to the subscription fulfillment agreement, include caging (receiving orders), entering transactions (orders, payments, address changes, etc.), editing transactions, maintaining the master file, billing and accounts receivable, mailing regular renewal promotions and other promotions, printing mailing labels and sorting labels, keeping track of postal service forms and payments, providing lettershop services, answering correspondence, and completing several operating reports. The information CDS maintained for MEN includes the subscriber's name and address, any premium codes, and promotional and historical data. CDS also developed customized software programs for MEN (billing 570 program hours since 1987, according to John Meneough, CDS vice-president), which allowed MEN to extract the data it found useful. Under the terms of the subscription fulfillment agreement, CDS bills MEN the first week of each calendar month for services it performed in the preceding month. Payment is due on or before the 10th of the month following the month in which MEN receives the invoice. CDS performed all of its services for MEN in Iowa, and retains possession of the list in Iowa. The subscription fulfillment agreement states that the agreement "shall be construed under and governed by the laws of the State of New York."

On or about June 23, 1988, MEN and Chemical entered into a credit agreement and a security agreement pursuant to which Chemical made loans to MEN totaling $14,975,000. The security agreement states that MEN grants Chemical a first priority security interest in, among other things, all of MEN's "general intangibles," specifically including the subscription list. At the time of Chemical's loan to MEN, MEN paid CDS for services performed through April 1988, but not for services performed in May or June 1988. On or before June 30, 1988, Chemical duly filed Uniform Commercial Code financing statements with the secretaries of state and local filing offices in New York, Illinois, and North Carolina. The financing statements described Chemical's collateral as including the subscription list. Chemical did not file a financing statement in Iowa.

MEN is currently in default of its obligations to Chemical under the Credit Agreement in the outstanding principal amount of $14,975,000. The value of the subscription list is less than $14.9 million. MEN currently owes CDS $394,588.44 for fulfillment services performed, invoiced and billed monthly from September 1989 through December 31, 1990.

The last published issue of Mother Earth News Magazine was the November-December 1990 issue. Newsstand copies were sent out, but subscriber copies were not mailed. The magazine staff was laid off in late November or early December 1990.

Owen Lipstein, general partner of MEN, has been trying to market MEN since 1989, with only one prior serious negotiation which did not result in a sale. Lipstein has been conducting sale negotiations with the Japanese Independent Communications Company (JICC) since May 1990. At the time of this writing, JICC and Lipstein have not consummated a sale, but Lipstein testified that JICC has orally agreed to purchase MEN if certain terms and conditions are met, namely: (1) Chemical's acceptance of $5,750,000 in satisfaction of MEN's loan obligations; (2) settlement with state and federal taxing authorities regarding $1.7 million in tax liability; and (3) delivery of a balance sheet from unsecured creditors reducing the unsecured debt from over $10 million to approximately $3 million. JICC would also pay $500,000 cash in transaction fees. As of March 20, 1991, according to Lipstein, the settlement negotiations with the taxing authorities were still ongoing; vendors representing 4 percent of the total unsecured debt had agreed formally to the JICC terms; and nearly all of the 25 major vendors (representing about 75 percent of the total unsecured debt) had agreed in non-binding letters of intent. Chemical offered no testimony about these negotiations from JICC personnel or any of the vendors.

* * *

First, I must consider the question of which state's lien law applies. CDS argues that New York's lien law applies because the agreement between CDS and MEN provides that the laws of the state of New York shall govern the agreement. This case, however, does not involve a contract dispute between

CDS and MEN, but rather a dispute between creditors as to lien priority. The law which parties to a bailment contract select to govern their agreement does not control the question of which law applies to the validity and priority of an artisan's lien. In re Stookey Holsteins, Inc., 112 B.R. 942, 948 n. 8 (Bankr.N.D.Ind.1990). An artisan's lien is governed by the law of the state in which the property is located and possessed. See A.L.U. Textile Combining Corp. v. First Hartford Corp., 25 B.R. 563, 564 (Bankr.S.D.N.Y.1982), aff'd, 33 B.R. 126 (S.D.N.Y.1983); 8 Am.Jur.2d, Bailments § 243. Because CDS possessed the subscription list and performed services on it in Iowa, and the list remains in Iowa, Iowa's lien law applies.

The second inquiry is whether CDS has an artisan's lien under Iowa law. I conclude that it does. The Iowa artisan's lien statute provides:

> Any person who renders any service or furnishes any material in the making, repairing, improving, or enhancing the value of any inanimate personal property, with the assent of the owner, express or implied, shall have a lien thereon for the agreed or reasonable compensation for the service and material while such property is lawfully in the person's possession, which possession the person may retain until such compensation is paid, but such lien shall be subject to all prior liens of record, unless notice is given to all lien holders of record and written consent is obtained from all lien holders of record to the making, repairing, improving, or enhancing the value of any inanimate personal property and in this event the lien created under this section shall be prior to liens of record.

Iowa Code § 577.1. Chemical argues that the services CDS provided were merely clerical. I disagree. The services CDS performed for MEN involve taking raw data supplied from various sources, and transforming the data into a form CDS could use for a multitude of purposes for the benefit of MEN. By updating and maintaining the list, and by manipulating the data with customized software, CDS provided a current and valuable product to MEN. These services improved or enhanced the value of the list within the meaning of section 577.1. See American Consumer, Inc. v. Anchor Computers, Inc., 93 Misc.2d 452, 453, 402 N.Y.S.2d 734 (Sup.Ct.N.Y.1978) (computer services performed on customer mailing list enhanced the value of the computer tapes, giving service provider artisan's lien under New York law). CDS also meets the other requirements of an artisan's lien: The owner of the list expressly assented to the services, the list is and has been in the lawful possession of CDS, and CDS has not received the agreed upon compensation for all of the services it has performed for MEN.

The third issue is whose lien takes priority over the other. The Iowa Uniform Commercial Code states: When a person in the ordinary course of his business furnishes services or materials with respect to goods subject to a security interest, a lien upon goods in the possession of such person given by statute or rule of law for such materials or services takes priority over a perfected security interest unless the lien is statutory and the statute expressly provides otherwise. Iowa Code § 554.9310. The Iowa artisan's lien statute does expressly provide otherwise when the perfected security interest (or other lien) is a "prior lien of record." § 577.1.[1] Chemical's lien is a "prior lien of record" within the meaning of section 577.1 only if Chemical perfected its lien (i.e., filed appropriate financing statements under the UCC) before CDS performed services improving or enhancing the value of the subscription list. See Municipal Equip. v. Butch & Son Deep Rock, 185 N.W.2d 756, 759 (Iowa 1971) (lien on a car, perfected before the holder of an artisan's lien had possession of or performed services on the car, held superior under Iowa law). CDS obtained an artisan's lien on the subscription list in 1979 by taking possession of the list and performing services on it. See id. at 758. CDS, therefore, obtained its lien well before Chemical perfected its lien.

Chemical argues that it holds the prior lien because at the time it perfected its security interest in the list, MEN had fully paid the invoices that were outstanding, and payment for the services performed in May and June of 1988 was not yet due. An artisan's lien, however, arises on rendering the service, not on some later date when payment for the service falls due. CDS began providing services long before Chemical obtained its security interest, continued to constantly provide services after that intervening event, and at no time did MEN fully pay CDS for all the services it had rendered.

Chemical also argues that because CDS has now been paid for all services rendered before June 23, 1988, and the artisan's lien CDS currently asserts is security only for payment of services performed after that date, Chemical's lien is a prior lien. I do not agree. Once CDS's lien arose in 1979, it remained in effect by virtue of CDS's continuous possession of the list and continuous performance of services on it for MEN. Chemical's lien cannot meet the statutory requirement of being "prior" to CDS's lien, because Chemical did not perfect its lien before CDS began performing services on the list in its possession. Chemical's position that an intervening lien becomes a hybrid-subordinate to the artisan's lien for prior services but prior to the artisan's lien for subsequent services-finds no support in the language of the lien statute. Furthermore, such a construction of the lien statute would put an extremely unfair and highly burdensome obligation on the artisan, requiring that it constantly check the public lien records (in this case, in other states) to see if the property on which it is performing services has suddenly been mortgaged. On the other hand, the party lending money and taking a mortgage has only the minimal burden of checking the physical location of the property mortgaged to ascertain whether it is in the hands of an artisan. Because Chemical's lien is not a prior lien of record under Iowa law, it is subordinate to the lien of CDS.

Irreparable Harm to Plaintiff

Chemical argues that the sale of the subscription list by CDS would drastically reduce the value of MEN as a going business for sale purposes, and thereby would cause irreparable harm to Chemical by decreasing the value of its collateral. Owen Lipstein, however, has been trying to sell MEN for nearly two years and has not yet succeeded. Lipstein currently has only one negotiation

---

1 The parties dispute whether Chemical had to file a financing statement in Iowa * * *. I need not address that issue now, and for purposes of this ruling I assume without even tentatively deciding that Chemical did not have to file in Iowa.

going, and that began almost a year ago. The evidence regarding the status of that negotiation indicates that the possibility of actually consummating a sale is extremely unlikely. Therefore, only a very slim chance of harm to Chemical exists if the preliminary injunction does not issue. Furthermore, Chemical can totally avoid even that slim chance of harm by buying the subscription list at CDS's foreclosure sale. By purchasing the subscription list, Chemical would keep open whatever possibility exists of a sale to JICC or another interested party, thereby precluding irreparable harm.

* * *

Applying and weighing the four * * * factors for issuance of preliminary injunctive relief leads me to conclude that the preliminary injunction sought by Chemical should not be granted. The funds from any foreclosure sale of the subscription list should, however, be held in escrow pending the final decision in this case. The parties raise other arguments, but I need not decide those issues at the preliminary injunction stage.

CURRY GRAIN STORAGE, INC. v. HESSTON CORP.

Supreme Court of Idaho, 1991.
120 Idaho 328, 815 P.2d 1068.

[Ida-Man, Inc. held an ownership interest in grass seed, which it delivered to Curry who cleaned and processed the seed and stored it against warehouse receipts. Hesston Corporation granted credit to Ida-Man in return for a security interest in the seed. This is an action by Curry in the nature of interpleader to determine whether Hesston's security interest defeats Curry's lien under section 7-209.]

JOHNSON, Justice.

* * *

III

CURRY'S LIEN IS NOT EFFECTIVE AGAINST HESSTON'S SECURITY INTEREST IN THE SEED.

Curry asserts that its lien is effective against Hesston's security interest in the seed. We disagree.

Pursuant to I.C. § 28-7-209(1), Curry had a lien against Ida-Man and the harvesters for its charges for cleaning, processing, and storing the seed. The issue presented for our resolution is whether Curry's lien is effective against Hesston under I.C. § 28-7-209(3)(a). The pertinent part of this section provides: (3)(a) A warehouseman's lien for charges and expenses under subsection (1) * * * is also effective against any person who so entrusted the bailor with possession of the goods that a pledge of them by [the bailor] to a good faith purchaser for value would have been valid but is not effective against a person as to whom the document confers no right in the goods covered by it under section 28-7-503. I.C. § 28-7-209(3)(a).

Curry argues that priority is determined under I.C. § 28-9-310. * * *

Under this statute, Curry's lien pursuant to I.C. § 28-7-209(1) takes priority over Hesston's perfected security interest unless I.C. § 28-7-209(3)(a) expressly provides otherwise. We conclude that I.C. § 28-7-209(3)(a) does expressly provide otherwise.

Pursuant to I.C. § 28-7-209(3)(a), Curry's lien is effective against Hesston only if Hesston so entrusted Ida-Man with possession of the seed that a pledge of the seed by Ida-Man to a good faith purchaser for value would have been valid. Also, Curry's lien is not effective against Hesston if under I.C. § 28-7-503, the weight tickets confer no right in the seed to Hesston. These express provisions of I.C. § 28-7-209(3)(a) take precedence over the priority provided in I.C. § 28-9-310.

We have frequently considered the comments to the official text of the UCC in determining the meaning of the text. We are supported in our conclusion here by the comment to the official text of I.C. § 28-7-209(3)(a), which includes this statement: Where the third party is the holder of a security interest, the rights of the warehouseman depend on the priority given to a hypothetical bona fide pledgee by Article [Chapter] 9, particularly Section 9-312. Thus the special priority granted to statutory liens by Section 9-310 does not apply to liens under subsection (1) of this section, since subsection (3) "expressly provides otherwise" within the meaning of Section 9-310.

We must then turn to the question whether Hesston so entrusted Ida-Man with the possession of the seed that a pledge of the seed to a hypothetical bona fide pledgee would have given the pledgee priority over Hesston. A pledge is defined as "a bailment; it is a bailment made for the purpose of security. Usually it secures a debt * * *." R. Braucher & A. Sutherland, Commercial Transactions 135 (2d ed. 1958).

I.C. § 28-9-312 states the priorities among conflicting security interests in the same collateral. In all cases not governed by other rules stated in this section, conflicting security interests rank according to priority in time of filing or perfection. I.C. § 28-9-312(5)(a). None of the other rules stated in the section apply. Therefore, since Hesston's security interest in the seed was perfected before the seed was delivered to Curry, Hesston's security interest has priority.

Curry argues that the decision in Vollmer C. Co., v. Union Warehouse & Supply Co., 43 Idaho 37, 248 P. 865 (1926) dictates a different result than the one we have reached. In Vollmer, the Court said: A warehouseman has a lien "on goods deposited or on the proceeds thereof in his hands, for all lawful charges for storage * * * of the goods; * * *." (C.S., sec. 6145.) The statute does not make such a lien superior to that of the lien of a chattel mortgage on the stored goods. But a warehouseman's lien for storage takes precedence over the lien of a chattel mortgage where the mortgagee consents to the storage.

Curry would have us apply Vollmer as authority for the proposition that consent by the holder of a prior perfected security interest to storage constitutes entrustment as contemplated in I.C. § 28-7-209(3)(a). The basis of this argument is that at the time Vollmer was decided, § 6146 of the Idaho statutes provided similarly to I.C. § 28-7-209(3)(a), as follows: [A] warehouseman's lien may be enforced: * * *. 2. Against all goods belonging to others which have been deposited at any time by the person who is liable as debtor for the claims in regard to which the lien is asserted if such person had been so intrusted with the possession of the goods that a pledge of the same by him at the time of the deposit to one who took the goods in good faith for value would have been valid. C.S. § 6146.

Section 6146 was not cited in Vollmer, however. Section 6145 was the only statute cited. Section 6145 did not deal with priority of the warehouse lien, but only with the claims that were included in the lien. In addition, the California case cited in Vollmer—Schmidt v. Bekins Van & Storage Co.—did not cite California statutes in support of the statement at issue. In Schmidt, the California court cited 40 Cyc. 458 as the source of the rule: A warehouseman is not entitled to retain mortgaged property to enforce his lien for charges when it was stored in violation of the provisions of the mortgage, without the mortgagee's consent, and no promise can be implied from the mortgage's silence. 155 P. at 648.

Consent is not the issue in this case. The issue is whether Hesston so entrusted the seed to Ida-Man that Ida-Man could have pledged the seed to a hypothetical bona fide pledgee to defeat Hesston's perfected security interest. Our analysis of this issue is not affected by Vollmer.

IV.

CONCLUSION.

We affirm the order of the trial court and remand the case for further proceedings consistent with our opinion.

NOTE ON REVISED ARTICLE 9

Revised § 9-330 continues the rule of current § 9-310 with respect to possessory liens arising by operation of law. In addition, the revision originally proposed (through the draft that we used in preparing this text) to extend the scope of Article 9 to cover nonpossessory statutory liens, defined in Revised § 9-102(53A) as "an interest in personal property: (i) which secures payment or performance of an obligation; (ii) which is created by statute [in favor of a person that in the ordinary course of its business furnishes goods or services,]; (iii) and the effectiveness of which does not depend on the person's possession of personal property." During its November, 1997, meeting, however, the Drafting Committee decided to remove non-agricultural, nonpossessory statutory liens from the scope of Revised Article 9. Nevertheless, we think it is instructive to consider how priority issues would have been treated if they had been included.

Generally, statutory liens were to be perfected by filing, Revised § 9-309(a), and priority between a statutory lien and a conflicting security interest determined under the general first to file or perfect rule. Revised § 9-319A(a)(1). However, if the statute under which the statutory lien arose contained its own rule of priority, the revision would have deferred to that rule. Revised § 9-

319A(c). Finally, the enforcement of statutory liens was to have been governed by the terms of the statute under which the lien arose and, thus, excluded from the enforcement provisions in Part 6 of Revised Article 9. See Revised § 9-601(e).

Revised Article 9 does continue to bring within its scope "agricultural liens," which are farm products liens created by statute to secure payment or performance of an obligation for either goods or services supplied to a debtor engaged in farming operations or rent on real property leased to a debtor engaged in farming operations. Revised § 9-102(3). Pursuant to Revised § 9-309(a), agricultural liens must be perfected by filing. Revised § 9-319(a)(1) then establishes a first to file or perfect rule of priority among both multiple agricultural liens and as between an agricultural lien and a conflicting security interest. Also, enforcement of agricultural liens, unlike the treatment that had been proposed for other forms of statutory liens, is governed by Part 6 of Revised Article 9.

An agricultural lien is distinct from a "production money security interest,"* which is defined as a security interest in crops given to secure an obligation to enable the debtor to produce the crops. Revised § 9-105(a). Production money security interests are, under certain conditions, afforded priority over even an earlier filed security interest in the same crops. See Revised § 9-321. If a person holds both an agricultural lien and a production money security interest in the same collateral, Revised § 9-321(d) provides that the priority rules applicable to agricultural liens govern. However, the Reporters' Comments suggest that a creditor can avoid this result by waiving its agricultural lien. The production money security interest, although a new concept under the revision, obviously has its origins in current § 9-312(2). That provision establishes a limited purchase money priority for certain crop loans, but has generally been regarded as ineffective in accomplishing its purpose of encouraging credit to permit farmers to plant a new crop. See generally United States v. Minster Farmers Coop. Exchange, Inc., 430 F.Supp. 566 (N.D. Ohio 1977).

SECTION 5. REAL ESTATE OWNERS AND ENCUMBRANCERS

UCC § 9-313

(*see Selected Commercial Statutes*)

---

* At its November, 1997, meeting, the Drafting Committee also expressed its position that the provisions on production money security interests should be presented only as a "model" and that Revised Article 9 should take no position as to these provisions on the merits [eds.].

IN RE CLIFF'S RIDGE SKIING CORP.

United States Bankruptcy Court, Western District of Michigan, 1991.
123 B.R. 753.

[In July of 1980 Cliff's Ridge Development granted a mortgage in its ski slopes and security interest in fixtures on the slopes to First of America (FOA). FOA made a proper fixture filing.

In November of 1982 Cliff's Ridge Development sold its slopes to Cliff's Ridge Skiing (which later filed in bankruptcy and is the debtor in this proceeding) and retained a second mortgage on the real estate to secure the purchase price.

In December of 1982 First National made a purchase money loan to the debtor to acquire a chair lift. First National made a fixture filing with the Register of Deeds and a regular filing with the Secretary of State. The fixture filing recited that the goods were to be affixed on November 24, 1982. FOA agreed to subordinate its interest in the lift to First National's security interest.

The three creditors are here claiming the proceeds of the sale of the lift.]

JAMES D. GREGG, Bankruptcy Judge.

DISCUSSION

Is the Chairlift a Fixture?

Mich.Comp.Laws Ann. § 440.9313(1)(a) states: "Goods are 'fixtures' when they become so related to particular real estate that an interest in them arises under real estate law." Uniform Commercial Code § 9-313(1)(a) is "unhelpful" and "it is merely an invitation to read the real estate statutes and the local case law on what is and what is not a fixture." White & Summers, Uniform Commercial Code 1153 (3rd ed. 1988).

In Michigan, whether personal property becomes a fixture and thereby part of realty is determined by a three-part test: (1) is the property annexed or attached to the realty, (2) is the attached property adapted or applied to the use of the realty, and (3) is it intended that the property will be permanently attached to the realty? The three-part test remains valid under current Michigan law.

In this case, FOA and Cliff's Ridge Dev. each assert the chairlift is a fixture, was annexed to the realty, and is therefore subject to their respective prior recorded mortgages. FOA and Cliff's Ridge Dev. each implicitly assert that the three-part test has been satisfied. First National does not seriously dispute that the chairlift is a fixture. However, First National has not stipulated to such a determination. This court must therefore determine whether the chairlift is a fixture.

The chairlift was attached to the realty. Concrete pads were poured in the realty prior to the erection of the chairlift. Towers were then bolted to the concrete pads, cables were strung, and about 100 chairs were attached to the cables. The parties have stipulated that "chairlifts are part of ski hills but can be severed from the ski hills and sold." The court finds the chairlift was annexed or attached to the real property.

The parties have stipulated that the chairlift was engineered to be erected on the realty and the chairlift was specially modified to be attached to the realty. The court finds the chairlift was adapted to the ski hill real property for its use and purposes.

Very little testimony exists whether the parties intended to permanently affix the chairlift to the real estate. In the Project Plan, and other documents relating to the Debtor's request to obtain EDC financing, it is stated that the loan was intended to finance "construction" and "installation" of the chairlift "improvements" to the realty. Final approval of the requested financing was conditioned upon conveyance of the realty from Cliff's Ridge Dev. to the Debtor. In two financing statements dated December 14 and December 15, 1982, filed by First National, it is stated, "The goods are to become fixtures on 11-24-82." No other evidence regarding intent has been introduced by any party. Under Michigan law, attachments to realty to facilitate its use become part of the realty and, if done by the owner, are presumed to be permanent. Based upon the preponderance of the evidence, the court finds the Debtor intended to permanently affix the chairlift to the realty.

Under governing Michigan law, all requirements of the three-part test to determine whether personal property has become a fixture have been met. The court concludes that the chairlift in dispute is a fixture.

Creation and Perfection of an Interest in Fixtures.

Under Michigan law, there are two methods by which a creditor may create and perfect an interest in fixtures. A creditor may utilize procedures under Michigan real estate law. Alternatively, a creditor may take a security interest in a fixture and perfect that interest under the Uniform Commercial Code as adopted in Michigan ("U.C.C.").

Article 9 of the U.C.C. allows the creation of an interest in fixtures pursuant to state real estate law. Prior to adoption of the U.C.C., Michigan law was well-settled that once a fixture is annexed or attached to realty, the fixture became part of the realty and title to the fixture is subject to a real estate mortgage.

* * *

Once a mortgage creates an interest in fixtures under Michigan real estate law, the interest must be perfected. Perfection under state real estate law is accomplished by recordation of the mortgage in the county where the real property is located.

The second method by which a security interest in fixtures may be created and perfected is under the U.C.C. without reference to state real estate law. A "security interest" is defined very broadly to mean "an interest in personal property or *fixtures* which secures repayment of an obligation." Mich.Comp.Laws Ann. § 440.1201(37) (emphasis supplied). Article 9 of the U.C.C. applies "[t]o any transaction (regardless of its form) which is intended to create a security interest in personal property or *fixtures* * * *." Mich.Comp.Laws Ann. § 440.9102(1)(a) (emphasis supplied).

* * *

The financing statement which covers fixtures, or goods to become fixtures, must be filed where a mortgage on the real estate would be recorded. Mich.Comp.Laws Ann. § 440.9401(1)(b). In Michigan, an interest in real estate is properly recorded at the register of deeds in the county in which the real estate is located. Mich.Comp.Laws Ann. §§ 53.145; 565.1; 565.23. When a sufficient financing statement is filed in the proper place, a "fixture filing" occurs. Mich.Comp.Laws Ann. § 440.9313(1)(b). After a proper fixture filing, a secured party has a perfected interest in the fixtures and may enforce its security interest against other persons according to designated priorities. Mich.Comp.Laws Ann. § 440.9313(4), (5), (6) and (7).

Under the U.C.C., a mortgage may be effective as a fixture filing from the date of its recordation provided four specified requirements are met, including that the mortgage describes the goods by "item or type". An issue exists whether this U.C.C. subsection mandates that a mortgage creating an interest in fixtures under state real estate law must contain a sufficient description of the fixtures, or the goods to become fixtures, by "item or type". At the hearing, some argument was made that if a mortgage fails to include such a description, no valid interest in fixtures can be created under state real estate law. The court has been unable to discover any reported case which addresses this issue.

As discussed above, an interest in fixtures, or goods which become fixtures, may be created under state real estate law, or under the U.C.C. State real estate law creates real property interests in fixtures while the U.C.C. allows creation of personal property interests in fixtures. The U.C.C. establishes priorities resolving conflict between these distinct legal creatures on "turbulent waters * * * with difficulty". White & Summers, Uniform Commercial Code 1151 (3rd ed. 1988).

A "sufficient" fixture filing requires a "statement indicating the types or describing the items of collateral." Mich.Comp.Laws Ann. § 440.9402(1). A complying mortgage filed in lieu of a financing statement must also contain, among other things, a description of goods "by item or type". Mich.Comp.Laws Ann. § 440.9402(6). The U.C.C. requires, whether a fixture filing is accomplished by filing a financing statement or recording a complying mortgage, the information included must be the same. However, the U.C.C. also permits a valid security interest in fixtures to be created under state real estate law. Mich.Comp.Laws Ann. § 440.9313(3).

The U.C.C. requirement that the type or items of collateral be adequately described applies only to the creation and perfection of personal property interests in fixtures under the U.C.C.; this U.C.C. requirement does not apply to creation and perfection of real property interests in fixtures under state real estate law. U.C.C. law and state real estate law are separate and distinct methods by which interests in fixtures are created and perfected. The court therefore rejects any argument that the collateral must be explicitly described by item or type in a mortgage which otherwise creates an interest in fixtures under state real estate law.

Do the Creditors Hold a Valid Interest in the Chairlift and the Proceeds?

FOA's mortgage on the real property where the chairlift was affixed was granted on July 24, 1980; the mortgage was properly recorded on August 1, 1980. The mortgage granted FOA an interest in the real property together with "all improvements now or hereafter created on the property * * * and all fixtures now or hereafter attached to the property, all of which, including replacements and additions thereto, shall be deemed to be and remain a part of the property covered by this mortgage."

When a fixture becomes complemental to real property, it becomes a permanent accession and the fixture becomes part of the security with regard to any existing mortgage. The language in FOA's prior recorded mortgage is sufficient to create and perfect its interest in the chairlift fixture under state real estate law. FOA retained its interest in the proceeds pursuant to this court's order whereby valid liens would attach to the proceeds of the sale.

Cliff's Ridge Dev.'s mortgage on the real property where the chairlift was affixed was granted on November 22, 1982; the mortgage was properly recorded on November 23, 1982. The mortgage itself recognizes FOA's prior mortgage and states Cliff's Ridge Dev.'s interest is subordinate to FOA's prior mortgage. Cliff's Ridge Dev.'s mortgage grants an interest in the real property together "with the hereditaments and appurtenances thereunto belonging or in anywise appertaining." There is no language in the mortgage relating to "fixtures". An "appurtenance" is an "article adapted to the use of the property to which it is connected, and which was intended to be a permanent accession to the freehold." Black's Law Dictionary 94 (5th Ed. West Publishing Co.1979). An "appurtenance" is equivalent to a "fixture".

A mortgage covers fixtures even when they are not explicitly mentioned in the mortgage. If the chairlift became connected to the real property after the grant of Cliff's Ridge Dev.'s mortgage, Cliff's Ridge Dev. has an interest in the chairlift; the appurtenance or fixture becomes part of the security with regard to any existing mortgage. On the other hand, if the chairlift became connected to the real property before the grant of the mortgage, the chairlift would be covered by the subsequent mortgage without a special mention in the mortgage. Therefore, under state real estate law, Cliff's Ridge Dev. has an interest in the chairlift. Cliff's Ridge Dev. also has an interest in the proceeds from the chairlift sale in accordance with the court's prior order.

On December 13, 1982, the Debtor granted the EDC a security interest in the chairlift. On the same date, the EDC assigned its security interest to First National. As of December 13, 1982, the Debtor had signed a security agreement which described the collateral and rights in the collateral. On December 17, 1982, First National made its first loan disbursement of $100,000 to the Debtor. Since there was no agreement to postpone attachment of the security interest, First National's attachment of the security interest occurred on December 17, 1982. Mich.Comp.Laws Ann. § 440.9203(2).

On December 14, 1982, a financing statement regarding the chairlift was filed where mortgages are recorded with the Marquette County Register of

Deeds. The form of the financing statement meets all the necessary requirements under the U.C.C.Mich.Comp.Laws Ann. § 440.9402(1) and (5). A sufficient financing statement regarding the chairlift fixture was filed in the proper place and a "fixture filing" occurred. Mich.Comp.Laws Ann. §§ 440.9313(1)(b); 440.9401(1)(b). First National therefore holds a perfected personal property interest in the chairlift under the U.C.C. It now also holds an interest in the sale proceeds pursuant to this court's prior order.

If these were the only facts and law to be applied, the court would now easily apply the U.C.C. priority rules and determine entitlement to the sale proceeds. Unfortunately, sorting out commercial security transactions is not always so simple.

Does First National Hold a Purchase Money Security Interest in the Chairlift and the Proceeds?

First National asserts it held a purchase money security interest in the chairlift. First National therefore argues it is entitled to the sale proceeds because it holds an interest which is superior to FOA's and Cliff's Ridge Dev.'s mortgage interests.

The general rule of priority is that a security interest in fixtures is subordinate to a conflicting interest held by a mortgagee of the related real estate. Mich.Comp.Laws Ann. § 440.9313(7). Under the general rule, FOA's and Cliff's Ridge's mortgage interests would be superior to First National's interest in the chairlift fixture.

One exception to the general rule governs where the security interest in fixtures is (1) a purchase money security interest, (2) the interest of the mortgagee arose before the goods became fixtures, (3) a valid fixture filing occurred before the goods became fixtures or within 10 days thereafter, and (4) the debtor has an interest of record in the real estate. Mich.Comp.Laws Ann. § 440.9313(4)(a).

The first requirement raises the threshold issue: Does First National hold a purchase money security interest? Mich.Comp.Laws Ann. § 440.9107 states: A security interest is a "purchase money security interest" to the extent that it is (a) taken or retained by the seller of the collateral to secure all or part of its price; or (b) taken by a person who by making advances or incurring an obligation gives value to enable the debtor to acquire rights in or the use of collateral if such value is in fact so used. The Debtor purchased the chairlift from the Breckenridge Ski Area sometime after April or May, 1982 on a cash-on-delivery basis. Therefore, First National was not the "seller of the collateral" and no purchase money security interest arose under Mich.Comp.Laws Ann. § 440.9107(a).

First National advanced funds to the Debtor pursuant to the loan transaction—$100,000 was disbursed on December 17, 1982 and $49,864.34 was disbursed on December 23, 1982. The chairlift was delivered in August, 1982. The parties have stipulated that the sale was to be on a cash-on-delivery basis although it is also stipulated that the time that Breckenridge was actually paid is not known. Because delivery of the chairlift occurred approximately four months before First National made any loan advance, the court concludes the value given by First National did not "enable" the Debtor to acquire the chairlift. Further, there are no facts in the record to support that the value, i.e., the funds disbursed by First National, was "in fact so used" by the Debtor to purchase the chairlift. Although the Debtor paid $65,000 for the chairlift, the Debtor also paid $10,000 for shipping, $7,500 for engineering, and approximately $80,000 for erection of the chairlift. Given the stipulated facts that (1) the chairlift was delivered in August, 1982; (2) the erection of the chairlift towers commenced in September, 1982; (3) the erection of the towers was completed by November 15, 1982; (4) the cable was strung in November, 1982; (5) the cable was spliced on December 2, 1982; and (6) the chairlift was tested with the chairs in place on December 7, 1982—it thus appears that the costs were either paid, or incurred, by the Debtor prior to the time First National made the advances.

First National has the burden of proof, by preponderance of evidence, to demonstrate that it holds a purchase money security interest pursuant to the statutory requirements of Mich.Comp.Laws Ann. § 440.9107(b). Based upon the court's findings of fact, First National has failed to meet its burden of proof. The court concludes it does not hold a purchase money security interest in the chairlift.

* * *

Resolution of Priority to Chairlift Proceeds.

Priority of competing or conflicting interests in a fixture is governed by the U.C.C. In certain specified instances, a holder of a perfected security interest in a fixture will have priority over a prior encumbrancer under real estate law. Mich.Comp.Laws Ann. § 440.9313(4). An encumbrancer includes the holder of a real estate mortgage. Mich.Comp.Laws Ann. § 440.9105(1)(g). In other instances, a holder of a perfected security interest in a fixture will be subordinate to a conflicting interest of an encumbrancer of the related real estate. Mich.Comp.Laws Ann. § 440.9313(7).

A leading commentator has succinctly stated the U.C.C. fixture priority general rule which is germane to this dispute. This court sees no need to attempt to improve the comment or restate the general rule. "The first-in-time-first-in-right rule runs throughout Article Nine, and 9-313 is no different * * *. If the fixture lender perfects by a fixture filing before the real estate creditor files a mortgage on the real estate to which the goods have become affixed, the fixture lender has priority. If the mortgagee files first, he wins." White & Summers, Uniform Commercial Code 1156 (3rd ed. 1988).

In accordance with this court's factual findings, the general fixture priority rule initially governs. First National does not hold a perfected purchase money security interest in the chairlift. Cliff's Ridge Dev., as an encumbrancer, did not consent in writing to First National's security interest or disclaim its interest in the chairlift as a fixture. No other specific exception to the general fixture priority rule is applicable. Therefore, absent FOA's subordination, the priority of the parties' interests in the chairlift would be: First, FOA as a real estate encumbrancer; second, Cliff's Ridge Dev. as a real estate encumbrancer; and third, First National as holding a perfected security interest.

As a result of the Subordination Agreement between FOA and First National, the respective initial priorities have been consensually altered. However, Cliff's Ridge Dev.'s priority has not been affected because it was not a party to the subordination. Based upon the subordination, the priority is altered as follows: (1) FOA is prior to Cliff's Ridge Dev.; (2) Cliff's Ridge Dev. is prior to First National; and (3) First National is prior to FOA. The classic circular priority conundrum (of the kind briefly addressed, but seldom resolved, in law school) therefore exists. How should the circular priority be resolved? The parties and the court have been unable to discover any Michigan reported cases discussing circular priorities.

* * *

The court believes that the effect of the Subordination Agreement should be construed as FOA and First National having "traded places" to the extent of the money advanced by First National to the Debtor for the chairlift loan which remains unpaid or the remaining mortgage balance owed to FOA by the Debtor, whichever is less. By so doing, Cliff's Ridge Dev.'s interest and its original priority position will not be adversely or beneficially affected by the other parties' subordination agreement.

After a careful review of the case law cited by the parties and after conducting independent research, this court has determined to follow the circular priority formula set forth in ITT Diversified Credit Corp. v. First City Capital Corp., 737 S.W.2d 803, 804, 4 U.C.C.Rep.Serv.2d 927, 929 (1987): For example, A, B and C have claims against the debtor which are entitled to priority in alphabetical order. "A" subordinates his claim to "C." After foreclosure of the secured interest, the resulting fund is insufficient to satisfy all three claims. The proper distribution of the fund is as follows. 1. Set aside from the fund the amount of "A"'s claim. 2. Out of the money set aside, pay "C" the amount of its claim, pay "A" to the extent of any balance remaining after "C"'s claim is satisfied. 3. Pay "B" the amount of the fund remaining after "A"'s claim has been set aside. 4. If any balance remains in the fund after "A"'s claim has been set aside and "B"'s claim has been satisfied, distribute the balance to "C" and "A". See Gilmore, Security Interests in Personal Property § 39.1 at 1021 (1965). Thus, "C", by virtue of the subordination agreement, is paid first, but only to the amount of "A"'s claim, to which "B" was in any event junior. "B" receives what it had expected to receive, the fund less "A"'s prior claim. If "A"'s claim is smaller than "C"'s, "C" will collect the balance of its claim, in its own right, only after "B" has been paid in full. "A", the subordinator, receives nothing until "B" and "C" have been paid except to the extent that its claim, entitled to first priority, exceeds the amount of "C"'s claim, which, under its agreement, is to be first paid.

Cliff's Ridge Dev. argues that the subordination by FOA to First National mandates that FOA's initial first priority status should be entirely relegated to a third position behind both Cliff's Ridge Dev. and First National [citations omitted]. If this argument is accepted, Cliff's Ridge Dev. would be beneficially elevated to the first priority and become entitled to receive the chairlift sale proceeds.

This court declines to follow those cases cited by Cliff's Ridge Dev. and rejects its argument. FOA did not subordinate its entire real estate mortgage to First National; FOA only subordinated its mortgage interest to the extent it covered the chairlift to be attached as a fixture. The partial subordination by FOA is more akin to the facts of ITT Diversified rather than those cases relied upon by Cliff's Ridge Dev. More importantly, this court strongly believes that the better reasoned resolution of the circular priority dilemma mandates that Cliff's Ridge Dev.'s initial priority should not be altered, either beneficially or adversely, as a result of a subordination agreement to which it was not a party.

FOA, Cliff's Ridge Dev. and First National each hold claims in amounts in excess of the proceeds realized from the sale of the chairlift. Applying the circular priority formula set forth in ITT Diversified, after paying "C" (First National) a portion of the amount of its claim, the fund is completely exhausted. No remaining funds are available for distribution to either "A" (FOA) or "B" (Cliff's Ridge Dev.).

* * *

PROBLEMS

1. Homer Owner purchased a new dishwasher from AAA Appliances on credit. AAA had Homer sign a security agreement granting AAA a security interest in the dishwasher to secure the unpaid balance of the purchase price. AAA did not file a financing statement. Homer installed the dishwasher in the kitchen of his home under one of the counters. Two months later, Homer files a chapter 7 bankruptcy petition. AAA has filed a claim as a secured creditor in Homer's bankruptcy case, and the trustee has moved to set aside AAA's security interest under § 544(a) of the Bankruptcy Code. Assuming the dishwasher is not a fixture, will the trustee prevail? What result assuming the dishwasher is a fixture? See § 9-313(4)(d).

2. Assume the same facts as above, except that two months after installing the dishwasher, Homer grants First Fidelity a mortgage on the property. The mortgage, which is promptly recorded with the County Recorder of Deeds, contains a clause indicating that the lien created by the mortgage extends to "all improvements, accessions, appurtenances, and fixtures," located on the property. If Homer later defaults on both obligations, which party has priority in the dishwasher?

3. Assume the same facts as above except that: (i) the First Fidelity Mortgage is granted and recorded five days after the dishwasher is installed by Homer, and (ii) two days later AAA does a proper fixture filing with respect to the dishwasher. If Homer later defaults on both obligations, which creditor is prior? See § 9-313(4)(a) and (b).

4. Assume the same facts as Question 1 above, except that: (i) Homer leases the house from Lucy Lessor, and (ii) AAA filed a financing statement on the day

after the sale referring to Homer as the debtor and containing a description of both the dishwasher and the property on which it was to be installed. AAA filed the financing statement in the UCC records and in the office where a mortgage on the property would be recorded where it was indexed under Homer's name. Two months later, Homer vacated the premises and was never heard from again. When AAA demanded access to the property to repossess the dishwasher, Lucy objected, claiming that the dishwasher was part of the real estate which had reverted to her upon Homer's default. Consult §§ 9-402(5), 9-313(5) and analyze whether Lucy is right. See also Lewiston Bottled Gas Company v. Key Bank of Maine, 601 A.2d 91 (Me. 1992).

5. Assume the same facts as Question 4 except that: (i) the financing statement filed by AAA showed Lucy as the record owner of the property and was cross-indexed under her name, and (ii) two years earlier Lucy had granted a mortgage to Solidarity State Bank which contained a standard "fixtures" clause. If AAA seeks to repossess the dishwasher after Homer's default, will it be entitled to priority over Solidarity? If so, what are Lucy and Solidarity's rights if removal of the dishwasher causes damage to the counter under which it had been installed? See § 9-313(8).

6. Assume the same facts as above except that, prior to any default by Homer, Lucy defaults on the Solidarity mortgage and Solidarity brings foreclosure proceedings. Upon learning of this action, AAA brings an action seeking a declaration that its debt is prior to Solidarity's mortgage and that, therefore, it should be entitled to priority in the funds received on foreclosure to the extent due on its debt from Homer. Will AAA prevail in this action? In answering this question consider the following Note.

NOTE ON REVISED ARTICLE 9

When an Article 9 fixture financer has priority in goods which have become fixtures, she is entitled under § 9-313(8) to remove the goods from the real estate, but must reimburse any encumbrancer or owner other than the debtor for damages to the premises caused by the removal. In some instances, those damages could be considerable. Thus, the question has arisen whether the fixture financer can proceed by means of a judicial foreclosure under state real property law or simply assert her interest in a foreclosure proceeding commenced by another party with an interest in the property. Several courts have answered this question in the negative. These courts reason that since § 9-313 does not provide a remedy against the realty itself, the fixture financer's right of removal in § 9-313(8) should be construed as an exclusive remedy. See Maplewood Bank v. Sears, Roebuck & Co., 625 A.2d 537 (N.J. 1994). Therefore, to permit a fixture financer to either conduct its own judicial foreclosure or assert a claim to proceeds in another party's real property foreclosure would undermine that remedial scheme. The drafters of Revised Article 9 were cognizant that this interpretation may work to deprive a fixture financer of a meaningful remedy when the goods in question are specially manufactured to fit the property or so integrated as impossible to remove except at great expense. Consequently,

Revised § 9-604(b) contains a provision, absent from current § 9-313, that expressly authorizes a fixture financer with priority to proceed *either* under Article 9 or state real property law.

Chapter 10

BANKRUPTCY AND RELATED INSOLVENCY LAWS

SECTION 1. STATE INSOLVENCY PROCEEDINGS

OVERVIEW

State debt collection law is frequently characterized, in contrast to federal bankruptcy law, as "grab law." The term colorfully captures the fact that in most instances the creditors who are first to reduce their claims to judgment and seize the debtor's assets will be paid in full, while other creditors whose claims share the same legal priority may go completely unsatisfied. In some instances, however, an insolvent debtor's principal creditors will voluntarily agree to a private arrangement under the terms of which the participating creditors will share equally in the proceeds from a voluntary liquidation of the debtor's assets. These agreements may provide for *extension* of the time for payment of participating creditor claims as well as *composition*, entailing only partial payment of creditor claims. In addition, many states by statute or common law recognize a debtor's right to assign all of the debtor's assets to a custodian for purposes of liquidation and distribution to creditors on a pro rata basis. Commonly referred to as "assignments for the benefit of creditors" (or "ABCs"), these procedures are useful for business debtors that intend to dissolve, are not entitled to discharge in bankruptcy, and are unable to obtain the requisite consensus among major creditors in order to make a private out-of-court arrangement effective. Like most collective remedies, the theory of ABCs is that if individual creditor execution efforts can be halted and the assigned assets sold off in a orderly fashion, the return for creditors as a group will be higher than if the assets were sold off piecemeal in uncoordinated forced sales by individual creditors. ABC statutes and procedures vary widely from state to state, with the New York law (N.Y. DEBTOR & CREDITOR LAW, Art. 2, §§ 2-24 (McKinney 1990)) offering one of the more comprehensive regulatory structures. In general, if a debtor makes an assignment of assets that does not comply with the prevailing state scheme, creditors seeking to levy on assets may obtain a court order declaring the assignment void.

In addition to state assignment statutes, placing a debtor's assets in the hands of a court-appointed receiver is another technique for winding-up the affairs of a financially distressed debtor. The precursor of modern-day reorganization under the Bankruptcy Code, today, receiverships are typically utilized in cases where the debtor is an entity, such as a railroad, bank or insurance company, that is statutorily ineligible to file for relief under the federal bankruptcy law. See Bankruptcy Code § 109(b). In addition, creditors that wish to impose a collective regime on a debtor who is immune from being involuntarily forced into bankruptcy (consisting, by virtue of Bankruptcy Code § 303(a), of not-for-profit organizations, farmers, and various other forms of non-business entities) may bring an equitable action in state court for the appointment of a receiver. In most instances, however, the lack of uniformity among the states, the absence of provision for debtor discharge, and the uncertain nature of judicial supervision over the process, make assignments and receiverships inferior alternatives to a federal bankruptcy proceeding from the perspective of both debtors and creditors. It is important to recognize, however, that even in a federal bankruptcy proceeding, state law continues to play an important role in defining a claimant's rights against the estate, including the validity, enforceability, and priority of security interests and other liens on the debtor's property.

SECTION 2. INTRODUCTION TO BANKRUPTCY

S. SNYDER & L. PONOROFF, COMMERCIAL BANKRUPTCY LITIGATION § 1.02 (1989, 1997).

Objectives of Bankruptcy Cases

A bankruptcy case is the process that is set into motion by the filing of a petition seeking relief under the Bankruptcy Code. Generally speaking, two types of relief are available upon the filing of a bankruptcy petition. That is, through bankruptcy (1) the debtor may obtain a discharge of burdensome and oppressive debts; and (2) creditors may obtain an orderly method of repayment of the debtor's obligations to them. While the discharge is central to modern bankruptcy law and policy, at its core, bankruptcy is still a collective debt collection device designed to maximize the overall return to multiple claimants against the assets of an insolvent debtor. As such, whether in a liquidation or a rehabilitative mode, bankruptcy is considered more efficient than parallel state and other federal non-bankruptcy law debt collection systems which contemplate uncoordinated, individual creditor collection actions and remedies.

A bankruptcy case may be filed under any one of the five operative chapters of the Bankruptcy Code. Each of these debtor-relief chapters differs both in terms of the purposes and consequences of bankruptcy and in the manner by which they provide for debtor relief and creditor repayment.

A case filed under chapter 7 of the Bankruptcy Code is a liquidation case. A bankruptcy trustee is appointed, or on occasion elected, in every chapter 7 case to take or acquire possession of all property in which the debtor had a legal or equitable interest as of the time the bankruptcy petition was filed. The trustee may avoid invalid liens that encumber the property as well as any improper exemptions that the debtor claims with respect to that property. On the other hand, when property is fully secured by valid liens or is properly exempt from the bankruptcy estate, it may be abandoned by the trustee. After collecting all of the assets comprising the bankruptcy estate, the trustee will liquidate unencumbered and partially encumbered property and, after paying valid liens and the costs of bankruptcy, will distribute the proceeds of sale to nonpriority unsecured creditors on a pro rata basis. Certain unsecured creditor claims are entitled to priority in chapter 7 liquidation and, therefore, must be paid in full before any distribution to other unsecured claims can occur.

An individual debtor in a chapter 7 case receives a general discharge unless it is determined that the debtor committed one of the acts or satisfies one of the conditions that can result in the denial of discharge. The discharge covers all debts existing as of the time the petition was filed, except for certain categories of debts which are statutorily excepted from discharge.

Corporations and other entities do not receive a discharge in a chapter 7 case and, partly for that reason, typically do not file for relief under chapter 7. Additionally, since a chapter 7 filing results in immediate liquidation, it ordinarily produces nothing for the owners of a business which they could not have produced for themselves under conventional state law dissolution procedures. Occasionally, however, a corporation or other business entity will file a chapter 7 petition so that management can avoid having to spend the time and avoid the risk that may result from liquidating a business that has some unencumbered assets.

A chapter 11 case is a reorganization case. By permitting reorganization, Congress expressed a clear and decided preference for rehabilitation as an alternative to liquidation for business debtors experiencing financial trouble. A business debtor will ordinarily file a voluntary chapter 11 case to attempt to preserve some portion of the going concern value of the business for its owners, which value would otherwise be lost through piecemeal liquidation of the firm's productive assets. Specifically, chapter 11 provides the owners of a business with an opportunity to salvage some share of that going concern value by creating an environment under which such a business, although temporarily ailing, can continue to operate free from the potentially crushing pressures of individual debt-collection efforts. In theory, by enforcing the conditions necessary in order for the business to remain intact while it rescales its operations, restructures its finances and, hopefully, returns to economic viability, greater value will be realized in the long run for all concerned.

Upon filing of a chapter 11 petition, the debtor automatically becomes the so-called debtor-in-possession. The debtor-in-possession has all of the powers of a bankruptcy trustee and continues to operate the business during bankruptcy. The debtor can be ousted from managerial control over its business only if the court for cause, such as fraud or gross mismanagement, appoints a chapter 11 trustee.

General creditors are repaid in a chapter 11 case by means of a plan of reorganization that they or their representative, the creditors' committee, negotiate with the debtor while the debtor is attempting to restructure its business operations. Initially, only the debtor may file the plan of reorganization.

However, this period of exclusivity may lapse, after which a plan may be filed by any party in interest.

The typical plan of reorganization provides for repayment over an extended period of time of the entire amount of fully secured creditors' claims and of a ratable portion of the aggregate claims of unsecured creditors. When (as is usually the case) unsecured creditors are not repaid in full, the plan will provide for conversion of all or some portion of their claims into an equity position in the reorganized business. Thus, the owners of a business that files for relief under chapter 11 must be prepared to accept the fact that the cost of a successful reorganization may be the dilution or, on occasion, even the elimination, of their ownership interest.

If the court confirms the plan of reorganization, all of the debtor's debts are subject to repayment only in accordance with the terms of the plan and, with certain exceptions, the debtor is discharged from those debts. While the plan will ordinarily be confirmed by means of acceptance by each class of creditors whose claims are proposed to be altered under the plan, the proponent of a plan of reorganization may also request confirmation over the dissent of one or more creditor classes if certain requirements are met. This alternative method of confirmation is commonly referred to as "cramdown."

In recent years, several academic commentators, writing mostly from an economics-based perspective of the law, have argued for the repeal of chapter 11 on the ground that conflicts between failing businesses and their creditors could be more efficiently resolved by the market utilizing private, contracts-based systems of priorities rather than through a court-supervised reorganization process. This call for the repeal of chapter 11 has evoked a strong and vociferous response in the literature from other commentators who view the goals or purposes of chapter 11 in broader terms than wealth maximization for corporate security holders. Perhaps the sanest, and certainly the most realistic, approach is one that recognizes the existing flaws in chapter 11, but proposes reform rather than abandonment of the system.

Cases brought under chapters 9, 12, and 13 of the Bankruptcy Code are designed for special types of debtors. Chapter 9 is a debt adjustment case for municipalities ineligible to seek relief under chapter 7 of the Bankruptcy Code. Chapter 12 is a debt adjustment proceeding which permits family farmers with limited amounts of debt to reorganize their farming operations without incurring the expense and delays that result from the filing of a chapter 11 case. Chapter 12 has a sunset provision. Unless extended by Congress, chapter 12 will be automatically repealed on October 1, 199[8].* Chapter 13 is a debt adjustment case designed to permit an individual with regular income to pay his or her debts out of future income as an alternative to chapter 7 liquidation.

Relief under the Bankruptcy Code is available by voluntary or involuntary petition. An eligible debtor can initially request relief under any one of the five operative chapters of the Bankruptcy Code by means of a voluntary petition.

---

* Legislation is currently pending that would make chapter 12 a permanent part of the Bankruptcy Code [eds.].

Additionally, with some restrictions, a case may be converted from one chapter of the Bankruptcy Code to any other chapter of the Code under which the debtor is eligible for relief. Unsecured creditors, particularly when concerned about the dissipation of a debtor's assets resulting from transfers to preferred creditors or insiders, can request relief under chapters 7 and 11 by means of an involuntary petition. Like the debtor in a voluntary case, creditors will file an involuntary chapter 11 petition when they perceive that the business may have some going concern value that can be preserved and realized through reorganization. Otherwise, they will file an involuntary chapter 7 case.

NOTE ON SECURED CLAIMS IN BANKRUPTCY

Outside of bankruptcy we speak of a creditor as being "secured" without regard to the relationship between the value of the collateral and the amount of the obligation secured. Not so in bankruptcy. Section 506(a) of the Bankruptcy Code defines a claim as secured to the extent of the lesser of the amount owed by the debtor or *the value of the collateral.* This means that when the collateral is worth less than the debt a secured creditor will really have two claims if the debtor files for bankruptcy: a secured claim measured by the value of the collateral and an unsecured claim for the deficiency. This bifurcation of the secured creditor's claim has important implications in chapters 11, 12, and 13 where, generally speaking, a debtor's plan may be confirmed as long as it proposes to provide the secured party with a stream of payments over the life of the plan having a present value equal to the amount of the secured claim. With respect to the unsecured portion of its claim the secured creditor simply shares pro rata in whatever distributions are made to unsecured creditors as a group. Often these distributions will be for considerably less than full value of the unsecured claims.

Bifurcation is of less consequence in chapter 7 liquidation cases because of the principle that valid liens against the debtor's property are unaffected by the bankruptcy case, except to the extent subject to avoidance by the trustee as discussed in the next two sections. The effect of having the lien "pass through" bankruptcy is that after the case is closed, the secured creditor's interest in the property remains in full force and effect notwithstanding the debtor's discharge from personal liability under § 727(b). Thus, the secured creditor may foreclose on the property and apply the proceeds of sale to the entire unpaid portion of the debt, even though the debtor has been released from personal liability by the discharge. This principle was enunciated by the Supreme Court over a hundred years ago in the case of Long v. Bullard, 117 U.S. 617 (1886), and was reaffirmed much more recently in the Court's decision in Dewsnup v. Timm, 502 U.S. 410 (1992). While some commentators have argued that this principle rests on a constitutional foundation derived from the Fifth Amendment's prohibition against the taking of property without just compensation, the actual basis for the rule is not entirely clear. See In re Penrod, 50 F.3d 459, 463 (7th Cir.1995) (noting that liens pass through bankruptcy "unless they are brought within the bankruptcy proceeding and dealt with there").

Finally, it bears noting that even if the interest of a lienholder in property of the estate is not divested by a bankruptcy filing, this does not mean that it is business as usual for the secured party. The act of filing bankruptcy operates as an automatic stay against all collection efforts against the debtor. Code § 362(a). This includes actions by a secured creditor to obtain possession of its collateral or otherwise initiate foreclosure proceedings. However, if the secured party is undersecured and the value of its collateral is depreciating, it is entitled to "adequate protection" under § 361, usually in the form of periodic payments from the estate to ensure that the value of its secured claim is not reduced beyond the amount of the claim as of the date of filing. If the debtor is unable to provide collateral, the secured creditor is entitled to relief from the stay in order to pursue its state law remedies against the property. See § 362(d). If the value of the collateral is not threatened in any way, however, the stay remains in place and the secured creditor is not entitled to interest during the period it must wait before being able to proceed against the collateral. Section 506(b) contains an exception to the rule concerning post-petition interest to the extent the value of the collateral exceeds the debt. In addition, even in chapter 7, the property may be sold or otherwise disposed of, subject only to the requirement, once again, that the secured party's interest in the property be adequately protected. See §§ 363(b), (e), and (f). Also, as noted earlier, in cases filed under chapters 11, 12, and 13, the debtor may retain the collateral, subject to the secured party's lien, provided that the secured party is paid the value of its claim over the life of the plan. By far, however, the biggest threat to the secured party in a bankruptcy case is that the trustee will be able to exercise one of her avoiding powers to have the lien set aside entirely.

SECTION 3. THE TRUSTEE'S STRONG-ARM POWERS

(a) THE TRUSTEE AS LIEN CREDITOR—§ 544(a)(1)

BARWELL, INC. v. FIRST OF AMERICA BANK

United States District Court, Northern District of Indiana, 1991.

Page 297, supra

JONES v. SMALL BUSINESS ADMINISTRATION (IN RE COHUTTA MILLS, INC.)

United States District Court, Northern District of Georgia, 1989.
108 B.R. 815.

HAROLD L. MURPHY, District Judge.

Facts and Procedural History

Bankruptcy Trustee Jones appeals the Bankruptcy Court's decision that the Small Business Administration (SBA) has a perfected security interest in personalty of Bankruptcy Debtor Cohutta Mills, Inc. The trustee had honored the SBA's claim to a security interest in realty, but objected to the SBA's claim to a security interest in personalty on the ground that it was not perfected.

The Bankruptcy Court held a hearing on the trustee's objection, where it heard argument from counsel and testimony from a representative of SBA, and received documentary evidence. The proof adduced shows that, in 1977, King's Tuft, Inc. borrowed money from Cohutta Banking Company (Cohutta Bank), and the loan was guaranteed by SBA. Cohutta Bank secured the note with equipment, machinery, and after-acquired property of King's Tuft and filed financing statements that perfected its interests.

In 1979, Cohutta Bank assigned the note and security interests to SBA, and filed statements reflecting those assignments.

Subsequently, to resolve financial problems of King's Tuft, its owners created a new corporation, Cohutta Mills, and transferred King's Tuft's assets to Cohutta Mills. On April 22, 1980, Cohutta Mills entered into an "Assumption Agreement" wherein it assumed King's Tuft's obligations under SBA's note. In the same document, SBA consented to the transfer on the condition that Cohutta Mills assumed those obligations. King's Tuft ceased to exist at that point.

Cohutta Mills had the same president as King's Tuft and pursued the same line of business at the same location using the same machinery and equipment. SBA did not file new financing statements when the new corporation was formed, although it did send letters to King's Tuft's creditors. Approximately two years later, on August 16, 1982, SBA filed a continuation statement indicating that it retained a security interest in the property of King's Tuft. Cohutta Mills filed for bankruptcy on February 6, 1987.

Issue on Appeal

Under 11 U.S.C. § 544(a)(1), a bankruptcy trustee has the rights of a hypothetical lien creditor as of the filing of the bankruptcy petition. The rights of a lien creditor are determined pursuant to state law. Under Georgia's version of the Uniform Commercial Code (hereinafter referred to as "UCC"), a lien creditor has priority over an unperfected, though secured, creditor. Ga.Code Ann. § 11-9-301(1)(b), (3). In the bankruptcy context, therefore, if the secured creditor's interest is not perfected, the creditor "stands as [a] general unsecured creditor who must defer to the trustee." In re Merts Equipment Co., 438 F.Supp. 295, 298 (M.D.Ga.1977).

The Parties' Arguments

The trustee argues that SBA's interest is unperfected because SBA filed the continuation statement in the name of King's Tuft instead of Cohutta Mills. He stresses that Cohutta Mills was a new corporation, as opposed to change of name of King's Tuft, and reasons that a prospective creditor searching the files under the name of Cohutta Mills would not locate SBA's interest.

The trustee argues further that Cohutta Mills assumed SBA's note and not the security agreement and that, in any event, a security interest would not attach to after-acquired property of Cohutta Mills. Lastly, the trustee claims the SBA breached a contractual agreement to file financing statements in the name of Cohutta Mills.

SBA responds that it was not required to file a new financing statement when the property was transferred and that its continuation statement was effective. SBA contends further that this Court cannot consider the trustee's argument concerning after-acquired property because the trustee did not develop a factual record thereon.

* * *

[The court then held that sections 9-306(2) and 9-402(7) should be construed to provide "that a security interest terminates upon the transfer of the collateral unless the secured creditor unambiguously authorized the disposition subject to its security interest" and that the SBA had consented to the transfer but had preserved its rights.]

2. Was the Filed Financing Statement Effective to Perfect SBA's Security Interest in the Property After the Property had been Transferred to Cohutta Mills?

Under Georgia law, a financing statement, among other things, must give the correct name of the debtor. Ga.Code Ann. § 11-9-402(1). A financing statement that misnames the debtor is nevertheless effective so long as the error is not "seriously misleading." See § 11-9-402(8) ("A financing statement that substantially complies with the requirements of this Code section is effective even though it contains minor errors which are not seriously misleading."). Conversely, if the financing statement misnames the debtor "so substantially that it is misleading, the filing has no effect and does not perfect the security interest."

If a financing statement is effective when filed but it becomes seriously misleading due to the subsequent name change or restructuring of the debtor, the secured party, under the second sentence of § 11-9-407(2), is nevertheless protected as to collateral covered through that time and, if applicable under the security agreement, to property acquired by the debtor through four months thereafter. § 11-9-402(7); In re Taylorville Eisner Agency, Inc., 445 F.Supp. 665, 668 (S.D.Ill.1977); Uniform Commercial Code § 9-402(7) comment 7 ("[t]he old financing statement, if legally still valid under the circumstances, would continue to protect collateral acquired before the change and * * * acquired within the four months.").

If, on the other hand, the financing statement is effective when filed but the collateral is transferred by the debtor, then, under the third sentence of § 11-9-402(7), the secured party's interest is perfected as to that collateral only. § 11-9-402(7) ("a filed financing statement remains effective with respect to collateral transferred by the debtor even though the secured party knows of or consents to the transfer.").

In sum, therefore, once the secured party files an effective financing statement, it is relieved, to a certain extent, of the burden of correcting misleading errors, and a prospective creditor is obligated to inquire into the debtor's source of title. Taylorville, 445 F.Supp. at 669; Franchise Systems, 46 B.R. at 162, quoting Uniform Commercial Code § 9-402(7) comment 8.

In the instant case, the financing statement was effective when filed in 1977 as it correctly named King's Tuft as the debtor. In 1980, however, when the collateral was transferred to Cohutta Mills, the statement became seriously misleading: because the two names are completely dissimilar, a searcher of Cohutta Mills' interests would not be alerted to inquire into King's Tuft's interests.

The effect of the filed financing statement is more difficult to resolve because the creation of Cohutta Mills was both a transfer of assets and a restructuring of King's Tuft's business to avoid financial problems. The UCC itself does not explain how a court should distinguish between those situations for purposes of § 9-402(7) and, as the Taylorville Court noted, "[i]n practically all cases of transfer of secured collateral the transferee would have a different name, identity or corporate organization." Taylorville, 445 F.Supp. at 669.

The Ninth Circuit has discussed the vagueness of the UCC in this regard and, after reviewing the sparse authority on point, determined that "the drafters intended the third sentence to apply to bona fide transfers to third parties unrelated to the transferor." Bank of the West v. Commercial Credit Financial Services, Inc., 852 F.2d 1162, 1168-71 & n. 6 (9th Cir.1988) (emphasis added).

In the instant case, based on the facts found by the Bankruptcy Court, which are not "clearly erroneous," the transaction in question seems closer to a restructuring of the corporation than a transfer of assets. Specifically, the Bankruptcy Court found that the two corporations had the same president and that Cohutta Mills pursued the same line of business at the same location using the same machinery and equipment as King's Tuft. Rather than merely a transfer of assets between two corporations, King's Tuft essentially became Cohutta Mills as a result of the transactions. The third sentence does not apply because the transfer was not between unrelated parties. See Bank of the West, 852 F.2d at 1168-71.

Under the second sentence of § 9-402(7), therefore, SBA's filed financing statement became seriously misleading upon the transfer of assets to Cohutta Mills, and covered property owned and acquired by Cohutta Mills through four months from the date of transfer only.

Having resolved that issue, the Court must determine whether the continuation statement filed in the name of King's Tuft renewed SBA's perfected interest in that property.

3. Was the Continuation Statement Effective to Renew SBA's Perfected Security Interest?

A financing statement is effective for five years from its filing date. Ga.Code Ann. § 11-9-403(2). If the creditor wishes to extend the perfection, it must file a "continuation statement" within the six month period that precedes the expiration of that five year period. § 11-9-403(3). The continuation statement must "be signed by the secured party, identify the original statement by file number, [and] state the original statement is still effective." Id. A continuation statement is effective for 5 years, and succeeding continuation statements may be filed indefinitely. Id.

The statute expressly requires that a continuation statement reflect a change in the debtor's address or in the location of the collateral if such a change causes the statement to be filed in a different office from the financing statement. The statute does not, however, expressly require that a continuation statement reflect a change in the name of the debtor.

Arguably, SBA's continuation statement in the name of King's Tuft was valid because the statement met the core requirements of § 11-9-403: the financing statement, as discussed, was effective to perfect SBA's security interest in collateral owned and acquired by Cohutta Mills through four months after the transfer of assets, and the continuation statement stated that the original statement was still effective.

On the other hand, the financing statement statute provides that a seriously misleading statement at the time of filing is ineffective whereas a financing statement that becomes seriously misleading is effective to a limited extent. See § 11-9-402. The statutes do not contain a similar provision for continuation statements. Some cases, however, have noted that because the mutual purpose of financing and continuation statements is to give notice to creditors, the "seriously misleading" test of § 9-402(8) applies to determining whether errors in continuation statements render the statement ineffective.

The * * * cases stand for the proposition that a continuation statement must substantially comply with the requirements of § 9-403(3) to be effective, but they do not resolve whether a continuation statement must, in addition to the explicit statutory requirements, reflect a change in the debtor.

* * *

Although § 9-403 is silent about such a requirement, the purpose of the financing and continuation statements is to provide notice of security interests to prospective creditors, and an umbrella provision of the UCC mandates that every duty be performed in "good faith." If a debtor changes its name such that a filed financing statement becomes seriously misleading, it would be incongruous to permit the limited effectiveness of that filing to be renewed by a seriously misleading continuation statement. The better rule is that upon the lapse of a seriously misleading, though partially effective, financing statement, the secured party, acting in good faith, must file a continuation statement under the new debtor's name if it wishes to sustain its perfected status.

SBA argues that because § 9-402(7) imposes a burden on prospective creditors to search in the name of the former owner of collateral, its continuation statement was valid. First, that duty is imposed when the debtor's situation changes during the five year term of the financing statement, and the UCC is silent about whether that duty continues once that term has lapsed. Second, as the trustee argues, continuation statements can be filed indefinitely, and requiring prospective creditors to search in the name of a former owner can in certain circumstances become an unduly burdensome task. From a practical perspective, the rule fashioned by the Court is more reasonable.

Under the rules discussed and on the facts presented in this case, the Court concludes that the continuation statement was seriously misleading when it was filed and is therefore ineffective to sustain SBA's perfected status in the property of Cohutta Mills.

* * *

ACCORDINGLY, the decision of the Bankruptcy Court is REVERSED.

(b) THE TRUSTEE AS BONA FIDE PURCHASER OF REAL ESTATE—§ 544(a)(3)

BRIGGS v. KENT (IN RE PROFESSIONAL INVESTMENT PROPERTIES OF AMERICA)

United States Court of Appeals, Ninth Circuit, 1992.
955 F.2d 623, cert. denied, 506 U.S. 818.

T.G. NELSON, Circuit Judge.

* * *

FACTS AND PROCEEDINGS BELOW

In October, 1985, the Briggs lent $50,000 to the debtor, Professional Investment Properties. They received a promissory note and a deed of trust on the debtor's real property as security for the loan. The deed of trust was not recorded.

When the Briggs learned of the debtor's financial difficulties, they filed a petition to force the debtor into involuntary bankruptcy on May 28, 1986. Simultaneously, they filed a Motion for Appointment of Trustee, and the real property became an asset of the bankruptcy estate pursuant to 11 U.S.C. § 541. In anticipation of a sale of the real property by the trustee, the Briggs attempted to impose an equitable lien on the proceeds. The bankruptcy court denied their motion for summary judgment and held that the Briggs were unsecured creditors of the estate.

The Briggs appealed to the district court which remanded for further findings of fact. Specifically, the district court questioned whether the trustee had constructive notice of the Briggs' interest in the real property. On remand, the Briggs presented expert testimony "that the contents of the petition constituted constructive notice of the Briggs' interest in the real property." Nevertheless, the bankruptcy court granted summary judgment in favor of the trustee concluding that "any constructive notice of plaintiffs' interest achieved by filing the original bankruptcy pleadings comes too late to secure their interest in a position prior to that acquired by the trustee."

The district court reversed, reaching the opposite conclusion: "It is the judgment of the court that the quoted language constituted constructive notice of a prior claim by the Briggs."

* * *

Analysis

The bankruptcy trustee holds "strong arm powers" provided by 11 U.S.C. § 544(a)(3) which states the trustee is to be considered:

> A bona fide purchaser of all real property * * * from the debtor, against whom applicable law permits such transfer to be perfected, that attains the status of a bona fide purchaser and has perfected such transfer at the time of the commencement of the case, whether or not such a purchaser exists.

11 U.S.C. §544(a)(3)

State law determines whether a party is a bona fide purchaser. In re Washburn and Roberts, Inc., 795 F.2d 870, 872 (9th Cir.1986). In Washington, a bona fide purchaser is defined as "one who without notice of another's claim of right to, or equity in, the property prior to his acquisition of title, has paid the vendor a valuable consideration." Miebach v. Colasurdo, 102 Wash.2d 170, 175, 685 P.2d 1074, 1078 (1984). Washington, which is a race-notice state, generally holds that a bona fide purchaser prevails over a prior transferee who has failed to record. RCW 65.08.070; Paganelli v. Swendsen, 50 Wash.2d 304, 308, 311 P.2d 676, 678 (1957). Since the strong arm powers elevate the trustee to a level of a bona fide purchaser, a trustee without notice can generally avoid any unrecorded transfer of land in the State of Washington. Washburn at 872.

The Briggs admit that their deed of trust was unrecorded. This case turns on whether the petition itself put the trustee on sufficient inquiry or constructive notice of their prior security interest. Miebach stated:

> It is a well-settled rule that where a purchaser has knowledge of information of facts which are sufficient to put an ordinarily prudent man upon inquiry, and the inquiry, if followed with reasonable diligence, would lead to the discovery of defects in the title or of equitable rights of others affecting the property in question, the purchaser will be held chargeable with knowledge thereof and will not be heard to say that he did not actually know of them. In other words, knowledge of facts sufficient to excite inquiry is constructive notice of all that the inquiry would have disclosed.

Miebach, 102 Wash.2d at 175-76, 685 P.2d at 1078 (quoting Peterson v. Weist, 48 Wash. 339, 341, 93 P. 519, 519 (1908)).

The bankruptcy court found factually that a diligent title search would disclose a bankruptcy filing. Secondly, it found that "a reasonably prudent purchaser of the debtor's property would be placed on notice of the contents of bankruptcy pleadings from the time of their being filed." It determined, as a matter of law, however, that "any constructive notice of plaintiffs' interest achieved by filing the original bankruptcy pleadings comes too late to secure their interest in a position prior to that acquired by the trustee."

It is the Briggs' contention, obviously, that the bankruptcy court was wrong; that the debtor's involuntary petition contained facts sufficient to put the trustee on at least inquiry notice that they had a prior claim. Secondly, they assert that notice simultaneous with filing is sufficient.[1]

A trustee does not become a hypothetical bona fide purchaser if she has been put on constructive or inquiry notice. In re Marino, 813 F.2d 1562, 1565 (9th Cir.1987). McCannon v. Marston, 679 F.2d 13, 16 (3rd Cir.1982) clarified the distinction by noting, "[t]he reference to the trustee's or creditors' knowledge appears to have originated out of a concern that actual knowledge might affect the trustee's status as a hypothetical lien creditor." Id. at 16. McCannon pointed out, however, that "Congress was careful to modify the status of bona fide purchasers by inserting the words 'against whom applicable law permits such transfer to be perfected.'" Id. at 17.

The trustee argues that inquiry notice is insufficient because it is a species of actual notice which is irrelevant in this context. See McCannon note 2. He cites Sands v. United States, 198 F.Supp. 880, 884 (W.D.Wash.1960) aff'd, First Federal Sav. & Loan Ass'n of Bremerton v. United States, 325 F.2d 481 (9th Cir.1961), which states "actual notice may also consist of implied or inquiry notice."

This explanation directly conflicts with Marino which clearly mandated that a trustee may still be held accountable if put on inquiry notice. Marino controls, not simply because it is more recent, but because it discusses the relationship of section 544(a)(3) with state property law. Moreover, decisions such as Probasco discuss the trustee's notice requirement in terms of a constructive notice that encompasses inquiry notice. "A prudent purchaser inquiring as to the unity of ownership of all three parcels 'might have learned' of Probasco's interest in [the property]." Id. at 1356. See also In re Tleel, 876 F.2d 769, 772 (9th Cir.1989) (discussing the failure in that case to provide constructive or inquiry notice).

The trustee argues that even if inquiry notice could preclude him from invoking the avoidance powers, the information in the Briggs petition was insufficient to provide such notice. He contends further that any information or

---

1 The trustee's actual notice is of no consequence. Section 544(a) states that the trustee shall have the rights and powers of a bona fide purchaser "without regard to actual knowledge." Probasco and In re Marino, 813 F.2d 1562, 1565 (9th Cir.1987) have consequently held that "actual knowledge is irrelevant." See McCannon v. Marston, 679 F.2d 13, 16-17 (3d Cir.1982).

notice which he attained after that period did not bear on his status as a bona fide purchaser at the time of filing of the case.[2]

The Briggs Involuntary Creditors' Petition makes one reference to the deeds of trust:

2. The nature and amount of Petitioners' claims are as follows:

(a) ROBERT BRIGGS: Purchase of various Promissory Notes supposedly secured by assignments of Deeds of Trust with interest-only monthly payments which are now delinquent, some with said Notes have matured and are unpaid, in the aggregate amount of approximately $137,500.

E.R. at 17.

While the bankruptcy court held that this petition came too late to secure the Briggs' position ahead of the trustee's, the district court determined that under Washington law:

> this language is sufficient to put an ordinarily prudent person on inquiry of the Briggs' interest in the real property in the form of Deed of Trust. Certainly, the language creates a circumstance which raises a duty to require further inquiry by the trustee to determine if there is a Deed of Trust. A reasonably diligent inquiry would have disclosed the unrecorded deeds of trust.

E.R. at 17-18.

While the bankruptcy court determined as a matter of law that inquiry notice that is simultaneous with filing "comes too late," the district court held that the filing would put the trustee, once appointed, on inquiry notice.

We are persuaded by the district court's holding. There is no practical reason why a trustee should not be put on inquiry notice by the very petition that created his position. A trustee who has not yet been appointed can hardly argue that he has been prejudiced by being charged with notice by the petition. Secondly, there is an abundance of authority making clear that state law determines a bona fide purchaser's status.[3] If the petition satisfies Washington law, the trustee has been put on inquiry notice.

"The burden of establishing that a purchaser had prior notice of another's claim, right, or equity, rests upon the one who asserts such prior notice." Glaser v. Holdorf, 56 Wash.2d 204, 209, 352 P.2d 212, 215 (1960) (citations omitted). In Miebach, the court noted that because the plaintiff was an experienced businessman and the debtors still had possession of the property, making continuous improvements on it, the plaintiff was on at least inquiry notice of their

---

2 This is true. In re Gurs, 27 B.R. 163 (9th Cir.BAP1983), defined a § 544(a)(3) hypothetical bona fide purchaser as one who is without actual knowledge "at the instant the petition is filed," and purchases property from the debtor for value and in good faith. Consequently, we will only discuss the ramifications of the petition itself.

3 See In re Washburn and Roberts, 795 F.2d at 872; In re Tleel, 876 F.2d at 772; In re Marino, 813 F.2d at 1565; In re Torrez, 63 B.R. 751, 754 (9th Cir.BAP1986), aff'd, 827 F.2d 1299 (9th Cir.1987).

claim to the property. Id. 685 P.2d at 1077-78.

In Peterson v. Weist, 48 Wash. 339, 93 P. 519 (1908), the deed delivered to the plaintiff's vendor contained a reservation clause which stated:

> Saving and reserving therefrom all the timber of every kind and character now thereon, except cedar, reserving also the right to pass over the premises wherever necessary to remove the timber herein reserved; possession to be given of the timber and roads when A.C. Mowry's time is up upon the timber, viz.: 3 years from Feb. 10, 1902.

Id. at 340, 93 P. at 519.

The appellants in Peterson conceded they were aware of the reservation but did not know of the time allowed for removal. The court had no sympathy: "If they had no notice of the time allowed for removal of the timber it was solely because they made no inquiry. They could not blindly rely on the statement of their vendors and they made no inquiry from any other source." Id. (citations omitted).

This case is similar. The involuntary petition indicated the very people who instigated the bankruptcy proceedings held a deed of trust. This petition should have raised the trustee's suspicions and compelled him to inquire further. Since this was an involuntary petition, the trustee need only have contacted the Briggs to determine their specific interest. In fact, the trustee had a duty to inquire as to the nature of the Briggs' claim once he was appointed.

The bankruptcy court's findings of fact support this holding even if its conclusions of law do not. The court determined that "a reasonably prudent purchaser of the debtor's property would be placed on notice of the bankruptcy pleadings from the time of their being filed." This statement is consistent with the district court's holding that the petition simultaneously provided notice to the trustee. Consequently, while we adopt the bankruptcy's court's findings of fact, we hold that the district court arrived at the correct legal conclusion.

* * *

NOTES AND QUESTIONS

1. Section 544(a)(1) gives the trustee the status of a hypothetical judicial lien creditor, while § 544(a)(3) confers the status bona fide purchaser of real property. Bearing in mind that the rights of a party occupying each such position are determined under applicable state law, what power does the trustee's entitlement to the rights of a BFP of real property add that the trustee did not already possess as a judicial lien creditor under § 544(a)(1)? Also, how do the rights and powers of the trustee under § 544(a) differ from those conferred by § 544(b), discussed in Section 1 of Chapter 3, supra?

2. The strong-arm powers in § 544(a) occasionally come into conflict with the provisions of § 541(d) which exclude from the bankruptcy estate property in which the debtor holds legal, but not equitable, title. Specifically, the courts

have differed in their analysis of whether the trustee may use her powers under § 544(a) to avoid the third party's equitable interest and thereby acquire the property for the estate. Some courts hold that § 541(d) prevails over the trustee's strong-arm powers, while others take the position that § 541(d) should not be construed as imposing a limit on the trustee's avoiding powers. The problem has manifested itself in circumstances where the creditor, having failed to acquire or perfect a security interest in the debtor's property, contends that the property was "wrongfully" appropriated, and therefore should be made subject to a constructive trust in the creditor's favor. In rejecting this argument, at least in situations where the property had not earlier been impressed with a constructive trust either by virtue of a separate prepetition proceeding or specific state statute, the Sixth Circuit observed:

> "The equities of bankruptcy are not the equities of the common law. Constructive trusts are an anathema to the equities of bankruptcy since they take from the estate, and thus directly from competing creditors, not from the offending debtor. [footnote omitted.] "Ratable distribution among all creditors" justifies the Code's placement of the trustee in the position of first-in-line judgment creditor and bona fide purchaser for value, empowered to avoid certain competing interests (and even to nullify the debtor's "preferential" prepetition payments to otherwise entitled creditors) so as to maximize the value of the estate."

XL/Datacomp, Inc. v. Wilson (In re Omega Group, Inc.), 16 F.3d 1443, 1452 (6th Cir. 1994). But see Sanyo Electric, Inc. v. Howard's Appliance Corp. (In re Howard Appliance Corp.), 874 F.2d 88 (2d Cir. 1989) (resolving the conflict between §§ 541(d) and 544(a) in favor of a secured creditor, whose perfection had lapsed prior to the bankruptcy filing, based on the argument that the creditor was entitled to the benefit of a constructive trust over the collateral). See generally Sherwin, *Constructive Trusts in Bankruptcy*, 1989 U. Ill. L. Rev. 297, 320 *et seq.* (1989).

3. Section 551 of the Bankruptcy Code provides that a transfer avoided under, *inter alia*, § 544(a) "is preserved for the benefit of the estate, but only with respect to property of the estate." Under what circumstances would this provision benefit the estate? Consider a debtor who has granted two liens on the same property, the senior lien avoidable under § 544(a) but the junior lien beyond challenge. Without § 551, what would the result be of the trustee's exercise of her avoiding power? Can such a situation ever arise? See UCC § 9-401(2).

SECTION 4. BANKRUPTCY PREFERENCES

(a) IN GENERAL

PONOROFF, NOW YOU SEE IT, NOW YOU DON'T: AN UNCEREMONIOUS ENCORE FOR TWO-TRANSFER THINKING IN THE ANALYSIS OF INDIRECT PREFERENCES, 69 Am. Bankr. L.J. 203, 236-40 (1995).

Historically, bankruptcy law has exhibited an almost schizophrenic confusion when it comes to locating, articulating, and implementing the purposes of the preference law. The very use of the term *preference* connotes an *intent* to confer an advantage over other creditors. Nonetheless, the [Bankruptcy] Code's formulation of a voidable preference deliberately omits reference to any requirement of a culpable state of mind on the part of either the debtor or the preferred creditor. Instead, in contrast to prior law, the focus under the Code has shifted to effect; the essence of modern preference doctrine is no longer in the *act* of preferring by the debtor, but in the preferential *consequence* to the transferee-creditor.

When viewed in the context of the historical evolution leading to the wholesale elimination of any subjective elements in the statutory formulation of a preferential transfer, this emphasis on preferential effect marks a watershed in the long struggle for hegemony between the two most frequently quoted justifications for preference law: (i) deterrence of precipitous collection activity which leads to dismemberment of a financially beleaguered debtor, and (ii) equality of distribution among similarly situated creditors. In its current incarnation, bankruptcy law serves the equality policy first and foremost. * * *

Closely aligned with the ideal that the primary purpose of the preference law is to preserve bankruptcy distribution policies is the imaginative conceptualization of the estate as a pot of assets existing as of a certain point in time prior to bankruptcy and inviolate except as necessary to implement public policies of equal weight and import. Under pre-Code law, this idea found expression in the diminution of the estate doctrine which operated to some extent as an independent requirement of a voidable preference. When the Code was adopted, some commentators argued that the diminution doctrine no longer had any place in preference analysis and that its continued application would serve only to undermine the structural integrity of § 547. Courts, however, have continued to employ the doctrine as both a mechanism for explaining why particular transactions contravene key bankruptcy purposes and as a benchmark for distinguishing those transfers on the fringe of existing doctrine which are subject to avoidance under § 547 from those that are not. Despite the appeal and the systemic benefits of a purely mechanical rule, it is impossible to deal in a consistent, principled way with the variety of transactions that give rise to preference issues without resort to the underlying consequential objective. The joining of equality policy with the diminution concept points to such an objective in preference cases.

McCoid, Bankruptcy, Preferences, and Efficiency: An Expression of Doubt, 67 Va. L. Rev. 249, 270-73 (1981).

An alternative to more regulation is less of it. What would be the consequences of "deregulation" or the abolition of preference law?

Abolition of preference law would eliminate uncertainty costs. Creditors could rely on transfers made to pay or secure antecedent debts, at least in the absence of fraud. The argument that preference law is "unfair" because it retroactively changes the rules of the game for creditors also makes abolition attractive. Nonbankruptcy law tells a creditor that he is in a race with other creditors. Receiving payment first or getting a prior lien is the creditor's only protection against the possibility that a debtor's assets will prove inadequate to satisfy all claims against him. Bankruptcy stops the race for priority and replaces it with the principle of equality. Preference law makes that change retroactive by applying the equality principle to the period immediately preceding bankruptcy. Although creditors are on notice that this may occur, a transfer that was perfectly legitimate when made may nevertheless be invalidated. Ordinarily, setting aside a transaction implies that it never should have occurred. Fraudulent conveyance law is illustrative: the debtor's fraudulent intent and the grantee's knowledge taint the conveyance when it is made.

The unfairness of retroactively changing the rules of behavior can only be justified on the ground that it is necessary to achieve fairness of another sort—equality among creditors. Without preference law, the argument runs, there would be nothing left to distribute equally. Although abolition would eliminate recapture and deterrence, these are not the only avenues to distributional equality and to maximization of estate value. In theory, at least, those goals may also be achieved by filing a bankruptcy petition promptly on the debtor's insolvency. Filing deprives the debtor of the power to make transfers satisfying or securing an antecedent debt, and it automatically stays further creditor collection efforts. The 1978 Act makes filing easier and more attractive. It is easier because an act of bankruptcy is no longer required. An involuntary petition requires only the debtor's failure to pay his debts as they come due. It is more attractive because rehabilitation is generally available in involuntary proceedings. Moreover, liquidation proceedings initiated under chapter 7 can be converted to reorganization proceedings under chapter 11 and vice versa.

The efficacy of filing would depend on the willingness of creditors to file and on their ability to do so promptly. Desire for equality in distribution and maximization of estate value would seem to argue for filing. The individual creditor, however, acting out of self-interest, might elect instead to accept or seek a preference where one is available and file only when it is not and when there is a danger of others receiving preferences. Thus, the same considerations that prevent effective deterrence under current law would seemingly inhibit willingness to file. Presumably, those considerations would also grant undue advantage to the knowledgeable creditor. There is, however, one difference. The recapture feature of existing preference law allows a creditor to defer filing while he explores the possibility of obtaining a preference. Abolition would eliminate that breathing space. For the risk-averse creditor, that would increase the incentive to file to prevent preferences favoring others. Perhaps, however, the inability to recapture if for some reason there was delay would counterbalance this increased incentive. The need to file promptly would require knowledge of the debtor's situation. The new standard for filing makes that easier, but there might still be some delay and thus room for prefiling preference transfers. In sum, were preferences law abolished, prompt filing, although an avenue to equality and maximum estate value, would not lead to greater efficacy.

Additionally, dependence on filing would entail the costs of proceeding formally in cases that creditors currently handle informally. Informal collective action has its own costs, but it seems clear that the expenses of a formal proceeding are greater. Delay, restrictions imposed by chapter 11 on the nature of a "work-out," and the problems generated by the stigma of a filing are the kinds of costs that may lead creditors to prefer informal proceedings. That view may be due, at least in part, to the fact that, before the 1978 Act, involuntary rehabilitation was unavailable in most cases; thus, it may be outdated.

The increased cost of formal proceedings seems to provide the most powerful argument against abolition because abolition would require prompt filing to achieve distributional equality and maximization of estate value. It seems impossible to quantify that increase, and in any event, to be instructive, that increase would have to be compared with the uncertainty costs of preference law.

FINK v. FIDELITY FINANCIAL SERVICES, INC. (IN RE BEASLEY)

United States Bankruptcy Court, Western District of Missouri, 1995.
183 B.R. 857, aff'd, 102 F.3d 334 (8th Cir. 1996), aff'd, 118 S. Ct. 651 (1998).

FRANK W. KOGER, Chief Judge.

Debtor filed for relief under 11 U.S.C. Chapter 7 on November 18, 1994. At the § 341 meeting and from documentation and claims filed, the Chapter 7 Trustee determined that there was a problem with the alleged secured position of Fidelity Financial Services. For that reason the Trustee demanded that the debtor deliver possession of a 1994 Ford Probe which debtor had purchased and which debtor and Fidelity Financial Services thought was secured by a perfected lien in favor of said financial institution based on the monies advanced to debtor by said institution. Faced with the alternative of either turning the car over and letting the Trustee fight with Fidelity Financial Services or paying off the car in some fashion, debtor chose to convert to a Chapter 13. Debtor was then in effect a debtor in possession and the Chapter 13 Trustee engaged debtor's counsel to be his counsel to seek determination of the validity of Fidelity Financial's lien.

In this proceeding therefore, it would seem that debtor is basically somewhat of a stake holder and nothing more. If the Chapter 13 Trustee is successful and the lien is avoided, debtor by virtue of 11 U.S.C. § 1325(a)(4) has to pay the value of the vehicle (less exemption) into the Chapter 13 plan for the unsecured creditors. If, on the other hand, the lien of Fidelity Financial is determined to be impregnable, debtor has to pay Fidelity Financial the balance due on the lien, at least to the value of the collateral.

With this background then, the Court will recite the facts which are basically stipulated to by the parties. Debtor purchased the 1994 Probe on August 17, 1994, and delivered at that time to Fidelity Financial Services, Inc. her promissory note for $14,090.80 with interest at the rate of 20.85%. Debtor also delivered to Fidelity Financial a security agreement which has been introduced into evidence.

On September 7, 1994, or 21 days later, Fidelity mailed an application for Missouri Title and License to the Missouri Department of Revenue together with the requisite fee for the imposition of the lien on the face of the title. A copy of that application has also been submitted into evidence.

The so called "blue slip" which is the secured party's copy of the application was processed by the Department of Revenue and returned to Fidelity with a file date of September 23, 1994. However, a search of the records determined, and the parties have agreed, that the Department of Revenue received Fidelity's application for title and imposition of lien on September 12, 1994. Putting all the dates together what is obvious already to informed readers is that Fidelity filed the necessary paper work and same was received by the Department of Revenue 26 days after the date debtor signed the note and security agreement and delivered same to Fidelity. The date of the filing of the petition was 93 days after August 17, 1994, and therefore outside the magic preference period because, of course, there is no claim that Fidelity is an insider. Nevertheless, the date that Fidelity mailed the application to the Department of Revenue that would procure for it a secured position, the date that same was received by the Department of Revenue, the date that the "blue slip" was returned to Fidelity, were all within the magic 90 day preference period. Informed readers will also note, of course, that as of October 22 or October 24, 1994, whichever date one prefers, Congress had decreed that 11 U.S.C. § 547(c)(3) would allow a snap back of 20 days from the date of purchase to the date of perfection under the so called purchase money security interest exception to preference law. The State of Missouri, on the other hand, allows a secured party 30 days to perfect a purchase money security interest and provides that if a secured party does transmit the title application and lien imposition paper work to the Department of Revenue within 30 days of the purchase, the lien is valid as a purchase money security interest against all parties obtaining any interest within the time period between purchase and receipt of application. See Mo.Rev.Stat. § 301.600.2 (1994), which provides in relevant part:

> A lien or encumbrance on a motor vehicle or trailer is perfected by the delivery to the director of revenue of the existing certificate of ownership, if any, an application for a certificate of ownership containing the name and address of the lienholder and the date of his security agreement, and the required certificate of ownership fee. It is perfected as of the time of its creation if the delivery of the aforesaid to the director of revenue is completed within thirty days thereafter, otherwise as of the time of the delivery.

Thus, we find the problem. Is it the bankruptcy law of 20 days that controls, or is it the state law of 30 days that controls?

There is a split in authority among the courts that have considered this exact issue. In In re Hamilton, 892 F.2d 1230, 1234-35 (5th Cir.1990), and in In re Loken, 175 B.R. 56, 61 (9th Cir. BAP 1994), the Fifth Circuit Court of Appeals and the Ninth Circuit Bankruptcy Appellate Panel concluded that state law grace, or relation-back, periods are inapplicable for purposes of determining whether a transfer is preferential under section 547. * * *

On the other hand, in In re Hesser, 984 F.2d 345, 348-49 (10th Cir.1993), and in In re Busenlehner, 918 F.2d 928, 930-31 (11th Cir.1990), cert. denied, Moister v. General Motors Acceptance Corp., 500 U.S. 949, 111 S.Ct. 2251, 114 L.Ed.2d 492 (1991), the Tenth Circuit Court of Appeals and Eleventh Circuit Court of Appeals concluded that state law relation-back periods are applicable under a section 547 analysis. * * *

This Court is persuaded that the reasoning of the appellate courts in Hamilton and Loken and other courts which have determined that state law relation-back periods are inapplicable when deciding whether a preferential transfer has occurred is correct. The court in Loken discussed the split in authority and opined:

> Looking at the plain language of Section 547(e)(1), taken as a whole, we find that an ambiguity does not exist. The term "perfected" must be viewed in the context of the rest of the Section and with regard for the usual usage of that term. Section 547(e)(1) states that a transfer is perfected when a creditor "cannot" acquire a superior interest. This Section directs courts to determine when a judicial lienholder is not able to obtain a position superior to that of the transferee in question. See In re Lane, 980 F.2d 601, 605 (9th Cir.1992) (applying Section 547(e)(1)(A)—the definition of transfer is "unambiguous;" a transfer is perfected when a subsequent purchaser cannot acquire a superior interest.) If a judicial lienholder could still obtain superior rights, then the transfer has not been perfected such that the lien holder "cannot" obtain superior rights. Essentially, under Section 547(e)(1), the court must determine the moment in time when a judicial lien creditor is barred from obtaining superior rights. This is a natural reading of the complete Code Section. The courts that have reached a different conclusion have taken the word "perfected" out of the context of the remaining words of the statute. We hold that a creditor on a simple contract is barred from acquiring a judicial lien superior to the interest of the transferee when the transferee takes the last step required by state law to perfect its security interest. Until that last step is taken, other creditors could potentially obtain superior rights. Until this last step, it is not possible to say that other creditors "cannot" obtain superior rights.

This interpretation, that the term "perfected" refers to that single date, or moment in time, when the state perfection statute is satisfied, is also consistent with the general usage of the term. See In re Holloway, supra, 132 B.R. at 774 ("[I]n the real world perfection is actually accomplished on a particular date by doing a particular act."). A perfect example is the Oregon statute at issue here. The Oregon statute requires that an application for notation of the interest on the certificate of title be sent to the DMV. The application must be accompanied by certain documentation. The application is marked when it is received by the DMV. The final act required by the Oregon statute is the submission of a completed application and supporting documentation. If everything is in order, "the security interest is perfected as of the date marked by the [DMV] on the application." O.R.S. § 803.097(3). The last act required by Oregon law is the submission of a completed application and supporting documentation to the DMV. Once it is confirmed that this has been done properly, Oregon treats this last required act as the moment the security interest is perfected. This is simply how the term perfected is used in common usage.

Since this issue has produced such divergent views we also will look at the history of this Code section and the legislative intent behind it. The first thing we note is that Congress intended to harmonize the preference statute with the Uniform Commercial Code.

> [T]he adoption of the Uniform Commercial Code radically altered the terminology of secured transactions, and the courts have applied the new terminology to the preference sections, which uses certain of the same words as the Uniform Commercial Code but in different senses and with different meanings. It is time to bring the two statutes into harmony, and H.R. 8200 does that by adopting the more modern terminology of the Uniform Commercial Code, and providing for specific treatment of transfers by the Code.

H.Rep. No. 595, 95th Cong., 1st Sess. 179 (footnotes deleted). This statement is consistent with our holding that Section 547(e)(1) must be read in accordance with general commercial usage.

The Bankruptcy Act ("Act") set a twenty-one day time limit for perfection of transfers. Under Section 60(a)(7) of the Act, the time period would be shorter if state law provided for less time to perfect. However, while state law might provide for less time, Section 60(a)(7) clearly prohibited the use of a state statute to expand the twenty-one days maximum time limit. Congress's reason for changing the timing of Section 60(a)(7) to the ten day time period of Code Section 547(e)(2) is clear. Congress made the change to create a uniform rule throughout the country and it did not intend for state grace periods to be relevant under Section 547. In re Burnette, supra, 14 B.R. at 801. Congress set the grace period at ten days to correspond with the grace period provided under the Uniform Commercial Code. See In re Walker, supra, 161 B.R. at 495 (quoting White and Summers, Uniform Commercial Code § 25-7, 447-48 (3d ed.1988)). See also Burnette, supra, 14 B.R. at 800. Congress could have provided that each state's own version of Uniform Commercial Code Section 9-310(2) would be applicable. Then states, such as Oregon, could have adopted changes as they saw fit. However, Congress did not do this. Instead, it created one uniform grace period of ten days.

We also take note of Congress's enactment of the Bankruptcy Reform Act of 1994, which was signed into law on October 22, 1994. The Reform Act now allows a creditor twenty days to perfect its purchase money security interest while still qualifying for the enabling loan exception found in Section 547(c)(3). By this change, Congress acknowledged that states were enacting grace periods greater than ten days for such security interests. Congress could have deferred completely to the states by incorporating each state's own timing into the Code. Instead, it chose to continue having the Code itself dictate the applicable grace period. Furthermore, Congress did not amend Section 547(e)(1), which provides the definition for "perfection" as used in Section 547.

Even under the Reform Act then, if a creditor perfects its interest more than ten days after the transfer is effective between the parties, the transfer will be deemed made on the date of perfection, and a preference may therefore exist. If it is perfected within ten days, the transfer is deemed made as of the day it became effective between the parties. Under such circumstances, there will have been no transfer on account of an antecedent debt, and hence, no preference. The only difference under the new law is that lienholders asserting purchase money security interests, who perfect their interest within twenty days of the debtor taking possession of the property in question, may now be able to interpose Section 547(c)(3) as a defense to a preference action. For all purposes of Section 547 though, be it to determine if there was a transfer on account of an antecedent debt or if the enabling loan exception applies, perfection is still determined pursuant to Section 547(e), and is still determined without any reference to state grace periods.

The Panel now applies this law to the facts at hand. The parties agree that Romania's application for a notation of the security interest on the certificate of title was marked October 31, 1991. Clearly then, since there is no other mark on it, the application was received by the DMV on that date, it contained all the required information and it was accompanied by all necessary documentation. The security interest was perfected on October 31, 1991. See O.R.S. 803.097(3). On that date, Romania cut off any possibility that a judicial lien creditor could obtain superior rights in the collateral. The relation back effect of O.R.S. § 79.3010(2) is inapplicable.

The plain language of Section 547(e)(2) provides that a secured creditor will have a ten day grace period for perfecting its security interest. Pursuant to Section 547(e)(1), courts must look to state law to determine the moment in time in which the last step is taken to perfect a security interest. Varying grace periods provided for under state law are irrelevant. If the last necessary act was done within the ten day period of Section 547(e)(2)(A), the transfer will have been made when it became effective between the parties. If it is made after the ten day period, it will have been made when perfected under Section 547(e)(2)(B).

The security interest was effective between Loken and Romania on October 19, 1991. The DMV stamped Romania's application as received on October 31, 1991. The security interest was perfected on that date. This was beyond the ten day grace period allowed. Therefore, under Section 547(e)(2)(B), the transfer of the security interest is treated as made on October 31, 1991, and not October 19, 1991. Consequently, the transfer was made on account of an antecedent debt under Section 547(b)(2) and that essential element of the preference claim was met.

Loken, 175 B.R. at 61-64.

The recent amendment to section 547(c)(3)(B), which extended the time period in which a lender may perfect its security interest from 10 to 20 days after the debtor receives possession of the property, is further support for the Court's conclusion that state law relation-back periods do not apply. As astutely noted by the bankruptcy court in Walker, 161 B.R. at 499, n. 18:

> Interestingly, Senate Bill No. 540, a comprehensive set of amendments to the Bankruptcy Code is currently under consideration in Congress. One such change proposed by the bill would be to extend the Section 547(c)(3) grace period to 20 days from the present 10 days because most states have now adopted longer periods for perfection of purchase money security interests. If Defendant's position is correct, and state relation back statutes are already operative under the statute, it is curious that some in Congress feel the need for an amendment to the Code. S.Rep. No. 103-168, 103d Cong. (1993).

See also H.R.Rep. 103-834, 103d Cong., 2d Sess. 20 (Oct. 4, 1994); 140 Cong.Rec. H10767 (Oct. 4, 1994), reprinted in Norton Bankruptcy Code Pamphlet p. 596 (1994-95 ed.) (The amendment to section 547(c)(3)(B) "conforms bankruptcy law practices to most States' practice by granting purchase-money security lenders a 20-day period in which to perfect their security interest."). [Footnote omitted]

Here, there is no dispute that Beasley received possession of the 1994 Ford Probe on August 17, 1994. Pursuant to Missouri law, the security interest was perfected at the earliest on September 7, 1994, or 21 days later, when Fidelity Financial mailed an application for Missouri Title and License noting the lien together with the requisite fee to the Missouri Department of Revenue. See In re Schalk, 592 F.2d 993, 996-97 (8th Cir.1979) (applying Missouri law) (The security interest is perfected at the earliest when the lender sends an application for a certificate of ownership noting the lien with the required fee to the Missouri Department of Revenue.); Mo.Rev.Stat. § 301.600.2 (1994). The 30-day relation-back period prescribed in Mo.Rev.Stat. § 301.600.2 is inapplicable. Fidelity Financial perfected its lien beyond the 20-day relation-back period provided in section 547(c)(3)(B). Fidelity Financial's security interest in the 1994 Ford Probe is deemed avoided pursuant to section 547(b). The Court will set aside Fidelity Financial's lien as a voidable preference.

CONCLUSION

Based on the above discussion, the Chapter 13 Trustee's request for relief in his complaint is GRANTED. Fidelity Financial Services's lien is set aside as a voidable preference.

The foregoing Memorandum Opinion constitutes Findings of Fact and Conclusions of Law as required by Fed.R.Bankr.P. 7052. So ORDERED.

NOTE ON *BEASLEY*

The bankruptcy court's decision in *Beasley* was affirmed first by the district court (which sits in review of final orders entered by the bankruptcy court), then by the Eighth Circuit, and eventually by the United States Supreme Court. Fidelity Financial Services, Inc. v. Beasley, 118 S. Ct. 651 (1998). In its opinion, the Supreme Court agreed that while state law may determine *how* perfection is accomplished, it is wholly inapplicable to the determination of *when* a transfer occurs for purposes of avoidance as a preferential transfer under § 547 of the Bankruptcy Code. To maintain any measure of integrity, the time of transfer for preference purposes must be established on a uniform basis by federal law. Consequently, even though the lender in *Beasley* was deemed timely perfected under state law as of the date of the debtor's purchase of the automobile, that could not protect the lender from the trustee's ability to set aside the transfer because the physical act of perfection occurred not only beyond the 10-day period of § 547(e)(2), but also beyond the 20-day period in § 547(c)(3)(B), thus rendering the transfer preferential within the meaning of § 547(b), and unprotected by the defense in § 547(c)(3) for purchase money loans.

PROBLEMS

As illustrated by *Beasley*, the interaction between § 547(e), which determines the time when a transfer is deemed to occur for preference analysis purposes, and § 547(c)(3), which protects certain purchase money security interests from the trustee's preference avoiding power, is interesting and complex. Consider each of the problems below in light of the following common facts and referring to Bankruptcy Code § 547(b) and (e):

On June 1, Debtor borrows $50,000 from Bank and grants Bank a security interest in Debtor's existing and after-acquired equipment. On September 15, Debtor files a petition under chapter 7 of the Bankruptcy Code. At all times relevant, Debtor is insolvent.

1. If Bank files its financing statement on June 20, can its security interest be set aside as a preference?
2. Does your answer change if the financing statement is filed on June 9? Does it matter if the bankruptcy petition is filed on July 15 rather than September 15?
3. Suppose the same facts as Question #2 except that the loan was made on May 15. Is the security interest voidable as a preference?
4. Assume now that the loan occurred and the security interest was granted and perfected back in January. If, in August, the month before filing for bankruptcy, the debtor acquires a new piece of equipment, can the trustee avoid all or any portion of Bank's security interest?
5. Assume the same facts as Question #4 except that what happens in August is that the Debtor makes a $10,000 payment to Bank. Has there been a preference? See § 547(b)(5).

(b) PREFERENCE DEFENSES

PONOROFF, EVIL INTENTIONS AND AN IRRESOLUTE ENDORSEMENT FOR SCIENTIFIC RATIONALISM: BANKRUPTCY PREFERENCES ONE MORE TIME, 1993 Wis. L. Rev. 1439, 1480-82.

The idea of formally excepting certain kinds of preferential transfers from the reach of the trustee's avoidance power is of relatively recent origin as well. In fact, of the seven exceptions [now eight] carved out by section 547(c), only the exception which now appears as section 547(c)(4) had a specific statutory counterpart under the former Bankruptcy Act. The inclusion in the Bankruptcy Code of an integrated system of statutorily prescribed exceptions to the preference provision of section 547(b) can be explained, in part, by the need to temper the vastly expanded scope of the trustee's preference power resulting from the simultaneous elimination of a *mens rea* test and the incorporation of a statutory presumption of insolvency. That need, in turn, can be explicated in either or both of two ways. The exceptions in section 547(c) can be regarded as a "backdoor" way of reintroducing a moral standard into preference law. Alternatively, they can be seen as reconciling with the "equity is equality" principle the equally important but potentially antonymous policy of encouraging business concerns to continue to engage in credit transactions with a financially distressed debtor.

It would be difficult and perhaps unfair to disassociate completely the scheme of preference exceptions in section 547(c) from the sentiment that these transactions do not involve the sort of deliberate "eve of bankruptcy" grab which colored earlier preference law. Nevertheless, the central theme running through the preference exceptions is return to the transferor of equivalent new value such that, as a result of the transfer, there has not been any net diminution in the aggregate value of the estate available for distribution to general creditors. In this sense, the integrated scheme of exceptions in section 547(c) further coheres with the equality of distribution theme underlying the Bankruptcy Reform Act's approach to preferences generally.

NOTE ON PREFERENCE DEFENSES

Section 547(c)(3), which was the defense at issue in *Beasley*, supra, is a good illustration of the policy seeking to encourage creditors to continue to do business with a financially troubled debtor. By offering broad protection for loans that enable the debtor to acquire new assets, the theory is that the odds are improved that the debtor will be able to turnaround its financial misfortunes and avoid bankruptcy entirely. Moreover, since commensurate value has been added to the estate in the form of the purchase money collateral, the preferential effect of the transfer is *de minimus*. In many instances, of course, the transaction will not give rise to a preference at all since the security interest will have been given on account of new value. In other cases, however, the debtor may not receive the new property until several days or more have passed from the time the debt is incurred. The transfer of the security interest will now be on account of an antecedent debt. Thus, it is in the latter circumstances where § 547(c)(3) might be available to protect the purchase money seller or lender from the trustee's preference avoiding power.

Two other preference defenses tend to be important to secured lenders. Section 547(c)(1) protects transfers that are *intended to be*, and in fact *are*, in return for substantially contemporaneous new value. This provision tempers the harshness and inflexibility of the definition of a voidable preference in § 547(b). Because the term "substantially contemporaneous" is not defined, there is some disagreement over whether § 547(c)(1) can ever be invoked to prevent avoidance of a security interest perfected more than ten days following attachment. In W.T. Vick Lumber Co. v. Chadwick (In re W.T. Vick Lumber Co.), 179 B.R. 283, 291-92 (Bankr. N.D. Ala. 1995), the court announced its intention to follow the "strict rule" barring application of § 547(c)(1) to permit an increase in the 10-day period of § 547(e)(2) as the longest gap allowed between attachment and perfection. In contrast to *W.T. Vick Lumber Co.*, in Kepler v. Security Pacific Housing Servs. Corp. (In re McLaughlin), 183 B.R. 171 (Bankr. W.D. Wis. 1995), the court rejected the trustee's argument that perfection of the security interest can *never* be contemporaneous unless it occurs within 10 days of its creation. The Seventh Circuit, the *McLaughlin* court noted, follows a different rule on the ground that "the modifier 'substantial' makes clear that contemporaneity is a flexible concept which requires a case by case inquiry into all the relevant circumstances (e.g., length of delay, reason for delay, nature of the transaction, intentions of the parties, possible risk of fraud) surrounding an allegedly preferential transfer." Id. at 175 (citing Pine Top Ins. v. Bank of Am. Nat'l Trust & Sav., 969 F.2d 321, 328 (7th Cir. 1992)).

The other defense of major import to secured lenders is § 547(c)(5), which protects a "floating lien" in the debtor's inventory and receivables from the rule that, for preference purposes, a transfer of an interest in the debtor's property cannot occur until the debtor has acquired rights in the property transferred. The exception accomplishes its goal by insulating the inventory and receivables financer's lien from attack to the extent that the lender's position is not improved during the preference period. The theory of § 547(c)(5) is sound. It derives from the view that if there has been no financial improvement in the lender's position during the preference period, then any transfers of an interest in new collateral acquired within the preference period were merely in substitution of inventory or receivables in which the lender claimed a perfected interest prior to the commencement of the preference period. Correspondingly, there is no net diminution in the value of the debtor's property available for distribution to other creditors. This theory has its origin in case law addressing the issue under the preference provision (§ 60(a)(2)) of the former Bankruptcy Act which contained no statutory exception for floating liens. In DuBay v. Williams, 417 F.2d 1277 (9th Cir. 1969), Judge Hufstedler reasoned as follows:

> Section 60a(2) of the Bankruptcy Act provides that 'a transfer of property * * * shall be deemed to have been made or suffered at the time when it became so far perfected that no subsequent lien upon such property obtainable by legal or equitable proceedings on a simple contract could become superior to the rights of the transferee.'

Congress did not state that a 'transfer' occurs when a security interest attaches or when state law says a conveyance has been made. Congress provided that a transfer is 'deemed' to have been made when it became 'so far perfected' that no subsequent lien creditor could achieve priority. 'Transfer' for the purpose of section 60a(2) is thus equated with the act by which priority over later creditors is achieved and not with the event which attaches the security interest to a specific account.

We look to state law, therefore, only to decide the point at which Rose City's claim to the future accounts was sufficiently asserted to prevent a subsequent lien creditor from achieving priority over it in those accounts. That time was the date upon which Rose City filed its financing statement. (Grain Merchants of Indiana, Inc. v. Union Bank & Savings Co., Bellevue, Ohio (7th Cir. 1969) 408 F.2d 209.) Because Rose City filed its financing statement long before the four-month period anteceding bankruptcy, its security interest is immune from the trustee's preference challenge.

There is no conflict between this result and the federal policy expressed in section 60 of the Bankruptcy Act. From the inception of section 60 in 1898, through its amendments, including the adoption of the present version in 1950, Congress intended to achieve two aims: (1) to prevent an insistent creditor from harvesting more than his fair share of the insolvent's assets by obtaining transfers from the debtor on the eve of bankruptcy, and (2) to discourage extension of credit to debtors under circumstances which concealed from general creditors the precarious financial condition of the debtor.

* * *

Nothing in the legislative history of section 60a(2) suggests that Congress intended to permit a trustee to upset floating liens on accounts receivable which, as here, were automatically perfected and which involved none of the symptoms of last minute favoritism characterizing true preferences. On the contrary, the history of the section shows that Congress knew how important accounts receivable financing was to the business community, particularly to small-business men, and one of Congress' principal objectives in amending section 60a(2) was to loosen the flow of credit to small-business men whose financing had been seriously impaired by the old bona fide purchaser test. * * *

The next case illustrates the operation of § 547(c)(5) of the Bankruptcy Code.

______

GALLOWAY v. FIRST ALABAMA BANK (IN RE WESLEY INDUSTRIES)

United States Courts of Appeals, Eleventh Circuit, 1994.
30 F.3d 1438.

BARKETT, Circuit Judge.

[In this case, the bank had established a revolving line of credit cash collateral account into which the debtor deposited proceeds from the sale of its accounts receivable, and from which the debtor made payments to the bank on a promissory note secured by, among other collateral, inventory and accounts receivable. The trustee specifically challenged three payments made during the extended one-year insider-preference period determined to be applicable in this case. The court agreed that the payments in question were preferential within the meaning of § 547(b), and then turned its attention to the exception in § 547(c)(5).]

Section 547(c)(5) provides in pertinent part:

> (c) The trustee may not avoid under this section a transfer—
>
> (5) that creates a perfected security interest in inventory or a receivable or the proceeds of either, except to the extent that the aggregate of all such transfers to the transferee caused a reduction, as of the date of the filing of the petition and to the prejudice of other creditors holding unsecured claims, of any amount by which the debt secured by such security interest exceeded the value of all security interests for such debt on the later of—
>
> (A) * * *
>
> (ii) with respect to a transfer to which subsection (b)(4)(B) of this section applies, one year before the date of the filing of the petition. * * *

The Bankruptcy Reform Act of 1978 ("the Act") established that a lender's perfected security interest in property later acquired independently by the debtor might not be insulated from preferential attack. Section 547(c)(5) of the Act carves out an exception for inventory or accounts receivable that protects the transfer of a security interest in after-acquired property, i.e., a "floating lien," provided that the creditor does not improve its position within the vulnerable period prior to bankruptcy. This exception:

> permits a creditor with, say, a 'floating lien' on the 'receivables' of such a company to maintain that lien as the specific accounts receivable are paid off, and replaced by new ones, without fear that a future bankruptcy trustee will mount a preference attack on new accounts receivable arising during the 'preference' period * * * . Insofar as the grant of a security interest in the new collateral (receivables or inventory that comes into existence during the preference period) improves the creditor's position (compared to his position at the beginning of the preference period), the grant of security constitutes a preference to the extent of the improvement.
>
> Braunstein v. Karger (In re Melon Produce, Inc.), 976 F.2d 71, 75 (1st

Cir.1992) (citation omitted). The bankruptcy judge recognized that the secured transaction at issue in this case was a "floating lien." We adopt this determination and now apply the "improvement in position" test.

To determine whether a creditor improves its position, the factfinder must compare the amount of debt outstanding to the value of collateral securing the debt (i.e., inventory and accounts receivable) at the beginning and end of the appropriate preference period. Roemelmeyer v. Walter E. Heller & Co., Southeast, Inc. (In re Lackow Bros., Inc.), 752 F.2d 1529, 1531-32 (11th Cir.1985). At each point in time, the difference between debt outstanding and collateral is deemed a "deficiency." There is no "improvement in position" so long as the deficiency at the beginning of the preference period is equal to or smaller than the deficiency at the end of the preference period.

If on February 21, 1989 (the date one year prior to Debtor's filing for bankruptcy), the amount of First Alabama's deficiency was greater than it was on the date of filing, the Trustee could recover the payments Debtor made from its cash collateral fund to First Alabama. If, however, the amount of the deficiency was smaller, reflecting no relative improvement in position, then § 547(c)(5) provides First Alabama with a complete defense to the Trustee's attempt to avoid the cash collateral transfers.

The bankruptcy judge applied the "improvement in position" test by calculating the deficiency at the two relevant points in time. The bankruptcy court found that on February 21, 1989, First Alabama's collateral was valued at $363,048, securing an obligation of $1,300,000. The court determined the deficiency on that date to be $936,952. The court then looked to the date the Debtor filed the bankruptcy petition and found that on February 21, 1990, First Alabama's collateral was valued at $70,442, securing an obligation of $1,034,815 and resulting in a $964,373 deficiency. Applying the "improvement in position" test, the bankruptcy judge found an increase in the amount of the deficiency between the two relevant points in time.

It is clear from these numbers that First Alabama did not improve its position with regard to the cash collateral account during the one year immediately preceding the Chapter 11 filing to the prejudice of the debtor's unsecured creditors. The amount by which the debt exceeded the value of the collateral increased rather than decreased during this time. * * *

Discovering no error in the factual findings of the lower courts, and no abuse of discretion, we affirm the judgment of the district court in its entirety.

AFFIRMED.

QUESTIONS

1. The "improvement in position" test in § 547(c)(5) requires valuing the debtor's inventory at both the onset of the preference period and as of the date of filing. The method of valuation chosen will tend to have a significant effect on the portion of the inventory and receivables security interest that

can be set aside by the trustee. For example, if the lender is fully secured as of the commencement of the preference period there can never be an improvement in position because it would be impossible for the unsecured deficiency to be reduced from $0. The question then becomes what method of valuing the inventory should be used? "On-going concern" value? Cost? Liquidation value? For differing approaches to the question, see Smith v. Associates Commercial Corp. (In re Clark Pipe & Supply Co.), 893 F.2d 693, 698 (5th Cir. 1990); Samson v. Alton Bank & Trust Co. (In re Ebbler Furniture & Appliances, Inc.), 804 F.2d 87 (7th Cir. 1986); and Roemelmeyerv. Walter E. Heller & Company, Southeast (In re Lackow Brothers, Inc.), 752 F.2d 1529 (11th Cir. 1985).

2. Assume that a secured party has a first lien security interest on all of the debtor's inventory. At the beginning of the preference period, the debt is $100,000 and there is $50,000 in inventory. On the date of filing the debt is still $100,000, but the value of the inventory is now $60,000 as a result of an increase in the market value of goods of that kind. Has there been an improvement in the lender's position? Can any portion of the lien be set aside as a preference? Why or why not?

IN RE COMPTON CORP.

United States Court of Appeals, Fifth Circuit, 1987.
831 F.2d 586, modified, 835 F.2d 584 (1988).

JERRE S. WILLIAMS, Circuit Judge.

This is a bankruptcy preference case in which a bankruptcy trustee seeks to recover a transfer made via a letter of credit for the benefit of one of the debtor's unsecured creditors on the eve of bankruptcy. The bankruptcy court and the district court found there to be no voidable preference. We reverse.

I. Factual Background

In March 1982, Blue Quail Energy, Inc., delivered a shipment of oil to debtor Compton Corporation. Payment of $585,443.85 for this shipment of oil was due on or about April 20, 1982. Compton failed to make timely payment. Compton induced Abilene National Bank (now MBank-Abilene) to issue an irrevocable standby letter of credit in Blue Quail's favor on May 6, 1982. Under the terms of the letter of credit, payment of up to $585,443.85 was due Blue Quail if Compton failed to pay Blue Quail this amount by June 22, 1982. Compton paid MBank $1,463.61 to issue the letter of credit. MBank also received a promissory note payable on demand for $585,443.85. MBank did not need a security agreement to cover the letter of credit transaction because a prior 1980 security agreement between the bank and Compton had a future advances provision. This 1980 security agreement had been perfected as to a variety of Compton's assets through the filing of several financing statements. The most recent financing statement had been filed a year before, May 7, 1981. The letter of credit on its face noted that it was for an antecedent debt due Blue Quail.

On May 7, 1982, the day after MBank issued the letter of credit in Blue Quail's favor, several of Compton's creditors filed an involuntary bankruptcy petition against Compton. On June 22, 1982, MBank paid Blue Quail $569,932.03 on the letter of credit after Compton failed to pay Blue Quail.

In the ensuing bankruptcy proceeding, MBank's aggregate secured claims against Compton, including the letter of credit payment to Blue Quail, were paid in full from the liquidation of Compton's assets which served as the bank's collateral. Walter Kellogg, bankruptcy trustee for Compton, did not contest the validity of MBank's secured claim against Compton's assets for the amount drawn under the letter of credit by Blue Quail. Instead, on June 14, 1983, trustee Kellogg filed a complaint in the bankruptcy court against Blue Quail asserting that Blue Quail had received a preferential transfer under 11 U.S.C. § 547 through the letter of credit transaction. The trustee sought to recover $585,443.85 from Blue Quail pursuant to 11 U.S.C. § 550.

Blue Quail answered and filed a third party complaint against MBank. On June 16, 1986, Blue Quail filed a motion for summary judgment asserting that the trustee could not recover any preference from Blue Quail because Blue Quail had been paid from MBank's funds under the letter of credit and therefore had not received any of Compton's property. On August 27, 1986, the bankruptcy court granted Blue Quail's motion, agreeing that the payment under the letter of credit did not constitute a transfer of debtor Compton's property but rather was a transfer of the bank's property. The bankruptcy court entered judgment on the motion on September 10, 1986. Trustee Kellogg appealed this decision to the district court. On December 11, 1986, the district court affirmed the bankruptcy court ruling, holding that the trustee did not establish two necessary elements of a voidable transfer under 11 U.S.C. § 547. The district court agreed with Blue Quail and the bankruptcy court that the trustee could not establish that the funds transferred to Blue Quail were ever property of Compton. Furthermore, the district court held that the transfer of the increased security interest to MBank was a transfer of the debtor's property for the sole benefit of the bank and in no way benefitted Blue Quail. The district court therefore found no voidable preference as to Blue Quail. The trustee is appealing the decision to this Court.

II. The Letter of Credit

It is well established that a letter of credit and the proceeds therefrom are not property of the debtor's estate under 11 U.S.C. § 541. When the issuer honors a proper draft under a letter of credit, it does so from its own assets and not from the assets of its customer who caused the letter of credit to be issued. As a result, a bankruptcy trustee is not entitled to enjoin a post petition payment of funds under a letter of credit from the issuer to the beneficiary, because such a payment is not a transfer of debtor's property (a threshold requirement under 11 U.S.C. § 547(b)). A case apparently holding otherwise, In re Twist Cap., Inc., 1 B.R. 284 (Bankr.Fla. 1979), has been roundly criticized and otherwise ignored by courts and commentators alike.

Recognizing these characteristics of a letter of credit in a bankruptcy case is necessary in order to maintain the independence principle, the cornerstone of letter of credit law. Under the independence principle, an issuer's obligation to the letter of credit's beneficiary is independent from any obligation between the beneficiary and the issuer's customer. All a beneficiary has to do to receive payment under a letter of credit is to show that it has performed all the duties required by the letter of credit. Any disputes between the beneficiary and the customer do not affect the issuer's obligation to the beneficiary to pay under the letter of credit.

Letters of credit are most commonly arranged by a party who benefits from the provision of goods or services. The party will request a bank to issue a letter of credit which names the provider of the goods or services as the beneficiary. Under a standby letter of credit, the bank becomes primarily liable to the beneficiary upon the default of the bank's customer to pay for the goods or services. The bank charges a fee to issue a letter of credit and to undertake this liability. The shifting of liability to the bank rather than to the services or goods provider is the main purpose of the letter of credit. After all, the bank is in a much better position to assess the risk of its customer's insolvency than is the service or goods provider. It should be noted, however, that it is the risk of the debtor's insolvency and not the risk of a preference attack that a bank assumes under a letter of credit transaction. * * *

The trustee in this case accepts this analysis and does not ask us to upset it. The trustee is not attempting to set aside the post petition payments by MBank to Blue Quail under the letter of credit as a preference; nor does the trustee claim the letter of credit itself constitutes debtor's property. The trustee is instead challenging the earlier transfer in which Compton granted MBank an increased security interest in its assets to obtain the letter of credit for the benefit of Blue Quail. Collateral which has been pledged by a debtor as security for a letter of credit is property of the debtor's estate. The trustee claims that the direct transfer to MBank of the increased security interest on May 6, 1982, also constituted an indirect transfer to Blue Quail which occurred one day prior to the filing of the involuntary bankruptcy petition and is voidable as a preference under 11 U.S.C. § 547. This assertion of a preferential transfer is evaluated in Parts III and IV of this opinion.

It is important to note that the irrevocable standby letter of credit in the case at bar was not arranged in connection with Blue Quail's initial decision to sell oil to Compton on credit. Compton arranged for the letter of credit after Blue Quail had shipped the oil and after Compton had defaulted in payment. The letter of credit in this case did not serve its usual function of backing up a contemporaneous credit decision, but instead served as a back up payment guarantee on an extension of credit already in jeopardy. The letter of credit was issued to pay off an antecedent unsecured debt. This fact was clearly noted on the face of the letter of credit. Blue Quail, the beneficiary of the letter of credit, did not give new value for the issuance of the letter of credit by MBank on May 6, 1982, or for the resulting increased security interest held by MBank. MBank, however, did give new value for the increased security interest it obtained in Compton's collateral: the bank issued the letter of credit.

When a debtor pledges its assets to secure a letter of credit, a transfer of debtor's property has occurred under the provisions of 11 U.S.C. § 547. By subjecting its assets to MBank's reimbursement claim in the event MBank had to pay on the letter of credit, Compton made a transfer of its property. The broad definition of "transfer" under 11 U.S.C. § 101(50) is clearly designed to cover such a transfer. Overall, the letter of credit itself and the payments thereunder may not be property of debtor, but the collateral pledged as a security interest for the letter of credit is.

Furthermore, in a secured letter of credit transaction, the transfer of debtor's property takes place at the time the letter of credit is issued (when the security interest is granted) and received by the beneficiary, not at the time the issuer pays on the letter of credit.

The transfer to MBank of the increased security interest was a direct transfer which occurred on May 6, 1982, when the bank issued the letter of credit. Under 11 U.S.C. § 547(e)(2)(A), however, such a transfer is deemed to have taken place for purposes of 11 U.S.C. § 547 at the time such transfer "takes effect" between the transferor and transferee if such transfer is perfected within 10 days. The phrase "takes effect" is undefined in the Bankruptcy Code, but under Uniform Commercial Code Article 9 law, a transfer of a security interest "takes effect" when the security interest attaches. Because of the future advances clause in MBank's 1980 security agreement with Compton, the attachment of the MBank's security interest relates back to May 9, 1980, the date the security agreement went into effect. The bottom line is that the direct transfer of the increased security interest to MBank is artificially deemed to have occurred at least by May 7, 1981, the date MBank filed its final financing statement, for purposes of a preference attack against the bank. This date is well before the 90 day window of 11 U.S.C. § 547(b)(4)(A). This would protect the bank from a preference attack by the trustee even if the bank had not given new value at the time it received the increased security interest. MBank is therefore protected from a preference attack by the trustee for the increased security interest transfer under either of two theories: under 11 U.S.C. § 547(c)(1) because it gave new value and under the operation of the relation back provision of 11 U.S.C. § 547(e)(2)(A). The bank is also protected from any claims of reimbursement by Blue Quail because the bank received no voidable preference.

The relation back provision of 11 U.S.C. § 547(e)(2)(A), however, applies only to the direct transfer of the increased security interest to MBank. The indirect transfer to Blue Quail that allegedly resulted from the direct transfer to MBank occurred on May 6, 1982, the date of issuance of the letter of credit. The relation back principle of 11 U.S.C. § 547(e)(2)(A) does not apply to this indirect transfer to Blue Quail. Blue Quail was not a party to the security agreement between MBank and Compton. So it will not be able to utilize the relation back provision if it is deemed to have received an indirect transfer resulting from the direct transfer of the increased security interest to MBank. Blue Quail, therefore, cannot assert either of the two defenses to a preference attack which MBank can claim. Blue Quail did not give new value under § 547(c)(1), and it received a transfer within 90 days of the filing of Compton's bankruptcy petition.

III. Direct/Indirect Transfer Doctrine

The federal courts have long recognized that "[t]o constitute a preference, it is not necessary that the transfer be made directly to the creditor." National Bank of Newport v. National Herkimer County Bank, 225 U.S. 178, 184, 32 S.Ct. 663, 635, 56 L.Ed. 1042 (1912). "If the bankrupt has made a transfer of his property, the *effect* of which is to enable one of his creditors to obtain a greater percentage of his debt than another creditor of the same class, circuity of arrangement will not avail to save it." Id. (Emphasis added). To combat such circuity, the courts have broken down certain transfers into two transfers, one direct and one indirect. The direct transfer to the third party may be valid and not subject to a preference attack. The indirect transfer, arising from the same action by the debtor, however, may constitute a voidable preference as to the creditor who indirectly benefitted from the direct transfer to the third party.

This is the situation presented in the case before us. The term "transfer" as used in the various bankruptcy statutes through the years has always been broad enough to cover such indirect transfers and to catch various circuitous arrangements.

* * *

IV. The Direct/Indirect Doctrine in the Context of a Letter of Credit Transaction

The case at bar differs from the cases discussed in Part III supra only by the presence of the letter of credit as the mechanism for paying off the unsecured creditor. Blue Quail's attempt to otherwise distinguish the case from the direct/indirect transfer cases does not withstand scrutiny.

In the letter of credit cases discussed in Part II supra, the letters of credit were issued contemporaneously with the initial extension of credit by the beneficiaries of the letters. In those cases the letters of credit effectively served as security devices for the benefit of the creditor beneficiaries and took the place of formal security interests. The courts in those cases properly found there had been no voidable transfers, direct or indirect, in the letter of credit transactions involved. New value was given contemporaneously with the issuance of the letters of credit in the form of the extensions of credit by the beneficiaries of the letters. As a result, the 11 U.S.C. § 547(c)(1) preference exception was applicable.

The case at bar differs from these other letter of credit cases by one very important fact: the letter of credit in this case was issued to secure an antecedent unsecured debt due the beneficiary of the letter of credit. The unsecured creditor beneficiary gave no new value upon the issuance of the letter of credit. When the issuer paid off the letter of credit and foreclosed on the collateral securing the letter of credit, a preferential transfer had occurred. An unsecured creditor was paid in full and a secured creditor was substituted in its place.

The district court upheld the bankruptcy court in maintaining the validity of the letter of credit issued to cover the antecedent debt. The district court held that MBank, the issuer of the letter of credit, could pay off the letter of credit and foreclose on the collateral securing it. We are in full agreement. But we also look to the impact of the transaction as it affects the situation of Blue Quail in the bankrupt estate. We hold that the bankruptcy trustee can recover from Blue Quail, the beneficiary of the letter of credit, because Blue Quail received an indirect preference. This result preserves the sanctity of letters of credit and carries out the purposes of the Bankruptcy Code by avoiding a preferential transfer. MBank, the issuer of the letter of credit, being just the intermediary through which the preferential transfer was accomplished, completely falls out of the picture and is not involved in this particular legal proceeding.

MBank did not receive any preferential transfer—it gave new value for the security interest. Furthermore, because the direct and indirect transfers are separate and independent, the trustee does not even need to challenge the direct transfer of the increased security interest to MBank, or seek any relief at all from MBank, in order to attack the indirect transfer and recover under 11 U.S.C. § 550 from the indirect transferee Blue Quail.

We hold that a creditor cannot secure payment of an unsecured antecedent debt through a letter of credit transaction when it could not do so through any other type of transaction. The purpose of the letter of credit transaction in this case was to secure payment of an unsecured antecedent debt for the benefit of an unsecured creditor. This is the only proper way to look at such letters of credit in the bankruptcy context. The promised transfer of pledged collateral induced the bank to issue the letter of credit in favor of the creditor. The increased security interest held by the bank clearly benefitted the creditor because the bank would not have issued the letter of credit without this security. A secured creditor was substituted for an unsecured creditor to the detriment of the other unsecured creditors.

We also hold, therefore, that the trustee can recover under 11 U.S.C. § 550(a)(1) the value of the transferred property from "the entity for whose benefit such transfer was made." In the case at bar, this entity was the creditor beneficiary, not the issuer, of the letter of credit even though the issuer received the direct transfer from the debtor. The entire purpose of the direct/indirect doctrine is to look through the form of a transaction and determine which entity actually benefitted from the transfer.

The fact that there was a prior security agreement between the issuing bank and the debtor containing the future advances clause does not alter this conclusion. As we pointed out in Part II supra, this prior security agreement gave MBank an additional shield from preferential attack because of the relation back mechanism of 11 U.S.C. § 547(e)(2)(A). 11 U.S.C. § 547(e)(2)(A), however, does not avail Blue Quail to shield it from a preferential attack for the indirect transfer. The indirect transfer to Blue Quail occurred on May 6, 1982, when the letter of credit was issued and the increased security interest was pledged. This was the day before the involuntary bankruptcy petition was filed. For purposes of 11 U.S.C. § 547, a transfer of Compton's property for the benefit of Blue Quail did occur within 90 days of the bankruptcy filing. The bankruptcy and district courts erred in failing to analyze properly the transfer of debtor's property that occurred when Compton pledged its assets to obtain the letter of credit. This transfer consisted of two aspects: the direct transfer to MBank which is not a voidable preference for various reasons and the indirect transfer to Blue Quail which is a voidable preference.

All of the requirements of 11 U.S.C. § 547(b) have been satisfied in the trustee's preferential attack against Blue Quail. There was (1) a transfer of Compton's property for the benefit of Blue Quail (2) for an antecedent debt owed by Compton (3) made while Compton was insolvent (4) within 90 days before the date of the filing of the petition (5) that enabled Blue Quail to receive more than it would receive under a Chapter 7 liquidation. The net effect of the indirect transfer to Blue Quail was to remove $585,443.85 from the pool of assets available to Compton's unsecured creditors and substitute in its place a secured claim for the same amount.

The precise holding in this case needs to be emphasized. We do not hold that payment under a letter of credit, or even a letter of credit itself, constitute preferential transfers under 11 U.S.C. § 547(b) or property of a debtor under 11 U.S.C. § 541. The holding of this case fully allows the letter of credit to function. We preserve its sanctity and the underlying independence doctrine. We do not, however, allow an unsecured creditor to avoid a preference attack by utilizing a letter of credit to secure payment of an antecedent debt. Otherwise the unsecured creditor would receive an indirect preferential transfer from the granting of the security for the letter of credit to the extent of the value of that security. Our holding does not affect the strength of or the proper use of letters of credit. When a letter of credit is issued contemporaneously with a new extension of credit, the creditor beneficiary will not be subject to a preferential attack under the direct/indirect doctrine elaborated in this case because the creditor will have given new value in exchange for the indirect benefit of the secured letter of credit. Only when a creditor receives a secured letter of credit to cover an unsecured antecedent debt will it be subject to a preferential attack under 11 U.S.C. § 547(b).

V. Liability of MBank for the Preferential Transfer

Blue Quail has no valid claim against MBank for reimbursement for any amounts Blue Quail has to pay the trustee under the trustee's preference claim, just as the trustee has no preference challenge against MBank. Blue Quail received the preferential transfer, not MBank. MBank gave new value in exchange for the increased security interest in its favor. Thus, it is insulated from any assertion of a voidable preference. The bank in no way assumed the risk of a preference attack by issuing the letter of credit. For these reasons, we affirm the district court's dismissal of Blue Quail's request to proceed against MBank for reimbursement.

In addition, the trustee may not set aside the $1,463.61 fee Compton paid MBank to issue the letter of credit. This payment is not a preferential transfer. MBank has fully performed its duties under the terms of the letter of credit and has earned this fee. The services MBank rendered in issuing and executing the letter of credit constitute new value under the 11 U.S.C. § 547(c)(1) preference exception.

VI. Conclusion

Blue Quail Energy received an indirect preferential transfer from Compton Corporation on May 6, 1982, one day prior to the filing of Compton's bankruptcy petition. We reverse the district court and render judgment in favor of Trustee Kellogg against Blue Quail Energy, Inc. in the amount of $585,443.85 plus interest to be fixed by the district court pursuant to 11 U.S.C. §§ 547, 550. The district court's dismissal of Blue Quail's claim against MBank for reimbursement is affirmed.

REVERSED IN PART, AFFIRMED IN PART, AND REMANDED.

MORE ON *COMPTON* AND THE "TWO-TRANSFER" THEORY

In a 1989 decision, the Seventh Circuit rejected the "two-transfer" theory espoused in *Compton* in a case involving a payment on a corporate debt that had been guaranteed by an insider. Levit v. Ingersoll Rand Financial Corp., 874 F.2d 1186 (7th Cir. 1989). The payment was made to a noninsider creditor and occurred outside of the standard 90-day preference period. However, the transfer "benefited" the insider whose contingent liability on the guarantee had been reduced proportionately by the amount of the payment. Therefore, the extended one-year preference period applied. Because Bankruptcy Code § 550(a)(1) permits an avoided transfer to be recovered from *either* the transferee *or* the "entity for whose benefit such transfer was made," the trustee sought recovery from the solvent noninsider creditor. The creditor argued that since the transfer was only preferential as to the insider, recovery should be limited to the insider. The court disagreed, observing that avoidability is an attribute of the transfer, not the identity of the recipient. *Levit*, which was subsequently followed by several other circuit courts, evoked a hue and cry from the established lending community. The industry then put sufficient pressure on Congress so that in 1994, § 550 was amended to add a provision which provides:

> (c) If a transfer made between 90 days and one year before the filing of the petition—
> (1) is avoided under section 547(b) of this title; and
> (2) was made for the benefit of a creditor that at the time of such transfer was an insider;
>
> the trustee may not recover under subsection (a) from a transferee that is not an insider.

Although new § 550(c) unquestionably overrules the result in *Levit* it is unclear whether by adopting this provision Congress also intended to establish that *Levit* was not a proper interpretation of the preference law as it existed at the time the case was decided. The issue is of more than passing interest because § 550(c)'s protection is limited to transfers made for the benefit of a creditor that is also an *insider* of the debtor. Thus, it has no bearing one way or the other on whether *Compton* remains good authority or whether the reasoning employed by the court in *Levit* might be applied to a letter of credit issuing bank in the position of MBank in *Compton*. In fact, there are important distinctions between the letter of credit transaction at issue in *Compton* and the insider-guarantee scenario involved in *Levit.* These differences might influence the outcome one way or the other. For the time being, however, it seems fair to say that § 550(c) cannot be described as an outright rejection of two-transfer theory employed in *Compton.* Therefore, in indirect or triangular preferences involving non-insider creditors, the issue of whether the transaction should be viewed as involving one transfer or two remains an unsettled one. See generally Ponoroff, *Now You See It, Now You Don't: An Unceremonious Encore for Two-Transfer Thinking in the Analysis of Indirect Preferences*, 69 Am. Bankr. L.J. 203 (1995).

SECTION 5. OTHER MEANS OF AFFECTING SECURITY INTERESTS IN BANKRUPTCY

(a) EQUITABLE SUBORDINATION

BANKRUPTCY CODE § 510(c)

Notwithstanding subsections (a) and (b) of this section, after notice and a hearing the court may—

(1) under principles of equitable subordination, subordinate for purposes of distribution all or any part of an allowed claim to all or any part of another allowed claim * * *; or

(2) order that any lien securing such a subordinated claim be transferred to the estate.

SUMMIT COFFEE COMPANY v. HERBY'S FOODS, INC. (IN RE HERBY'S FOODS, INC.)

United States Court of Appeals, Fifth Circuit, 1993.
2 F.3d 128.

POLITZ, Chief Judge.

* * *

Background

Herby's Foods, Inc. produced and distributed fast foods to convenience stores. The Summit Coffee Company, Inc., Dunnam-Snyder Company, and The Snyder Company, Inc. (collectively, the Insiders) are interrelated companies that advanced funds to Herby's and possess claims as unsecured creditors in the Herby's bankruptcy.

The corporate "food chain" was as follows: (1) Herby's was a wholly owned subsidiary of Summit; (2) all of the voting securities of Summit were owned by Dunnam; (3) Dunnam is a partnership composed of seven trusts for the benefit of William Snyder's ex-wife and children; and (4) the managing agent for Dunnam at the time of Summit's acquisition of Herby's was Snyder Co., owned by William Snyder's ex-wife and children. In addition to the commonality of ownership interests, these companies enjoyed a commonality of management. At various times, William Snyder personally held several management positions, including president of Snyder Co., managing agent of Dunnam, an officer of Summit, and president of Herby's. The Insiders stipulated that they are "insiders" of Herby's as defined in the Bankruptcy Code.

Summit purchased Herby's on October 26, 1987 pursuant to a Stock Purchase Agreement. The purchase price was $5,500,000, $2,800,000 of which was actually a loan to Herby's to pay off an intercompany debt to its previous owner. Herby's executed a note and security agreement in favor of Summit for $2,800,000. Like the Stock Purchase Agreement, these documents were dated October 26, 1987; the security interest, however, was not perfected at that time.

In addition, Dunnam provided a working capital line of credit to Herby's in the amount of $4,000,000. The parties have stipulated that no third-party lender would make a working capital loan to Herby's on any terms. The line of credit was evidenced by Herby's promissory note and security agreement, both dated October 26, 1987. Once again, the security interest was not timely perfected. Through a series of draws, Herby's eventually borrowed the maximum amount available under this line of credit.

Summit did not file a UCC-1 to perfect its security interest under the purchase money loan until November 10, 1988, 13 months after the note and security agreement had been executed. Similarly, Dunnam did not file a UCC-1 to perfect its security interest under the working capital loan until June 9, 1989, 20 months after the date of the underlying note and security agreement. According to Snyder, both of these security agreements covered "basically everything" owned by Herby's. Snyder also admitted that, "[w]e delayed putting in the UCC's because we were hoping to get a secured lender."

Between Summit's acquisition of Herby's and the filing of its petition in bankruptcy on September 7, 1989, the amount that Herby's owed to its unsecured creditors (other than the Insiders) increased fivefold, from $929,550.23 to $4,635,675. Further, between January 6, 1989 and September 1, 1989, Snyder Co. made unsecured advances to Herby's exceeding $579,000, advances which were not evidenced by loan agreements or any other documentation and which apparently bore no interest.

After Herby's filed its voluntary Chapter 11 bankruptcy petition, the Insiders, as unsecured creditors, submitted these proofs of claims:

Summit	$3,086,394.52
Dunnam	$4,054,696.12
Snyder Co.	$579,276.47

The Official Unsecured Creditors Committee (the Committee) responded with a Complaint to Subordinate Claims, Avoid Liens and Object to Claims. In its complaint the Committee sought to subordinate and object to the claims of the Insiders and to avoid the liens of Summit and Dunnam. Neither Summit nor

Dunnam asserted liens, nor did they oppose their avoidance, apparently in recognition of their avoidability under 11 U.S.C. § 547. The Insiders opposed the avoidance of their claims and, alternatively their subordination to a level below that of general unsecured creditors.

The bankruptcy court applied the test for equitable subordination which we detailed in In re Mobile Steel Co. Under that test, equitable subordination is justified only if: (1) the claimant engaged in inequitable conduct; (2) the misconduct resulted in injury to the creditors or conferred an unfair advantage on the claimant; and (3) equitable subordination of the claim would not be inconsistent with the provisions of the Bankruptcy Act (now Bankruptcy Code). The bankruptcy court found in the affirmative on each of the three Mobile Steel inquiries and subordinated the claims of the Insiders to the level of equity holders, finding that this ranking was necessary to offset the harm that the debtor and its non-insider creditors had suffered as a result of the inequitable conduct of the Insiders. 134 B.R. 207 (Bkrtcy.N.D.Tex.1991).

Timely appealing the affirmance by the district court, the Insiders assert five points of error: (1) the finding that Herby's was undercapitalized on the date of Summit's acquisition; (2) the finding that the late perfection by Summit and Dunnam of their security interests constituted inequitable conduct; (3) the characterization of the sums advanced to Herby's by Summit, Dunnam, and Snyder Co. as equity contributions rather than loans; (4) the finding that the Insiders' actions harmed the other creditors sufficiently to warrant subordination; and (5) the affirmance of the extent of the equitable subordination ordered by the bankruptcy court.

Analysis

B. Principles of Equitable Subordination

The Bankruptcy Code provides that the bankruptcy court may "under principles of equitable subordination, subordinate for purposes of distribution all or part of an allowed claim to all or part of another allowed claim or all of part of an allowed interest to all or part of another allowed interest." The legislative history of this provision reflects that Congress "intended that the term 'principles of equitable subordination' follow existing case law and leave to the courts development of this principle." The equitable powers of a bankruptcy court, including the power to subordinate, may be "invoked to the end that fraud will not prevail, that substance will not give way to form, that technical considerations will not prevent substantial justice from being done."

In Mobile Steel we established the test to determine when equitable subordination is appropriate. In addition to the tripartite test noted above, we further held in Mobile Steel that three additional principles must be considered in determining whether the three prongs of the subordination test have been satisfied. First, the inequitable conduct by the claimant may be sufficient to warrant subordination whether or not the misconduct related to the acquisition or assertion of the claim. Second, a claim should be subordinated only to the extent necessary to offset the harm that the bankrupt and its creditors suffered as a result of the inequitable conduct. Third, the claims arising from the dealings between the debtor and its fiduciaries must be subjected to rigorous scrutiny, and, if sufficiently challenged, the burden shifts to the fiduciary to prove both the good faith of the transaction and its inherent fairness.

Subsequent to Mobile Steel, we expanded the class of claims that are subject to rigorous scrutiny to include insider claims. Additionally, if the claimant is an insider, less egregious conduct may support equitable subordination. The determination of insider status is a question of fact subject to the clearly erroneous standard of review.

Although the exact parameters of inequitable conduct have not been comprehensively or precisely delineated, such conduct does encompass: (1) fraud, illegality, breach of fiduciary duties; (2) undercapitalization; and (3) the claimant's use of the debtor corporation as a mere instrumentality or alter ego.

Undercapitalization generally refers to the insufficiency of capital contributions made to the debtor corporation. Inadequate capitalization may be established by the testimony of a skilled financial analyst that the capitalization "would definitely be insufficient to support a business of the size and nature of the bankrupt in light of the circumstances existing at the time the bankrupt was capitalized." Capitalization is also inadequate "if, at the time when the advances were made, the bankrupt could not have borrowed a similar amount of money from an informed outside source."

Even though undercapitalization alone generally does not justify equitable subordination, evidence of additional inequitable conduct may do so. For example, if an insider makes a loan to an undercapitalized corporation, the combination of undercapitalization and the insider loan may allow the bankruptcy court to recharacterize the loan as a capital contribution, or to equitably subordinate the loan to the claims of other creditors.

C. Equitable Subordination of Appellants' Claims

1. Undercapitalization

The record contains evidence to support the finding that Herby's was undercapitalized on the date of Summit's purchase. An expert financial witness tendered by the Committee testified that as of the date of its acquisition by Summit, Herby's capital was not sufficient to support its operations. The testimony of a former financial officer of Herby's corroborated the fact that on the date of its acquisition, Herby's was incapable of paying its debts as they became due and therefore was insolvent. William Snyder conceded that Herby's was insolvent on the date of acquisition.

We need not rely solely on the first prong of the Mobile Steel test for inadequate capitalization, however. The Insiders stipulated before trial that:

Prior to the closing, Snyder [Co.] on behalf of Dunnam, solicited certain financial institutions seeking a loan to complete the acquisition. No independent third-party lender, after reviewing the financial position of the Debtor and Summit, would lend Dunnam or the Debtor money secured by the assets of the debtor on terms acceptable to the Insider Claimants. Indeed, only one lender offered financing but it required personal guarantees * * * . The Debtor was not able to obtain working capital from a third-party lender after the Acquisition.

As evidenced by this stipulation, Herby's could not have borrowed a similar amount from an informed outside source on acceptable terms, either to complete the acquisition or to obtain working capital. We find no error in the bankruptcy court's determination that Herby's was undercapitalized on the date of acquisition. The finding is fully supported by the evidence.

2. Delayed Perfection as Inequitable Conduct

As stated, undercapitalization alone generally is insufficient to justify equitable subordination. The Insiders contend that the bankruptcy court erroneously treated the untimely perfection of their security interests as sufficient additional inequitable conduct to warrant subordination. We need not decide, however, whether the combination of undercapitalization plus merely the late perfection of security for the avowed purpose of "hoping to get a secured lender" constitutes sufficient inequitable conduct to support subordination; the Insiders herein did more.

The Insiders never injected any equity capital into Herby's, electing instead to advance funds through tardily perfected secured loans made at times when no bona fide third-party lender would have done so. With full knowledge that Herby's was undercapitalized and insolvent, the Insiders persisted with their practice of advancing funds only in the form of loans.

Further, the loan from Summit was not initially reflected on Herby's books. When finally booked, it was listed as an unsecured loan. Similarly, the Dunnam debt was never definitively identified on Herby's books. Finally, the purported working capital loans from Snyder Co., totaling over one-half million dollars, were never evidenced by any form of loan agreement.

Summit received only minimal interest payments and no principal payments on its note. It perfected its security position only after Herby's stopped making the interest payments. Likewise, Dunnam received only five interest payments and did not perfect its security interest until seven months after Herby's stopped payments. The working capital advances from Snyder Co. apparently never purported to bear any interest. We find more than adequate evidence of inequitable conduct on the part of the Insiders to support the court's equitable subordination of their claims.

3. Recharacterization

The Insiders also charge that the bankruptcy court erred in recharacterizing as equity contributions the sums advanced by the Insiders as loans, citing as support Tomlinson v. 1661 Corporation. They also complain that the Committee did not seek recharacterization, but only equitable subordination.

This point of error need not long detain us. We affirm the bankruptcy court's decision to subordinate the Insiders' claims to the level of equity, not any decision it might have made to recharacterize these advances from loan to equity. The Insiders concede in their brief that a court is authorized to recharacterize a loan as an equity contribution even when circumstances do not warrant equitable subordination. They further concede that in the instant case the practical effects of recharacterization on the one hand and equitable subordination to the level of equity on the other would be the same.

The judgment of the bankruptcy court declares that the claims of the Insiders "are hereby fully subordinated to those of the other unsecured creditors in this case." Even though that ranks the Insiders below the level of all other unsecured creditors, thereby putting the claims of the Insiders on the same level as equity holders, no mention of recharacterizing the Insiders' loans is made in the bankruptcy court's judgment. We recognize that language in the Memorandum Opinion and Order could be read to support the suggestion that the court recharacterized the claims at issue; however, such an implicit recharacterization was not essential to the bankruptcy court's judgment. Consequently, we need not decide whether the bankruptcy court in fact recharacterized the loans as equity and, if so, whether such recharacterization was proper. The court a quo expressly subordinated the Insiders' claims to a position below the level of unsecured creditors and we find that such subordination was fully justified in this case.

4. Harm to Other Creditors

The Insiders next maintain that their conduct did not harm the creditors of Herby's sufficiently to warrant subordination. They acknowledge, however, that the aggregate size of Herby's unsecured debt to its trade creditors increased from approximately $900,000 to over $4,600,000, and that the average number of days outstanding for trade payables increased almost elevenfold, from approximately seven to approximately seventy-five, between the date of Summit's acquisition of Herby's and its filing for relief in bankruptcy. Nevertheless, they insist that no evidence was presented to the bankruptcy court that any specific creditor was deceived or lured into extending additional unsecured credit by the actions as required by Fabricators. The Insiders' reliance on this argument is misplaced.

The Fabricators court found that inducing other creditors to extend additional credit through misrepresentations to be one form of inequitable conduct. In this point of error, the Insiders are not contesting the existence of inequitable conduct but, rather, whether such misconduct either produced injury to the arms-length creditors of the bankrupt or secured an unfair advantage for the miscreant claimants. Both injury and unfair advantage may be established by proving that a specific creditor was deceived or lured into extending additional credit to the bankrupt. "It is well established that actual fraud need not be shown for equitable subordination." Mere good faith on the part of the Insiders would not negate the harm sustained by Herby's creditors; neither would it lessen the advantage gained by the Insiders.

The bankruptcy court found that the Insiders' conduct harmed Herby's outside creditors by significantly increasing their trade credit exposure and by reducing their ultimate dividend in the liquidation. Most importantly, the court found that the Insiders had secured an unfair advantage by structuring their cash contributions to Herby's as loans, rather than as equity capital. If the Insiders were allowed to retain their ranking as unsecured creditors, they would have gained an advantage in the priority scheme by encouraging outside creditors to increase their credit exposure to Herby's. Their efforts were successful; those trade creditors substantially increased their credit to Herby's during the period in question. We are persuaded that the inequitable conduct of the Insiders produced sufficient injury to the unsecured trade creditors and secured a sufficiently unfair advantage for the Insiders to warrant equitable subordination.

5. Cure by Nonassertion

The Insiders argue that they cured any prior inequitable conduct by not trying to enforce their liens in bankruptcy and by seeking only the status of general unsecured creditors. They previously admitted, however, in their answer to the Complaint to Subordinate Claims, that Summit's and Dunnam's liens were avoidable, that they could only assert unsecured claims against the estate, and that they had no security interest in the proceeds of the sale of Herby's assets. They also admitted that Snyder never had a security interest to perfect. We cannot accept the proposition that the nonassertion of invalid claims results in the legal legerdemain suggested by the Insiders.

Even assuming that the Insiders had arguably valid claims as secured parties, their failure to file secured claims would not have cured what appears to be a previously obtained advantage. One might suggest that if the trade creditors had known that the Insiders early on had made secured loans to Herby's (thereby signaling that security was essential), the larger trade creditors would have declined to extend credit or would have sought secured status for themselves. The facts of the instant case support the proposition that the Insiders were able to lull the trade creditors into extending more unsecured credit to Herby's than they would have had they understood the Insiders' own assessment of Herby's financial health. The fact that the Insiders now seek only to be treated as unsecured creditors would not cure the effect of such deception of the trade creditors.

6. Degree of Subordination

The Insiders finally contend that their claims should have been subordinated only to the level of general unsecured creditors. "The prerogative to relegate claims to inferior status on equitable grounds, though broad, is not unlimited." As noted earlier, a claim should be subordinated only to the extent necessary to correct the harm or unfair advantage caused by the inequitable conduct.

The harm or unfair advantage that resulted from the Insiders' inequitable conduct is not limited to whatever may have resulted from their late perfection of Summit's and Dunnam's security interests. Both the harm and the unfair advantage are much more pervasive. Herby's was undercapitalized from the date of Summit's acquisition, and the Insiders did nothing to rectify that situation. Further, the advances from Summit and Dunnam were neither accurately nor timely reflected on Herby's financial records and the purported loans from Snyder Co. were never evidenced on the records or by any form of a loan agreement.

While these deceptive practices were being perpetrated, the aggregate sums owed by Herby's to its trade creditors increased by 3.7 million dollars. According to the record before us, the total amount distributable from Herby's estate will approximate 2.1 million dollars. If the claims of the Insiders are allowed a ranking equal to that of the unsecured trade creditors, the Insiders would receive approximately 75% of Herby's estate. This cannot be permitted. Even with subordination, the harm to the trade creditors will not be completely rectified. Anything less than full subordination would lend judicial approval to the unfair advantage secured by the Insiders. This we will not do.

AFFIRMED.

S. SNYDER & L. PONOROFF, COMMERCIAL BANKRUPTCY LITIGATION § 10.11 (1989, 1997).

From the individual creditor point of view, the implications of having its interest in the debtor's property set aside as a preference under section 547 or its claim equitably subordinated under section 510(c) may be the same—an advantage over competing creditors has been lost. However, both philosophically and procedurally, the two doctrines are quite different * * * . [R]egardless of effect, section 510(c) is not an avoiding power.

In a proper case, [however] preference law and the doctrine of equitable subordination may operate in tandem. For example, by means of conduct sufficient to justify subordination, a creditor may obtain payment of its claim or otherwise improve its position in advance of the bankruptcy filing. While the payment or advantage may be restored to the estate if the elements of section 547(b) can be satisfied, absent further sanction by the court the reproachable creditor will simply line up for payment along with all the blameless creditors in the order of priority established by the Bankruptcy Code. Therefore, if a complete remedy is to be provided for creditors harmed (beyond the loss resulting from the preference) by the preferred creditor's fraudulent or inequitable conduct, the guilty creditor's remaining unsecured claim also must be subject to subordination under section 510(c).

NOTES AND QUESTIONS

1. In *Herby's Foods* the relationship between the debtor and the creditors against whom subordination was sought was not limited to that of debtor and creditor. Because these creditors were also owners and managers of the debtor their interaction with the debtor was subject to exacting fiduciary standards. The "inequitable conduct" forming the basis for the subordination order was the breach of those duties. Ordinarily, a disinterested, arms-length creditor undertakes no fiduciary obligations to the debtor. Thus, the sort of self-interested behavior that might be grounds for subordination of an insider's claim is usually acceptable behavior for a noninsider creditor. This is why, traditionally, most equitable subordination cases have involved insiders. However, Berquist v. First National Bank of St. Paul (In re American Lumber Co.), 7 B.R. 519 (D. Minn. 1979), involved a conventional lender that, after the debtor became delinquent on

its loan, directed the debtor to continue business as usual while it began foreclosure of its receivables security interest. After the debtor filed for bankruptcy, the trustee argued that the lender's claim should be subordinated to the claims of other unsecured creditors on the ground that the business had been operated solely for the purpose of generating new receivables to apply to the lender's claim. Citing the lender's near total control over the debtor's operations, coupled with the failure to deal fairly and forthrightly with vendors and suppliers that all the while continued to extend new credit to the debtor oblivious of its imminent demise, the court ordered the subordination. *American Lumber* generated a great deal of criticism from banks and other traditional lenders that argued they should not have to risk subordination of their claims as the price for taking reasonable and customary steps to protect their credits and maximize their return after a debtor begins experiencing financial problems. Where is the line between the exercise of control sufficient to impose fiduciary-like obligations on the outside lender and a bank's exercise of what amounts to nothing more than prudent lending practices? For further discussion, see Smith v. Associates Commercial Corp. (In re Clark Pipe & Supply Co.), 893 F.2d 693 (5th Cir. 1990).

2. Should insiders ever be permitted to make loans to a debtor that share the same legal priority as the loans of arms-length creditors? Even if so, should insiders be permitted to make secured loans?

3. Although the court never reached the issue in *Herby's Foods*, why did the plaintiff argue that, and why did the bankruptcy court treat, the delayed perfection of the insiders' security interests as sufficiently inequitable conduct to warrant subordination?

4. In a nonbankruptcy situation, do the state courts have authority to adjust creditor priorities based on equitable considerations? See UCC § 1-103; Ninth District Production Credit v. Duggan, 821 P.2d 788 (Colo. 1991).

(b) CRAM-DOWN

KENNEDY, SECURED CREDITORS UNDER THE BANKRUPTCY REFORM ACT, 15 Ind. L. Rev. 477, 492-93 (1982).

The Bankruptcy Reform Act consolidates provisions that deal with rehabilitation as distinguished from liquidation. Reorganization of corporations, partnerships, and individually owned enterprises may be effected under Chapter 11, and secured claims as well as unsecured claims may be dealt with in a plan proposed and confirmed under that chapter. An official creditors' committee appointed in a Chapter 11 case, * * * can represent only the unsecured creditors, but there is authority for the appointment of additional committees, including one or more committees for secured creditors. A plan of reorganization under Chapter 11 may modify any secured debt with the consent of the creditor or of prescribed majorities of secured creditors in the same class. If the plan leaves the secured creditor or a class of secured creditors unimpaired, acceptance is presumed without the necessity of any solicitation. If the provisions of a plan affecting a secured debt are neither accepted nor deemed accepted, the court may nevertheless confirm a plan if it is found by the court to be "fair and equitable" and does not "discriminate unfairly." The standard of "fair and equitable" is satisfied with respect to secured claims if the plan provides as follows:

(i) (I) that the holders of such claims retain the lien securing such claims, whether the property subject to such lien is retained by the debtor or transferred to another entity, to the extent of the allowed amount of such claims; and

(II) that each holder of a claim of such class receive on account of such claim deferred cash payments totaling at least the allowed amount of such claim, of a value, as of the effective date of the plan, of at least the value of such holder's interest in the estate's interest in such property;

(ii) for the sale, subject to section 363(k) of this title, of any property that is subject to the lien securing such claims, free and clear of such lien, with such lien to attach to the proceeds of such sale, and the treatment of such lien on proceeds under clause (i) or (iii) of this subparagraph; or

(iii) for the realization by such holders of the indubitable equivalent of such claims.

IN RE NEFF

United States Bankruptcy Court, Northern District of Texas, 1985.
60 B. R. 448, aff'd w/o opinion, 785 F.2d 1033 (5th Cir. 1986).

MICHAEL A. McCONNELL, Bankruptcy Judge.

On January 12, 1984, Tom Stanley Neff ("Neff" or "the Debtor"), an individual engaged in the business of farming and ranching in Mitchell County, Texas filed a Petition for Reorganization under Chapter 11 of the Bankruptcy Code. Approximately one year later, Neff presented a plan to the Court for repayment of his debts which Neff now asks the Court to confirm.

* * *

Cram-Down on Secured Creditors—11 U.S.C. § 1129(b)(2)(A)

A plan can be forced on or "crammed down" on a class of secured creditors which rejects it if: 1. The holders of the secured claims in the class will continue to have a lien in the property subject to the lien whether that property is retained by the reorganized Debtor or transferred by it. 2. The holders of the secured claims in the class are to receive deferred cash payments under the plan totalling at least the allowed amount of the secured claim and of a present value at least equal to the value of the lien such holders have. 3. The holders of the secured claims receive the "indubitable equivalent" of their secured claim.

In general, the Debtor desiring to retain property subject to valid liens for a reorganization under Section 1129 can do so provided that (1) the Debtor has sufficient cash to pay off the secured debt in full; (2) the Debtor can negotiate the secured creditor into a bifurcated claim by the prospects of a better return on any unsecured deficiency under the plan; or (3) the Debtor has sufficient financial strength and future cash flow to establish that it can handle the increased debt service on a restructured, extended pay-out to the secured creditor. The last option requires restructuring in which the secured creditor can require total cash payment equalling his debt and also principal amount, amortization, and interest rates which will discount back to the present value of his collateral. Finally, the Debtor may offer the secured creditor the "indubitable equivalent" of his claim. 10 Broken Bench Review 69, October 1983.

The Claim of Sweetwater PCA

Because Class 8 (whose sole member is the Sweetwater Production Credit Association) voted against acceptance of the Plan of Reorganization, the plan of reorganization cannot be confirmed unless the "cram-down" provisions of Section 1129(b) have been met. The Plan of Reorganization provides that the Sweetwater Production Credit Association will retain all of its liens in (1) all of the Debtor's equipment and vehicles in which the Sweetwater Production Credit Association had a lien prior to the filing of this case, plus a replacement lien for any equipment purchased after the effective date of the plan, to provide adequate protection against depreciation; (2) the 450 to 500 head of cattle presently owned by the estate; and (3) the land in Mitchell and Dickins Counties, Texas. The Court further finds that for voting purposes the secured claim of Sweetwater Production Credit Association is approximately $2,147,382.00 and is fully secured.

The Debtor proposes to pay 100% of the secured portion of the Sweetwater Production Credit Association claim as follows. Neff will create a reserve for 1985 operating expenses and for taxes anticipated to be due and owing for 1984 income out of the proceeds from crops and cattle sold for the 1984 crop year. Additionally, the crop proceeds will be used to pay those classes of creditors entitled to payment at or immediately after confirmation. The remaining proceeds remaining after the creation of the reserves and the immediate payments will be applied to the Sweetwater Production Credit Association debt.

The principal amount of the Sweetwater Production Creditor Association claim remaining after the payment from crop proceeds of 1984 will be calculated by the value of the property securing the Sweetwater Production Credit Association as of the date the Plan is confirmed (approximately $2,147,382.00 as of November 15, 1984). The debt will be evidenced by a new note to be executed by Debtor and will be secured by all of the property in which the PCA has a presently existing valid lien, with the exception of the Ruidoso home. The note will be in the amount equal to the equity available to PCA in the properties securing the note. The PCA's claim for interest in excess of the value of property securing its claim is not recoverable under the Bankruptcy Code.

Neff will be obligated to make an annual payment on the secured note in at least the amount of interest which accrues on the principal amount of the note at a floating rate equal to the floating rate charged by the PCA to all its customers. At the end of the fifth full year after confirmation, all unpaid principal will be due in full as a "balloon payment" to the PCA.

During the five years after confirmation, Debtor shall have the right to seek permission to sell any of the properties securing the PCA secured note free and clear of liens as permitted by Section 1123(a)(5)(D) of the Code. The PCA's lien shall attach to any proceeds from such sale. Any unsecured portion of the claim will be paid on the same basis and in the same proportion as the claim of all Class 11 unsecured creditors.

As stated previously, Section 1129(b) allows a debtor to cram down a plan over the objection of a secured creditor if the secured creditor will receive deferred cash payments under the plan of a present value at least equal to the value of its collateral. As noted by Judge Lavien in In re Fi-Hi Pizza, Inc., 40 B.R. 258, 11 BCD 1209 (Bankr.D.Mass.1984):

> "In any case, the critical term to be analyzed is the elusive phrase "present value," also known as present discounted value. Present value is not necessarily a legal concept, but rather a term of art used by the economic and financial communities. In re Fisher, 29 B.R. 542, 543 (Bankr.D.Kansas 1983). One author has defined it as: 'the value today of a future payment or stream of payments, discounted at the appropriate discount rate.' Brigham, Financial Management Theory and Practice, 916 (1st Ed.1977); see also, Samuelson, Economics 596, 613-14 (9th Ed.1973); In re Fisher, 29 B.R. 542, 543. Put another way, present value reflects the financial reality that a dollar that is received in the future, is not worth the same as a dollar in hand today. Not only does inflation deflate the value of what a dollar may purchase in the future, but a party that has a dollar today may invest it in a variety of investments that would yield a return."

The factors relevant to determining an appropriate (discount) interest rate are catalogued in 5 Collier on Bankruptcy, P 1129.03, at 1129-65 (1982) as follows:

> "The appropriate discount (interest) rate must be determined on the basis of the rate of interest which is reasonable in light of the risks involved. Thus, in determining the discount (interest) rate, the court must consider the prevailing market rate for a loan of a term equal to the payout period, with due consideration of the quality of the security and the risk of subsequent default."

In the instant case, the Court finds that a floating rate of interest equal to the rate charged by Sweetwater PCA on all of its loans to other customers will give the PCA the "present value" of its claim, and, therefore, the Plan can be crammed down on the PCA over its objections. Moreover, in any event, the Court specifically finds that Sweetwater PCA has been given the "indubitable equivalent" of its claim.

* * *

NOTE ON "CRAM-DOWN" UNDER CHAPTERS 7 AND 13

Secured claims can also be modified (crammed-down) in chapter 13. Under § 1325(a)(5) a plan may be confirmed, over the objection of a secured creditor, provided that the secured creditor (i) retains its lien on the property, and (ii) the *value* of the payments to be distributed to that creditor under the plan is not less than the amount of the secured claim. Because under § 506(a) a claim is only secured to the extent of the value of the collateral, the latter requirement means that, at a minimum, the secured creditor must receive in present value terms the lesser of the value of the collateral or the amount of the indebtedness. The exercise entails first determining the value of the collateral, next establishing the payout term (usually 3 or 5 years), and finally applying the appropriate interest or discount rate to determine the monthly payment amount. This means that depending on prevailing market conditions, the chapter 13 debtor will be able not only to extend the term of the loan, but also to reduce the effective rate of interest and, in the case of a partially secured debt, reduce the principal amount of the note to the value of the collateral. In that event, the creditor will also have an unsecured claim for the deficiency, but the requirements relating to unsecured claims are far less demanding to satisfy. Bankruptcy Code § 1325(a)(4). The one exception to the foregoing is for claims secured solely by a mortgage on the debtor's principal residence. Section 1322(b)(2) prohibits modification of such claims (unless the last scheduled payment on the loan is due before the final payment under the plan). This means that the debtor's plan must provide for the continuation of regularly scheduled mortgage payments during the life of the plan, and the debt will *not* be discharged from personal liability on the mortgage note after completion of all payments provided for by the plan. Bankruptcy Code § 1328(a)(1). What policies justify the exclusion of home mortgage loans from secured debts subject to modification in chapter 13? In light of this exclusion, does chapter 13 offer any benefits to a debtor whose primary financial problem involves arrearages on her home mortgage loan? See Bankruptcy Code § 1322(b)(5).

There is no provision for cram-down in chapter 7. However, prior to 1992, one way in which chapter 7 debtors in some jurisdictions had managed to reduce the amount of liens encumbering their property was through the technique known as "lien stripping" under § 506(d). That provision provides that "to the extent a lien secures a claim against the debtor that is not an allowed secured claim, such lien is void." Relying on a literal reading of this language, some courts permitted a debtor who owned perhaps a home subject to a mortgage debt in an amount greater than the value of the home to nullify the portion of the lien that exceeded the value of the house. See Gaglia v. First Federal Savings & Loan Association, 889 F.2d 1304 (3d Cir. 1989). However, after a split in the circuits developed, the Supreme Court agreed to review the issue and ruled that lien stripping is not authorized in chapter 7. Over a strong dissent from Justice Scalia, the majority opinion concluded that § 506(d) only applies where the claim is *both* not allowed under § 502 *and* secured. Dewsnup v. Timm, 502 U.S. 410 (1992). In order to reach this result the Court was required to interpret the phrase "allowed secured claim" under § 506(d) as meaning something quite different from the indisputable meaning of the term under § 506(a). This unusual interpretation is open to serious question on both doctrinal and policy grounds. See Ponoroff & Knippenberg, *The Immovable Object Versus the Irresistible Force: Rethinking the Relationship Between Secured Credit and Bankruptcy Policy*, 95 Mich. L. Rev. ___ (1997).

SECTION 6. THE RIGHT OF RECLAMATION

COUNTRYMAN, THE CONCEPT OF A VOIDABLE PREFERENCE IN BANKRUPTCY, 38 Vand. L. Rev. 713, 822-23 (1985). "As I struggled through this extensive process of manufacturing contractual 'expectation interests' for many parties not given to these rarefied expectations, and as I recalled that section 547(c)(5) has proved to be the least important exception in section 547(c), I recalled also that I was experiencing a reaction similar to one I once provoked in my onetime colleague and longtime friend, Professor Gilmore. I once labored mightily to prove that U.C.C. section 2-502, giving a buyer of goods who had paid in advance a right to recover the goods from an insolvent seller, and section 2-702, giving an unpaid seller of goods on credit a right to reclaim them from an insolvent buyer, should not be applied in bankruptcy cases. Shortly thereafter, I received a brief note from Professor Gilmore. I have not preserved the note, but I am certain that I remember it exactly. Those who knew him will recognize it as pure Gilmore: 'I was surprised to learn that you were so exercised about § 2-502,' he wrote. 'It was drafted merely to placate Karl Llewellyn and was meant to be meaningless.'"

IN RE FEDERAL'S, INC.

United States Court of Appeals, Sixth Circuit, 1977.
553 F.2d 509.

ENGEL, Circuit Judge.

In this appeal we consider whether Section 2-702(2) of the Uniform Commercial Code, as enacted in Michigan, grants to a seller of goods a right of reclamation superior to the right of the insolvent buyer's trustee in bankruptcy and if so, whether that right must be invalidated as conflicting with Sections 64 and 67c(1)(A) of the Bankruptcy Act. 11 U.S.C. §§ 104 and 107c(1)(A). * * *

The facts were stipulated in the district court. On August 10, 1972 Matsushita Electric Corporation (Panasonic) delivered to Federal's, Inc. on credit electronic goods valued at approximately $64,000. On August 16, 1972 Federal's filed a petition under Chapter XI of the Bankruptcy Act and a receiver was appointed. Two days later, on August 18, 1972, Panasonic made timely demand, pursuant to Section 2-702(2) of the Uniform Commercial Code, M.C.L.A. § 440.2702, for the return of the merchandise delivered to Federal's. It was stipulated that Federal's intended to pay for the goods at the time they were ordered and received.

Upon these facts the district judge in a carefully considered opinion ruled in favor of the bankruptcy trustee on all issues, In the Matter of Federal's, Inc., 402 F.Supp. 1357 (E.D.Mich.1975).

I. PANASONIC'S RIGHT OF RECLAMATION UNDER SECTION 2-702(2)

In seeking to reclaim its merchandise, Panasonic relies upon the right of reclamation granted by § 2-702(2) of the Uniform Commercial Code as enacted in Michigan, M.C.L.A. § 440.2702(2). In resisting that right, the trustee in bankruptcy first asserts that the status conferred upon him by § 70c[1] of the Bankruptcy Act makes him a "lien creditor" under § 2-702(3) to which Panasonic's rights are subordinate.

The district court recognized, as do we, that any resolution of the issue as it arises in this circuit must commence with our decision in In re Mel Golde Shoes, Inc., 403 F.2d 658 (6th Cir. 1968). In that case Johnston & Murphy Shoes delivered a shipment of merchandise to Mel Golde Shoes, only to find them subject to an attachment levied against Golde's inventory by one of Golde's creditors. On February 2, Mel Golde filed a petition under Chapter XI of the Bankruptcy Act, but only after Johnston & Murphy, exercising the right of reclamation under § 2-702(2) as enacted in Kentucky, KRS § 355.2-702(2), made timely demand for the return of the merchandise.

On petition for review the district court ruled that under the Code, Johnston & Murphy possessed an unperfected security interest in the goods within the meaning of U.C.C. § 9-301 and that its right was therefore inferior to the rights of a lien creditor. On appeal this court reversed and rejected the claim that a seller of goods under § 2-702(2) is to be treated as a creditor with an unperfected security interest. Instead, we held that the rights of an unpaid seller under the Code are tantamount to those of a defrauded seller of goods under common law, a view consistent with the Official Comment to § 2-702 that the subsection "takes as its base line the proposition that any receipt of goods on credit by an insolvent buyer amounts to a tacit business misrepresentation of solvency and therefore is fraudulent as against the particular seller". In re Mel Golde Shoes, supra, at 660, quoting the Official Comment. The question then was whether in Kentucky the rights of a defrauded seller of goods were superior to the rights of a lien creditor. Because we reasoned that the question was not resolved by any provision in the Kentucky Code, it was necessary to repair to the pre-Code common law of Kentucky. We concluded that Kentucky conformed to the general rule that a defrauded seller's right to reclaim his goods is superior to that of an attaching creditor.

Despite some dissatisfaction expressed by the bankruptcy judge and the district court concerning the requirement of Mel Golde that the rights of a lien creditor are to be determined by reference to pre-Code state law, see In the Matter of Federal's, supra, at 1359 n. 1, we adhere to that view here. See also, In re Kravitz, 278 F.2d 820 (3rd Cir. 1960).

---

[1] Section 70c of the Bankruptcy Act was the predecessor of section 544 of the Bankruptcy Code [eds.].

Michigan's enactment of § 2-702, like Kentucky's, does not provide any express guidance concerning the relative priorities of a seller under § 2-702(2) and the trustee of the bankrupt buyer. As in Mel Golde, we are therefore put to the task of examining pre-existing Michigan law, of applying it to the extent we can ascertain it and making an educated determination of how Michigan courts would deal with the question to the extent it has not been precisely answered.

The district court correctly observed that there are no reported cases in Michigan which involve the competing claims of a buyer's judicial lien creditor and a reclaiming defrauded seller. In a review of numerous early Michigan decisions, the district court concluded that Michigan makes a distinction between lien creditors on the basis of whether the consideration for the lien was advanced before or after the seller had delivered the goods to the insolvent buyer. It concluded that at least to the extent that the consideration was advanced after the delivery of the goods, the rights of the lien creditor were superior to the rights of the reclaiming seller. This line of reasoning, however, required a further inquiry into whether the hypothetical lien creditor under § 70c is to be construed as one whose judgment is based upon a consideration which arose before or after the delivery of the goods.

* * *

[The court then held that section 70c did not give the trustee the rights of a lien creditor that extends credit after the delivery of the goods.]

B. PRIORITY UNDER MICHIGAN LAW

Even if the trustee is assumed to have extended credit subsequent to the delivery of the goods to the insolvent buyer, it would still be necessary to decide whether under Michigan law the trustee then would prevail over the defrauded seller. Once again we disagree with the district court in its analysis of the problem. While it is true that the cases cited by the district court indicate that the rights of a defrauded vendor may be inferior to those of a chattel mortgagee who without notice obtained his mortgage for present value from the purchaser, nevertheless it is significant that, with the possible exception of Hoffman v. Lake Shore & Michigan Southern R.R., supra, each case involved not a judicial lien, but rather a consensual lien granted by the bankrupt to one who, without knowledge of the rights of the defrauded seller, had advanced present consideration. However, § 70c requires us to look to the assumed powers of the trustee based on liens obtained by legal proceedings, not liens obtained consensually.

The common law of Michigan is generally that an execution sale passes only whatever title the judgment debtor had in the property. In French v. DeBow, 38 Mich. 708, 712 (1878), the court held that a levy of execution did not "give to the creditor any rights analogous to those of a bona fide purchaser . . . The creditor, when he makes sale on his execution and becomes the purchaser, may thereby acquire new equities; but until that time he stands in the rights of his debtor and the levy may be defeated by equities which the debtor is unable to resist."

This rule has been observed in the decisions of our circuit noting the scope of a trustee's power in the State of Michigan. In In re Toms, 101 F.2d 617, 619 (6th Cir. 1939), we held that the trustee takes such property not as an innocent purchaser but subject to all valid claims, liens and equities enforceable against the bankrupt, except in cases where there has been a conveyance or encumbrance which is void or voidable as to the trustee by some positive provision of the Bankruptcy Act.

* * *

Reversed and remanded for further proceedings consistent herewith.

IN RE KRAVITZ

United States Court of Appeals, Third Circuit, 1960.
278 F.2d 820.

GOODRICH, Circuit Judge.

This is a reclamation proceeding in which a seller of goods to the bankrupts seeks to reclaim them from the trustee in bankruptcy. The goods have been sold under stipulation and the claim is now against the fund. Both the referee and the learned district court have denied reclamation and the seller of the goods appeals.

On January 16, 1958, the bankrupts purchased goods on credit from the seller, The Wilcox-Gay Corporation; the goods were delivered to the bankrupts on January 17. On January 20, 1958, an involuntary petition in bankruptcy was filed and on January 21, 1958, the seller took the necessary steps to rescind the sale.

Whether the bankrupts in obtaining the goods had made 'materially false statements (relied on by the seller) as to their solvency and ability to pay' was a matter on which the referee and the district court differed in approach. The referee said that he would, if necessary, find that there was ample evidence to support the allegation that the 'bankrupts knew at the time of the purchase and delivery that they were hopelessly insolvent and could not pay for said merchandise and knowingly concealed their insolvency from' the seller. But he refused to decide whether there had been a positive misrepresentation which induced the credit. The district court, on the other hand, found that there was insufficient proof, as a matter of law, to support a finding of 'a positive misrepresentation which induced the credit,' and held that such proof was a necessary element of the seller's case. We agree with the referee that the answer to the question of 'positive misrepresentation' is immaterial for, in either event, the seller cannot prevail over the trustee.

The rights of a seller to reclamation of goods because of the insolvency of a buyer are, in Pennsylvania, stated in the Uniform Commercial Code, Pa.Stat.Ann.tit. 12A. Section 2-702(1) says that 'where a seller discovers the buyer to be insolvent he may * * * (b) subject to the rights of a buyer in ordinary course * * * or lien creditor under this Article (Section 2-403), and within ten days after receipt, reclaim any goods received by the buyer on credit * * * .'

Section 2-403(4) refers the rights of lien creditors to, inter alia, Article 9 and Section 9-301(3) says that the term 'lien creditor' includes 'a trustee in bankruptcy from the date of the filing of the petition * * * .'

Then when we come to the federal law, Section 70, sub. c of the Bankruptcy Act, 11 U.S.C.A. § 110, sub. c, states that 'the trustee, as to all property * * * upon which a creditor of the bankrupt could have obtained a lien by legal or equitable proceedings at the date of bankruptcy, shall be deemed vested as of such date with all the rights * * * of a creditor then holding a lien thereon by such proceedings, whether or not such a creditor actually exists.' This, of course, is the so-called 'strong-arm clause' of the statute by which the trustee becomes 'the ideal creditor, irreproachable and without notice, armed cap-a-pie with every right and power which is conferred by the law of the state upon its most favored creditor who has acquired a lien by legal or equitable proceedings.'

We think the correct way to put the matter is that by federal law the trustee in bankruptcy is made a lien creditor and that this right thus given him is recognized by the Uniform Commercial Code which simply states the power of the trustee as created by the prevailing law, that is, the federal law of bankruptcy.

It is perfectly clear that, while Section 70, sub. c of the Bankruptcy Act makes the trustee an ideal lien creditor, what such a lien creditor gets is determined by the law of the state involved, here Pennsylvania.

Then what right does an ideal lien creditor have in Pennsylvania? We think that the Pennsylvania law gives certain lien creditors a higher claim than that of a defrauded seller and that such precedent governs this case even assuming the seller to have been defrauded in fact. In Schwartz v. McCloskey, 1893, 156 Pa. 258, 263, 27 A. 300, 301, the court said: 'It has never been held, in this state, that, as against an attachment or execution on a debt contracted subsequent to the alleged voidable sale, the vendor could rescind, and reclaim the goods. On the contrary, in Smith v. Smith, 21 Pa.St. 367, the rule that he cannot do so is approvingly recognized. * * * Mann v. Salsberg, 1901, 17 Pa.Super. 280, 285, is an authority to the same effect and this principle, so far as we can ascertain, has never been overruled or modified in Pennsylvania. The Uniform Commercial Code does not change this rule. It seems to us, therefore, that, in Pennsylvania, the seller's right of rescission is not an absolute right at all but is subject to the right of a lien creditor who extended credit subsequent to the sale. By virtue of Section 70, sub. c of the Bankruptcy Act, the trustee in bankruptcy has the rights of such a lien creditor and is, in this case, entitled to the proceeds from the sale of the goods in question.

The judgment of the district court will be affirmed.

BRAUCHER, RECLAMATION OF GOODS FROM A FRAUDULENT BUYER, 65 Mich. L. Rev. 1281, 1282-84 (1967).

The Uniform Sales Act contained no provision on reclamation by a seller by reason of insolvency or fraud of the buyer. It was generally assumed that a defrauded seller could replevy the goods sold as against the buyer himself, but that insolvency without fraud was not a basis for rescission and replevin. Amid some dispute, there was substantial authority that a hopelessly insolvent buyer who received goods on credit was fraudulent if he knew payment was extremely unlikely and failed to disclose that fact, even though he intended to pay if he could.

The right of the seller to reclaim from the insolvent buyer himself is largely academic, since control of the goods could also be obtained by a levy under a judgment for the price. The question whether there is a right to reclaim ordinarily becomes critical only when there is a third-party claimant. Bona fide subpurchasers from the insolvent buyer have long been protected against avoidance of the buyer's voidable title. But it has been widely held that a levying creditor of the fraudulent buyer is not such a purchaser, at least where he extends credit before the fraudulent sale. Even where credit is extended after the sale, the orthodox rule would protect the levying creditor only if he purchases at an execution sale and pays the purchase price without notice of the fraud, or if there is an estoppel. The defrauded seller is estopped if by words or conduct he induces the creditor to believe that the fraudulent buyer is the owner of the goods, if he has reason to know that the creditor is likely to extend credit in reliance on the apparent ownership, and if the creditor does extend credit in reliance thereon.

A few cases, however, have applied a flat rule that creditors who extend credit to the buyer after he has taken possession under his fraudulent purchase and who levy on the goods are not subject to the seller's right to reclaim. Pennsylvania decisions to this effect were relied on in *In re Kravitz*, and there are a few decisions in other states suggesting a similar rule. Some decisions seem to treat any levying creditor without notice of the fraud as a bona fide purchaser, and occasionally an assignee for the benefit of creditors has been treated as a purchaser for value.

BANKRUPTCY CODE § 546(c)

Except as provided in subsection (d) of this section, the rights and powers of a trustee under sections 544(a), 545, 547, and 549 of this title are subject to any statutory or common-law right of a seller of goods that has sold goods to the debtor, in the ordinary course of such seller's business, to reclaim such goods if the debtor has received such goods while insolvent, but—

(1) such a seller may not reclaim any such goods unless such seller demands in writing reclamation of such goods—

(A) before 10 days after receipt of such goods by the debtor; or

(B) if such 10-day period expires after the commencement of the case, before 20 days after receipt of such goods by the debtor;

* * *

NOTES AND QUESTIONS

1. Section 546(c)(1) was adopted with a view toward clearing up the confusion over whether a seller's state-created right to reclaim goods was subject to the trustee's avoiding powers. Does it accomplish that goal?

2. There are some important differences between the state law requirements for reclamation in § 2-702(2) and § 546(c). For example, § 2-702 relieves the seller of the ten-day demand rule if the buyer made a written misrepresentation of solvency within three months before delivery of the goods. Section 546(c)(1) contains no such exclusion. If a seller can establish compliance with § 2-702(2) but not § 546(c) can the seller maintain a claim to the goods? If so, would such claim be subject to the trustee's avoiding powers?

3. Both §§ 2-702(2) and 546(c) require that the buyer be *insolvent* at the time the goods were received in order for the seller to establish a valid reclamation claim. However, the UCC's definition of when a person is "insolvent" in § 1-201(23) is broader than the Bankruptcy Code definition of the term in § 101(32). Can a reclaiming seller under § 546(c) rely on the UCC's definition? See Pike Tool & Grinding v. Storage Technology Corp. (In re Storage Technology Corp.), 48 B.R. 862 (D. Colo. 1985).

4. As earlier discussed, a reclaiming seller's rights under § 2-702(2) are still subject to the rights of a "good faith purchaser." What happens in a bankruptcy case when the goods in dispute become subject to the claim of a prior security interest in the debtor's property under the terms of a valid after acquired property clause? Can an Article 9 secured party be a good faith purchaser? If so, what happens to the reclaiming seller's claim? See American Saw & Mfg. Co. v. Bosler Supply Group (In re Bosler Supply Group), 74 B.R. 250 (N.D. Ill. 1987).

PART IV

COMMERCIAL SYSTEMS

INTRODUCTORY NOTE

(1) Avoiding the Transaction Costs of Contract

The effort to streamline commercial transactions entails three objectives. The first is avoiding two sources of transaction cost: (a) the cost of fashioning the relationships merchants enter into and (b) the cost of structuring obligations. The doctrines of consideration and promissory estoppel and the Statute of Frauds, one might conclude, are peculiarly nonmerchant, though courts have correctly applied them to many merchant transactions. The fact is, however, that these doctrines and the statute along with virtually the entire mass of contract formation law is cumbersome baggage that impedes the celerity often necessary in mercantile transactions. We cannot say that commercial law is a refuge from contract formation law, because contract formation law post-dates the commercial law concept of the specialty that is the subject of payments systems law. Rather, contract formation law [offer, acceptance, revocation, and the like] and the doctrines of consideration and promissory estoppel may be attempts to escape commercial law's preoccupation with celerity and certainty, for those features of commercial law sometimes yield harsh results.

Commercial law continues, nonetheless, to fashion obligations that are unlike contract obligations and does so for the reason that commerce demands them.

(2) Avoiding Litigation

It is easy to see in the litigation age that some merchants and their bankers might be leery of "going to law." Hiring lawyers, drafting pleadings, engaging in and suffering one's opponent's discovery efforts, trying the case before a jury of persons unfamiliar with the industry, and above all paying the opportunity costs of litigating instead of manufacturing or selling constitute an unappealing option. A merchant's balance sheet consists normally of the premier commercial assets: inventory and receivables. These are assets that the financial markets can assess and buy or lend against quickly and inexpensively. The merchant with a portfolio of causes of action will not be surprised when his banker demonstrates little interest in lending the merchant cash, for everyone in commerce knows that a cause of action is a problematic asset.

Merchants, then, are anxious to fashion their relationships in ways that keep them from the courthouse and to make those infrequent trips to the courthouse quick ones.

The idea that a merchant dispute might take two or three years to resolve is, with all due respect, risible. Merchants dispute claims, but they often continue to do business with each other while the claims are being resolved. In the model commercial dispute resolution, the dispute arises in the morning; the parties continue to do business throughout the day; and their fellow merchants resolve the matter in a 20-minute session before everyone goes home for dinner.

All right, we are exaggerating; but this exaggeration is closer to the prototypical commercial arbitration than it is to a full-blown lawsuit in the Southern District of New York. In a commercial arbitration, there is usually no discovery; rules of evidence do not apply; there is no jury; the fact finders are usually merchants themselves; the matter is resolved in a fraction of the time it takes to try a lawsuit; and the costs are far lower. Merchants will tell you, moreover, that the results are superior.

Sometimes merchants cannot arbitrate. In that case, they prefer an obligation that is simple and concise. Simple, concise obligations can be enforced with a minimum of lawyering.

(3) Abstracting or Merging the Obligation

The merger of equity with the common law and the rise of Contract introduced into commercial relations the notion that obligations arise out of relationships or out of agreements. Enforcement of relationary obligations and agreements generally rests on full analysis of the relationship or the agreement. One cannot deny that that analysis is often necessary for a proper allocation of liabilities, but neither can one deny that the analysis is cumbersome.

There are times, moreover, when encumbering the obligation with relationary and agreement analysis renders the obligation unmarketable. A merchant who holds obligations free of underlying contract or relationship equities can market, i.e., sell or borrow against, those obligations more quickly and at better prices (or lower interest) than the merchant holding obligations subject to those equities.

This Part IV is a study of commercial law's response to these three problems. Chapter 11 introduces responses to the first problem. Chapter 12 introduces responses to the second and third. Chapter 13 deals with commercial limits on the enforcement of obligations, and Chapter 14 studies commercial law remedies when a party breaches a commercial obligation.

Chapter 11

CREATING COMMERCIAL OBLIGATIONS

SECTION 1. PROMISES UNDER SEAL AND THE LIKE

HOLMES, STATURE AND STATUS OF A PROMISE UNDER SEAL AS A LEGAL FORMALITY, 29 Willamette L. Rev. 617, 618-21 (1993).

Common sense dictates that if a person desires to make a legally enforceable promise, the law should provide a means for accomplishing that end. However, our modern contract law may not be so accommodating. We do not submit to the ideal of *pacta sunt servanda* (promises must be kept), and our society chooses not to enforce all promises. Because promises are not per se legally enforceable in our society, the preeminent question is what types of promises should the law enforce. Some fact or factor must surround a promise to make it legally enforceable. At least five theories of contractual obligations (bargain, reliance, will, efficiency, and fairness) have been advanced for explaining which promises merit legal enforcement. However, these theories will not enforce all promises for which the promisors intended to be legally bound.

Donative promises illustrate this problem. Gratuitous promises, unbargained for or unrelied on, generally are not legally enforceable. Scholars continue to probe for felicitous approaches to make gift promises binding when this fulfills the promisor's intent. Other promises that may not be legally enforceable include promises: To modify an obligation, to keep an offer open, to release a debt, to pay for past favors, to convey land, to assume the obligation of another, promises made within the family and promises by bailees.

The formal method is one means to underwrite the legal enforceability of promises. For example, the formality of a promise under seal is an efficient, trustworthy method of channeling a person's deliberate intent to be legally obligated. With the exception of the consent theory, the problem with theories such as bargain, reliance, efficiency, and fairness is that they do not provide an adequate theoretical justification for formal promises. As a result, current legal scholars ignore the formal approach. As Randy Barnett observes: "Formal contracts ought to be an 'easy' case of contractual enforcement, but prevailing theories that require bargained-for consideration, induced reliance, or even economic 'efficiency' would have a hard time explaining why." The promissory basis of contract gives us that theory. Although we ultimately may discard it, the formal method merits our serious consideration, especially when promisors intend to be legally obligated.

At early common law, form took precedence over substance. Thus, a promise was not binding unless surrounded by certain formalities. Modern contract law continues to recognize the validity and legal enforceability of certain promises based on their formal characteristics. There are five acknowledged categories of legally binding formal contracts: recognizances, negotiable instruments, negotiable documents, letters of credit, and contracts under seal.

A.I. TRADE FINANCE, INC. v. PETRA BANK

United States Court of Appeals, Second Circuit, 1993.
989 F.2d 76.

JACOBS, Circuit Judge.

* * *

The January 1989 transaction at issue involves a species of trade finance known as "forfaiting."[1] Our understanding of this subject is drawn from the limited record materials that generically describe the uses, mechanics and conventions of forfaiting transactions. Forfaiting is an inventive means of facilitating exports to troubled or debt-laden countries. Forfaiting transactions involve the sale of goods or services for promissory notes or bills of exchange. In a forfaiting transaction of the kind at issue here, involving the sale of goods for promissory notes, the forfaiter finances the sale by paying the exporter (usually at a substantial discount) and receives in return the importer's promissory notes. The exporter relinquishes any further claim for payment and has no further role in the transaction other than to deliver the goods or services and guarantee their quality.

A forfaiting transaction involves at least one other essential party: a guarantor bank. In the ordinary course, forfaiters will not finance any trade debts without an unconditional and irrevocable guaranty from a bank or other substantial guarantor. The forfaiter and guarantor usually become involved in the transaction shortly after the commercial terms are worked out between the exporter and the importer. The importer arranges for the bank to guarantee the payment of the note to the forfaiter, at which time the forfaiter becomes fully responsible for payment to the exporter. All burdens of debt collection fall upon the forfaiter, without recourse to the exporter. Upon maturity of the notes, the forfaiter typically presents them to the guarantor for payment.

---

1 Forfaiting is a term derived from the French *a forfait*, which means to surrender or relinquish the rights to a thing. Aside from plaintiff's ongoing disputes concerning the forfaited notes at issue here, we have found no American case law that deals with forfaiting. This form of financing apparently arose in response to the trade crisis created by the installing of communist regimes in Eastern European countries, and is used as well in developing and Third World nations. According to record materials, in past years forfaiting reportedly has accounted for between 0.5 and 1.0% of world trade. See Forfaiting, Euromoney, Feb.1988, at Special Supplement 3.

The guaranty employed in a forfaiting transaction often consists of a two-word endorsement, "*per aval*," recorded on the note itself and followed by one or more authorized signatures of the guarantor bank. This endorsement is known as an "aval."[1] As brief and cryptic as the aval may be, the customs and practices of the forfaiting industry make it a fully articulated contractual obligation.

The record informs us that forfaiting institutions control their risks in several ways. First, forfaiters purchase the notes at a substantial discount that reflects the interest cost, the importer's credit rating and the credit-risk factor for the importer's country. Second, the notes must be in a fully convertible currency, usually dollars, Swiss francs or Deutschmarks, and the guaranty must be in the currency stipulated on the face of the notes. Third, the notes are usually payable in a commercial center, where there is an expectation of regularity in financial dealings. Fourth, most forfaiters spread risk by buying and selling forfaited trade paper among each other, also without recourse, in a secondary market.

PILLANS v. VAN MIEROP

Court of King's Bench, 1765.
97 Eng. Rep. 1035.

[White, who was a merchant in Ireland, incurred a debt due Pillans and Rose, the plaintiffs, a merchant house in Holland. For reimbursement of that debt, on February 16, 1762, White offered to send the plaintiffs a remittance or to arrange for them to draw a draft or drafts on a house of standing in London. The plaintiffs chose the latter course. Subsequently, White, as well as the Dutch plaintiffs, wrote the defendants, Van Mierop and Hopkins, a London merchant house, requesting the defendants to issue a letter of credit in favor of Pillans and Rose, so that Pillans and Rose would know in advance that when they drew their drafts they would be accepted and, later, paid. On March 19, 1762, Van Mierop and Hopkins issued their letter of credit to Pillans and Rose. In the credit they undertook to honor Pillans and Rose's drafts on Van Mierop and Hopkins for the account of White.

The judgment of Lord Mansfield follows, the judgments of Wilmot and Aston being omitted.]

LORD MANSFIELD.

This is a matter of great consequence to trade and commerce, in every light.

If there was any kind of fraud in this transaction, the collusion and mala fides would have vacated the contract. But from these letters, it seems to me clear, that there was none. The first proposal from White, was "to reimburse the plaintiffs by a remittance, or by credit on the house of Van Mierop:" this was the

---

1 The French word *aval* is a commercial term meaning "backing" or "endorsement." The derivation is disputed. The Oxford English Dictionary says the term "aval" comes from *a val*, meaning "at the bottom," which is presumably where the guarantee of payment was normally affixed. Webster's New International Dictionary (2d ed. 1956) says it comes from *a valoir*, meaning "to be accepted as valid."

alternative he proposed. The plaintiffs chose the latter. Both the plaintiffs and White wrote to Van Mierop and Company. They answered "that they would honour the plaintiffs draughts." So that the defendants assent to the proposal made by White, and ratify it. And it does not seem at all that the plaintiffs then doubted of White's sufficiency, or meant to conceal any thing from the defendants.

If there be no fraud, it is a mere question of law. The law of merchants, and the law of the land, is the same: a witness can not be admitted, to prove the law of merchants. We must consider it as a point of law. A nudum pactum does not exist, in the usage and law of merchants.

I take it, that the ancient notion about the want of consideration was for the sake of evidence only: for when it is reduced into writing, as in covenants, specialties, bonds, &c. there was no objection to the want of consideration. And the Statute of Frauds proceeded upon the same principle.

In commercial cases amongst merchants, the want of consideration is not an objection.

This is just the same thing as if White had drawn on Van Mierop and Hopkins, payable to the plaintiffs: it had been nothing to the plaintiffs, whether Van Mierop and Co. had effects of White's in their hands, or not: if they had accepted his bill. And this amounts to the same thing:—"I will give the bill due honour," is, in effect, accepting it. If a man agrees that he will do the formal part, the law looks upon it (in the case of an acceptance of a bill) as if actually done. This is an engagement "to accept the bill, if there was a necessity to accept it; and to pay it, when due:" and they could not afterwards retract. It would be very destructive to trade, and to trust in commercial dealing, if they could. There was nothing of nudum pactum mentioned to the jury; nor was it, I dare say, at all in their idea or contemplation.

I think the point of law is with the plaintiffs.

UCC § 5-105

Consideration is not required to issue, amend, or cancel a letter of credit, advice, or confirmation.

Official Comment

This section dispenses with [proof of consideration] and validates the position of Lord Mansfield in Pillans v. Van Mierop.

Farber & Matheson, Beyond Promissory Estoppel: Contract Law and the "Invisible Handshake," 52 U. Chi. L. Rev. 903, 945-46 (1985).

The traditional view of contract law divides promissory liability into two categories. By far the larger category involves the bargained-for exchange of promises for other consideration. These bargains are enforced, even in the absence of reliance, in order to protect the parties' expectation that future conduct will be governed by present commitments. The other, much smaller category, is that of promissory estoppel. Here, liability is imposed to remedy the injury to promisees who have relied on promises in vain.

Based on our survey of recent promissory estoppel cases, we believe that promissory estoppel is losing its link with reliance. In key cases promises have been enforced with only the weakest showing of any detriment to the promisee. Reliance-based damages are the exception, not the rule. With the decline of reliance, promissory estoppel is moving away from tort law. It has become a means of enforcing promises differing in doctrinal detail from traditional contract law but sharing a common goal. That goal, we have argued is to foster trust between economic actors. Trust is a moral good, but it is also an economic asset. It allows coordination and planning between economic actors and fosters the formation of valuable economic institutions.

Perhaps in an earlier age traditional contract law was adequate to foster the degree of trust society needed in economic activities. Today, an increasingly interdependent society needs to foster trust in a variety of relationships not readily organized through the device of the formal contract. Promissory estoppel is one of several mechanisms courts have used to try to close what we have called the "relational gap" in contract law.

In our view, recent cases expansively applying promissory estoppel are steps on the road to a broader rule of promissory obligation. We have proposed as a new standard for enforcement that all promises made in furtherance of economic activities be enforced without regard to the presence of consideration or reliance. Although we recognize that courts have not yet articulated this standard, we believe they are moving in this direction.

We do not wish to overstate our claims for our approach. Like Corbin, we are skeptical of claims that the common law can be reduced to a simple set of rules, as well as claims that the proper resolution of contracts issues can be deduced from some set of abstract principles. And although we think our description of the cases we surveyed is a fair one, we certainly do not claim that every case can be neatly fit within our framework. Law is much too untidy for that. Perhaps most importantly, our rule does not pretend to be an eternal verity. It is tailored to provide for enforcement of promises in the kinds of relationships that are central to the contemporary economy.

SECTION 2. NEGOTIABLE INSTRUMENTS AND DOCUMENTS

INTRODUCTORY NOTE

There are two kinds of negotiable instrument: orders to pay money and promises to pay money. § 3-104(a) & (e). Each of these has a subcategory.

Orders to pay are either checks or drafts; promises are either notes or certificates of deposit. Everyone is familiar with the check. A buyer issues one when she orders her bank to pay the seller the purchase price of the goods or services that the buyer purchased from the seller. Less often but still often enough for us to study the transaction, a seller issues a draft that orders his buyer to pay him. This order, being drawn on a buyer and not a bank, is not a check but simply a draft. § 3-104(f). The *United Overseas Bank* case in section 2(b) of Chapter 12 illustrates the documentary draft transaction; and section 3(b), infra, discusses the draft in the commercial letter of credit transaction.

In order to be negotiable, instruments must conform to somewhat ancient style. Above all, they must contain words of negotiability, i.e., they must be payable to bearer or order. § 3-104(a)(1). Note that checks need not contain the words of negotiability. § 3-104(a) & (c). You cannot avoid the rules of negotiability, then, by striking the words of negotiability from the printed check forms your bank insists you use.

Of the four negotiable instruments, this chapter deals mostly with checks and promissory notes, the two negotiable instruments most common in domestic commerce. There are four parties to these instruments that incur obligations when they sign the instrument. No one incurs instrument liability without signing the instrument. § 3-401(a). Three of these parties appear in check and draft transactions. They are the drawer, the indorser, and the acceptor. In note transactions, the parties incurring liability are the issuer and the indorser. Sections 3-412 through 3-415 delineate the undertakings of these parties. Note that the undertakings are conditional, i.e., the party enforcing the obligation must satisfy conditions before he can require the obligor to pay.

Negotiable instruments respond to the three problems identified in the introductory note to Part IV of this casebook. Here we see how they reduce transaction costs. The two cases that follow illustrate the operation of the liability rules for, in the first, an indorser of a check, and, in the second, the issuer and the guarantor of a note.

BRANNONS NUMBER SEVEN, INC. v. PHELPS

Court of Appeals of Oklahoma, 1983.
665 P.2d 860, 36 U.C.C. Rep. Serv. 225.

MEANS, Judge.

This is an appeal by the defendant, Robert Phelps, from an order of the trial court which granted summary judgment in favor of the plaintiff, Brannons Number Seven.

The issues involved are (1) whether Brannons, as the holder of two insufficient payroll checks, was required to give notice of dishonor to Phelps as the endorser, and (2) whether a disputed notice of dishonor is a substantial material fact precluding the granting of summary judgment.

We answer both questions in the affirmative and reverse.

The basic facts are not in dispute. Phelps was in the employment of Jet Service Company. Jet issued two payroll checks to Phelps in the amounts of $454.49 and $350.05. Brannons, a grocery store, cashed the two checks for Phelps. Phelps had endorsed the two checks, placing his telephone number on the back of each check, below his endorsement. Phelps received the proceeds from the checks. Upon presentment by Brannons to the drawee bank, notice of dishonor due to insufficient funds in the drawer's account was given to Brannons.

Brannons, by way of affidavit attached to its motion for summary judgment, states that it "requested Robert Phelps to pay Plaintiff [Brannons]" the sums of the two checks. Attached to Phelps' response to Brannons' motion for summary judgment is his affidavit which states that Brannons never requested him to pay the sums of the checks "by either verbal or written demand." Again in Phelps' answers to Brannons' request for admissions, Phelps denied that Brannons requested him to pay the sums of the checks.

The trial court granted plaintiff Brannons' summary judgment for the sum of $804.64, plus attorney's fees and costs.

I.

The requirement of notice of dishonor to an endorser is clear.

Title 12A O.S.1981 § 3-501(2)(a), states that unless notice is excused under § 3-511:

> "(a) notice of any dishonor is necessary to charge any endorser;"

> The contractual duties and liabilities of an endorser and holder when an uncertified check passes between the parties are found in 12A O.S.1981 § 3-414(1) * * * [The court then quotes the section.]

> The holder's rights are stated in 12A O.S.1981 § 3-507(2):

> "Subject to any necessary notice of dishonor * * * the holder has upon dishonor an immediate right of recourse against the drawers and endorsers."[1]

An endorser's liability is contingent and does not become fixed unless and until the holder complies with the requirement of notice of dishonor. This notice is an element of Brannons' cause of action and Brannons thus has the burden of proving that it gave notice.

II.

The affidavits, briefs and exhibits to the pleadings relied upon by the trial judge in granting summary judgment present a substantial controversy as to a material fact as to whether notice of dishonor of the checks was given to the endorser Phelps. Assuming arguendo, that requesting payment by Phelps of the checks in question constituted notice of dishonor, Phelps denies that such a request

---

[1] The court's references are to the pre-revised version of Article 3 [eds.].

occurred. This presents a question of fact to be proved by Brannons to the satisfaction of the trier of facts before recovery is permissible.

Reversed and remanded for trial on the issue of notice of the dishonor.

NOTE ON BANK COLLECTIONS

The domestic and international bank collection systems involve an extraordinary and complex series of relationships among commercial banks; Federal Reserve Banks; and, now, a service industry applying advanced information storage, retrieval, and transmission technology. It is unnecessary, however, for the student of commercial law to study the intricacies of that system, which collects about fifty billion checks a year and a similarly large number of credit card orders and makes wire transfers that exceed in amount the money transferred by all of the checks and credit card transfers together.

It is enough to know that essentially collections fall into one of two categories: those that "pull" the funds to the payee, and those that "push" the funds to the payee. The check and credit card collection systems involve "pull orders." Wire transfers are usually "push orders."

Check collections involve three entities: the depositary bank, intermediary banks, and the payor bank. § 4-105(2), (3), & (4). In check transactions, the buyer, as everyone knows, sends the check to the seller, who deposits it at his own bank, the depositary bank. Using the intermediary banks, the depositary bank forwards the check to the payor bank, which we call the drawee bank, i.e., the bank that the buyer orders to pay the seller. Thus the depositary bank is the seller's bank; the drawee bank the buyer's bank.

Note that in the check collection system, the buyer orders her bank to pay the seller but does not send the order to her bank. She sends it to the seller, who uses the check to "pull" the funds into his account at the depositary bank. The same is true of drafts, which sellers use to order their buyers (or their buyers' banks) to pay the seller. Drawers of drafts deposit the drafts and use the collection system to "pull" the funds into the seller's account.

"Push orders," we will see, are generally more efficient than "pull orders." Because wire transfers are usually "push orders," many predict that they will eventually replace the check collection system. The European system of "giro" accounts is a "push order" system. Europeans use giros far more often than they use checks. Reeducating millions of check writers and retrofitting the pull order technology of the banking system to adapt it to push orders is occurring, but gradually.

A.I. TRADE FINANCE, INC. v. LAMINACIONES DE LESACA, S.A.

United States Court of Appeals, Second Circuit, 1994.
41 F.3d 830.

KEARSE, Circuit Judge.

Defendants Laminaciones de Lesaca, S.A. ("Laminaciones"), and its parent company, Altos Hornos de Vizcaya, S.A. ("Altos Hornos"), appeal from a final judgment of the United States District Court for the Southern District of New York, Michael B. Mukasey, Judge, awarding plaintiff A.I. Trade Finance, Inc. ("AITF"), $1,434,692.70, plus interest and costs, against defendants as the maker and guarantor, respectively, of promissory notes issued for the purchase of equipment. Notwithstanding defendants' contention, inter alia, that the seller of the equipment had breached the underlying commercial contract, the district court granted summary judgment to AITF on the ground that it was a holder in due course within the meaning of § 3-302(1) of the pre-1990 version of the Uniform Commercial Code ("UCC") as adopted in New York (McKinney 1991) ("NYUCC" or "Code"),[1] and hence was not subject to defendants' defenses against the seller. On appeal, defendants contend principally that AITF is not a holder in due course * * * . For the reasons below, we disagree and affirm the judgment of the district court.

I. BACKGROUND

The events are not in dispute. In August 1990, defendants agreed to purchase certain steel processing machinery called a "slitting line" from Delta Brands, Inc. ("Delta"), a Texas-based exporter, for Laminaciones's factory in Spain. Delta asked AITF, a trade finance company specializing in international transactions, to finance the transaction.

A. The Agreements

During negotiations with respect to the terms of the transaction, AITF representative Richard Tull traveled to Spain to attend a two-day series of meetings between Delta and defendants. The meetings concerning the underlying commercial transaction between Delta and defendants were conducted in Spanish without an interpreter. Tull, who did not speak Spanish, met separately with a Delta official and representatives of Altos Hornos's finance department to discuss in English the specific terms for financing the transaction.

The meetings culminated in, inter alia, an August 8, 1990 agreement between Laminaciones and Delta (the "equipment contract" or "commercial contract"), pursuant to which Delta was to deliver and install the machinery, and Laminaciones was to pay Delta 15 percent of the contract price within 60 days of the effective date of the contract, and to pay the balance in 10 semi-annual installments dating from shipment, plus interest calculated at 12 percent per annum on the outstanding balance. As evidence of the debt, Laminaciones was to issue to Delta 10 promissory notes for the appropriate amounts, with Altos Hornos cosigning as guarantor, to be payable at intervals commencing six months from the date of Delta's shipment of the equipment from Texas. Laminaciones agreed to deliver the notes, signed but with their maturity dates left blank, to a United States bank, with

[1] The court's references are to the pre-revised version of Article 3 [eds.].

irrevocable instructions for the notes' completion and their delivery to Delta "against shipping documents for the equipment contemplated by the Contract."

AITF agreed to buy the Laminaciones notes from Delta. This agreement was eventually formalized in a November 27, 1990 letter of commitment signed by AITF and Delta (the "commitment letter"). The commitment letter provided that shipment of the machinery would occur on approximately March 20, 1991, "with promissory notes to be available to AITF for discounting not later than 4.12.91."

AITF furnished defendants with standard promissory note forms to be used, one of which was annexed to the commercial contract. It also furnished Altos Hornos with a letter dated August 8, 1990, referring to the "financing which we are providing to Altos Hornos de Vizcaya, S.A. on behalf of Delta Brands, Inc.," and stating that in the event that AITF elected to sell the notes after acquiring them from Delta, Altos Hornos would have a right of first refusal. Laminaciones and Altos Hornos, by letter to AITF dated March 25, 1991, "confirm[ed] that nothing in the commercial contract impairs the negotiability of the financial obligation." In the same letter, Laminaciones and Altos Hornos also "consent[ed] to the financial obligation being governed by New York law and the place of non-exclusive jurisdiction being the state and federal courts located therein."

B. Performance and Non-Performance

In February 1991, Laminaciones delivered its 10 promissory notes to its bank in New York, Banco Bilbao Vizcaya ("Banco Bilbao"), with irrevocable instructions to enter the appropriate maturity dates and release the notes to Delta upon Delta's presentation of documents showing that all of the equipment had been shipped. Laminaciones instructed Banco Bilbao that the maturity date of the first note was to be 182 days from the date on the bill of lading for "the last departure which completes the total value of the . . . contract."

On February 27, 1991, AITF sent Delta a letter reminding it that, in accordance with the commitment letter, the promissory notes "must be presented to A.I. Trade Finance, Inc. in acceptable form by April 12, 1991." AITF's February 1991 letter stated that AITF would not extend its commitment beyond the April 12 date.

In April 1991, Delta presented to Banco Bilbao, inter alia, a bill of lading dated April 1, 1991, and an invoice indicating that a "slitting line with new shear" had been shipped to Laminaciones and showing the entire balance of the purchase price as due. Based on the documents presented, Banco Bilbao filled in the maturity dates of the 10 promissory notes, with the first note bearing a maturity date of September 30, 1991, i.e., 182 days from the bill-of-lading date, and released the notes to Delta. On receipt of the notes, Delta immediately endorsed and sold them to AITF for $3,081,438.68. When AITF presented the first note on or about its September 30, 1991 maturity date, Laminaciones promptly paid the amount of that note without objection.

However, at the time the invoice, bill of lading, and other documents were presented to Banco Bilbao in April 1991, Delta had not in fact shipped all of the machinery due Laminaciones under the equipment contract. Several shipments were made after the date indicated in the bill of lading. In a September 1991 letter to Delta, Altos Hornos stated that the maturity dates on the notes should not have been calculated prior to the date of Delta's final shipment, and it asked Delta to pay the excess interest accrued under the notes. With respect to the first note, Delta complied with Altos Hornos's request by paying an adjustment of interest totaling $24,000.

Some of the machinery called for by the equipment contract was never delivered, and in March 1992, Laminaciones canceled the contract. When AITF presented Laminaciones's second note for payment after it matured on April 1, 1992, Laminaciones declined to pay it. AITF thereafter demanded payment from Altos Hornos pursuant to the guarantee; Altos Hornos responded by telex dated June 4, 1992, stating that "due to a temporary break on the part of Delta Brands Inc [sic] in complying with its obligations, payment of the due promissory note number 2/10 has been suspended as a precaution." Since then, additional notes have reached maturity; no further payments have been made.

C. The Present Lawsuit and the District Court's Ruling

When further efforts to collect proved unsuccessful, AITF commenced the present action against Laminaciones and Altos Hornos to enforce the notes. Defendants took the position, inter alia, that no payments were due on the promissory notes (1) because Banco Bilbao had not followed Laminaciones's instructions to make the first maturity date 182 days after Delta's "last" shipment, and (2) because Delta had submitted fraudulent shipping documents in order to procure the notes. Both sides moved for summary judgment.

AITF, in support of summary judgment in its favor, contended that as a good-faith purchaser of the notes from Delta, AITF was a holder in due course under NYUCC § 3-302(1) and was entitled to payment from the maker and guarantor of the notes notwithstanding any defenses the maker and guarantor might have against Delta. Defendants contended that they were entitled to summary judgment in their favor principally on the grounds (1) that the notes were not negotiable instruments, and (2) that even if they were negotiable and AITF were a holder in due course, AITF was subject to the defenses defendants could assert against Delta * * * .

In an Opinion and Order dated December 27, 1993, published at 840 F.Supp. 271, the district court denied defendants' motion and granted that of AITF, holding that AITF was a holder in due course within the meaning of NYUCC § 3-302(1) and was therefore not subject to any defenses defendants might have against Delta. The court concluded that the limiting language of NYUCC § 3-305(2) does not apply to a party that was involved only in the financing aspects of a commercial transaction. It further noted that the present case concerned a transnational "forfait" transaction, in which a trade finance company commonly " 'become[s] involved * * * shortly after the commercial terms are worked out' " between the importer and the exporter, and thereafter negotiates the credit terms with the maker and guarantor of the documents evidencing the debt. 840 F.Supp. at 274 (quoting A.I. Trade Finance, Inc. v. Petra Bank, 989 F.2d 76, 78 (2d Cir.1993)). The court concluded that a rule limiting the scope of AITF's rights as a holder-in-due-course would force forfaiters generally to alter their established practices, thereby reducing the availability of commercial credit, contrary to the underlying objectives of the UCC.

In sum, the district court held that, because AITF had not participated in negotiating the terms of the underlying commercial transaction between Delta and Laminaciones and Altos Hornos, and because AITF had satisfied the other requirements for holder-in-due-course status, Laminaciones and Altos Hornos must make payment on those notes that had matured. This appeal followed.

II. DISCUSSION

On appeal, defendants pursue their contention that AITF is subject to their defenses against Delta for breach of the equipment contract, arguing chiefly that (1) under established New York law, AITF is not a holder-in-due-course * * * and hence is deprived of normal holder-in-due-course immunity from those defenses. In addition, defendants argue that AITF could not be a holder in due course because it had "close connections" with Delta. We find no merit in these contentions.

A. "Negotiability" and AITF's Status as a Holder in Due Course

To be "negotiable" under the NYUCC, an instrument must (1) "be signed by the maker or drawer," (2) "contain an unconditional promise or order to pay a sum certain in money and no other promise, order, obligation or power given by the maker or drawer except as authorized by [NYUCC Article 3]," (3) "be payable on demand or at a definite time," and (4) be payable to the payee's "order" or to the instrument's "bearer." NYUCC § 3-104(1). A purchaser of a negotiable instrument becomes a holder in due course if he "takes the instrument (a) for value; and (b) in good faith; and (c) without notice that it is overdue or has been dishonored or of any defense against or claim to it on the part of any person." NYUCC § 3-302(1). Section 3-305 provides, subject to certain exceptions not pertinent here, that a holder in due course "takes the instrument free from (1) all claims to it on the part of any person; and (2) all defenses of any party to the instrument with whom the holder has not dealt." Id. §§ 3-305(1) and (2).

Defendants contend that AITF is not a holder in due course because (a) the promises reflected in Laminaciones's notes, being premised on Delta's satisfaction of several requirements before the notes could issue, were "conditional," and the notes were therefore nonnegotiable; (b) AITF did not show that it purchased the notes in good faith; and (c) AITF did not show that it had no notice of Delta's breach. These contentions must be rejected.

1. Negotiability

The requirements for negotiability set out in § 3-104(1) of the Code concern the form and content of the instrument itself. See, e.g., DH Cattle Holdings Co. v. Smith, 195 A.D.2d 202, 209-10, 607 N.Y.S.2d 227, 231-32 (1st Dep't 1994); see also NYUCC § 3-105 cmt. 8 (holder of a negotiable instrument must be able to "ascertain all of its essential terms from its face"). While the indicia of negotiability must be visible on the face of the instrument, a note containing an otherwise unconditional promise is not made conditional merely because it refers to, or states that it arises from, a separate agreement or transaction. See NYUCC §§ 3-105(1)(b), (c); id. cmt. 3 (reference to separate agreement does not limit terms of payment "in the absence of any express statement to that effect").

Further, the Code provides that an instrument may subsequently become negotiable even though it lacks a prerequisite of negotiability at the time it is signed. Section 3-115(1) states: When a paper whose contents at the time of signing show that it is intended to become [a negotiable] instrument is signed while still incomplete in any necessary respect it cannot be enforced until completed, but when it is completed in accordance with authority given it is effective as completed. Id. § 3-115(1). See also id. § 3-304(4)(d) (purchaser's knowledge that an incomplete instrument was completed after signing but prior to purchase does not constitute notice of a defense or claim, "unless the purchaser has notice of any improper completion"). Thus, a condition precedent to the completion of a note does not preclude its ultimate negotiability, provided that the note is otherwise negotiable and is eventually "completed in accordance with authority given." Id. § 3-115(1).

Similarly, the failure of a condition that is not visible on the face of a completed promissory note does not make the note nonnegotiable; rather, the failure creates a defense that is available only against a holder who is not a holder in due course. See NYUCC § 3-306(c) (non-due-course holder takes instrument subject to, inter alia, defense of nonperformance of condition precedent).

The district court correctly rejected defendants' contention that the promissory notes issued by Laminaciones were not negotiable. The 10 notes were signed by Laminaciones and by Altos Hornos; each note contained an unconditional promise to pay a precise sum to the order of Delta, and contained no other promise; and, after completion by defendants' agent Banco Bilbao, each note showed the precise date on which payment of the specified sum was due. Banco Bilbao had authority from defendants to fill in each note's maturity date upon presentation by Delta of evidence that all of the machinery called for by the contract had been shipped, and to set the due dates at specified intervals from the date of Delta's bill of lading. Upon Delta's presentation of the documentation required by defendants, the notes were completed by Banco Bilbao in accordance with this authority and thereby became fully effective. The notes themselves do not refer to any condition in the underlying equipment contract; nor is any necessary term determinable only by reference to an extrinsic fact that is not revealed on the face of the notes. Given the precise terms on the face of the notes, the mere reference to the bill-of-lading date did not impair the notes' negotiability.

2. <u>Notice and Good Faith</u>

If the maker of a negotiable instrument has shown the existence of a defense, a holder who wishes to cut off that defense by claiming holder-in-due course immunity has the ultimate burden of establishing by a preponderance of the total evidence that he purchased the instrument for value, in good faith, and without notice. See NYUCC § 3-307(3) & cmt. 3. The holder's initial burden on the issues of notice and good faith, however, is "a slight one" that may be satisfied by his affidavit disclaiming any knowledge of the maker's defense when the notes were negotiated. First International Bank, Ltd. v. L. Blankstein & Son, Inc., 59 N.Y.2d 436, 444, 465 N.Y.S.2d 888, 892, 452 N.E.2d 1216, 1220 (1983). Such an affidavit, "[w]hile necessarily conclusory in form," may nevertheless be enough to place on the maker the burden of coming forward with evidence sufficient to raise a genuine issue as to the holder's notice of defenses. Id. Since documentary proof as to notice will ordinarily be in the hands of the maker, the holder will be entitled to summary judgment based on such an affidavit unless the maker proffers evidence of facts that, if accepted, would establish the holder's notice of a valid defense. See id.

The purchaser of a note has notice of a claim or defense if, at the time he purchases the instrument, he has "knowledge of the claim or defense or knowledge of such facts that his action in taking the instrument amounts to bad faith." NYUCC § 3-304(7). In determining whether a party had notice, the New York Court of Appeals has held that this section, a nonuniform provision of the pre-1990 version of the UCC, requires application of "a subjective test of actual knowledge rather than an objective test which might involve constructive knowledge." See Carrefour U.S.A. Properties Inc. v. 110 Sand Co., 918 F.2d 345, 347 (2d Cir.1990) (quoting Hartford Accident & Indemnity Co. v. American Express Co., 74 N.Y.2d 153, 162, 544 N.Y.S.2d 573, 578, 542 N.E.2d 1090, 1094-95 (1989)). "Holders in due course are to be determined by the simple test of what they actually knew, not by speculation as to what they had reason to know, or what would have aroused the suspicion of a reasonable person in their circumstances * * *." Id. at 163, 544 N.Y.S.2d at 578, 542 N.E.2d at 1094.

An equivalent standard governs the Code's requirement of "good faith." That term is defined as "honesty in fact in the conduct or transaction concerned." NYUCC § 1-201(19). In evaluating a party's good faith, "the inquiry is what [the holder] actually knew." Chemical Bank v. Haskell, 51 N.Y.2d at 92, 432 N.Y.S.2d at 480, 411 N.E.2d at 1341. If a holder "did not have actual knowledge of some fact which would prevent a commercially honest individual from taking up the instruments, then its good faith [is] sufficiently shown." Id.

Within this framework, the district court correctly concluded that AITF had satisfied its burden of proving that it took the notes in good faith and without notice of any valid defenses. AITF supported its summary judgment motion with the affirmations of two of its assistant vice presidents, who had approved AITF's payment for the notes to Delta. Both officers stated that AITF had purchased the notes in good faith, paying $3,081,438.68 for them, and that neither they nor, to their knowledge, any other AITF employee or agent knew of any defenses that defendants might have had against Delta at the time AITF purchased the notes from Delta. This sufficed to meet AITF's initial burden of proving its good faith and its lack of actual notice of Delta's breach.

Defendants' contention that AITF purchased the notes with notice of Delta's breach was not supported by evidence sufficient to create a genuine issue to be tried. Although, as defendants argue, AITF was aware that the release of the notes to Delta was subject to a condition precedent, the awareness of the existence of a condition is insufficient to suggest an awareness that the condition was not fulfilled. Defendants also point to AITF's February 27, 1991 letter to Delta, which stated that AITF would not extend its agreement to purchase the notes beyond the April 12 date set by the commitment letter; they apparently argue that it can be inferred from the February 1991 letter that AITF knew Delta was having difficulty in meeting its obligations under the equipment contract. Even assuming that such an inference were justified, however, under New York law AITF had no responsibility to inquire whether Delta thereafter in fact performed. The facts cited by defendants thus failed to create any triable issue concerning AITF's actual knowledge at the time it purchased the notes.

In sum, we find no error in the district court's conclusion that AITF purchased the notes from Delta as a holder in due course.

* * *

C. The "Close-Connectedness" Theory

Finally, defendants contend that AITF could not have become a holder in due course because it had "close connections" with Delta. This contention need not detain us long. Under the so-called "close-connectedness" doctrine, which has not been recognized in New York, some states have endorsed the view that a transferee who has an " 'unusually close relationship with the transferor' " may not take an instrument from the transferor as a holder in due course. Vitols v. Citizens Banking Co., 10 F.3d 1227, 1233 (6th Cir.1993) (quoting Arcanum National Bank v. Hessler, 69 Ohio St.2d 549, 549, 433 N.E.2d 204, 206 (1982)); see also Leasing Service Corp. v. River City Construction, Inc., 743 F.2d 871, 875-77 (11th Cir.1984) (discussing cases). At least one state court, however, noting the intimate relationship between the concepts of "close connectedness" and notice as defined in the UCC, has rejected the doctrine as "only a substitute for a proper analysis" of a party's holder-in-due-course status under UCC § 3-302(1). Cessna Finance Corp. v. Warmus, 159 Mich.App. 706, 712, 407 N.W.2d 66, 69 (1987).

Further, even the courts that have adopted this doctrine have generally applied it only in cases involving consumer credit transactions in which the seller and the financing entity are intertwined or have an ongoing relationship encompassing many transactions. See, e.g., Unico v. Owen, 50 N.J. 101, 111-15, 232 A.2d 405, 410-12 (1967); see also Leasing Service Corp. v. River City Construction, Inc., 743 F.2d at 876 (concluding that doctrine has been applied "only where there is a consumer involved who has been given a 'raw deal' "). But see St. James v. Diversified Commercial Finance Corp., 102 Nev. 23, 26, 714 P.2d 179, 181 (1986) (adopting doctrine "with respect to all transactions where the buyer can demonstrate a close connection between the seller and lender").

We need not consider in this case whether or to what extent the New York courts would apply the "close-connectedness" doctrine where a seller and a lender have such a close relationship, or whether the doctrine would be applied to commercial credit transactions, for in the present case defendants have not pointed to any evidence suggesting that AITF and Delta had a close relationship. To the contrary, they concede that AITF had purchased notes from Delta on only one other occasion and that the two companies had no common management. Hence, even if recognized under New York law, the doctrine would afford defendants no basis for relief.

CONCLUSION

We have considered all of defendants' arguments on this appeal and have found them to be without merit. The judgment of the district court is affirmed.

BANK OF NEW YORK v. AMOCO OIL CO.

United States District Court, Southern District of New York, 1993.
831 F. Supp. 254.

TENNEY, District Judge.

The plaintiff Bank of New York ("BNY") brought this action in March of 1990 seeking damages incurred because the defendant, Amoco Oil Company ("Amoco"), allegedly wrongfully refused to turn over certain platinum to BNY. By the time BNY obtained the platinum, it was able to sell the metal only at a reduced price. BNY bases its rights to the platinum on holding certificates issued by Amoco, which were given to BNY as collateral for loans to Drexel Burnham Lambert Trading Corp. ("DBL Trading").

* * *

BNY bases its conversion claim on the alleged superior rights that it had to the platinum under Article 7 of the U.C.C. If the holding certificates were negotiable documents of title that DBL Trading duly negotiated to BNY, then BNY obtained title to the platinum, and Amoco was under an obligation "to hold or deliver the goods according to the terms of the document free of any defense or claim by [it] except those arising under the terms of the document." N.Y. U.C.C. Law § 7-502(1)(d) (McKinney 1990).

I. The Holding Certificates as Documents of Title

The holding certificates come under the purview of Article 7 only if they fall within the definition of a document of title. The U.C.C. states that the following are documents of title:

> Bill of lading, dock warrant, dock receipt, warehouse receipt or order for the delivery of goods, and also any other document which in the regular course of business or financing is treated as adequately evidencing that the person in possession of it is entitled to receive, hold and dispose of the document and the goods it covers. To be a document of title a document must purport to be issued by or addressed to a bailee and purport to cover goods in the bailee's possession which are either identified or are fungible portions of an identified mass. U.C.C. § 1-201(15).

A. Holding Certificates as "Other Documents" under Section 1-201(15)

The parties agree that the holding certificates are not bills of lading, warehouse receipts, or anything else specifically enumerated in section 1-201(15). However, BNY contends that they fall within the broad language describing "other documents" that constitute documents of title, and the court agrees.

Mr. Van Den Hogen's testimony demonstrated his belief that the holding certificates gave BNY the right, as required by the definition, to receive the platinum in the event of default. He testified that he interpreted the language of the holding certificates to mean "that in the event of a default by [DBL Trading], we would be able to endorse the certificates and present [them] to, in this case, Amoco and to obtain the goods immediately."

When Mr. Van Den Hogen was asked whether he would have accepted the holding certificates as collateral if he could not call them in and receive the platinum at any time, and on demand, he stated that BNY would not have accepted them as collateral. Moreover, the General Loan and Security Agreement between BNY and DBL Trading provided that BNY had the immediate right to liquidate collateral in the event of default.

In addition to Mr. Van Den Hogen's testimony, the bank also presented testimony from two people outside of BNY who worked in the commodities industry. Michael D. Magidson, who is presently a Vice President and Chief Financial Officer at Gerald Metals, Inc., testified concerning Gerald Metals' use and issuance of holding certificates as collateral. Mr. Magidson was at times responsible for obtaining short term loans from a number of international banks. Gerald Metals issued holding certificates like those at issue here, and Mr. Magidson testified that he believed they were accepted by all the banks with which Gerald Metals did business.[1] He estimated that Gerald Metals has, in the last two decades, used between three and five hundred holding certificates as collateral for loans, some of which were issued by Amoco.

As to the companies who issued holding certificates, Mr. Magidson stated that "the major industrial companies of nonferrous and precious metals in the United States" customarily issue holding certificates as collateral. He testified that he understood a holding certificate to grant a bank the right to immediate possession in the event of default on a loan.

BNY also presented the testimony of Terrence P. Sweeney, who is the Executive Director of Legal Affairs at Swiss Bank Corp. Mr. Sweeney testified that Swiss Bank is involved in commodities lending that includes loans secured by precious metals; one of the firms to which Swiss Bank made such loans was DBL Trading. In short term financing,[2] Swiss Bank—along with other banks—accepted holding certificates as one form of collateral. Mr. Sweeney testified that prior to the inception of this lawsuit against Amoco by BNY, Swiss Bank accepted as collateral documents similar to the holding certificates at issue here.

Amoco presented the testimony of Daniel A. Mahni, who is currently employed at Republic National Bank of New York. Mr. Mahni testified that, as one involved in commodities lending, he would not have accepted holding certificates as collateral for overnight loans from DBL Trading. He stated that as a matter of practice in the industry, holding certificates are not considered a form of possessory collateral, and that they are not regarded as documents of title. The court finds that Mr. Mahni's testimony was undercut significantly by his admission on cross-examination that he had not seen a holding certificate such as those at issue in this litigation until speaking with Amoco's attorneys last year. He had no first hand

---

1 The following banks were named over the course of Mr. Magidson's testimony: BNY, Chase Manhattan Bank, Chemical Bank, Citibank, French American Bank, Israel Discount Bank, Mellon Bank, Swiss Bank Corp., and Union Bank of Switzerland.

2 Swiss Bank often arranged such financing through intercreditor agreements, in which two or more banks would lend to a borrower on a secured basis. An intercreditor agreement serves to delineate the order of the banks' claims against that borrower, which clarifies priority of creditors in the event of default.

knowledge of banking practices at other banks, such as Swiss Bank, Chemical Bank, or BNY. Moreover, he stated that he would not be willing to accept as collateral a warehouse receipt or a bill of lading—which clearly constitute documents of title, see U.C.C. § 1-201(15)—unless it was issued by an authorized depository.

Mr. Mahni had until 1988 worked for Chase Manhattan Bank in the commodities division, on the precious metals "team." Although he did not accept holding certificates as collateral on that team, he testified that, for example, the "nonferrous team," which presumably coordinated lending with holders of nonferrous metals, did accept holding certificates for use as collateral. Mr. Mahni's testimony fell far short of its presumed goal of showing that industry practice in the late 1980s was not to accept holding certificates as collateral for overnight loans. This court did not find his testimony persuasive, either as to individual practices at particular banks or as to industry practice.

In sum, the court finds that BNY did treat the holding certificates as "adequately evidencing that [BNY] is entitled to receive, hold and dispose of the document and the goods it covers." U.C.C. § 1-201(15). Moreover, industry practice was to accept holding certificates as well, at least in some circumstances, as documents of title. Notwithstanding Amoco's objections, discussed below, the holding certificates here did constitute documents of title and fall within the purview of Article 7.

B. Amoco's Status as a Bailee

Amoco argues that the holding certificates are not documents of title because it was not a bailee under section 1-201(15). It claims that it was not holding the platinum for purposes of storage or transportation—the two traditional functions of bailees within the meaning of Article 7. Amoco also points to the definition of a bailee as "the person who by a * * * document of title acknowledges possession of goods and contracts to deliver them." U.C.C. § 7-102(1)(a). Amoco claims that under the agreement between DBL Trading and Amoco, there was no contract for anything other than a lease of the platinum from DBL Trading to Amoco, and thus no contract to deliver the platinum.

* * *

Even if Amoco does not satisfy the technical definition of a bailee under section 7-102(1)(a), the requirements of section 1-201(15) may still be met. Under that section, Amoco need not be a bailee, but only must purport to be a bailee, in order to render the holding certificates documents of title. By changing the holding certificates to add language in which Amoco acknowledged that it was holding the goods, and would deliver them on surrender of the holding certificate "properly endorsed," Amoco changed its own function. It thus purported to be a bailee.

The fact that there was an underlying lease transaction rather than a contract for storage or transportation does not vitiate this conclusion. There was no language in the holding certificates themselves to indicate the nature of the underlying transaction. In the certificates, Amoco states that it is holding a specific quantity and grade of platinum, for the account or order of DBL Trading, and it agrees to release the platinum "on surrender of this certificate properly endorsed."

BNY also points out that "the essential purpose of Amoco's holding certificates was to put lenders on notice that DBL Trading had unencumbered inventory that it wished to pledge as collateral," and consequently their function was equivalent to documents of title. The court believes this to be the case; Amoco did change the wording of the holding certificates by adding order language and specifically stating that the platinum was free of all liens and encumbrances.

While there is strong support for BNY's argument that Amoco was in fact a bailee, it is not necessary to so hold. Amoco purported to be a bailee, which suffices to bring it within the definition of a bailee as that term is used in section 1-201(15).

* * *

II. Negotiability

In order to be negotiable, a document of title must state "by its terms [that] the goods are to be delivered to bearer or to the order of a named person." U.C.C. § 7-104(1)(a). The comment to the section states: [Here the court quotes § 7-104 cmt. 1 (2d para.).]

BNY asserts that the certificates were negotiable, although they did not quote the language of the section verbatim. It argues that an instrument is negotiable if, when looked at in its entirety, it evidences the intention of being negotiable. Amoco, on the other hand, advocates a strict interpretation of the wording of the document. It claims that the holding certificates should not be deemed negotiable because (1) they provide for the "holding" of the goods, rather than their "delivery," and do not quote the suggested language verbatim; (2) Amoco never intended that the documents be negotiable; and (3) the language of release on surrender does not create negotiability.

While there is little authority on point, cases decided before the U.C.C. was adopted have applied a broad definition of negotiability. See, e.g., Gerard v. Bank of New York & Trust Co., 265 N.Y. 336, 340, 193 N.E. 165 (1934) (stating that an instrument is negotiable, even if order or bearer language is omitted, when "it is apparent from the whole nature of the instrument and the language employed that such was intended to be its character"), reh'g denied, 266 N.Y. 544, 195 N.E. 192 (1935); Manny v. Wilson, 137 A.D. 140, 143, 122 N.Y.S. 16, 19 (1st Dep't 1910) ("any words importing an intention that the instrument shall be negotiable suffice"), aff'd, 203 N.Y. 535, 96 N.E. 1121 (1911).[1]

BNY also relies upon In re George B. Kerr, Inc., 25 B.R. 2 (Bankr.D.S.C.1981), aff'd, 696 F.2d 990 (4th Cir.1982), to support the contention that the section should be liberally construed. The bankruptcy court, holding that certain warehouse receipts were negotiable despite the lack of "order" or "bearer" language on their face, stated:

---

1 The prior uniform acts required a document to state plainly "non-negotiable" or "not negotiable" if it was to be treated as such. See Uniform Warehouse Receipts Act, § 7, 3 U.L.A. 44 (1959); Uniform Bills of Lading Act, § 8, 4 U.L.A. 20 (1922). While this point is hardly decisive, it implies that the presumption is one of negotiability, even if a document fails to adhere exactly to the language in the statute.

The warehouse receipts * * * were negotiable because they represented absolute title to the goods, were issued by the debtor, were endorsed by the debtor in blank, and were delivered [to the current holder]. Since the goods represented by the receipts could be obtained only upon presentation and surrender of the receipts, the goods were to be delivered to the bearer of the receipts. The receipts thus meet the requirements for negotiability. Id. at 7.

The court also rejected any notion that a document of title must contain the exact words as stated in section 7-104; the court found "no support for this assertion in the Uniform Commercial Code or the case law described thereunder." Id.

The reasoning of the bankruptcy court in In re Kerr is persuasive here. Although the holding certificates did not literally comply with section 7-104(1)(a), they represented title to the goods on their face, stating that there were no liens or encumbrances and that the metal was being held for DBL Trading's account or order. They were signed by Amoco's representative, and stated that the goods would be delivered when the certificates were properly endorsed.

Amoco has produced no law to show that its intent as to the certificates has any bearing on negotiability; yet it strongly denies that it intended the documents to be negotiable. However, even if intent is relevant, the testimony at trial merely demonstrated to this court Amoco's apathy about the documents' significance, until this suit was brought. For example, Mr. Sloss stated that he did not know what the documents signified overall; he did not know what the specific word "encumbered" meant, id.; and he added the "order" language only because Susan Gold requested it. Yet once the certificates were changed explicitly to add "order" language, the nature of the documents changed. Even if Amoco did not intend to change the significance of the holding certificates, it issued holding certificates that were in fact negotiable. There was nothing on the face of the certificates to indicate to outsiders any other intent on Amoco's part.

The official comment to section 7-104 notes that use of the words "Deliverable on proper indorsement and surrender of this receipt" does not render a document negotiable, because bailees may require such language to insure that a non-negotiable receipt is returned—i.e., to maintain records. Yet Mr. Sloss testified that the holding certificates were not always returned, and if a platinum lease was extended, he did not issue a new holding certificate but allowed the old one to remain outstanding. This casual manner of recordkeeping certainly indicates that Amoco did not put the language in purely for administrative purposes. Moreover, the fact that such language, standing alone, fails to render a document negotiable does not mean that the presence of these words automatically renders a document non-negotiable.

III. Due Negotiation

Section 7-501(4) lays out the requirements for due negotiation. It states:

A negotiable document of title is "duly negotiated" when it is negotiated * * * to a holder who purchases it in good faith without notice of any defense against or claim to it on the part of any person and for value, unless it is established that the negotiation is not in the regular course of business or financing or involves receiving the document in settlement or payment of a money obligation. Id.

DBL Trading, by placing its indorsement on the back of the holding certificates, and then delivering the certificates to BNY, negotiated them to BNY. See U.C.C. § 7-501(1). BNY gave value for the certificates by providing credit of 95 percent of the platinum's value. See id. § 1-201(44)(a). The factual question involved, however, is whether BNY had notice of Amoco's claims to the document—i.e., whether BNY knew about Amoco's lease.

The parties dispute whether the term "notice" required Amoco to show that BNY had actual knowledge of the lease, or if it must show merely that BNY should have known about it. Amoco cites to the definition of notice in section 1-201(25). It argues that the term "notice" includes reason to know, and that BNY had reason to know of the lease because information about the leases was given to Mr. Van Den Hogen at BNY. Under this definition, BNY potentially could be charged with constructive knowledge of Amoco's involvement.

BNY argues that Amoco is required to prove actual knowledge; the bank refers to "notice" as defined in Articles Three and Eight—in the context of the phrase "notice of claims or defenses . . .," which only holds a party responsible if it has actual knowledge.

In the cross-references accompanying section 7-501, the reader is referred to the definition of notice in section 1-201(25). Although BNY presented a compelling argument that notice should only include actual knowledge, the court is inclined to adopt the definition in Article 1 to which the cross-references refer. However, even under this standard, the court finds that Amoco has failed to show that BNY had notice of Amoco's claim to the platinum.

[The court then quoted the definition of notice in UCC § 1-201(25).]

BNY did not have actual knowledge under subsection (a). Mr. Van Den Hogen testified that he was never told that Amoco's leases overrode the bank's right to the platinum. Furthermore, Ms. Murray, one of DBL Trading's representatives who worked with BNY, testified that she did not tell Mr. Van Den Hogen that the leases would prevent BNY from recovering the platinum in the event of default. To her knowledge, Mr. Van Den Hogen was never made aware of Amoco's lease by DBL Trading.

Moreover, Mr. Van Den Hogen's behavior indicates that he believed the holding certificates gave BNY the right to immediate possession in the event of default. He filed financing statements in all jurisdictions where platinum was located. He rejected three holding certificates that did not comply.

* * *

CONCLUSION

The court finds that the holding certificates issued by Amoco constituted negotiable documents of title that were duly negotiated to BNY by DBL Trading. Plaintiff is to be awarded $550,000.00, as the agreed upon limit, and prejudgment interest thereupon from April 4, 1990. Plaintiff to submit judgment in accordance herewith.

SECTION 3. INDEPENDENT BANK UNDERTAKINGS

(a) CASHIER'S CHECKS

NATIONAL NEWARK & ESSEX BANK v. GIORDANO, 268 A.2d 327, 329 (N.J. Super. 1970). The purchaser's obligation on the check becomes secondary and the bank is both the drawer and drawee. It undertakes to draw the amount represented from its own resources. It must therefore of necessity be said that issuance of the cashier's check constitutes an acceptance of it by the issuing bank. In drawing the instrument the bank represents that as drawee it will honor the draft when presented. The requirements for an acceptance as set forth in N.J.S.A. 12A:3-410(1) are fulfilled by the affixing of the signature of the agent of the issuing bank. The rule may thus be stated that a cashier's check is accepted for payment when issued. See Mellon National Bank v. Citizens Bank & Trust Co., 88 F.2d 128 (8 Cir. 1937), cert. denied, 302 U.S. 702, 58 S.Ct. 21, 82 L.Ed. 542.

Under the provisions of N.J.S.A. 12A:4-303 a stop-order, whether or not effective under other rules of law to terminate or suspend the bank's right or duty to pay an item, comes too late to terminate or suspend such right or duty if it is received after the bank has accepted or certified the item. Since a cashier's check is accepted when issued, N.J.S.A. 12A:4-303 in effect makes it impossible to stop payment on a cashier's check once is has been issued.

LAWRENCE, MAKING CASHIER'S CHECKS AND OTHER BANK CHECKS COST-EFFECTIVE: A PLEA FOR REVISION OF ARTICLES 3 AND 4 OF THE UNIFORM COMMERCIAL CODE, 64 Minn. L. Rev. 275, 282 (1980). Commentators discussing the rights of bank check obligors have focused mainly on the problem of determining when these obligors may resist payment under the provisions of the Uniform Commercial Code. These commentators have failed, however, to examine the appropriate role of bank checks in our economy, and the question of whether treating them under the existing provisions of the Code strips them of their independent function as cash substitutes. Cashier's checks and certified checks are well suited to serve as cash substitutes. Given the business community's need for such an instrument, there is no reason why these checks should not be permitted to fill this role.

UCC § 3-411 and Official Comment 1
(*see Selected Commercial Statutes*)

(b) LETTERS OF CREDIT AND ACCEPTANCES

MCCURDY, COMMERCIAL LETTERS OF CREDIT, 35 Harv. L. Rev. 539, 564-66 (1922).

Three objections may be made to the recognition of letters of credit as self-sufficing instruments of the law merchant. In the first place, these letters have not reached that point of uniformity that bills of exchange and promissory notes have attained. There are many types, some of which are considered in the business world as creating binding obligations upon issue, and others of which are looked upon as revocable at will. If business ideas on the subject are not uniform, judicial ideas are chaotic. Moreover, letters of credit vary in formality from telegraphic communications and simple memoranda to letters written in ordinary epistolary form. There is considerable variation in the forms and in the transaction which gives rise to the letter. For an instrument to be a specialty it must have reached a high degree of formality. In the second place, even if a letter of credit be recognized as a mercantile specialty, it does not follow that consideration is unnecessary. The trend of the common law has been to give effect to the custom of merchants which makes certain *choses in action* negotiable, but not to give effect to the custom of merchants which makes specialty promises binding without consideration. There is an essential difference between recognizing, in furtherance of commerce, that certain *choses in action* are assignable so as to confer upon the assignee original in distinction to derivative rights, and in recognizing that certain promises need no consideration to be legally enforceable. In the one case the question relates to the transferability of an existing legal right; in the other case the question concerns the creation of that right. To some extent, to be sure, especially in the matter of negotiable instruments, the common law has expanded and modified its strict conception of what constitutes consideration. But the law has never abolished its necessity. There was a time when consideration was thought to be a matter of evidence rather than a requirement of substantive law. Lord Mansfield in *Pillans v. Van Mierop*, confusing in a strange way consideration with the Statute of Frauds, tried to abolish the requirement of consideration, in so far as written commercial promises were concerned, on the theory that the writing is sufficient proof of the existence of the contract. He was soon overruled, and this conspicuous failure of a great judge has been a warning to all later judges. The conception that the doctrine of *nudum pactum* does not apply to mercantile contracts is entirely exploded, and it is now settled that even for negotiable instruments consideration is required as between the immediate parties. In the third place, the tendency, legislative as well as judicial, is toward consideration and not away from it. The efficacy of seals has been almost everywhere abolished. At the same time there is a legislative tendency, evidential and procedural, not substantive, to give *prima facie* effect to any promise in writing.

The doctrine of consideration is due to accidents of history; it is peculiar to the common law; it may be thought of as provincial; it may not be desirable; but it exists as a firmly established principle of English and American law. Courts might well modify the common-law conception of what constitutes consideration. This would be legitimate judicial extension of and deduction from established principle. But to abolish it is surely not within the province of the courts. In the past, no court has decided that a letter of credit needs no consideration. In the future, courts may treat these letters as mercantile specialties. But the opinion may be ventured that no court will, without legislative enactment, openly and consciously declare that they need no consideration for their support. The legal analysis of letters of credit must therefore be made according to common-law principles, but it is submitted that, once the correct business analysis is made in the particular case, the common law is adequate to deal with them.

FIRST COMMERCIAL BANK v. GOTHAM ORIGINALS, INC.

Court of Appeals of New York, 1985.
64 N.Y.2d 287, 486 N.Y.S.2d 715, 475 N.E.2d 1255.

SIMONS, Judge.

This is a special proceeding instituted pursuant to CPLR 6221 to determine adverse claims to attached property. The disputed property consists of funds and assets held by respondent Bank Leumi Trust Company of New York. Petitioner, First Commercial Bank, claims the proceeds because Bank Leumi accepted drafts it presented in the amount of $70,978.50 which had been drawn in connection with a letter of credit. Respondent Gotham Originals, Inc., the customer of Bank Leumi which obtained the letter of credit, claims that Bank Leumi may not transfer the proceeds because the court enjoined it from doing so before it honored the drafts. Petitioner bases its claim to the funds on the provisions of Uniform Commercial Code § 4-303(1)(a)[1] which provides that legal process comes too late to suspend the bank's duty to pay an item if it comes, as this order did, after the bank has accepted it. Gotham contends, however, that the restraining order was timely under section 5-114(2)(b) of the Code because the order was served upon the Bank before it honored the drafts. The Code defines honor as "to pay or to accept and pay" (Uniform Commercial Code § 1-201[21]). Thus, the order was untimely under section 4-303 because Bank Leumi had accepted the drafts before enjoined but timely under section 5-114 because it had not yet honored them. The Appellate Division held that under these circumstances section 4-303 prevails. We agree and therefore affirm its order.

I.

In June 1981 respondent Gotham Originals, Inc. agreed to purchase approximately 24,000 pairs of ladies leather and snakeskin shoes from Teng Shih Industries Company, Ltd., and other Taiwanese shoe manufacturers. To finance the purchase, it obtained an irrevocable letter of credit from Bank Leumi designating Teng Shih Industries as beneficiary and petitioner First Commercial Bank, a banking corporation organized under the laws of the Republic of China and having its principal place of business in Taipei, as advising bank. The total amount of the letter of credit, as amended, was $172,026. It was transferrable and contained an expiration date of September 5, 1981. On September 10, 1981, R. Bore International, Inc., a transferee beneficiary of Teng Shih Industries, negotiated to petitioner two drafts in the amount of $70,978.50, payable on sight 60 days from date, together with the other documents required by the letter of credit. Petitioner paid for the drafts in Taiwanese currency and credited the amounts to R. Bore's checking account although it did so "under reserve" because the letter of credit had expired on September 5, 1981. On September 21st, Bank Leumi received from petitioner the two drafts, the required documentation and transmittal letters and a request for payment of the drafts on Gotham's letter of credit. Petitioner disclosed the discrepancy in the expiration date, noted that it had negotiated the drafts "under

---

1 All of the court's references are to the pre-revised UCC [eds.].

reserve" and requested advice as to when it could lift the reserve and make final payment to R. Bore. Bank Leumi subsequently obtained a waiver of the discrepancy in the expiration date from Gotham and on September 24th it notified petitioner by letter that the drafts had been accepted and that payment would be made on November 23, 1981.

After Bank Leumi had accepted the drafts, but before it had paid them, Gotham instituted an action against Teng Shih, R. Bore and the other shoe manufacturers-sellers in Supreme Court, New York County, claiming they had sold it worthless merchandise and charging them with fraud and breach of contract. It simultaneously obtained a temporary restraining order enjoining Bank Leumi from transferring the letter of credit or any moneys or assets of the sellers and sought orders attaching the proceeds of the drafts. After the restraining order was served on Bank Leumi and the attachment was perfected, Bank Leumi refused to pay petitioner.

Petitioner first attempted to recover the funds by a plenary action against Bank Leumi and the bank, in turn, impleaded Gotham. Petitioner then moved for summary judgment and when its motion was denied it commenced this proceeding. In it petitioner seeks to vacate and discharge the restraining order and the orders of attachment, to void the Sheriff's levy and to obtain a determination that section 4-303 of the Code controls this transaction and requires Bank Leumi to pay the accepted drafts. * * *

On November 15, 1983 Special Term granted Gotham's motion and dismissed the petition * * * .

The Appellate Division, First Department, unanimously reversed and granted the petition (101 A.D.2d 790, 476 N.Y.S.2d 835). It held that there were no procedural bars to reaching the merits and, on the merits, it held that the attachment order was untimely under Uniform Commercial Code § 4-303 and was therefore ineffective to terminate or suspend Bank Leumi's duty to pay the accepted drafts.

II.

The purpose of a letter of credit is to substitute for, and therefore support, an engagement to pay money. Letters of credit are used in various ways in modern business practice, but when used in the traditional manner to finance a sale of goods, the credit subsumes a separate agreement by a buyer to pay money to a seller. By issuing a letter of credit, the issuer undertakes an obligation to pay the beneficiary, or his transferee if the letter is negotiable, from the account of its customer. Thus, a commercial letter of credit transaction involves three separate contractual relationships and undertakings: first, the underlying contract for the purchase and sale of goods between the customer (the buyer, Gotham in this case) and the beneficiary (the seller Shih): second, the agreement between the issuer (Bank Leumi), customarily a bank but frequently some other institution or person, and its customer (Gotham) in which the issuer typically agrees to issue the letter of credit in return for its customer's promise to reimburse it for any payments made under the credit plus a commission; and third, the letter of credit itself which is an engagement by the bank or other issuer that it will honor drafts or other demands for payment presented by the beneficiary or a transferee beneficiary upon compliance with the terms and conditions specified in the credit.

The fundamental principle governing these transactions is the doctrine of independent contracts. It provides that the issuing bank's obligation to honor drafts drawn on a letter of credit by the beneficiary is separate and independent from any obligation of its customer to the beneficiary under the sale of goods contract and separate as well from any obligation of the issuer to its customer under their agreement. Stated another way, this principle stands for "the fundamental proposition * * * that all parties [to a letter of credit transaction] deal in documents rather than with the facts the documents purport to reflect." (H. Harfield, Letters of Credit 76 [ALI-ABA Uniform Commercial Code Practice Handbook 1979]). Thus, the issuer's obligation to pay is fixed upon presentation of the drafts and the documents specified in the letter of credit. It is not required to resolve disputes or questions of fact concerning the underlying transaction.

A limited exception to this rule of independence is provided in section 5-114 of the Code (see also, Sztejn v. Schroder Banking Corp., 177 Misc. 719, 31 N.Y.S.2d 631). Under the general rule the issuer must honor the draft when the documents presented comply with the terms of the letter of credit. But when a required document does not conform to the necessary warranties or is forged or fraudulent or there is fraud in the transaction, an issuer acting in good faith may, but is not required to, refuse to honor a draft under a letter of credit when the documents presented appear on their face to comply with the terms of the letter of credit. Further than that, a customer may also enjoin an issuer from honoring such a draft if the issuer fails to do so on its own. Notwithstanding this exception, if the person presenting a draft drawn on a letter of credit is a holder in due course, the issuer must pay the draft, whether it has notice of forgery or fraud or not.

Thus, if petitioner had taken the drafts under circumstances which made it a holder in due course, it would have acquired greater rights than the beneficiary and Bank Leumi would be obligated to honor the drafts despite Gotham's allegations of fraud in the transaction. Petitioner has neither pleaded nor proved its status as a holder in due course, however. Indeed it asserts that its status as such is irrelevant and maintains that it is entitled to recover on the facts presented in any event.

Petitioner was initially designated as an advising bank and stood in a neutral position; its only obligation was to convey accurate information of the issuance, amendment and terms and conditions of the credit to its beneficiaries. By purchasing the signed drafts drawn under the letter of credit by the transferee-beneficiary, R. Bore, it became a negotiating bank and because of Bank Leumi's express engagement in the letter of credit to honor drafts presented by a negotiating bank, petitioner acquired rights against Bank Leumi, as issuer, "to the same extent as if it were named as beneficiary of the credit" (H. Harfield, Letters of Credit 14).

Thus, although the parties agree subdivision (2)(b) is the provision of section 5-114 pertinent to this appeal because petitioner does not claim to be a holder in due course, they disagree on its significance. Gotham contends that the court was authorized to enjoin payment of the drafts pursuant to it because there was fraud in the transaction. Petitioner asserts that section 4-303 prevails in the case of conflict and that because the drafts were accepted before the restraining order was issued or served on Bank Leumi, its rights became fixed and are paramount to Gotham's, notwithstanding its status and the statutory authorization to enjoin payment found in section 5-114.

III.

Section 4-102 of the Code specifically provides that if the provisions of article 4 conflict with those of article 3 then article 4 shall govern and that if they conflict with the provisions of article 8 then the provisions of article 8 shall govern. It contains no similar provision with respect to a conflict with the provisions of article 5 nor does any section in article 5 deal with the conflict. The controlling language must be found in section 4-303(1). It states that any legal process served upon a payor bank, "whether or not effective under other rules of law" to terminate or suspend the bank's duty to pay the item comes too late to terminate or suspend that duty if the bank has previously accepted the item (Uniform Commercial Code § 4-303[1][a]). Section 5-114 contains no similar provision. Indeed, the Legislature made clear that article 5 and the UCP do not control every aspect of a transaction that involves a letter of credit when it provided that article 5 was intended to deal "with some but not all of the rules and concepts of letters of credit" (Uniform Commercial Code § 5-102[3]; see, J. White & R. Summers, Handbook on Uniform Commercial Code § 18-2, at 711 [2d ed.]). Accordingly, section 4-303, by its terms, supersedes section 5-114 and when Bank Leumi accepted the drafts on September 24, 1981, it became directly, primarily and unconditionally obligated to the holder to pay them at maturity (Uniform Commercial Code § 3-413[1]; for the definition of "acceptance" see Uniform Commercial Code § 3-410[1]). Because the restraining order was served on it on October 30, 1981, 36 days after the act of acceptance, it came "too late" to prevent payment to petitioner.

* * *

Important policy considerations suggest the result also. Letters of credit provide a quick, economic and predictable means of financing transactions for parties not willing to deal on open accounts by permitting the seller to rely not only on the credit of the buyer but also on that of the issuing bank. By its terms, the credit often reflects a conscious negotiation of risk allocation between customer and beneficiary and its utility rests heavily on strict adherence to the agreed terms and the doctrine of independent contract. It is this predictability of credit arrangements which permits not only the financing of sale of goods transactions between widely separated parties in different jurisdictions but also has permitted the development of a market in trade or bankers' acceptances of time drafts. Once a draft payable in the future is accepted by a bank, it becomes known as a bankers' acceptance, and such acceptances can be, and regularly are, sold in conjunction with letter of credit transactions to obtain financing prior to the date of maturity in a market sanctioned by the Federal Reserve Board. If the courts intervene to enjoin issuing banks from paying drafts they have previously accepted they seriously undermine this market and limit the use of acceptances as a financing tool.

Accordingly, the order of the Appellate Division should be affirmed, with costs.

NOTE ON ACCEPTANCES

No one is liable on a negotiable instrument unless he signs it. § 3-401. A drawee/payor bank, therefore, is not liable on a check merely by virtue of the fact that the buyer orders the bank to pay; nor is a buyer liable on a draft just because a seller has drawn the draft on the buyer. Anyone can draw a draft on anyone else, but the drawee is not liable without signaling that liability with a signature. Checks and drafts, moreover, are not assignments. § 3-408. True, as we shall see in § 1(b) of Chapter 14, the buyer may have a cause of action against her bank if it does not pay a properly payable check. The drawee bank's liability, however, does not arise out of the negotiable instrument but out of the bank/customer relationship. § 4-402(b).

It is important to commerce, however, that drawees be able to make themselves liable on a draft, usually a draft that is payable a time, say, sixty days, after acceptance or after some other date. They make that undertaking by signing the draft on its face. Such a signature renders the drawee an acceptor and gives rise to acceptor liability. §§ 3-409, 3-413. Sometimes holders of checks want to enhance the acceptability of the check by having the drawee bank accept or "certify" it.

Acceptances are useful in credit situations. A seller that agrees to give a buyer sixty days to pay for goods may want to borrow against the buyer's promise to pay before the sixtieth day. Bankers and other investors will buy or lend against the buyer's acceptance more readily than they will buy or lend against the buyer's naked promise to pay. An acceptance is a commercial obligation, the buyer's promise to pay is only a contractual obligation. Sometimes, large borrowers engage in acceptance financing, under which their banks accept drafts payable a number of days after acceptance. The acceptances, banker's acceptances, are easy to sell in the money markets and generate funds that the borrower can use until the acceptances come due. Banker's acceptances also arise in commercial letter of credit transactions.

(c) INTERNATIONAL BANK GUARANTEES

ICC UNIFORM RULES FOR DEMAND GUARANTEES Art. 2(a) & (b) (1992)

(a) For the purpose of these Rules, a demand guarantee (hereinafter referred to as "Guarantee") means any guarantee, bond or other payment undertaking, however named or described, by a bank, insurance company or other body or person (hereinafter called the "Guarantor") given in writing for the payment of money on presentation in conformity with the terms of the undertaking of a written demand for payment and such other document(s) (for example, a certificate by an architect or engineer, a judgment or an arbitral award) as may be specified in the Guarantee, such undertaking being given

i) at the request or on the instructions and under the liability of a party (hereinafter called "the Principal"); or

ii) at the request or on the instructions and under the liability of a bank, insurance company or any other body or person (hereinafter called "the Instructing Party") acting on the instructions of a Principal to another party (hereinafter the "Beneficiary").

(b) Guarantees by their nature are separate transactions from the contract(s) or tender conditions on which they may be based, and Guarantors are in no way concerned with or bound by such contract(s), or tender conditions, despite the inclusion of a reference to them in the Guarantee. The duty of a Guarantor under a Guarantee is to pay the sum or sums therein stated on the presentation of a written demand for payment and other documents specified in the Guarantee which appear on their face to be in accordance with the terms of the Guarantee.

UNITED NATIONS CONVENTION ON INDEPENDENT BANK GUARANTEES AND STAND-BY LETTERS OF CREDIT Art. 3 "For the purposes of this Convention, an undertaking is independent where the guarantor/issuer's obligation to the beneficiary is not subject to the existence or validity of an underlying transaction, or to any other undertaking (including stand-by letters of credit or independent guarantees to which confirmations or counter-guarantees relate), or to any term or condition not appearing in the undertaking, or to any future, uncertain act or event except presentation of documents or another such act or event within a guarantor/issuer's sphere of operations."

SECTION 4. SURETYSHIP OBLIGATIONS

TWOMBLEY v. WULF

Supreme Court of Oregon, 1971.
258 Ore. 188, 482 P.2d 166.

[Plaintiff, the owner of two companies, sold their assets to defendants for cash and for the defendants' agreement to assume a debt due a bank. The debt was secured by a lien on a checker cab. The defendants did not pay the debt; the bank repossessed the cab, sold it, and made a claim for the deficiency against the plaintiff. The plaintiff responded by executing a promissory note in favor of the bank's assignee, Bonded Credit. Plaintiff then sued the defendants to recover the amount of the note.]

BRYSON, Justice.

The defendants' first assignment of error is that the trial court erred in allowing plaintiff to recover for a loss she never sustained. Their contention is that mere execution and delivery of the promissory note to Bonded Credit does not support the judgment in favor of the plaintiff in the amount of the note; in defendants' words, '(p)laintiff paid nothing. Plaintiff sustained no damages.'

The defendants' contention must be considered in the context of the relationship which arose between them and the plaintiff upon execution of the written contract for the sale of plaintiff's businesses and assets. That relationship is: Upon executing the contract wherein defendants agreed to assume plaintiff's indebtedness to the bank on the retail installment sales contract covering the Checker cab, the parties to the contract, with respect to that covenant, created a relationship of involuntary suretyship whereby the defendants became the principal obligors on the indebtedness due for the balance of the cab, and the plaintiff acquired the privileges of a surety. As surety on the indebtedness, plaintiff's right of action against defendants accrued at the time she paid the indebtedness for which defendants were primarily liable.

> The rule is quoted in 72 C.J.S. Principal and Surety § 309, p. 772:
> '(f)or purposes of reimbursement from the principal, payment may be sufficiently made by a surety by the passing of a Negotiable security, and payment will be deemed to have been made by the surety if he gives his own Note * * * where it is accepted by the creditor as payment; and The surety is entitled to reimbursement from the principal before the instrument so accepted by the creditor has been paid.'
>
> Restatement 281, Security § 107, is to the same effect:
> 'Where a creditor accepts from the surety in discharge of the principal's matured duty a negotiable instrument on which the surety is liable for an amount equal to or less than the amount due from the principal, the principal is under an immediate duty to reimburse the surety to the amount of the instrument.'

Thus, it only remains to be established that the creditor, Bonded Credit, accepted plaintiff's negotiable promissory note as payment of the deficiency balance owed by plaintiff on the installment sales contract covering the Checker cab. We believe that was established by the testimony of Mr. Hearn, the operator of Bonded Credit. On direct examination, Mr. Hearn testified that plaintiff had paid him $1,065.20. On cross-examination he testified that plaintiff had paid him in that amount by executing and delivering to him, her promissory note.

* * *

The court did not err, as contended in the defendants' first assignment of error.

RESTATEMENT (THIRD) OF SURETYSHIP AND GUARANTY § 2(e) (1996). The secondary obligation may be created * * * by contract between an obligor and another person pursuant to which, without a novation, the other person assumes a duty of the obligor to the obligee, with the result that the other person becomes the principal obligor and the original obligor becomes the secondary obligor.

SECTION 5. WARRANTIES

(a) PURPOSE

PRIEST, A THEORY OF THE CONSUMER PRODUCT WARRANTY, 90 Yale L.J. 1297, 1307-10, 1313 (1981), as reprinted in **V. P. GOLDBERG, READINGS IN THE ECONOMICS OF CONTRACT LAW** 174-77 (1989).

Let us * * * [try] to predict the contents of warranties where the costs of extending product life and of insuring product losses are the sole determinants of their contents. Imagine that consumers are perfectly informed about the likelihood of a product defect and about the losses that will be suffered should a product become defective. Imagine also that consumers somehow make their preferences regarding warranty terms known to manufacturers and that manufacturers are responsive to those preferences. Imagine that warranty contracts are standardized only to reduce negotiation costs and thus that the standardized form itself does not affect the substantive obligations of consumers relative to manufacturers. Finally, imagine that all products are manufactured under conditions of perfect competition, so that each characteristic of a product—including warranty terms—serves to optimize the welfare of some dominant class of consumers. What would be the terms of product warranties?

In the common view, a warranty serves as both an insurance policy and a repair contract. As an insurance policy, a warranty provides that if, within a certain period, the product or some part of the product becomes defective, the manufacturer will compensate the buyer for the loss by repair, replacement, or refund of the purchase price. As a repair contract, a warranty fixes an obligation upon the manufacturer for some period of time to provide, without charge, services necessary to repair a defect in order to prolong the useful capacity of the product.

* * *

As a repair contract, a warranty reflects the respective costs to the consumer and the manufacturer of repair services. Repair by the consumer and manufacturer are substitutes, and the consumer can be expected to purchase repair services as part of the warranty wherever the manufacturer's price is less than the consumer's cost of providing the repair himself. Obviously, a consumer can (and frequently does) provide many repair services more cheaply than a manufacturer. It is plausible, for example, that where shelves fall in a refrigerator, repair by the consumer is cheaper. Of course, since the consumer and manufacturer are always free after the purchase of the good to negotiate for the provision of services of this kind, the warranty itself is valuable only if it reduces transaction costs for future agreements. Thus, a warranty may be expected to allocate responsibility to the manufacturer for those types of repairs that most frequently are difficult or burdensome for consumers to provide themselves.

Although the above example, as well as most uses of the word "repair," refers to investments designed to return a product to a condition it enjoyed at some previous period of time, it is worthwhile to consider "repair service" to a product more broadly as any investment designed to optimize the performance of the product over time. Viewed in this light, for example, restraining young children from swinging on a refrigerator door represents an investment in a form of "repair" that may well be less costly than hiring a serviceman at a later date to install new hinges. Similarly, a manufacturer may anticipate future repair services by technological investments in the design of the product that make its operation less susceptible to interruption—designing brackets to hold refrigerator shelves more securely, for example—or by investments to control a consistent quality of production.

With respect to repair investments of this nature, however, a warranty serves a role beyond that of reducing transaction costs. The warranty promise establishes and enforces the obligation of the manufacturer to make investments in the design of the good or in quality control. Such an agreement between the parties subsequent to the sale could not achieve the same result as easily, so that there are advantages to "tying" the warranty to the sale of the product. The warranty in this regard operates as a performance bond of the manufacturer. The value of the bond is equal to the costs to the manufacturer of defective product claims. As long as the manufacturer makes appropriate investments, the bond will not be forfeited. The decision to allocate repair investments of this nature between the manufacturer and consumer, however, is identical to the decision of who should bear typical repair costs As before, we would expect the parties to allocate between themselves, according to relative costs, all investments in "repair," whether in the form of direct reconditioning services, of product design, or of a consumer's care for or maintenance of the product so as to extend its useful life.

It is evident that the various activities described as repair are substitutes for insurance. Repair, like insurance, is a means of reducing the magnitude of a loss from an unexpected event such as a defect. It is important now, however, to depart from the common view of the warranty and to distinguish more clearly between repair as a redistribution of wealth over time, like insurance, and repair as an allocative investment which alters the productive capacity of the good. The first example of repair—the reinstallation of the refrigerator shelves by the consumer—is a form of self-insurance for the loss. The owner bears the full cost of time and energy necessary to replace the shelves after the event occurs, which, in this case, appears to be cheaper than buying market insurance requiring the manufacturer to replace the shelves. But neither repair by the consumer nor by the manufacturer directly alters the probability of the loss occurring and, thus, is like insurance. The second example—restraining the child from swinging on the refrigerator door—is an allocative investment by a consumer that extends the useful life of the product by reducing the probability of a future loss. Certainly, the burdens of a parent increase as the discipline of children becomes more strict or specific. But again, it may well be cheaper for a consumer to restrain his child than either to buy market insurance for repair of the door or to pay the manufacturer to design a refrigerator with hinges as sturdy as playground equipment.

Thus, in this terminology, a consumer's decision to accommodate himself to a scratch in the surface of an appliance is an example of self-insurance of the defect. The consumer's earlier efforts to reduce the likelihood of the scratch, for example, by increasing the level of his care or by isolating the appliance, is an allocative investment by the consumer. The manufacturer's promise in a warranty to repair the scratch after it occurs is market insurance. And the manufacturer's production decision to make the surface more resistant to abrasion is an example of an allocative investment by the manufacturer.

* * *

A warranty in this view is the instrument that expresses consumer preferences for allocative or insurance investments. It is a contract that divides responsibility for allocative investments and insurance between the consumer and the manufacturer. The content of the contract is determined by the respective costs to the two parties of allocative investments or insurance. According to this approach, a manufacturer makes investments to prolong product life up to the point at which the marginal cost of such investments equals the marginal benefit. A manufacturer, then, offers market insurance for those losses or items of service for which market insurance is less costly than insurance or allocative investments by the consumer himself.

To the extent that a manufacturer disclaims liability or excludes or limits warranty coverage, however, it shifts to the consumer the obligation to make allocative investments to preserve the product or to self-insure for its loss. A disclaimer or an exclusion of coverage is the functional equivalent of provisions, common in other contracts, that explicitly require one of the parties to take certain actions to prevent breach or to insure for losses from uncertain events. The theory predicts that disclaimers of liability and exclusions of coverage will be observed in consumer product warranties for those specific allocative or insurance investments that the consumer can provide more cheaply than the manufacturer. In this view, disclaimers and exclusions can be said to be demanded by consumers because of the relative cheapness of consumer allocative investments or of self-insurance.

(b) WARRANTIES AS TO GOODS

UCC § 2-314(1)

(*see Selected Commercial Statutes*)

REITZ, A HISTORY OF CUTOFF RULES AS A FORM OF *CAVEAT EMPTOR*: PART 1—THE 1980 U.N. CONVENTION ON THE INTERNATIONAL SALE OF GOODS, 36 Am. J. Comp. L. 437, 437-43 (1988).

"*Qui vend le pot, dit le mot.*"
French Proverb

Caveat Emptor is a venerable rule of sales law. It appears that both the early Roman law and the early Germanic law permitted the buyer to be parted from his money for substandard goods with no more protection than whatever inspection and express contractual guarantees the buyer had the foresight to insist upon. The development of the warranty of quality, especially the implied warranty of quality, may be viewed as a movement toward a significant measure of protection for the unwary buyer that corrects the worst excesses of *caveat emptor* by holding the seller, in the absence of explicit agreement, to quality standards matching the expectations buyers in the particular market reasonably have in light of the seller's behavior and the context of the transaction. Like the rules of financial disclosure for sales of corporate stock, warranty law may be justified as a tool to minimize transaction costs and secure buyer confidence in the marketplace, thereby promoting commerce. It apparently accords with widespread notions of fairness because it has been widely adopted.

The capacity of warranty law to curb the sharp practices associated with *caveat emptor* and to secure confidence in the marketplace is undercut if the buyer's rights to obtain a remedy for breach of warranty are subject to rules that cut off the buyer's rights too quickly. Instead of hoping that unwary buyers will fail to bargain for specific quality terms in the contract, the seller of shoddy goods can hope that unwary buyers will fail either to notice defects in the delivered goods or to pursue their remedies before the cutoff give the seller immunity. Short cutoff rules thus constitute another form, albeit attenuated, of *caveat emptor*.

It is striking how many special cutoff rules limiting the buyer's right to a remedy for the breach of the warranty of quality there are in various national systems of sales law. They include special limitations periods that are shorter than the limitations period generally applicable to claims between buyer and seller, notice rules that cut off buyers' claims unless the buyer gives the seller notice within some short period, and even acceptance rules that cut off buyers' remedies upon acceptance. Short cutoffs are particularly prevalent in civil law systems, including virtually all of Western Europe except the United Kingdom, all of Latin America, and many of the Soviet-bloc countries. The civil law tends to employ all three types of cutoffs in combination and imposes the same cutoff rule on both of the buyer's principal remedies for breach of warranty, "avoidance" and damages, often in very short time periods. Short cutoffs are not as common in the common law tradition. Nevertheless, the American UCC limits both the buyer's damage and avoidance remedies by separate but similar notice rules and uses an acceptance rule to cut off the avoidance remedy for defects of which the buyer knew or should have known at delivery. The British Sale of Goods Act (SGA) employs only one special short cutoff, an acceptance rule affecting the remedy of avoidance only, but for all defects, latent or patent.

This study seeks to understand why so many legal systems have adopted special cutoff rules that, absent an agreement to the contrary, limit the buyer's remedies for breach of the warranty of quality in a way that favors sellers. Three theses will be considered. First, the functional justification for cutoff rules argues that the cutoff rules minimize transaction costs by assigning risks to the parties best able to bear those risks. Second, the political thesis suggests that cutoff rules are the product of political conflict in which sellers' representatives have simply tended to prevail over buyer's representatives. Third, the conceptual thesis explains cutoff rules as products of the ways in which we have conceptualized sales transactions and the institution of warranty.

Part I of the article focuses on the political thesis. After first arguing that the functional justification is inadequate to explain the prevalence of special cutoff rules, Part I then examines the process of negotiations that led up the 1980 U.N. Convention on Contracts for the International Sale of Goods (CISG). Of the entire history of warranty, from Roman times until now, this recent attempt at international unification of sales law provides the clearest evidence, outside of the consumer context, that cutoff rules have been imposed over objection by representatives of buyers' interests. At the 1980 diplomatic conference in Vienna to negotiate the final text of the CISG, representatives from a number of developing countries strongly objected to a notice rule cutting off the buyer's damage remedy on the grounds that it would be prejudicial to their interests as buyers of complex machinery, their main import. The issue of the notice rule was one of the few points that divided the developing countries from the developed countries and "one of the Conference's most difficult problems." The result of this challenge by Third World buyers was amendment of the notice rule by the addition of some obscure compromise language. Part I offers, as a by-product of the inquiry into the politics of cutoff rules, an interpretation of the compromise struck with regard to the notice rule.

After describing the politics of cutoff rules during the international unification of sales law, Part I will offer a political thesis to fit that experience. The thesis must account for the apparent lack of opposition from buyer groups in developed countries. It must also account—as Part II of this Article, to be published in a subsequent issue, will show—for a striking lack of commercial buyer opposition in the entire historical development of cutoff rules in various national legal systems prior to the international unification efforts. Indeed, Part II will show that commercial interests have constituted the primary support for cutoff rules and that the only group of buyers who have tended to oppose these rules have been consumers, who have tended to gain exemption from at least the notice rule. A major aspect of the political thesis developed in Part I of this article is therefore that the processes by which sales law is generally formulated are structurally biased to underrepresent the interest of commercial buyers in a way that did not apply in the negotiation of the CISG. The conclusion to Part I explores the political thesis's implication that caution should be exercised in using merchants' customs and usages (*lex mercatoria*) as a basis for international commercial legislation.

Part II of this article will chronicle the history of cutoff rules from their inception in Roman law through medieval and modern civil and common law developments to show how the development of cutoff rules has been an integral part of the history of warranty. Besides providing historical data for testing the political thesis developed in Part I, Part II will examine the conceptual thesis. The historical record is replete with evidence of two types of conceptualizations that have influenced the development of special cutoff rules. One is deep ambivalence about the justification for the institution of warranty itself, especially implied warranty. The other is a tendency that can be traced from Roman times to today to conceptualize the sales transaction in a way that attributes decisive importance to acceptance for determining the buyer's rights. Final evaluation of the political thesis will thus have to await evaluation of the potentially competing conceptual thesis. Part II will argue that both theses are necessary to account for the historical development of special cutoffs on buyers' warranty rights.

ALLSTATES LEASING CO. v. BASS

Supreme Court of Idaho, 1975.
96 Idaho 873, 538 P.2d 1177.

[Defendant (Respondent) contacted the manufacturer of a car wash system and agreed to buy one. The manufacturer's representatives told defendant that he should finance the arrangement through plaintiff leasing company, and they asked him to sign a lease application agreement and a lease, both of which forms had been provided to the manufacturer by plaintiff. Subsequently, plaintiff sent defendant a substitute lease form in order to correct a $.10 error in the monthly payment figure. The substitute lease contained a warranty disclaimer.]

McQUADE, Chief Justice.

Respondent made two monthly payments on the lease with the last monthly payment being made in October, 1969, but thereafter refused to make additional payments. In November and again in December of 1969, respondent wrote to appellant requesting that it take the Budg-O-Matic unit back. In the November letter respondent informed appellant that the car wash machine wasn't producing enough revenue to make its payments, and that he told the salesmen from appellant's organization that if it didn't make its payments and show a profit, he would not keep it. In the December letter, respondent reaffirmed his wish that appellant remove the car wash system and for the first time referred to the system's inability to function without freezing up in the cold weather. Appellant responded to these letters in a correspondence dated, December 10, 1969, whereupon it informed respondent that 'The dealer who sold this unit to you originally is presently out of town and will return sometime next week, at which time we will contact him for help in disposing of your unit.' Respondent testified that he was never contacted by anyone after receiving this letter, nor did anyone pick up the machine as of the date of trial.

On October 12, 1970, appellant brought this action against the respondent for rentals due under the lease agreement after respondent refused to make further payments. Respondent in his answer to the complaint contended that the lease was null and void because of alleged misrepresentations concerning the quality and expected performance of the car wash system made on the part of the two salesmen, who solicited his business. Respondent maintained that these two salesmen were agents and representatives of appellant. Respondent also asserted in his answer that the lease was of no force and effect because the leased equipment was defective, thereby breaching the implied warranties of fitness and merchantability which accompanied the delivery of the equipment. Respondent counterclaimed for compensatory and punitive damages which he alleged he suffered as a result of appellant's action.

The trial court rejected appellant's claim for damages resulting from the alleged breach by respondent of the lease agreement. It found that the car washing unit leased by appellant to respondent was defective in design and manufacture; was not as represented nor up to the standards as represented so that the defects were sufficient to entitle respondent to relief as against the manufacturer, Auto Laundry Manufacturing Co. However, it did not find that the representations made by the agents of the manufacturer were binding upon appellant so as to hold it liable under an express warranty theory. Rather it held appellant liable as a lessor under a theory of breach of implied warranties in the nature of fitness. The Court therefore rescinded the lease agreement, relieving respondent of further liability under the lease. It did, however, allow appellant to retain the past rentals paid to it as the value of the use of the defective equipment while in respondent's possession, and ordered that the equipment be returned to appellant. Respondent's counterclaim for damages was denied. The appellant appeals from the trial court's judgment.

Appellant contends that it is unsettled in Idaho whether the lease of personal property has the same legal effect with respect to implied warranties as does a sale of goods. Appellant concedes that there is authority in other jurisdictions to that effect, but maintains that even if this be the rule of law in this state, the trial court committed reversible error when it concluded that under the facts of this case there existed either an implied warranty of fitness for a particular purpose or an implied warranty of merchantability. In the alternative, appellant argues that any warranties which may have been applicable were effectively disclaimed by it.

* * *

In ruling that the implied warranty doctrine applies by analogy to lease transactions, we are not saying that the implied warranty of fitness for a particular purpose (I.C. § 28-2-315) or the implied warranty of merchantability (I.C. s 28-2-314) will arise in all lease transactions as a matter of law. Rather, what we are saying is that the implied warranties of fitness for a particular purpose or merchantability will be imposed in lease transactions when there are present those factors which justify the imposition of either of these warranties in the seller-buyer situation. Thus, before an implied warranty for a particular purpose will be imposed upon a lessor, the lessee must demonstrate that the requirements set forth in I.C. § 28-2-315 have been satisfied. Similarly, before an implied warranty of merchantability will be imposed upon a lessor, the lessee has the burden of showing that the requirements set forth in I.C. § 28-2-314 have been met. Our ruling does not restrict the lessor from making use of the right to disclaim warranties as permitted under I.C. § 28-2-316. We will now proceed to review the trial court's decision within this framework of analysis.

* * *

By analogy in a lease transaction, in order for such an implied warranty [of fitness for particular purpose] to arise it must be shown that: (1) the lessor was made aware of the lessee's need, (2) that the lessor recommended a product, and (3) that the lessee leased the product as recommended.

In the instant case, the record indicates that while appellant lessor may have been aware of respondent lessee's need, it made no suggestion or recommendation as to a choice of car wash system to meet this need. Furthermore there is no evidence that respondent made his selection on any basis other than his own inspection of the manufacturer's literature describing the equipment and his impressions of the equipment based upon the statements made by the manufacturer's salesmen which the trial court correctly found did not bind appellant lessor. This being the case, we conclude that no implied warranty of fitness for a particular purpose existed.

Turning our inquiry next to the question of whether appellant impliedly warranted that the car wash system would be of merchantable quality, we conclude that no such implied warranty existed in the instant case. I.C. § 28-2-314 sets forth in pertinent part the following definition of an implied warranty of merchantability in a sales transaction: [The court then quoted § 2-314 and comment.]

It is true that prior to the execution of the lease in issue, appellant handled between forty to fifty transactions over a period of six to eight months, concerning the same Budg-O-Matic Car Wash System that is the subject of this dispute. However, this in our mind does not make All-States Leasing a 'merchant' for purposes of the Code. The record discloses that appellant does not build, manufacture or sell any equipment or machines of any kind, but rather is in the business of purchasing or financing the purchase of equipment specifically selected and specified by an approved lessee. Mr. Lorenz, the Chairman of the Board of Directors and Vice President of appellant company testified:

Q. Now, what business-what is the business nature of All-States Leasing Company?

A. We are a capital equipment lessor. We provide equipment to people who make application to use for a lease, if we grant it, we buy the equipment that they specify from the people that they want us to buy it from and we lease it to them.

Q. Does All-States Leasing Company manufacture any kind of equipment?

A. No.

Q. Does All-States Leasing Company broker or distribute any kind of equipment?

A. No.

Q. Do you distribute any kind of merchandise at all?

A. None.

Q. Do you manufacture any kind of merchandise?

A. None.

Q. In other words, your business or All-States Leasing Company is strictly a company that leases or buys equipment that people specify and, then, lease that to them?

A. That's correct.

* * *

In light of our conclusion that appellant was a finance lessor and not a merchant for purposes of I.C. § 28-2-314, it is unnecessary to pass upon the validity of the disclaimer clause, as it has no bearing on the merits of this appeal.

We do not have to decide whether respondent would have a cause of action against the manufacturer, as the manufacturer was not joined as a party to this action.

Judgment reversed.

DONALDSON and BAKES, JJ., concur.

SHEPARD, Justice (dissenting).

I disagree with that portion of the majority opinion that holds that the lessor is not a 'merchant.' I cannot agree that the appellant who purchased and thereafter leased large numbers of car wash systems was not 'a person who deals in goods of the kind.' Although the appellant here did not build or manufacture such equipment, neither do most retailers. The sole distinction in this case is that appellant, being a lessor rather than a vendor, retained title to the equipment. The majority's purported change in rule permitting a lessor, in some circumstances, to be held to an implied warranty of merchantability is in reality no change at all. If a person must 'sell' and divest himself of title to become a 'merchant' and thus subject himself to implied warranty liability a lessor can never be subjected to such liability on implied warranty.

UCC §§ 2A-103(e) & (g), 2A-212(1), 2A-213
(*see Selected Commercial Statutes*)

(c) Negotiable Instrument Warranties

INTRODUCTORY NOTE

The major arena for negotiable instrument warranties is the check collection system. There, three warranties are important. The first is the warranty that the party transferring or enforcing the instrument is entitled to enforce it. Negotiable instruments law fashions a complex of rules for determining whether a party may enforce the instrument. Generally, those rules, which are set out in Part 2 of Article 3, provide that an instrument payable to order must be indorsed and delivered for the party holding it to be authorized to enforce it. If the instrument is payable to bearer, delivery alone is sufficient to make the holder an authorized enforcer. The net effect of the rules is that generally, the forgery of a necessary indorsement renders the holder unauthorized. Thus the first warranty is a warranty that there are no forgeries of necessary indorsements.

The second important warranty is the warranty against alterations. A party seeking to transfer or enforce an instrument warrants in effect that there have been no alterations to it. Fraudulently raising the amount of an instrument is the common alteration.

The third important warranty is that against forgery of the drawer's signature. This warranty originates in rather quaint historical fashion but survived revision of Articles 3 and 4 with surprising vigor. It only applies when a person transfers an instrument but not when she seeks to enforce it.

In modern check collections, the chief warranty rules are those against forged indorsements and alterations. The warranty against forged drawer's signatures arises infrequently. The problem arises when the drawee/payor bank honors a check with a forged indorsement or an alteration. In those events, the check is not properly payable, and the drawee must recredit its customer's account when she discovers the forgery or alteration and reports it to her bank. Usually, then, it is the drawee/payor bank that makes the breach of warranty claim; and it makes it most of the time against the depositary bank.

In a manner consistent with the warranty theory Professor Priest explains in the excerpt in the article beginning on page 507, the negotiable instrument warranty rules impose the warranty on the party best situated to prevent the loss that a forgery or alteration entails. It makes sense to impose the warranty against forged indorsements on the depositary bank, if it is in the best position to prevent the loss by asking the indorser for identification. Presumably, the depositary bank is also in the best position to prevent alterations either by examining the instrument carefully or by refusing to give credit to shady customers.

If the depositary bank must reimburse the drawee/payor bank for breaching a warranty, the depositary bank will usually have a cause of action for breach of warranty against its customer, the depositor, if it can find him.

PRICE v. NEAL

Court of King's Bench, 1762.
3 Burr. 1354.

Case for money had and received for plaintiff's use: on non assumpsit pleaded, verdict for plaintiff on this special case.

A bill of 40£ was drawn in the name of one Sutton on the plaintiff, dated 22d November, 1760, which in the course of trade was indorsed to the defendant for a valuable consideration, and notice of it left at plaintiff's house the day it became due. Plaintiff sent his servant to take up the bill, who did so, and paid the money. A second bill was drawn, 1st February, 1761, on plaintiff, in the same name, which plaintiff accepted, and wrote an order thereon for his banker to pay it; and being so accepted, it was indorsed to the defendant for a valuable consideration, and was paid by such order of the plaintiff. It appeared afterwards, that both bills were forged by one Lee, who was since hanged for other forgeries. The defendant acted innocently and bonâ fide, without the least privity or suspicion, and paid the full value of both bills. The question was, whether the plaintiff can recover back from the defendant the money paid on the said bills or either of them.

The counsel for the plaintiff gave up the accepted bill, on the authority of *Jenys and Fawler*, Tr. 2 Geo. 2, Stra. 946, where it is held, that proof of forgery shall not be admitted on behalf of the acceptor of a bill, because it would hurt the negotiation of paper credit; unless a difference could be allowed as to the admission of evidence on a trial, and the determining law, after the fact is settled. As to the first bill, which was never accepted, they insisted the case was different. No credit had been given to that bill by an acceptance; therefore the same inconvenience would not follow.

Per Cur.—This is an action for money had and received; the condictio indebiti in the Roman law; the most liberal species of actions on the case. If a man pays money bona fide due, after the Statute of Limitation has run upon it, or pays money fairly won at play, it will not lie to recover it back. It will lie if paid on a mistake, or without consideration, and the like. In the present case, nobody knows the hand of the drawer but the plaintiff. The first bill is taken up by him; the second is accepted by him, before it comes to the defendant. The negligence in the plaintiff is greater than can possibly be imputed to the defendant. Where the loss has fallen, there it must lie. One innocent man must not relieve himself by throwing it on another.

Postea delivered to the defendant, with judgment of nonsuit.

NOTE ON *PRICE v. NEAL*

In the eighteenth century, the larger merchant houses extended credit to the smaller merchants who did business with them. In *Price*, Lord Mansfield held that the merchant houses were in the best position to know the drawer's signature.

Today, banks honor drafts drawn on them without looking at the signatures. When the fifty billion checks arrive at the drawee banks, their sorter machines read the magnetic ink character recognition symbols on the check to determine the account to be charged, the number of the check, and the amount. The first two data are imprinted on the check. The last is encoded by the depositary bank's key punch operators, usually the night after the payee deposits the check. Drawees do examine some checks, those over a certain amount, say $50,000; but they do not examine the signature (nor the date, nor the indorsements) on the vast majority of checks that they honor.

While it made sense in the eighteenth century to assume that the drawee would examine the draft to determine the authenticity of the drawer's signature, it makes little sense to make that assumption today. Yet, during the revision of Articles 3 and 4 in the late 1980s, the banks themselves expressed satisfaction with the *Price* rule, whose costs they had allocated in what they felt was a satisfactory way.

PROBLEM

On May 1 Seller deposited at his bank, Second National Bank, three checks ostensibly drawn by Buyer on First National Bank. The first was in the amount of $100 but Seller had fraudulently raised it to $1,000. The second was payable to the order of Seller and Jones. Seller had forged Jones' signature on the back of the check. The third was not drawn by Buyer. Seller had found one of Buyer's checks and forged her signature as drawer. All three checks went through the collection system, and when they arrived at First National Bank, the drawee/payor bank, Second's reader sorter machines paid them and charged Buyer's account.

When Buyer received her checks and statement at the end of the month, she discovered the alteration and the forgeries. When she notified First, First recredited her account for the amount of the checks, except for the $100 on the first check, as it must under the bank/customer rules. § 4-401.

(a) Does First have a cause of action against Second for breach of warranty? See §§ 3-417(a)(1) & (2), 4-208(a)(1) & (2).

(b) If Second must reimburse First for any of the checks, does Second have a cause of action against Seller for breach of warranty? See §§ 3-416(a)(1), (2) & (3), 4-207(a)(1), (2) & (3).

(c) Could First have recovered from Seller for breach of warranty? Id.

(d) LETTERS OF CREDIT

INTRODUCTORY NOTE

The Code's letter of credit warranties are similar to its negotiable instrument warranties. The Code imposes the warranties on parties in order to provide an incentive for them to avoid losses they are in the best position to avoid. But the warranty rules are not gratuitous. In the negotiable instruments setting, Lord Mansfield would not impose on the presenter a warranty against a forged drawer's signature. That rule made sense when the drawee was in a position to know the drawer's signature, as the drawees were in the eighteenth century. The drawee did not need the warranty, so the law did not provide it, else the loss would fall on a party less able to avoid it.

In letter of credit law, there has been some confusion over the scope of the presenter's warranty to the bank that issued the letter of credit. Under letter of credit law, the issuer of the credit must examine the documents to determine whether they comply on their face with the terms of the credit. The following case read the Code's warranty rule as one against facial defects. The issuer, of course, can see the facial defects, and the *Philadelphia Gear* case is surely wrong, as the revised version of the Article 5 warranty suggests. Section 5-110 clearly does not cover facial conformity of the presenter's documents. *Philadelphia Gear*, however, is something of a leading case under old Article 5.

PHILADELPHIA GEAR CORP. v. CENTRAL BANK

United States Court of Appeals, Fifth Circuit, 1983.
717 F.2d 230.

GEE, Circuit Judge.

The terrain of the present appeal is a failed business transaction, one that culminated in several and mutual allegations of failure to honor contractual obligations. The contract at issue is a documentary letter of credit. The district court determined that the issuing bank wrongfully dishonored drafts presented pursuant to the letter of credit. In consequence, it ordered the issuer to pay the face value of all drafts presented. Because we conclude that the district court did not strike the correct balance between the parties' competing duties and obligations, we reverse its judgment.

Background

On April 23, 1981, Central Bank, appellant, issued a document entitled "Irrevocable Commercial Letter of Credit No. 02408" in the amount of 4.5 million dollars (hereinafter "credit" or "letter of credit"). The credit was issued on behalf of Central's customer United Machinery Services, Inc. ("United") in favor of Philadelphia Gear Corporation ("Philadelphia") as beneficiary. The record reflects that the credit was issued to support Central's obligations to Philadelphia under a sale of goods contract. By its terms, the credit could accommodate individual drafts in maximum amounts of 75 thousand dollars; thereafter to be automatically reinstated to a limit of 4.5 million dollars. Each draft presented pursuant to the credit was required to bear the notation: "DRAWN UNDER LETTER OF CREDIT OF CENTRAL BANK." The record also reveals that each draft was to be accompanied by a copy of the credit. In addition, payment was conditioned upon presentation by Philadelphia's intermediary, Provident National Bank of Philadelphia ("Provident"), of an "inland bill of lading evidencing shipment of any of the above described units to United Machinery, Inc." Contrary to this provision, the credit did not specify the exact nature of the goods to be delivered. More, the credit was expressly subject to the Uniform Customs and Practices for Commercial Documentary Credits fixed by the Thirteenth Congress of the International Chamber of Commerce (1974 Revision Publication 290) (hereinafter "I.C.C. Pub. 290").

Sometime during the latter half of 1981 relations between United and Philadelphia soured. United refused to pay for goods which it claimed were not ordered; and Philadelphia, in contradiction, demanded payment—maintaining that the goods were delivered pursuant to contractual agreement. As a result of this dispute Philadelphia, through Provident, tendered six drafts on the letter of credit in late December of 1981. Several days later Central decided that it would not pay the drafts and returned them to Provident with notice to that effect. The notice stated that the drafts were being returned "due to their non-compliance with the terms of the relevant credit." In early January of 1982 Philadelphia tendered three additional drafts on the credit. Again Central refused to pay, in each case citing as its reason general noncompliance with the credit's terms. Undeterred, Philadelphia wired Central requesting a more definite statement of Central's reasons. Central responded that "[t]he reasons for dishonor are as previously stated."

Oblivious to the manifest logic of Central's position, on February 10, 1982, Philadelphia instituted this diversity action for breach of contract in the Western District of Louisiana. Specifically, Philadelphia sought a declaratory judgment that the drafts were payable under the credit, damages for wrongful dishonor, and—because the credit remained a valid contractual obligation—a preliminary and permanent injunction ordering that future drafts be timely paid. Without result the district court attempted to reconcile the parties' differences at pretrial conference. By this time Philadelphia had been made aware of the exact defect in each of the drafts previously tendered. On the eve of trial Philadelphia presented to Central eleven additional drafts with supporting documentation. These were placed in the registry of the court. The record also reflects that throughout trial Philadelphia presented additional drafts; each was placed in the registry.

At the conclusion of all the evidence the district court found: (1) Each of Philadelphia's tendered drafts failed in some respect to conform to the letter of credit; (2) all the defects were curable; (3) some of the deficiencies were known to agents of Philadelphia and Provident; and (4) Central neither returned the supporting documentation to Philadelphia's drafts (submitted before institution of suit) nor informed Philadelphia that it would hold the documentation on file for its inspection. Applying to these findings what it perceived to be the relevant statutory and case law, the district court determined that Central was liable for the face value of all drafts presented and entered judgment in a corresponding amount. Central now appeals that judgment.

Relevant Standard

Because the resolution of all other issues flows from its determination, the crucial issue of this appeal is whether the district court struck the proper balance between the parties' competing duties and obligations under the credit. We conclude that it did not. The district court characterized the present case as an action for wrongful dishonor. So doing, it relied extensively on the following provisions of the Louisiana Uniform Commercial Code (hereinafter the "Code") and I.C.C. Pub. 290: * * *.

> (1) A bank to which a documentary draft or demand for payment is presented under a credit may without dishonor of the draft of credit
>
> (a) defer honor until the close of the third banking day following receipt of the document * * * .
>
> La.R.S. 10:5-112.
>
> (c) If, upon receipt of the documents, the issuing bank considers that they appear on their face not to be in accordance with the terms and conditions of the credit, that bank must determine, on the basis of the documents alone, whether to claim that payment, acceptance or negotiation was not effected in accordance with the terms and conditions of the credit.
>
> (d) The issuing bank shall have a reasonable time to examine the documents and to determine as above whether to make such a claim.
>
> (e) If such claim is to be made, notice to that effect, stating the reasons therefor, must, without delay, be given by cable or other expeditious means to the bank from which the documents have been received (the remitting bank) and such notice must state that the documents are being held at the disposal of such bank or are being returned thereto.
>
> (f) If the issuing bank fails to hold the documents at the disposal of the remitting bank, or fails to return the documents to such bank, the issuing bank shall be precluded from claiming that the relative payment, acceptance or negotiation was not effected in accordance with the terms and conditions of the credit.

I.C.C. Pub. 290 art. 8(c)-(f).

Against the background of these provisions, the district court first reasoned that at all times pertinent to the present case Provident was a presenter as defined by La.R.S. 10:5-112 and a remitting bank as defined by article 8(e) of I.C.C. Pub. 290. In consequence, Central was obliged to inform Provident of the precise reasons it considered the tendered documents to be nonconforming. See I.C.C. Pub. 290, arts. 8(c), (e). Concluding in each instance that Central failed to meet this obligation, the district court determined that Central was estopped to raise the documents' deficiencies as a defense, the requirement of strict compliance with the terms of letters of credit notwithstanding. More, the district court reasoned that estoppel was proper because Central's failure either to return the drafts' supporting documentation or to give notice that it was being held at Provident's disposal violated article 8(f) of I.C.C. Pub. 290, thwarting any attempt to cure the drafts' defects.

While the above analysis is plausible, it is incomplete. The primary flaw in this analysis is its approach to the concept of dishonor in credit transactions. The district court focused upon the duty of the issuer to pay, finding Central's performance wanting in this respect. It appears to us, however, that in the first instance dishonor puts at issue the adequacy of the beneficiary's performance under the letter of credit. While the adequacy of that performance must be examined in light of the issuer's corresponding duties, it must always remain the primary focus of analysis. We reach this conclusion by tracing the contours of a credit transaction.

Such a transaction usually comprises three separate contracts: "[f]irst, the issuing bank enters into a contract with its customer to issue the letter of credit. Second, there is a contract between the issuing bank and the party receiving the letter of credit. Third, the customer who procured the letter of credit signs a contract with the person receiving it, usually involving the sale of goods or the provision of some service." The obligations and duties created by the contract between the issuer and the credit's beneficiary are completely separate from the underlying transaction, with absolutely no consequence given the underlying transaction unless the credit expressly incorporates its terms. See La.R.S. 10:5-109. In consequence, the issuer's duty to pay is conditioned solely upon the credit's terms: usually, as here, the beneficiary's presentation of facially conforming documents. Id., 10:5-114; see also Harfield, Bank Credits and Acceptances at 73-86 (1975) (hereinafter cited as "Bank Credits and Acceptances"). More, the issuer has no obligation to go beyond a facial examination of the tendered documents in determining whether payment is warranted and, in fact, may incur liability if he does so. In addition, the issuer's promise to pay under the credit is irrevocable. In concert, these features facilitate economic exchange by providing the beneficiary a source certain of payment in the event the issuer's customer refuses to pay.

Since an issuer's duty to pay arises exclusively from the terms of the credit, with no defenses beyond those terms, its liability turns on whether the beneficiary has performed in accordance with the terms and conditions of the credit. The documentation necessary to support payment has the beneficiary as its source and must conform exactly to the requirements of the credit; otherwise the issuer is entitled to refuse payment.

This doctrine of strict compliance is firmly grounded in commercial reality. In the event payment is made upon presentations that do not conform to the credit, the issuer loses its right to reimbursement from its customer. In this event the beneficiary's debt is satisfied and the customer escapes liability on both the underlying and letter of credit contracts while the issuer incurs a corresponding liability—without defense or recourse. More, the rejection of strict compliance as a doctrine would vitiate the economic value of a credit transaction; for not only would the issuer be compelled to assume the risks of the underlying contract's nonperformance, it would also be required to assume the additional risks of judicial realignment of its obligations under the credit. * * *

There can be no wrongful dishonor where the drafts presented are nonconforming and the issuer gives timely and sufficient notice to that effect. See La.R.S. 10:5-112, 114. Because it is undisputed that Philadelphia received timely notice of nonpayment, accompanied in each instance by a statement that payment was refused because of Philadelphia's noncompliance with the terms of the credit, our inquiry must focus upon the sufficiency of Central's notice.

Central contends and the district court found that there were substantial irregularities in Philadelphia's first ten presentations. The record reflects that six were accompanied by photocopies of "shipping evidences" or "shipping notices" rather than the required inland bills of lading. In addition, the shipping documents accompanying the first ten presentations were stale. Article 41 of ICC Pub. 290, incorporated by reference into the credit, provides that "[i]f no * * * period of time is stipulated in the credit, banks will refuse documents presented to them more than 21 days after the issuance of the Bills of Lading or other shipping documents." The district court found that Philadelphia was aware of "some" of these defects at the time of presentation. With respect to the drafts that Philadelphia knew to be defective, we hold that Central's notice was not deficient and that the district court erred in concluding that it wrongfully dishonored these drafts.

Philadelphia does not seriously dispute the facts we have stated. Instead, it presents a three-tiered argument designed to vitiate their impact. First, it urges that because the shipping documents were stale by virtue of an agreement between it and United, Central was required to seek United's approval prior to dishonor. Next, it contends that the defects were curable because it could have reshipped the goods, generating fresh bills of lading, had Central permitted United to return the shipped merchandise. Finally, Philadelphia urges that Central possessed an unqualified duty to notify it of the precise defects within its drafts and that absent such notice liability must attach. We believe this argument to be without merit.

As noted above, a letter of credit and the underlying contract are completely separate agreements, and the issuer may not use the terms of the underlying transaction as a defense unless the credit expressly incorporates its terms. It follows that an underlying contract may not be used to amplify the terms of a credit not expressly incorporating them. It further follows that because the underlying transaction does not affect the credit, any proof concerning a particular custom or course of dealing between the issuer's customer and the beneficiary within the underlying transaction cannot cure the apparent nonconformity of a required document. See La.R.S. 10:5-109. Nor are we persuaded that custom requires an issuer, in every instance, to notify its customer before rejecting nonconforming drafts. We find nothing in the Code or I.C.C. Pub. 290 that warrants such a result.

Louisiana law provides that: "[a] course of dealing between parties and any usage of trade in the vocation or trade in which they are engaged or of which they are or should be aware give particular meaning to and supplement or qualify terms of an agreement." La.R.S. 10:1-205(3). Concomitantly, that law imposes an obligation of good faith in the performance of every contract. Id., 10:1-203. Here it is undisputed that I.C.C. Pub. 290 reflects a codification of accepted banking practice. Article 3(c) of that publication provides that "[an irrevocable letter of credit] can neither be amended nor cancelled without the agreement of all parties thereto." This language is precise in its meaning and requires no interpretation. Because Central has obviously chosen to decline Philadelphia's invitation to modify the credit, the only inquiry is whether good faith—required by the law of Louisiana—imposes a duty beyond both custom and the credit's terms. We believe not. Good faith "means honesty in fact in the conduct or transaction concerned." La.R.S. 10:1-201(9). Nothing in the record suggests that Central acted dishonestly in any aspect of the present transaction. We are not prepared to hold that the timely rejection of a facially nonconforming draft constitutes an act of bad faith. Nor are we prepared to lay it down that good faith imposes a duty to rewrite a contract where there is no hint of unconscionability or fraud. We recognize that issuers often consult their customers before rejecting nonconforming drafts submitted under a credit. Doubtless such a course of action is good commercial etiquette; we cannot, however, require it where the terms of the credit do not.

Appellee's second and third points we treat together, since even assuming that the defects in the documentation submitted to Central were curable, we are unable to conclude that the district court's judgment was correct. To answer these compounded issues we must determine the legal consequences where a beneficiary knowingly submits nonconforming documents. The credit clearly permits the issuer to refuse payment on drafts accompanied by bills of lading more than 21 days old. See I.C.C. Pub. 290, article 41. Central refused payment on the ground that each draft failed to comply with the credit and declined to furnish Philadelphia with any amplifying information. At oral argument, Central asserted that the drafts were rejected because the bills of lading were stale. By the district court's analysis, however, although Philadelphia knew at least some of the drafts to be nonconforming when tendered, Central was required to specify its reasons for refusing payment irrespective of Philadelphia's knowledge.

Our reading of the relevant case law and commentaries confirms that at its essence a credit is a peculiar form of executory contract, one whereby the issuer makes a continuing offer to pay upon the beneficiary's performance of the terms and conditions stipulated in the credit. In consequence, an issuer's obligation to pay is wholly conditioned upon the beneficiary's performance, here, the delivery of specified documents. Further, nonpayment by the issuer gives rise to an action by the beneficiary for breach of contract in which the beneficiary must plead and prove due performance on its part. As stated above, due performance may be demonstrated only by a showing of compliance with the credit's terms.

As we have noted above, the Code incorporates a standard of good faith in every contract made pursuant to its injunctions. La.R.S. 10:1-203. That standard requires honesty in fact in the conduct or transaction concerned. Id., 10:1-201(9). Section 10:5-111 of the Code provides that a beneficiary warrants, in presentation, that its drafts conform to the conditions of the credit. By knowingly tendering nonconforming drafts, Philadelphia breached both of these provisions. It would be a strange rule indeed under which a party could tender drafts containing defects of which it knew and yet attain recovery on the ground that it was not advised of them. For these reasons, we conclude that the district court's judgment was in error regarding those drafts in which the deficiencies were known. We do not hold today that a beneficiary may never prevail where its supporting documentation fails to meet the credit's requirements but only that, upon the present facts, the beneficiary has failed so abysmally in meeting its contractual obligations that no inquiry beyond that failure is required.

* * *

As noted above, the district court found only that Philadelphia knew of "some" of the defects in the presented drafts:

> All drafts submitted to Central by Philadelphia failed to conform to the requirements of the letter of credit in various respects. Some of the deficiencies were known to agents of Philadelphia and Provident. All of these defects were curable.

Our review of the record indicates that the court did not clearly focus on this aspect of the case. In Philadelphia's brief to us, it twice speaks of the "fact" that it knew that the documents accompanying the earlier drafts were stale, and the district court's opinion observes that Philadelphia did not seriously dispute that it knew of defects in all the drafts. Since knowledge of the defects is crucial under our holding, we think the best course is to remand. We do so, directing the district court to determine which, rather than some, of the presentations contained deficiencies known to the presenter at the time of presentation, and to enter judgment accordingly.

For the reasons stated above, the judgment of the district court is reversed and remanded for further proceedings. In consequence, we do not reach the parties' arguments concerning the proper allocation of damages in credit transactions.

* * *

GOLDBERG, Circuit Judge, dissenting.

Ever mindful of the persuasive force of the majority opinion, I must, nonetheless, dissent. The majority faults the district court for being unduly attentive to the issuing bank's duty to pay a draft under a letter of credit rather than the beneficiary's duty to comply strictly to the terms of the letter of credit. I fear that the majority has similarly been unduly attentive to the facts of this case and has uttered a rule insufficiently sensitive to the day-to-day use of letters of credit.

Briefly stated, the case's present posture is as follows: Central Bank issued a letter of credit of which Philadelphia Gear was the beneficiary. The letter of credit incorporated by reference two important terms:

> (e) If [the issuing bank claims a draft is not in compliance with the terms of the letter], notice to that effect, stating the reasons therefore, must, without delay, be given by cable or other expeditious means to the bank from which the documents have been received (the remitting bank) and such notice must state that the documents are being held at the disposal of such bank or are being returned thereto.
>
> (f) If the issuing bank fails to hold the documents at the disposal of the remitting bank, or fails to return the documents to such bank, the issuing bank shall be precluded from claiming that the relative payment acceptance or negotiation was not effected in accordance with the terms and conditions of the credit.

International Chamber of Commerce Pub. 290 art. 8(e), (f). Philadelphia Gear submitted defective drafts to Central Bank under this letter of credit, knowing that "some" of the drafts were defective. Central Bank dishonored the drafts, offering no explanation other than noting that the drafts were not in compliance with the letter of credit; Central Bank also failed to return promptly the drafts with supporting documentation or to hold them at the disposal of the remitting bank.

Philadelphia Gear sued Central Bank for wrongful dishonorment. The district court held that Central Bank was estopped from asserting defects in the drafts as a defense for two separate reasons. First, Central Bank failed to give notice to Philadelphia Gear of the specific defects; second, Central Bank did not return or hold at the disposal of the remitting bank the drafts and supporting documentation. The panel today holds that a knowing tender of defective drafts absolves the issuing bank of its duty to give notice of the defects and of its duty to return the drafts and supporting documentation; the panel remands for a determination of which drafts were knowingly defectively submitted. I believe this rule to be inadvisable for two reasons.[1]

First, although the majority's rule might be an equitable treatment of the present litigants, it introduces a factor treading on the toes of principles basic to letters of credit. Letters of credit are near-mechanical forms of payment designed to facilitate commercial exchange. The terms of letters of credit and applicable laws choreograph an elaborate dance. As long as the steps are followed, payment also follows. There is no need to make inquiries into the underlying transaction; the parties need merely pirouette down the path prescribed by the letter and applicable statutes. Facial compliance is the watchword.

The procedures relating to dishonoring a draft are equally choreographed. One of the important turns in that dance is providing the beneficiary an opportunity to correct a defective draft. I.C.C.Pub. 290 arts. 8(e), (f) delineates two steps in this turn: an issuing bank must return the defective draft and give specific notice of the

---

1 The majority rule contains some ambiguities that are undesirable, but that are not pertinent to my major objections. First, it is not clear to me what type of knowledge is required. Consider the following situations:

1. The supporting documents are voluminous and the beneficiary knows to a moral certainty that they must contain some errors somewhere.
2. The beneficiary suspects that a term in the draft is not in compliance, but is not sure.
3. The day after presentment the beneficiary discovers an error.

I am not sure what result the majority rule would command in these three instances.

A second problem may arise if the negative pregnant of the majority rule is true—if the beneficiary did not know of an error, the issuing bank is estopped from relying on that defect to justify dishonorment. Consider the situation in which (1) a draft contains two errors; (2) the beneficiary knows of error # 1; (3) the issuing bank dishonors the draft without notice of reasons; (4) the beneficiary cures error # 1 and resubmits the draft. Is the bank then estopped from dishonoring because of the unknown and uncured error # 2? Presumably, these are questions the majority would postpone for cases in which they are outcome determinative. That postponement, however, merely contributes to the uncertainty that the majority has injected into a device specifically created to remove uncertainty from commercial transactions.

defects. These two steps are crucial to allowing an innocent beneficiary an opportunity to cure an inadvertent error in a draft. Though this motivation is less compelling when the beneficiary knew beforehand of the defects, the steps are still part of the dance.

An inherent advantage of letters of credit is that questions regarding dishonorment are easily answered—a court or potential litigant need merely look to the choreography and see if the dancers took the proper steps. This usually poses an objective question, with the answer obvious from the face of the documents and the terms of the letter of credit. The rule the majority has chosen to apply to this case injects into the otherwise mechanical and simple inquiry that most subjective issue of the knowledge of the beneficiary.

The result of the majority's rule does not clearly offend me in the case in which the beneficiary in fact knowingly presented defective drafts—as I mentioned earlier, the opportunity-to-cure rationale is not overly compelling in such cases. What deeply disturbs me is that the majority has encouraged dishonoring banks to remain silent as to their reasons, stonewalling and injecting a complex, subjective, litigable issue into every wrongful dishonorment. Henceforth defendant issuing banks will include in their responsive pleadings the boilerplate Philadelphia Gear defense: "Furthermore, the beneficiary knew of the defects at the time of submission." What was once a rigidly choreographed dance now contains a grand jete to the psychoanalyst's couch to look inside the beneficiary's head.

My second major objection to the majority opinion is that it judicially alters the terms of the agreement between the parties before us. I.C.C.Pub. 290 art. 8(e) specifically requires a dishonoring issuing bank to give notice of the reasons for dishonorment and to return the draft and documentation. Article 8(f) even prescribes a sanction for failure to return the draft and documentation (upon which the trial court understandably based its decision). Nowhere is the issuing bank excused from its obligations by the state of mind of the beneficiary. The majority rule has simply engrafted a new term into the parties' agreements. This judicially imposed condition renders somewhat suspect the majority's nominal obeisance to the principle of free contracting.

Though the instant case is a diversity case and "writing in diversity we write on the wind," Thompson v. Johns-Manville Sales Corp., 714 F.2d 581 at 583 (5th Cir.1983) (Gee, J.), the precedential force of the majority opinion is likely to be great considering the field of law and the stature of the author. It distresses me to think that the once useful device of letters of credit may be a less reliable device now. The previously impossible possibility of contentious litigation of a subjective element can now arise in every suit for wrongful dishonorment. Accordingly, I must leave the majority to their pas de deux and glissade offstage, dissenting.

NOTE ON COMMON LAW WARRANTIES

The criticism here of *Philadelphia Gear* should not be taken as a suggestion that the Code's warranty rules are exclusive. Rather, the criticism rests on the idea that the warranty in *Philadelphia Gear* conflicts with warranty theory. There is no need for the warranty in *Philadelphia Gear*. The issuer can see facial defects. The issuer cannot see fraud and cannot take the time to investigate underlying contract breach. The Code, therefore, imposes the obligation to guard against such conduct on the presenter, either the beneficiary of the credit or his bank. Those parties are better able to prevent the losses fraud or underlying contract breach cause.

As the following case suggests, there may be reason to impose warranties in addition to those of the Code.

BAYERISCHE VEREINSBANK ALKIENGESELLSCHAFT v. NATIONAL BANK OF PAKISTAN

Queens Bench Division (Commercial Court), 1996.
[1997] 1 Lloyd's Rep. 59.

[Plaintiff, a Bavarian bank, had, through its London branch, confirmed a credit issued by the defendant. The credit ran to the benefit of Meredith Jones & Co., the English seller of cotton, on behalf on Suhail Jute Mills Ltd., the Pakistani buyer. When the beneficiary presented its documents at the counters of the confirmer, the confirmer paid and sought reimbursement from the issuer. The issuer refused to reimburse for two reasons. First, it appeared that the confirmer had accepted the documents after the credit's stated expiry, as it was authorized to do under article 44(a) of the Uniform Customs that the parties had incorporated into the credit, but the confirmer had not notified the issuer that it had so acted, as article 44(c) of the Uniform Customs requires it to do, or at least had not so notified the issuer until well after the issuer rejected the documents. Second, the issuer claimed that the documents were defective, but the issuer did not give timely notice and specification of the defects, as article 14 of the Uniform Customs require. The plaintiff resorted to the cotton but realized a deficiency after sale of $249,636.50 and now sues the issuer to recover the loss.]

MANCE, J.

* * *

The factual position has already been set out. The plaintiffs on Aug 1, 1994 communicated the presentation of the documents to the defendants by a telex which stated that the beneficiary had presented documents "in order and in time". On Aug 9, 1994, at the defendants' request the plaintiffs reaffirmed that the documents had been presented "in order". Mr. Tozzi was however prepared to accept that art 44(c) required a statement drawing express attention, in whatever words, to the fact that the documents had been presented within the time limits extended in accordance with art 44(a), and that the telex of Aug 1, 1994 did not meet this requirement. I am prepared for present purposes to proceed on the basis that this is correct. It is worth noting, however, that compliance with the requirement in the present case added little or nothing relevant to the information available to the defendants. The telex itself showed that the documents had been presented by at latest Aug 1, 1994. One would expect the defendants to have been aware that Saturdays and Sundays are not working days in London. Suhail Jute were certainly aware of this, and were able to deduce from the shipping documents that they must have been presented after the end of July, 1994, a matter about which they complained in their letter dated Aug

13, 1994. Their letter however overlooked art 44(a), about which the defendants as bankers should have been aware. If the defendants had considered the matter at all, they would, despite the absence of an express notice under art 44(c), have come to the conclusion that the documents must have been presented in time, either prior to the stated expiry date, or in any event not later than an extended date of Aug 1, 1994. On Sept 14, 1994 the fact that the documents had been negotiated under art 44(a) was expressly communicated to them. Even then this does not appear to have struck them as having any significance. When proceedings were issued in May, 1995, neither the plaintiffs (who pleaded that presentation was "on or about 30th July 1994") nor the defendants (who responded that it was on July 30, 1994) were evidently focussing on the date of presentation at all. The very recent amended defence based on the plaintiffs' failure to provide a statement under art 44(c) has overall a somewhat technical appearance on the facts of this case.

On Miss Andrews' analysis, none of this would matter. She submits that the provision of a statement under art 44(c) constitutes a condition precedent to a confirming bank's right to reimbursement. She also submits that the condition precedent is one which can only be fulfilled within a very short time. Failing that, the issuing bank can treat itself as discharged from any obligation at all to take up the documents or to reimburse the confirming bank under the letter of credit. Mr. Tozzi in contrast relies on the absence of any prescribed time, procedure or sanction in art 44(c). He contrasts the specific provisions, albeit in a different context, of art 14(e). In many situations, including the present, the consequences of non-compliance with art 44(c) could be insignificant. Significant consequences could be appropriately compensated in damages if art 44(c) were treated as a simple warranty or indeterminate obligation. In any event, he submits, the defendants are in this case precluded from relying on art 44(c) by failure to act in accordance with the provisions of art 14.

I start by considering the rationale of art 44(c). This is not easy to fit into any coherent overall scheme. Whether documents have been presented for negotiation within the validity of a letter of credit is something that one would expect to be considered by, and to be clear one way or the other to, a confirming bank such as the plaintiffs here. It is not a matter about which a confirming bank would be required or necessarily expected to make any express statement to the issuing bank although a confirming bank might choose to do so. Nor would it necessarily appear from the documents themselves or from the date of their transmittal to the issuing bank, particularly in cases where the documents were presented for negotiation near the expiry date of the credit. The instructions given by an issuing to a confirming bank are, however, limited to taking up documents presented in time under the credit. An issuing bank which was aware that the documents had been presented late could refuse to reimburse a confirming bank which had paid regardless of the late presentation. It appears to me that an issuing bank which reimbursed the confirming bank in ignorance of the late presentation, and later learned of it, could recover the moneys paid on the ground of mistake of fact. Generally speaking, a confirming bank gives to an issuing bank no warranty as to the genuineness or accuracy of documents. However, the time of presentation stands on a different footing. It is a matter within the direct scope of the instructions given to the confirming bank and which it is the duty of that bank to check. If it fails to do so, it must be answerable to the issuing bank. By asking the issuing bank to take up the documents in circumstances where the issuing bank normally has no means of knowing the precise date of presentation, it seems to me that a confirmation bank represents or states implicitly that the presentation was in time.

Against this background of general principle, art 44(c) may be easier to understand. It provides for a statement to be made expressly in any case where the presentation has only been in time by reason of an extension of the stated expiry date under art 44(a). One view of the purpose of the statement may thus be that it serves to give the issuing bank assurance in circumstances where the credit has in fact been invoked at the last possible moment, and to provide a clear basis for recourse if the assurance proves incorrect. However, if this is the scheme, then, as I have already indicated, it has not been completely carried through in UCP 500. It is obvious that there can be cases where a credit has been invoked on or just before its stated expiry date. In such cases, an issuing bank might be doubtful about the position and wish to have a similar express assurance, but UCP 500 contains no such requirement. Unless the confirming bank is prepared to volunteer an assurance, the issuing bank must simply rely on the confirming bank's performance of its functions and on the implicit assurance that probably arises on the transmittal of the documents for payment. Another possible purpose is to provide the issuing bank with a clear statement which it can itself use in claiming reimbursement from its customer, the applicant for the credit. Once again, so far as this is the purpose, it has not been carried through completely, since no such express statement is required generally.

Assuming the purpose or purposes of a statement under art 44(c) to be as I have stated, it is a fair inference that the draftsman of UCP 500 had in mind a statement to be provided prior to or on transmittal of the documents to the issuing bank. However, since no statement is required except in circumstances where the documents have been presented under art 44(a), the paradox arises that the very failure to provide such a statement is likely in many cases to mean that the issuing bank remains unaware that the documents were presented under art 44(a). It is only with hindsight, or where the precise date of negotiation of the documents by the issuing bank is for some reason apparent, that the issuing bank can actually complain about the absence of such a statement. In any other case, the issuing bank will receive documents and will be bound on their face to take them up and pay for them, on the faith of the confirming bank's due performance of its duties. It appears to me difficult to view compliance with art 44(c) as a condition precedent to the issuing bank's liability in circumstances when (i) the issuing bank commonly has no means of knowing of any non-compliance with art 44(c), (ii) in circumstances where the issuing bank is aware that art 44(a) applies, any statement would simply confirm this, and (iii) the statement required under art 44(c) would do no more than express what is anyway implicit in the transmittal of documents by the confirming bank to the issuing bank, namely that they were presented to the confirming bank for negotiation before the expiry of the credit.

* * *

The above conclusions make it unnecessary to consider whether art 14 can apply to documents which are discrepant in the sense that they have been presented out of time. I say only a few provisional words about the point. Articles 13 and 14 deal with discrepancies on the face of documents. The precise date of presentation will not, in the usual course, appear upon examination from the face of the documents. Presentation and the right to refuse documents presented late under the credit are matters dealt with separately in UCP 500: cf. Arts 42-45. Between the beneficiary and the bank to which the beneficiary presents documents, there is thus much to say for the view that arts 13 and 14 have no application. As between banks, if it comes to the attention of an issuing bank that the confirming bank has without authority accepted late presented documents, the issuing bank can no doubt hold the confirming bank responsible, although the documents give no indication of the breach of duty on their face. Where the documents do, unusually, state or enable any firm deduction to be made about the date of their presentation to the confirming bank, then, if art 14 has no application, questions of waiver or ratification may still arise at common law, if an issuing bank takes up the documents without demur. There seems to me even greater difficulty about applying art 14 to a case where documents are otherwise in order but it can be deduced from their dates that they have been presented on an extended expiry date, without any statement having been provided under art 44(c). The information to be derived from the documents would in such a case confirm that the documents had been presented within time under art 44(a) and would render any statement under art 44(c) a mere formality. I can at present see little basis for treating such documents as discrepant on their face within art 14 for lack of a statement under art 44(c). A statement under art 44(c) is, I think, a separate matter from the documents themselves, even as between banks. It is, as I have said, unnecessary for me to decide any of these points. The defendants' defence based on the absence of a statement under art 44(c) fails on the grounds previously indicated: either the provision of such a statement is not a condition precedent to an issuing bank's obligation to take up the documents, or, if it is a condition precedent, it was satisfied on this particular case on Sept 14, 1994.

[The court then held that the issuer, by failing to specify the documentary defects in a timely manner as UCP 500 art. 14(d) requires, was precluded under art. 14(e) from raising the defects against the confirmer.]

Chapter 12

REIFYING AND ABSTRACTING COMMERCIAL OBLIGATIONS

INTRODUCTORY NOTE

Contract law recognizes the reality that obligations arise out of relationships and agreements, so it looks at parties and sees manufacturers and dealers, buyers and sellers, owners and brokers. Above all, Contract law determines obligations by looking at the agreement of the parties. Commercial law on the other hand, eschews reality at times and characterizes parties only in terms of their obligations: issuers, drawers, payees, drawees, and beneficiaries.

Generally, a written contract represents the agreement of the parties. It is not itself the agreement; it is a record of it or of part of it. § 1-201(3) & (11). One of the chief distinctions between commercial law and Contract lies in the fact that commercial law's obligations are generally separate from relationships and agreements.

Commercial law effects that separation in two ways. First, it reifies obligations. Reification is the notion that a piece of paper or other record is the obligation itself, that is, the paper does not represent the obligation; it is the obligation.

The second step in commercial law's separation process is the principle of abstraction. This principle teaches that an obligation is independent of the agreement or relationship out of which it arose. More than the reification principle, abstraction conflicts with Contract dogma; and it has been something of a struggle for merchants and bankers to convince courts that the principle has any integrity.

There are, moreover, exceptions to the abstraction principle; and advocates of it must constantly justify the principle, or the exceptions will swallow it. There is healthy tension here. The abstraction principle can yield harsh results, and there are times when commerce fails to justify those results. The consumer promissory note debacle referred to in section 2(b) below illustrates such failure. When the justification for abstraction fails, the obligation must be dependent, as Contract law teaches. In the commercial setting, however, the abstraction results are usually justifiable. Abstraction yields efficiencies that all parties enjoy; and it is not unfair to enforce an abstract obligation against a party that freely entered into it and enjoyed its benefits before the fact (ex ante, as the economists say) but wants to avoid the abstraction consequences after the fact (or ex post).

SECTION 1. REIFICATION OR MERGER

BULLER v. CRIPS, 87 Eng. Rep. 793 (Q.B. 1694). This was an action by an indorsee against the maker of a note payable to "John Smith, or order [for] the sum of one hundred pounds, on account of wine had from him." Id. Lord Holt, Chief Justice, was disinclined to permit the indorsee to sue. The note was "only an invention of the goldsmiths in Lombard-Street, who had a mind to make a law to bind all those that did deal with them * * *." Id. The chief justice consulted with "two of the most famous merchants in London, to be informed of the mighty ill consequences that it was pretended would ensue" if the court did not recognize the merchant practice of indorsee enforcement of the note. Ultimately, the court denied the plaintiff's standing and concluded that the merchants would just have to use drafts, which the English and other Commonwealth countries call "bills of exchange."

NOTE ON PROMISSORY NOTE CONTROVERSY

In the early part of the eighteenth century, London merchants waged a campaign in favor of the promissory note, which they wanted to use as a substitute for scarce specie. The common law courts had accepted the draft (bill of exchange), which served the same purpose; but Lord Holt drew the line at the note campaign, which he correctly saw as an attempt by the merchants to dictate law to Guildhall. There were a number of cases, some containing colorful language, that earned Holt the reputation, which persists to this day, of peevish curmudgeon. Ultimately, the matter was resolved in Parliament with the Statute of Anne, 1704, 3 & 4 Anne, ch. 8 (Eng.), which accorded the promissory note the features of negotiability that Queen's Bench had denied it in *Buller v. Crips* and companion cases. As a peer, Holt probably participated in the statute's enactment. Some historians claim that the evidence, though equivocal, suggests that he favored the measure, coming as it did from the Parliament and not from "the goldsmiths in Lombard-Street."

SMITH v. GENTILOTTI

Supreme Judicial Court of Massachusetts, 1977.
371 Mass. 839, 359 N.E.2d 953.

BRAUCHER, Justice.

The plaintiffs, mother and son, sued the father's executrix on an instrument in the form of a check payable to the order of the son for $20,000, executed by the father in 1969 and delivered to the mother, postdated November 4, 1984. The check was indorsed by the father as follows: "For Edward Joseph Smith Gentilotti My Son If I should pass away The amount of $20000.00 dollars Shall be taken from My Estate at death. S. Gentilotti 11-25-69". A judge of the Probate Court reported the case under G.L. c. 215, § 13, and we brought it here on our own motion. We hold that judgment should be entered for the plaintiffs.

We summarize the judge's findings, based on stipulations of the parties and the testimony of the mother. The father's will is dated August 1, 1962. The son was born in Michigan on November 4, 1964. From August 1, 1964, to September 15, 1972, the father paid the mother more than $14,000 by forty-nine checks and paid her additional sums in cash; she also received stock later sold for $1,500. From time to time the father asked the mother whether she still had the check in suit, expressed approval that she still had it, and requested her to keep it. Both mother and father expected it to be enforceable. She did not transfer or negotiate the check, and did not bring any paternity proceedings against the father. He died May 31, 1973. Demand for payment has been duly made and refused.

The case is governed by the Uniform Commercial Code, G.L. c. 106. Under § 3-104,[1] the instrument in question is on its face a check drawn on a bank in Milford, Massachusetts, payable on demand, and a negotiable instrument. Its negotiability is not affected by the fact that it was postdated fifteen years; the time when it is payable is determined by the stated date. § 3-114(1), (2). The indorsement modifies the check by providing for acceleration of the time of payment and for direct payment by the drawer's estate. The acceleration provision is authorized by § 3-109(1)(c). As for direct payment, the drawee bank was not authorized to pay the check more than ten days after the drawer's death, if it knew of the fact of death. § 4-405. Hence presentment to that bank was entirely excused as a futile gesture. § 3-511(2). Thus, the provision for direct payment merely restates the result prescribed by law. §§ 3-413(2), 3-507(1)(b). We need not consider the plaintiff's argument that the indorsement is a draft drawn on the drawer, effective as a note under § 3-118(a).

The principal contentions of the defendant are, first, that the instrument sued on is not a negotiable instrument, and, second, that it is unenforceable for want of consideration or reliance. We hold that the instrument was a negotiable instrument. The plaintiffs, unless they have the rights of a holder in due course, took the instrument subject to the defense of want of consideration. §§ 3-306(c), 3-408. But the signatures were admitted, and in such cases 'production of the instrument entitles a holder to recover on it unless the defendant establishes a defense.' § 3-307(2). The judge here did not find that the defense of want of consideration had been established, and neither his findings nor the stipulation and evidence compel such a finding.

The defendant suggests that the instrument was given in lieu of an inheritance. She does not argue that, if otherwise valid, it fails because it is testamentary in character. Such an argument could not prevail, since a valid contract may properly serve as a substitute for a will.

Judgment is to be entered for the plaintiffs.

So ordered.

---

[1] All of the court's references are to the pre-revised Code [eds.].

BALDWIN v. CHILDS

Court of Appeals of New York, 1928.
249 N.Y. 212, 163 N.E. 737.

CARDOZO, C. J.

Plaintiffs, manufacturers, made contracts in October, 1921, for the sale to Childs & Joseph of 574 bales of cotton goods, to be marked and numbered in a stated way, payment to be made within 70 days following delivery. The buyers were then hopelessly insolvent; their liabilities being $2,518,000 in excess of their assets.

The goods were not delivered till December 20, 23, and 26. Before that date, however, negotiable bills of lading, identifying the goods by marks and numbers and calling for their transportation to a foreign country, had been issued to the buyers by the defendants Norton, Lilly & Co., agents for a steamship company. These bills of lading, dated November 29 and December 5, were issued in violation of law, since the goods they represented were not aboard the vessel and were not even in existence. The bills were at once negotiated to banks, who took them in good faith and in return for present value.

Upon the delivery of the bales in the latter part of December, the buyers promptly sent them to the defendants Norton, Lilly & Co., the agents for the steamship line, who held them as bailees for the account of the holders of the outstanding bills of lading. By this time the financial condition of Childs & Joseph had become more desperate than ever. A few days later, on December 29, a committee of creditors began an examination of their books. The plaintiffs gave notice of rescission on January 5, 1922, and demanded back the goods, then in the possession of Norton, Lilly & Co., as bailees for the banks, the holders of the bills of lading. This action of replevin followed. A judgment in favor of the plaintiffs was reversed by the Appellate Division (223 App. Div. 781, 227 N. Y. S. 626), and the complaint dismissed, upon two grounds: First, that the evidence was insufficient to justify a finding that the goods were bought and accepted with fraudulent intent; and, second, that, even though fraud had been made out, the holders of the bills of lading had gained the better title.

We think a jury might fairly find, not merely that Childs & Joseph were insolvent, but that they bought the goods and accepted delivery with the preconceived intent to refuse payment when due. As to this we content ourselves with stating our conclusion. No useful end would be promoted by an analysis of the evidence, for we agree with the Appellate Division that the effect of the delivery of the goods to the agents of the steamship company before notice of rescission was to validate the bills of lading and confirm the title of the banks as purchasers for value.

The bills of lading, when issued, did not pass the title to the goods, for the goods, as we have seen, were not aboard the vessel nor even manufactured. Even so, the effect of delivery when subsequently made was to give vitality to the bills by relation and estoppel, and confirm the title of the holders. The case would be different if, between the making of the bills and the delivery at the steamship, another lien or title had intervened. The sale by the plaintiffs to Childs & Joseph was voidable, not void, and delivery was made upon the vessel, to feed the bills of lading, before notice of rescission had given birth to hostile rights.

We think the banks did not cease to be purchasers for present value because, when value was thus given, the bills that they bought and paid for were not yet united to the goods. Their standing as such purchasers may have added nothing to their title until the union was effected. Once it was effected, title to the goods was theirs perforce of title to the bills, and for the bills they had paid cash. Their rights would be no less, however, if the bills of lading were to be taken as coming into being when the goods were on the vessel, and till then as empty simulacra. The cash paid by the banks was then an antecedent debt, but the continuing duty rested on the carrier to validate the existing documents or to issue new ones as a substitute. The transportation was to a foreign country, with the result that the bills of lading were subject to the federal statute (U. S. Code, title 49, §§ 81, 111; Federal Uniform Bills of Lading Act of August 29, 1916, c. 415; 39 Stat. 538). An antecedent debt is value within the ruling of the federal courts.

* * *

The judgment should be affirmed with costs.

ROGERS, THE IRRELEVANCE OF NEGOTIABLE INSTRUMENTS CONCEPTS IN THE LAW OF THE CHECK-BASED PAYMENT SYSTEM, 65 Tex. L. Rev. 929, 933-34 (1987).

The evolution in recent years of alternatives to the check system, such as credit card systems and electronic funds transfer systems, has prompted considerable interest in the law of payment systems. In 1977 the Permanent Editorial Board for the Uniform Commercial Code responded to the many changes in technology and commercial practice by creating a committee to suggest revisions to Articles 3, 4, and 8 of the Uniform Commercial Code (U.C.C.). The work of the so-called 3-4-8 Committee culminated in the draft of a proposed Uniform New Payments Code (U.N.P.C.) covering all payment systems other than cash. The U.N.P.C., however, was not received favorably by many influential sectors of the bar and essentially has been abandoned. Instead, the Permanent Editorial Board now proposes to draft a separate article for wire transfers as well as various amendments to the existing Articles 3 and 4.

The opposition to the unified approach of the U.N.P.C. stems in part from an implicit assumption that, so far as the present check-based system is concerned, there is nothing wrong with Articles 3 and 4 of the U.C.C. Expressed in slightly different terms, the popular assumption is that present law is well adapted to the technology and practice of the check-based payment system, and that problems are created only by the development of new and different technologies. This Article suggests that this assumption is unfounded; that the system of law in Articles 3 and 4 of the U.C.C. is generations behind the development of commercial practice; and that the basic conceptual structure of Articles 3 and 4 is fundamentally ill-suited even to the paper-based check system.

The core of much of the present law of the check system is the proposition that checks are negotiable instruments; that is, that the concepts of negotiable instruments law provide a sensible foundation on which to erect a system of law specifying the rights and duties of participants in check transactions. What I shall refer to as the "negotiable instruments law approach" rests on three assumptions concerning the design of legal rules for the check-based payment system:

First, it is important to specify certain standardized liabilities incurred by the parties to checks, independent of their obligations arising out of the underlying transactions.

Second, it is important that these independent liabilities, along with the instructions given by the checks to the banking system for making payment, be "reified" in the pieces of paper used, so that checks may be regarded as items of property subject to property law concepts like transfer, title, and conversion.

Third, it is important to apply to checks the rule of transfer that permits a transferee to become a holder in due course, taking free of most claims and defenses.

Briefly stated, the thesis of this Article is that these assumptions are false; for that reason negotiable instruments law concepts are at best irrelevant, and often misleading, in understanding the law of the check system.

II. Checks as Instruments of Bank Credit Transfer

In assessing the soundness of the view that checks should be regarded as negotiable instruments, it is important initially to clarify the role of checks in the monetary system. Aside from electronic funds transfers, the bulk of the payments in the modern economy are made by checks and the bulk of the money supply consists of bank deposits subject to transfer by check. Currency forms only a small part of the monetary system. In a sense, therefore, checks are a substitute for currency, just as in earlier times bank notes and notes issued by nonfinancial entities were substitutes for specie. To those interested in "macro" matters of monetary policy and economic history, this is an important truth. To those interested in the "micro" matter of the law governing the rights and obligations of participants in the payment systems, however, the similarity of economic function between checks and other specie substitutes can be misleading.

Consider first the sort of legal categories and concepts appropriate to the relatively simple monetary system in which specie is the only form of money. One may puzzle at great length over the complex social phenomenon of the use of precious metals as money; for purposes of legal analysis, though, most of that interesting line of inquiry is not significant. The important characteristic of a specie-based monetary system is that money is completely reified. A gold or silver coin that the sovereign has minted and declared to be current coin of the realm is money—it does not represent money or substitute for money; it is money. Accordingly, fairly simplistic property notions will suffice as the basis of payment system law. For example, deciding what counts as payment in such a system requires merely specifying the appropriate rules for the transfer of ownership of coins. Moreover, the set of property transfer rules that evolved in the specie-based system are simple: possession here is ten-tenths of the law. Relatively little modification of basic legal concepts is required to pass from a specie-based system to a bank note system, that is, a monetary system in which payments are made by transferring not specie itself but paper bank notes that are not themselves legal tender but embody the promise of a bank to pay in specie. The essence of a bank note system is that bank credit is used as a substitute for specie as a medium of exchange. The use of promises to pay money as substitutes for money is, to be sure, an innovation of major economic significance, and a sophisticated legal structure is required to control the dangers inherent in the use of bank credit as money. Nonetheless, the use of credit as money in the bank note system requires little modification of the basic legal concepts of payment systems law.

Just as in a specie system the individual items of minted precious metal are complete reifications of money, so too in a bank note system the individual paper bank notes are complete reifications of the money substitute, bank credit. Accordingly, the same set of property and property transfer concepts used in analyzing payment transactions between participants in the specie system can be employed in the bank note system. As in the specie system, the ownership of money can be viewed as a relationship between a person and a thing; the only difference is that the thing, a bank note, is of symbolic rather than inherent value. Nonetheless, so long as the symbol serves as a complete reification of the bank's promise to pay money, basic property and property transfer concepts remain useful; only the object of the concepts changes. Establishing a legal framework for the bank note monetary system is only a matter of applying the property transfer rules used in a specie system to the pieces of paper representing banks' promises to pay money. Thus, in the Anglo-American legal system, the significant steps were the recognition of the free transferability of debts embodied in written promises to pay; and second, the application to those writings of the rule that good title to currency can be derived even from a thief.

The transition from a payment system based on bank notes to a payment system based on deposit accounts subject to transfer by check is, in an odd sense, both a simple and a complex matter. To modern students of economics and banking, nothing seems simpler than the notion that bank deposits are every bit as much a money substitute as bank notes. Even the narrowest measure of money stock, for example, includes commercial bank demand deposits as well as currency. Students of banking and economic history, however, know what a long struggle this modern recognition represents. Scholars of the history of American banking theory and policy have been struck by the obsession of eighteenth-and nineteenth-century thinkers and politicians with bank note issue, and their failure to recognize that bank deposits play essentially the same economic role. Given this background, I can anticipate roars of protest—or, more likely, laughter—at the suggestion that there is an important difference between a monetary system based on bank note issue and a monetary system based on demand deposits subject to checks. Nonetheless, the difference, although of little or no concern from the perspective of monetary theory and policy, is of major concern for payment systems law.

In both a bank note system and a check system, payments are made by the transfer of bank credit from one person to another. The two systems, however, differ significantly in the role played by the pieces of paper. In the bank note system, the bank notes themselves are reifications of bank credit. The holder of a bank note is, by virtue of holding that note, the creditor of the issuing bank. When payment is made by transferring a bank note from one person to another, the act of transferring possession of the bank note effects the transfer of the bank credit. For that reason, a system of legal rules governing such a payment system can be erected appropriately on a foundation of ordinary property concepts. In such a system, it is entirely sensible to discuss questions of good title, transfer, and conversion, because the note, which represents the bank credit, is a reification of money.

In the check system, however, the check is not a reification, embodiment, or representation of bank credit. In the usual case of an uncertified check, the drawee bank never incurs any contractual liability on the instrument. Although the drawer of the check incurs secondary liability under section 3-413(2) [now § 3-414], the bank on which the check is drawn has no contractual obligation to the payee or any other holder of the check. The transfer of bank credit through check payment occurs not as the instrument passes from person to person but when the instrument ultimately is presented to and paid by the drawee bank. In short, a check is simply an instruction directing the transfer of bank credit, not a medium for the transfer of bank credit.

SECTION 2. THE NEGOTIABILITY PREROGATIVE

INTRODUCTORY NOTE

In 1992 the state government in California faced a fiscal crisis. The legislature and the governor could not agree on budget legislation, and the fiscal year began without any budget. In order to prevent the government from shutting down, the state issued registered warrants to some of its creditors. The warrants were, in effect, IOUs, the state's promises to pay what it owed the creditor when the state finally collected the taxes for that fiscal year.

State creditors, then, held something of value—warrants from the state. Holding something of value, however, was not enough. The creditors were not interested in collecting money from the state in the future; they were interested in paying their bills right away. They could not pay their bills, however, unless they had access to what we all use to pay our bills—bank credit, which we transfer from our bank accounts to our creditors' bank accounts by check, credit card, or wire transfer.

When the state was fashioning its warrants program to cover the emergency, state financial officers knew that when creditors took their warrants to the banks and asked the banks to credit their accounts, the banks would resist for a number of reasons. First, they would be concerned that they might not get their money for some time. Second, the banks would have to consider the risk that there might be claims or defenses on the warrants. Suppose a creditor sold office supplies to a state agency, and the agency decided the supplies were substandard? In that case, the state would resist paying the warrant that creditor held. Or, suppose a creditor obtained a warrant from the state by selling goods to the state that were subject to a security interest. In that case the secured party could claim the warrant as proceeds from the sale of collateral.

In order to allay these fears and enhance the value of the warrants, the state resorted to two very old credit devices: First, it issued the warrants at an attractive interest rate; second, it issued the warrants under a provision of California law that rendered the warrants negotiable. At that point, the state was assured that the banks would take the warrants, for they were then marketable.[1]

This story illustrates the value of the negotiability prerogative. Negotiability is not some kind of trap created by banks to snare unwary debtors. The treasury officials of the state of California, the debtor/obligor on these warrants, knew what they were doing when they elected to make their warrants negotiable. They were willing to reify their obligations and to render them free of claims and defenses in order to make them more marketable in the hands of their creditors. By rendering them marketable, they made the warrants more valuable. That value benefitted the debtor on the warrant, the state; and it benefitted the creditor, the holder of the warrant. The warrant's negotiability helped the state out of its financial crisis.

In many commercial transactions, debtors want credit and find it more accessible if they first reify their obligations and then render them free of claims and defenses, that is, render them negotiable.

(a) CUTTING OFF CLAIMS

BANK OF NEW YORK v. AMOCO OIL CO.

United States District Court, Southern District of New York, 1993.
831 F. Supp. 254.

[See page 492 supra for the facts of this case and the portion of the decision finding that the "holding certificates" in the plaintiff's possession were negotiable documents of title covering platinum held by Amoco and that the receipts were duly negotiated to the plaintiff bank. The portion of the opinion reproduced here relates to Amoco's attempt to avoid conversion liability on the grounds that it did not know which of two parties: (1) the plaintiff which had

---

[1] In fact, the warrants ran into another problem. Because they were not in a form easily amenable to bank collection equipment and because there were counterfeit risks, banks found it expensive to take the warrants and claimed that the 5% interest rate, though well above the market rate, was not sufficient to make the investment attractive. Also, many banks were concerned that they would themselves face a liquidity problem if they found all of their lendable funds tied up in the warrants. The governor and the legislature reached a compromise before all of the banks reached that point, but many banks had refused to take the warrants, which amounted to more than $3.5 billion before the compromise.

taken the documents by due negotiation or (2) the original owner of the platinum (Drexel Burnham Lambert Trading Corp.) from whom Amoco had leased it, was entitled to the platinum.]

* * *

IV. Amoco's Defense of Reasonableness

Amoco claims that it acted reasonably in holding the platinum while attempting to ascertain who had ownership rights in the platinum; it argues that this reasonableness precludes a finding in BNY's favor on the conversion claim.

Amoco's in-house counsel, Matthew Gallo, and Rosanne Witmer, a senior Vice President at BNY, testified about communications between Amoco and BNY after DBL Trading defaulted on its overnight loans on February 13, 1990. At Ms. Witmer's direction, Barbara Hyland initially sent a letter to DBL Trading demanding payment on behalf of the bank. BNY also immediately began to liquidate the collateral that it held on DBL Trading's loans.

On February 15, Ms. Hyland spoke with Mr. Sloss at Amoco, as she had been advised to do by DBL Trading. Mr. Sloss testified that he "was very surprised by the call. You know, I tried to be polite and tell her that my agreement for the metal was with [DBL Trading], but that I would certainly discuss it with the law firm." He also claimed that Ms. Hyland only asked about reclaiming the platinum after the leases expired. In her testimony, on the other hand, Ms. Hyland claimed, "I do believe * * * [Mr. Sloss] could have mentioned lease and I said that I had not seen any of the underlying lease transactions nor was I aware that there were specific leases tied to these holding certificates."

Ms. Hyland also sent a letter requesting the metal to Mr. Sloss on February 15. This letter eventually made its way to Mr. Gallo. He apparently was confused by her letter, although it seems to the court to be fairly straightforward. In connection with the possibility of selling the platinum, Mr. Van Den Hogen had DBL Trading send Mr. Sloss a letter amending delivery instructions and told Mr. Sloss to deliver to Johnson Matthey to the account and order of BNY. In the meantime, on February 23, Mr. Van Den Hogen called Mr. Muscarella at DBL Trading, asking him to provide copies of the leases between Amoco and DBL Trading.

After at least a week, Ms. Hyland had not heard from Mr. Sloss; she called him and again demanded the release of the platinum. Mr. Sloss told her he would advise her of a decision on or about March 6. Ms. Hyland wrote to Mr. Sloss again on March 2, 1990, this time asking that Amoco transfer the metal by issuing new holding certificates, and offering to allow Amoco to hold the metal until the expiration of each lease. Mr. Van Den Hogen testified that BNY offered this concession "in view of the business relationship that the Bank of New York maintained with Amoco." BNY required new holding certificates and specific release dates in order to try to sell the platinum in a futures transaction. The bank made this offer "[w]ithout waiving any claim or right which the Bank may have as a result of Amoco's refusal to honor the Bank's earlier request * * *." Presumably some conversation took place between BNY and Amoco after Amoco received this letter; for Ms. Hyland wrote to Amoco yet again on March

5, 1990. Her letter again stressed that the bank had an unencumbered right of ownership in the metal, but she offered Amoco indemnification if it would release the metal or issue new holding certificates in the bank's name. Ultimately, Amoco agreed to deliver the platinum on condition that BNY seek damages in this action of only $550,000, and a transfer of platinum was made on April 4, 1990—well over a month after DBL Trading's default on the loan from BNY.

Under the circumstances, the court is not convinced that Amoco's refusal was reasonable. First, Mr. Gallo's failure to understand BNY's requests does not indicate confusion so much as a lack of research on his part. Mr. Gallo had only passing familiarity with Article 7 of the U.C.C., as he testified at trial. While Amoco may have faced some confusion at the outset, its own internal procedures—the issuance of holding certificates—caused BNY to have a document giving it ownership of the platinum. Despite the fact that Amoco was leasing from DBL Trading, the conflicting claim from BNY did not give Amoco the right to ignore that claim when in fact its own holding certificates were what transferred that right. Any conduct by Amoco other than immediate surrender of the platinum was unreasonable.

V. Damages Calculation

After bringing this lawsuit, BNY made a partial settlement agreement with Amoco, in which BNY agreed to seek no more than $550,000.00 in this action. The parties have stipulated that BNY would have been able to sell the platinum on February 15, when it was entitled to the metal. Given the listings for the sale of platinum at that time, it appears that BNY could have sold the metal at a price of $522.90 per ounce. In fact, BNY was not able to sell until April 4, 1990, when it sold the 22,230 ounces platinum it obtained from Amoco at a price of $471.70 per troy ounce. Thus BNY sustained a loss of $51.20 per ounce, which when multiplied by the total 22,230 ounces leads to damages of $1,138,176.00. Of course, this amount well exceeds the $550,000 limitation in this action, and BNY consequently is entitled to the full amount of $550,000.00, with interest from April 4, 1990.

NOTE ON NEGOTIABLE FORM AND DOCUMENTS OF TITLE

As the *Baldwin v. Childs* case, supra, indicates, merchants found merit in reifying the obligation of a bailee to redeliver goods. Goods valued in the billions of dollars are subject to "bailment," a legal term that includes the relationship that arises in the commercial storage and transport of goods and in the lease of them too. While those goods are stored, transported, or leased, their owners may want to sell them or may need credit. In either event, they often will want to transfer an interest (the title in a sale, a security interest in the event of a loan) in the goods without interrupting the bailment. It makes no sense for the law to require delivery of goods when commercial parties want the goods to stay where they are. A farm producer who has stored 100,000 bushels of soybeans in Iowa should not have to deliver the beans to a broker buyer when the broker wants the beans to stay in Iowa until the broker finds a sub-buyer who wants to take delivery. Banks should be able to take a possessory security interest in goods at sea without requiring the ship's captain to attorn that he holds the goods for the bank.

By reducing bailed goods to mere simulacra and reifying the goods in pieces of paper (warehouse receipts and bills of lading), merchant practices permitted easy transfer of interests in the bailed goods.

Not all bailments give rise to negotiable documents, however, just as not all obligations are reified in a negotiable instrument. Commercial law has been chary about according its special protections willy nilly. Only transactions that are quite regular merit the protections of negotiability; and merchants can reify goods or documents only with paper that is unmistakably negotiable in form. §§ 3-104, 7-501. Negotiability is not to arise by accident.

In the event the parties do not use negotiable paper, purchasers cannot qualify for the special protections.

PHILADELPHIA NATIONAL BANK v. IRVING R. BOODY & CO.

1 U.C.C. Rep. Serv. (Callaghan) 560 (Funk, Arbitrator 1963)

[SAWCO granted Boody, its seller, a perfected security interest in wool. Thereafter, SAWCO stored the wool with a warehouse and caused the warehouse to issue a nonnegotiable receipt to Wagman, to whom SAWCO granted a security interest in the wool. When SAWCO became insolvent, Boody and Wagman claimed the wool.

Boody argued that its security interest ranked first by virtue of the rules of Article 9. SAWCO argued that it had special rights under Article 7 by virtue of the fact that it took a security interest by a warehouse receipt.

The matter was submitted to arbitration before Carl Funk, one of the drafters of the Code; and the opinion was published in Callaghan's UCC Reporting Service.]

The issue presented by this case is of importance to banks and other financial institutions. Documents of title covering goods worth millions of dollars are released every day by banks relying on the perfected security interest they obtain through the use of trust receipts and the filing of financing statements. Conversely, millions of dollars are loaned by banks on the security of non-negotiable documents of title issued in the name of the lending bank. It is essential for everyone engaged in banking and commerce to know the relative value of the two security interests if they should come into conflict, as they did in this case. It is suggested that the Uniform Commercial Code is either ambiguous or conflicting in dealing with this question.

* * *

The parties agree that this is a conflict between two perfected security interests. Boody's interest arose through the release of a delivery order of the wool to SAWCO against a trust receipt on September 13, 1960, at a time when a financing statement had been duly filed, and hence Boody's security interest was perfected at the time of such release. [Sections 9-304(5), 9-302, 9-303.] Thereafter, Wagman obtained a perfected security interest by the pledge to it of a non-negotiable warehouse receipt for the wool, issued in its name. [Section 9-304(3).] Boody's interest was perfected by filing, Wagman's by the issuance of the non-negotiable receipt. The perfection of Boody's interest occurred first in point of time.

* * *

So far as Article 9 is concerned, therefore, Boody should prevail and its counsel claims that Article 9 alone should be considered. Counsel for Wagman, on the other hand, contends that there is a conflict between Article 9 and Article 7 on Documents of Title, and that the provisions of Article 7 should control. An examination of that article, however, fails to reveal such a conflict. On the contrary, Article 7 is consistent with Article 9 and under it Boody likewise must prevail.

Throughout the Code there is a clear distinction between negotiable and non-negotiable documents of title, and there are situations where the holder to whom a negotiable document has been duly negotiated is in a stronger position than the holder, under otherwise identical circumstances, of a non-negotiable document. For example, under Section 7-502, a holder to whom a negotiable document of title has been duly negotiated acquires thereby * * * title to the document and title to the goods and certain other rights, whereas under Section 7-504, a transferee of a document, whether negotiable or non-negotiable, to whom the document has been delivered by not duly negotiated, acquires only the title and rights which his transferor had or had actual authority to convey. "Due negotiation" is the key to this paramount position; but only a negotiable document of title can be negotiated or duly negotiated. All the references in Article 7 to negotiation and due negotiation are limited to negotiable documents. This is true even of subsection 7-501(2)(b), which reads:

> "(b) When a document running *to the order of a named person* is delivered to him the effect is the same as if the document had been negotiated." (Emphasis added.)

since a non-negotiable document does not run to the order of a named person and therefore does not come within this subsection.

So far, therefore, Article 7 is consistent with Article 9. If Wagman's warehouse receipt had been negotiable its delivery to Wagman by SAWCO would have constituted a due negotiation and it would have prevailed over Boody's security interest, but there is nothing in Article 7 which makes the non-negotiable receipt issued in Wagman's name and delivered to it the equivalent of a negotiable receipt.

* * *

Great stress is laid upon the importance to commerce of sustaining the position of the holder of a non-negotiable warehouse receipt. It is true that such receipts are preferred over negotiable receipts by banks and other lenders for practical reasons, primarily because goods can be released to their customers without the surrender of the receipt itself, which would be required if the receipt were negotiable. It is undoubtedly true that banks and others advance large sums of money relying on such non-negotiable receipts issued in the name of the bank without making any check to determine whether financing statements covering the goods are on file. In doing so, banks should recognize that while they thereby obtain protection against unsecured creditors of their customer and his trustee in bankruptcy, they do not get full protection against the type of double financing that occurred in this case; and they must weigh the risk of loss against the practical advantages of using non-negotiable receipts.

It is of some significance, moreover, that no similar case has been found by counsel or by the Arbitrator under either the Uniform Commercial Code or under its predecessors, the Uniform Warehouse Receipts Act and the Uniform Trust Receipts Act. Under Section 42 of the Warehouse Receipts Act, a person to whom a receipt had been transferred but not negotiated, acquired no better title to the goods than that possessed by his transferor, and the Act drew a distinction similar to that of the Code between the due negotiation of a negotiable receipt and the transfer of a receipt without negotiation. Under the Uniform Trust Receipts Act, entrusting goods or documents exposed the entruster to loss if the trustee should obtain and wrongfully negotiate a negotiable document, to a purchaser, including a pledgee; but it made no similar provision where the document was not negotiated. It also gave protection similar to that of the Code to "buyers in ordinary course of trade," but this term, like "buyer in ordinary course of business," did not include a pledgee. Hence, it appears that in giving priority to Boody in the present situation, the Code did not change the earlier law. If, as a matter of policy, the rule should now be changed to meet the demands of commerce, and non-negotiable receipts issued in the name of a bank and delivered to it should be given the same protection as negotiable receipts similarly delivered, this must be done by amendment to the Code.

The Arbitrator therefore holds that Boody's security interest has priority over that of Wagman and of The Philadelphia National Bank as Wagman's assignee.

UCC § 9-309

Nothing in this Article limits the rights of a holder in due course of a negotiable instrument (Section 3-302) or a holder to whom a negotiable document of title has been duly negotiated (Section 7-501) or a protected purchaser of a security (Section 8-303) and the holders or purchasers take priority over an earlier security interest even though perfected. Filing under this Article does not constitute notice of the security interest to such holders or purchasers.

HENDRIES, INC. v. AMERICAN EXPRESS CO.

Supreme Court of New York, Appellate Division

Page 183, supra

QUESTIONS

1. Does a bank that honors a documentary draft, as the bank did in *Hendries*, become the owner of the documents of title accompanying the draft? Section 7-502(1) suggests that it does, but is it more accurate to say that the bank only holds a security interest? If the bank's interest is only a security interest, what would happen to the proceeds from the sale of the goods if they exceed the amount of the bank's loan? Should the bank get more out of the goods than it has loaned (plus interest and fees, of course)? Do banks speculate in ice cream mix?
2. If the letter of credit issuer that honors the draft and takes the documents of title by due negotiation only holds a security interest, can it be cut off under article 9? See § 9-309.

(b) Cutting Off Defenses

INTRODUCTORY NOTE

The earliest distinct features of negotiable obligations were (1) the right of the holder to sue on the obligation in his own name (a reification feature) and (2) the ability to defeat prior claims (a negotiability feature). Later, there developed in negotiable instruments law the idea that the holder of the instrument defeated defenses that might have been good against the original payee in the underling transaction.

Probably, this feature, the cutting off of defenses, is the one that excites the most opposition to negotiable instruments law. That opposition rests in part on the fact that merchants unwisely used the feature against unsuspecting consumers with an attendant brouhaha that nearly brought down the whole negotiability edifice. Fortunately for commerce, as we shall see in this section, the consumer protection movement and the legislatures saved commercial law from its own folly by carving out exceptions for consumer transactions.

Before we can consider the exceptions, however, it is necessary to examine the doctrine of cutting off defenses more closely.

The first point to make in that study is that the doctrine only applies to commercial defenses: the right of recoupment, failure of consideration, and fraud in the inducement. These are the principal commercial defenses that arise when shipments are short, late, or nonconforming or services are not up to par. Commercial law gladly suffers the costs of fraud in the execution, infancy, incompetence, and illegality. Good faith purchasers of negotiable paper generally take subject to these noncommercial and (happily) rare defenses. § 3-305(a) & (b).

There remains another important defense, discharge in bankruptcy or state insolvency proceedings. Here, the legislatures have mandated relief for debtors; and merchants must live with that command. Insolvency is an ubiquitous risk. Commerce suffers from it, but there are rewards here too, for by putting the loss on the solvent party that trusted the insolvent party, the law encourages efficient allocation of credit.

UNITED OVERSEAS BANK v. VENEERS, INC.

United States District Court, District of Maryland, 1974.
375 F. Supp. 596.

BLAIR, District Judge.

Plaintiff, United Overseas Bank, a Swiss corporation, filed this suit under the diversity jurisdiction of the federal courts, seeking to recover from defendant, Veneers, Inc., a Maryland corporation, on a bill of exchange dishonored by Veneers. The case is presently before the court on cross-motions for summary judgment. * * *

On or about May 16, 1968, Madera S.A., a corporation with a banking account in United Overseas Bank, presented to United Overseas Bank for collection a bill of exchange drawn by Madera with Madera as payee and Veneers as payor. As requested by Madera, United Overseas forwarded the bill of exchange to Maryland National Bank in Baltimore for presentation to and acceptance by Veneers. The bill of exchange called for the payment by Veneers to the order of Madera of $42,478.40 on July 21, 1968. Upon its receipt by Maryland National Bank in Baltimore the bill of exchange was presented to Veneers for acceptance. On May 24, 1968, John Williamson, President of Veneers, signed the printed acceptation form on the bill of exchange, signifying that Veneers had accepted it for payment at Maryland National Bank, Baltimore, Maryland, on July 21, 1968.

The accepted bill of exchange remained in the hands of Maryland National Bank which, on May 31, 1968, forwarded a notice to United Overseas that Veneers had accepted it for payment on July 21, 1968. On June 7, 1968, United Overseas, acting on the notice that Veneers had accepted, discounted the bill by making available for Madera's immediate withdrawal $41,853.88. On July 22, 1968, the bill of exchange was presented by Maryland National Bank to Veneers for payments. Veneers, however, refused to honor it, asserting that Madera was indebted to it on a separate account (apparently in the amount of $36,941.72) and that Veneers would not honor the bill of exchange until Madera had settled this account. That same day, July 22, Maryland National Bank protested the nonpayment and had notices of the nonpayment sent to Veneers, United Overseas Bank and Madera. A series of telex interchanges between Maryland National Bank and United Overseas Bank ensued. When it became obvious to United Overseas that Veneers was not going to pay the bill of exchange, it enlisted the aid of its parent, Bank of America, which retained counsel to press the matter in the courts. On July 29, 1969, on the advice of counsel, United Overseas, through its Director, Pierre Jeandin, placed a collection bank endorsement upon the back of the bill of exchange. Until that time, the bill of exchange had upon it no endorsement whatsoever. United Overseas affixed the endorsement in the belief that it, as a collection bank, was entitled to place its depositor's endorsement upon negotiable instruments placed with it for collection. Until sometime before

United Overseas affixed the collection endorsement in Switzerland, the bill of exchange had been in the possession of Maryland National Bank in Baltimore, Maryland. It should be noted at this point that the endorsement by United Overseas was placed upon the bill of exchange approximately one year after it had been dishonored by Veneers. At a time shortly after United Overseas received notice of acceptance by Veneers but before it received notice of dishonor, Madera availed itself of the cash credit on hand in United Overseas Bank and withdrew the money. Apparently Madera is bankrupt and there is little hope of collection from Madera of either the amount Veneers alleges is due it or the amount which is in question in this present suit.

Until it received notice of the dishonorment by Veneers, United Overseas had no knowledge of any claim of Veneers against Madera and at the time it made credits available for withdrawal by Madera, it was under the confirmed impression that Madera was a solvent, viable concern. Madera had done banking business with United Overseas for a period of years and the transaction leading to this suit was not a single isolated transaction but was done in the normal course of business with a regular customer of the bank.

* * *

What must now be determined is what the effect of the transfer was and whether, under the U.C.C., plaintiff became a holder in due course.

[The court then determined that because the late indorsement was ineffective, the indorsements on the draft did not run to plaintiff. Plaintiff was not, therefore, a holder and perforce could not be a holder in due course.]

These conclusions necessitate a determination of whether Veneers has a defense assertable against Madera. Defendant, in its motion for summary judgment, has not conclusively established by affidavit or record to the court's satisfaction the existence, nature, or extent of the claim it allegedly has against Madera. In fact, all indications are that plaintiff's claim against defendant is larger than defendant's claim against Madera. Hence, further proceedings consistent with this opinion are required.

Therefore, for the reasons herein stated, it is ordered this 10th day of October, 1973, that:

1. Plaintiff's Motion for Summary Judgment be and hereby is denied;

2. Defendant's Motion for Summary Judgment be and hereby is denied.

GILMORE, THE GOOD FAITH PURCHASE IDEA AND THE UNIFORM COMMERCIAL CODE: CONFESSIONS OF A REPENTANT DRAFTSMAN, 15 Ga. L. Rev. 605, 612-13, 619 (1981).

Let me suggest some quite different conclusions that we could have deduced from our premises. In a society that recognizes property as something more than theft, you do not go around lightly destroying property rights; you must have a compelling reason for awarding A's property to C. Even in a contract-oriented law, you do not go around lightly telling people who have been tricked, cheated, and defrauded that they must nevertheless pay up in full; you must have a compelling reason for doing that, too. So, what could the compelling reasons have been which led the courts to reach, the better part of two hundred years ago, these extraordinary conclusions? Are those reasons equally compelling today?

In the case of the negotiable instrument construct, the answers appear to be clear. In the late eighteenth century, mercantile bills of exchange and bank notes, a sort of unofficial currency which the merchants and bankers had invented, served as an indispensable supplement to the official currencies, which were in short supply. Without these bills and notes, the primitive banking system could not possibly have coped with the enormously increased number of transactions that followed the industrial revolution. This commercial paper typically passed from hand to hand in a long series of transfers, ending up in the hands of strangers who knew nothing about the original transaction or about earlier transfers of the bill or note and had no way of finding out about them. The need to protect the strangers who bought the paper in the market, even at the cost of doing harm to the obligors and earlier holders, was the compelling reason that led the courts to elaborate the good faith purchaser, or holder in due course, idea in negotiable instruments law.

After the middle of the nineteenth century, currency reforms and modern uses of bank credit made this mercantile currency unnecessary and obsolete. Mercantile paper, to the extent that it remained in use, no longer circulated in anything that could be described as a market; the strangers who had once bought the paper had by 1900 become an extinct species. There are clear indications in the late nineteenth-century case law that the courts—responding to the new situation, as courts, for reasons that escape us, always do—had set about dismantling the structure of the pre-1850 law of negotiable instruments. That discernible trend was interrupted by the codification of the pre-1850 law in the Negotiable Instruments Law (N.I.L.), which was strongly supported by the bankers and their allies and was enacted within the space of a few years throughout the country.

* * *

I shall not go into any detail about article 3 of the Code, which deals with negotiable instruments, renamed commercial paper. I once commented that article 3 is the N.I.L. doubled in spades—negotiability *in excelsis*—and went on to say that the article gravely reviews each of the pressure points that had emerged in the N.I.L. case law and resolves the issue in favor of negotiability and the holder in due course. The most outrageous thing about article 3, a statute drafted in the 1940's, is that there is no reference, in text or comment, to the then rapidly developing body of case law holding that finance companies and banks to which consumer notes were negotiated could not hold the notes free of the consumer's contract defenses because of their close connection with the dealer-sellers. That omission has been remedied by an intricate network of state and federal statutes and regulations, but it should never have been tolerated in the first place.

NYQUIST, A SPECTRUM THEORY OF NEGOTIABILITY, 78 Marq. L. Rev. 897, 897-903 (1995).

> The first law course I had a chance to teach was Bills and Notes. Yale was very gentle with the unbroken colt: Bills and Notes three times a week at 8 A.M.—and nothing else. And I had John Edgerton's copy of Smith & Moore's Cases: "'My face is my fortune, Sir,' it said," was his observation on *Miller v. Race*. "Notes make music, once you learn to play." That was inside the cover * * *. "Why 'Equities'? It is the bfp who has the equities." There was time and occasion to fall really in love with the subject, and I have never fallen out.
>
> Karl Llewellyn

Negotiable instruments scholarship rests on four interconnected and largely untested propositions. Llewellyn, with an instinct for the jugular, touches on three of them in his brief reminiscence. The other premise has evolved in a handful of theoretical commercial paper articles published over the past twenty-five years, and all four assumptions underlie virtually the entire contemporary discourse on negotiable instruments.

"My face is my fortune." Negotiable instruments are seen to inhabit a separate and exclusive enclave where basic principles of contract and property law do not apply. Entrance to his domain is entirely a matter of form. Documents satisfying the requirements of Article 3 of the Uniform Commercial Code gain admission. Documents failing the formal tests are deemed "simple" contracts and relegated to rules of contract assignment and property transfer that reduce their value to purchasers. A corollary of the separate enclave premise is that negotiable instrument principles are viewed as having limited applicability outside Article 3.

"Notes make music once you learn to play." Negotiable instruments statutes have invariably preferred rigid rules over flexible standards. For the past one hundred years American negotiable instruments law has been embodied in two successive rules-based uniform statutes; the now antiquated Uniform Negotiable Instruments Law and Article 3 of the Uniform Commercial Code. Pursuing Llewellyn's music analogy, the drafters of Article 3 deployed an intricate twelve-tone scale, and "learning to play" can be a daunting task. Moreover, the structure of Article 3 contributes to rigid either/or thinking about negotiable instruments. In Article 3 an instrument is either negotiable or it is not. Negotiable instruments are either promises or orders, payable on demand or at a definite time, and payable to order or bearer. A holder of a negotiable instrument is either a holder in due course or she is not. Disputes involve either defenses or claims or both. Disappointed purchasers may have a cause of action either in contract or warranty or both. Defenses to contract liability are either personal or real.

The inflexible dualism of negotiable instruments logic contributes to the view that most issues are resolvable by the application of predictable rules: "[T]here is little room for the chancellor's foot to rotate in the law of bills and notes." Furthermore, commercial paper literature seldom investigates or even sees connections to other subjects. Negotiable instruments law is viewed as self-contained and self-sufficient. Similarly, non-commercial paper legal scholarship shows little interest in negotiability principles.

"It is the bfp who has the equities." It is conventional wisdom that a transfer of property vests in the transferee only the right, title, and interest of the transferor. As a consequence, a transferee takes a position no better than her transferor. An assignee of rights under a simple contract takes subject to all defenses and claims that would be effective against the assignor. This "same as" position is seen as a fundamental and almost inviolable principle—as natural as water seeking its own level. A holder in due course, on the other hand, *can* take a position that is better than his transferor. A holder in due course takes free of all claims to the instrument and most defenses. Holder in due course rights are considered an unnatural and extraordinary violation of the basic principle. In U.C.C. Article 3, water flows upstream.

The final premise of negotiable instrument scholarship has become apparent in a succession of articles whose very titles leave little doubt about the authors' opinions: *Negotiability—Who Needs It?, The Good Faith Purchase Idea and the Uniform Commercial Code: Confessions of a Repentant Draftsman, Formalism and the Law of Negotiable Instruments, The Holder in Due Course and Other Anachronisms in Consumer Credit, The Last Nail in the Coffin of the Holder in Due Course Doctrine, and Codification of Negotiable Instruments Law: A Tale of Reiterated Anachronism.*

This scholarship is based on the proposition that negotiability serves a single policy. It argues that the "better than" position evolved in the nineteenth century to encourage commercial transactions in negotiable instruments and similar documents. A better than position enhances the price purchasers will be willing to pay by eliminating the need to discount for the possibility of claims and defenses. A holder in due course is subject only to the problems arising from her particular transaction of purchase, a transaction over which she has control and whose details she knows. Problems arising out of prior transactions, whether the initial issuance of the instrument or transfers subsequent to issuance, are of no concern except to the extent they give rise to real defenses.

It is further argued that the negotiability principle would have been abandoned in the late nineteenth century except for the "apparent accident of codification." The Negotiable Instruments Law and Uniform Commercial Code perpetuated an archaic and exhausted concept that, although wounded, is still dangerous when applied to modern transactions. Negotiability operates to cut off legitimate consumer defenses, confers on banks undeserved rights against third parties, and is generally seen to place the weak at the mercy of the strong.

This Article examines all four assumptions: that the negotiability principle inhabits a special enclave, is rigidly dualistic, is self-contained, and promotes a single antiquated policy. Part I argues that the negotiability concept is one of the fundamental ways of thinking about transfers of property and a "better than" position is an option generally available to courts and legislatures. While a "better than" position may not be chosen in a particular case or statutory section, it is more widely used than the literature recognizes. Moreover, negotiability is not rigidly dualistic with alternatives limited to a "same as" position or full holder in due course rights. Instead, the negotiability principle offers an entire spectrum of possibilities—from positions only marginally better than "same as," through numerous intermediate positions, to a full Article 3 holder in due course position, and then beyond, to negotiability positions even more radical than those found in U.C.C. Article 3. The negotiability principle displays flexibility, diversity, and subtlety, and is so firmly imbedded in the idea of transfer it often goes unnoticed.

Part II explores one of the major symptoms of commercial paper scholarship's inflexible dualism. While the literature has devoted tremendous energy explicating holder in due course rights and contrasting those rights with a "same as" position, it has entirely failed to explore a third alternative: the transferee might take a position that is worse than her transferor. A "worse than" position displays a range of possibilities similar to the negotiability spectrum, from outright prohibitions of transfer to positions only marginally less than a "same as" position. The "worse than" alternative is in many ways as important as negotiability and demonstrates a comparable richness and variety.

Part III demonstrates that negotiability, far from being self-contained, developed in an atmosphere of borrowing and reverse-borrowing across property lines. Analogies to goods, bank notes, and coin were particularly important. Furthermore, negotiable instruments law still exists as part of a complex network with numerous connections to other types of property. The negotiability principle is not, nor has it ever been, restricted to negotiable instruments. A general failure to recognize this network of connections has produced peculiar anomalies such as negotiable instruments being treated as less negotiable than other kinds of property and documents being first banished from Article 3 and then readmitted with little thought to the consequences.

The "same as" position is neither natural nor fundamental—it is constructed like any other legal principle. It is no more nor less important than the "better than" and "worse than" alternatives. It is often either ignored or unseen and in many instances it appears as mere argument joined to a "better than" or "worse than" counterargument.

Throughout, this Article claims that negotiability serves not one policy but many policies. While negotiability clearly can have disastrous consequences for consumers, it can also protect consumers, guard against secret liens, defend the integrity of a filing system, encourage ordinary course transactions in goods, speed bank collections and payments, and even insulate Samuel Williston from tax liability for the interest coupons he gave as gifts to his daughter during the Christmases of 1934 and 1935. Negotiability cannot be identified with a single interest; it has been an ally and a foe of many interests. Negotiability is not a closed system but rather a fundamental principle at work in many systems.

J. DOLAN, FUNDAMENTALS OF COMMERCIAL ACTIVITY § 22A (Supp. 1995)

The promissory note * * * achieved a measure of prominence in domestic commerce during the 19th century. Prior to the advent of open-account sales, many merchant sellers accommodated their buyers' need for credit with a time draft in the documentary draft transaction * * *. The buyer's acceptance of the draft gave the seller a negotiable instrument, which the seller could negotiate to a bank or other lender as security for a loan, often at a discounted price. The negotiability feature of the draft made it attractive to the lender since the instrument was abstract from the underlying transaction, that is, it was free of that transaction's equities. If the goods that the seller sold the buyer were not merchantable, short, or otherwise non-complying, the buyer, as acceptor of the draft, could not raise those objections against the holder when the draft came due.

The documentary draft transaction entailed more detail and cost than the merchants were willing to bear. First, of course, the transaction required the seller to obtain a document of title; and there were times when it was otherwise unnecessary for the parties to use a document. Second, merchants designed the draft for presentation through the banking system twice: first for acceptance and second for payment.

If the seller and the buyer did not use a document of title, as they apparently did not on many occasions, and if they wanted to avoid the need to present the negotiable instrument for acceptance and, in fact, wanted the buyer's signature on a negotiable instrument before they shipped the goods, the promissory note was the preferred instrument.

Eastern seaboard sellers, then, might take a promissory note from their customers in the midwest and ship goods via their factors from time to time until the amount of the note was exhausted. The note, being negotiable, was designed for discount, having the same attractive abstraction feature that characterized the draft.

Although not all of the reasons for the growth of the note are clear, we know that it gained a measure of prominence in the 19th century for it appeared in the banking system with considerable frequency and reflected a large volume of commerce.

The 20th century witnessed the note's comparative demise, as it witnessed the demise of the documentary draft in domestic commerce. As reliable credit reporting made open-account selling an attractive alternative to both the promissory note transaction and the documentary draft transaction, the two negotiable instruments largely disappeared from domestic commercial sales, though they have both survived in other transactions and in some international sales.

* * *

In the 20th century, a dramatic change in consumer buying practices brought the note back into commerce in a role for which, it is now clear, the note was ill suited. That change was the advent of consumer credit.

In more than one way, Henry Ford's manufacturing, employment, and marketing practices have changed the face and commerce of America. For our purposes, an important change arose when he made automobiles available to the mass market. That event, especially when it combined with the prosperity that followed the First World War, made it necessary for consumers to obtain credit. Similarly, after the Second World War, the increase in automobile sales and the rise of consumer durable sales (washing machines, refrigerators, and the like) increased that need exponentially.

Understandably, the merchants that sold automobiles and consumer durables resorted to the negotiable promissory note. They were familiar with the note, and they understood the advantage of presenting an abstracted obligation to the financial intermediaries that were ultimately the financers of these consumer transactions.

The merchant buyer who signed the note understood its implications, especially its negotiability feature that rendered the merchant buyer's defenses unavailable against the holder. The consumer buyer, however, was unaware of those implications; and when the consumer's refrigerator failed to keep the ice cream frozen, he could not understand why the law forced him to pay for the refrigerator. Thus, the law surprised a party; it worked a result contrary to that party's reasonable expectations. Law that effects that kind of surprise is a prime candidate for change.

The consumer credit transaction suffered from another disability. It lent itself too readily to fraud or other sharp practices. Unscrupulous, often fly-by-night dealers employed the note in a way that shocked the legal and commercial communities. Such dealers would sell shabby services or merchandise to unsuspecting consumer buyers on credit, take a promissory note from the consumers, discount the notes at a local lending institution, and then move on to the next county. When the consumer learned that the services or goods were not as warranted, the dealer was gone; and the finance company was asserting its holder-in-due-course right to cut off the consumer's fraud or breach-of-warranty defense. Consumers were and remain less sophisticated buyers than their merchant counterparts. Unscrupulous sellers to merchant buyers were never able to use the note with the success that attended its use in the consumer setting.

Courts, legislatures, and regulators ultimately responded to the situation but not until considerable time had elapsed and until the practices gave impetus to a consumer movement that is still with us. The result was twofold. First, the law extirpated the negotiable note from the consumer transaction. Second, there arose a measure of odium in the minds of many toward the note, the effect of which has been a lingering suspicion that it is not an honest, efficient, commercial device, but a trap laid by unscrupulous sellers and lenders for unwary buyers or borrowers.

FEDERAL TRADE COMMISSION HOLDER-IN-DUE-COURSE REGULATIONS

16 C.F.R. 433.1-433.3

(*see Selected Commercial Statutes*)

SECTION 3. THE INDEPENDENCE PRINCIPLE

(a) IN GENERAL

INTRODUCTORY NOTE

We have already seen the independence principle in operation in this chapter's section 2(a) (cutting off claims) and section 2(b) (cutting off defenses). Negotiable instruments law protects the holder in due course, and the law of negotiable documents protects the holder by due negotiation by cutting off claims and defenses. These rules render the obligations (negotiable instruments and negotiable documents) independent of the transactions out of which they arise. This section deals with the independence principle in a different context, that of credit enhancement.

Often a debtor needs to enhance her credit. If a buyer's credit rating is weak, the market will not accept her promise to pay. If a dealer's credit is weak, suppliers will not sell on credit. If a developer's credit is weak, banks will not lend money for the development. Debtors use their property to enhance credit obligations. Security interests and mortgages are probably the most common credit enhancers.

Commercial law has devised a number of quite different credit enhancement mechanisms, however. These mechanisms involve third parties. Under them, parties other than the debtor in some way undertake to pay the debtor's obligation. There are two categories of these third party enhancements: (1) dependent enhancements and (2) independent enhancements. Generally, though locution can be quite imprecise here, when we speak of suretyship or guaranty, we are referring to dependent credit enhancement; when we speak of letters of credit or international bank guarantees (N.B. spelling difference), we are speaking of independent credit enhancement.

ITEK CORP. v. FIRST NATIONAL BANK, 730 F.2d 19, 23 (1st Cir. 1984). "Parties to a contract may use a letter of credit in order to make certain that contractual disputes wend their way towards resolution with money in the beneficiary's pocket rather than in the pocket of the [applicant]."

EAKIN v. CONTINENTAL ILLINOIS NATIONAL BANK & TRUST CO., 875 F.2d 114, 115 (7th Cir. 1989). "Letters of credit are designed to avoid complex disputes about how much the [applicants] really owe. The promise and premise are 'pay now, argue later.'"

UCC § 5-103(d)

Rights and obligations of an issuer to a beneficiary or a nominated person under a letter of credit are independent of the existence, performance, or nonperformance of a contract or arrangement out of which the letter of credit arises or which underlies it, including contracts or arrangements between the issuer and the applicant and between the applicant and the beneficiary.

INTERNATIONAL CHAMBER OF COMMERCE, UNIFORM CUSTOMS AND PRACTICE FOR DOCUMENTARY CREDITS (UCP 500) Article 3(a) (1993). "Credits, by their nature, are separate transactions from the sales or other contract(s) on which they may be based * * *."

UNCITRAL CONVENTION ON INDEPENDENT GUARANTEES AND STAND-BY LETTERS OF CREDIT art. 3 (1995). "For purposes of this Convention, an undertaking is independent where the guarantor/issuer's obligation to the beneficiary is not subject to the existence or validity of an underlying transaction, or to any other undertaking * * * or to any term or condition not appearing in the undertaking * * *."

COMPTROLLER OF THE CURRENCY, INTERPRETIVE RULING, 12 C.F.R. § 7.71016 (1997). "A national bank may issue * * * letters of credit and other independent undertakings * * *. Under such letters of credit and other independent undertakings, the bank's obligation to honor depends upon the presentation of specified documents and not upon non-conditions of resolution of questions of fact or law at issue between the account party and the beneficiary."

INTERNATIONAL CHAMBER OF COMMERCE, ICC UNIFORM RULES FOR DEMAND GUARANTEES art. 2(c) (1992). "Guarantees by their nature are separate transactions from the contract(s) or tender conditions on which they may be based * * *."

PROBLEMS

California Creditor holds two $1 million promissory notes from Saudi Developer. The notes are due on April 1, and Developer has not paid them. Creditor fears that if Developer is not already insolvent, it soon will be.

The first note is enhanced by the guaranty of Global Guaranty Corp., a French insurance company. Under the terms of the guaranty, Global undertakes to pay the amount of the note in the event Developer defaults. The second note is enhanced by First New York Bank's standby letter of credit. Under the terms of the standby, First agrees to honor Creditor's draft up to $1 million if it is presented on or before May 1 along with Creditor's statement that it has not been paid.

Developer, which is not subject to jurisdiction in the United States, claims that it is not in default under the note by virtue of the fact that Creditor has breached its loan agreement with Developer to lend funds for the development. Creditor disputes Developer's argument, which rests on interpretation of voluminous contract documents, development construction records, and conflicting opinions of architects.

(a) If Creditor makes a claim on the guaranty on May 1, when will it get its money? Do you think it might have to litigate? Where will the litigation occur? Who will be the plaintiff? Who will hold the $1 million during the litigation?

(b) If Creditor draws on the credit, what should First do? If First pays, might there still be litigation? Where will it be? Who will hold the $1 million during the litigation?

(c) If you represent Creditor the next time it lends to a developer in a distant forum, which of the two credit enhancement mechanisms would you recommend, the dependent guaranty or the independent letter of credit? Do you suppose that in a development such as this one the parties agree to commercial arbitration in a neutral city? Will that term in the underlying contract erase the distinction between the dependent and the independent enhancing mechanism?

(b) THE STRICT COMPLIANCE RULE

INTERNATIONAL CHAMBER OF COMMERCE, UNIFORM CUSTOMS AND PRACTICE FOR DOCUMENTARY CREDITS art. 4 (1995). "In Credit operations all parties concerned deal with documents, and not with goods, services and/or other performances to which the documents may relate."

NOTE ON THE STRICT COMPLIANCE RULE

The strict compliance rule is the first and a necessary corollary to the independence principle. If an independent undertaking issuer may or must investigate the underlying transaction, the independence of the undertaking shatters. Issuers must pay on the basis of documents presented to the issuer by the beneficiary or its agent. The issuer's examination of the documents, moreover, must be ministerial. Document checkers determine facial conformity, not actual conformity.

There are limits to the strict compliance rule, but the limits are surprisingly narrow, as the following cases indicate.

EQUITABLE TRUST CO. v. DAWSON PARTNERS, [1927] 27 Lloyd's List LR 49. "[T]here is no room for documents which are almost the same, or which will do just as well."

CORPORACION DE MERCADEO AGRICOLA v. MELLON BANK INTERNATIONAL

United States Court of Appeals, Second Circuit, 1979.
608 F.2d 43.

LUMBARD, Circuit Judge.

Plaintiff Corporacion de Mercadeo Agricola (CMA) appeals from an order entered by Judge Leval in the Southern District of New York on December 7, 1978 and reported at 464 F.Supp. 88 (S.D.N.Y.1978) dismissing CMA's contract claim against Mellon Bank International (Mellon). CMA alleged that Mellon unjustifiably refused to honor CMA's draft drawn under Mellon's letter of credit 5171. Mellon moved for summary judgment and showed that CMA failed to tender documentation in conformity with the specifications contained in the letter of credit. The district court granted Mellon's motion and CMA appealed. We affirm.

This case arises out of dealings between CMA and the Pan American Fruit and Produce Corporation (Pan American). In March, 1974, CMA and Pan American entered into Contract No. 84 which provided that CMA would sell to Pan American approximately 30,000 metric tons of Venezuelan paddy rice at a price of $9,630,000. The ninth paragraph of the contract provided for payment of the purchase price by means of an irrevocable letter of credit. This first letter of credit was to be issued in CMA's favor in the above amount within five days after execution of the contract of sale.

To ensure performance of its contractual obligations, including execution of the first letter of credit as required by paragraph nine, Pan American agreed to provide CMA upon execution of the contract with a guaranty of ten percent of the total purchase price, of $963,000. The contract further provided that this guaranty would become payable "by virtue of the sole fact of nonfulfillment" by Pan American of any of its obligations under the agreement. Accordingly, Pan American purchased from Mellon Bank on March 18, 1974 a second letter of credit (LC 5171) in CMA's favor which provided liquidated damages totalling $963,000 should Pan American default.

* * *

This guaranty was designed to compensate the seller for any losses incurred as the result of the buyer's insolvency or as the result of any other contingency leading to the buyer's default. The letter of credit called for statements from both the buyer and the seller acknowledging the buyer's default, but the contract did not specify any circumstances under which the buyer would be required to issue a statement. However, in the event of default, the seller could have sought a court order requiring the production by the buyer of the necessary statement in order to enforce the good faith intentions of the parties. No such court order was sought here until after the letter of credit expired.

As of April, 1974, Pan American had failed to obtain the first irrevocable letter of credit which was to be used for payment of the purchase price, in violation of paragraph nine of the contract. CMA therefore advised Mellon in late April, 1974 that it planned to exercise its right to obtain liquidated damages under the second letter of credit. Mellon agreed, at Pan American's request, to extend the expiration date of the second letter of credit from April 30, 1974 to June 30, 1974, in order to allow more time for Pan American to cure its default. Pan American, however, failed to cure its default. Accordingly, on June 5, 1974, CMA presented Mellon Bank with a draft on the second letter of credit in the amount of $963,000, accompanied by documents which CMA claims satisfied the requirements of the letter of credit. These documents included:

> 1. A document written by one Sr. Valera on April 29, 1974, in which Valera asserts that he is the representative of Pan American and that Pan American has not fulfilled its obligations under the contract;
>
> 2. A copy of Pan American's letter of February 13, 1974, authorizing Valera to sign Contract No. 84 on behalf of Pan American (see infra);
>
> 3. A statement by CMA that Pan American had not fulfilled its obligations under the contract; and
>
> 4. A copy of Contract No. 84 bearing Valera's signature for Pan American.

Since Valera's authority to sign on behalf of Pan American for payment on the letter of credit is at the center of this controversy, we shall review the nature and extent of that authority in some detail.

[The court concluded that Valera did not have authority to sign the document on behalf of Pan American.]

* * *

When CMA demanded payment on the letter of credit, Valera's lack of authority immediately attracted attention. After reviewing the documents and noting Valera's lack of authority, Mellon Bank checked with Pan American to see if it should nevertheless honor CMA's draft on the basis of Valera's signature. Pan American advised Mellon that Valera was not authorized to prepare a statement of facts or sign for Pan American and that Mellon should therefore not pay on the draft.

On June 11, 1974, Mellon advised CMA that it would not honor the draft because:

> "* * * Sr. Gonzalo Sanchez Valera is not authorized to sign on behalf of the accountee, Pan American Fruit and Produce Corporation. The accountee informs us the authority which was previously granted to him was revoked prior to the opening of our credit. Consequently, the requirement for a statement of facts by the accountee has not been fulfilled."

CMA never submitted the required statement of facts to Mellon. The letter of credit expired June 30, 1974.

CMA commenced no action seeking injunctive relief against Mellon or Pan American, such as an order requiring Pan American to provide a statement of facts, prior to the June 30, 1974 expiration of the letter of credit. Nor did CMA seek to cure the defect in the original documentation by submitting revised or new documents. Instead, CMA commenced this suit against Mellon on November 26, 1974, seeking damages for breach of contract and alleging that Mellon breached its contract with CMA by failing to pay on the letter of credit. On April 5, 1975, CMA filed a second complaint seeking equitable relief in the form of an order directing Pan American to deliver a proper statement of facts to Mellon or adjudging Mellon Nunc pro tunc to have received a proper statement of facts.

Pan American moved for dismissal of the second action pursuant to Rule 12(b) (6) of the Federal Rules of Civil Procedure. Treating the motion as one for summary judgment, Judge Cannella of the Southern District of New York ordered dismissal as to Pan American on April 21, 1976, on the ground that it was by then too late to compel Pan American to provide a statement of facts. CMA has not appealed that ruling. On the same day, Judge Cannella also granted CMA's cross-motion for consolidation.

On July 8, 1976, Mellon moved for summary judgment, on the ground that Valera was not authorized to sign for Pan American and that the refusal to pay on the letter of credit was therefore proper. On May 10, 1977, Judge Cannella denied Mellon's motion in a two-sentence order on the ground that there were disputed factual issues regarding the effectiveness of Pan American's alleged revocation of Valera's authority and the parties' knowledge of that purported revocation.

After additional discovery, Mellon again moved for summary judgment, asserting that further discovery made such a motion proper once again. That same day, without request by the parties, the action was transferred to Judge Leval. There ensued several pretrial conferences with Judge Leval, who raised additional issues and afforded the parties the opportunity to respond to these issues with supplemental briefs and affidavits. Judge Leval granted Mellon's motion for summary judgment on December 6, 1978.

Judge Leval granted Mellon's motion for summary judgment for two reasons. First, since a power which is neither stated to be revocable nor coupled with an interest is revocable at will, he concluded that Mellon could not be required to honor a statement by a representative without fresh confirmation of that representative's authority. Second, Judge Leval concluded that Valera's original authorization did not include any authority "to make on behalf of Pan American a statement to its banker amounting to a confession of liability authorizing payment of an indemnity of nearly a million dollars." Since it is black letter law that the terms and conditions of a letter of credit must be strictly adhered to, Judge Leval concluded that Mellon had followed the only proper course available in refusing payment.[1]

---

[1] Judge Leval's conclusion with respect to the propriety of Mellon's refusal to honor CMA's draft on the letter of credit tracks Judge Cannella's conclusions on the same issue when he granted Pan American's motion to dismiss on April 21, 1976. In his opinion, Judge Cannella had written:

> "A bank's obligation in a letter of credit transaction is defined by the contract between the bank and its customer. It is obliged to pay only if the documents

* * *

CMA also claims that Judge Leval should not have granted summary judgment because whether Mellon acted in good faith in denying the draft is a factual matter which can only be resolved at trial. But Mellon's good faith is not a relevant issue on this record. The contract among the parties required that Mellon pay on the letter of credit only after CMA presented conforming documents. CMA never presented conforming documents. Accordingly, Mellon was never obligated to pay on the draft and the question of good faith does not arise. See, e. g., Key Appliance, Inc. v. First National City Bank, 37 N.Y.2d 826, 377 N.Y.S.2d 482, 339 N.E.2d 888 (1975); AMF Head Sports Wear, Inc. v. Ray Scott's All-American Sports Club, Inc., 448 F.Supp. 222, 224 (D.Ariz.1978) ("Dishonor of a demand for payment when the demand does not comply with the terms of the letter of credit cannot constitute bad faith").

Finally, CMA contends that if its legal arguments fail, this court should nevertheless issue an equitable Nunc pro tunc order either adjudging Mellon to have received a proper statement of facts or directing Pan American to deliver a proper statement of facts. But since Mellon has not been shown guilty of any wrongdoing or bad faith, and its legal obligations under the letter of credit have expired, there is no basis for awarding an equitable decree. CMA, moreover, has not been without a remedy at law. Rather, CMA has slept on whatever rights it has. Once the letter of credit expired, CMA's proper remedy was to sue Pan American directly, a remedy which CMA has not chosen to pursue.

There can be no doubt, as our Brother Gurfein so persuasively points out, that the terms of the letter of credit accepted by CMA proved to be unfortunate for it because they required it, before payment could be made, to present to Mellon a "statement of facts", signed by CMA and Pan American, with respect to Pan American's failure to perform its obligations under the rice-purchase contract "in accordance with conditions agreed upon by buyers and sellers". We find nothing ambiguous about this plain requirement, which was clearly intended to protect the bank against becoming involved in any dispute that might develop between the beneficiary and accountee over whether the underlying conditions had been met.

CMA, presumably a sophisticated business organization, had been put on notice by the plain language of the letter of credit and by the express written limitation on Valera's authority, which was restricted to representation before organizations of the Republic of Venezuela and did not extend to the letter of credit, that it would have to rely upon Pan American to join in any statement of

---

submitted strictly comply with the essential requirements of the letter of credit. Here Mellon obligated itself to honor plaintiff's drafts against the letter of credit until June 30, 1974. When Mellon did not receive the proper documents prior to that date, whether due to its customer's wrongful acts or otherwise, its obligation to pay terminated. Whatever rights plaintiff may now have against Pan American for its alleged wrongful refusal to submit a statement of facts, they do not include an enlargement of Mellon's obligations under the letter of credit, absent some wrongful act on its part. Any other result would have serious ramifications throughout the banking community."

default if that should become necessary. This reliance turns out to have been misplaced. However, CMA's predicament is not attributable to Mellon but to Pan American. Thus CMA failed to avoid the harm to it by negotiating a more advantageous letter of credit in the first place or by seeking relief against Pan American before the letter of credit expired.

Under the circumstances, it is hardly appropriate for a federal court to supply the protection which CMA thought it had at the expense of the Mellon Bank which was within its rights in strictly construing the agreement. Any claims CMA may have as a result of its bad bargain lie against Pan American, not against the bank.

Affirmed.

GURFEIN, Circuit Judge, dissenting:

* * *

In issuing a letter of credit allowing a veto by its customer, the bank took neither collateral from its customer, Pan American, nor even a personal indemnity from Pan American's principal. It has been asserted by affidavit on the summary judgment motion that Pan American had only two officers and employees, no apparent credit line except from Mellon, no visible capital, consequential resources or active accounts, and was operated from the office of its lawyer. We must take these assertions as unrebutted for purposes of summary judgment. In sum, when payment on the letter of credit was demanded, the bank was "defending in its own interest."

That a hoax was perpetrated on CMA is obvious. It was led to believe that it had the guaranty of an American bank when, in fact, it had nothing, according to the majority.

* * *

BEYENE v. IRVING TRUST CO.

United States Court of Appeals, Second Circuit, 1985.
762 F.2d 4.

KEARSE, Circuit Judge.

Plaintiffs Dessaleng Beyene and Jean M. Hanson appeal from a final judgment of the United States District Court for the Southern District of New York, Morris E. Lasker, Judge, dismissing their complaint seeking damages for the alleged wrongful refusal of defendant Irving Trust Company ("Irving") to honor a letter of credit. The district court granted Irving's motion for summary judgment dismissing the complaint on the ground that, since the bill of lading presented to Irving misspelled the name of the person to whom notice was to be given of the arrival of the goods and thereby failed to comply with the terms of the letter of credit, Irving was under no duty to honor the letter of credit. On appeal, plaintiffs contend, inter alia, that the mere misspelling of a name should not relieve a bank of its duty to honor a letter of credit. We agree with the district court that the misspelling in this case was a material discrepancy that relieved Irving of its duty to pay the letter of credit, and we affirm the judgment.

FACTS

The material undisputed facts may be stated briefly. In March 1978, Beyene agreed to sell to Mohammed Sofan, a resident of the Yemen Arab Republic ("YAR"), two prefabricated houses. Sofan attempted to finance the purchase through the use of a letter of credit issued by the Yemen Bank for Reconstruction and Development ("YBRD") in favor of Beyene. YBRD designated Irving as the confirming bank for the letter of credit and Irving subsequently notified Beyene of the letter's terms and conditions. Beyene designated the National Bank of Washington ("NBW") as his collecting bank.

In May 1979, NBW sent Irving all of the documents required under the terms of the letter of credit. Thereafter, Irving telephoned NBW to inform it of several discrepancies in the submitted documents, including the fact that the bill of lading listed the party to be notified by the shipping company as Mohammed Soran instead of Mohammed Sofan. The NBW official contacted testified at deposition that Irving never waived the misspelling discrepancy and continued to assert that it was a discrepancy, though it undertook to request authorization from YBRD to pay the letter of credit despite the discrepancy. Such authorization was not forthcoming, and Irving refused to pay.

Plaintiffs instituted the present suit seeking damages for Irving's failure to pay the letter of credit. Irving moved for summary judgment dismissing the complaint on a variety of grounds. The district court granted the motion on the sole ground that the misspelling of Sofan's name in the bill of lading constituted a material discrepancy that gave Irving the right to dishonor the letter of credit. This appeal followed.

DISCUSSION

On appeal, plaintiffs contend principally that (1) the district court's ruling is unsound as a matter of precedent and of policy, and (2) Irving should be required to pay the letter of credit on grounds of waiver and estoppel. We find merit in none of plaintiffs' contentions. We need discuss only the first.

The nature and functions of commercial letters of credit have recently been explored by this Court, see Voest-Alpine International Corp. v. Chase Manhattan Bank, N.A., 707 F.2d 680, 682-83 (2d Cir.1983); Marino Industries Corp. v. Chase Manhattan Bank, N.A., 686 F.2d 112, 114-15 (2d Cir.1982), and will not be repeated in detail here. The terms of a letter of credit generally require the beneficiary of the letter to submit to the issuing bank documents such as an invoice and a bill of lading to provide "the accredited buyer [with] some assurance that he will receive the goods for which he bargained and arranged payment." H. Harfield, Bank Credits and Acceptances 57 (5th ed. 1974). The issuing bank, or a bank that acts as confirming bank for the issuer, takes on an absolute duty to pay the amount of the credit to the beneficiary, so long as the beneficiary complies with the terms of the letter. In order to protect the issuing or confirming bank, this absolute duty does not arise unless the terms of the letter have been complied with strictly. Literal compliance is generally "essential so as not to impose an obligation upon the bank that it did not undertake and so as not to jeopardize the bank's right to indemnity from its customer." Voest-Alpine International Corp. v. Chase Manhattan Bank, 707 F.2d at 683; see H. Harfield, Letters of Credit 57-59 (1979).

While some variations in a bill of lading might be so insignificant as not to relieve the issuing or confirming bank of its obligation to pay, we agree with the district court that the misspelling in the bill of lading of Sofan's name as "Soran" was a material discrepancy that entitled Irving to refuse to honor the letter of credit. First, this is not a case where the name intended is unmistakably clear despite what is obviously a typographical error, as might be the case if, for example, "Smith" were misspelled "Smithh." Nor have appellants claimed that in the Middle East "Soran" would obviously be recognized as an inadvertent misspelling of the surname "Sofan." Second, "Sofan" was not a name that was inconsequential to the document, for Sofan was the person to whom the shipper was to give notice of the arrival of the goods, and the misspelling of his name could well have resulted in his nonreceipt of the goods and his justifiable refusal to reimburse Irving for the credit. (Indeed, the record includes a telex from Beyene, stating that Sofan had not been notified when the goods arrived in YAR and that as a result demurrage and other costs had been incurred.) In the circumstances, the district court was entirely correct in viewing the failure of Beyene and NBW to provide documents that strictly complied with the terms of the letter of credit as a failure that entitled Irving to refuse payment.

Plaintiffs do not contend that there was any issue to be tried as to the fact of the misspelling of Sofan's name. Their assertions that Irving waived the admitted discrepancy or was estopped from relying on it were not supported sufficiently to withstand a motion for summary judgment and were properly rejected by the district court for the reasons stated in its opinion.

CONCLUSION

The judgment of the district court is affirmed.

NEW BRAUNFELS NATIONAL BANK v. ODIORNE

Court of Appeals of Texas, 1989.
780 S.W.2d 313, 10 U.C.C. Rep. Serv.2d 1352.

JONES, Judge.

This appeal presents the question of how strictly a beneficiary of a letter of credit must comply with a condition of the credit in order to require payment by the issuer. New Braunfels National Bank (Bank) filed this suit (1) to obtain a judgment declaring that it had properly refused to honor a draft on a $250,000 letter of credit it had issued, and (2) to obtain an injunction prohibiting, until the parties' rights under the credit could be determined, the account party from withdrawing its $250,000 certificate of deposit which had been purchased from the Bank to guarantee reimbursement in the event the Bank paid on the credit. * * *

On April 29, 1986, the Bank issued its irrevocable letter of credit number 86-122-S. The "86" represented the year in which the credit was issued; the "122" represented the numerical sequence of all credits ever issued by the Bank, regardless of the year of issuance; the "S" indicated that the credit was a "standby" letter of credit. The only condition for Bates's drawing on the credit was that any draft be marked as follows: "Drawn under New Braunfels National Bank Irrevocable Letter of Credit Number 86-122-S * * *." The expiry date of the credit was April 29, 1987.

* * *

One year later, on the morning of April 29, 1987, Clive Harris, a representative of Bates, presented to the president of the Bank a letter of introduction and instruction from Bates, a draft signed by Bates, and the original letter of credit. After some study and consultation with its lawyers, the Bank refused to honor the draft because the draft's legend referred to "Irrevocable Letter of Credit No. 86-122-<u>5</u> " instead of "86-122-<u>S</u>." (Emphasis added.) The Bank refused to allow Harris to change the "5" to an "S" without written authorization from Bates. When Bates attempted to wire such authorization, the cable was misdirected and finally arrived—by mail—several days later, after Harris had returned to the Cayman Islands with the original letter of credit. When the error was eventually corrected a week later, the Bank refused to honor the corrected draft on the ground that the credit had expired.

* * *

Most commentators agree that maintaining the integrity of the strict compliance rule is important to the continued usefulness of letters of credit as a commercial tool. That does not mean, however, that strict compliance demands an oppressive perfectionism. For example, one * * * commentator has recognized a logical distinction between discrepancies that relate to the business of the underlying transaction and those that relate to the banker's own business:

> The strict-compliance rule rests on the judgment that issuers should not be forced into the position of determining whether a documentary discrepancy is significant. The rule assumes that issuers are not in a position to know whether discrepancies matter to the commercial parties. Nothing in that assumption requires courts to absolve issuers from knowing the significance of discrepancies for their own business; while it is consistent with the strict-compliance rule to say that an issuer should not be charged with knowledge of whether an air bill, rather than an ocean bill, covering computer components is a significant defect, it is not consistent with the rule to say that a bank issuer is absolved from knowing whether the abbreviation of the word "number" to "No." in the legend on a draft is a significant defect. Banks presumably know nothing about the shipment of computer components, but they know a great deal about legends on drafts—legends that credits require, usually because the banks insist on them.

* * *

Two cases exemplify defects in legends, which, as far as we can tell, will always be "noncommercial" defects. In Tosco Corp. v. FDIC, 723 F.2d 1242 (6th Cir.1983), the credit required that a draft on the credit contain the following legend: "drawn under Bank of Clarksville Letter of Credit Number 105." The bank refused to honor the draft presented by the beneficiary because the legend in the draft

(1) added the word "Tennessee" after "Clarksville"; (2) used a lower case "l" in the term "letter of Credit"; and (3) abbreviated "Number" to "No." In First Bank v. Paris Savings & Loan Association, 756 S.W.2d 329 (Tex.App.1988, writ denied), the credit required that a draft contain the following legend: "Drawn under Paris Savings and Loan Association Letter of Credit No. 1033." The bank refused to honor the draft presented because the legend stated: "Drawn under Paris Savings and Loan Association Letter of Credit No. 1033, dated June 12, 1986, i/a/o $250,000." In both cases, the beneficiary prevailed.

* * *

We think the distinction * * * is a sensible and salutary one. Indeed, although Texas courts have not expressly recognized the distinction in those terms, they seem to have done so implicitly. In virtually every recent case in which the defect was a "commercial" one, the issuer has prevailed. On the other hand, in virtually every recent case in which the defect was a "noncommercial" one, the beneficiary has prevailed.

In the present case, the only defect challenged by the Bank was that the required legend stated it was drawn under New Braunfels National Bank Irrevocable Letter of Credit Number "86-122-5" instead of "86-122-S." By itself, this discrepancy might or might not be of significance. (It was undisputed that none of the reference numbers for credits issued by the Bank ended with a numeral and that Bank officers had no doubt which credit Bates was attempting to draw on.) Here, however, there was more: the draft in question was accompanied by and attached to the original letter of credit, which naturally had the correct credit number prominently displayed. Accompanying documents may be considered in determining whether the presentment made by the beneficiary has strictly complied with the terms of the credit. Temple-Eastex, 672 S.W.2d at 796. Considering both the draft and the original credit together, it would be obvious to any bank document examiner, prudent or otherwise, that the discrepancy in the present case was merely a typographical or clerical error and of no possible significance.

We therefore sustain Bates's points of error one and three. In so holding, we do not hold that a beneficiary may satisfy noncommercial conditions in a credit by mere "substantial compliance"; we hold only that for such conditions "strict compliance" means something less than absolute, perfect compliance. We make no holding with respect to defects relating to commercial conditions.

SECTION 4. OTHER EFFORTS TO ABSTRACT PROMISES

(a) HELL OR HIGH WATER CLAUSES

COLORADO INTERSTATE CORP. v. CIT GROUP/EQUIPMENT FINANCING, INC.

United States Court of Appeals, Tenth Circuit, 1993.
993 F.2d 743.

McKAY, Chief Judge.

In this diversity action, Plaintiffs Colorado Interstate Corporation and Colorado Interstate Gas Company (hereinafter collectively referred to as "Colorado Interstate") appeal from a district court order granting summary judgment to Defendant, The CIT Group/Equipment Financing, Inc. (hereinafter referred to as "CIT") on Colorado Interstate's restitution and breach of contract claims. The claims arise from Colorado Interstate's lease of computer equipment.

In 1985, Colorado Interstate leased computer equipment from CMI Corporation (hereinafter referred to as "CMI"). The lease between CMI and Colorado Interstate (hereinafter referred to as the Master Lease) contained what is known as a "hell or high water clause" and provided for the assignment of rent payments.

* * *

In 1986, Colorado Interstate decided to upgrade its mainframe computer system. In order to effectuate this upgrade, CMI entered into a lease with Electronic Data Systems Leasing Corporation (hereinafter "EDS") on December 4, 1986, whereby EDS leased the equipment to CMI (hereinafter referred to as the Prime Lease). CMI subsequently leased this equipment to Colorado Interstate on December 11, 1986, pursuant to an Equipment Schedule which incorporated by reference the terms of the Master Lease.

In June of 1987, CMI assigned its right to payments under the Master Lease to CIT. Preparatory to the assignment, Colorado Interstate signed a Consent and Agreement to assignment which provided in pertinent part:

> The Company [Colorado Interstate] agrees:
>
> (i) To remit and deliver all Moneys directly to [CIT] * * * with identification of the source and application of the funds, without abatement, reduction, counterclaim or offset * * *.
>
> * * *
>
> [CIT] hereby agrees that so long as no Event of Default as defined in the lease shall have occurred and be continuing, it [CIT] will not disturb [Colorado Interstate's] quiet and peaceful possession of the Equipment and its unrestricted use of the Equipment for its intended purpose under the terms of the Lease.

As a result, Colorado Interstate unconditionally agreed to pay all rents to CIT until the Master Lease expired in August of 1989.

In November of 1988, CMI ceased making payments to EDS under the Prime Lease. In January of 1989, CMI filed a petition under Chapter 11 of the Bankruptcy Code. CMI and EDS subsequently entered into an agreement approved by the bankruptcy court declaring the Prime Lease terminated as of November 8, 1988.

Because it was no longer receiving rent payments from CMI, EDS demanded the return of the equipment from Colorado Interstate and threatened a replevin action. In order to avoid being dispossessed of the equipment, Colorado Interstate began paying EDS the amounts owed by CMI under the Prime Lease. Colorado Interstate also continued making payments to CIT in accordance with the assignment.

In May of 1991, Colorado Interstate initiated this action against CIT seeking to recoup the rents paid to CIT after the termination of the Prime Lease in November 1988. Colorado Interstate also sought damages for breach of an agreement not to disturb Colorado Interstate's quiet enjoyment. The district court granted summary judgment in CIT's favor and awarded costs and attorney fees. Colorado Interstate brought this appeal.

* * *

B.

Colorado Interstate also argues that the district court erred in holding that the obligation to pay rent under the hell or high water clause continued notwithstanding the fact that Colorado Interstate's right of quiet enjoyment was disturbed. Colorado Interstate argues that it was only obligated to pay rent under the hell or high water clause as long as it was obligated to pay rent at all, and that the duty to pay ceased when its quiet enjoyment was disturbed. Essentially, Colorado Interstate argues that its obligation to pay rent under the hell or high water clause and the covenant of quiet enjoyment are mutual or interdependent obligations under the contract.

CIT argues that even assuming, arguendo, that Colorado Interstate's quiet enjoyment was disturbed, under the hell or high water clause its right to uninterrupted rent payments continued because Colorado Interstate's unconditional obligation to pay rent was independent from the obligations of both CMI and CIT.

A review of the unambiguous language of the lease reveals that Colorado Interstate did in fact agree to an unconditional obligation to pay rent that was separate from any duty or obligation of CMI or CIT. The lease states that

> the rights of Lessor and Assignee in and to such Rent, are absolute and unconditional and are not subject to any abatement, reduction, setoff, defense, counterclaim or recoupment due or alleged to be due to, or by reason of, any past, present or future claims which Lessee may have against Lessor, Assignee, the manufacturer or seller of the equipment, or against any person for any reason whatsoever.

Likewise, Colorado Interstate agreed in the Consent and Agreement "to remit and deliver all [rents] directly to [CIT] * * * without abatement, reduction, counterclaim or offset. * * *."

Colorado Interstate's assertion that its duty to pay rent only continued as long as its quiet enjoyment remained undisturbed is without merit. When Colorado Interstate agreed to the terms of the Master Lease which contained the hell or high water clause, it agreed to continue making rent payments despite any claim it might have against either CMI or CIT. Colorado Interstate's sole remedy was limited to bringing an action against CMI while continuing to make rent payments. Neither the assignment nor CMI's status as debtor in bankruptcy relieved Colorado Interstate of this obligation. Essentially, Colorado Interstate assumed the risk of CMI's nonperformance.

Colorado Interstate attempts to circumvent this result by citing Texas constructive eviction cases for the proposition that breach of the covenant of quiet enjoyment relieves a tenant from the duty to pay rent. See Downtown Realty, Inc. v. 509 Tremont Bldg., Inc., 748 S.W.2d 309, 312-13 (Tex.Ct.App.1988); Fidelity Mut. Life Ins. Co. v. Kaminsky, 768 S.W.2d 818, 819 (Tex.Ct.App.1989). Assuming that Colorado Interstate's right of quiet enjoyment was disturbed in a manner cognizable under Texas law, Colorado Interstate's reliance on these cases is still misplaced. Downtown and Fidelity are clearly distinguishable in that the leases at issue did not contain a hell or high water clause that effectively separated the parties' respective duties and obligations. Accordingly, Colorado Interstate's reliance on these cases for the proposition that the right of quiet enjoyment is inseparable from the duty to pay rent is without merit.

Although the Texas courts have not expressly ruled on the enforceability of the hell or high water clause at issue in this case, they have as a general matter recognized the enforceability of an unconditional obligation to pay rent. In Stewart v. United States Leasing Corp., 702 S.W.2d 288 (Tex.Ct.App.1985), Stewart arranged for United States Leasing to purchase a copy machine from Salt and Pepper Copiers and then lease it to him. Stewart agreed to an unconditional obligation to pay rent to the defendant, regardless of any claim plaintiff might have against the vendor. When the vendor failed to deliver the copier to Stewart, he ceased making rent payments and United States Leasing brought suit. The court noted:

> An examination of the lease reveals that Salt and Pepper Copiers was not an agent of [defendant], the lessor, and that any claims regarding the equipment were to be made solely against the vendor, Salt and Pepper Copiers. It further expressly provided that regardless of claims against Salt and Pepper Copiers, Stewart was to pay all rents payable under the lease. Id. at 290.

The court went on to reject Stewart's claim of lack of consideration and enforced Stewart's unconditional obligation to pay rent.

Other courts that have considered the enforceability of hell or high water clauses have enforced such provisions in analogous situations. See, e.g., American Computer v. Jack Farrell Implement, 763 F.Supp. 1473, 1484 n. 9 (D.Minn.1991), aff'd, 967 F.2d 1208 (8th Cir.1992), cert. denied, 506 U.S. 956, 113 S.Ct. 414, 121 L.Ed.2d 338 (1992); Philadelphia Sav. Fund Soc'y v. Deseret Management Corp., 632 F.Supp. 129, 135-36 (E.D.Pa.1985); In re CLE Corp., No. 85-06877-SWC, slip op. at 15-18 (Bankr.N.D.Ga., April 5, 1989); West Virginia v. Hassett (In re O.P.M. Leasing Services, Inc.), 21 B.R. 993, 1006-07 (Bankr.S.D.N.Y.1982).

In O.P.M., after reviewing the effect of a similar hell or high water clause, the court reasoned as follows:

> To deny this clause its full force and effect would effectively reconstruct the contract contrary to the intent of the parties, which reconstruction would be impermissible.
>
> Moreover, it is a well-settled principle that "parties to a contract are given broad latitude within which to fashion their own remedies for breach of contract * * *. It follows that contractual limitations upon remedies are generally to be enforced unless unconscionable.
>
> * * *
>
> The essential practical consideration requiring liability as a matter of law in these situations is that these clauses are essential to the equipment leasing industry. To deny their effect as a matter of law would seriously chill business in this industry because it is by means of these clauses that a prospective financier-assignee of rental payments is guaranteed meaningful security for his outright loan to the lessor. Without giving full effect to such clauses, if the equipment were to malfunction, the only security for this assignee would be to repossess equipment with substantially diminished value. O.P.M., 21 B.R. at 1006-07 (citations omitted).

The court went on to enforce the provisions of the hell or high water clause and held that despite the lessor's breach of an obligation to maintain the equipment, the lessee's unconditional obligation to pay rent continued.

As one commentator has noted:

> Under the hell or high water provision, the lessee undertakes to pay rentals * * * once the lessee has formally accepted the property * * *. Whether the property functions satisfactorily, is useful to the lessee, is suitable for the purposes intended, or is lost, stolen, condemned, or destroyed, and whether the lessee has any right of offset against the lessor or the lenders, is irrelevant. In short, rent payments continue to come hell or high water, without any reduction or offset, even if the lessee is wrongfully dispossessed of the equipment by the lessor * * *. 1 Bruce E. Fritch et. al., Equipment Leasing-Leveraged Leasing 152-53 (3d ed. 1988).

Where sophisticated parties enter into an agreement setting forth their rights and obligations, the terms of the agreement should control unless the agreement would otherwise be void under state law. E.g., Graham Const. Co. v. Walker Process Equip., Inc., 422 S.W.2d 478, 483 (Tex.Civ.App.1967). As noted by the O.P.M. court, there are significant policy reasons for upholding hell or high water clauses where, as in the equipment leasing industry, the enforceability of the provision aids the parties in obtaining financing that would not otherwise be available.[1] Such policy justifications are particularly important in the computer leasing industry where advances in technology significantly decrease the value of equipment that is quickly becoming obsolete. Cf., O.P.M., 21 B.R. at 1007 (noting that in the absence of a hell or high water clause, if the equipment malfunctioned, the only security available to the assignee would be the repossession of equipment having substantially reduced value).

In the instant case, sophisticated and well-represented parties entered into an agreement which detailed their rights and obligations. The agreement was advantageous to all parties involved and provided Colorado Interstate with equipment it may not have been able to obtain absent the unconditional obligation to pay rent. In the absence of fraud or deceit which is not claimed here, it is our view that under Texas law the parties should be held to their agreement. We are of the view that Colorado Interstate assumed the risk of CMI's nonperformance and should not be relieved of its obligations under the agreement simply because CMI happens to be a debtor in bankruptcy. See Fritch at 153. We hold that pursuant to the terms of the hell or high water clause, Colorado Interstate's obligation to pay rent continued notwithstanding CMI's default and the threat of a replevin action by EDS.

* * *

E.

Colorado Interstate also argues that the policy justifications for enforcing the hell or high water clause in the O.P.M. case are not present in this case because the record would not support the conclusion that CIT was a finance lessor. In O.P.M., the court noted that other courts had distinguished between finance lessors and merchant lessors in considering the enforceability of a hell or high water clause.[1] See O.P.M., 21 B.R. at 1007. Colorado Interstate does not argue that CIT is a merchant lessor or that the same policy would not apply to a financier-assignee such as CIT; rather, it merely asserts the record would not support a finding that CIT is a finance lessor.

As an initial matter it is important to note that the distinction between merchant and finance lessors in the context of determining the enforceability of hell or high

---

1 As evidence of the growing acceptance of a hell or high water provisions in the equipment leasing industry, we note that § 2A-407 of the U.C.C. provides that in all finance leases other than those involving a consumer, "the lessee's promises under the lease contract become irrevocable and independent upon the lessee's acceptance of the goods." Id. As the Comments note, "[t]his section is self-executing; no special provision need be added to the contract." Id., cmt. To date, the Texas legislature has not adopted § 2A of the U.C.C.

1 The court defined finance and merchant lessors as follows: "[A] finance lessor [is one] whose only service is to provide funds and who is not [a] merchant lessor. A merchant lessor is one who deals in goods and holds itself out as having specialized knowledge about the design, operation and repair of the chattel leased." O.P.M., 21 B.R. at 1007. The significance of being classified as a merchant lessor is that merchant lessors may be charged with statutory warranties of merchantability and suitability for a particular purpose under 2A of Uniform Commercial Code, or by applying the provisions of article 2 by analogy in those jurisdictions that have yet to adopt article 2A. See Fritch, supra, at 48-49, 63-64, 66-68.

water clauses in O.P.M. was but part of the court's reasoning. In any event, the rationale for enforcing a hell or high water clause in a case involving a financier-assignee clearly applies, as noted by the O.P.M. court.

The essential practical consideration requiring liability as a matter of law in these situations is that these clauses are essential to the equipment leasing industry. To deny their effect as a matter of law would seriously chill business in this industry because it is by means of these clauses that a prospective financier-assignee of rental payments is guaranteed meaningful security for his outright loan to the lessor. O.P.M. 21 B.R. at 1007.

Moreover, we are of the view that the policy reasons for distinguishing between merchant lessors and finance lessors when determining the enforceability of a hell or high water clause should not apply where, as in this case, the lessor has expressly disclaimed all warranties of merchantability and suitability, and the lessee has expressly assumed responsibility, vis-a-vis the lessor, for the suitability and functioning of the leased equipment. Accordingly, Colorado Interstate's attempt to distinguish this case on this ground is without merit.

F.

Additionally, Colorado Interstate asserts the enforcement of the hell or high water clause under the circumstances of this case would amount to an impermissible penalty under Texas law.

* * *

Under Texas law, "[t]he right of competent parties to make their own bargains is not unlimited." Stewart v. Basey, 150 Tex. 666, 245 S.W.2d 484, 486 (1952). One such limitation is where a stipulated damage provision is viewed to constitute a penalty. See id. 245 S.W.2d at 486-87. "The universal rule for measuring damages for breach of contract is just compensation for the loss or damages actually sustained," and "[a] party has no right to have a court enforce a stipulation which violates that rule." Id. at 486. Thus, where an "agreement contains several matters of different degrees of importance, and yet the sum named is payable for the breach of any, even the least[,] * * * the sum stipulated to be paid has been treated as a penalty." Id.

Although there is no stipulated damage provision at issue in the instant case, Colorado Interstate nonetheless contends that the effect of the hell or high water clause in this case amounts to a penalty because Colorado Interstate was required to pay twice for the computer equipment to avoid having it repossessed. In support of this position, Colorado Interstate cites Texas case law holding a lessor could not enforce a liquidated damage provision requiring full payments for future rents where the lessor had also repossessed the equipment. See American Lease Plan v. Ben-Kro Corp., 508 S.W.2d 937, 943-44 (Tex.Civ.App.1974); Southwest Park Outpatient Surgery, Ltd. v. Chandler Leasing Div., 572 S.W.2d 53 (Tex.Civ.App.1978).

Because there is no stipulated damage provision at issue in this case, an analysis under penalty law does not lend itself to the present inquiry. See id. at 55 (the question of whether a contractual provision provides for a penalty may be determined entirely from the face of the contract). In any event, Colorado Interstate's assertion in this regard is unavailing because the primary focus of a penalty inquiry is just compensation. Unlike the facts in American Lease and Southwest Park, there is no issue of unjust compensation in this case. Furthermore, Colorado Interstate had a cause of action against CMI when it ceased making payments to EDS. Because the reasonableness of a stipulated damage provision is determined at the time the parties entered into the agreement, the fact that CMI is presently in bankruptcy should not affect the determination of the issue of just compensation in this case. In contrast, in American Lease and Southwest Park there was never an available cause of action to recover damages for the repossession of the leased equipment.

Although Colorado Interstate may have been forced to choose between making double payments or having the equipment repossessed, this does not create an unenforceable penalty under Texas law. By agreeing to the terms of the Master Lease and Equipment Schedule, Colorado Interstate assumed the risk of CMI's nonperformance. Accordingly, Colorado Interstate's argument in this regard is without merit.

* * *

UCC § 2A-407

(*see Selected Commercial Statutes*)

UCC § 9-206(1)

(*see Selected Commercial Statutes*)

(b) Asset Securitization

INTRODUCTORY NOTE

Disintermediation is the phenomenon of taking funds out of the traditional financial intermediaries, banks, and lending them directly to borrowers. Traditionally, a short term investor, i.e., someone with more cash than he currently needs, deposited the cash in a bank. The funds were available on demand, so that the investor could get them back with short notice; and the investment was safe. The deposit was insured. The rate of return, however, was usually low. The bank, in turn, functioning as an intermediary, reloaned the funds to its borrowers, people with short term cash needs.

Large industrial borrowers realized that they could borrow at better rates by cutting the banks out of the transaction. They achieved that efficiency in a number of ways, usually by enhancing the borrower's obligations, so that rating agencies would give then investment grade ratings, so that the obligations could be packaged and sold in financial markets.

Short term commercial paper borrowing is an example of an early and quite effective device for avoiding the banks and borrowing directly from the investing public. It consists of the issuance by a borrower, say, a national retailer, of promissory notes, usually in a series. The notes are backed by the financial guaranty of a large institution, e.g., the bond of an insurance company or the standby letter of credit of a bank or consortium of banks. Because the paper is enhanced by institutions that are familiar with the creditworthiness of the borrower, the retailer, the rating agencies give the notes a high rating; and investors who know little about the retailer other than what they read in the Wall Street Journal, are willing to buy the notes.

Another method of cutting banks out of the profit picture is asset securitization. This phenomenon involves the sale of assets to a special purpose vehicle (a trust) that carves the assets up into parts (tranches). An automobile credit company has large cash needs and may want to borrow against its chattel paper, the retail installment contracts it has purchased from automobile dealers or that it has generated itself by lending directly to automobile buyers. The credit company can sell the chattel paper to a trust, which will sell notes or bonds to the investing public through money market brokers. Those notes or bonds are securitized by the chattel paper.

Asset securitization requires abstraction in a sense different from the abstraction we have seen earlier in this chapter. The abstraction in asset securitization is abstraction from the credit company. The rating agencies and the investors do not want to invest, i.e., make the loan, if they are lending to the credit company. The company has other creditors and sometimes has bad financial reports that may depress the investment rating of the paper the investors are buying. Thus, the special purpose vehicle, the trust, buys the financial assets from the company, thereby abstracting the assets from the company's balance sheet, so that the company's creditors (and trustee in bankruptcy if things really get bad) will have no claim against the asset.

A problem arose, however, by virtue of the fact that the company, the ultimate borrower, often sells the assets (the chattel paper) with recourse; and that arrangement gives the company/trust relationship some of the trappings of a loan, making the special purpose vehicle a lender and not a buyer, a lender that may have only a claim in bankruptcy similar to the company's other creditors rather than full ownership of the assets.

PANTALEO ET AL., RETHINKING THE ROLE OF RECOURSE IN THE SALE OF FINANCIAL ASSETS, 52 Bus. Law. 159, 159-63 (1996).

What does it mean to "sell" a financial asset? The answer has confounded courts and commentators for some time. The question has taken on increased importance with the rise of the securitization industry. A financial asset is a right to payment of money. Examples include trade receivables (rights to payment for goods sold or services rendered), lease rentals, mortgage and other loans, license and franchise fees, and any other legal or contractual right to payment.

Transfers of financial assets in which the parties state that they intend a sale, and in which all the benefits and risks commonly associated with ownership are transferred for fair value in an arm's-length transaction, are easily identifiable as sales. The issue becomes complicated if the buyer retains recourse to the seller such that less than all of the risks of ownership are transferred. In that case, an issue can arise over whether to view the transaction as a sale or a secured loan. But why?

Under contract law, parties generally are free to enter into and enforce any contract that is not illegal or against public policy; there is nothing about recourse, for example, that either is illegal or in violation of public policy. Common law favors the free transfer of rights to receive money where there are no significant externalities that have consequences to third parties. There is no legal or public policy which precludes a transferor from improving the value of an asset sold by adding its own guarantee. When a financial asset represented by a check or other draft is transferred, recourse is the common, accepted, and sometimes mandatory consequence of transfer. Indorsement with recourse has never been viewed as precluding the existence of a sale.

A seller might agree to some kind of recourse because it wants the benefits of the sale and is prepared to incur recourse in order to induce someone to buy the asset. The most common example is the sale of goods backed by warranties. The Official Comments to the U.C.C. recognize that "there may be a true sale of accounts, [or] chattel paper * * * although recourse exists."

The complication arises most often when a buyer of a financial asset attempts to enforce or has to defend its ownership rights to an asset in the seller's subsequent bankruptcy case. In bankruptcy, for example, if the sale were treated as a sale, the buyer would enjoy greater rights and privileges than if the sale were treated as a loan. The asset would belong to the buyer. It would not be part of the seller's bankruptcy estate, and the buyer would not have to worry about the automatic stay, turnover, or any interference with its property rights. This result is good for the buyer, but some might argue that it damages the debtor's chances for rehabilitation and creditors' expectations of equal treatment. Because of this tension between the buyer's interest and those of the debtor and its creditors, recharacterization issues often arise in bankruptcy cases. When they do, they appear largely to turn on whether the existence of recourse turns a "sale" into a "loan."

But if, as the U.C.C. comment states, there may be a true sale even with recourse, then under what circumstances should a bankruptcy court recharacterize a sale as a loan? Furthermore, is it a question of state law, federal law, or both?

The authors of this Article try to answer these questions by rethinking the role of recourse in the sale of financial assets. The concept of "true sale" is profoundly significant in today's commercial world Defining true sale is the holy grail of the securitization market, a market in which hundreds of billions of dollars flow in transactions structured around constantly evolving ideas of what true sale means. In structuring true sale transactions, tension often arises between the desire for a certain amount of recourse and the belief that "too much" recourse will prevent true sale treatment.

There is no single case that presents a comprehensive theory of the effect of recourse in a true sale. Little thought has been given, for example, to the competing policy issues of balancing the need for clarity, fairness, and simplicity in commercial transactions with those bankruptcy law policies that may be affected by treating a transfer with recourse as a sale rather than a loan. Yet, sale characterization has important consequences.

> If the transfer of the future payment stream from the originator [seller] to the third party [purchaser] fails to constitute a true sale under §541 of the Bankruptcy Code, the transfer would be deemed an advance of funds by the third party to the originator secured by the payment stream, *i.e.*, a secured loan. The third party would then be a creditor of the originator and have a security interest, but not an ownership interest, in the payment stream. In such a case, the originator's bankruptcy would, under §362 of the Bankruptcy Code, automatically result in a stay of all actions by creditors to foreclose on or otherwise obtain property of the originator. The third party may not be able to obtain payments collected on the payment stream until the stay is modified. Further, under §363 of the Bankruptcy Code, a court, after notice to creditors and the opportunity of a hearing, could order the cash collections of the payment stream to be used by the originator in its business as working capital if the originator or its trustee in bankruptcy provides adequate protection for the interest of the third party in the payment stream. "Adequate protection," though, does not always translate into an alternative cash source.
>
> In addition, § 364 of the Bankruptcy Code also would permit the originator, if credit is not otherwise available to it and if adequate protection is given to the third party, to raise cash by granting to new lenders a lien that is either *pari passu* with that of the third party, or if a *pari passu* lien cannot attract new financing, a lien having priority over the third party's lien.[1]

Because the law fails to define clearly the effect of recourse in a sale, virtually all of the securitization transactions that involve noninvestment grade originators or the issuance of publicly traded securities require a two-tier structure to avoid the risk that recourse might disqualify true sale treatment for a transfer.

In this Article, the authors analyze the caselaw and define, in their view, the consequences of the presence of recourse in sales of financial assets. The analysis in this Article assumes an arm's-length transaction in which the buyer has taken all requisite steps to perfect its interest in the asset it buys. The authors conclude that:

(i) A distinction in law can be made between two types of recourse, which are identified by this Article as recourse for collectibility and economic recourse. Recourse for collectibility is the equivalent of warranting that the asset will perform in accordance with its terms. Economic recourse is the equivalent of warranting a return to the buyer of its investment plus an agreed upon yield unrelated to the

---

1 Steven L. Schwarcz, The Parts Are Greater than the Whole: How Securitization of Divisible Interests Can Revolutionize Structured Finance and Open the Capital Markets to Middle-Market Companies, 1993 Colum. Bus. L. Rev. 139. 144 n.16.

asset's payment terms. As a matter of state law, the transfer of a financial asset in an arm's-length transaction should be treated as a sale if the parties so state, even if the buyer retains partial or full recourse for collectibility against the seller. If the buyer retains economic recourse against the seller, however, the transaction is susceptible to recharacterization as a loan. The rationale underlying the case law is that when recourse relates only to the quality of the asset being sold, that type of recourse is consistent with a sale (similar to a warranty on sale); but when the recourse goes beyond the quality of the asset and ensures an economic rate of return to the purported buyer that is unrelated to the payment terms of the underlying asset, the asset serves merely as collateral and the transaction is susceptible to being recharacterized as a loan.

(ii) A sale under state law should be treated as a sale in bankruptcy, even if the buyer has partial or full recourse for collectibility against the seller. Although bankruptcy policies may require a bankruptcy court to determine independently whether recharacterization is appropriate, state law principles of recharacterization must govern the analysis. The U.S. Supreme Court has specifically found that following state contract law is necessary to reduce uncertainty by treating interests uniformly within a state and to prevent a party from receiving a windfall by the happenstance of bankruptcy. State law is determinative of contractual rights when the contract for the sale of financial assets is formed, and to preempt state law by reason of the occurrence of a bankruptcy upsets the economic bargain reached between the parties.

This Article then applies these principles to a variety of transaction structures that are used, or potentially useful, in the marketplace. It illustrates that, in many cases involving the sale of financial assets, a true sale determination can be made even if the buyer were to have full or partial recourse to the seller for collectibility.

SHENKER & COLLETTA, ASSET SECURITIZATION: EVOLUTION, CURRENT ISSUES AND NEW FRONTIERS, 69 Tex. L. Rev. 1369, 1376-80 (1991).

* * *

B. The Basics of a Securitized Transaction: A Model

Securitization transactions generally involve some or all of the following parties: (1) the initial owner of the asset (the "sponsor"); (2) the issuer of the debt or equity instruments; (3) the investment bankers who assist in structuring the transaction and who underwrite or place the securities; (4) the rating agencies, who assess the credit quality of certain types of instruments and assign a credit rating; (5) a credit enhancer, possibly a bank, surety company, or insurer, who provides credit support through a letter of credit, guarantee, or other assurance that there will be a source of funds available for payments as they become due on the securities; (6) a servicer, usually the sponsor or an affiliate, who collects payments due on the underlying assets and, after retaining a servicing fee, pays them over to the security holders or their trustee; (7) a trustee, who deals with the credit enhancer, servicer, and issuer on behalf of the security holders; and (8) legal counsel, who participate in the structuring of the transaction and who may provide advice to the rating agencies or others in the form of legal opinions. With these players in mind, an outline of the typical asset securitization transaction can be constructed from our definition.

First, the asset to be securitized is generally an income-producing asset, and the cash flow produced by the asset is used as the source of funds for the payments to be made to the purchasers of the debt or equity instruments. Most transactions involve large numbers of homogeneous assets pooled together. Assets most suitable for securitization are those with standardized terms, delinquency and loss experience that can support an actuarial analysis of expected losses, and uniform underwriting standards and servicing procedures satisfactory; to rating agencies and investors. Assets that do not satisfy these criteria, however, such as individual commercial real property, may also be securitized.

Second, the asset being securitized generally must be segregated from the sponsor's other assets in order to insulate the securitized asset from certain risks associated with the sponsor's other assets—principally, the risk that their owner or an affiliate may become subject to a bankruptcy proceeding—and to help ensure that the transaction is treated as a sale for tax or accounting purposes or both, if such treatment is desired. Segregation is usually accomplished by transferring the assets to a distinct entity, frequently referred to as a "special purpose vehicle," that is restricted from engaging in any activity other than owning, and perhaps servicing, the securitized assets. In addition, various steps must be taken to ensure that the transfer will be effective as against third parties, including creditors of the sponsor or its affiliates. The special purpose vehicle is the actual issuer of the instruments and may be a trust, corporation, or partnership. In securitizations involving the issuance of debt interests, entities that cannot become a debtor in a Bankruptcy Code proceeding, such as banks or thrifts, can effectively segregate an asset by pledging it either to the issuer of the interests or directly to the debt holders.

Third, the instruments sold in a securitized transaction may be either debt or equity and will usually, though not necessarily, constitute "securities" for purposes of federal securities laws.

Fourth, in addition to the steps taken to minimize risks associated with a bankruptcy proceeding, a securitized transaction is structured both to reduce or reallocate certain risks inherent in the underlying assets, such as prepayment risk and concentration risk, and to permit, to the greatest extent feasible, the ready resale of the securities issued. With reduced or reallocated risks and greater liquidity, the securities will be more appealing to a wider range of purchasers and, consequently, the yield required to sell them will be lower.

An asset securitization can take a number of forms consistent with this prototype. A wide variety of assets have been securitized utilizing this basic format, including: office buildings, shopping centers and other commercial real estate (both for construction and permanent financing); credit card receivables; automobile, recreational vehicle, and truck loans; boat and mobile home loans; computer, automobile, equipment, and other leases; Small Business Administration loans; loans to franchisees of fast food restaurants and motels; loans against the cash value of life and casualty insurance policies and loans to insureds to pay for insurance policy premiums; problem bank loans; loans to Third World countries; junk bonds and health care receivables. The most familiar asset securitization is the mortgage-backed security, which, although experiencing significant growth only quite recently, has roots dating back more than a century.

SECTION 5. EFFECT OF REIFICATION ON UNDERLYING TRANSACTIONS

INTRODUCTORY NOTE

The abstraction and the independence principle are not eternal verities. They rest on a purpose. Generally, the purpose is to permit commercial parties to fashion a credit enhancement device that reduces some costs and allocates others. Their chief impact is on the undertaking's payment, which they render more certain, and they thereby make capital available to parties that need it and deserve it, in a creditworthy sense.

There are instances, however, when fairness demands that the abstraction concept not apply and when the cost to the device is minimal.

UCC § 3-310

(*see Selected Commercial Statutes*)

PROBLEM

Seller and Buyer entered into a contract for the sale of shipments of toluene, payment to be made thirty days after invoice. The agreement stipulated that Seller would invoice Buyer upon shipment.

Seller invoiced Buyer each month in the amount of $100,000.

(1) What is the effect on Buyer's contract obligation to pay in each of the following cases:

  (a) Buyer gave Seller a cashier's check for $50,000 in part payment of one invoice. See § 3-310(a).

  (b) Buyer gave Seller a certified check for $100,000 for one of the invoices. See § 3-310(a).

  (c) Buyer gave seller a thirty day promissory note for $100,000 for one of the invoices. See § 3-310(b)(2) & (4).

  (d) Buyer gave Seller Buyer's personal check for $100,000 for one of the invoices. See § 3-310(b)(1) & (4).

(e) Buyer caused First National Bank to issue a letter of credit payable against Seller's presentation of a draft on the bank accompanied by the invoice and a signed certificate that the invoice is unpaid. See § 3-310(c) [Is a letter of credit an "instrument?" No, "instrument" means negotiable instrument, § 3-104(b); and a letter of credit does not contain words of negotiability. § 3-104(c). See UCC § 2-325 and the following case.]

(2) What happens in each of the cases, if the instrument, or, in the last case, the letter of credit, is not honored?

SHAMSHER JUTE MILLS LTD. v. SETHIA (LONDON) LTD.

Queen's Bench Division (Commercial Court), 1986.
[1987] 1 Lloyd's Rep. 388.

Mr. Justice BINGHAM.

This case raises a novel problem. If an fob seller who has contracted for payment under a letter of credit to be opened by the buyer ships the goods but fails to obtain payment under the credit because of a failure on his part to comply with its terms, may he recover the contract price or damages for non-acceptance against the buyer? The bank which opened the relevant credit is not a party to the action and no claim is made against it. The plaintiffs accept that the documents which they presented under the credit contained discrepancies and that the bank was entitled to refuse payment.

* * *

On about Dec 20, 1984 Oriental Credit Ltd. of London opened an irrevocable letter of credit no DC 4180 in favour of the sellers. It does not appear that this was confirmed. After amendment, it was for US $40,000 available by the sellers' draft at sight drawn on the buyers accompanied by a number of documents in duplicate, quadruplicate or sextuplicate. These documents included a certificate of packing issued by the manufacturer in quadruplicate and a certificate of weight and quality by the sellers and authenticated by the Dhaka Chamber of Commerce confirming that the goods conformed to the stated specification, also in quadruplicate. The credit provided that the latest shipment date should be Feb 28, 1985, that the expiry date should be Mar 15, 1985, in Bangladesh and that documents must be presented for negotiation within 15 days of the bill of lading. Documents were to be forwarded in one lot by DHL courier. The Uniform Customs and Practice (1983 Revision) were incorporated, and the credit expressly provided:

> Payment will be effected in accordance with the negotiating bank instructions upon presentation documents to ourselves which conform to all terms and conditions of the letter of credit.

* * *

The sellers' central contention is that a letter of credit is conditional payment only. If, therefore, a seller duly ships the goods and fails to obtain payment under the letter of credit he is entitled to recover the price directly from the buyer, at any rate once the letter of credit has expired. If this were open to doubt, cl 13 of the

BJMA terms would in this case resolve the doubt in the sellers' favour. Reliance was placed on WJ Alan & Co. Ltd. v El Nasr Export and Import Co., [1972] 1 Lloyd's Rep 313; [1972] 2 QB 189, particularly on the judgment of Lord Denning MR, and on ED & F Man Ltd. v Nigerian Sweets & Confectionery Co. Ltd., [1977] 2 Lloyd's Rep 50.

The buyers agree that a letter of credit is conditional payment only, but contend that it is under the parties' contract the sole method of payment agreed. While it may well be open to a seller to claim against the buyer if the agreed method of payment fails through no fault of the seller, this is not so where the failure to obtain payment results from the seller's failure to operate the prescribed machinery in the agreed manner. Clause 13 makes plain that a letter of credit is not absolute payment (a point which was unclear when the rule was promulgated) but does no more than that. Reliance was also placed on the Alan case, particularly on the judgment of Lord Justice Megaw, and on Ficom SA v Sociedad Cadex Limitada [1980] 2 Lloyd's Rep 118.

On the facts as I have summarized them the authorities in my judgment lead to the following conclusions:

1. If I am correct that Oriental's Credit was never confirmed, it was a credit which did not conform with the requirements of the contract. But the sellers were content to accept the credit at the time as meeting the buyers' contractual obligation, and cannot now be heard to object, which indeed they have not tried to do. So the credit must be treated as if it did conform.

2. There were other inconsistencies between the terms of the contract and the terms of Oriental Credit's letter of credit. But by accepting the credit terms the sellers must be taken to have varied the contract in accordance with the terms of the credit they have accepted, or at least to have waived any right to rely on the earlier contract terms. This, again, is something the sellers have not tried to do.

3. The contract here made no reference at all to the documents which the sellers were to give the buyers nor to how or when documents were to be given nor to the terms of the letter of credit. This is therefore, I think, a case of the kind envisaged by Mr. Justice Robert Goff (as he then was) in the Ficom case (at 131)

> * * * where the parties do not, in their sale contract, define the terms of the proposed letter of credit. Where that occurs the letter of credit, as subsequently agreed between the parties, may fill the contractual gap and so supplement the terms of the sale contract * * *.

In the present case the contractual gap was a big one, but it seems clear that the terms of the letter of credit, as agreed, filled it.

4. The language of Lord Justice Megaw in the Alan case (at pp. 326 and 217A) is apposite here:

> The contract of sale contained its own express provision for payment, which I have already quoted in full. I repeat the essential words: "Payment: By confirmed, irrevocable letter of credit * * *." There is nothing else in the contract, at least in its express term, which adds to,

> subtracts from or qualifies that contractual provision as to payment of the price * * *.

In this case the position is even clearer, since "L/C at sight" was also included in the price clause.

5. The parties are right to agree in the present case that the letter of credit is, on Lord Denning's classification in Alan, conditional payment. The sellers never agreed that they would only look to Oriental Credit for payment whatever happened. Nor is the credit to be regarded as no payment at all but only a means by which payment may be obtained, a form of collateral security. But to speak of a letter of credit as conditional payment of the price does not perhaps make very clear what the condition is or how it works. If the buyer establishes a credit which conforms or is to be treated as conforming with the sale contract, he has performed his part of the bargain so far. If the credit is honoured according to its terms, the buyer is discharged even though the credit terms differ from the contract terms: that was the Alan case. If the credit is not honoured according to its terms because the bank fails to pay, the buyer is not discharged because the condition has not been fulfilled: that was the Nigerian Sweets case. This makes good sense:

> * * * For the buyer promised to pay by letter of credit, not to provide by a letter of credit a source of payment which did not pay [as Lord Justice Stephenson put it in the Alan case at pp. 329 and 220G.]

If the seller fails to obtain payment because he does not and cannot present the documents which the terms of the credit, supplementing the terms of the contract, require, the buyer is discharged: that was the Ficom case. In the ordinary case, therefore, of which the present is an example, the due establishment of the letter of credit fulfils the buyer's payment obligation unless the bank which opens the credit fails for any reason to make payment in accordance with the credit terms against documents duly presented. I know of no case where a seller who has failed to obtain payment in accordance with the credit terms against documents duly presented. I know of no case where a seller who has failed to obtain payment under a credit because of failure on his part to comply with its terms has succeeded in recovering against a buyer personally. If this were an available road to recovery, many of the familiar arguments about discrepancies in documents would be unnecessary. Bearing in mind the likelihood that buyers will (as here) sell on to sub-buyers, such a result would, I think, throw the course of international trade into some confusion. It must in my view follow that the sellers here, not having complied with the credit terms, cannot recover against the buyers personally.

6. I do not think that cl 13 of the BJMA terms alters this result. The buyer is under the clause to remain responsible for payment of the full value of all goods shipped in accordance with the contract. But this cannot be read quite literally, since plainly a seller who had shipped goods in accordance with the contract but never made documents available to the buyer to enable the buyer to get possession of the goods could not recover the price. So "this contract" in the clause must mean the whole contract, as varied or supplemented by the agreed terms of the letter of credit. The clause then makes plain, as may before the Alan decision have been doubtful, that the establishment of the credit is not absolute payment; and the clause is in line with the law as I understand it, that a seller who has duly performed all the

contract terms, including the presentation of all the documents required by the credit, but who has not obtained payment, may continue to look to the buyers. That is not this case.

7. Even if everything I have said so far is wrong, and the sellers are in principle entitled to seek payment from the buyers despite Oriental Credit's justified refusal to make payment under the credit, I would have the greatest doubt whether the sellers on the facts were able to do so. It must be a prerequisite of recovery that the sellers should have presented the documents to the buyers and demanded payment. Here, the documents were presented to Oriental Credit with a request for payment under the credit but they were never presented to the buyers themselves and I do not think Oriental Credit were the buyers' agents to receive the documents otherwise than under the letter of credit. If, however, my earlier conclusions are right this point does not arise.

8. It follows from the conclusions already expressed that the sellers are not entitled to recover the price of these two consignments from the buyers. It also follows, by parity of reason, that their alternative claim for damages for non-acceptance must fail, because there never was a wrongful non-acceptance. Even if there had been, I should be unable to award damages in the absence of any particularized claim for damages supported by evidence.

* * *

The result is that the action fails. This is a harsh result for the sellers, who appear to have set out to perform the contract in an honest, efficient and businesslike way. It was not, I gather, their usual practice to sell against letters of credit, which was a requirement imposed by the government of Bangladesh. The trouble here may therefore be the result of some unfamiliarity. I describe the result as harsh, because the sellers parted with the goods and have received no payment from anyone (although they could, of course, on rejection of the documents, have re-sold). But I hope that they, and in particular Mr. Mohammad Ạli, who made a good impression as a witness, will understand that the law and practice of international commerce cannot be modified by the Courts to meet particular cases, however hard.

Chapter 13

COMMERCIAL DEFENSES

INTRODUCTORY NOTE

Tension in the law begets compromise. Rules admit of exceptions. One doctrine or principle gives way to a countervailing doctrine or principle. Observers strive to find equipoise where in reality there is dynamism. Sometimes one principle erodes another completely. Eventually patterns tend to emerge; and we define new rules out of the compromise or, perhaps, out of the detritus of a vanquished principle.

In commercial law many principles find their limits in defenses and remedies. The law establishes a rule of liability and then erodes the rule, principally with doctrines such as estoppel and good faith. At other times, the law fashions a rule of liability but reduces its harshness with limited remedies.

This chapter and the next deal with limits on the doctrines we studied in Chapters 11 and 12. In addition, we see here creative use of common law concepts, so creative that one might say that they are not the common law concepts at all. Fraud, for example, is an old idea. Commercial law first bifurcated it into fraud in the execution and fraud in the inducement and treated the two quite differently in negotiable instruments law, as we have already seen. In this chapter, we learn of another kind of fraud, letter of credit fraud, which is neither fraud in the inducement nor fraud in the execution but which becomes a fulcrum on which the independence principle rests, some would say precariously

SECTION 1. ESTOPPEL AND THE LIKE

INTRODUCTORY NOTE

There are two kinds of estoppel. The first is the classic rule. It rests on culpability evaluation. Conduct that prompts another to rely reasonably to his detriment yields an estoppel that prevents the actor from doing or saying something. This is equitable estoppel. It has a cousin, promissory estoppel. Both of them rest on evaluation of all of the circumstances with attendant investigation of the facts and the relationships of the parties.

A second kind of estoppel is much stricter. First it eschews the reliance and even the detriment components of classic estoppel. Under the second kind of estoppel, often called "preclusion," moreover, there is little factual analysis. If *A* does such and such, *B* can estop *A* from raising certain arguments. If *C*'s employee does such and such, *C* cannot impose liability on *D*.

The first kind of estoppel (reliance and detriment estoppel) is more at home in Contract; the second (Preclusion) in commercial law.

OHIO & MISSISSIPPI RY. v. MCCARTHY, 96 U.S. 258 (1878). In this case the plaintiff sued the railroad for gross negligence in letting his cattle die. Originally, the railroad argued that the delays that caused the deaths stemmed from a shortage of rolling stock. Later, at trial, the railroad's lawyers argued that West Virginia's sabbath law prevented it from transshipping the cattle promptly. The Court was not impressed with this later argument, which it considered "an afterthought, suggested by the pressures and exigencies of the case." Id. at 267. "He is not permitted thus to mend his hold. He is estopped from doing it by a settled principle of law." Id. at 267-68. There was no evidence in the *McCarthy* case that the plaintiff had relied on the first argument to his detriment.

FPI DEVELOPMENT, INC. v. NAKASHIMA, 282 Cal. Rptr. 508, 530 (Cal. Ct. App. 1991). "Where a party participates in a sham [and] the intention is that the note be taken as a jural act by the one upon whom the sham is perpetrated * * *. [, i]t will not lie in the mouth of the participant to say that there was no execution of the note."

UCC § 4A-202(b)
(*see Selected Commercial Statutes*)

(a) NEGOTIABLE INSTRUMENTS AND THE BANK/CUSTOMER RELATIONSHIP

INTRODUCTORY NOTE

There are a number of estoppel rules in Articles 3 and 4 and one in Article 1. Section 1-103 provides that the law of estoppel shall supplement the rules of the Code unless those rules displace it. That estoppel rule, presumably, is classic estoppel. The rules in Articles 3 and 4 are more in the nature of preclusion rules.

Section 3-406 is the least commercial of these. It raises an estoppel against a party whose negligence substantially contributes to an unauthorized signature or an alteration. In the event the fact finder determines that such negligence occurred, the negligent party may not claim that the signature or alteration are unauthorized. Note that this rule and others in Article 3 are subject to a comparative fault rule. Sections 3-404 and 3-405 relate to impostors, fictitious payees, and faithless employees. There is also an important estoppel rule in Article 4. Section 4-406(d) raise an estoppel against a customer that fails to examine her checking account statement promptly. Each of these rules allocates the loss under comparative fault.

Thus here we see the law swaying first one way, then the other, then back the first way. The Code posits liability rules for those who sign negotiable instruments. §§ 3-412 to 3-415. It relieves them of liability, of course, if the signatures are unauthorized. § 3-403. But, if parties are negligent, it precludes them from saying the signatures are unauthorized. Finally it relieves them of some of their liability if their counterparty was also negligent.

The second of the two cases that follow arose under the old versions of Articles 3 and 4. The excerpt from Professor Rubin's article summarizes the state of affairs.

TEXAS STADIUM CORP. v. SAVINGS OF AMERICA

Court of Appeals of Texas, 1996.
933 S.W.2d 616, 32 U.C.C. Rep. Serv.2d 490.

WHITTINGTON, Justice.

* * *

BACKGROUND

TSC is the lessee of Texas Stadium in Irving, Texas. Candace Pratt worked as an accounts payable clerk for TSC from late 1988 until August 1993. As part of her job, Pratt prepared TSC checks, which were later signed by authorized officers of TSC.

While employed at TSC, Pratt embezzled money from TSC. As part of her embezzlement scheme, Pratt established a d/b/a account at SOA in the name of Candace A. Pratt d/b/a AAA Lawn Maintenance Service and Repair ("AAA"). To effect her embezzlement scheme, Pratt would prepare a check for an actual vendor, and after having the check signed by an authorized officer of TSC, Pratt would alter the check by either changing the payee name to a version of the AAA name or by adding the AAA name above the original payee name. Pratt also used other methods to embezzle money from TSC. One such method was to prepare a TSC check in a version of the AAA name and then deposit it into her account once it was signed. Once Pratt obtained the appropriate signatures and deposited the checks in her d/b/a account, SOA then forwarded the checks to TSC's bank, and the checks were paid in due course. In all, Pratt deposited 206 checks in her account, totalling $1,060,052.10.

After discovering Pratt's scheme, TSC filed suit against Pratt and SOA to recover the money Pratt embezzled. TSC alleged causes of action against Pratt and SOA for negligence, conversion, money had and received, and breach of warranty. In July 1994, SOA moved for summary judgment on all of TSC's claims. In its motion, SOA asserted it was entitled to judgment as a matter of law because: (1) Texas law is well settled that losses resulting from a faithless employee are the burden of the employer; (2) TSC did not have standing to assert warranty claims against SOA; (3) the final payment rule precluded TSC's common law causes of action; and (4) the statute of limitations barred TSC's claims. After hearing the evidence and arguments of counsel, the trial judge granted summary judgment in favor of SOA without specifying the basis for his ruling. TSC and Pratt then entered into an agreed judgment. TSC appeals the summary judgment granted in favor of SOA.

* * *

INTENDED PAYEE DEFENSE

In its summary judgment motion, SOA alternatively asserted that section 3.405(a)(3) precluded TSC from recovering on its causes of action. In its ninth point of error, TSC contends the trial judge erred in granting summary judgment because fact issues exist on SOA's intended payee defense. Specifically, TSC contends that section 3.405(a)(3) of the Texas UCC, commonly known as the padded payroll rule, does not apply to the facts of this case, and the trial judge erred in concluding otherwise. We disagree.

Under the padded payroll rule, an indorsement by any person in the name of a named payee is effective if an agent or employee of the maker or drawer has supplied the maker with the name of the payee intending the latter to have no such interest. Tex. Bus. & Com.Code Ann. § 3.404 (Vernon Supp.1996). Application of section 3.405 precludes causes of action for negligence, conversion, and money had and received. Comment four[1] to section 3.405(a)(3) indicates that the purpose behind the rule is to place the loss resulting from a faithless employee on the employer as a risk of its business. The reason for allocating the loss on the employer is two-fold. First, the employer is normally in a better position to prevent such forgeries by reasonable care in the selection and supervision of its employees. Second, the employer is normally in a better position to cover any potential losses with fidelity insurance and the cost of such insurance is more appropriately an expense of the employer's business.

In its summary judgment motion, SOA contended that this was a classic case of the faithless employee and the ideal case for application of section 3.405(a)(3). TSC countered that section 3.405 was not applicable for three reasons. First, the record contained no summary judgment evidence indicating Pratt intended the payee to have no interest at the time the TSC officer signed the check. Second, when Pratt prepared checks payable to a version of the AAA name, she in fact intended for the AAA entity to have an interest. Third, many of the indorsements were not in the name of the named payee as required by section 3.405(a). On appeal, TSC makes the same arguments it made in its summary judgment response. For the reasons that follow, we cannot agree with TSC's contentions.

For section 3.405(a)(3) to apply, Pratt must have (1) supplied the name of the payee to TSC and (2) intended for the payee not to have an interest in the check. Two types of checks are present in this case. First, there are checks prepared in some version of the AAA name. Second, there are checks prepared in the name of an actual vendor for an actual indebtedness. We will address the two groups separately.

With respect to the first group of checks, TSC argues section 3.405 does not cover these checks because AAA Lawn Maintenance Service & Repair did in

---

1 Comment one in the Official Version [eds.].

fact exist. We disagree. The fact that AAA existed does not preclude application of section 3.405. In a case similar to this one, an employee arranged to have dividend checks made payable to two dummy corporations he controlled. Prudential-Bache Sec., Inc. v. Citibank, N.A., 4 U.C.C. Rep. Serv.2d 533, 533-34, 1987 WL 257803 (N.Y.Sup.Ct.1987), aff'd, 141 A.D.2d 353, 529 N.Y.S.2d 983 (N.Y.App.Div.1988), order aff'd. as modified, 73 N.Y.2d 263, 539 N.Y.S.2d 699, 536 N.E.2d 1118 (1989). The employee deposited the funds in the accounts of the dummy corporations at the defendant collecting bank. The court held that section 3.405(a)(3) applied even though the corporations actually existed and the employee intended for the corporations to receive these funds. Id. at 535.

A similar conclusion was reached by the court in Dorsey v. Houston National Bank, 338 S.W.2d 540, 542 (Tex.Civ.App.—Waco 1960, writ ref'd). There, an employee was one of two required signatories on company checks. The employee prepared checks to former employees who were owed nothing and obtained the other required signature on the checks. The employee then indorsed the checks and cashed them. The company sued the bank that cashed the checks. In arguing it was not liable for the amount of the underlying checks, the bank relied on the predecessor to section 3.405 which made an instrument a bearer instrument when it is payable to the order of a fictitious person, and such fact is known to the person making it so payable. Id. at 542. Although the employer argued that section 3.405's predecessor was inapplicable because the payees, former employees, were not fictitious, the Waco Court disagreed, holding that the payees were fictitious because they were not legitimate payees. Id. at 542.

As with the dummy corporations in Prudential-Bache and the former employees in Dorsey, AAA was merely a conduit for Pratt's embezzlement. The fact that AAA was an entity on paper misses the point of section 3.405. The critical fact is that AAA was not a legitimate payee of TSC, and TSC did not intend for AAA to have any funds. See Dorsey, 338 S.W.2d at 542. Thus, we conclude, based on the reasoning in Prudential-Bache and Dorsey, that the first group of checks was covered under section 3.405.

We reach a similar conclusion with respect to the second group of checks—i.e., those that were prepared in the name of an actual vendor for an actual indebtedness. Although TSC argues that section 3.405(a)(3) does not cover these checks because there is no summary judgment evidence that Pratt did not intend the named vendor to have an interest in the checks at the time the checks were signed, we disagree. A similar argument was raised and rejected in Clinton Weilbacher Builder, 643 S.W.2d at 476. In that case, an employee at Clinton Weilbacher Builder forged the payees' signatures on thirty-two checks drawn on the company account and made payable to various creditors. Id. at 474. Clinton Weilbacher Builder sued its bank, and the bank defended on the basis of the padded payroll rule. Id. Like TSC, Clinton Weilbacher Builder claimed section 3.405(a)(3) did not apply because there was no evidence the employee intended that the payees have no interest in the proceeds at the time she supplied their names to Clinton Weilbacher Builder. See id. at 475. The court disagreed. In reaching its decision, the court noted that the summary judgment evidence showed that the payees had already been paid for services rendered and that this evidence could lead to only one conclusion—that the employee did not intend the named payees to have an interest in the proceeds at the time she supplied their name to her employer. Id. at 476.

Evidence similar to that in Clinton Weilbacher Builder exists in this case. Robert Nunez, TSC's controller at the time of Pratt's embezzlement, testified in his deposition that the vendors whose names appeared on the subject checks had already been paid. According to Nunez, Pratt simply recycled invoices so they were put through the system twice. We hold based on this record that the summary judgment evidence conclusively established that Pratt did not intend for the vendors to have an interest in the proceeds at the time she supplied their names.

TSC next contends the padded payroll rule does not apply because the indorsements are not in the name of the named payees. A discrepancy between the payee and the indorsement does not preclude application of section 3.405(a)(3). See British Caledonian Airways, 819 F.2d at 599-600. Applying section 3.405 even where slight discrepancies between the named payee and the indorsement exist furthers the policy of the section to place the risk of loss for a faithless employee on the employer. Id. Accordingly, we reject TSC's argument that the rule does not apply because the indorsements were not in the named payees' names.

We conclude that the padded payroll rule applies in this case. The trial judge properly concluded that section 3.405(a)(3) places the loss on TSC for all of the indorsed checks. Like section 3.418, section 3.405 precludes TSC's causes of action for negligence, conversion and money had and received. We overrule TSC's ninth point of error.

* * *

We affirm the trial court's judgment.

NOTE ON THE BANK/CUSTOMER RELATIONSHIP

The following case arises by virtue of the fact that under Part 4 of Article 4, banks may not charge a customer's account unless the checks the bank receives through the bank collection system or over its own counters are "properly payable." § 4-401(a). Checks bearing forged drawer's signatures or forged necessary indorsements are not properly payable. Checks bearing an alteration are properly payable only according to their original tenor.

Two rules reduce the loss this rule puts on drawee banks. First, as § 5(c) in Chapter 11 explains, the drawee probably has a cause of action against a depositary bank or the depositor who warrant that there are no forged necessary indorsements and no alterations. If the drawer's signature is forged, however, under the rule of *Price v. Neal,* supra, the drawee must take the loss. The second limitation on the liability rule on improperly payable checks is the preclusion of § 4-406, which is not the broadest rule in any event.

SIMCOE & ERIE GENERAL INSURANCE CO. v. CHEMICAL BANK

United States District Court, Southern District of New York, 1991.
770 F. Supp. 149.

SWEET, District Judge.

Defendant Chemical Bank, New York Trust Company ("Chemical") has moved pursuant to Rule 56, Fed.R.Civ.P., for summary judgment dismissing the diversity action of plaintiffs Simcoe & Erie General Insurance Company ("Simcoe") and its subrogee, the Guarantee Insurance Company of North America ("Guarantee"). For the reasons set forth below, the motion is granted in part and denied in part.

* * *

The Facts

This action arises from a check forgery scheme perpetrated by Lily Lee ("Lee"), Simcoe's employee, over the period March 14, 1985 through July 30, 1986.

Between March 1985 and August 1986, Simcoe maintained a checking account (the "operating account") with Chemical.

Simcoe hired Lee in January 1985. On January 3, 1985, Simcoe filed a Representative Card with Chemical. The card read, in pertinent part, as follows:

> Please cash any checks bearing my/our signature (or endorsement) when presented by my/our representative whose signature appears below. These instructions remain in effect until written revocation is received by you.

The card bore Lee's signature, identifying her as Simcoe's representative, and was issued in the name of and signed by Raymond J. Morton ("Morton"), Simcoe's vice president-secretary and treasurer during the relevant period. The representative card remained effective until July 31, 1985.

On June 22, 1982, Simcoe had executed a resolution (the "Resolution") signed by Morton and Shang C. Lee, Simcoe's assistant treasurer and Lee's mother, that stated:

> that the Secretary or any Assistant Secretary * * * is hereby authorized and directed to certify, * * * to the Bank * * * the names of the officers and other representatives of this Corporation * * * and specimens of the respective signatures, and that the Bank may conclusively assume that persons at anytime certified by it to be * * * representatives of this Corporation continue as such until receipt by the Bank of written notice to the contrary.

Of the employees of Simcoe's New York office, Lee alone drew the checks, made all the entries in Simcoe's books, and reconciled the checks against the bank statements when they were returned by Chemical.

At the beginning of the forgery scheme, Lee would present the checks to the Chemical representative listing herself as payee and containing Morton's signature forged by Lee. After the checks were returned by Chemical, Lee would alter the payee of the check to reflect the names of legitimate companies with which Simcoe regularly did business. Lee also altered the voucher copies in Simcoe's ledgers. Later in the course of the scheme, Lee returned the checks to Simcoe's files leaving her name as payee.

After the forgery scheme was uncovered, Morton upon examining the checks was unable to discern which checks contained his signature and which were forgeries.

In 1985, Simcoe's actual expenses exceeded its budgeted expenses by $82,392. The amount of forged checks for 1985 totalled $95,704.

The Coopers & Lybrand audit of Simcoe's books during the period 1985-86 did not reveal the forgeries. During the relevant period Coopers & Lybrand did not perform a full audit for Simcoe, which would have included an audit of Simcoe's bank accounts.

Chemical sent Simcoe monthly statements of its operating account and returned to Simcoe the checks drawn on the account. The statement for the period March 6 through April 3, 1985 was received by Simcoe on April 11, 1985.

All Chemical statements bore the warning: "Please examine at once. Except for electronic transfers, account will be considered correct if no report is received within 14 days." Simcoe failed to notify Chemical within 14 days of April 11, 1985.

On July 30, 1986, upon checking the signatures on a check drawn on Simcoe's operating account, Chemical called Simcoe and asked Morton to verify his signature on the check. Simcoe & Erie first notified Chemical of the forgeries on August 13, 1986 based on the statement received for the period ending July 31, 1986.

Chemical refunded $862.59 to Simcoe. This amount represented the four forged checks paid by Chemical in March 1985 before Simcoe had an opportunity to review its first statement.

Guarantee paid Simcoe $109,585.76 ($152,202.54 Canadian dollars). In exchange for such payment, Simcoe assigned its claim to Guarantee, and fully released all rights it had against any party for compensation in connection with Lee's forgeries.

Discussion

* * *

II. Duty to Discover Unauthorized Signatures

Section 4-406 of the Uniform Commercial Code, "Customer's Duty to Discover and Report Unauthorized Signature and Alteration," (McKinney's 1990) ("§ 4-406"), which both parties agree governs the instant dispute, provides, in pertinent part: [The court here quoted § 4-406 of the pre-revised Article 4. Cf. UCC 4-406.]

Thus, if Chemical can establish, to the exclusion of any genuine issue of material fact, that Simcoe, either through its own negligence or through its failure to notify within the time prescribed by the statute, is precluded from asserting a claim against the bank with respect to each of the checks at issue, then Chemical should be granted summary judgment as a matter of law. If, however, Simcoe raises an issue of fact with respect to the above or with respect to Chemical's standard of care in paying the checks, then summary judgment will be denied.

A. Simcoe's Exercise of Due Care

In support of its position that Simcoe failed to use due care in examining the returned checks for unauthorized signatures, Chemical points to Simcoe's failure to notify the bank of any unauthorized signatures within fourteen days of the receipt of the statement relating to the checks until its notification of Chemical on August 13, 1986.

The customer's duty to notify the bank within fourteen days is set forth in § 4-406(2)(b) of the statute as well as on each statement. Courts have upheld the failure to meet the fourteen day notification requirement imposed under § 4-406 as a basis for a grant of summary judgment in favor of the bank.

In addition to this undisputed failure to notify, Simcoe did not maintain vigilance over the accounts after the statements had been returned. Simcoe neither detected Lee's tampering with the payee line of the checks to reflect legitimate vendors before placing them in the file nor her alteration of the voucher copies in its ledgers.

Simcoe also allowed the same person to be responsible for drawing the checks, keeping the books, and reconciling statements with the book entries. Chemical shows that such practices were not standard at Simcoe by adducing Morton's deposition testimony as well as a memorandum from E.H. Swindall ("Swindall"), Simcoe's chief financial officer, showing that immediately after the discoveries of the forgeries, headquarters in Canada directed the use of new procedures relating to the reconciliation of the account and the reporting of budget variances.

Simcoe and Guarantee for their part adduce no evidence showing Simcoe's exercise of due care in reviewing the checks in question, asserting merely that its use of due care is a question of fact. Chemical has therefore established to the exclusion of any question of fact that Simcoe failed to use due care to examine the statements and to discover any unauthorized signatures as required by § 4-406(1).

B. Chemical's Exercise of Due Care

1. Before the Expiration of the Authorization Card

Simcoe's representative card authorizing Lee to present checks for cashing bearing Morton's signature, which Chemical had on file, was in effect from January 1985 until its expiration on July 31, 1985.

Chemical adduces further evidence relevant to the period the representative card was in effect in support of its position that it was not negligent in failing to recognize that Morton's signatures as presented by Lee were forgeries. Morton's deposition testimony shows that a person exercising reasonable care could believe the signatures were Morton's, since even Morton could not later distinguish the checks he had signed from the forgeries.

In support of its position that Chemical was negligent in cashing the checks on which Morton's signatures were forged, Simcoe and Guarantee adduce testimony that cards bearing a sample of Morton's signature, as well as those of other officers of Simcoe, were on file at the branch at which the operating account was maintained, a few feet away from the teller. However no evidence has established that it is routine practice for tellers at Chemical, or at other banks, to pull the signature specimen from the file each time a check bearing that signature was presented.

2. After the Expiration of the Representative Card

With respect to the forgeries that occurred after the expiration of Lee's representative card on July 31, 1985, an issue of fact remains as to Chemical's negligence, where Chemical has adduced no evidence that establishes that it is customary for banks to cash checks presented by employees of customers after the expiration of the representative card. Morton's deposition testimony establishes that it is not Chemical's practice to require tellers to ask for a representative card after the representative employee became familiar to the teller at the branch at which the account was maintained. Such evidence does not address directly the issue of the expired representative card.

C. The March 6—April 3, 1985 Forgeries

Given that Chemical has established to the preclusion of any genuine issue of material fact Simcoe's lack of due care, § 4-406 may preclude Simcoe's and Guarantee's claims as a matter of law. With respect to those checks forged from March 6 through April 3, 1985—the subject of the statement received by Simcoe on April 11, 1985—§ 4-406(2)(a) provides that Simcoe and Guarantee are precluded from asserting a claim if Chemical establishes Simcoe's lack of due care; its own exercise of due care; and that Chemical suffered a loss by reason of Simcoe's failure to exercise due care.

There is no dispute that Chemical reimbursed Simcoe in the amount of $862.59, the sum of the checks containing unauthorized signatures paid by Chemical from March 6 through April 3, 1985.

Based on the undisputed facts and on the lack of an issue of fact as to Simcoe's failure to use due care and as to Chemical's use of due care with respect to these checks, Simcoe is precluded under § 4-406(2)(a) from asserting a claim against Chemical based on the checks paid from March 6 through April 3, 1985. Therefore, summary judgment is granted dismissing those claims based on the checks forged during this period.

D. The Checks Presented from April 3, 1985—July 31, 1985

Chemical's showing, to the preclusion of any genuine issue of material fact, that Simcoe failed to use ordinary care and promptness in examining the statements and that Chemical itself exercised ordinary care in cashing the checks as long as the representative card was in effect requires summary judgment, pursuant to § 4-406(2)(b), dismissing the claims based on forgeries subsequent to April, 1985, and up to and including July 31, 1985.

There is no dispute that (1) Chemical paid the checks in good faith;[1] (2) Simcoe received a statement on April 11, 1985; (3) Simcoe failed to notify Chemical of the unauthorized signatures within 14 days of the receipt of such statement.

Nor does Simcoe's and Guarantee's contention, in the face of a showing by Chemical to the contrary, that regardless of its own use of due care in examining the checks, Chemical failed to exercise due care in allowing them to be cashed require a contrary holding. Sussman, 140 A.D.2d at 668, 529 N.Y.S.2d at 327. In Sussman, the Appellate Division affirmed the trial court's grant of summary judgment in favor of the bank where plaintiff had failed to notify the bank within the fourteen days required pursuant to § 4-406 where the court found that the bank had exercised reasonable care. Id., 529 N.Y.S.2d at 328.

Therefore, given Simcoe's undisputed failure to report unauthorized signatures within fourteen days, it is precluded from bringing any claims against Chemical based on checks paid subsequent to its receipt of the first statement relating to checks forged by Lee and up to and including the date of the expiration of the representative card. Therefore, summary judgment dismissing these claims is required as a matter of law.

* * *

Conclusion

For the reasons set forth above, Chemical's motion for summary judgment is granted with respect to the checks paid before the expiration of the representative card on July 31, 1985. With respect to the claims based on checks paid after that date, the motion for summary judgment is denied.

RUBIN, EFFICIENCY, EQUITY AND THE PROPOSED REVISION OF ARTICLES 3 AND 4, 42 Ala. L. Rev. 551, 561-63, 564-65, 566-70 (1991).

No sane person engages in payment activities for the intrinsic pleasure of doing so. Payments are a means to an independently determined end. In order to obtain goods or services in a commercial culture like our own, one must pay for them. This involves the use of a mechanism such as cash, a credit card, an electronic fund transfer, or a check. The more inexpensive this mechanism is to use, the more efficient it is; that is, the fewer extraneous expenses it imposes on the underlying transaction. Economists describe such extraneous expenses as transaction costs; a working definition of efficiency, therefore, is the minimization of these transaction costs. In the payment context, this means minimizing the cost of the payment mechanism as a whole.

---

[1] There is no dispute as to Chemical's good faith, defined in § 1-201 as "honesty in fact in the conduct or transaction concerned," in paying the checks, a matter distinct from Chemical's care or lack of care in making such payments.

A perfectly functioning market will minimize transaction costs, such as the cost of payments, by competitive pressure; that is, the parties will negotiate an efficient payment contract. Efficiency will suffer, however, if there is a market failure. There are three main sources of market failure: monopoly, or some other limit on the number of competitors; externalities, or costs imposed on those who are not parties to the transaction; and information asymmetry between the parties. With respect to the payment system, monopoly can probably be eliminated from consideration, since the American banking industry is highly competitive; there may often be too many competitors as a result of regulatory barriers, but there are rarely too few. Externalities do not appear to be a major problem either. There has been some fear that a bank failure in the electronic fund transfer system could cause a chain reaction of other failures, but there has never been such an event, and it would be virtually impossible with checks, which transfer smaller sums and move at more manageable velocities. The third type of market failure, information asymmetry, occurs when one party to the transaction has better information than another and thus is able to obtain benefits or allocate costs to an extent that decreases the overall efficiency of the contract. This type of market failure is a major problem in the checking system.

The problem arises when consumers, rather than businesses, are involved. Most businesses can obtain the information they need, since they are repeat players, and they generally have the necessary staff and economic resources. Large firms, moreover, tend to have professional cash mangers whose life work involves the details of the payment system. But consumers have neither the resources nor the experience to obtain the necessary information. Deposit contracts are complex, involving a variety of different price items—interest rate, minimum balance, printing charges, item charges, stop payment charges, bounced check charges and the like. Consider how much information and knowledge would be required to determine whether an account that pays 4% interest on amounts over $500, with a $10 stop payment and bounced check fee, is a better deal than one which pay 6% interest on amounts over $1000, charges 10¢ per check and $15 for stop payments and bounced checks. Some of these items are not only difficult to compute, but difficult to evaluate. Most people, for example, would have difficulty predicting how many checks they will stop in a given year. Loss allocation provisions are even worse; they involve unfamiliar legal concepts, and virtually no consumer can estimate the likelihood of falling victim to a bank error or fraud.

Where a market failure occurs, private contract will not effectuate the social goal of economic efficiency and there is an economic justification for imposing substantive legal rules. If efficiency is the goal, these legal rules should be designed to reallocate costs in a manner that approximates the contract that the parties would have reached had they possessed the necessary information. In doing so, the law would be attempting to minimize the total cost of the payment. This is not always easy to do, but it represents a guiding principle. Neither former Articles 3 and 4 nor the revisions follow this principle.

* * *

The final area of market failure is loss allocation. Here the market failure is probably the most extreme, given the unpredictability of the occurrence and the complexity of the issue. The most efficient way to allocate losses, which usually appears in negotiated contracts between parties with equivalent information, is to place liability for clearly avoidable losses on the party responsible for the loss and divide liability for other losses between the customer and the financial institution. The bulk of the loss would generally be allocated to the financial institution, because the financial institution can spread it through the price it charges to all users of the system, and because the institution is in the best position to decide how much money to spend on avoiding the loss. The customer would generally be assigned enough of the loss to give it an incentive to take reasonable precautions but no more. Assigning excessive liability to the customer is inefficient. It may induce the customer to take excessive precautions against the loss—that is, precautions that are more costly than spreading the loss among all customers. Alternatively, it might impose heavy losses on a single customer. Given the general principle of risk aversion—that people will pay small amounts to avoid a small chance of losing a large amount—the cost to customers of such losses is greater, in a real sense, than the cost of spreading the loss to all customers.

An even more important element of economic efficiency is to avoid large expenditures in allocating the loss. This means avoiding litigation and other elaborate forms of adjudication. Suppose someone writes a fraudulent check for $50,000 and absconds with the money. There is one optimal allocation of this loss. Assigning the loss to the wrong party will produce greater costs to the system as a whole—perhaps $55,000 of real losses, instead of $50,000. But litigating to find this optimal loss allocation will cost $20,000, or a total of $70,000 in losses, instead of the sub-optimal $55,000. Unless the amount of the loss is extraordinarily large or the facts of the case extraordinarily simple, the costs of finding the optimal loss allocation by litigation will dwarf the savings realized by that process, even assuming that it always achieves the efficient result.

Private contracts between knowledgeable parties tend to follow these rules. Both the Visa and MasterCard companies, for example, impose losses on member banks for an explicit failure to follow their precautionary rules. Losses which occur despite these precautions are absorbed by the company (and, of course, spread to customers through the pricing system). The company then decides on the level of precaution it wants to take and the amount of anti-loss technology, like holograms on cards, that it wants to develop. If there is a dispute about a particular loss allocation, it is resolved by a simple arbitration, which generally consists of a one-page letter from each side and a one paragraph decision by a private arbitrator.

* * *

The original loss allocation rules in Articles 3 and 4 did not embody these principles of economic efficiency, and the revisions do little to alter this situation. The concept of loss spreading does not occur in the revised Code at all; parties are assigned liability on the basis of their actions, with no regard to their economic status. Revised Article 3, which still contains the bulk of the loss allocation rules does not even acknowledge that banks are involved. It continues to use the generic terminology of "person," "drawee" or "payor," as if we still had a group of individuals with interchangeable roles, as we did in eighteenth century mercantile practice. This obscures the basic policy choice of loss spreading. When we assign liability to a bank, we are not imposing a loss on that "person" as an individual entity. Instead, we are deciding that the loss should be spread across the entire customer base, instead of letting it fall on the particular customers who happened to be victimized. In many cases, such loss spreading will be more efficient, but the Code does not reflect that fact.

The Code and its revision do embody the second principle of economic efficiency in loss allocation—that the loss should be assigned to the party who is in the best position to avoid it. This is achieved through use of the fault principle. If there is a forged drawer's signature, liability is assigned to the drawee; if there is a forged indorsement, liability is initially assigned to the drawee, but can be shifted to the person who first took the fraudulent instrument from the thief. This is the venerable rule of *Price v. Neal*. It is preserved in sections 3-416, 3-418, and 3-419, which replace former section 3-417 with mercifully clearer language and a separate treatment of transfer and presentment warranties. Although this rule imposes strict liability on banks in certain circumstances, the banks remained faithful to the sponsors' agreement and made no attempt to eliminate this liability.

The fault principle enters, however through former sections 3-405 and 3-406, which are essentially preserved in sections 3-404 to 3-406 of the revision. Former section 3-406 allowed the drawee bank to shift liability to any person who contributes to a fraud or forgery by failing to exercise ordinary care. Here (and in revised section 3-405), the bankers were unable to resist temptation and demanded a new provision that relieves them of the obligation to examine checks. The revision achieves this result by declaring that failure to examine does not constitute a lack of ordinary care, thus overruling Medford Irrigation District v. Western Bank. In addition, certain actions are deemed negligent per se, and automatically shift liability to the party at fault. In former Article 3, these actions are defined in section 3-405. The revision retains this definitional approach and also adds a new section on employer liability. Unlike the treatment of fictitious payees in former Article 3, this new section is clear, but it does expand the existing liability of employers. That may well be efficient, however, given that an entity with employees is generally a business, and is thus unlikely to suffer from information asymmetries. But the relationship of this section to the other liability provisions is obscure. The revision now contains a general negligence section, a more particularized section directed at employers, and a still more particularized section directed at specific kinds of frauds, some of which affect employers and others which tend to be practiced upon individuals. One thing that does seem clear, amidst this proliferation of liability rules, is that banks wanted a broad and overlapping arsenal for shifting liability for check frauds to their customers.

An even more serious problem with these liability provisions, however, is that fault does not quite correspond to the economic principle that the loss should be assigned to the party who could have avoided it most readily. To begin with, the U.C.C. fault principles impose unnecessarily large losses on consumers—larger than is necessary to induce them to take whatever precautions they are likely to take. For example, consumers can avoid losses by taking precautions against the theft of their checkbooks, and they will do so if they are at risk of losing some meaningful sum of money, for example a hundred dollars, and of undergoing the inconvenience of closing their old account and opening a new one. Providing that they can lose the entire account balance, as the U.C.C.'s fault principle does, is unlikely to induce any additional precaution. The person who carelessly leaves a checkbook on the hardware store counter will still do so, even with all this additional liability, because his action is the result of carelessness, not a conscious weighing of the costs and benefits. Beyond a certain point, liability simply punishes the consumer without achieving any increased level of loss reduction.

The second way that the fault principle deviates from economic efficiency is by ignoring the role of systematic planning. Consumers virtually never devise long-range loss avoidance strategies, and they have no opportunity to alter the nature of the check collection system. Banks design the system, and banks can avoid losses by restructuring it, by training their employees, or by developing new technologies. For example, banks assert that they cannot check the signatures of all checks drawn upon them, but they are currently experimenting with optical scanning devices that may ultimately do exactly that. Such precautions will often be the most cost-effective means of loss reduction, but they are not captured by our concept of fault. Courts rarely hold that a bank was at fault, in a particular case, because it failed to engage in a five year planning process to develop a new security device.

But the most serious problem with the fault principle that Article 3 embodies, and that the revision perpetuates, is the enormous cost of its effectuation. Determining fault requires a complex, fact-based adjudication that will rapidly devour the amount at issue in all but the largest cases. The reporters were aware of this problem. While they never abandoned the fault principle, they did propose that the loss simply be divided in half in situations where both parties were negligent. Even this modest effort to reduce loss imposition costs troubled the banking industry, and the provisions were dropped. Instead, sections 3-405 and 3-406 now contain a comparative negligence provision to deal with cases where both parties are at fault. This is even worse, of course; with the contributory negligence or dual contributory negligence of the existing law, only the fact of negligence must be established. Under the revision the precise amount of negligence becomes important, so every fact is relevant, and the agonizingly expensive process of discovery and trial can go on even longer.

This is a market failure of its own, a market failure generated by the structure of the legal system. It means that consumers can virtually never enforce their rights against a bank because it will simply be too expensive to do so. What makes this particularly serious is that consumers almost always end up with the loss if there is a dispute. The bank is holding the consumer's money, and can simply debit the account for the amount in question. This power, virtually unique among businesses, means that the consumer must generally initiate the lawsuit. Since the suit cannot be economically pursued, the consumer has to "lump it." The result is inefficient because the consumer is not necessarily the party who should bear the loss, even according to the rather limited precaution-based rules of Article 3, and certainly not according to more general principles of economic efficiency that include loss spreading. But the only thing that is more inefficient than failing to bring suit is bringing it; then the loss may be allocated in accordance with economic efficiency, but the expense of allocating it will outweigh any allocational advantage.

(b) LETTERS OF CREDIT

BARCLAYS BANK D.C.O. v. MERCANTILE NATIONAL BANK

United States Court of Appeals, Fifth Circuit, 1973.
481 F.2d 1224.

[This case involves early litigation of a confirmer's liability under a standby letter of credit, a type of credit not often confirmed and one, in this case, issued by a mortgage broker (Allied), not a bank. The confirmer was a bank, but the banker that signed the confirmation language did not appreciate the import of the confirmation he was issuing. In a thorough and thoughtful portion of the opinion not reproduced here, the court held that there were no policy reasons not to apply the pre-revised version of Article 5 to a confirmation of a standby issued by a non-bank. Revised Article 5 codifies that holding. See 5-102(a)(9). The balance of the opinion deals with defenses the confirmer raised when the beneficiary of the credit sued for wrongful dishonor. Barclays is the beneficiary; Mercantile the confirmer.]

INGRAHAM, Circuit Judge.

* * *

In the spring of 1970 Bay Holding Company Ltd., of Trinidad, W.I., began negotiations with Barclays Bank D.C.O. of New York for a loan of about $400,000 to help finance a real estate development in the Caribbean. Barclays apparently was reluctant to rely solely on the security furnished by Bay Holding because in late May of 1970 Allied Mortgage Consultants, Inc., an Atlanta mortgage broker, issued to Barclays its irrevocable letter of credit in a sum not to exceed $400,000 for the account of Bay Holding. This letter of credit was to expire on June 15, 1971. Allied was at that time (May 1970) a customer of Mercantile National Bank of Atlanta. At Allied's insistence Mercantile simultaneously wrote the letter which underlies this litigation. The full text of this letter is set out in the margin,[1] but the third paragraph-on which this appeal turns-provides:

---

[1] The text of the letter is deleted [eds.].

"We hereby confirm the letter of credit and undertake to honor any drafts presented to us on or before expiration date of the letter of credit in accordance with the terms and conditions of said letter of credit.

Very truly yours

/s/ Carl M. Harris

Executive Vice President"

This paragraph was not a part of the first letter which Mercantile sent to Barclays. It was added by Mr. Harris, the Executive Vice President of Mercantile, after Allied's first letter of credit and Mercantile's accompanying letter were not accepted by Barclays, allegedly because neither conformed to standard banking practice.

Barclays subsequently received a demand note executed by Bay Holding for $350,000 and thereafter transferred this sum to Bay's checking account at Barclays. On August 4, 1970, Allied wrote a letter to Barclays concerning an earlier telephone conversation in which Allied told Barclays that Bay had failed to comply with its agreement with Allied relative to the underlying real estate transaction. This letter "instructed" Barclays "that no further funds are to be drawn against the letter of credit without the written authorization from Allied Mortgage Consultants." Because it had previously transferred the entire $350,000 to Bay's account and believing that no action on its part was necessary, Barclays did nothing with respect to this letter.

There were no further developments until March 3, 1971, when Barclays notified Allied, pursuant to the terms of Allied's letter of credit, that it intended after ninety days to present its draft to Allied for any unpaid indebtedness of Bay Holding on its previously executed promissory note. On May 31, 1971, Barclays presented this note to Bay and demanded payment; it was dishonored and protested. Barclays then exercised its right of set-off by applying funds of Bay Holding on deposit with Barclays against the amount of the note. The resulting unpaid balance was $280,011.65. Thereafter Barclays timely presented its draft for the unpaid amount to Allied under the letter of credit, but this draft was dishonored. Barclays then presented the draft to Mercantile, demanding payment on the theory that Mercantile was a confirming bank on Allied's letter of credit by virtue of its June 1, 1970 letter to Barclays. Mercantile denied liability and this law suit followed.

The district court reasoned that Mercantile's letter was an unambiguous confirmation of Allied's letter of credit, the result of which left Mercantile, after Bay's default and Allied's dishonor, primarily liable for the full $280,011.65 under § 5-107(2)[1] of the U.C.C. as adopted in Georgia. As an alternative holding, the court opined that the letter also made Mercantile an issuer of credit under § 5-103(1)(a), which would also render Mercantile primarily liable. Judgment was entered accordingly and Mercantile appeals.

* * *

[1] All of the court's UCC citations are to pre-revised Article 5 [eds.].

Even though we have concluded that under the U.C.C. a bank may confirm a non-bank credit, we must still determine whether Mercantile's letter of June 1, 1970, was, in fact, a confirmation of the credit issued to Barclays by Allied. The thrust of Mercantile's argument is that the question of the intent of the parties concerning this letter should have been submitted to the jury. We agree with the district court that there is not present in this case any dispute for a jury to resolve.

The pertinent provisions of the June 1 letter are as follows:

> "We [Mercantile] hereby confirm the letter of credit and undertake to honor any drafts presented to us on or before expiration date of the letter of credit in accordance with the terms and conditions of said letter of credit."

The letter was signed by Carl M. Harris, the Executive Vice President of Mercantile, who handled this transaction. It appears from his deposition that he did not consult anyone at the bank regarding the language used in the letter or the legal effect of that language. Even though there is a dispute surrounding the manner in which the language was added—Barclays said that its representative, Mr. Swart, quoted the language to Mr. Harris over the telephone while Mr. Harris stated that the language is that given to him by Mr. Vano, a representative of Allied, who had apparently received the language from Mr. Swart—there is no dispute concerning the words used, and it is undisputed that the source of the language was Barclays Bank. Mercantile argues that it only intended to confirm the signatures on Allied's letter of credit, that it was only obligating itself as a "collecting bank" (whatever that means in this context), and that it did not agree to pay Barclays from its own funds. According to Mercantile, there is thus a disputed factual issue, the intent of the parties, on which it should have been allowed to present extrinsic evidence supporting its view to a jury.

We agree with Mercantile that as a general rule interpretation of a written agreement is a question of fact. Agreement on this point, however, does not compel the conclusion that a jury question is always created when parties supposedly differ regarding the meaning of terms used in a writing.

* * *

In determining whether to permit the introduction of extrinsic evidence of the parties' intent relative to meaning to the jury, the court must first determine that reasonable differing inferences as to meaning are raised by the words used in the context and circumstances of their use. The issue here then is whether the meaning attached to the third paragraph of Mercantile's letter by Barclays—that Mercantile confirmed Allied's letter of credit—is subject to a factual dispute entitled to be submitted to the jury.

In the circumstances of this case there was no dispute for the jury to resolve. One important factor is simply Mercantile's participation in this transaction. Barclays is entitled to assume that when dealing with another bank in a commercial undertaking that bank is competent to conduct its own affairs. Mr. Harris's deposition reveals that he did not completely understand what he was doing when he added the confirmatory language. But there are no allegations that Barclays deceived Mr. Harris or tricked him into adding the third paragraph of the letter. Mr. Harris's lack of understanding and failure of knowledge in this area of banking business cannot furnish an out for his employer, Mercantile. Barclays was entitled to rely on the statement in the letter which would justify a reasonable banker in concluding that Mercantile confirmed Allied's letter of credit. The language used conforms to that commonly employed in banking circles to confirm a letter of credit. Having employed words which give of but one meaning in the community of their use, Mercantile cannot escape the legal liability flowing from the use of those words by the assertion that it did not use them as they are commonly understood in banking circles.

In determining whether to allow extrinsic or parol evidence regarding the meaning of the June 1, 1970 letter to go to a jury, the district court was bound to apply the parol evidence rule, a rule of the substantive law of contract, as would a Georgia court. Harville Rose Service v. Kellogg Co., 448 F.2d 1346, 1349 (5th Cir. 1971). Applying the standard for the admissibility of parol evidence as formulated by the Georgia courts, we hold that the district court properly granted Barclays' motion for summary judgment.

Mercantile advances three additional theories on which to escape liability: (1) that Mercantile's obligation was a guaranty and as such is ultra vires for a national bank; (2) that Barclays failed to provide the necessary documentation accompanying its draft to Mercantile; and (3) that Barclays had a duty on the day Allied allegedly repudiated its letter of credit to withhold payment to Bay Holding of additional funds under the credit. We reject these contentions.

Mercantile's relationship to this transaction has been established as that of a confirming bank. "A confirming bank by confirming a credit becomes directly obligated on the credit to the extent of its confirmation as though it were its issuer and acquires the rights of an issuer." Section 5-107(2). "It may seem that a letter of credit is in the nature of a guaranty. In fact, there is a vast difference between a guaranty and a letter of credit. The issuer of a credit assumes a primary obligation to the beneficiary as opposed to a secondary liability under a guaranty."[1] It is clear that Mercantile's obligation here is not a guaranty.[2]

Mercantile next argues that it has no duty to pay the draft presented by Barclays because the draft was not accompanied by the proper documentation. The crucial, undisputed fact in this regard is that following the receipt of Barclays' draft Mercantile wrote a letter to Barclays on June 9, 1971, which although stating that the draft was being dishonored, acknowledged that the draft was accompanied "with all required documentation called for in the said Letter of

---

1 J. Halls, The Uniform Commercial Code in Minnesota: Article 5—Letters of Credit, 50 Minn. L. Rev. 453, 454 n.3 (1966).

2 As one commentator has noted:

> "A letter of credit always serves as a guaranty. This does not mean that it is a guaranty. A letter of credit is an identical twin to a guaranty, but the fact that the two things look alike and may be used for the same purpose and are difficult to distinguish one from the other, does not mean that they are the same thing, and does not mean that there are not differences, which, however subtle, are of major importance." H. Harfield, Uniform Commercial Code: Symposium-Code Treatment of Letters of Credit, 48 Corn. L.Q. 92, 93 (1963).

Credit." Mercantile now endeavors to escape liability by confessing that it made a mistake in the letter because hindsight reveals that Barclays did not furnish the proper documentation.

As did the district court, we will assume that the documentation furnished by Barclays was faulty. We nonetheless agree with the district court that it is too late in the journey to raise this defect. Since Allied's letter of credit did not expire until June 15, 1971, if Mercantile had notified Barclays on June 9, 1971, that the documentation furnished was improper, Barclays might have remedied the defect. To allow Mercantile to raise this defense, founded upon its own admitted mistake and after affirmatively stating that all required documentation was present, would not comport with our abstract sense of justice, nor, and more importantly, with the rule applied in cases involving letters of credit that "[b]y formally placing its refusal to pay on one ground, the defendant must be held to have waived all others." Bank of Taiwan v. Union National Bank, 1 F.2d 65, 66 (3rd Cir. 1924). See also Continental National Bank v. National City Bank, 69 F.2d 312, 318-319 (9th Cir. 1934).

Mercantile points out that this rule has not heretofore been applied by this circuit nor by the courts of Georgia. The more significant fact, however, is that it has not been rejected. Under Erie R. R. Co. v. Tompkins, 304 U.S. 64, 58 S.Ct. 817, 82 L.Ed. 1188 (1938), we are therefore free to apply this rule because we believe that it would be applied by the Georgia Supreme Court.

It is apparent from Mercantile's June 9 letter that its refusal to pay the draft was not premised on the absence of the proper documents. The letter states affirmatively that the documentation was satisfactory. Payment was refused because Mercantile did not believe that it was liable to pay the draft from its own funds. In addition, Mercantile's appellate brief reveals that Mr. Harris did not even examine the documents to determine if, in fact, they did conform. According to the brief, he simply took Barclays' word that all required documentation accompanied the draft. Mercantile again seems to be of the view that Barclays should bear the brunt of Mr. Harris's failure to ascertain what was going on, that, for some unexplainable reason, Barclays is to blame for Mercantile's failure to adequately perform its banking duties. Mercantile cannot lull Barclays into believing that there was no problem with the documentation when there was still time for Barclays to have attempted to cure the technical defect and then turn around and assert the lack thereof as a defense to the suit on the draft. Having informed Barclays that the documentation was proper, Mercantile must, on the facts of this case, be held to have waived the alleged faulty documentation as a defense.

There are no provisions in Article 5 which would indicate a belief on the part of the drafters that this doctrine of waiver should be inapplicable under the U.C.C. Absent a disavowal of the rule, a section providing to the contrary, or a section which conflicts with the purpose of this rule, § 5-102(3) provides an adequate source for the conclusion that this rule of waiver may be applied in appropriate cases. "Subsection (3) [§ 5-102(3)] recognizes that in the present state of the law and variety of practices as to letters of credit, no statute can effectively or wisely codify all the possible law of letters of credit without stultifying further development of this useful device." Section 5-102(3), Comment 2. Our decision that the rule should be applied to Mercantile is in accord with a court's duty to construe Article 5, as well as the other rules relating to letters of credit not codified in this Article, in such a manner as to conform the rules to an underlying sense of fair play so that the expectations of the parties to a business transaction will not be frustrated by the application of a rule which is not grounded in sound policy considerations.

* * *

The purpose served by ruling that this transaction is within the Code is that commercial undertakings are facilitated if businessmen (and perhaps also their lawyers) can be reasonably certain of the set of rules which will govern their activity. As a particular transaction is planned, there are, of course, many considerations other than the legal aspects of a specific course of action. But a businessman would be derelict in his planning if he did not ask the question: What rules will apply if this transaction goes sour or fails to meet expectations? The instant case is an example of both adequate and inadequate planning. Instead of merely relying on the promissory note of Bay Holding and the security accompanying it, Barclays sought a letter of credit from a party who was apparently in better financial condition and more easily accessible than Bay Holding. The relationship with Allied was thus born. Allied was willing to issue its letter of credit because of its expectation of receiving a monetary reward from Bay for aiding Bay in obtaining the money from Barclays. It is most significant that the device chosen by Barclays and Allied to be the basis of their relationship was the letter of credit which results in the creation of a relationship independent of the underlying transaction between the issuer of the credit and its customer, or between the customer and the beneficiary of the credit.

Mercantile came into the picture because Barclays was not completely satisfied with its relationship with Allied and because Allied sought help from its banker in carrying the commercial undertaking through to completion. The tool used to involve Mercantile was a letter confirming Allied's credit. The pains taken by Barclays to assure that Mercantile's letter met the common requirements of a letter of confirmation is unmistakably indicative of a purpose to create an independent relationship with Mercantile Bank. In short, Barclays was planning for the contingency which did in fact occur. Mercantile has not presented, and we are unable to discern, any reason to frustrate this planning.

The judgment of the district court is affirmed.

MACINTOSH, LETTERS OF CREDIT: CURBING BAD FAITH DISHONOR, 25 U.C.C. L.J. 3, 3-4, 29-32 (1992).

[In the article excerpted below, Professor Macintosh identified three responses for dealing with letter of credit issuers that dishonor a beneficiary's demand for payment on the pretext that the documents did not conform when in reality it is the issuer's loss of a right of reimbursement that drives the decision. First, some courts and commentators argued that imposing a broadened good faith standard on the issuer and giving the beneficiary a cause of action if the issuer acted in violation of the standard would alleviate the problem. The second suggested response was to relax the strict compliance rule of letter of credit law, so that issuers could not dishonor the beneficiary's draft unless documentary defects were substantial.

Professor Macintosh argued that these responses would destroy the letter of credit as an efficient commercial device because both would require the issuer's document examiners to make complex commercial or legal judgments rather than the ministerial judgments that the strict compliance rule allows. She concluded that there was a third and better way.]

Recent studies reveal an astonishing fact: Up to 90 percent of documents initially presented for payment under letters of credit do not comply with stated terms and conditions for payment. Fortunately, most documentary defects are waived by customers or cured by beneficiaries, so that issuers ultimately dishonor only one percent of all presentations. Nevertheless, disputes regarding documentary compliance still account for most letter-of-credit litigation.

In the last few years, beneficiaries have unleashed a powerful new weapon in such litigation: the bad-faith claim. Unwilling to accept defeat, even in cases where the presence of documentary defects would ordinarily justify dishonor, beneficiaries are alleging that issuers dishonored defective presentations for ulterior reasons or that issuers deliberately prevented them from curing documentary defects. Moreover, beneficiaries are no longer satisfied with the limited statutory remedy for wrongful dishonor and are supplementing complaints with allegations of bad-faith conduct in an attempt to recover enormous punitive damage awards.

Bad-faith conduct that frustrates the beneficiary's reasonable expectation of prompt and reliable payment defeats the basic purpose of the letter of credit. The purpose of this article is to discover and recommend some means of effectively curbing such conduct, without inadvertently impairing the commercial utility of the letter of credit.

* * *

There is [an] indirect method of curbing pretextual dishonor that does not compromise the commercial utility of the letter of credit: facilitation of documentary cure. Given enough time and information, the beneficiary can often cure documentary defects before the credit expires, leaving the issuer with no choice but to honor his complying second presentation.

Existing statutory law requires every issuer to dishonor promptly and return documents to the beneficiary. The Code gives an issuer only three banking days following receipt of documents to decide whether to honor or dishonor. An issuer cannot delay its decision beyond these three days, for any such delay constitutes dishonor. Moreover, upon dishonor, the issuer must either return the draft or other demand for payment together with accompanying documents, or hold the documents at the disposal of the presenter while sending him an advice to that effect. If the issuer fails to do so within three banking days following receipt of the documents, it is accountable to the beneficiary for the amount of his draft or demand.

Unfortunately, the Code does not expressly require the issuer to identify the documentary defects that compel dishonor. Without this vital information, the beneficiary does not know what he must do to cure. However, many letters of credit incorporate the Uniform Customs and Practice for Documentary Credits (UCP), a statement of international customs and practice. The UCP gives an issuer a reasonable time to examine documents and decide whether to honor or dishonor. Notice of dishonor must be given without delay to the presenting bank, or to the beneficiary if the documents were received directly from him. Significantly, this notice must identify the defects that led the issuer to dishonor and state whether the documents will be returned or held at the disposal of the presenting bank or beneficiary. If the issuer fails to comply with these requirements, it is strictly precluded from claiming that the documents are not in accordance with the credit terms, leaving the beneficiary with an ironclad claim for wrongful dishonor.

Of course, not all letters of credit incorporate the UCP. Some courts have used equitable principles to impose similar requirements, holding that an issuer is estopped to assert documentary defects when it deprives the beneficiary of the opportunity to cure before the credit expires by waiting too long to dishonor or return documents. Other courts have held that an issuer that fails to adequately identify documentary defects waives any defects that the beneficiary could have cured with proper notice.

Although few courts have recognized its significance, the good-faith obligation can help to facilitate documentary cure in two important ways. First, the obligation prohibits the issuer from deliberately attempting to *thwart* cure. Under the Code, the issuer has an obligation to perform the letter-of-credit contract in good faith (i.e., honestly). Surely, honest performance excludes deliberate efforts to cheat the beneficiary out of the opportunity to present complying documents and receive payment under the credit. Therefore, if an issuer delays dishonor, withholds documents, or fails to identify defects for the purpose of preventing cure, it acts in bad faith under the Code. Similarly, under the common law, when one party evades the spirit of the bargain, he breaches the covenant of good faith and fair dealing implied in every contract. From the beneficiary's point of view, the very heart of the letter-of-credit bargain is the opportunity to present complying documents and obtain prompt, reliable payment. Thus, if an issuer delays dishonor, withholds documents, or fails to identify defects for the purpose of preventing cure, it acts in bad faith under the common law.

Second, the good-faith obligation imposes an affirmative obligation upon the issuer to *cooperate* with the beneficiary in his attempt to cure documentary defects. Summers theorizes that failure to cooperate in the other party's performance can constitute bad faith. To illustrate this point, he cites a case holding that an insurer has a good-faith obligation to identify deficiencies in the insured's notice and proof of loss, and give the insured an opportunity to correct the deficiencies. Reasoning by analogy, when a beneficiary presents noncomplying documents, the issuer has a good-faith obligation to promptly identify defects, so that the beneficiary has the opportunity to correct them before the credit expires. Significantly, the good-faith obligation requires such cooperation *even in cases where the letter of credit does not incorporate the UCP or otherwise expressly require identification of documentary defects.*

* * *

NOTE ON REVISED RULES

Professor Macintosh's prescription for preventing bad faith dishonor is now the law. Revised Article 5 requires the issuer or nominated bank to examine the documents and to notify the beneficiary of defects within a reasonable time after presentation, not to exceed seven banking days. See UCC § 5-108(b). Many bankers will tell you that three days is usually enough time to examine routine presentations. The section, moreover, precludes the issuer from raising defects if it does not examine the documents and give the notice of defects within a reasonable period of time. UCC § 5-108(c). UCP 500 contains a similar rule. Courts generally enforce the preclusion and time rules against issuers vigorously.

UCC § 5-108(b) &(c)
(*see Selected Commercial Statutes*)

NOTE ON THE UNIFORM CUSTOMS

The Committee on Banking Technique and Practice of the International Chamber of Commerce has, from time to time, promulgated the Uniform Customs and Practice for Documentary Credits, commonly referred to as the UCP. The current version of the UCP is UCP 500, which was promulgated in 1993. Most letters of credit issued throughout the world, including most credits issued by U.S. banks, incorporate the UCP by reference.

Originally, the ICC drafted the UCP in order to rationalize practices involving commercial letters of credit. Those letters of credit support the international sale of goods and traditionally involve an invoice from the foreign seller, the bill of lading covering transport of the goods to the buyer, insurance documents and various other documents relating to the goods. With the rise of the standby letter of credit, which supports virtually any executory promise, the ICC extended the UCP to the standby; and the letter of credit industry incorporated the UCP into the standby.

Generally, UCP 500 sets out rules of practice, rather than legal rules. The UCP, then, supplements a statutory regime such as Article 5 or the UN Convention on Independent Bank Guarantees and Stand-by Letters of Credit. Article 5 refers to the UCP and acknowledges that where the credit incorporates UCP 500, in the event of a conflict between Article 5 and the UCP, the UCP will govern unless the conflict is with one of Article 5's few nonvariable provisions. § 5-116(c).

One of the rules in UCP 500 requires the issuer of a credit to examine the beneficiary's documents promptly. UCP 500 art. 13(a) & (b). Article 14(d) requires the issuer to notify the beneficiary without delay if the issuer decides that the documents do not conform to the conditions of the credit. In that event, the issuer may have elected to dishonor the beneficiary's draft; and the notice must recite the defects in the documents. The obvious purpose of the notice is to permit the beneficiary to correct defects, if there is still time under the credit to do that, or to make other arrangements for the sale of the goods, if the credit is a commercial credit. The rule, then, is very pro-beneficiary, for coupled with it is a preclusion rule, as the following excerpt and case illustrate.

UNIFORM CUSTOMS AND PRACTICE FOR DOCUMENTARY CREDITS (UCP 500) art. 14(e).

"If the Issuing Bank and/or Confirming Bank, if any, fails to act in accordance with the provisions of this Article and/or fails to hold the documents at the disposal of, or return them to the presenter, the Issuing Bank and/or the Confirming Bank, if any, shall be precluded from claiming that the documents are not in compliance with the terms and conditions of the credit."

QUESTION

Why would a committee of international bankers fashion pro-beneficiary rules in their Uniform Customs and Practice and then put teeth into them by creating a strict estoppel, i.e., preclusion, rule for banks that do not observe the pro-beneficiary rules?

KUNTAL, S.A. v. BANK OF NEW YORK

United States District Court, Southern District of New York, 1989.
703 F. Supp. 312.

WALKER, District Judge.

* * *

The relevant facts can be summarized in brief. On October 14, 1986, the Bank of New York ("the Bank") issued letter of credit no. I 23825 (the "LC") for the account of a New York buyer, Six Continents Ltd. ("Six Continents") in favor of Kuntal, S.A. ("Kuntal"), a Uruguayan seller of sweaters to Six Continents. Hispano Americana Casa Bancaria of Montevideo, Uruguay ("Hisbank") acted as the presenting bank on the credit, and subsequently assigned its rights under the LC to Kuntal. By its terms, the LC falls under the Uniform Customs and Practice for Documentary Credits (1983 Revision), International Chamber of Commerce Publication 400 ("UCP 400").

Six Continents, a New York corporation, sought to purchase cotton sweaters from Kuntal in Montevideo, Uruguay. On January 20, 1987, the cotton sweaters were shipped by air from Uruguay to New York. On February 12, 1987, Six

Continents requested that the Bank release the goods to Six Continents. On that same day, the Bank issued an air release and Six Continents received the goods. Neither Kuntal nor Hisbank authorized the Bank to issue an air release to Six Continents for the goods.

On February 19, 1987, the Bank received the shipping documents. There were three discrepancies between the LC and the shipping documents: (1) shipment was effected to New York instead of Boston as in the LC; (2) the LC called for shipment of a greater number of sweaters than was actually shipped; and (3) the airway bill was consigned to the Bank instead of to the account party as required by the LC. On March 4, 1987, the Bank first gave Hisbank notice of the Bank's refusal of the documents for the three reasons above, and informed Hisbank that the Bank was holding the documents at Hisbank's disposal.

The parties further agree that both the shipping documents and the February 12 air release reflect 38 cartons of sweaters. On March 9, 1987, Six Continents placed 29 cartons of sweaters in a bonded warehouse. By letter dated March 18, 1987, Six Continents informed the Bank not only that 38 cartons of sweaters were repacked into 29 cartons, but also that Six Continents had requested a packing list from Six Continents' customer.

To date, the Bank has refused payment under the LC to either Hisbank or Kuntal. Kuntal brought this action seeking payment pursuant to the terms of the LC. Plaintiff recognizes that the discrepancies in the documents would, in the ordinary course of business, justify the Bank's refusal to honor the letter of credit. Before this Court, however, plaintiff presents two discrete legal questions, arguing in the alternative that a favorable answer to either compels judgment in its favor. First, did the Bank, by its release of the goods to its customer, waive its objections to the discrepancies in the documents? And, second, did the Bank, by its two week delay not only in determining whether to accept or refuse the documents but also in giving notice of its refusal of the documents, waive its objections to the discrepancies in the documents? It is unnecessary to address plaintiff's first argument; the Court concludes that plaintiff's second argument supports its request for summary judgment.

DISCUSSION

Under the UCP 400, if an issuing bank decides to refuse letter of credit documents, it "must give notice to that effect without delay by telecommunication or, if that is not possible, by other expeditious means, to the bank from which it received the documents * * * or to the beneficiary * * *." UCP 400, Article 16(d). The UCP 400 further provides that if the issuing bank fails to act in accordance with Article 16(d), then the bank "shall be precluded from claiming that the documents are not in accordance with the terms and conditions of the credit." Id. Article 16(e).

Plaintiff argues that the Bank's two week delay in giving Kuntal notice of the Bank's decision to refuse the documents waives the discrepancies therein. The Bank presents essentially the same story under a slightly different light. The documents, the Bank states, arrived at the Bank on February 19, 1987.

Under UCP 16(c), an issuing bank is allowed a reasonable time to examine the documents, and the Bank examined the submitted documents two business days later on February 23, 1987. 9 days later on March 4, 1987, the Bank gave notice to Hisbank [which, as noted above, has assigned its rights in this matter to Kuntal] under Article 16(d) of the UCP.

The Bank explains that "the delay in giving Article 16(d) notice was for the purpose of allowing Six Continents to decide whether it would accept a deal that been altered unilaterally by Kuntal."

Nowhere, however, does the Bank suggest why Six Continents needed 9 full days to reach a decision on whether or not to accept the deal. Furthermore, its position is "at odds with the basic letter of credit tenet that banks deal solely with documents, not in goods." Bank of Cochin Ltd. v. Manufacturers Hanover Trust, 612 F.Supp. 1533, 1543 (S.D.N.Y.1985), aff'd, 808 F.2d 209 (2d Cir.1986).[1]

The Bank correctly notes that UCP 400 does not specifically define the terms "reasonable time" or "without delay." However, "the phrase ['without delay'] is akin to 'immediate (at once), instant, instantaneous, instantly, prompt.' All of these synonyms connote a sense of urgent action within the shortest interval of time possible." Cochin, 808 F.2d at 213 (citation omitted) (holding that "a twelve to thirteen day lapse of time cannot be considered notification 'without delay' under any reasonable definition of that phrase"). In addition, the Bank's "argument would defeat the letter of credit's function of being a swift, fluid and reliable financing device." Cochin, 612 F.Supp. at 1543 (citation omitted).

Although the facts of this case admittedly are not as compelling as those that were present in Cochin—which involved large scale fraud—the same principle animates both decisions. In the absence of any persuasive and reasonable justification for the Bank's 9 day delay following its examination of the documents, this Court concludes that the delay waived the issuing bank's right to object to discrepancies between the LC and the relevant shipping documents. As the Second Circuit Court of Appeals explained, "[i]n this era of near instantaneous international communications, we can find no rationale to justify [the Bank's] delay in informing [the beneficiary] of the specific defects and of its intention to return the documents." Cochin, 808 F.2d at 213. In this case, the Bank has offered no convincing rationale to justify its delay.

CONCLUSION

Accordingly, the Court grants plaintiff's motion for summary judgment.

PRICE & PIERCE INTERNATIONAL, INC. v. CIMEX, U.S.A., INC., LETTER OF CREDIT UPDATE 35 (July 1987) (N.Y. Sup. Ct. 1987), aff'd w/o op. sub nom., PRICE & PIERCE INTERNATIONAL, INC. v. HANIL BANK

---

1 The Cochin case addressed Articles 8(d) and (e) of the 1974 version of the UCP, the predecessor to UCP 400. Articles 16(c) and (d) from the 1983 revision are virtually identical to Articles 8(d) and (e), a fact neither side in this case disputes.

LTD., 523 N.Y.S.2d 333 (App. Div.), appeal denied, 528 N.E.2d 521 (1988). In this case the issuer had failed to notify the beneficiary promptly of its decision to dishonor, but the beneficiary had failed to show detriment caused by the delay. The court ruled for the beneficiary, that failure notwithstanding. In the course of its opinion, the trial court referred to testimony by an expert witness, Henry Harfield, who had authored the leading letter of credit treatise at the time and who, as a partner in a New York law firm, had represented the nation's then largest credit issuer, Citibank. Harfield testified that banks should give prompt notice to the beneficiary of the bank's decision to dishonor in order to avoid waste. Prompt notice permits the beneficiary of a commercial credit to make different shipping arrangements and to see to the disposal of the rejected goods. Delays can be exceedingly costly.

UCC § 5-108(b)(3) & (c)

(*See Selected Commercial Statutes*)

NOTE ON WAIVER

Regrettably, some courts dealing with estoppel or preclusion rules fall into "waiver" rhetoric. They hold that by conduct that gives rise to an estoppel a party waives its rights. Waiver is the intentional relinquishment of a known right and is about as closely related to estoppel as badminton is to lacrosse.

(c) Documents of Title

UCC § 7-503(1)(a) & (b)

(*see Selected Commercial Statutes*)

PROBLEM

Doctor Cleveland, who lived in the city, leased the family farm he inherited to Jack McNabb under a lease that provided for payment to Cleveland by McNabb of $50 for every acre planted in cotton and $10 for every acre planted in beans. McNabb had been farming under the lease for some time, and it was his practice to harvest the crops, store them against negotiable warehouse receipts, sell the receipts to grain companies or cotton gins, and remit the rent to his landlord. One year, times were hard; and McNabb used the cash he received from the sale of the receipts to pay creditors other than Doctor Cleveland.

McNabb is insolvent. Cleveland is suing the cotton gin and grain company for his rent. Under state law, the crops are subject to a landlord's lien. What result? See UCC § 7-503(1)(a) & (b).

SECTION 2. BAD FAITH

INTRODUCTORY NOTE

This is an area of hot debate. How can anyone argue that he is not subject to a requirement of honesty and observance of standards of fair dealing? Well, many lawyers make the arguments, some of which are reproduced in the law review excerpts and cases that follow.

Essentially, the pro-good faith forces want an end to sharp practices, especially by "big" guys against "little" guys. The anti-good faith people generally deny that there are standards of fair dealing in the trade or that fact finders will be able to figure out what they are. Both sides usually, though not always, agree that parties must behave honestly—a subjective rule. The debate is mostly over the standards of fair dealing, an objective rule.

The debate is hot in part because lawyers know that language matters, but the fact is that although the pro-good faith forces are winning most of the legislative battles, the anti-good faith forces are winning most of the cases. In late 1997, the lender liability war appears to have gone to the lenders. Courts are happy to award grand judgments in favor of tort claimants who suffer personal injury; but are rather cheap with commercial claimants who argue that some banker used sharp practices against them.

Perhaps the courts are just more conservative than formerly. Perhaps the rash of bank insolvencies and the savings and loan debacle of the 1980s convinced the courts that large judgments against financial intermediaries are not always cost free. Whatever the reason, the courts seem to be saying that the commercial world is a rough and tumble place with considerable heat and that if you can't stand the heat . . . .

SUMMERS, "GOOD FAITH" IN GENERAL CONTRACT LAW AND THE SALES PROVISIONS OF THE UNIFORM COMMERCIAL CODE, 54 Va. L. Rev. 195, 196-99 (1968).

[T]his Article will deal with * * * requirements of good faith recognized in contract case law and in Code provisions on sales, a much neglected area of study. The focus will be on three questions. First, what meaning have the courts and the Code draftsmen given to the phrase "good faith"? It will be argued that good faith, as used in the case law, is best understood as an "excluder"—it is a phrase which has no general meaning or meanings of its own, but which serves to exclude many heterogeneous forms of bad faith. It will also be suggested that if the Code draftsmen had perceived this, they would not have given the term the general, invariant meaning: "honesty in fact in the conduct or transaction concerned."

The second question is: In what circumstances do case law and the Code provisions on sales impose obligations of good faith? Although it has not been possible to do a comprehensive survey of the cases, it can be seen from the ones reviewed here that the duties judges have imposed in the name of contractual good faith are more varied and numerous than anyone has yet recognized in print. On the other hand, it will be seen that the Code's explicit requirements of good faith in sales transactions are less extensive than some scholars would have us believe. It will also be suggested that extra-Code law on good faith—via section 1-103, which states that "general principles" are to supplement the Code's specific provisions—will prove a more fertile source of Code requirements of good faith than will the Code sections which use these very words.

The theories on which courts have afforded relief against contractual bad faith include contract, tort and quasi-contract. And the forms of such relief are highly varied, ranging from denial of any recovery to the award of punitive damages. Our final question is: What adjustments might be made in these theories and forms to provide more adequate relief? Several modest proposals will be set forth, not as final solutions, but as suggestions worthy of further consideration. Among other things, it will be argued that courts should resort to tort law more often than they have to combat bad faith.

Before taking up the first question, it is appropriate to explain in some detail why the imposition and refinement of legal standards of good faith are of potentially great significance in contractual contexts, commercial and noncommercial. First of all, in these contexts good faith has pervasive and distinctive relevance. It is natural for two parties to assume that each will act in good faith toward the other throughout the course of their contractual dealings. Moreover, morals obligate them to act this way. Yet, in one sense their interest will remain essentially antagonistic, for each will be expecting to get something from the other on advantageous terms. And, in a given case, misunderstandings may arise, unforeseen events occur, expected gains disappear or dislikes develop which may motivate one party to act in bad faith. If, however, such a party is legally as well as morally obligated to act in good faith, he will be significantly less likely to break faith.

Good faith is not only peculiarly and pervasively relevant in contractual matters, it is also part of a family of general legal doctrines, including implied promise, custom and usage, fraud, negligence and estoppel, which perform significant functions in this field. These doctrines supplement, limit and qualify specific legal rules and contact terms, and some of them also serve as substantive bases of liability independent of contract. The functions they perform further the most fundamental policy objectives of any legal system—justice, and justice according to law. By invoking good faith, implying a promise or working an estoppel it may be possible for a judge to do justice *and* do it according to law. Without legal resources of this general nature he might, in a particular case, be unable to do justice at all, or he might be able to do it only at the cost of fictionalizing existing legal concepts and rules, thereby snarling up the law for future cases. In begetting snarl, fiction may introduce inequity, unclarity or unpredictability. In addition, fiction can divert analytical focus or even cast aspersions on an innocent party.

It should be emphasized that in the foregoing family of general doctrines, good faith has its own distinctive potential. For example, a judge may resort to it as an independent theory of liability for misconduct which is neither fraudulent nor negligent. He may rely on it to enforce the unspecified "inner logic" of a deal when custom and usage are silent and when the true basis for implying a promise is that good faith requires as much. He can also invoke it to help prevent the abuse of powers conferred by contract when the elements of estoppel are absent. Thus good faith is both a pervasively relevant and an independently significant doctrine in the fields of contracts and sales.

UCC § 1-201(22), Revised UCC Article 1
[Discussion Draft—September 1997]

"Good Faith," except as provided in Article 5, means honesty in fact and the observance of reasonable commercial standards of fair dealing.

JUENGER, LISTENING TO LAW PROFESSORS TALK ABOUT GOOD FAITH: SOME AFTERTHOUGHTS, 69 Tul. L. Rev. 1253, 1255-56 (1995).

To be sure, concepts such as good faith and abuse of rights did grow on civilian soil, yet there are analogies in the common-law world, the most notable being the chancellor who assumed the task of dispensing equity as a necessary antidote to the common law's rigidity and formalism. The chancellor's "good conscience" is but another verbal variant of justice, the basic ingredient of good faith.

* * *

But the fact that the term "good faith" is essentially meaningless does not furnish a good reason for rejecting it. American constitutional law would be considerably poorer absent vague terms such as "due process" and "equal protection" phrases that—like good faith—invite judges to heed tenets of fundamental fairness when making their decisions.

DIMATTEO, THE COUNTERPOISE OF CONTRACTS: THE REASONABLE PERSON STANDARD AND THE SUBJECTIVITY OF JUDGMENT, 48 S. Car. L. Rev. 293, 330 (1997). "The importance and complexity of trade usage and commercial practice led Llewellyn to believe that the reasonable person as applied by a judge or jury was ill-equipped to make such determinations of fact. '[F]ew judges have the specialized skill in such matters * * * and juries are notoriously out of touch with such matters.' The reasonable person does not possess the highly technical and specialized knowledge needed to determine what was considered a reasonable practice or usage in a given trade or profession. Llewellyn believed that such decisions should be abdicated to a merchant tribunal or to expert arbitrators. His idea for a merchant tribunal was never adopted despite his strong advocacy. The reasonable person remains the final arbiter of commercial reasonableness."

UCC § 5-108(e)
(See Selected Commercial Statutes)

K.M.C. CO. v. IRVING TRUST CO.

United States Court of Appeals, Sixth Circuit, 1984.
757 F.2d 752.

KENNEDY, Circuit Judge.

Irving Trust Company (Irving) appeals from a judgment entered against it in this diversity action for breach of a financing agreement. K.M.C. is a Tennessee corporation headquartered in Knoxville and engaged in the wholesale and retail grocery business. In 1979, Irving and K.M.C. entered into a financing agreement, whereby Irving held a security interest in all of K.M.C.'s accounts receivable and inventory and provided K.M.C. a line of credit to a maximum of $3.0 million, increased one year later to $3.5 million at a lower rate of interest, subject to a formula based on a percentage of the value of the inventory plus eligible receivables. On March 1, 1982, Irving refused to advance $800,000 requested by K.M.C. This amount would have increased the loan balance to just under the $3.5 million limit. K.M.C. contends that Irving's refusal without prior notice to advance the requested funds breached a duty of good faith performance implied in the agreement and ultimately resulted in the collapse of the company as a viable business entity. Irving's defense is that on March 1, 1982, K.M.C. was already collapsing, and that Irving's decision not to advance funds was made in good faith and in the reasonable exercise of its discretion under the agreement.

* * *

The jury found Irving liable for breach of contract and fixed damages at $7,500,000 plus pre-judgment interest. Defendant's motions to dismiss and for a directed verdict and post-trial motions for judgment n.o.v., a new trial or a remittitur were denied.

* * *

Irving contends that the Magistrate erred in instructing the jury with respect to its obligations under the financing agreement, that K.M.C. failed to sustain its burden of showing that Irving acted in bad faith and that the jury's verdict was against the weight of the evidence. We conclude that the jury instructions were not in error and that the jury's verdict was supported by substantial evidence.

* * *

The essence of the Magistrate's instruction to the jury was that there is implied in every contract an obligation of good faith; that this obligation may have imposed on Irving a duty to give notice to K.M.C. before refusing to advance funds under the agreement up to the $3.5 million limit; and that such notice would be required if necessary to the proper execution of the contract, unless Irving's decision to refuse to advance funds without prior notice was made in good faith and in the reasonable exercise of its discretion. Irving contends that the instruction with respect to notice gave undue emphasis to K.M.C.'s theory of the case and was an erroneous explanation of its contractual obligations, in that the decision whether to advance funds under the financing agreement was solely within the bank's prerogative. It reasons further that an implied requirement that the bank provide a period of notice before discontinuing financing up to the maximum credit limit would be inconsistent with the provision in the agreement that all monies loaned are repayable on demand.

As part of the procedure established for the operation of the financing agreement, the parties agreed in a supplementary letter that all receipts of K.M.C. would be deposited into a "blocked account" to which Irving would have sole access. Consequently, unless K.M.C. obtained alternative financing, a refusal by Irving to advance funds would leave K.M.C. without operating capital until it had paid down its loan. The record clearly established that a medium-sized company in the wholesale grocery business, such as K.M.C., could not operate without outside financing. Thus, the literal interpretation of the financing agreement urged upon us by Irving, as supplemented by the "blocked account" mechanism, would leave K.M.C.'s continued existence entirely at the whim or mercy of Irving, absent an obligation of good faith performance. Logically, at such time as Irving might wish to curtail financing K.M.C., as was its right under the agreement, this obligation to act in good faith would require a period of notice to K.M.C. to allow it a reasonable opportunity to seek alternate financing, absent valid business reasons precluding Irving from doing so. Hence, we find that the Magistrate's instructions were an accurate statement of the applicable law. See Wells v. Alexandre, 130 N.Y. 642, 29 N.E. 142, 143 (1891) ("[I]f a notice was requisite to its proper execution, a covenant to give such notice will be inferred, for any other construction would make the contract unreasonable, and place one of the parties entirely at the mercy of the other." (citations omitted)); cf. U.C.C. § 2-309 comment 8 ("[T]he application of principles of good faith and sound commercial practice normally call for such notification of the termination of a going contract relationship as will give the other party reasonable time to seek a substitute arrangement.").

* * *

Nor are we persuaded by Irving's reasoning with respect to the effect of the demand provision in the agreement. We agree with the Magistrate that just as Irving's discretion whether or not to advance funds is limited by an obligation of good faith performance, so too would be its power to demand repayment. The demand provision is a kind of acceleration clause, upon which the Uniform Commercial Code and the courts have imposed limitations of reasonableness and fairness. See U.C.C. § 1-208; Brown v. AVEMCO Investment Corp., 603 F.2d 1367, 1375-80 (9th Cir.1979). The Magistrate did not err in refusing the requested charge on the demand provision.

Irving did not object to the good faith portion of the Magistrate's instruction. Nevertheless, on appeal it suggests for the first time that before liability can be imposed, the proof must establish not only abuse of discretion but also bad faith, which it defines as synonymous with dishonesty. Even if such an argument were timely at this stage in the proceedings, which it is not, none of the cases cited by Irving are on point.

* * *

Irving contends that the sole factor determinative of whether it acted in good faith is whether it, through its loan officer Sarokin, believed that there existed valid reasons for not advancing funds to K.M.C. on March 1, 1982. It quotes Blaine v. G.M.A.C., 82 Misc.2d 653, 655, 370 N.Y.S. 2d 323, 327 (1975), for the proposition that under applicable New York law, it is the bank's "actual mental state" that is decisive. The Magistrate observed that there was competent evidence that a personality conflict had developed between Sarokin and Butler of K.M.C. He suggested that the jury may have concluded that Sarokin abused his discretion in refusing without notice to advance funds despite knowing that he was fully secured because of his disapproval of Butler's management philosophy.

Were the outcome of this case solely dependent upon Sarokin's subjective state of mind, we might feel constrained, despite the conclusions of the Magistrate above, to hold that the evidence was insufficient to support the verdict. However, to a certain extent the conduct of Irving must be measured by objective standards. While it is not necessary that Sarokin have been correct in his understanding of the facts and circumstances pertinent to his decision not to advance funds for this court to find that he made a valid business judgment in doing so, there must at least be some objective basis upon which a reasonable loan officer in the exercise of his discretion would have acted in that manner.[1]

James Kuharski was executive vice president and manager of secured lending activities for Irving, and two levels above Sarokin in Irving's management hierarchy. Kuharski acknowledged that Irving owed its clients a duty of good faith, that it was not a policy of Irving to terminate financing without notice, and that if Sarokin believed that Irving was adequately secured he would not have been acting in accordance with that duty of good faith to have refused without notice to advance funds to K.M.C.

William Calloway was president of the Park National Bank in Knoxville, which was the depository bank for K.M.C.'s "blocked account" and a 20% participant with Irving in the financing agreement. He also acknowledged that he believed that there is a duty of good faith from a banker to his client that would require a period of notice prior to termination of financing if a loan was well secured. He testified further that on March 1, he believed that the loan to K.M.C. was fully secured as to both interest and principal, and that any reasonable banker looking at the loan would agree that it was fully secured.

Gerald Connolly was an attorney in Milwaukee, Wisconsin, one of whose clients was a large wholesaler named Gateway Foods. In response to a call from Butler on March 1, Gateway's president requested that Connolly assist K.M.C. in

---

1 While the appellee suggests in its brief that the Magistrate charged the jury on a wholly subjective standard, we do not read the charge that way. The jury was charged "that what is important in connection with the requirement of good faith is the actual mental state of the officers and agents of Irving Trust." The definition of an arbitrary and capricious decision that followed, as one "having no rational basis," is consonant with our analysis. * * * There is ample evidence in the record to support a jury finding that no reasonable loan officer in the same situation would have refused to advance funds to K.M.C. without notice as Sarokin did on March 1, 1982.

any way he could. Connolly testified that pursuant to that request he called Sarokin, who acknowledged in their conversation that Irving was adequately secured and that terminating financing would destroy K.M.C., and that Sarokin ultimately agreed to advance the funds requested by K.M.C., in part to give Connolly the opportunity to come to Knoxville and evaluate K.M.C. for the purpose of acquisition by Gateway Foods. Connolly testified that he called Irving the next day enroute to Knoxville and was told by a subordinate that Sarokin had changed his mind about advancing funds, and that in a telephone conversation that night Sarokin stated that he had changed his mind and decided to "proceed with his game plan."

In fact, counsel for Irving conceded in his summation to the jury that the bank was adequately secured on March 1, 1982. He argued, however, that what is important is not the amount of security, but the capacity of the debtor to pay back the loan. The jury was entitled to find that a reasonable notice period would not change the ability of K.M.C. to pay the loan. The nature of the security was such that the loan would rapidly be paid down on demand. Irving's quarterly audits and other memoranda regarding K.M.C. consistently stated that the strength of its position was in the inventory, which was readily marketable. As late as two months before the events in question, the quarterly audit had concluded that even in the event of a liquidation of the company no loss would be sustained by Irving.

Generally, there was ample evidence in the record from which the jury could have concluded that March 1 simply was not that unusual a day in the history of the relationship between Irving and K.M.C. Such factors as payables and receivables, cited by Sarokin as the basis for his conclusion that K.M.C. was in a state of financial collapse, were closely monitored by Irving. Moreover, three days later, on March 4, Sarokin agreed to advance $700,000 to K.M.C., increasing its outstanding balance to $3.3 million. While the evidence was in conflict whether K.M.C.'s overall financial condition was deteriorating or improving, there is ample evidence belying Irving's characterization that on March 1, Sarokin was faced with a sudden crisis of unprecedented proportions. On this basis alone, the jury could have found that Irving did not fulfill its obligation of good faith performance to K.M.C. when it cut off financing without prior notice.

Irving also argues that it was entitled to a directed verdict on the ground that Sarokin reasonably believed that even if he advanced the $800,000 requested on March 1, K.M.C.'s checks to its suppliers would bounce in significant number and amount and K.M.C. would fold anyway. The events of March 1 were triggered by K.M.C.'s request the previous Friday for an extension of its line of credit to $4 million. Sarokin testified that he believed that K.M.C. would have required this extension, in addition to its request for $800,000 up to its $3.5 million line, to cover all of its outstanding checks. The evidence was substantially in conflict on whether with the $800,000 all of K.M.C.'s checks would have been honored when presented. The jury, by its verdict, resolved this fact issue in favor of K.M.C. In awarding damages to K.M.C. it found that Irving's breach caused K.M.C.'s injury. Irving does not object that the jury was improperly charged on causation. It necessarily follows from the jury's award of damages to the plaintiff that it found that checks would not have bounced. There was ample evidence in the record from which the jury could have so found. However, the question of whether checks in fact would have bounced is distinct from the question of whether Sarokin reasonably could have believed that they would bounce. On the record before us we do not think that the jury could find that Sarokin could not reasonably have held such a belief. Therefore, the question that we must address is whether such a belief in itself would constitute a valid business reason for Irving to refuse to advance the funds requested by K.M.C. without prior notice. We hold, on the particular facts before us, that it would not.

Whether or not the $800,000 requested would have been sufficient to cover all of K.M.C.'s outstanding checks, Sarokin's abrupt refusal to advance funds to K.M.C. on March 1 amounted to a unilateral decision on his part to wind up the company. If Sarokin had agreed to advance the $800,000 but no more, and checks still had bounced, we would have a different case. But, given that Sarokin knew or should have known that the bank was adequately secured, and that if adequately secured it was Irving's policy that some period of notice would be due before financing was denied, Sarokin's action could only be justified if in some way he reasonably believed that it was necessary to protect the bank's interests. There was ample evidence—in particular, the conclusion of Irving's auditors that no losses would be sustained by the bank in the event of liquidation, and Sarokin's decision on March 4 to advance almost the full amount requested just three days earlier, despite the fact the K.M.C. was in much worse condition because of the intervening damage to its credit standing—from which the jury could have concluded that Sarokin had no such reason in mind and hence that his action was arbitrary and capricious.

Finally, Irving contends that even if a period of notice were required, it would be unreasonable to impose upon it an obligation to continue financing K.M.C. for the length of time that would have been necessary to arrange alternative financing or a sale of the company. If Irving had given K.M.C. 30 days, 7 days, even 48 hours notice, we would be facing a different case. However, no notice was given. Until Sarokin told Butler on the phone the afternoon of March 1 that the $800,000 requested would not be advanced, not even Calloway of the Park Bank or Lipson, who had been sent down to Knoxville by Sarokin the previous Friday to gather information, both of whom lunched with Butler immediately before the call to New York, had any inkling that Sarokin might act as he did. Based upon the reasoning above, whether alternative financing could have been found or a sale arranged is pertinent to causation rather than whether Sarokin acted reasonably and in good faith, and there was ample evidence in the record from which the jury could find that either would have been possible.

* * *

We are not insensitive to Irving's complaint that K.M.C.'s value on March 1, 1982, was less than the jury's award of $7,500,000. It is plain from the record that the company was heavily leveraged, its heavy losses in 1981 had eroded stockholder equity, and it had a substantial amount of uncollectible receivables in excess of its bad debt reserve. Nevertheless, the Magistrate concluded that the damage award was not outside the limits of the reasonable range, and we are constrained to agree. Plaintiff's witness Ronnenberg valued K.M.C. at $10,351,200, and Wampler at $11 to 13 million. It is noteworthy that Irving's witness Randal Smith, executive vice president for Scrivener, Incorporated, a large food wholesaler, testified that on November 21, 1979, he offered $3.5 million for K.M.C.'s stock. Scrivener's internal analysis of this offer estimated that with the assumption of K.M.C.'s net liabilities the total cost of acquisition would be $8.9 million. Moreover, Smith almost immediately raised Scrivener's offer to $4.5 million, and was authorized to go to $5.0 million. This $4.5 million offer would have amounted to a total price of $9.9 million.

The judgment is affirmed.

NOTE ON DEMAND OBLIGATIONS

Traditionally, much of commercial bank lending to businesses was under demand notes. A demand note is payable simply on demand and, therefore, is quite different from time or installment obligations, which fix a date for repayment of the loan. Usually, lenders under demand obligations would not "call" the note unless something untoward happened: the borrower got into financial difficulty, markets declined, a guarantor of the note died, or collateral diminished in value. In those events, the bank required the borrower to refinance; and they initiated the refinancing by calling the note, which was callable without notice and without reason, being on demand. *KMC* miscites § 1-208 as authority for the rule that a lender must have good reason and must give notice before calling a demand obligation. See § 1-208, cmt. (2d para.).

Commercial lending has always been more complex than the model the preceding paragraph describes; and today it is very complex; but even under revolving inventory financing or working capital lending, many banks use the demand note, a simple one-paragraph obligation that permits the bank to call the loan whenever it feels like it.

The introduction of good faith analysis into commercial lending renders the demand note risky business. Bankers still use them, but they are now aware that judges and juries may second guess them and may make that second guess under impressions fostered by the imperfections of our fact finding system of litigation.

One of the consequences of the changed state of affairs is the greater use of notes that are not payable on demand but that can be called only on certain conditions. Those conditions include the traditional grounds for calling a loan and sometimes add every conceivable situation that might render the loan risky.

In fact, loan officers and their borrowers now often spend considerable time with their lawyers negotiating these terms and fashioning lengthy language for what used to be a simple note. Thus in the interest of protecting a few from bank bad faith, the many must pay the extra transaction costs the lender liability rules have fostered.

KMC is the leading lender liability case, but it has not spawned the rash of lawsuits or borrower victories that some in the banking profession feared when the Sixth Circuit decided it. Few appellate courts have followed it; more have criticized or questioned it; and perhaps a lot more have ignored it.

KHAM & NATE'S SHOES NO. 2, INC. v. FIRST BANK

United States Court of Appeals, Seventh Circuit, 1990.
908 F.2d 1351.

EASTERBROOK, Circuit Judge.

Kham & Nate's Shoes No. 2, Inc., ran four retail shoe stores in Chicago. It has been in bankruptcy since 1984, operating as a debtor in possession. First Bank of Whiting, one of Kham & Nate's creditors, appeals from the order confirming its plan of reorganization. This order not only reduces the Bank's secured claim to unsecured status but also allows Khamolaw Beard and Nathaniel Parker, the debtor's principals, to retain their equity interests despite the firm's inability to pay its creditors in full. The bankruptcy judge subordinated the Bank's claims after finding that it behaved "inequitably", and he allowed Beard and Parker to retain their interests on the theory that their guarantees of new loans to be made as part of the reorganization are "new value".

I.

The Bank first extended credit to the Debtor in July 1981. This $50,000 loan was renewed in December 1981 and repaid in part in July 1982. The balance was rolled over until late 1983, when with interest it came to $42,000. In September 1983 Bank issued several letters of credit in favor of Debtor's customers. Debtor furnished a note to support these letters of credit; the Bank's security interest was limited to the goods the suppliers furnished. In late 1983 Debtor, experiencing serious cash-flow problems, asked for additional capital, which Bank agreed to provide if the loan could be made secure. That was hard to do, for Debtor had lost money the previous two years and owed more than $440,000 to tax collectors; any new loan from Bank would stand behind the back tax liabilities. The parties discussed two ways to make Bank secure: a guarantee by the Small Business Administration, and a bankruptcy petition followed by an order giving a post-petition loan super-priority.

While waiting for the SBA to act on its application, Debtor filed its petition under Chapter 11 of the Bankruptcy Code in January 1984. Judge Toles granted its application for an order under 11 U.S.C. § 364(c)(1) giving a loan from Bank priority even over the administrative expenses of the bankruptcy. Debtor and Bank then signed their loan agreement, which opens a $300,000 line of credit. The contract provides for cancellation on five days' notice and adds for good measure that "nothing provided herein shall constitute a waiver of the right of the Bank to terminate financing at any time".

The parties signed the contract on January 23, 1984, and Debtor quickly took about $75,000. Suppliers began to draw on the letters of credit. On February 29 Bank mailed Debtor a letter stating that it would make no additional advances after March 7. Although the note underlying the line of credit required payment on demand, Bank did not make the demand. It continued honoring draws on the letters of credit. Debtor's ultimate indebtedness to Bank was approximately $164,000: $42,000 outstanding on the loan made in 1981, $47,000 on the letters of credit, and $75,000 on the line of credit. Debtor paid $10,000 against the line of credit in April 1985 but has made no further payments. Debtor did not ask the court to order Bank to make further advances or to grant super-priority to another creditor to facilitate loans from another source.

There matters stood until the spring of 1988, when Debtor proposed its fourth plan of reorganization. Although the previous three plans had called for Bank to be paid in full, the fourth plan proposed to treat Bank's claims as general unsecured debts. This fourth plan also proposed to allow the shareholders to keep their stock, in exchange for guaranteeing new loans to Debtor.

Bankruptcy Judge Coar held an evidentiary hearing and concluded that Bank had behaved inequitably in terminating the line of credit and inducing Debtor's suppliers to draw on the letters of credit. These draws, the judge concluded, converted Bank from an unsecured lender (the position it held before the bankruptcy) to a super-secured lender under Judge Toles' financing order. Judge Coar first vacated the financing order and then subordinated Bank's debt, on the authority of 11 U.S.C. § 510(c). Finally, Judge Coar confirmed the plan of reorganization, including the provision allowing the stockholders of Debtor to retain their interests. He found that their guarantees were "new value" equivalent to the worth of the interests they would retain, which the judge thought small. The district judge affirmed, 104 B.R. 909 (N.D.Ill.1989).

II.

Appellate jurisdiction is our initial hurdle. Bank filed an appeal but now contends that we lack jurisdiction. It observes that although Judge Coar has confirmed the plan of reorganization, he has not quantified Bank's entitlements. Debtor filed a counterclaim against Bank, contending that it is entitled to more than $300,000 in damages because of Bank's refusal to provide extra credit. After Bank stopped making loans, Debtor closed its head office in a snazzy building on Michigan Avenue; a deterioration in the prestige of its address made suppliers less willing to deliver shoes on credit, Debtor insists, with the result that it shrunk from four stores (two in ritzy locations) to one on Chicago's south side. Judge Coar entered an order finding Bank liable to Debtor, essentially for the reasons he subordinated Bank's claims. After taking evidence on Debtor's damages in the spring of 1990, however, the judge issued an order requiring the parties to brief anew the question whether the finding of liability—and implicitly the subordination of Bank's claims—was proper. Pending counterclaims usually prevent a bankruptcy order from being final, see In re Berke, 837 F.2d 293 (7th Cir.1988), so Bank asks us to dismiss the appeal. (Why does Bank not just withdraw its notice of appeal? Appellate jurisdiction in bankruptcy cases is a murky subject. Bank fears that if the order confirming the plan turns out to be "final" after all, then it will forfeit its rights if it does not press all claims now. * * *)

[The court then held that it had jurisdiction.]

Judge Coar gave two principal reasons for subordinating Bank's claim. One is that the "Bank was fully aware of the Debtor's plight, and its reliance upon the line of credit, and disregarded the consequences for the Debtor and its creditors." The other is that Bank obtained an "unfair advantage" by inducing suppliers to draw on the letters of credit after the financing order, thus promoting its position on these advances from unsecured to supersecured. Bank has made our analysis of the second reason simple by disclaiming priority for either the $47,000 advanced to satisfy the letters of credit or the $42,000 outstanding on the loan made in 1981. These are, and always have been, unsecured loans. Orders under § 364(c) do not allow a creditor to boost the priority of existing loans. Section 364(c) speaks of "obtaining of credit or the incurring of debt"; prior loans and sums disbursed on prior firm commitments fit neither category. Sums paid out after bankruptcy on letters of credit issued before bankruptcy are pre-bankruptcy loans, to which § 364(c) cannot apply, because the bank is committed before the bankruptcy to honor sight drafts tendered with conforming draws. Priority under § 364 is not necessary to obtain this credit for the debtor. So although the financing order appears to give Bank priority on all of its loans, pre- and post-filing, Bank wisely concedes that the order could not properly have done so. The 1981 loan and the advances in 1984 to honor the letters of credit always were unsecured. The plan of reorganization properly treats them as unsecured.

Subordination matters only for the $65,000 outstanding on advances under the line of credit authorized by the financing order. Section 510(c) lets bankruptcy judges subordinate claims but does not provide criteria for the exercise of this power. Absence of statutory criteria commits the subject to the courts, to be worked out in the common law fashion. * * * Courts require the insiders to return to their position at the end of the line. * * * But Bank is neither an insider nor a person seeking to collect a penalty, and it has not delayed without justification. It contributed new value under a contract, and it wants no more than the priority Judge Toles promised as the lure.

Cases subordinating the claims of creditors that dealt at arm's length with the debtor are few and far between. Benjamin v. Diamond, 563 F.2d 692 (5th Cir.1977) (Mobile Steel Co.), suggests that subordination depends on a combination of inequitable conduct, unfair advantage to the creditor, and injury to other creditors. Debtor submits that conduct may be "unfair" and "inequitable" for this purpose even though the creditor complies with all contractual requirements, but we are not willing to embrace a rule that requires participants in commercial transactions not only to keep their contracts but also do "more"—just how much more resting in the discretion of a bankruptcy judge assessing the situation years later. Contracts specify the duties of the parties to each other, and each may exercise the privileges it obtained. Banks sometimes bind themselves to make loans (commitment letters and letters of credit have this effect) and sometimes reserve the right to terminate further advances. Courts may not convert one form of contract into the other after the fact, without raising the cost of credit or jeopardizing its availability. Unless pacts are enforced according to their terms, the institution of contract, with all the advantages private negotiation and agreement brings, is jeopardized.

"Inequitable conduct" in commercial life means breach plus some advantage-taking, such as the star who agrees to act in a motion picture and then, after $20 million has been spent, sulks in his dressing room until the contract has been renegotiated. Firms that have negotiated contracts are entitled to enforce them to the letter, even to the great discomfort of their trading partners, without being mulcted for lack of "good faith". Although courts often refer to the obligation of good faith that exists in every contractual relation, e.g., UCC § 1-201; Jordan v. Duff & Phelps, Inc., 815 F.2d 429, 438 (7th Cir.1987), this is not an invitation to the court to decide whether one party ought to have exercised privileges expressly reserved in the document. "Good faith" is a compact reference to an implied undertaking not to take opportunistic advantage in a way that could not have been contemplated at the time of drafting, and which therefore was not resolved explicitly by the parties. When the contract is silent, principles of good faith—such as the UCC's standard of honesty in fact, UCC § 1-201(19), and the reasonable expectations of the trade, UCC § 2-103(b) (a principle applicable, however, only to "merchants", which Bank is not)—fill the gap. They do not block use of terms that actually appear in the contract.

We do not doubt the force of the proverb that the letter killeth, while the spirit giveth life. Literal implementation of unadorned language may destroy the essence of the venture. Few people pass out of childhood without learning fables about genies, whose wickedly literal interpretation of their "masters'" wishes always leads to calamity. Yet knowledge that literal enforcement means some mismatch between the parties' expectation and the outcome does not imply a general duty of "kindness" in performance, or of judicial oversight into whether a party had "good cause" to act as it did. Parties to a contract are not each others' fiduciaries; they are not bound to treat customers with the same consideration reserved for their families. Any attempt to add an overlay of "just cause"—as the bankruptcy judge effectively did—to the exercise of contractual privileges would reduce commercial certainty and breed costly litigation. The UCC's requirement of "honesty in fact" stops well short of the requirements the bankruptcy judge thought incident to contractual performance. "[I]n commercial transactions it does not in the end promote justice to seek strained interpretations in aid of those who do not protect themselves." James Baird Co. v. Gimbel Bros., Inc., 64 F.2d 344, 346 (2d Cir.1933) (L. Hand, J.).

Bank did not break a promise at a time Debtor was especially vulnerable, then use the costs and delay of obtaining legal enforcement of the contract as levers to a better deal. Debtor and Bank signed a contract expressly allowing the Bank to cease making further advances. The $300,000 was the maximum loan, not a guarantee. The Bank exercised its contractual privilege after loaning Debtor $75,000; it made a clean break and did not demand improved terms. It had the right to do this for any reason satisfactory to itself. In re Prima Co., 98 F.2d 952, 965 (7th Cir.1938); CTS Truss. See also UCC § 1-208 (official comment stating that the statutory obligation of good faith in accelerating a term note does not apply to a bank's decision to call demand notes). The principle is identical to that governing a contract for employment at will: the employer may sack its employee for any reason except one forbidden by law, and it need not show "good cause".

Although Bank's decision left Debtor scratching for other sources of credit, Bank did not create Debtor's need for funds, and it was not contractually obliged to satisfy its customer's desires. The Bank was entitled to advance its own interests, and it did not need to put the interests of Debtor and Debtor's other creditors first. To the extent K.M.C., Inc. v. Irving Trust Co., 757 F.2d 752, 759-63 (6th Cir.1986), holds that a bank must loan more money or give more advance notice of termination than its contract requires, we respectfully disagree. First Bank of Whiting is not an eleemosynary institution. It need not throw good money after bad, even if other persons would catch the lucre.

Debtor stresses, and the bankruptcy judge found, that Bank would have been secure in making additional advances. Perhaps so, but the contract did not oblige Bank to make all advances for which it could be assured of payment. Ex post assessments of a lender's security are no basis on which to deny it the negotiated place in the queue. Risk must be assessed ex ante by lenders, rather than ex post by judges. If a loan seems secure at the time, lenders will put up the money; their own interests are served by making loans bound to be repaid. What is more, the bankruptcy judge's finding that Bank would have been secure in making additional advances is highly questionable. The judgment of the market vindicates Bank. If more credit would have enabled Debtor to flourish, then other lenders should have been willing to supply it. Yet no one else, not even the SBA, would advance additional money to Debtor.

Both the bankruptcy and district judges characterized as inequitable Bank's decision in December 1983 not to extend additional credit unless Kham & Nate's filed a petition in bankruptcy (or obtained a guarantee from the SBA). According to the courts, this forced the firm into bankruptcy; having propelled it there, Bank was obliged to help. This is insufficient on two levels—first because filing for bankruptcy often helps rather than injures the firm (the automatic stay keeps the wolves and tax collectors from the door), and second because linking an offer of extra credit to a bankruptcy petition does not "force" a firm to file one. A bank may insist on security before lending; bankruptcy followed by an order under § 364 was one device for providing it. If Kham & Nate's Shoes did not like that option, it was entitled to shop around. Conditioning new money on higher security no more obliges a Bank to "lend a helping hand" (in excess of contractual promises) than does setting a high rate of interest or taking security in receivables, other ways to deal with a lower probability of repayment.

Although Debtor contends, and the bankruptcy judge found, that Bank's termination of advances frustrated Debtor's efforts to secure credit from other sources, and so propelled it down hill, this is legally irrelevant so long as Bank kept its promises. It is factually questionable too. Why would Bank shoot itself in the foot—spurning what the bankruptcy judge thought to be sure repayment while leaving an outstanding balance of $164,000 that it could not expect to collect if Debtor collapsed? At all events, Debtor could have asked for further orders under § 364 making potential lenders secure and ensuring a flow of credit; it did not. It could have asked Judge Toles to clarify his financing order, so that other creditors would know that Bank's priority was limited to $75,000; it did not. A straightforward inference is that even high priority would not have induced other institutions to put up money—just as high priority did not make Bank feel sufficiently secure.

The only breach on Bank's part that Debtor has identified is a technical one: the contract calls for five calendar days' telephonic and written notice, while Bank gave only written notice. (An officer of Bank testified that he gave telephonic notice, but the bankruptcy court's contrary finding is not clearly erroneous.) This offense was trivial. Clauses requiring notice by telephone are designed to ensure that the borrower has five real days to find a new lender, that delays in the mail do not diminish the time available. So Bank was obliged to extend credit until five days after Debtor received actual notice—that is, five days after the letter arrived. Bank mailed the letter February 29, 1984, terminating advances as of March 7. If the letter took two days to arrive, Debtor still had five days between notice and the cutoff. If Debtor got less, then an award would be in order for the loss attributable to the inadequate notice. It is safe to assume that the damages would be substantially less than the difference between the value of the $65,000 balance with super-priority and the amount that Bank will receive if the loan is lumped with other unsecured credit. Equitable subordination under § 510(c) is not a device to magnify the damages available for inconsequential breaches of contract.

* * *

PATTERSON, A FABLE FROM THE SEVENTH CIRCUIT: FRANK EASTERBROOK ON GOOD FAITH, 76 Iowa L. Rev. 503, 511-12, 520-21 (1991).

Judge Coar's decision to subordinate the amount owed to First under its line-of-credit agreement with Kham is grounded in an argument about reliance and reasonable expectations. Fully aware of Kham's need for financing, and knowing all too well that Kham was relying upon this financing to fund its postpetition operations, First's decision to refuse to make further advances under the line of credit "disregarded the consequences for [Kham] and its creditors." Finding no valid business reason for terminating Kham's line of credit, Judge Coar held that First breached the implied covenant of good faith and fair dealing. On the basis of this breach of contract, First's claim under the line-of-credit agreement was subordinated.

In reaching his decision under the good faith standard, Judge Coar relied upon the Sixth Circuit's decision in *K.M.C. Co., Inc. v. Irving Trust Co.* In *K.M.C.*, as in *Kham*, the creditor under a line-of-credit agreement suddenly and inexplicably refused to make further advances to a debtor in a type of business that required ready access to cash reserves. The unexpected termination of credit resulted in catastrophic losses to each of the debtor firms. As in *Kham*, the note signed by the parties in *K.M.C.* was a demand instrument. Despite this fact, the Sixth Circuit held that demand for payment in full without any prior warning was a "literal interpretation of the financing agreement [which] * * * would leave K.M.C.'s continued existence at the whim or mercy of Irving [the creditor], absent an obligation of good faith performance." This aspect of the decision has generated a torrent of commentary and debate. More to the point, Judge Easterbrook directed his attention in *Kham* to this aspect of the *K.M.C.* decision.

* * *

Judge Coar found that by shutting off Kham's line of credit at a time when it was particularly vulnerable, First violated its good faith obligation to Kham. In making this decision, Judge Coar explicitly followed the reasoning in *K.M.C.* to the effect that a line-of-credit agreement (or more broadly, a contract) cannot be terminated without notice unless there is a valid business reason for so doing. Judge Coar and the district court agreed that First had no valid business reason for shutting off Kham's flow of cash, fully secured by property of Kham. It is precisely this reasoning and the holding to which it led that Judge Easterbrook rebukes and vacates.

OVERBY, BONDAGE, DOMINATION, AND THE ART OF THE DEAL: AN ASSESSMENT OF JUDICIAL STRATEGIES IN LENDER LIABILITY GOOD FAITH LITIGATION, 61 Fordham L. Rev. 963, 1023-24, 1028-29 (1993).

The lender liability experience, however, discredits concerns that the obligation of good faith licenses judges to superimpose extracontractual obligations upon the parties. The interventionist and relational approaches appear the least employed. Generally, courts have been sensitive to the parties' contract and agreement. Moreover, the failure of the cases to generate the body of "good faith law" necessary to provide certainty and consistency exemplifies the limitations of those approaches in providing workable standards for the obligation of good faith. The plane of debate in the courts, rather, lies in differences over the amount of sensitivity which courts should have to the parties' agreement. Hence, the choice devolves to one between the interpretivist and passive approaches to good faith. In the lending context, the "effectiveness of express terms" approach, as set out in Kham & Nate's, is the preferable methodology to use in enforcing the parties' agreement.

In addition to being supported by strong precedent, the "effectiveness of express terms" approach is further strengthened by persuasive policy considerations. First, the approach enforces the basic principle of contract interpretation that express terms control over implied terms. When a lending agreement asserts that amounts due thereunder are payable upon demand or upon acceleration by the lender upon a specified event of default, or that a lender may discontinue financing as provided by the agreement, any interpretation otherwise necessarily contravenes this principle. To the extent that the interventionist, interpretivist, or relational approaches impose requirements of fair play in demanding payment, of restraint in accelerating under the agreement, or of notice prior to discontinuation of financing, those requirements inexorably lead to the conclusion that demand does not mean demand, acceleration does not mean acceleration, or a right to discontinue does not mean a right to discontinue. Just because the borrower blindly hoped the lender would not exercise those rights does not create an interpretive event.

Second, The interpretive methods mandate judicial intervention in, and review of, every lender decision in order to determine the broadly construed "agreement" of the parties. Regardless of whether that effort could lead to determinable results, it conflicts with other principles bearing upon the enforcement of contracts beyond those of promoting autonomy or enforcing expectations in the particular case before the court. The interpretivist approaches increase the cost of contracting through invocation of the judicial dispute resolution mechanism in every case. Further, the interpretivist approaches rely upon transaction-specific facts which generate little information upon which transactors may rely in structuring their own affairs, and, by interjecting the state into every dispute, threaten to alter the social relationship between lender and borrower.

* * *

One significant concern raised in the debates over introduction of the obligation of good faith and fair dealing in the Restatement focused on the obligation's potential to invoke widespread "judicial remaking of contracts." A comprehensive analysis of the history of lender liability litigation indicates that, for the most part, United States courts are resisting that temptation. Although not entirely unprecedented, judicial activism which uses the obligation of good faith to impose standards of conduct irrespective of the parties' agreement is rare. The recent shift in some courts to a vocally passive strategy toward good faith issues in lending reaffirms that the initial concerns over the introduction of the obligation of good faith ought not be a source of extreme apprehension. Accordingly, lenders may rest a little easier knowing that they are winning in the courts and their agreements generally will be enforced.

MANNESMAN HANDEL AG v. KAUNLARAN SHIPPING CORP.

Queen's Bench Division (Commercial Court), 1992.
[1993] 1 Lloyd's Rep. 89.

[The facts are moderately complex. Mannesman, a German company, agreed to sell a quantity of pig iron of Russian origin to a Bermuda middleman, which arranged to resell it to a Chinese buyer. There were two letters of credit. A Hong Kong bank issued the first on behalf of the Chinese buyer in favor of the Bermuda middleman. A Swiss bank issued the second on behalf of the Bermuda middleman in favor of the German seller. The Bermuda middleman used the first letter of credit to secure its reimbursement obligation to the second issuer by assigning the proceeds of the first credit to the issuer of the second.

Because of Chinese import restrictions against Russian goods, the commercial parties arranged to falsify a bill of lading in order to hide the Russian origin of the iron. The Bermuda middleman presented the false bill of lading to the first issuer, which honored its credit and, pursuant to the assignment, paid the proceeds to the second issuer. Using the false bill, the Chinese buyer was able to bring the goods through Chinese customs.

When the German seller sought payment under the second issuer's credit, the second issuer, which had obtained payment under the first credit, in part by virtue of the fact that the German seller had provided the pig iron to the Bermuda middleman, dishonored the German seller's request for payment. The Swiss bank dishonored on the grounds that the German seller's documents did not conform with the terms of the second letter of credit.

The Bermuda middleman is insolvent, and the German seller's assignee sues the second issuer, Swiss bank, for wrongful dishonor.]

SAVILLE, J.

The rights and obligations of the Swiss bank and the German company under the letter of credit issued by the Swiss bank are, it is common ground, governed by Swiss law. Under that law and the terms of the letter of credit the Swiss bank were legally obliged to make payment against documents which conformed to the terms of the letter of credit. As is the case in English law, there is a doctrine of strict compliance: the documents must conform in all respects with the requirements of the letter of credit. As the Swiss bank expert called by the Swiss bank stated, Swiss commentators and the established case law would agree with Lord Sumner's well known statement:

There is no room for documents which are almost the same or which will do just as well * * * as the documents required by the credit.

However, it is equally clearly established in Swiss law that the doctrine of strict compliance can be displaced where it is established that reliance on this document would be contrary to art 2 of the Swiss Civil Code. This article provides as follows:

1. *Chacun est tenu d'exercer ses droits et d'executer ses obligations selon les regles de la bonne foi.*[1]

2. *L'abus manifeste d'un droit n'est pas protege par la loi.*[2]

The expert called by the Swiss bank expressed the view that in Swiss law this principle of good faith is extremely narrowly confined in the context of letters of credit. In his words, the principle would only apply to preclude a bank from relying upon discrepancies that were "wholly insignificant". Since in this expert's view many of the discrepancies in the present case could not be so described, art 2 did not displace the doctrine of strict compliance and the Swiss bank were not obliged to make payment under the letter of credit.

I do not accept this view of Swiss law. In the first place, I can find nothing in the cases and commentaries shown to me that limits the application of art 2 in this way. Of course in Swiss law art 2 will only be applied in exceptional cases, where it is demonstrated that insistence on strict adherence to the conditions of the letter of credit would indubitably be regarded to good faith—but none of the cases or commentaries suggested that even if this is demonstrated, nonetheless art 2 cannot be applied if the discrepancies are somehow to be regarded as other than "wholly insignificant".

---

1 "Everyone is obliged to exercise his rights and perform his obligation according to the rule of good faith." [eds.].

2 "Manifest abuse of right is not protected by the law." [eds.].

In the second place, with great respect to this expert, I do not follow his classification of discrepancies into those that are "wholly insignificant" and others. The expert accepted that by a "wholly insignificant" discrepancy he nevertheless meant a discrepancy that (apart from art 2) would entitle a bank to refuse to accept the documents. How then is one to determine whether a discrepancy is to be treated as "wholly insignificant"? This can hardly be done by looking at the letter of credit alone: a discrepancy is a discrepancy and it is unlikely (to say the least) that a letter of credit would itself stipulate or indicate what is to be regarded as significant or insignificant; yet this expert was reluctant to accept that Swiss law allowed one to look outside the letter of credit at the surrounding circumstances. In the end I formed the view that what this expert was really doing was criticizing the leading case on the subject in Swiss law, namely the decision of the Supreme Court in Societe de Banque Suisse v Societe Generale Alsacienne de Banque, [1989] JT 1342, where to my mind at least it is clear that the Court was prepared to look and did look at all the circumstances when judging whether or not art 2 was applicable; and where, as I have already indicated, there is no suggestion that art 2 could only be applied after it is determined that the discrepancy is "wholly insignificant". Of course, if having looked at all the circumstances the Court concludes that it would be in bad faith for the bank to rely on strict compliance then at that stage (ex hypothesi) the discrepancies will indeed be of no significance of materiality.

It was strongly urged on me that to widen the application of art 2 beyond the suggested concept of "wholly insignificant" discrepancies would be calculated to undermine if not destroy the doctrine of strict compliance and to blur if not extinguish the distinction between transactions concerning goods and transactions concerning goods [documents? Eds.], letter of credit falling within the former and not the latter category. Thus much reliance was placed upon the fact that in the case cited, the Court was clearly of the view that the mere fact that the goods in question had been duly delivered to the buyers did not entail that the bank had to take up non-conforming documents.

I was not persuaded by these arguments for it seems to me that they simply miss the point, which is whether in all the circumstances it would be contrary to good faith for a bank to insist on strict compliance. Obviously, the mere fact that the goods had been delivered to the buyer can hardly, in itself, demonstrate that it would not be in good faith for the bank to reject non-conforming documents, since the bank is concerned with documents not goods. This said, if circumstances exist which do demonstrate that it would be contrary to good faith for a bank to insist on strict compliance, I can see no adverse affects on the general doctrine of strict compliance or indeed any blurring or extinguishing of the distinction between documents and goods. Indeed to my mind to argue the contrary leads logically to the proposition (unacceptable in any civilised society) that it is lawful to act in bad faith. It is indeed the very purpose of art 2 to avoid that state of affairs.

For these reasons I reject the views of the Swiss law expert called by the Swiss bank and prefer the view of the expert called by the demise charterers, that the question is simply whether in all the circumstances Swiss law would regard as contrary to art 2 the refusal of the Swiss bank to accept the documents on the grounds that they did not comply with the terms of the letter of credit.

I agree with this expert that Swiss law would so regard the refusal in the present case. By the time the documents were rejected the Swiss bank knew (as was admitted in evidence) that the Bermudan company had acted dishonestly in preparing and using false documents while the true documents were still in circulation; and must have appreciated that by such means the Bermudan company had not only obtained payment in respect of the goods but had also disposed or helped to dispose of the goods whilst the German company remained unpaid. Despite the Bermudan company obtaining the proceeds by doing the very things the Swiss bank witnesses told me they would not have countenanced, the Swiss Bank took advantage of the Bermudan company's dishonesty by claiming and receiving those proceeds as due under their assignment—and did so believing (or at least hoping) that the unpaid German company would be unable to present conforming documents.

Furthermore, it is not suggested (indeed it is difficult to see how it could be suggested) that in these circumstances the discrepancies in the documents were in fact of any significance whatever to the Bermudan company—indeed on the evidence it is clear that they were not. The receiver, of course, was properly concerned that there should be no preference of creditors (though the Bermudan company itself wanted the Swiss bank to pay the German company) but as a master [matter? Eds.] of Swiss law (which governed the relationship between the Swiss bank and the Bermudan company) it is clear that in the circumstances there was no question of the Bermudan company having any legitimate complaint or indeed any rights against the Swiss bank if the latter did pay against non-conforming documents.

To my mind in these wholly exceptional circumstances the insistence of the Swiss bank that it would withhold payment because the documents did not comply with the conditions of the letter of credit is, as a matter of Swiss law, bound to be regarded as contrary to good faith; that the case falls within the principles applied by the Supreme Court in Société de Banque Suisse v. Société Generale Alsacienne de Banque; and that accordingly the Swiss bank failed to perform its obligations to the German company under the letter of credit.

* * *

GOODE, ABSTRACT PAYMENT UNDERTAKINGS IN INTERNATIONAL TRANSACTIONS, 22 Brook. J. Int'l L. 1, 9-10 (1996).

2. *The concept of good faith*

There is another, and potentially more serious, challenge to the principle of strict compliance, namely the concept of good faith. A general concept of good faith has long been a tenet of the civil law and has been spreading rapidly to other legal families. It is featured, for example, in the American Uniform Commercial Code, the Vienna Sales Convention, the EC Directives on self-employed commercial agents and unfair terms in consumer contracts, the UNCITRAL

Convention, and the UNIDROIT Conventions on International Factoring and International Financial Leasing, as well as in the UNIDROIT Principles for International Commercial Contracts and the separate Principles of European Contract Law issued by the Commission on European Contract Law. Only two years ago an English court, applying Swiss law, held that it would be contrary to the principles of good faith to allow a bank to rely on discrepancies to refuse payment under a letter of credit when it had received the proceeds of a back-to-back letter of credit.

English law does not as yet possess any general principle of good faith in contracts. Its courts, conscious of London's position as a world financial centre, are wary of such open-textured concepts and the degree of unpredictability perceived as likely to result from their introduction. It is not clear how long this approach will be maintained. Once the courts have become accustomed to handling good faith in the context of the EC Directive on unfair terms in consumer contracts, they may find that they can live with it after all. Even so, it is not clear what implications this would have for the bank's right to reject non-conforming documents tendered under a letter of credit. Where, in contrast to the Swiss bank case, the bank has no interest of its own in the outcome of the presentation, is its own good faith to be determined by whether a rejection of the documents by its customer would be in good faith, or is some other criterion to be applied? And how far should the requirement of good faith incline the court towards adopting a substantial compliance standard?

UCC § 5-102(a)(7) & Official Comment 3
(*see Selected Commercial Statutes*)

NOTE ON GOOD FAITH IN COMMERCIAL TRANSACTIONS

The drafting of Article 5 prompted some vigorous debate on the good faith question including a modicum of heat and a surfeit of verbiage. The following is an excerpt from a letter one adviser, who was against a subjective good faith rule in Article 5, wrote to another adviser, a strong advocate for an expanded definition of good faith. The compromise referred to was to make the credit issuer responsible for a standard of good faith in the letter of credit transaction that was the equivalent of the standard that applied to the commercial parties in the underlying transaction.

"The law of voluntary obligations at its best is binary. Formation rules are clear. Liability is strict. Duties, terms, and conditions are explicit. Unlike the continuum of tort law, contracts in general and commercial specialties in particular do not need a third party (court or jury) to determine their existence and scope.

That description of voluntary obligations law is not accurate, of course. Courts and legislatures have introduced imprecision into voluntary obligations law, sometimes with good cause and minor damage, sometimes without good cause and with major damage. The damage, of course, redounds to the benefit of lawyers who make money out of the confusion and to the detriment of commercial parties who pay the lawyers.

Introduction of a good-faith standard into the law of contracts, negotiable instruments, and letters of credit adds to the imprecision of that law. That addition is costly. The benefit, in my judgment, is largely illusory. In theory, it is nice to say that we have law that requires commercial parties to behave in accordance with reasonable standards of fairness in their industry. I doubt, however, that there are such standards in many settings; and, if there are, I am confident that juries and courts will be unable to discern them. I base that skepticism on ten years of practicing law, a good part of it in courtrooms before judges and juries. That there is a culture in some industries, in some settings, and at some times one cannot deny. But cultures are difficult to capture and impossible to replicate in the courtroom.

Your compromise does not avoid these failings; it only narrows the scope of them. The law already provides, furthermore, a tort remedy for beneficiary misbehavior and a tort remedy for applicant misbehavior. The applicant may sue the beneficiary that draws fraudulently. The beneficiary may recover for tortious interference from the applicant that prevails upon the issuer to dishonor wrongfully. True, the tort thresholds are higher than your good-faith threshold would be. But the reason for the relatively higher tort threshold is to protect the contract relationships from the erosion your good-faith standard will effect.

Section 2-103(1)(b) may have made sense in the 1940s sale-of-goods setting. In those days sellers and buyers held large stocks of inventory; the rate of product obsolescence was slow; markets were regional; and the number of players and pace of entry and exit from the trade was low. All that has changed. Just-in-time inventory practices, high obsolescence rates, and international markets with new faces constantly appearing may make the section problematic. In the 1940s merchants in the garment industry knew whether it was bad faith for a Chicago buyer to reject a New York seller's shipment of forty gross of shirts because the sleeves on four cartons were faded or whether five percent contaminants in a shipment of vegetable oil from a Des Moines grain company to a Jersey City chemical concern rendered the shipment non-conforming. Whether Llewellyn's presumption is valid today when garments come from Taiwan and vegetable oil goes to Holland is something I cannot answer, but I hope [the committee drafting Article 2 and its chair] are taking a good look at it. I do know, however, that there are no standards of fair dealing in the trade when a Saudi bank draws on a standby issued in New York to secure the Saudi bank's guarantee and that there is no such standard when a seller of apples draws on a commercial credit after some starlet calls a press conference to announce that the growers' fungicide is carcinogenic.

In short, the problem is that you cannot do what it is you want to do. Instead of raising the standards of commercial practice, you will have standards in the courtroom when there are none in the market place, ersatz standards when there are, imprecise obligations, and a continuum of liability. Certainty, a precious commodity in commercial law, will suffer."

SECTION 3. FRAUD

INTRODUCTORY NOTE

Fraud losses in commercial transactions are enormous, easily in the billions of dollars annually. The systems we study, commercial bank lending, credit cards, check collections, consumer sales, and letters of credit, are particularly vulnerable. But it is really the entire commercial structure that suffers, and it suffers dearly. Ultimately, we all pay for fraud—more or less. It is this "more or less" part of the fraud costs that concerns commercial law.

Federal and state agencies and many private industries engage in expensive efforts to police fraudulent activity and render it less profitable by punishing the fraudster. Commercial law does its part too, but in a less normative, more amoral way. Commercial law seldom punishes the fraudulent party. Its formula for deterring fraud is one of allocating fraud losses, and often it must allocate them among "innocent" parties.

Fraud is a defense, of course, always against the party that perpetrates the fraud. That is as it should be in any rational system. The problem arises when we must allocate the loss when the fraudulent party has fled ("skipped" in commercial jargon) or has the ill grace to become insolvent. In those cases, generally, though not always, commercial law allocates the loss to the party that deals with the fraud. The first assumption is that the party dealing with the fraud is in the better position to prevent it than a later party. The second assumption, consistent with the first, is that the system of financial intermediation, i.e., the banking system or the financial markets, should not bear the cost of recurring market fraud, just as that system generally does not bear the loss of market fluctuation. There are, of course, exceptions.

(a) A CLASSIC DISTINCTION

UCC § 3-305(a)(1 & 2) & (b)
(*see Selected Commercial Statutes*)

FR. WINKLER KG v. STOLLER

United States Court of Appeals, Third Circuit, 1988.
839 F.2d 1002.

ROSENN, Circuit Judge.

The principal issue in this diversity action requires us to determine the effect of the parol evidence rule on plaintiff-appellee Fr. Winkler KG's ("Winkler") attempt to recover on two promissory notes guaranteed by defendant-appellant Gene Stoller. By order dated February 24, 1987, the United States District Court for the District of New Jersey granted plaintiff's motion for summary judgment on the notes, and permitted defendant leave to file a counterclaim. Thereafter, the court denied Stoller's motion for reconsideration and dismissed his counterclaim. The defendant appeals and we affirm.

* * *

In 1968, Winkler, a West German manufacturer of bakery equipment, entered into an exclusive North American dealership agreement with Bakers Equipment Winkler, Inc. ("BEW"), a New York corporation engaged in the sale and service of bakery machinery. The agreement extended for a fifteen year period unless either party gave notice of termination one year prior to the termination date. In 1973, Stoller became BEW's chief executive officer.

As consideration for the bakery equipment that it purchased, BEW executed a series of promissory notes payable to Winkler, who, in turn, discounted them with its lender, Deutche Bank. In May 1980, Winkler began requiring Stoller's personal guarantee on all subsequent promissory notes. The plaintiff explained that Deutche Bank would no longer discount BEW's notes without Stoller's guarantee. In compliance with Winkler's request, Stoller guaranteed seven notes on September 2, 1980.

On August 4, 1982, Stoller guaranteed two additional notes on BEW's behalf in consideration for the purchase of equipment. These notes, which form the basis of this appeal, had an aggregate value of $671,485.88. On the front of each note, Stoller signed his name followed by the designation "chief executive officer" to indicate his representative capacity. However, on the back of each note, Stoller signed only his name with no additional designation. The words "per aval Gene Stoller" were printed under each signature. Stoller admits to executing the notes in this fashion.[1]

* * *

In further support of his contention, Stoller relies upon Westmont Nat. Bank v. Payne, 108 N.J.L. 133, 156 A. 652 (E & A 1931), and upon Chera v. The Shores, 145 N.J.Super. 19, 366 A.2d 994 (1976). In Westmont, the New Jersey Court of Errors and Appeals held that the parol evidence rule did not preclude defendants from demonstrating that their signatures on a note were procured by fraud. 156 A. at 654-55. Kirkbride, the cashier of the Westmont National Bank, obtained defendants' signature on two blank sheets of paper by assuring them that "no harm would come" to either themselves or their home. The defendants claimed that they did not even know that they were signing a note. Westmont, therefore, involved fraud in the very execution of an instrument. In this case, however, Stoller knowingly executed two notes but alleged that they were not to be enforced against him. We conclude that Westmont is distinguishable from the instant action based upon Stoller's inability to establish fraud. * * *

---

1 By August 1982, BEW was in precarious financial condition. Helmut Winkler, one of Winkler's general partners, asserted that the plaintiff would never have advanced BEW the equipment without Stoller's guarantee.

PROBLEM

Seller provided services to Buyer and sent Buyer an invoice for $500, the agreed upon price. Buyer duly mailed her check for $500 to Seller, who artfully and fraudulently raised it to $5,000, deposited it at his bank, Second Bank, which sent it through the check collection system to First Bank, the drawee/payor bank.

(a) If the drawee/payor bank pays the $5,000 to Second, may the drawee charge Buyer's account? If so, for how much. See § 4-401.

(b) If Second gives value to Seller and if the drawee/payor dishonors, may Second enforce the instrument against Buyer? If so, for how much? See § 3-407(c).

(c) If Second does not give value to Seller and if the drawee dishonors, may Seller enforce the instrument against Buyer for $5,000? For $500? See § 3-407(b)

(d) If Seller may not enforce the instrument against Buyer, may Seller recover from Buyer on the underlying service contact? See § 3-310(b)(3). If not, is Buyer getting the services for free? Can Seller recover on a theory of unjust enrichment? See § 1-103. Assume that Seller is a corporation and that its treasurer, without authority, made the alteration to the check. Would these facts alter your analysis of the company's right to recover from the buyer?

(b) LETTER OF CREDIT FRAUD

INTRODUCTORY NOTE

As section 3 in Chapter 12 explains, letters of credit work only if they are independent of the transactions out of which they arise. If law or practice entangle the credit with related transactions, the letter of credit becomes a dependent obligation in the nature of suretyship; commercial parties lose a useful device; and commercial banks lose a product.

When a beneficiary of a credit presents his draft and documents to the issuer, the applicant for the credit, the bank's customer, knows that the game may soon be up. If the issuer pays, the money will be in the beneficiary's hands and in the beneficiary's forum; and if the draw is improper as a matter of contract law by virtue of the underlying agreement, the applicant will have to litigate in unfavorable circumstances, i.e., not having the funds and, perhaps, in a distant jurisdiction.

A Boston buyer of cotton shirts from a Malaysian seller is never happy to see her bank wire the $80,000 purchase price to Kuala Lumpur if the shirts are defective or the shipment is short. The buyer can make a claim against the seller, but she would prefer to have the $80,000 rather than defective shirts and a claim against a seller in a foreign city.

The independence principle teaches, however, that the buyer in this illustration is in the less favorable position. Because she agreed in the underlying sales contract to a sale with payment by letter of credit, there is little she can do. Perhaps she can avail herself of an arbitration clause, and one would hope she has a responsible seller to make a claim against. Otherwise, she has simply learned an $80,000 lesson.

There are circumstances in which the buyer may avoid this painful result. If, rather than breach of the warranty of merchantability defense, the buyer has a fraud defense, she may be able to stop the issuer from paying. Then the seller will have to sue, probably in Boston. There is a fraud exception to the independence principle, but the fraud defense is not simply a matter of shouting "fraud!"

SZTEJN v. J. HENRY SCHRODER BANKING CORP.

Supreme Court of New York, 1941.
177 Misc. 719, 31 N.Y.S.2d 631.

SHIENTAG, J.

This is a motion by the defendant, the Chartered Bank of India, Australia and China, (hereafter referred to as the Chartered Bank), made pursuant to Rule 106(5) of the Rules of Civil Practice to dismiss the supplemental complaint on the ground that it fails to state facts sufficient to constitute a cause of action against the moving defendant. The plaintiff brings this action to restrain the payment or presentment for payment of drafts under a letter of credit issued to secure the purchase price of certain merchandise, bought by the plaintiff and his coadventurer, one Schwarz, who is a party defendant in this action. The plaintiff also seeks a judgment declaring the letter of credit and drafts thereunder null and void. The complaint alleges that the documents accompanying the drafts are fraudulent in that they do not represent actual merchandise but instead cover boxes fraudulently filled with worthless material by the seller of the goods. The moving defendant urges that the complaint fails to state a cause of action against it because the Chartered Bank is only concerned with the documents and on their face these conform to the requirements of the letter of credit.

On January 7, 1941, the plaintiff and his coadventurer contracted to purchase a quantity of bristles from the defendant Transea Traders, Ltd. (hereafter referred to as Transea) a corporation having its place of business in Lucknow, India. In order to pay for the bristles, the plaintiff and Schwarz contracted with the defendant J. Henry Schroder Banking Corporation (hereafter referred to as Schroder), a domestic corporation, for the issuance of an irrevocable letter of credit to Transea which provided that drafts by the latter for a specified portion of the purchase price of the bristles would be paid by Schroder upon shipment of the described merchandise and presentation of an invoice and a bill of lading covering the shipment, made out to the order of Schroder.

The letter of credit was delivered to Transea by Schroder's correspondent bank in India, Transea placed fifty cases of material on board a steamship, procured a bill of lading from the steamship company and obtained the customary invoices. These documents describe the bristles called for by the letter of credit. However, the complaint alleges that in fact Transea filled the fifty crates with cowhair, other worthless material and rubbish with intent to simulate genuine merchandise and defraud the plaintiff and Schwarz. The complaint then alleges that Transea drew a draft under the letter of credit to the order of the Chartered Bank and delivered the draft and the fraudulent documents to the 'Chartered Bank at Cawnpore, India, for collection for the account of said defendant Transea'. The Chartered Bank has presented the draft along with the documents to Schroder for payment. The plaintiff prays for a judgment declaring the letter of credit and draft thereunder void and for injunctive relief to prevent the payment of the draft.

For the purposes of this motion, the allegations of the complaint must be deemed established * * *. Therefore, it must be assumed that Transea was engaged in a scheme to defraud the plaintiff and Schwarz, that the merchandise shipped by Transea is worthless rubbish and that the Chartered Bank is not an innocent holder of the draft for value but is merely attempting to procure payment of the draft for Transea's account.

It is well established that a letter of credit is independent of the primary contract of sale between the buyer and the seller. The issuing bank agrees to pay upon presentation of documents, not goods. This rule is necessary to preserve the efficiency of the letter of credit as an instrument for the financing of trade. One of the chief purposes of the letter of credit is to furnish the seller with a ready means of obtaining prompt payment for his merchandise. It would be a most unfortunate interference with business transactions if a bank before honoring drafts drawn upon it was obliged or even allowed to go behind the documents, at the request of the buyer and enter into controversies between the buyer and the seller regarding the quality of the merchandise shipped. If the buyer and the seller intended the bank to do this they could have so provided in the letter of credit itself, and in the absence of such a provision, the court will not demand or even permit the bank to delay paying drafts which are proper in form. Of course, the application of this doctrine presupposes that the documents accompanying the draft are genuine and conform in terms to the requirements of the letter of credit.

However, I believe that a different situation is presented in the instant action. This is not a controversy between the buyer and seller concerning a mere breach of warranty regarding the quality of the merchandise; on the present motion, it must be assumed that the seller has intentionally failed to ship any goods ordered by the buyer. In such a situation, where the seller's fraud has been called to the bank's attention before the drafts and documents have been presented for payment, the principle of the independence of the bank's obligation under the letter of credit should not be extended to protect the unscrupulous seller. It is true that even though the documents are forged or fraudulent, if the issuing bank has already paid the draft before receiving notice of the seller's fraud, it will be protected if it exercised reasonable diligence before making such payment. However, in the instant action Schroder has received notice of Transea's active fraud before it accepted or paid the draft. The Chartered Bank, which under the allegations of the complaint stands in no better position than Transea, should not be heard to complain because Schroder is not forced to pay the draft accompanied by documents covering a transaction which it has reason to believe is fraudulent.

Although our courts have used broad language to the effect that a letter of credit is independent of the primary contract between the buyer and seller, that language was used in cases concerning alleged breaches of warranty; no case has been brought to my attention on this point involving an intentional fraud on the part of the seller which was brought to the bank's notice with the request that it withhold payment of the draft on this account. The distinction between a breach of warranty and active fraud on the part of the seller is supported by authority and reason. As one court has stated: 'Obviously, when the issuer of a letter of credit knows that a document, although correct in form, is, in point of fact, false or illegal, he cannot be called upon to recognize such a document as complying with the terms of a letter of credit.' Old Colony Trust Co. v. Lawyers' Title & Trust Co., 2 Cir., 297 F. 152 at page 158, certiorari denied 265 U.S. 585, 44 S.Ct. 459, 68 L.Ed. 1192.

No hardship will be caused by permitting the bank to refuse payment where fraud is claimed, where the merchandise is not merely inferior in quality but consists of worthless rubbish, where the draft and the accompanying documents are in the hands of one who stands in the same position as the fraudulent seller, where the bank has been given notice of the fraud before being presented with the drafts and documents for payment, and where the bank itself does not wish to pay pending an adjudication of the rights and obligations of the other parties. While the primary factor in the issuance of the letter of credit is the credit standing of the buyer, the security afforded by the merchandise is also taken into account. In fact, the letter of credit requires a bill of lading made out to the order of the bank and not the buyer. Although the bank is not interested in the exact detailed performance of the sales contract, it is vitally interested in assuring itself that there are some goods represented by the documents.

On this motion only the complaint is before me and I am bound by its allegation that the Chartered Bank is not a holder in due course but is a mere agent for collection for the account of the seller charged with fraud. Therefore, the Chartered Bank's motion to dismiss the complaint must be denied. If it had appeared from the face of the complaint that the bank presenting the draft for payment was a holder in due course, its claim against the bank issuing the letter of credit would not be defeated even though the primary transaction was tainted with fraud. This I believe to the better rule despite some authority to the contrary.

The plaintiff's further claim that the terms of the documents presented with the draft are at substantial variance with the requirements of the letter of credit does not seem to be supported by the documents themselves.

Accordingly, the defendant's motion to dismiss the supplemental complaint is denied.

INTRAWORLD INDUSTRIES, INC. v. GIRARD TRUST BANK, 336 A.2d 316, 324-25 (1975). "In light of the basic rule of the independence of the issuer's engagement and the importance of this rule to the effectuation of the purposes of the letter of credit, we think that the circumstances which will justify an injunction against honor must be narrowly limited to situations of fraud in which the wrongdoing of the beneficiary has so vitiated the entire transaction that the legitimate purposes of the independence of the issuer's obligation would no longer be served. A court of equity has the limited duty of

> 'guaranteeing that (the beneficiary) not by allowed to take unconscientious advantage of the situation and run off with plaintiff's money on a pro forma declaration which has *absolutely no basis in fact*.' Dynamics Corp. of America v. Citizens and Southern National Bank, 356 F.Supp. 991, 999 (N.D.Ga.1973) (emphasis supplied)."

ELLINGER, FRAUD IN DOCUMENTARY CREDIT TRANSACTIONS, 1981 J. Bus. L. 258, 262. Professor Ellinger argues that under the American cases, courts may issue an injunction only when "the beneficiary acts without any shred of honest belief in his rights."

UNITED TRADING CORP. v. ALLIED ARAB BANK LTD., [1985] 2 Lloyd's Rep. 554, 561 (C.A.). In this case the court fashioned the English rule for injunctions against payment of a letter of credit. The rule requires the party seeking the injunction to show fraud by clear evidence and to show clear evidence that the issuer knows there is fraud. With respect to the petitioner's allegation of fraud, the court required "strong corroborative evidence of the allegation, usually in the form of contemporary documents" and stipulated that fraud must be "the only realistic inference to draw."

LES MUTUELLE DU MANS VIE v. LIFE ASSURANCE CO., 128 F.R.D. 233, 241 (N.D. Ill. 1989). When an applicant sought to enjoin draws on a letter of credit, the court denied the relief and awarded Rule 11 sanctions to the defendant, observing that the plaintiff, ignoring applicable law had sought "to override the fundamental nature of letters of credit as an arm's length allocation of risk distribution."

UCC § 5-109(a) & Official Comment 1 (3d para.)

(*see Selected Commercial Statutes*)

NOTE ON LIMITS TO THE FRAUD EXCEPTION

The preceding cases and § 5-109(a) indicate that commercial law has fashioned an elevated level of fraud that a party must show before he can stop payment under a credit. That elevated level is often a barrier to injunctive relief and goes far in protecting the letter of credit's independence.

There are additional protections. First, as a matter of common law, most states require that a party alleging fraud prove it not by the usual preponderance of the evidence standard (more probably true than not true) but by "clear and convincing" evidence. Second, in order to obtain injunctive relief, the Code and most jurisdictions as a matter of civil procedure require the petitioner to satisfy certain prerequisites established by the law of equity that can be difficult to meet. Section 2(b) in the next chapter deals with those equity prerequisites. Third, as the following problem indicates, letter of credit law has created an exception to the fraud rule in favor of various protected parties that applies even if the petitioner (1) establishes the elevated level of fraud, (2) shows it by clear and convincing evidence, and (3) satisfies the equity prerequisites.

PROBLEM

[This problem explains a rather subtle distinction in letter of credit law that bankers universally recognize but that U.S. courts have not observed with rigor. Happily, the drafters of revised Article 5 have codified the distinction, but even the codification is moderately recondite.

The problem is one of deciding whom to protect when the applicant for the credit demonstrates clearly that the beneficiary is practicing egregious fraud, delivering, say, bricks in the cartons instead of telecommunications equipment.

Letter of credit law, at some risk to the credit as a commercial device, has crafted an exception to the independence principle in these circumstances and accommodates the applicant's request for an injunction against payment, assuming, of course, that the applicant has no adequate remedy at law.

But, and this is a big "but", letter of credit law will not let the defrauded applicant stop payment if certain innocent parties suffer by virtue of the injunction. The problem is that of identifying the protected parties. Not all innocent parties get the protection.

The key to the Article 5 resolution of the problem lies in the definition of "nominated person" in § 5-102(11). Under that section, the credit issuer, in effect, designates the parties who will be protected from the applicant's injunction against payment. The following problem illustrates the Code's correct understanding of what is the universal view of international bankers.]

On May 1, at the request of Buyer Co., Issuer Bank issued its $248,000 letter of credit in favor of Seller Co. The credit was payable against Seller Co.'s presentation of documents including an invoice and a bill of lading covering the shipment of 248 cartons of telecommunications equipment. The credit also designated Second Bank in Seller's city as the place where Seller should present its documents and draft and authorized Second Bank to pay Seller if the documents complied facially with the terms of the credit. The credit was payable in fractions, so that Seller could ship part of the 248 cartons at one point, draw on the credit and be paid, and later ship another part (or the balance) of the 248 cartons, draw, and be paid.

On May 20, Seller presented at the counters of Second Bank a draft for $100,000 and accompanying documents, including an invoice and a bill of lading describing the merchandise as "telecommunications equipment." Second Bank's document examiners reviewed the documents, determined that they were in facial conformity with the terms of the credit, and paid Seller $100,000. The next day, Seller presented at the counters of Third Bank for collection a second set of documents and a draft for $148,000. Third took the documents, reviewed them for facial conformity with the terms of the credit, passed them on to Second Bank for collection, and credited Seller's loan account for $148,000. Second gave Third only a provisional credit (i.e., no value) and sent both sets of documents to Issuer Bank on May 23. As Issuer Bank's document examiners were reviewing the documents, Buyer brought uncontrovertible evidence to the attention of Issuer Bank that the bills of lading and invoices were false and that the cartons contained bricks instead of telecommunications equipment.

Issuer Bank suggested to Buyer that Buyer seek to have reimbursement of the two banks enjoined. Buyer has petitioned the court for an injunction against payment. How should the bank rule? [See § 5-109(a)(1).]

UCC § 5-109(a)(1)
(*see Selected Commercial Statutes*)

(c) CREDIT CARD FRAUD

FIRST NATIONAL CITY BANK v. MULLARKEY

Civil Court of the City of New York, 1976.
87 Misc.2d 1, 385 N.Y.S.2d 473.

BARDY, Judge.

Plaintiff sues the defendant for $581.26, principal balance due on a credit card, and for an additional 20% or $116.25 counsel fees.

Defendant in his answer denies owing 90% of the credit card claim made by plaintiff.

On the trial the plaintiff called the defendant solely to ask if he requested a credit card to which defendant responded affirmatively. The plaintiff then called as witness its auditor who testified that, according to the account records of the plaintiff, the defendant owed a credit card balance of $581.26 and thereupon rested.

The defendant testified that six charges dated December 16, 1973 totaling $498.63 were charges not made by him, and that said charges were due to an 'unauthorized use of his credit card.' He testified that on January 23, 1974 he reported his credit card was lost and received from a Miss Berlin a number 55575 in connection with such report.

The General Business Law of the State of New York, Section 512, L.1971 incorporates and makes an integral part of the state's law with respect to credit cards the 'Truth in Lending Act' and the regulations thereunder, enacted by the Congress (Chapter 41 of the Consumer Credit Protection Laws—15 U.S.C.A., Section 1601 et seq.).

Pursuant to statute 15 U.S.C.A.—Section 1643, subdivisions 'b', 'c', and 'd', the burden of proof is on the card issuer to show that the use was authorized or, if the use was unauthorized, then the burden of proof is on the card issuer to show that the conditions of liability for the unauthorized use of a credit card as set forth in subsection (a) of this section, have been met.

In subdivision 'a' referred to above, the conditions of liability for the unauthorized use of a credit card which plaintiff has the burden to meet are:

a) That the defendant accepted the credit card;

b) That the liability is not in excess of $50;

c) That the card issuer gives adequate notice to the cardholder of the potential liability;

d) That the card issuer has provided the cardholder with a self-addressed, prestamped notification to be mailed by the cardholder in the event of loss or theft of the credit card;

e) That the unauthorized use occurs before the cardholder has notified the card issuer that an unauthorized use of the credit card has occurred or may occur as the result of loss, theft, or otherwise;

f) The card issuer has provided a method whereby the user of such card can be identified as the person authorized to use it.

The said section 1643 goes on further to say that '(f)or the purposes of this section, a cardholder notifies a card issuer by taking such steps as may be reasonably required in the ordinary course of business to provide the card issuer with the pertinent information whether or not any particular officer, employee, or agent of the card issuer does in fact receive such information.'

The express intent of the Congress in enacting the 'Truth in Lending Act' was to protect the consumer or cardholder against charges for unauthorized use of his or her credit card, and to limit his or her liability for such unauthorized use to a maximum of $50.00 providing, however, that the credit card issuer has complied with certain conditions precedent as set forth in the statute.

Certainly there is room for fraud if a cardholder is unscrupulous or dishonest, and in a multi-million dollar enterprise—such as credit extension—credit card issuers are or should be aware of the existence of individuals who are credit risks, and should make the necessary investigation prior to the issuance of credit cards.

However, the 'Truth in Lending Act' (15 U.S.C.A., section 1601 et seq.; New York State General Business Law, section 512) was intended to protect the vast majority of credit cardholders who, in the main, are honest and should not be penalized for the dishonesty of a few.

Accordingly, it is the Court's opinion based upon the evidence herein and the pertinent Federal and State statutes and case law, that the limit of the defendant's liability with respect to the unauthorized charges of December 16, 1973 totaling $498.63—is $50. On the evidence herein, the plaintiff is entitled to the sum of $82.63 credit card charges which the defendant has not disputed, plus the additional sum of $50. (the statutory limit of liability on the unauthorized charges) as hereinbefore indicated, for a total sum of $132.63.

Judgment for the plaintiff in the sum of $132.63.

CONSUMER CREDIT PROTECTION ACT

15 U.S.C.A. § 1643

(*see Selected Commercial Statutes*)

QUESTION

What would be the general policy of an efficiency seeking bank when its customer claims that several purchases amounting to $250 are unauthorized? What would its policy be when the same customer keeps reporting such small dollar unauthorized purchases? What would its policy be when a customer reports $10,000 in unauthorized purchases?

SECTION 4. UNCONSCIONABILITY

UCC § 2-302

(*see Selected Commercial Statutes*)

UCC § 2-719(3)

(*see Selected Commercial Statutes*)

MURRAY, THE REVISION OF ARTICLE 2: ROMANCING THE PRISM, 35 Wm. & Mary L. Rev. 1447, 1497-99 (1994).

Others may be startled to learn that section 2-302, which Arthur Leff once called "an emotionally satisfying incantation" demonstrating that "it is easy to say nothing with words" requires no revision. The statutory language is devoid of any test to determine what is and what is not unconscionable. Leff was correct. It is emotionally satisfying, but that's it. If it is desirable to state a relatively clear parol evidence test in the statutory language rather than in the comments to section 2-202, as the Study Project Committee suggests, it certainly seems desirable to state the basic unconscionability tests in section 2-302. Notwithstanding the substantial drafting challenge, the basic concepts of unfair surprise and oppression could be stated as the fundamental concepts of unconscionability. The comments then could elaborate and illustrate these concepts to further explain the unexpected and adhesive forms of unconscionability. If the basic tests were set forth in the revised section, the application of unconscionability could be elaborated in the comments. Certainly, the application of the doctrine to merchant contracts should be clarified, and I believe expanded, at least in the comments. The argument that adherence to the formulas required to disclaim implied warranties precludes unconscionability should be expressly rejected with clear statements that such adherence merely meets the threshold standards for recognition of such disclaimers.

There is a serious question as to whether consumers should be bound by material risk-shifting clauses which they would have little if any opportunity to understand. For example, where a preprinted form contains an exclusion of consequential damages, it may be desirable to view such a clause as prima facie unconscionable with respect to a consumer buyer. The Study Group, however, has recommended the deletion of language in section 2-719(3) that declares a limitation on consequential damages in the case of consumer goods prima facie unconscionable where there is injury to the person. This is consistent with the Study Group's earlier recommendation that privity be reincarnated in section 2-318, even in cases involving injury to the person. Under my recommendation, the implied warranty of merchantability should not be disclaimable with respect to a consumer. Consumer buyers should never lose that warranty.

If consumers retained the implied warranty of merchantability without limitation and if limitations on consequential damages were prima facie unconscionable as to consumers, that protection, along with remedial assistance such as that already afforded by other state and federal legislation, finally would provide a level of protection consonant with a consumer's reasonable expectations and inability to understand or bargain out of material risk-shifting clauses. The reactions to such changes from some manufacturers would range from alarm to hysteria. Such reactions would be baseless.

We have moved from the ninety day and (later) one-year and 12,0000 mile warranty on new automobiles to three-year "bumper-to-bumper" express warranties and even longer express warranties against specified defects. The total consumer protection legislation in America has not caused this change. The cause was something called competition—essentially competition from the Japanese. The quality of American automobiles has improved substantially because of this competition and not because of our legislation. We continue to live with ridiculously poor warranty protection with respect to electronic devices because Americans do not manufacture these products and there is no competition with the Japanese and Pacific Rim manufacturers.

American business is now consumed with a "total quality" concept to ascertain global competitiveness. Precluding disclaimers of implied warranties or exclusions of consequential damages at least in consumer products would further fuel the incentive to American corporations to create total quality products for sale throughout America and the world.

DIMATTEO, THE COUNTERPOISE OF CONTRACTS: THE REASONABLE PERSON STANDARD AND THE SUBJECTIVITY OF JUDGMENT, 48 S. Car. L. Rev. 293, 338-41 (1997).

The role of the reasonable person has expanded with the advent of form contracts. The standardization of contracts has removed the narrow focus of the reasonable person from the four corners of the contract. The rationalization of this narrower focus was premised upon the sanctity of the written contract and the duty of the contracting parties to read any instrument upon which they affix their signatures. This traditional focus holds that the act of signing a standard form is evidence that the signer intended to accept all of its terms. The full totality of the circumstances analysis is shunted. The reasonable person determines contractual consent based solely upon a four corners reading of the contract.

This approach became increasingly untenable when it became apparent that in reality there was no such actual consent. A rational application of the reasonable person standard would recognize the flaw in this notion of consent. The fact of the matter was that at least one of the parties did not read or understand the fine print of the preprinted form. There is no true manifestation of intent because there has been no conscious agreement to accept the unread terms. This unawareness of the forms' content is akin to the doctrine of mistake where one party is unaware of a certain fact. It became increasingly difficult for the reasonable person to conclude that the parties had consented to all the terms in the form. The role of the reasonable person was thus expanded to determine what reasonable terms would be included and what unreasonable terms would be jettisoned from the contract. In order to accomplish this task the reasonable person was placed in the shoes of the recipient of the form, generally the ordinary consumer, to determine the person's reasonable expectations regarding the intent of the terms to be found in the form. "Courts must examine the circumstances surrounding the transaction to determine the consumer's objective understanding." The reasonable expectations of the ordinary consumer are used to supplement the actual writing in the courts enforcement decisions. Professor Meyerson asserts that this reasonable expectation analysis can also be performed from the perspective of the form-giver. "A consumer's assent to a contract should be determined by how a reasonable person in the other party's position would ascertain the consumer's intent as manifested through words and deeds." Whether from the perspective of the consumer or the form-giver, the final guide to enforcement is not the written form but what the signing party knew and what a reasonable consumer would have known.

Professor Llewellyn devised a solution to the dilemma of determining the reasonable intention of the parties in the area of form contracts. He bifurcated form contracts: the dickered deal and the supplementary boilerplate deal.

Instead of thinking about "assent" to boiler-plate clauses, we can recognize that so far as concerns the specific, there is no assent at all. What has in fact been assented to, specifically, are the few dickered terms, and the broad type of the transaction, and but one thing more. That one thing more is a blanket assent (not a specific assent) to any not unreasonable or indecent terms the seller may have on his form, which do not alter or eviscerate the reasonable meaning of the dickered terms. The reasonable person is given two tasks in Llewellyn's dichotomy: (1) to interpret the meaning of the terms expressly negotiated by the parties, and (2) to determine what non-dickered terms are to be reconstructed or expelled due to unreasonableness or what reasonable terms are to be implied to fill in gaps.

The notion of blanket assent was reanalyzed by Professor Fried. He asks whether it is the task of the courts to construct "a kind of nonconsensual penumbra around the consensual core." The reasonable person can perform this task by looking to the type or essence of the contract. For purposes of determining reasonableness, the reasonable person looks to the terms generally found in such contracts. The test becomes "whether the consumer, as a reasonable man, should have been aware of the material risk allocated to him" or whether the terms of the form contract were "fundamentally different in its purport from what [a reasonable person would have] believed to be the case." The reasonable person is called on to conform the boilerplate terms to the spirit of the contract as represented by the dickered terms and the type of transaction being undertaken. A second-order conformity is often performed as well. This is the conformity best engineered by the communal reasonable person. It is based upon the assumption that the party's blanket assent was made with the implied understanding that the other party's boilerplate did not contain any unreasonable or unfair terms. This indicates a transformation of the reasonable person from being a creation of objective fact to being a creation of values. The focus is not on what was considered to be reasonable at the time of formation as perceived by the contracting parties. Instead, the focus has shifted forward to what the reasonable person considers to be reasonable from the perspective of the court. Professor Horwitz summarized this conversion of the reasonable person: "Objectivism was the legal expression of this quest for uniformity. It shifted legal inquiry away from a focus on actual intent or will toward a concern with reasonable, average, or customary practices."

BROWN v. INVESTORS MORTGAGE CO.

United States Court of Appeals, Ninth Circuit, 1997.
121 F.3d 472.

PER CURIAM.

Plaintiff Catherine Brown borrowed $28,800 on her home. She fell behind in her payments. The lender initiated foreclosure proceedings.

To prevent foreclosure, Brown borrowed another $50,000 on her home from defendant CLS Mortgage, Inc. The debt carried 16% interest, required monthly payments of $666.67 for three years, and was then payable in full. The maximum interest permitted by state usury law was 12.22%. Brown again fell behind, and CLS commenced foreclosure.

To pay off the CLS loan, Brown borrowed $74,000 from defendant Investors Mortgage Company (IMC). The debt carried interest of 15%, exceeding the existing 12% limit under state law. Brown defaulted. IMC commenced nonjudicial foreclosure. Brown filed for bankruptcy and sued the lenders and others to invalidate the loans, alleging violations of state usury law and the Washington Consumer Protection Act. Defendants moved for summary judgment. The bankruptcy court ordered dismissal. The district court affirmed.

* * *

Brown argues the IMC loan was procedurally unconscionable because (1) Brown had no meaningful choice regarding the terms of the loan, and (2) IMC raised Brown's proposed monthly payments after she complained the proposed payments were too high. While Brown was in difficult straits, the facts she alleges in support of her first arguments do not rise to the level of unfairness required to sustain a claim of unconscionability. We reject Brown's second argument because IMC raised Brown's subsequent payments after lowering the initial payments at her request.

Brown argues the loan was substantively unconscionable. The cases cited by Brown are unpersuasive. The interest rate on the IMC loan, while high, was not unusual for loans made to high-risk borrowers.

* * *

Chapter 14

COMMERCIAL REMEDIES

INTRODUCTORY NOTE

Remedies inform causes of action, which inform rights and obligations. Remedies, then, tell us a lot about what commercial law really thinks of the obligations and rights commercial parties have bestowed on each other. We study remedies last not because they are least important in the understanding of commercial law but simply because it is difficult to study them without knowing all that comes before.

For some, this is a sad ending, for others a happy one. By now, students should know that commercial law is susceptible to the tensions that manifest themselves in most areas of human endeavor, the tension between conservative and liberal, trader and raider, nonactivist and activist, right and left, believer and skeptic.

In this chapter, the liberal may see commercial law taking away with one hand what it claims to have given with another; the conservative may see it protecting party autonomy. The fact is that the commercial law of remedies is generally a story of limiting the causes of action that commercial law recognizes for breach of commercial obligations.

Of course, this is neither a happy nor a sad ending, for it is no ending at all. Commercial law is dynamic. It has to be; it serves a dynamic culture; and the lawyer who thinks he has the answers can only say he has them for today or, maybe, for yesterday. This book is a study in commercial law basics in part because the authors despair of teaching anything else. Commercial law is far too vast to teach in the three to eight credit hours most students can afford to allocate to it; and, whatever heroic efforts teachers may make, the most we can provide is a snapshot of a rolling storm of tidal motion.

In short, this chapter is another effort to illustrate the tensions in commercial law and some of the current resolutions. You will note contrast here similar to the contrast you have seen in earlier chapters. On the one hand, commercial law limits recovery with rules of privity and then abrogates the limits with doctrines of unjust enrichment and subrogation; it grants a cause of action against financial intermediaries and then denies recovery for consequential damages, though we all know the aggrieved party suffers them.

All of this could be resolved easily if we could only find that philosopher king Plato wrote about.

SECTION 1. DAMAGES IN GENERAL

UCC § 1-106

(*see Selected Commercial Statutes*)

(a) ELECTRONIC FUNDS TRANSFER

EVRA CORP. v. SWISS BANK CORP.

United States Court of Appeals, Seventh Circuit, 1982.
673 F.2d 951 (7th Cir.), cert. denied, 459 U.S. 1017.

POSNER, Circuit Judge.

The question—one of first impression—in this diversity case is the extent of a bank's liability for failure to make a transfer of funds when requested by wire to do so. The essential facts are undisputed. In 1972 Hyman-Michaels Company, a large Chicago dealer in scrap metal, entered into a two-year contract to supply steel scrap to a Brazilian corporation. Hyman-Michaels chartered a ship, the Pandora, to carry the scrap to Brazil. The charter was for one year, with an option to extend the charter for a second year; specified a fixed daily rate of pay for the hire of the ship during both the initial and the option period, payable semi-monthly "in advance"; and provided that if payment was not made on time the Pandora's owner could cancel the charter. Payment was to be made by deposit to the owner's account in the Banque de Paris et des Pays-Bas (Suisse) in Geneva, Switzerland.

The usual method by which Hyman-Michaels, in Chicago, got the payments to the Banque de Paris in Geneva was to request the Continental Illinois National Bank and Trust Company of Chicago, where it had an account, to make a wire transfer of funds. Continental would debit Hyman-Michaels' account by the amount of the payment and then send a telex to its London office for retransmission to its correspondent bank in Geneva—Swiss Bank Corporation—asking Swiss Bank to deposit this amount in the Banque de Paris account of the Pandora's owner. The transaction was completed by the crediting of Swiss Bank's account at Continental by the same amount.

When Hyman-Michaels chartered the Pandora in June 1972, market charter rates were very low, and it was these rates that were fixed in the charter for its entire term-two years if Hyman-Michaels exercised its option. Shortly after the agreement was signed, however, charter rates began to climb and by October 1972 they were much higher than they had been in June. The Pandora's owners were eager to get out of the charter if they could. At the end of October they thought they had found a way, for the payment that was due in the Banque de Paris on October 26 had not arrived by October 30, and on that day the Pandora's owner notified Hyman-Michaels that it was canceling the charter because of the breach of the payment term. Hyman-Michaels had mailed a check for the October 26 installment to the Banque de Paris rather than use the wire-transfer method of payment. It had done this in order to have the use of its money for the period that it would take the check to clear, about two weeks. But the check had not been mailed in Chicago until October 25 and of course did not reach Geneva on the twenty-sixth.

When Hyman-Michaels received notification that the charter was being canceled it immediately wired payment to the Banque de Paris, but the Pandora's owner refused to accept it and insisted that the charter was indeed canceled. The matter was referred to arbitration in accordance with the charter. On December 5, 1972, the arbitration panel ruled in favor of Hyman-Michaels. The panel noted that previous arbitration panels had "shown varying degrees of latitude to Charterers"; "In all cases, a pattern of obligation on Owners' part to protest, complain, or warn of intended withdrawal was expressed as an essential prerequisite to withdrawal, in spite of the clear wording of the operative clause. No such advance notice was given by Owners of M/V Pandora." One of the three members of the panel dissented; he thought the Pandora's owner was entitled to cancel.

Hyman-Michaels went back to making the charter payments by wire transfer. On the morning of April 25, 1973, it telephoned Continental Bank and requested it to transfer $27,000 to the Banque de Paris account of the Pandora's owner in payment for the charter hire period from April 27 to May 11, 1973. Since the charter provided for payment "in advance," this payment arguably was due by the close of business on April 26. The requested telex went out to Continental's London office on the afternoon of April 25, which was nighttime in England. Early the next morning a telex operator in Continental's London office dialed, as Continental's Chicago office had instructed him to do, Swiss Bank's general telex number, which rings in the bank's cable department. But that number was busy, and after trying unsuccessfully for an hour to engage it the Continental telex operator dialed another number, that of a machine in Swiss Bank's foreign exchange department which he had used in the past when the general number was engaged. We know this machine received the telexed message because it signaled the sending machine at both the beginning and end of the transmission that the telex was being received. Yet Swiss Bank failed to comply with the payment order, and no transfer of funds was made to the account of the Pandora's owner in the Banque de Paris.

No one knows exactly what went wrong. One possibility is that the receiving telex machine had simply run out of paper, in which event it would not print the message although it had received it. Another is that whoever took the message out of the machine after it was printed failed to deliver it to the banking department. Unlike the machine in the cable department that the Continental telex operator had originally tried to reach, the machines in the foreign exchange department were operated by junior foreign exchange dealers rather than by professional telex operators, although Swiss Bank knew that messages intended for other departments were sometimes diverted to the telex machines in the foreign exchange department.

At 8:30 a.m. the next day, April 27, Hyman-Michaels in Chicago received a telex from the Pandora's owner stating that the charter was canceled because payment for the April 27-May 11 charter period had not been made.

Hyman-Michaels called over to Continental and told them to keep trying to effect payment through Swiss Bank even if the Pandora's owner rejected it. This instruction was confirmed in a letter to Continental dated April 28, in which Hyman-Michaels stated: "please instruct your London branch to advise their correspondents to persist in attempting to make this payment. This should be done even in the face of a rejection on the part of Banque de Paris to receive this payment. It is paramount that in order to strengthen our position in an arbitration that these funds continue to be readily available." Hyman-Michaels did not attempt to wire the money directly to the Banque de Paris as it had done on the occasion of its previous default. Days passed while the missing telex message was hunted unsuccessfully. Finally Swiss Bank suggested to Continental that it retransmit the telex message to the machine in the cable department and this was done on May 1. The next day Swiss Bank attempted to deposit the $27,000 in the account of the Pandora's owner at the Banque de Paris but the payment was refused.

Again the arbitrators were convened and rendered a decision. In it they ruled that Hyman-Michaels had been "blameless" up until the morning of April 27, when it first learned that the Banque de Paris had not received payment on April 26, but that "being faced with this situation," Hyman-Michaels had "failed to do everything in (its) power to remedy it. The action taken was immediate but did not prove to be adequate, in that (Continental) Bank and its correspondent required some 5/6 days to trace and effect the lost instruction to remit. (Hyman-Michaels) could have ordered an immediate duplicate payment-or even sent a Banker's check by hand or special messengers, so that the funds could have reached owner's Bank, not later than April 28th." By failing to do any of these things Hyman-Michaels had "created the opening" that the Pandora's owner was seeking in order to be able to cancel the charter. It had "acted imprudently." The arbitration panel concluded, reluctantly but unanimously, that this time the Pandora's owner was entitled to cancel the agreement. The arbitration decision was confirmed by a federal district court in New York.

Hyman-Michaels then brought this diversity action against Swiss Bank, seeking to recover its expenses in the second arbitration proceeding plus the profits that it lost because of the cancellation of the charter. The contract by which Hyman-Michaels had agreed to ship scrap steel to Brazil had been terminated by the buyer in March 1973 and Hyman-Michaels had promptly subchartered the Pandora at market rates, which by April 1973 were double the rates fixed in the charter. Its lost profits are based on the difference between the charter and subcharter rates.

Swiss Bank impleaded Continental Bank as a third-party defendant, asking that if it should be ordered to pay Hyman-Michaels, then Continental should be ordered to indemnify it. Continental filed a cross-claim against Hyman-Michaels seeking to shift back to Hyman-Michaels the cost of any judgment that Swiss Bank might obtain against it, on the ground that any errors by Continental were caused by Hyman-Michaels' negligence. Hyman-Michaels in turn counterclaimed against Continental, alleging that Continental had both been negligent and broken its contract with Hyman-Michaels in failing to effect payment on April 26, and was therefore liable to Hyman-Michaels along with Swiss Bank.

The case was tried to a district judge without a jury. In his decision, 522 F.Supp. 820 (N.D.Ill.1981), he first ruled that the substantive law applicable to Hyman-Michaels' claim against Swiss Bank was that of Illinois, rather than Switzerland as urged by Swiss Bank, and that Swiss Bank had been negligent and under Illinois law was liable to Hyman-Michaels for $2.1 million in damages. This figure was made up of about $16,000 in arbitration expenses and the rest in lost profits on the subcharter of the Pandora. The judge also ruled that Swiss Bank was not entitled to indemnification from Continental Bank, which made Continental's cross-claim moot; and lastly he dismissed Hyman-Michaels' counterclaim against Continental on the ground that Continental had not breached any duty to Hyman-Michaels. The case comes to us on Swiss Bank's appeal from the judgment in favor of Hyman-Michaels and from the dismissal of Swiss Bank's claim against Continental Bank, and on Hyman-Michaels' appeal from the dismissal of its counterclaim against Continental Bank.

* * *

When a bank fails to make a requested transfer of funds, this can cause two kinds of loss. First, the funds themselves or interest on them may be lost, and of course the fee paid for the transfer, having bought nothing, becomes a loss item. These are "direct" (sometimes called "general") damages. Hyman-Michaels is not seeking any direct damages in this case and apparently sustained none. It did not lose any part of the $27,000; although its account with Continental Bank was debited by this amount prematurely, it was not an interest-bearing account so Hyman-Michaels lost no interest; and Hyman-Michaels paid no fee either to Continental or to Swiss Bank for the aborted transfer. A second type of loss, which either the payor or the payee may suffer, is a dislocation in one's business triggered by the failure to pay. Swiss Bank's failure to transfer funds to the Banque de Paris when requested to do so by Continental Bank set off a chain reaction which resulted in an arbitration proceeding that was costly to Hyman-Michaels and in the cancellation of a highly profitable contract. It is those costs and lost profits—"consequential" or, as they are sometimes called, "special" damages—that Hyman-Michaels seeks in this lawsuit, and recovered below. It is conceded that if Hyman-Michaels was entitled to consequential damages, the district court measured them correctly. The only issue is whether it was entitled to consequential damages.

If a bank loses a check, its liability is governed by Article 4 of the Uniform Commercial Code, which precludes consequential damages unless the bank is acting in bad faith. See Ill.Rev.Stat. ch. 26, § 4-103(5). If Article 4 applies to this transaction, Hyman-Michaels cannot recover the damages that it seeks, because Swiss Bank was not acting in bad faith. Maybe the language of Article 4 could be stretched to include electronic fund transfers, see section 4-102(2), but they were not in the contemplation of the draftsmen. For purposes of this case we shall assume, as the Second Circuit held in Delbrueck & Co. v. Manufacturers Hanover Trust Co., 609 F.2d 1047, 1051 (2d Cir. 1979), that Article 4 is inapplicable, and apply common law principles instead.

Hadley v. Baxendale, 9 Ex. 341, 156 Eng.Rep. 145 (1854), is the leading common law case on liability for consequential damages caused by failure or delay in carrying out a commercial undertaking. The engine shaft in plaintiffs' corn mill had broken and they hired the defendants, a common carrier, to transport the shaft to the manufacturer, who was to make a new one using the broken shaft as a model. The carrier failed to deliver the shaft within the time promised. With the engine shaft out of service the mill was shut down. The plaintiffs sued the defendants for the lost profits of the mill during the additional period that it was shut down because of the defendants' breach of their promise. The court held that the lost profits were not a proper item of damages, because "in the great multitude of cases of millers sending off broken shafts to third persons by a carrier under ordinary circumstances, such consequences (the stoppage of the mill and resulting loss of profits) would not, in all probability, have occurred; and these special circumstances were here never communicated by the plaintiffs to the defendants." 9 Ex. at 356, 156 Eng.Rep. at 151.

The rule of Hadley v. Baxendale—that consequential damages will not be awarded unless the defendant was put on notice of the special circumstances giving rise to them—has been applied in many Illinois cases, and Hadley cited approvingly. See, e.g., Underground Constr. Co. v. Sanitary Dist. of Chicago, 367 Ill. 360, 369, 11 N.E.2d 361, 365 (1937); Western Union Tel. Co. v. Martin, 9 Ill.App. 587, 591-93 (1882); Siegel v. Western Union Tel. Co., 312 Ill.App. 86, 92-93, 37 N.E.2d 868, 871 (1941); Spangler v. Holthusen, 61 Ill.App.3d 74, 80-82, 18 Ill.Dec. 840, 378 N.E.2d 304, 309-10 (1978). In Siegel, the plaintiff had delivered $200 to Western Union with instructions to transmit it to a friend of the plaintiff's. The money was to be bet (legally) on a horse, but this was not disclosed in the instructions. Western Union misdirected the money order and it did not reach the friend until several hours after the race had taken place. The horse that the plaintiff had intended to bet on won and would have paid $1650 on the plaintiff's $200 bet if the bet had been placed. He sued Western Union for his $1450 lost profit, but the court held that under the rule of Hadley v. Baxendale Western Union was not liable, because it "had no notice or knowledge of the purpose for which the money was being transmitted." 312 Ill.App. at 93, 37 N.E.2d at 871.

The present case is similar, though Swiss Bank knew more than Western Union knew in Siegel; it knew or should have known, from Continental Bank's previous telexes, that Hyman-Michaels was paying the Pandora Shipping Company for the hire of a motor vessel named Pandora. But it did not know when payment was due, what the terms of the charter were, or that they had turned out to be extremely favorable to Hyman-Michaels. And it did not know that Hyman-Michaels knew the Pandora's owner would try to cancel the charter, and probably would succeed, if Hyman-Michaels was ever again late in making payment, or that despite this peril Hyman-Michaels would not try to pay until the last possible moment and in the event of a delay in transmission would not do everything in its power to minimize the consequences of the delay. Electronic funds transfers are not so unusual as to automatically place a bank on notice of extraordinary consequences if such a transfer goes awry. Swiss Bank did not have enough information to infer that if it lost a $27,000 payment order it would face a liability in excess of $2 million.

It is true that in both Hadley and Siegel there was a contract between the parties and here there was none. We cannot be certain that the Illinois courts would apply the principles of those cases outside of the contract area. As so often in diversity cases, there is an irreducible amount of speculation involved in attempting to predict the reaction of a state's courts to a new issue. The best we can do is to assume that the Illinois courts would look to the policies underlying cases such as Hadley and Siegel and, to the extent they found them pertinent, would apply those cases here. We must therefore ask what difference it should make whether the parties are or are not bound to each other by a contract. On the one hand, it seems odd that the absence of a contract would enlarge rather than limit the extent of liability. After all, under Swiss law the absence of a contract would be devastating to Hyman-Michaels' claim. Privity is not a wholly artificial concept. It is one thing to imply a duty to one with whom one has a contract and another to imply it to the entire world.

On the other hand, contract liability is strict. A breach of contract does not connote wrongdoing; it may have been caused by circumstances beyond the promisor's control-a strike, a fire, the failure of a supplier to deliver an essential input. And while such contract doctrines as impossibility, impracticability, and frustration relieve promisors from liability for some failures to perform that are beyond their control, many other such failures are actionable although they could not have been prevented by the exercise of due care. The district judge found that Swiss Bank had been negligent in losing Continental Bank's telex message and it can be argued that Swiss Bank should therefore be liable for a broader set of consequences than if it had only broken a contract. But Siegel implicitly rejects this distinction. Western Union had not merely broken its contract to deliver the plaintiff's money order; it had "negligently misdirected" the money order. "The company's negligence is conceded." 312 Ill.App. at 88, 91, 37 N.E.2d at 869, 871. Yet it was not liable for the consequences.

Siegel, we conclude, is authority for holding that Swiss Bank is not liable for the consequences of negligently failing to transfer Hyman-Michaels' funds to Banque de Paris; reason for such a holding is found in the animating principle of Hadley v. Baxendale, which is that the costs of the untoward consequence of a course of dealings should be borne by that party who was able to avert the consequence at least cost and failed to do so. In Hadley the untoward consequence was the shutting down of the mill. The carrier could have avoided it by delivering the engine shaft on time. But the mill owners, as the court noted, could have avoided it simply by having a spare shaft. 9 Ex. at 355-56, 156 Eng.Rep. at 151. Prudence required that they have a spare shaft anyway, since a replacement could not be obtained at once even if there was no undue delay in carting the broken shaft to and the replacement shaft from the manufacturer. The court refused to imply a duty on the part of the carrier to guarantee the mill owners against the consequences of their own lack of prudence, though of course if the parties had stipulated for such a guarantee the court would have enforced it. The notice requirement of Hadley v. Baxendale is designed to assure that such an improbable guarantee really is intended.

This case is much the same, though it arises in a tort rather than a contract setting. Hyman-Michaels showed a lack of prudence throughout. It was imprudent for it to mail in Chicago a letter that unless received the next day in Geneva would put Hyman-Michaels in breach of a contract that was very profitable to it and that the other party to the contract had every interest in canceling. It was imprudent thereafter for Hyman-Michaels, having narrowly avoided cancellation and having (in the words of its appeal brief in this court) been "put * * * on notice that the payment provision of the Charter would be strictly enforced thereafter," to wait till arguably the last day before payment was due to instruct its bank to transfer the necessary funds overseas. And it was imprudent in the last degree for Hyman-Michaels, when it received notice of cancellation on the last possible day payment was due, to fail to pull out all the stops to get payment to the Banque de Paris on that day, and instead to dither while Continental and Swiss Bank wasted five days looking for the lost telex message. Judging from the obvious reluctance with which the arbitration panel finally decided to allow the Pandora's owner to cancel the charter, it might have made all the difference if Hyman-Michaels had gotten payment to the Banque de Paris by April 27 or even by Monday, April 30, rather than allowed things to slide until May 2.

This is not to condone the sloppy handling of incoming telex messages in Swiss Bank's foreign department. But Hyman-Michaels is a sophisticated business enterprise. It knew or should have known that even the Swiss are not infallible; that messages sometimes get lost or delayed in transit among three banks, two of them located 5000 miles apart, even when all the banks are using reasonable care; and that therefore it should take its own precautions against the consequences—best known to itself—of a mishap that might not be due to anyone's negligence.

* * *

We could remand for new findings based on the proper legal standard, but it is unnecessary to do so. The undisputed facts, recited in this opinion, show as a matter of law that Hyman-Michaels is not entitled to recover consequential damages from Swiss Bank.

Since Hyman-Michaels' complaint against Swiss Bank must be dismissed, Swiss Bank's third-party complaint against Continental Bank and Continental Bank's cross-claim against Hyman-Michaels are moot. That leaves only Hyman-Michaels' counterclaim against Continental Bank still to be considered.

* * *

On the merits, we agree with the district judge that Hyman-Michaels did not prove its case. Continental did not break any contract with Hyman-Michaels. All it undertook to do on April 25 was to transmit a telex message to Swiss Bank, and it did so. All it undertook to do on April 27, by the evidence of Hyman-Michaels' own confirming letter, was to advise its correspondent—that is, Swiss Bank—to "persist in attempting to make * * * payment," and it did so advise its correspondent. Nor was Continental negligent on either occasion. Its telex operator had used the machine in Swiss Bank's foreign department before, for the same purpose and without incident; he had no reason to expect a mishap. And Continental used due care in assisting Swiss Bank in the latter's vain hunt for the missing telex. The district court's findings on these issues were skimpy but the facts are clear and a remand is unnecessary.

No other issues need be decided. The judgment in favor of Hyman-Michaels against Swiss Bank is reversed with directions to enter judgment for Swiss Bank. The judgment in favor of Continental Bank on Swiss Bank's third-party complaint is vacated with instructions to dismiss that complaint as moot. The judgment dismissing Continental's cross-claim against Hyman-Michaels as moot, and the judgment in favor of Continental on Hyman-Michaels' counterclaim, are affirmed. The costs of the appeals shall be borne by Hyman-Michaels (Evra Corporation).

UCC § 4A-305(a), (b) & (c) & cmt. 2
(*see Selected Commercial Statutes*)

SECURITIES FUND SERVICES, INC. v. AMERICAN NATIONAL BANK & TRUST COMPANY

United States District Court, Northern District of Illinois, 1982.
542 F. Supp. 323.

[The plaintiff (SFS), a corporate transfer agent acting upon what it believed to be written instructions of a shareholder, redeemed stock it was holding for the shareholder, and caused its bank (NEMB) to wire the proceeds to defendant bank (ANB) for the account of "John Bushman, Trustee // 204471." Upon receipt of the transfer notice, the ANB banker observed that there was no account in the name of Bushman, though there was an account bearing the number on the transfer order in the name of Gerald S. Haberkorn, Inc. The defendant thereupon credited the Haberkorn account with more than $2 million. In fact, the directions to plaintiff were forged; and Haberkorn, in reliance on notice of the deposit, parted with merchandise, presumably, to the fraudster's co-conspirator. Having made Bushman whole, SFS argued that the money was gone and that defendant should restore it. The complaint contained causes of action in negligence among other things.]

LEIGHTON, District Judge.

This is a civil diversity action for damages arising out of a wire transfer transaction. New England Merchants National Bank of Boston (NEMB), at the direction of plaintiff Security Fund Services (SFS), requested, by wire, a transfer of funds disbursed by SFS to an account purportedly in the American National Bank and Trust Company of Chicago (ANB), the defendant. The dispute arises from questions now being raised concerning crediting of the funds by ANB.

* * *

Under Illinois law, negligence must be proved by the existence of a duty owed to plaintiff by defendant, a breach of that duty, and an injury proximately resulting from that breach. The existence of such a duty is a question of law. Evra Corp., 522 F.Supp. at 828, citing Cunis v. Brennan, 56 Ill.2d 372, 308 N.E.2d 617 (1974). For a legal duty to exist, the occurrence must not be simply foreseeable but "reasonably foreseeable." Evra Corp., Id. at 959. The plaintiff in Evra contended that the defendant Swiss Bank owed plaintiff a duty to transmit the wire transfer accurately and timely. The court found that Swiss Bank owed a duty of care to Evra to maintain a system of receiving and disposing of telex messages upon which plaintiff could rely, and that Swiss Bank breached that duty. The court stated that the facts indicated "an appalling lack of regard on the part of Swiss Bank for the more than reasonably foreseeable possibility that the negligent maintenance of its foreign exchange telex machines could result in substantial damage to one of its customers." Id. at 829. Thus, Evra, as one of Swiss Bank's "customers," could anticipate due care to be exercised by Swiss Bank in the handling of the wire transfer. In its opinion reversing the lower court, the Seventh Circuit held that this type of "general foreseeability" is insufficient to support an award of consequential damages. Evra Corp., 673 F.2d 951, at 959 (7th Cir. 1982). However, the circuit court noted that a different case was presented where, as here, direct damages are sought. Id. at 955.

In this case, SFS can likewise be deemed to be a "customer" of ANB. Section 4-104(e) of the U.C.C. defines a customer as "any person having an account with a bank or for whom a bank has agreed to collect items and includes a bank carrying an account with another bank." Through the agency relation discussed, ANB was acting essentially as a collecting bank for NEMB which in turn was the custodial agent of the funds disbursed by SFS. Furthermore, the official comment to U.C.C. 4-203, dealing with the effect of instructions given to a collecting bank by the transferor, states that the collecting bank is liable for failure to exercise good faith or ordinary care. Thus, reading the complaint in the light most favorable to SFS, it was a "customer" of ANB which owed it a duty to use due care in handling the wire transfer. Further, the loss of the transferred funds is the reasonably foreseeable result of a deposit made where the name on the transfer instructions differs from the name on the account into which the funds are deposited. Thus, plaintiff has stated a claim in negligence, therefore, the motion to dismiss Counts I-III is denied.

LLOYD'S PLC v. LYNCH, 702 F. Supp. 157, 158 (N.D. Ohio 1988). When a bank clerk failed to deliver "a cryptic details of payment message," accompanying an international wire transfer over the S.W.I.F.T. system, the sender claimed that a planned merger failed and that it suffered damages in the amount of $100,000,000. The court dismissed the claim, holding as a matter of law that the damages were not foreseeable.

UCC § 4A-207

(*see Selected Commercial Statutes*)

DOLE, RECEIVING BANK LIABILITY FOR ERRORS IN WHOLESALE WIRE TRANSFERS, 69 Tul. L. Rev. 877, 912-16 (1995).

Under Article 4A, the general immunity of receiving banks from liability for errors made by prior senders may well have been a conscious decision to facilitate machine processing of payment orders upon the basis of numerical identifiers. In any event, this general immunity has the effect of protecting receiving banks that engage in automated processing from liability for errors that would be apparent only upon visual inspection of a payment order.

UNCITRAL commenced work on the Model Law in response to the development of electronic transmission, but early in the project decided not to emphasize the method of communicating a payment order. Nevertheless, by obligating receiving banks to give notice to identified senders only of inconsistencies that have been detected, the Model Law accommodates automated processing. Because payment orders that are processed by automation are not visually inspected, inconsistencies that do not preclude automated processing will not be detected.

Article 4A also has two special provisions protecting reliance by receiving banks upon numbers identifying intermediary banks, beneficiaries' banks, and beneficiaries in the automated processing of payment orders. The protection with respect to identifiers of a beneficiary's bank and a beneficiary is most important. A misidentification of an intermediary bank alone is more likely to delay a funds transfer than to preclude a payment order from reaching the intended beneficiary.

Notwithstanding a deviation from a sender's subjective intention, the applicability of a protective provision makes a "right" bank or beneficiary out of persons that a sender subjectively considers to be "wrong" and prevents both activation of the money-back guarantee and receiving bank liability for error. For example, consider an originator's payment order that designates "John Jones" as the beneficiary, but the account identified as belonging to John Jones is in fact owned by Mary Smith. Then, in reliance upon the accuracy of the account number, the beneficiary's bank pays the transferred funds into Mary Smith's account. In this situation, a protective provision can deem the funds transfer properly completed. Proper completion would require the originator to recover the mistaken payment from Mary Smith and entitle the beneficiary's bank that relied upon the mistaken account number without verifying its accuracy to retain the payment received from its sender.

The Model Law has no express protective provisions. However, the limitation of the Model Law notice obligation to "detected inconsistencies" has the effect of conferring broad immunity upon receiving banks from liability for their sender's errors in payment orders that are processed automatically. The Article 4A protective provisions, on the other hand, have both express exceptions and omissions.

For an originator's bank to be entitled to rely upon numerical identifiers under Article 4A, a nonbank originator, who may be unfamiliar with automated processing, for example, must have been given prior notice that an identifying number might be relied upon without verification. The signing of a general funds-transfer agreement containing this notice prior to acceptance of a nonbank originator's order would suffice for the duration of the agreement. The other express exceptions to immunity involve a receiving bank's actual knowledge that a mismatched identifying number and name refer to different persons, which is unlikely to exist with respect to orders processed by automation, and an identification of a beneficiary that refers either to a nonexistent or an unidentifiable person or account, which will cause an order to be rejected by an automated processing system.

Although the Article 4A protective provisions are intended to facilitate automated processing, the statutory text is not so limited, and the Official Comments note that receiving banks engaging in manual processing are also covered. In fact, the aspects of the protective provisions that allow receiving banks to rely upon names are relevant only to manually processed orders.

Nevertheless, it is reasonable to apply the protective provisions more liberally with respect to payment orders that are processed by automation. In the absence of a receiving bank's waiver of the protective provisions by express contract or the applicability of an express statutory exception, the courts should deem a bank to have exercised due care with respect to errors by processing a payment order with a type of automation that has become accepted in the banking industry. Thus, an originator's bank's failure to give a nonbank originator notice of possible reliance upon numerical identifiers, which is covered by an express statutory exception, would make the originator's bank responsible for losses due to errors in the numerical identifiers. But, identification of a beneficiary solely by an erroneous number that in fact identifies a different account holder is omitted from the protective provisions. With respect to an erroneous number that is the sole identification of a beneficiary, automation policy justifies deeming a receiving bank to have exercised due care in engaging in automated processing. If receiving banks could incur negligence liability because of errors in the terms of a payment order that was processed without visual inspection, automated processing would be penalized and discouraged.

ELECTRONIC FUND TRANSFER ACT § 909

Consumer Liability for Unauthorized Transfers

(15 U.S.C.A. § 1693g (Tit. IX Consumer Credit Protection Act))

GAFFNEY v. COMMUNITY FEDERAL SAVINGS & LOAN ASSOCIATION

Court of Appeals of Missouri, 1986.
706 S.W.2d 530.

KELLY, Judge.

Defendant, Community Federal Savings and Loan Association, appeals from an adverse judgment in the St. Louis County Circuit Court awarding plaintiffs, Michael and Marilyn Gaffney, $2,600 plus interest for actual damages, and $10,000 for punitive damages in an action by plaintiffs against defendant for unauthorized withdrawals and the subsequent failure to re-credit funds to plaintiffs' savings account.

* * *

In November, 1978 plaintiffs opened a trust account at Community Federal Savings and Loan Association. Plaintiffs were designated as trustees on the account for Marilyn Gaffney's mother. Plaintiffs were issued pass cards and PIN numbers pursuant to a request form signed by Marilyn Gaffney. The pass card and PIN number are used to withdraw money from an automated teller machine, or from Schnucks stores.

Michael Gaffney testified he destroyed his pass card and PIN number the day he received the card, and before ever using them. Marilyn Gaffney testified she put her pass card in her wallet and her PIN number in the drawer of the nightstand in the couple's bedroom. She also testified that she had never used her pass card or PIN number to withdraw money from an automated teller machine or from Schnucks stores.

Prior to April 4, 1980 there had been a total of eight withdrawals from plaintiffs' account since they opened it in November of 1978. However, between April 5, 1980 and April 13, 1980, thirteen withdrawals were made each in the amount of $200. These withdrawals were either made from an [ATM] or from various Schnucks stores.

Plaintiffs received a statement from defendant on May 9, 1980 reflecting the thirteen withdrawals. Marilyn Gaffney, upon receiving the statement, checked her purse to verify that her pass card was still in her wallet. She also checked her nightstand drawer to make sure her PIN number was not missing. Both items were in the correct places. After being informed of the discrepancy in the bank statement by Marilyn Gaffney, Michael Gaffney immediately notified defendant by telephone of the thirteen unauthorized withdrawals. The next day on May 10, 1980 plaintiffs went to a branch of defendant's bank to discuss the problem with its representatives.

* * *

There are no Missouri cases or statutes dealing directly with the issues surrounding unauthorized transfers of funds by the use of an automated teller machine. Automated teller machines are a new device used by the banking industry, consequently the legal issues stemming from their use have not been fully litigated or resolved. There is a federal statute which governs automated teller machine transactions. The Electronic Fund Transfer Act, 15 U.S.C. Section 1693 et seq. sets out guidelines as well as the liabilities of the banks and the customer concerning the use of the automated teller machine. However, this statute is not controlling in this case as plaintiffs did not bring this action under the statute. Nevertheless it is a helpful guide in resolving the issues in this case since the issues revolve around transactions involving the use of automated teller machines. The federal statute provides for the re-crediting of a customer's account when it is found that an unauthorized electronic fund transfer or an incorrect electronic fund transfer involving their account has occurred. 15 U.S.C. Section 1693f. Therefore there is precedent in other jurisdictions for the existence of causes of action and recovery for improper electronic fund transfer transactions. See Ognibene v. Citibank, N.A., 112

Misc.2d 219, 446 N.Y.S.2d 845 (N.Y. City Civ. Ct.1981). In Ognibene the New York Court adopted the 15 U.S.C. Section 1693 et seq. as the governing body of law regarding automated teller machine transactions as New York had not passed any legislation governing this area. Ognibene v. Citibank, N.A., 446 N.Y.S.2d at 847. However, since we cannot rely on this statute as a cause of action as formed by the evidence in this case we must consider other bases for relief.

The relationship between a bank and a depositor is one of debtor and creditor grounded in contract; and the bank's contractual duty to charge a depositor's account only on the depositor's authentic order is absolute.

* * *

Defendant contends in his third point on appeal that a verdict should have been directed for defendant on the issue of punitive damages in that no evidence was submitted that defendant acted intentionally, without justification and with the knowledge such action was wrongful.

* * *

The jury found that there was sufficient evidence to prove plaintiffs' claim that there had been thirteen unauthorized withdrawals amounting to $2,600. We agree plaintiffs made their case on this claim. However we find insufficient evidence to support the award of $10,000 in punitive damages. There was nothing in the record to indicate that defendant knew its charging of the account was wrongful when it performed this act nor was there evidence to conclude defendant unjustifiably failed to re-credit the account. It was later determined that defendant's actions regarding plaintiffs' account were wrongful but at the time defendant acted it did so with the belief its actions were lawful. Moon v. Tower Grove Bank & Trust Co., supra. Therefore we find no malice, and conclude that the award of punitive damages was error.

The judgment is affirmed as to the $2,600 plus interest in actual damages but reversed as to the $10,000 in punitive damages.

OGNIBENE v. **CITIBANK, N.A.,** 112 Misc. 2d 219, 446 N.Y.S.2d 845 (N.Y. Civ. Ct. 1981). Plaintiff depositor testified that he went to one of the defendant bank's automated teller facilities, where a person was using the telephone between two of the machines. The person, a fraud, posed as an employee of the bank and induced plaintiff into letting him use plaintiff's ATM card to "test" the terminal. It turned out that the fraud had effected two $200 withdrawals from plaintiff's account. Plaintiff sued to have his account recredited, and defendant argued that plaintiff had authorized the withdrawals by letting the imposter use his card. The court disagreed and entered judgment for the customer. For the view that negligence of the customer cannot increase liability as imposed by the statute, see Official Staff Interpretations, [Reg. E; EFT-2], 12 C.F.R. Part 205, Supp. II 172 (1986).

(b) CHECKS

UCC § 4-103(e)

(*see Selected Commercial Statutes*)

DUNNIGAN v. FIRST BANK

Supreme Court of Connecticut, 1991.
271 Conn. 205, 585 A.2d 659.

BORDEN, Associate Justice.

In this appeal, we are called upon to define the meaning and scope of General Statutes § 42a-4-403(3) of the Uniform Commercial Code (Code) as applied to the facts of this case. The defendant bank appeals, after a court trial, from the judgment of the trial court in favor of the plaintiff, the trustee in bankruptcy of Cohn Precious Metals, Inc. (Cohn), a customer of the bank. We transferred the appeal to this court pursuant to Practice Book § 4023, and we now reverse the trial court's judgment.

The plaintiff brought this action against the bank for wrongfully paying a check issued by Cohn over Cohn's valid stop payment order. The trial court determined that the plaintiff had established a loss within the meaning of § 42a-4-403(3) as a result of the bank's payment of the check, and that the subrogation provisions of General Statutes § 42a-4-407 did not defeat the rights of Cohn. The court accordingly rendered judgment for the amount of the check. This appeal followed.

The bank claims that judgment was improperly rendered for the plaintiff because (1) as a matter of law, Cohn did not suffer a loss within the meaning of § 42a-4-403(3), and (2).[1] * * *

The parties stipulated to the following facts. On November 8, 1978, pursuant to purchase order 1142, Lamphere Coin, Inc. (Lamphere), a trader in coins and precious metals, delivered to Cohn certain silver dollars with a unit price of $1.71 and with a total value of $27,492.07. Cohn's bookkeeper incorrectly recorded the unit price of those coins, however, as $17.10, resulting in an erroneous total value of $47,098.93. On November 9, 1978, Cohn paid Lamphere $47,098.93 by wire transfer to Lamphere's bank account, resulting in an overpayment to Lamphere by Cohn of $19,606.86. On November 10, 1978, Lamphere delivered three and one-half bags of silver dollars to Cohn pursuant to Cohn's purchase order 1145. The value of the silver dollars was $21,175. On the same day, Cohn issued two checks drawn on its account at the bank to Lamphere, one in the amount of $12,175 and one in the amount of $9000, totaling $21,175.

Between November 10 and November 15, Cohn discovered its bookkeeper's error and, on November 14, 1978, directed the bank to stop payment on the two checks totaling $21,175 that had been issued on November 10, 1978. The bank stopped payment on the $9000 check, but on or about November 20, 1978, the bank inadvertently honored the $12,175 check over the valid stop payment order. Cohn

---

[1] Throughout the court's references are to pre-revised Article 4 [eds.].

retained the three and one-half bags of silver dollars, but never recovered its overpayment from Lamphere. As of November 20, 1978, the date of the improper payment of the check by the bank, and at all times thereafter Lamphere owed Cohn in excess of $13,000 as a result of these transactions.

The merits of this controversy revolve around the meaning of § 42a-4-403(3), which provides that "[t]he burden of establishing the fact and amount of loss resulting from the payment of an item contrary to a binding stop order is on the customer." The bank argues that where there is good consideration for a particular check, or where the check was given as payment on a binding contract, the bank that paid the check over a valid stop payment order is not liable to its customer, because there was no "loss resulting from [its] payment* * *." General Statutes § 42a-4-403(3). Thus, in the bank's view a customer cannot establish a loss under this provision of the code by relying on the loss of credits due the customer from prior unrelated transactions between the customer and the payee of the check. The plaintiff argues, as the trial court concluded, that whether a customer has incurred a "loss" within the meaning of § 42a-4-403(3) cannot be determined solely by focusing on the transaction underlying the particular check involved, but must be determined by focusing on the entire relationship between the customer and the payee of the check. The plaintiff contends that it is unreasonable to disregard the relative positions of the parties, especially where they have demonstrated a continuing course of business dealings, where there are likely to be such credits. Under such circumstances, the plaintiff claims that focusing on a single transaction is contrary to the intent of the Code. Thus, in the plaintiff's view, Cohn would have had a good "defense" to a claim by Lamphere on the check because of the overpayment, and by paying the check the bank caused Cohn a loss within the meaning of § 42a-4-403(3).

The issue, therefore, is whether, on the facts of this case, the bank customer who sought to establish "the fact and amount of loss resulting from the payment of an item contrary to a binding stop payment order" pursuant to § 42a-4-403(3) was entitled to do so by resorting to credits from prior transactions unrelated to that for which the check was issued, or whether the customer was limited to the facts of the particular transaction for which the check was issued. We conclude that the customer was limited to the facts of the particular transaction for which the check was issued, and that § 42a-4-403(3) does not contemplate taking into account a loss by the customer of credits that arose from prior unrelated transactions.

* * *

Under § 42a-4-403(1), a bank customer has the right to order his bank to stop payment on a check, so long as he does so in a timely and reasonable manner, and, under § 42a-4-403(2), an oral stop payment order is binding on the bank for a limited period of time. The fact that the bank has paid the check over the customer's valid stop payment order does not mean, however, that the customer is automatically entitled to repayment of the amount of the check. Under § 4-403(3), the customer must also establish "the fact and amount of loss resulting from" the bank's improper payment.

The case law makes clear that "[t]he loss * * * must be more than the mere debiting of his account." Grego v. South Carolina National Bank, 283 S.C. 546,

549, 324 S.E.2d 94 (1984) Otherwise, § 42a-4-403(3) would be superfluous. Furthermore, whether the customer has suffered such a loss is in the first instance a question of fact.

The cases and commentators also agree that where the check in question was supported by good consideration, or where the payee has enforceable rights against the maker based on the transaction underlying the check, the customer has suffered no loss within the meaning of § 42a-4-403(3). * * *

Applying these principles to the facts of this case, we conclude that as a matter of law Cohn suffered no "loss" within the meaning of § 42a-4-403(3). The check was supported by good consideration because it was issued in payment for the silver coins that Lamphere delivered to Cohn. Furthermore, on the basis of that underlying transaction Lamphere had enforceable rights to payment by Cohn for those coins.

The plaintiff argues, however, that, although the particular check was supported by valid consideration and although there were no defenses available to it arising out of that particular transaction, the previous transaction between Cohn and Lamphere had supplied Cohn with a defense to payment of the check based on Cohn's overpayment to Lamphere. We disagree.

First, the language of § 42-4-403(3) suggests a narrower reading than would be required by the plaintiff's position. Section 42a-4-403(3) places on the bank's customer the "burden of establishing the fact and amount of loss resulting from the payment of an item contrary to a binding stop payment order * * *." By contrast, § 42a-4-402, which deals with a bank's liability to its customer for a wrongful dishonor, as opposed to a wrongful payment, provides as follows: "A payor bank is liable to its customer for damages proximately caused by the wrongful dishonor of an item. When the dishonor occurs through mistake liability is limited to actual damages proved. If so proximately caused and proved damages may include damages for an arrest or prosecution of the customer or other consequential damages. Whether any consequential damages are proximately caused by the wrongful dishonor is a question of fact to be determined in each case." Thus, pursuant to § 42a-4-402 the wrongfully dishonoring bank may be liable for all consequential damages proximately caused by its wrongful conduct, including damages resulting from arrest or prosecution of the customer, whereas there is a conspicuous absence from § 42a-4-403(3) of language indicating such a broad scope of liability for wrongful payment.

This difference in the scope of the language used in § 42a-4-403(3), as compared to that used in § 42a-4-402, is consistent with the notion that § 42a-4-403(3) is intended to impose a limited, rather than broad, form of liability on banks.

* * *

In this case, the plaintiff seeks more than to establish a loss caused by the bank's failure to honor Cohn's stop payment order. That "loss" occurred in fact on November 9, 1978, when Cohn overpaid for the coins it had received. Rather, the plaintiff seeks to recoup a loss resulting from a prior transaction separate from and independent of the stopped check. Thus, the plaintiff's position would permit the customer to establish a "loss" based on offsets or counterclaims against the payee based on prior unrelated transactions, no matter how remote from the check in question or from the transaction underlying it. We do not believe that the intent of § 42a-4-403(3) ranges that far.

* * *

The judgment is reversed, and the case is remanded with direction to render judgment for the defendant.

[The dissent is omitted.]

UCC § 4-402(b)

(*see Selected Commercial Statutes*)

UCC § 4-403

(*see Selected Commercial Statutes*)

PROBLEM

Seller delivered $50,000 worth of apples to Buyer on May 1, and Buyer sent Seller a check for the purchase price on May 2. On May 3, Activist announced to the media that the insecticide used on the apples causes serious illness, a claim that is untrue. On May 2 Buyer stopped payment on the check. On May 3, Buyer's bank inadvertently paid the check.

(a) If Buyer alleges the foregoing facts in a claim against the bank, should the court deny the bank's motion to dismiss for failure to state a claim?

(b) Would your answer differ if Activist's claim had been true and Buyer had alleged that additional fact?

BEARD, EFFECTUATING THE CUSTOMER'S RIGHT TO STOP PAYMENT OF A CHECK: THE FORGOTTEN SECTION 4-401, 37 Wayne L. Rev. 1815, 1815-19 (1991).

The provisions of Article 4 of the Uniform Commercial Code relating to a customer's right to stop payment of an item appear, at first blush, to be clear and straightforward. In fact, these provisions have generated confusion and left the customer at the tender mercies of his bank. When the bank properly honors a stop payment order, the mechanism of the Code works splendidly. The bank returns the item unpaid, and has no liability to its customer or the holder. Ultimate liability in the underlying transaction is resolved between the drawer and holder.

Serious problems arise, however, when the bank fails to honor a valid and effective stop payment order. Upon payment of the item, the bank will inevitably charge the customer's account. As a result of this charge, the customer loses the use of the funds until the bank recredits the account. The customer's belief in the effectiveness of the stop order exacerbates the situation because the customer is likely to continue drawing checks against funds he assumes are available, with the distinct possibility that these checks will be dishonored for insufficient funds.

Current constructions of the Code frustrate the customer's ability to obtain an immediate recredit to his account. The Code imposes no explicit obligation on the bank to recredit the customer's account, and expressly places the burden of proving the fact and amount of loss on the customer. Accordingly, the bank can maintain the charge against the customer's account and force the customer to bear the burden of commencing litigation to recover. This state of affairs unfairly penalizes the customer and runs contrary to the Code policies underlying the right to stop payment.

Although recent decisions have attempted to ease the customer's burden of proving loss once litigation has commenced, the benefits of such analyses remain unavailable to the customer who does not or cannot litigate. To fully effectuate the right to stop payment, the customer must have the ability to force the bank to recredit his account without the necessity of litigation.

* * *

Under prevailing interpretations of section 4-403, the customer confronted with a payment over a valid stop order faces two, interrelated problems. First, the customer has lost the use of funds debited from his account following payment of the stopped item. This results from the lack of an express duty on the part of the bank to recredit the account when presented with evidence by the customer of the bank's failure to honor the valid stop order.

This inability to obtain a pre-litigation recredit leads to the customer's second problem. If the bank's payment discharged a valid obligation of the customer, prevailing interpretations of section 4-403(3) indicate that the customer will be unable to prove the requisite "loss" under that subsection in order to recover from the bank. Such a narrow interpretation of "loss" under section 4-403(3) fails to recognize the bank's breach of the bank-depositor contract, and forecloses recovery of "secondary losses," such as loss of credit or subsequent check dishonors resulting from the bank's initial wrongful payment of the stopped item.

By recognizing and giving effect to the forgotten section 4-401, the bank's initial wrong is corrected through recredit. If the bank does not recredit voluntarily, the bank's breach continues to afford the customer the ability to recover all damages flowing therefrom.

The simplest solution to the customer's plight is to amend the Code to provide for an explicit duty on the part of the bank to recredit the customer's account following payment over a valid stop order. Unfortunately, the recently proposed revisions to Articles 3 and 4 do not include such a provision. Accordingly, this article will provide an analytical pathway through the maze of apparently conflicting Code provisions which impact a customer's right to stop payment. The text of the Code provides the customer with a right to have his account immediately recredited following payment over a valid stop order without the burden of litigation, while protecting the rights of the bank to recover the amount paid in order to avoid unjust enrichment of the customer or other parties. Such application of the

Code protects the rights of both the customer and the bank, simultaneously preserving and advancing the policies of the Code.

(c) LETTERS OF CREDIT

H. HARFIELD, BANK CREDITS AND ACCEPTANCES 109 (5th ed. 1974).

[I]t is a cardinal precept, as we have seen, that banks deal in documents and not in merchandise. Therefore, a defect in the merchandise or a nonconformity of the merchandise to the terms of the documents which results in consequential damages is not the kind of risk a bank bargains for, or assumes by implication, when it issues a commercial credit.

If the rule were otherwise and the issuing bank thereby placed in the normal mercantile position with respect to consequential damages, the bank would be undertaking risks which it could not in the nature of things adequately evaluate or control. It would accordingly be necessary for the bank to protect itself, after a period of experience, by increasing its commercial credit rates to a point which would in effect insure it against these mercantile risks which are not properly a part of the banking business. This would indeed be a disservice to the mercantile community, because an essence of the commercial credit is its low cost. In practice, the overwhelming majority of commercial credits are performed precisely as stipulated and the transactions clear with no adverse effect. On this basis, banks are able to finance tremendously valuable shipments for a very small fraction of one percent of the amount involved. If the banks were liable for consequential damages, the added liability would have to be directly reflected in the commercial credit rates, with the result that the skillful and prudent members of the mercantile community would be paying, through increased rates, for the ineptitude or recklessness of marginal operators.

UCC § 5-111(a), (b) & (c)
(*see Selected Commercial Statutes*)

COMPTROLLER OF THE CURRENCY, INTERPRETIVE RULING
12 C.F.R. § 7.7016(b).

As a matter of safe and sound banking practice, banks that issue independent undertakings should not be exposed to undue risk. At a minimum, banks should consider the following:

* * *

(ii) The undertaking should be limited in amount.

(d) THE ECONOMIC LOSS DOCTRINE

MOORMAN MFG. CO. v. NATIONAL TANK CO.

Supreme Court of Illinois, 1982.
91 Ill.2d 69, 435 N.E.2d 443.

MORAN, Justice.

* * *

On July 26, 1978, plaintiff filed a three-count complaint containing the following allegations. Defendant designed, manufactured and sold storage tanks. In 1966, plaintiff purchased a bolted-steel grain-storage tank from defendant for use at its feed-processing plant in Alpha, Illinois. In the last few months of 1976 or the first months of 1977, a crack developed in one of the steel plates on the second ring of the tank. Count I alleged that the tank was not reasonably safe due to certain design and manufacturing defects. Count II asserted that defendant had made certain representations, which were in fact untrue, in connection with the sale of the tank. Count III accused defendant of negligently designing the tank. * * * [P]laintiff sought damages representing the cost of repairs and reinforcement as well as loss of use of the tank. The trial court granted defendant's motion to dismiss the first three counts, concluding that the cost of repair and loss of profits or income were economic losses which could not be recovered under the tort theories named in the complaint.

* * *

The appellate court recognized this court's reliance upon [§ 402A of the Restatement of Torts] * * *, but determined that the policy behind section 402A should be fulfilled without the court being bound by the section's precise language. Subsequent decisions of this court involving strict liability in tort have applied section 402A as well as comments to section 402A regarding the unreasonably dangerous nature a defect must possess. Contrary to the conclusion reached by the appellate court, we believe the language limiting section 402A to unreasonably dangerous defects resulting in physical harm to the ultimate user or consumer, or to his property, reflects sound policy reasons.

First, the law of sales has been carefully articulated to govern the economic relations between suppliers and consumers of goods. The framework provided by the UCC includes the parol evidence rule [UCC § 2-202], express warranties [UCC § 2-313], implied warranties [UCC § 2-314], rules on disclaimers [UCC § 2-316], notice requirements [UCC § 2-607], limitations on the extent of a manufacturer's liability [UCC §§ 2-718, 2-719] and a statute of limitations [UCC § 2-725]. Although warranty rules frustrate just compensation for physical injury, they function well in a commercial setting. These rules determine the quality of the product the manufacturer promises and thereby determine the quality he must deliver.

We note, for example, section 2-316 of the UCC, which permits parties to a sales contract to limit warranties in any reasonable manner, or to agree that the buyer possesses no warranty protection at all. The parties may even agree to exclude the implied warranties of merchantability and fitness if they do so in writing, and may modify the implied warranty by clear and conspicuous language. Yet, a manufacturer's strict liability for economic loss cannot be disclaimed because a manufacturer should not be permitted to define the scope of its own responsibility for defective products. Thus, adopting strict liability in tort for economic loss would effectively eviscerate section 2-316 of the UCC.

Further, application of the rules of warranty prevents a manufacturer from being held liable for damages of unknown and unlimited scope. If a defendant were held strictly liable in tort for the commercial loss suffered by a particular purchaser, it would be liable for business losses of other purchasers caused by the failure of the product to meet the specific needs of their business, even though these needs were communicated only to the dealer. Finally, a large purchaser, such as plaintiff in the instant case, can protect itself against the risk of unsatisfactory performance by bargaining for a warranty. Or, it may choose to accept a lower purchase price for the product in lieu of warranty protection. Subsequent purchasers may do likewise in bargaining over the price of the product. We believe it is preferable to relegate the consumer to the comprehensive scheme of remedies fashioned by the UCC, rather than requiring the consuming public to pay more for their products so that a manufacturer can insure against the possibility that some of his products will not meet the business needs of some of his customers.

* * *

Plaintiff argues that economic loss is not sought in this case. It asserts in its brief that a product defect existed that posed an "extreme threat to life and limb, and to property of plaintiff and others, a defect which resulted in a sudden and violent ripping of plaintiff's tank, and which only fortunately did not extend the full height of the tank." Plaintiff further asserts that, because costs of repairs are not economic losses, consequential damages resulting from the loss of use of the tank during repairs does not constitute economic loss either.

"Economic loss" has been defined as "damages for inadequate value, costs of repair and replacement of the defective product, or consequent loss of profits-without any claim of personal injury or damage to other property * * *." (Note, Economic Loss in Products Liability Jurisprudence, 66 Colum.L.Rev. 917, 918 (1966) (Economic Loss)) as well as "the diminution in the value of the product because it is inferior in quality and does not work for the general purposes for which it was manufactured and sold." (Comment, Manufacturers' Liability to Remote Purchasers for "Economic Loss" Damages-Tort or Contract ? 114 U.Pa.L.Rev. 539, 541 (1966).) These definitions are consistent with the policy of warranty law to protect expectations of suitability and quality.

The demarcation between physical harm or property damage on the one hand and economic loss on the other usually depends on the nature of the defect and the manner in which the damage occurred.

* * *

We * * * hold that, where only the defective product is damaged, economic losses caused by qualitative defects falling under the ambit of a purchaser's disappointed expectations cannot be recovered under a strict liability theory. Here, count I of the complaint alleged that during the last few months of 1976 and the first few months of 1977, "a crack developed in one of the steel plates on the second ring of (the) tank; such crack was not discovered by plaintiff * * * until such tank was being emptied on or about August 24, 1977." This was not the type of sudden and dangerous occurrence best served by the policy of tort law that the manufacturer should bear the risk of hazardous products. Rather, * * * the harm resulted from a qualitative defect relating to the purchaser's expectation in terms of the product's fitness to perform its intended function. Plaintiff suffered a commercial loss of the type that the law of warranty is designed to protect. Consequently, repair and reinforcement of the tank and loss of the tank's use constitute economic losses for which plaintiff cannot recover under a theory of strict liability in tort.

Our conclusion that qualitative defects are best handled by contract, rather than tort, law applies whether the tort theory involved is strict liability or negligence. Tort theory is appropriately suited for personal injury or property damage resulting from a sudden or dangerous occurrence of the nature described above. The remedy for economic loss, loss relating to a purchaser's disappointed expectations due to deterioration, internal breakdown or nonaccidental cause, on the other hand, lies in contract.

* * *

We note that there are some cases in which the courts have allowed recovery in negligence for economic loss. Yet, the vast majority of commentators and cases support the view against allowing recovery in negligence for economic losses.

The policy considerations against allowing recovery for solely economic loss in strict liability cases apply to negligence actions as well. When the defect is of a qualitative nature and the harm relates to the consumer's expectation that a product is of a particular quality so that it is fit for ordinary use, contract, rather than tort, law provides the appropriate set of rules for recovery. Moreover, as was true with strict liability, if a manufacturer were held liable in negligence for the commercial loss suffered by a particular purchaser, it would be liable for business losses of other purchasers caused by the failure of its product to meet the specific needs of their businesses, even though the needs were communicated only to the dealer. Thus, a manufacturer could be held liable for damages of unknown and unlimited scope, even though the product is not unreasonably dangerous and even though there is no damage to person or property.

* * *

This court has held that economic loss is recoverable where one intentionally makes false representations (Soules v. General Motors Corp. (1980), 79 Ill.2d 282, 37 Ill.Dec. 597, 402 N.E.2d 599), and where one who is in the business of supplying information for the guidance of others in their business transactions makes negligent representations (Rozny v. Marnul (1969), 43 Ill.2d 54, 250 N.E.2d 656). Neither of these cases, however, implied that economic loss was recoverable for innocent misrepresentation. Holding a manufacturer liable for economic loss for misrepresentations that were neither intentionally nor negligently made would, in effect, be an imposition of strict liability. The manufacturer would be accountable for all economic losses suffered by purchasers pursuant to such a misrepresentation.

We have already discussed extensively the policy reasons militating against allowing recovery in strict liability for solely economic loss.

* * *

Due to the already discussed nature of economic losses, a purchaser's remedy for those losses by virtue of a seller's innocent misrepresentation appropriately lies under the warranty provisions of the UCC. Thus, in this case, plaintiff cannot recover in tort its purely economic losses for any innocent misrepresentations made by defendant.

In summary, extension of the tort theories of strict liability, negligence or innocent misrepresentation to cover solely economic losses would, in effect, make a manufacturer the guarantor that all of its products would continue to perform satisfactorily throughout their reasonably productive life. Subjecting a manufacturer to liability under those tort theories for a purchaser's solely economic losses would encroach upon the decision by our legislature to enact the sales provisions, sections 2-101 to 2-725, of the Uniform Commercial Code.

* * *

GREAT LAKES HIGHER EDUCATION CORP. v. AUSTIN BANK

United States District Court, Northern District of Illinois, 1993.
837 F. Supp. 892.

[Great Lakes drew 224 checks totaling $273,152.88 on its account at First Wisconsin. Although the opinion is not clear on the point, it appears that a malefactor obtained the checks, deposited them at Austin, the defendant, and absconded with the proceeds. First Wisconsin paid the checks after Austin sent them for collection through the bank collection system. None of the checks were indorsed, so they were not properly payable; and one would assume that First Wisconsin was not able to charge Great Lakes' account. First Wisconsin sued Austin for, among other things, common law negligence.]

GEORGE M. MAROVICH, District Judge.

* * *

Plaintiffs invoke the law of common law negligence against Austin in their third count. In response, Austin cites Moorman Mfg. Co. v. National Tank Co., 91 Ill.2d 69, 61 Ill.Dec. 746, 753-54, 435 N.E.2d 443, 450-51 (1982), for the proposition that under Illinois law, the parties to a commercial transaction cannot recover in tort for economic losses (the "Moorman doctrine"). In Moorman, the plaintiff sued the company that designed, manufactured and sold him a defective storage tank, asserting damages for the cost of repair and reinforcement as well as loss of use of the tank. Id. 61 Ill.Dec. at 753, 435 N.E.2d at 450. The Illinois Supreme Court held that the plaintiff had suffered "a commercial loss of the type that the law of warranty is designed to protect" rather than a "sudden and dangerous occurrence best served by the policy of tort law." Id. The court held that its conclusion applied to cases of negligence as well as strict liability, noting that "allowing an aggrieved party to recover under a negligence theory for solely economic loss would constitute an unwarranted infringement upon the scheme provided by the UCC." Id. 61 Ill.Dec. at 754-55, 435 N.E.2d at 451-52.

The Seventh Circuit has upheld Moorman in applying Illinois law. In Valenti v. Qualex, Inc., 970 F.2d 363, 369 (7th Cir.1992), the court held that the Moorman decision has been upheld consistently in Illinois and by the Seventh Circuit. The court explained that "the basic principle of Moorman is that the type of loss, not the defendant's conduct, is critical. When only economic loss is incurred, the plaintiff may only raise contract theories even if the defendant's alleged conduct constituted a tort as well as a breach of contract." Id. quoting Bethlehem Steel Corp. v. Chicago Eastern Corp., 863 F.2d 508 (7th Cir.1988). See also Nielsen v. United Servs. Automobile Ass'n, 244 Ill.App.3d 658, 183 Ill.Dec. 874, 881, 612 N.E.2d 526, 533 (1993) (stating that the Moorman doctrine applied to fire insurance policy coverage so that defendant had no duty in negligence to plaintiffs apart from their contractual undertakings).

Plaintiffs' argument is not persuasive that because the UCC clearly intended that it would be supplemented by common-law principles (§ 1-103), it follows that a claim for negligence may be asserted unless a specific provision of the UCC expressly overrules the common law. No section of the UCC expressly displaces any common law remedy. It is by implication that an alternative remedy under the UCC exists for such a factual situation that the common law is displaced on that same point. Here, First Wisconsin and Great Lakes have other remedies under the UCC which they have alternatively plead in their complaint, thus showing that a common law action for negligence is unnecessary and may not be alleged here.

We also do not accept Plaintiffs' contention that there is a need for further investigation in order to determine whether there existed a "commercial or contractual relationship" between the disputed parties, so as to invoke the Moorman doctrine. It is clear that the relationship is a commercial one because the transactions and damages involved in this case are financial in nature. Thus, there is nothing further to establish and Plaintiffs' negligence claim may not be properly asserted under Illinois law because of the Moorman doctrine.

* * *

SECTION 2. EXTRAORDINARY REMEDIES (SPECIFIC PERFORMANCE, INJUNCTIONS, AND THE LIKE)

(a) Specific Performance

NOTE ON EXTRAORDINARY REMEDIES

It ought to be clear from the outset that the common law, unlike its civil law cousin, does not look fondly on what we term the extraordinary remedies. Articles 2 and 2A will permit specific performance only if the goods are unique. We know from study of Contract remedies, moreover, that expectation damages, though they are often exceedingly difficult to prove, are the normal measure of recovery for breach of contract.

These lessons are well enough learned by now that we need not dwell on them, but it is worth remembering that this state of affairs has dramatic consequences. Economists teach us that breach will be efficient in the event that the aggrieved party can recover his damages. Most lawyers are convinced, however, that the aggrieved party usually cannot prove those damages, be they reliance or expectation or that in those cases that award damages the award bears at least an attenuated relation to reality. Even when the plaintiff recovers a grand award, some of us view the damages portion of the trial (expert testimony, graphs, and charts) as an elaborate fib.

In short, the absence of specific performance as the primary remedy in breach of contract cases is a limitation on the aggrieved party's right of recovery. It is a strong indication that commercial law does not regard litigation with favor. As we are seeing, it is not the only such indication.

UCC §§ 2-709, 2-716, 2A-521, & 2A-529
(*see Selected Commercial Statutes*)

(b) INJUNCTIONS

INTRODUCTORY NOTE

The injunction is a powerful remedy. Unrestrained, it can upset commercial law's general antipathy to court interference with party autonomy. Thus the law restrains it. First, commercial law is suspicious that the system of litigation will not get it right. Second, litigation delays and costs reallocate party allocation of risk. Both consequences are anathema to commerce. Courts have fashioned a number of prerequisites for the extraordinary relief that equity created in response to the rigidity of the common law. Thus we see the usual paradigm. The common law is harsh, so equity fashions equitable relief. Equitable relief creates uncertainty and costs, so the courts fashion limits on the relief.

Normally, courts describe the limits on preliminary injunctions as including some or all of the following: (1) no adequate remedy at law, (2) a threat of irreparable injury, (3) a likelihood that the petitioner will succeed on the merits, (4) a balance of hardships tipping in favor of granting relief, and (5) no indication that the public interest will be adversely affected by granting the relief.

In practice, the first and second prerequisites are essentially the same; and those two plus the third are the prerequisites that usually give the petitioner trouble. If she can satisfy those elements of the rule, courts normally enter the preliminary injunction.

The order entering that injunction is often the whole ball game. Recall that commerce's attitude toward protracted litigation is similar to nature's attitude toward a vacuum, and the reallocation of risks that the preliminary injunction effects prompts a settlement. There is no need for a trial on the merits; the petitioner has already won.

The following cases illustrate the risk of that reordering when the parties are using a cashier's check or a letter of credit. They also illustrate the law's reluctance to entertain the remedy precisely because it effects that reordering.

PROBLEM

This morning Seller of real estate closed a real estate sale with Buyer. Seller gave Buyer a warranty deed covering the property, and Buyer gave Seller a cashier's check for $50,000. Later in the day Buyer learned that, contrary to Seller's express warranties, there was a tenant on the property claiming a right to stay there at a rent significantly below market. The rights of the tenant are superior to those of Buyer as a matter of real estate law. Buyer immediately sought an injunction against the issuer of the check, First Bank. Should the court enter the injunction? Would it matter whether Seller had deposited the check at his bank and received value?

NOTE ON CASHIER'S CHECKS

Traditionally, the cashier's check played a major role at closings, the events that mark the performance by the parties of the executory promises they made when they entered into the contract. If a seller agrees to sell a buyer a piece of real estate, the closing is the time at which the seller performs by delivering a sufficient warranty deed for the property, and the buyer pays the purchase price. By delivering the deed, the seller empowers the buyer to cause the real estate records to reflect buyer's ownership and gives the buyer the power to sell to a bona fide purchaser. The seller, therefore, should not give the deed to the buyer until the seller is satisfied that the buyer will pay. The buyer's delivery of a cashier's check does the job.

While cashier's checks still play a role in commerce, wire transfers and letters of credit often play the role the cashier's check formerly played.

FOXBORO CO. v. ARABIAN AMERICAN OIL CO.

United States Court of Appeals, First Circuit, 1986.
805 F.2d 34.

TORRUELLA, Circuit Judge.

This appeal concerns the propriety of a preliminary injunction to prevent the honoring of an international letter of credit. Because plaintiff has failed to demonstrate irreparable harm, we reverse the district court and vacate the preliminary injunction.

I. The Contract and Letter of Credit

In March 1984 plaintiff, The Foxboro Company ("Foxboro"), a Massachusetts corporation, contracted with the Arabian American Oil Company ("Aramco"), a Delaware corporation, to provide a process control system for the Qasim Refinery in Saudi Arabia. Under the agreement Foxboro was to receive certain scheduled payments upon reaching specified contractual milestones. Foxboro had the option of allowing Aramco to retain a percentage of the payments as security, or of providing a bank guarantee to Aramco equal to the amount Aramco could retain. The contract provided that disputes be governed by Saudi Arabian law and be subject to arbitration.

Foxboro elected to provide the bank guarantee, which was issued by Saudi American Bank ("Samba") to Aramco. The Samba guarantee was itself secured by a letter of credit issued by Citibank on Foxboro's behalf. This "four-way" security is a typical commercial arrangement for American contractors doing business in the Middle East.

In March 1985 Aramco terminated the contract for "convenience," as it was authorized to do under the contract. In February 1986, after eleven months of negotiation over post-termination obligations, Aramco made a demand on the Samba bank guarantee, and Samba, in turn, made a demand on the Citibank letter of credit. Foxboro sought a temporary restraining order to prevent the execution of the letter of credit or bank guarantee. Foxboro alleged that the demand on the guarantee was fraudulent. The district court granted the restraining order, 634 F.Supp. 1226, and thereafter issued the preliminary injunction which is the subject of the appeal in this case.

II. Review of the Preliminary Injunction

To obtain a preliminary injunction a plaintiff must show: (1) that plaintiff will suffer irreparable injury if the injunction is not granted; (2) that such injury outweighs any harm which granting injunctive relief would inflict on the defendant; (3) that plaintiff has exhibited a likelihood of success on the merits; and (4) that the public interest will not be adversely affected by the granting of the injunction. We may reverse a district court's order granting a preliminary injunction only for an abuse of discretion or a clear error of law. We find that the district court did commit such an error in its assessment of Foxboro's "irreparable injury." Accordingly, we find it unnecessary to reach the other factors enumerated * * * .

Foxboro and Aramco are disputing their financial obligations under the contract. Honoring Aramco's demand on the bank guarantee, and Samba's demand on the letter of credit, will transfer money from Foxboro to Aramco, but will not change the merits of the underlying claim. The principal legally cognizable injury to Foxboro is that it will have to seek recovery of these sums through the contractually agreed upon forum. We do not find irreparable injury where only money is at stake and where the plaintiff has a satisfactory remedy at law to recover the money at issue. See Itek Corp. v. First Nat'l Bank, 730 F.2d 19, 22 (1st Cir.1984).

In Itek we affirmed the granting of a preliminary injunction to prevent the honoring of a letter of credit. But Itek involved a contract with the imperial government of Iran that was interrupted by the Iranian revolution and the seizing of the American hostages. Allowing the letter of credit to be honored in that case would have created irreparable harm; the plaintiff would have had no adequate remedy at law during the throes of the revolution. This case presents a far different situation.

The parties contracted to be bound by Saudi Arabian law and to use Saudi Arabian arbitration in resolving disputes between them. International arbitration provides Foxboro an adequate remedy. Indeed, the underlying contract dispute is currently being arbitrated at Foxboro's behest.

Foxboro may also sue Aramco in federal court for any harm done to it by the allegedly fraudulent demand on the bank guarantee and letter of credit. Aramco is a Delaware corporation wholly owned by four United States corporations. Foxboro has not demonstrated that Aramco would be unwilling or unable to pay any judgment debt, or that Aramco lacks sufficient assets in the United States to cover any such debt. Foxboro thus has several avenues open to recover any money due from the allegedly fraudulent demand.

The district court found that Foxboro would suffer two forms of irreparable injury if the demand on the bank guarantee and letter of credit were honored. First, Aramco would achieve on "unfair advantage in the ongoing negotiations * * * between the parties". And second, Foxboro's business reputation would suffer. Neither of these harms, nor the two combined, are sufficient to constitute irreparable injury in this case.

The contract clearly contemplates that Aramco would have an advantage in negotiations. That advantage was the purpose of the retainage or bank guarantee provision. Whether that advantage is "unfair" in this case depends on whether the Aramco demand on the bank guarantee was "fraudulent." If the demand was fraudulent, Foxboro may recover the damages flowing from the fraud in federal court. Thus, an unfair negotiating advantage will not irreparably harm Foxboro.

The claimed harm to Foxboro's business reputation presents a more interesting issue. Foxboro claims that Aramco's fraudulent demand will make it more expensive for Foxboro to obtain letters of credit in the future. Whether the demand on the bank guarantee and letter of credit does so depends on how courts treat these credit instruments. If an injunction against an allegedly fraudulent demand can be easily obtained, then the party who is unable to secure such an injunction may be presumed to be subject to a proper demand and, thus, a credit risk in the future. But, if such injunctions are difficult to obtain, the failure to obtain one says nothing about the propriety of the demand on the letter of credit.

As we indicated in Itek, an injunction to impede the honoring of a letter of credit is an extraordinary remedy that should rarely be granted. This is so because their near inviolableness is an important element of trust underlying a large segment of international commerce. In contrast, however, the failure to obtain injunctive relief should have little or no consequence for Foxboro's reputation. In fact, it could very well be argued that seeking to prevent payment of an irrevocable letter of credit could have more drastic consequences on the movant's long range business reputation. The district court's contrary finding was speculative. Like the Fifth

Circuit, "we are reluctant to accept the district court's inferences that payment on a letter of credit will embroider a permanent 'scarlet letter' on the bodice of the bank's customer." Enterprise International, Inc. v. Corporacion Estatal Petrolera Ecuatoriana, 762 F.2d 464, 474-75 (5th Cir.1985).

We fail to see how the demand on the letter of credit will prejudice Foxboro in future business deals. Letters of credit are independent of the underlying contract. Aramco's demand says no more about the merits of any dispute based on the underlying contract than would a complaint filed in court.

Accordingly, the order of the district court below is reversed and the preliminary injunction vacated.

RECON OPTICAL, INC. v. STATE OF ISRAEL, 816 F.2d 854 (2d Cir. 1987). "Recon/Optical, Inc. ("Recon") appeals from Judge Griesa's denial of its application for a preliminary injunction. Recon sought to prevent the Government of Israel ("Israel") from drawing $21.5 million against a letter of credit pending arbitration of the parties' contractual disputes.

* * *

Under our well-established standard for determining whether to grant the extraordinary remedy of a preliminary injunction, the moving party must establish irreparable harm and either (1) likelihood of success on the merits or (2) sufficiently serious questions going to the merits to make them a fair ground for litigation and a balance of hardships tipping decidedly toward the party requesting preliminary relief. On appeal, review is limited to determining whether the district court abused its discretion in denying a preliminary injunction. Because Recon has failed to show either a likelihood of success or serious questions going to the merits, we affirm."

* * *

LAYCOCK, THE DEATH OF THE IRREPARABLE INJURY RULE, 103 Harv. L. Rev. 688, 689-92 (1990).

The irreparable injury rule has received considerable scholarly attention. In 1978, Owen Fiss examined the possible reasons for the rule and found them wanting. A vigorous debate over the economic wisdom of applying the rule to specific performance of contracts began about the same time, and soon came to center on the transaction costs associated with the two remedies. Both Fiss and Dan Dobbs have noted that the rule is often ignored, and in a review of Fiss' book, I argued that the stringent definition of adequacy pulls most of the rule's teeth. The Restatement (Second) of Torts dropped the traditional version of the rule from the black letter and condemned it as misleading, but replaced it only with a long and unstructured list of factors to be considered. Doug Rendleman and Gene Shreve offered separate defenses of the rule, arguing that equitable remedies are generally more troublesome than legal remedies. But Rendleman conceded that the usual formulations of the rule divert analysis from the real policies at issue, and Shreve also seemed to think the rule is generally misunderstood.

* * *

Courts have escaped the rule by defining adequacy in such a way that damages are never an adequate substitute for plaintiff's loss. Thus, our law embodies a preference for specific relief if plaintiff wants it. The principal doctrinal expression of this preference is the rule that damages are inadequate unless they can be used to replace the specific thing that plaintiff lost. Damages can be used in this way for only one category of losses: to replace fungible goods or routine services in an orderly market. In that context, damages and specific relief are substantially equivalent. Either way, plaintiff winds up with the very thing he wanted, and the preference for specific relief becomes irrelevant. In all other context, there is ample basis in precedent and principle for holding that damages are inadequate. I document these claims with a large sample of cases; the sample is described below.

Courts ignore this body of precedent, and find damages adequate, only when there is some identifiable reason to deny specific relief in a particular case. Most of these cases arise on motions for preliminary relief. Although the vocabulary of adequate remedy and irreparable injury is common to both preliminary and permanent relief, the competing considerations are quite different at the two stages of litigation. Denying relief at the preliminary stage protects defendant's right to a full hearing, and a stringent variation of the irreparable injury rule lets the court openly balance the risks to each side. Preliminary relief is best considered as a separate issue, only distantly related to the choice of remedy at final judgment.

At the stage of permanent relief, specific relief is problematic only occasionally. Sometimes it imposes undue hardship or interferes with countervailing rights. Sometimes it interferes with the authority of another tribunal or bypasses a more particularized remedy. Sometimes it is impractical to supervise; sometimes the case is moot or not yet ripe; sometimes the court does not really want to grant any relief at all. Courts may deny specific relief in all these cases, and they may offer the irreparable injury rule in support of these results, but that rationale is misleading. The meanings of "irreparable" and "adequate" must constantly be manipulated to achieve sensible results. "Irreparable" and "adequate" are labels for conclusions reached on other grounds.

These real reasons for denying equitable remedies are not derived from the adequacy of the legal remedy or from any general preference for damages. Some of the reasons are based on the cost of the equitable remedy in particular circumstances; others apply equally to legal remedies in similar cases. Sometimes there are good reasons to deny legal relief and grant equitable relief instead. But there is no general presumption against equitable remedies.

I conclude that the irreparable injury rule is dead. It does not describe what the cases do, and it cannot account for the results. Injunctions are routine, and damages are never adequate unless the court wants them to be. Courts can freely turn to the precedents granting injunctions or the precedents denying injunctions, depending on whether they want to hold the legal remedy adequate or inadequate. Whether they want to hold the legal remedy adequate depends on whether they have some other reason to deny the equitable remedy, and it is these other reasons that drive the decisions.

SECTION 3. PRIVITY

INTRODUCTORY NOTE

The privity requirement disappeared in the law of product liability, but it survives in much of commercial law. Note that in *Evra*, page 650, the Seventh Circuit declined to let Hyman-Michaels sue Swiss Bank on a contract theory. "Privity is not a wholly artificial concept," said the *Evra* court.

Also, in sections of the *Moorman* opinion not reproduced here, the court made much of the fact that extending tort liability for product defects to economic losses would diminish the role of privity, whose role, let's face it, is to limit the number of people that can recover for loss. The letter of credit case that follows the Note is illustrative.

NOTE ON BANKS IN LETTER OF CREDIT TRANSACTIONS

In many letter of credit transactions, especially those involving the international sale of goods, banks other than the issuer of the credit play important roles. Most international bank departments issue their letters of credit over S.W.I.F.T. (Society for Worldwide Interbank Financial Telecommunications), a service that permits banks to identify each other quickly and to communicate cheaply and by means of an advanced technology called EDI (electronic data interchange).

A bank in Frankfurt issuing a letter of credit on behalf of a German buyer of agricultural commodities from a New York exporter, will not send any notice to the exporter, who is the beneficiary of the credit. Rather, the Frankfurt bank sends a S.W.I.F.T. message to its New York correspondent, which then "advises" the exporter that the credit is established. The Frankfurt bank is the issuer of the credit. The New York bank is the adviser. § 5-102(a)(1). Sometimes, the exporter wants a local bank to be on the hook and will insist in the underlying sales agreement with the buyer that the credit be "confirmed." A confirmed credit is a credit that carries the direct obligation not only of the issuer (usually in the buyer's city) but also of a bank in the seller's market, the New York bank in this illustration. § 2-325(3). If the buyer has agreed to supply a confirmed credit, the Frankfurt issuer will ask its correspondent not only to advise the credit but to confirm it too. When the New York bank issues its confirmation, it becomes obligated on the credit as if it were the issuer. § 5-102(a)(4).

At this point, there are four parties in the transaction, the seller, the buyer, the issuer, and the confirmer. Sometimes there are two more. A seller seeking to draw on a letter of credit may use its own bank to collect the funds. In that case, the seller prepares the documents necessary to comply with the terms of the credit, draws a draft on the issuer or the confirmer, as the credit directs, and takes the draft and documents to his own bank for collection. The collecting bank then presents them to the bank nominated by the issuer to honor the draft. In the case of a confirmed credit, that bank, the nominated or paying bank, will almost always be the confirmer.

On occasion, usually when the credit is not confirmed, the issuer may direct the beneficiary to draw not on the issuer but on a bank in the seller's market. This arrangement may be simpler for all parties. It permits the seller/beneficiary to present documents locally and correct defects quickly, and it often facilitates payment in the seller's local currency. Often the issuer nominates the adviser to honor the beneficiary's draft, but the bank's role as adviser is completed when it advises the credit. When it reappears in the transaction as the drawee of the beneficiary's draft, it is a nominated bank, in this case, nominated to honor the draft.

There has been, as you would suspect, some controversy over the relationships among these parties. If the applicant for the credit, the German buyer in this illustration, is unhappy with the confirmer's performance, she may seek to recover from the confirmer. Generally, as the following case suggests, courts have not been receptive to the applicant's suit.

AUTO SERVICIO SAN IGNACIO, S.R.L. v. COMPANIA ANONIMA VENEZOLANA DE NAVEGACION

United States Court of Appeals, Fifth Circuit, 1985.
765 F.2d 1306.

PATRICK E. HIGGINBOTHAM, Circuit Judge.

This case concerns an international letter of credit issued by the Banco de Maracaibo of Venezuela on behalf of plaintiff Auto Servicio San Ignacio, S.R.L., a Venezuelan corporation. We must decide whether an advising, confirming, and paying bank on such a letter of credit owes any duty of care under Louisiana tort law to the customer of the bank that issued the credit; whether one to two years is a reasonable length of time for the issuing bank to wait before asserting a claim against the advising, confirming, and paying bank that the credit was paid on non-conforming documents; and whether the advising, confirming, and paying bank must look beyond the face of documents complying with the terms of the credit to ascertain facts that only such a bank can determine. We answer all three questions in the negative and affirm the district court's grant of summary judgment.

* * *

Auto Servicio wished to purchase $106,098.48 worth of tires from an American corporation, Worldwide Tire, and arranged for payment to Worldwide with a letter of credit. Defendant Hibernia National Bank of New Orleans acted as the advising, confirming, and paying bank for the Banco de Maracaibo. Under the terms of the credit, Hibernia was to release to Worldwide a draft paying for the tires upon Worldwide's presentment of bills of lading and certain additional documents which would verify that the tires were insured and loaded aboard a ship bound for Venezuela.

The credit was issued by Banco on March 25, 1982, and on March 26, Hibernia so notified Worldwide. On April 8, one "David Smith," a representative from Worldwide, presented Hibernia with documents which seemingly complied with those required by the credit, and Hibernia issued him a draft for the required sum. Hibernia then notified Banco that it had done so, and forwarded the presented documents to Banco.

The documents, as it turned out, were forged. There were no tires, Worldwide was a sham corporation, and David Smith had cashed the draft and skipped town. On April 23, immediately after Auto Servicio discovered the fraud, Banco cabled Hibernia asking it to cancel the credit. Hibernia had debited Banco's account weeks earlier and accordingly, refused the request, explaining that it had come too late.

Auto Servicio apparently did not contest Banco's right to debit its account. Instead Auto Servicio sought relief in the federal district court in New Orleans against Hibernia Bank for its role in the transaction. This appeal concerns the district court's grant of summary judgment in favor of Hibernia on Auto Servicio's claims against it.

Although the district court conceded that there were arguably issues of material fact on the question whether Hibernia had exercised the standard of care required by [UCC § 5-109][1] in honoring the documents presented on the letter of credit, it granted summary judgment in favor of Hibernia, concluding that the duty of care owed by Hibernia as advising, confirming, and paying bank ran only to its customer, Banco, the issuer of the credit, and not to Banco's customer, Auto Servicio. In short, the court held that in light of the relationships in the letter of credit transaction as defined by Article 5 of the U.C.C., Auto Servicio's claim should have been brought against Banco, not Hibernia. The court then refused to circumvent this statutory scheme by allowing Auto Servicio to state a tort claim against Hibernia, reasoning again that although section 5-109 imposed on Hibernia a duty to examine the credit documents with care and to observe general banking usage, this duty did not run to Auto Servicio.

* * *

Auto Servicio first reurges its argument that Hibernia should be liable to it under Louisiana tort principles because Auto Servicio was one foreseeably injured by Hibernia's failure to exercise the proper care in examining the documents presented on the letter of credit. Like the district court, we are unconvinced. The district court correctly determined that to the extent there is a duty under Louisiana tort law, it is the duty of care defined by section 5-109, owed by Hibernia only to its customer on the letter of credit, Banco. The reasons given by the court for its refusal to expand the confirming bank's liability on a negligence theory are sound: "[It] would disrupt the letter of credit transaction as structured by [Article 5] and would hinder the commercial viability of the letter of credit. A bank in Hibernia's position would not be nearly so willing to provide its services if liability were extended to parties with whom it never dealt." 586 F.Supp. at 264. The exchange function of the letter of credit rests upon objective predictable standards with defined expectations and risks. Injecting the uncertainty of the tort principles contended for is inconsistent with these necessities and is not supported by the Code, which implicitly rejects them.

---

1 All of the court's references are to pre-revised Article 5 [eds.].

The only authority in support of Auto Servicio's theory, Instituto National etc. v. Continental Illinois, 530 F.Supp. 279 (N.D.Ill.1982), has been criticized, see U.C.C. Survey, 38 The Business Lawyer, 1169, 1176-78 (1983), and differs factually from the instant case. The Continental court recognized a negligence action by the customer of the issuer against the confirming bank, but not on the basis that the confirming bank failed to exercise due care in examining the documents required by the letter of credit. Rather, the theory was that the confirming bank was negligent when it supervised the beneficiary's revision of those documents. While we are unpersuaded by its reasoning, the case is, in any event, distinguishable.

In sum, we affirm the district court's decision that Auto Servicio had no cause of action under the Louisiana tort law against Hibernia, the advising, confirming, and paying bank on the letter of credit.

[The balance of the opinion denying recovery to Auto Servicio as assignee of the rights of Banco against Hibernia is omitted.]

SECTION 4. SUBROGATION

(a) In General

INTRODUCTORY NOTE

Subrogation is a remedy to rectify unjust enrichment. The remedy does not apply automatically. First, the court must find unjust enrichment; then it invokes the remedy. Some people have forgotten the unjust enrichment exercise.

Subrogation does more than avoid loss for a party whose funds have satisfied an obligation. It also reallocates burdens. At times, it gives collateral to a party that extended credit without a thought to collateral; at other times it gives collateral to a party that probably did think about collateral but didn't want to pay the price of getting it.

---

3 G. PALMER, THE LAW OF RESTITUTION 344 (1978). "[Subrogation] is properly used only as a means of preventing unjust enrichment."

COMPANIA ANONIMA VENEZOLANA DE NAVEGACION v. A.J. PEREZ EXPORT CO., 303 F.2d 692, 697 (5th Cir. 1962). "[Subrogation] is now a mechanism so universally applied in new and unknown circumstances that it is easy to overlook that it originates in equity. Every facet, whether substantive or procedural, is controlled by the equitable origin and aim of subrogation. * * * It is not an absolute right, but one which depends upon the equities and attending facts and circumstances of each case. * * * It is a matter of grace to be granted or withheld as the equities of the case demand."

NATIONAL SHAWMUT BANK v. NEW AMSTERDAM CASUALTY CO.

United States Court of Appeals, First Circuit, 1969.
411 F.2d 843.

COFFIN, Circuit Judge.

* * *

The critical question which this appeal raises is one which has been, and continues to be, the cause of some uncertainty in the wake of enactment of Article 9 of the Uniform Commercial Code (U.C.C.). It is: to what extent, if any, does the doctrine of subrogation survive the passage of Article 9 of the U.C.C.?

Our effort will be to see what subrogation means in the transaction before us, to see what extent Article 9 is devised to deal with such a transaction, and to apply relevant case law. Subrogation is an old term, rooted in equity, and semantically stemming from words meaning 'ask under'. Today we use the parallel phrase, 'stand in the shoes of'. The equitable principle is that when one, pursuant to obligation—not a volunteer, fulfills the duties of another, he is entitled to assert the rights of that other against third persons.

In this case there is confusion because the tendency is to think of the surety on Miller Act payment and performance bonds as standing in the shoes only of the entity it 'insures'—the contractor. So long as this one-dimensional concept prevails, logic compels the surety to be assessed as merely one of the contractor's creditors, and to be subject to the system of priorities rationalized by the Uniform Commercial Code. But the surety in cases like this undertakes duties which entitle it to step into three sets of shoes. When, on default of the contractor, it pays all the bills of the job to date and completes the job, it stands in the shoes of the contractor insofar as there are receivables due it; in the shoes of laborers and material men who have been paid by the surety—who may have had liens; and, not least, in the shoes of the government, for whom the job was completed.

This unique accumulation of subrogation rights serves to induce a function that is neither ordinary insurance nor ordinary financing. The business of a construction contract surety is not one of ordinary insurance, for the risk is not actuarially linked to premiums, nor is there a pooling of risks. Neither is the business one of ordinary financing, for while the surety extends its credit to the owner (the government), as the ultimate guarantee that the job will be done, this is a credit that may either never have to be drawn upon or, if it is drawn upon at all, will in all likelihood be overdrawn. That is, if a contractor defaults, 'payment' of the credit depends upon the surety's competence in economically finishing what somebody else has started. In this hermaphroditic situation, the 'security' for the surety is not the fee but a compound of its confidence in the contractor and the opportunity to prevent or minimize its ultimate loss by its right to salvage the debacle by its own performance. Assuming that its confidence is misplaced, the surety receives very little from the contractor but the right to complete the job. Unlike a bank, it does not face specific requests for funds which it is able to link to suitable collateral with subsequent requests determined by assessment of current management and currently available additional security. In case of default, the bank takes its security; the surety must go ahead and perform.

All of this, we think, is relevant background to an interpretation of the Uniform Commercial Code as applied to the kind of security interest at issue. We commence by saying that appellant makes a respectable argument based on the Code. At best, however, we deem the Code not compelling and, on balance, not focused or directed to the surety's problem. To begin with, we have the exculpatory general principle that 'Unless displaced by the particular provisions of this chapter, the principles of law and equity * * * shall supplement its provisions.' M.G.L.A. § 1-103. As we shall see, the Massachusetts Supreme Judicial Court gives impressive weight to this canon in French Lumber Co., Inc. v. Commercial Realty & Finance Co., Inc., 346 Mass. 716, 719, 195 N.E. 507 (1964).

Going on to specifics, we note the definition of 'security interest' in M.G.L.A. § 1-201(37) as 'an interest in personal property or fixtures which secures payment or performance of an obligation * * * (and which) includes any interest of a buyer of accounts * * * or contract rights * * *.' Neither clause seems to fit the construction contract surety. What secures its payment is really the opportunity, on default, to finish the job and apply any available funds against its cost of completion. This kind of right does not readily settle under the rubric of 'personal property' or 'fixtures'. Nor does the surety easily fit the description of a 'buyer of * * * contract rights'. We make a similar comment about M.G.L.A. § 9-102(1)(a) which applies the Code 'to any transaction * * * which is intended to create a security interest in personal property or fixtures including * * * contract rights; and * * * (b) to any sale of * * * contract rights'. While one may strain to say that the right to finish a job in an emergency and thus minimize damages is a contract right, we think it is not the kind of independently valuable asset that such synonyms as 'goods, documents, instruments, general intangibles, (and) chattel paper' suggest.

There are other hurdles. Section 9-102(2) requires 'security interests' to be 'created by contract'. In this case the real security is not the assignment of accounts receivable—which could be, failing the completion of performance, set off by the government—but the eventual right to be in the shoes of the government upon job completion. This is not 'created by contract' but rather by the status, resulting from a contract, inhering in a surety, quite independently of the expressed terms of the contract.

We add to this our difficulties with § 9-106 which defines 'account' as 'any right to payment * * * not evidenced by an instrument' and 'contract right' as 'any right to payment under a contract not yet earned by performance'. As to the former, when the contractor defaults, there is no right to payment, see infra. As to the latter, we think of a right to receive payments from one who continues with the performance (as rents receivable by a landlord), rather than a right conditioned on performance by the transferee of the 'right'.

We have, finally, the historic fact of the rejection of a proposed § 9-312(7) to the Code which would have provided that 'A security interest which secures an obligation to reimburse a surety * * * secondarily obligated to complete performance is subordinate to' a later lender which perfects its security interest. * * * Contrary to appellant's argument, we do not feel that this signalized an admission by surety companies that theirs was a 'security interest' within the meaning of the Code, but simply that they had won the battle to defend the preserve of subrogation. The cases cited by the Board would seem to underscore this conclusion.

Finally, the Bank asserts that even if the surety may claim as a subrogee, the Bank has a superior claim in equity. This is so, according to the Bank, where earned progress payments are involved and where the surety has benefitted from the contractor's application of the loan proceeds to contracts bonded by the surety.

The position espoused by the Bank originated in cases where earned progress payments had been paid to an assignee bank and the surety was attempting, after the default of the contractor, to recover the amounts paid.

Here the payments were earned but unpaid prior to the contractor's default. Prior to default, the contractor had the right to assign progress payments and had the Bank received payment, it could not (absent circumstances amounting to fraud) have been divested by the surety. But upon default, the surety which is obligated to complete the work steps into the shoes of the government—not of the contractor which on default has forfeited its rights. It is subrogated not only to the right of the government to pay laborers and materialmen from funds retained out of progress payments, but also to the government's right to apply to the cost of completion the earned but unpaid progress payments in its hands at the time of default. The Massachusetts Supreme Judicial Court has specifically recognized that a mere assignee of a contractor, such as appellant here, receives the right to moneys due the latter subject, however, to the dominant right of the owner to recoup the damages suffered by default. American Bridge Co. of New York v. City of Boston, 202 Mass. 374 (1909).

While appellant has cited many cases where a bank was allowed to retain progress payments made to it, which we have noted supra, its only authority for the proposition that a bank has priority over a surety with regard to earned but unpaid progress payments is General Casualty Co. v. Second National Bank of Houston, 178 F.2d 679 (5th Cir. 1949). Any distinction between the surety's rights to retainage and those to unpaid progress payments, however, was eliminated by the later Fifth Circuit case of Trinity Universal Insurance Co. v. United States, 382 F.2d 317 (5th Cir. 1967).

Our analysis has centered on the interpretation of the Code and of the doctrine of subrogation as developed by the cases. We have found no basis for injecting other general equitable or policy considerations. We are unmoved by the claims of either the Bank or the surety to inherently superior status. The Bank loan undoubtedly helped minimize the surety's cost of completion. But completion by the surety was necessary to preserve the fund which is here in issue. The surety could concededly have avoided this litigation by perfecting its filing, but so could the Bank by making inquiry of the arrangements between contractor and surety. It may well be—although we express no opinion—that to subject sureties to the filing requirements of the Code would improve and rationalize the system of financing public contracts. But equitable subrogation is too hardy a plant to be uprooted by a Code which speaks around but not to the issue.

RINN v. FIRST UNION NATIONAL BANK

United States District Court, District of Maryland, 1995.
176 B.R. 401.

[First Union refinanced a loan that Maryland National had made to the debtor. Maryland National had a perfected security interest in debtor's accounts, and the court found that the parties intended that First would take an assignment of the security interest from Maryland; but when the parties completed the refinancing, they neglected to assign the Maryland security interest to First Union. First Union never perfected a security interest of its own. When the debtor filed in bankruptcy, the trustee challenged First Union's claim to the collateral as an unperfected security interest or no security interest at all.]

GARBIS, District Judge.

* * *

III. DISCUSSION

A. Subrogation

Broadly defined, subrogation is the substitution of one person in the place of another with reference to a lawful claim or right. 73 Am.Jur.2d Subrogation § 1 at 598 (1974); Sheldon, The Law of Subrogation, § 1 (1st ed. 1882). Originating in equity, the doctrine's operation at law is governed by equitable principles. Compania Anonima Venezolana de Navegacion v. A.J. Perez Export Co., 303 F.2d 692, 697 (5th Cir.1962), cert. denied, 371 U.S. 942, 83 S.Ct. 321, 9 L.Ed.2d 276 (1962). Subrogation is intended to provide relief against loss to a meritorious creditor who has paid the debt of another, Bachmann v. Glazer, 316 Md. 405, 559 A.2d 365, 368 (1989), and to obtain an equitable adjustment between parties "by securing the ultimate discharge of a debt by the person who in equity ought to pay it." Collins v. Blue Cross of Virginia, 213 Va. 540, 193 S.E.2d 782, 784 (1973).

There are two kinds of subrogation: legal and conventional. Security Ins. Co. v. Mangan, 250 Md. 241, 242 A.2d 482, 485 (Md.1968). Legal subrogation is a construct of equity and does not depend upon a contract. Conventional subrogation, by contrast, is founded upon some understanding or agreement, express or implied, and is often treated as synonymous with assignment. Id. In essence, conventional subrogation is the result of an agreement that the liens existing as security for the debt shall be kept alive for the lender's benefit. Bachmann v. Glazer, 316 Md. 405, 559 A.2d 365, 368 (1989) ("The doctrine is a legal fiction whereby an obligation extinguished by a payment made by a third person is treated as still subsisting for the benefit of this third person."); Levenson v. Capital Mortgage, 101 Md.App. 122, 643 A.2d 505, 509 (1994) (same). It may be invoked "where one having no interest or any relation to the matter pays the debt of another, and by agreement is entitled to the rights and securities of the debtor so paid."[1] Mangan, 242 A.2d at 485.

Founded on principles of natural reason and justice, subrogation is a highly favored doctrine and expansively applied. D'Angelo v. Cornell Paperboard Products Co., 19 Wis.2d 390, 120 N.W.2d 70, 76-77 (1963); 3105 Grand Corp. v. New York, 288 N.Y. 178, 42 N.E.2d 475, 477 (1942); see also Compania Anonima Venezolana de Navegacion v. A.J. Perez Export Co., 303 F.2d 692, 697 (5th Cir.1962), cert. denied, 371 U.S. 942, 83 S.Ct. 321, 9 L.Ed.2d 276 (1962) ("These principles [of subrogation are] so well established that to cite cases would be an affectation"). Indeed, subrogation has been consistently upheld by courts in each of the states in which the subsidiaries' assets are located—Maryland, Delaware, and Virginia—and thus whose laws control this proceeding. See e.g., Collins v. Blue Cross of Virginia, 213 Va. 540, 193 S.E.2d 782, 785 (1973) ("The general right of subrogation has long been recognized and favored in Virginia"); Bachmann v. Glazer, 316 Md. 405, 559 A.2d 365 (1985); Willis v. Continental Cas. Co., 649 F.Supp. 707, 709 (D.Del.1986) ("Delaware courts have long recognized that '[s]ubrogation is a creature of equity, historically cognizable in our [courts]' ").

Once applied, subrogation places the party subrogated in the shoes of the creditor. Levenson v. Capital Mortgage, 101 Md.App. 122, 643 A.2d 505, 510 (1994). The party subrogated acquires all rights, securities, and remedies the creditor has against the debtor and is "[regarded] as constituting one and the same person with the creditor whom he succeeds." Peek v. Wachovia Bank & Trust Co., 242 N.C. 1, 86 S.E.2d 745, 755 (1955). As the Supreme Court summarized: "One who rests on subrogation stands in the place of one whose claim he has paid, as if the payment giving rise to the subrogation had not been made." United States v. Munsey Trust Co., 332 U.S. 234, 242, 67 S.Ct. 1599, 1603, 91 L.Ed. 2022 (1947).

B. Subrogation of First Union

First Union claims it is entitled to conventional subrogation based on the express or implied agreement that First Union would assume a first priority security interest of equal dignity as that possessed by the previous creditor, Maryland National, in exchange for its refinancing of the Maryland National debt. It is undisputed that First Union extended its January, 1989, loan to the Ruppert Brothers subsidiaries on the express condition that it receive the identical security interest in the subsidiaries' inventory and accounts receivables that Maryland National possessed at that time. The November, 1988, commitment letter set forth this condition, and the Trustee does not deny that the debtors readily agreed to the condition. It was pursuant to this mutual agreement that First Union directly paid Maryland National funds necessary to refinance the subsidiaries' debt.

Courts have traditionally applied the doctrine of subrogation in the context of one who pays off a mortgage or encumbrance which the principal debtor has

---

1 In this respect, a party's right under conventional subrogation is somewhat broader than legal subrogation, for the right is granted irrespective of whether the payment was necessary for the protection of the person seeking subrogation.

failed to discharge. As the court stated in Levenson v. Capital Mortgage, 101 Md.App. 122, 643 A.2d 505, 510 (1994):

> [T]he weight of authority extends the application of the doctrine of equitable subrogation to situations in which the initial and refinancing lenders are not the same, provided the refinancing lender's money is intended to be used, and is used, to eliminate a specific encumbrance, and the refinancing lender intended "to get as security for his loan either the land free and clear of the encumbrance or else the benefit of the encumbrance itself" rather than rely upon the general credit of the mortgagor.

Id. 643 A.2d at 510 (emphasis added), quoting 4 American Law of Property § 16.149 at 349 (1952). See also, Kaplan v. Walker, 164 N.J.Super. 130, 395 A.2d 897, 900 (1978) ("As to the * * * rule of subrogation of a refinancing lender to the position of the lender whose lien is discharged by the proceeds of the later loan, there being no prejudice to or justified reliance by a party in adverse interest, there can be no doubt"); French Lumber Co. v. Commercial Realty & Finance Co., 346 Mass. 716, 195 N.E.2d 507 (1964). In these cases, "equity, speaking from the standpoint of good conscience, substitutes the person so paying the debt to the place of the original creditor, so far as to enable him to enforce the security for the purpose of reimbursement." Martin v. Hickenlooper, 90 Utah 150, 59 P.2d 1139, 1152 (1936), quoting Jackson Trust Co. v. Gilkinson, 147 A. 113, 114 (N.J.Eq.1929). Likewise, the equities in the case at bar dictate that conventional subrogation be applied to keep the Maryland National first-priority perfected lien alive in favor of First Union, which loaned the subsidiaries funds to pay off the Maryland National debt on the express condition that it assume this lien.

It is not necessary that the one to whose rights another is subrogated make a formal assignment of the securities or other rights to the subrogee. * * * Therefore, it was not necessary for Maryland National to formally assign its perfected security interest to First Union; as long as First Union and the debtors intended to pledge personal property as security for their obligation to First Union, and this property—the subsidiaries inventory and receivables—was sufficiently described or identified, the equitable lien followed as of course. Moreover, equity, regarding that as done which ought to have been done, treats the assignment as being made as soon as the right to subrogation arises, which is ordinarily the time at which the subrogee pays the debt. Accordingly, the equitable assignment of Maryland National's perfected security interest was made in January, 1989, the time at which First Union paid the Maryland National debt.

* * *

Trustee argues that because First Union failed to follow the proper procedures to obtain and perfect its security interests, equitable subrogation should be denied. To perfect a security interest in property, Title 9 of the Uniform Commercial Code ("U.C.C."), which has been adopted by each of the states involved in this case, requires the filing of a financial statement in the appropriate registries. U.C.C. § 9-403. First Union did not file financial statements regarding its security interest in the debtors' inventory and accounts receivables until February 12, 1992.

Section 1-103 of the U.C.C. provides, however, that "[u]nless displaced by the particular provisions of [the U.C.C.] * * * the principles of law and equity * * * shall supplement its provisions." Courts have consistently held that "[n]othing in the provisions of Title 9 regarding secured transactions expressly or implicitly refutes the application of subrogation." Therefore, the formal procedures mandated by the U.C.C. may be supplemented by the principles of equitable subrogation. In other words, First Union failure to satisfy the statutory filing requirements becomes immaterial once it is equitably subrogated to the position of Maryland National, which had properly obtained and recorded financial statements for a security interest in the debtors' inventory and accounts receivable.

* * *

(b) CHECKS

UCC § 4-407

If a payor bank has paid an item over the order of the drawer or maker to stop payment, or after an account has been closed, or otherwise under circumstances giving a basis for objection by the drawer or maker, to prevent unjust enrichment and only to the extent necessary to prevent loss to the bank by reason of its payment of the item, the payor bank is subrogated to the rights

(1) of any holder in due course on the item against the drawer or maker;

(2) of the payee or any holder of the item against the drawer or maker either on the item or under the transaction out of which the item arose; and

(3) of the drawer or maker against the payee or any holder of the item with respect to the transaction out of which the item arose.

PROBLEM

On May 1 Buyer gave Seller a $50,000 check to cover Seller's delivery of corn to Buyer's chemical facility. Buyer later discovered that the moisture content of the corn exceeded industry standards and that the corn had a market value of only $10,000. Buyer notified its bank to stop payment on the check. Seller, in the meantime took the check, properly indorsed, to Second National Bank, which credited Seller's checking account. On May 3, First Bank, the drawee bank, by mistake paid the check over Buyer's stop payment order.

How would subrogation apply in the following cases?

(a) If on May 2, Second Bank had allowed Seller to withdraw the $50,000? See § 4-407(1). [Hint: Has Second given value?] See §§ 3-302, 3-303, 4-210, 4-211.

(b) If the funds are still on deposit at Second Bank? See § 4-407(3).

(c) If, contrary to the recited facts, the corn is in fact conforming to industry standards. See § 4-407(2).

(c) LETTERS OF CREDIT

TUDOR DEVELOPMENT GROUP, INC. v. UNITED STATES FIDELITY & GUARANTY CO.

United States Court of Appeals, Third Circuit, 1991.
968 F.2d 357.

[Associates, a developer, entered into a contract with Susquehenna (SCC) for construction work in connection with a subdivision development. SCC obtained two bonds from USF&G to guarantee SCC's performance. The $594,000 in proceeds from these bonds are the subject of this complex litigation. In order to obtain permits for the development from the township, Associates had to agree to construct public improvements, and the township insisted that Associates obtain a bond or a letter of credit to secure the public improvements obligation. Dauphin issued the letter of credit at Associates' request and obtained from Associates (1) an assignment of proceeds from bonds other than the USF&G bonds and (2) the promissory note of Associates' general partner.

SCC defaulted, and Associates made a claim on the USF&G bonds. Tudor claims the bond settlement proceeds by virtue of an assignment of them from Associates. The township drew on the letter of credit, and Dauphin paid. Dauphin claims the proceeds under the doctrine of equitable subrogation.]

COWEN, Circuit Judge.

The most salient feature of a letter of credit and the principal reason for its use in commercial transactions is the "independence principle." This means that the letter of credit is a commercial instrument completely separate from the underlying contract between the customer and the beneficiary. The independence principle obliges the issuer to honor the draft when the beneficiary presents conforming documents without reference to compliance with the terms of the underlying contract between the customer and the beneficiary. This "independence" means that should disagreement arise between customer and beneficiary, the dispute is resolved with the money already in the pocket of the beneficiary. It also means that when an issuer makes payment under a letter of credit, the issuer is satisfying its own primary obligation to the beneficiary, without reference to the rights of its customer under the underlying contract with the beneficiary.

In contrast, a guarantor is subject to liability only if the beneficiary has sought and has been unable to obtain payment from the party who is primarily liable on the debt. Therefore a guarantor is actually liable for the debt of another party which that party has failed to satisfy.

In this case, the customer in the letter of credit transaction was Associates. The contract underlying the letter of credit was the subdivision agreement entered into by Associates and the Township, and the Township was the beneficiary of the letter of credit. Dauphin Deposit, the issuer, was obligated under the terms of the letter to honor the Township's demand for payment when the Township certified that the agreed upon improvements had not been made by Associates. Once Dauphin Deposit honored the letter, Associates, as its customer, had an immediate statutory obligation to reimburse Dauphin, the issuer and was also obligated to do so under the terms of the reimbursement agreement.

While section 5114(c)[1] states that the issuer shall be reimbursed, there are no comparable statutory provisions indicating the manner in which such reimbursement shall occur. The method of reimbursement is a matter left to negotiations between the parties. In this case, the reimbursement obligation was memorialized contractually in the reimbursement agreement entered into by Associates and Dauphin Deposit. In addition, Dauphin Deposit negotiated for assignment rights in certain collateral held by Associates, namely its rights under the Wausau performance bonds and also looked to the Tudor promissory note as collateral in its dealings with Associates.

III.

The classic explanation of the doctrine of equitable subrogation is as follows:

> Where property of one person is used in discharging an obligation owed by another or a lien upon property of another, under such circumstances that the other would be unjustly enriched by the retention of the benefit thus conferred, the former is entitled to be subrogated to the position of the obligee or lien-holder.

Generally, the following five prerequisites must be satisfied before a claimant may avail itself of the remedy of equitable subrogation: (1) the claimant paid the creditor to protect his own interests; (2) the claimant did not act as a volunteer; (3) the claimant was not primarily liable for the debt; i.e., secondary liability; (4) the entire debt has been satisfied; and (5) allowing subrogation will not cause injustice to the rights of others.

Pennsylvania law offers little guidance, however, on the question of whether the doctrine is applicable in the context of letters of credit. This dearth of state case law is best explained by the simple fact that the question of subrogation usually arises in the bankruptcy setting. The issuer which has honored a demand for payment under a letter of credit has an immediate and unconditional statutory right to reimbursement from its customer and has usually secured adequate collateral to make itself whole in the event of honor.

* * *

Courts grappling with this issue have generally concluded that while there are some superficial similarities between guarantees and letters of credit, their "legal" characteristics remain quite distinct and thus the remedies available should remain distinct as well. As noted by the district court, the key distinction between letters of credit and guarantees is that the issuer's obligation under a letter of credit is primary whereas a guarantor's obligation is secondary—the guarantor is only obligated to pay if the principal defaults on the debt the principal owes. In contrast, while the

---

1 The court's references are to pre-revised Article 5 (eds.)

issuing bank in the letter of credit situation may be secondarily liable in a temporal sense, since its obligation to pay does not arise until after its customer fails to satisfy some obligation, it is satisfying its own absolute and primary obligation to make payment rather than satisfying an obligation of its customer. Having paid its own debt, as it has contractually undertaken to do, the issuer "cannot then step into the shoes of the creditor to seek subrogation, reimbursement or contribution from the [customer]. The only exception would be where the parties reach an agreement to the contrary." In re Kaiser Steel, 89 B.R. at 153.

The distinct nature of the obligations which arise with respect to letters of credit and guarantees is also reflected in a number of provisions of the UCC itself. See 13 Pa. Cons.Stat.Ann. § 5103 cmt. ("[t]he issuer is not a guarantor of the performance of these underlying transactions"); 13 Pa.Cons.Stat.Ann. § 5101 cmt. ("[t]he other source of law respecting letters of credit is the law of contracts with occasional unfortunate excursions into the law of guaranty"); 13 Pa.Cons.Stat.Ann. § 5109 cmt. ("issuer receives compensation for a payment service rather than for a guaranty of performance"). While we recognize that arguments may be made and have been made in support of allowing subrogation, we believe that Article 5 of the UCC, when viewed in its entirety, evinces an intent to keep the law of guarantee and the law of letters of credit separate. In our view, the Uniform Commercial Code Committee, rather than the federal courts, is best equipped to address this problem.

* * *

The UCC does contain one direct reference to the possibility of subrogation in the letter of credit context: "[t]he customer will normally have direct recourse against the beneficiary if performance fails, whereas the issuer will have such recourse only by assignment of or in a proper case subrogation to the rights of the customer." 13 Pa.Cons.Stat.Ann. § 5109 cmt. This comment, however, is clearly limited to the possibility of the issuer being subrogated to the customer's rights against the beneficiary. In the present case, rather than seeking subrogation rights against the beneficiary of the letter, Dauphin Deposit seeks subrogation rights against a stranger to the letter of credit issued in favor of the Township. In any event, this comment merely suggests rather than mandates the availability of subrogation in certain cases.

Finally, we note that some courts have determined that equitable subrogation is not available to a bank which has honored a letter of credit, but has not been reimbursed. These courts have rejected the remedy of equitable subrogation in the belief that allowing subrogation would abrogate the independence principle which is the cornerstone of letter of credit law. The district court in this case disagreed with that assessment and concluded that "the independence principle is technically not violated by allowing Dauphin Deposit to proceed against its customer." App. at 1144. We agree with the district court that the vitality of the independence principle is unlikely to be substantially diminished were we to allow subrogation in this situation. However, as noted, one of the principal requirements of equitable subrogation has not been satisfied here—that the party seeking subrogation have satisfied the debt of another—and therefore we conclude that the district court correctly determined that the remedy cannot be invoked in this case. Moreover, as will be discussed, the equities do not favor granting subrogation rights in this case.

IV.

Even if we were to ignore the fact that Dauphin Deposit has failed to meet the technical requirements to avail itself of the remedy of subrogation since it was satisfying its own primary obligation in paying under the letter of credit, we would nevertheless be compelled to reject its claimed right to the remedy of equitable subrogation on these facts. As the district court concluded, the equities do not favor subrogation in this case.

When Dauphin Deposit agreed to issue a letter of credit on behalf of its customer, Associates, it was in a position to bargain for whatever security it thought appropriate. It chose to contract for an assignment of rights in the Wausau bonds and received a promissory note from Tudor. In addition, Dauphin Deposit received a large annual fee for the service of issuing the credit based upon the face amount of the letter. It could have contracted for an assignment of rights in the USF&G bonds but did not do so.

Presumably, at the time these arrangements were made Dauphin was satisfied with the collateral it received and the creditworthiness of its customer. However, now that Dauphin has discovered that it made a poor business decision in not contracting for an assignment of rights in the USF & G bonds, it seeks our help in gaining additional rights. As the district court properly concluded, there is no apparent reason why the court should exercise its equitable powers to rewrite the contract between the parties to give Dauphin Deposit more security than it bargained to receive. * * *

In assessing the equities of the situation, we must also look to the other parties who could or would be affected by a decision to allow subrogation in this case. Those parties who engaged in business dealings with Associates subsequent to the issuance of the letter of credit, including Investors, to whom Associates assigned its rights in the USF & G bonds, assumed they would be free from any future claims by Dauphin Deposit with respect to the letter of credit. We do not believe the equities favor treating Dauphin Deposit in a manner which would be detrimental to those parties who had subsequent dealings with Associates.

Finally, we note that as a general matter, equitable relief is not appropriate where a party has an adequate legal or statutory remedy. Here, Dauphin Deposit appears to have two legal remedies and one statutory remedy: (1) seek judgment against Tudor on the promissory note; (2) sue Associates directly under the Reimbursement Agreement; and (3) seek reimbursement under 13 Pa.Cons.Stat.Ann. § 5114(c) which provides that an issuer is entitled to immediate reimbursement from its customer in the event of honor. In determining whether a remedy is "adequate," we must look to its availability and not to the likelihood of its success. Thus the fact that the remedies set forth above might not make Dauphin Deposit whole does not mandate a finding that such remedies are inadequate, thereby requiring this court to grant equitable relief.

V.

In sum, we conclude that equitable subrogation is not an appropriate remedy in this situation, both because an issuing bank which honors a letter of credit makes good its own primary obligation, rather than fulfilling the obligation of another, and because the equities of the case before us do not warrant it. We will affirm the judgment of the district court granting summary judgment in favor of Investors.

BECKER, Circuit Judge, dissenting.

This appeal presents a close, difficult, and important question that has divided both courts and scholars. The majority concludes that, under Article 5 of the Uniform Commercial Code and the common law, a bank that has issued a standby letter of credit may never qualify for equitable subrogation to the rights of its defaulting customer in the underlying commercial transaction. The majority opinion is a fine piece of advocacy for a respectable position, one that has been adopted by a majority of the courts to face the issue (although rejected by the only federal appellate court that has reached the question). Nevertheless, I believe that the majority has backed the wrong horse. I would hold that an issuer of a standby letter of credit may, in proper circumstances, obtain equitable subrogation to the rights of its customer.

The majority also concludes that, even assuming that equitable subrogation is available in some cases, the equities in this case do not warrant it. Because I believe that genuine issues of material fact remain on this issue, I would not decide it on summary judgment. I would instead remand the case to the district court for further proceedings to determine whether the facts and equities here weigh in favor of or against Dauphin Deposit's claim. I therefore respectfully dissent.

* * *

2. Interference with the Independence Principle

The recent American Bar Association/U.S. Council on International Banking Task Force on the Study of U.C.C. Article 5 reached no definitive conclusion on when and whether subrogation is available in the letter of credit context, although it agreed that statutory resolution of the question would be useful. See its report, An Examination of U.C.C. Article 5 (Letters of Credit) 21 (Sept. 29, 1989), reprinted in 45 Bus.Law. 1527 (1990). The task force did agree, however, that "the question of the availability of subrogation is one which must be regarded as being essentially outside of credit law and the letter of credit transaction," and that "the primary factor in determining [subrogation's] availability should be whether it would affect the integrity of principles vital to letter of credit law." Id.

As noted above, the cornerstone of the law of letters of credit is the independence principle, and thus if granting subrogation to issuers of letters of credit would undermine the independence principle, then such subrogation must not be permitted. In my view, allowing the issuer of a letter of credit to subrogate to the rights of its customer would not undermine the independence principle.

The independence principle ensures the beneficiary of prompt payment and basically determines that the beneficiary will have the dollars in its pocket if there is a dispute between it and the customer over the underlying transaction. As discussed above, this distinguishes a letter of credit from an ordinary guaranty: a guaranty is not independent in this sense, and guarantors may generally assert defenses available to the party whose obligation is guaranteed.

Investors suggests that the independence principle must be viewed as a wall between the letter of credit side and the underlying transaction side. Some courts have similarly argued that allowing subrogation would permit an issuer to interfere with the underlying contract. But the point of the independence principle is not to set up a wall for the sake of a wall, but to serve certain purposes. The independence principle undoubtedly requires the issuer to pay first, without looking through to the underlying transaction. Subrogation should therefore be unavailable before the issuer has paid the beneficiary. Once the issuer has done so, however, as Dauphin Deposit has here, the purpose of the independence principle has been served: the beneficiary has the money.

Insistence on perpetual separation is thus pointless formalism. On a more pragmatic level, I would agree that if the possibility of subsequent subrogation would discourage issuers from honoring already-issued letters of credit, then subrogation should not be permitted, because that would undercut the purposes of Article 5. But I cannot see why that would be so. If anything, the unavailability of subsequent subrogation might discourage issuers from honoring the letters because they would have one less means of obtaining reimbursement.

In sum, the policies underlying Article 5 of the U.C.C. do not require courts to deny subrogation to all issuers of standby letters of credit. The remaining question is whether other policy considerations commend the per se rule argued by Investors and adopted by the majority.

C. Other Policy Considerations

1. The Issuer's Ability to Protect Itself Contractually

In my view, Investors' (and the majority's) best argument is that the issuer of a letter of credit is perfectly able to protect itself contractually. That is, the issuer receives a payment for its services and may also demand assignment rights to collateral in the event that it is forced to pay on the letter. Investors argues that Dauphin Deposit made a deal with Associates and received certain collateral rights, including assignment rights to the other bonds involved in the Green Hill Project (the "Wausau bonds"). It is certainly fair to ask why Dauphin Deposit should receive the additional right of subrogation, simply because it made a bad gamble or wasn't wary enough when negotiating its reimbursement agreement with Associates. Many courts have voiced similar concerns.

Nevertheless, this argument, although powerful, proves too much. Generally applied, the same argument would virtually eliminate equitable subrogation altogether, for it would apply to every guaranty or suretyship contract. Moreover, in many cases this may lead to the customer receiving an undeserved windfall. A customer may default on both its obligation on the underlying transaction and its obligation to reimburse the issuer of the letter of credit, yet retain any income deriving from the original transaction. In short, the issuer's ability to protect itself may be a strong equity against it, as is the fact that it receives a fee for its services, but countervailing equities may outweigh these considerations in certain cases.

* * *

For the foregoing reasons, I would reverse the judgment of the district court and remand for further proceedings.

UCC § 5-117

(*see Selected Commercial Statutes*)

QUESTIONS

(a) Does § 5-117 mean that a credit issuer is always subrogated to the beneficiary's rights in the applicant's property?

(b) Does it mean that the issuer is presumptively subrogated?

(c) What does it mean?

PROBLEM

Rogers Corp. is a construction company that hoped to profit from the construction contracts to be let by Valley Vue Joint Venture, a partnership that was developing a subdivision. The partnership borrowed the money from a mortgage lender to buy the real estate to be developed. The mortgage lender insisted that in addition to the mortgage, which secured repayment of the loan, the developer obtain a standby letter of credit in the amount of $1,000,000 running to the benefit of the mortgage lender, which would have the right to draw on the credit in the event the developer defaulted on the loan.

Being short of capital, the partnership was unable to obtain the letter of credit without Rogers' help. At that point, Rogers, in order to get Security Bank to issue the standby credit, agreed to reimburse the issuer in the event of a draw.

The developer defaulted and is in bankruptcy; the mortgage lender drew on the issuer of the standby; and Rogers reimbursed the issuer.

Rogers presumably has a claim against the partnership in bankruptcy, but the claim is unsecured. Rogers did not get any collateral from the partnership. The mortgage lender did obtain collateral, however, the mortgage; and Rogers now seeks to subrogate itself to the mortgage lender's mortgage, thereby transmuting its unsecured claim into a secured claim.

(a) Did Rogers' reimbursement of the issuer enrich general creditors in the partnership bankruptcy? [Assume that the mortgage loan is fully paid and that the real property is an asset of the bankruptcy estate free and clear of all liens.]

(b) Are the unsecured creditors of the partnership unjustly enriched by Rogers' payment?

NOTE ON CONFIRMER'S CLAIM AGAINST THE APPLICANT

If, as the *Auto Servicio* case holds, the applicant may not sue the confirmer when the confirmer misbehaves, it makes sense to hold that the confirmer should not be able to sue the applicant when the issuer fails to reimburse the confirmer. In *In re Glade Springs, Inc.*, 826 F.2d 440 (6th Cir. 1987), however, we see that by using subrogation, a confirmer did just that successfully.

Glade Springs allowed a confirmer to subrogate itself to the issuer's rights against the issuer's customer, the applicant for the credit. Both the issuer and the applicant were insolvent. Evaluation of *Glade Springs*, requires comparison of its outcome with the outcome in the event the court had not allowed subrogation. Without subrogation, the receiver of the failed issuer would have had full recovery from the applicant; and the confirmer would have had less than full recovery, the dividend at the end of the receivership.

Arguably, insolvency laws serve a disciplinary function: those who extend credit to parties that become insolvent suffer losses. The confirmer in *Glade Springs* extended credit to the issuer when the confirmer confirmed the issuer's credit. By giving the confirmer full recovery, subrogation interrupts the discipline of the bank insolvency regime—an unwise confirmer gets paid in full.

SECTION 5. CONVERSION

INTRODUCTORY NOTE

Conversion, a tort, is the act of officiously intermeddling with the property of another. Under the tort, moreover, liability is strict. It matters not whether the tortfeasor's conduct is an innocent or intentional interference. An auctioneer that sells stolen property is liable to the true owner, the auctioneer's ignorance of the fact that the property was stolen notwithstanding. The grain elevator that buys grain from a farmer after the farmer grants the bank a properly perfected security interest is liable to the bank at common law. A bank that takes a stolen check with a forged indorsement and collects it for the forger is liable in conversion to the check's true owner, so does a bank that holds a person's check and does nothing with it. In short, conversion is a claim that a propertied person who has suffered interference with a property interest brings against the converter.

The tort has broad use in many areas of commercial activity: secured transactions, transport and storage, and bank collections. This section takes a look at those features of conversion law that affect the latter two areas.

(a) CHECKS

UCC § 3-420
(*see Selected Commercial Statutes*)

PROBLEMS

(1) Buyer gave Seller a $5,000 check payable to the order of Seller. Forger took the check, forged Seller's indorsement, and deposited the check at Second Bank, which sent the check to First Bank, the drawee/payor bank, which paid it.

(a) May Buyer recover from anyone in conversion?

(b) May Seller recover in conversion from Thief? From Second Bank? From First Bank?

(2) Assume in the foregoing example (i) that Forger was an employee of Seller and that Seller, under the preclusion rule of § 3-405(b), is precluded from asserting the forgery against the banks and (ii) that both banks acted with due care.

(a) May Seller recover in conversion from Forger? From Second Bank? From First Bank?

(b) If Second has given value to Thief, is Second a holder in due course? Does a holder in due course take subject to claims? See § 3-306. Is an action in conversion a claim?

(b) TRANSPORT AND STORAGE

R.E. HUNTLEY COTTON CO. v. FIELDS

Court of Civil Appeals of Texas, 1977.
551 S.W.2d 472, 21 U.C.C. Rep. Serv. 1157.

JAMES A. ELLIS, Chief Justice.

The trial court temporarily enjoined defendants Allenberg Cotton Company, Inc., R. S. Tapp, d/b/a R. S. Tapp & Co., Adolph Hanslik Cotton Company, Inc., and R. E. Huntley Cotton Company, d/b/a Panhandle Warehouse and Compress Company from removing 1640 bales of cotton grown by Welton Fields and several other plaintiff cotton farmers and stored in the defendant Panhandle's warehouse. The trial court required an injunction bond in the amount of $1,500. All affected defendants have appealed and by their respective points of error have raised issues concerning (1) the adequacy of plaintiffs' legal remedies, (2) the plaintiffs' probable right of relief and (3) the adequacy of the injunction bond. Reversed and rendered.

The principal controversy in this suit arises out of the plaintiffs' sale of 1765 warehouse receipts to Vaughn B. Nowlin, an F.O.B. cotton buyer. These sales occurred during the early months of 1976, and the plaintiffs were paid with checks drawn on the First State Bank of Childress, Texas (hereinafter referred to as the Bank). The cotton represented by the warehouse receipts was stored at the warehouse of the defendant R. E. Huntley Cotton Company d/b/a Panhandle Warehouse and Compress Company in Cottle County. The Bank dishonored Nowlin's checks to the plaintiffs. At about the same time (February 25 to March 10, 1976), Nowlin sold the warehouse receipts to the three defendant cotton companies. At the time these transfers were effected, none of the defendants had any actual knowledge that the plaintiffs had not been paid. In quick succession, Nowlin came within the jurisdiction of the federal bankruptcy court and the plaintiffs filed this lawsuit seeking return of the warehouse receipts in the defendants' hands, damages from the Bank and an injunction restraining the defendants from removing 1640 bales of cotton stored in the warehouse. The trial court temporarily enjoined the defendants from disposing of, selling, encumbering, giving away or otherwise removing the cotton from Cottle County. * * * In their appeal, all four defendants have presented similar arguments as to why the injunction should be dissolved.

* * *

The defendants have presented another ground for dissolution of the injunction. They have argued that the plaintiffs failed to demonstrate a probable right of recovery in the trial court. A basic question is whether the warehouse receipts were negotiable. If the warehouse receipts were negotiable and duly negotiated to the defendants, the plaintiffs failed to prove that they had a probable right of recovery because the defendants would have received title to the cotton. Tex.Bus. & Comm.Code Ann. § 7.502. Moreover, if the warehouse receipts are negotiable instruments, there is no justification for a temporary injunction, and the plaintiffs have not pleaded a cause of action against the respective defendants. The plaintiffs have argued that the warehouse receipts were not negotiable documents and/or not duly negotiated to the defendant cotton companies.

[The court then held that the receipts were negotiable.]

The plaintiffs, however, have argued that even though the warehouse receipts were negotiable, they were not "duly negotiated" to the defendants within the meaning of Tex.Bus. & Comm.Code Ann. § 7.501(d). * * *

At the temporary injunction hearing, no evidence was produced tending to prove that the cotton companies did not pay value for the warehouse receipts, or that the transaction was not in the regular course of business, or that they had actual notice of any claims to the warehouse receipts. Furthermore, there is no evidence that the defendants did not act in good faith. Although the plaintiffs presented some evidence that the defendants had access to information sufficient to put them on notice of claims to the cotton, that knowledge is immaterial unless defendants had actual knowledge of facts and circumstances that would amount to bad faith. There is no evidence of such actual knowledge, and we have concluded that the plaintiffs failed to prove their probable right to relief.

The points of error * * * to the extent that they contend that the court erred in granting the injunctive relief on the grounds that the plaintiffs failed to establish * * * their probable right to recover against the defendants on the merits, are sustained. It is therefore our opinion that the injunction should be dissolved.

UCC § 7-404

(*see Selected Commercial Statutes*)

QUESTION

At common law, if a thief bailed goods with a warehouse and if the warehouse returned the goods to the thief at the end of the bailment, the warehouse had converted the true owner's goods and was liable. Similarly, at common law an auctioneer that sold stolen goods was liable to the true owner in conversion. Section 7-404 changes the common law rule for warehouses? Why doesn't the Code change the conversion liability rule for auctioneers?

(c) WIRE TRANSFERS

MRF RESOURCES LTD. v. MERCHANTS BANK OF NEW YORK

Court of Appeals of New York, 1996.
89 N.Y.2d 674, 652 N.Y.S.2d 601, 674 N.E.2d 1366.

SIMONS, Judge.

Galit Diamond, Inc., the third-party defendant in this action, has asserted a counterclaim against defendant The Merchants Bank of New York seeking to recover damages allegedly sustained when the bank delayed execution of a funds transfer to Galit's diamond supplier in Israel. The delay occurred when Merchants wrongfully placed a hold on Galit's bank account. Galit does not claim that it suffered any direct damages, only consequential damages due to the supplier's subsequent refusal to conduct further business with it because of the delay. Supreme Court considered the bank's conduct under articles 3 and 4 of the Uniform Commercial Code and found Merchants liable under UCC 4-402. It granted Galit judgment for $531,168. The Appellate Division reversed, holding that the matter was governed solely by UCC article 4-A which regulates funds transfers and that section 4-A-305(3) does not authorize consequential damages absent an express agreement between the parties. We granted Galit leave to appeal so that we could review the dismissal of its counterclaim.

Before this Court, Galit contends that the Appellate Division erred because it did not acknowledge that the events involved more than just a funds transfer transaction. It maintains that article 4-A does not control this case because the delay in executing the funds transfer was caused by the wrongfully placed hold on Galit's account and that it was the hold which precipitated the delay in the funds transfer and caused damage. Under these circumstances, Galit contends the provisions of UCC article 4 may be applied and consequential damages awarded. Stated another way, Galit claims that because the bank's wrongful conduct did not occur within the scope of a funds transfer, article 4-A does not exclusively govern the parties' rights even though the ultimate result of the bank's conduct was a delay in executing the funds transfer.

The underlying events and transactions occurred in 1993 at a Manhattan branch of Merchants. Plaintiff MRF Resources Limited maintained a checking account at that office, as did Galit Diamond, Inc. On May 20, 1993, the bank certified a check drawn by MRF, payable to Galit Diamond, Inc. in the amount of $58,958. Upon receipt of the check, Galit presented it to Merchants for payment, and the bank posted the funds to Galit's account on that same day. Shortly thereafter, MRF's president informed Merchants that the certified check was forged. As a result, the bank placed a hold on Galit's account which continued from June 4 through June 8, 1993. Supreme Court found, and Merchants now concedes, that it had no legal basis for doing so.

Meanwhile, on June 1, Galit presented Merchants with a funds transfer application accompanied by a check drawn on its Merchants account in the amount of $30,030. The check was intended to cover a funds transfer for $30,000 and the bank's fee for that service. The application directed a credit to the Israeli bank account of Ilan Gertler, the supplier of approximately 60% of Galit's diamond inventory. Without rejecting the application or informing Galit that a hold had been placed on its account, Merchants held onto the funds transfer application and check. Gertler eventually received the funds, but a week later than expected. Because the late transfer tainted Galit's creditworthiness, Gertler severed its business relationship with Galit greatly damaging Galit's ability to conduct its business profitably.

In its counterclaim, Galit alleged that Merchants Bank was liable in damages for "wrongful[ly] freezing" its account and claimed at trial that Merchants' handling of the certified check violated various provisions of article 3 of the Uniform Commercial Code giving rise to liability under article 4. It does not dispute that if article 4-A governs the transaction, it is not entitled to consequential damages flowing from a delayed transfer of funds because Merchants, the receiving bank of the payment order, did not agree to be liable for consequential damages (see, UCC 4-A-305[3]; see generally, UCC 4-A-103). But Galit maintains that article 4-A is not exclusive when the case involves something more than a funds transfer. Specifically, it argues that articles 3 and 4 of the Uniform Commercial Code govern Merchants' conduct with respect to the certified check and the hold on Galit's account, and that the bank is liable to Galit for consequential damages pursuant to UCC 4-402. Assuming, without deciding, that article 4-A is not controlling in these circumstances, we address the merits of Galit's article 4 claim.

Under UCC 4-402, "[a] payor bank is liable to its customer for damages proximately caused by the wrongful dishonor of an item." Galit contends that since it is a customer of Merchants Bank, UCC 4-402 entitles it to consequential damages arising from the bank's attempt to decertify the certified check, and the unjustified hold placed on Galit's account. The claims do not withstand analysis.

Uniform Commercial Code § 4-104(1)(e) defines a "customer" as "any person having an account with a bank." Assuming the payee of a check is a customer within the meaning of UCC 4-402, UCC 4-402 does not provide a customer with an automatic basis to hold a bank liable simply because it is a customer or because there was a negotiable instrument involved somewhere in the chain of transactions; section 4-402 permits the customer to recover damages when a payor bank wrongfully dishonors an item. Accordingly, to be entitled to damages under that section Galit must establish that Merchants Bank wrongfully dishonored an item, and that the dishonored item was an "instrument for the payment of money" (UCC 4-104[1][g]).

The check drawn on MRF's account was certified by Merchants, and Merchants does not now dispute that Galit was a holder in due course. That check is an instrument within the meaning of UCC articles 3 and 4 (see, UCC 3-102 [1][e]; 4-104[1][g]), and it was finally paid to Galit no later than when Merchants Bank posted it to Galit's account on May 20, 1993 (see, UCC 3-411, 3-418). Galit contends that the hold placed on its account was an attempt to decertify or dishonor the certified check. But the hold placed on Galit's account deprived it of access to the account and all of its funds. Merchants did not dishonor nor "decertify" the certified check, and it did not attempt to debit or withdraw from Galit's account the $58,958. Accordingly, Merchants did not "dishonor" an item within the meaning of UCC 4-402.

Galit's contention that Merchants is liable under UCC 4-402 because it wrongfully placed a hold on the account also fails. An account is not an instrument or item within the meaning of articles 3 and 4 (see, UCC 3-102[1][e]; 4-104[1][g]), and a hold placed on an account is not a wrongful dishonor of an item within the meaning of UCC 4-402. Thus, notwithstanding Merchants wrongful conduct, Galit's chosen course of litigation—that it is entitled to consequential damages under section 4-402—does not provide a basis for such liability.

Accordingly, the order of the Appellate Division should be affirmed, with costs.

IMPULSE TRADING, INC. v. NORWEST BANK MINNESOTA, N.A.

United States District Court, District of Minnesota, 1995.
907, F. Supp. 1284 (D. Minn. 1995).

SPENCER WILLIAMS, District Judge:

* * *

Impulse asserts claims against Norwest for: (1) violation of Article 4A of the Uniform Commercial Code * * *; (2) wrongful setoff; (3) conversion; and (4) negligence. The Court will address each claim in turn.

* * *

1. This action is governed by Article 4A of the U.C.C. which covers electronic funds transfers. Impulse Trading v. Norwest Bank Minnesota, N.A., 870 F.Supp. 954, 959 (D.Minn.1994). Minnesota adopted Article 4A of the U.C.C. in 1991.

2. The comment to Article 4A states the following:

> In the drafting of Article 4A, a deliberate decision was made to write on a clean slate and to treat a funds transfer as a unique method of payment to be governed by unique rules that address the particular issues raised by this method of payment * * *.
>
> The rules that emerged represent a careful and delicate balancing of [various] interests and are intended to be the exclusive means of determining the rights, duties and liabilities of the affected parties in any

> situation covered by particular provisions of the Article. Consequently, resort to principles of law or equity outside of Article 4A is not appropriate to create rights, duties and liabilities inconsistent with those stated in this Article.

3. In the only case the Court has located specifically addressing the scope of Article 4A's preemption, the court found common law tort claims to be preempted by Article 4A. See Donmar Enterprises, Inc. v. Southern Nat'l Bank of North Carolina, 828 F.Supp. 1230, 1235-36 (W.D.N.C.1993) (finding that Federal Reserve Board Regulation J which adopts Article 4A of the U.C.C. preempts both contradictory and duplicative causes of action for wrongful payment and negligence), aff'd, 64 F.3d 944 (4th Cir.1995). Preemption is also in accord with the Minnesota courts' general interpretation of the U.C.C. as barring all common law tort claims arising out of commercial transactions except those involving personal injury. See Hapka v. Paquin Farms, 458 N.W.2d 683, 688 (Minn.1990) (finding that in cases involving commercial transactions the U.C.C. preempts tort claims for strict products liability and negligence); Superwood Corp. v. Siempelkamp Corp., 311 N.W.2d 159, 162 (Minn.1981) ("To allow tort liability in commercial transactions would totally emasculate * * * the U.C.C. Clearly the legislature did not intend for tort law to circumvent the statutory scheme of the U.C.C.").

4. Therefore, Article 4A preempts Impulse's common law claims for conversion, wrongful setoff and negligence as they relate to the funds transfer.

INDEX

References are to Page Numbers

ISBN 0-314-21117-9

9 780314 211170 90000